THE CMPTR SOLUTION

Every 4LTR Press solution includes:

Visually Engaging Textbook + **Online Study Tools** + **Tear-out Review Cards** + **Interactive eBook**

Heading Numbers Connect Print & eBook

STUDENT RESOURCES:

- Interactive eBook
- Auto-Graded Quizzes
- Flashcards
- Games
- Additional Assignments
- Videos
- Interactive Infographics
- Student Review Cards

Students sign in at **www.cengagebrain.com**

INSTRUCTOR RESOURCES:

- All Student Resources
- Engagement Tracker
- LMS Integration
- Instructor's Resource Manual
- Test Bank
- PowerPoint® Slides
- Instructor Prep Cards

Instructors sign in at **www.cengage.com/login**

D1127783

JULY 2010

4LTR Press adds eBooks in response to a 10% uptick in digital learning preferences.

Engagement Tracker launches, giving faculty a window into student usage of digital tools.

1 out of every 3 (1,400) schools has adopted a 4LTR Press solution.

750,000 students are IN.

AUGUST 2010

NOVEMBER 2010

Third party research confirms that 4LTR Press digital solutions improve retention and outcomes.

CourseMate

Students access the 4LTR Press website at 4x's the industry average.

IN 2011

60 unique solutions across multiple course areas validates the 4LTR Press concept.

2,000

1 out of every 2 (2,000) schools has a 4LTR Press adoption.

APRIL 2011

Over 1 million students are IN.

We're always evolving. Join the 4LTR Press In-Crowd on Facebook at www.facebook.com/4ltrpress

AUGUST 2011

2012 AND BEYOND

CENGAGE
Learning·

CMPTR, 2nd Edition
Katherine T. Pinard
Robin M. Romer

Vice President, General Manager: Dawn Gerrain

Senior Director of Development: Marah
    Bellegarde

Senior Product Team Manager: Donna Gridley

Associate Product Manager: Amanda Lyons

Product Development Manager: Leigh Hefferon

Senior Content Developer: Emma F. Newsom

Content Developer: Julia Leroux-Lindsey

Associate Content Developer: Katherine Russillo

Editorial Assistant: Melissa Stehler

Senior Brand Manager: Elinor Gregory

Market Development Managers: Kristie Clark,
    Gretchen Swann

Marketing Coordinator: Amy McGregor

Developmental Editors: Katherine T. Pinard,
    Robin M. Romer

Senior Content Project Manager:
    Jennifer Goguen McGrail

Compositor: GEX Publishing Services

Art Director: GEX Publishing Services

Cover Art: © Image Source/Getty Images

Copyeditor: Pamela Hunt

Proofreader: Kim Kosmatka

Indexer: Alexandra Nickerson

For product information and technology assistance, contact us at
Cengage Learning Customer & Sales Support, 1-800-354-9706.

For permission to use material from this text or product,
submit all requests online at **www.cengage.com/permissions**.
Further permissions questions can be e-mailed to
permissionrequest@cengage.com

Some of the product names and company names used in this book have been used for identification purposes only and may be trademarks or registered trademarks of their respective manufacturers and sellers.

Microsoft and the Office logo are either registered trademarks or trademarks of Microsoft Corporation in the United States and/or other countries. Cengage Learning is an independent entity from the Microsoft Corporation, and not affiliated with Microsoft in any manner.

Disclaimer: Any fictional data related to persons or companies or URLs used throughout this book is intended for instructional purposes only. At the time this book was printed, any such data was fictional and not belonging to any real persons or companies.

Library of Congress Control Number: 2013940147

ISBN-13: 978-1-285-09619-3
ISBN-10: 1-285-09619-3

Cengage Learning
200 First Stamford Place, 4th Floor
Stamford, CT 06902
USA

Cengage Learning is a leading provider of customized learning solutions with office locations around the globe, including Singapore, the United Kingdom, Australia, Mexico, Brazil, and Japan. Locate your local office at: **international.cengage.com/global**

Cengage Learning products are represented in Canada by Nelson Education, Ltd.

To learn more about Cengage Learning, visit **www.cengage.com**

Purchase any of our products at your local college store or at our preferred online store **www.cengagebrain.com**

Printed in the United States of America
2 3 4 5 6 7 8 9 17 16 15 14 13

Brief Contents

© iStockphoto.com/track5

Supri Suharjoto/Shutterstock.com

Andresr/Shutterstock.com; Used with permission from Microsoft Corporation

jannoon028/Shutterstock.com

Pressmaster/Shutterstock.com

WORD 2013

Monkey Business Images/Shutterstock.com

EXCEL 2013

Dmitriy Shironosov/Shutterstock.com

ACCESS 2013

mitya73/Shutterstock.com

POWERPOINT 2013

Clara/Shutterstock.com

INTEGRATION

INDEX 750

Table of Contents

Andresr/Shutterstock.com

Shutterstock 58277284

Networks and the Internet

4 Computer Networks 106

5 Introducing the Internet and Email 138

6 Computer, Network, and Internet Security and Privacy 162

Tom Wang/Shutterstock.com

Courtesy of Citrix Online

WINDOWS 8

7 Exploring Windows 8 and Managing Files 196

Spectral-Design/Shutterstock.com

BROWSERS AND EMAIL

8 Using Internet Explorer and the Mail and People Apps 238

AlexAranda/Shutterstock.com

EXCEL 2013

13 Creating a Workbook 422

silver-john/Shutterstock.com

14 Working with Formulas and Functions 454

Cybrain/Shutterstock.com

15 Creating an Advanced Workbook 492

Falconia/Shutterstock.com

16 Inserting and Formatting Charts 520

ACCESS 2013

17 Creating a Database 556

18 Maintaining and Querying a Database 590

19 Creating Forms and Reports 620

POWERPOINT 2013

20 Creating a Presentation 646

Goal !?!

viviamo/Shutterstock.com

21 Enhancing a Presentation 682

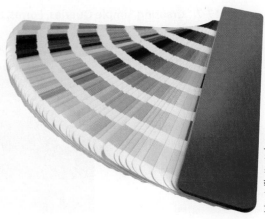

joingate/Shutterstock.com

iofoto/Shutterstock.com

Introduction to Computers and the Internet

© iStockphoto.com/track5

Computers and other forms of technology impact your daily life in many ways. You encounter computers in stores, restaurants, and other retail establishments. You probably use computers and the Internet regularly to obtain information, find entertainment, buy products and services, and communicate with others. You might carry a mobile phone or another mobile device at all times so you can remain in touch with others and access Internet information as you need it. You might even use these portable devices to pay for purchases, play online games with others, watch TV and movies, and much, much more.

Businesses also use computers extensively, such as to maintain employee and customer records, manage inventories, maintain online stores and other Web sites, process sales, control robots and other machines in factories, and provide executives with the up-to-date information they need to make decisions. The government uses computers to support the nation's defense systems, for space exploration, for storing and organizing vital information about citizens, for law enforcement and military purposes, and other important tasks. In short, computers and computing technology are used in an endless number of ways.

Learning Objectives

After studying the material in this chapter, you will be able to:

1-1 Explain what computers do

1-2 Identify types of computers

1-3 Describe computer networks and the Internet

1-4 Understand how computers impact society

1-1 What Is a Computer?

A **computer** is a programmable, electronic device that accepts data, performs operations on that data, presents the results, and stores the data or results as needed. The fact that a computer is programmable means that a computer will do whatever the instructions tell it to do. The programs used with a computer determine the tasks the computer is able to perform.

1-1a Primary Operations of a Computer

The four primary operations of a computer are referred to as input, processing, output, and storage. These operations can be defined as follows:

▶ **Input**—entering data into the computer

▶ **Processing**—performing operations on the data

▶ **Output**—presenting the results

▶ **Storage**—saving data, programs, or output for future use

The progression of input, processing, output, and storage is sometimes called the IPOS cycle or the information processing cycle.

For a computer that has been programmed to add two numbers, as shown in Exhibit 1-1, input occurs when data (in this example, the numbers 2 and 5) is entered into the computer, processing takes place when the computer program adds those two numbers, and output happens when the sum of 7 is displayed on the computer screen. The storage operation occurs any time the data, a change to a program, or the output is saved for future use.

Another example of a computer is a supermarket barcode reader. First, the grocery item being purchased is passed over the barcode reader—input. Next, the description and price of the item are looked up—processing. Then, the item description and price are displayed on the cash register and printed on the receipt—output. Finally, the inventory, ordering, and sales records are updated—storage.

Today's computers also typically perform communications functions, such as sending or retrieving data via the Internet, accessing information located in a shared company database, or exchanging email messages. Therefore, **communications**—technically an input or output operation, depending on which direction the information is going—is considered the fifth primary computer operation.

> A user inputs raw data into a computer; the computer processes, or modifies, it into meaningful information.

1-1b Data vs. Information

Raw, unorganized facts are called **data**. A user inputs data into a computer, and then the computer processes it. When **data** is modified, or **processed**, into a meaningful form, it becomes **information**. Information is frequently generated to answer some type of question, such as how many of a restaurant's employees work fewer than 20 hours per week, how many seats are available on a particular flight from Los Angeles to San Francisco, or what is Hank Aaron's lifetime home run total.

Of course, you don't need a computer system to process data into information. For example, anyone can go through time cards or employee files and

---

computer A programmable, electronic device that accepts data input, performs processing operations on that data, and outputs and stores the results.

input The process of entering data into a computer; can also refer to the data itself.

processing Performing operations on data that has been input into a computer to convert that input to output.

output The process of presenting the results of processing; can also refer to the results themselves.

storage The operation of saving data, programs, or output for future use.

communications The transmission of data from one device to another.

data Raw, unorganized facts.

process To modify data.

information Data that has been processed into a meaningful form.

Exhibit 1-1 Information processing cycle

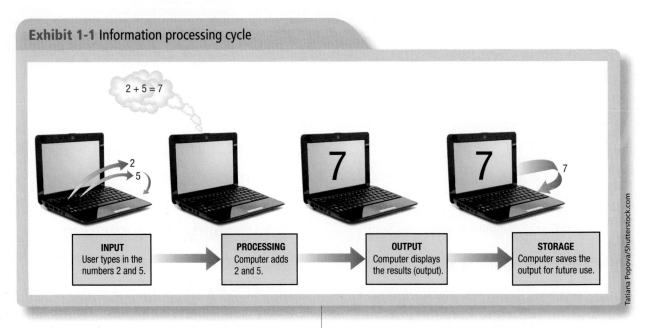

INPUT	PROCESSING	OUTPUT	STORAGE
User types in the numbers 2 and 5.	Computer adds 2 and 5.	Computer displays the results (output).	Computer saves the output for future use.

Tatiana Popova/Shutterstock.com

make a list of people who work a certain number of hours. This work could take a lot of time when done by hand, especially for a company with many employees. Computers, however, can perform such tasks almost instantly, with accurate results. Information processing (the conversion of data into information) is a vital activity today for all computer users, as well as for businesses and other organizations.

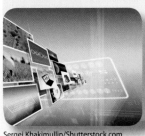
hardware The physical parts of a computer.

software Programs or instructions used to tell the computer what to do to accomplish tasks.

end user A person who uses a computer to perform tasks or obtain information.

programmer A computer professional who writes the programs that computers use.

1-1c Hardware and Software

The physical parts of a computer (the parts you can touch) are called **hardware**. Hardware components can be internal (located inside the computer) or external (located outside the computer and connected to the computer via a wired or wireless connection). Exhibit 1-2 illustrates typical computer hardware.

The term **software** refers to the programs or instructions used to tell the computer hardware what to do and to allow people to use a computer to perform specific tasks, such as creating letters, preparing budgets, managing inventory and customer databases, playing games, watching videos, listening to music, scheduling appointments, editing digital photographs, designing homes, viewing Web pages, burning DVDs, and exchanging email. In Exhibit 1-2, the software being used allows you to look at information on the Internet.

1-1d Computer Users and Professionals

Computer users, often called **end users**, are the people who use computers to perform tasks or obtain information. This includes an accountant electronically preparing a client's taxes, an office worker using a word processing program to create a letter, a supervisor using a computer to check whether manufacturing workers have met the day's quotas, a parent emailing his or her child's teacher, a college student researching a topic online, a child playing a computer game, and a person shopping.

Programmers, on the other hand, are computer professionals who write the programs that computers use.

Exhibit 1-2 Typical computer hardware and software

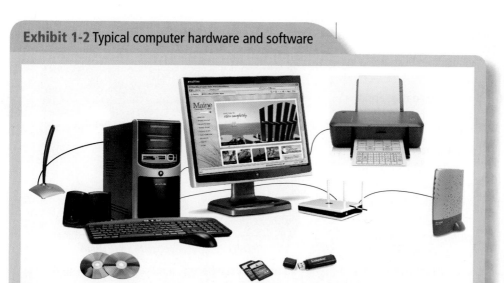

Exhibit 1-2 Typical computer hardware and software

Courtesy of Gateway, Inc.; Courtesy, Hewlett-Packard Company; Courtesy of Logitech; Courtesy D-Link Systems; Courtesy of Kingston Technology Company, Inc.; Nomad_Soul/Shutterstock.com; © 2014 Cengage Learning

Other computer professionals include systems analysts, who design computer systems to be used within their companies; computer operations personnel, who are responsible for the day-to-day computer operations at a company, such as maintaining systems or troubleshooting user-related problems; and security specialists, who are responsible for securing the company computers and networks against hackers and other intruders.

1-2 Types of Computers

The types of computers available today vary from the tiny computers embedded in consumer products, to the pocket-sized mobile devices that do a limited number of computing tasks, to the powerful and versatile computers found in homes and businesses, to the superpowerful computers used to control the country's defense systems. Computers are generally classified by category, based on size, capability, and price.

> Computers are classified by size, capability, and price.

1-2a Embedded Computers

An **embedded computer** is a tiny computer embedded into a product designed to perform specific tasks or functions for that product. For example, computers are often embedded into household appliances, such as dishwashers, microwaves, ovens, and coffee makers, as well as into other everyday objects, such as thermostats, answering machines, treadmills, sewing machines, DVD players, and televisions, to help those appliances and objects perform their designated tasks. Cars also use many embedded computers to assist with diagnostics, to notify the user of important conditions (such as an underinflated tire or an oil filter that needs changing), to facilitate the car's navigational or entertainment systems, to help the driver perform tasks, and to control the use of the airbag and other safety devices, such as cameras that alert a driver that a vehicle is in his or her blind spot, as shown in Exhibit 1-3. Because embedded computers are designed for specific tasks and specific products, they cannot be used as general-purpose computers.

Exhibit 1-3 Embedded computer in a car

A camera located under the mirror detects moving vehicles in the driver's blind spot.

A light indicates that a moving vehicle is in the driver's blind spot.

Courtesy Volvo Cars of North America

embedded computer A tiny computer embedded in a product and designed to perform specific tasks or functions for that product.

Cloud Computing

In general, **cloud computing** refers to data, applications, and even resources stored on computers that users access over the Internet—in a "cloud" of computers—rather than on users' computers, and they access only what they need when they need it. This type of network has been used for several years to create the supercomputer-level power needed for research and other power-hungry applications, but it was more typically referred to as *grid computing* in this context. Today, cloud computing typically refers to accessing Web-based applications and data using a personal computer, mobile phone, or any other Internet-enabled device (see the accompanying illustration). Although many of today's cloud applications (such as Google Apps, Windows Live, Facebook, and YouTube) are consumer-oriented, other cloud applications (such as computing power or storage space available on demand, and online sales or service applications) are designed specifically for businesses. Businesses often use applications available in the *public cloud*; they also frequently create a *private cloud* just for data and applications belonging to their company.

The biggest advantages of cloud computing include the ability to access data from anywhere the user has access to an active Internet connection and, because data is stored online instead of on the device being used, the data is safe if the device is lost, stolen, or damaged.

Tablet computer accessing the cloud

In addition, Web-based applications are often less expensive than installed software. Disadvantages of cloud computing include a possible reduction in performance of applications if they run more slowly via the cloud than they would run installed locally, and the potentially high expense related to data transfer for companies and individuals using high-bandwidth applications. There are also security concerns about how safe the stored online data is from unauthorized access and data loss.

Despite the potential risks, many people believe that cloud computing is the wave of the future and will consist of millions of computers located in data centers around the world that are connected via the Internet. They also view cloud computing as a way to enable all of an individual's devices to stay synchronized, allowing an individual to work with his or her data and applications on a continual basis.

1-2b Mobile Devices

A **mobile device** is loosely defined as a very small device, typically pocket-sized, that has built-in computing or Internet capability. Mobile devices are commonly used to make telephone calls, send text messages, view Web pages, take digital photos, play games, download and play music, watch TV shows, and access calendars and other personal productivity features. Most mobile phones today include computing and Internet capabilities; these phones, such as the one in Exhibit 1-4, are called smartphones. Small tablet devices designed for Web browsing, playing movies and other multimedia content, gaming, and similar activities are also typically considered mobile devices. Handheld gaming devices, such as the Nintendo 3DS, and portable digital media players, such as the iPod touch,

Exhibit 1-4 Smartphone

that include Internet capabilities can also be referred to as mobile devices, though they have fewer overall capabilities

cloud computing To use data, applications, and resources stored on computers accessed over the Internet rather than on users' computers.

mobile device A very small device with built-in computing or Internet capability.

than conventional mobile devices. Mobile devices are almost always powered by a rechargeable battery system.

Mobile devices tend to have small screens and keyboards. Because of this, mobile devices are more appropriate for individuals who want continual access to email; timely Web content such as breaking news, weather forecasts, driving directions, and updates from Web sites like Facebook; and music collections than for those individuals wanting general Web browsing and computing capabilities. This is beginning to change, however, as mobile devices continue to grow in capabilities, wireless communications continue to become faster, and as mobile input options, such as voice and touch input, continue to improve. For instance, some mobile devices can perform Internet searches and other tasks via voice commands, some can be used to pay for purchases while you are on the go, many can view virtually any Web content, and many can view and edit documents stored in a common format, such as Microsoft Office documents.

> PC usually refers to a personal computer that uses Microsoft Windows.

1-2c Personal Computers (PCs)

A **personal computer** (**PC**) is a small computer designed to be used by one person at a time. Personal computers are widely used by individuals and businesses today.

Conventional personal computers that are designed to fit on or next to a desk, as shown in Exhibit 1-5, are often referred to as **desktop computers**. Desktop computers can be housed in different types of cases. A tower case is a system unit designed to sit vertically, typically on the floor. A desktop case is designed to be placed horizontally on a desk's surface. An all-in-one case incorporates the monitor and system unit into a single piece of hardware.

Desktop computers usually conform to one of two standards or platforms: PC-compatible or Mac. PC-compatible computers evolved from the original IBM PC—the first personal computer that was widely accepted for business use. In general, PC-compatible hardware and software can be used with all brands of PC-compatible computers, such as those made by Dell, Hewlett-Packard, NEC, Acer, Lenovo, Fujitsu, and Gateway. These computers typically run the Microsoft Windows operating system. Mac computers are made by Apple, run the Mac OS operating system, and use different software than PC-compatible computers. Mac computers are traditionally the computer of choice for artists, designers, and others who require advanced graphics capabilities.

Portable computers are small personal computers that are designed to be carried around easily. This portability makes them very flexible. They can be used at home or in the office; they can also be used at school, while on vacation, at off-site meetings, and at other locations. Portable computers are essential for many workers, such as salespeople who make presentations or take orders from clients off-site, agents who collect data at remote locations, and managers who need computing and communications resources as they travel. They are also often the computer of choice for students and for individuals buying a new home computer.

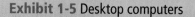

Exhibit 1-5 Desktop computers

PC-COMPATIBLE TOWER COMPUTER   MAC ALL-IN-ONE COMPUTER

Courtesy, Hewlett-Packard Company; © iStockphoto.com/ecxn; © iStockphoto.com/seaskylab

personal computer (**PC**) A type of computer based on a microprocessor and designed to be used by one person at a time.

desktop computer A personal computer designed to fit on or next to a desk.

portable computer A small personal computer designed to be carried around easily.

Computers Then and Now

The history of computers is often referred to in terms of generations, with each new generation characterized by a major technological development.

Precomputers and Early Computers (before approximately 1946)

Early computing devices include the abacus, the slide rule, the mechanical calculator, and Dr. Herman Hollerith's Punch Card Tabulating Machine and Sorter (shown here). This was the first electromechanical machine that could read punch cards. It was used to process the

Hollerith's Punch Card Tabulating Machine and Sorter

Courtesy IBM Corporate Archives

1890 U.S. Census data. Hollerith's company eventually became International Business Machines (IBM).

First-Generation Computers (approximately 1946–1957)

The first computers were enormous, often taking up entire rooms. First-generation computers could solve only one problem at a time because they needed to be physically rewired with cables to be

ENIAC computer

Courtesy U.S. Army

reprogrammed. Paper punch cards and tape were used for input, and output was printed on paper. Completed in 1946, ENIAC (shown here) was the world's first large-scale, general-purpose computer. UNIVAC, released in 1951, was initially built for the U.S. Census Bureau and was used to analyze votes in the 1952 U.S. presidential election. UNIVAC became the first computer to be mass produced for general commercial use.

Second-Generation Computers (approximately 1958–1963)

The second generation of computers, such as the IBM 1401 mainframe (shown here), were physically smaller, less expensive, more powerful, more energy-efficient, and more reliable than

IBM 1401 mainframe

Courtesy IBM Corporate Archives

first-generation computers. Programs and data were input on punch cards and magnetic tape, output was on punch cards and paper printouts, and magnetic tape was used for storage. Hard drives and programming languages, such as FORTRAN and COBOL, were developed and implemented during this generation.

Third-Generation Computers (approximately 1964–1970)

Integrated circuits (ICs) marked the beginning of the third generation of computers, such as the IBM System/360 mainframe (shown here). Integrated circuits incorporate many transistors and electronic circuits on a single tiny silicon chip, making

IBM Systems/360 mainframe

Courtesy IBM Corporate Archives

computers even smaller and more reliable than the earlier computers.

Fourth-Generation Computers (approximately 1971–present)

The invention of the microprocessor in 1971 ushered in the fourth generation of computers. In essence, a microprocessor contains the core processing capabilities of an entire computer on one single chip. The original IBM PC

Original IBM PC

Courtesy IBM Corporate Archives

(shown here) and Apple Macintosh computers, and most of today's modern computers, fall into this category.

Fifth-Generation Computers (Now and the Future)

Fifth-generation computers have no precise classification because experts disagree about a definition. One common opinion is that fifth-generation computers will be based on artificial intelligence, allowing them to think, reason, and learn. Voice and touch are expected to be a primary means of input, and computers may be constructed in the form of optical computers that process data using light instead of electrons, tiny computers that utilize nanotechnology, or as entire general-purpose computers built into desks, home appliances, and other everyday devices.

Exhibit 1-6 Portable computers

NOTEBOOK

TABLET

NETBOOK

Courtesy Belkin International, Inc.; © iStockphoto.com/uchar; Robert Kneschke/Shutterstock.com

Portable computers (see Exhibit 1-6) are available in the following configurations:

▶ **Notebook computers (laptop computers)**—computers that are about the size of a paper notebook and open to reveal a screen on the top half of the computer and a keyboard on the bottom. They are comparable to desktop computers in features and capabilities.

▶ **Tablet computer**—typically notebook-sized computers that are designed to be used with a digital pen, a digital stylus, or touch input. Most tablet computers are slate tablets, which are one-piece computers with a screen on top and no keyboard, such as the one shown in Exhibit 1-6. Convertible tablets use the same clamshell design as notebook computers but their top half can be rotated and folded shut so they can be used as either a notebook or a tablet computer.

▶ **Netbooks**—also called mini-notebooks, mini-laptops, and ultraportable computers; notebook computers that are smaller (a 10-inch-wide screen is common), lighter (typically less than three pounds), less expensive, and have a longer battery life than conventional notebooks. They are especially appropriate for students and business travelers. They usually do not include a CD or DVD drive, and they have a smaller keyboard than a notebook computer.

Most personal computers today are sold as stand-alone, self-sufficient units that are equipped with all the hardware and software needed to operate independently. In other words, they can perform input, processing, output, and storage without being connected to a network, although they can be networked. In contrast, a device that must be connected to a network to perform processing or storage tasks is referred to as a **dumb terminal**. Two types of personal computers that may be able to perform a limited amount of independent processing (like a desktop or notebook computer) but are designed to be used with a network (like a dumb terminal) are thin clients and Internet appliances.

A **thin client**—also called a network computer (NC)—is a device that is designed to be used with a company network. Instead of using local hard drives for storage, programs are accessed from and data is stored on a network server. A thin client might be installed in a hotel lobby to provide guests with Internet access, hotel and conference information, room-to-room calling, and free phone calls via the Internet. The main advantage of thin clients over desktop computers is lower cost because hardware needs to be replaced less frequently and because computer maintenance, power, and air-conditioning are less expensive. Additional benefits

notebook computer (laptop computer)
A portable computer that is about the size of a paper notebook that is comparable to a desktop computer in features and capabilities.

tablet computer A portable computer about the size of a notebook that is designed to be used with a digital pen, a digital stylus, or touch input.

netbook A very small notebook computer that usually does not include a CD or DVD drive.

dumb terminal A computer that must be connected to a network to perform processing or storage tasks.

thin client A device designed to access a network for processing and data storage instead of performing those tasks locally.

include increased security because data is not stored locally, and easier maintenance because all software is located on a central server. Disadvantages include having limited or no local storage and not being able to function as a stand-alone computer when the network is not working.

Network computers or other devices designed primarily for accessing the Internet and/or exchanging email are called **Internet appliances** (sometimes referred to as Internet devices or Internet displays). Some Internet appliances are designed to be located in the home. They can be built into another product, such as a refrigerator or telephone console, or they can be a stand-alone device, such as the one shown in Exhibit 1-7, that is designed to deliver news, sports scores, weather, music, and other Web-based information. Gaming consoles, such as the Nintendo Wii, the Xbox 360 shown in Exhibit 1-8, and the Sony PlayStation 3, that can be used to view Internet content in addition to their gaming abilities can be classified as Internet appliances when they are used to access the Internet. Internet capabilities are also being built into television sets, which make these Internet appliances, as well.

> Internet appliances are everywhere—built into refrigerators, gaming consoles, and even TV sets.

Exhibit 1-8 Xbox 360 gaming console

Barone Firenze/Shutterstock.com

1-2d Midrange Servers

A **midrange server** (sometimes called a **minicomputer**) is a medium-sized computer used to host programs and data for a small network. Typically larger, more powerful, and more expensive than a desktop computer, a midrange server is usually located in an out-of-the-way place and can serve many users at one time. Users connect to the server through a network, using their desktop computer, portable computer, thin client, or dumb terminal consisting of just a monitor and keyboard (see Exhibit 1-9). Midrange servers are often used in small- to medium-sized businesses such as medical or dental offices, as well as in school computer labs. There are also special home servers designed for home use, which are often used to back up (make duplicate copies of) the content located on all the computers in the home and to host music, photos, movies, and other media to be shared via a home network.

One trend involving midrange servers, as well as mainframe computers (discussed next), is **virtualization**—the creation of virtual (rather than actual) versions of a computing resource. Server virtualization uses separate server environments that are physically located on the same computer but function as separate servers and do not interact with each other. For instance, all applications for an organization can be installed in virtual environments on a single physical server instead of using a separate server for each application. Using a separate server for each application wastes resources because the servers are often not used to full capacity—one estimate is that about only 10 percent of server capability is frequently utilized. With virtualization, companies can fulfill their computing needs with

Exhibit 1-7 Stand-alone Internet device

12:00 PM

epi

Courtesy of Sony Electronics, Inc.

Internet appliance A specialized network computer or device designed primarily for Internet access and/or email exchange.

midrange server (**minicomputer**) A medium-sized computer used to host programs and data for a small network.

virtualization The creation of virtual versions of a computing resource.

10   Chapter 1: Introduction to Computers and the Internet

Exhibit 1-9 Midrange server

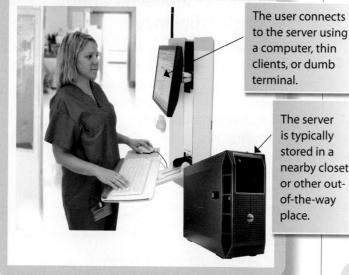

The user connects to the server using a computer, thin clients, or dumb terminal.

The server is typically stored in a nearby closet or other out-of-the-way place.

Courtesy Ergotron Inc.; Courtesy Dell Inc.

fewer servers, which results in lower costs for hardware and server management, as well as lower power and cooling costs. Consequently, one of the most significant appeals of server virtualization today is increased efficiency.

1-2e Mainframe Computers

A **mainframe computer**, such as the one shown in Exhibit 1-10, is a powerful computer used in many large organizations that need to manage large amounts

Exhibit 1-10 Mainframe computer

Courtesy of IBM Corporation

of centralized data. Larger, more expensive, and more powerful than midrange servers, mainframes can serve thousands of users connected to the mainframe via personal computers, thin clients, or dumb terminals in a manner similar to the way users connect to midrange servers. Mainframe computers are typically located in climate-controlled data centers and connect to the rest of the company computers via a computer network. During regular business hours, a mainframe runs the programs needed to meet the different needs of its wide variety of users. At night, it commonly performs large processing tasks, such as payroll and billing. Today's mainframes are sometimes referred to as high-end servers or enterprise-class servers.

1-2f Supercomputers

Some applications require extraordinary speed, accuracy, and processing capabilities—for example, sending astronauts into space, controlling missile guidance systems and satellites, forecasting the weather, exploring for oil, breaking codes, and designing and testing new products. **Supercomputers**—the most powerful and most expensive type of computer available—were developed to fill this need. Some relatively new supercomputing applications include hosting extremely complex Web

mainframe computer A powerful computer used in large organizations to manage large amounts of centralized data and run multiple programs simultaneously.

supercomputer The fastest, most expensive, and most powerful type of computer.

sites, such as search sites and social networks, and three-dimensional applications, such as 3D medical imaging, 3D image projections, and 3D architectural modeling. Unlike mainframe computers, which typically run multiple applications simultaneously to serve a wide variety of users, supercomputers generally run one program at a time as fast as possible.

Conventional supercomputers can cost several million dollars each. To reduce the cost, supercomputers are often built by connecting hundreds of smaller and less expensive computers (increasingly midrange servers) into a **supercomputing cluster** that acts as a single supercomputer. The computers in the cluster usually contain multiple processors and are dedicated to processing cluster applications. For example, the Tianhe-1A supercomputer, which is shown in Exhibit 1-11, contains 14,336 processors and is one of the fastest computers in the world. This supercomputing cluster is installed at China's National Lab Supercomputer Center in Tianjin and is used for a variety of research applications, including petroleum exploration, medical research, and simulation of large aircraft design. At 2.57 petaflops (quadrillions of floating point operations per second). Tianhe-1A is one of the fastest computers in the world. A new IBM supercomputer named Sequoia that is currently under development for the Lawrence Livermore National Laboratory is expected to use approximately 1.6 million processors and perform at 20 petaflops.

Exhibit 1-11 Supercomputer

Courtesy of NVIDIA

supercomputing cluster A group of numerous smaller computers connected together to act as a single supercomputer.

network Computers and other devices that are connected to share hardware, software, and data.

1-3 Computer Networks and the Internet

A **network** is a collection of computers and other devices that are connected to enable users to share hardware, software, and data, as well as to communicate electronically. Computer networks exist in many sizes and types. For instance, home networks are commonly used to allow home computers to share a single printer and Internet connection, as well as to exchange files. Small office networks enable workers to access company records stored on a network server, communicate with other employees, share a high-speed printer, and access the Internet, as shown in Exhibit 1-12. School networks allow students and teachers to access the Internet and school resources, and large corporate networks often connect all of the offices or retail stores in the corporation, creating a network that spans several cities or states. Public wireless networks, such as those available at some coffeehouses, restaurants, public libraries, and parks, provide Internet access to individuals via their portable computers and mobile devices. Mobile telephone networks provide Internet access and communications capabilities to smartphone users.

Exhibit 1-12 Example of a computer network

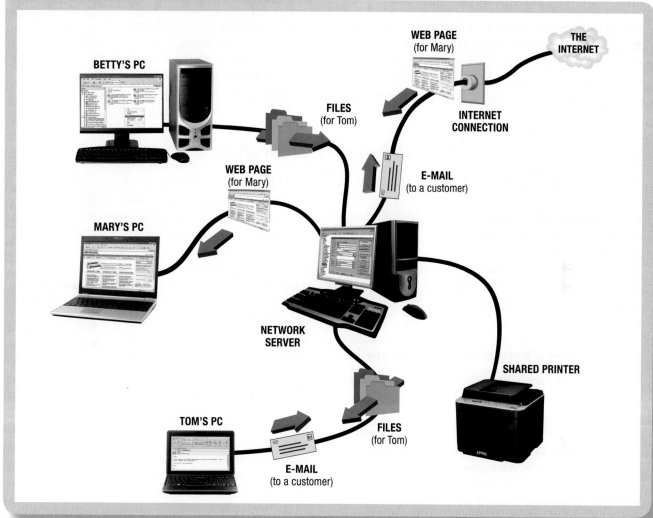

BETTY'S PC

WEB PAGE
(for Mary)

THE INTERNET

FILES
(for Tom)

INTERNET CONNECTION

WEB PAGE
(for Mary)

E-MAIL
(to a customer)

MARY'S PC

NETWORK SERVER

SHARED PRINTER

TOM'S PC

FILES
(for Tom)

E-MAIL
(to a customer)

1-3a The Internet and the World Wide Web

The **Internet**, the largest and most well-known computer network in the world, is technically a network of networks because it consists of thousands of networks that can access each other. Individual users connect to the Internet by connecting their computers or other devices to servers belonging to an **Internet service provider** (**ISP**)—a company that provides Internet access. ISPs—which include conventional and mobile telephone companies like AT&T, Verizon, and Sprint; cable providers like Comcast and Time Warner; and stand-alone ISPs like NetZero and EarthLink—function as onramps to the Internet, providing Internet access to their subscribers. ISP servers are continually connected to a larger network, called a regional network, which, in turn, is connected to one of the major high-speed networks within a country, called a backbone network.

Backbone networks within a country are connected to each other and to backbone networks in other countries, forming the Internet.

While the term *Internet* refers to the physical structure of that network, the **World Wide Web** (**Web** or **WWW**) refers to one resource—a collection of documents called **Web pages**—available through the Internet. A group of

> **Internet** The largest and most well-known computer network, linking millions of computers all over the world.
>
> **Internet service provider** (**ISP**) A business or other organization that provides Internet access to others, usually for a fee.
>
> **World Wide Web** (**Web** or **WWW**) The collection of Web pages available through the Internet.
>
> **Web page** A document located on a Web server.

Web pages belonging to one individual or company is called a **Web site**. Web pages are stored on computers called **Web servers** that are continually connected to the Internet; they can be accessed at any time by anyone with a computer or other Web-enabled device and an Internet connection. A wide variety of information is available via Web pages, such as company and product information, government forms and publications, maps, telephone directories, news, weather, sports results, airline schedules, and much, much more. You can also use Web pages to shop and perform other types of online financial transactions; access social networks like Facebook and MySpace; and listen to music, play games, watch television shows, and perform other entertainment-oriented activities (see Exhibit 1-13). Web pages are viewed using a **Web browser**, such as Internet Explorer (IE), Chrome, Safari, Opera, or Firefox.

> A wide variety of information is available via Web pages.

1-3b Accessing a Network or the Internet

To access a local computer network, you need to use a network adapter, either built into your computer or attached to it, to connect your computer to the network. With some computer networks you need to supply information, such as a username and a password, to connect to the network. After you are connected to the network, you can access network resources, including the network's Internet connection. If you are connecting to the Internet without going through a computer network, your computer needs to use a modem to connect to the communications media, such as a telephone line, a cable connection, or a wireless signal, used by your ISP to deliver Internet content.

Web site A collection of related Web pages.

Web server A computer continually connected to the Internet that stores Web pages accessible through the Internet.

Web browser A program used to view Web pages.

Internet address A unique address that identifies a computer, person, or Web page on the Internet, such as an IP address, a domain name, a URL, or an email address.

IP address A numeric Internet address used to uniquely identify a computer on the Internet.

domain name A text-based Internet address used to uniquely identify a computer on the Internet.

To request a Web page or other resource located on the Internet, its **Internet address**—a unique numeric or text-based address—is used. The most common types of Internet addresses are IP addresses and domain names (to identify computers), URLs (to identify Web pages), and email addresses (to identify people).

IP addresses and their corresponding **domain names** are used to identify computers available through the Internet. IP (short for Internet Protocol) addresses are numeric, such as 207.46.197.32, and are commonly used by computers to refer to other computers. A computer that hosts information available through the Internet, such as a Web server hosting Web pages, usually has a unique text-based domain name, such as microsoft.com, that corresponds to that computer's IP address to make it easier for people to request Web pages located on that computer.

IP addresses and domain names are unique; that is, no two computers on the Internet use the exact same IP address or the exact same domain name. To ensure this, specific IP addresses are allocated to each network, such as a company network or an ISP, to be used with the computers on that network. There is a worldwide registration system for domain name registration. When a domain name is registered, the IP address of the computer that will be hosting the Web site associated with that domain name is also registered. The Web site can be accessed using either its domain name or the corresponding IP address.

LEARN MORE

IPv6

IPv4 was never designed to be used with the billions of devices that access the Internet today. Because the maximum number of IPv4 unique addresses—2^{32}—are expected to run out soon, a newer version of IP—IPv6—was developed. IPv6 allows for 2^{128} unique addresses. Although IPv4 and IPv6 are expected to coexist for several years until IPv6 eventually replaces IPv4, the U.S. government has mandated that all federal agencies be capable of switching to IPv6 and to purchase only IPv6-compatible new hardware and software. Experts suggest that businesses perform a network audit to determine what hardware and software changes will be needed to switch to IPv6 so that the business is prepared when the change is deemed necessary.

Exhibit 1-13 Examples of common Web activities

ACCESSING PRODUCT INFORMATION

LOOKING UP REFERENCE INFORMATION

READING NEWS

SHOPPING

ACCESSING SOCIAL NETWORKS

WATCHING TV SHOWS AND MOVIES

When a Web site is requested by its domain name, the corresponding IP address is looked up using one of the Internet's domain name system (DNS) servers, and then the appropriate Web page is displayed.

Although most IP addresses (called IPv4) have four parts separated by periods, the newer IPv6 addresses have six parts separated by colons. The transition fromIPv4 to IPv6 is necessary because of the vast number of devices now connecting to the Internet.

Domain names typically reflect the name of the individual or organization associated with that Web site. The different parts of a domain name are separated by a period. The far right part of the domain name (which begins with the rightmost period) is called the top-level domain (TLD) and traditionally identifies the type of organization or its location, such as .com for businesses, .edu for educational institutions, .jp for Web sites located in Japan, or .fr for Web sites located in France. The part of the domain name that precedes the TLD is called the second-level domain name and typically reflects the

name of a company or an organization, a product, or an individual. Only the legitimate holder of a trademarked name, such as Microsoft, can use that trademarked name as a domain name, such as microsoft.com. There were seven original TLDs used in the United States; additional TLDs and numerous two-letter country code TLDs have since been created. See Exhibit 1-14 for some examples.

Similar to the way an IP address or domain name uniquely identifies a computer on the Internet, a **Uniform Resource Locator** (**URL**) uniquely identifies a Web page by specifying the protocol—or standard—being used to display the Web page, the Web server hosting the Web page, the name of any folders on the Web server in which the Web page file is stored, and, finally, the Web page's file name, if needed.

Kaspri/Shutterstock.com

Uniform Resource Locator (URL) Uniform Resource Locator (URL) An Internet address that uniquely identifies a Web page.

Exhibit 1-14 Sample top-level domains (TLDs)

Original TLDs	Intended use
.com	Commercial businesses
.edu	Educational institutions
.gov	Government organizations
.int	International treaty organizations
.mil	Military organizations
.net	Network providers and ISPs
.org	Noncommercial organizations
Newer TLDs	**Intended use**
.aero	Aviation industry
.biz	Businesses
.fr	French businesses
.info	Resource sites
.jobs	Employment sites
.mobi	Sites optimized for mobile devices
.name	Individuals
.pro	Licensed professionals
.uk	United Kingdom businesses

The most common Web page protocols are Hypertext Transfer Protocol (http://) for regular Web pages or Hypertext Transfer Protocol Secure (https://) for secure Web pages that can be used to transmit sensitive information safely, such as credit card numbers. File Transfer Protocol (ftp://) is sometimes used to upload and download files. The file extension used in the Web page file name, such as .html or .htm for standard Web pages, indicates the type of Web page that will be displayed. For example, looking at the URL for the Web page shown in Exhibit 1-15 from right to left, you can see that the Web page called *index.html* is stored in a folder called *working-with-us* inside another folder called *careers* on the Web server associated with the *cengage.com* domain, and is a regular (nonsecure) Web page because the standard *http://* protocol is being used.

1-3c Using Email

Email is the process of exchanging messages between computers over a network—usually the Internet. Email is one of the most widely used Internet applications—Americans alone send billions of email messages daily—and email sent via a mobile device is growing at an astounding rate. You can send an email message from any Internet-enabled device, such as a desktop computer, portable computer, or mobile device, to anyone who has an Internet email address.

To contact someone using the Internet, you most often use his or her **email address**. An email address consists of a **username** (a unique identifying name), followed by the @ symbol, followed by the domain name for the computer that will be handling that person's email (called a mail server). For example, jsmith@cengage.com is the email address assigned to John Smith, a hypothetical employee at Cengage Learning, the publisher of this textbook.

1-3d Surfing the Web

Once you have an Internet connection, you are ready to begin **surfing the Web**—that is, using a Web browser to

Exhibit 1-15 URL for a Web page

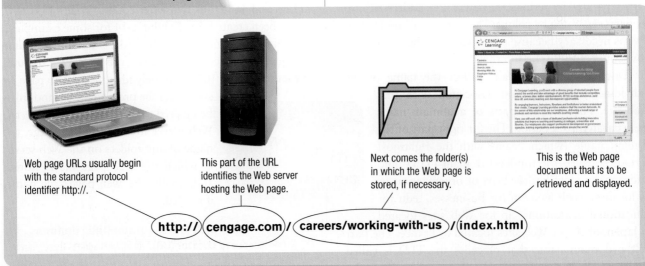

Web page URLs usually begin with the standard protocol identifier http://.

This part of the URL identifies the Web server hosting the Web page.

Next comes the folder(s) in which the Web page is stored, if necessary.

This is the Web page document that is to be retrieved and displayed.

http:// cengage.com / careers/working-with-us / index.html

Exhibit 1-16 Web page open in the Chrome Web browser

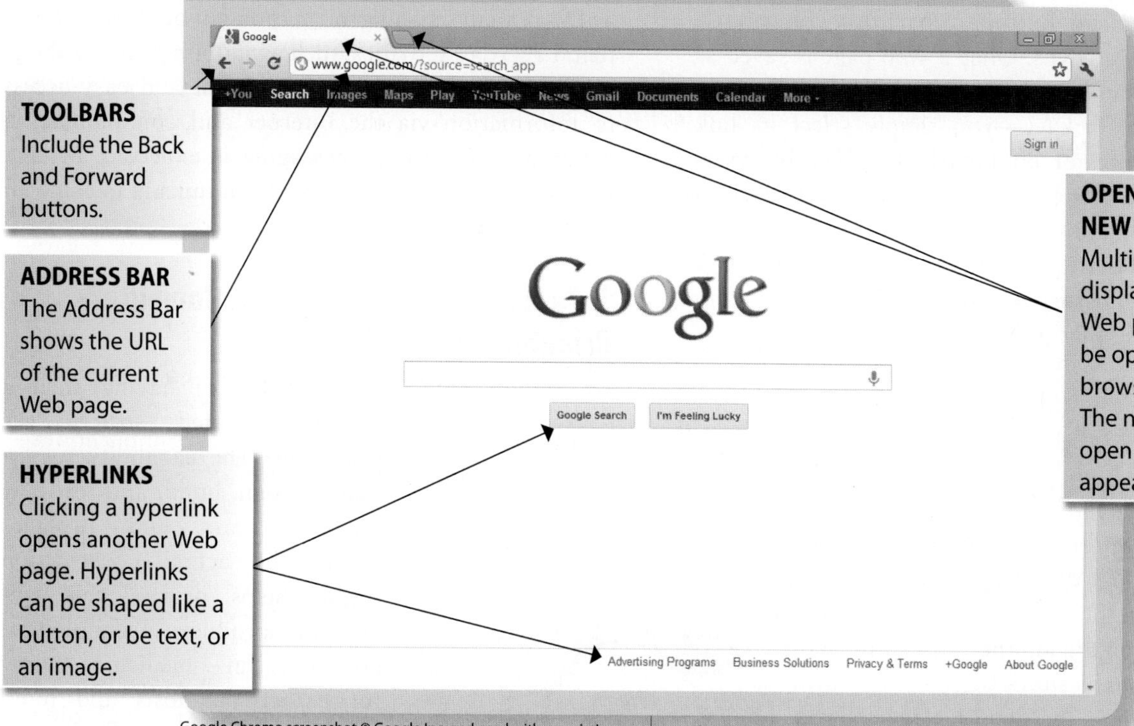

TOOLBARS
Include the Back and Forward buttons.

ADDRESS BAR
The Address Bar shows the URL of the current Web page.

HYPERLINKS
Clicking a hyperlink opens another Web page. Hyperlinks can be shaped like a button, or be text, or an image.

OPEN TAB AND NEW TAB BUTTON
Multiple tabs displaying different Web pages can be open in one browser window. The name of the open Web page appears in the tab.

Google Chrome screenshot © Google Inc. and used with permission.

view Web pages. The first page that your Web browser displays when it is opened is your browser's starting page, or home page. From your browser's home page, you can move to other Web pages.

FYI

Pronouncing Internet Addresses

Because Internet addresses are frequently given verbally, it is important to know how to pronounce them. Keep in mind the following tips when you say an Internet address:

▶ If a portion of the address forms a recognizable word or name, it is spoken; otherwise, it is spelled out.

▶ The @ sign is pronounced *at*.

▶ The period (.) is pronounced *dot*.

▶ The forward slash (/) is pronounced *slash*.

Type of address	Sample address	Pronunciation
Domain name	berkeley.edu	berkeley dot e d u
URL	microsoft.com/windows /ie/default.asp	microsoft dot com slash windows slash i e slash default dot a s p
Email address	president@whitehouse.gov	president at white house dot gov

To navigate to a new Web page for which you know the URL, type that URL in the browser's Address bar, as shown in Exhibit 1-16, and then press the Enter key. After that page is displayed, you can use the hyperlinks—graphics or text linked to other Web pages—on that page to display other Web pages.

The most commonly used Web browsers include Internet Explorer, Chrome (shown in Exhibit 1-16), Safari, and Firefox. Most browsers include tabbed browsing so you can open multiple Web pages at the same time, the ability to search for Web pages using the Address bar, and tools for bookmarking and revisiting Web pages.

email Messages sent from one user to another over the Internet or other network.

email address An Internet address consisting of a username and computer domain name that uniquely identifies a person on the Internet.

username A name that uniquely identifies a user on a specific computer network.

surf the Web To use a Web browser to view Web pages.

All Web browsers have a feature (usually called Favorites or Bookmarks that is accessed via a Favorites or Bookmarks menu, button, or bar) that you can use to save Web page URLs. Once a Web page is saved as a favorite or a bookmark, you can redisplay that page without typing its URL—you simply select its link from the Favorites or Bookmarks list. Web browsers also maintain a History list, which is a record of all Web pages visited during the period of time specified in the browser settings. You can revisit a Web page located on the History list by displaying the History list and selecting that page.

FYI

Searching the Web

Many people turn to the Web to find specific information. Special Web pages, called search sites, are available to help you locate what you are looking for on the Internet. One of the most popular search sites—Google—is shown in Exhibit 1-16. To conduct a search, you type one or more keywords into the search box on a search site, and a list of links to Web pages matching your search criteria is displayed. Also, numerous reference sites are available on the Web to look up addresses, phone numbers, ZIP codes, maps, and other information. To find a reference site, type the information you are looking for (such as "ZIP code lookup" or "topographical maps") in a search site's search box to see links to sites with that information.

1-4 Computers and Society

The vast improvements in technology over the past decade have had a distinct impact on daily life. Computers have become indispensable tools at home and work. Related technological advancements have changed the way everyday items—cars, microwaves, coffee pots, toys, exercise bikes, telephones, televisions, and more—look and function. As computers and everyday devices become smarter, they work faster, better, and more reliably than ever before, as well as take on additional capabilities. Computerization and technological advances have also changed society as a whole. Without computers, banks would be overwhelmed by the job of tracking all the transactions they process,

moon exploration and the space shuttle would still belong to science fiction, and scientific advances such as DNA analysis and gene mapping would be nonexistent. Everyday activities, such as shopping and banking, are increasingly automated, and fast and easy access to information via the Internet and communication via email and instant messaging is expected. In fact, the Internet and its resources have quickly become an integral part of our society.

1-4a Benefits and Risks of a Computer-Oriented Society

The benefits of having such a computer-oriented society are numerous. The capability to virtually design, build, and test new buildings, cars, and airplanes before the actual construction begins helps professionals create safer products. Technological advances in medicine allow for earlier diagnosis and more effective treatment of diseases than ever before. The ability to shop, pay bills, research products, participate in online courses, and look up vast amounts of information 24 hours a day, 7 days a week, 365 days a year via the Internet is a huge convenience. In addition, a computer-oriented society generates new opportunities. For example, technologies, such as speech recognition software and Braille input and output devices, enable physically or visually challenged individuals to perform necessary job tasks and to communicate with others more easily.

Technology has also made a huge number of tasks in our lives go much faster. Instead of experiencing a long delay for a credit check, an applicant can get approved for a purchase, loan, or credit card almost immediately. Documents and photographs can be emailed or faxed in moments, instead of taking at least a day to be mailed physically. Viewers can watch favorite TV shows online and access up-to-the-minute news at their convenience. And we can download information, programs, music, files, movies, and more on demand when we want or need them, instead of having to order them and then wait for delivery or go to a physical store to purchase the items.

Although there are a great number of benefits from having a computer-oriented society, there are risks as well. A variety of problems have emerged from our extensive computer use, ranging from stress and health concerns, to the proliferation of unsolicited emails and harmful programs that can be installed on our computers without our knowledge, to security and privacy issues, to legal and ethical dilemmas. Many security and privacy concerns stem from the fact that so much personal business takes place online—or at least ends up as data in a computer database somewhere—and the potential for misuse of this data is enormous.

> Data about our activities is stored on computers accessible via the Internet, putting privacy at risk.

Another concern is the repercussions of collecting such vast amounts of information electronically. Some people worry about creating a "Big Brother" situation, in which the government or another organization is watching everything that we do. And some Internet behavior, such as downloading music or movies from an unauthorized source or viewing pornography on an office computer, can get you arrested or fired.

Some people view the potential risk to personal privacy as one of the most important societal issues. As more and more data about our everyday activities is collected and stored on computers accessible via the Internet, our privacy is at risk because the potential for privacy violations increases. Today, data is collected about practically anything we buy online or offline, although offline purchases may not be associated with our identity unless we use a credit card or a membership or loyalty card. The issue is not that data is collected—with virtually all organizations using computers for recordkeeping, that is unavoidable—but how the collected data is used and how secure it is. Data collected by businesses may be used only by that company or shared with others. Data shared with others often results in spam—unsolicited emails. Spam is an enormous problem for individuals and businesses today, and it is considered by many to be a violation of personal privacy.

1-4b Understanding Intellectual Property Rights

All computer users should be aware of **intellectual property rights**, which are the legal rights to which the creators of intellectual property—original creative works—are entitled. Examples of intellectual property include music and movies; paintings, computer graphics, and other works of art; poetry, books, and other types of written works; symbols, names, and designs used in conjunction with a business; architectural drawings; and inventions. The three main types of intellectual property rights are copyrights, trademarks, and patents.

A **copyright** is a form of protection available to the creator of an original artistic, musical, or literary work, such as a book, movie, software program, musical composition, or painting. It gives the copyright holder the exclusive right to publish, reproduce, distribute, perform, or display the work. Immediately after creating a work, the creator automatically owns the copyright of that work. Copyrights apply to both published and unpublished works and remain in effect until 70 years after the creator's death. Copyrights for

CAUTION

Protecting Your Computer

To help protect your computer, never open an email attachment from someone you do not know or that has an executable file extension (the last three letters in the file name preceded by a period), such as .exe, .com, or .vbs, without first checking with the sender to make sure the attachment is legitimate. You should never click a link in an email message. You should also be careful about what files you download from the Internet. In addition, it is crucial to install security software on your computer and to set up the program to monitor your computer on a continual basis and detect or block any harmful programs.

intellectual property rights The legal rights to which creators of original creative works are entitled.

copyright The legal right to sell, publish, or distribute an original artistic or literary work; it is held by the creator of a work as soon as it exists in physical form.

Protecting Digital Content

To protect their rights, some creators of digital content (such as art, music, photographs, and movies) use **digital watermarks**—a subtle alteration of digital content that is not noticeable when the work is viewed or played but that identifies the copyright holder. For instance, the digital watermark for an image might consist of slight changes to the brightness of a specific small portion of the image that are imperceptible to people but are easily read by software. Digital watermarks can be added to images, music, video, TV shows, ebooks, and other digital content. The purpose of digital watermarking is to give digital content a unique identity that remains intact even if the work is copied, edited, compressed, or otherwise manipulated.

Another rights-protection tool used with digital content is **digital rights management (DRM) software**, which is used to control the use of a work. For instance, DRM used in conjunction with business documents (called enterprise rights management) can protect a sensitive business document by controlling usage of that document, such as by limiting who can view, print, or copy it. DRM used with digital content, such as movies, ebooks, and music, downloaded via the Internet can control whether the downloaded file can be copied to another device, as well as make a video-on-demand movie or a rented ebook unviewable after the rental period expires.

Robin Lund/Shutterstock.com

works registered by an organization or as anonymous works last 95 years from the date of publication or 120 years from the date of creation, whichever is shorter. Although works created in the United States after March 1, 1989, are not required to display a copyright notice to retain their copyright protection, displaying a copyright statement on a published work, such as the ones shown in Exhibit 1-17, reminds others that the work is protected by copyright law and that any use must comply with copyright law.

Anyone wishing to use copyrighted materials must first obtain permission from the copyright holder and pay any required fee. One exception is the legal concept of **fair use**, which permits limited duplication and use of a portion of copyrighted material for specific purposes, such as criticism, commentary, news reporting, teaching, and research. For example, a teacher may legally read a copyrighted poem for discussion in a poetry class, and a news crew may videotape a small portion of a song at a concert to include in a news report of that concert.

A **trademark** is a word, phrase, symbol, or design (or a combination of words, phrases, symbols, or designs) that identifies one product or service. A trademark used to identify a service is also called a service mark. Trademarks that are claimed but not

digital watermark A subtle alteration of digital content that identifies the copyright holder.

digital rights management (DRM) software Software used to protect and manage the rights of creators of digital content.

fair use Permits limited duplication and use of a portion of copyrighted material for specific purposes, such as criticism, commentary, news reporting, teaching, and research.

trademark A word, phrase, symbol, or design that identifies a good or service.

Exhibit 1-17 Copyright statements

© 2014 Course Technology, Cengage Learning

ALL RIGHTS RESERVED. No part of this work covered by the copyright herein may be reproduced, transmitted, stored or used in any form or by any means graphic, electronic, or mechanical, including but not limited to photocopying, recording, scanning, digitizing, taping, Web distribution, information networks, or information storage and retrieval systems, except as permitted under Section 107 or 108 of the 1976 United States Copyright Act, without the prior written permission of the publisher.

BOOK COPYRIGHT NOTICES

© 2012 Throw The Fight - All Rights Reserved.

WEB SITE COPYRIGHT NOTICES

© 2014 Cengage Learning; Courtesy Throw the Fight www.myspace.com/throwthefight, www.throwthefight.com.

Ethics

The term **ethics** refers to standards of moral conduct. For example, telling the truth is a matter of ethics. An unethical act is not always illegal, but an illegal act is usually viewed as unethical by most people. For example, purposely lying to a friend is unethical but usually not illegal, whereas perjuring oneself in a courtroom as a witness is both illegal and unethical.

Ethical beliefs can vary widely from one individual to another. Ethical beliefs can also vary based on religion, country, race, or culture. In addition, different ethical standards can apply to different areas of one's life. For example, personal ethics guide an individual's personal behavior and business ethics guide an individual's workplace behavior.

Ethics with respect to the use of computers are referred to as **computer ethics**. Computer ethics have taken on more significance in recent years because the proliferation of computers in the home and the workplace provides more opportunities for unethical acts than in the past. The Internet also makes it easy to distribute information such as computer viruses, spam, and spyware that many people would view as unethical, as well as to distribute copies of software, movies, music, and other digital content in an illegal and unethical manner.

Whether at home, at work, or at school, ethical issues crop up every day. For example, you may need to make ethical decisions such as whether to accept a relative's offer of a free copy of a downloaded song or movie, whether to have a friend help you take an online exam, whether to upload a photo of your friend to Facebook without asking permission, or whether to post a rumor on a campus gossip site.

Employees may need to decide whether to print their birthday party invitations on the office color printer, whether to correct the boss for giving them credit for another employee's idea, or whether to sneak a look at information that they can access but have no legitimate reason to view. IT employees, in particular, often face this latter ethical dilemma because they typically have both access and the technical ability to retrieve a wide variety of personal and professional information about other employees, such as their salary information, Web surfing history, and email.

Businesses also deal with a variety of ethical issues in the course of normal business activities—from determining how many computers a particular software program should be installed on, to identifying how customer and employee information should be used, to deciding business practices. **Business ethics** are the standards of conduct that guide a business's policies, decisions, and actions.

Petr Malyshev/Shutterstock.com

registered with the U.S. Patent and Trademark Office (USPTO) can use the mark™; nonregistered service marks can use the symbol℠. The symbol® is reserved for registered trademarks. Trademarked words and phrases—such as iPod®, Chicken McNuggets®, Google Docs™, and Walmart. com℠—are widely used today. Trademarked logos are also common.

Businesses and individuals should be very careful when copying,

sharing, or otherwise using copyrighted material to ensure that the material is used in both a legal and an ethical manner. Students, researchers, authors, and other writers need to be especially careful when using literary material as a resource for papers, articles, books, and so forth, to ensure the material is used appropriately and is properly credited to the original

ethics Overall standards of moral conduct.

computer ethics Standards of moral conduct as they relate to computer use.

business ethics Standards of moral conduct that guide a business's policies, decisions, and actions.

Exhibit 1-18 Examples of what is and what is not plagiarism

Plagiarism	Not plagiarism
A student including a few sentences or a few paragraps written by another author in his term paper without crediting the original author.	A student including a few sentences or a few paragraps written by another author in his term paper, either indenting the quotation or placing it inside quotation marks, and crediting the original author with a citation in the text or with a footnote or endnote.
A newspaper reporter changing a few words in a sentence or paragraph written by another author and including the revised text in an article without crediting the original author.	A newspaper reporter paraphrasing a few sentences or paragraphs written by another author without changing the meaning of the text, including the revised text in an article, and crediting the original author with a proper citiation.
A student copying and pasting information from various online documents to cretate her research paper without crediting the original authors.	A student copying and pasting information from various online documents and using those quotes in her research paper either indented or enclosed in quotation marks with the proper citations for each author.
A teacher sharing a poem with a class, leading the class to believe the poem was his original work.	A teacher sharing a poem with a class, clearly identifying the poet.

author. To present someone else's work as your own is **plagiarism**, which is a violation of copyright law and an unethical act. It can also get you fired, as some reporters have found out after faking quotes or plagiarizing content from other newspapers. Examples of acts that would normally be considered or not considered plagiaristic are shown in Exhibit 1-18.

With the widespread availability of online articles and fee-based online term paper services, some students might be tempted to create their papers by copying and pasting excerpts of online content into their documents to pass off as their original work. But these students should realize that this is plagiarism, and instructors can usually tell when a paper is created in this manner. There are also online sources instructors can use to test the originality of student papers. Most colleges and universities have strict consequences for plagiarism, such as automatically failing the assignment or course or being expelled

from the institution. As Internet-based plagiarism continues to expand to younger and younger students, many middle schools and high schools are developing strict plagiarism policies as well.

1-4c Computers and Health

Common physical conditions caused by computer use include eyestrain, blurred vision, fatigue, headaches, backaches, and wrist and finger pain. Some conditions are classified as **repetitive stress injuries** (**RSIs**), in which hand, wrist, shoulder, or neck pain is caused by performing the same physical movements over and over again. For instance, extensive keyboard and mouse use has been associated with RSIs, although RSIs can be caused by non-computer-related activities as well. One RSI related to the repetitive finger movements made when using a keyboard is **carpal tunnel syndrome** (**CTS**)—a painful and crippling condition affecting the hands and wrists. CTS occurs when the nerve in the carpal tunnel located on the underside of the wrist is compressed. An RSI associated with typing on the tiny keyboards commonly found on mobile phones and mobile devices is **DeQuervain's tendonitis**—a condition in which the tendons on the thumb side of the wrists are swollen and irritated. Computer vision syndrome (CVS) is a collection of eye and vision problems, including eyestrain or eye fatigue, dry eyes, burning eyes, light sensitivity, and blurred vision. Extensive computer use can also lead to headaches and pain in the shoulders, neck, or back.

plagiarism Presenting someone else's work as your own.

repetitive stress injury (RSI) A type of injury, such as carpal tunnel syndrome, that is caused by performing the same physical movements over and over again.

carpal tunnel syndrome (CTS) A painful and crippling condition affecting the hands and wrists that can be caused by computer use.

DeQuervain's tendonitis A condition in which the tendons on the thumb side of the wrist are swollen and irritated.

Repetitive stress and other injuries related to the work environment are estimated to account for one-third of all serious workplace injuries.

Some recent physical health concerns center on heat. For instance, one study measured the peak temperature on the underside of a typical notebook computer at over 139° Fahrenheit. Consequently, many portable computer manufacturers now warn against letting any part of a computer touch your body, and a variety of laptop desks or notebook cooling stands are available for those occasions when your lap must be used as your work surface. Noise-induced hearing loss from extensive use of earbud headsets connected to mobile devices is another growing concern.

1-4d Environmental Concerns

The increasing use of computers in our society has created a variety of environmental concerns. The term **green computing** refers to the use of computers in an environmentally friendly manner. Minimizing the use of natural resources, such as energy and paper, is one aspect of green computing. In 1992, the U.S. Environmental Protection Agency (EPA) introduced ENERGY STAR as a voluntary labeling program designed to identify and promote energy-efficient products in an effort to reduce greenhouse gas emissions. An ENERGY STAR–qualified computer will use between 30 percent and 65 percent less energy, depending on how it is used. Today, the ENERGY STAR label appears on office equipment, residential heating and cooling equipment, major appliances, lighting, home electronics, and more. **Eco-labels**—environmental performance certifications—are used in other countries as well (see Exhibit 1-19).

The high cost of electricity and the recent increase in data center energy usage has made power consumption and heat generation by computers key concerns for businesses and individuals. Although computers have become more energy efficient, they can still draw quite a bit of power in standby and sleep modes—particularly with a screen saver enabled. Devices like computers, home electronics, and appliances that draw power even when they are turned off are sometimes called energy vampires. The average U.S. household spends an estimated $100 per year powering devices that are turned off or in standby mode.

U.S. Environmental Protection Agency, ENERGY STAR program; Courtesy of the European Commission; Directorate-General Courtesy of Korea Environmental Labeling Association (KELA); Courtesy of ABNT - ASSOCIAÇÃO BRASILEIRA DE NORMAS TÉCNICAS; Courtesy Good Environmental Choice Australia

Exhibit 1-19 Eco-labels from several countries

> To save on vampire power costs, unplug your devices whenever you are not using them.

Green computing can have tremendous financial benefits. In fact, EPA estimates that even a 10 percent reduction in energy consumption by U.S. data centers would save enough energy to power up to 1 million homes per year and save U.S. businesses $740 million annually.

In addition to more energy-efficient hardware, alternate power sources are being developed for greener computing. For instance, solar power is a growing alternative for powering electronic devices, including computers and mobile phones. With solar power, solar panels convert sunlight into electricity, which is then stored in a battery. Improvements in

green computing The use of computers in an environmentally friendly manner.

eco-label A certification, usually issued by a government agency, that identifies a device as meeting minimal environmental performance specifications.

Workspace Design

Ergonomics is the science of fitting a work environment to the people who work there. With respect to computer use, it involves designing a safe and effective workspace, which includes properly adjusting furniture and hardware and using ergonomic hardware when needed. As shown in the illustration, a proper work environment—used in conjunction with good user habits and procedures—can prevent many physical problems caused by computer use. Proper placement and adjustment of furniture is a good place to start when evaluating a workspace from an ergonomic perspective.

The desk should be placed where the sun and other sources of light cannot shine directly onto the screen or into the user's eyes. The monitor should be placed directly in front of the user about an arm's length away, and the top of the screen should be no more than 3 inches above the user's eyes once the user's chair is adjusted. The desk chair should be adjusted so that the keyboard is at, or slightly below, the height at which the user's forearms are horizontal to the floor (special ergonomic chairs are also available). A footrest should be used, if needed, to keep the user's feet flat on the floor after the chair height has been set. The monitor settings should be adjusted to make the screen brightness match the brightness of the room and to have a high amount of contrast; the screen should also be periodically wiped clean of dust. Some setups allow the user to raise the workspace in order to work while standing, when desired.

Portable computer users should either connect their computer to a secondary monitor or use a notebook stand to elevate the display screen of a notebook computer to the proper height. Notebook stands and docking stations can also be used to easily connect peripheral devices (such as a keyboard, printer, and monitor) to a portable computer at a home or office workspace.

In addition to workspace devices, a variety of ergonomic hardware can be used to help users avoid or alleviate physical problems associated with computer use. These include:

- Ergonomic keyboards designed to lessen the strain on the hands and wrist.
- Trackballs that are essentially upside-down mice that can be more comfortable to use than a mouse.
- Document holders to allow the user to see both the document and the monitor without turning his or her head.
- Antiglare screens that cover the monitor and lessen glare and resulting eyestrain.
- Keyboard drawers that lower the keyboard and enable the user to keep his or her forearms parallel to the floor.
- Wrist supports to keep wrists straight while using the mouse or keyboard and to support the wrists and forearms when not using those devices.
- Computer gloves designed to prevent and relieve RSIs by supporting the wrist and thumb while allowing the full use of hands.

These devices can help users to avoid and reduce discomfort while working on a computer. In addition, computer users should take frequent breaks from typing, use good posture, stretch from time to time, and periodically refocus their eyes on a distant object for a minute or so.

TILT-AND-SWIVEL MONITOR
Adjusts for a comfortable viewing angle; top of screen should be no higher than 3 inches above the user's eyes.

DOCUMENT HOLDER
Keeps documents close to the monitor so the user does not have to turn his or her head.

PROPER USER POSITION
Sit straight with shoulders back, about 24 inches away from the monitor; keep forearms, wrists, and hands straight; keep forearms and thighs parallel to the floor.

ADJUSTABLE TABLE/DESK
Optimal height is between 25 and 29 inches tall. Keyboard and mouse should be at or just below elbow height; use a keyboard drawer if needed.

FOOTREST
Can be used, if needed, to keep legs properly positioned.

ADJUSTABLE CHAIR
Height is adjustable and has support for the lower back.

© 2014 Cengage Learning

Proper setup of an ergonomic workspace

ergonomics The science of fitting a work environment to the people who work there.

solar technology are making its use increasingly more feasible and economical.

Another environmental concern is the amount of trash—and sometimes toxic trash—generated by computer use. One concern is paper waste. It now appears that the so-called paperless office that many visionaries predicted would arrive is largely a myth. Instead, research indicates that global paper use has grown more than sixfold since 1950, and one-fifth of all wood harvested in the world today ends up as paper. The estimated number of pages generated by computer printers worldwide is almost one-half billion a year. If all this paper were stacked, it would create a pile 25,000 miles high. In addition to paper-based waste, computing refuse includes electronic hardware such as used toner cartridges, obsolete or broken hardware, and discarded CDs, DVDs, and other storage media. Much of this **e-waste** ends up in landfills.

Picsfive/Shutterstock.com

Compounding the problem of the amount of e-waste generated is that computers, mobile phones, and related hardware contain a variety of toxic and hazardous materials. For instance, a desktop computer may contain up to 700 different chemical elements and compounds, many of which (such as arsenic, lead, mercury, and cadmium) are hazardous and expensive to dispose of properly.

A global concern regarding e-waste is where it all eventually ends up. Much of it ends up in municipal landfills that are not designed for toxic waste. Even worse, the majority of all computer equipment sent to recyclers in developed countries (at least 80 percent,

according to most estimates) ends up being exported to developing countries, such as China, India, and Nigeria, with more lax environmental standards, legislation, or enforcement than in the United States. Much of the e-waste exported to these countries is simply dumped into fields or processed with primitive and dangerous technologies that release toxins into the air and water. Unaware of the potential danger of these components, rural villagers are often employed to try to repair equipment. Hardware that cannot be repaired is often burned or treated with acid baths to try to recover precious metals, but such processes release very dangerous pollutants.

Basel Action Network

Nigerian boy trying to repair electronic equipment for resale

Recycling computer equipment is difficult because of toxic materials and poor product design; however, proper recycling is essential to avoid pollution and health hazards. Some recycling centers will accept computer equipment, but many charge a fee for this service. Many computer manufacturers have voluntary take-back programs that will accept obsolete or broken computer equipment from consumers at a minimal cost. Expired toner cartridges and ink cartridges can sometimes be returned to the manufacturer or exchanged when ordering new cartridges; the cartridges are then refilled and resold. Cartridges that cannot be refilled can be sent to a recycling facility. In addition to helping to reduce e-waste in landfills, using refilled or recycled printer cartridges saves the consumer money because they are less expensive than new cartridges. Other computer components—such as CDs, DVDs, USB flash drives, and hard drives—can also be recycled through some organizations, such as GreenDisk, that reuse salvageable items and recycle the rest.

e-waste Electronic trash, such as discarded computer components.

In lieu of recycling, older equipment that is still functioning can be used for alternate purposes, such as for a child's computer, a personal Web server, or a DVR. Or it can be donated to schools and nonprofit groups. Some organizations accept and repair donated equipment and then distribute it to disadvantaged groups or other individuals in need of the hardware. However, be sure to completely remove any data stored on computer equipment before you dispose of, recycle, or donate it so that someone else cannot recover your information from that device.

LEARN MORE

Going Green

In addition to being more energy efficient, computers today are being built to run quieter and cooler, and they are using more recyclable hardware and packaging. Many computer manufacturers are also reducing the amount of toxic chemicals such as cadmium, mercury, and lead, being used in personal computers. In the United States, computer manufacturers are beginning to produce more environmentally friendly components, such as system units made from recyclable plastic, nontoxic flame-retardant coatings, and lead-free solder on the motherboard. Recycling programs to reuse and salvage components are becoming more available.

pryzmat/Shutterstock.com

Quiz Yourself

1. Define computer.

2. What are the four primary operations of a computer?

3. Describe the difference between data and information.

4. What is the difference between hardware and software?

5. What is an end user?

6. Explain cloud computing.

7. List the six general types of computers.

8. What is the difference between a desktop computer and a portable computer?

9. What is a mainframe computer?

10. What is a network?

11. What is the largest and most well-known computer network in the world?

12. Explain the difference between the Internet and the World Wide Web.

13. Describe the three most common types of Internet addresses.

14. Identify the three parts of the email address jsmith@cengage.com.

15. What is a copyright?

16. Define computer ethics.

17. Why are repetitive stress injuries associated with computer use?

18. How does ergonomics relate to computer use?

Practice It

Practice It 1-1

A computer along with the Internet and World Wide Web are handy tools that you can use to research topics covered in this book, complete projects, and perform the online activities available at the book's Web site that are designed to enhance your learning and understanding of the content covered in this book. Use an Internet-enabled computer to access the CMPTR Web site located at www.cengagebrain.com.

1. What types of information and activities are available on the CMPTR Web site?

2. Select an activity and use your mouse to click its link, and then explore the activity. Repeat the process to explore at least two more activities.

3. Evaluate the usefulness of the available resources in enhancing your learning experience.

4. Evaluate your experience using the CMPTR Web site.

5. Prepare a one-page summary that answers these questions, and then submit it to your instructor.

Practice It 1-2

A great deal of obsolete computer equipment eventually ends up in a landfill, even though there may be alternative actions that could be taken instead.

1. Research what options are available to discard the following:

   a. a 10-year-old computer that is no longer functioning
   b. a four-year-old cell phone that still works but is too slow to meet your needs
   c. a used-up toner cartridge for a laser printer

2. Which local schools and charitable organizations, if any, would accept any of these items?

3. Check with at least one computer manufacturer and one recycling company to see if they would accept the computers. If so, what would the procedure and cost be?

4. Check with at least one vendor selling refilled toner cartridges to see if it buys old cartridges or requires a trade-in with an order. If the vendor purchases old cartridges, how much will it pay per cartridge?

5. Prepare a one-page summary that describes your findings, answers these questions, and presents your recommendations, and then submit it to your instructor.

On Your Own

On Your Own 1-1

Some aspects of an ergonomic workspace, such as a comfortable chair and nonglaring light, may feel good right from the beginning. Others, such as using an ergonomic keyboard or a wrist rest, may take a little getting used to.

1. Go to a local store that has some ergonomic equipment—such as adjustable office chairs, desks with keyboard drawers, ergonomic keyboards, or notebook stands—on display that you can try out.

2. Test each piece, adjusting it as needed, and evaluate how comfortable it seems.

3. Evaluate your usual computer workspace. Are there any adjustments you should make? Is there any new equipment you would need to acquire to make your workspace setup more comfortable?

4. Create a list of any changes you could make for free, as well as a list of items you would need to purchase and the estimated cost. Which changes and items do you think would most increase your comfort?

5. Prepare a one-page summary that describes your findings and answers these questions, and then submit it to your instructor.

Chapter 1

ADDITIONAL STUDY TOOLS

IN THE BOOK
▶ Complete end-of-chapter exercises
▶ Study tear-out Chapter Review Card

ONLINE
▶ Complete additional end-of-chapter exercises

▶ Take practice quiz to prepare for tests
▶ Review key term flash cards (online, printable, and audio)
▶ Play "Beat the Clock" and "Memory" to quiz yourself
▶ Watch the videos to learn more about the topics taught in this chapter

Answers to Quiz Yourself

1. A computer is a programmable, electronic device that accepts data, performs operations on that data, presents the results, and stores the data or results as needed.

2. The four primary operations of a computer are input, processing, output, and storage.

3. Data is raw, unorganized facts. Information is data that has been processed or modified into a meaningful form.

4. The physical parts of a computer, such as the keyboard, monitor, and printer, are called hardware. Software refers to the programs or instructions that are used to tell the computer hardware what to do and to allow people use a computer to perform specific tasks, such as creating letters, preparing budgets, managing inventory and customer databases, playing games, watching videos, listening to music, scheduling appointments, editing digital photographs, designing homes, viewing Web pages, burning DVDs, and exchanging email.

5. An end user is a person who uses a computer to perform tasks or obtain information.

6. In general, cloud computing refers to data, applications, and even resources stored on computers accessed over the Internet—in a "cloud" of computers—rather than on users' computers, and you access only what you need when you need it.

7. The six general types of computers are embedded computers, mobile devices, personal computers (PCs), midrange servers, mainframe computers, and supercomputers.

8. Conventional personal computers that are designed to fit on or next to a desk are often referred to as desktop computers. Portable computers are small personal computers that are designed to be carried around easily.

9. A mainframe computer is a powerful computer used in many large organizations that need to manage large amounts of centralized data. Larger, more expensive, and more powerful than midrange servers, mainframes can serve thousands of users connected to the mainframe via personal computers, thin clients, or dumb terminals.

10. A network is a collection of computers and other devices that are connected to enable users to share hardware, software, and data, as well as to communicate electronically.

11. The Internet is the largest and most well-known computer network in the world.

12. The Internet refers to the physical structure of the largest network in the world. The World Wide Web (Web or WWW) refers to one resource—a collection of documents called Web pages—available through the Internet.

13. The three most common types of Internet addresses are IP addresses and domain names (to identify computers), URLs (to identify Web pages), and email addresses (to identify people).

14. The email address jsmith@cengage.com consists of the username jsmith, followed by the @ symbol, followed by the domain name cengage.com for the computer that will be handling that person's email (called a mail server).

15. A copyright is the legal right to sell, publish, or distribute an original artistic or literary work; it is held by the creator of a work as soon as it exists in physical form.

16. Computer ethics are standards of moral conduct as they relate to the use of computers.

17. Repetitive stress injuries (RSIs) occur when hand, wrist, shoulder, or neck pain is caused by performing the same physical movements over and over again, such as extensive keyboard and mouse use.

18. Ergonomics is the science of fitting a work environment to the people who work there. With respect to computer use, it involves designing a safe and effective workspace, which includes properly adjusting furniture and hardware and using ergonomic hardware when needed. A proper work environment—used in conjunction with good user habits and procedures—can prevent many physical problems caused by computer use.

Computer Hardware

© Fancy Collection/SuperStock

When most people think of computers, images of hardware usually fill their minds. Hardware includes the system unit, keyboard, mouse, monitor, and all the other pieces of equipment that make up a computer system. This chapter describes the hardware located inside the system unit, which is the main box of the computer and where most of the work of a computer is performed. It discusses the different types of devices that can be used for data storage. It also covers the wide variety of hardware that can be used for input and output. Keep in mind that hardware needs instructions from software in order to function. Hardware without software is like a car without a driver or a canvas and paintbrush without an artist. Software is discussed in the next chapter.

Learning Objectives

After studying the material in this chapter, you will be able to:

2-1 Understand how data is represented to a computer

2-2 Identify the parts inside the system unit

2-3 Explain how the CPU works

2-4 Describe different types of storage systems

2-5 Identify and describe common input devices

2-6 Identify and describe common output devices

2-1 Digital Data Representation

Virtually all computers today are digital computers. Most digital computers are binary computers, which can understand only two states, represented by the digits 0 and 1 and usually thought of as off and on. Consequently, all data processed by a binary computer must be in binary form. When you enter data into a computer, the computer translates the natural-language symbols you input into binary 0s and 1s, processes that data, and then translates and outputs the results in a form that you can understand. The 0s and 1s used to represent data can be represented in a variety of ways, such as with an open or closed circuit, the absence or presence of electronic current, two different types of magnetic alignment on a storage medium, and so on, as shown in Exhibit 2-1.

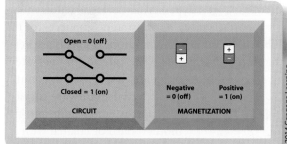

Exhibit 2-1 Ways of representing 0 and 1

© 2014 Cengage Learning

Regardless of their physical representations, these 0s and 1s are commonly referred to as bits, a computing term derived from the phrase *binary digits*. A **bit** is the smallest unit of data that a binary computer can recognize. The input you enter via a keyboard, the software program you use to play your music collection, the term paper stored on your computer, and the digital photos located on your mobile phone are all just groups of bits. A bit by itself typically represents only a fraction of a piece of data. Eight bits grouped together are collectively referred to as a **byte**. A named collection of bytes that represent something such

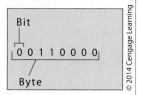

8 bits = 1 byte

© 2014 Cengage Learning

as a written document, a computer program, a digital photo, a song, or virtually any other type of data is called a **file**. Because the numbers of bytes needed to represent a file can be in the thousands or millions of bytes, prefixes are commonly used with the term byte to represent larger amounts of data.

LEARN MORE

A Bit about Bytes

Prefixes are combined with the term *byte* to describe data that is large than a byte:

▶ **1 kilobyte (KB)** is equal to 1,024 bytes but is usually thought of as approximately 1,000 bytes.

▶ **1 megabyte (MB)** is about 1 million bytes.

▶ **1 gigabyte (GB)** is about 1 billion bytes.

▶ **1 terabyte (TB)** is about 1 trillion bytes.

▶ **1 petabyte (PB)** is about 1,000 terabytes.

▶ **1 exabyte (EB)** is about 1,000 petabytes.

▶ **1 zettabyte (ZB)** is about 1,000 exabytes.

▶ **1 yottabyte (YB)** is about 1,000 zettabytes.

2-2 Inside the System Unit

The **system unit** is the main case of a computer. It houses the computer's processing hardware, as well as a few other devices, such as storage devices, the power supply, and cooling fans. The system unit for a desktop computer is often a rectangular box, although other shapes and sizes are available. The inside of a system unit for a desktop computer is shown in Exhibit 2-2.

bit The smallest unit of data that a binary computer can recognize.

byte Eight bits grouped together.

file A named collection of bytes that represent virtually any type of data.

system unit The main case of a computer.

Exhibit 2-2 Inside a typical system unit

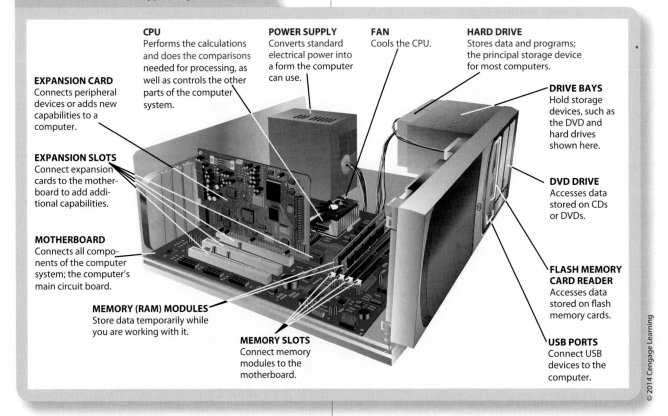

CPU
Performs the calculations and does the comparisons needed for processing, as well as controls the other parts of the computer system.

POWER SUPPLY
Converts standard electrical power into a form the computer can use.

FAN
Cools the CPU.

HARD DRIVE
Stores data and programs; the principal storage device for most computers.

EXPANSION CARD
Connects peripheral devices or adds new capabilities to a computer.

EXPANSION SLOTS
Connect expansion cards to the motherboard to add additional capabilities.

MOTHERBOARD
Connects all components of the computer system; the computer's main circuit board.

MEMORY (RAM) MODULES
Store data temporarily while you are working with it.

MEMORY SLOTS
Connect memory modules to the motherboard.

DRIVE BAYS
Hold storage devices, such as the DVD and hard drives shown here.

DVD DRIVE
Accesses data stored on CDs or DVDs.

FLASH MEMORY CARD READER
Accesses data stored on flash memory cards.

USB PORTS
Connect USB devices to the computer.

© 2014 Cengage Learning

2-2a The Motherboard

A **circuit board** is a thin board containing computer chips and other electronic components. **Computer chips** are very small pieces of silicon or other semiconducting material that contain integrated circuits, which are collections of electronic circuits containing microscopic pathways that electrical current can travel along, and transistors, which are switches controlling the flow of electrons along the pathways. The main circuit board inside the system unit is called the **motherboard**.

All devices used with a computer need to be connected via a wired or wireless connection to the motherboard. Typically, external devices such as monitors, keyboards, mice, and printers connect to the motherboard by plugging into a port. A **port** is a special connector accessible through the exterior of the system unit case that is used to connect an external hardware device. The port is either built into the motherboard or created with an expansion card inserted into an expansion slot on the motherboard. Wireless external devices typically use a transceiver that plugs into a port on the computer to transmit data between the wireless device and the motherboard, or they use wireless networking technology, such as Bluetooth, built into the motherboard.

> The main circuit board inside the system unit is called the motherboard.

circuit board A thin board containing computer chips and other electronic components.

computer chip A very small piece of silicon or other semiconducting material that contains integrated circuits and transistors.

motherboard The main circuit board inside the system unit.

port A connector on the exterior of the system unit case that is used to connect an external hardware device.

2-2b The Power Supply

The power supply inside a desktop computer connects to the motherboard to deliver electricity to the computer. Portable computers almost always contain a rechargeable battery pack to power the computer when it is not connected to a power outlet, as well as an external power supply adapter that connects the computer to a power outlet to recharge the battery when needed.

2-2c The CPU

The **central processing unit** (**CPU** or **processor**) is a computer chip that performs the calculations and comparisons needed for processing; it also controls the computer's operations. The CPU is the main processing device for a computer and is often considered the "brain" of the computer. The CPU consists of a variety of circuitry and components that are packaged together and are connected directly to the motherboard. Most personal computers and servers today use Intel or Advanced Micro Devices (AMD) CPUs. Netbook and mobile devices might instead use processors manufactured by other companies, such as ARM. Some examples of common processors are shown in Exhibit 2-3.

Most CPUs today are **multi-core CPUs**, which are CPUs that contain the processing components or cores of multiple independent processors in a single CPU. For example, dual-core CPUs contain two cores and quad-core CPUs contain four cores. Multi-core CPUs allow computers to work on more than one task simultaneously, such as burning a DVD while surfing the Web, as well as to work faster within a single application.

One measurement of the processing speed of a CPU is the **clock speed**, which measures the number of instructions that can be processed per second. Clock speed is typically rated in megahertz (MHz) or gigahertz (GHz). A CPU with a higher clock speed can process more instructions per second than the same CPU with a lower clock speed. CPUs for the earliest personal computers ran at less than 5 MHz; the fastest CPUs have a clock speed of more than 3 GHz.

Although clock speed is important to computer performance, factors such as the number of cores, the amount of RAM and cache memory, the speed of external storage devices, and the bus width and bus speed greatly affect the overall processing speed of the computer. As a result, computers are beginning to be classified less by clock speed and more by the computer's overall processing speed or performance.

Exhibit 2-3 Examples of CPUs

Four cores

Shared Level 3 cache memory

DESKTOP PROCESSORS
Typically have 2 to 6 cores and are designed for performance.

SERVER PROCESSORS
Typically have 4 to 12 cores and are designed for very high performance.

MOBILE PROCESSORS
Typically have 2 to 4 cores for notebook computers (left) or 1 to 2 cores for netbook computers and mobile devices (right), and are designed for performance and increased battery life.

Courtesy of Intel Corporation; © 2003, 2005, 2006, 2007 Advanced Micro Devices, Inc., Reprinted with permission. AMD, the AMD Arrow logo, AMD Opteron, and combinations thereof are trademarks of Advanced Micro Devices, Inc.; Courtesy of ARM

central processing unit (CPU or processor) The chip located on the motherboard of a computer that performs the processing for the computer.

multi-core CPU A CPU that contains the processing components or cores of multiple independent processors.

clock speed A measurement of the number of instructions that a CPU can process per second.

A computer **word** is the amount of data (typically measured in bits or bytes) that a CPU can manipulate at one time. Just a few years ago, CPUs used 32-bit words (referred to as 32-bit processors). Today, most CPUs are 64-bit processors, which means that they can simultaneously process 64 bits, or eight bytes, at one time. Usually, a larger word size allows for faster processing, provided the software being used is written to take advantage of 64-bit processing.

Cache memory is a special group of very fast memory circuitry located on or close to the CPU that is used to speed up processing by storing the data and instructions that may be needed next by the CPU in handy locations. When cache memory is full and the CPU calls for additional data or a new instruction, the system overwrites as much data in cache memory as needed to make room for the new data or instruction. This allows the data and instructions that are most likely still needed to remain in cache memory.

> Multi-core CPUs allow computers to work on more than one task simultaneously.

word The amount of data (typically measured in bits or bytes) that a CPU can manipulate at one time.

cache memory A group of very fast memory circuitry located on or close to the CPU to speed up processing.

memory Chips located inside the system unit used to store data and instructions while the computer is working with them.

RAM (random access memory) Memory used to store data and instructions while the computer is running.

2-2d Memory

In a computer, **memory** is chips located inside the system unit that the computer uses to store data and instructions while it is working with them. **RAM (random access memory)** is used to store the essential parts of the operating system while the computer is running, as well as the programs and data that the computer is currently using. The term *memory* in reference to computers usually means RAM. Because RAM is volatile, its content is erased when the computer is shut off. Data in RAM is also deleted when it is no longer needed, such as when the program using that data is closed.

Like the CPU, RAM consists of electronic circuits etched onto chips. As shown in Exhibit 2-4, these chips are arranged onto circuit boards called memory modules, which, in turn, are plugged into the motherboard. Most personal computers sold today have slots for two to four memory modules, and at least one slot is filled. For example, the motherboard shown in Exhibit 2-2 has two memory modules installed and room to add two more modules. If you want to add more RAM to a computer and no empty slots are available, you must replace at least one of the existing memory modules with a higher capacity module.

Exhibit 2-4 RAM memory modules

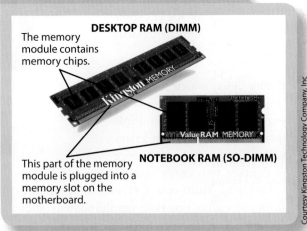

DESKTOP RAM (DIMM)

The memory module contains memory chips.

NOTEBOOK RAM (SO-DIMM)

This part of the memory module is plugged into a memory slot on the motherboard.

Courtesy Kingston Technology Company, Inc

Cooling Components

One byproduct of packing an increasing amount of technology in a smaller system unit is heat, an ongoing problem for CPU and computer manufacturers. Because heat can damage components and cooler chips can run faster, virtually all computers today employ fans, heat sinks (small components typically made of aluminum with fins that help to dissipate heat), or other methods to cool the CPU and system unit, including liquid-filled tubes that draw heat away from processors. Notebook computer users can use a notebook cooling stand if the built-in fan is not sufficient to cool the computer.

Fans on the back of the system unit

Fan on top of the CPU

Water cooling tubes

FANS AND WATERCOOLING SYSTEMS
These cooling methods and heat sinks are used with computers today to cool the inside of the computer.

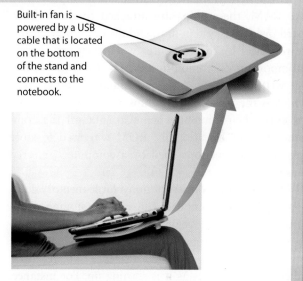

Built-in fan is powered by a USB cable that is located on the bottom of the stand and connects to the notebook.

NOTEBOOK COOLING STANDS
These stands cool the underside of a notebook computer by allowing for better air circulation; some stands also include a fan.

RAM capacity is measured in bytes. The amount of RAM that can be installed in a computer system depends on the CPU in that computer and the operating system being used. For instance, while computers using 64-bit CPUs can utilize a virtually unlimited amount of RAM (older 32-bit CPUs can use up to only 4 GB of RAM), a 64-bit operating system is needed to use more than 4 GB of RAM. In addition, different versions of a 64-bit operating system might support different amounts of RAM. Consequently, when adding RAM to a computer, it is important to determine whether the computer can support it. Having more RAM allows more applications to run at one time and the computer to respond more quickly when a user switches from task to task. Most new computers have at least 2 GB of RAM; 2 to 8 GB of RAM is considered normal for home computers.

It is also important to select the proper type and speed of RAM when adding new memory. Most personal computers today use SDRAM (synchronous dynamic RAM). SDRAM is commonly available in DDR (double-data rate), DDR2, and DDR3 versions. DDR memory sends data twice as often as ordinary SDRAM to increase throughput, DDR2 transmits twice as much data in the same time period as DDR, and DDR3 is about twice as fast as the highest-speed DDR2 memory available today. Each type of SDRAM is typically available in a variety of speeds (measured in MHz).

To further improve memory performance, memory today typically uses a dual-channel memory architecture, which has two paths that go to and from memory, so it can transfer twice as much data at one time as single-channel memory architecture of the same speed. Tri-channel (three paths) and quad-channel (four paths) memory architecture are also beginning to be used for higher performance. Multi-channel RAM typically needs to be installed in matched sets, such as two 1 GB dual-channel memory modules instead of a single 2 GB dual-channel memory module.

A **register** is high-speed memory built into the CPU that temporarily stores data during processing. Registers are used by the CPU to store data and intermediary results temporarily during processing. Registers are the fastest type of memory used by the CPU, even faster than Level 1 cache. Generally, more registers and larger registers result in increased CPU performance. Most CPUs contain multiple registers that are used for specific purposes.

ROM (**read-only memory**) consists of nonvolatile chips that permanently store data or programs. Like RAM, these chips are attached to the motherboard inside the system unit, and the data or programs are retrieved by the computer when they are needed. An important difference, however, is that you can neither write over the data or programs in ROM chips (which is the reason ROM chips are called read-only) nor erase their content when you shut off the computer's power. Traditionally, ROM was used to store permanent instructions used by a computer (referred to as firmware).

Flash memory consists of nonvolatile memory chips that the user or computer can use for storage. Flash memory chips have begun to replace ROM for storing system information, such as a computer's **BIOS**, or basic input/output system—the sequence of instructions the computer follows as it is starting up. For instance, one of the computer's first activities when you turn on the power is to perform a power-on self-test, or POST. The POST takes an inventory of system components, checks each component to see whether it is functioning properly, and initializes system settings, which produces the beeps you may hear as your computer boots. Traditionally, the instructions for the POST have been stored in ROM. By storing this information in flash memory instead of ROM, however, the BIOS information can be updated as needed.

register High-speed memory built into a CPU.

ROM (read-only memory) Nonvolatile chips on the motherboard that permanently store data or programs.

flash memory Nonvolatile memory chips that can be used for storage by a computer or a user.

BIOS (basic input/output system) The sequence of instructions the computer follows as it is starting up.

expansion slot A location on the motherboard into which an expansion card is inserted to connect it to the motherboard.

expansion card (interface card) A circuit board used to give desktop computers additional capabilities.

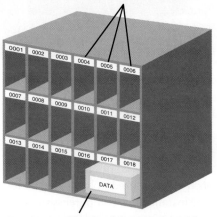
2-2e Expansion Slots, Expansion Cards, and ExpressCard Modules

Expansion slots are locations on the motherboard into which expansion cards can be inserted to connect those cards to the motherboard. **Expansion cards** (also called **interface cards**) are circuit boards that are used to give desktop—and to a limited extent,

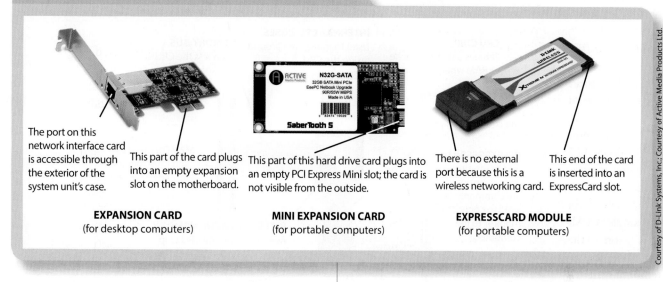

Exhibit 2-5 Expansion cards and an ExpressCard module

The port on this network interface card is accessible through the exterior of the system unit's case.

This part of the card plugs into an empty expansion slot on the motherboard.

N32G-SATA
32GB SATA Mini PCIe
EeePC Netbook Upgrade
90R/55W MBPS
Made in USA
SaberTooth S

This part of this hard drive card plugs into an empty PCI Express Mini slot; the card is not visible from the outside.

There is no external port because this is a wireless networking card.

This end of the card is inserted into an ExpressCard slot.

EXPANSION CARD
(for desktop computers)

MINI EXPANSION CARD
(for portable computers)

EXPRESSCARD MODULE
(for portable computers)

Courtesy of D-Link Systems, Inc.; Courtesy of Active Media Products Ltd.

notebook—computers additional capabilities, such as to connect the computer to a network, to add a TV tuner to allow you to watch and record television shows on the computer, to add a hard drive to a computer, or to connect a monitor to the computer. Most desktop computers come with a few empty expansion slots so new expansion cards can be added as needed. Each type of expansion slot is designed for a specific type of expansion card.

Notebook computers and other portable computers do not use the same expansion cards as desktop computers. Traditionally, PC Cards were used for notebook expansion, but today many notebook and netbook computers use the newer ExpressCard modules. **ExpressCard modules** are inserted into the computer's ExpressCard slot. They can also be used with any desktop computer that has an ExpressCard slot. Exhibit 2-5 shows two expansion cards and an ExpressCard module.

2-2f Buses

A **bus** is an electronic path over which data can travel. Buses are located within the CPU to move data between CPU components. A variety of buses are also etched onto the motherboard to tie the CPU to memory and to peripheral devices.

You can picture a bus as a highway with several lanes; each wire in the bus acts as a separate lane, transmitting one bit at a time. The number of bits being transmitted at one time depends on the bus width, which is the number of wires in the bus over which data can travel (see Exhibit 2-6). The bus speed is also a very

important factor because the bus width and bus speed together determine the bus's **throughput** or **bandwidth**, which is the amount of data that can be transferred via the bus in a given time period.

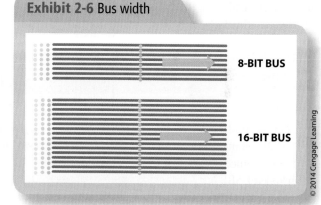

Exhibit 2-6 Bus width

8-BIT BUS

16-BIT BUS

© 2014 Cengage Learning

The buses that connect peripheral (typically input and output) devices to the motherboard are often called **expansion buses**. Expansion buses connect directly to ports on the system unit case or to expansion slots on the motherboard. Some of the most common expansion

ExpressCard module A module that can be inserted into a computer's ExpressCard slot to add additional functionality or to connect a peripheral device to that computer; commonly used with notebook computers.

bus An electronic path over which data travels.

throughput (bandwidth) The amount of data that can be transferred, such as via a bus, in a given time period.

expansion bus A bus on the motherboard used to connect peripheral devices.

buses and expansion slots are illustrated in Exhibit 2-7.

One of the more versatile bus architectures is the **Universal Serial Bus** (**USB**). The USB standard allows 127 different devices to connect to a computer via a single USB port on the computer's system unit. At 12 Mbps (millions of bits per second), the original USB 1.0 standard is slow. However, the newer USB 2.0 standard supports data transfer rates of 480 Mbps, and the newest 4.8 Gbps (billions of bits per second) USB 3.0 standard (also called SuperSpeed USB) is about 10 times faster than USB 2.0. The convenience and universal support of USB have made it one of the most widely used standards for connecting peripheral devices today.

FireWire (also known as **IEEE 1394**) is a high-speed bus standard developed by Apple for connecting devices—particularly multimedia devices like digital video cameras—to a computer. Like USB, FireWire can connect multiple external devices via a single port. FireWire is relatively fast—the original FireWire standard supports data transfer rates of up to 320 Mbps, the newer FireWire standard (called FireWire 800) supports data transfer rates up to 800 Mbps, and the emerging FireWire 3200 standard is expected to support 3.2 Gbps transfer rates.

2-2g Ports and Connectors

As already mentioned, ports are the connectors located on the exterior of the system unit that are used to connect external hardware devices. Each port is attached to the appropriate bus on the motherboard so that when a device is plugged into a port, the device can communicate with the CPU and other computer components. Typical ports for a desktop computer and the connectors used with those ports are shown in Exhibit 2-8.

Exhibit 2-7 Buses and expansion slots

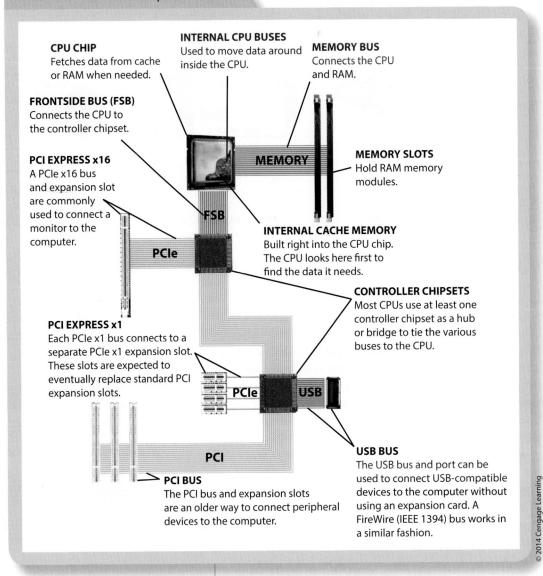

CPU CHIP
Fetches data from cache or RAM when needed.

INTERNAL CPU BUSES
Used to move data around inside the CPU.

MEMORY BUS
Connects the CPU and RAM.

FRONTSIDE BUS (FSB)
Connects the CPU to the controller chipset.

PCI EXPRESS x16
A PCIe x16 bus and expansion slot are commonly used to connect a monitor to the computer.

MEMORY SLOTS
Hold RAM memory modules.

INTERNAL CACHE MEMORY
Built right into the CPU chip. The CPU looks here first to find the data it needs.

PCI EXPRESS x1
Each PCIe x1 bus connects to a separate PCIe x1 expansion slot. These slots are expected to eventually replace standard PCI expansion slots.

CONTROLLER CHIPSETS
Most CPUs use at least one controller chipset as a hub or bridge to tie the various buses to the CPU.

PCI BUS
The PCI bus and expansion slots are an older way to connect peripheral devices to the computer.

USB BUS
The USB bus and port can be used to connect USB-compatible devices to the computer without using an expansion card. A FireWire (IEEE 1394) bus works in a similar fashion.

© 2014 Cengage Learning

Universal Serial Bus (USB) A versatile bus architecture widely used for connecting peripheral devices.

FireWire (IEEE 1394) A high-speed bus standard used to connect devices—particularly multimedia devices like digital video cameras—to a computer.

Exhibit 2-8 Typical ports and connectors for desktop computers

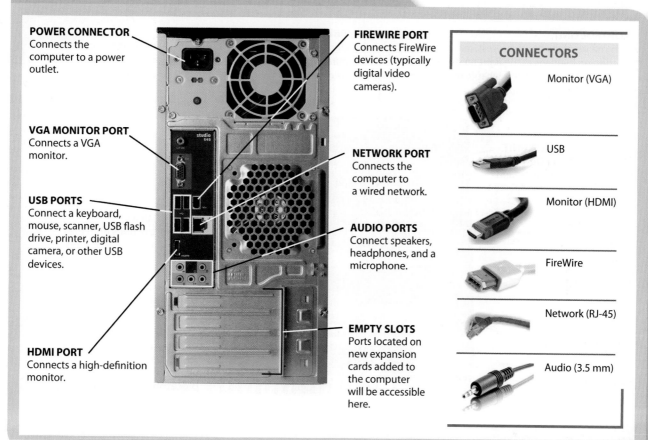

POWER CONNECTOR
Connects the computer to a power outlet.

VGA MONITOR PORT
Connects a VGA monitor.

USB PORTS
Connect a keyboard, mouse, scanner, USB flash drive, printer, digital camera, or other USB devices.

HDMI PORT
Connects a high-definition monitor.

FIREWIRE PORT
Connects FireWire devices (typically digital video cameras).

NETWORK PORT
Connects the computer to a wired network.

AUDIO PORTS
Connect speakers, headphones, and a microphone.

EMPTY SLOTS
Ports located on new expansion cards added to the computer will be accessible here.

CONNECTORS

Monitor (VGA)

USB

Monitor (HDMI)

FireWire

Network (RJ-45)

Audio (3.5 mm)

Courtesy Dell Inc.; Courtesy Belkin International, Inc.

Portable computers have ports similar to desktop computers but often have fewer of them. Smartphones and other mobile devices have a more limited amount of expandability. However, these devices usually come with at least one built-in expansion slot—typically a USB port.

LEARN MORE

Plug and Play

Most computers today support the Plug and Play standard, which means the computer automatically configures new devices as soon as they are installed and the computer is powered up. If you want to add a new device to your desktop computer and a port is available for the device you want to add, then you just need to plug it in. However, you should shut down the computer first unless the device uses a USB or FireWire port. USB and FireWire devices are hot-swappable, meaning they can be plugged into their respective ports while the computer is powered up. Hot swappable devices are recognized by the computer as soon as they are connected to it; other devices are recognized by the computer when the computer is first powered up after the device has been added.

2-3 How the CPU Works

A CPU consists of a variety of circuitry and components packaged together into a single component. The key element of the CPU is the **transistor**—a device made of semiconductor material that controls the flow of electrons inside a chip. CPUs contain hundreds of millions of transistors.

transistor A device made of semiconductor material that controls the flow of electrons inside a chip.

Exhibit 2-9 CPU components

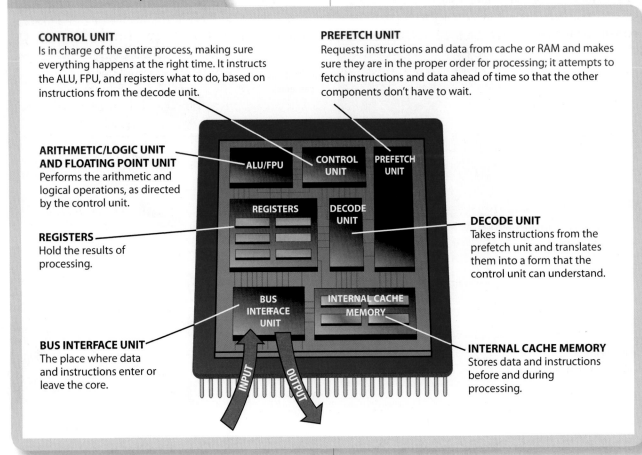

CONTROL UNIT
Is in charge of the entire process, making sure everything happens at the right time. It instructs the ALU, FPU, and registers what to do, based on instructions from the decode unit.

PREFETCH UNIT
Requests instructions and data from cache or RAM and makes sure they are in the proper order for processing; it attempts to fetch instructions and data ahead of time so that the other components don't have to wait.

ARITHMETIC/LOGIC UNIT AND FLOATING POINT UNIT
Performs the arithmetic and logical operations, as directed by the control unit.

REGISTERS
Hold the results of processing.

DECODE UNIT
Takes instructions from the prefetch unit and translates them into a form that the control unit can understand.

BUS INTERFACE UNIT
The place where data and instructions enter or leave the core.

INTERNAL CACHE MEMORY
Stores data and instructions before and during processing.

ALU/FPU • CONTROL UNIT • PREFETCH UNIT • REGISTERS • DECODE UNIT • BUS INTERFACE UNIT • INTERNAL CACHE MEMORY • INPUT • OUTPUT

2-3a Typical CPU Components

To begin to understand how a CPU works, you need to know how the CPU is organized and what components it includes. A simplified example of the principal components that might be included in a single core of a typical CPU is shown in Exhibit 2-9. Additional components are also typically located inside the CPU, but not within each core. For instance, there are buses to connect the CPU cores to each other, buses to connect each core to the CPU's memory controller (which controls the communication between the CPU cores and RAM), and buses to connect each core to any cache memory that is shared between the cores. If the CPU contains a graphics processing unit (GPU), as the most recent CPU designs from Intel and AMD do, it would be located inside the CPU package as well.

arithmetic/logic unit (ALU) The part of a CPU core that performs integer arithmetic and logical operations.

floating point unit (FPU) The part of a CPU core that performs decimal arithmetic.

control unit The part of a CPU core that coordinates its operations.

The **arithmetic/logic unit** (**ALU**) is the section of a CPU core that performs arithmetic (addition, subtraction, multiplication, and division) involving integers and logical operations (such as comparing two pieces of data to see if they are equal or determining if a specific condition is true or false). Arithmetic requiring decimals is usually performed by the **floating point unit** (**FPU**). Arithmetic operations are performed when mathematical calculations are requested by the user, as well as when many other common computing tasks are performed. For example, editing a digital photograph in an image editing program, running the spell checker in a word processing program, and burning a music CD are all performed by the ALU, with help from the FPU when needed, using only arithmetic and logical operations. Most CPUs today have multiple ALUs and FPUs that work together to perform the necessary operations.

The **control unit** coordinates and controls the operations and activities taking place within a CPU core, such as retrieving data and instructions and passing them on to the ALU or FPU for execution. In other words, it directs the flow of electronic traffic within the core, much like a traffic cop controls the flow of vehicles on a roadway. Essentially, the control unit tells the ALU and FPU what to do and makes sure that everything happens at the right time in order for the appropriate processing to take place.

The **prefetch unit** orders data and instructions from cache or RAM based on the current task. The prefetch unit tries to predict what data and instructions will be needed and retrieves them ahead of time, to help avoid delays in processing.

The **decode unit** takes the instructions fetched by the prefetch unit and translates them into a form that can be understood by the control unit, ALU, and FPU. The decoded instructions go to the control unit for processing.

The **bus interface unit** allows the core to communicate with other CPU components, such as the memory controller and other cores. As previously mentioned, the memory controller controls the flow of instructions and data going between the CPU cores and RAM.

2-3b The System Clock and the Machine Cycle

To synchronize all of a computer's operations, a **system clock**—a small quartz crystal located on the motherboard—is used. The system clock sends out a signal on a regular basis to all other computer components, similar to a musician's metronome or a person's heartbeat. Each signal is referred to as a cycle. The number of cycles per second is measured in hertz (Hz). One megahertz (MHz) is equal to one million ticks of the system clock. Many personal computers have system clocks that run at 200 MHz, and all devices (such as CPUs) that are synchronized with these system clocks run at either the system clock speed or at a multiple of or a fraction of the system clock speed. During each clock tick, the CPU can execute one or more instructions.

Whenever the CPU processes a single basic instruction, it is referred to as a **machine cycle**. Each machine cycle consists of four general operations, as shown in Exhibit 2-10.

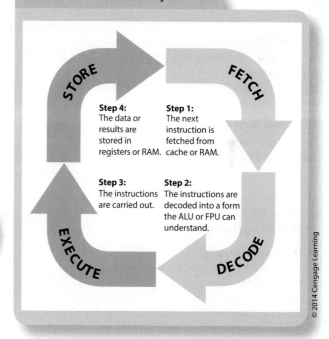

Exhibit 2-10 Machine cycle

Step 1: The next instruction is fetched from cache or RAM.

Step 2: The instructions are decoded into a form the ALU or FPU can understand.

Step 3: The instructions are carried out.

Step 4: The data or results are stored in registers or RAM.

© 2014 Cengage Learning

prefetch unit The part of a CPU core that attempts to retrieve data and instructions before they are needed for processing to avoid delays.

decode unit The part of a CPU core that translates instructions into a form that can be processed by the ALU and FPU.

bus interface unit The section of a CPU core that allows the core to communicate with other CPU components.

system clock A small quartz crystal located on the motherboard that synchronizes a computer's operations.

machine cycle The series of steps performed by a computer when the CPU processes a single basic instruction.

2-4 Storage Systems

When you first create a document on a computer, both the program you are using to create the document and the document itself are temporarily stored in RAM. But when the program is closed, both are erased from RAM. Consequently, anything that needs to be preserved for future must be stored on a more permanent medium.

Storage systems make it possible to save programs, data, and processing results for later use. They provide nonvolatile storage, so that when the power is shut off, the data stored on the storage medium remains intact. All storage systems involve two physical parts: A **storage medium** is the hardware where data is actually stored, and its corresponding **storage device** in which the storage medium is inserted to be read from or written to.

Letters or names are assigned to each storage device so that the user can identify a device (see Exhibit 2-11). Some drive letters, such as the letter C typically used with the primary hard drive, are usually consistent from computer to computer. The rest of the drive letters on a computer might change as new devices are added. When a new storage device is detected, the computer assigns and reassigns drive letters, as needed.

2-4a Hard Drives

With the exception of computers designed to use only network storage devices (such as network computers and some Internet appliances), virtually all personal computers come with a **hard drive** that is used to store most programs and data. Internal hard drives are located inside the system unit and are not designed to

be removed unless they need to be repaired or replaced. External hard drives typically connect to a computer via a USB or FireWire port and are frequently used for additional storage (such as for digital photos, videos, and other large multimedia files), to move files between computers, and for backup purposes.

Most hard drives are magnetic. **Magnetic hard drives** contain one or more metal hard disks or platters that are coated with a magnetizable substance. These hard disks are permanently sealed inside the hard drive case, along with the read/write heads used to store (write) and retrieve (read) data and an access mechanism used to move the read/write heads in and out over the surface of the hard disks (see Exhibit 2-12). One hard

storage medium The hardware where data is actually stored.

storage device The hardware used to read from or write to a storage medium.

hard drive Hardware used to store most programs and data on a computer.

magnetic hard drive A hard drive consisting of one or more metal magnetic disks permanently sealed, along with an access mechanism and read/write heads, inside its drive.

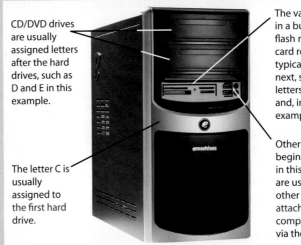

Exhibit 2-11 Storage device identifiers

CD/DVD drives are usually assigned letters after the hard drives, such as D and E in this example.

The letter C is usually assigned to the first hard drive.

The various slots in a built-in flash memory card reader are typically assigned next, such as the letters F, G, H and, in this example.

Other letters, beginning with J in this example, are used for any other storage devices attached to the computer, such as via these USB ports.

Courtesy of Gateway, Inc.

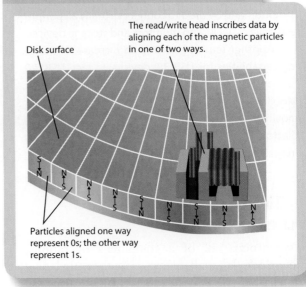

Exhibit 2-12 How data is stored on magnetic disks

Disk surface

The read/write head inscribes data by aligning each of the magnetic particles in one of two ways.

Particles aligned one way represent 0s; the other way represent 1s.

© 2014 Cengage Learning

Exhibit 2-13 Magnetic hard drives

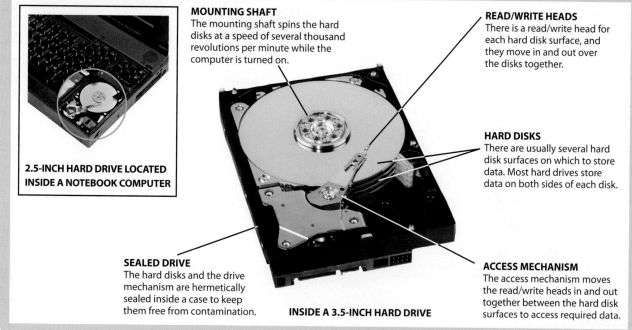

MOUNTING SHAFT
The mounting shaft spins the hard disks at a speed of several thousand revolutions per minute while the computer is turned on.

READ/WRITE HEADS
There is a read/write head for each hard disk surface, and they move in and out over the disks together.

2.5-INCH HARD DRIVE LOCATED INSIDE A NOTEBOOK COMPUTER

HARD DISKS
There are usually several hard disk surfaces on which to store data. Most hard drives store data on both sides of each disk.

SEALED DRIVE
The hard disks and the drive mechanism are hermetically sealed inside a case to keep them free from contamination.

INSIDE A 3.5-INCH HARD DRIVE

ACCESS MECHANISM
The access mechanism moves the read/write heads in and out together between the hard disk surfaces to access required data.

drive usually contains a stack of several hard disks. If so, there is a read/write head for each hard disk surface (top and bottom), as illustrated in Exhibit 2-13, and these heads move in and out over the disk surfaces simultaneously.

A magnetic hard drive's read/write heads never touch the surface of the hard disks at any time, even during reading and writing. If the read/write heads do touch the surface—for example, if a desktop computer is bumped while the hard drive is spinning or if a foreign object gets onto the surface of a hard disk—a head crash occurs, which can typically do permanent damage to the hard drive. Because the read/write heads are located extremely close to the surface of the hard disks (less than one-half millionth of an inch above the surface), the presence of a foreign object the width of a human hair or even a smoke particle on the surface of a hard disk is like placing a huge boulder on a road and then trying to drive over it with your car.

The surface of a hard disk is organized into **tracks** (concentric rings) and pie-shaped groups of **sectors**, as shown in Exhibit 2-14. On most computer systems, the smallest storage area on a hard disk is a **cluster**—one or more adjacent sectors. Because a cluster is the smallest area on a hard disk that a computer can access, everything stored on a hard disk always takes

up at least one cluster. In addition to tracks, sectors, and clusters, hard disks are also organized into cylinders (refer again to Exhibit 2-14). A **cylinder** is the collection of one specific track located on each hard disk surface.

A newer type of hard drive is the **solid-state drive (SSD,** also called a **flash memory hard drive)**, which is a hard drive that uses flash memory technology instead of spinning hard disk platters and magnetic technology. Consequently, data is stored as electrical charges on flash memory media, and SSDs have no moving parts. See Exhibit 2-15. These characteristics mean that SSDs are not subject to mechanical failures like magnetic hard drives and are, therefore, more resistant to shock and vibration. They also consume less power, generate less heat, make no noise,

track A concentric ring on the surface of a hard disk where data is recorded.

sector A pie-shaped section on the surface of a hard disk.

cluster The smallest storage area on a hard disk formed by one or more adjacent sectors.

cylinder The collection of one specific track located on each hard disk surface.

solid state drive (SSD, or **flash memory hard drive)** A hard drive that uses flash memory technology.

Exhibit 2-14 Organization of a magnetic hard disk

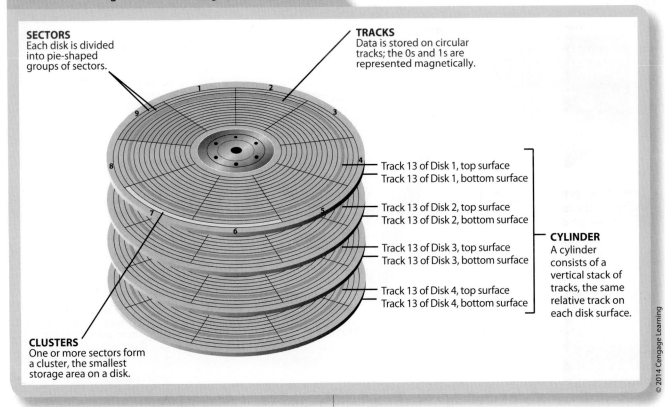

SECTORS
Each disk is divided into pie-shaped groups of sectors.

TRACKS
Data is stored on circular tracks; the 0s and 1s are represented magnetically.

Track 13 of Disk 1, top surface
Track 13 of Disk 1, bottom surface

Track 13 of Disk 2, top surface
Track 13 of Disk 2, bottom surface

Track 13 of Disk 3, top surface
Track 13 of Disk 3, bottom surface

Track 13 of Disk 4, top surface
Track 13 of Disk 4, bottom surface

CYLINDER
A cylinder consists of a vertical stack of tracks, the same relative track on each disk surface.

CLUSTERS
One or more sectors form a cluster, the smallest storage area on a disk.

© 2014 Cengage Learning

Exhibit 2-15 Solid-state drive

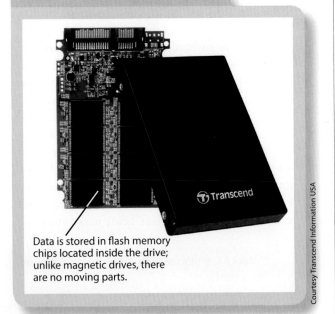

Data is stored in flash memory chips located inside the drive; unlike magnetic drives, there are no moving parts.

Courtesy Transcend Information USA

and are faster. Although previously too expensive for all but specialty applications, prices of SSDs have fallen significantly over the past few years, and they

disk access time The total time that it takes for a hard drive to read or write data.

are becoming the norm for netbooks, mobile devices, and other very portable devices. One disadvantage of SSDs is that flash memory cells can wear out with repeated use.

Hard drives can be internal or external. Internal hard drives are permanently located inside a computer's system unit and typically are not removed unless a problem occurs with them. Virtually all computers have at least one internal hard drive that is used to store programs and data. In addition, a variety of external hard drives are available, as shown in Exhibit 2-16. External hard drives are commonly used to transport a large amount of data from one computer to another, for backup purposes, and for additional storage.

The total time that it takes for a hard drive to read or write data is called the **disk access time** and requires the following:

1. **Seek time**—The read/write heads move to the cylinder that contains (or will contain) the desired data.

2. **Rotational delay**—The hard disks rotate into the proper position so that the read/write heads are located over the part of the cylinder to be used.

Exhibit 2-16 External hard drives

FULL-SIZED EXTERNAL HARD DRIVES
Are about the size of a 5 by 7-inch picture frame, but thicker; this drive holds 3 TB.

PORTABLE HARD DRIVES (MAGNETIC)
Are about the size of a 3 by 5-inch index card, but thicker; this drive holds 1.5 TB.

PORTABLE HARD DRIVES (SSD)
Are about the size of a credit card, but thicker; this drive holds 256 GB.

EXPRESSCARD HARD DRIVES
Fit into an ExpressCard slot; this drive holds 32 GB.

Image courtesy of Iomega an EMC company; Courtesy Transcend Information USA

3. **Data movement time**—The data moves, such as reading the data from the hard disk and transferring it to memory, or transfers from memory and is stored on the hard disk.

A typical disk access time is around 8.5 milliseconds (ms). To minimize disk access time, magnetic hard drives usually store related data on the same cylinder. This strategy reduces seek time and, therefore, improves the overall access time. Because SSDs do not have to move any parts to store or retrieve data, they do not require seek time or rotational delay, and their access time is much faster than magnetic hard drives—essentially instantaneous at about 0.1 ms on some benchmark tests.

To speed up magnetic hard drive performance, disk caching is often used. A **disk cache** stores copies of data or programs that are located on the hard drive and that might be needed soon in memory to avoid having to retrieve the data or programs from the hard drive when they are requested. Because the hard disks do not have to be accessed if the requested data is located in the disk cache, and because retrieving data from memory is much faster than from a magnetic hard disk, disk caching can speed up performance. Disk caching also saves wear and tear on the hard drive and, in portable computers, can also extend battery life. Memory used for disk caching typically consists of memory chips located on a circuit board inside the hard drive case. It can also be a designated portion of RAM.

Most conventional magnetic hard drives today include a flash memory-based disk cache ranging in size from 8 MB to 64 MB built into the hard drive case. However, **hybrid hard drives**—essentially a combination flash memory/magnetic hard drive (see Exhibit 2-17)—use a much larger amount of flash memory (typically 4 GB). In addition to using the flash memory to reduce the number of times the hard disks in a hybrid hard drive need to be read, hybrid hard drives can also use the flash memory to temporarily store (cache) data to be written to the hard disks, which can further extend the battery life of portable computers and mobile devices. The additional flash memory in a hybrid hard drive can also allow encryption or other security measures to be built into the drive.

> # Disk caching saves wear and tear on the hard drive.

disk cache Memory used in conjunction with a magnetic hard drive to improve system performance.

hybrid hard drive A combination flash memory/magnetic hard drive.

Exhibit 2-17 Hybrid hard drive

MAGNETIC HARD DRIVE
This drive contains 2 hard disks and 4 read/write heads that operate in a manner similar to a conventional hard drive.

FLASH MEMORY DISK CACHE
This drive contains 4 GB of flash memory to duplicate data as it is stored on the hard disks so the data can be accessed when the hard disks are not spinning.

Courtesy of Seagate Technology LLC

2-4b Optical Discs

Optical discs are thin circular discs made out of polycarbonate substrate—essentially a type of very strong plastic—that are topped with layers of other materials and coatings used to store data and protect the disc. Data on optical discs is stored and read optically using laser beams. Data can be stored on one or both sides of an optical disc, depending on the disc design, and some types of discs use multiple recording layers on each side of the disc to increase capacity. An optical disc contains a single spiral track (instead of multiple tracks like magnetic disks), and the track is divided into sectors to keep data organized. As shown in Exhibit 2-18, this track (sometimes referred to as

optical disc A storage medium in the shape of a thin circular disc made out of polycarbonate substrate that is read from and written to using a laser beam.

a *groove* to avoid confusion with the term *tracks* that refers to songs on an audio CD) begins at the center of the disc and spirals out to the edge of the disc. Optical discs include CDs, DVDs, and high-capacity Blu-ray Discs (BD), and discs can be read-only, recordable (can be written to once), or rewritable (can be written to, erased, and rewritten as needed). Optical discs are the current standard for software delivery. They are also commonly used for backup purposes and for storing and/or transporting music, photo, video, and other large files.

CAUTION

Back Up Data

Because you never know when a head crash or other hard drive failure will occur—there may be no warning whatsoever—be sure to back up the data on your hard drive on a regular basis. Backing up data—that is, creating a second copy of important files—is critical not only for businesses but also for individuals. If a hard drive becomes damaged, a data recovery firm might be able to help retrieve the data.

Exhibit 2-18 How recorded optical discs work

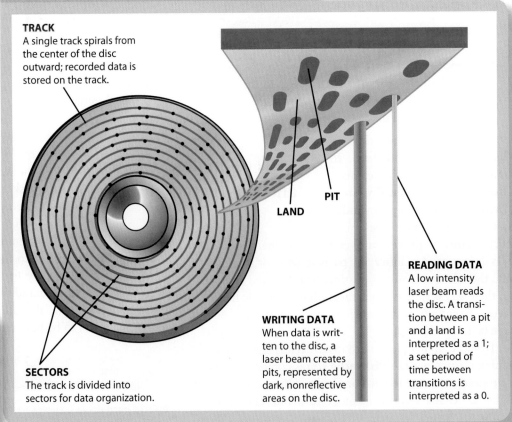

TRACK
A single track spirals from the center of the disc outward; recorded data is stored on the track.

PIT

LAND

READING DATA
A low intensity laser beam reads the disc. A transition between a pit and a land is interpreted as a 1; a set period of time between transitions is interpreted as a 0.

WRITING DATA
When data is written to the disc, a laser beam creates pits, represented by dark, nonreflective areas on the disc.

SECTORS
The track is divided into sectors for data organization.

© 2014 Cengage Learning

One of the biggest advantages of optical discs is their large capacity. To further increase capacity, many discs are available as dual-layer (DL) discs that store data in two layers on a single side of the disc, so the capacity is approximately doubled. For an even larger capacity, discs with more than two layers are in development. Discs can also be double sided, which doubles the capacity, but the disc must be turned over to access the second side. Double-sided discs are most often used with movies and other prerecorded content, such as to store a widescreen version of a movie on one side of a DVD disc and a standard version on the other side. Optical discs can also use the + or – standard. See Exhibit 2-19 for examples of recordable discs.

Exhibit 2-19 Recordable optical discs

CD-R DISCS
Hold 650 MB.

DVD+R DL DISCS
Hold 8.5 GB.

BD-R DL DISCS
Hold 50 GB.

Another advantage of optical discs is durability. They are more durable than magnetic media and do not degrade with use, as some magnetic media does. However, the discs should be handled carefully and stored in their cases when not in use to protect the recorded surfaces of the discs from scratches, fingerprints, and other marks that can interfere with the usability of the discs.

Optical discs are designed to be read by **optical drives**, such as CD, DVD, and BD drives, and the type of optical drive being used must support the type of optical disc being used. Most optical drives today support multiple types of optical discs—some support all possible types. Optical drives are almost always downward-compatible, meaning they can be used with lower (older) types of discs but not higher (newer) ones. So, while a DVD drive would likely support all types of CDs and DVDs, it cannot be used with BDs; but most BD drives today support all types of CDs, DVDs, and BDs.

The process of recording data onto a recordable or rewritable optical disc is called burning. To burn an optical disc, the optical drive being used must support burning and the type of disc being used. In addition, CD-burning or DVD-burning software is required. Many burning programs are available commercially, and recent versions of operating systems (including Windows and Mac OS) include burning capabilities. In addition, most CD and DVD drives come bundled with burning software.

Data is written to an optical disc in one of two ways. With read-only optical discs like movie, music, and software CDs and DVDs, the surface of the disc is molded or stamped appropriately to represent the data. To accomplish this, tiny depressions (when viewed from the top side of the disc) or bumps (when viewed from the bottom) are created on the disc's surface. These bumps are called *pits*; the areas on the disc that are not changed are called *lands*. With recordable or rewritable optical discs that can be written to using an optical drive such as a CD drive or DVD drive, the reflectivity of the disc is changed using a laser to represent the data stored there—dark, nonreflective areas are pits; reflective areas are lands, as was illustrated in Exhibit 2-18. In either case, the disc is read with a laser and the computer interprets the reflection of the laser off the disc surface as 1s and 0s.

optical drive A drive designed to read optical discs.

Creative Marketing with Optical Discs

Optical discs are available in a variety of sizes, appearances, and capacities. Some businesses have adopted the practice of using optical discs to replace ordinary objects, such as business cards and mailed advertisements. Business card CDs are discs with business card information printed on the outside that contain a résumé, a portfolio, or other digital documents. Optical discs can also be scented to have a specific aroma, such as a particular perfume, popcorn, pine trees, or a specific fruit. The scent is added to the disc's label and is released when the surface of the disc is rubbed. In addition, optical discs can be made into a variety of sizes and shapes—such as a heart, a triangle, an irregular shape, or a hockey-rink shape appropriate for business card CDs—because the track starts at the center of a disc and just stops when it reaches an outer edge of the disc. However, an ongoing patent battle about changing the shape of any normally round storage media (a process an individual claims to have patented) has resulted in these shapes not being available by any CD or DVD manufacturer until the patent issue is resolved.

Different types of optical discs use different types of laser beams. Conventional CDs use infrared lasers; conventional DVDs use red lasers, which allow data to be stored more compactly on the same size disc; and high-definition Blu-ray discs (BD) use blue-violet lasers, which can store data even more compactly on a disc.

Most recordable optical discs have a recording layer containing organic light-sensitive dye embedded between the disc's plastic and reflective layers. One exception to this is the BD-R, which has a recording layer consisting of inorganic material. When data is written to a recordable disc, the recording laser inside the recordable optical drive burns the dye (for CDs and DVDs) or melts and combines the inorganic material (for BD-Rs), creating nonreflective areas that function as pits. In either case, the marks are permanent, so data on the disc cannot be erased or rewritten.

To write to, erase, or overwrite rewritable optical discs, phase change technology is used. With this technology, the rewritable CD or DVD is coated with layers of a special metal alloy compound that can have two different appearances after it has been heated and then cooled, depending on the heating and cooling process used. With one process, the material crystallizes and that area of the disc is reflective. With another process, the area cools to a nonreflective amorphous state. Before any data is written to a rewritable optical disc, the disc is completely reflective. To write data to the disc, the recording laser heats the metal alloy in the appropriate locations on the spiral track and then uses the appropriate cooling process to create either the nonreflective areas (pits) or the reflective areas (lands). To erase the disc, the appropriate heating and cooling process is used to change the areas to be erased back to their original reflective state.

2-4c Flash Memory Storage Systems

As discussed previously, flash memory is a chip-based storage medium that represents data using electrical charges. It is used in a variety of storage systems, such as the SSDs and hybrid hard drives already discussed as well as the additional storage systems discussed next.

> Flash memory cards are the most common type of storage media for portable devices.

Because flash memory media are physically very small, they are increasingly being embedded directly into a variety of consumer products—such as portable digital media players, digital cameras, handheld gaming devices, GPS devices, mobile phones, and even sunglasses and wristwatches—to provide built-in data storage. **Embedded flash memory** refers to flash memory chips embedded into products. Flash memory is also increasingly being integrated into mobile devices, such as small tablet computers and smartphones. Although embedded flash memory can take the form of small SSDs or memory cards, it is increasingly being implemented with small stand-alone chips, such as the one shown in Exhibit 2-20.

embedded flash memory Flash memory chips embedded into products.

Exhibit 2-20 Embedded flash memory

PORTABLE TABLET
Contains 16 GB of embedded flash memory.

EMBEDDED FLASH MEMORY

One of the most common types of flash memory media is the **flash memory card**—a small, rectangular card containing one or more flash memory chips, a controller chip, other electrical components, and metal contacts to connect the card to the device or reader with which it is being used. Flash memory cards are available in a variety of formats, as shown in Exhibit 2-21. These formats are not interchangeable, so the type of flash memory card used with a device is determined by the type of flash media card that device can accept. Flash memory cards are the most common type of storage media for digital cameras, portable digital media players, mobile phones, and other portable devices. They can also be used to store data for a personal computer, as well as to transfer data from a portable device to a computer. Consequently, most desktop and notebook computers today come with a flash memory card reader capable of reading flash memory cards; an external flash memory card reader (that typically connects via a USB port) can be used if a built-in reader is not available. The capacity of flash memory cards is continually growing and is up to about 2 GB for standard cards and 32 GB for high-capacity cards; extended capacity cards are expected to reach capacities of 2 TB by 2014.

Exhibit 2-21 Flash memory cards

FLASH MEMORY CARD READER
Can be built-in or external and usually support several different types of flash memory media; external readers such as this one typically connect to a computer via a USB port.

COMPACTFLASH (CF) CARD

MEMORY STICK

SECURE DIGITAL (SD) CARDS

XD PICTURE CARD

flash memory card A small, rectangular flash memory medium.

USB flash drives (sometimes called USB flash memory drives, thumb drives, or jump drives) consist of flash memory media integrated into a self-contained unit that connects to a computer or other device via a standard USB port and is powered via the USB port. As shown in Exhibit 2-22, USB flash drives can take a variety of sizes, colors, and appearances. USB flash drives are designed to be very small and very portable. Because they are becoming so widely used, additional hardware related to USB flash drives is becoming available, such as USB duplicator systems used by educators to copy assignments or other materials to and from a large collection of USB flash drives at one time.

Exhibit 2-22 USB flash drives

CONVENTIONAL DRIVE

CUSTOM CONVENTIONAL DRIVE

CUSTOM WRISTBAND DRIVE

CUSTOM WALLET DRIVE

USB flash drive Flash memory media integrated into a self-contained unit that plugs into a USB port.

remote storage A storage device that is not connected directly to the user's computer.

network attached storage (NAS) A high-performance storage system connected individually to a network to provide storage for computers on that network.

storage area network (SAN) A network of hard drives or other storage devices that provide storage for another network.

To read from or write to a USB flash drive, you just plug it into a USB port. If the USB flash drive is being used with a computer, it is assigned a drive letter by the computer, just like any other type of attached drive, and files can be read from or written to the USB flash drive until it is unplugged from the USB port. The capacity of most USB flash drives today ranges from 2 GB to 256 GB.

2-4d Network Storage and Online/Cloud Storage Systems

Remote storage refers to using a storage device that is not connected directly to the user's computer; instead, the device is accessed through a local network or through the Internet. Using a remote storage device via a local network (referred to as network storage) works in much the same way as using local storage (the storage devices and media that are directly attached to the user's computer). To read data from or write data to a remote storage device (such as a hard drive in another computer being accessed via a network), the user just selects it and then performs the necessary tasks in the usual fashion. Network storage is common in businesses. It is also used by individuals with home networks for backup purposes or to share files with another computer in the home.

Because of the vast amount of data shared and made available over networks, network storage has become increasingly important. There are two common types of network storage. **Network attached storage (NAS)** consists of high-performance storage systems that are connected individually to a network to provide storage for the computers connected to that network. They can be large storage systems designed for a large business, or smaller NAS devices designed for a home or a small business. A growing trend, in fact, is home NAS devices designed to store multimedia data to be distributed over a home entertainment network. A **storage area network (SAN)** also provides storage for a network, but it consists of a separate

USB Flash Drive PCs

USB flash drives are a great way to transport documents from one location to another. But what about using one to take a personalized computer with you wherever you go? It is possible and easy to do with the use of portable applications (also called portable apps)—computer programs that are designed to be used with portable devices like USB flash drives. When the device is plugged into the USB port of any computer, you have access to the software and personal data (including your browser bookmarks, calendar, email and instant messaging contacts, and more) stored on that device, just as you would on your own computer. And when you unplug the device, none of your personal data is left behind because all programs are run directly from the USB flash drive. Many portable applications, such as the PortableApps suite, are free and include all the basics you might want in a single package. For instance, Portable Apps includes a menu structure, antivirus program, Web browser, email program, calendar program, the OpenOffice.org office suite, and more.

1. USB flash drive is plugged into a computer.

2. This menu is displayed; all programs run off the USB flash drive.

network of hard drives or other storage devices, which is connected to the main network.

The primary difference between network attached storage and a storage area network is how the storage devices interface with the network—that is, whether the storage devices act as individual network nodes, just like computers, printers, and other devices on the network (NAS), or whether they are located in a completely separate network of storage devices that is accessible to the main network (SAN). However, in terms of functionality, the distinction between NAS and SANs is blurring because they both provide storage services to the network. Typically, both NAS and SAN systems are scalable, so new devices can be added as more storage is needed, and devices can be added or removed without disrupting the network.

Remote storage devices accessed via the Internet are often referred to as **online storage** or **cloud storage**. Although these terms are often used interchangeably, some view cloud storage as a specific type of online storage that can be accessed on demand by various Web applications. Most online applications, such as Google Docs, the Flickr photo-sharing service, and social networking sites like Facebook, provide online storage for these services. There are also sites whose primary objective is to allow users to store documents online, such as Box.net or Windows Live SkyDrive. Typically, online/cloud storage sites are password-protected and allow users to specify uploaded files as private files or as shared files that designated individuals can access.

> Some smart cards store biometric data that is used to ensure the authenticity of the card's user.

2-4e Smart Cards

A **smart card** is a credit card–sized piece of plastic that contains computer circuitry and components—typically a processor, memory, and storage. Smart cards store a relatively small amount of data (typically 64 KB or less). Smart cards are commonly used for national and student ID cards, credit and debit cards, and cards that store identification data for accessing facilities or computer networks.

To use a smart card, it must either be inserted into a smart card reader (if it is the type of card that requires contact) or placed close to a smart card reader (if it is a contactless card) built into or attached to a

online storage (cloud storage) Remote storage devices accessed via the Internet.

smart card A credit card–sized piece of plastic that contains a chip and computer circuitry that can store data.

Storing Documents in the Cloud

The ability to store documents online (or "in the cloud") is growing in importance as more applications are becoming Web based and as more individuals want access to their files from anywhere with any Internet-enabled device, such as a portable computer or mobile phone. Online storage is also increasingly being used for backup purposes—some online storage sites have an automatic backup option that uploads the files from designated folders on your computer to your online account at regular, specified intervals as long as your computer is connected to the Internet. Many Web sites providing online storage to individuals offer the service for free (for instance, SkyDrive gives each individual 25 GB of free storage space); others charge a small fee, such as $10 per month for 50 GB of storage space.

computer, keyboard, vending machine, or other device (see Exhibit 2-23). Once a smart card has been verified by the card reader, the transaction—such as making a purchase or unlocking a door—can be completed. For an even higher level of security, some smart cards store biometric data in the card and use that data to ensure the authenticity of the card's user before authorizing the smart card transaction.

2-4f Storage Systems for Large Computer Systems

Businesses and other organizations have tremendous storage needs that are growing exponentially. In addition to regular business data storage (such as employee files, customer and order data, business documents, and Web site content), new regulations are continually increasing the types of and amounts of data that many businesses need to archive. These documents must be stored in a manner in which they can be readily retrieved as needed. One forecast predicts that digital storage needs will increase by 50 percent annually through 2014.

For large computer systems, instead of finding a single hard drive installed within the system unit, you are most likely to find a large storage system (sometimes called a storage server)—a separate piece of hardware containing multiple high-speed hard drives—connected to the computer system or network. Large storage systems typically contain drawers of hard drives for a large total capacity. For

Exhibit 2-23 Smart card uses

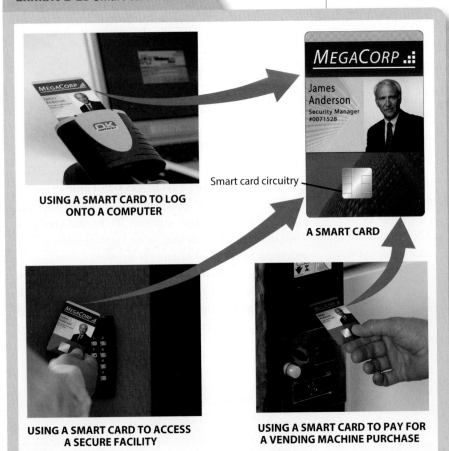

USING A SMART CARD TO LOG ONTO A COMPUTER

A SMART CARD

Smart card circuitry

USING A SMART CARD TO ACCESS A SECURE FACILITY

USING A SMART CARD TO PAY FOR A VENDING MACHINE PURCHASE

instance, the storage system shown in Exhibit 2-24 can include up to 1,280 hard drives for a total capacity of 800 TB.

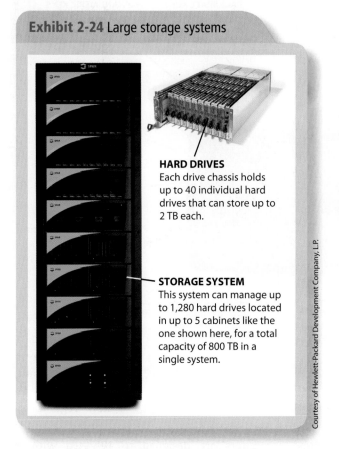

Exhibit 2-24 Large storage systems

HARD DRIVES
Each drive chassis holds up to 40 individual hard drives that can store up to 2 TB each.

STORAGE SYSTEM
This system can manage up to 1,280 hard drives located in up to 5 cabinets like the one shown here, for a total capacity of 800 TB in a single system.

Courtesy of Hewlett-Packard Development Company, L.P.

In addition to being used as stand-alone storage for large computer systems, large storage systems may also be used in network attached storage (NAS), storage area network (SAN), and RAID (redundant array of independent disks) systems. **RAID (redundant array of independent disks)** is a method of storing data on two or more hard drives that work together. Although RAID can be used to increase performance, it is most often used to protect critical data on a large storage system. Because RAID usually involves recording redundant (duplicate) copies of stored data, the copies can be used, when necessary, to reconstruct lost data. This helps to increase the fault tolerance—the ability to recover from an unexpected hardware or software failure, such as a system crash—of a storage system.

Most storage servers are based on magnetic hard disks, although magnetic tape storage systems are also possible. **Magnetic tape** consists of plastic tape coated with a magnetizable substance that represents the bits and bytes of digital data, similar to magnetic hard disks. Although magnetic tape is no longer used for everyday storage applications because of its sequential-access property, it is still used today for business data archiving and backup. One advantage of magnetic tape is its low cost per terabyte.

Which Type of Storage Do You Need?

With so many storage alternatives available, it can be overwhelming to decide which devices and media are most appropriate for your personal situation. In general, you will need a hard drive for storing programs and data; some type of recordable or rewritable optical drive for installing programs, backing up files, and sharing files with others; and a flash memory card reader for transferring photos, music, and other content between portable devices and the computer. If you plan to transfer music, digital photos, and other multimedia data on a regular basis between devices—such as a computer, digital camera, mobile phone, and printer—you will want to select and use the flash memory media that are compatible with the devices you are using. You will also need to obtain the necessary adapter for your computer if it does not include a compatible built-in flash memory reader. You will also need at least one convenient free USB port to use to connect external hard drives, USB flash drives, and other USB-based storage hardware, as well as USB devices that contain storage media, such as digital cameras and portable digital media players. Fewer storage options are available for mobile devices, so evaluate the available options when selecting a mobile device to ensure that it can perform the functions you need, such as the ability to back up data and contacts in the cloud or on a medium you can access with another device, the ability to transfer photos and other data to a computer or printer, and so forth.

RAID (redundant array of independent disks) A method of storing data on two or more hard drives that work together.

magnetic tape Storage media consisting of plastic tape coated with a magnetizable substance.

Exhibit 2-25 Typical desktop keyboard

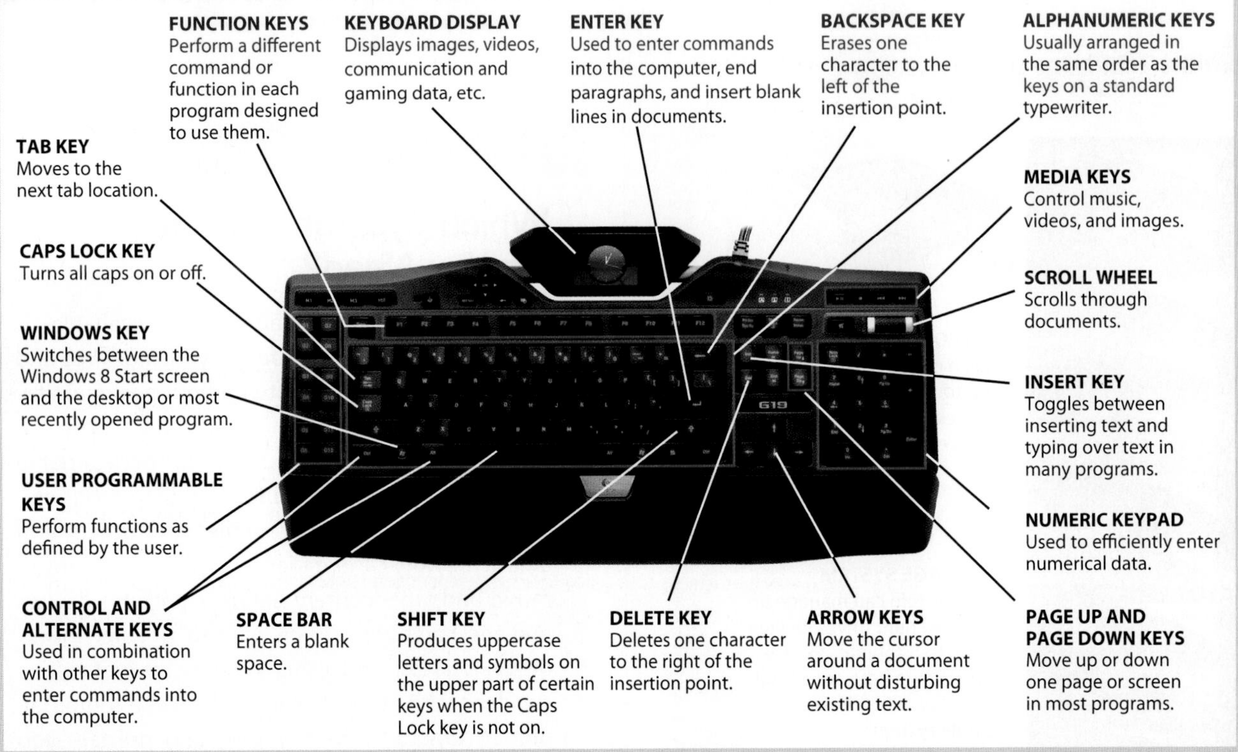

FUNCTION KEYS
Perform a different command or function in each program designed to use them.

KEYBOARD DISPLAY
Displays images, videos, communication and gaming data, etc.

ENTER KEY
Used to enter commands into the computer, end paragraphs, and insert blank lines in documents.

BACKSPACE KEY
Erases one character to the left of the insertion point.

ALPHANUMERIC KEYS
Usually arranged in the same order as the keys on a standard typewriter.

TAB KEY
Moves to the next tab location.

MEDIA KEYS
Control music, videos, and images.

CAPS LOCK KEY
Turns all caps on or off.

SCROLL WHEEL
Scrolls through documents.

WINDOWS KEY
Switches between the Windows 8 Start screen and the desktop or most recently opened program.

INSERT KEY
Toggles between inserting text and typing over text in many programs.

USER PROGRAMMABLE KEYS
Perform functions as defined by the user.

NUMERIC KEYPAD
Used to efficiently enter numerical data.

CONTROL AND ALTERNATE KEYS
Used in combination with other keys to enter commands into the computer.

SPACE BAR
Enters a blank space.

SHIFT KEY
Produces uppercase letters and symbols on the upper part of certain keys when the Caps Lock key is not on.

DELETE KEY
Deletes one character to the right of the insertion point.

ARROW KEYS
Move the cursor around a document without disturbing existing text.

PAGE UP AND PAGE DOWN KEYS
Move up or down one page or screen in most programs.

Courtesy of Logitech; © 2014 Cengage Learning

2-5 Input Devices

An **input device** is any piece of equipment that is used to enter data into the computer. The most common input devices used with personal computers are keyboards and pointing devices, such as a mouse or pen. There are also input devices designed for touch input, for capturing and reading data in electronic form, and for inputting audio data.

Some keyboards contain special keys to control the speaker volume or launch an email program.

2-5a Keyboards

Most computers are designed to be used with a **keyboard**—a device containing keys used to enter characters on the screen. Keyboards can be built into a device, attached using a wired cable, such as via a USB port, or connected via a wireless connection. A typical desktop computer keyboard is shown in Exhibit 2-25. Like most keyboards, this keyboard contains standard alphanumeric keys to input text and numbers, as well as additional keys used for various purposes such as to control the speaker volume or to launch an email program. Keyboards, such as the one in Exhibit 2-25, are increasingly using illuminated keys to light up the characters on the keyboard to allow individuals to work under a variety of lighting conditions, such as in a dark living room or in an airplane.

input device Any piece of equipment that is used to enter data into the computer.

keyboard An input device containing keys used to enter characters on the screen.

Keyboards on Clothing

One possibility for the future is printing keyboards directly on clothing and other products that can connect wirelessly to the devices being used. For example, keyboards might be printed on jackets to allow consumers to wirelessly input data or otherwise control their mobile phones while on the go, or keyboards might be printed on soldiers' uniforms to be used with netbooks or other small computers while in the field.

2-5b Pointing Devices

In addition to a keyboard, most computers are used in conjunction with some type of pointing device. **Pointing devices** are used to select and manipulate objects, to input certain types of data, such as handwritten data, and to issue commands to the computer. The **mouse** (see Exhibit 2-26) is the most common pointing device for a desktop computer. It typically rests on the desk or other flat surface close to the computer, and the user slides it across the surface in the appropriate direction to point to and select objects on the screen. As it moves, an on-screen mouse pointer—usually an arrow—moves accordingly. Once the mouse pointer is pointing to the desired object on the screen, the user clicks the buttons on the mouse to perform actions on that object (such as to open a hyperlink, to select text, or to resize an image). Similar to keyboards, mice typically connect via a USB port or via a wireless connection. Older mechanical mice have a ball exposed on the bottom surface of the mouse to control the pointer movement. Most mice today are optical mice or laser mice that track movements with light.

Exhibit 2-26 Examples of mice

LASER MICE   3D MICE

Courtesy of Logitech; Courtesy 3Dconnexion

Similar to an upside-down mechanical mouse, a **trackball** has the ball mechanism on top, instead of on the bottom. The ball is rotated with the thumb, hand, or finger to move the on-screen pointer. Because the device itself does not need to be moved, trackballs take up less space on a desk than mice. They also are easier to use for individuals with limited hand or finger mobility.

Many devices, including some desktop computers and many tablet computers and mobile devices, can accept pen input, which is input by writing, drawing, or tapping on the screen with a penlike device called a **stylus** or a **digital pen**. Sometimes, the stylus (also called an electronic pen or tablet pen) is simply a plastic device with no additional functionality. Other times, it is a pressure-sensitive device that transmits the pressure applied by the user to the device that the stylus is being used with to allow more precise input. These more sophisticated styluses also are typically powered by the device that they are being used with; have a smooth, rounded tip so they do not scratch the screen; and contain buttons or switches to perform actions such as erasing content or right-clicking.

Special Mice

For use with virtual worlds, animation programs, and other 3D applications, 3D mice are available that are designed to make navigation through a 3D environment easier. For example, the 3Dconnexion SpaceNavigator 3D mouse shown in Exhibit 2-26 has a controller cap, which can be lifted up to move an object up, rotated to "fly" around objects, or tilted to "look" up. In addition to being used with desktop computers, mice can also be used with portable computers (such as notebook and netbook computers) as long as an appropriate port (such as a USB port) is available. Also, special cordless presenter mice can be used to control on-screen slide shows.

pointing device An input device that moves an on-screen pointer used to select and manipulate objects and to issue commands to the computer.

mouse A common pointing device that the user slides along a flat surface to move the pointer on the screen.

trackball A pointing device similar to an upside-down mechanical mouse with the ball mechanism on top.

stylus (digital pen) A penlike device used for input by writing, drawing, or tapping on the screen.

A variety of gaming devices today, such as the joystick, gamepad, and steering wheels shown in Exhibit 2-27, can be used as controllers to supply input to a computer. Other input devices are intended to be used with gaming consoles, including guitars, drums, and other musical instruments; dance pads and balance boards, and other motion-sensitive controllers; and proprietary controllers such as the Wii Remote, Xbox Kinect, and PlayStation Move.

Exhibit 2-27 Other common pointing devices

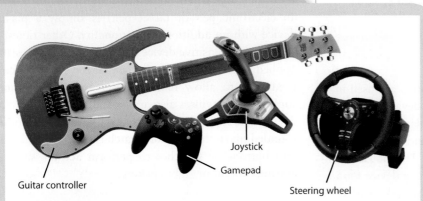

Guitar controller

Joystick

Gamepad

Steering wheel

GAMING DEVICES
Most often used for gaming applications.

CONTROL BUTTONS
Commonly found on portable digital media players and other consumer devices.

TOUCH PADS
Commonly found on notebook and netbook computers.

Courtesy Logitech; Courtesy of SanDisk Corporation; Vladiro09/Shutterstock.com

Many consumer devices, such as portable digital media players, GPS devices, and handheld gaming devices, use special control buttons and wheels to select items and issue commands to the device. For instance,

the portable digital media player shown in Exhibit 2-27 contains buttons on the front and sides that are used to access music and other content stored on the device, navigate through songs, and adjust the volume.

2-5c Touch Devices

Touch screens allow the user to touch the screen with his or her finger as a pointing device to select commands or otherwise provide input to the computer associated with the touch screen. Their use is becoming common with personal computers, as well as with mobile phones and other mobile devices (see Exhibit 2-28) to provide easy input. Many touch screens are multi-touch, which means they can recognize input from more than one finger at a time. Similar multi-touch products are used for large wall displays, such as for use in museums, government command centers, and newsrooms. Touch screens are also used in consumer kiosks, restaurant order systems, and other point-of-sale (POS) systems. They are also useful for on-the-job applications (such as factory work) where it might be impractical to use a keyboard or mouse. A growing trend is to use touch screens that provide tactile feedback—a slight movement or other physical sensation in response to the users' touch so they know their input has been received by the computer. Although touch screens make many devices more convenient for most people to use, these devices and their applications are not accessible to blind individuals, users with limited mobility, and other individuals with a disability.

A **touch pad** is a rectangular pad across which a fingertip or thumb slides to move the on-screen pointer; tapping the touch pad or its associated buttons performs clicks and other mouse actions. Although most often found on notebook and netbook computers (refer back to Exhibit 2-27), touch pads are also available as stand-alone devices to be used with desktop computers and are built into some keyboards.

touch screen An input device that is touched with the finger to select commands or otherwise provide input to the computer.

touch pad A rectangular pad across which a fingertip or thumb slides or taps to control the pointer.

Exhibit 2-28 Touch screens

DESKTOP COMPUTERS   **PORTABLE COMPUTERS**

MOBILE DEVICES   **SURFACE COMPUTING DEVICES**

Courtesy, Hewlett-Packard Company; Courtesy TabletKiosk; Courtesy of Samsung; Courtesy Microsoft Corporation

Touch screens are also used in consumer kiosks, restaurant order systems, and other point-of-sale (POS) systems.

2-5d Scanners and Readers

A variety of input devices are designed to capture data in digital form so a computer can manipulate it.

LEARN MORE

Surface Computing

A new trend in touch screens is surface computing, which uses a combination of multi-touch input from multiple users and object recognition to interact with computers that are typically built into tabletops and other surfaces. One example is Microsoft Surface. This product, shown in Exhibit 2-28, uses touch and gestures performed via the screen, as well as objects placed on the screen, as input. It can recognize input from multiple users and multiple objects placed on the table simultaneously.

A **scanner**, more officially called an optical scanner, captures an image of an object—usually a flat object, such as a printed document, photograph, or drawing—in digital form and then transfers that data to a computer. Typically, the entire document is input as a single graphical image that can be resized, inserted into other documents, posted on a Web page, emailed to someone, printed, or otherwise treated like any other graphical image. The text in the scanned image, however, cannot be edited unless optical character recognition (OCR) software is used in conjunction with the scanner to input the scanned text as individual text characters.

The quality of scanned images is indicated by optical resolution, usually measured in **pixels per inch (ppi)**, although this is often mistakenly referred to as **dots per inch (dpi)**. (The quality of *printed* images is measured in dots per inch.) If you scanned the same image at 96 ppi, 300 ppi, and 600 ppi, the three versions would display at different sizes on a computer monitor: The 96ppi image would display at the smallest size, and the 600 ppi image would display at the largest size. If you resize the images scanned at the lower resolutions so they display larger on the computer monitor, these images would appear blocky (sometimes referred to as pixelated). Therefore, the image should be scanned at a size that is equal to or larger than the display size to achieve the best results. Exhibit 2-29 shows an image scanned at different resolutions and then resized to the same dimensions.

A variety of readers are available to read the different types of codes and marks used to represent data on products, advertising material, packages,

scanner An input device that reads printed text or captures an image of an object and then transfers that data to a computer.

dots per inch (dpi) A measurement of resolution that indicates the quality of an image or output.

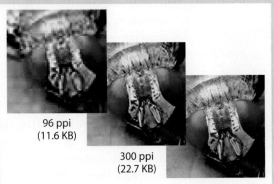

96 ppi
(11.6 KB)

300 ppi
(22.7 KB)

600 ppi
(448 KB)

RESOLUTION
Most scanners let you specify the resolution (in dpi) to use for the scan. High-resolution images look sharper but result in larger le sizes.

StudioNewmarket/Shutterstock.com; © 2014 Cengage Learning

ABC123
ISBN CODES

1 40002 66162 2
UPC (UNIVERSAL PRODUCT CODE) CODES

DATABAR CODES

INTELLIGENT MAIL CODES

ISBN-13: 978-1-111-52799-0
ISBN-10: 1-111-52799-7
90000

9 781111 527990
CODE 39 CODES

QR CODES

Courtesy of Motorola Solutions; © 2014 Cengage Learning

and other items. A **barcode** is an optical code that represents data with bars of varying widths or heights (see Exhibit 2-30). Two of the most familiar barcodes are UPC (Universal Product Code), the type of barcode found on packaged goods in supermarkets and other retail stores, and ISBN (International Standard Book Number), the barcode used with printed books. Businesses and organizations can also create and use custom barcodes to fulfill their unique needs. For instance, shipping organizations such as FedEx and UPS use custom barcodes to mark and track packages, retailers such as Target and Walmart use custom barcodes added to customer receipts to facilitate returns, hospitals use custom barcodes to match patients with their charts and medicines, libraries and video stores use custom barcodes for checking out and checking in books and movies, and law enforcement agencies use custom barcodes to mark evidence.

> Mobile phones can download a coupon by capturing a QR code with the camera.

Another type of barcode is the QR (Quick Response) code that represents data with a matrix of small squares. These are usually designed to be used by consumers with mobile phones with cameras. For instance, capturing the image of a QR barcode located on a magazine or newspaper ad with a mobile phone's camera could enable the consumer's mobile phone to load a Web page, dial a phone number, display a video clip, or download a coupon or ticket. QR codes can also be used to transfer contact information to a phone or add an event to an online calendar.

Barcodes are read with **barcode readers**. Barcode readers use either light reflected from the barcode or imaging technology to interpret the bars contained in the barcode as the numbers or letters they represent. Then, data associated with that barcode—typically identifying data, such as data used to uniquely identify a product, shipped package, or other item—can be retrieved. Fixed barcode readers are frequently used in point-of-sale (POS) systems (see Exhibit 2-31). Portable barcode readers are also available for people who need to scan barcodes while on the go, such as while walking through a warehouse, retail store, hospital, or other facility. Barcode-reading capabilities are now also included in many mobile phones.

Radio frequency identification (RFID) is a technology that can store, read, and transmit data located

barcode Machine-readable code that represents data as a set of bars.

barcode reader An input device that reads barcodes.

radio frequency identification (RFID) A technology that can store, read, and transmit data in RFID tags.

Exhibit 2-31 Barcode readers

FIXED BARCODE READERS
Used most often in retail point-of-sale applications.

PORTABLE BARCODE READERS
Used when portability is needed.

INTEGRATED BARCODE READERS
Used most often for consumer applications.

Exhibit 2-32 RFID tag

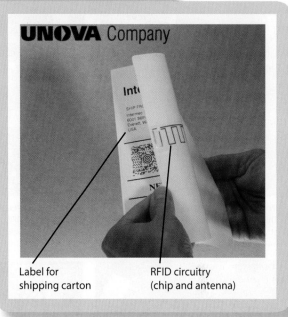

Label for
shipping carton

RFID circuitry
(chip and antenna)

more. The data in RFID tags is read by **RFID readers**. Whenever an RFID-tagged item is within range of an RFID reader (from two inches to up to 300 feet or more, depending on the type of tag and the radio frequency being used), the tag's built-in antenna allows the information located within the RFID tag to be sent to the reader. Because RFID technology can read numerous items at one time, it is also possible that, someday, RFID will allow a consumer to perform self-checkout at a retail store by just pushing a shopping cart past an RFID reader, which will ring up all items in the cart at one time. RFID is used today for many different applications; Exhibit 2-33 shows some examples.

Despite all its advantages, a number of privacy and security issues need to be resolved before RFID gains widespread use at the consumer level. Precautions against fraudulent use—such as using high-frequency tags that need to be within a few inches of the reader and requiring a PIN code, a signature, or another type of authorization when an RFID payment system is used—are being developed. Currently, a price limit (such as $25) for completely automated purchases (without a signature or other authorization), similar to many credit cards today, is being debated as a compromise between convenience and security. Privacy

in RFID tags. **RFID tags** contain tiny chips and radio antennas, as shown in Exhibit 2-32, and can be attached to objects, such as products, price tags, shipping labels, ID cards, assets (such as livestock, vehicles, computers, and other expensive items), and

RFID tag A tiny chip and radio antenna attached to an object so it can be identified using RFID technology.

RFID reader A device that reads the data in an RFID tag.

Exhibit 2-33 RFID applications

INVENTORY TRACKING
This RFID reader reads all of the RFID tags attached to all of the items on the palette at one time.

TICKETING APPLICATIONS
This stationary RFID reader is used to automatically open ski lift entry gates for valid lift ticket holders at a ski resort in Utah.

MOBILE PAYMENTS
This stationary RFID reader is used at checkout locations to quickly process payments via RFID-enabled credit cards or mobile phones.

BORDER SECURITY
This stationary RFID reader is used at the U.S.-Mexico border crossing located in San Diego to reduce wait time.

Courtesy LARA SOLT/KRT/Newscom; Courtesy of teamaxess.com; Courtesy MasterCard Worldwide; AP Images/Denis Poroy

advocates are concerned about linking RFID tag data with personally identifiable data contained in corporate databases, such as to track consumer movements or shopping habits. No long-term solution to this issue has yet been reached.

Optical mark readers (OMRs) input data from special forms to score or tally exams, questionnaires, ballots, and so forth. Typically, people use a pencil to fill in small circles or other shapes on the form to indicate their selections, and then the form is inserted into an optical mark reader such as shown in Exhibit 2-34

to be scored or tallied. The results can be input into a computer system if the optical mark reader is connected to a computer.

Optical character recognition (OCR) refers to the ability of a computer to recognize text characters. The characters are read by a compatible scanning device, such as a scanner, barcode reader, or dedicated OCR reader, and then OCR software is used to identify each character and convert it to editable text. While OCR systems can recognize many different types of printed characters, optical characters—which are characters specifically designed to be identifiable by humans as well as by an OCR device—are often used in documents intended to be processed by an OCR system. For example, optical characters are widely used in processing turnaround documents, such as the monthly bills for credit card and utility companies (see Exhibit 2-35). These documents contain optical characters in certain places on the bill to aid processing when consumers send it back with payment—or "turn it around."

optical mark reader (OMR) A device that inputs data from special forms to score or tally the data on those forms.

optical character recognition (OCR) The ability of a computer to recognize scanned text characters.

Exhibit 2-34 Optical mark reader

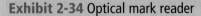

Courtesy Scantron Corporation®

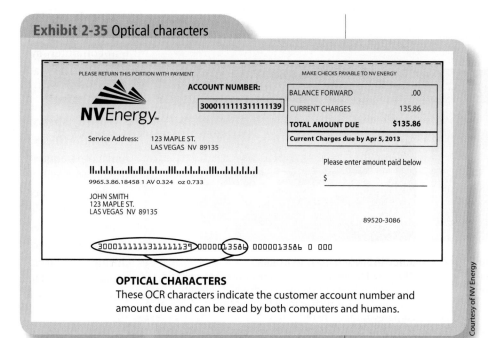

Exhibit 2-35 Optical characters

PLEASE RETURN THIS PORTION WITH PAYMENT   MAKE CHECKS PAYABLE TO NV ENERGY

NVEnergy™

ACCOUNT NUMBER:

3000111111311111139

BALANCE FORWARD	.00
CURRENT CHARGES	135.86
TOTAL AMOUNT DUE	**$135.86**
Current Charges due by Apr 5, 2013	

Service Address: 123 MAPLE ST.
LAS VEGAS NV 89135

9965.3.86.18458 1 AV 0.324   oz 0.733

JOHN SMITH
123 MAPLE ST.
LAS VEGAS NV 89135

Please enter amount paid below

$ _____

89520-3086

3000111111311111139 000001358b 0000013586 0 000

OPTICAL CHARACTERS
These OCR characters indicate the customer account number and amount due and can be read by both computers and humans.

Courtesy of NV Energy

Magnetic ink character recognition (MICR) is a technology used primarily by the banking industry to facilitate check processing. MICR characters, such as those located on the bottom of a check that represent the bank routing number, check number, and account number, are inscribed on checks with magnetic ink when the checks are first printed. These characters can be read and new characters, such as to reflect the check's amount, can be added by an MICR reader (also called a check scanner) when needed. High-volume MICR readers are used by banks to process checks deposited at the bank. Smaller units, such as the one shown in Exhibit 2-36, are used by many businesses to deposit paper checks remotely. MICR readers are also incorporated in most

Exhibit 2-36 Magnetic ink character recognition readers

Courtesy Epson America

new ATMs to enable the MICR information located on checks inserted into the ATM to be read at the time of the deposit.

Biometrics is the science of identifying individuals based on measurable biological characteristics. **Biometric readers** are used to read biometric data about a person so that the individual's identity can be verified based on a particular unique physiological characteristic, such as a fingerprint or a face, or personal trait, such as a voice or a signature. As shown in Exhibit 2-37, a biometric reader can be stand-alone or built into another piece of hardware, such as a keyboard, a mobile device, an external hard drive, or a USB flash drive. Biometric readers can be used to allow only authorized users access to a computer or facility or to the data stored on a storage device, as well as to authorize electronic payments, log on to secure Web sites, or punch into and out of work.

CAUTION

RFID and Privacy

Keep your enhanced driver's license and passport in the supplied protective sleeve when not in use to protect against unauthorized reading or tracking via RFID technology. Although no personal data is stored in the RFID chips used in these documents, hackers have demonstrated the ability to read the RFID chips used in these documents if they are not properly shielded. Because of this, privacy advocates recommend taking this precaution with any RFID-enabled identity document.

2-5e Audio Input

Audio input is the process of entering audio data into the computer. The most common types of audio input are voice and music. Voice input—inputting spoken

biometric reader A device used to input biometric data, such as an individual's fingerprint or voice.

Exhibit 2-37 Biometric readers

STAND-ALONE FINGERPRINT READERS
Often used to control access to facilities or computer systems, such as to the notebook computer shown here.

BUILT-IN FINGERPRINT READERS
Often used to control access to the device into which the reader is built or to verify an individual's identity using that device, such as for law enforcement purposes as shown here.

©iStockphoto.com/Sami Suni; Courtesy of Motorola Solutions

words and converting them to digital form—is typically performed via a microphone or headset (a set of headphones with a built-in microphone). It can be used in conjunction with sound recorder software to store the voice in an audio file as well as with Voice over IP (VoIP) systems that allow individuals to place telephone calls from a computer over the Internet. It can also be used in conjunction with speech recognition software to provide spoken instructions to a computer. **Speech recognition systems** enable the computer to recognize voice input as spoken words. It requires appropriate software, such as Dragon Naturally Speaking or Windows Speech Recognition, in addition to a microphone. See Exhibit 2-38. To enable hands-free operation, speech recognition capabilities are increasingly incorporated into mobile phones, GPS systems, and other mobile devices. They are also commonly built into cars to enable hands-free control of navigation systems

and sound systems, as well as to allow hands-free mobile phone calls to take place via the car's voice interface. Specialty speech recognition systems are frequently used to control machines, robots, and other electronic equipment, such as by surgeons during surgical procedures. They can also be used by individuals who cannot use a keyboard to input data and control the computer.

Music input systems are used to input music into a computer, such as to create an original music composition or arrangement or to create a custom music CD. Existing music can be input into a computer via a music CD or a Web download. For original compositions, microphones and keyboard

speech recognition system Hardware and software that enable a computer to recognize voice input.

Exhibit 2-38 Speech recognition systems

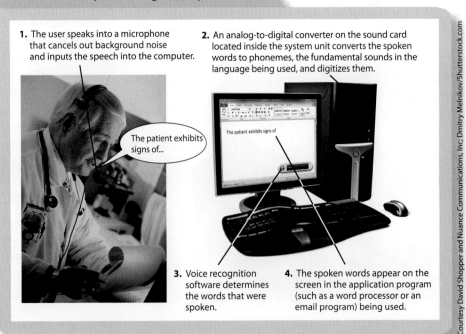

1. The user speaks into a microphone that cancels out background noise and inputs the speech into the computer.

2. An analog-to-digital converter on the sound card located inside the system unit converts the spoken words to phonemes, the fundamental sounds in the language being used, and digitizes them.

The patient exhibits signs of...

The patient exhibits signs of

3. Voice recognition software determines the words that were spoken.

4. The spoken words appear on the screen in the application program (such as a word processor or an email program) being used.

Courtesy David Shopper and Nuance Communications, Inc; Dmitry Melnikov/Shutterstock.com controllers—essentially piano keyboards connected to a computer—can be used (see Exhibit 2-39). Original music compositions can also be created using a conventional computer keyboard with appropriate software or a special device (such as a microphone or digital pen) designed to input music and convert it to a printed musical score. Once the music is input into the computer, it can be saved, modified, played, inserted into other programs, or burned to a CD or DVD.

Exhibit 2-39 Music input system

Courtesy Ergotron Inc.

LEARN MORE

Digital Cameras

Digital cameras record images on a digital storage medium, such as a flash memory card, built-in hard drive, or DVD disc. Digital cameras are usually designated either

Tungphoto/Shutterstock.com

as still cameras (which take individual still photos) or video cameras (which capture moving video images), although many cameras can take both still images and video. They are also available as stand-alone devices (commonly called PC cams or Webcams) to connect to a desktop computer or a network. In addition to stand-alone still and video cameras, digital camera capabilities are integrated into many portable computers and mobile devices. The images taken with a digital camera can be transferred to a computer for editing, printing, or inclusion in a document.

2-6 Output Devices

An **output device** accepts processed data from the computer and presents the results to the user, most of the time on the computer screen, on paper, or through a speaker.

2-6a Display Devices

A **display device**—the most common form of output device—presents output visually on some type of screen. The display device for a desktop computer is more formally called a **monitor**. The display device for a notebook computer, netbook, tablet, mobile phone, or other device for which the screen is built into the device is typically called a **display screen**. In addition to being used with computers and mobile devices, display screens are also built into handheld gaming devices; home entertainment devices, such as remote controls, televisions, and portable DVD players; automobile windshields; and kitchen appliances. They are also an important component in digital photo frames, e-book readers, portable digital media players, and other consumer products. See Exhibit 2-40.

The **CRT monitor** used to be the norm for desktop computers. CRT monitors use the same cathode-ray tube technology used in conventional televisions in which an electron gun sealed inside a large glass tube projects an electron beam at a screen coated with red, green, and blue phosphor dots; the beam lights up the appropriate colors in each **pixel**—the smallest colorable areas on a display device—essentially tiny dots on a display screen—to display the image. As a result, CRTs are large, bulky, and heavy.

> **output device** A device that accepts processed data from the computer and presents the results to the user.
>
> **display device** An output device that contains a viewing screen.
>
> **monitor** A display device for a desktop computer.
>
> **display screen** A display device built into a notebook computer, netbook, or other device.
>
> **CRT monitor** A display device that uses cathode-ray tube technology.
>
> **pixel** The smallest colorable areas on a display device.

Exhibit 2-40 Uses for display devices

PORTABLE COMPUTERS

HANDHELD GAMING DEVICES

DIGITAL PHOTO FRAMES

MOBILE DEVICES

DIGITAL SIGNAGE SYSTEMS

Andrew Buckin/Shutterstock.com; Courtesy of Samsung; Photo courtesy of Nokia; Courtesy of Clear Channel Spectacolor; Courtesy of Sony Electronics Inc.;

Most computers (as well as most television sets, mobile phones, and other consumer devices containing a display screen) use the thinner and lighter **flat panel displays**. Flat panel displays form images by manipulating electronically charged chemicals or gases sandwiched between thin panes of glass or other transparent material. Flat panel displays take up less desk space, which makes it possible to use multiple monitors working together to increase the amount of data the user can view at one time (see Exhibit 2-41), increasing productivity. Flat panel displays also consume less power than CRTs, and most use digital signals to display images (instead of the analog signals used with CRT monitors), which allows for sharper images. To use multiple monitors, you must have the necessary hardware to support them, such as a monitor port on a notebook computer or an appropriate video adapter, as discussed shortly. One disadvantage to a flat panel display is that the images sometimes cannot be seen clearly when viewed from certain angles.

flat panel display A slim display device that that uses electronically charged chemicals or gases to display images.

Exhibit 2-41 Flat panel displays

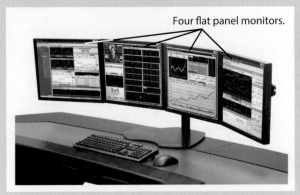

Four flat panel monitors.

Courtesy CineMassive Displays

One of the most common flat panel technologies is **liquid crystal display** (**LCD**), which uses charged liquid crystals located between two sheets of clear material (usually glass or plastic) to light up the appropriate pixels to form the image on the screen. Several layers of liquid crystals are used, and, in their normal state, the liquid crystals are aligned so that light passes through the display. When an electrical charge is applied to the liquid crystals (via an electrode grid layer contained within the LCD panel), the liquid crystals change their orientation, or "twist," so that light cannot pass through the display, and the liquid crystals at the charged intersections of the electrode grid appear dark. Color LCD displays use a color filter that consists of a pattern of red, green, and blue subpixels for each pixel. The voltage used controls the orientation (twisting) of the liquid crystals and the amount of light that gets through, affecting the color and shade of that pixel—the three different colors blend to make the pixel the appropriate color.

LCD displays can be viewed only with reflective light, unless light is built into the display. Consequently, LCD panels used with computer monitors typically include a light inside the panel, usually at the rear of the display—a technique referred to as backlighting. LCDs are currently the most common type of flat panel technology used for small- to medium-sized computer monitors. The monitors shown in Exhibit 2-41 are LCD monitors.

Another common flat panel technology is **LED** (**light-emitting diode**), which is also commonly used with consumer products, such as alarm clocks, Christmas lights, car headlights, and more. LEDs are also used to backlight LCD panels, although **organic light-emitting diode** (**OLED**) might eventually replace LCD technology entirely. OLED displays use layers of organic material that emit a visible light when electric current is applied. Because they emit a visible light, OLED displays do not use backlighting. This characteristic makes OLEDs

more energy efficient than LCDs and lengthens the battery life of portable devices using OLED displays. Other advantages of OLEDs are that they are thinner than LCDs, they have a wider viewing angle than LCDs so displayed content is visible from virtually all directions, and their images are brighter and sharper than LCDs. OLED displays are incorporated into many digital cameras, mobile phones, portable digital media players, and other consumer devices (see Exhibit 2-42). They are also beginning to appear in television and computer displays.

Exhibit 2-42 How OLED displays work

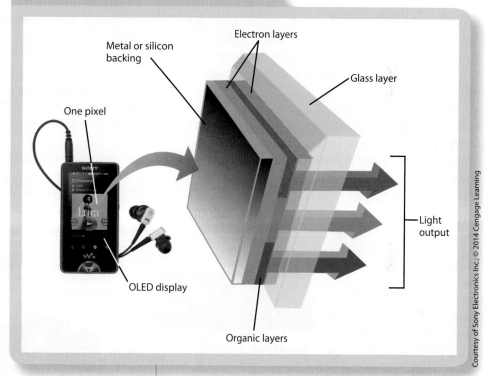

Metal or silicon backing

Electron layers

Glass layer

One pixel

Light output

OLED display

Organic layers

Courtesy of Sony Electronics Inc.; © 2014 Cengage Learning

Plasma displays use a layered technology like LCDs and look similar to LCD displays, but they use a layer of gas between two plates of glass instead of a layer of liquid crystals or organic material. A phosphor-coated

liquid crystal display (LCD) A type of flat panel display that uses charged liquid crystals to display images.

LED (light-emitting diode) A common flat panel technology.

organic light-emitting diode (OLED) A type of flat panel display that uses emissive organic material to display brighter and sharper images.

plasma display A flat panel display technology that uses a layer of gas between two plates of glass instead of a layer of liquid crystals or organic material.

screen (with red, green, and blue phosphors for each pixel) is used, and an electron grid layer and electronic charges are used to make the gas atoms light up the appropriate phosphors to create the image on the screen. Although plasma technology has traditionally been used with the very large displays used by businesses and many large screen televisions, it is slowly being replaced by LCDs.

Display devices form images by lighting up the proper configurations of pixels. A variety of technologies can be used to lighten up the pixels needed to display a particular image. Display devices can be monochromatic displays, in which each pixel can only be one of two colors, such as black or white, or color displays, in which each pixel can display a combination of three colors—red, green, and blue—in order to display a large range of colors. Most monitors and display devices today are color displays.

The number of pixels used on a display screen determines the screen resolution, which affects the amount of information that can be displayed on the screen at one time. When a higher resolution is selected, such as 1,600 pixels horizontally by 900 pixels vertically for a standard computer monitor (written as 1,600 × 900 and read as 1600 by 900), more information can fit on the screen, but everything will be displayed smaller than with a lower resolution, such as 1,280 × 768. The screen resolution on many computers can be changed by users to match their preferences and the software being used.

Display device size is measured diagonally from corner to corner. Most desktop computer monitors today are between 17 inches and 30 inches (though larger screens—up to 60 inches and more—are becoming increasingly common); notebook and tablet displays are usually between 14 inches and 17 inches; netbooks typically have 10-inch displays; and tablet displays are typically between 7 inches and 10 inches. To better view DVDs and other multimedia

content, many monitors are widescreen, which conforms to the 16:9 aspect ratio of widescreen televisions, instead of the conventional 4:3 aspect ratio.

The video card installed inside a computer or the integrated graphics component built directly into the motherboard of the CPU of the computer houses the graphics processing unit (GPU)—the chip devoted to rendering images on a display device. The video card or the integrated graphics component determines the graphics capabilities of the computer, including the screen resolutions available, the number of bits used to store color information about each pixel (called the bit depth), the total number of colors that can be used to display images, the number of monitors that can be connected to the computer via that video card or component, and the types of connectors that can be used to connect a monitor to the computer. Video cards typically contain a fan and other cooling components to cool the card. Most video cards also contain memory chips (typically called video RAM, or VRAM) to support graphics display, although some do not and are designed to use a portion of the computer's regular RAM as video RAM instead. Most video cards today contain between 256 MB and 1 GB of video RAM. A typical video card is shown in Exhibit 2-43.

Exhibit 2-43 Video card

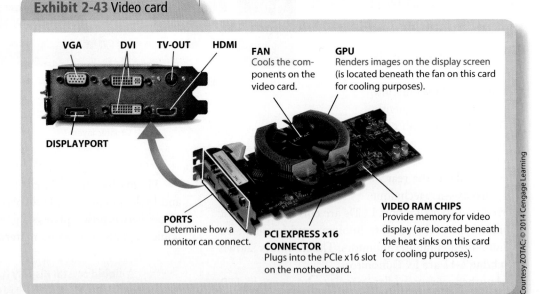

VGA   DVI   TV-OUT   HDMI

FAN
Cools the components on the video card.

GPU
Renders images on the display screen (is located beneath the fan on this card for cooling purposes).

DISPLAYPORT

PORTS
Determine how a monitor can connect.

PCI EXPRESS x16 CONNECTOR
Plugs into the PCIe x16 slot on the motherboard.

VIDEO RAM CHIPS
Provide memory for video display (are located beneath the heat sinks on this card for cooling purposes).

The three most common types of interfaces used to connect a monitor to a computer are VGA (Video Graphics Array), DVI (Digital Visual Interface), and HDMI (High-Definition Multimedia Interface). VGA uses a 15-pin D-shaped connector and it is commonly used with CRT monitors and many flat-panel monitors to transfer analog images to the

3D Flat Panel Displays

Recent improvements in flat panel display technology and graphics processing have led to several emerging 3D output devices. The newest 3D products use filters, prisms, multiple lenses, and other technologies built into the display screen to create the 3D effect and, as a result, do not require 3D glasses. Some 3D displays resemble conventional monitors; others are shaped differently, such as the dome-shaped Perspecta 3D display. Other 3D displays are designed to be wearable, such as the eyeglasses-based display shown in the photo. This device projects the image from a mobile device to a display screen built into the glasses. The technology allows the user to see the image as if it is on a distant large screen display, and many 3D wearable displays overlay the projected image on top of what the user is seeing in real time to provide situational awareness while the display is being used. Wearable 3D displays are also designed for soldiers and other mobile workers.

Display is built into eyeglasses, which connect to a mobile device.

Images from the source device (a text message in this example) are displayed on top of the user's normal vision.

Hi Jack,
Contract is approved and ready to sign. Need your signature ASAP.
John

Wearable 3-D display

Courtesy Lumus Ltd.

monitor. DVI uses a more rectangular connector and it is frequently used with flat panel displays to allow the monitor to receive clearer, more reliable digital signals than is possible with a VGA interface. HDMI uses a smaller connector and can be used with display devices that support high-definition content. A newer type of connector is DisplayPort, which is designed to eventually replace VGA and DVI ports on computers, video cards, and monitors. In fact, Apple already includes a smaller version—referred to as a Mini DisplayPort—on its newest MacBooks. The ports used with each of these possible connections are illustrated in Exhibit 2-43.

A video card or integrated video component in a desktop computer has at least one port exposed through the system unit case to connect a monitor. Notebook computers and other computers with a built-in display typically contain a monitor port to connect a second monitor to the computer. A

Display devices are measured diagonally from corner to corner.

Leelaryonkul/Shutterstock.com

relatively new option for connecting multiple monitors to a computer is using the computer's USB port. USB monitors (monitors designed to connect via a USB port) can be added to a computer even if that computer does not have a video card that supports multiple monitors.

Most computer monitors are physically connected to the system unit via a cable. Some display devices, such as digital photo frames, e-book readers, and some computer monitors and television sets, however, are designed to be wireless.

2-6b Data and Multimedia Projectors

A **data projector** is used to display output from a computer onto a wall or projection screen. Conventional data projectors are often found in classrooms, conference rooms,

data projector A display device that projects computer output onto a wall or projection screen.

and similar locations and can be freestanding units or permanently mounted onto the ceiling. Although most data projectors connect via cable to a computer, wireless projectors are available. Some projectors also include an iPod or iPhone dock for connecting an iPod to project videos stored on that device.

For projecting content to a small audience while on the go, small pico projectors are available. These pocket-sized projectors typically connect to a mobile phone, a portable computer, or a portable digital media player to enable the device to project an image onto a wall or other flat surface from up to 12 feet away. Pico projectors typically create a display up to 10 feet wide in order to easily share information stored on the device without everyone having to crowd around a tiny screen. Another type of data projector is designed to project actual 3D projections or holograms. For instance, holograms of individuals and objects can be projected onto a stage for a presentation. Hologram display devices can be used in retail stores, exhibitions, and other locations to showcase products or other items in 3D.

2-6c Printers

Instead of the temporary, ever-changing soft copy output that a monitor produces, printers produce **hard copy**, which is a permanent copy of the output on paper. Most desktop computers are connected to a printer. Portable computers can use printers as well.

Printers produce images through either impact or nonimpact technologies. Impact printers, like old ribbon typewriters, have a print mechanism that actually strikes the paper to transfer ink to the paper. For example, a dot-matrix printer such as the one shown in Exhibit 2-44 uses a print head consisting of pins that strike an inked ribbon to transfer the ink to the paper—the appropriate pins are extended (and, consequently, strike the ribbon) as the print head moves across the paper to form the appropriate words or images. Impact printers are used primarily for producing multipart forms, such as invoices, packing slips, and credit card receipts.

Most printers today are nonimpact printers, meaning they form images without the print mechanism actually touching the paper. Nonimpact printers usually

Exhibit 2-44 Dot-matrix printer

Courtesy InfoPrint Solutions Company

produce higher-quality images and are much quieter than impact printers. The two most common types of printers—laser printers and ink-jet printers—are both nonimpact printers. Both impact and nonimpact printers form images with dots, in a manner similar to the way monitors display images with pixels. Because of this, printers are very versatile and can print text in virtually any size, as well as print photos and other graphical images. In addition to paper, both impact and nonimpact printers can print on transparencies, envelopes, mailing labels, and more. Both color and black-and-white printers are available.

Most printing technologies today form images with dots of liquid ink or flecks of toner powder. The print resolution is measured in dots per inch (dpi). Guidelines for acceptable print resolution are typically 300 dpi for general purpose printouts, 600 dpi for higher-quality documents, 1,200 dpi for photographs, and 2,400 dpi for professional applications.

Print speed is typically measured in **pages per minute** (**ppm**). How long it takes a document to print depends on the actual printer being used, the selected print resolution, the amount of memory inside the printer, and the content being printed. For instance, pages containing photographs or other images typically take longer

Exhibit 2-45 How black-and-white laser printers work

1. The paper enters the printer, and then it is given an electrical charge so the toner can stick to the paper, as explained in step 5.

2. The printer's microprocessor decodes page data sent from the computer.

3. Instructions from the printer's micro-processor control a laser beam that charges the appropriate locations on the drum so the toner will stick to the drum, as explained in step 4.

4. Toner powder is applied to the drum and sticks only to the charged areas on the drum.

5. The paper rolls over the drum and the toner is transferred to the paper, forming the image for the entire page.

6. The paper goes through the fusing unit, at which point the toner is permanently affixed to the paper through heat and pressure.

7. The paper exits the printer.

© 2014 Cengage Learning

to print than pages containing only text, and full-color pages take longer to print than black-and-white pages. Common speeds for personal printers range from about 20 to 35 ppm; network printers used by businesses typically print from 30 to 65 ppm.

Most personal printers today connect to a computer via a USB connection. Many also have the option of connecting via a wired or wireless network connection. In addition, many personal printers can receive data to print via a flash memory card, a cable connected to a digital camera, or a camera docking station (a device connected to a printer into which a digital camera is placed so images stored in the camera can be printed).

Laser printers form images with toner powder (essentially ink powder) and are the standard for business documents. To print a document, the laser printer uses a laser beam to charge the appropriate locations on a drum to form the page's image, and then toner powder is released from a toner cartridge and sticks to the drum. The toner is transferred to a piece of paper when the paper is rolled over the drum, and a heating unit fuses

> Laser printers and ink-jet printers are both nonimpact printers.

the toner powder to the paper to permanently form the image, as illustrated in Exhibit 2-45. Common print resolutions for laser printers are between 600 and 2,400 dpi; speeds for personal laser printers range from about 15 to 35 ppm.

Ink-jet printers form images by spraying tiny drops of liquid ink from one or more ink cartridges onto the page, one line at a time, as illustrated in Exhibit 2-46. Some printers print with one single-sized ink droplet; others print using different-sized ink droplets and using multiple nozzles or varying electrical charges for more precise printing. The printhead for an ink-jet printer typically travels back and forth across the page, which is one reason why ink-jet printers are slower than laser printers. However, an emerging type of ink-jet printer uses a printhead that

laser printer An output device that forms images with toner powder (essentially ink powder).

ink-jet printer An output device that forms images by spraying tiny drops of liquid ink from one or more ink cartridges onto paper.

Each ink cartridge is made up of multiple tiny ink-filled firing chambers; to print images, the appropriate color ink is ejected through the appropriate firing chamber.

INK-JET PRINTER

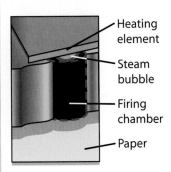

- Heating element
- Steam bubble
- Firing chamber
- Paper

1. A heating element makes the ink boil, which causes a steam bubble to form.

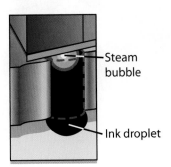

- Steam bubble
- Ink droplet

2. As the steam bubble expands, it pushes ink through the firing chamber.

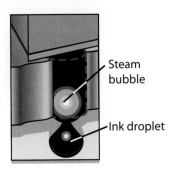

- Steam bubble
- Ink droplet

3. The ink droplet is ejected onto the paper and the steam bubble collapses, pulling more ink into the firing chamber.

is the full width of the paper, which allows the print-head to remain stationary while the paper feeds past it. These printers are very fast, printing up to 60 ppm for letter-sized paper.

Because ink-jet printers are relatively inexpensive, have good-quality output, and can print in color, ink-jet printers are usually the printer of choice for home use. With the use of special photo paper, ink-jet printers can also print photograph-quality digital photos. Starting at less than $50 for a simple home printer, ink-jet printers are affordable, although the cost of the replaceable ink cartridges can add up, especially if you do a lot of color printing.

Barcode printers enable businesses and other organizations to print custom barcodes on price tags, shipping labels, and other documents for identification or pricing purposes. Most barcode printers can print labels in a variety of barcode standards; some can also encode RFID tags embedded in labels.

Portable printers are small, lightweight printers that can be used on the go, usually with a notebook computer or a mobile device, and they connect via either a wired or wireless connection. Portable printers that can print on letter-sized (8½ by 11-inch) paper are used by businesspeople while traveling. Portable receipt, label, and barcode printers are used in some service professions. Printers can also be integrated into other devices. For instance, some digital cameras contain an integrated

barcode printer A printer used to print barcodes.

portable printer A small, lightweight printer that can be used on the go, such as with a notebook computer or a mobile device.

printer that is based on a new technology developed by ZINK (for "zero ink") Imaging. This printer uses no ink; instead, it uses special paper that is coated with color dye crystals. Before printing, the embedded dye crystals are clear, so ZINK Paper looks like regular white photo paper. The ZINK printer uses heat to activate and colorize these dye crystals when a photo is printed, creating a full-color image. In addition to being integrated into a variety of consumer electronics devices, including digital cameras and digital picture frames, stand-alone printers that use ZINK paper are also available.

To print charts, drawings, maps, blueprints, posters, signs, advertising banners, and other large documents in one piece, a larger printer is needed. Most large-format printers (sometimes called plotters) are wide-format ink-jet printers, which are designed to print documents from around 24 inches to 60 inches in width. Although typically used to print on paper, some wide-format ink-jet printers can print directly on fabric and other types of materials.

When 3D output is required, such as to print a 3D model of a new building or prototype of a new product, **3D printers** can be used. Instead of printing on paper, these printers typically form output in layers using molten plastic during a series of passes to build a 3D version of the desired output—a process called fused deposition modeling (FDM®). Some printers can produce multicolor output; others print in only one color and need to be painted by hand, if color output is desired.

LEARN MORE

Multifunction Devices

Some printers today offer more than just printing capabilities. These units—referred to as **multifunction devices (MFDs)**, or all-in-ones—typically copy, scan, fax, and print documents. MFDs can be based on ink-jet printer or laser printer technology, and they are available as both color and black-and-white devices. Although multi-function devices have traditionally been desktop units used in small offices and home offices, larger workgroup multifunction devices are now available that are designed for multiple users, either as stand-alone stations or as networked units.

Courtesy Epson America

2-6d Audio Output

Audio output includes voice, music, and other audible sounds. Computer speakers, the most common type of audio output device, connect to a computer and provide audio output for computer games, music, video clips and TV shows, Web conferencing, and other applications. Computer speaker systems resemble their stereo system counterparts and are available in a wide range of prices. Some speaker systems (such as the one shown in Exhibit 2-47) consist of only a pair of speakers. Others include additional speakers and a subwoofer to create better sound (such as surround sound) for multimedia content. Instead of being stand-alone units, the speakers for some desktop computers are built directly into, or are permanently attached to, the monitor.

Exhibit 2-47 Audio output device

COMPUTER SPEAKERS
Used to output sound from a computer.

Courtesy of Altec Lansing

Portable computers and mobile devices typically have speakers integrated into the device; mobile devices can also be connected to a stereo system or other consumer device that contains an iPod/MP3 dock and integrated speakers designed to be used to play music stored on a portable digital media player. In addition, many cars can connect a portable digital media player or other mobile device to the car's stereo system. Typically, mobile devices are connected to a speaker system via

3D printer A printer that uses molten plastic during a series of passes to build a 3D version of the desired output.

multifunction device (MFD) An output device that can copy, scan, fax, and print documents.

the device's headphone jack, dock connection, or USB port. There are also wireless speakers available to play audio obtained from a home entertainment system or to deliver (via a home network) music from your digital music library or the Internet.

Headphones can be used instead of speakers when you do not want the audio output to disturb others (such as in a school computer lab or public library). Headsets are headphones with a built-in microphone and are often used when dictating to a computer and when making telephone calls or participating in Web conferences using a computer; wireless headsets are commonly used in conjunction with mobile phones. Even smaller than headphones are the earphones and earbuds often used with portable digital media players, handheld gaming devices, and other mobile devices.

Quiz Yourself

1. How is data represented in a computer?

2. What is a bit?

3. What is a byte?

4. What is the main circuit board inside the system unit?

5. What is the main processing device for a computer?

6. Explain the difference between RAM and ROM.

7. What is an expansion card?

8. What is Plug and Play?

9. What does the ALU do?

10. Describe the difference between a storage medium and a storage device.

11. How is the surface of a hard disk organized?

12. How does a disk cache speed up performance?

13. List the three types of optical discs.

14. What is cloud storage?

15. Define input device and output device.

16. What is the most common pointing device?

17. How is the quality of scanned images and printed output measured?

18. What is one of the most common types of flat panel technologies in use today?

Practice It

Practice It 2-1

Adding additional RAM to a computer is one of the most common computer upgrades. Before purchasing additional memory, however, it is important to make sure that the memory about to be purchased is compatible with the computer.

1. Select a computer (your own computer, a school computer, or a computer at a local store), and then determine the manufacturer and model number, the CPU, the operating system, the current amount of memory, the total number of memory slots, and the number of available memory slots. (You can look at the computer or ask an appropriate individual—such as a lab aide in the school computer lab or a salesperson at the local store. If you look inside the computer, be sure to unplug the power cord first and do not touch any components inside the system unit.)

2. Use the information you learned and a memory supplier's Web site to determine the appropriate type of memory needed for your selected computer.

3. What choices do you have in terms of capacity and configuration?

4. Can you add just one memory module, or do you have to add memory in pairs?

5. Can you keep the old memory modules, or do they have to be removed?

6. Prepare a one-page summary of your findings and recommendations, and submit it to your instructor.

Practice It 2-2

USB flash drives can be used to bring your personal software and settings with you to any computer with which you use that drive. In addition, USB flash drives can be used to securely store files, grant access to a computer, and more.

1. Research two features that USB flash drives can provide in addition to data storage.

2. For your selected features, determine what each feature does, how it works, and what benefits it provides.

3. What are some examples of USB flash drives that are currently being sold that include those features?

4. Is there an additional cost for drives that contain these features? If so, do you think it is worth the extra cost?

5. Do you think the features are beneficial? Why or why not?

6. Prepare a one- or two-page summary of your findings and opinions, and submit it to your instructor.

On Your Own

On Your Own 2-1

The choice of an appropriate input device for a product is often based on both the type of device being used and the target market for that device. For instance, a device targeted to college students and one targeted to older individuals may use different input methods. Suppose that you are developing a device to be used primarily for Internet access that will be marketed to senior citizens.

1. What type of hardware would you select as the primary input device? Why?

2. What are the advantages of your selected input device?

3. What are the disadvantages of your selected input device?

4. How could the disadvantages be minimized?

5. Prepare a one-page summary of your opinions and submit it to your instructor.

Chapter 2

ADDITIONAL STUDY TOOLS

IN THE BOOK
▶ Complete end-of-chapter exercises
▶ Study tear-out Chapter Review Card

ONLINE
▶ Complete additional end-of-chapter exercises

▶ Take practice quiz to prepare for tests
▶ Review key term flash cards (online, printable, and audio)
▶ Play "Beat the Clock" and "Memory" to quiz yourself
▶ Watch the videos to learn more about the topics taught in this chapter

Answers to Quiz Yourself

1. Data is represented in a computer as binary digits—a series of 0s and 1s.

2. A bit is the smallest unit of data that a computer can recognize.

3. A byte is a series of eight bits.

4. The main circuit board inside the system unit is the motherboard.

5. The main processing device for a computer is the CPU (or processor or central processing unit).

6. RAM is volatile memory used to store data and instructions while the computer is running. ROM is nonvolatile memory that permanently stores data or programs.

7. An expansion card is a circuit board used to give desktop computers additional capabilities.

8. Plug and Play means the computer automatically configures new devices as soon as they are installed and the computer is powered up.

9. The ALU is the part of a CPU core that performs logical operations and integer arithmetic.

10. A storage medium is the hardware where data is actually stored. A storage medium is inserted into its corresponding storage device in order to be read from or written to.

11. The surface of a hard disk is organized into concentric tracks and pie-shaped groups of sectors.

12. A disk cache stores copies of data or programs that are located on the hard drive and that might be needed soon in memory chips to avoid having to retrieve the data or programs from the hard drive when they are requested.

13. The three types of optical discs are CD, DVD, and BD.

14. Cloud storage refers to remote storage devices accessed via the Internet.

15. An input device is any piece of equipment that is used to enter data into the computer. An output device accepts processed data from the computer and presents the results to the user, most of the time on the computer screen, on paper, or through a speaker.

16. The most common pointing device is the mouse.

17. The quality of scanned images and printed output is measured in dots per inch (dpi).

18. One of the most common types of flat panel technologies in use today is LCD technology.

Computer Software

Courtesy Dana Hursey/Masterfile

All computers require software to operate and perform basic tasks. System software is the software used to run a computer. It runs in the background at all times, making it possible for you to use your computer. Application software is the software that performs the specific tasks users want to accomplish using a computer. Different application software is available to meet virtually any user need, and individuals and businesses use software to perform hundreds of tasks. Some of the most common types of application software used today are word processing, spreadsheet, database, presentation graphics, and multimedia software. This chapter discusses system software, including the operating systems that are the primary component of system software and the utility programs that perform support functions for the operating system. It also covers the various types of application software you may encounter in your personal and professional life.

Learning Objectives

After studying the material in this chapter, you will be able to:

3-1 Explain system software and operating systems

3-2 Identify operating systems for personal computers

3-3 Identify operating systems for mobile devices and larger computers

3-4 Describe common types of application software

3-5 Describe application software used for business

3-6 Describe application software used for working with multimedia

3-7 Describe other types of application software

3-1 Introduction to System Software and Operating Systems

System software consists of the operating system and utility programs that control a computer and allow you to use it. These programs enable the computer to boot, to launch application programs, and to facilitate important jobs, such as transferring files from one storage medium to another, configuring the computer to work with the hardware connected to it, managing files on the hard drive, and protecting the computer from unauthorized use. All computers require software to operate and perform basic tasks. Without system software and application software, a computer is just a pile of hardware.

A computer's **operating system** is a collection of programs that manages and coordinates the activities taking place within the computer; it is the most critical piece of software installed on the computer. The operating system is loaded into memory during the **boot process**, which is the first thing that occurs when you turn on a computer. The operating system then completes the boot process, provides access to application software, and ensures that all actions requested by a user are valid and processed in an orderly fashion. For example, when you issue the command for your computer to store a document on your hard drive, the operating system must perform the following steps:

1. Make sure that the specified hard drive exists.
2. Verify that there is adequate space on the hard drive to store the document, and then store the document in that location.
3. Update the hard drive's directory with the file name and disk location for that file so that the document can be retrieved when needed.

In addition to managing all of the resources associated with your computer, the operating system also facilitates connections to the Internet and other networks.

3-1a Functions of the Operating System

In general, the operating system serves as an intermediary between the user and the computer, as well as between application programs and the computer's

> Without software, a computer is just a pile of hardware.

FYI

Current Software

Writing about software is like writing about clouds. By the time you have finished writing, the software version or cloud formation has changed. This chapter provides an overview about the types of computer software available. It is intended to be a starting point. Although sometimes specific software versions are mentioned, they are not necessarily the most current versions (though they were as this chapter was being written). If you want or need information about the latest software available, you should research the specific software in which you are interested.

hardware, as shown in Exhibit 3-1. Without an operating system, no other program can run, and the computer cannot function. Many tasks performed by the operating system, however, go unnoticed by the user because the operating system works in the background much of the time.

As Exhibit 3-1 illustrates, one principal role of every operating system is to translate user instructions into a form the computer can understand. It also translates any feedback from hardware—such as a signal that the printer has run out of paper or that a new hardware device has been connected to the computer—into a form that the user can understand. The means by which an operating system or any other program interacts with the user is called the **user interface**.

> **system software** Programs such as the operating system and utility programs that control a computer and its devices and enable application software to run on the computer.
>
> **operating system** A collection of programs that manages and coordinates the activities taking place within the computer.
>
> **boot process** The actions taken by programs built into the computer's hardware to start the operating system.
>
> **user interface** The means by which an operating system or other program interacts with the user.

CONCEPTS

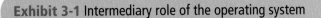

Exhibit 3-1 Intermediary role of the operating system

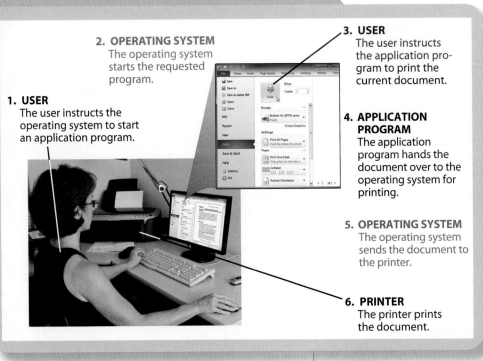

2. OPERATING SYSTEM
The operating system starts the requested program.

1. USER
The user instructs the operating system to start an application program.

3. USER
The user instructs the application program to print the current document.

4. APPLICATION PROGRAM
The application program hands the document over to the operating system for printing.

5. OPERATING SYSTEM
The operating system sends the document to the printer.

6. PRINTER
The printer prints the document.

JHDT Stock Images LLC/Shutterstock.com; Courtesy of Microsoft

During the boot process, the essential portion, or core, of the operating system (called the **kernel**) is loaded into memory. The kernel remains in memory while the computer is on so that it is always available, and other parts of the operating system are retrieved from the hard drive and loaded into memory when needed. Before the boot process ends, the operating system determines the hardware devices that are connected to the computer and whether they are configured properly, and reads an opening batch of instructions. These start-up instructions are tasks the operating system carries out each time the computer boots, such as prompting the user to sign in to an instant messaging program or launching a security program to run continually in the background to detect possible threats.

Typically, many programs are running in the background at any one time, even before the user launches any application software. Exhibit 3-2 lists all the programs running on one computer immediately after it boots. These programs are launched automatically by the operating system. In Windows, users can see some of the programs that are running in the background by looking at the icons in the notification area.

The operating system also configures all devices connected to a computer. Small programs called **device drivers** (or simply **drivers**) are used to communicate with peripheral devices, such as monitors, printers, portable storage devices, and keyboards. Most operating systems include the drivers needed for the most common peripheral devices. In addition, drivers often come on a CD packaged with the peripheral device, or they can be downloaded from the manufacturer's Web site. Most operating systems look for and recognize new devices each time the computer boots, using the Plug and Play standard. If a new device is found, the operating system tries to install the appropriate driver to get the new

kernel The essential portion, or core, of the operating system.

device driver (**driver**) A small program used to communicate with a peripheral device, such as a monitor, printer, portable storage device, or keyboard.

		0%	30%	0%	0%

Task Manager

File Options View

Processes | Performance | App history | Startup | Users | Details | Services

Name	Status	CPU	Memory	Disk	Network
Apps (2)					
Microsoft Word		0%	39.7 MB	0 MB/s	0 Mbps
Task Manager		0.2%	9.9 MB	0 MB/s	0 Mbps
Background processes (51)					
ACEngSvr Module (32 bit)		0%	0.8 MB	0 MB/s	0 Mbps
ACMON (32 bit)		0%	0.4 MB	0 MB/s	0 Mbps
Acresso Software Manager (32 b...		0%	0.9 MB	0 MB/s	0 Mbps
ASLDR Service (32 bit)		0%	0.6 MB	0 MB/s	0 Mbps
AsScrPro (32 bit)		0%	0.6 MB	0 MB/s	0 Mbps
ASUS FastBoot		0%	5.9 MB	0 MB/s	0 Mbps
ASUS InstantOn Program (32 bit)		0%	1.0 MB	0 MB/s	0 Mbps
ASUS InstantOn Program (32 bit)		0%	0.9 MB	0 MB/s	0 Mbps
ASUS Live Update (32 bit)		0%	2.4 MB	0 MB/s	0 Mbps
ATK Media (32 bit)		0%	0.6 MB	0 MB/s	0 Mbps

Fewer details   End task

list of programs

amount of memory used by each program

Courtesy of Microsoft

hardware ready to use. For instance, Exhibit 3-3 shows the message displayed when a new USB drive is identified by the Windows 8 operating system.

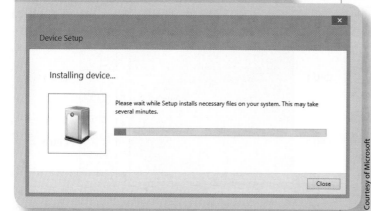

Exhibit 3-3 Message that Windows found new hardware

Courtesy of Microsoft

As you work on a computer, the operating system continuously manages the computer's resources and makes them available to devices and programs when needed. If a problem occurs—such as if a program stops functioning or too many programs are open for the amount of memory installed—the operating system notifies you and tries to correct the problem, often by closing the offending program. If the problem cannot be corrected by the operating system, you typically need to reboot the computer.

The operating system performs is **file management**, which involves keeping track of the files stored on a computer so that they can be retrieved when needed.

3-1b Processing Techniques for Increased Efficiency

Operating systems often utilize various processing techniques to operate more efficiently and increase the amount of processing the computer can perform in any given time period. One way computers operate more efficiently is to multitask. **Multitasking** refers to the ability of an operating system to have more than one program (also called a task) open at one time. For example, multitasking allows you to edit a spreadsheet file in one window while loading a Web page in another window, or to retrieve new email messages in one window while a word processing document is open in another window.

A **thread** is a sequence of instructions within a program that is independent of other threads. Examples include spell checking, printing, and opening documents in a word processing program. Operating systems that support multithreading can rotate between multiple threads so that processing is completed faster and more efficiently, even though only one thread is executed by a single core at one time.

If a computer has two or more CPUs (or multiple cores in a single CPU), techniques that perform operations simultaneously are possible. **Multiprocessing** and **parallel processing** are both techniques that use multiple processors or cores that work together to perform tasks more efficiently. With multiprocessing, each CPU or core typically works on a different job. With parallel processing, the CPUs or cores usually work together to complete one job more quickly. In either case, tasks are performed simultaneously (at exactly the same time). In contrast, multitasking and multithreading use a single CPU or core and process tasks sequentially (by rotating through tasks). Exhibit 3-4 illustrates the difference between simultaneous and sequential processing, using tasks typical of a desktop computer.

Multiprocessing is supported by most operating systems and is used with personal computers that have multi-core CPUs, as well as with servers and mainframe computers that have multi-core CPUs and/ or multiple CPUs. Parallel processing is used most often with supercomputers and supercomputing clusters.

Because many programs are memory-intensive, good memory management, which involves optimizing the use

> Because an operating system can multitask, you can edit a spreadsheet file while loading a Web page.

file management The task of keeping track of the files stored on a computer so they can be retrieved when needed.

multitasking The ability of an operating system to have more than one program open at one time.

thread A sequence of instructions within a program that is independent of other threads.

multiprocessing A processing technique in which multiple processors or multiple processing cores in a single computer each work on a different job.

parallel processing A processing technique in which multiple processors or multiple processing cores in a single computer work together to complete one job more quickly.

Exhibit 3-4 Sequential vs. simultaneous processing

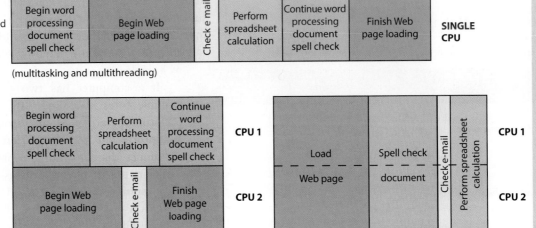

SEQUENTIAL PROCESSING Tasks are performed one right after the other.	Begin word processing document spell check	Begin Web page loading	Check e-mail	Perform spreadsheet calculation	Continue word processing document spell check	Finish Web page loading	SINGLE CPU

(multitasking and multithreading)

SIMULTANEOUS PROCESSING
Multiple tasks are performed at the exact same time.

		CPU 1
Begin word processing document spell check	Perform spreadsheet calculation	Continue word processing document spell check

Begin Web page loading	Check e-mail	Finish Web page loading	CPU 2

(multiprocessing)

Load Web page	Spell check document	Check e-mail	Perform spreadsheet calculation	CPU 1
				CPU 2

(parallel processing)

© 2014 Cengage Learning

of main memory (RAM), can help speed up processing. The operating system allocates RAM to programs as needed and then reclaims that memory when the program is closed. Each additional running program or open window consumes memory. One memory management technique frequently used by operating systems is **virtual memory**, which uses a portion of the computer's hard drive as additional RAM. When the amount of RAM required exceeds the amount of RAM available, the operating system moves portions of data or programs from RAM to the virtual memory area of the hard drive, which is called the **page file** or **swap file**. See Exhibit 3-5. Consequently, as a program is executed, some of the program may be stored in RAM and some in virtual memory. This paging or swapping process continues until the program finishes executing. Virtual memory allows you to use more memory than is physically available on your computer, but using virtual memory is slower than using just RAM.

Some input and output devices are exceedingly slow, compared to CPUs. If the CPU had to wait for these slower devices to finish their work, the computer system would experience a horrendous bottleneck. To avoid this problem, most operating systems use buffering and spooling. A **buffer** is an area in RAM or on the hard drive designated to hold input and output on their way into or out of the system. For instance, a keyboard buffer

virtual memory
A memory management technique frequently used by operating systems that uses a portion of the computer's hard drive as additional RAM.

page file (swap file)
The virtual memory area of a hard drive.

buffer An area in RAM or on the hard drive designated to hold input and output on their way into or out of the system.

Exhibit 3-5 How virtual memory works

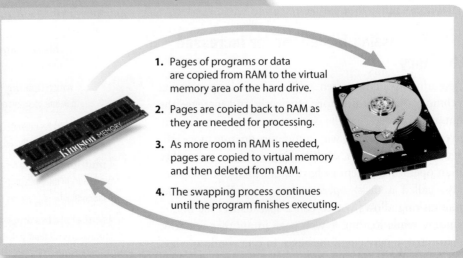

1. Pages of programs or data are copied from RAM to the virtual memory area of the hard drive.

2. Pages are copied back to RAM as they are needed for processing.

3. As more room in RAM is needed, pages are copied to virtual memory and then deleted from RAM.

4. The swapping process continues until the program finishes executing.

Courtesy of Kingston Technology, Inc.; Courtesy Western Digital; © 2014 Cengage Learning stores characters as they are entered via the keyboard, and a print buffer stores documents that are waiting to be printed. The process of placing items in a buffer so they can be retrieved by the appropriate device when needed is called **spooling**. The most common use of buffering and spooling is print spooling. Print spooling allows multiple documents to be sent to the printer at one time and to print, one after the other, in the background while the computer and user are performing other tasks. The documents waiting to be printed are in a print queue, which designates the order in which the documents will be printed. It is also common for computers to use buffers to assist in redisplaying images on the screen and to temporarily store data that is in the process of being burned onto a CD or DVD.

3-1c Differences Among Operating Systems

Different types of operating systems are available to meet different needs. Some of the major distinctions among operating systems include the type of user interface utilized, whether the operating system is targeted for personal or network use, and what type of processing the operating system is designed for.

Most operating systems today use a **graphical user interface** (**GUI**), in which users can click icons or commands on the screen to issue instructions to the computer. The older DOS operating system and some versions of the UNIX and Linux operating systems use a **command line interface**, which requires users to type commands to issue instructions to the computer. See Exhibit 3-6. Graphical versions of the UNIX and Linux operating systems are also available.

Operating systems used with personal computers are typically referred to as **personal operating systems** (also called **desktop operating systems**), and they are designed to be installed on a single computer. In contrast, **server operating systems** (also called **network operating systems**) are designed to be installed on a network server to grant multiple users access to a network and

Exhibit 3-6 Command line interface vs. graphical user interface

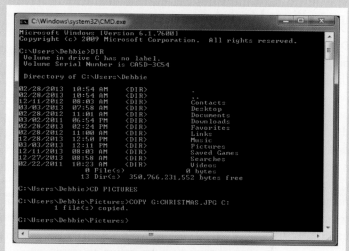

COMMAND LINE INTERFACE
Commands are entered using the keyboard.

GRAPHICAL USER INTERFACE
Tiles, icons, buttons, and other objects are selected with the mouse or finger on a touch screen to issue commands to the computer.

Courtesy of Microsoft

spooling The process of placing items in a buffer so they can be retrieved by the appropriate device when needed.

graphical user interface (**GUI**) A graphically based user interface that allows a user to communicate instructions to the computer by clicking icons or commands on the screen.

command line interface A text-based user interface that requires the user to communicate instructions to the computer by typing commands.

personal operating system (**desktop operating system**) An operating system designed to be installed on a single computer.

server operating system (**network operating system**) An operating system designed to be installed on a network server to grant multiple users access to a network and its resources.

Detecting Problems and Installing Updates

Once a device and its driver have been installed properly, they usually work fine. If the device driver file is deleted, becomes corrupted, or has a conflict with another piece of software, then the device will no longer work. Usually, the operating system detects problems like this during the boot process and then notifies you and tries to reinstall the driver automatically. If the operating system is unable to correct the problem, you can reinstall the driver manually. You may also need to update or reinstall some device drivers if you upgrade your operating system to a newer version. To keep your system up to date, many operating systems have an option to check for operating system updates automatically—including updated driver files—on a regular basis. Enabling these automatic updates is a good idea to keep your system running smoothly and protected from new threats, such as computer viruses.

Courtesy of Microsoft

its resources. Each computer on a network has its own personal operating system installed (just as with a stand-alone computer), and that operating system controls the activity on that computer, while the server operating system controls access to network resources. Computers on a network may also need special client software to access the network and issue requests to the server. An overview of how a typical personal operating system and a server operating system interact on a computer network is illustrated in Exhibit 3-7.

Exhibit 3-7 How operating systems are used in a network environment

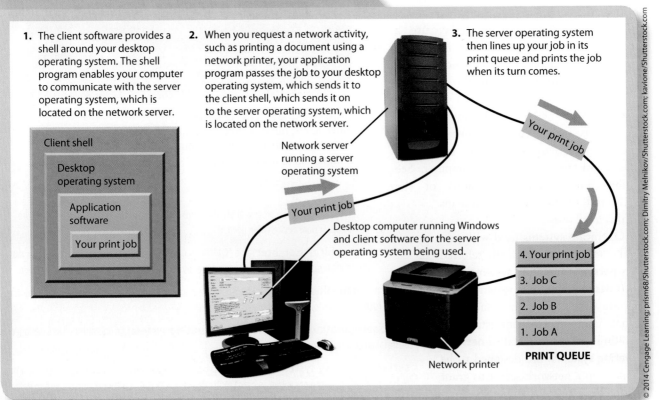

1. The client software provides a shell around your desktop operating system. The shell program enables your computer to communicate with the server operating system, which is located on the network server.

2. When you request a network activity, such as printing a document using a network printer, your application program passes the job to your desktop operating system, which sends it to the client shell, which sends it on to the server operating system, which is located on the network server.

3. The server operating system then lines up your job in its print queue and prints the job when its turn comes.

Client shell
Desktop operating system
Application software
Your print job

Network server running a server operating system

Your print job

Desktop computer running Windows and client software for the server operating system being used.

Your print job

4. Your print job
3. Job C
2. Job B
1. Job A

PRINT QUEUE

Network printer

© 2014 Cengage Learning; prism68/Shutterstock.com; Dimitry Melnikov/Shutterstock.com; kavione/Shutterstock.com

In addition to personal operating systems and server operating systems, **mobile operating systems** are designed to be used with mobile phones and other mobile devices, and **embedded operating systems** are built into consumer kiosks, cash registers, cars, consumer electronics, and other devices.

As new technologies or trends (such as new types of buses, virtualization, power consumption concerns, touch and gesture input, and Web-based software, for example) emerge, operating systems must be updated to support them. On the other hand, as technologies become obsolete, operating system manufacturers need to decide when to end support for those technologies. Likewise, hardware manufacturers also need to respond to new technologies introduced by operating systems. For instance, the latest versions of Windows and Mac OS support multi-touch input. When a new operating system feature, such as multi-touch input, is introduced, hardware manufacturers—monitor manufacturers in this case—must decide whether to adapt their hardware to support the new feature.

supported a menu-driven interface. The two primary forms of DOS are PC-DOS and MS-DOS. PC-DOS was created originally for IBM PCs (and is owned by IBM); MS-DOS was created for use with IBM-compatible PCs. Both versions were originally developed by Microsoft Corporation, but neither version is updated any longer. DOS is considered obsolete because it does not utilize a graphical user interface and does not support modern processors and processing techniques. Some computers, such as computers running the Windows operating system, however, can still execute DOS commands and users can issue these commands using the Command Prompt window, as shown in Exhibit 3-8.

Exhibit 3-8 DOS commands issued via the Command Prompt window

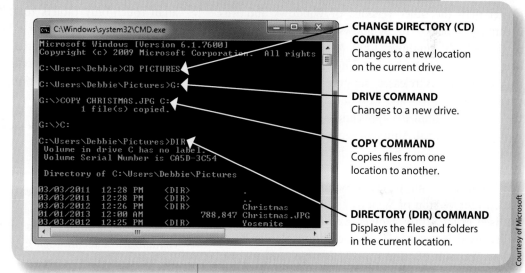

CHANGE DIRECTORY (CD) COMMAND
Changes to a new location on the current drive.

DRIVE COMMAND
Changes to a new drive.

COPY COMMAND
Copies files from one location to another.

DIRECTORY (DIR) COMMAND
Displays the files and folders in the current location.

3-2 Operating Systems for Personal Computers

Many operating systems today are designed either for personal computers (such as desktop and notebook computers) or for network servers. The original operating system for personal computers and the four personal and server operating systems most commonly used today are discussed next.

3-2a DOS

During the 1980s and early 1990s, **DOS (Disk Operating System)** was the dominant operating system for personal computers. DOS traditionally used a command line interface, although later versions of DOS

3-2b Windows

Windows has been the predominant operating system for personal computers for many years, and holds about 90 percent of the market. Microsoft created the original version of Windows—Windows 1.0—in 1985 in an effort to meet the needs of users frustrated by having to learn and use DOS commands. Windows 1.0 through Windows 3.x (where x stands for the version number of

> **mobile operating system** An operating system designed to be used with mobile phones and other mobile devices.
>
> **embedded operating system** An operating system that is built into devices such as consumer kiosks, cash registers, cars, and consumer electronics.
>
> **DOS (Disk Operating System)** The dominant operating system for personal computers during the 1980s and early 1990s.
>
> **Windows** The predominant operating system for personal computers.

the software, such as Windows 3.0, 3.1, or 3.11) were not, however, full-fledged operating systems. Instead, they were operating environments for the DOS operating system—that is, they were graphical shells that operated around the DOS operating system—which were designed to make DOS easier to use.

In 1994, Microsoft announced that all versions of Windows after 3.11 would be full-fledged operating systems instead of just operating environments. The next three versions of Windows designed for personal computers were Windows 95 (released in 1995), Windows 98 (released in 1998), and Windows Me (Millennium Edition) (released in 2000). Windows NT (New Technology) was the first 32-bit version of Windows designed for high-end workstations and servers. It was built from the ground up using a different kernel than the other versions of Windows and was eventually replaced by Windows 2000. Windows XP replaced both Windows 2000 (for business use) and Windows Me (for home use). Throughout this progression of Windows releases, support for new hardware (such as DVD drives and USB devices), networking and the Internet, multimedia applications, and voice and pen input were included. Although support for all of the early versions of Windows has been discontinued, Microsoft plans to support Windows XP until 2014.

Windows Vista replaced Windows XP and was the current version of Windows until Windows 7 was released in late 2009. However, Windows Vista is still widely used. It comes in four basic editions (Home Basic, Home Premium, Business, and Ultimate) and in both 32-bit and 64-bit versions. One of the most obvious changes in Windows Vista is the Aero interface, which uses transparent windows and dynamic elements such as Live Thumbnails of taskbar buttons. Windows Vista also introduced the Sidebar feature, which contains gadgets—small applications that are used to perform a variety of tasks, such as displaying weather information, a clock, a calendar, a calculator, sticky notes, news headlines, personal photos, email messages, and stock tickers. The Vista Start menu introduced an Instant Search feature that allows users to search for and open programs and documents stored on their computers. Other features new to Vista include security features and much improved networking, collaboration, and synchronization tools.

Windows 7, released in 2009, is available in both 32-bit and 64-bit versions and in four main editions, including Home Premium (the primary version for home users) and Professional (the primary version for businesses). Windows 7 requires less memory and processing power than previous versions of Windows, and it is designed to start up and respond faster than Vista. Microsoft states that all versions of Windows 7 run well on netbooks and mobile tablets.

The latest version of Windows, Windows 8, was released in 2012. According to Microsoft, it is a "reimaging of Windows, from the chip to the interface." Windows 8 includes support for ARM processors, which are used primarily with portable devices but which may be used more with PCs in the future. Windows 8 is designed to be used with a wide range of devices, from small touch-only tablets to full-size desktop systems, as well as with or without a keyboard or mouse. The Windows 8 Start screen is tile based, instead of the traditional Windows Start menu, and it uses live tiles to show up-to-date information and notifications from your apps.

3-2c Windows Server and Windows Home Server

Windows Server is the version of Windows designed for server use. Windows Server 2008 includes Internet Information Services 7.0, which is a powerful Web platform for Web applications and Web services; built-in virtualization technologies; a variety of new security tools and enhancements; and streamlined configuration and management tools. The latest version of Windows Server 2008 is called Windows Server 2008 R2 and includes features that are designed specifically to work with client computers running Windows 7.

A related operating system designed for home use is Windows Home Server, which is preinstalled on home server devices and designed to provide services for a home network. For instance, a home server can serve as a central storage location for all devices in the home, such as computers, gaming consoles, and portable digital media players. Home servers can also be set up to back up all devices in the home on a regular basis, as well as to give users of the home network access to the data on the home server and to allow parents or other authorized individuals to control the home network from any computer via the Internet.

Windows Server The version of Windows designed for server use.

3-2d Mac OS and Mac OS X Server

Mac OS is the proprietary operating system for Mac computers made by Apple, Inc. It is based on the UNIX operating system and set the original standard for graphical user interfaces. Many of today's operating systems follow the trend that Mac OS started and, in fact, use GUIs that highly resemble the one used with Mac OS.

Recent versions of Mac OS, such as Mac OS X Snow Leopard (shown in Exhibit 3-9), are part of the Mac OS X family. Mac OS X allows multithreading and multitasking, supports dual 64-bit processors, and has a high level of multimedia functions and connectivity. In addition, it includes the Safari Web browser, a Dashboard containing widgets that can be displayed or hidden as desired, a Stacks feature that allows you to store files (documents, programs, and so on) in a Stack on the Dock, and a Quick Look feature that shows you previews of files without opening them.

Exhibit 3-9 Mac OS X Leopard

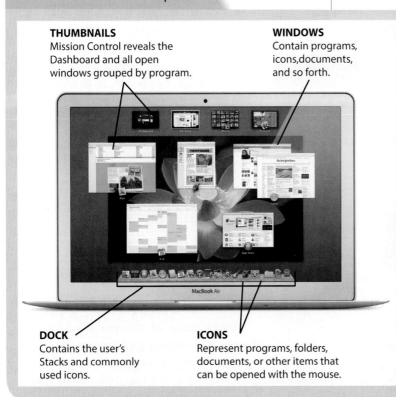

THUMBNAILS
Mission Control reveals the Dashboard and all open windows grouped by program.

WINDOWS
Contain programs, icons, documents, and so forth.

DOCK
Contains the user's Stacks and commonly used icons.

ICONS
Represent programs, folders, documents, or other items that can be opened with the mouse.

Mac OS X Server is the server version of Mac OS X. The latest version—Mac OS X Lion Server—is a full 64-bit operating system that is up to twice as fast as earlier server versions. New capabilities built into Lion Server include file sharing for iPad users (so users can access, copy, and share documents on the server) and push notifications (so users can be notified immediately when they receive new email messages, calendar invitations, changes to meetings, or updates to contact information).

3-2e UNIX

UNIX was developed in the late 1960s at AT&T Bell Laboratories as an operating system for midrange servers. UNIX is a multiuser, multitasking operating system. Computer systems ranging from personal computers to mainframes can run UNIX, and it can support a variety of devices from different manufacturers. This flexibility gives UNIX an advantage over competing operating systems in some situations. However, UNIX is more expensive, requires a higher level of technical knowledge, and tends to be harder to install, maintain, and upgrade than most other commonly used operating systems.

Many versions of UNIX are available, as are many operating systems based on UNIX. These operating systems—such as Mac OS—are sometimes referred to as UNIX flavors. In fact, the term UNIX, which initially referred to the original UNIX operating system, has evolved to refer to a group of similar operating systems based on UNIX. Many UNIX flavors are incompatible, which creates some problems when a program written for one UNIX computer system is moved to another computer system running a different flavor of UNIX. To avoid this incompatibility problem, the Open Group consortium has overseen the development of the Single UNIX Specification—a standardized programming environment for UNIX applications—and certifies UNIX systems if they conform to the Single UNIX Specification.

3-2f Linux

Linux (pronounced with a short *i* sound) is an operating system developed by Linus Torvalds in 1991 when he was a student at the University of Helsinki in Finland. Linux was developed independently from

Courtesy of Apple

Mac OS The proprietary operating system for computers made by Apple, Inc.

Mac OS X Server The server version of Mac OS X.

UNIX A multiuser, multitasking operating system developed in the late 1960s at AT&T Bell Laboratories as an operating system for midrange servers.

Linux An open source operating system developed by Linus Torvalds in 1991 that is available without charge over the Internet.

it. Linux was released to the public as **open source software**, which is a program that the program owners allow anyone to modify. Over the years, the number of Linux users has grown, and volunteer programmers from all over the world have collaborated to improve it, sharing their modified code with others over the Internet. Although Linux originally used a command line interface, most recent versions of Linux programs use a graphical user interface, as shown in Exhibit 3-10. Linux is widely available as a free download via the Internet. Companies are also permitted to customize Linux and sell it as a retail product. Commercial Linux distributions, such as those available from Red Hat and Novell, come with maintenance and support materials (something that many of the free versions do not offer), making the commercial versions more attractive for corporate users.

> Linux is pronounced with a short i sound—*lih-nuks.*

one Linux-based operating system (Android) developed for mobile phones is also now used with mobile tablets, as well as netbooks and other very portable personal computers.

One reason individuals and organizations are switching to Linux and other open source software is cost. Using the Linux operating system and a free or low-cost office suite, Web browser program, and email program can save hundreds of dollars per computer.

3-3 Operating Systems for Mobile Devices and Larger Computers

Although notebook, netbook, and other portable personal computers typically use the same operating systems as desktop computers, mobile phones and other mobile devices usually use mobile operating systems—either mobile versions of personal operating systems (such as Windows or Linux) or special operating systems (such as Android, Apple iOS, or BlackBerry OS) that are designed specifically for mobile devices. There are also embedded operating systems designed to be used with everyday objects, such as home appliances, gaming consoles, digital cameras, toys, watches, GPS systems, home medical devices, voting terminals, and cars. Most users select a mobile phone by considering the mobile provider, hardware, and features associated with the phone, instead of considering the operating system used. However, the operating system used with a phone or other device determines some of the phone's capabilities (such as whether it can accept touch input or its display can rotate automatically as the phone changes orientation), the interface used, and the applications that can run on that device.

Exhibit 3-10 Linux with a 3D graphical user interface

Courtesy of Novell

Over the years, Linux has grown from an operating system used primarily by computer techies who disliked Microsoft to a widely accepted operating system with strong support from mainstream companies such as IBM, HP, Dell, and Novell. Linux is available in both personal and server versions. It is also widely used with mobile phones. The use of Linux with inexpensive personal computers is growing. In fact,

3-3a Mobile and Embedded Versions of Windows

Windows Phone is the version of Windows designed for mobile phones. Recent versions of Windows Phone are designed primarily for touch input and feature a tile-based interface (see Exhibit 3-11). Tiles contain real-time

open source software A program that the program owners allow anyone to modify.

Windows Phone The version of Windows designed for mobile phones.

Exhibit 3-11 Examples of operating systems for mobile devices

WINDOWS PHONE 7

ANDROID

APPLE iOS

HP webOS

Windows Embedded is a family of operating systems based on Windows that is designed primarily for consumer and industrial devices that are not personal computers, such as cash registers, digital photo frames, GPS devices, ATMs, medical devices, and robots. The current versions of Windows Embedded are based on Windows 7 and include a variety of products (such as Compact, Standard, Enterprise, Automotive, and Thin Client) to match the type of device being used.

3-3b Other Mobile Phone Operating Systems

Android (shown in Exhibit 3-11) is a Linux-based operating system developed by the Open Handset Alliance, a group that includes Google and more than 30 technology and mobile companies. As a relatively new operating system, it was built from the ground up with current mobile device capabilities in mind, which enables developers to create mobile applications that take full advantage of all the features a mobile device has to offer. It is an open platform, so anyone can download and use Android, although hardware manufacturers must adhere to certain specifications to be called "Android compatible."

The mobile operating system designed for Apple mobile phones and mobile devices, such as the iPhone and the iPod Touch, is **iOS** (see Exhibit 3-11). This operating system is based on Apple's Mac OS X operating system, supports multi-touch input, and has hundreds of applications available via the App Store. The current version of iOS is iOS5. It supports multitasking and includes the Safari Web browser and apps for email, messaging, music, search, and video calling via FaceTime. It also includes a Notifications Center to view all notifications in one location, as well as a Find My iPhone app to help users locate, lock, or remotely wipe a lost or stolen iPhone.

BlackBerry OS is the operating system designed for BlackBerry devices. It supports multitasking and, like other mobile operating systems, it includes email and Web browsing support, music management, video recording, calendar tools, and more. In addition, BlackBerry OS includes a voice note feature that allows you to send a voice note via email or text message and has an integrated maps feature.

information about missed calls, unread messages, social networking updates, and other timely content of interest to mobile users. Tiles can be customized by the user, and they can be linked to a photo gallery, Web site, or app. In addition to tiles, Windows Phone has hubs, which are used to tie together related experiences from different apps. For instance, the People Hub shows your contacts, as well as status updates from Facebook friends. Other hubs include Games (featuring xBox Live), Pictures, and Music + Video. Windows Phone phones include some apps, such as mobile versions of Internet Explorer and Microsoft Word, Excel, and PowerPoint; additional apps can be downloaded from the Windows Phone Marketplace. Windows Phone supports multitasking, and you can sync your Windows Phone phone with a computer.

> **Windows Embedded** A family of operating systems based on Windows that is designed primarily for consumer and industrial devices that are not personal computers.
>
> **Android** A Linux-based operating system designed for mobile phones developed by the Open Handset Alliance.
>
> **iOS** The mobile operating system designed for Apple mobile phones and mobile devices.
>
> **BlackBerry OS** The operating system designed for BlackBerry devices.

HP webOS (known as Palm webOS before Hewlett-Packard acquired Palm) is a Linux-based mobile operating system developed for Palm mobile phones, such as the Palm Pre and HP Veer (see Exhibit 3-11). HP webOS supports full multitasking; it also includes a Web browser, an email app, and an integrated messaging system to show instant messages, texts, and pictures from contacts in one combined view. Additional apps are available through the App Catalog.

Symbian OS is a mobile operating system that has been the most widely used mobile operating system worldwide, running on nearly half of the world's mobile phones, primarily outside North America, for many years. However, use has been declining and is expected to decline further as one of Symbian's biggest supporters—Nokia—began using Windows 7 on some of its phones in 2011.

3-3c Operating Systems for Larger Computers

Larger computers—such as high-end servers, mainframes, and supercomputers—sometimes use operating systems designed solely for that type of system. For instance, IBM's z/OS is designed for IBM mainframes. In addition, many servers and mainframes today run conventional operating systems, such as Windows, UNIX, and Linux. Linux in particular is increasingly being used with both mainframes and supercomputers; often a group of Linux computers are linked together to form a Linux supercomputing cluster. Larger computers may also use a customized operating system based on a conventional operating system. For instance, many IBM mainframes and Cray supercomputers use versions of UNIX developed specifically for those computers (AIX and UNICOS, respectively).

3-4 Introduction to Application Software

Application software includes all the programs that allow you to perform specific tasks on a computer, such as writing a letter, preparing an invoice, viewing a Web page, listening to a music file, checking the inventory of a particular product, playing a game, preparing financial statements, and designing a home.

3-4a Software Categories

The four basic categories of software are commercial software, shareware, freeware, and public domain software, which are described in Exhibit 3-12. Each type of software has different ownership rights. In addition, software that falls into any of these four categories can also be open source software. An open source program can be copyrighted, but individuals and businesses are allowed to modify the program and redistribute it—the only restrictions are that changes must be shared with the open source community and the original copyright notice must remain intact.

The ownership rights of a software program specify the allowable use of that program. After a software program is developed, the developer (typically an

HP webOS A Linux-based mobile operating system developed for Palm/HP devices.

Symbian OS A mobile operating system historically used with mobile phones, primarily used outside North America.

application software The programs that allow you to perform specific tasks on a computer.

Exhibit 3-12 Types of software

Category	Description	Examples
Commercial software	A software program that is developed and sold for a profit.	Microsoft Office (office suite) Norton AntiVirus (antivirus program) Adobe Photoshop (image editing program) World of Warcraft (game)
Shareware	A software program that is distributed on the honor system; typically available free of charge but may require a small registration fee.	WinZip (file compression program) Ulead Video ToolBox (video editing/ conversion program) Image Shrinker (image optimizer) Deluxe Ski Jump 3 (game)
Freeware	A software program that is given away by the author for others to use free of charge.	Internet Explorer (Web browser) OpenOffice.org (office suite) QuickTime Player (media player) Yahoo! Messenger (instant messaging program)
Public domain software	A software program that is not copyrighted.	Lynx (text-based Web browser) Pine (email program)

individual or an organization) holds the ownership rights for that program and decides whether the program can be sold, shared with others, or otherwise distributed. When you purchase a software program, you are not actually buying the software. Instead, you are acquiring a **software license** that permits you to use the software. This license specifies the conditions under which the buyer can use the software, such as the number of computers on which it may be installed (many software licenses permit the software to be installed on just one computer). See Exhibit 3-13. In addition to being included in printed form inside the packaging of most software programs, the licensing agreement is usually displayed and must be agreed to by the end user at the beginning of the software installation process.

Commercial software includes any software program that is developed and sold for a profit. When you buy a commercial software program (such as Microsoft Office, TurboTax, or GarageBand), it typically comes with a single-user license, which means you cannot legally make copies of the installation CD to give to your friends and you cannot legally install the software on their computers using your CD. You cannot even install the software on a second computer that you own, unless allowed by the license. For example, some software licenses state that the program can be installed on one desktop computer and one portable computer belonging to the same individual. Schools or businesses that need to install software on a large number of computers or need to

have the software available to multiple users over a network can usually obtain a site license or network license for the number of users needed.

In addition to their full versions, some commercial software is available in a demo or trial version. Typically, these versions can be used free of charge and distributed to others, but often they are missing key features such as the ability to save or print a document or they will not run after the trial period expires. Because these programs are not designed as replacements for the fee-based version, it is ethical to use them only to determine whether you want to buy the full program. If the decision is made against purchasing the product, you should uninstall the demo or trial version from your computer.

Recent trends in computing—such as multiprocessing, virtualization, and cloud computing—are leading to new software licensing issues for commercial software companies. For example, software companies must decide whether the number of installations allowed by the license is counted by the number of computers on which the software is installed or by the total number of processors or CPU cores used by those computers, as well as decide how to determine the number of users in a virtualized environment. Software vendors are expected to develop and implement new licensing models to address these and other trends in the future.

Shareware programs are software programs that are distributed on the honor system. Most shareware programs are available to try free of charge but typically require a small fee if you choose to use the program

---

software license A permit that specifies the conditions under which a buyer can use the software.

commercial software A software program that is developed and sold for a profit.

shareware program A software program that is distributed on the honor system; typically available free of charge but may require a small registration fee.

Exhibit 3-13 Examples of software licenses

This statement explains that you are accepting the terms of the license agreement by installing the software.

This statement explains that the program can be tried for 14 days and then it needs to be either registered or uninstalled.

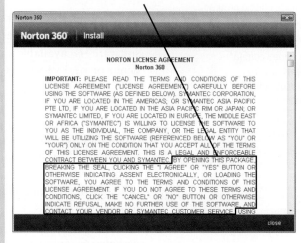

COMMERCIAL SOFTWARE PROGRAM

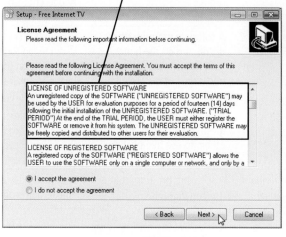

SHAREWARE PROGRAM

Courtesy of Symantec; Courtesy Holersoft

regularly. By paying the requested registration fee, you can use the program for as long as you want to use it and may be entitled to product support, updates, and other benefits. You can legally and ethically copy shareware programs to pass along to friends and colleagues for evaluation purposes, but those individuals are expected to pay the shareware fee if they decide to keep the product.

Many shareware programs have a specified trial period, such as one month. Although it is not illegal to use shareware past the specified trial period, it is unethical to do so. Shareware is typically much less expensive than commercial versions of similar software because it is often developed by a single programmer and because it uses the shareware marketing system to sell directly to consumers (usually via a variety of software download sites, such as the one shown in Exhibit 3-14) with little or no packaging or advertising expenses. Shareware authors stress that the ethical use of shareware helps to cultivate this type of software distribution. Legally, shareware and demo versions of commercial software are similar, but shareware is typically not missing key features.

freeware program A
software program that is given away by the author for others to use free of charge.

Exhibit 3-14 Shareware and freeware programs are typically downloaded via the Web

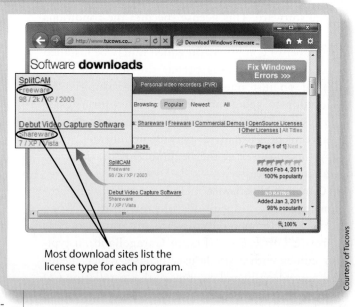

Most download sites list the license type for each program.

Courtesy of Tucows

Freeware programs are software programs that are given away by the author for others to use free of charge. Although freeware is available without charge and can be shared with others, the author retains the ownership rights to the program, so you cannot do anything with it—such as sell it or modify it—that is not expressly allowed by the author. Freeware programs are frequently developed by individuals. Commercial software companies sometimes release freeware as well, such as Microsoft's Internet Explorer and RealNetworks' RealPlayer. Like shareware programs, freeware programs are widely available over the Internet.

Public domain software is not copyrighted; instead, the ownership rights to the program have been donated to the public domain. Consequently, it is free and can be used, copied, modified, and distributed to others without restrictions.

3-4b Desktop vs. Mobile Software

Mobile phones, iPads and other tablets) usually require mobile software, also called apps, which are software programs designed for a specific type of mobile phone or other mobile device. See Exhibit 3-15.

In addition to having a more compact, efficient appearance, many mobile apps include features for easier data input, such as an on-screen keyboard, a phrase list, or handwriting recognition capabilities. Some mobile apps are designed to be compatible with popular desktop software, such as Microsoft Office, to facilitate sharing documents between the two platforms. The number of mobile applications is growing all the time, and many are available free of charge.

3-4c Installed vs. Web-Based Software

Software also differs in how it is accessed by the end user. It can be installed on and run from the end user's computer (or installed on and run from a network server in a network setting), or it can be Web-based and accessed by the end user over the Internet.

Installed software must be installed on a computer before it is run. Desktop software can be purchased in physical form (such as on a CD or DVD) or downloaded from the Internet (see Exhibit 3-16). Mobile software is almost always downloaded from an app store, such as Apple's App

Exhibit 3-15 Mobile apps

Exhibit 3-16 Installed software

public domain software A software program that is not copyrighted.

installed software A software program that must be installed on a computer before it is run.

Exhibit 3-17 Web-based software

BUSINESS SAAS APPLICATIONS
This program allows you to share documents and collaborate on projects online (available in both desktop and mobile versions, as shown here).

ONLINE APPLICATIONS
This program allows you to create Office documents online.

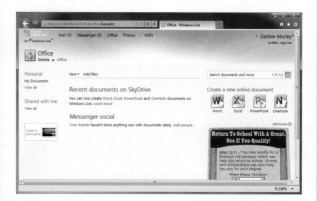

WEB DATABASE APPLICATIONS
This application allows you to retrieve property information, such as home values and homes for sale.

Store, BlackBerry's App World, or the Google Play Store. In either case, the program is installed using its installation program, which typically runs automatically when the software CD or DVD is inserted into the drive or when the downloaded program is opened. After the software is installed, it is ready to use. Whether installed software requires a fee depends on whether the program is a commercial, demo/trial, shareware, freeware, or public domain program.

Web-based software (**Software as a Service** (**SaaS**) or **cloudware**) A software program that is run directly from the Internet.

Instead of being available in an installed format, some software is run directly from the Internet as **Web-based software**, also referred to as **Software as a Service** (**SaaS**) and **cloudware**. See Exhibit 3-17. A Web-based software program is delivered on demand via the Web to wherever the user is at the moment, provided he or she has an Internet connection (and has paid to use the software if a payment is required). The use of Web-based software is growing rapidly. In fact, research firm Gartner estimates that Web-based software is growing by 20 percent per year and predicts the market will exceed $150 billion by 2013. Typically, documents created using Web-based software are stored online, which makes them accessible via any Internet-enabled device.

Open Source Software

The use of open source software has grown over the past few years, primarily for cost reasons. One of the first widely known open source programs was the Linux operating system. However, low-cost or no-cost open source alternatives are also available for a wide selection of application programs. For instance, the free LibreOffice office suite can be used as an alternative to Microsoft Office, and the free GIMP program can be used to retouch photos instead of Adobe Photoshop or another pricey image editing program. In addition to saving money, these alternative programs often require less disk space and memory than their commercial software counterparts do. Other possible benefits of using open source software include increased stability and security (because they are tested and improved by a wide variety. of programmers and users), and the ability to modify the application's code.

Perceived risks of using open source software include lack of support and compatibility issues. An emerging trend is applying open source principles to hardware—some hardware designers are releasing designs for new hardware to the public in hopes that manufacturing companies will use the designs in new products and credit them as the original designer.

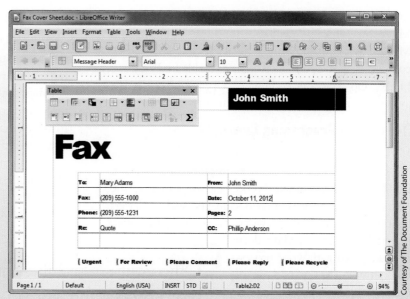

Courtesy of The Document Foundation

3-5 Application Software for Business

Sometimes, related software programs (such as a group of graphics programs, utility programs, or office-related software) are sold bundled together as a **software suite**. Businesses and individuals often use office suites, sometimes called productivity software suites, to produce written documents. Typically, office suites contain the following programs, and many also contain additional productivity tools—such as a calendar, an email or a messaging program, or collaboration tools:

▶ **Word processing software**—allows users to create and edit complex text-based documents that can also include images and other content.

▶ **Spreadsheet software**—provides users with a convenient means of creating documents containing complex mathematical calculations.

▶ **Database software**—allows users to store and organize vast amounts of data and retrieve specific information when needed.

▶ **Presentation graphics software**—allows users to create visual presentations to convey information more easily to others.

One of the most widely used office software suites is Microsoft Office. The latest version is Microsoft Office 2013. Similar suites are available from Corel (WordPerfect Office) and Apple (iWork). Free alternative office suites are LibreOffice and OpenOffice.org; a free Web-based office suite is Google Docs. Many office suites are available in a variety of versions, such as a home or student version that contains fewer programs than a professional version. Not all software

Courtesy Microsoft Corporation; Box shot reprinted with permission of Corel Corporation; PRNewsFoto/Apple

> **software suite** Related software programs (such as a group of graphics programs, utility programs, or office-related software) that are sold bundled together.

suites are available for all operating systems. For example, Microsoft Office is available for both Windows and Mac OS computers; iWork is available only for Mac OS computers; and OpenOffice.org is available for Windows, Linux, and Mac OS computers. OpenOffice.org is also available in more than 30 different languages.

3-5a Word Processing Concepts

Virtually all formal writing today is performed using a word processing program. **Word processing** refers to using a computer and word processing software to create, edit, save, and print written documents, such as letters, contracts, manuscripts, newsletters, invoices, marketing material, and reports. Many documents created with word processing software also include photos, drawn objects, clip art images, hyperlinks, video clips, and text in a variety of sizes and appearances. Like any document created with software instead of paper and pencil, word processing documents can be retrieved, modified, and printed as many times as needed. The most frequently used word processing programs are Microsoft Word, Corel WordPerfect, and Apple Pages.

Word processing programs typically include improved collaboration, security, and rights-management tools (tools used to protect original content from misuse by others). They also typically include a variety of Web-related tools, as well as support for speech and pen input. Web-related features include the ability to send a document as an email message via the word processing program, the inclusion of hyperlinks in documents, and the ability to create or modify Web pages or blogs. The latest versions of Office also include the ability to collaborate with others online.

> Office suites typically contain word processing, spreadsheet, database, and presentation graphics programs.

3-5b Spreadsheet Concepts

Another widely used application program is spreadsheet software. **Spreadsheet software** is the type of application software used to create computerized spreadsheets. A **spreadsheet** is a group of values and other data organized into rows and columns. Most spreadsheets include formulas that are used to compute calculations based on data entered into the spreadsheet.

In spreadsheets created with spreadsheet software, all formula results are updated automatically whenever any changes are made to the data. Consequently, no manual computations are required, which increases accuracy.

In addition, the automatic recalculation of formulas allows individuals to modify spreadsheet data as often as necessary either to create new spreadsheets or to experiment with various possible scenarios (called what-if analysis) to help make business decisions. Spreadsheet software typically includes a variety of data analysis tools, as well as the ability to generate charts. The most widely used spreadsheet programs today are Microsoft Excel, Corel Quattro Pro, and Apple Numbers—again, all are part of their respective software suites. Spreadsheet software is commonly used by a variety of businesses and employees, including CEOs, managers, assistants, analysts, and sales representatives.

Most spreadsheet programs have built-in Web capabilities. Although they are used less commonly to create Web pages, many spreadsheet programs include the option to save the current worksheet as a Web page and insert hyperlinks into worksheet cells. Microsoft Excel includes the ability to collaborate online, as well as to copy ranges of cells to a Web publishing or word processing program to insert spreadsheet data into a document as a table.

3-5c Database Concepts

People often need to retrieve specific data rapidly while on the job. For example, a customer service representative may need to locate a customer's order status quickly while the customer is on the telephone. The type of software used for such tasks is a database management system. A **database** is a collection of related data that is stored on a computer and organized in a way that enables information to be retrieved as needed. A **database management system** (**DBMS**)—also called **database software**—is the type of program used to

word processing The use of a computer and word processing software to create, edit, save, and print written documents.

spreadsheet software The type of application software used to create computerized spreadsheets.

spreadsheet A group of values and other data organized into rows and columns.

database A collection of related data that is stored on a computer and organized in a way that enables information to be retrieved as needed.

database management system (DBMS or database software) The type of program used to create, maintain, and organize data in a database, as well as to retrieve information from it.

create, maintain, and organize data in a database, as well as to retrieve information from the database. The most commonly used database management systems include Microsoft Access, Oracle Database, and IBM DB2.

Databases are often used on the Web. For instance, many Web sites use one or more databases to keep track of inventory; to allow searching for people, documents, or other information; and to place real-time orders. In fact, any time you type keywords in a search box on a search site or hunt for a product on a retail store's Web site using its search feature, you are using a Web database.

3-5d Presentation Graphics Concepts

If you try to explain to others what you look like, it may take several minutes. Show them a color photograph, on the other hand, and you can convey the same information within seconds. The saying "a picture is worth a thousand words" is the cornerstone of presentation graphics. A **presentation graphic** (see Exhibit 3-18) is an image designed to visually enhance a presentation such as an electronic slide show or a printed report, to convey information more easily to people. A variety of software including spreadsheet programs, image editing programs, and presentation graphics software can be used to create presentation graphics. Presentation graphics often take the form of electronic slides containing images, text, video, and more that are displayed one after the other in an electronic slide show. Electronic slide shows are created with **presentation graphics software** and can be run on individual computers or presented to a large group using a data projector; for instance, they are frequently used for business and educational presentations. Some of the most common presentation graphics programs are Microsoft PowerPoint, Corel Presentations, and Apple Keynote—again, all part of their respective software suites.

Presentation graphics programs can be used to generate Web pages or Web page content, and slides can include hyperlinks.

3-6 Application Software for Working with Multimedia

Graphics are images, such as digital photographs, clip art, scanned drawings, and original images created using a software program. **Multimedia** technically refers to any application that contains more than one type of media but usually means audio and video content. A variety of software programs are designed to help individuals create or modify graphics, edit digital audio or video files, play media files, burn CDs and DVDs, and so forth, as discussed next. Some programs focus on just one task; others are designed to perform multiple tasks, such as to import and edit images, audio, and video, and then create a finished DVD.

presentation graphic An image designed to visually enhance a presentation, such as an electronic slide show or a printed report.

presentation graphics software The type of program used to create electronic slide shows that can be run on individual computers or presented to a large group using a data projector.

graphic An image, such as a digital photograph, clip art, a scanned drawing, or an original image created using a software program.

multimedia Any application that contains more than one type of media; often used to refer to audio and video content.

Exhibit 3-18 Examples of presentation graphics

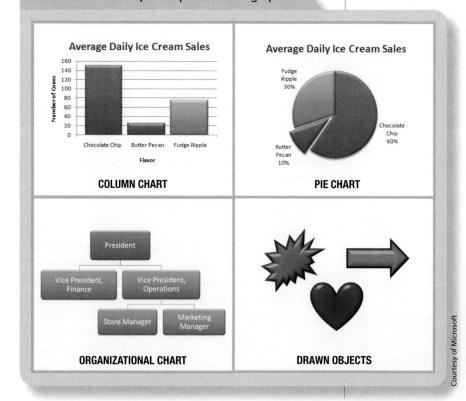

Courtesy of Microsoft

Exhibit 3-19 Graphics software

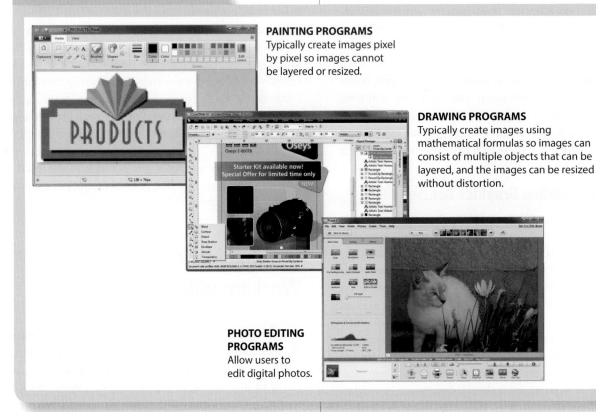

PAINTING PROGRAMS
Typically create images pixel by pixel so images cannot be layered or resized.

DRAWING PROGRAMS
Typically create images using mathematical formulas so images can consist of multiple objects that can be layered, and the images can be resized without distortion.

PHOTO EDITING PROGRAMS
Allow users to edit digital photos.

3-6a Graphics Software

Graphics software—also called digital imaging software—is used to create or modify images. Graphics software programs are commonly distinguished by whether they are primarily oriented toward painting, drawing, or image editing, although these are general categories, not strict classifications. See Exhibit 3-19.

Painting programs traditionally create **bitmap images**, which are created by coloring the individual pixels in an image. One of the most common painting programs is Microsoft Paint. Painting programs are often used to create and modify simple images, but, unless the painting program

> ## Multimedia usually means audio and video content.

supports layers and other tools discussed shortly, use for these programs is relatively limited. This is because when something is drawn or placed on top of a bitmap image, the pixels in the image are recolored to reflect the new content, and whatever was beneath the new content is lost. In addition, bitmapped images cannot be enlarged and still maintain their quality, because the pixels in the images just get larger, which makes the edges of the images look jagged. Some painting programs, such as Corel Painter, do support layers and so are more versatile. Painting tools are also increasingly included in other types of software, such as in office suites and drawing programs.

Drawing programs (also referred to as illustration programs) typically create **vector graphics**, which use mathematical formulas to represent image content instead of pixels. Unlike bitmap images, vector images can be resized and otherwise manipulated without loss of quality. Objects in drawing programs can also typically be layered. So, if you place one object on top of another, you can later separate the two images if desired. Drawing programs are often used by individuals and small

graphics software A program used to create or modify images; also called digital imaging software.

bitmap image A graphic created by coloring the individual pixels in an image.

vector graphic A graphic that uses mathematical formulas to represent image content instead of pixels.

business owners to create original art, logos, business cards, and more. They are also used by professionals to create corporate images, Web site graphics, and so forth. Popular drawing programs include Adobe Illustrator and CorelDRAW.

Image editing or photo editing programs are drawing or painting programs that are specifically designed for touching up or modifying images, such as original digital images and digital photos. Some widely used consumer image editing and photo editing programs are Adobe Photoshop Elements, Apple iPhoto, Corel Paint Shop Photo Pro, Microsoft Office Picture Manager, and the free Picasa program. For professional image editing, Adobe Photoshop is the leading program.

3-6b Audio Capture and Editing Software

For creating and editing audio files, audio capture and audio editing software is used. To capture sound from a microphone, sound recorder software is used; to capture sound from a CD, ripping software is used. In either case, after the audio is captured, it can then be modified as needed with audio editing software. See Exhibit 3-20. For instance, background noise or pauses can be removed, portions of the selection can be edited out, multiple segments can be spliced together, and special effects such as fade-ins and fade-outs can be applied. Also available are specialized audio capture and editing programs designed for specific applications, such as creating podcasts or musical compositions. Professional audio capture and editing software (such as Sony Creative Software Sound Forge Pro and Adobe

Audition) is used to create professional audio for end products, Web pages, commercial podcasts, presentations, and so forth. Common consumer audio capture and editing programs include Windows Sound Recorder, Apple GarageBand, the free Audacity program, and Sony Creative Software Sound Forge Audio Studio software.

3-6c Video Editing and DVD Authoring Software

Digital video can be imported directly into a video editing program by connecting the camera to the computer or by inserting the storage media containing the video (such as a DVD) into the computer. After the video has been imported, video editing (such as deleting or rearranging scenes, adding voice-overs, and adding other special effects) can be performed, as shown in Exhibit 3-21. Some video editing software today can edit video in high-definition format.

DVD authoring refers to organizing content to be transferred to DVD, such as importing video clips and then creating the desired menu structure for the DVD to control the playback of those videos. (Refer again to Exhibit 3-21.) DVD burning refers to recording data (such as a collection of songs or a finished video) on a recordable or rewritable DVD. DVD authoring and burning capabilities are commonly included with video editing capabilities in video creation software; there are also stand-alone DVD authoring programs, and DVD burning capabilities are preinstalled on computers containing a recordable or rewritable optical drive. Many file management programs (such as Windows Explorer) include CD and DVD burning capabilities as well. Consumer video editing software includes Adobe Premiere Express, Serif MoviePlus, Roxio Creator, Apple iMovie and iDVD, Windows Live Movie Maker, Corel VideoStudio Express, and Sony Creative Software Vegas Movie Studio HD. Professional products include Adobe Premiere Pro, Roxio Creator Pro, Corel VideoStudio Pro, and Sony Creative Vegas Pro.

3-6d Media Players

Media players are programs designed to play audio and video files available via a computer—such as music

media player A program designed to play audio and video files available via a computer.

Exhibit 3-20 Audio editing software

Exhibit 3-21 Video editing software

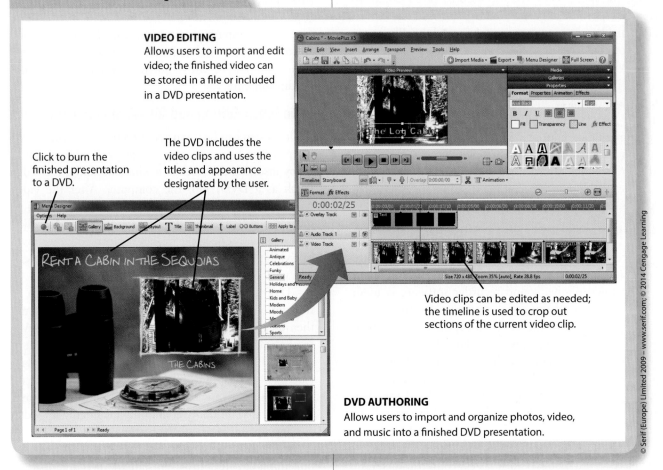

VIDEO EDITING
Allows users to import and edit video; the finished video can be stored in a file or included in a DVD presentation.

Click to burn the finished presentation to a DVD.

The DVD includes the video clips and uses the titles and appearance designated by the user.

Video clips can be edited as needed; the timeline is used to crop out sections of the current video clip.

DVD AUTHORING
Allows users to import and organize photos, video, and music into a finished DVD presentation.

© Serif (Europe) Limited 2009 – www.serif.com; © 2014 Cengage Learning

CDs, downloaded music, or video streamed from the Internet. Many media players are available for free, such as RealPlayer, Windows Media Player, and iTunes Player (see Exhibit 3-22). Media players typically allow you to arrange your stored music and videos into playlists and then transfer them to CDs or portable digital music players. Some also include the ability to download video from the Web and purchase and download music via an associated music store.

3-6e Graphics, Multimedia, and the Web

Graphics and multimedia software is often used by individuals and businesses to create content to be included on a Web site or to be shared via the Web. For instance, company logos, Web site banners, games, tutorials, videos, demonstrations, and other multimedia content available on the Web are created with multimedia software.

Exhibit 3-22 Typical media player program

Use to view the media files stored on your computer.

Use to buy more media or review your purchases.

Use to access content on a CD or portable device.

Use to view or access your playlists.

Courtesy of Apple

3-7 Other Types of Application Software

Many other types of application software are available. Some are geared for business or personal productivity; others are designed for entertainment or educational purposes. Still others are intended to help users with a particular specialized application, such as preparing financial reports, issuing prescriptions electronically, designing buildings, controlling machinery, and so forth.

3-7a Desktop and Personal Publishing Software

Desktop publishing refers to using a personal computer to combine and manipulate text and images to create attractive documents that look as if they were created by a professional printer (see Exhibit 3-23). Although many desktop publishing effects can be produced using a word processing program, users who frequently create publication-style documents usually find a desktop publishing program a more efficient means for creating those types of documents. Some popular desktop publishing programs are Adobe InDesign, Microsoft Publisher, and Serif PagePlus. Personal publishing refers to creating desktop publishing–type documents—such as greeting cards, invitations, flyers, calendars, certificates, and so forth—for personal use. Specialized personal publishing programs are available for particular purposes, such as to create scrapbook pages, cross-stitch patterns, and CD and DVD labels.

3-7b Educational, Entertainment, and Reference Software

A wide variety of educational and entertainment application programs are available. **Educational software** is designed to teach one or more skills, such as reading, math, spelling, a foreign language, or world geography, or to help prepare for standardized tests. **Entertainment software** includes games, simulations, and other programs that provide amusement. A hybrid of these two categories is called edutainment—educational software that also entertains. **Reference software** includes encyclopedias, dictionaries, atlases, mapping/travel programs, cookbook programs, nutrition or fitness programs, and other software designed to provide valuable information. Although still available as stand-alone software packages, reference information today is also obtained frequently via the Internet.

> Many types of application software are available.

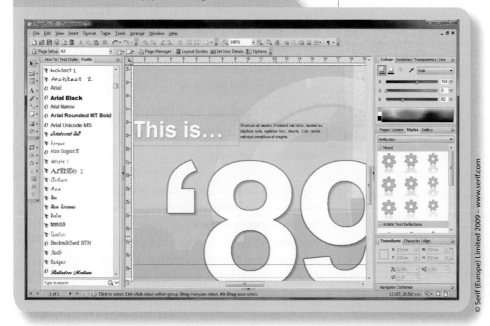

Exhibit 3-23 Desktop publishing software

© Serif (Europe) Limited 2009 – www.serif.com

desktop publishing The use of a personal computer to combine and manipulate text and images to create attractive documents that look as if they were created by a professional printer.

educational software An application program designed to teach one or more skills.

entertainment software An application program that provides amusement, such as a game or simulation.

reference software An application program designed to provide information, such as an encyclopedia, a dictionary, or an atlas.

3-7c Note Taking Software and Web Notebooks

Note taking software is used by both students and businesspeople to take notes during class lectures, meetings, and similar settings. It is used most often with tablet computers and other devices designed to accept pen input. Typically, note taking software, such as Microsoft OneNote or Circus Ponies NoteBook, supports both typed and handwritten input; handwritten input can usually be saved in its handwritten form as an image or converted to typed text. See Exhibit 3-24. The NoteBook program also includes a voice recorder so you can record a lecture or meeting—tapping the speaker icon next to a note replays the voice recorded at the time that particular note was taken. Note taking software typically contains features designed specifically to make note taking—and, particularly, retrieving information from the notes—easier. Like in a paper notebook, you can usually create tabbed sections (such as one tab per course); files, notes, Web links, and any other data are then stored under the appropriate tabs. In addition, search tools that allow you to find the information you need quickly and easily are usually included. Online versions of these programs, such as Zoho Notebook, are referred to as **Web notebooks** and are designed to help organize your online research, including text, images, Web links, search results, and other content located on Web pages.

3-7d CAD and Other Types of Design Software

Computer-aided design (CAD) software enables users to design objects on the computer. For example, engineers or architects can create designs of buildings or other objects and modify the designs as often as needed. Increasingly, CAD programs are including capabilities to

Exhibit 3-24 Note taking software

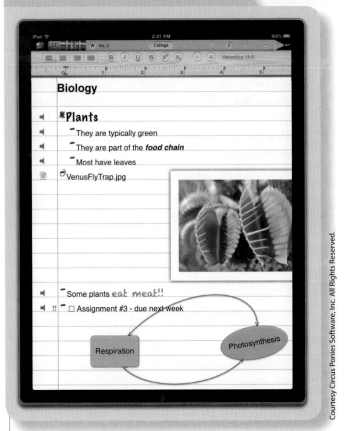

analyze designs in terms of how well they meet a number of design criteria, such as testing how a building design will hold up during an earthquake or how a car will perform under certain conditions. Besides playing an important role in the design of finished products, CAD is also useful in fields such as art, advertising, law, architecture, and movie production. In addition to the powerful CAD programs used in business, design programs are available for home and small business use, such as for designing new homes and for making remodeling plans, interior designs, and landscape designs.

3-7e Accounting and Personal Finance Software

Accounting software is used to automate common accounting activities, such as managing inventory, creating payroll documents and checks, preparing financial statements, and tracking business expenses (see Exhibit 3-25). **Personal finance software** is commonly used at home by individuals to write checks and balance checking accounts, track personal expenses, manage stock portfolios, and prepare income taxes. Increasingly, personal finance activities

note taking software An application program used by both students and businesspeople to take notes during class lectures, meetings, and similar settings.

Web notebook An online version of a note taking software program.

computer-aided design (CAD) software An application program that enables users to design objects on the computer.

accounting software An application program that is used to automate some accounting activities.

personal finance software Accounting software that is commonly used at home by individuals.

Exhibit 3-25 Accounting software

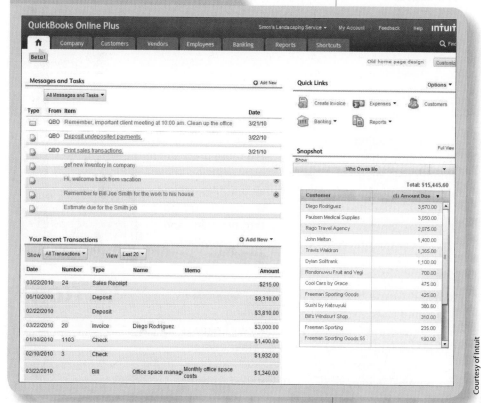

Slingbox product gives you access to and control over your cable box and DVR via the Internet, and GoTo-MyPC software (shown in Exhibit 3-26) allows you to access a computer (such as a home or office PC) from any Web-enabled device while you are away from home, including controlling the computer and accessing files and email. Other remote access software automatically backs up all data files on your main computer to a secure Web server so they can be accessed from any Web-enabled device (such as a portable computer or mobile phone, in some

are becoming Web-based, such as the online banking and online portfolio management services available through many banks and brokerage firms.

3-7f Project Management, Collaboration, and Remote Access Software

Project management software is used to plan, schedule, track, and analyze the tasks involved in a project, such as the construction of a building or a large advertising campaign for a client. Project management capabilities are often included in **collaboration software**—software that enables a group of individuals to work together on a project—and are increasingly available as Web-based software programs.

Remote access software enables individuals to access content on another computer they are authorized to access, via the Internet. Some programs allow you to control the remote computer directly; others allow you to access your media files (such as recorded TV shows or music) from any Web-enabled device while you are away from home. For instance, the

Exhibit 3-26 Remote access software

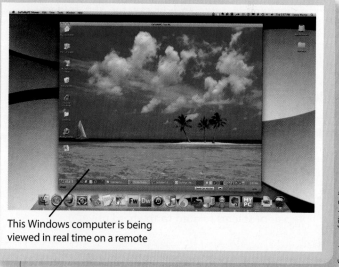

This Windows computer is being viewed in real time on a remote

project management software An application program used to plan, schedule, track, and analyze the tasks involved in a project.

collaboration software An application program that enables a group of individuals to work together on a project.

remote access software An application program that enables individuals to access content on another computer they are authorized to access, via the Internet.

cases), as well as shared with others for collaboration purposes. To make it easier to share single large files with others, you can use Web-based **file sending applications**, such as YouSendIt.

Utility Programs

A **utility program** is a software program that performs a specific task, usually related to managing or maintaining the computer system. Many utility programs—such as programs for finding files, diagnosing and repairing system problems, cleaning up a hard drive, viewing images, playing multimedia files, and backing up files—are built into operating systems. Many stand-alone utility programs are also available as an alternative to the operating system's utility programs (such as a backup program) or to provide additional utility features not built into the operating system being used (such as a registry cleaner or a file compression program). Stand-alone utility programs are often available in a suite of related programs (such as a collection of maintenance programs or security programs). Some of the most commonly used integrated and stand-alone utility programs include:

▶ **File management programs**—perform file management tasks so you can see the folders and files stored on a drive as well as copy, move, rename, and delete them. The file management program in the Windows operating system is Windows Explorer.

▶ **Search tools**—search for documents and other files on a storage medium that meet specific criteria.

▶ **Diagnostic programs**—evaluate your computer system, looking for problems and making recommendations for fixing any errors that are discovered.

▶ **Disk management programs**—diagnose and repair problems related to the hard drive.

▶ **Uninstall programs**—remove the programs along with related extraneous data, such as references to those programs in the system files.

▶ **Cleanup utilities**—delete temporary files (such as deleted files still in the Recycle Bin, temporary Internet files, and temporary installation files) to free up disk space, and sometimes locate unnecessary information in the Windows registry and other system files (such as from uninstalled programs) and delete it.

Courtesy of Symantec

▶ **File compression programs**—reduce the size of files so they take up less storage space; also used to decompress or restore the files to their original size. The most common format used for compressed files in the Windows environment is the .zip format.

▶ **Backup and recovery programs**—make a copy of important files, and then restore them in case of a power outage, hardware failure, accidental deletion, or overwriting of files.

▶ **Security programs**—protect against malicious software being installed on the computer and against someone accessing the computer via the Internet or a wireless connection.

file sending application
A Web-based program used to share single large files with others.

utility program A software program that performs a specific task, usually related to managing or maintaining the computer system.

Quiz Yourself

1. What is the purpose of system software?

2. Explain multitasking.

3. What is the difference between multiprocessing and parallel processing?

4. List the four most widely used personal operating systems.

5. What is a utility program?

6. What is application software?

7. Explain the difference between commercial software and shareware programs.

8. Explain the function of a software license.

9. Describe what a software suite is.

10. What types of programs do office suites typically contain?

11. What does multimedia refer to?

12. Explain the difference between a bitmap image and a vector graphic.

13. What are media players?

14. Explain desktop publishing.

15. Why would an individual use personal finance software?

16. What type of software enables a group of people to work together on a project?

Practice It

Practice It 3-1

A number of new operating systems have been developed in the past few years, such as Android, HP webOS, and Google Chrome OS.

1. Select one new or emerging operating system and research it.

2. What is the purpose and targeted market for this operating system?

3. What advantages does it have over any current competition for this market?

4. If the operating system was developed to fulfill a new need, are there other operating systems that are being adapted or being developed as a result?

5. Do you think your selected operating system will succeed? Why or why not?

6. Prepare a one- or two-page summary that answers these questions, and submit it to your instructor.

Practice It 3-2

Many online tours and tutorials are available for application programs. Some are available through the software company's Web site; others are located on third-party Web sites.

1. Select one common software program, such as Word, Excel, PowerPoint, Chrome, Google Docs, or Paint. Locate a free online tour or tutorial for the program you selected, and then work your way through one tour or tutorial.

2. What features of the application program do you think are most interesting?

3. How helpful is the tour or tutorial? Is the tour or tutorial easy to use and understand?

4. Did you encounter any errors or other problems as you worked through the tour or tutorial?

5. Are there multiple versions for varying levels of difficulty? If so, how did you choose which version to review?

6. Would you recommend this tour or tutorial to others? Why or why not?

7. Prepare a one-page summary that answers these questions, and submit it to your instructor.

On Your Own

On Your Own 3-1

No matter which operating system you have, it is likely you will eventually need to get some help resolving a problem. Support options typically include the following: searchable knowledge bases, technical support phone numbers and email addresses, online chat, FAQs, and user discussion groups.

1. Research the different types of support options that are typically available (listed above).

2. Select one operating system and go to the manufacturer's Web site. Which of the support options listed in the previous paragraph are available?

3. Select one support option. How it is used? What type of information can be obtained?

4. Which support option would you prefer if you encountered a problem with your operating system? Why?

5. Prepare a one-page summary that answers these questions, and submit it to your instructor.

Chapter 3

ADDITIONAL STUDY TOOLS

IN THE BOOK

▶ Complete end-of-chapter exercises
▶ Study tear-out Chapter Review Card

ONLINE

▶ Complete additional end-of-chapter exercises

▶ Take practice quiz to prepare for tests
▶ Review key term flash cards (online, printable, and audio)
▶ Play "Beat the Clock" and "Memory"
▶ Watch the videos to learn more about the topics taught in this chapter.

Answers to Quiz Yourself

1. System software consists of the operating system and utility programs that control a computer and allow you to use a computer. These programs enable the computer to boot, to launch application programs, and to facilitate important jobs, such as transferring files from one storage medium to another, configuring the computer to work with the hardware connected to it, managing files on the hard drive, and protecting the computer system from unauthorized use.

2. Multitasking refers to the ability of an operating system to have more than one program (also called a task) open at one time.

3. The primary difference between multiprocessing and parallel processing is that with multiprocessing each CPU typically works on a different job, whereas with parallel processing, the CPUs usually work together to complete one job more quickly.

4. The four most widely used personal operating systems are Windows, Mac OS, UNIX, and Linux.

5. A utility program is a software program that performs a specific task, usually related to managing or maintaining the computer system.

6. Application software includes all the programs that allow you to perform specific tasks on a computer, such as writing a letter, preparing an invoice, viewing a Web page, listening to a music file, checking the inventory of a particular product, playing a game, preparing financial statements, and designing a home.

7. Commercial software includes any software program that is developed and sold for a profit. Shareware programs are software programs that are distributed on the honor system. Most shareware programs are available to try free of charge but typically require a small fee if you choose to use the program regularly.

8. When a software program is purchased, the buyer is acquiring a software license that permits him or her to use the software. This license specifies the conditions under which the buyer can use the software, such as the number of computers on which it may be installed.

9. A software suite is a group of related software programs (such as graphics programs, utility programs, or office-related software) that are sold bundled together.

10. Office suites typically contain word processing software, spreadsheet software, database software, and presentation graphics software.

11. Multimedia technically refers to any application that contains more than one type of media but is often used to refer to audio and video content.

12. A bitmap image is a graphic created by coloring the individual pixels in an image. A vector graphic uses mathematical formulas to represent image content instead of pixels.

13. Media players are programs designed to play audio and video files available via a computer—such as music CDs, downloaded music, or video streamed from the Internet.

14. Desktop publishing refers to using a personal computer to combine and manipulate text and images to create attractive documents that look as if they were created by a professional printer.

15. Personal finance software is commonly used at home by individuals to write checks and balance checking accounts, track personal expenses, manage stock portfolios, and prepare income taxes.

16. Collaboration software enables a group of individuals to work together on a project.

Computer Networks

Supri Suharjoto/Shutterstock.com

From telephone calls to home and business networks to Web surfing and online shopping, networking and the Internet are deeply embedded in our society. Because of this, it is important to be familiar with basic networking concepts and terminology, as well as with the variety of activities that take place today via networks—including the Internet, the world's largest network. It is also important to be aware of the potential problems and risks associated with networks and our networked society. This chapter introduces basic networking principles, including what a computer network is, how it works, and what it can be used for.

Learning Objectives

After studying the material in this chapter, you will be able to:

4-1 Explain what networks are

4-2 Identify network characteristics

4-3 Understand how data is transmitted over a network

4-4 Describe common types of networking media

4-5 Identify protocols and networking standards

4-6 Describe networking hardware

4-1 What Is a Network?

Recall that a **computer network** is a collection of computers and other hardware devices that are connected so users can share hardware, software, and data, as well as communicate with each other electronically. Today, computer networks are converging with telephone networks and other communications networks, with both data and voice being sent over these networks. Computer networks range from small, private networks to the Internet and are widely used by businesses and individuals. Common uses include:

▶ Sharing an Internet connection among several users

▶ Sharing application software, printers, and other resources

▶ Facilitating Voice over IP (VoIP), email, videoconferencing, messaging, and other communications applications

▶ Working collaboratively, such as sharing a company database or using collaboration tools to create or review documents

▶ Exchanging files among network users and over the Internet

▶ Connecting the computers and the entertainment devices, such as TVs, gaming consoles, and stereo systems, located within a home

In most businesses, computer networks are essential. They enable employees to share expensive resources, access the Internet, and communicate with each other as well as with business partners and customers. They facilitate the exchange and collaboration of documents, and they are often a key component of the ordering, inventory, and fulfillment systems used to process customer orders. In homes, computer networks enable individuals to share resources, access the Internet, and communicate with others. In addition, they allow people to access a wide variety of information, services, and entertainment, as well as share data, such as digital photos, downloaded movies, and music, among the networked devices in a home. On

the go, networks enable individuals to work from remote locations, locate information whenever and wherever it is needed, and stay in touch with others.

4-2 Network Characteristics

Networks can be identified by a variety of characteristics, including whether they are designed for wired or wireless access, their topology, their architecture, and their size or coverage area.

4-2a Wired vs. Wireless Networks

Networks can be designed for access via wired and/or wireless connections. With a **wired network** connection, the computers and other devices on the network are physically connected via cabling to the network. With a **wireless network** connection, wireless (usually radio) signals are used to send data through the air between devices, instead of using physical cables. Wired networks include conventional telephone networks, cable TV networks, and the wired networks commonly found in schools, businesses, and government facilities. Wireless networks include conventional television and radio networks, cellular telephone networks, satellite TV networks, and the wireless networks commonly found in homes, schools, and businesses. Wireless networks are also found in many public locations, such as coffeehouses, businesses, airports, hotels, and libraries, to provide Internet access to users while they are on the go via public wireless **hotspots**.

> Many networks are accessible through both wired and wireless connections.

computer network Computers and other hardware devices that are connected to share hardware, software, and data.

wired network A network in which computers and other devices are connected to the network via physical cables.

wireless network A network in which computers and other devices are connected to the network without physical cables.

hotspot A location that provides wireless Internet access to the public.

Networking Applications

Businesses and individuals use a wide variety of networking applications for communications, information retrieval, and other applications. Some of the most common are:

▶ **Internet**—The Internet is the largest computer network in the world. Many networking applications today, such as information retrieval, shopping, entertainment, and email, take place via the Internet.

▶ **Telephone**—The original telephone network is one of the first communications networks. This network is still used today to provide telephone service to conventional landline phones and is used for some types of Internet connections. **Mobile phones** (also called **wireless phones**) use a wireless network for communications instead of the regular telephone network. The most common type of mobile phone is the **cellular (cell) phone**, which communicates via cellular technology. Another, but less common, type of mobile phone is the **satellite phone**, which communicates via satellite technology.

Courtesy of Iridium

Soldier using satellite phone

▶ **Television and Radio Broadcasting**—Broadcast television networks and radio networks are two other original communications networks. Other networks involved with television content delivery are cable TV networks, satellite TV networks, and the private closed-circuit television (CCTV) systems used by businesses for surveillance and security purposes.

▶ **Global Positioning System (GPS) Applications**—The global positioning system (GPS) network consists of 24 Department of Defense GPS satellites (in orbit approximately 12,000 miles above the earth). A GPS receiver measures the distance between the receiver and four GPS satellites simultaneously to determine the receiver's exact geographic location.

▶ **Monitoring Systems**—Monitoring systems use networking technology to determine the current location or status of an object, such as where a vehicle was driven and how fast it was driven, the vital signs of elderly or infirm individuals, and the temperature and relative humidity in pharmaceutical plants during the drug development process. Monitoring systems are also in homes to manage and control smart devices such as smart appliances and home automation systems.

▶ **Multimedia Networking**—A growing use of home networks is to deliver digital multimedia content, such as digital photos, digital music, home movies, downloaded movies, and recorded TV shows, to devices such as computers, televisions, and home entertainment systems on that network.

▶ **Collaborative Computing**—Workgroup or collaborative computing uses networking technology with collaborative software tools to enable individuals to work together on documents and other project components.

▶ **Telecommuting**—**Telecommuting** is when individuals work from a remote location (typically their homes) and communicate with their places of business and clients via networking technologies.

▶ **Videoconferencing**—**Videoconferencing** is the use of networking technology to conduct real-time, face-to-face meetings between individuals physically located in different places.

Courtesy Cisco Systems, Inc.

▶ **Telemedicine**—Telemedicine uses networking technology to provide medical information and services. It includes Web sites that patients can access to contact their physicians, make appointments, view lab results, and more. More complex telemedicine systems are most often used to provide care to individuals who may not otherwise have access to that care, such as allowing people living in remote areas to consult with a specialist. Telesurgery is a form of robot-assisted surgery in which at least one of the surgeons performs the operation by controlling the robot remotely over the Internet or another network.

Many networks are accessible via both wired and wireless connections. For instance, a business may have a wired main company network to which the computers in employee offices are always connected and provide wireless access to the network for visitors and employees to use while in waiting rooms, conference rooms, and other locations. A home network may have a wired connection between one computer and the devices needed to connect that computer to the Internet, plus wireless access for other devices that may need to access the home network wirelessly.

Wired networks tend to be faster and more secure than wireless networks. Wireless networks allow easy connections in locations where physical wiring is impractical or inconvenient, as well as provide much more freedom about where you can use your computer. With wireless networking, for example, you can surf the Web on your notebook or tablet computer from anywhere in your house, access the Internet with your portable computer or mobile phone while on the go, and create a home network without having to run wires among the rooms in your house.

4-2b Network Topologies

The physical topology of a computer network indicates how the devices in the network are arranged. The three most common physical topologies are star, bus, and mesh, as shown in Exhibit 4-1.

▶ **Star network**—A network in which all the networked devices connect to a central device through which all network transmissions are sent. If the central device fails, the network cannot function.

▶ **Bus network**—A network that uses a central cable to which all network devices connect. All data is transmitted down the bus line from one device to another so if the bus line fails, the network cannot function.

▶ **Mesh network**—A network that uses a number of different connections between network devices so that data can take any of several possible paths from source to destination. Consequently, if one device on a mesh network fails, the network can still function, assuming an alternate path is available. Mesh networks are used most often with wireless networks.

Many networks, however, do not conform to a standard topology. Some networks combine topologies and connect multiple smaller networks, in effect turning several smaller networks into one larger one. For example, two star networks may be joined together using a bus cable.

4-2c Network Architectures

Networks also vary by their **architecture**, the way they are designed to communicate. The two most common network architectures are client-server and peer-to-peer.

Client-server networks include both **clients**, which are computers and other devices on the network that request and use network resources, and **servers**, which are computers that are dedicated to processing client requests. Network servers are typically powerful computers with lots of memory and a very large hard drive. They provide access to software, files, and other resources that are being shared via the network. Servers typically perform a variety of tasks. For example, a single server can act as a network server to manage network traffic, a file server to manage shared files, a print server to handle printing-related activities, and/or a mail server or Web server to manage email and Web page requests, respectively. Only one server appears in the network

---

mobile phone (wireless phone) A phone that uses a wireless network for communications instead of the regular telephone network.

cellular (cell) phone A type of mobile phone that communicates via cellular technology.

satellite phone A type of mobile phone that communicates via satellite technology.

telecommute The act of working from a remote location by using computers and networking technology.

videoconference A real-time, face-to-face meeting between individuals physically located in different places conducted through the use of networking technology.

star network A network that uses a host device connected directly to several other devices.

bus network A network that uses a central cable to which all network devices connect.

mesh network A network that uses multiple connections between network devices.

architecture The way computers are designed to communicate.

client-server network A network that includes both clients and servers.

client A computer or other device on a network that requests and uses network resources.

server A computer that is dedicated to processing client requests.

Exhibit 4-1 Common network topologies

STAR NETWORKS
Use a central device to connect each device directly to the network.

BUS NETWORKS
Use a single central cable to connect each device in a linear fashion.

MESH NETWORKS
Each computer or device is connected to multiple (sometimes all of the other) devices on the network.

download To retrieve files from a server to a client.

upload To transfer files from a client to a server.

peer-to-peer (P2P) network A network in which the computers on the network work at the same functional level, and users have direct access to the network devices.

illustrated in Exhibit 4-2, and it is capable of performing all server tasks for that network. When a client retrieves files from a server, it is called **downloading**; transferring data from a client to a server is called **uploading**.

With a **peer-to-peer (P2P) network**, a central server is not used. As shown in Exhibit 4-3, all the computers on the network work at the same functional level, and users have direct access to the computers and other devices attached to the network. For instance, users can access files stored on a peer computer's hard drive and print using a peer computer's printer, provided those devices have been designated as shared devices. Peer-to-peer networks are less expensive and less complicated to implement than client-server networks because there are no dedicated servers, but they may not have the same performance as client-server networks under heavy use. Peer-to-peer capabilities are built into many personal operating systems and are often used in conjunction with small office or home networks.

Another type of peer-to-peer networking—sometimes called Internet peer-to-peer (Internet P2P) computing—is performed via the Internet. Instead of placing content on a Web server for others to view via the Internet, content is exchanged over the Internet directly between individual users via a peer-to-peer network. For instance, one user can copy a file from another user's hard drive to his or her own computer via the Internet. Internet P2P networking is commonly used for exchanging music and video files with others over the Internet—an illegal act if the content is copyright-protected and the exchange is unauthorized, although legal Internet P2P networks exist.

CAUTION

Sharing Folders on a Network

Do not enable sharing for folders that you want to keep private from others on your network. When you enable sharing for a folder, other people on your network can see it. If you choose to use a P2P network, be sure to designate the files in your shared folder as read-only to prevent your original files from being overwritten by another P2P user.

4-2d Network Size and Coverage Area

Networks are also classified by their size and their coverage area. This impacts the types of users the network is designed to service. The most common categories of networks can use both wired and wireless connections.

Exhibit 4-2 Client-server network with one server

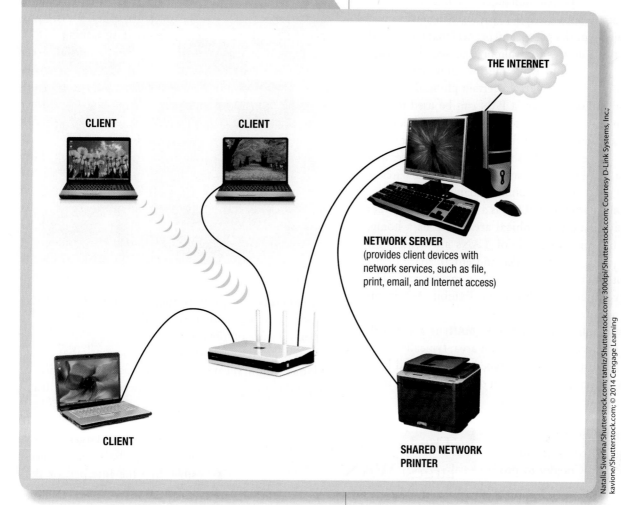

CLIENT

CLIENT

THE INTERNET

NETWORK SERVER
(provides client devices with
network services, such as file,
print, email, and Internet access)

CLIENT

SHARED NETWORK
PRINTER

Natalia Siverina/Shutterstock.com; tatniz/Shutterstock.com; 300dpi/Shutterstock.com; Courtesy D-Link Systems, Inc.; kavione/Shutterstock.com; © 2014 Cengage Learning

Exhibit 4-3 Peer-to-peer networks

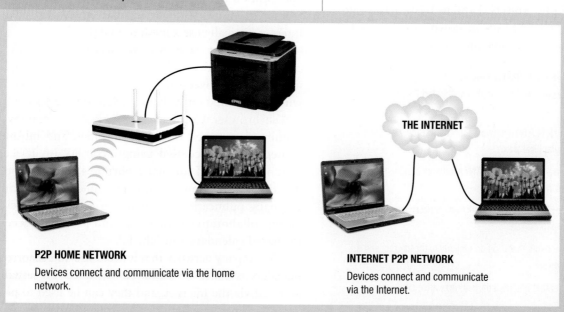

THE INTERNET

P2P HOME NETWORK
Devices connect and communicate via the home
network.

INTERNET P2P NETWORK
Devices connect and communicate
via the Internet.

Natalia Siverina/Shutterstock.com; Courtesy D-Link Systems, Inc.; kavione/Shutterstock.com; tatniz/Shutterstock.com; © 2014 Cengage Learning

A **personal area network** (**PAN**) is a network of personal devices for one individual (such as his or her portable computer, mobile phone, headset, digital camera, portable digital media player, and printer) that is designed to enable those devices to communicate and share data. PANs can be set up to work together automatically as soon as the devices get within a certain physical distance of each other. For instance, a PAN can be used to synchronize mobile devices automatically with a desktop computer as soon as the individual returns home or to the office. The range of a PAN is very limited, so devices in a PAN must be physically located close together. Wireless PANs (WPANs) are more common than wired PANs.

A **local area network** (**LAN**) is a network that covers a relatively small geographical area, such as a home, an office building, or a school. LANs allow users on the network to exchange files and email, share printers and other hardware, and access the Internet. The client-server network shown in Exhibit 4-2 is an example of a LAN.

A **metropolitan area network** (**MAN**) is a network designed to service a metropolitan area, typically a city or county. Most MANs are owned and operated by a city or by a network provider in order to provide individuals in that location access to the MAN. Some wireless MANs are created by cities or large organizations (including Microsoft and Google) to provide free or low-cost Internet access to area residents. These projects are typically supported by local taxes and are sometimes referred to as municipal Wi-Fi projects. Exhibit 4-4 shows a sign identifying a wireless MAN in downtown Riverside, California. In addition, some Internet service providers

Exhibit 4-4 Sign describing a MAN in Riverside, California

are experimenting with setting up free wireless MANs in select metropolitan areas for their subscribers to use when they are on the go.

A **wide area network** (**WAN**) is a network that covers a large geographical area. Typically, a WAN consists of two or more LANs that are connected together using communications technology. The Internet, by this definition, is the world's largest WAN. WANs may be publicly accessible, like the Internet, or they may be privately owned and operated. For instance, a company may have a private WAN to transfer data from one location to another, such as from each retail store to the corporate headquarters. Large WANs, like the Internet, typically use a mesh topology.

An **intranet** is a private network, such as a company LAN, that is designed to be used by an organization's employees and is set up like the Internet with data posted on Web pages that are accessed with a Web browser. Consequently, little or no employee training is required to use an intranet, and intranet content can be accessed using a variety of devices. Intranets are used for many purposes, such as coordinating internal email and communications, making company publications available to employees, facilitating collaborative computing, and providing access to shared calendars and schedules.

A company network that is accessible to authorized outsiders is called an **extranet**. Extranets are usually accessed via the Internet, and they can be used to provide customers and business partners with access to

> The Internet is the world's largest WAN.

personal area network (**PAN**) A network that connects an individual's personal devices that are located close together.

local area network (**LAN**) A network that connects devices located in a small geographical area.

metropolitan area network (**MAN**) A network designed to service a metropolitan area.

wide area network (**WAN**) A network that connects devices located in a large geographical area.

intranet A private network that is set up similarly to the Internet and is accessed via a Web browser.

extranet An intranet that is at least partially accessible to authorized outsiders.

Connecting to a Wi-Fi Hotspot

To connect to a Wi-Fi hotspot, all you need is a device, such as a mobile phone or a notebook computer, with a Wi-Fi adapter installed and enabled. On a Windows computer that has a Wi-Fi adapter installed, an icon representing your wireless network connection should appear in the notification area. When you are within range of a Wi-Fi hotspot, an asterisk appears on the icon to indicate that wireless networks were found. Click this icon to see all of the Wi-Fi access points in the area. If more than one hotspot is listed, click the network to which you want to connect. If the network is an unsecured network, it does not require a passphrase and you may see a warning that any information you send might be visible to others. To connect to the selected network, click the Connect button. For free hotspots, you should be connected shortly. For some free hotspots, you need to start your browser and then click a button to indicate that you agree with the network usage terms. Then you can use your browser and email program as usual. For secured networks, you will need to supply the appropriate passphrase before you can connect to the Internet via that hotspot. For most fee-based hotspots, a logon screen appears. You need to enter a username and password and then agree with the network usage terms before being connected.

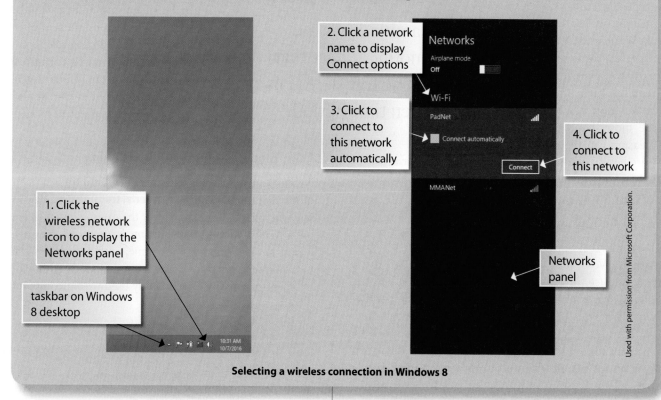

2. Click a network name to display Connect options

3. Click to connect to this network automatically

4. Click to connect to this network

1. Click the wireless network icon to display the Networks panel

taskbar on Windows 8 desktop

Networks panel

Networks
Airplane mode
Off

Wi-Fi

PadNet
Connect automatically
Connect

MMANet

10:31 AM
10/7/2016

Used with permission from Microsoft Corporation.

Selecting a wireless connection in Windows 8

the data they need. Access to intranets and extranets is typically restricted to employees and other authorized users, similar to other company networks.

A **virtual private network** (**VPN**) is a private, secure path across a public network (usually the Internet) that is set up to allow authorized users private, secure access to the company network. VPNs allow an organization to provide secure, remote access to the company network without the cost of physically extending the private network. For instance, a VPN can allow a traveling employee, a business partner, or an employee located at a satellite office or public wireless hotspot to connect securely to the company network via the Internet. A process called tunneling is typically used to carry the data over the Internet; special encryption technology is used to protect the data so it cannot be understood if it is intercepted during transit.

virtual private network (**VPN**) A private, secure path over the Internet used for accessing a private network.

4-3 Data Transmission

Data transmitted over a network has specific characteristics, and it can travel over a network in various ways. The amount of data that can transfer during a given time period, how the data is transmitted, how it is timed, and how it is delivered all factor into the transmission.

4-3a Bandwidth

Bandwidth (also called **throughput**) is the amount of data that can be transferred in a given time period. Just as a wide fire hose allows more water to pass through it per unit of time than a narrow garden hose allows, a networking medium with a high bandwidth allows more data to pass through it per unit of time than one with a low bandwidth. Text data requires the least amount of bandwidth; video data requires the most. Bandwidth is usually measured in the number of bps (bits per second), Kbps (thousands of bits per second), Mbps (millions of bits per second), or Gbps (billions of bits per second).

> Bandwidth is the amount of data that can be transferred in a given time period.

4-3b Analog vs. Digital Signals

Data can be represented as either analog or digital signals. Voice and music data in its natural form, for instance, is analog. Data stored on a computer is digital. Most networking media send data using **digital signals**, in which data is represented by only two discrete states: 0s and 1s. **Analog signals**, such as those used by the conventional telephone system, represent data with continuous waves. The data to be transmitted over a

networking medium must match the type of signal—analog or digital—that the medium supports. If it doesn't, then the data must be converted before it is transmitted. For instance, analog data that is to be sent using digital signals, such as analog music broadcast by a digital radio station,

ANALOG SIGNALS

DIGITAL SIGNALS
Analog vs. digital signals

© 2014 Cengage Learning

must first be converted into digital form. Likewise, digital data to be sent using analog signals, such as computer data sent over a conventional analog telephone network, must first be converted into analog form. The conversion of data between analog and digital form is performed by networking hardware.

4-3c Transmission Type and Timing

Networking media can also use either serial transmission or parallel transmission. With **serial transmission**, data is sent one bit at a time, one after the other along a single path. When **parallel transmission** is used, the message is sent at least one byte at a time, with each bit in the byte taking a separate path. See Exhibit 4-5. Although parallel transmission is frequently used within computer

bandwidth (throughput) The amount of data that can be transferred in a given time period.

digital signal A type of signal where the data is represented by 0s and 1s.

analog signal A type of signal where the data is represented by continuous waves.

serial transmission A type of data transmission in which the bits in a byte travel down the same path one after the other.

parallel transmission A type of data transmission in which bytes of data are transmitted at one time with the bits in each byte taking a separate path.

Exhibit 4-5 Serial vs. parallel transmissions

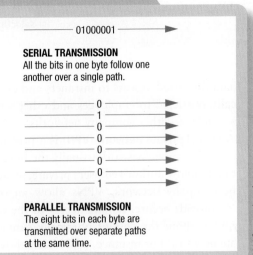

Exhibit 4-6 Transmission timing

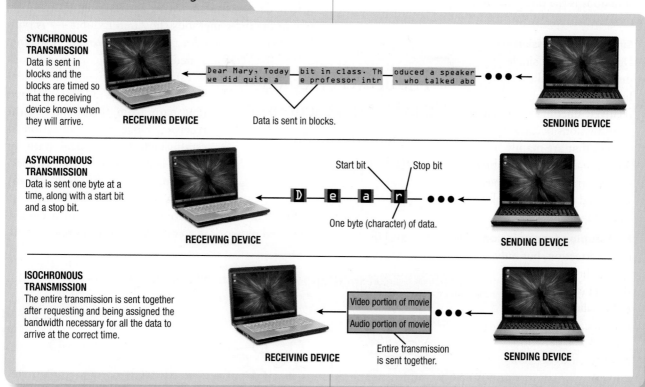

SYNCHRONOUS TRANSMISSION
Data is sent in blocks and the blocks are timed so that the receiving device knows when they will arrive.

RECEIVING DEVICE

Dear Mary, Today we did quite a | bit in class. Th e professor intr | oduced a speaker , who talked abo

Data is sent in blocks.

SENDING DEVICE

ASYNCHRONOUS TRANSMISSION
Data is sent one byte at a time, along with a start bit and a stop bit.

RECEIVING DEVICE

Start bit · Stop bit

D e a r

One byte (character) of data.

SENDING DEVICE

ISOCHRONOUS TRANSMISSION
The entire transmission is sent together after requesting and being assigned the bandwidth necessary for all the data to arrive at the correct time.

RECEIVING DEVICE

Video portion of movie
Audio portion of movie

Entire transmission is sent together.

SENDING DEVICE

Natalia Siverina/Shutterstock.com; atniz/Shutterstock.com; © 2014 Cengage Learning

components, such as for buses, and is used for some wireless networking applications, networking media typically use serial transmission.

When data is sent using serial transmission, one of the following three techniques is used to organize the bits being transferred so the data can be reconstructed after it is received:

▶ **Synchronous transmission**—Data is organized into groups or blocks of data, which are transferred at regular, specified intervals. Because the transmissions are synchronized, both devices know when data can be sent and when it should arrive. Most data transmissions within a computer and over a network are synchronous transmissions.

▶ **Asynchronous transmission**—Data is sent when it is ready to be sent, without being synchronized. To identify the bits that belong in each byte, a start bit and stop bit are used at the beginning and end of the byte, respectively. This overhead makes asynchronous transmission less efficient than synchronous transmission, and so it is not as widely used as synchronous transmission.

▶ **Isochronous transmission**—Data is sent at the same time as other related data to support types of real-time applications that require the different types of data to be delivered at the proper speed for that application. For example, when transmitting a video file, the audio data must be received at the proper time in order for it to be played with its corresponding video data. To accomplish this with isochronous transmission, the sending and receiving devices first communicate to determine the bandwidth and other factors needed for the transmission, and then the necessary bandwidth is reserved just for that transmission.

Although all three of these methods send data one bit at a time, the three methods vary with respect to how the bits are organized for transfer, as shown in Exhibit 4-6.

synchronous transmission A type of serial data transmission in which data is organized into groups or blocks of data that are transferred at regular, specified intervals.

asynchronous transmission A type of serial data transmission in which data is sent when it is ready to be sent without being synchronized.

isochronous transmission A type of serial data transmission in which data is sent at the same time as other related data.

Chapter 4: Computer Networks   **115**

Another distinction between the different types of transmissions is the direction in which transmitted data can move.

▶ **Simplex transmission—** Data travels in a single direction only (like a door-bell). Simplex transmission is relatively uncommon in data transmissions because most devices that are mainly one-directional, such as a printer, can still transmit error messages and other data back to the computer.

▶ **Half-duplex transmission—**Data can travel in either direction, but only in one direction at a time (like a walkie-talkie where only one person can talk at a time). Some network transmissions are half-duplex.

▶ **Full-duplex transmission—**Data can move in both directions at the same time (like a telephone). Many network and most Internet connections are full-duplex; sometimes two connections between the sending device and receiving device are needed to support full-duplex transmissions.

> The delivery method used for data sent over the Internet is packet switching.

4-3d Delivery Method

When data needs to travel across a large network, one of the three methods shown in Exhibit 4-7 is typically used. With **circuit switching**, a dedicated path over a network is established between the sender and receiver, and all data follows that path from the sender to the receiver. Once the connection is established, the physical path or circuit is dedicated to that connection and cannot be used by any other device until the transmission is finished. The most common example of a circuit-switched network is a conventional telephone system.

Exhibit 4-7 Circuit-switched, packet-switched, and broadcast networks

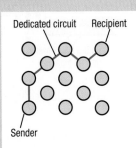

CIRCUIT-SWITCHED NETWORK
Data uses a dedicated path from the sender to the recipient.

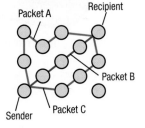

PACKET-SWITCHED NETWORK
Data is sent as individual packets, which are assembled at the recipient's destination.

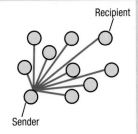

BROADCAST NETWORK
Data is broadcast to all nodes within range; the designated recipient retrieves the data.

© 2014 Cengage Learning

simplex transmission A type of data transmission in which data travels in a single direction only.

half-duplex transmission A type of data transmission in which data can travel in either direction but only in one direction at a time.

full-duplex transmission A type of data transmission in which data can move in both directions at the same time.

circuit switching A method of transmitting data in which messages travel along a dedicated network path.

packet switching A method of transmitting data in which messages are separated into packets that travel along the network separately and then are reassembled in the proper order at the destination.

broadcasting A method of transmitting data in which data is sent out to all nodes on a network and is retrieved only by the intended recipient.

The delivery method used for data sent over the Internet is packet switching. With **packet switching**, messages are separated into small units called packets. Packets contain information about the sender and the receiver, the actual data being sent, and information about how to reassemble the packets to reconstruct the original message. Packets travel along the network separately, based on their final destination, network traffic, and other network conditions. When the packets reach their destination, they are reassembled in the proper order. Another alternative is **broadcasting**, in which data is sent out, typically in packets, to all nodes on a network and is retrieved only by the intended recipient. Broadcasting is used primarily with LANs.

Exhibit 4-8 Wired network transmission media

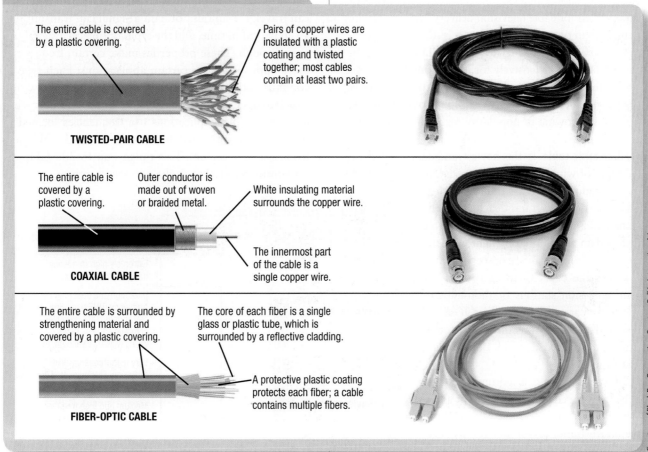

The entire cable is covered by a plastic covering.

Pairs of copper wires are insulated with a plastic coating and twisted together; most cables contain at least two pairs.

TWISTED-PAIR CABLE

The entire cable is covered by a plastic covering.

Outer conductor is made out of woven or braided metal.

White insulating material surrounds the copper wire.

The innermost part of the cable is a single copper wire.

COAXIAL CABLE

The entire cable is surrounded by strengthening material and covered by a plastic covering.

The core of each fiber is a single glass or plastic tube, which is surrounded by a reflective cladding.

A protective plastic coating protects each fiber; a cable contains multiple fibers.

FIBER-OPTIC CABLE

Courtesy of Black Box Corporation; Courtesy Belkin International, Inc.

4-4 Networking Media

To connect the devices in a network, either wired media (physical cables) or wireless media (typically radio signals) can be used. The most common wired and wireless networking media are discussed next.

4-4a Wired Networking Media

The most common types of wired networking media are twisted-pair, coaxial, and fiber-optic cable, which are shown in Exhibit 4-8.

A **twisted-pair cable** is made up of pairs of thin strands of insulated wire twisted together. Twisted-pair is the least expensive type of networking cable and has been in use the longest. In fact, it is the same type of cabling used inside most homes for telephone communications. Twisted-pair cabling can be used with both analog and digital data transmission and is commonly used for LANs. Twisted-pair cable is rated by category, which indicates the type of data, speed, distance,

and other factors that the cable supports. Category 3 (Cat 3) twisted-pair cabling is regular telephone cable; higher speed and quality cabling—such as Category 5 (Cat 5), Category 6 (Cat 6), and Category 7 (Cat 7)—is frequently used for home or business networks. The pairs of wires in twisted-pair wire are twisted together to reduce interference and improve performance. To further improve performance, it can be shielded with a metal lining. Twisted-pair cables used for networks have different connectors than those used for telephones.

A **coaxial cable** (also known as **coax**) consists of a relatively thick center wire surrounded by insulation and then covered with a shield of braided wire to block electromagnetic signals from entering the cable. Coaxial cable was originally developed to carry a large number of high-speed video transmissions at one time, such as to deliver

twisted-pair cable A networking cable consisting of insulated wire strands twisted in sets of two and bound into a cable.

coaxial cable (**coax**) A networking cable consisting of a center wire inside a grounded, cylindrical shield, capable of sending data at high speeds.

cable TV service. It is commonly used today in computer networks, for short-run telephone transmissions outside of the home, and for cable television delivery. Although more expensive than twisted-pair cabling, it is much less susceptible to interference and can carry more data more quickly. Although not used extensively for networking home computers at the moment, that may change with the relatively new option of networking via the existing coax in a home. Coax is also growing in popularity for home multimedia networks.

Fiber-optic cable is the newest and fastest of these three types of wired transmission media. It contains multiple—sometimes several hundred—clear glass or plastic fiber strands, each about the thickness of a human hair. Fiber-optic cable transfers data represented by light pulses at speeds of billions of bits per second. Each strand has the capacity to carry data for several television stations or thousands of voice conversations. However, each strand can send data in only one direction, so two strands are needed for full-duplex data transmissions.

Fiber-optic cable is commonly used for the high-speed backbone lines of a network, such as to connect networks housed in separate buildings or for the Internet infrastructure. It is also used for telephone backbone lines and, increasingly, is being installed by telephone companies all the way to the home or business to provide super-fast connections directly to the end user. The biggest advantage of fiber-optic cabling is speed; the main disadvantage of fiber-optic cabling is the initial expense of both the cable and the installation.

4-3b Wireless Networking Media

Wireless networks usually use radio signals to send data through the airwaves. All wireless applications in the United States—such as wireless networks, mobile phones, radio and TV broadcasts, sonar and radar applications, and GPS systems—use specific frequencies as assigned by the Federal Communications Commission (FCC). Frequencies are measured in hertz (Hz). The frequencies that make up the electromagnetic spectrum—the range of common electromagnetic radiation—are

shown in Exhibit 4-9. Different parts of the spectrum have different properties, such as the distance a signal can travel, the amount of data a signal can transmit in a given period of time, and the types of objects a signal can pass through. These properties make certain frequencies more appropriate for certain applications. Each type of communication is assigned specific frequencies within which to operate. As illustrated in Exhibit 4-9, most wireless networking applications use frequencies located in the radio frequency (RF) band at the low end of the electromagnetic spectrum. This range—up to 300 GHz—is sometimes referred to as the wireless spectrum.

Exhibit 4-9 The electromagnetic spectrum

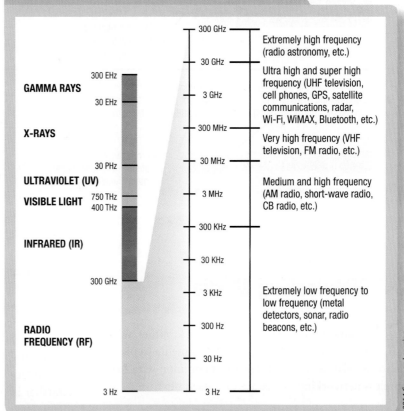

© 2014 Cengage Learning

The frequencies assigned to an application, such as FM radio or cell phone service, typically consist of a range of frequencies to be used as needed for that application. For instance, FM radio stations broadcast on frequencies from 88 MHz to 108 MHz, and each radio station in a particular geographic area is assigned its own frequency. Most radio frequencies in the United States are licensed by the FCC and can be used only for that specific application by the licensed individuals in their specified geographic areas. However, the 900 MHz, 2.4 GHz, 5 GHz, and 5.8 GHz frequencies used by many cordless landline phones, garage door openers, and other consumer devices—as well as for Wi-Fi,

---

fiber-optic cable A networking cable that contains hundreds of thin, transparent fibers over which lasers transmit data as light.

Exhibit 4-10 How cellular phones work

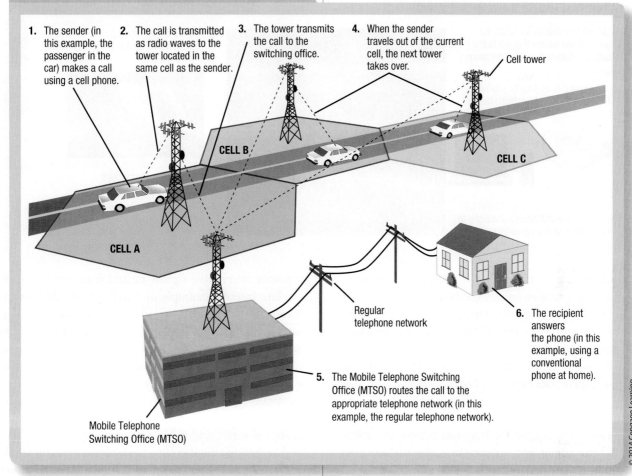

1. The sender (in this example, the passenger in the car) makes a call using a cell phone.

2. The call is transmitted as radio waves to the tower located in the same cell as the sender.

3. The tower transmits the call to the switching office.

4. When the sender travels out of the current cell, the next tower takes over.

Cell tower

CELL B

CELL C

CELL A

Regular telephone network

6. The recipient answers the phone (in this example, using a conventional phone at home).

5. The Mobile Telephone Switching Office (MTSO) routes the call to the appropriate telephone network (in this example, the regular telephone network).

Mobile Telephone Switching Office (MTSO)

© 2014 Cengage Learning

WiMAX, and Bluetooth wireless networking—fall within an unlicensed part of the spectrum and, therefore, can be used by any product or individual. A frequency range can be further broken down into multiple channels, each of which can be used simultaneously by different users. There are also ways to combine multiple signals to send them over a transmission medium at one time to allow more users than would otherwise be possible.

Because the number of wireless applications is growing all the time and the parts of the spectrum appropriate for today's wireless networking applications are limited, the wireless spectrum is relatively crowded and frequencies are in high demand. One benefit of the 2009 switch from analog to digital television broadcasts is that it freed up some of the VHF and UHF frequencies for other applications.

Cellular radio transmissions are used with cell phones and are sent and received via cellular (cell) towers—tall metal poles with antennas on top. Cellular service areas

> Wireless networks usually use radio signals to send data through the airwaves.

are divided into honeycomb-shaped zones called cells; each cell contains one cell tower. When a cell phone user begins to make a call, it is picked up by the cell tower located in the cell in which the cell phone is located and that belongs to the user's mobile phone provider. That cell tower then forwards the call to the mobile phone company's Mobile Telephone Switching Office (MTSO), which routes the call to the recipient's telephone via his or her mobile or conventional telephone service provider, depending on the type of phone being used by the recipient. See Exhibit 4-10. When a cell phone user moves out of the current cell into a new cell, the call is passed automatically to the appropriate cell tower in the

cellular radio transmission A type of data transmission used with cell phones in which the data is sent and received via cell towers.

Exhibit 4-11 How satellite Internet works

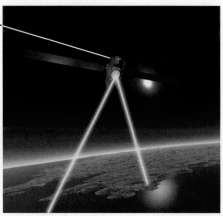

3. An orbiting satellite receives the request and beams it down to the satellite dish at the ISP's operations center.

2. The request is sent up to a satellite from the individual's satellite dish.

1. Data, such as a Web page request, is sent from the individual's computer to the satellite dish via a satellite modem.

4. The ISP's operations center receives the request (via its satellite dish) and transfers it to the Internet.

THE INTERNET

5. The request travels over the Internet as usual. The requested information takes a reverse route back to the individual.

cell that the user is entering. The transmission of data, such as email and Web page requests, sent via cell phones works in a similar manner. The speed of cellular radio transmissions depends on the type of cellular standard being used.

Microwaves are high-frequency radio signals that can send large quantities of data at high speeds over long distances. Microwave signals can be sent or received using microwave stations or communications satellites, but they must travel in a straight line from one station or satellite to another without encountering any obstacles because microwave signals are line of sight. **Microwave stations** are earth-based stations that can transmit microwave signals directly to each other over distances of up to about 30 miles. To avoid buildings, mountains, and the curvature of the earth obstructing the signal, microwave stations are usually placed on tall buildings, towers, and mountaintops. Microwave stations typically contain both a dish-shaped microwave antenna and a transceiver. When one station receives a transmission from another, it amplifies it and passes it on to the next station. Microwave stations can exchange data transmissions with communications satellites, as well as with other microwave stations.

Communications satellites are space-based devices launched into orbit around the earth to receive and

transmit microwave signals to and from earth (see the satellite Internet example in Exhibit 4-11). Microwave stations designed specifically to communicate with satellites, such as for satellite TV and Internet services, are typically called satellite dishes. Communications satellites were originally used to facilitate microwave transmission when microwave stations were not economically viable, such as over large, sparsely populated areas, or were physically impractical, such as over large bodies of water, and were used primarily by the military and communications companies, such as for remote television news broadcasts. Today, communications satellites are used to send and receive transmissions to and from a variety of other devices, such as personal satellite dishes used for satellite television and Internet service, GPS receivers, satellite radio receivers, and satellite phones. They are also used for earth observation (EO), such as for weather observation, mapping, and government surveillance purposes.

Traditional communications satellites maintain a geosynchronous orbit 22,300 miles above the earth. Because these satellites are so far above the surface of the earth, there is a slight delay while the signals travel from earth, to the satellite, and back to earth again. This delay—less than one half-second—is not normally noticed by most users, such as individuals who receive Internet or TV service via satellite, but it does make geosynchronous satellite transmissions less practical for voice, gaming, and other real-time communications. Because of this delay factor, low earth orbit (LEO) satellite systems were developed for use with satellite telephone systems. LEO satellites typically are located anywhere from 100 to 1,000 miles above the earth and, consequently, provide faster transmission

microwaves High-frequency radio signals that can send large quantities of data at high speeds over long distances.

microwave station A device that sends and receives high-frequency, high-speed radio signals.

communications satellite A device that orbits the earth and relays communications signals over long distances.

than traditional satellites. Medium earth orbit (MEO) systems typically use satellites located about 1,000 to 12,000 miles above the earth and are used most often for GPS.

One type of wireless networking that does not use signals in the RF band of the electromagnetic spectrum is **infrared (IR) transmission**, which sends data as infrared light rays over relatively short distances. Like an infrared television remote control, infrared technology requires line-of-sight transmission. Because of this limitation, many formerly infrared devices, such as wireless mice and keyboards, now use RF radio signals instead. Infrared transmissions are still used with remote controls, such as for computers that contain TV tuners. They are also used to beam data between some mobile devices, as well as between some game consoles, handheld gaming devices, and other home entertainment devices.

FYI

Radio Signals

Radio signals can be short range (such as to connect a wireless keyboard or mouse to a computer), medium range (such as to connect a computer to a wireless LAN or public hotspot), or long range (such as to provide Internet access to a large geographic area or to broadcast a TV show).

Christian Delbert/Shutterstock.com

4-5 Communications Protocols and Networking Standards

A **protocol** is a set of rules to be followed in a specific situation. In networking, for instance, communications protocols determine how devices on a network communicate. The term standard refers to a set of criteria or requirements that has been approved by a recognized standards organization, such as the American National Standards Institute (ANSI), which helps to develop standards used in business and industry, or the Institute of Electrical and Electronics Engineers (IEEE), which develops networking standards, or is accepted as a de facto standard by the industry. Standards help manufacturers ensure their hardware and software products work with other computing products.

> Standards help manufacturers ensure their hardware and software products work with other computing products.

Networking standards typically address both how the devices in a network physically connect, such as the types of cabling that can be used, and how the devices communicate, such as the communications protocols that can be used.

4-5a TCP/IP and Other Communications Protocols

The most widely used communications protocol today is TCP/IP. **TCP/IP** is the protocol used for transferring data over the Internet and actually consists of two protocols: Transmission Control Protocol (TCP), which is responsible for the delivery of data, and Internet Protocol (IP), which provides addresses and routing information. TCP/IP uses packet switching to transmit data over the Internet; when the packets reach their destination, they are reassembled in the proper order (see Exhibit 4-12). Support for TCP/IP is built into virtually all operating systems, and IP addresses are commonly used to identify the various computers and devices on networks such as LANs.

The first widely used version of IP—Internet Protocol Version 4 (IPv4)—was standardized in the early 1980s. IPv4 uses 32-bit addresses, which allows for 2^{32} possible unique addresses. Although still widely used today, IPv4 was never designed to be used with the billions of devices that access the Internet today, and IPv4 addresses are expected to run out soon. Consequently, a newer version of IP (IPv6) was developed. IPv6 uses 128-bit addresses, which allows for 2^{128} possible unique addresses and adds many improvements to IPv4 in areas such as routing, data security, and network autoconfiguration. While IPv4 and IPv6 are expected to coexist for

infrared (IR) transmission A wireless networking medium that sends data as infrared light rays.

protocol A set of rules to be followed in a specific situation.

TCP/IP A networking protocol that uses packet switching to facilitate the transmission of messages; the protocol used with the Internet.

Exhibit 4-12 How TCP/IP works

1. Each message is split into packets.

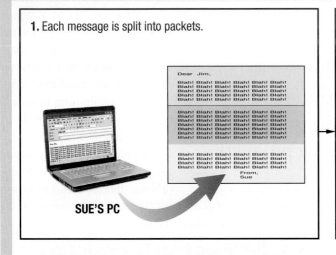

SUE'S PC

2. The packets are addressed to the same destination.

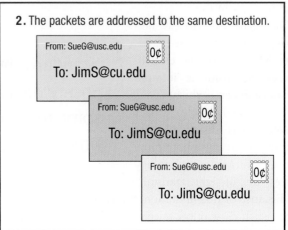

From: SueG@usc.edu 0¢
To: JimS@cu.edu

From: SueG@usc.edu 0¢
To: JimS@cu.edu

From: SueG@usc.edu 0¢
To: JimS@cu.edu

4. The packets are reassembled into the message at the destination.

JIM'S PC

3. The packets may travel the same or different routes to the destination.

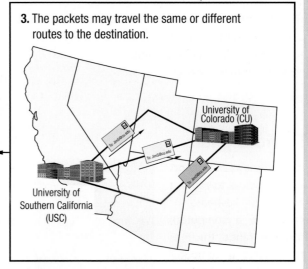

University of Colorado (CU)

University of Southern California (USC)

Natalia Siverina/Shutterstock.com; tatniz/Shutterstock.com; © 2014 Cengage Learning

several years until IPv6 eventually replaces IPv4, the U.S. government has mandated that all federal agencies be capable of switching to IPv6 and to purchase only IPv6-compatible new hardware and software.

While TCP/IP is used to connect to and communicate with the Internet, other protocols are used for specific Internet applications. Some examples are:

▶ **HTTP (Hypertext Transfer Protocol)**—used to display Web pages

▶ **HTTPS (Secure Hypertext Transfer Protocol)**—used to display Web pages

▶ **FTP (File Transfer Protocol)**—used to transfer files over the Internet

▶ **SMTP (Simple Mail Transfer Protocol)**—used to deliver email over the Internet

▶ **POP3 (Post Office Protocol)**—used to deliver email over the Internet

4-5b Ethernet (802.3)

Ethernet (**802.3**) is the most widely used standard for wired networks. It is typically used with LANs that have a star topology, though it can also be used with WANs and MANs and can be used in conjunction with twisted-pair, coaxial, or fiber-optic cabling.

Ethernet has continued to evolve since it was invented in the mid-1970s. About every three years, the new approved amendments are incorporated into

Ethernet (**802.3**) The most widely used standard for wired networks.

the existing IEEE 802.3 Ethernet standard to keep it up to date. Exhibit 4-13 summarizes the various Ethernet standards. Of these, the most common are Fast Ethernet, Gigabit Ethernet, and 10 Gigabit Ethernet. The 40 Gigabit Ethernet and 100 Gigabit Ethernet standards were ratified in 2010, and products are expected to be available soon. The even faster Terabit Ethernet standard is under development and is expected to be used for connections between servers, as well as for delivering video, digital X-rays and other digital medical images, and other high-speed, bandwidth-intensive networking applications.

Exhibit 4-13 Ethernet standards

Standard	Maximum Speed
10BASE-T	10 Mbps
Fast Ethernet (100BASE-T or 100BASE-TX)	100 Mbps
Gigabit Ethernet (1000BASE-T)	1,000 Mbps (1 Gbps)
10 Gigabit Ethernet (10GBASE-T)	10 Gbps
40 Gigabit Ethernet	40 Gbps
100 Gigabit Ethernet	100 Gbps
Terabit Ethernet*	1,000 Gbps (1 Tbps)
* Expected by 2015	

© 2014 Cengage Learning

Devices connected to an Ethernet network need to have an Ethernet port either built in or added using an expansion card. Ethernet networks can contain devices using multiple Ethernet speeds, but the slower devices will operate only at their respective speeds.

A recent Ethernet development is Power over Ethernet (PoE), which allows electrical power to be sent along the cables in an Ethernet network along with data. These cables are often referred to as Ethernet cables. Consequently, in addition to sending data, the Ethernet cable can be used to supply power to the devices on the network. PoE is most often used in business networks with remote wired

devices, such as outdoor networking hardware, security cameras, and other devices, that are not located near a power outlet. It can also be used to place networked devices near ceilings or other locations where a nearby power outlet may not be available. Using PoE requires special hardware and devices designed for PoE, but it eliminates the need for access to power outlets for that portion of the network. Regular Ethernet-enabled devices can be powered via PoE if a special PoE adapter, such as the one shown in Exhibit 4-14, is used.

4-5c Phoneline, Powerline, G.hn, and Broadband over Powerline (BPL)

Two alternatives to the Ethernet standard for wired home networks are the Phoneline and Powerline standards. Phoneline (also called the HomePNA standard) allows computers to be networked through ordinary telephone wiring and telephone jacks without interfering with voice telephone calls, as well as over existing home coaxial cable wiring. The newest version of this standard—HomePNA 3.1—supports speeds up to 320 Mbps and is designed to network both the computers and the home entertainment devices within a home. The Powerline (also called HomePlug) standard allows computers to be networked over existing power lines using conventional electrical outlets. Similar to Phoneline networks, Powerline networks are quick and easy to set up and are relatively fast (up to 200 Mbps). In addition, they have the advantage that houses usually have many more power outlets than phone outlets. Similar to the newest Phoneline standard, the

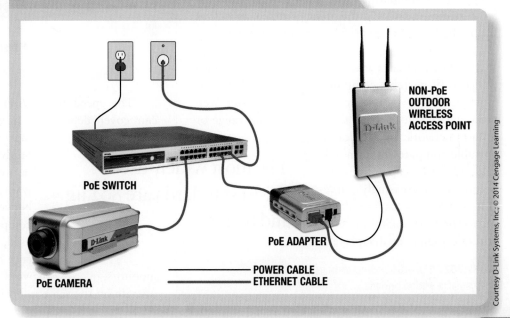

Exhibit 4-14 Ethernet-enabled devices powered via PoE

PoE SWITCH

PoE CAMERA

PoE ADAPTER

NON-PoE OUTDOOR WIRELESS ACCESS POINT

——— POWER CABLE
——— ETHERNET CABLE

Courtesy D-Link Systems, Inc.; © 2014 Cengage Learning

newest Powerline standard—named HomePlug AV—can be used to network home entertainment devices in addition to computers. The emerging HomePlug AV2 standard is expected to be five times faster than HomePlug AV, which will allow it to support streaming HD video throughout the home. HomePlug AV2 capabilities are expected to be built into home entertainment devices, as well as into stand-alone products for computers and other electronic devices that do not have HomePlug capabilities built in.

The G.hn standard is a standard designed as a unified worldwide standard for creating home networks over any existing home wiring—phone lines, power lines, and coaxial cable. It is being promoted by the HomeGrid Forum and is supported by HomePNA. Once the standard is finalized, products that support all three types of home networking connections discussed in this section can be developed.

An emerging technology based on the Powerline standard that is under development and that is designed to deliver broadband Internet to homes via the existing outdoor power lines (with the addition of some new hardware at the power poles) is broadband over Powerline (BPL). Currently, BPL service is available only in limited areas through the area's power company, but BPL has great potential for delivering broadband Internet access to virtually any home or business that has access to electricity.

4-5d Wi-Fi (802.11)

One of the most common networking standards used with wireless LANs is **Wi-Fi** (**802.11**), which is a family of wireless networking standards that use the IEEE 802.11 standard. Wi-Fi is the current standard for wireless networks in the home or office, as well as for public Wi-Fi hotspots. It is sometimes called wireless Ethernet because it is designed to easily connect to a wired Ethernet network. Wi-Fi hardware is built into virtually all portable computers sold today. It is also built into many mobile devices to allow faster Web browsing via Wi-Fi when the user is within range of a Wi-Fi network. In addition to portable computers and mobile devices, Wi-Fi capabilities are becoming increasingly integrated into everyday products, such as printers, digital cameras, portable digital media players,

> The most widely used Wi-Fi standards are 802.11g and 802.11n.

Wi-Fi (802.11) A widely used networking standard for medium-range wireless networks.

handheld gaming devices, gaming consoles, and Blu-ray Disc players (see Exhibit 4-15), to allow those devices to wirelessly network with other devices or to access the Internet.

Exhibit 4-15 Wi-Fi–enabled products

MOBILE TABLET

MUSIC PLAYER

BLU-RAY DISC PLAYER

Courtesy of Motorola; Courtesy of Logitech; Courtesy of Sony Electronics Inc.

The speed of a Wi-Fi network and the area it can cover depend on a variety of factors, including the Wi-Fi standard and hardware being used, the number of solid objects—such as walls, trees, or buildings—between the access point and the computer or other device being used, and the amount of interference from cordless phones, baby monitors, microwave ovens, and other devices that also operate on the same radio frequency as Wi-Fi (usually

2.4 GHz). In general, Wi-Fi is designed for medium-range data transfers—typically between 100 and 300 feet indoors and 300 to 900 feet outdoors. Usually both speed and distance degrade with interference. The distance of a Wi-Fi network can be extended using additional antennas and other hardware designed for that purpose.

A summary of the different Wi-Fi standards in use today is shown in Exhibit 4-16. The most widely used of these are 802.11g and 802.11n.

Courtesy Wi-Fi Alliance. The Wi-Fi CERTIFIED logo is a registered trademark of the Wi-Fi Alliance

Exhibit 4-16 Wi-Fi standards

Wi-Fi Standard	Description
802.11b	An early Wi-Fi standard; supports data transfer rates of 11 Mbps.
802.11a	Supports data transfer rates of 54 Mbps, but uses a different radio frequency (5 GHz) than 802.11g/b (2.4 GHz), making the standards incompatible.
802.11g	A current Wi-Fi standard; supports data transfer rates of 54 Mbps and uses the same 2.4 GHz frequency as 802.11b, so their products are compatible.
802.11n	The newest Wi-Fi standard; supports speeds up to about 300 Mbps and has twice the range of 802.11g. It can use either the 2.4 GHz or 5 GHz frequency.

© 2014 Cengage Learning

The 802.11n standard is currently the fastest Wi-Fi standard. Its use of MIMO (multiple in, multiple out) antennas to transfer multiple streams of data at one time, in addition to other improvements, allows for data transmissions typically about five times as fast as 802.11g and about twice the range.

Typically, 802.11g and 802.11n products can be used on the same network, and the products are backward compatible (so computers using older 802.11g hardware can connect to 802.11n networks, for instance, though they will connect only at 802.11g speeds). To ensure that hardware from various vendors will work together, consumers can look

for products that are certified by the Wi-Fi Alliance.

Wi-Fi is very widely used, but it does have some limitations—particularly its relatively limited range. For instance, a person using a Wi-Fi hotspot inside a coffeehouse will lose that Internet connection when he or she moves out of range of that network and will need to locate another hotspot at his or her next location. In addition, many businesses may be physically too large for a Wi-Fi network to span the entire organization. Although hardware can be used to extend a Wi-Fi network, an emerging possibility for creating larger wireless networks is WiMAX.

4-5e WiMAX (802.16)

WiMAX (**802.16**) is a series of standards designed for longer range wireless networking connections, typically MANs. Similar to Wi-Fi, fixed WiMAX (also known as 802.16a) is designed to provide Internet access to fixed locations, sometimes called hotzones. However, WiMAX hotzones are significantly larger than Wi-Fi hotspots. A typical hotzone radius is between two and six miles, though WiMAX can transmit data as far as 10 miles or more. With fixed WiMAX, it is feasible to provide coverage to an entire city or other geographical area by using multiple WiMAX towers, similar to the way cell phone cells overlap to provide continuous cell phone service. See Exhibit 4-17. WiMAX can use

Exhibit 4-17 WiMAX vs. Wi-Fi

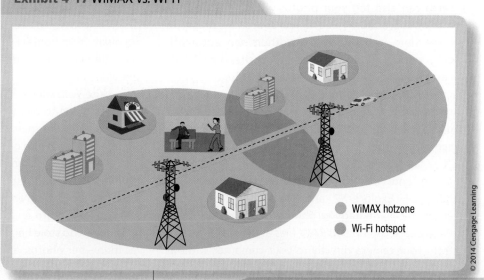

○ WiMAX hotzone
● Wi-Fi hotspot

© 2014 Cengage Learning

WiMAX (**802.16**) An emerging wireless networking standard that is faster and has a greater range than Wi-Fi.

licensed radio frequencies, in addition to unlicensed frequencies like Wi-Fi, to avoid interference issues.

Mobile WiMAX (802.16e) is the mobile version of the WiMAX wireless networking standard. It is designed to deliver broadband wireless networking to mobile users via a mobile phone, portable computer, or other WiMAX-enabled device. Specifications for a new version of mobile WiMax (802.16m, or WiMax Release 2) have been finalized. This new technology is faster than original WiMAX.

WiMAX capabilities are beginning to be built into portable computers and other devices, and WiMAX is currently being used to provide Internet access to more than one billion people in about 150 countries. In the United States, for instance, WiMAX leader Clearwire offers both fixed and mobile WiMAX-based Internet service to businesses and individuals in more than 75 cities.

4-5f Cellular Standards

Cellular standards have evolved over the years to better fulfill the demand for mobile Internet, mobile multimedia delivery, and other relatively recent mobile trends. The original first-generation phones were analog and designed for voice only. Newer cell phones, starting with second-generation (2G) phones, are digital, support both data and voice, and are faster. Common 2G wireless standards include GSM (Global System for Mobile communications) and CDMA (Code Division Multiple Access). Both of these standards are designed for voice traffic, and both support speeds up to 14.4 Kbps, though some wireless providers have developed technologies such as EDGE (Enhanced Data Rates for GSM Evolution) that can be used with 2G networks to provide faster service; for instance, EDGE supports speeds up to 135 Kbps. These interim developments are sometimes referred to as 2.5G cellular standards. Both GSM and CDMA are used in the United States, although they are not compatible with each other. (Phones that can be used with both standards are available.) GSM is also widely used overseas, though with different frequencies so international travelers will need to ensure their 2G phone supports the frequencies used in their destination location—some 2G phones support multiple frequencies to permit international roaming.

Wi-Fi SD Cards

One interesting, relatively new Wi-Fi product is the Wi-Fi SD card. These cards are designed to upload photos wirelessly and automatically from your camera to your computer via a Wi-Fi network. Some cards can also tag your photos with location information based on geographic coordinates as you take them (called geotags); others can automatically upload your photos to Web sites like Flickr, Facebook, YouTube, and Picasa.

For instance, all four Eye-Fi cards in the accompanying photo wirelessly transfer the photos from your digital camera to your home computer as soon as the camera is within range of your home Wi-Fi network. They can also wirelessly upload photos to your favorite photo- and video-sharing Web sites. The Eye-Fi Geo X2, Eye-Fi Explore X2, and Eye-Fi Pro X2 cards also automatically geotag your photos. In addition, the Eye-Fi Pro X2 card can upload RAW files and transfer images from your camera directly to your computer without requiring Wi-Fi access, and both the Eye-Fi Explore X2 and Eye-Fi Pro X2 cards come with one year of HotSpot Access to enable you to send images to photo-sharing

Web sites and your home computer via a wireless hotspot when you are away from home. Eye-Fi users can also download a free iPhone app that enables them to upload photos and videos taken with their iPhone to their computer or favorite Web sites.

In addition to allowing you to share your photos immediately with others, using a Wi-Fi SD card for your digital photos can also give you the peace of mind that your photos are backed up on your home computer and/or online. This is especially beneficial if your camera is stolen or the card becomes damaged. In fact, using an Eye-Fi card enabled one woman to catch the individual who stole her camera gear while she was on vacation—her photos, along with images of the thief with the camera gear, were uploaded to her home computer, and the police were able to apprehend the thief and recover the stolen gear.

The current standard for cellular networks today in the United States and many other countries is 3G (third generation), with 4G (fourth generation) networks emerging. 3G and 4G networks use packet switching instead of circuit switching. Users of both 3G and 4G mobile phones and mobile devices can access broadband Internet content (such as online maps, music, games, TV, videos, and more—see Exhibit 4-18). Because 3G and 4G speeds are equivalent to the speeds many home broadband Internet users experience, Internet access via a 3G or 4G network is often referred to as mobile broadband.

Virtually all mobile phone providers today have a 3G network, and most are moving to 4G networks. The 3G standard used with a network depends on the type of cellular network. For instance, GSM mobile networks, such as AT&T Wireless and T-Mobile, typically use the HSDPA (High Speed Downlink Packet Access)/ UMTS (Universal Mobile Telecommunications System) 3G standards for their 3G networks; CDMA networks, such as Verizon Wireless and Cricket Wireless, typically use the EV-DO (Evolution Data Optimized) 3G standard instead.

There are two primary standards for 4G networks today: the mobile WiMAX standard already discussed and Long Term Evolution (LTE), supported by AT&T Wireless, Verizon Wireless, and T-Mobile. Although mobile WiMAX is not technically a cellular standard, it is being used by some companies, such as Sprint, to provide 4G mobile phone service to subscribers, in addition to Internet service.

4-5g Bluetooth, Ultra Wideband (UWB), and Other Short-Range Wireless Standards

Several wireless networking standards are in existence or being developed that are designed for short-range wireless networking connections. Most of these are used to facilitate PANs or very small, special-purpose home networks, such as connecting home entertainment devices or appliances within a home.

Exhibit 4-18 Mobile broadband

Courtesy of Motorola

LEARN MORE

Personal Mobile Hotspots

You can access Wi-Fi hotspots in many locations. You can also create your own hotspot whenever you need it. This is possible with several emerging products designed to create personal mobile hotspots that can be used with any Wi-Fi device, such as notebook computers, mobile phones, mobile tablets, and portable gaming devices. One such product is Verizon Wireless's MiFi Intelligent Mobile Hotspot, shown in the accompanying illustration. The MiFi, about the size of several stacked credit cards, creates a mobile hotspot by just powering up the device. The MiFi device connects to Verizon Wireless's 3G mobile network and provides access to that network for up to five Wi-Fi devices. To those devices, the MiFi hotspot appears as any other Wi-Fi hotspot, so users connect as they usually would. There is currently no unlimited data plan, so users need to keep an eye on their total data usage to avoid overage fees.

For travelers and other individuals who might want to create a hotspot only periodically, Virgin Mobile sells a version of MiFi that is used with prepaid data plans, such as $40 per month for unlimited access or $10 for 10 days of data service capped at 100 MB per day. This option can allow families and other travelers to all access the Internet while in the car, in the airport, or at a hotel, without paying pricey hotel and airport Internet fees. For these travelers, mobile hotspots might be just the ticket.

Courtesy Verizon Wireless

Bluetooth is a wireless standard that was originally designed for very short-range connections. Current Bluetooth connections work up to 10 meters—approximately 33 feet—or less; the newest specification—Bluetooth 4.0—has a longer range, up to 200 feet. It is designed to replace cables between devices, such as to connect a wireless keyboard or mouse to a desktop computer, to send print jobs wirelessly from a portable computer to a printer, or to connect a mobile phone to a wireless headset. Bluetooth devices automatically recognize and network with each other when they get within transmission range. Bluetooth signals can transmit through clothing and other nonmetallic objects, so a mobile phone or other device in a pocket or briefcase can connect with Bluetooth hardware, such as a headset, without having to be removed from the pocket or briefcase. Bluetooth is increasingly being used with consumer devices, such as to connect pedometers, heart rate monitors, and other health and fitness devices to a watch or mobile phone, and to connect 3D glasses to a 3D television set.

Bluetooth works using radio signals in the frequency band of 2.4 GHz, the same as Wi-Fi. The latest Bluetooth specifications can utilize 802.11 technology when transferring large amounts of data to support transfers up to 24 Mbps. Bluetooth 4.0 devices can also use their low-energy capabilities to wirelessly connect to other devices while being powered (potentially for years) by a single button-sized battery. When two Bluetooth-enabled devices come within range of each other, their software identifies each

> A mobile phone can connect with a Bluetooth headset even when the phone is in your pocket.

other using their unique identification numbers and establishes a link. Because there may be many Bluetooth devices within range, up to 10 individual Bluetooth networks (called **piconets**) can be in place within the same physical area at one time. See Exhibit 4-19. Each piconet can connect up to eight devices, for a maximum of 80 devices within any 10-meter radius. To facilitate this, Bluetooth divides its allocated radio spectrum into multiple channels of 1 MHz each. Each Bluetooth device can use the entire range of frequencies, jumping randomly (in unison with the other devices in that piconet) on a regular basis to minimize interference between piconets, as well as from other devices, such as garage door openers, Wi-Fi networks, and some cordless phones and baby monitors, that use the same frequencies.

Another standard that is designed to connect peripheral devices, similar to Bluetooth, but that transfers data more quickly is **wireless USB**. The speed of wireless USB depends on the distance between the devices being used, but it is approximately 100 Mbps at 10 meters (about 33 feet) or 480 Mbps at 3 meters (about 10 feet).

Bluetooth A networking standard for very short-range wireless connections.

piconet A Bluetooth network.

wireless USB A wireless version of USB designed to connect peripheral devices.

Exhibit 4-19 Piconets

The desktop computer, keyboard, and mouse form a piconet to communicate with each other. The headset and cell phone (not shown in this photo) belong to another piconet.

The headset and cell phone form a piconet when they are within range to communicate with each other.

© iStockphoto.com/Ben Blankenburg; © Stockbyte/Getty Images

Several wireless technologies are being developed to transfer multimedia content quickly between nearby devices. One example is **Ultra Wideband** (**UWB**), which is similar to wireless USB. UWB speeds vary from 100 Mbps at 10 meters (about 33 feet) to 480 Mbps at 2 meters (about 6.5 feet).

Another possibility is **WirelessHD** (**WiHD**). Similar to UWB, WiHD is designed for fast transfers of high-definition video between home consumer electronic devices, but it is faster. Backed by seven major electronics companies, WiHD is designed to transfer full-quality uncompressed high-definition audio, video, and data within a single room at speeds up to 25 Gbps, though those speeds have not been obtained yet. WiHD operates at 60 GHz and incorporates a smart antenna system that allows the system to steer the transmission, allowing for non-line-of-sight communications.

A wireless standard designed for very fast transfers between devices that are extremely close together (essentially touching each other) is **TransferJet**. Developed by Sony, TransferJet is designed to quickly transfer large files, such as digital photos, music, and video, between devices as soon as they come in contact with each other. For example, you can use TransferJet to transfer data between mobile phones or between digital cameras, to download music or video from a consumer kiosk or digital signage system to a mobile phone or other mobile device, or to transfer images or video from a digital camera to a TV set or printer. At a maximum speed of 560 Mbps, TransferJet is fast enough to support the transfer of video files.

One networking standard designed for inexpensive and simple, short-range networking (particularly sensor networks) is ZigBee (802.15). ZigBee is intended for applications that require low data transfer rates and several years of battery life. For instance, ZigBee can be used for home and commercial automation systems to connect a wide variety of devices (such as appliances and lighting, heating, cooling, water, filtration, and security systems) and allows for their control from anywhere in the world. ZigBee is also used in industrial plant manufacturing, personal home healthcare, device tracking, telecommunications, and wireless sensor networks.

ZigBee is designed to accommodate more than 65,000 devices on a single network and supports speeds from 20 Kbps to 250 Kbps, depending on the frequency being used (several different frequencies

are available for ZigBee networks). ZigBee has a range of 10 to 100 meters (about 33 to 328 feet) between devices, depending on power output and environmental characteristics. A wireless mesh configuration can be used to greatly extend the range of the network.

Another wireless networking standard that can connect your home electronic devices together is Z-Wave. Devices with Z-Wave capabilities built-in or connected via a Z-Wave module can communicate with each other and can be controlled via home control modules, as well as remotely via a computer or mobile phone. There can be up to 232 devices on a single Z-Wave network, and each device has its own unique code. Devices can control each other, such as your garage door opener turning on your house lights when you arrive home, and sequences of actions can be programmed to be performed with a single button, such as turning off the house lights, activating the security system, locking the doors, and programming the coffee pot for breakfast when a single button designated for bedtime is pressed. Z-Wave signals have a range of about 90 feet indoors.

For a summary of wireless networking standards, see Exhibit 4-20.

Ultra Wideband (**UWB**) A networking standard for very short-range wireless connections among multimedia devices.

WirelessHD (**WiHD**) An emerging wireless networking specification designed for connecting home consumer devices.

TransferJet A networking standard for wireless connections between devices that are touching.

Exhibit 4-20 Common wireless networking standards

Category	Examples	Intended Purpose	Approximate Range
	Bluetooth Wireless USB	To connect peripheral devices to a mobile phone or computer.	33–200 feet
Short range	Ultra Wideband (UWB) WirelessHD (WiHD) TransferJet WiGig	To connect and transfer multimedia content between home consumer electronic devices (computers, TVs, DVD players, etc.).	1 inch–33 feet
	ZigBee Z-Wave	To connect a variety of home, personal, and commercial automation devices.	33 feet–328 feet
Medium range	Wi-Fi (802.11)	To connect computers and other devices to a local area network.	100–300 feet indoors; 300–900 feet outdoors
	Wi-Fi Direct	To connect computers and other devices directly together.	600 feet
Long range	WiMAX Mobile WiMAX	To provide Internet access to a large geographic area for fixed and/or mobile users.	6 miles non-line of sight; 30 miles line of sight
	Cellular standards	To connect mobile phones and mobile devices to a cellular network for telephone and Internet service.	10 miles

4-6 Networking Hardware

Various types of hardware are necessary to create a computer network, to connect multiple networks together, or to connect a computer or network to the Internet. The following sections discuss the most common types of networking hardware used in home and small office networks.

4-6a Network Adapters and Modems

A **network adapter**, also called a **network interface card** (**NIC**) when it is in the form of an expansion card, is used to connect a computer to a network (such as a home or business network). A **modem** (derived from the terms *modulate* and *demodulate*) is used to connect a computer to a network over telephone lines. Technically, to be called a modem, a device must convert digital signals, such as those used by a computer, to modulated analog signals, such as those used by conventional telephone lines, and vice versa. However, in everyday use, the term *modem* is also used to refer to any device that connects a computer to a broadband Internet connection, such as a cable modem used for cable Internet service. In addition, the term *modem* is often used interchangeably with *network adapter* when describing devices used to obtain Internet access via certain networks, such as cellular or WiMAX networks.

Most computers and mobile devices come with a built-in network adapter and modem. The type of network adapter and modem depends on the type of network and Internet access being used. When selecting a network adapter or modem, the type of device being used and the expansion slots and ports available on that device need to be considered as well. For example, network adapters and modems for desktop computers typically come in PCI, PCI Express (PCIe), or USB format, and network adapters and modems for portable computers usually connect via USB or an ExpressCard slot. In addition, the network adapter or modem needs to support the type of networking media, such as twisted-pair cabling, coaxial cabling, or wireless signal, being used. Some examples of network adapters and modems are shown in Exhibit 4-21.

network adapter A device used to connect a computer to a network.

network interface card (**NIC**) A network adapter in the form of an expansion card.

modem A device that is used to connect a computer to a network over telephone lines.

Exhibit 4-21 Network adapters and modems

PCI EXPRESS GIGABIT ETHERNET ADAPTER FOR DESKTOP COMPUTERS
- Port for twisted-pair Ethernet cable

USB WI-FI ADAPTER FOR DESKTOP OR NOTEBOOK COMPUTERS
- Connects to USB port

USB POWERLINE ADAPTER FOR DESKTOP OR NOTEBOOK COMPUTERS
- Connects via a cable to USB port
- Connects to a power outlet

EXPRESSCARD WI-FI ADAPTER FOR NOTEBOOK COMPUTERS
- Slides into ExpressCard slot

USB 4G MODEM FOR DESKTOP OR NOTEBOOK COMPUTERS
- Connects to USB port

USB/ETHERNET CABLE MODEM
- Incoming coaxial cable from cable provider and either a USB or Ethernet cable coming from the computer or router connect to the back of the modem.

Courtesy D-Link Systems, Inc.; Courtesy Belkin International, Inc.; Courtesy Verizon Wireless

FYI

Fixing a Slow or Stopped Internet Connection

If your Internet connection slows down or stops working altogether, try power cycling your modem and router. Unplug the modem and router for 30 seconds, then plug in the modem and wait 30 seconds, then plug in the router.

4-6b Switches, Routers, and Other Hardware for Connecting Devices and Networks

A variety of networking hardware is used to connect the devices on a network, as well as to connect multiple networks together. For instance, as mentioned earlier in this chapter, networks using the star topology need a central device to connect all of the devices on the network. In a wired network, this device was originally a hub. A hub transmits all data received to all network devices connected to the hub, regardless of which device the data is being sent to, so the bandwidth of the network is shared and the network is not extremely efficient. Today, the central device in a wired network is usually a switch. A **switch** contains ports to which the devices on the network connect (typically via networking cables) and facilitates communications between the devices, similar to a hub. But, unlike a hub, a switch identifies which device connected to the switch is the one the data is intended for and sends the data only to that device, rather than sending data out to all connected devices. Consequently, switches are more efficient than hubs.

To connect multiple networks (such as two LANs, two WANs, or a LAN and the Internet), a **router** is used. Routers pass data on to the intended recipient only and can plan a path through the network to ensure the data reaches its destination in the most efficient manner possible. They are also used to route traffic over the Internet.

switch A device that connects multiple devices on a wired network and forwards data only to the intended recipient.

router A device that connects multiple networks together and passes data to the intended recipient using the most efficient route.

A **wireless access point** is a device on a wireless network used to grant network access to wireless client devices. In home and small business networks, typically the capabilities of a switch, router, and wireless access point are integrated into a single wireless router device. A **wireless router** (such as the one shown in Exhibit 4-22) is commonly used to connect both wireless (via Wi-Fi) and wired (via Ethernet cables) devices to a network and to connect that network to an Internet connection via the appropriate broadband modem. Some broadband modems today include wireless router capabilities, which you can use to create a wireless network and obtain Internet access using a single piece of hardware. To connect just two LANs together, a **bridge** can be used. The most common use for a bridge in a home network is to wirelessly connect a wired device (such as a home audio/video system, DVR, or gaming console) to a home network via a wireless connection.

There are also routers and other devices used to connect multiple devices to a cellular network. For instance, 3G mobile broadband routers are used to share a 3G mobile wireless Internet connection with multiple devices (such as your cell phone, personal computer, and handheld gaming device)—essentially creating a Wi-Fi hotspot that connects to your 3G Internet connection. Other devices can be used to route cell phone calls over a broadband network to provide better cellular coverage while indoors.

4-6c Other Networking Hardware

Additional networking hardware is often needed to extend the range of a network and to share networking media.

Repeaters are devices that amplify signals along a network. They are necessary whenever signals have to travel farther than would be otherwise possible over the networking medium being used. Repeaters are available for both wired and wireless networks; repeaters for a wireless network are often called range extenders. **Range extenders** usually connect wirelessly to the network and repeat the wireless signal to extend coverage of that network outside or to an additional floor of a building, or to eliminate dead spots—areas within the normal network range that do not have coverage. Some WDS (Wireless Distribution System) wireless access points can be used as range extenders by extending the network coverage from one access point to another.

Exhibit 4-22 Wireless routers

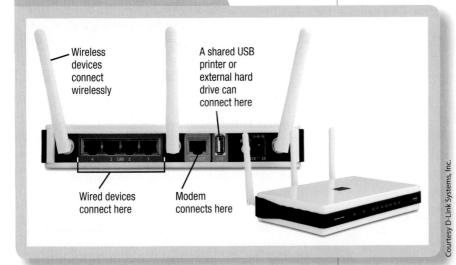

Wireless devices connect wirelessly

A shared USB printer or external hard drive can connect here

Wired devices connect here

Modem connects here

Courtesy D-Link Systems, Inc.

wireless access point A device on a wireless network used to grant network access to wireless client devices.

wireless router A router with a built-in wireless access point.

bridge A device used to connect two LANs.

repeater A device on a network that amplifies signals along a network.

range extender A repeater for a wireless network.

Another alternative for increasing the range of a Wi-Fi network is using a higher-gain (stronger) **antenna**. The MIMO antennas used by many 802.11n routers allow for faster connections and a greater range than typically experienced by 802.11g wireless networks, but sometimes this still isn't enough. Using a network adapter designed for the router being used typically helps the network range to some extent; so does replacing the antenna on the router with a higher-gain antenna or adding an external antenna to a networking adapter, if the adapter contains an antenna connector.

Antennas come in a variety of formats and are classified as either directional antennas (antennas that concentrate the signal in a particular area) or omnidirectional antennas (antennas that are equally effective in all directions). Directional antennas have a farther range than omnidirectional antennas but a more limited delivery area. The strength of an antenna is measured in decibels (dB). For applications where a large Wi-Fi coverage area is needed (such as in a large business or a hotel), high-gain outdoor antennas can be used (in conjunction with outdoor range extenders and access points, if needed) to enable the network to span a larger area than the hardware would normally allow.

> High-speed communications lines are expensive and almost always have far greater capacity than a single device can use.

High-speed communications lines are expensive and almost always have far greater capacity than a single device can use. Because of this, signals from multiple devices are often combined and sent together to share a single communications medium. A **multiplexer** combines the transmissions from several different devices and sends them as one message. Regardless of how the signals are sent, when the combined signal reaches its destination, the individual messages are separated from one another. Multiplexing is frequently used with fiber-optic cables and other high-capacity media to increase data throughput. For instance, if eight signals are multiplexed and sent together over each fiber in one fiber-optic cable, then the throughput of that cable is increased by a factor of eight.

A **concentrator** is a type of multiplexer that combines multiple messages and sends them via a single transmission medium in such a way that all the individual messages are simultaneously active, instead of being sent as a single combined message. For example, ISPs often use concentrators to combine the signals from their conventional dial-up modem customers to be sent over faster communications connections to their Internet destinations.

antenna A device used for receiving or sending radio signals and often used to increase the range of a network.

multiplexer A device that combines the transmissions from several different devices and sends them as one message.

concentrator A multiplexer that combines multiple messages and sends them via a single transmission medium in such a way that of all the individual messages are simultaneously active, instead of being sent as a single combined message.

Devices in a Network

This example shows how the devices discussed in this chapter might be used in a network. As you can see, many different types of hardware are used to connect networking devices.

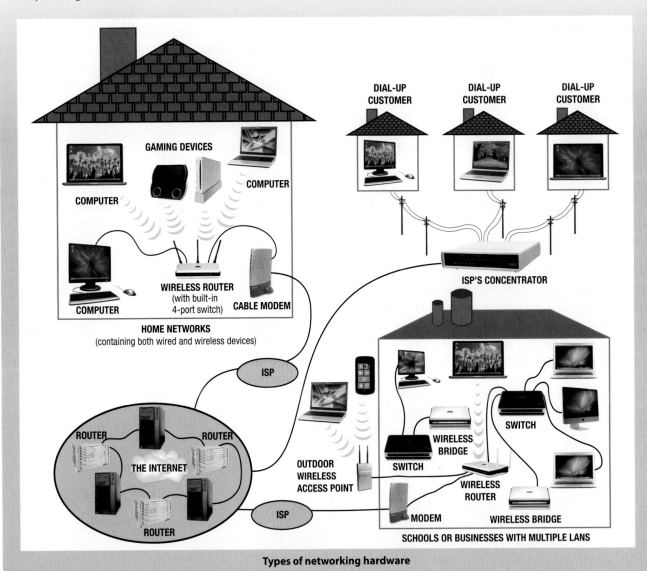

Types of networking hardware

Gjermund Alsos/Shutterstock.com; © iStockphoto/Sara Winter; Courtesy of DCB; Ruslan Ivantsov/Shutterstock.com; Natalia Siverina /Shutterstock.com; Sergey Furtaev/Shutterstock.com; Courtesy of Samsung; Courtesy D-Link Systems, Inc.; Courtesy of Sony Electronics Inc.; © 2014 Cengage Learning

1. Define computer network.

2. Describe telecommuting.

3. What are the three most common network topologies?

4. What is the difference between a client-server network and a peer-to-peer network?

5. What is a small network designed to connect the personal devices for an individual (such as via Bluetooth) called?

6. What is the world's largest WAN?

7. What is a virtual private network (VPN)?

8. Describe the difference between digital and analog signals.

9. What are the three most common types of cables used to create wired networks?

10. What is TCP/IP?

11. What is the most widely used standard for wired networks?

12. What is the current standard for wireless networks?

13. What is an emerging wireless networking standard that is faster and has a greater range than Wi-Fi?

14. What is Bluetooth?

15. What is a switch?

16. What does a router do?

17. What is a repeater?

18. Why are signals from multiple devices often combined and sent together to share a single communications medium?

Practice It

Practice It 4-1

Home networks—particularly wireless home networks—are becoming very common. Suppose that you have a desktop computer and a notebook computer, and you want to network the two computers wirelessly. You also want to use a printer with both computers.

1. Determine the hardware you will need to wirelessly network the two computers and the printer.

2. Create a labeled sketch of the network.

3. Create a list of the hardware you need to acquire.

4. Research the approximate cost of the hardware to determine the overall cost of creating the wireless network (excluding the cost of the computers and the printer). Record the model numbers of the hardware items and the sources where you found the prices.

5. Prepare a one-page summary of your findings that includes your sketch, and submit it to your instructor.

Practice It 4-2

WiMAX and Wi-Fi are both wireless networking standards.

1. Research WiMAX and Wi-Fi to determine their current status and the differences between the two standards.

2. Are they designed for the same or different purposes? Explain your answer.

3. How are they being used today?

4. Do you think the standards will coexist in the future or one will eventually replace the other? Explain your answer.

5. Prepare a one-page summary that answers these questions, and submit it to your instructor.

On Your Own

On Your Own 4-1

Internet peer-to-peer (P2P) networking involves sharing files and other resources directly with other computers via the Internet. While some content is legally exchanged via an Internet P2P network, some content (such as movies and music) is exchanged illegally.

1. Should Internet P2P networks be regulated to ensure they are used only for legal activities? Why or why not?

2. If a P2P network set up for legitimate use is used for illegal purposes, should the organization or person who set up the P2P network be responsible? Explain your answer.

3. Would you want to use an Internet P2P network? Why or why not?

4. Use the Web to research more about BitTorrent and Gnutella's LimeWire. Do you think these are legitimate P2P networks? Why or why not?

5. Prepare a one-page summary that answers these questions, and submit it to your instructor.

Chapter 4

ADDITIONAL STUDY TOOLS

IN THE BOOK
▶ Complete end-of-chapter exercises
▶ Study tear-out Chapter Review Card

ONLINE
▶ Complete additional end-of-chapter exercises

▶ Take practice quiz to prepare for tests
▶ Review key term flash cards (online, printable, and audio)
▶ Play "Beat the Clock" and "Memory" to quiz yourself
▶ Watch the videos to learn more about the topics taught in this chapter

Answers to Quiz Yourself

1. A computer network is a collection of computers and other hardware devices that are connected so users can share hardware, software, and data, as well as communicate with each other electronically.

2. Telecommuting allows individuals to work from a remote location (typically their homes) and communicate with their places of business and clients via networking technologies.

3. The three most common network topologies are star, bus, and mesh.

4. A client-server network includes both clients, which are computers and other devices on the network that request and use network resources, and servers, which are computers that are dedicated to processing client requests. A peer-to-peer network connects all the computers on the network at the same functional level without using a server, and users have direct access to the computers and other devices attached to the network.

5. A small network designed to connect the personal devices for an individual is a personal area network (PAN).

6. The world's largest WAN is the Internet.

7. A virtual private network (VPN) is a private, secure path across a public network (usually the Internet) that is set up to allow authorized users private, secure access to the company network.

8. In a digital signal, data is represented by 0s and 1s. In an analog signal, data is represented by continuous waves.

9. The three most common types of cables used to create wired networks are twisted-pair cable, coaxial cable, and fiber-optic cable.

10. TCP/IP is the protocol used for transferring data over the Internet.

11. The most widely used standard for wired networks is Ethernet.

12. The current standard for wireless networks is Wi-Fi.

13. The emerging wireless networking standard that is faster and has a greater range than Wi-Fi is WiMAX.

14. Bluetooth is a wireless standard that is designed for very short-range connections.

15. A switch contains ports to which the devices on the network connect and facilitates communications between the devices by identifying which device connected to the switch is the one that specific data is intended for and sending the data only to that device.

16. A router passes data on to the intended recipient by planning a path through a network to ensure the data reaches its destination in the most efficient manner possible.

17. A repeater is a device that amplifies signals along a network.

18. Signals from multiple devices are often combined and sent together to share a single communications medium because high-speed communications lines are expensive and almost always have far greater capacity than a single device can use.

Introducing the Internet and Email

Daniel Fleck/Shutterstock.com

With the prominence of the Internet in our personal and professional lives, it is hard to believe that not too long ago few people had even heard of the Internet, let alone used it. But technology is continually evolving. In fact, only relatively recently has technology evolved enough to allow the use of multimedia applications—such as downloading music and movies, watching TV and videos, and playing multimedia interactive games—over the Internet to become everyday activities. Today, *Internet* and *Web* are household words that have redefined how people think about computers, communications, and the availability of news and information.

Despite the popularity of the Internet, many users cannot answer some basic questions about it. What makes up the Internet? Is it the same thing as the Web? How did the Internet begin, and where is it heading? How can the Internet be used to find specific information? This chapter addresses these types of questions and more.

5-1 Evolution of the Internet

The Internet is a worldwide collection of separate, but interconnected, networks accessed daily by millions of people using a variety of devices to obtain information, disseminate information, access entertainment, or communicate with others. Although *Internet* has become a household word only during the past two decades or so, it has actually operated in one form or another for much longer than that.

5-1a From ARPANET to Internet2

The roots of the Internet began with an experimental project called ARPANET. In 1969, the U.S. Department of Defense Advanced Research Projects Agency (ARPA) connected four supercomputers to form the first computer network and called it **ARPANET**. Exhibit 5-1 is a sketch of ARPANET that was drawn in 1969.

One objective of the ARPANET project was to create a computer network that would allow researchers located in different places to communicate with each other. Another objective was to build a computer network capable of sending or receiving data over a variety of paths to ensure that network communications could continue even if part of the network was destroyed, such as in a nuclear attack or by a natural disaster. As the project grew during the next decade, students were granted access to ARPANET as networks at hundreds of colleges and universities that were doing research for the Department of Defense. These networks consisted of a mixture of different computers so, over the years, protocols were developed for tying this mix of computers and networks together, for transferring data over the network, and for ensuring that data was transferred intact.

In the early 1980s, the Computer Science Network (CSNET) was created so that computers at computer science departments at colleges and universities that were not allowed to connect to ARPANET could connect to each other. This project was funded by the National Science Foundation (NSF). Another network, called BITNET, was created to enable computers at colleges and universities to exchange email. Then, in 1986, the NSF created NSFNET, using the knowledge they gained from building CSNET. NSFNET became the foundation of the Internet as it is today.

> The roots of the Internet began with an experimental project called ARPANET.

Exhibit 5-1 Hand-drawn sketch of ARPANET from 1969

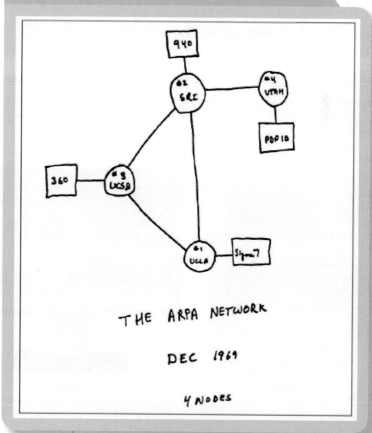

ARPANET The predecessor of the Internet, named after the Advanced Research Projects Agency (ARPA), which sponsored its development.

The Internet infrastructure can be used for a variety of purposes, such as researching topics of interest; exchanging email and other messages; participating in videoconferences and making telephone calls; downloading software, music, and movies; purchasing goods and services; watching TV and video online; accessing computers remotely; and sharing files with others. Most of these activities are available through the primary Internet resource—the World Wide Web.

5-1b The World Wide Web

In its early years, the Internet was used primarily by the government, scientists, and educational institutions. Despite its popularity in academia and with government researchers, the Internet went virtually unnoticed by the public and the business community for over two decades because (1) it required a computer and (2) it was hard to use (see the left image in Exhibit 5-2). As always, however, computer and networking technology improved, and new applications quickly followed. Then, in 1989, a researcher named Tim Berners-Lee proposed the idea of the World Wide Web. He envisioned the Web as a way to organize information in the form of pages linked together through selectable text or images (today's hyperlinks) on the screen. Although the introduction of Web pages did not replace all other Internet resources, such as email and collections of downloadable files, it became a popular way for researchers to provide written information to others.

browser. Soon after, use of the Web began to increase dramatically because Mosaic's graphical user interface and its ability to display images on Web pages made using the Web both easier and more fun than in the past. Today's Web pages are a true multimedia, interactive experience, as shown in the right image in Exhibit 5-2. They can contain text, graphics, animation, sound, video, and three-dimensional virtual reality objects.

A growing number of today's Web-based applications and services are referred to as Web 2.0 applications. Although there is no precise definition, Web 2.0 generally refers to applications and services that use the Web as a platform to deliver rich applications that enable people to collaborate, socialize, and share information online. Some Web 2.0 applications include cloud computing, social networking sites, podcasts, blogs, and wikis.

The Web is only part of the Internet, but it is by far the most widely used part. Today, most companies regard their use of the Internet and their Web presence as indispensable competitive business tools, and many individuals view the Internet—and especially the Web—as a vital research, communications, and entertainment medium.

5-1c Internet2

Internet2 is a consortium of researchers, educators, and technology leaders from industry, government, and the international community who are dedicated to the development of revolutionary Internet technologies. Internet2 uses high-performance networks linking over 200 member institutions to deploy and test new network applications and technologies. Designed as a research and development tool to help create technologies that ensure the Internet can handle tomorrow's applications, Internet2 is working to deploy advanced applications and technologies that might not be possible otherwise with today's Internet—it is not a new network that is intended to replace the Internet. Much of Internet2 research is focused on speed. In fact, the Internet2 network is currently in the process of being upgraded to support 8.8 Tbps. Once that upgrade is complete, Internet2 will be used to offer advanced telemedicine and distance learning programs across the country via its network.

Exhibit 5-2 The Internet: Then and Now

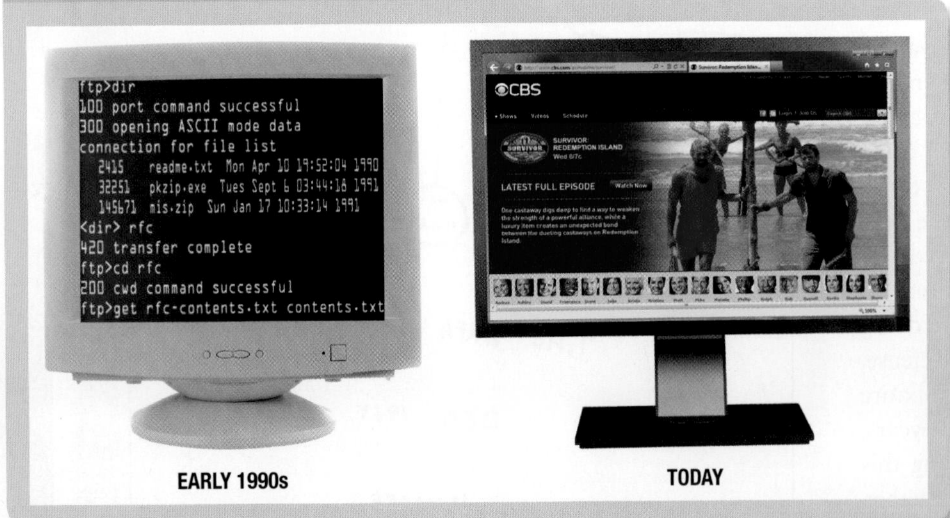

EARLY 1990s TODAY

In 1993, a group of professors and students at the University of Illinois National Center for Supercomputing Applications (NCSA) released the Mosaic Web

The Internet Is Not the Web

Even though many people use the terms *Internet* and *Web* interchangeably, they are not the same thing. Technically, the Internet is the physical network, and the Web is the collection of Web pages accessible over that network. A majority of Internet activities today take place via Web pages, but Internet resources other than the Web are not accessed via a Web browser. For instance, files can be uploaded and downloaded using an FTP (File Transfer Protocol) program, and conventional email can be accessed using an email program.

5-1d The Internet Community Today

The Internet community today consists of individuals, businesses, and a variety of organizations located throughout the world. According to the Pew Internet & American Life Project, the Internet is used by approximately 80% of the U.S. population. Virtually anyone with a computer or other Web-enabled device can be part of the Internet, either as a user or as a supplier of information or services. Most members of the Internet community fall into one or more of the following groups:

> The Internet is used by approximately 80 % of the U.S. population.

▶ **Users**—people who use the Internet to retrieve content or perform online activities, such as to look up a telephone number, read the day's news headlines or top stories, browse through an online catalog, make an online purchase, download a music file, watch an online video, make a phone call, or send an email message.

▶ **Internet service providers (ISPs)**—businesses or other organizations, including telephone, cable, and satellite companies, that provide Internet access to others, typically for a fee. Exhibit 5-3 shows the logos of some of these companies. Regardless of their delivery method and geographical coverage, ISPs are the onramp to the Internet, providing their subscribers with access to the Web, email, and other Internet resources. Some ISPs also provide proprietary online services available only to their subscribers.

Exhibit 5-3 ISP logos

Use of the AT&T logo is granted under permission by AT&T Intellectual Property.; Courtesy of Verizon Communications; Courtesy Comcast; Photos(s) courtesy of Hughes Network Systems, LLC; Courtesy EarthLink, Inc.; Courtesy Clearwire

▶ **Internet content providers**—the suppliers of the information that is available through the Internet. Internet content providers can be commercial businesses, nonprofit organizations, educational institutions, individuals, and more.

▶ **Application service providers (ASPs)**—the companies that manage and distribute Web-based software services to customers over the Internet. Instead of providing access to the Internet like ISPs do, ASPs provide access to software applications via the Internet. Common ASP applications for businesses include office suites, collaboration and communications software, accounting programs, and e-commerce software.

Internet service provider (**ISP**) A business or other organization that provides Internet access to others, typically for a fee.

Internet content provider A person or an organization that provides Internet content.

application service provider (**ASP**) A company that manages and distributes software-based services over the Internet.

- **Infrastructure companies**—the enterprises that own or operate the paths or "roadways" along which Internet data travels, such as the Internet backbone and the communications networks connected to it. Examples of infrastructure companies include conventional and mobile phone companies, cable companies, and satellite Internet providers.

- **Hardware and software companies**—the organizations that make and distribute the products used with the Internet and Internet activities. For example, companies that create or sell the software used in conjunction with the Internet, such as Web browsers, email programs, e-commerce and multimedia software, and Web development tools, fall into this category. So, too, do the companies that make the hardware, such as network adapters, modems, cables, routers, servers, computers, and mobile phones, that is used with the Internet.

- **Governments**—the ruling bodies of countries that can pass laws limiting both the information made available via Web servers located in a particular country and the access individuals residing in that country have to the Internet.

  For example, in France, it is illegal to sell items or post online content related to racist groups or activities. In China, tight controls are imposed on what information is published on Web servers located in China, as well as on the information available to its citizens. And in the United States, anything illegal offline is illegal online.

- **Key Internet organizations**—other organizations that are responsible for many aspects of the Internet. For example, the Internet Society (ISOC) provides leadership in addressing issues that may impact the future of the Internet. It also oversees the groups responsible for Internet infrastructure standards, such as determining the protocols that can be used and how Internet addresses are constructed, as well as facilitating and coordinating Internet-related initiatives around the world. ICANN (Internet Corporation for Assigned Names and Numbers) coordinates activities related to the Internet's naming system, such as IP address allocation and domain name management. The World Wide Web Consortium (W3C) is an international community of over 450 organizations dedicated to developing new protocols and specifications to be used with the Web and to ensure its interoperability. In addition, many colleges and universities support Internet research and manage blocks of the Internet's resources.

FYI

Who's in Charge of the Internet and the Web?

One remarkable characteristic of both the Internet and Web is that they are not owned by any person or business, and no single person, business, or organization is in charge. Each network connected to the Internet is privately owned and managed individually by that network's administrator; the primary infrastructure that makes up the Internet backbone is typically owned by communications companies, such as telephone and cable companies. The closest the Internet comes to having a governing body is a group of organizations, including the ISOC, ICANN, and W3C, that are involved with issues such as establishing the protocols used on the Internet, making recommendations for changes, and encouraging cooperation between and coordinating communications among the networks connected to the Internet. Governments in each country have the power to regulate the content and use of the Internet within their borders, as allowed by their laws. However, legislators often face serious obstacles getting legislation passed into law—let alone getting it enforced. Making governmental control even harder is the "bombproof" design of the Internet itself. If a government tries to block access to or from a specific country or Web site, for example, users can use a third party, such as an individual located in another country or a different Web site, to circumvent the block.

5-2 Connecting to the Internet

Connecting to the Internet typically involves three decisions—determining the type of device you will use to access the Internet, deciding which type of connection you want, and selecting the Internet service provider to use. Once you have made these determinations, you can set up your computer to access the Internet.

5-2a Selecting the Type of Device

You can access the Internet using a variety of devices. The type of device you use depends on a combination of factors, such as the devices available, whether you need access just at home or while on the go, and what types of Internet content you want to access. Some possible devices are shown in Exhibit 5-4.

One advantage of using personal computers for Internet access is that they have relatively large screens for viewing Internet content, and they typically have a full keyboard for easier data entry. They can also be used to view or otherwise access virtually any Web page content, such as graphics, animation, music files, games, and video clips. In addition, they typically have a large hard drive and are connected to a printer so Web pages, email messages, and downloaded files can be saved or printed easily.

Exhibit 5-4 Devices used to access the Internet

PERSONAL COMPUTER

MOBILE PHONE

TELEVISION

Courtesy, Hewlett-Packard Company; Used with permission from Microsoft Corporation.; Eric Milos/Shutterstock.com; Courtesy of Yahoo! ® Connected TV

FYI

The Internet Is Not Free

The myth that the Internet is free stems from the fact that traditionally no cost has been associated with accessing online content—such as news and product information—or with email exchange, other than what Internet users pay ISPs for Internet access. But, someone somewhere has to pay to keep the Internet up and running.

Businesses, schools, public libraries, and most home users pay ISPs flat monthly fees to connect to the Internet. In addition, businesses, schools, libraries, and other large organizations might have to lease high-capacity communications lines, such as from a telephone company, to support their high level of Internet traffic. Mobile users who want Internet access while on the go typically pay hotspot providers or mobile phone providers for this access. ISPs, phone companies, cable companies, and other organizations that own part of the Internet infrastructure pay to keep their parts of the Internet running smoothly. ISPs also pay software and hardware companies for the resources they need to support their subscribers. Eventually, most of these costs are passed along to end users through ISP fees.

ISPs that offer free Internet access typically obtain revenue by selling on-screen ads that are displayed on the screen when the service is being used. Also, the growing trend of subscription or per-use fees to access Web-based resources negates the myth that the Internet is free. For instance, downloadable music and movies are very common, and some journal or newspaper articles require a fee to view them online. In fact, some newspapers and magazines have moved entirely online and most charge a subscription fee to view the level of content that was previously published in a print version. In lieu of a mandatory fee, some Web sites request a donation for use of the site. Many experts expect the use of fee-based Internet content to continue to grow at a rapid pace.

Creativa/Shutterstock.com

Mobile devices are increasingly being used to view Web page content, exchange email and other messages, and download music and other online content. Although mobile phones are convenient to use on the go, they have a relatively small display screen; mobile tablets typically have a larger screen size for easier viewing. Some devices include a built-in or sliding keyboard for easier data entry; others utilize pen or touch input instead.

Another option is using a gaming console or handheld gaming device to access Web content, in addition to using that device to play games. For instance, the Sony PlayStation 3, Sony PSP, Nintendo Wii, and Nintendo 3DS all have Web browsers that can be used to access Web content. Broadband-enabled TVs have Internet capabilities built in to display Web pages and other Web content, such as interactive polls and other show-specific information, social networking updates, and shopping opportunities, without any additional hardware.

> Wireless Web is one of the fastest growing uses of the Internet.

5-2b Choosing a Connection Type

To access the Internet, a device is connected to a computer or network, usually belonging to an ISP, a school, or an employer, that is continually connected to the Internet. The most common types of Internet connections for personal use are summarized in Exhibit 5-5 and are described below.

Conventional dial-up Internet access uses a dial-up modem connected to a standard telephone jack with regular twisted-pair telephone cabling. With a dial-up connection, a computer dials its modem and connects to a modem attached to an ISP's computer over standard telephone lines only when needed. While connected to an ISP, the computer can access Internet resources. To end that Internet session, the computer is disconnected from the ISP. Conventional dial-up Internet service is most often used with home computers for users who do not need, or do not want to pay for, faster broadband Internet service. Advantages include inexpensive hardware, ease of setup and use, widespread availability,

Exhibit 5-5 Typical home Internet connection options

Type of Internet Connection	Availability	Approximate Monthly Price	Approximate Maximum Speed*
Conventional dial-up	Anywhere there is telephone service	56 Kbps	Free–$20
Cable	Virtually anywhere cable TV service is available	10–25 Mbps	$30–55
DSL	Within three miles of a switching station that supports DSL	1–15 Mbps	$15–55
Satellite	Anywhere there is a clear view of the southern sky and where a satellite dish can be mounted and receive a signal	1–2 Mbps	$40–90
Fixed wireless	Selected areas where service is available	1–6 Mbps	$35–55
Broadband over fiber (BoF) Fiber-to-the-premises (FTTP)	Anywhere fiber has been installed to the building	5–50 Mbps	$55–145
Mobile wireless (3G/4G)	Virtually anywhere cellular phone service	600 Kbps–12 Mbps	Varies greatly; often bundled with mobile phone service

* Download speed; most connections have slower upload speeds.

© 2014 Cengage Learning

conventional dial-up Internet access
Dial-up Internet access via standard telephone lines.

and security (unauthorized access to the computer via the Internet is limited because the computer is not continually connected to the Internet). The primary disadvantages are the hassle of dialing up every time you want to connect to the Internet, the inconvenience of tying up that telephone line, and a much slower connection speed than other types of connections.

Most Internet connections are direct (or always-on) connections, which provide a continuous connection to the ISP. Direct connections keep devices continually connected to the ISP and, therefore, continually connected to the Internet. With a direct connection, such as cable, DSL, satellite, or fixed wireless, you access the Internet simply by opening a Web browser, such as Internet Explorer, Chrome, or Firefox, using your chosen device. Direct Internet connections are typically broadband connections, are commonly used in homes and businesses, and are often connected to a LAN to share the Internet connection with multiple devices within the home or business. In fact, more than two-thirds of all home Internet connections in the United States are broadband connections, according to a recent Pew Internet & American Life Project study.

Cable Internet access uses a direct connection and is the most widely used type of home broadband connection, with over half of the home broadband market. Cable connections are very fast, typically between 10 and 25 Mbps, though some faster services are available for a premium fee, and are available wherever cable TV access is offered as long as the local cable provider supports Internet access. Consequently, cable Internet is not widely available in rural areas. Cable Internet service requires a cable modem.

DSL (Digital Subscriber Line) Internet access is a direct connection that transmits via standard telephone lines, but it does not tie up your telephone line. DSL requires a DSL modem and is available only to users who are relatively close (within three miles) to a telephone switching station and who have telephone lines capable of handling DSL. DSL speeds are slower than cable speeds, and the speed of the connection degrades as the distance between the modem and the switching station gets closer and closer to the three-mile limit. Consequently, DSL is usually available only in urban areas. Download speeds are typically between 1 and 15 Mbps.

Satellite Internet access uses a direct connection but is slower and more expensive than cable or DSL access—typically up to around 2 Mbps. However, it is often the only broadband option for rural areas. In addition to a satellite modem, it requires a transceiver satellite dish mounted outside the home or building to receive and transmit data to and from the satellites being used. Installation requires an unobstructed view of the southern sky to have a clear line of sight between the transceiver and appropriate satellite. Performance might degrade or stop altogether during very heavy rain or snowstorms.

Fixed wireless Internet access uses a direct connection and is similar to satellite Internet in that it uses wireless signals, but it uses radio transmission towers—either stand-alone towers like the one shown in Exhibit 5-6 or transmitters placed on existing cell phone towers—instead of satellites. Fixed wireless Internet access requires a modem and, sometimes, an outside-mounted transceiver. Fixed wireless companies typically

Exhibit 5-6 WiMAX tower at the peak of Whistler Mountain in British Columbia

Courtesy Tranzeo Wireless USA

cable Internet access Fast, direct Internet access via cable TV lines.

DSL (Digital Subscriber Line) Internet access Fast, direct Internet access via standard telephone lines.

satellite Internet access Fast, direct Internet access via the airwaves and a satellite dish.

fixed wireless Internet access Fast, direct Internet access available in some areas via the airwaves.

use Wi-Fi and/or WiMAX technology to broadcast the wireless signals to customers. Speeds are typically up to about 6 Mbps, though the speed depends somewhat on the distance between the tower and the customer, the type and number of obstacles in the path, and the type and speed of the connection between the wireless transmitter and the Internet.

In areas where fiber-optic cabling runs all the way to the building, a new type of direct Internet connection is available to homes and businesses that is generically called **broadband over fiber** (**BoF**) or **fiber-to-the-premises** (**FTTP**), with other names being used by individual providers, such as Verizon's fiber-optic service (FiOS). These fiber-optic networks are most often installed by telephone companies to upgrade their overall infrastructures and, where installed, are used to deliver telephone and TV service in addition to Internet service. However, some cities are creating fiber-optic MANs that include connections to businesses and homes to provide very fast broadband Internet services. Where available, download speeds for BoF service typically range between 5 Mbps and 50 Mbps, and the cost varies accordingly. BoF requires a special networking terminal installed at the building to convert the optical signals into electrical signals that can be sent to a computer or over a LAN.

Mobile wireless Internet access is the direct connection most commonly used with mobile phones, mobile tablets, and other mobile devices to keep them connected to the Internet via a mobile phone network, even as they are carried from place to place. Some mobile wireless services can be used with notebook and netbook computers. The speed of mobile wireless depends on the cellular standard being used—3G networks typically have speeds between 600 Kbps and 1.7 Mbps; 4G networks are often between 5 and 12 Mbps. Costs for mobile wireless Internet access vary widely, with some packages including unlimited Internet, some charging by the number of minutes of Internet use, and some charging by the amount of data transferred.

A **Wi-Fi hotspot** is a location with a direct Internet connection and a wireless access point that allows users to connect wirelessly (via Wi-Fi) to the hotspot to use its Internet connection; see Exhibit 5-7. Public Wi-Fi hotspots are widely available today, such as at many coffeehouses and restaurants; at hotels, airports, and other locations frequented by business travelers; and in or nearby public areas such as libraries, subway stations, and parks. Some public Wi-Fi hotspots are free; others charge per hour, per day, or on a subscription basis. College campuses also typically have Wi-Fi hotspots to provide

> Public Wi-Fi hotspots are widely available.

Exhibit 5-7 Typical Wi-Fi hotspots

COFFEEHOUSES AND OTHER PUBLIC LOCATIONS
Often fee-based, though some are available for free.

HOSPITALS, BUSINESSES, AND OTHER ORGANIZATIONS
Usually designed for employees but are sometimes also available free to visitors.

COLLEGE CAMPUSES
Usually designed for students and faculty; sometimes used directly in class for student assignments, as shown here.

Anton Gvozdikov/Shutterstock.com; John Wollwerth/Shutterstock.com; Courtesy Abilene Christian University

broadband over fiber (BoF) or **fiber-to-the-premises (FTTP)**
Very fast, direct Internet access via fiber-optic networks.

mobile wireless Internet access
Internet access via a mobile phone network.

Wi-Fi hotspot A location that provides wireless Internet access to the public.

Internet access to students. Many businesses and other organizations have Wi-Fi hotspots for use by employees in their offices, as well as by employees and guests in conference rooms, waiting rooms, lunchrooms, and other onsite locations.

Most types of connections are broadband or high-speed connections. As applications requiring high-speed connections continue to grow in popularity, access to broadband Internet speeds are needed to take full advantage of these applications. For instance, high-definition television, video chat, video-on-demand (VOD), and other multimedia applications all benefit from fast broadband connections, as shown in Exhibit 5-8.

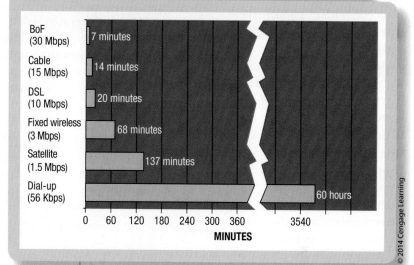

Exhibit 5-8 Length of time to download a 1.5 GB movie using different connection options

© 2014 Cengage Learning

LEARN MORE

ISP Bandwidth Limits

Internet traffic has increased tremendously recently as people are watching TV and videos online, downloading music and movies, playing online multiplayer games, participating in video phone calls, using online backup services, and otherwise performing high-bandwidth activities. This has created the issue of ISPs potentially running out of bandwidth available for customers, resulting in outages or delays. In response, some ISPs have, at times, blocked selected traffic to and from their customers, such as cable giant Comcast blocking the use of P2P sites like BitTorrent, which is often used to download movies, music, and other large files. Other ISPs are slowing down traffic to and from heavy users during peak Internet usage periods or experimenting with bandwidth caps as Internet usage management tools. For instance, AT&T recently implemented bandwidth caps for all home broadband customers. With a bandwidth cap, customers either temporarily lose Internet access or are charged an additional fee if they exceed their download limit (often 5 GB to 150 GB per month). Although common for mobile broadband, bandwidth caps for home Internet service were unusual until recently. Bandwidth caps have even spread to college campuses, due to the popularity of Netflix, YouTube, and other high-bandwidth applications that strain college networks.

For instance, Ohio University recently implemented a 5 Mbps download limit on all students.

Comcast, like most ISPs, includes a statement in its terms of service agreement that allows it to "efficiently manage its networks" to prevent customers from using a higher than normal level of bandwidth. However, many considered Comcast's blocking of P2P content to be a blatant net neutrality issue because Comcast was blocking access to multimedia from a source other than its own cable source, and the Internet is designed for all content to be treated equally. There are also concerns about bandwidth caps and that overcharges will grow to an unreasonable level—particularly by cable companies and other providers that may want to stifle Internet multimedia to protect their TV advertising revenues. It is unclear at this time whether bandwidth caps will be part of the future of home Internet service. However, it is clear that, as Internet usage by the average consumer continues to grow, the issue of a finite amount of Internet bandwidth versus an increasing demand for online multimedia content will remain.

ARENA Creative/Shutterstock.com

5-2c Selecting an ISP

The type of device you will use (such as a personal computer or mobile phone), the type of Internet connection and service you want (such as cable Internet or mobile wireless), and your geographical location (such as metropolitan or rural) determine your ISP options. The pricing and services available through any two ISPs will probably differ somewhat, based on the speed of the service, as well as other services available. The questions listed in Exhibit 5-9 can help you narrow your ISP choices and determine the questions you want answered before you decide on an ISP. A growing trend is for ISPs to offer a number of tiers, or different levels (speeds) of service for different prices so users requiring faster service can get it but at a higher price.

Exhibit 5-9 Questions to ask before choosing an ISP

Area	Questions to Ask
Services	Is the service compatible with my device?
	Is there a monthly bandwidth limit?
	How many email addresses can I have?
	What is the size limit on incoming and outgoing email messages and attachments?
	Do I have a choice between conventional and Web–based email?
	Is there dial–up service that I can use when I'm away from home?
	Are there any special member features or benefits?
	Does the service include Web site hosting?
Speed	How fast are the maximum and usual downstream (ISP to my PC) speeds?
	How fast are the maximum and usual upstream (my PC to ISP) speeds?
	How much does the service slow down under adverse conditions, such as high traffic or poor weather?
Support	Is 24/7 telephone technical support available?
	Is Web–based technical support (such as via email) available?
	Is there ever a charge for technical support?
Cost	What is the monthly cost for the service? Is it lower if I prepay a few months in advance? Are different tiers available?
	Is there a setup fee? If so, can it be waived with a 6–month or 12–month agreement?
	What is the cost of any additional hardware needed, such as modem or transceiver?
	Can the fee be waived with a long–term service agreement?
	Are there any other services (telephone service, or cable or satellite TV, for instance) available from this provider that I have or want and that can be combined with Internet access for a lower total cost?

© 2014 Cengage Learning

5-2d Setting Up Your Computer

The specific steps for setting up your computer to use the type of Internet connection you selected depend on the type of device, the type of connection, and the ISP you have chosen to use. Some types of Internet connections, such as satellite and broadband over fiber, require professional installation, after which you will be online. With other types, you can install the necessary hardware—typically a modem that connects to your computer or wireless router via an Ethernet cable—yourself. You will usually need to select a username and a payment method at some point during the ordering or setup process. This username is needed to log on to some types of Internet connections; it is also used in the email address that will be associated with that Internet service.

After one computer is successfully connected to the Internet, you may need to add additional hardware to connect other computers and devices that you want to be able to access the Internet. For instance, to share a broadband connection, you can connect other computers directly to the modem via an Ethernet cable or Wi-Fi connection if the modem contains a built-in switch or wireless router. If the modem does not include switching or wireless routing capabilities, you will need to connect a switch or wireless router to the modem, typically via an Ethernet cable, and then connect your devices to the switch or router, to share the Internet connection with those devices.

5-3 Searching the Internet for Information

Most people use the Internet to find specific information. For instance, you might want to find the lowest price for the latest *Pirates of the Caribbean* DVD, flights available from Los Angeles to New York on a particular day, a recipe for clam chowder, the weather forecast for the upcoming weekend, a video of the previous presidential inaugural address, or a map of hiking trails in the Grand Tetons. The Internet provides access to a vast array of interesting and useful information, but that information is worthless if you cannot find it when you need it.

Evaluating Web Sites

When you gather information from Web pages, you need to determine if the information can be trusted. This involves considering the following aspects about the Web page:

▶ Evaluate both the author and the source to determine if the information is reliable and unbiased.

▶ Check for a date to see how current the information is—many online articles are years old.

▶ Verify the information with a second source, if possible, if you will be using the information in a report, paper, or other document in which accuracy is important.

5-3a Using Search Sites

Finding information on the Internet is made easier through the power of search engines, available through search sites. **Search sites** are Web sites designed specifically to help users find information on the Web. Some popular search engines are Google, Bing, and Yahoo! Search. Most search sites use a **search engine**—a software program—in conjunction with a huge database of information about Web pages to help visitors find Web pages that contain the information they are seeking.

Search site databases are updated on a regular basis; for example, Google estimates that its entire index is updated about once per month. Typically, this occurs using small, automated programs (often called spiders or webcrawlers) that use the hyperlinks located on Web pages to jump continually from page to page. At each Web page, the spider program records important data about the page into the search site's database, such as the page's URL, its title, the keywords that appear frequently on the page, and the keywords and descriptive information added to the page's code by the Web page author when the page was created. In addition to spider programs, search site databases also obtain information from Web page authors who submit Web page URLs and keywords associated with their Web sites to the search site.

To conduct a search, type appropriate **keywords**—one or more words describing what you are looking for—into a search box on a search site. Many Web browsers allow you to type search terms directly in the Address bar instead of a URL and then perform the search using whichever search site is specified as the default search site. Multiple keywords are sometimes called a **search phrase**. The site's search engine then uses those keywords to return a list of links to Web pages (called **hits**) that match your search criteria (see Exhibit 5-10). Search sites differ in determining how close a match must be between the specified search criteria and a Web page before a link to that page is displayed, so the number of hits from one search site to another may vary.

Often, a search phrase returns millions of hits. To narrow the search, you can add words to the search phrase. For example, if you type *cooking* as the search

Exhibit 5-10 Using a search site

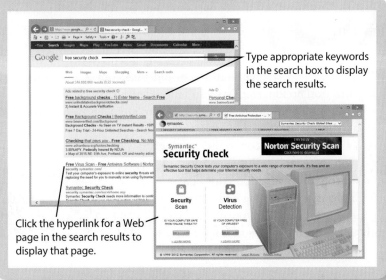

Type appropriate keywords in the search box to display the search results.

Click the hyperlink for a Web page in the search results to display that page.

Google screenshot © Google Inc. and used with permission.; Courtesy of Symantec; Used with permission from Microsoft Corporation.

search site A Web site designed to help users search for Web pages that match specified keywords or selected categories.

search engine A software program used by a search site to retrieve matching Web pages from a search database.

keyword A word typed in a search box on a search site or other Web page to locate information related to that keyword.

search phrase Multiple keywords.

hit A link that matches search criteria in a search site.

phrase, the list of results will include recipe sites, sites with definitions of cooking, links to books about cooking, and so on. To restrict the list of results to only Web sites that contain recipes for cooking in the fusion style with fish, you can add *fusion*, *fish*, and *recipes* to the search phrase.

5-3b Citing Internet Resources

Recall that a copyright is the legal right to sell, publish, or distribute an original artistic or literary work; it is held by the creator of a work as soon as it exists in physical form. Before you download or copy graphics, maps, images, sounds, or information from Web sites that you visit, you need to find out if and how you can use the materials and then, if necessary, get permission from the owner of the content. Some Web sites include their copyright and permission request information on their home pages. Some Web sites indicate that the material is free, but almost everything on the Internet is copyrighted.

Under the fair use policy, you can use copyrighted material for educational or nonprofit purposes, as opposed to commercial profit. Information that is considered factual and materials that are so old that copyright protection no longer exists also fall under the category of fair use. You should still give credit to any Web site that you use in your research. By carefully checking the copyright and permission policies of the Web sites you visit, you can ensure that you make the right decision regarding if and how you can use the content you find and avoid violating any copyright laws. For more information about copyrights in the United States, visit the U.S. Copyright Office Web site at www.copyright.gov.

© 2014 Cengage Learning

The guidelines for citing Web page content are similar to those for written sources. In general, the author, date of publication, and article or Web page title are listed along with a "Retrieved" statement listing the date the article was retrieved from the Internet and the URL of the Web page used to retrieve the article. If in doubt when preparing a research paper, check with your instructor as to the style manual, such as APA, Modern Language Association (MLA), or *Chicago Manual of Style*, he or she prefers you to follow and refer to that guide for direction.

5-4 Evolution of Email

Email is one of the most widely used Internet applications—Americans alone send billions of email messages daily—and email sent via a mobile device is growing at an astounding rate. An email message is a simple text document that you can compose and send using an email program, also called email client software, such as Mail, which is included with Windows 8.

5-4a Origins of Email

Email has actually existed for longer than the Internet. In the 1960s, a program called SNDMSG was written to allow computer users who shared time on the same computer to leave messages for each other on that computer. In 1971, Ray Tomlinson, one of the engineers who worked on ARPANET, combined SNDMSG with another program he had written called CPYNET that allowed people to send files from one networked computer to another to create the first email program. Tomlinson also created the addressing system still used today: the username followed by @ (the at symbol) followed by the computer name to which the message was being sent. For example, look at the address john_wynn@wynnco.biz. It begins with a username, or login ID, which in this case is john_wynn. The @ symbol signifies that the email server name will be provided next—which, in this case, is wynnco.biz.

Tom Wang/Shutterstock.com

> Email has actually existed for longer than the Internet.

Although many companies used their internal LANs to provide email service among employees, email service was not available to the public until 1988 when NSF-NET licensed MCI Mail to become the first commercial company allowed to provide email service to the public. CompuServe was licensed in 1989, and more companies followed in the next few years. Since then, email has become as ubiquitous as the telephone, and email service is available through a wide range of free and fee-based options. Like the telephone, email is commonly used for personal and business communication worldwide.

5-4b How Email Works

You can send an email message from any Internet-enabled device, such as a desktop computer, portable computer, or mobile device, to anyone who has an Internet email address. As illustrated in Exhibit 5-11, when you send a message, it travels from your computer, through a network, such as a LAN or the Internet, and arrives at the computer that has been designated and set up as your mail server, and then continues through the Internet to the mail server being used by the recipient's ISP, which stores the email message until the recipient's computer retrieves it. The server then forwards the message to the recipient's computer. Because email uses this store-and-forward technology, you can send messages to any users on the network, even if they do not have their computers turned on. When it is convenient, the recipients log on to the network and use their email programs to receive and read their messages. In addition to text, email messages can include attached files, such as documents, photos, and videos.

Email can be sent and received via an email program, such as Microsoft Outlook, that is installed on the computer being used or via a Web mail service, which is a Web page belonging to a Web mail provider such as Gmail or Windows Live Mail. Using an installed email program is convenient if you use email often and want to have copies of sent and received messages stored on your computer. Web-based email allows you to access your messages from any computer or device with an Internet connection by displaying the appropriate Web mail page and logging on to access your email account.

Exhibit 5-11 How email works

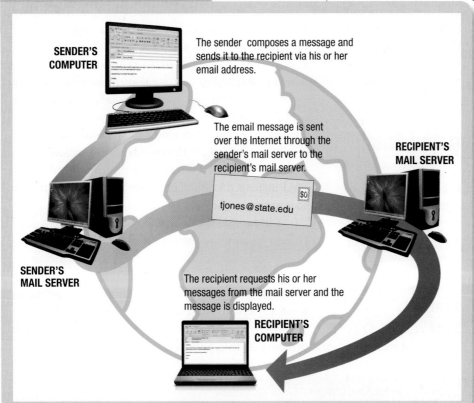

SENDER'S COMPUTER

The sender composes a message and sends it to the recipient via his or her email address.

The email message is sent over the Internet through the sender's mail server to the recipient's mail server.

tjones@state.edu

RECIPIENT'S MAIL SERVER

SENDER'S MAIL SERVER

The recipient requests his or her messages from the mail server and the message is displayed.

RECIPIENT'S COMPUTER

Ruslan Ivantsov/Shutterstock.com; 300dpi/Shutterstock.com; tatniz/Shutterstock.com; © 2014 Cengage Learning

LEARN MORE

Email Privacy

Many people mistakenly believe that the email they send and receive is private and will never be read by anyone other than the intended recipient. Because email is transmitted over public media, however, only encrypted (electronically scrambled) email can be transmitted safely. Although unlikely to happen to your personal email, nonencrypted email can be intercepted and read by someone else. Consequently, from a privacy standpoint, a nonencrypted email message should be viewed more like a postcard than a letter.

It is also important to realize that your employer and your ISP have access to the email you send through those organizations. Businesses and ISPs typically archive (keep copies of) email messages that travel through their servers and are required to comply with subpoenas from law enforcement agencies for archived email messages.

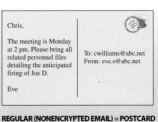

Chris,

The meeting is Monday at 2 pm. Please bring all related personnel files detailing the anticipated firing of Joe D.

Eve

To: cwilliams@abc.net
From: eve.s@abc.net

REGULAR (NONENCRYPTED EMAIL) = POSTCARD

From: eve.s@abc.net

To: cwilliams@abc.net

CONFIDENTIAL

ENCRYPTED EMAIL = SEALED LETTER

© 2014 Cengage Learning

The email address you use directs the message to its destination. Your email address is included as the return address in any message you send, so that the recipients can easily respond to your message. All email addresses must follow the format established by Ray Tomlinson, such as john_wynn@wynnco.biz. To ensure a unique email address for everyone in the world, usernames must be unique within each domain name. So, even though there could be a john_wynn at Wynn Company who is using the email john_wynn@wynnco.biz and a john_wynn at Cengage Learning who is using the email address john_wynn@cengage.com, the two email addresses are unique. It is up to each organization with a registered domain name to ensure that one—and only one—exact same username is assigned to its domain.

5-5 Beyond Browsing and Email

In addition to basic browsing and email, many other activities can take place via the Internet. Although the programs that supported these various types of online communications were originally dedicated to a single task, today's programs often can be used for a variety of types of online communications.

5-5a Online Written Communication

Instant messaging (**IM**), also commonly referred to as **chat**, allows you to exchange real-time typed messages with people on your contact list—a list of individuals such as family, friends, and business associates whom you specify or with whom you have already exchanged messages. Instant messages (IMs) can be sent via computers and mobile phones using installed messaging programs such as AIM, Windows Live Messenger, or Yahoo! Messenger, using Web-based messaging services such as Meebo.com or Web versions of AIM or Yahoo! Messenger, or using other online communications programs, such as Gmail and Skype or social networks like Facebook and MySpace, which support instant messaging. Originally a popular communications method among friends, IM has also become a valuable business tool. Instant messaging capabilities are also sometimes integrated into Web pages, such as to ask questions of a customer service representative or to start a conversation with one of your friends via a social networking site.

Text messaging is a form of messaging frequently used by mobile phone users. Also called Short Message Service (SMS), text messaging is used to send short (fewer than 160 characters) text-based messages via a cellular network. If the messages also include photos, audio, or video, Multimedia Message Service (MMS) is used instead. In either case, the messages are typically sent to the recipient via his or her mobile phone number.

A **blog**—also called a Web log—is a Web page that contains short, frequently updated entries in chronological order, typically as a means of expression or communication (see Exhibit 5-12). In essence, a blog is an online personal journal accessible to the public that is usually created and updated by one individual. Blogs are written by a wide variety of individuals—including ordinary people, as well as celebrities, writers, students,

instant messaging (IM) or **chat** A way of exchanging real-time typed messages with other individuals.

text messaging A way of exchanging real-time typed messages with other individuals via a cellular network and, typically, cell phones.

blog A Web page that contains short, frequently updated entries in chronological order, typically by just one individual.

Exhibit 5-12 An example of a blog

Courtesy of Carol Cram; Google screenshot © Google Inc. and used with permission.; Used with permission of Microsoft Corporation.

and experts on particular subjects—and can be used to post personal commentary, research updates, comments on current events, political opinions, celebrity gossip, travel diaries, television show recaps, and more.

Blogging software, available via blogging sites such as Blogger.com, is often used to easily create and publish blogs and blog updates to the Web. Blogs are also frequently published on school, business, and personal Web sites. Blogs tend to be updated frequently, and entries can be posted via computers, email, and mobile phones. Blogs often contain text, photos, and video clips.

With their growing use and audiences, bloggers are beginning to have increasing influence on businesses, politicians, and individuals. An ethical issue surrounding blogging relates to bloggers who are paid to blog about certain products. Although some Web sites that match bloggers with advertisers require that the blogger reveal that he or she receives payment for "sponsored" posts, some believe that commercializing blogging will corrupt the blogosphere. Others, however, view it as a natural evolution of word-of-mouth advertising.

Microblogging is the process of posting very short messages, called updates, to a microblogging service that others can read. Twitter is an extremely popular, free microblogging service that allows members (both individuals and businesses) to post short (up to 140 characters) updates—called Tweets—at any moment. The updates can be sent via text message, IM, email, or even Xbox (see Exhibit 5-13) and are posted to the member's Twitter.com page. Tweets can also be sent to others' mobile phones if they have set up their accounts to follow you via text updates. Members can also search the Twitter Web site to find Tweets of interest.

5-5b Online Audio and Video Communications

Another Web resource that can provide you with useful information is a **podcast**—a recorded audio or video file that can be downloaded via the Internet, such as the audio and video podcasts available for download via the Web site that accompanies this text. The term *podcast* is derived from the iPod portable digital media player (the first widely used device for playing digital audio files), although you can also listen to podcasts today using a computer or mobile phone.

Podcasting (or creating a podcast) enables individuals to create self-published, inexpensive Internet radio broadcasts to share their knowledge, express their opinions, or present their original poems, songs, or short stories with others. Podcasts are also created and distributed by businesses. For instance, some commercial radio stations are making portions of their broadcasts available via podcasts, and a growing number of news sites and corporate sites have regular podcasts available. In fact, some view podcasts as the new and improved radio because it is an easy way to listen to your favorite radio broadcasts on your own schedule. Podcasts are also used for educational purposes. Podcasts are typically uploaded to the Web on a regular basis.

> Bloggers are beginning to have increasing influence on businesses, politicians, and individuals.

Exhibit 5-13 Twitter via Xbox

What are you doing?

Ellena I overslept and missed yoga this morning, so annoying! June 1st from xbox

Michael Paterson Just finished a barbeque with my boys and the rest of my family. Hanging by the pool. It's Hot! 100 degrees in LA! June 1st from web

DawnRi Went to the movies with the dancers tonight. We saw I Love You, Man. SOOOO funny! June 1st from xbox

Stone Secord Who's up for Halo3 in 5... 4...3...2...1 June 1st from web

James Burns Just made the train... WHEW June 1st from web

twitter

Used with permission from Microsoft Corporation; Courtesy of Twitter.

microblog Very short messages, called updates, posted to a microblogging service that others can read.

podcast A recorded audio or video file that can be played or downloaded via the Web.

Internet telephony is the original industry term for the process of placing telephone calls over the Internet. Today, the standard term for placing telephone calls over the Internet or any other type of data network is **Voice over Internet Protocol (VoIP)**, and it can take many forms. At its simplest level, VoIP calls can take place from computer to computer, such as by starting a voice conversation with an online buddy using a messaging program and a headset or microphone connected to the computer. Computer-to-computer calls, such as via the popular Skype service, as well as via messaging programs that support voice calls, are generally free. Often calls can be received from or made to conventional or mobile phones for a small fee.

More permanent VoIP setups—sometimes referred to as digital voice, broadband phone, or Internet phone service—are designed to replace conventional landline phones in homes and businesses. VoIP is offered through some ISPs, such as cable, telephone, and mobile phone companies; it is also offered through dedicated VoIP providers, such as Vonage. Permanent VoIP setups require a broadband Internet connection and a VoIP phone adapter, also called an Internet phone adapter, which goes between a conventional phone and a broadband router, as shown in Exhibit 5-14. Once your phone calls are routed through your phone adapter and router to the Internet, they travel to the recipient's phone, which can be another VoIP phone, a mobile phone, or a landline phone. VoIP phone adapters are typically designed for a specific VoIP provider. With these more permanent VoIP setups, most users switching from landline phone service can keep their existing telephone number.

The biggest advantage of VoIP is cost savings, such as unlimited local and long-distance calls for as little as $25 per month, or basic cable and VoIP services bundled together for about $50 per month. One of the biggest disadvantages of VoIP is that it does not function during a power outage or if your Internet connection goes down.

Web conferences typically take place via a personal computer or mobile device and are used by businesses and individuals. Basic Web conferences, such as a video call between individuals as shown in Exhibit 5-15, can be performed via any online communications program, such as an instant messaging program, that supports video phone calls. Business Web conferences that require multiple participants or other communication tools, such as a shared whiteboard or the ability for attendees to share the content of their computer screens, may need to use Web conferencing software or services instead. Business Web conferencing is often used for meetings between

---

Exhibit 5-14 How VoIP works

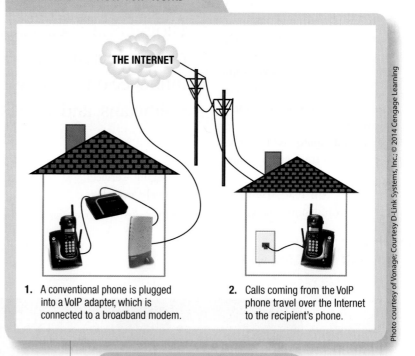

1. A conventional phone is plugged into a VoIP adapter, which is connected to a broadband modem.

2. Calls coming from the VoIP phone travel over the Internet to the recipient's phone.

Exhibit 5-15 Web conferencing

Voice over Internet Protocol (VoIP)
The process of placing telephone calls via the Internet or data network.

Web conference A face-to-face meeting that takes place via the Web.

individuals located in different geographical locations, as well as for employee training, sales presentations, customer support, and other business applications.

Webinars (Web seminars) are similar to Web conferences but typically have a designated presenter and an audience. Although interaction with the audience is usually included, a Webinar is typically more one-way communication than a Web conference.

5-5c Online Communities

A **social networking site** can be loosely defined as any site that creates a community of individuals who can communicate with and/ or share information with one another. Some examples are MySpace, Facebook, and Google+, which allow users to post information about themselves for others to read; Meetup, which connects people in specific geographic areas with common hobbies and interests; video-sharing sites like YouTube; and photo-sharing sites like Flickr and Fotki. Social networking can be performed via personal computers, though the use of mobile social networking—social networks accessed with a mobile phone or other mobile device—is growing rapidly, making social networking a real-time, on-the-go activity. Some reasons for this include that most individuals carry a mobile phone with them all the time, many individuals like to communicate with others via the Web while they are on the go, and mobile phones enable location applications to be integrated into the social networking experience.

Social networking sites are used most often to communicate with existing friends. Facebook, for instance, allows you to post photos, videos, music, and other content. You can also chat with Facebook friends who are currently online and publish notes and status updates on your Facebook wall, as well as the walls of your friends' Facebook pages.

In addition to being used for personal activities, social networking sites are also viewed as a business marketing tool. For instance, MySpace, Facebook,

and YouTube are often used by businesses, political candidates, emerging musicians, and other professionals or professional organizations to increase their online presence. There are also social networking sites designed for business networking. These sites (such as LinkedIn, shown in Exhibit 5-16) are used for recruiting new employees, finding new jobs, building professional contacts, and other business activities. Other specialized social networking sites include sites designed for children and families, such as to exchange messages, view online task lists, and access a shared family calendar.

Exhibit 5-16 LinkedIn business networking site

PERSONAL PROFILING SITES
Allow individuals to post information about themselves, view status information about their friends, exchange messages, and so forth.

BUSINESS NETWORKING SITES
Help businesspeople find business contacts, potential new employees and clients, dinner and traveling partners during business trips, and so forth.

Another form of information collaboration sometimes used for educational purposes is the wiki. **Wikis**—named for the Hawaiian phrase *wiki wiki*, meaning quick—are a way of creating and editing collaborative Web pages quickly and easily. Similar to a blog, the content on a wiki page can be edited and republished to the Web just by pressing a Save or Submit button. However, wikis are intended to be modified by others and so are especially appropriate for collaboration, such as for class Web pages or group projects. To protect the content of a wiki from sabotage, the entire wiki or editing privileges for a wiki can be password protected.

Webinar A seminar presented via the Web.

social networking site A site that enables a community of individuals to communicate and share information.

wiki A collaborative Web page that is designed to be edited and republished by a variety of individuals.

One of the largest wikis is Wikipedia (shown in Exhibit 5-17), a free online encyclopedia that contains over eight million articles written in 250 languages, is updated by more than 75,000 active contributors, and is visited by hundreds of thousands of individuals each day. Although most Wikipedia contributors edit articles in a responsible manner, there are instances of erroneous information being added to Wikipedia pages intentionally. As with any resource, you should carefully evaluate the content of a Wikipedia article before referencing it in a report, Web page, or other document.

Exhibit 5-17 Wikipedia

Courtesy of Wikipedia; Used with permission of Microsoft Corporation.

5-5d Online Entertainment

There are an ever-growing number of ways to use the Web for entertainment purposes, such as listening to music, watching TV and videos, and playing online games. Music can be listened to or downloaded via a computer, mobile phone, or portable digital media player. Music files downloaded to your computer can be played from your computer's hard drive; they can also be copied to a CD to create a custom music CD or transferred to a portable digital media player or mobile phone, provided the download agreement does not preclude it. Most (about 70%, according to one estimate) online music is accessed via a mobile device, and online subscription services are viewed as the fastest growing online music market.

Watching TV shows, videos, and movies online is another very popular type of online entertainment. Online videos have been available to watch for a number of years. YouTube alone streams one billion video views per day. Today, however, you also have the option of online TV and online movies. The availability of live online TV has been fairly limited in the past but is growing. Some Web sites, such as CNN.com Live, offer live news coverage, and some TV shows and sporting events can be delivered in real time to mobile phones (referred to as mobile TV and shown in Exhibit 5-18).

A wide variety of recorded TV content, such as episodes of current TV shows after they have been aired, is available through the respective television network Web sites for viewing online. A number of Web sites, such as Hulu, TV.com, Xfinity TV, and CastTV (shown in Exhibit 5-18), also provide free access to many prime-time TV shows, older TV shows, and full-length feature films. In addition, YouTube and Internet Movie Database (IMDb) have full-length TV shows and movies that visitors can watch for free, and Comcast offers TV subscribers free online TV content delivered to their TV or mobile devices. A new trend is the development of original TV series, sometimes referred to as telewebs, that are available only online. Typically, online TV and movies are streaming media, in which the video plays from the server when it is requested. Consequently, you need an Internet connection to view the video.

Online gaming is another common online entertainment activity. Many Web sites—especially children's Web sites—include games for visitors to play. There are also sites whose sole purpose is hosting games that can be played online. Some of the games are designed to be played alone or with just one other person. Others, called online multiplayer games, are designed to be played online against many other online gamers. Online multiplayer games, such as Doom, EverQuest, and Final Fantasy, are especially popular in countries such as South Korea that have readily available high-speed Internet connections and high levels of Internet use in

Exhibit 5-18 Online TV and movies

MOBILE TV
Both live and recorded TV shows can be delivered directly to a mobile phone.

ONLINE TV AND MOVIES
TV shows and movies can be watched online for free via a variety of Web sites.

Courtesy MobiTV; Courtesy CastTV; Used with permission of Microsoft Corporation.

general. Internet-enabled gaming consoles, such as the PlayStation 3, Xbox 360, and Wii, and portable gaming devices, such as the Sony PSP and Nintendo 3DS, that have built-in Internet connectivity can also be used for multiplayer online gaming.

5-5e E-Commerce

Online shopping and online investing are examples of **e-commerce**—online financial transactions. It is very common today to order products, buy and sell stock, pay bills, and manage financial accounts online. However, because online fraud, credit card fraud, and identity theft (a situation in which someone gains enough personal information to pose as another person) are continuing to grow rapidly, it is important to be cautious when participating in online financial activities. To protect yourself, use a credit card or online payment service such as PayPal whenever possible when purchasing goods or services online so that any fraudulent activities can be disputed. Also, be sure to

enter your payment information only on a secure Web page (look for a URL that begins with *https* instead of *http*). Online financial accounts should also be protected with strong user passwords that are changed frequently.

Online shopping is commonly used to purchase both physical products—such as clothing, books, DVDs, shoes, furniture, and more—and downloadable products—such as software, movies, music, and e-books—via Web pages like the one shown in Exhibit 5-19. Forrester Research predicts that U.S. online sales will reach approximately $250 billion by 2014.

Online auctions are the most common ways to purchase items online from other individuals. Sellers list items for sale on an auction site, such as eBay, and pay a small listing fee and a commission to the auction site if the item is sold. Individuals can visit the auction site and enter bids on auction items until the end of the auction. Another common way to purchase items from other

Exhibit 5-19 Online shopping site

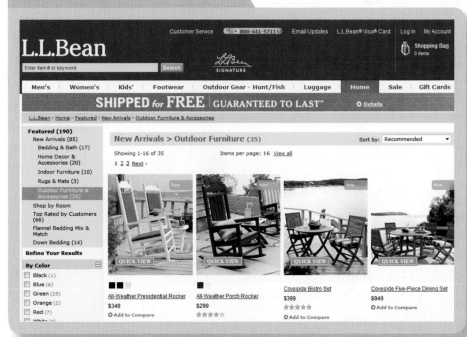

www.llbean.com. L.L.Bean® is a registered trademark of L.L.Bean Inc. Copyright 2011; Used with permission of Microsoft Corporation.

e-commerce Online financial transactions.

individuals is via online classified ads, such as those posted on the popular Craigslist site.

Many banks today offer online banking as a free service to their customers to enable customers to check balances on all their accounts, view cashed checks and other transactions, transfer funds between accounts, pay bills electronically, and perform other activities related to their bank accounts. Online banking is continually growing and can be performed via a computer or a mobile device. In fact, most banks allow users to view balances, transfer funds, and more via a mobile Web site, mobile banking app, or text message.

Buying and selling stocks, bonds, mutual funds, and other types of securities is referred to as online investing. Although it is common to see stock quote capabilities on many search and news sites, trading stocks and other securities requires an online broker. Common online investing services include the ability to order sales and purchases; access performance histories, corporate news, and other useful investment information; and set up an online portfolio that displays the status of the stocks you specify.

5-5f Product, Corporate, Government, and Other Information

The Web is a very useful tool for locating product and corporate information. Manufacturer and retailer Web sites often include product specifications, instruction manuals, and other information that is useful to consumers before or after they purchase a product. Numerous consumer review sites, such as Epinions.com, are also available to help purchasers evaluate their options before buying a product online or in a physical store. For investors and consumers, a variety of corporate information is available online, from both company Web sites and sites, such as hoovers.com, that offer free or fee-based corporate information.

An **e-portfolio**, also called an electronic portfolio or digital portfolio, is a collection of an individual's work accessible through a Web site. Typically, e-portfolios are linked to a collection of student-related information, such as résumés, papers, projects, and other original works. Some e-portfolios are used for a single course; others are designed to be used and updated throughout a student's educational career, culminating in a comprehensive collection of information that can be used as a job-hunting tool.

e-portfolio A collection of an individual's work accessible via the Web.

Quiz Yourself

1. What is ARPANET?

2. What is an Internet service provider?

3. What three decisions are typically involved before you connect to the Internet?

4. What is a direct Internet connection?

5. What is a Wi-Fi hotspot?

6. What three things determine your ISP options?

7. How are search site databases typically updated?

8. How do you use a search engine to conduct a search?

9. Is the number of hits returned for a particular search phrase always the same from one search site to another? Why or why not?

10. Before you download or copy graphics, maps, images, sounds, or information from Web sites that you visit, what should you do?

11. Describe how email works.

12. An ethical issue surrounding blogging relates to bloggers who are paid to blog about certain products. Explain the different sides of this issue.

13. What is a microblog?

14. List the biggest advantage and the biggest disadvantage of VoIP.

15. What is a Webinar?

16. What is a social networking site?

17. Which is more appropriate for collaborating with others—a blog or a wiki?

18. Why is it important to be cautious when participating in online financial activities?

Practice It

Practice It 5-1

An increasing number of public locations offer Wi-Fi hotspots for public use. You can often find them in public libraries, coffee shops, bookstores, and even some restaurants.

1. Find one location in your local area that offers public Wi-Fi access, and then either visit the location or contact the provider to find out the how the hotspot works, in terms of fees and access.

2. Is there a fee to use the hotspot?

3. If so, do you have to subscribe on a regular basis, or can you pay only when you want to use the hotspot?

4. Where and how is payment made?

5. Do you need any special software to access the hotspot?

6. Do you need to be assigned a username or key (such as a WEP, WPA, or WPA 2 key) before you can use the service?

7. Prepare a one-page summary that answers these questions and submit it to your instructor.

Practice It 5-2

Twitter became virtually an overnight sensation, but some question its usefulness.

1. Do you want to know the routine activities your friends (or other individuals you choose to follow) are doing at any moment? Why or why not?

2. Is it useful information to Tweet that you are stuck in traffic or having a bad day? Why or why not?

3. Do you regularly follow anyone on Twitter? Why or why not?

4. Because Twitter updates have to be very short, some may think that Tweeting on the job does not take up enough time to be a concern, but what about the distraction factor? Should employers allow employees to use Twitter, Facebook, and other popular online activities during work hours? Why or why not?

5. Prepare a one-page summary that answers these questions and submit it to your instructor.

On Your Own

On Your Own 5-1

Social networks (such as Facebook and MySpace) are very popular with individuals. However, it has become apparent recently that some individuals are moving from casual social networking use to compulsive or addictive behavior.

1. Investigate either Facebook addiction or Internet addiction.

2. How common is it?

3. What are some of the warning signs?

4. Is there an actual medical disorder associated with it? If so, what is it and how is it treated?

5. Find one example in a news or journal article of a person who was "addicted" to using a social networking site or other online activity. Why was that person's behavior considered addictive? Was that person able to modify his or her behavior?

6. Have you ever been concerned about becoming addicted to any Internet activities? Why or why not?

7. Prepare a one- or two-page summary that answers these questions and submit it to your instructor.

Chapter 5

ADDITIONAL STUDY TOOLS

IN THE BOOK

▶ Complete end-of-chapter exercises

▶ Study tear-out Chapter Review Card

ONLINE

▶ Complete additional end-of-chapter exercises

▶ Take practice quiz to prepare for tests

▶ Review key term flash cards (online, printable, and audio)

▶ Play "Beat the Clock" and "Memory" to quiz yourself

▶ Watch the videos to learn more about the topics taught in this chapter

Answers to Quiz Yourself

1. *ARPANET is the predecessor of the Internet, named after the Advanced Research Projects Agency (ARPA), which sponsored its development.*

2. *An Internet service provider is a business or other organization that provides Internet access to others, typically for a fee.*

3. *The three decisions typically involved before you connect to the Internet are (1) determining the type of device you will use to access the Internet, (2) deciding which type of connection you want, and (3) selecting the Internet service provider to use.*

4. *A direct Internet connection is an Internet connection that is always on, providing a continuous connection to the ISP.*

5. *A Wi-Fi hotspot is a location that provides wireless Internet access to the public.*

6. *The type of device you will use (such as a personal computer or mobile phone), the type of Internet connection and service you want (such as cable Internet or mobile wireless), and your geographical location (such as metropolitan or rural) determine your ISP options.*

7. *Search site databases are typically updated by small, automated programs (often called spiders or webcrawlers) that use the hyperlinks located on Web pages to jump continually from page to page and record important data about each page.*

8. *To use a search engine to conduct a search you type a keyword or a search phrase into the search box on the search site.*

9. *The number of hits returned for a particular search phrase is not always the same from one search site to another because search sites differ in determining how close a match must be between the specified search criteria and a Web page before a link to that page is displayed.*

10. *Before you download or copy graphics, maps, images, sounds, or information from Web sites that you visit, you need to find out if and how you can use the materials and then, if necessary, get permission from the owner of the content.*

11. *The following describes how email works: When you send a message, it travels from your computer, through a network, such as a LAN or the Internet, and arrives at the computer that has been designated and set up as your mail server, and then continues through the Internet to the mail server being used by the recipient's ISP, which stores the email message until the recipient's computer retrieves it. The server then forwards the message to the recipient's computer.*

12. *Although some Web sites that match bloggers with advertisers require that the blogger reveal that he or she receives payment for "sponsored" posts, some believe that commercializing blogging will corrupt the blogosphere. Others, however, view it as a natural evolution of word-of-mouth advertising.*

13. *A microblog is very short messages, called updates, posted to a microblogging service that other members can read, such as Tweets posted on Twitter.*

14. *The biggest advantage of VoIP is cost savings, such as unlimited local and long-distance calls for as little as $25 per month, or basic cable and VoIP services bundled together for about $50 per month. One of the biggest disadvantages of VoIP is that it does not function during a power outage or if your Internet connection goes down.*

15. *A Webinar is a seminar presented via the Web.*

16. *A social networking site can be loosely defined as any site that creates a community of individuals who can communicate with and/or share information with one another, such as MySpace, Facebook, and Google+.*

17. *A wiki is more appropriate than a blog for collaborating with others.*

18. *It is important to be cautious when participating in online financial activities because online fraud, credit card fraud, and identity theft (a situation in which someone gains enough personal information to pose as another person) are continuing to grow rapidly.*

Computer, Network, and Internet Security and Privacy

© Camilo Jimenez/iStockphoto

Networks and the Internet help many workers be more efficient and effective, as well as add convenience and enjoyment to our personal lives. However, the widespread use of home and business networks and the Internet increases the risk of unauthorized computer access, theft, fraud, and other types of computer crime. The vast amount of business and personal data stored on computers accessible via company networks and the Internet increases the chances of data loss due to crime or employee errors. In addition, our networked society has raised a number of privacy concerns. Although sometimes selected people or organizations have a legitimate need for some personal information, there is always the danger that information provided to others will be misused.

This chapter looks at a variety of security and privacy concerns stemming from the use of computer networks and the Internet and introduces safeguards for each concern. The chapter also looks at legislation related to network and Internet security.

Learning Objectives

After studying the material in this chapter, you will be able to:

6-1 Explain network and Internet security concerns

6-2 Identify and protect against unauthorized access and use

6-3 Identify and protect against computer sabotage

6-4 Identify and protect against online theft, online fraud, and other dot cons

6-5 Describe and protect against cyberstalking and other personal safety concerns

6-6 Assess personal computer security and identify precautions

6-7 Identify privacy concerns

6-8 Discuss current security and privacy legislation

6-1 Understanding Security Concerns

Security concerns related to computer networks and the Internet range from a program making your computer function abnormally, to a hacker using your personal information to make fraudulent purchases, to someone harassing you online in a discussion group.

Many Internet security concerns can be categorized as computer crimes. **Computer crime**—sometimes referred to as **cybercrime**—includes any illegal act involving a computer. Cybercrime is a multibillion-dollar business that is often conducted by seasoned criminals. According to the FBI, organized crime organizations in many countries are increasingly turning to computer crime to target millions of potential victims, and Internet scams are expected to increase in reaction to the recent troubled economy. Other types of computer crime do not include the Internet, such as using a computer to create counterfeit currency or stealing a computer or other hardware.

With some security concerns, such as when a program changes your browser's home page, the consequence may be just an annoyance. In other cases, such as when someone steals your identity and purchases items using your name and credit card number, the consequences are much more serious. In addition, with the growing use of wireless networks, social networking sites, cloud computing, and individuals accessing company networks remotely, paired with an increasing number of security and privacy regulations that businesses need to comply with, network and Internet security has never been more important. All computer users should be aware of the security concerns surrounding computer, network, and Internet use, and they should take appropriate precautions.

6-2 Unauthorized Access and Unauthorized Use

Unauthorized access occurs whenever an individual gains access to a computer, network, file, or other resource without permission—typically by hacking into the resource. **Unauthorized use** is using a computer resource for unauthorized activities, even if the user is authorized to access a particular computer or network. For instance, students may be authorized to access the Internet via a campus computer lab, but some use, such as viewing pornography, would likely be deemed off-limits. For employees, checking personal email or visiting personal Facebook pages at work might be classified as unauthorized use.

Unauthorized access and many types of unauthorized use are criminal offenses in the United States and many other countries. Whether a specific act constitutes unauthorized use or is illegal depends on the circumstances, as well as the specific company or institution involved. To explain acceptable computer use to their employees, students, or other users, many organizations and educational institutions publish guidelines for behavior, often called **codes of conduct** (see Exhibit 6-1).

6-2a Hacking

Hacking refers to the act of breaking into a computer or network. It can be performed in person if the hacker has physical access to the computer, but it is more often performed via the Internet or another network. Hacking in the United States and many other countries is a crime.

Typically, the motivation for hacking is to steal data, sabotage a computer system, or perform some other type of illegal act. In particular, the theft of consumer data, such as credit card numbers, has increased dramatically over the past several years. A growing trend is to hack into a computer and use it in an illegal or unethical act, such as generating spam or hosting pornographic Web sites.

In addition to being a threat to individuals and businesses, hacking is also considered a serious threat

---

computer crime (cybercrime) Any illegal act involving a computer.

unauthorized access Access gained to a computer, network, file, or other resource without permission.

unauthorized use Use of a computer resource for unauthorized activities.

code of conduct Guidelines for behavior that explain acceptable computer use.

hack To break into a computer or network.

Exhibit 6-1 Sample code of conduct

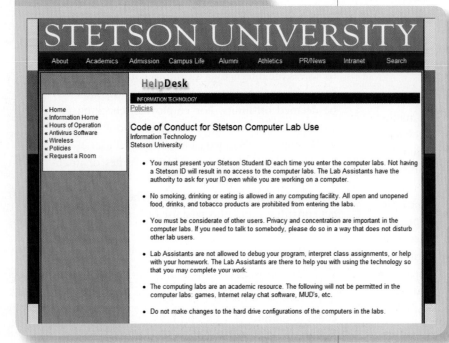

STETSON UNIVERSITY

About   Academics   Admission   Campus Life   Alumni   Athletics   PR/News   Intranet   Search

HelpDesk

« Home
« Information Home
« Hours of Operation
« Antivirus Software
« Wireless
« Policies
« Request a Room

INFORMATION TECHNOLOGY
Policies

Code of Conduct for Stetson Computer Lab Use
Information Technology
Stetson University

- You must present your Stetson Student ID each time you enter the computer labs. Not having a Stetson ID will result in no access to the computer labs. The Lab Assistants have the authority to ask for your ID even while you are working on a computer.

- No smoking, drinking or eating is allowed in any computing facility. All open and unopened food, drinks, and tobacco products are prohibited from entering the labs.

- You must be considerate of other users. Privacy and concentration are important in the computer labs. If you need to talk to somebody, please do so in a way that does not disturb other lab users.

- Lab Assistants are not allowed to debug your program, interpret class assignments, or help with your homework. The Lab Assistants are there to help you with using the technology so that you may complete your work.

- The computing labs are an academic resource. The following will not be permitted in the computer labs: games, Internet relay chat software, MUD's, etc.

- Do not make changes to the hard drive configurations of the computers in the labs.

to national security in the United States. The increased number of systems that are controlled by computers and are connected to the Internet, along with the continually improving abilities of hackers and the increasing availability of sets of tools that allow hackers to access a system, has led to an increased risk of **cyberterrorism**—where terrorists launch attacks via the Internet. Current concerns include attacks against the computers controlling vital systems, such as the nation's power grids, banks, and water filtration facilities, as well as computers related to national defense, the airlines, and the stock market.

Hackers often gain access via a wireless network. This is because wireless networks are becoming so common and it is easier to hack into a wireless network than a wired network. In fact, it is possible to gain access to a wireless network just by being within range of a

> As many as 70% of all Wi-Fi networks are left unsecured.

wireless access point, unless the access point is sufficiently protected. Although security features are built into wireless routers and other networking hardware, they are typically not enabled by default. As a result, many wireless networks belonging to businesses and individuals—some estimates put the number as high as 70% of all Wi-Fi networks—are left unsecured.

6-2b War Driving and Wi-Fi Piggybacking

Unauthorized use of a Wi-Fi network is called war driving or Wi-Fi piggybacking, depending on the location of the hacker at the time. **War driving** involves driving in a car with a portable computer looking for unsecured Wi-Fi networks to connect to. **Wi-Fi piggybacking** is accessing someone else's unsecured Wi-Fi network without authorization.

6-2c Interception of Communications

Some criminals gain unauthorized access to data, files, email messages, VoIP calls, and other content as it is being sent over the Internet. For instance, unencrypted messages, files, logon information, and more sent over an unsecured wireless network can be captured and read by anyone within range using software designed for that purpose. Proprietary corporate information and sensitive personal information is at risk if it is sent unsecured over the Internet or over a wireless home or corporate network. Data on mobile devices with Bluetooth capabilities enabled can be accessed by other Bluetooth devices that are within range. With more than 70% of smartphone owners using their smartphones to access sensitive data (such as banking and credit card accounts), according to Juniper Research, an increasing number of users may have sensitive data stored on their phones.

In a new trend, criminals are intercepting credit and debit card information during the card verification process, accessing the data

cyberterrorism An attack launched by terrorists via the Internet.

war driving Driving around an area with a Wi-Fi-enabled computer or mobile device to find a Wi-Fi network to access and use without authorization.

Wi-Fi piggybacking Accessing an unsecured Wi-Fi network without authorization.

War Driving and Wi-Fi Piggybacking: Legal and Ethical?

Both war driving and Wi-Fi piggybacking are ethically—if not legally—questionable acts. Both the hacker and the owner of the Wi-Fi network risk the introduction of programs that are harmful to their computers and unauthorized access of the data located on their computers. In addition, the network owner may experience reduced performance or even cancelled Internet service if the ISP limits bandwidth or the number of computers allowed to use a single Internet connection. In some countries, such as the U.K., laws are clear that unauthorized access of a Wi-Fi connection is illegal. In the United States, federal law is not as clear, although some states have made using a Wi-Fi connection without permission illegal. Advocates of war driving and Wi-Fi piggybacking state that individuals or businesses who do not protect their access points are welcoming others to use them. Critics compare that logic to that of an unlocked front door—you cannot legally enter a home just because the front door is unlocked. Some wireless network owners do leave their access points unsecured on purpose, and some communities are creating a collection of wireless access points to provide wireless Internet access to everyone in that community. However, it is difficult—if not impossible—to tell if an unsecured network is that way intentionally, unless the hotspot information states that it is a free public Wi-Fi hotspot.

Courtesy of JiWire

Wi-Fi finder lists hotspots for specific area

from a card in real time as a purchase is being authorized. In several recent cases, hackers installed software at payment terminals, such as restaurant cash registers or gas station credit/debit card readers to gather data during transactions and then send it to the hackers. The increased occurrence of real-time attacks may be partly because of the new Payment Card Industry Data Security Standard (PCI DSS) rules that require companies to limit the credit card data stored on company servers and to encrypt the data that is allowed to be stored.

6-2d Protecting Against Unauthorized Access and Unauthorized Use

The first step in protecting against unauthorized access and unauthorized use is to ensure that only authorized individuals can access an organization's facilities and computer networks. In addition, organizations must ensure that authorized individuals can access only the resources that they are supposed to access. Access control systems are used for these purposes. Specific types of access control systems include the following:

▶ **Possessed knowledge access system**—requires the person requesting access to provide information that only the authorized user is supposed to know, such as a password.

▶ **Possessed object access system**—requires the person requesting access to use physical objects for identification purposes, such as smart cards, RFID-encoded badges, and magnetic cards.

▶ **Biometric access system**—requires the person requesting access to provide a particular unique biological characteristic (such as a fingerprint, a hand, a face, or an iris) for identification.

Another way to control access to a computer or network is to use a **firewall**, which is a security system that essentially creates a barrier between a computer or a network and the Internet. Firewalls are typically two-way, so they check all incoming and outgoing traffic. Personal firewalls are software designed to protect home computers from hackers attempting to access those computers through their Internet connections. All computers with direct Internet connections (DSL, cable, satellite, or fixed wireless Internet access) should use a firewall; computers using dial-up Internet access only are relatively safe from hackers. Many routers, modems, and other pieces of networking hardware also include built-in firewall capabilities to help secure the networks these devices are used with. Firewalls designed to protect business networks may be software-based, hardware-based, or a combination of the two. They can be used both to prevent network access by hackers and other outsiders, and to control employee Internet access.

> **firewall** A collection of hardware and/or software that protects a computer or computer network from unauthorized access.

After installing and setting up a firewall, individuals and businesses should test their systems to determine if vulnerabilities still exist. Individuals can use online security tests—such as the Symantec Security Check shown in Exhibit 6-2 or the tests at Gibson Research's ShieldsUP! site—to check their computers; businesses may wish to hire an outside consultant to perform a comprehensive security assessment.

Exhibit 6-2 Online security scans check system for vulnerabilities

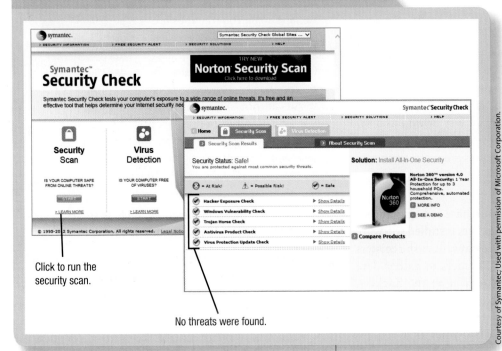

Click to run the security scan.

No threats were found.

Courtesy of Symantec; Used with permission of Microsoft Corporation.

To protect that data from being viewed by unauthorized individuals, you can use **encryption**, which is a way of temporarily converting data into a form of data that is unreadable until it is decrypted.

Secure Web pages use encryption so that sensitive data sent via the Web page is protected as it travels over the Internet. The most common security protocols used with secure Web pages are Secure Sockets Layer

(SSL) and Extended Validation Secure Sockets Layer (EV SSL). The URL for Web pages using either form of SSL begins with *https:* instead of *http:*. Sensitive information should be entered only on secure Web pages so that a criminal cannot intercept that data. Some Internet services, such as Skype and Hushmail, use built-in encryption. Encryption can also be added manually to a file or an email message before it is sent over the Internet to ensure that the content is unreadable if the file or message is intercepted during transit. In addition to securing files during transit, encryption can be used to protect the files stored on a hard drive so they will be unreadable if opened by an unauthorized person. Increasingly, computers and storage devices, particularly those used with portable computers, are self-encrypting, which means they encrypt all data automatically and invisibly to the user.

The two most common types of encryption are private key encryption and public key encryption. A key is essentially a password. **Private key encryption**, also called symmetric key encryption, uses a single, secret private key to both encrypt and decrypt a file or message being sent over the Internet. Private key encryption can be used to send files securely to others. The recipient must have the private key to access the file.

Public key encryption, also called asymmetric key encryption, uses two encryption keys to encrypt and decrypt documents. Specifically, public key encryption uses a private key and a public key that are related mathematically to each other and have been assigned to a particular individual. An individual's public key is not secret and is available for anyone to use, but the corresponding private key is secret and is used only by the individual to whom it was assigned. Exhibit 6-3 illustrates how public key encryption is used to secure an email message.

A **virtual private network** (**VPN**) is used when a continuous secure channel over the Internet is needed.

encryption A method of scrambling the contents of an email message or a file to make it unreadable if an unauthorized user intercepts it.

private key encryption A type of encryption that uses a single key to encrypt and decrypt a file or message.

public key encryption A type of encryption that uses key pairs to encrypt and decrypt a file or message.

virtual private network (**VPN**) A private, secure path over the Internet that provides authorized users a secure means of accessing a private network via the Internet.

Exhibit 6-3 How public key encryption secures an email message

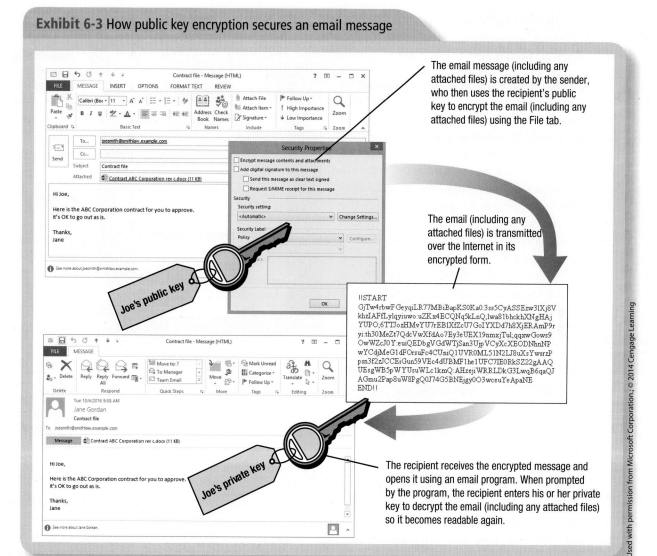

The email message (including any attached files) is created by the sender, who then uses the recipient's public key to encrypt the email (including any attached files) using the File tab.

The email (including any attached files) is transmitted over the Internet in its encrypted form.

!!START
GjTw4rbwFGeyqiLR77MBiBapKS0Ka0:3ss5CyASSEzw3IXj8V
khzIAFfLylqyiuwo:uZKx4ECQNq5kLnQ;lwa81bhckhXNgHAj
YUPO;6TTJozHMvYU7rEB1XfZcU7GoIYXDd7h8XjERAmP9r
yi:th30MeZt7QdcVwXfdAo7Ey3eUEX19nmxjTul;qqxwGows9
OwWZcJ0Y:euiQEDbgVGdWTjSan3UjpVCyXcXEODNhnNP
wYCdjMeG1dFOrsuFc4CUniQ1UVR0ML51N2LJ8uXsYwsrzP
psn3f2zJCCEiGun59VEc4dUBMF1he1UFC7IE0RkSZ22gAAQ
UEsgWB5pWYUsuWLc1kmQ:AHzejiWRRLDkG3LwqB6qaQJ
AGmu2Pap8uW8PgQ0J74G5BNEjgy0O3wceuYeApaNE
END!!

The recipient receives the encrypted message and opens it using an email program. When prompted by the program, the recipient enters his or her private key to decrypt the email (including any attached files) so it becomes readable again.

A VPN provides a secure private tunnel from the user's computer through the Internet to another destination and is most often used to provide remote employees with secure access to a company network. VPNs use encryption and other security mechanisms to ensure that only authorized users can access the remote network and that the data cannot be intercepted during transit. Because it uses the Internet instead of an expensive private physical network, a VPN can provide a secure environment over a large geographical area at a manageable cost.

6-3 Computer Sabotage

Computer sabotage—acts of malicious destruction to a computer or computer resource—is another common type of computer crime. Computer sabotage can take several forms, including launching a harmful program, altering the content of a Web site, or changing data or programs located on a computer. Computer sabotage is illegal in the United States and is estimated to cost billions of dollars per year, primarily for labor costs related to correcting the problems caused by the sabotage, lost productivity, and lost sales.

6-3a Botnets

A common tool used to perform computer sabotage is a botnet. A computer that is controlled by a hacker or other computer criminal is referred to as a **bot** or **zombie computer**; a group of bots that are controlled by

---

computer sabotage An act of malicious destruction to a computer or computer resource.

bot (zombie computer) A computer that is controlled by a hacker or other computer criminal.

Securing a Router

A home wireless network should be secured properly so unauthorized individuals cannot use it. Security settings are specified in the router's configuration screen, such as the one shown here. To open your router's configuration screen to check or modify the security settings, type the IP address assigned to that device (such as 192.168.0.1—check your router's documentation for its default IP address and username) in your browser's Address bar. Use the default password to log on the first time, and then change the password using the configuration screen to prevent unauthorized individuals from changing your router settings. To secure the router, enter the network name (SSID) you want associated with the router, select the appropriate security mode, such as WEP, WPA, or WPA2, and then type a secure passphrase to use to log on to the network.

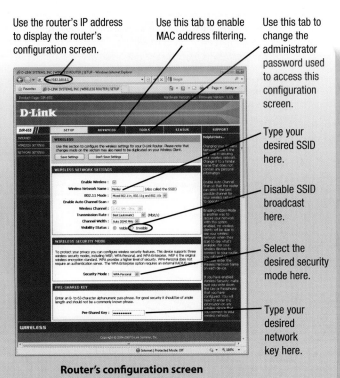

Use the router's IP address to display the router's configuration screen.

Use this tab to enable MAC address filtering.

Use this tab to change the administrator password used to access this configuration screen.

Type your desired SSID here.

Disable SSID broadcast here.

Select the desired security mode here.

Type your desired network key here.

Router's configuration screen

Courtesy D-Link Systems, Inc.; Used with permission from Microsoft Corporation

one individual and can work together in a coordinated fashion is called a **botnet**. Millions of U.S. computers are unknowingly part of a botnet.

6-3b Computer Viruses and Other Types of Malware

Malware is a generic term that refers to any type of malicious software. Malware programs are intentionally written to perform destructive acts, such as damaging programs, deleting files, erasing a hard drive, or slowing the performance of a computer. This damage can take place immediately after a computer is infected, or it can begin when a particular condition is met.

Writing malware or posting the malware code on the Internet is not illegal, although it is highly unethical and irresponsible behavior. Distributing malware, on the other hand, is illegal.

botnet A group of bots that are controlled by one individual.

malware Any type of malicious software.

virus A software program installed without the user's knowledge that is designed to alter the way a computer operates or to cause harm to the computer system.

worm A malicious program designed to spread rapidly to a large number of computers by sending copies of itself to other computers.

One type of malware is a **virus**—a software program that is installed without the permission or knowledge of the computer user, that is designed to alter the way a computer operates, and that can replicate itself to infect any new media to which it has access. Computer viruses are often embedded into program or data files, such as games, videos, and music files downloaded from Web pages or shared via a P2P service. They are spread when an infected file is downloaded, transferred to a new computer via an infected removable storage medium, or emailed to another computer (see Exhibit 6-4). Viruses can also be installed when a recipient clicks a link in an instant message or an email, such as an email that contains a link to view an electronic greeting card. Once a copy of the infected file reaches a new computer, it embeds itself into program, data, or system files on the new computer and remains there, affecting that computer according to its programmed instructions until it is discovered and removed.

Another common form of malware is a **worm**, which is a malicious program that is designed to cause damage by creating copies of its code and sending those copies to other computers via a network. Often, a worm is sent to other computers as an email attachment. Usually, after the infected email attachment is opened by an individual, the worm inflicts its damage and then automatically sends copies of itself to other computers via the Internet or a private network, using addresses in the email address book located on the newly infected computer.

Exhibit 6-4 How a computer virus might spread

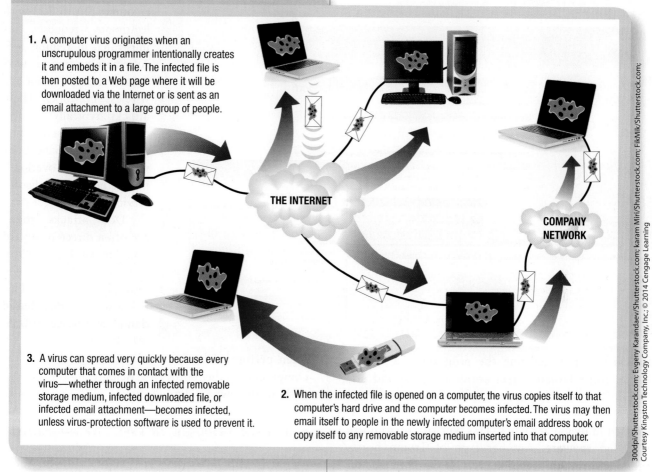

1. A computer virus originates when an unscrupulous programmer intentionally creates it and embeds it in a file. The infected file is then posted to a Web page where it will be downloaded via the Internet or is sent as an email attachment to a large group of people.

THE INTERNET

COMPANY NETWORK

3. A virus can spread very quickly because every computer that comes in contact with the virus—whether through an infected removable storage medium, infected downloaded file, or infected email attachment—becomes infected, unless virus-protection software is used to prevent it.

2. When the infected file is opened on a computer, the virus copies itself to that computer's hard drive and the computer becomes infected. The virus may then email itself to people in the newly infected computer's email address book or copy itself to any removable storage medium inserted into that computer.

Some worms do not require any user action to infect the user's computer. Instead, the worm scans the Internet looking for computers that are vulnerable to that particular worm and sends a copy of itself to those computers to infect them. Other worms just require the user to view an infected email message or insert an infected removable storage medium into the computer to infect the computer. Still other worms are specifically written to take advantage of newly discovered security holes in operating systems and email programs.

A **Trojan horse** is a type of malware that masquerades as something else—usually an application program. When the seemingly legitimate program is downloaded or installed, the Trojan horse infects the computer. Many recent Trojan horses masquerade as normal, ongoing activities when they are installed, such as the Windows Update service or a warning from a program that is supposed to protect a computer

> Writing malware code is unethical, but not illegal. Distributing malware is illegal.

against malware, to try to trick unsuspecting users into downloading another malware program or buying a useless program. For instance, after a rogue antivirus program like the one shown in Exhibit 6-5 is installed, the malware takes over the computer, displaying warning messages or scan results indicating the computer is infected with malware. The rogue program typically prompts the user to buy a fake protection program to get rid of the "malware."

Unlike viruses and worms, Trojan horses cannot replicate themselves. Trojan horses are usually spread by being downloaded from the Internet, though they may also be sent as an email attachment, either from the Trojan horse author or from individuals who

> **Trojan horse** A malicious program that masquerades as something else.

Exhibit 6-5 Rogue antivirus program

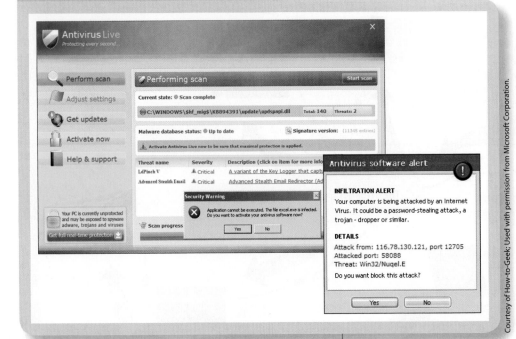

useless traffic is generated, the server has no resources left to deal with legitimate requests, as illustrated in Exhibit 6-6. An emerging trend is DoS attacks aimed at mobile wireless networks. These attacks typically involve repeatedly establishing and releasing connections with the goal of overloading the network to disrupt service.

DoS attacks today are often directed toward popular sites and typically are carried out via multiple computers. This is known as a **distributed denial of service (DDoS) attack**. DDoS attacks are often performed by botnets created by hackers; the computers in the botnet participate in the attacks without the owners' knowledge.

forward it, not realizing the program is a Trojan horse. Some Trojan horses are designed to find private information located on infected computers and then send that information to the malware creator to be used in illegal activities. This type of Trojan horse is called **spyware**. Another type of Trojan horse, called a **keylogger**, records every keystroke made on the infected computer and then sends the sensitive information it recorded to criminals.

6-3c Denial of Service (DoS) Attacks

A **denial of service (DoS)** attack is an act of sabotage that attempts to flood a network server or Web server with so many requests for action that the server shuts down or simply can no longer handle requests. If enough

6-3d Data, Program, or Web Site Alteration

Another type of computer sabotage occurs when a hacker breaches a computer system to delete or alter the data and programs located there. For example, a student might try to hack into the school database to change his or her grade, or a hacker might change a program located on a company server to steal money or information.

Data on Web sites can also be altered by hackers. For instance, individuals sometimes hack into and alter other people's social networking accounts. It is also becoming more common for hackers to compromise legitimate Web sites and then use those sites to perform malware attacks. For example, a hacker can alter a Web site to display an official-looking message that informs the user that a particular software program must be downloaded to use the site, or the hacker might post a rogue ad on a legitimate site that redirects the user to a malware site instead of the site for the product featured in the ad.

6-3e Protecting Against Computer Sabotage

To protect against becoming infected with a computer virus or other type of malware, computers and other

---

spyware A program designed to find private information on a computer and then send that information to the creator of the malware program.

keylogger A malware program that records every keystroke on a computer and then sends the sensitive information it recorded to criminals.

denial of service (DoS) attack An act of sabotage that attempts to flood a network server or a Web server with so much activity that it is unable to function.

distributed denial of service (DDoS) attack A DoS attack carried out by multiple computers.

Exhibit 6-6 How a DoS attack might work

1. Hacker's computer sends several simultaneous requests; each request asks to establish a connection to the server but supplies false return information. In a distributed DoS attack, multiple computers send multiple requests at one time. **Hello? I'd like some info...**

Hello? I'd like some info...

I'm busy. I can't help you right now.

LEGITIMATE COMPUTER

2. The server tries to respond to each request but can't locate the computer because false return information was provided. The server waits for a short period of time before closing the connection, which ties up the server and keeps others from connecting. **I can't find you. I'll wait and try again...**

HACKER'S COMPUTER

3. The hacker's computer continues to send new requests so, as a connection is closed by the server, a new request is waiting. This cycle continues, which ties up the server indefinitely. **Hello? I'd like some info...**

4. The server becomes so overwhelmed that legitimate requests cannot get through and, eventually, the server usually crashes.

WEB SERVER

devices used to access the Internet or a company network should have security software installed. **Security software** typically includes a variety of security features, including a firewall, protection against spyware and bots, and protection against some types of online fraud. One of the most important components is **antivirus software**, which protects against computer viruses and other types of malware. Antivirus software runs continuously to monitor the computer and incoming email messages, instant messages, Web page content, and downloaded files to prevent malicious software from executing. See Exhibit 6-7. Many antivirus programs also scan devices when they are connected to a USB port. Antivirus software helps prevent malware from being installed on your computer because it deletes or quarantines any suspicious content as it arrives. Regular full-system scans can detect and remove any viruses or worms that find their way onto your computer.

Exhibit 6-7 Security software

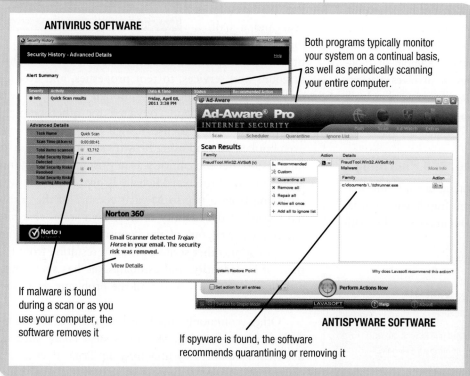

ANTIVIRUS SOFTWARE

Both programs typically monitor your system on a continual basis, as well as periodically scanning your entire computer.

Email Scanner detected *Trojan Horse* in your email. The security risk was removed.

If malware is found during a scan or as you use your computer, the software removes it

If spyware is found, the software recommends quarantining or removing it

ANTISPYWARE SOFTWARE

security software
Software, typically a suite of programs, used to protect a computer against a variety of threats.

antivirus software Software used to detect and eliminate computer viruses and other types of malware.

6-4 Online Theft, Online Fraud, and Other Dot Cons

A booming area of computer crime involves online theft, fraud, scams, and related activities designed to steal money or other resources from individuals or businesses. These are collectively referred to as **dot cons**.

6-4a Theft of Data, Information, and Other Resources

Data theft or **information theft** is the theft of data or information located on or being sent from a computer. It can be committed by stealing an actual computer, or it can take place over the Internet or a network by an individual gaining unauthorized access to that data by hacking into the computer or by intercepting the data in transit. Common types of data and information stolen via the Internet or another network include customer data (such as Web site passwords or credit card information) and proprietary corporate information.

Money is another resource that can be stolen via a computer. Company insiders sometimes steal money by altering company programs to transfer small amounts of money—for example, a few cents worth of bank account interest—from a very large number of transactions to an account controlled by the thieves. Added together, the amounts can be substantial. Another example of monetary theft performed via computers involves hackers electronically transferring money illegally from online bank accounts, traditional bank accounts, credit card accounts, or accounts at online payment services such as PayPal.

6-4b Identity Theft, Phishing, and Pharming

A growing dot con trend is obtaining enough information about an individual to perform fraudulent financial transactions. Often, this is carried out in conjunction with

> Dot cons are a booming area of computer crime.

identity theft. **Identity theft** occurs when someone obtains enough information about a person to be able to masquerade as that person—usually to buy products or services in that person's name, as illustrated in Exhibit 6-8. Typically, identity theft begins when a thief obtains a person's name, address, and Social Security number, often from a discarded or stolen document, such as a preapproved credit card application that was sent in the mail; from information obtained via the Internet, such as a résumé posted online; from information located on a computer, such as on a stolen computer or hacked server; or from information sent from a computer via a computer virus or spyware program installed on that computer. The thief may then order a copy of the individual's birth certificate, obtain a "replacement" driver's license, make purchases and charge them to the victim, or open credit or bank accounts in the victim's name. Identity theft is illegal, and, in 1998, the federal government passed the Identity Theft and Assumption Deterrence Act, which made identity theft a federal crime.

Identity theft can be extremely distressing for victims, take years to straighten out, and be very expensive. For example, for a year and a half, a thief used the identity of victim Michelle Brown to obtain over $50,000 in goods and services, to rent properties, and even to engage in drug trafficking. Although the culprit was eventually arrested and convicted for other criminal acts, she continued to use Brown's identity and was even booked into jail using Brown's stolen identity. As a final insult after the culprit was in prison, U.S. Customs agents detained the real Michelle Brown when she was returning from a trip to Mexico because of the criminal record of the identity thief. Brown states that she has not traveled out of the country since, fearing an arrest or some other serious problem resulting from the theft of her identity, and estimates she has spent over 500 hours trying to correct all the problems related to the identity theft.

Other commonly used techniques are skimming and social engineering. Skimmers steal credit card or debit card numbers by attaching an illegal device to a credit card reader or an ATM that reads and stores

dot con A fraud or scam carried out through the Internet.

data theft (information theft) The theft of data or information located on or being sent from a computer.

identity theft Using someone else's identity to purchase goods or services, obtain new credit cards or bank loans, or otherwise illegally masquerade as that individual.

Exhibit 6-8 How identity theft works

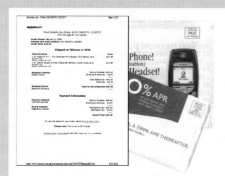

1. The thief obtains information about an individual from discarded mail, employee records, credit card transactions, Web server files, or some other method.

2. The thief uses the information to make purchases, open new credit card accounts, and more in the victim's name. Often, the thief changes the address on the account to delay the victim's discovery of the theft.

3. The victim usually finds out by being denied credit or by being contacted about overdue bills generated by the thief. Clearing one's name after identity theft is time consuming and can be very difficult and frustrating for the victim.

© 2014 Cengage Learning; © Ryan McVay/Getty Images

the card numbers. They also position a hidden camera to capture ATM PINs. Social engineering involves pretending—typically via phone or email—to be a bank officer, potential employer, or other trusted individual to get the potential victim to supply personal information.

Dmitry Kalinovsky/Shutterstock.com

Phishing (pronounced "fishing") is the use of an email message that appears to come from a legitimate organization such as eBay, PayPal, or a bank, but is actually sent from a phisher to trick the recipient into revealing sensitive personal information, such as Web site logon information or credit card numbers. Once obtained, this information is used in identity theft and other fraudulent activities. A phishing email looks legitimate and contains links that appear to go to the Web site of the legitimate business. However, these links go to the phisher's **spoofed Web site**, which is set up to look like the legitimate site. Phishing emails are typically sent to a wide group of individuals and usually include an urgent message stating that the individual's credit card or account information needs to be updated and instructing the recipient of the email to click the link provided in the email to keep the account active, as shown in Exhibit 6-9. If the victim clicks the link and supplies the requested information via the spoofed site, the criminal gains access to all information provided by the victim. Phishing attempts can also occur via instant messages, text messages, fake messages sent via eBay or MySpace, Tweets, and pop-up security alert windows. Phishers also frequently

use spyware; clicking the link in the phishing email installs the spyware on the victim's computer where it remains, transmitting sensitive data to the phisher, until it is detected and removed.

Spear phishing is a new trend in which emails are targeted to a specific individual and appear to come from an organization or person that the targeted individual has an association with. These emails often include personalized information, such as the potential victim's name, to make them seem more legitimate. Spear phishers target employees of selected organizations by posing as someone within the company, such as a human resources or technical support employee. These spear phishing emails often request confidential information or direct the employee to click a link to validate an account. The goal of corporate spear phishing attacks is usually to steal intellectual property, such as software source code, design documents, or schematics.

Pharming is a scam that uses spoofed domain names to reroute traffic intended for a commonly used Web site to a spoofed Web site set up by the pharmer in an

phish To use of spoofed email messages to gain credit card numbers and other personal data to be used for fraudulent purposes.

spoof To set up a Web site that looks like a legitimate site but that collects private information from an unsuspecting user.

spear phishing A personalized phishing scheme targeted at an individual.

pharming The use of spoofed domain names to obtain personal information to use in fraudulent activities.

Exhibit 6-9 Phishing email

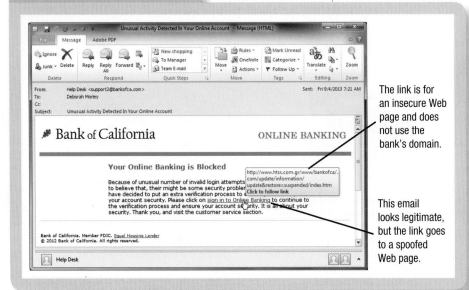

The link is for an insecure Web page and does not use the bank's domain.

This email looks legitimate, but the link goes to a spoofed Web page.

effort to obtain users' personal information. Sometimes pharming takes place using malicious code sent to a computer via an email message or other distribution method. More often, it takes place through changes made to a DNS server—a computer that translates URLs into the appropriate IP addresses needed to display the Web page corresponding to a URL. After hacking into a company's DNS server, the pharmer changes the IP addresses used in conjunction with a particular

company's URL (called DNS poisoning) so any Web page requests made to the legitimate company URL are routed via the company's poisoned DNS server to a phony spoofed Web page located on the pharmer's Web server. So, even though a user types the proper URL to display the legitimate company Web page in his or her browser, the spoofed page is displayed instead. Because spoofed sites are set up to look like the legitimate sites, the user typically does not notice any difference.

6-4c Online Auction Fraud and Other Internet Scams

Online auction fraud (sometimes called **Internet auction fraud**) occurs when an online auction buyer pays for merchandise that is never delivered or that is delivered but is not as represented. In addition, a wide range of other scams can occur via Web sites or unsolicited emails. Common types of scams include loan scams, work-at-home cons, pyramid schemes, bogus

online auction fraud (Internet auction fraud) When an item purchased through an online auction is never delivered or delivered but not as represented by the seller.

digital certificate Electronic data used to verify the identity of a person or an organization; includes a key pair that can be used for encryption and digital signatures.

digital signature A unique digital code that can be attached to a file or an email message to verify the identity of the sender and guarantee the file or message has not been changed since it was signed.

LEARN MORE

Digital Certificates and Digital Signatures

The purpose of a **digital certificate** is to authenticate the identity of an individual or organization. Digital certificates are granted by certificate authorities and contain the name of the person, organization, or Web site being certified along with a certificate serial number, an expiration date, and a public/private key pair. These keys and the digital certificate are used with secure Web pages to guarantee the Web pages are secure and actually belong to the stated organization.

The keys included in a digital certificate can also be used to authenticate the identity of a person sending an email message or other document. To digitally sign an email message or other document, the sender's private key is used, and that key, along with the contents of the document, generates a unique **digital signature**. When a digitally signed document is received, the recipient's computer uses the sender's public key to verify the digital signature. The digital signature will be deemed invalid if even one character of the document is changed after it is signed, digital signatures guarantee that the document was sent by a specific individual and that it was not tampered with after it was signed.

credit card offers and prize promotions, and fraudulent business opportunities and franchises. These offers try to sell potential victims nonexistent services or worthless information, or they try to convince potential victims to voluntarily supply their credit card details and other personal information, which are then used for fraudulent purposes.

One ongoing Internet scam is the Nigerian letter fraud scheme. This scheme involves an email message that appears to come from the Nigerian government and that promises the potential victim a share of a substantial amount of money in exchange for the use of the victim's bank account. Supposedly the victim's bank account information is needed to facilitate a wire transfer, but the victim's account is emptied instead, or up-front cash is needed to pay for nonexistent fees, which the con artist keeps while giving nothing in return. See Exhibit 6-10. The theme of these scams often changes to fit current events.

private information by sending sensitive information via secure Web servers only and not disclosing personal information—especially a Social Security number or your mother's maiden name—unless it is absolutely necessary and you know how the information will be used and that it will not be shared with others. In addition, never give out sensitive personal information to anyone who requests it over the phone or by email; businesses that legitimately need personal information such as bank account or credit card numbers will not request that information via phone or email.

In addition to disclosing personal information only when it is necessary and only via secure Web pages, you should use security software and keep it up to date to guard against computer viruses, spyware, and other malware that can be used to send information from your computer or about your activities to a criminal.

To avoid phishing schemes, never click a link in an email message to go to a secure Web site; instead, always type the URL for that site in your browser (not necessarily the URL shown in the email message).

You can also use browser-based antiphishing tools and digital certificates to help guard against identity theft and the phishing and pharming schemes used in conjunction with identity theft. Antiphishing tools are built into many email programs and Web browsers to help notify users of possible phishing Web sites. For instance, some email programs will disable links in email messages identified as questionable, unless the user overrides it; many browsers warn users when a Web page associated with a possible phishing URL is requested (see Exhibit 6-11); and antiphishing capabilities are included in many recent security suites.

The best protection against many dot cons is common sense. Be extremely cautious of any unsolicited email messages you receive. Realize that if an offer sounds too good to be true, it probably is. Before bidding on an auction item, check out the feedback rating of the seller to see comments written by other auction sellers and buyers. Always pay for auctions and other online

Exhibit 6-10 Nigerian letter fraud email

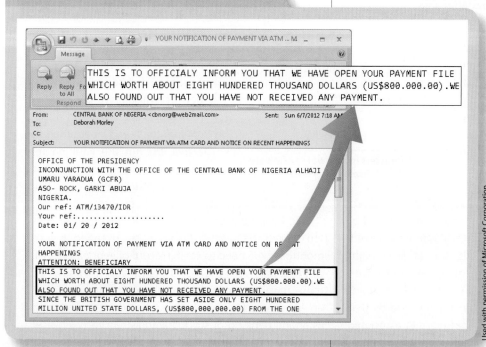

6-4d Protecting Against Identity Theft and Online Threats

The best protection against many dot cons is protecting your identity—that is, protecting any identifying information about you that could be used in fraudulent activities. You should be vigilant about protecting

Exhibit 6-11 Unsafe Web site alert

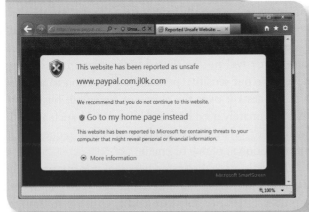

This website has been reported as unsafe
www.paypal.com.jl0k.com

We recommend that you do not continue to this website.

⊘ Go to my home page instead

This website has been reported to Microsoft for containing threats to your computer that might reveal personal or financial information.

⊙ More information

Microsoft SmartScreen

purchases using a credit card or an online payment service such as PayPal that accepts credit card payments so you can dispute the transaction through your credit card company, if needed. For expensive items, consider

using an escrow service, which allows you to ensure that the merchandise is as specified before your payment is released to the seller.

It is important to act quickly if you think you have been a victim. For instance, you should work with your local law enforcement agency, credit card companies, and the three major consumer credit bureaus—Equifax, Experian, and TransUnion—to close any accessed or fraudulent accounts, place fraud alerts on your credit report, and take other actions to prevent additional fraudulent activity while the fraud is being investigated.

6-5 Cyberstalking and Other Personal Safety Concerns

Cybercrime, in addition to being expensive and inconvenient, can also be physically dangerous. Although most of us may not ordinarily view using the Internet as a potentially dangerous activity, cases

LEARN MORE

Safeguarding Passwords

Passwords are secret words or character combinations associated with an individual. They are typically used in conjunction with a username. Username/password combinations are often used to restrict access to networks, computers, Web sites, routers, and other computing resources—the user is granted access to the requested resource only after supplying the correct information. Passwords usually appear as asterisks or dots as they are being entered so they cannot be viewed.

To create strong passwords, use at least eight characters; use a combination of upper- and lowercase letters, numbers, and symbols; do not form words found in the dictionary; and do not use words that match the username that the password is associated with. One way to create a strong password is to create a passphrase that you can remember and use corresponding letters and symbols, such as the first letter of each word, for your password. For instance, the passphrase "My son John is five years older than my daughter

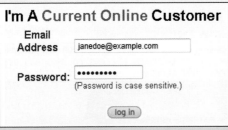

I'm A Current Online Customer

Email Address: janedoe@example.com

Password: ●●●●●●●●
(Password is case sensitive.)

(log in)

Characters in passwords often are displayed as dots

Abby" could be used to remember the corresponding strong password "Msji5yotMd@". Or you can choose an abbreviation or unusual words you will remember, and then add a mix of numbers and special characters. Do not use your name, your kids' or pets' names, your address, your birthdate, or any other public information as your password.

To keep your passwords safe, do not keep a written copy of the password in your desk or taped to your monitor. If you need to keep a record of your passwords, create a password-protected file on your computer or use a password manager program. Also, use a different password for your highly sensitive activities, such as online banking or stock trading, than for Web sites that remember your settings or profile, such as online news, auction, or shopping sites. If a hacker determines your password on a low-security site, he or she can use it on an account containing sensitive data if you use the same password on both accounts.

password A secret word or character combination associated with an individual.

of physical harm due to Internet activity do happen. For example, children and teenagers have become the victims of pedophiles who arranged face-to-face meetings by using information gathered via email, message boards, social networking sites, or other online sources. Also, a growing number of incidents have occurred in which children are threatened by classmates via email, posts on social media sites, or text messages. Adults may fall victim to unscrupulous or dangerous individuals who misrepresent themselves online, and the availability of personal information online has made it more difficult for individuals to hide from people who may want to do them harm, such as abused women trying to hide from their abusive husbands.

6-5a Cyberbullying and Cyberstalking

Two of the most common ways individuals are harassed online are cyberbullying and cyberstalking. Bullying others via the Internet, such as through email, text messaging, a social networking site, or other online communications method, is referred to as **cyberbullying**. Unfortunately, cyberbullying is common, and is especially prevalent among teens. By some estimates, it affects as many as half of all U.S. teenagers. Many states and schools have reviewed their harassment statutes and bullying policies and, as a result, implemented new laws or amended existing harassment laws to address cyberbullying.

Although incidents of online harassment between adults can be referred to as cyberharassment, repeated threats or other malicious behavior that pose a credible threat of harm carried out online between adults is referred to as **cyberstalking**. Cyberstalkers sometimes find their victims online—for instance, someone in a discussion group who makes a comment or has a screen name that the cyberstalker does not like, or bloggers who are harassed and threatened with violence or murder because of their blogging activities. Other times, the attack is more personal, such as employers who are stalked online by former employees who were fired and celebrities who are stalked online by fans. Cyberstalking typically begins with online harassment, such as sending harassing or threatening email messages to the victim, posing as the victim to sign the victim up for pornographic or otherwise offensive email newsletters, publicizing the victim's home address and telephone number, or hacking into the victim's social networking pages to alter the content. Cyberstalking can also lead to offline stalking and possibly physical harm.

Although there are as yet no specific federal laws against cyberstalking, all states have made it illegal, and some federal laws do apply if the online actions include computer fraud or another type of computer crime, suggest a threat of personal injury, or involve sending obscene email messages.

6-5b Online Pornography

A variety of controversial and potentially objectionable material is available on the Internet. Although there have been attempts to ban this type of material from the Internet, they have not been successful. Like its printed counterpart, online pornography involving minors is illegal. Because of the strong link experts believe exists between child pornography and child molestation, many experts are very concerned about the amount of child pornography that can be found and distributed via the Internet. They also believe that the Internet makes it easier for sexual predators to act out, such as by striking up "friendships" with children online and convincing these children to meet them in real life.

6-5c Protecting Personal Safety

The increasing amount of attention paid to cyberbullying and cyberstalking is leading to more efforts to improve safeguards. For instance, social networking sites have privacy features that can be used to protect the private information of their members. In addition, numerous states in the United States have implemented cyberbullying and cyberstalking laws. Although no surefire way exists to completely protect against cyberbullying, cyberstalking, and other online dangers, some common-sense precautions can reduce the chance of a serious personal safety problem occurring due to online activities. The following can help you protect yourself against cyberstalking and other types of online harassment:

▶ Use gender-neutral, nonprovocative identifying names, such as *jsmith*, instead of *janesmith* or *iamcute*.

> # Cyberbullying affects as many as half of all U.S. teenagers.

cyberbullying Children or teenagers bullying other children or teenagers via the Internet.

cyberstalking Repeated threats or harassing behavior between adults carried out via email or another Internet communications method.

- Be careful about the types of photos you post of yourself online, and do not reveal personal information, such as your real name, address, or telephone number, to people you meet online.

- Do not respond to any insults or other harassing comments you receive online.

- Consider requesting that your personal information be removed from online directories, especially those associated with your email address or other online identifiers.

6-6 Personal Computer Security

Some computer security issues are not related to networks and the Internet. These include having your computer stolen, losing a document because the storage medium it was stored on becomes unreadable, or losing your mobile phone containing your entire contact list and calendar.

6-6a Hardware Loss

Hardware loss can occur when a personal computer, USB flash drive, mobile device, or other piece of hardware is stolen or is lost by the owner. Hardware loss, as well as other security issues, can also result from hardware damage—both intentional and accidental—and system failure.

One of the most obvious types of hardware loss is hardware theft, which occurs when hardware is stolen from an individual or from a business, school, or other organization. Although security experts stress that the vast majority of hardware is stolen to obtain the value of the hardware itself, corporate executives and government employees may be targeted by computer thieves for the information contained on their computers. Even if the data on a device is not the primary reason for a theft, any unencrypted sensitive data stored on the stolen device is at risk of being exposed or used for fraudulent purposes, which is happening at unprecedented levels.

Hardware loss also occurs when hardware is being transported in luggage or in a package that is lost by an airline or shipping company, or when an individual misplaces or otherwise loses a piece of hardware. If any sensitive data was contained on the lost hardware, individuals risk identity theft. Businesses hosting sensitive data that is breached have to deal with the numerous issues and potential consequences of that loss, such as notifying customers that their personal information was exposed, responding to potential lawsuits, and trying to repair damage to the company's reputation.

6-6b System Failure and Other Disasters

Although many of us may prefer not to think about it, **system failure**—the complete malfunction of a computer system—and other types of computer-related disasters do happen. From accidentally deleting a file to having

system failure
The complete malfunction of a computer system.

FYI

Public Hotspot Precautions

Using firewall software, secure Web pages, VPNs, and encryption is a good start for protecting against unauthorized access and unauthorized use at a public Wi-Fi hotspot. The following additional precautions can help you to avoid data on your computer or data sent over the Internet from being compromised:

zmkstudio/Shutterstock.com

- Turn off automatic connections, and pay attention to the list of available hotspots to make sure you connect to a legitimate access point.

- Enter passwords, credit card numbers, and other data only on secure Web pages using a VPN.

- If you are not using a VPN, encrypt all sensitive files before transferring or emailing them.

- If you are not using a VPN, avoid online shopping, banking, and other sensitive transactions.

- Turn off file sharing so others cannot access the files on your hard drive.

- Turn off Bluetooth and Wi-Fi when you are not using them.

- Disable ad hoc capabilities to prevent another computer from connecting to your computer directly without using an access point.

- Use antivirus software, and make sure your operating system and browser are up to date.

Disaster Recovery Plan

To supplement backup procedures, businesses and other organizations should have a **disaster recovery plan** (also called a **business continuity plan**)—a plan that spells out what the organization will do to prepare for and recover from a disruptive event, such as a fire, natural disaster, terrorist attack, power outage, or computer failure. Disaster recovery plans should include information about who will be in charge immediately after the disaster has occurred, what alternate facilities and equipment can be used, where backup media is located, the priority of getting each operation back online, disaster insurance coverage information, emergency communications methods, and so forth. If a **hot site**—an alternate location equipped with the computers, cabling, desks, and other equipment necessary to keep a business's operations going—is to be used following a major disaster, it should be set up ahead of time, and information about the hot site should be included in the disaster recovery plan. Businesses that cannot afford to be without email service should also consider making arrangements with an emergency mail system provider to act as a temporary mail server if the company mail server is not functioning. Copies of the disaster recovery plan should be located off-site.

your computer just stop working, computer problems can be a huge inconvenience, as well as cost a great deal of time and money. System failure can occur because of a hardware problem, software problem, or computer virus. It can also occur because of a natural disaster, sabotage, or terrorist attack. Computer hardware consists of relatively delicate components that can be damaged easily by power fluctuations, heat, dust, static electricity, water, and abuse. For instance, fans clogged by dust can cause a computer to overheat; dropping a computer will often break it; and spilling a drink on a keyboard or leaving a mobile phone in the pocket of your jeans while they go through the wash will likely cause some damage.

Exhibit 6-12 Cable locks secure computers and other hardware

 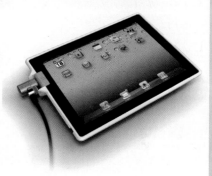

NOTEBOOK LOCK
This combination cable lock connects via a security slot built into the notebook computer.

SECURITY CASE
This iPad security case includes a keyed cable lock.

Courtesy of Kensington Computer Products Group

6-6c Protecting Against Hardware Loss, Hardware Damage, and System Failure

Locked doors and equipment can be simple deterrents to computer theft. To secure computers and other hardware to a table or other object that is difficult to move, you can use cable locks, such as the ones shown in Exhibit 6-12. As an additional precaution with portable computers, you can use laptop alarm software that emits a very loud alarm noise if the computer is unplugged, if USB devices are removed, or if the computer is shut down without the owner's permission.

Encryption can be used to prevent a file from being readable if it is intercepted or viewed by an unauthorized individual. **Full disk encryption** (**FDE**) provides an easy way to protect the data on an entire computer in case it is

> **disaster recovery plan (business continuity plan)** A written plan that describes the steps a company will take following the occurrence of a disaster.
>
> **hot site** An alternate location equipped with the computers and other equipment necessary to keep a business's operations going.
>
> **full disk encryption (FDE)** A technology that encrypts everything stored on a storage medium without any user interaction.

lost or stolen. FDE systems encrypt everything stored on the drive (the operating system, application programs, data, temporary files, and so forth), so users do not have to remember to encrypt sensitive documents, and the encryption is always enabled. A hard drive that uses FDE, which is often referred to as a **self-encrypting hard drive**, typically needs a user-name and password, biometric characteristic, or other authentication control before the computer containing the drive will boot.

Encryption can also be used to protect the data stored on removable storage media; a strong password, a biometric feature, or a PIN (such as is used with the device shown in Exhibit 6-13) is used to provide access to the data on the drive.

> The recovery rate of a lost or stolen computer is about 2 or 3%.

Exhibit 6-13 Encrypted USB flash drive

LOK-IT Secure Flash Drive®

Some software tools are designed to aid in hardware recovery, once a device has been lost or stolen. This can be beneficial because, according to FBI statistics, the recovery rate of a stolen or lost computer is about 2 or 3%. One software tool that can be used to help increase the chances of a stolen or lost computer being recovered is computer tracking software. When a computer with tracking software installed is reported lost or stolen, the computer tracking software sends identifying information, such as location information determined from nearby Wi-Fi networks, to the computer tracking software company on a regular basis when the computer is connected to the Internet so current location information can be provided to law enforcement agencies to help them recover the computer. Some software can even take video or photos with the computer's video camera of the person using the stolen computer to help identify and prosecute the thief.

Often any sign that computer tracking software is running on the computer or is sending information via the Internet is hidden from the user, so the thief is usually not aware that a computer tracking system is installed on the computer. An alternative is tracking software that displays a message on the screen when the computer is lost or stolen, such as a plea to return the device for a reward or a simple statement of "THIS COMPUTER IS STOLEN" in a big, bright banner on the desktop. Some software can also remotely lock the computer and display a message that the device is locked and will not function without the appropriate password.

Another antitheft tool is the use of asset tags on hardware and other expensive assets. These labels usually identify the owner of the asset and are designed to be permanently attached to the asset. Some tags are designed to be indestructible; others are tamper-evident labels that change appearance if someone tries to remove them.

Keep in mind the following precautions when using portable computers and other mobile devices:

▷ Install and use encryption, antivirus, antispyware, and firewall software.

▷ Secure computers with boot passwords; set your mobile phone to autolock after a short period of time, and require a passcode to unlock it.

▷ Use only secure Wi-Fi connections, and disable Wi-Fi and Bluetooth when they are not needed.

▷ Do not store usernames or passwords attached to a computer or inside its case.

▷ Use a plain case to make a portable computer less conspicuous.

▷ Keep an eye on your devices at all times, especially when traveling.

▷ Use a cable lock to secure devices to a desk or other object whenever you must leave them unattended.

▷ Regularly back up your data.

▷ Do not store unencrypted, sensitive data on your device.

self-encrypting hard drive A hard drive that uses full disk encryption (FDE).

Exhibit 6-14 Protective cases

MOBILE PHONE CASE   MOBILE TABLET CASE

Courtesy of OtterBox

Proper care of hardware can help prevent serious damage to a computer system. An obvious precaution is to not harm your hardware physically, such as by dropping a portable computer. To help protect portable devices against minor abuse, use protective cases, as shown in Exhibit 6-14. These cases are typically padded or made from protective material; they also often have a thin, protective layer over the device's display to protect against scratches.

If you need more protection than a case can provide, **ruggedized devices** are designed to withstand much more physical abuse than conventional devices and range from semi-rugged to ultrarugged. See Exhibit 6-15. Ruggedized devices are used most often by individuals who work outside of an office, such as field workers, construction workers, outdoor technicians, military personnel, police officers, and firefighters.

To protect hardware from damage due to power fluctuations, use a **surge suppressor** with a computer whenever it is plugged into a power outlet, as shown in Exhibit 6-16. The surge suppressor prevents electrical power spikes from harming your system. For the best protection, surge suppressors should be used with all of the powered components connected to the computer. Small surge suppressors designed for use on the go are also available as are surge suppressors designed for business and industrial use.

Users who want their desktop computers to remain powered up when the electricity goes off should use an **uninterruptible power supply** (**UPS**), such as the one shown in Exhibit 6-16, which contains a built-in battery. The length of time that a UPS can power a system depends on the type and number of devices connected to the UPS, the power capacity of the UPS device, and the age of the battery. Most UPS devices also protect against power fluctuations.

Exhibit 6-16 Surge suppressors and UPSs

SURGE SUPPRESSOR   UPS

Courtesy of Schneider Electric

Exhibit 6-15 A ruggedized computer

Courtesy General Dynamics Itronix

ruggedized device A device that is designed to withstand much more physical abuse than a conventional device.

surge suppressor A device that protects a computer system from damage due to electrical fluctuations.

uninterruptible power supply (**UPS**) A device containing a built-in battery that provides continuous power to a computer and other connected components when the electricity goes out.

Self-Destructing Devices

Some people or businesses are less concerned about recovering a stolen device than about ensuring the data located on the computer is not compromised. In these instances, devices that self-destruct on command are a viable option. Kill switch capabilities, which are available both as part of some computer tracking software programs and as stand-alone utilities, destroy the data on a device, typically by overwriting preselected files multiple times, rendering them unreadable, when instructed. Kill switches are activated upon customer request when the device is determined to be lost or stolen. Once the kill switch is activated, all data on the computer is erased whenever it next connects to the Internet or when another predesignated remote trigger is activated, such as a certain number of unsuccessful logon attempts.

Lookout app kill switch activated

UPSs designed for use by individuals usually provide power for a few minutes to keep the system powered up during short power blips, as well as to allow the user to save open documents and shut down the computer properly in case the electricity remains off. Industrial-level UPSs typically run for a significantly longer time (up to a few hours) but not long enough to power a facility during an extended power outage.

Dust, heat, static electricity, and moisture can also be dangerous to a computer, so do not place computer equipment in direct sunlight or in a dusty area. You can use a small, handheld vacuum made for electrical equipment periodically to remove the dust from the keyboard and from inside the system unit, but be very careful when vacuuming inside the system unit. Also, be sure the system unit has plenty of ventilation, especially around the fan vents. To help reduce the amount of dust that is drawn into the fan vents, raise your desktop computer several inches off the floor. You should also avoid placing a portable computer on a soft surface, such as a couch or blanket, to help prevent overheating. Unless your computer is ruggedized, do not get it wet or otherwise expose it to adverse conditions.

privacy The state of being concealed or free from unauthorized intrusion.

information privacy The rights of individuals and companies to control how information about them is collected and used.

6-7 Understanding Privacy Concerns

Privacy is usually defined as the state of being concealed or free from unauthorized intrusion. The term **information privacy** refers to the rights of individuals and companies to control how information about them is collected and used. Computers, with their ability to store, duplicate, and manipulate large quantities of data, combined with the fact that databases containing our personal information can be accessed and shared via the Internet, present challenges for protecting personal privacy.

Many people are concerned about the privacy of their Web site activities and email messages. Recently, an unprecedented number of high-profile data breaches have occurred—some via hacking and other network intrusions; others due to lost or stolen hardware, or carelessness with papers or storage media containing Social Security numbers or other sensitive data. Because every data breach is a risk to information privacy, protecting the data stored in databases is an important concern for everyone. Additional privacy concerns are spam and other marketing activities, electronic surveillance, and electronic monitoring.

6-7a Databases, Electronic Profiling, Spam, and Other Marketing Activities

Information about individuals can be located in many different databases. For example, educational institutions have databases containing student information, organizations use databases to hold employee information, and most physicians and health insurance providers maintain databases containing individuals' medical information. If these databases are adequately protected from hackers and other unauthorized individuals, and if the data is not transported on a portable computer or other device that may be vulnerable to loss or theft, these databases do not pose a significant privacy concern to consumers because the information can rarely be shared without the individuals' permission. However, the data stored in these types of databases is not always sufficiently protected and has been breached quite often in the past. Consequently, these databases, along with marketing databases and government databases that are typically associated with a higher risk of personal privacy violations, are of growing concern to privacy advocates.

Marketing databases contain marketing and demographic data about people, such as where they live and what products they buy. This information is used for marketing purposes, including sending advertisements that fit each individual's interests via regular mail or email or trying to sign up people over the phone for some type of service. Almost any time you provide information about yourself online or offline—when you subscribe to a magazine, fill out a product registration card, or buy something using a credit card—there is a good chance that the information will find its way into a marketing database.

Marketing databases are also used in conjunction with Web activities, such as social networking activities and searches performed via some personalized search services. For instance, the data stored on Facebook, MySpace, Google+, and other social networking sites can be gathered and used for advertising purposes by marketing companies, and the activities of users of personalized search services (where users log in to use the service) can be tracked and that data can be used for marketing purposes.

Information about individuals is also available in **government databases**. Some information, such as Social Security earnings and income tax returns, is confidential and can legally be seen only by authorized individuals. Other information, such as birth records, marriage certificates, and divorce information, as well as property purchases, assessments, liens, and tax values, is available to the public, including to the marketing companies that specialize in creating marketing databases.

In the past, the data about any one individual was stored in a variety of separate locations, such as at different government agencies, individual retail stores, the person's bank and credit card companies, and so forth. Because it would be extremely time consuming to locate all the information about one person from all these different places, there was a fairly high level of information privacy. Today, however, most of an individual's data is stored on computers that can communicate with each other via the Internet, which means accessing personal information about someone is much easier than it used to be. For example, a variety of public information about individuals is available free through the Internet, as demonstrated in Exhibit 6-17; paid services are also available that can perform online database searches for you.

Collecting in-depth information about an individual is known as **electronic profiling**. Electronic profiles are generally designed to provide specific information and can include an individual's name, current and previous addresses, telephone number, marital status, number and age of children, spending habits, and product preferences. The information retrieved from electronic profiles is then sold to companies upon request to be used for marketing purposes, as illustrated in Exhibit 6-18. For example, one company might request a list of all individuals in a particular state whose street addresses are considered to be in an affluent area and who buy baby products. Another company might request a list of all SUV owners in a particular city who have not purchased a car in five years.

> Every data breach is a risk to information privacy.

marketing database A collection of data about people that is stored in a large database and used for marketing purposes.

government database A collection of data about people that is collected and maintained by the government.

electronic profiling Using electronic means to collect a variety of in-depth information about an individual, such as name, address, income, and buying habits.

Exhibit 6-17 Searchable databases available via the Internet

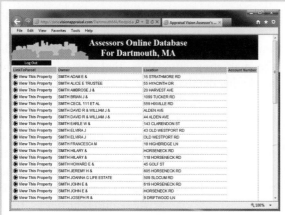

PROPERTY VALUE SEARCH

Some states permit searches for property located in that state, such as displaying the owner's name, address, and a link to additional information including property value for the supplied owner name.

VITAL RECORDS SEARCH

Some counties and states allow searches for documents related to marriages, divorces, births, legal judgments, deeds, liens, powers of attorney, and so forth.

ADDRESS NUMBER AND PHONE NUMBER SEARCH

Any information listed in a U.S. telephone book can be found using this site. You can search either by name or telephone number to view the available information.

Exhibit 6-18 How electronic profiling might work

When you make an electronic transaction, information about who you are and what you buy is recorded, usually in a database.

Databases containing the identities of people and what they buy are sold to marketing companies.

The marketing companies add the new data to their marketing databases; they can then reorganize the data in ways that might be valuable to other companies.

The marketing companies create lists of individuals matching the specific needs of companies; the companies buy the lists for their own marketing purposes.

Most businesses and Web sites that collect personal information have a **privacy policy** that discloses how the personal information you provide will be used (see Exhibit 6-19). As long as their actions do not violate their privacy policy, it is legal for businesses to sell the personal data that they collect. However, privacy policies are sometimes difficult to decipher, and most people do not take the time to read them before using a site. In addition, many businesses periodically change their privacy policies without warning, requiring consumers to reread privacy policies frequently or risk their personal information being used in a manner that they did not agree to when the information was initially provided.

Spam refers to unsolicited email sent to a large group of individuals at one time. The electronic equivalent of junk mail (see Exhibit 6-20), spam is most often used to sell products or services to individuals. Spam is also used in phishing schemes and other dot cons and is sent frequently via botnets. The text message spam shown in Exhibit 6-20 is an example of a phishing spam message. A great deal of spam involves health-related products, counterfeit products, pornography, and fraudulent business opportunities and stock deals. Spam can also be generated by individuals forwarding email messages they receive to everyone in their address books. Spam can also be sent through instant messages, text messages, and fax messages, and via social networking sites such as Facebook and Twitter.

The sheer volume of spam is staggering. Symantec MessageLabs recently estimated that more than 90%

Exhibit 6-19 Web site privacy policy

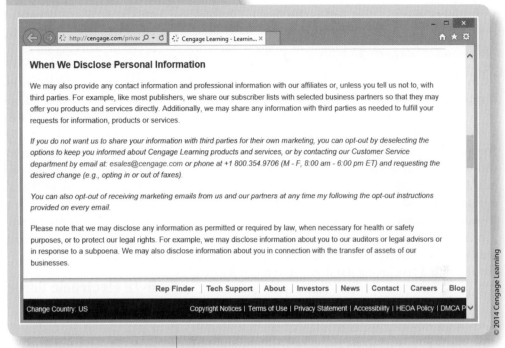

Exhibit 6-20 Examples of spam

EMAIL SPAM

TEXT MESSAGE SPAM

of all email messages is now spam. At best, large volumes of spam are an annoyance to recipients and can slow a mail server's delivery of important messages. At worst, spam can disable a mail network completely,

privacy policy A policy, commonly posted on a company's Web site, that explains how personal information provided to that company will be used.

spam Unsolicited, bulk email sent over the Internet.

or it can cause recipients to miss or lose important email messages because those messages have been caught in a spam filter or were accidentally deleted by the recipient while he or she was deleting a large number of spam email messages. Most Internet users spend several minutes each day dealing with spam, making spam expensive for businesses in terms of lost productivity, consumption of communications bandwidth, and drain of technical support. Spam sent to a mobile phone, either via text message or email, is also expensive for end users who have a limited data or text message allowance.

One of the most common ways of getting on a spam mailing list is by having your email address entered into a marketing database, which can happen when you sign up for a free online service or use your email address to register a product or make an online purchase. Spammers also use software to gather email addresses from Web pages, message board posts, and social networking sites.

To comply with truth-in-advertising laws, an unsubscribe email address included in an unsolicited email must be a working address. If you receive a marketing email from a reputable source, you may be able to unsubscribe by clicking the supplied link or otherwise following the unsubscribe instructions. Because spam from less-legitimate sources often has unsubscribe links that do not work or that are present only to verify that your email address is genuine—a very valuable piece of information for future use—many privacy experts recommend never replying to or trying to unsubscribe from any spam.

6-7b Electronic Surveillance and Monitoring

Electronic tools can be used in many ways to watch individuals, listen in on their conversations, or monitor their activities. Some of these tools, such as devices used by individuals to eavesdrop on wireless telephone conversations, are not legal. Other products and technologies, such as GPS devices that are built into some cars so they can be located if stolen or monitoring ankle bracelets used for offenders sentenced to house arrest, are used solely for law enforcement purposes. Other electronic tools can be used legally by individuals, by businesses in conjunction with employee monitoring, and by law enforcement agencies.

Computer-monitoring software records keystrokes, logs the programs or Web sites accessed, or otherwise monitors someone's computer activity. These programs are typically marketed toward parents, spouses, law enforcement agencies, or employers. Although it is legal to use computer-monitoring software on your own computer or on the computers of your employees, installing it on other computers without the owners' knowledge to monitor their computer activity is usually illegal.

Video surveillance is the use of closed-circuit security cameras to monitor activities taking place at facilities for security purposes. It is routinely used at retail stores, banks, office buildings, and other privately

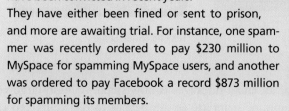
computer-monitoring software
Software that can be used to record an individual's computer usage, such as recording the actual keystrokes used or creating a summary of Web sites and programs accessed.

video surveillance The use of video cameras to monitor activities of individuals for work-related or crime-prevention purposes.

owned facilities that are open to the public, as well as public locations such as streets, parks, airports, sporting arenas, and subway systems for law enforcement purposes.

Public video surveillance systems are often used in conjunction with face recognition technology to try to identify known terrorists and other criminals, to identify criminals when their crimes are caught on tape, and to prevent crimes from occurring. Many privacy advocates object to the use of video surveillance and face recognition technology in public locations; their concerns are primarily based on how the video captured by these systems will be used.

Employee monitoring is the act of recording or observing the actions of employees while on the job. Common employee-monitoring activities include screening telephone calls, reviewing email, and tracking computer and Internet usage. Although many employees feel that being watched at work is an invasion of their personal privacy, it is legal and very common in the United States.

Presence technology is the ability of one computing device on a network to identify another device on the same network and determine its status. It can be used to tell when someone on the network is using his or her computer or mobile phone, as well as the individual's availability for communications, such as whether the individual is able and willing to take a call or respond to an IM at the present time.

6-7c Protecting Personal Privacy

Any business that stores personal information about employees, customers, or other individuals must take adequate security measures to protect the privacy of that information. Secure servers and encryption can protect the data stored on a server; firewalls and access control systems can protect against unauthorized access. To prevent personal information from being sent intentionally or inadvertently in an email message, organizations can use email encryption systems.

A final consideration for protecting the privacy of personal information for both individuals and businesses is protecting the information located on paper documents and hardware that are to be disposed of. Papers, CDs, DVDs, and other media containing sensitive data should be shredded. Because data deleted from a hard drive remains on the drive and can be recovered using special software, the hard drives of computers to be disposed of should be **wiped**—overwritten several times using disk-wiping or disk-erasing software so that the data on it cannot be recovered—before they are sold or recycled. Unlike the data on a drive that has merely been erased or even reformatted (which can still be recovered), data on a properly wiped drive is very difficult or impossible to recover.

Courtesy Fellowes, Inc.

Wiping is typically viewed as an acceptable precaution for deleting sensitive data such as Web site passwords

employee monitoring Observing or reviewing employees' actions while they are on the job.

presence technology Technology that enables one computing device to locate and identify the current status of another device on the same network.

wipe To overwrite a disk several times so that the data on it cannot be recovered.

and tax returns from hard drives and other storage media. However, before disposing of storage media containing sensitive data, businesses should consider physically destroying the media, such as by shredding or melting the hardware. To help with this process, data destruction services can be used.

Protecting your personal information is critical to safeguarding your privacy. Consequently, it makes sense to be cautious about revealing private information to anyone. The following privacy tips can help you safeguard personal information:

> Read a Web site's privacy policy, if one exists, before providing any personal information. If the Web site reserves the right to share your information unless you specifically notify them otherwise, it is best to assume that any information you provide will eventually be shared with others.

> Avoid putting too many personal details on your Web site or on a social networking site. If you want to post photos or other personal documents on a Web site for friends and family members to see, use a photo-sharing site that allows you to restrict access to your photos, such as Flickr, Snapfish, or Fotki. Avoid using location-based services that share your location information with strangers.

> When you sign up for free trials or other services that may result in spam, use a throw-away email address.

> Consider using privacy software, such as Anonymizer Universal or Privacy Guardian, to hide your personal information as you browse the Web so it is not revealed and your activities cannot be tracked by marketers. Also check the privacy settings of the online services that you use to see what control you have over what personal data is collected and shared.

> Supply only the required information when completing an online form. Just because a Web site or registration form asks for personal information, that does not mean you have to give it.

> If you are using a public computer, remove any personal information and settings stored on the computer during your session. You can use browser options to delete this data manually from the computer before you leave. To prevent the deleted data from being recovered, run the Windows Disk Cleanup program on the hard drive, making sure that the options for Temporary Internet Files and the Recycle Bin are selected during the Disk Cleanup process. An easier option is using the private browsing mode offered by some browsers (see Exhibit 6-21) that allows you to browse the Web without leaving any history on the computer you are using. In either case, be sure to log out of any Web sites you were using before leaving the computer.

Data on a properly wiped drive is very difficult or impossible to recover.

Protecting your email address is one of the best ways to avoid spam. One way to accomplish this is to use one private email address for family, friends, colleagues, and other trusted sources. For online shopping, signing up for free offers, message boards, product registration, and other activities that typically lead to junk email, use a disposable or **throw-away email address** (a second address obtained from your ISP or a free email address from a service such as Microsoft Outlook.com or Google Gmail). Another advantage of using a throw-away email address for only noncritical applications is that you can quit using it and obtain a new one if spam begins to get overwhelming or too annoying.

Although keeping your personal information as private as possible can help to reduce spam and other direct marketing activities, filtering can also be helpful. Some ISPs automatically block all email messages originating from known or suspected spammers so those email messages never reach individuals' mailboxes; other ISPs flag suspicious email messages as possible spam, based on their content or subject lines, to warn individuals that those messages may contain spam. To deal with spam that makes it to your computer, you can use an **email filter**—a tool for automatically sorting incoming email messages.

throw-away email address An email address used only for nonessential purposes and activities that may result in spam; the address can be disposed of and replaced if spam becomes a problem.

email filter A tool that automatically sorts incoming email messages based on specific criteria.

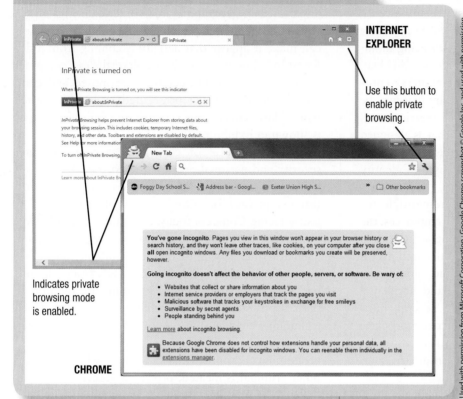

Exhibit 6-21 Private browsing can protect your privacy

INTERNET EXPLORER

Use this button to enable private browsing.

InPrivate is turned on

When InPrivate Browsing is turned on, you will see this indicator

InPrivate Browsing helps prevent Internet Explorer from storing data about your browsing session. This includes cookies, temporary Internet files, history, and other data. Toolbars and extensions are disabled by default.

See Help for more information.

To turn off InPrivate Browsing...

Learn more about InPrivate Br...

Indicates private browsing mode is enabled.

CHROME

You've gone incognito. Pages you view in this window won't appear in your browser history or search history, and they won't leave other traces, like cookies, on your computer after you close all open incognito windows. Any files you download or bookmarks you create will be preserved, however.

Going incognito doesn't affect the behavior of other people, servers, or software. Be wary of:

- Websites that collect or share information about you
- Internet service providers or employers that track the pages you visit
- Malicious software that tracks your keystrokes in exchange for free smileys
- Surveillance by secret agents
- People standing behind you

Learn more about incognito browsing.

Because Google Chrome does not control how extensions handle your personal data, all extensions have been disabled for incognito windows. You can reenable them individually in the extensions manager.

Email filters used to capture spam are called **spam filters**, or sometimes **junk email filters**. Many email programs have built-in spam filters that identify possible spam and either flag it or move it to a Spam or Junk Email folder.

Custom email filters are used to route messages automatically to particular folders based on stated criteria. For example, you can specify that email messages with keywords frequently used in spam subject lines, such as *free*, *porn*, *opportunity*, *last chance*, *weight*, and *pharmacy*, be routed into a folder named Possible Spam, and you can specify that all email messages from your boss's email address be routed into an Urgent folder. Filtering can help you find important messages in your Inbox by preventing it from becoming cluttered with spam. Be sure to check your Junk or Spam folder periodically to locate any email messages mistakenly filed there—especially before you permanently delete those messages.

Another way to reduce the amount of spam you receive is to opt out. **Opting out** refers to following a predesignated procedure to remove yourself from marketing lists or otherwise preventing your personal information from being obtained by or shared with others. By opting out, you instruct companies you do business with not to share your personal information

with third parties. You can also opt out of being contacted by direct and online marketing companies.

Opting-out procedures are confusing and time consuming, and they do not always work well. Consequently, some privacy groups are pushing to change to an **opt-in** process, in which individuals would need to opt in—request participation in—to a particular marketing activity before companies can collect or share any personal data. This is already the case in the European Union. In fact, Walmart recently changed its privacy policy to share information with third parties only if customers opt in. However, the general practice in the U.S. business community is to use your information as allowed for by each privacy policy unless you specifically opt out.

FYI

Chief Privacy Officer

Ensuring that the private data stored by a business is adequately protected is increasingly the responsibility of a chief privacy officer (CPO)—a rapidly growing position in business. CPOs are responsible for ensuring privacy laws are complied with, identifying the data in a company that needs to be protected, developing policies to protect that data, and responding to any incidents that occur. CPOs must also deal with the changing definition of what information is regarded as personal and, therefore, needs to be safeguarded.

spam filter (junk email filter) An email filter used to redirect spam from a user's Inbox.

opt out To request that you be removed from marketing activities or that your information not be shared with other companies.

opt in To request that you be included in marketing activities or that your information be shared with other companies.

There are few options for protecting yourself against computer monitoring by your employer or the government or against video surveillance systems. However, businesses should take the necessary security measures to ensure that employee activities are not being monitored by a hacker or other unauthorized individual. People should also secure their home computers to protect against computer-monitoring software that may be inadvertently installed via an electronic greeting card, game, or other downloaded file, and that is designed to provide a hacker with account numbers, passwords, and other sensitive data that could be used in identity theft or other fraudulent activities.

Businesses and organizations are responsible for keeping private information about their employees, the company, and their customers safe. Strong security measures can help to protect against unauthorized access by hackers. Businesses and organizations should take precautions against both intentional and accidental breaches of privacy by employees. In general, businesses must maintain a safe and productive workplace environment and protect the privacy of their customers and employees, while at the same time ensure the company is not vulnerable to lawsuits.

Employees are responsible for reading a company's employee policy that specifies what personal activities are allowed during company time or on company equipment, as well as what activities, such as Web surfing, email, telephone calls, and downloading files, may be monitored when initially hired. They should review it periodically to ensure that they understand the policy and do not violate any company rules while working for that organization. Because employers can legally monitor at-work activities, it is wise—from a privacy standpoint—to avoid personal activities at work.

6-8 Security and Privacy Legislation

Although new legislation is passed periodically to address new types of computer crimes, it is difficult for the legal system to keep pace with the rate at which technology changes. In addition, both domestic and international jurisdictional issues occur because many computer crimes affect businesses and individuals located in geographic areas other than the one in which the computer criminal is located, and hackers can make it appear that activity is coming from a different location than it really is. Nevertheless, computer crime legislation continues to be proposed and computer crimes are being prosecuted. A list of selected federal laws concerning network and Internet security is shown in Exhibit 6-22.

The high level of concern regarding computer security and personal privacy has led state and federal legislators to pass a variety of laws since the 1970s. Internet privacy is viewed as one of the top policy issues facing Congress today, and numerous bills have been proposed in the last several years regarding spam, telemarketing, spyware, online profiling, and other important privacy issues. However, Congress has had difficulty passing new legislation. In addition to the reasons stated above, including the rate at which technology changes and the jurisdictional issues when computer crimes affect businesses and individuals in geographic areas other than the one in which the computer criminal is located, privacy is difficult to define, and there is a struggle to balance freedom of speech with the right to privacy.

Another issue is weighing the need to implement legislation versus the use of voluntary methods to protect computer security and personal privacy. For instance, the Child Online Protection Act (COPA) has been controversial since it was passed in 1998, and, in fact, it has never been implemented. This legislation prohibited making pornography or any other content deemed harmful to minors available to minors via the Internet. This law was blocked by the U.S. Supreme Court several times, based on the likelihood that it violates the First Amendment and that less restrictive alternatives such as Internet filtering can be used instead to prevent the access of inappropriate materials by minors. A list of selected federal laws related to computer security and privacy are shown in Exhibit 6-23.

Exhibit 6-22 Computer network and Internet security legislation

Date	Law and Description
2004	**Identity Theft Penalty Enhancement Act** Adds extra years to prison sentences for criminals who use identity theft (including the use of stolen credit card numbers) to commit other crimes, including credit card fraud and terrorism.
2003	**CAN-SPAM Act** Implements regulations for unsolicited email messages.
2003	**Fair and Accurate Credit Transactions Act (FACTA)** Amends the Fair Credit Reporting Act (FCRA) to require, among other things, that the three nationwide consumer reporting agencies (Equifax, Experian, and TransUnion) provide to consumers, upon request, a free copy of their credit report once every 12 months.
2003	**PROTECT Act** Includes provisions to prohibit virtual child pornography.
2003	**Health Insurance Portability and Accountability Act (HIPAA)** Includes a Security Rule that sets minimum security standards to protect health information stored electronically.
2002	**Homeland Security Act** Includes provisions to combat cyberterrorism, including protecting ISPs against lawsuits from customers for revealing private information to law enforcement agencies.
2002	**Sarbanes-Oxley Act** Requires archiving a variety of electronic records and protecting the integrity of corporate financial data.
2001	**USA PATRIOT Act** Grants federal authorities expanded surveillance and intelligence-gathering powers, such as broadening the ability of federal agents to obtain the real identity of Internet users, intercept email and other types of Internet communications, follow online activity of suspects, expand their wiretapping authority, and more.
1998	**Identity Theft and Assumption Deterrence Act of 1998** Makes it a federal crime to knowingly use someone else's means of identification, such as name, Social Security number, or credit card, to commit any unlawful activity.
1997	**No Electronic Theft (NET) Act** Expands computer piracy laws to include distribution of copyrighted materials over the Internet.
1996	**National Information Infrastructure Protection Act** Amends the Computer Fraud and Abuse Act of 1984 to punish information theft crossing state lines and to crack down on network trespassing.
1984	**Computer Fraud and Abuse Act of 1984** Makes it a crime to break into computers owned by the federal government. This act has been regularly amended over the years as technology has changed.

Exhibit 6-23 Federal legislation related to computer security and privacy

Date	Law and Description
2009	**American Recovery and Reinvestment Act** Requires HIPAA covered entities to notify patients and/or customers when protected health information has been compromised.
2006	**U.S. SAFE WEB Act of 2006** Grants additional authority to the FTC to help protect consumers from spam, spyware, and Internet fraud and deception.
2005	**Real ID Act** Establishes national standards for state-issued driver's licenses and identification cards.
2005	**Junk Fax Prevention Act** Requires unsolicited faxes to have a highly-visible opt-out notice.
2003	**CAN-SPAM Act** Implements regulations for unsolicited email messages and lays the groundwork for a federal Do Not E-Mail Registry.
2003	**Do Not Call Implementation Act** Amends the Telephone Consumer Protection Act to implement the National Do Not Call Registry.
2003	**Health Insurance Portability and Accountability Act (HIPAA)** Includes a Security Rule that sets minimum security standards to protect health information stored electronically.
2002	**Sarbanes-Oxley Act** Requires archiving a variety of electronic records and protecting the integrity of corporate financial data.
2001	**USA PATRIOT Act** Grants federal authorities expanded surveillance and intelligence-gathering powers, such as broadening the ability of federal agents to obtain the real identity of Internet users and to intercept email and other types of Internet communications.
1999	**Financial Modernization (Gramm-Leach-Bliley) Act** Extends the ability of banks, securities firms, and insurance companies to share consumers' non-public personal information, but requires them to notify consumers and give them the opportunity to opt out before disclosing any information.
1998	**Child Online Protection Act (COPA)** Prohibits online pornography and other content deemed harmful to minors; has been blocked by the Supreme Court.
1998	**Children's Online Privacy Protection Act (COPPA)** Regulates how Web sites can collect information from minors and communicate with them.
1998	**Telephone Anti-Spamming Amendments Act** Applies restrictions to unsolicited, bulk commercial email.
1991	**Telephone Consumer Protection Act** Requires telemarketing companies to respect the rights of people who do not want to be called.
1988	**Computer Matching and Privacy Protection Act** Limits the use of government data in determining federal-benefit recipients.
1988	**Video Privacy Protection Act** Limits disclosure of customer information by video-rental companies.

1. How do many organizations and educational institutions explain acceptable computer use to their employees, students, or other users?

2. What is the typical motivation for hacking?

3. Why might hackers be moving away from targeting data stored on company servers and focusing on stealing data in real time during credit card and debit card transactions?

4. Define botnet.

5. What is malware?

6. How does a DoS attack disable a server?

7. What does antivirus software do?

8. Define phishing.

9. What is online auction fraud?

10. Why are many states and schools reviewing their harassment statutes and bullying policies?

11. How does a firewall help protect a computer?

12. What is a full-disk encryption?

13. What is a secure Web page?

14. What does information privacy refer to?

15. What is electronic profiling?

16. What does computer-monitoring software do?

17. Why would you use a throw-away email address?

18. What is the difference between opt-out and opt-in?

Practice It

Practice It 6-1

New computer viruses and other types of malware are released all the time. Most security companies, such as Symantec and McAfee, list the most recent security threats on their Web sites. In addition to the valid reports about new viruses found in the news and on antivirus software Web sites, reports of viruses that turn out to be hoaxes abound on the Internet. Besides being an annoyance, virus hoaxes waste time and computing resources. Also, they may eventually lead some users to routinely ignore all virus warning messages, leaving them vulnerable to a genuine, destructive virus.

1. Visit the Web site of a security company, and then identify a current virus or worm.

2. When was that virus or worm introduced? What does it do? How is it spread?

3. How many computers have been affected so far?

4. Is there an estimated cost associated with that virus or worm?

5. Is that virus or worm still in existence?

6. On the same Web site, find information about a recent virus hoax.

7. Identify the name of the hoax, when it was discovered, what it purports to do, and what you should do about it.

8. Research general guidelines for identifying virus hoaxes and other types of online hoaxes.

9. Prepare a one- or two-page summary of your findings, and submit it to your instructor.

Practice It 6-2

Some people view using live surveillance cameras as a valid crime-prevention tool; other people think it is an invasion of privacy.

1. Is it ethical for businesses to use video cameras to record customers' activities? If so, for what purposes?

2. Does a government have the responsibility to use every means possible to protect the country and its inhabitants, or do people have the right not to be watched in public?

3. One objection stated about these systems is, "It is not the same as a cop on the corner. This is a cop on every corner." What if it were a live police officer at each public video camera location instead of a camera? Would that be more acceptable from a privacy standpoint?

4. If people do not plan to commit criminal acts in public, should they be concerned that law enforcement personnel may see them? Why or why not?

5. Does the risk of being recorded deter some illegal or unethical acts?

6. Prepare a one- or two-page summary that answers these questions, and submit it to your instructor.

On Your Own

On Your Own 6-1

Although a company's privacy policy may look acceptable when you read it before submitting personal information to that company, no guarantee exists that the policy will not be changed.

1. Locate three different privacy policies on Web sites, and then analyze and compare them.

2. Do the policies specify what personal information might be shared and with whom?

3. Do the organizations reserve the right to change their policies at a later time without notice? If so, will they try to notify consumers?

4. Do any of the policies allow for any sharing of data with third-party organizations? If so, is the data personally identifiable, and can customers opt out?

5. What type of impact do you think a change in a company's privacy policy would have on customer loyalty?

6. Prepare a one- or two-page summary that answers these questions, and submit it to your instructor.

Chapter 6

ADDITIONAL STUDY TOOLS

IN THE BOOK

▶ Complete end-of-chapter exercises
▶ Study tear-out Chapter Review Card

ONLINE

▶ Complete additional end-of-chapter exercises

▶ Take practice quiz to prepare for tests
▶ Review key term flash cards (online, printable, and audio)
▶ Play "Beat the Clock" and "Memory" to quiz yourself
▶ Watch the videos to learn more about the topics taught in this chapter

Answers to Quiz Yourself

1. *Many organizations and education institutions publish codes of conduct to explain acceptable computer use to their employees, students, or other users.*

2. *The typical motivation for hacking is to steal data, sabotage a computer system, or perform some other type of illegal act.*

3. *Hackers might be moving away from targeting data stored on company servers and focusing on stealing data in real time during credit card and debit card transactions due to the Payment Card Industry Data Security Standard (PCI DSS) rules that require companies to limit the credit card data stored on company servers and to encrypt the data that is allowed to be stored.*

4. *A botnet is a group of bots that is controlled by one hacker or other computer criminal.*

5. *Malware is the generic term that refers to any type of malicious software that is written to perform destructive acts.*

6. *A DoS attack disables a server by flooding a network server or Web server with so many requests for action that it shuts down or can no longer handle legitimate requests, causing legitimate users to be denied service.*

7. *Antivirus software protects a computer against computer viruses and other types of malware.*

8. *Phishing is the use of a spoofed email message—an email that appears to come from a legitimate organization but is actually sent from a phisher—to trick the recipient into revealing sensitive personal information that is then used in identity theft and other fraudulent activities.*

9. *Online auction fraud (also called Internet auction fraud) occurs when an online auction buyer pays for merchandise that is never delivered or that is delivered but is not as represented.*

10. *Many states and schools are reviewing their harassment statues and bullying policies because cyberbullying is so common today, affecting as many as half of all U.S. teenagers.*

11. *A firewall helps to protect a computer by essentially creating a barrier between a computer or network and the Internet to protect against unauthorized use.*

12. *Full-disk encryption is a technology that encrypts everything stored on a storage medium without any user interaction.*

13. *A secure Web page is a Web page that uses encryption to protect information transmitted via that Web page.*

14. *Information privacy refers to the rights of individuals and companies to control how information about them is collected and used.*

15. *Electronic profiling uses electronic means to collect a variety of in-depth information about an individual, such as name, address, income, and buying habits.*

16. *Computer-monitoring software records keystrokes, logs the programs or Web site accessed, or otherwise monitors someone's computer activity.*

17. *You would use a throw-away email address for activities that typically lead to junk email to protect your private email address from spam.*

18. *Opting out refers to following a predesignated procedure to remove yourself from marketing lists or otherwise preventing your personal information from being obtained by or shared with others. Opting in refers to requesting participation in a particular marketing activity before companies can collect or share any personal data.*

CAPSTONE

Computer Concepts

Technology is changing our world at an explosive pace. Older technology becomes obsolete very quickly, and new technology is being introduced all the time. Think about some of the technological advances you have seen in the last several months as well as recent technologies that have become obsolete.

1. Discuss the impact of new technology regularly and quickly replacing existing technology. Be sure to consider the personal, business, societal, economic, global, and environmental impacts of the new technology.

2. What benefits does new technology provide? Be sure to consider individuals, businesses, local communities, the country, and the world.

3. What risks are involved or related to new technology? Who is affected by these risks? Can these risks be minimized? If so, how? If not, why not?

4. Do the benefits of new technology outweigh the risks? Who should have the ultimate decision about this—Consumers? Government? Businesses? Explain your answer.

5. What ethical concerns are related to the introduction of new technology?

6. Prepare a two- or three -page summary that answers these questions, and then submit it to your instructor.

Exploring Windows 8 and Managing Files

Andresr/Shutterstock.com; Used with permission from Microsoft Corporation; © 2014 Cengage Learning

Many personal computers use the **Microsoft Windows 8** operating system—Windows 8 for short. *Windows* is the name of the operating system; *8* indicates the version. Windows 8 manages and coordinates activities on your computer and helps your computer perform essential tasks.

In this chapter, you will learn the basics of working with Windows 8 and strategies for organizing files and folders. You will start Windows 8, learn about its features, and then explore its various elements, including windows, apps, file system, and Help. Along the way, you will practice navigating files and folders on your computer, and you will learn how to create, name, copy, move, and delete files and folders. You will also work with compressed files.

Microsoft Windows 8 An operating
system from Microsoft used by many personal computers.

Microsoft product screenshots used with permission from Microsoft Corporation.

Learning Objectives

After studying the material in this chapter,
you will be able to:

7-1 Use the Windows 8 Start screen
and desktop

7-2 Work with windows on the desktop

7-3 Switch between open windows
and running apps

7-4 Work with the Windows 8 file system

7-5 Work with files

7-6 Delete files and work with the
Recycle Bin

7-7 Close apps and windows

7-8 Get help

7-9 Shut down Windows

7-1 Using the Windows 8 Start Screen and Desktop

As the operating system, Windows 8 is the starting point of everything you do on your computer. After you start Windows 8, you need to know how to manipulate the user interface so that you can use your computer to accomplish tasks and activities.

7-1a Starting Windows 8

To start Windows 8, you simply turn your computer on. After completing the boot process, the screen that appears next depends on who last used the computer and whether the computer had been properly shut down or was just sleeping. Once you log in to Windows 8, the Start screen appears, as shown in Exhibit 7-1. The **Start screen** is where you access programs and features of your computer.

CAUTION

Save Your Files

Read each of the steps in the next activity carefully. If the screen described in a step is not the one you see on your computer, read all of the text, but do not do the actions described in that step, and then continue with the next step.

Begin Activity

Start Windows 8.

1 Turn on your computer. After a moment, Windows 8 starts. You might see the lock screen, which displays the current date and time.

2 If the lock screen appears, click anywhere on the screen or press any key to display the next screen. The screen that appears varies.

- If the last person who used the computer signed out of his or her Windows 8 user account, the Welcome screen appears listing all of the user names on the computer.

- If there is only one user account on the computer and the user signed out, the Welcome screen appears showing the user name. If a password is associated with the user account, the password box appears as well.

- If the last person who used the computer did not log out and has a password associated with his or her user account, the Welcome screen appears listing that person's user name and a password box, as well as a Back button.

- If the last person who used the computer did not log out and does *not* have a password associated with his or her user name, the Welcome screen appears briefly, listing that person's user name, and then either the Start screen or the desktop appears, depending on which screen was displayed when that user stopped using the computer.

3 If the Welcome screen appears listing your user name or all the user names on the computer, click your user name if necessary, type the password associated with your user account if any, and then press the **Enter key**. If the Start screen appears (refer to Exhibit 7-1), skip the rest of the steps in this Activity. If the Start screen does not appear, skip Step 4 and continue with Step 5.

4 If the Welcome screen appears listing only the previous user's user name, a password box, and a Back button, click the **Back button** to the left of the user name. All of the user names on the computer appear. Go back to Step 3.

5 If any other screen appears instead of the Start screen (the Start screen is shown in Exhibit 7-1), press the Windows key on the keyboard.

6 On the Start screen, if the user name in the upper-right corner indicates that another user is signed in, click the user name, click **Sign out**, and then go back to Step 3.

End Activity

Start screen The screen on Windows 8 where you can access programs and features of your computer.

Exhibit 7-1 Windows 8 Start screen

your user name

icon

live tile

tile

you might see different tiles or they might be arranged differently on your screen

7-1b Exploring the Start Screen

The Start screen includes multicolored rectangles called **tiles**, which represent applications or other resources, such as Web pages. Some tiles display an **icon**, a small picture that represents a resource available on your computer, such as an application or a file. Other tiles display pictures that preview the contents of the tile. For example, the Weather tile might display current weather conditions in cities around the world. A tile that displays content that is updated on a regular basis is called a **live tile**; the Weather tile is a live tile.

To interact with the Start screen, you use the keyboard and the pointing device. As you learned in Chapter 2, pointing devices come in many shapes and sizes. The most common pointing device is the mouse, so this book uses that term. If you are using a different pointing device, such as a trackball, or if you are using a touch pad or touch screen and your finger is the pointing device, substitute your device whenever you see the term *mouse*.

The **pointer** is a small object, such as an arrow, that moves on the screen when you move your mouse. The pointer is usually shaped like an arrow, although it changes shape depending on the pointer's location on the screen and the tasks you are performing. When you drag the mouse on a surface (or roll the trackball or slide your finger on a touch pad), the pointer on the screen moves in the corresponding direction. If you are using a touch screen, no pointer appears on the screen; you simply touch the part of the screen you want to interact with.

You use the mouse to perform specific actions:

▶ **Point**—to position the pointer directly on top of an item.

▶ **Click**—to press the left mouse button and immediately release it. (On a touch pad or touch screen, tap the screen with your finger.)

tile A rectangle on the Windows 8 Start screen that represents an application or another resource.

icon A small picture that represents a resource on your computer.

live tile A tile that displays content that is regularly updated.

pointer A small object, such as an arrow, that moves on the screen when you move your mouse.

point To position the pointer directly on top of an item.

click To press the left mouse button and immediately release it.

Exhibit 7-2 Scroll bar and Zoom button on the Start screen

scroll bar

Zoom button

▶ **Right-click**—to click the right mouse button and immediately release it. (On a touch screen, press and hold your finger in a spot on the screen.)

▶ **Double-click**—to click the left mouse button twice in quick succession. (On a touch pad or touch screen, double-tap the screen with your finger.)

▶ **Drag**—to position the pointer on top of an item, and then press and hold the left mouse button while moving the pointer. (On a touch screen, swipe your finger over the item or items you want to drag to select them, and then press and hold your finger over the selected item or items and slide your finger on the screen.)

If the Start screen contains more tiles than fit on one screen, you can point to the right edge of the Start screen to scroll, which shifts the screen display to show any tiles that are out of view. When you move the pointer, a scroll bar appears at the bottom of the screen indicating that the screen includes content that is out of view. See Exhibit 7-2. (Some screens display both vertical and horizontal scroll bars.) You can drag the scroll bar or click the arrows at either end of the scroll bar to scroll. If you are using a tablet or a computer with a touch screen, you touch a blank area of the screen and drag to the left.

You can also zoom the Start screen so the tiles appear smaller and more tiles fit on the screen at once. See Exhibit 7-3. You do so by clicking the Zoom button ▬, which appears in the lower-right corner of the Start screen, to the right of the scroll bar, when you move the pointer. If you are using a touch screen, you move two fingers closer together (pinch) on the screen.

When you position the pointer in the upper- or lower-right corner of the screen, icons called charms appear on the right edge of the Start screen, as shown in Exhibit 7-3. **Charms** are commands that you click to perform common tasks in Windows 8. Charms are located on the **Charms bar**. When you move the pointer onto the Charms bar, its background turns black and a black status box appears on the bottom-left corner of

the screen displaying the date and time. The status box might also display other status information, such as the strength of your network connection or battery level. See Exhibit 7-4.

Begin Activity

Explore the Start screen.

1 Move the pointing device so that the pointer moves to the right edge of the Start screen—that is, point to the right edge of the screen. Make sure you do not point to the upper- or lower-right corner of the screen. (If you are using a touch screen, drag a blank area of the screen from right to left.) The screen scrolls to display additional tiles.

2 Move the pointer so that the scroll bar appears at the bottom of the screen, and then click the **left scroll arrow** ◀ . (If you are using a touch screen, drag a blank area of the screen from left to right.) The screen scrolls back to the left.

> **Problem?** If the screen does not scroll, make sure you position the pointer on the very edge of the Start screen. If your Start screen contains additional tiles and the screen still does not scroll, click the **right scroll arrow** ▶ on the scroll bar at the bottom of the screen to scroll to the right.

right-click To click the right mouse button and immediately release it.

double-click To click the left mouse button twice in quick succession.

drag To position the pointer on top of an item, and then press and hold the left mouse button while moving the pointer.

charm A command that appears on the Charms bar.

Charms bar A bar that appears on right edge of the Start screen that contains commands for interacting with Windows 8.

Exhibit 7-3 Start screen zoomed out and the Charms bar

Charms bar

tiles are smaller so more are displayed on the Start screen

Exhibit 7-4 Active Charms bar and status box

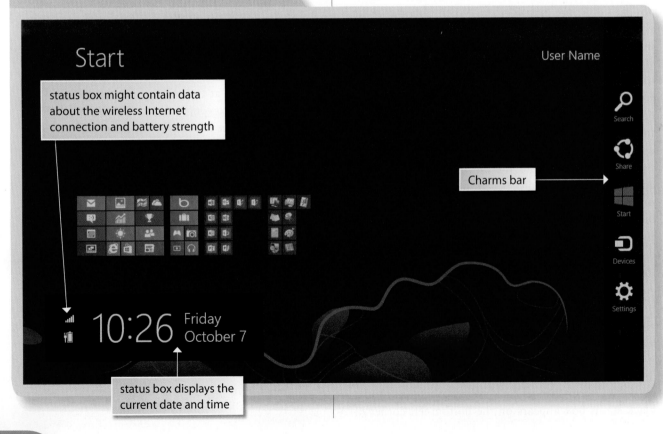

status box might contain data about the wireless Internet connection and battery strength

Charms bar

status box displays the current date and time

3 Move the pointer so that the scroll bar appears, and then click the **Zoom button** ▬. (If you have a touch screen, pinch two fingers closer together.) The tiles on the screen shrink to a smaller size so that you can see all of the tiles on the screen at once and blank space appears around the tiles.

4 Point to the upper-right corner of the screen. The Charms bar appears along the right edge of the screen. Refer back to Exhibit 7-3.

5 Move the pointer on top of the **Charms bar** so that its background turns black and the status box appears in the bottom-left corner of the screen. Refer back to Exhibit 7-4.

6 Click the **Settings charm**. The Settings panel appears in place of the Charms bar. You can adjust various settings for your computer from here, including connecting to a wireless network and adjusting the volume of your speakers.

> **Tip:** You can also press and hold down the Windows key and then press C to display the Charms bar.

7 Click a blank area of the screen. The Settings panel closes.

8 Click a **blank spot** on the Start screen. (If you are using a touch screen, spread (stretch) two fingers apart.) The tiles return to their original size.

End Activity

LEARN MORE

Using a Microsoft Account

A **Microsoft account** is a free account that you can create that associates an email address and password with Microsoft cloud services, such as Outlook.com for email, SkyDrive for file storage, and Xbox Live for games. If you sign into Windows 8 with an email address and password, you are using a Microsoft account. If you are not signed in to Windows 8 with a Microsoft account, you can sign in to your Microsoft account to use apps that require it, such as Mail (an app used to send and receive email messages) and Messaging (an app used to send and receive instant messages). You can also sign in to your Microsoft account to access and share files and other data stored on SkyDrive, which is free storage space provided on Microsoft's server. For example, you can store photos in a folder on your SkyDrive, and you can use the Photos app to display those photos on your PC and share them with others.

7-1c Switching Between the Start Screen and the Desktop

The **desktop** is the work area for using applications designed to run in Windows and where you manage files and folders. See Exhibit 7-5. Desktop applications do not use the Windows 8 interface. To switch to the desktop from the Start screen, you can click the Desktop tile on the Start screen. To return to the Start screen from the desktop, you can point to the lower-left corner of the screen to display a **thumbnail** (a miniature image) of the Start screen, as shown in Exhibit 7-6, and then click the thumbnail, or you can click the Start charm on the Charms bar. You can also press the Windows key on the keyboard.

Pressing the Windows key is an example of using a **keyboard shortcut**, which means you press one or more keys on the keyboard to perform an action. If you press the Windows key when the Start screen is displayed, you return to your previous location.

Begin Activity

Switch between the Start screen and the desktop.

1 On the Start screen, click the **Desktop tile** to display the desktop. (The Desktop tile is usually at the bottom of the first column of tiles.) The desktop appears in place of the Start screen. Refer to Exhibit 7-5. Your desktop might contain additional or different items, and you might see a different background.

2 Point to the lower-left corner of the screen. A thumbnail of the Start screen appears. Refer to Exhibit 7-6.

3 Click the **Start screen thumbnail**. The Start screen reappears.

> **Microsoft account** A free account that you can create that associates an email address and password with Microsoft cloud services.
>
> **desktop** The work area for using applications designed to run in Windows and for managing files and folders.
>
> **thumbnail** A miniature image.
>
> **keyboard shortcut** A key or combination of keys that performs a command.

Exhibit 7-5 Windows 8 desktop

Exhibit 7-6 Start screen thumbnail displayed on the desktop

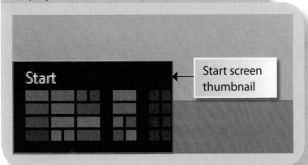

Start screen thumbnail

4 Press the **Windows key** ⊞. The desktop appears again.

Tip: When the desktop is displayed, press the Windows key to display the Start screen.

taskbar The horizontal bar containing buttons that provide quick access to common tools and running programs and buttons to start some programs.

button An object that you click to execute a command or perform a task.

5 Point to the upper-right corner of the screen. The Charms bar appears.

6 On the Charms bar, click the **Start charm** ⊞. The Start screen appears again.

7 Display the desktop again.

End Activity

7-1d Exploring the Desktop

Most of the features you use on the Start screen are available on the desktop. For example, you can point to the upper- or lower-right corners to display the Charms bar. In addition, the desktop includes the following features, as shown in Exhibit 7-7:

▶ **Taskbar**—the horizontal bar containing buttons that provide quick access to common tools and running programs and buttons to start some programs.

▶ **Button**—an object that you click to execute a command or perform a task.

Exhibit 7-7 Windows 8 desktop with a ScreenTip displayed

Recycle Bin

buttons

taskbar

ScreenTip

Friday, October 07, 2016

7:49 AM
10/7/2016

notification area

▶ **Notification area**—the area on the right end of the taskbar containing icons that provide information about the computer and some of the programs that are running, as well as display the current date and time.

▶ **Recycle Bin**—the icon for a folder that stores items deleted from the hard drive until you remove them permanently.

The graphic on the screen when the desktop is displayed and the colors used in the background are part of a **theme**, which, in Windows, is a set of desktop backgrounds, colors, sounds, and screen savers.

Interacting with the desktop is a little different from interacting with the Start screen. When you want more information about an item on the desktop, you can use the mouse to point to that item to make a **ScreenTip** appear, which identifies the name or purpose of the item. (ScreenTips do not appear on a touch screen.) In Exhibit 7-7, the ScreenTip for the date on the taskbar is displayed.

When you want to work with an item on the desktop, you need to select that item by clicking it. Clicking sends a signal to the computer that you want to perform an action on the object you clicked. When you right-click an item, the object is selected and a

shortcut menu opens. A **menu** is a group or list of commands that you click to complete tasks. A **shortcut menu** lists actions you can take with the item you right-clicked. You can right-click practically anything on the desktop, including a blank area of the desktop, to view commands associated with that item. Shortcut menus provide the commands you need where you need them. Exhibit 7-8 shows the shortcut menu for the Recycle Bin.

notification area The part of the taskbar that displays icons that provide information about the computer and programs that are running.

Recycle Bin Storage for items deleted from the hard drive until you remove them permanently.

theme In Windows, a set of desktop backgrounds, colors, sounds, and screen savers.

ScreenTip A box that appears when you point to an item that displays information about the item, such as its name or purpose.

menu A group or list of commands that you click to complete tasks.

shortcut menu A menu that lists actions you can take with the item you right-clicked.

Exhibit 7-8 Recycle Bin shortcut menu

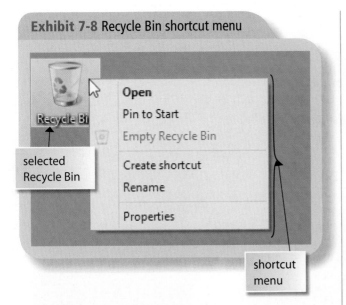

selected
Recycle Bin

Open
Pin to Start
Empty Recycle Bin

Create shortcut
Rename

Properties

shortcut
menu

LEARN MORE

Changing the Desktop Theme

The default desktop you see after you first install Windows 8 has a blue background with a picture of two daisies, as shown in Exhibits 7-7 and 7-8. You can easily change the appearance of the desktop. To change the desktop theme, right-click a blank area of the desktop to open the desktop shortcut menu, and then click Personalize to open the Personalization window. Click a theme in the box to select it, and then close the Personalization window. The desktop will be updated to show the theme you selected.

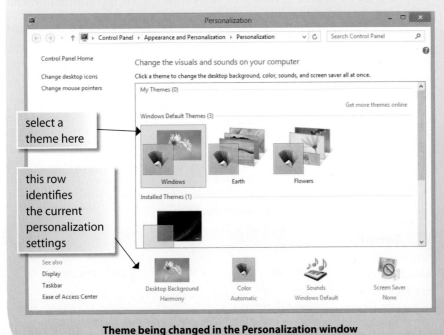

select a
theme here

this row
identifies
the current
personalization
settings

Theme being changed in the Personalization window

app A program designed to use the Windows 8 interface and work with touch screen devices.

Begin Activity

Explore the desktop.

1 On the taskbar, in the notification area, point to the **date and time**. Its ScreenTip appears showing the long version of the current date. Refer back to Exhibit 7-7.

2 On your desktop, point to the **Recycle Bin icon**. A light shaded box appears around it.

3 Point to the **desktop**. The box disappears from around the Recycle Bin.

4 Click the **Recycle Bin**, and then point to the **desktop**. The Recycle Bin is selected as indicated by the shaded box around it.

5 Right-click the **Recycle Bin**. The Recycle Bin shortcut menu opens. Refer back to Exhibit 7-8. The commands on this menu are actions you can take with the Recycle Bin.

6 Click a blank area of the desktop. The shortcut menu closes without you selecting a command.

7 Right-click a blank area of the desktop. The desktop shortcut menu opens. The commands differ from the commands that you saw on the Recycle Bin shortcut menu.

8 Press the **Esc key**. The shortcut menu closes without selecting a command.

9 Switch back to the **Start screen**.

End Activity

7-1e Starting Apps and Applications

Two types of programs run on Windows 8. Windows 8 **apps** are designed to use the Windows 8 interface (they will not work with earlier versions of Windows) and work with

Exhibit 7-9 Apps screen and the Search panel

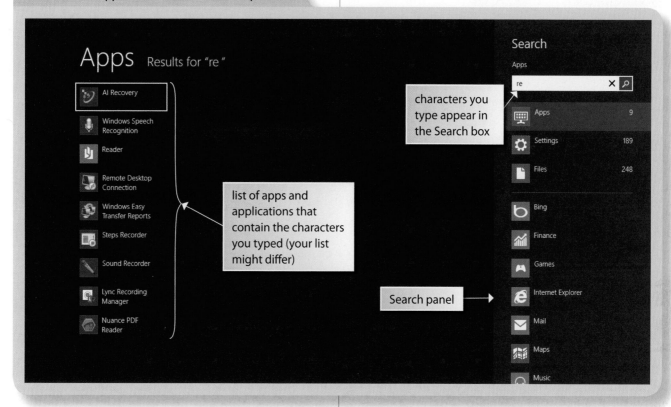

touch screen devices. **Desktop applications** are programs designed to run on the desktop in a window, and most will run on earlier versions of Windows. A **window** is a rectangular work area on the desktop that contains a program, text, files, or other data and tools for performing tasks. The programs included with Microsoft Office 2013 are desktop applications.

To start an app or a desktop application whose tile is on the Start screen, you can click it. If you do not see a tile for the app or application you want to start, you can simply start typing its name. When you begin typing, the Start screen is replaced by the Apps screen and the Search panel opens on the right, as shown in Exhibit 7-9. All the programs whose names contain the characters you are typing are listed, and the characters you type appear in the Search box. You can also click the Search charm to display the Apps screen with the Search panel open.

When you start an app, it fills the screen. The Weather app is shown in Exhibit 7-10. When you start a desktop application, the desktop appears and the application opens in a window. Exhibit 7-11 shows the Paint and Calculator windows open on the desktop.

Begin Activity

Start apps and applications.

1 On the Start screen, click the **Weather tile**. The Weather app opens. Refer to Exhibit 7-10.

2 Point to the lower-left corner of the screen, click the **Start screen thumbnail**, and then type **re.** The Apps screen appears with a list of programs that contain the letters *re.* Refer back to Exhibit 7-9. The Search panel also appears, and the letters you typed appear in the Search box. The search results include the Reader app. Reader is an app that lets you read and manage PDF documents, which are files in the Portable Document Format.

Problem? If settings or files appear in the search results, in the Search panel, click Apps in the Search panel, and then repeat Step 2 if necessary.

> **desktop application (application)** A program designed to run in a window on the desktop.
>
> **window** A rectangular work area on the desktop that contains a program, text, files, or other data and tools for performing tasks.

Exhibit 7-10 Weather app

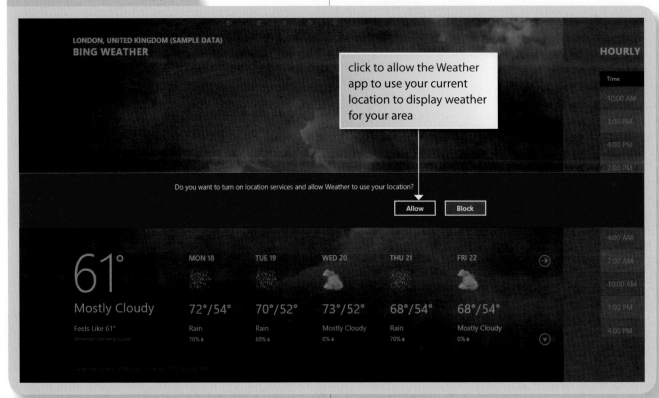

LONDON, UNITED KINGDOM (SAMPLE DATA)
BING WEATHER

HOURLY

Time

10:00 AM

1:00 PM

4:00 PM

7:00 PM

click to allow the Weather
app to use your current
location to display weather
for your area

Do you want to turn on location services and allow Weather to use your location?

[Allow]   [Block]

4:00 AM

7:00 AM

61°   MON 18   TUE 19   WED 20   THU 21   FRI 22

10:00 AM

Mostly Cloudy   72°/54°   70°/52°   73°/52°   68°/54°   68°/54°   1:00 PM

Feels Like 61°   Rain   Rain   Mostly Cloudy Rain   Mostly Cloudy   4:00 PM
Weather Underground 70%   60%   0%   70%   0%

Exhibit 7-11 Paint and Calculator application windows open on the desktop

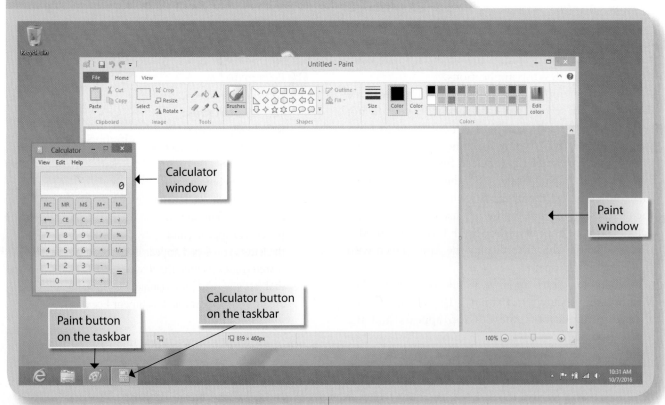

Recycle Bin

Untitled - Paint

Calculator
window

Paint
window

Calculator button
on the taskbar

Paint button
on the taskbar

10:31 AM
10/7/2016

3 In the list of search results on the Apps screen, click **Reader**. The Reader app starts. Now two apps are running.

4 Switch to the **Start screen**, type **paint**, and then click **Paint** in the list of search results on the Apps screen. Paint is a desktop application that you use to draw, color, and edit pictures. The desktop appears, and the Paint application window opens. The text *Untitled – Paint* appears at the top of the open window. A button corresponding to the Paint window appears on the taskbar.

5 Switch to the **Start screen** again, type **calc**, and then click **Calculator** in the list of search results. The desktop appears, the Calculator application window appears on top of the Paint application window, and its button appears on the taskbar. Refer back to Exhibit 7-11.

End Activity

LEARN MORE

Using the Search Panel

You use the Search panel to search for anything stored on your computer including documents, pictures, music, videos, and settings as well as apps and applications. Below the Search box in the Search panel is a list of the three categories of items you can search for: Apps, Settings, and Files. You have already used the Search panel to find apps by typing the app's name and then selecting the app on the Apps screen. When you enter text in the Search box, a number appears to the right of each category indicating the number of results related to the search text in Apps, Settings, and Files. To locate settings related to the text already entered, click Settings in the category list to display the Settings screen. To locate files related to the search text, click Files in the category list. The Files screen opens and displays files that contain the text you typed in their file names, contents, or file details. You can also click the appropriate category, and then type the text you want to search for in the Apps, Settings, or Files category.

Tip: To display the Apps screen without displaying the Search panel, right-click a blank area of the Start screen, and then click All apps on the Apps bar at the bottom of the screen.

desktop application starts and display commands for working with the program and the program's workspace. You opened two application windows when you started the desktop applications—Paint and Calculator. You use **File Explorer windows** to navigate, view, and work with the contents and resources on your computer. **Dialog boxes** are a special kind of window in which you enter or choose settings for how you want to perform a task.

All windows have a **title bar** at the top of the window that displays the name of the window. They also have a Close button [×] at the right end of the title bar that you can click to close the window.

application window A window that opens when an application starts and displays commands for working with the program and the program's workspace.

File Explorer window A window you use to navigate, view, and work with the contents and resources on your computer.

dialog box A window that opens when you need to enter or choose settings for how you want to perform a task.

title bar A banner at the top of a window that displays the window title and contains the Close button and sizing buttons.

7-2 Resizing and Moving Windows on the Desktop

When you work on the desktop, you interact with windows. There are three types of windows: application windows, File Explorer windows, and dialog boxes. **Application windows** open when a

Exhibit 7-12 Common window elements

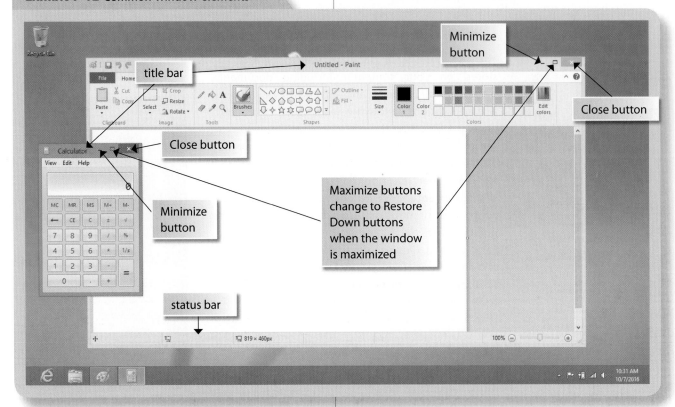

Application windows and File Explorer windows also have **sizing buttons**, located to the left of the Close button on the title bar, to enlarge or shrink a window. Most application and File Explorer windows have a **status bar** at the bottom of the window that displays information or messages about the task you are performing or the selected item. See Exhibit 7-12.

When more than one window is open on the desktop, only one can be the **active window**, the window to which the next keystroke or command is applied. If two or more windows overlap, the active window appears in front of the other windows. The button for the active window is highlighted on the taskbar.

After you open a window, you can change its size and position. The sizing buttons appear on the right end of the title bar. The first button is the Minimize button ⬛, which shrinks a window to its button on the taskbar. A minimized window is still open. You can redisplay a minimized window by clicking the window's button on the taskbar or by pointing to the button on the taskbar and then clicking the thumbnail that appears.

The next sizing button changes depending on the state of the window. If the window is not as large as it can be on the screen, the button is the Maximize button ⬜ . When you click the Maximize button, the window resizes to fill the screen. When the window is maximized, the button is the Restore Down button ⬜. Clicking the Restore Down button returns the window to the size it was before you maximized it.

You can also resize a window manually, if it not maximized. When you point to a window border, the pointer changes to a two-headed arrow. Using the two-headed arrow pointer, you drag the window border until the window is the size you want. To move a window to a new position on the screen, you drag the window by its title bar. You cannot reposition a maximized window.

sizing buttons The buttons used to enlarge or shrink a window.

status bar A banner at the bottom of a window that displays information or messages about the task you are performing or the selected item.

active window The window to which the next keystroke or command is applied.

Modifying the Start Screen

You can add tiles to the Start screen for any app, application, or folder installed on your computer and for commands such as the Shut down command. This is called **pinning**, which means the tile is permanently displayed, as if it were pinned in place. Likewise, removing a tile from the Start screen is called **unpinning**. You can also rearrange tiles and remove tiles for the apps you don't use. To pin an app or application to the Start screen, display the program on the Apps screen, and then right-click the app or application on the Apps screen. The Apps bar opens at the bottom of the screen, and the app or application you clicked is highlighted with a check mark. This means it is selected. On the Apps bar, click the Pin to Start button.

You can arrange the tiles on the Start screen into groups. For example, you might want to keep folders in one group, entertainment apps such as Music and Games in another group, and apps for keeping in touch with people, such as Mail, Messaging, and People, in a different group. You can also rearrange tiles within a group.

After organizing tiles into groups, you can move groups to different locations on the Start screen. To do so, zoom the Start screen to display all of the tiles at once, right-click a tile on the zoomed Start screen to select the group, and then drag the selected group to its new position.

Begin Activity

Resize and move windows.

1 On the Calculator window title bar, click the **Minimize button** −. The Calculator window shrinks to its button on the taskbar.

2 Minimize the Paint window.

3 On the taskbar, point to the **Paint button** . A thumbnail of the Paint window appears.

> **Problem?** If the Paint window fills the entire screen, click the Restore Down button . If the Paint window fills the screen and the Maximize button appears, point to a screen border so that the pointer changes to or , drag the border in to make the window smaller, and then click the Calculator window title bar.

4 Move the pointer on top of the **Paint window thumbnail**. A small Close button X appears on the thumbnail, and the Paint window reappears on the desktop.

5 Move the pointer off the **Paint window thumbnail**. The thumbnail and the Paint window on the desktop disappear.

6 Point to the **Paint button** , and then click the Paint **window thumbnail**. The Paint window reappears on the desktop.

7 On the Paint window title bar, click the **Maximize button** . The Paint window expands to fill the screen.

8 On the Paint window title bar, click the **Restore Down button** . The Paint window returns to its previous size.

9 Point to the **Paint window title bar**, press and hold down the left mouse button, and then drag in one direction. The window moves as you move the mouse.

10 Position the Paint window anywhere on the desktop, and then release the mouse button. The Paint window stays in its new location.

11 Point to the left border of the Paint window so that the pointer changes to ↔, and then drag the border to the left about an inch. The window widens by the amount you dragged.

12 Drag the left border of the Paint window to the right about an inch to return the window to its previous size.

13 Drag the Paint window by its title bar to reposition it in its original location.

End Activity

7-3 Switching Between Open Windows and Running Apps

Because only one window is active at a time, you must switch between windows if you want to work in another window. To make a window active, you can click in it or you can click its button on the taskbar.

> **pin** To permanently display an item.
>
> **unpin** To remove a pinned item so that it is no longer displayed.

Likewise, only one app can be active at a time. When more than one app is running, the apps that are not visible are running in the background. To switch between open apps, point to the upper-left corner of the screen to display a thumbnail of the most recently used app, and then slide the pointer down to display the **Switch List**, a list containing a thumbnail for each running app except the current one. You can click a thumbnail in the Switch List to switch to that app. Exhibit 7-13 shows the Switch List open on the desktop. The Switch List includes thumbnails for only Windows 8 apps, not desktop applications. Because Windows 8 treats the desktop as an app, the Switch List displays one thumbnail for the desktop.

Exhibit 7-13 Switch List displayed on the desktop

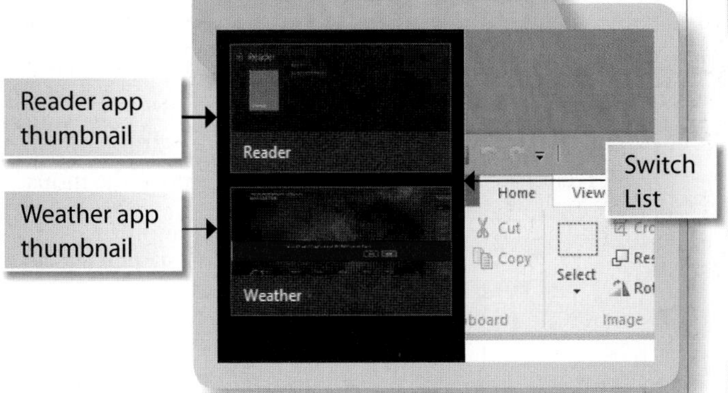

Reader app thumbnail

Weather app thumbnail

Switch List

You can also use a keyboard shortcut to switch from one open window and running app to another. With either the desktop or the Start screen displayed, you can press and hold the Alt key, and then press and release the Tab key to display all the open windows and running programs as thumbnails in the center of the screen. See Exhibit 7-14. Each time you press the Tab key, the selection box moves from one thumbnail to the next and the screen corresponding to that window or program appears behind the thumbnails.

Begin Activity

Switch between open windows and running apps.

1 Point to the upper-left corner of the screen. A thumbnail of the Reader app appears.

Switch List A list that contains all of the apps that are currently running.

snap To display an app on the left or right side of the screen and leave it open as you work in other apps.

2 Slide the pointer down the screen. The Switch List appears containing thumbnails of the Reader app and the Weather app. The Start screen thumbnail appears at the bottom of the Switch List. Refer back to Exhibit 7-13.

3 Click the **Weather app thumbnail**. The Weather app becomes the current app.

4 Display the **Switch List** again. Notice that the Desktop app now appears on the Switch List.

5 Click the **Desktop app thumbnail**. The desktop becomes the current app.

6 On the taskbar, click the **Calculator button**. The Calculator window opens and is the active window.

7 Press and hold the **Alt key**, and then press and release the **Tab key** without releasing the Alt key. The two open desktop applications (Paint and Calculator) and the three open apps (Weather, Reader, and Desktop) appear as thumbnails in the center of the screen.

8 With the Alt key still pressed, press the **Tab key** as many times as needed to select the Weather app thumbnail and display the Weather app behind the thumbnails. Refer to Exhibit 7-14.

9 Release the **Alt key**. The Weather app is the current app.

10 Use the **Switch List** to redisplay the **Desktop app**.

End Activity

FYI

Snapping Apps

Windows 8 apps start and run as full-screen programs so you can focus on your task and the content of the app. If you need to refer to information in one app while you are working in another app and if you are using a high screen resolution (at least 1366 × 768), you can **snap** an app, which means you display an app on the left or right side of the screen and leave it open as you work in other apps. To do this, switch to an open app, and then display the Switch List. Right-click the thumbnail for the other app you want to work with, and then click Snap left or Snap right on the shortcut menu to snap the app to the other side of the screen. To unsnap apps, point to the top of a snapped app, and then drag the app to the bottom of the screen. This both unsnaps and closes the app.

Exhibit 7-14 Thumbnails showing open programs and windows

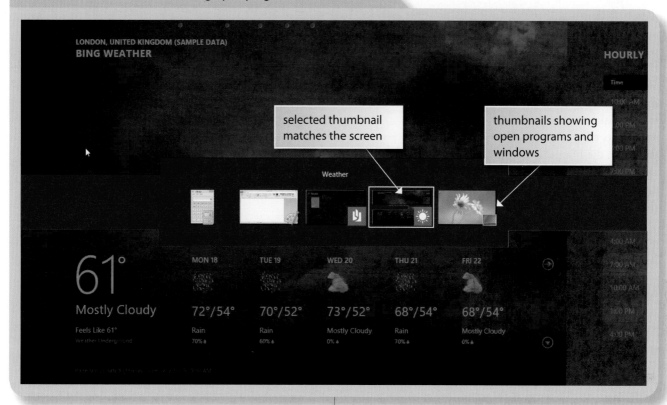

LONDON, UNITED KINGDOM (SAMPLE DATA)
BING WEATHER

HOURLY

selected thumbnail matches the screen

thumbnails showing open programs and windows

Weather

61°

Mostly Cloudy

Feels Like 61°

MON 18	TUE 19	WED 20	THU 21	FRI 22
72°/54°	70°/52°	73°/52°	68°/54°	68°/54°
Rain	Rain	Mostly Cloudy	Rain	Mostly Cloudy
70%	60%	0%	70%	0%

7-4 Working with the Windows 8 File System

A computer can store folders and files on different types of disks, ranging from removable media—such as USB drives, CDs, and DVDs—to hard disks, which are permanently stored on a computer. A computer distinguishes one disk drive from another by assigning each a drive letter. The hard disk is usually assigned to drive C. The remaining drives can have any other letters but are usually assigned in the order that the drives were installed on the computer. For example, your USB drive might be drive D or drive G.

Drives are organized into folders. A **folder** is a container that helps to organize files on a computer, just like a paper folder is used to organize files in a file cabinet. When you open a Files Explorer window, you are looking at the contents of the computer, a drive, or a folder. In Windows 8, files and folders are also organized into libraries. **Libraries** are a feature of Windows by which files and folders are recognized by category—documents, videos, pictures, and music. Windows recognizes

which category a file fits into based upon its file type. In File Explorer, a library organizes your files by these categories so you can easily locate them. For example, if you store some music files on your hard drive and others on an external drive, such as a digital music player attached to your computer, they all appear in the Music library.

Windows stores thousands of files in many folders on the hard disk of your computer. These are system files that Windows needs to display the desktop, use drives, and perform other operating system tasks. To ensure system stability and to find files quickly, Windows 8 organizes the folders and files on your drives in a hierarchy, or **file system**. At the top of the hierarchy, Windows stores folders and files that it needs when you turn on the computer. This location is called the **root directory** and is usually drive C (the hard disk). The term *root* refers to a

folder A container that helps to organize files on a computer.

library A feature of Windows by which files and folders are recognized by category.

file system The hierarchy of how files and folders are organized.

root directory The top of the file system where Windows stores folders and files that it needs when you turn on the computer.

popular metaphor for visualizing a file system—an upside-down tree, which reflects the file hierarchy that Windows uses. In Exhibit 7-15, the tree trunk corresponds to the root directory, the branches to the folders, and the leaves to the files.

Some folders contain other folders. An effectively organized computer contains a few folders in the root directory, and those folders contain other folders, also called **subfolders**.

The root directory, or top level, of the hard disk is only for system files and folders. You should not store your own work here because it could interfere with Windows or a program.

7-4a Opening a File Explorer Window

Remember that you use File Explorer windows to navigate, view, and work with the contents and resources on your computer. In addition to the title bar, sizing buttons, and status bar, File Explorer windows

Exhibit 7-15 Windows file hierarchy

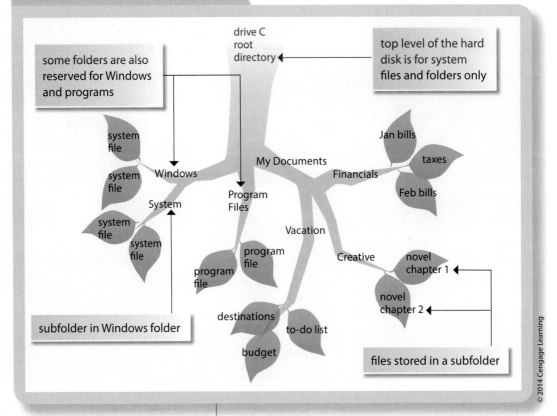

some folders are also reserved for Windows and programs

top level of the hard disk is for system files and folders only

drive C root directory

system file

system file

Windows

System

system file

system file

program file

Program Files

My Documents

Financials

Jan bills

taxes

Feb bills

Vacation

Creative

novel chapter 1

novel chapter 2

program file

subfolder in Windows folder

destinations

budget

to-do list

files stored in a subfolder

© 2014 Cengage Learning

contain the following elements, which are called out in Exhibit 7-16:

- **Quick Access Toolbar**—contains buttons for frequently used commands.

- **Ribbon**—contains commands for working with the contents of the window organized into tabs of related activities or tasks. Each tab is organized into groups of related commands. As you open different folders and navigate with File Explorer, new tabs appear at the top of the window to the right of the existing tabs. This type of tab is called a contextual tab, and it contains options related to your current task. For example, the Picture Tools Manage tab appears when you navigate to the Pictures library and contains options for working with pictures.

- **Help button**—accesses Windows Help.

- **Navigation buttons**—returns the display to a previously viewed window.

- **Address bar**—lists the location of the currently displayed folder.

- **Search box**—locates an item in the current location that matches the key words you typed in it.

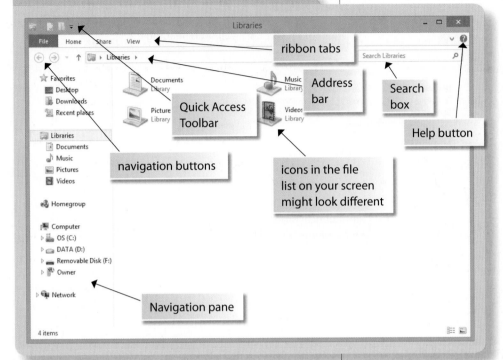

Exhibit 7-16 File Explorer window in Tiles view

ribbon tabs

Quick Access Toolbar

Address bar

Search box

navigation buttons

icons in the file list on your screen might look different

Help button

Navigation pane

▶ **Navigation pane**—contains icons and links to locations on your computer and your network organized into five categories: Favorites (for locations you access frequently), Libraries (for the Windows default libraries), Homegroup (for your shared home network, if any), Computer (for the drives and devices on your computer), and Network (for network locations your computer can access).

▶ **File list**—displays the contents of the current location or the results found after using the Search box.

Begin Activity

Open File Explorer windows.

1 On the taskbar, point to the **File Explorer button** to see its ScreenTip.

2 Click the **File Explorer button** . A File Explorer window named Libraries opens. Refer back to Exhibit 7-16.

3 On the taskbar, right-click the **File Explorer button** . A shortcut menu opens.

> **Tip:** You can also click the File tab on the ribbon, and then on the menu that opens, click Open new window.

4 Click **File Explorer**. A second Libraries window opens.

End Activity

7-4b Changing the View of File Explorer Windows

You can change the appearance of folder windows to suit your preferences. Windows 8 provides a variety of ways to view the contents of a folder—Extra large icons, Large icons, Medium icons, Small icons, List, Details, Tiles, and Content. Exhibit 7-16 in the previous section shows a folder in Tiles view, which displays folders and files as thumbnails with the file type listed below the name of the file, and Exhibit 7-17 shows a folder in Details view, which displays a small icon and lists information about each file. The icon provides a visual cue about the file type.

CAUTION

Don't Delete or Move System Files

Do not delete or move any files or folders from the root directory of the hard disk—doing so could disrupt the system so that you cannot run or start the computer. In fact, you should not reorganize or change any folder that contains installed software because Windows expects to find the files for specific programs within certain folders. If you reorganize or change these folders, Windows cannot locate and start the programs stored in that folder. Likewise, you should not make changes to the folder (usually named Windows) that contains the Windows operating system.

Navigation pane An area on the left side of File Explorer windows that contains icons and links to locations on your computer and your network.

To change the view, click one of the buttons in the status bar of the window, right-click a blank area of the window and then point to View, or use the View tab on the ribbon in the window. Exhibit 7-18 shows the Libraries folder with the View tab on the ribbon selected.

No matter which view you use, you can sort the file list by file name or another detail, such as size, type, or date. In Exhibit 7-17, the file list is sorted alphabetically by the file names, as indicated by the upward pointing triangle in the Name column heading. If you are viewing music files, you can sort by details such as contributing artists or album title. If you are viewing picture files, you can sort by details such as date taken or size. Sorting helps you find a particular file in a long file listing. In any view that shows column headings, such as Details view, you can click a column heading to sort the list by the information in that column. You can also right-click a blank area of the window, and then use the Sort by command on the shortcut menu to change the sort order.

Begin Activity

Change the view and sort order of the file list in a File Explorer window.

Exhibit 7-17 Libraries folder in Details view

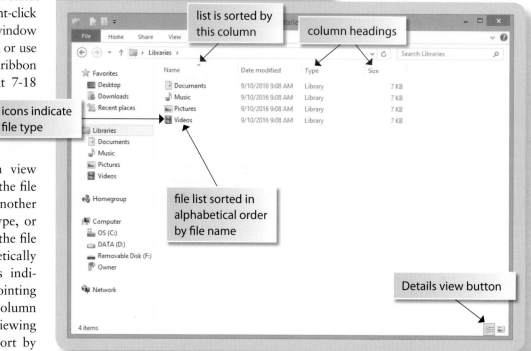

Exhibit 7-18 Libraries folder window with the View tab selected

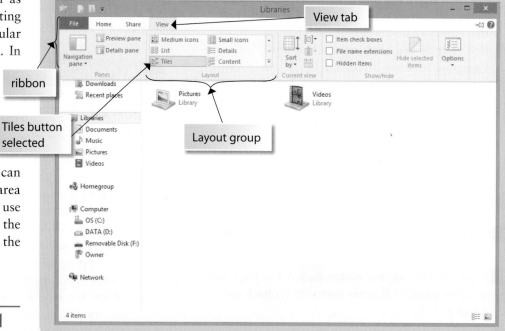

1 In the active Libraries folder window, click the **View tab** on the ribbon. The commands on the View tab appear. Refer to Exhibit 7-18.

2 In the Layout group on the View tab, click the **List button.** The View tab closes, and the libraries are displayed as a list.

3 On the status bar, click the **Large icons button** . The folder now shows the file list as large icons with only the file name below each icon.

4 On the status bar, click the **Details button** . The file list is displayed in Details view. Refer back to Exhibit 7-17.

5 In the file list, click the **Name column heading**. The triangle in the column heading changes to a downward pointing arrow, and the sort order changes to reverse alphabetical.

6 Right-click a blank area in the window, and then point to **Sort by** on the shortcut menu. A square with a black dot next to Name and Descending indicates the current sort order.

7 Click **Ascending**. The shortcut menu closes, and the list is resorted in alphabetical order by file name.

End Activity

7-4c Developing an Organizational Strategy

It is important to develop a strategy for organizing your folders and files. First, determine which files seem to belong together. Then, develop an appropriate file structure. Exhibit 7-19 shows how you could organize your files on a hard disk if you were taking distance-learning classes. To duplicate this organization, you would open the main folder for your documents, create four folders—one each for the Accounting, Computer Concepts, Management Skills, and Business Writing courses—and then store the writing assignments you complete in the Business Writing folder.

If you store your files on removable media, such as a USB drive or rewritable CD, you can use a simpler

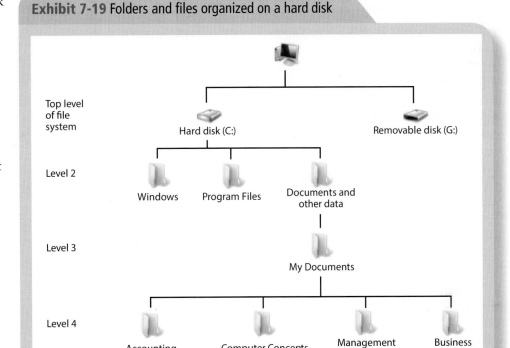

Exhibit 7-19 Folders and files organized on a hard disk

Top level of file system — Hard disk (C:) — Removable disk (G:)

Level 2 — Windows, Program Files, Documents and other data

Level 3 — My Documents

Level 4 — Accounting, Computer Concepts, Management Skills, Business Writing
Folders created for each course

Level 5 — Memo, Procedure, Proposal, Report
Files for the Business Writing course

© 2014 Cengage Learning

organization because you do not have to account for system files. In general, the larger the medium, the more levels of folders you should use because large media can store more files and, therefore, need better organization. For example, if you are organizing files on a USB drive, you could create folders in the top level of the USB drive for each general category of documents you store—one each for Courses, Creative, Financials, and Vacation. The Courses folder could then include one folder for each course, and each of those folders could contain the appropriate files.

7-4d Navigating to Folders

You explore, or navigate, your computer to work with its contents and resources. In this context, **navigate** means to move from one location to another on your computer, such as from one window or folder to another. To successfully navigate your computer, you need to understand a bit about how your computer is organized.

navigate To move from one location to another on your computer.

Exhibit 7-20 Relationship between your computer and the Computer window

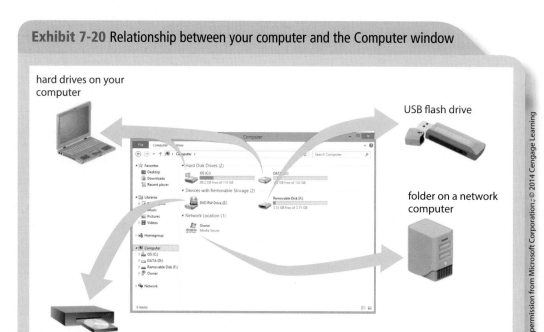

hard drives on your computer

USB flash drive

folder on a network computer

DVD drive

The Computer window represents your computer and its storage devices by displaying an icon for each object. See Exhibit 7-20. Recall that the first hard drive in a computer is usually drive C. If you add additional hard drives, they are usually designated D, E, and so on. If you have a DVD drive or a USB flash drive plugged into a USB port, it usually has the next letter in the alphabetic sequence. If you can access hard drives on other computers in a network, those drives sometimes (although not always) have letters associated with them as well.

To navigate to the files you want, it helps to know the file path. The **path** shows the location of a file on a computer and leads you through the file and folder organization to the file. For example, a file named Letterhead is stored in the Chapter subfolder of the Chapter 7 folder included with your data files. If you are working on a USB drive, the path to this file might be:

G:\Chapter 7\Chapter\Letterhead.docx

This path has four parts, and each part is separated by a backslash (\ ):

▶ **G:**—the drive name; for example, drive G might be the name for the USB drive

▶ **Chapter 7**—a top-level folder on drive G

▶ **Chapter**—a subfolder in the Chapter 7 folder

▶ **Letterhead.docx**—the name of the file

path A notation that indicates a file's location on a computer.

If someone tells you to find the file G:Chapter 7\Chapter\Letterhead.docx, you must navigate to drive G, open the Chapter 7 folder, and then open the Chapter folder to find the Letterhead file.

You can use any File Explorer window to navigate to the data files you need for the rest of these chapters. You can double-click a folder or drive in the file list to display the contents of that folder or drive, or you can click a folder or drive in the Navigation pane to navigate directly to that folder or drive and display its contents in the file list. When you move the pointer into the Navigation pane or when a folder is selected in the Navigation pane, triangles appear next to some icons, as shown in Exhibit 7-21. Right-pointing, white triangles ▷—called expand arrows—indicate that a folder contains other folders that are not currently displayed in the Navigation pane. Downward-pointing

FYI

Customizing File Explorer Windows

In addition to changing the way the file list is displayed and changing the sort order, you can make other changes to the layout of your folder windows. You can hide the Navigation pane to devote more space to file lists. You can display the Preview pane on the right side of a File Explorer window to display the contents of a picture file and some other types of files, or you can display the Details pane on the right to display information about a selected file, such as the author and file type. (You cannot display both the Details and the Preview panes at the same time.) To make these changes, click the appropriate buttons in the Panes group on the View tab on the ribbon.

Exhibit 7-21 Collapse and expand arrows in the Navigation pane

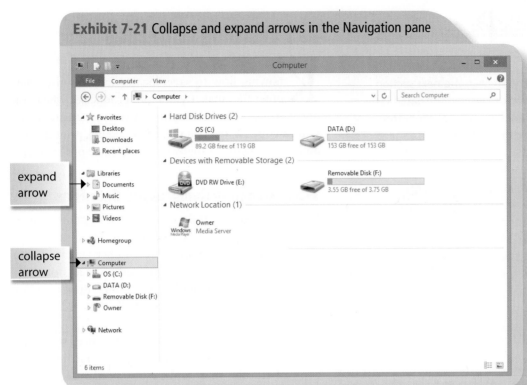

expand arrow

collapse arrow

black triangles ◢ —collapse arrows—indicate the folder is expanded, and its subfolders are listed below the folder name. Exhibit 7-21 shows Computer selected in the Navigation pane.

Begin Activity

Navigate to folders.

1 In the Navigation pane of the active Libraries window, if the Computer folder is not expanded, click the **Computer folder expand arrow** ▷ . The drives on your computer are listed below the Computer folder in the Navigation pane. Refer back to Exhibit 7-21.

2 In the Navigation pane, click **Computer**. The drives and network locations on your computer appear in the window, and the Home and Share tabs that were on the ribbon are replaced with the Computer tab.

3 If your data files are on your hard drive, in the Computer window, in the Navigation

pane, click **Documents**. If your data files are on a USB drive, in the Navigation pane, click **Removable Disk (drive letter:)**, where *drive letter* is whatever letter your removable drive is, such as E, F, or G. If your data files are on a network drive, in the Navigation pane, click the drive under **Network location**. The window now shows the list of folders on the drive you selected.

4 In the list of folders, double-click the folder that contains the data files, if necessary. You should see a folder named Chapter 7. (You might see additional chapter folders as well.)

End Activity

FYI

Determining Where to Store Files

When you create and save files on your computer's hard disk, you should store them in subfolders. The top level of the hard disk is off-limits for your files because they could interfere with system files. If you are working on your own computer, store your files within the My Documents folder, which is where many programs save files by default. When you use a computer on the job, your employer might assign a main folder to you for storing your work. In either case, if you simply store all your files in one folder, you will soon have trouble finding the files you want. Instead, you should create subfolders within a main folder to separate files in a way that makes sense for you. Even if you store most of your files on removable media, such as USB drives, you should organize those files into folders and subfolders.

Download

LEARN MORE

Navigating with the Address Bar

The Address bar displays your current location as a series of links separated by arrows. You can click a folder name in the Address bar to display the contents of that folder. You can also click an arrow to open a drop-down list with the names of each folder in that location. To display the contents of one of those folders, click the folder name in the list. You can also click the icon at the left end of the Address bar to change the hierarchy in the Address bar so each folder is separated by a backslash. You can then type a path directly in the Address bar.

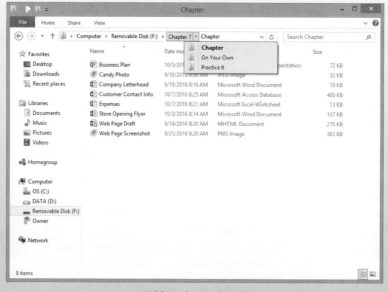

Address bar navigation

compressed (zipped) folder A folder that stores files in a compact format.

extract To create an uncompressed copy of a compressed file.

7-5 Working with Files

Knowing how to save, locate, and organize computer files makes you more productive when you are working with a computer. After you create a file, you can open it and edit the file's contents, print the file, and save it again—usually using the same program you used to create it.

7-5a Extracting Compressed Data Files

If you transfer files from one location to another, such as from your hard disk to a removable disk or vice versa, or from one computer to another via email, you can store the files in a compressed (zipped) folder. A **compressed (zipped) folder** stores files in a compact format. In File Explorer windows, Windows displays a zipper on the folder icon.

To work with a compressed file, you need to **extract** it, which means that you create an uncompressed copy of the file in a folder you specify. To do this, you right-click the compressed folder, and then click Extract All on the shortcut menu, or you select the compressed folder, click the Compressed Folder Tools Extract tab on the ribbon, and then click the Extract all button to open the Extract Compressed (Zipped) Folders dialog box. See Exhibit 7-22. The path to the folder in which the compressed folder is stored and a suggested folder name for the new uncompressed folder appears in the box. You can keep this path and suggested name or change it.

Exhibit 7-22 Extract Compressed (Zipped) Folders dialog box

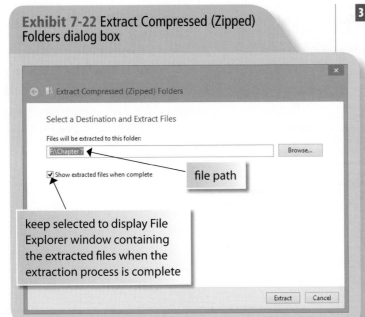

file path

keep selected to display File Explorer window containing the extracted files when the extraction process is complete

Begin Activity

Extract compressed files.

Read this before starting the next Activity: The data files that are provided with this book for Chapters 7 through 22 are provided as compressed folders, one per chapter. If you downloaded them yourself or if your instructor provided them to you as compressed folders, do the steps in the next Activity, "Extract compressed files." If the files were provided to you in uncompressed folders, read the steps in this Activity, but do not do them.

1 If you need to extract your data files from compressed folders, make sure the active File Explorer window contains the compressed folders for Chapters 7 through 22. If you do not need to extract your data files from compressed folders, read, but do not do, the steps in this Activity.

2 Right-click the **Chapter 7 compressed folder**. On the shortcut menu, click **Extract All**. The Extract Compressed (Zipped) Folders dialog box opens. The path to the folder the compressed folder is in and a suggested folder name of Chapter 7 is selected in the box in the middle of the dialog box. Refer back to Exhibit 7-22.

> **Tip:** You can also select the compressed folder, click the Compressed Folder Tools Extract tab on the ribbon, and then click the Extract all button.

3 If you do not need to change the location of the data files, skip to Step 4. If you need to change the location of the data files, click **Browse** to open the Select a destination dialog box, click the **expand arrow** ▷ next to Libraries to change the location to the hard drive on the computer, or click next to Computer or Network to select a location on an external or network drive, and then click the folder in which you want to store the Chapter 7 folder. Exhibit 7-23 shows a folder selected on a removable drive. Click **OK** to close the Select a destination dialog box. The Extract Compressed (Zipped) Folders dialog box is the active window again.

> **Problem?** If you need to create a new folder inside the currently selected folder in the list in the Select a destination box, click **Make New Folder**. A new folder is created in the list with the text *New folder* highlighted. Type the name of the new folder to replace the highlighted text with the new name.

Exhibit 7-23 Select a destination dialog box

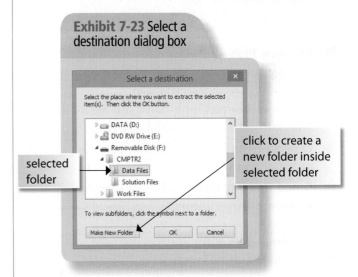

selected folder

click to create a new folder inside selected folder

4 Click **Extract**. A dialog box showing the progress of the extraction appears, and then the Chapter 7 folder window opens listing the Chapter, On Your Own, and Practice It folders.

5 Extract the files from the compressed folders containing the data files for Chapters 8 through Chapter 22.

End Activity

7-5b Creating a Folder or Subfolder

After you devise a plan for storing your files, you are ready to get organized by creating folders and subfolders that will hold your files and then moving the files into the appropriate folders. When you create a folder, you give it a name, preferably one that describes its contents. A folder name can have up to 255 characters but cannot include the / \ : * ? " < > or | characters. Exhibit 7-24 shows the files in the Chapter 7\Chapter folder. All of these files are related to a business named Cathy's Candy Shoppe. The files in this folder are described below:

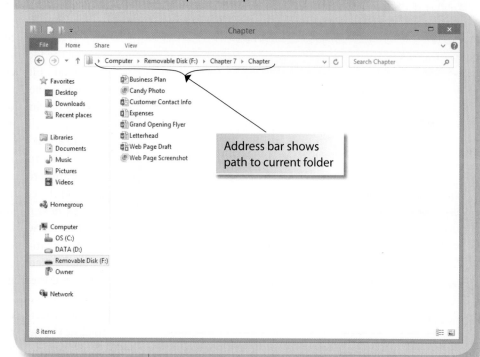

Exhibit 7-24 Files in the Chapter 7\Chapter folder in List view

- **Candy Photo** and **Web Page Screenshot**—graphics files. Candy Photo is a photograph of candy, and Web Page Screenshot is a graphic file in the file format PNG.

- **Business Plan**—a PowerPoint presentation that contains the beginning of a presentation to explain the store's business plan.

- **Customer Contact Info**—an Access file listing potential customer names and addresses.

- **Expenses**—an Excel file that lists projected expenses for the store.

- **Grand Opening Flyer**—a Word document that contains a flyer to announce the grand opening of the store.

- **Letterhead**—a Word document of (as the name implies) letterhead for the store.

- **Web Page Draft**—a Word document saved as a document that can be published to a Web server and accessed as a Web page.

One way to organize these files is to create the following three folders—one for graphics, one for the finances, and one for marketing—and then move the files into the appropriate folders:

- **Graphics folder**—Candy Photo and Web Page Screenshot

- **Finances folder**—Business Plan and Expenses

- **Marketing folder**—Customer Contact Info, Grand Opening Flyer, Letterhead, and Web Page Draft

When you are working on your own computer, you usually create folders within the My Documents folder, which is in the Documents library, and other standard folders, such as My Music and My Pictures, in the Music and Pictures libraries, respectively. If you are saving your files on a USB drive, you can create folders on it. To create a new folder, you can click the New folder button ▢ on the Quick Access Toolbar, or click the New folder button in the New group on the Home tab on the ribbon. When the new folder is created, the temporary folder name *New folder* is highlighted (selected), and a box appears around it, as shown in Exhibit 7-25. Text you type will replace the temporary name.

Begin Activity

Create folders.

1 Navigate to the Chapter 7\Chapter folder window using the techniques you learned earlier. This folder is included with your data files.

2 If the Chapter 7\Chapter folder window is not in Large icons view, click the **View tab** on the ribbon. In the Layout group, click the **Large icons button**.

Exhibit 7-25 New folder created in the current folder window

New folder button on the Quick Access Toolbar

selected temporary folder name for a new folder

3 On the Quick Access Toolbar, click the **New folder button** ▯. A folder icon with the selected temporary folder name *New folder* appears in the window. Refer back to Exhibit 7-25.

4 Type **Graphics** and then press the **Enter key**. *Graphics* replaces the temporary folder name, and the new Graphics folder is selected in the window.

5 On the ribbon, click the **Home tab**. In the New group, click the **New folder button**. Another new folder is created.

6 Type **Finances** to replace the temporary folder name, and then press the **Enter key**. The new folder is renamed.

7 Create a new folder named **Marketing**. The Chapter 7\Chapter folder now contains three subfolders.

End Activity

7-5c Moving or Copying Files and Folders

If you want to place a file into a folder from another location, you can move the file or copy it. Moving a file removes it from its current location and places it in a new location you specify. Copying also places the file in a new location but does not remove it from its current location. You can move and copy folders in the same way that you move and copy files. When you do, you move or copy all the files contained in the folder.

The easiest way to move files or folders is to drag them from one location to another. When you drag a file or folder from one location to another on the same drive, it is moved from its original location to the new location. Exhibit 7-26 shows the Business Plan file being moved from the Chapter 7\Chapter folder to the Chapter 7\Chapter\Finances folder. When you drag a file or folder from one drive to another drive, the file or folder is copied instead of moved.

Exhibit 7-26 File being moved between folders on the same drive

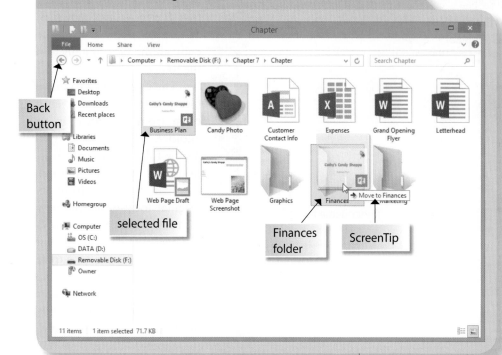

Back button

selected file

Finances folder

ScreenTip

Begin Activity

Move files or folders.

1 Drag the **Business Plan file** on top of the **Finances folder**, but do not release the mouse button. The ScreenTip identifies the action as moving the file to the Finances folder. Refer back to Exhibit 7-26.

2 Release the mouse button. A dialog box might briefly appear showing the progress as the file is moved. When the move is complete, the dialog box closes and the Business Plan file no longer appears in the window because you moved it to the Finances folder.

3 Double-click the **Finances folder**. The window changes to display the contents of the Finances folder, which now contains the Business Plan presentation file.

You can override the default behavior by dragging a file using the right mouse button (also referred to as right-dragging). When you drag a file or folder using the right mouse button, a shortcut menu appears as shown in Exhibit 7-27, and you can choose the Move here or the Copy here command, depending on what you want to do.

To move or copy more than one file at the same time, you select all the files you want to copy, and then drag them as a group. To select files and folders that are adjacent to each other in a window, click the first file or folder in the list, press and hold down the Shift key, click the last file or folder in the list, and then release the Shift key. To select files or folders that are not adjacent, click one file or folder, press and hold down the Ctrl key, click the other files or folders, and then release the Ctrl key.

Exhibit 7-27 Shortcut menu after right-dragging a file between folders

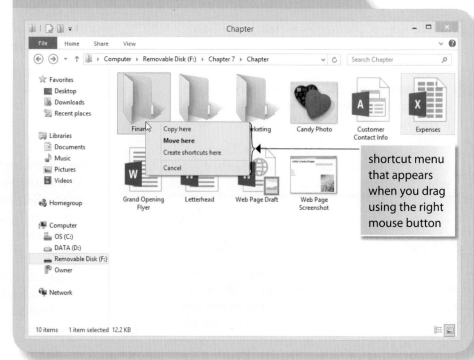

shortcut menu that appears when you drag using the right mouse button

4 To the left of the Address bar, click the **Back button** (←). The contents of the Chapter folder appear in the window. The folders now appear first in the window because the contents of the window automatically resorts alphabetically by name when you redisplay its contents, and folders appear before files in that sort order.

5 Right-click the **Expenses file**, but do not release the mouse button. Drag the **Expenses file** to the **Finances folder**, and then release the mouse button. A shortcut menu opens. Refer back to Exhibit 7-27.

6 On the shortcut menu, click **Move here**. The file is moved from the current folder to the Finances folder.

7 Click the **Customer Contact Info file**, and then press and hold the **Ctrl key**. Click the **Grand Opening Flyer file**, the **Letterhead file**, and the **Web Page Draft file**, and then release the **Ctrl key**. The four files you clicked are selected.

> **Tip:** You can also press and hold the Shift key, click the first file in the list, click the last file in the list, and then release the Shift key to select the first and last files you clicked as well as all of the files between them.

8 Point to any one of the four selected files, and then drag the four selected files into the **Marketing folder**.

9 Select the **Candy Photo file** and the **Web Page Screenshot file**, and then drag them into the **Graphics folder**.

10 Drag the **Graphics folder** into the **Marketing folder**.

11 In the Navigation pane, expand the drive containing your data files, expand subfolders until you

have expanded the **Chapter 7\Chapter folder**, and then expand the **Marketing folder**. The Graphics folder is listed below the Marketing folder in the Navigation pane.

End Activity

If you want to copy a file or folder from one location to another on the same drive, you can right-click and drag and then click Copy here, or you can press and hold the Ctrl key while you drag. The ScreenTip that appears indicates that you are copying the item. See Exhibit 7-28.

Exhibit 7-28 ScreenTip when pressing the Ctrl key while dragging a file

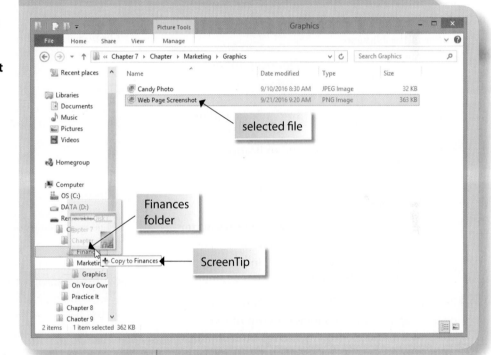

Begin Activity

Copy files or folders.

1 In the Navigation pane, click the **Graphics folder**. The two files in the Graphics folder appear in the folder window.

2 Press and hold the **Ctrl key**, and then drag the **Web Page Screenshot file** to the **Finances folder** in the Navigation pane, but do not release the Ctrl key. The ScreenTip indicates that the file will be copied to the Finances folder. Refer back to Exhibit 7-28.

3 Release the **mouse button**, and then release the **Ctrl key**. The file is copied to the Finances folder. Notice that the Web Page Screenshot file is still listed in the Graphics folder.

4 In the Navigation pane, click the **Finances folder**. The Web Page Screenshot file is listed in the folder window along with the other two files in the Finances folder.

5 In the Address bar, after Chapter, click the **right-pointing arrow** ▶ to display a list of folders in the Chapter folder, and then click **Marketing**. The contents of the Marketing folder appear in the folder window.

6 Right-click the **Web Page Draft file**, and then drag it to the **Finances folder** in the Navigation pane. When you release the mouse button, the same shortcut menu you saw when you were moving files appears.

> **Problem?** Even though you intend to copy the file, the ScreenTip *Move to Finances* appears. You can still choose the Copy here command on the shortcut menu when it appears.

7 On the shortcut menu, click **Copy here**. The file is copied to the Finances folder.

8 To the left of the Address bar, click the **Back button** ⬅. The contents of the previously viewed folder, the Finances folder, appear in the window, including the Web Page Draft file.

9 Press and hold the **Ctrl key**. In the Navigation pane, drag the **Graphics folder** on top of the **Chapter folder**. Release the **mouse button**, and then release the **Ctrl key**. The Graphics folder is copied to the Chapter folder and appears after the Finances folder in the folders list.

10 In the Navigation pane, click the **Graphics folder** in the Chapter folder (not the original Graphics folder in the Marketing folder). The two files in the original Graphics folder appear in the folder window because they were copied along with the folder.

End Activity

LEARN MORE

Moving and Copying Using the Ribbon and the Clipboard

You can also use the Cut, Copy, and Paste commands in the Clipboard group on the Home tab on the ribbon, or the Move to and Copy to commands in the Organize group on the Home tab. When you use the Cut, Copy, and Paste commands in the Clipboard group, you use the **Clipboard**, a temporary storage area in Windows on which files, folders, text, or other objects are stored when you copy or move them. To use these commands, click a file or folder to select it, click the Home tab, and then click the Cut command to remove the item from its current location and place it on the Clipboard, or click the Copy command to place a copy of the file or folder on the Clipboard. To paste the contents of the Clipboard, display the contents of the folder to which you want to place the item or the copy of the item, and then click the Paste button. If you cut or copy another item, the second item replaces the item currently on the Clipboard. Using the Move to or Copy to buttons is an alternative to dragging the items from one folder to another and nothing is placed on the Clipboard.

7-5d Naming and Renaming Files and Folders

As you work with files, pay attention to **file names**—they provide important information about the file, including its contents and purpose. A file name such as *Car Sales.docx* has three parts:

▶ **Title**—text you provide when you create a file that describes the content of the file and its purpose

---

Clipboard A temporary storage area in Windows on which objects are stored when you copy or move them.

file name A title that describes the content of the file and its purpose.

▶ **Dot**—the period (.) that separates the main part of the file name from the file extension

▶ **File extension**—three or four characters that follow the dot in the file name and that identify the file type

The main part of a file name can have up to 255 characters, which gives you plenty of space to name your file descriptively so that you will know its contents just by looking at the file name. You can use spaces and certain punctuation symbols in your file names. Like folder names, file names cannot contain the \ / ? : * " < > | symbols because these characters have special meaning in Windows.

The file extension helps you identify the type of file. For example, in the file name *Car Sales.docx*, the extension *docx* identifies the file as one created by Microsoft Office Word. You might also have a file called *Car Sales.jpg*—the *jpg* extension identifies the file as one created in a graphics program, such as Paint, or as a photograph. Though the main parts of these file names are identical, their extensions distinguish them as different files. You do not need to add extensions to file names because the program you use to create the file adds the file extension automatically.

Although Windows keeps track of extensions, not all computers are set to display them. The screenshots in this book do not show file extensions. You can, however, identify the file type of a file in a file list in a File Explorer window by pointing to it. The first line in the ScreenTip that appears tells you what type of file it is. Also, if the window is set to Details view, the Type column identifies the file type.

Guidelines for Naming Files

Be sure to give your files and folders meaningful names that help you remember their purpose and contents. You can easily rename a file or folder by using the Rename command on the file's shortcut menu. The following are a few suggestions for naming your files:

▶ **Use common names.** Avoid cryptic names that might make sense now but could cause confusion later, such as nonstandard abbreviations or imprecise names like Stuff2013.

▶ **Don't change the file extension.** When renaming a file, don't change the file extension. If you do, Windows might not be able to find a program that can open the file.

▶ **Find a balance between too short and too long.** Use file names that are long enough to be meaningful but short enough to read easily on the screen.

If you need to rename a file, right-click it in the file list, and then click Rename on the shortcut menu. You can also select a file, click the Home tab on the ribbon, and then click the Rename button in the Organize group. The file name becomes selected. Type the new name to replace the selected text. You do not need to type the file extension.

As you have already seen, folder names are also important. You might find that you need to rename an existing folder. You can do this using the same methods you use to rename files.

Begin Activity

Rename files or folders.

1 Display the contents of the **Marketing folder** in the window.

2 Right-click the **Grand Opening Flyer file**. On the shortcut menu, click **Rename**. The shortcut menu closes, and the file name is highlighted in the same manner as it was when you created a new folder.

> **Tip:** You can also select a file or folder, click the Home tab on the ribbon, and then in the Organize group, click the Rename button.

3 Type **Store Opening Flyer** and then press the **Enter key**. The file name changes to the name you typed.

> **Problem?** If your computer is set to display file extensions, only the file name is selected. The .docx file extension is not selected. If a dialog box opens asking if you are sure you want to change the file extension, click **No**, and then repeat Steps 2 and 3.

file extension Three or four characters that follow the dot in a file name and that identify the file type.

4 Click the **Letterhead file**, pause for a moment, and then click the **Letterhead file name**. The file name becomes highlighted.

5 Click immediately before the **L** in the file name, type **Company**, press the **Spacebar**, and then press the **Enter key**. The file is renamed to Company Letterhead.

6 On the Marketing folder title bar, click the **Minimize button** ▬ . The Marketing folder window minimizes to the File Explorer button on the taskbar.

7 Minimize the rest of the open windows.

End Activity

7-5e Working with Compressed Folders

You compress a folder so that the files it contains use less space on the disk. Compare two folders—a folder named Photos that contains about 8.6 MB of files and a compressed folder containing the same files but requiring only 6.5 MB of disk space. In this case, the compressed files use about 25 percent less disk space than the uncompressed files. You can also transfer the smaller compressed files more quickly.

To create a compressed folder, select all the files and folders you want to compress, click the Share tab on the ribbon, and then in the Send group, click the Zip button. The new, compressed folder appears in the same folder as the files and folders you compressed with a temporary folder name selected so that you can type a new name if you want. See Exhibit 7-29. You can also right-click one of the selected files or folders, point to Send to on the shortcut menu, and then click Compressed (zipped) folder. Note that the original folders are not removed. You can also right-click a single folder and use the same command to compress all the files stored in that folder. You can add additional files or folders to the compressed folder by dragging the files or folders to the compressed folder.

You can open a file from a compressed folder, although

you cannot modify the file. You can also move and copy files and folders in a compressed folder. To rename or edit a compressed file or folder, you must extract it first.

If a different compression program, such as WinZip, has been installed on your computer, the Send to Compressed (zipped) folder command might not appear on the shortcut menu. Instead, it might be replaced by the name of your compression program. In this case, refer to your compression program's Help system for instructions on working with compressed files.

As you have already seen, you can easily extract all the files from a compressed folder either by using the Extract All command on the shortcut menu or by clicking the Extract all button on the Compressed Folder Tools Extract tab on the ribbon. To extract one file from a compressed folder, open the compressed folder, click the file you want to extract, and then in the Extract To group on the Compressed Folder Tools Extract tab on the ribbon, click the button corresponding to the folder or library you want to put the extracted file into. If you do not see the folder you want, click the Desktop button, and the file will be extracted to the Desktop. Then you can open a File Explorer window and drag the extracted file into the correct folder or you can drag the compressed file from the compressed folder window into the window for the folder to which you want to extract the file. When you extract a file from a compressed folder, the compressed file remains in the compressed folder.

Exhibit 7-29 New compressed folder

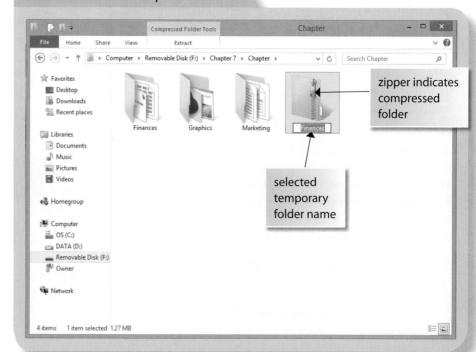

Backing Up Your Data

You should back up your data regularly so that you can restore the file s if something happens to your computer. Performing a backup can include backing up an entire computer (so it can be restored at a later date, if needed), backing up all data files (so they can be restored if the computer is lost or damaged), or backing up only selected files (so you have a clean copy of each selected file if the original is lost or destroyed). Depending on their size, backup data files can be placed on a recordable or rewritable CD or DVD, an external hard drive, a USB flash drive, or virtually any other storage medium. To protect against fires and other natural disasters, you should store backup media in a physical location other than where your computer is located or inside a fire-resistant safe. You can perform backups by manually copying files that change, but backup utility programs make the backup process easier. For convenience, many backup programs can be scheduled to back up specified files, folders, or drives on a regular basis (such as every night or once a week). You can also back up to the cloud using an online backup service, such as Carbonite or MozyHome. These services back up your files automatically to a secure Web server on a regular basis provided you have a broadband Internet connection.

Tatiana Popova/Shutterstock.com; © 2014 Cengage Learning

Begin Activity

Work with compressed folders.

1 On the taskbar, point to the **File Explorer button**. Thumbnails of all the open File Explorer windows appear.

2 Click the **Marketing thumbnail**. The Marketing folder window appears on the desktop.

3 Display the contents of the Chapter 7\Chapter folder in the window, and then select the **Finances folder** and the **Marketing folder**.

4 Click the **Share tab** on the ribbon. In the Send group, click the **Zip button**. A dialog box might open showing you the progress of the compression. After a few minutes, the dialog box closes and a new compressed folder with a zipper icon appears in the window with its temporary folder name selected. The temporary folder name is the same as the first folder you clicked when you selected the folders, so it will be Finances if you selected that folder first, and Marketing if you selected that folder first. The Finances and Marketing folders remain in the file list.

> **Problem?** If the Zip button does not appear in the Send group on the Share tab, a different compression program is probably installed on your computer. Read but do not perform the remaining steps.

5 Type **Compressed Folders** and then press the **Enter key** to rename the compressed folder.

6 Double-click the **Compressed Folders folder**. The Finances and Marketing folders are listed in the file list.

7 Double-click the **Finances folder**, and then click the **Business Plan file** in the file list to select it.

8 Click the **Compressed Folder Tools Extract tab** on the ribbon. The Extract To group includes buttons for the Desktop, the default libraries, and folders you recently opened.

9 Scroll the list of buttons in the Extract To group if necessary, and then click the **Desktop button**. The Business Plan file is extracted to the desktop. The compressed Business Plan file is still in the Compressed Folders folder.

> **Tip:** You can also display the Compressed Folders folder and the Chapter folder windows side by side, and then drag the Business Plan file from the Compressed Folders folder window to the Chapter folder window.

10 If you can't see the extracted Business Plan file on the desktop, drag the **Finances window** by its title bar until you can see the Business Plan file on the desktop.

11 Display the contents of the Chapter 7\Chapter folder in the window, point to the **Business Plan file** on the desktop, right-click it and drag it into the **Chapter folder window**, release the **mouse button**, and then on the shortcut menu, click **Move here**. The Business Plan file on the desktop is moved into the Chapter folder.

End Activity

7-6 Deleting Files and Working with the Recycle Bin

When you delete a file from a hard drive, it is not removed from your computer. Instead, it is moved to the Recycle Bin. The **Recycle Bin** holds deleted items until you remove them permanently.

7-6a Deleting Files and Folders

You should periodically delete unneeded files and folders so that your folders and drives do not get cluttered. When you delete a file or folder from the hard drive, the file or folder and all of its contents are moved to the Recycle Bin. When you delete a file or folder from removable media, such as a USB drive, or from a network drive, it is not moved to the Recycle Bin; instead, it is permanently deleted and cannot be recovered.

Used with permission from Microsoft Corporation.

Begin Activity

Delete files or folders.

1 Display the contents of the **Finances folder** in the folder window.

Recycle Bin A folder that holds items deleted from the computer until you remove them permanently.

2 Drag the **Web Page Screenshot** file on top of the Recycle Bin on the desktop so that the ScreenTip Move to Recycle Bin appears, and then release the mouse button. If your data files are stored on the hard drive, the file is moved to the Recycle Bin. If your data files are stored on removable media or a network drive, the Delete File dialog box opens asking if you are sure you want to permanently delete the file.

Problem? If you cannot see the Recycle Bin, drag the folder window covering it to a new location by its title bar.

3 If the Delete File dialog box is open, click **Yes**. The dialog box closes, and the file is deleted.

4 In the folder window, right-click the **Web Page Draft file**. On the shortcut menu, click **Delete**. If your data files are stored on removable media or a network drive, the Delete File dialog box opens.

Problem? If your data files are stored on the hard drive and a dialog box opens asking if you are sure you want to move the file to the Recycle Bin, click **Yes**.

5 If the Delete File dialog box is open, click **Yes**. The file is either moved to the Recycle Bin or permanently deleted.

6 Minimize the Finances folder window.

End Activity

7-6b Working with the Recycle Bin

You can double-click the Recycle Bin to open the Recycle Bin window and see the files that are ready to be permanently deleted. After you empty the Recycle Bin, you can no longer recover the files it contained. See Exhibit 7-30.

If you want to keep a file that is in the Recycle Bin instead of permanently deleting it, you can return the file to its previous location. To do this, right-click a file in the Recycle Bin window and then click Restore on the shortcut menu, or click the Recycle Bin Tools Manage tab on the Ribbon, and then click the Restore the selected items button.

Exhibit 7-30 Recycle Bin and Recycle Bin window

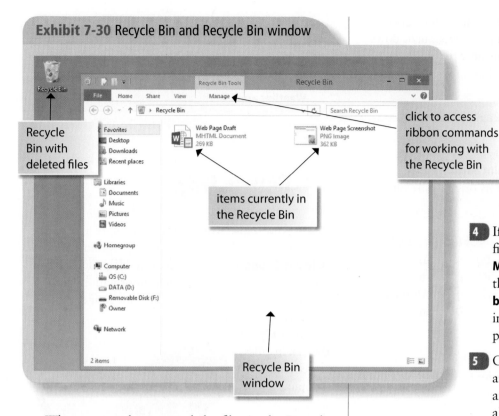

Recycle Bin with deleted files

click to access ribbon commands for working with the Recycle Bin

items currently in the Recycle Bin

Recycle Bin window

4 If the Recycle Bin contains files, click the **Recycle Bin Tools Manage tab** on the ribbon, and then click the **Empty Recycle Bin button**. A dialog box opens asking if you are sure you want to permanently delete the items.

5 Click **Yes**. The dialog box closes, and the files in the Recycle Bin are permanently deleted. They also disappear from the file list in the Recycle Bin window.

End Activity

When you no longer need the files in the Recycle Bin, you can permanently delete them. To do this, right-click the Recycle Bin and then click Empty Recycle Bin on the shortcut menu, or click the Empty Recycle Bin button on the Recycle Bin Tools Manage tab on the ribbon. Keep in mind that you cannot retrieve files that have been emptied from the Recycle Bin.

Make it a practice to regularly empty the Recycle Bin. Storing files in the Recycle Bin can slow down your computer's start-up time. The unneeded files also take up space on your computer. Files you want to keep should be stored in other folders, not in the Recycle Bin. Remember, permanently deleted files cannot be retrieved from the Recycle Bin.

Begin Activity

Work with the Recycle Bin.

1 Right-click the **Recycle Bin**. The Recycle Bin shortcut menu opens. If no files are currently in the Recycle Bin, the Empty Recycle Bin command will be gray, which means it is unavailable.

2 Press the **Esc key** to close the shortcut menu.

3 Double-click the **Recycle Bin**. The Recycle Bin window opens. Any files or folders currently in the Recycle Bin are listed in this window. Refer back to Exhibit 7-30.

7-7 Closing Apps and Windows

You should close an application when you are finished using it. Each application uses computer resources, such as memory, so Windows works more efficiently when only the applications you need are open. You should also close File Explorer windows that you are not using to keep your desktop uncluttered. You click the Close button ✕ at the right end of the title bar to close the window. If the window is a program window, clicking the Close button can also stop the program from running. (This is called *exiting* or *closing* the program.) You can also right-click a window's taskbar button, and then click Close window on the shortcut menu.

Windows 8 apps that are not actively being used are automatically placed in suspended mode, so they use far fewer resources, but it can still be a good idea to close apps that you are not using. To close a Windows 8 app, display the Switch List, right-click the app's thumbnail, and then click Close on the shortcut menu. You can also make the app active, position the pointer at the top of the screen so it changes to 🖑, and then drag straight down to the bottom of the screen. Remember that the desktop is an app, so you can close it just like any other app.

Begin Activity

Close apps and windows.

1 On the taskbar, click the **Paint button** 🖌. The Paint window is restored to its original size and becomes the active window.

2 On the Paint window title bar, click the **Close button** ✕. The Paint window and application close, and its button no longer appears on the taskbar.

> **Problem?** If a dialog box opens asking if you want to save changes to Untitled, click **Don't Save**.

3 On the taskbar, right-click the **Calculator button** 🖩. The shortcut menu for the Calculator taskbar button opens.

4 Click **Close window** on the shortcut menu. The Calculator window closes, and its button no longer appears on the taskbar.

5 On the taskbar, point to the **File Explorer button** 📁.

6 Point to the **Finances thumbnail**, and then click the **Close button** ✕ that appears in the upper-right corner of the thumbnail.

7 Right-click the **File Explorer button** 📁, and then on the shortcut menu, click **Close all windows**. The rest of the open File Explorer windows close.

8 Display the **Switch List**, and then right-click the **Reader thumbnail**. A shortcut menu opens.

9 On the shortcut menu, click **Close**. The Reader app closes.

10 Position the pointer at the top of the desktop screen so that it changes to 🖑, press and hold the left mouse button, and then quickly

> **Tip:** If windows are open on the desktop, they are *not* closed automatically when you close the Desktop app.

Windows Help and Support Help files stored on your computer as well as Help information stored on the Microsoft Web site.

drag all the way to the bottom of the screen. The Desktop app shrinks and then closes, and the Start screen appears.

11 Display the **Switch List**, and then close the **Weather app**.

End Activity

7-8 Getting Help

As you work, you might need more information about Windows or one of its programs. **Windows Help and Support** provides access to Help files stored on your computer as well as Help information stored on the Microsoft Web site. If you are not connected to the Web, you will have access only to the Help files stored on your computer.

7-8a
Opening Windows Help and Support

To start Windows Help and Support, type *help* on the Start screen, and then click Help and Support in the list of search results on the Apps screen. Windows Help and Support is a desktop application so its window opens on the desktop. The window that appears when you first start Help and Support is called the Home page. See Exhibit 7-31.

khz/Shutterstock.com

Begin Activity

Open Windows Help and Support.

1 On the Start screen, type **help**. The Apps screen appears, and Help and Support is listed in the search results.

> **Tip:** You can also start Windows Help and Support by pressing the F1 key or by clicking the Help button ❓ on the right end of the ribbon in a File Explorer window.

Find a Help topic using the Browse Help list.

1 At the top of the window under the Search box, click the **Browse help link**. A list of Windows Help topics appears.

2 Drag the vertical scroll bar on the right side of the window down as far as it can go. The list scrolls up. The topics at the bottom of the list that were not visible now appear in the window.

3 Click the **Files, folders, and search link**. The Files, folders, and search page in the Windows Help and Support window appears. A list of topics organized into categories related to files, folders, and searching appears.

4 Under the Work with your files category heading, click the **How to work with files and folders link**. The Windows Help and Support window displays information about that topic.

7-8c Using the Search Box

If you cannot find the topic you need by clicking a link or using the toolbar, or if you want to quickly find Help pages related to a particular topic, you can use the Search box. To do this, type a word or phrase about the topic you want to find to display a list of Help pages containing those words.

Use the Search box.

1 At the top of the window, click in the **Search box**. Refer back to Exhibit 7-31.

2 Type **shut down** and then click the **Search button**. A list of Help pages that contain the words *shut down* appears in the Windows Help and Support window.

3 Click the **How do I shut down (turn off) my PC link**. The Windows Help and Support window displays information about that topic.

4 Close the **Windows Help and Support window**.

Exhibit 7-31 Windows Help and Support window displaying the Home page

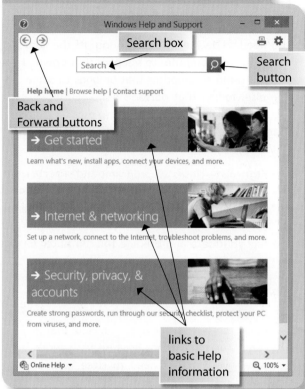

2 Click **Help and Support**. The Windows Help and Support window opens displaying the Home page. If you are not connected to the Web, the contents you see on the home page on your screen might differ.

7-8b Browsing Help Topics

The Browse help list organizes the information in Windows Help and Support into topics and categories. You can click a link to display the titles of related categories. You can click a topic under a specific category to get help about a particular task or feature.

To browse Help topics, you click the Browse help link near the top of the window. This opens the Windows Help topics page in the window. The list of topics in the window is too long to display all the topics at once. You use the vertical scroll bar to scroll the list up. To do this, you do one of the following actions:

▶ Drag the scroll box down the scroll bar

▶ Click the down scroll arrow as many times as needed to scroll one line at a time

▶ Click in the scroll bar below the scroll box to jump down one screen at a time

7-9 Shutting Down Windows

You should always shut down Windows before you turn off your computer. Doing so saves energy, preserves your data and settings, and makes sure your computer starts quickly the next time you use it. You can turn off Windows 8 by displaying the Charms bar, clicking the Settings charm, and then clicking the Power button on the Settings panel. When you click Shut down, your computer closes all open programs, including Windows itself, and then completely turns off your computer. Shutting down does not automatically save your work, so be sure to save your files before clicking the Shut down button.

Begin Activity

Shut down Windows 8.

1. Display the **Start screen**.
2. Do one of the following:
   - Display the **Charms bar**, click the **Settings charm** to display the Settings panel, click the **Power button**, and then click **Shut down** on the menu that opens.
   - Click your user name at the upper-right corner of the Start screen, and then click **Sign out**. Click the **lock screen** to display the list of user names, click the **Shut down button** in the lower-right corner, and then click **Shut down** on the menu that opens.

End Activity

LEARN MORE

Sign Out, Sleep, or Shut Down

When you are finished working on the computer, you need to decide whether to log off the computer, put the computer to sleep, or shut down. If you are using a computer that belongs to someone else, follow that person's policy. Otherwise, the best approach depends on who uses the computer and how long it will be idle. Consider the following as you make your decision:

- **Sign out**—closes all programs and signs you out of Windows 8 but leaves the computer turned on. If another person might use the computer shortly, log off Windows to protect your data and prepare the computer for someone else to use.
- **Sleep**—saves your work and then turns down the power to your monitor and computer. A light on the outside of the computer case blinks or turns yellow to indicate that the computer is sleeping. Because your work is saved, you do not need to close your programs or files before putting your computer to sleep. By default, Windows 8 is set to sleep after 15 to 30 minutes of idle time, depending on whether you are using a mobile or desktop computer. If you will be away from the computer for more than 15 minutes but less than a day, you can generally let the computer go to sleep on its own. To wake a desktop computer, you press any key or move the mouse. To wake a notebook computer, you might need to press the hardware power button on your computer case instead. After you wake a computer, the screen looks exactly as it did when you turned off your computer.
- **Shut down**—turns off the computer. If your computer is plugged in to a power outlet and you do not plan to use the computer for more than a day, shutting down saves wear and tear on your electronic components and conserves energy. You should also turn off the computer when it is susceptible to electrical damage, such as during a lightning storm, and when you need to install new hardware or disconnect the computer from a power source. If your mobile computer is running on battery power only and you do not plan to use it for a few hours, you should also shut it down to save your battery charge.

1. How do you display the Charms bar?

2. How do you start an app or an application?

3. How do you manually resize a window to a specific size?

4. How do you switch between open windows on the desktop? How do you switch to an open app?

5. What is a library?

6. What is the left pane in a File Explorer window called?

7. How do you change the view in a File Explorer window?

8. What is the root directory?

9. What is a path?

10. When you use the left mouse button to drag a file or folder from one location to another on a drive, what happens? What happens when you drag a file or folder from one drive to another drive?

11. Describe two ways to copy a file or folder from one location to another on the same drive using the mouse.

12. How many characters can a file name have?

13. How can you identify a compressed folder?

14. Is a file deleted from a compressed folder when you extract it?

15. How do you permanently delete files in the Recycle Bin from a drive?

16. How do you close a window? How do you close an app?

17. Describe two ways to use Windows Help and Support.

18. Why should you shut down Windows before turning off your computer?

Practice It

Practice It 7-1

1. Start Windows 8 and sign in, if necessary.

2. Start the Photos app and the Maps app.

3. Switch to the desktop, and then open the Libraries window.

4. Start the WordPad application.

5. Minimize the WordPad window.

6. Change the view of the Libraries window to Extra large icons.

7. Display the data files located in the Chapter 7\ Practice It folder in a new folder window, and then display the files as Large Icons.

8. In the Chapter 7\Practice It folder window, create three folders: **Marketing Info, Sales Dept,** and **Sales Meeting.**

9. Move the Photo1 for Brochure and Photo2 for Brochure files from the Chapter 7\Practice It folder into the Marketing Info folder.

10. Move the Meeting Agenda, Evaluation Form, and 2015 Sales files from the Chapter 7\Practice It folder into the Sales Meeting folder.

11. Move the New Bonus Plan file from the Chapter 7\Practice It folder into the Sales Dept folder.

12. Move the Sales Meeting folder from the Chapter 7\Practice It folder into the Sales Dept folder.

13. Copy the New Bonus Plan file located in the Sales Dept folder into the Sales Meeting folder, and then copy the 2015 Sales file located in the Sales Meeting folder into the Sales Dept folder.

14. Rename the Sales Meeting folder as **Spring Sales Meeting**.

15. In the Sales Dept folder, create a compressed (zipped) folder named **Sales Meeting Zipped** that contains all of the files and folders in the Spring Sales Meeting folder, and then move the zipped folder into the Chapter 7\Practice It folder.

16. Extract the contents of the Sales Meeting Zipped folder to a new folder named **Sales Meeting Extracted** in the Chapter 7\Practice It folder.

17. Delete the 2015 Sales file from the Spring Sales Meeting folder located in the Sales Dept folder.

18. Open the Recycle Bin window.

19. Empty the Recycle Bin, if necessary, and then close the Recycle Bin window.

20. Open the Windows Help and Support window, use the Browse help feature to display the list of Windows Help topics, click the Personalization link, and then click the Get started with themes link. Review this information.

21. Use the Search Help box to display a list of results for the word **libraries**. Click the Libraries: Frequently asked questions link, and then read the information in the window.

22. Make the Libraries window the active window. Change the view to Tiles.

23. Close all open windows and all running apps.

24. Sign out if needed, and then shut down Windows 8.

Practice It 7-2

1. Start Windows 8 and sign in, if necessary.

2. Start the News app, and then start the Notepad application.

3. Open a File Explorer window, and then open the Computer window. Identify the names of the drives on the computer.

4. In the Navigation pane, expand the Computer folder, and then expand the hard disk, such as Local Disk (C:) or OS (C:). Expand the Users folder, and then expand the Public folder.

5. Open a second File Explorer window, and display the contents of the Chapter 7\Practice It folder.

6. Change the view of the Practice It window to Details view.

7. Point to a file to display the ScreenTip, and compare the information in the ScreenTip with the details provided in Details view.

8. Create a copy of the Sales Flyer file located in the Chapter 7\Practice It folder in the same folder. (*Hint*: Use the right mouse button to drag the file to a blank area of the folder window.) Rename the Sales Flyer - Copy file as **Flyer for Ad**.

9. Create three copies of the Qtr1 Sales file located in the Chapter 7\Practice It folder to the same folder. Rename the copies as **Qtr2 Sales, Qtr3 Sales,** and **Qtr4 Sales**.

10. Create two folders in the Chapter 7\Practice It folder: **Auto Sales** and **Auto Advertising**.

11. Move the Sales Flyer and Flyer for Ad files into the Auto Advertising folder, and then move the Auto Advertising folder and the four Qtr Sales files into the Auto Sales folder.

12. Compress the four Qtr Sales files in the Auto Sales folder to a folder named **Quarter Sales Compressed** in the Auto Sales folder.

13. Extract only the Qtr1 Sales files from the Auto Sales Compressed folder to a folder named **Quarter Sales Extracted** folder located in the Chapter 7\Practice It folder.

14. Delete the Sales Flyer file from the Auto Sales\ Auto Advertising folder.

15. Rename the Auto Advertising folder as **Auto Advertising Info**.

16. Open the Windows Help and Support window, and then click the Get started link. In the list of topics, click Get to know Windows. Review this information.

17. Close all open windows and all running apps.

18. Sign out if needed and then shut down Windows 8.

On Your Own

On Your Own 7-1

1. Right-click a blank area of the Start screen, and then click All apps on the Apps bar that appears at the bottom of the screen. Scroll right until you see the apps listed under the category heading Windows Accessories, and then start the Windows Media Player application, which is an application that plays digital media.

2. Use Windows Help and Support to research the application you started in the previous step.

3. Start the Sticky Notes application.

4. Use ScreenTips to identify the two buttons on the note created on the desktop when you started the program in Step 3.

5. Close the Sticky Notes window.

6. Make the window containing the Windows Media Player application the active window.

7. Use Windows Help and Support to locate information on searching for files in File Explorer windows. Answer the following questions:

   a. Where is the Search box located?
   b. What is the name of the contextual tab that appears on the ribbon when you start searching?
   c. Do you need to type the entire file name to find a specific file?
   d. How do you clear your search history?

8. Display the contents of the Chapter 7\Chapter folder, and then display the full path in the Address bar. (*Hint*: Click the icon in the Address bar.) What is the full path?

9. Try to compress the Chapter 7\On Your Own folder. Describe what happens.

10. Close all open windows and running apps.

11. Sign out if needed, and then shut down Windows 8.

Chapter 7

ADDITIONAL STUDY TOOLS

IN THE BOOK
- ▶ Complete end-of-chapter exercises
- ▶ Study tear-out Chapter Review Card

ONLINE
- ▶ Complete additional end-of-chapter exercises

- ▶ Take practice quiz to prepare for tests
- ▶ Review key term flash cards (online, printable, and audio)
- ▶ Play "Beat the Clock" and "Memory" to quiz yourself
- ▶ Watch the videos to learn more about the topics taught in this chapter

Answers to Quiz Yourself

1. *To display the Charms bar, point to the upper- or lower-right corner of the screen.*

2. *To start an app or application, click its tile on the Start screen, or while on the Start screen, type the name of the app or application, and then click the program in the list of results that appears on the Apps screen.*

3. *To manually resize a window, point to a window border until the pointer changes to the two-headed arrow, and then drag the border.*

4. *To switch between open windows on the desktop, click in the window you want to make active or click the button on the taskbar that corresponds to the window you want to make active. To switch to an open app, point to the upper-left corner of the screen and then drag down to display the Switch List, and then click the thumbnail corresponding to the app you want to switch to.*

5. *A library is a central place to view and organize files and folders stored anywhere that your computer can access, such as those on your hard drive, removable drives, and network.*

6. *The left pane in a File Explorer window is called the Navigation pane.*

7. *To change the view in a File Explorer window, click one of the view buttons on the status bar or click the View tab on the ribbon, and then in the Layout group, click the desired view button.*

8. *The root directory is the topmost folder in a computer, and it stores the folders and files that the computer needs when you turn it on.*

9. *A path shows the location of a file on a computer.*

10. *When you use the left mouse button to drag a file or folder from one location to another on a drive, the file or folder is moved. When you drag a file or folder from one drive to another, the file or folder is copied.*

11. *To copy a file or folder from one location to another on the same drive, you can press and hold the Ctrl key and then drag the file or folder, or you can drag the file or folder using the right mouse button, and then on the shortcut menu, click Copy here.*

12. *A file name can have 255 characters.*

13. *You can identify a compressed folder by the zipper on the folder icon.*

14. *No, a file is not deleted from a compressed folder when you extract it.*

15. *To permanently delete files in the Recycle Bin from a drive, do one of the following: right-click the Recycle Bin, and then click Empty Recycle Bin on the shortcut menu; or double-click the Recycle Bin, click the file you want to permanently delete, click the Recycle Bin Tools Manage tab on the ribbon, and then the Empty Recycle Bin button.*

16. *To close a window, click the Close button on the title bar, right-click the window's button on the taskbar and then click Close window, or point to the window's button on the taskbar, point to the window's thumbnail, and then click the Close button on the thumbnail.*

17. *In the Windows Help and Support window, click the Browse help link to browse through a list of Help topics, or type key words in the Search box, and then click the Search button to display the list of topics that contain the words you typed.*

18. *You should shut down Windows before turning off your computer to save energy, preserve your data and settings, and make sure your computer starts quickly the next time you use it.*

Using Internet Explorer and the Mail and People Apps

jannoon028/Shutterstock.com

Windows 8 includes the Internet Explorer Web browser, which you can use to view and interact with Web pages. Windows 8 also includes two other apps to help you easily communicate with others: the Mail app and the People app. The Mail app lets you exchange email messages with others. The People app allows you to store information about the people with whom you communicate. In this chapter, you will work with Internet Explorer as well the Mail and People apps.

NOTE: This chapter was written for Windows 8 users. If you are using Windows 7, you will be able to do the steps for the Internet Explorer desktop application. This is all the steps in section 8-2, section 8-3b, and section 8-4b. You will also be able to complete the first Activity in section 8-4c, the second Activity in section 8-5, and Step 1 in the Activity in section 8-6.

Learning Objectives

After studying the material in this chapter, you will be able to:

8-1 Use the Internet Explorer app

8-2 Use the Internet Explorer desktop application

8-3 Use tabs in both the Internet Explorer app and the desktop application

8-4 Personalize Internet Explorer

8-5 Print Web pages

8-6 Close the Internet Explorer app and desktop application

8-7 Use the Mail app

8-8 Add information to the People app

8-1 Browsing the Web with Internet Explorer

Internet Explorer 10 is the current version of Microsoft's Web browser. Internet Explorer is available in two versions in Windows 8: as a Windows 8 app and as a desktop application. The Internet Explorer app is designed to be used with a touch screen, so it is more streamlined than the desktop application, most of the controls are hidden until you display them, and the controls are larger for easier touch access.

When you start either version of Internet Explorer, the page that appears is called the **home page** or the **start page**. The main page of a Web site is also called a **home page**. The home page appears when you type the domain name and top-level domain of a Web site, such as *www.nasa.gov*.

8-1a Starting the Internet Explorer App and Navigating to Web Pages

When you start the Internet Explorer app, your home page appears on the screen and the navigation bar appears at the bottom of the screen. The navigation bar contains the Address bar. To display a specific Web page, you enter its URL in the Address bar. (Recall from Chapter 1 that the URL is the address of a Web page.) For example, to display the home page of the Bing Web site, you type *www.bing. com* in the Address bar. Exhibit 8-1 shows the Bing home page in the Internet Explorer app. URLs are generally not case-sensitive. However, some operating systems used by Web servers do distinguish between uppercase and lowercase letters. So, if you are entering a URL that includes mixed cases, it is safer to enter the URL exactly as it was provided.

When you click in the Address bar in the Internet Explorer app, the navigation bar expands to include tiles under the headings Frequent and Favorites. See Exhibit 8-2. The tiles under Frequent are links to Web pages that have been visited recently on the computer you are using. The tiles under Favorites are links to Web pages that have been saved on the computer you are using so that you can easily load those pages.

To display the Web page whose URL you typed, you press the Enter key or click the Go button ➔ to the right of the Address bar. When a Web page appears, or **loads**, in a browser window, it is copied from the Web server to your computer.

CAUTION

The Dynamic Web

The Web is a dynamic medium, so the Web pages shown in the Exhibits will most likely differ from the Web pages that you see on your screen. You should still be able to identify the elements called out in the figures.

Begin Activity

Start the Internet Explorer app and the Internet Explorer desktop application.

1 On the Start screen, click the **Internet Explorer tile**. The Internet Explorer app starts, and your home page appears. For example, if your home page is the Bing home page, your screen will look similar to Exhibit 8-1.

2 On the navigation bar at the bottom of the screen, click anywhere in the **Address bar**. The URL in the Address bar is selected,

> **Problem?** If the Address bar isn't on the screen, right-click a **blank area** of the screen.

the Go button ➔ appears to the right of the Address bar, and the navigation bar expands to display the Frequent and Favorite Web pages. Refer to Exhibit 8-2. Anything you type will replace the selected URL.

Internet Explorer 10 The current version of Microsoft's Web browser.

home page (start page) The page that appears when a browser starts.

home page The main page of a Web site.

load To copy a Web page from a server to a computer.

Exhibit 8-1 Home page in the Internet Explorer app

background on your screen will differ

navigation bar

URL in the Address bar

Bing.com

Exhibit 8-2 Expanded navigation bar in the Internet Explorer app

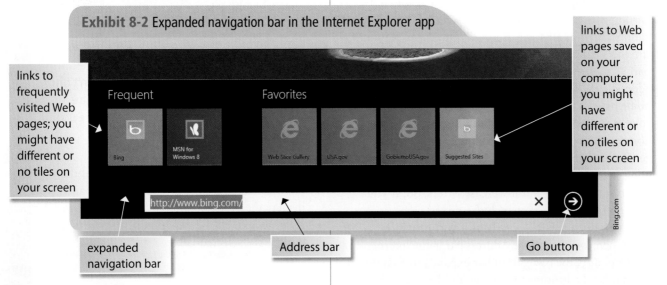

links to frequently visited Web pages; you might have different or no tiles on your screen

links to Web pages saved on your computer; you might have different or no tiles on your screen

Frequent

Favorites

http://www.bing.com/

expanded navigation bar

Address bar

Go button

Bing.com

3 Type **www.nasa.gov**. This is the URL for the home page for the NASA Web site. As you type, a list of Web sites that contain the same characters you are typing replaces the Frequent and Favorites tiles in the expanded navigation bar. If you see the URL you are typing, you can click it to display that Web page instead of finishing typing the URL.

4 Press the **Enter key**. Internet Explorer adds *http://* to the URL and then displays the page, in this case, the home page for the NASA Web site. Exhibit 8-3 shows the home page on the NASA Web site in the Internet Explorer app.

End Activity

Exhibit 8-3 NASA home page in the Internet Explorer app

ABOUT NASA link

NASA.gov

http:// added to the beginning of the URL you typed

Another way to navigate to Web pages is to click links on a Web page in the browser window. A **link** is text or a graphic formatted so that when you click it, another Web page loads in the browser window, you jump to another location on the same Web page, or you open a document stored on your computer or on a Web server. As you click different links, the URL in the Address bar changes.

Begin Activity

Use a link in the Internet Explorer app.

1 Near the top of the NASA home page, point to **ABOUT NASA**. The pointer changes to 🖑 to indicate that this text is a link, and the URL of the linked page appears above the left end of the status bar. See Exhibit 8-4. A list of links available on the

Problem? If the ABOUT NASA link is not at the top of the page, look elsewhere on the page. If you can't find it, point to any other link and substitute that page for the ABOUT NASA page in subsequent steps.

About Us page also appears. This happens because of the underlying design of this Web page; this does not always happen.

2 On the left, click the **What NASA Does link**. The What Does NASA Do? Web page loads, and the URL in the Address bar changes to the address for that page.

End Activity

8-1b Visiting Previously Viewed Web Pages

You can also point to the left or right sides of the screen to make Back and Forward arrows appear and then click those to move between recently viewed pages. (If you are using a touch screen, you can swipe a finger across the screen to move between recently viewed pages.) If the Back or Forward button on the navigation bar is dimmed, or if an arrow button does not appear when you point to the sides of the screen, it means that there is no recently viewed Web page to display. Exhibit 8-5 shows the Back arrow on the left side of the screen. The Back and Forward buttons and arrows track only your current browser session.

link Text or a graphic formatted to load a Web page, jump to another location on the same Web page, or open a document when it is clicked.

Exhibit 8-4 Pointing to a link on a Web page in the Internet Explorer app

ABOUT NASA link

links available on the ABOUT US page

ScreenTip with URL of the link being pointed to

pointer

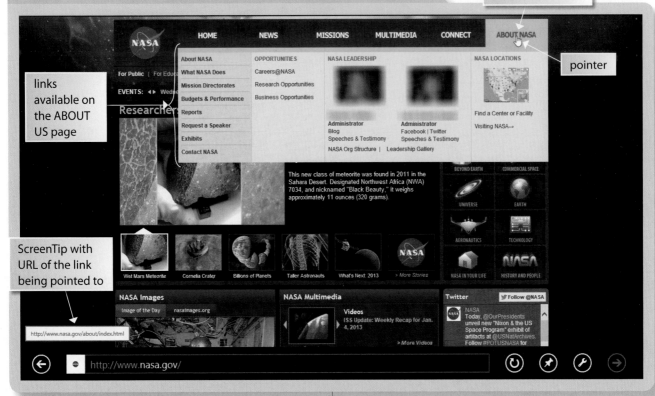

Exhibit 8-5 Back arrow and Back and Forward buttons in the Internet Explorer app

Back arrow

Back button

Forward button

Begin Activity

Go to previously viewed Web pages.

1 On the navigation bar, to the left of the Address bar, click the **Back button** ⬅. The previously viewed Web page—the NASA Web site home page—appears on the screen. Now the Forward button is available.

2 On the right side of the navigation bar, click the **Forward button** ➡. The What Does NASA Do? page loads again. The Forward button is again unavailable (dimmed) because that is the last page you viewed, and no more pages are available.

3 Point to the **right side of the screen**. The Forward arrow does not appear because no more pages are available after the current page.

4 Point to the **left side of the screen**. The Back arrow ◀ appears. Refer back to Exhibit 8-5.

5 Click the **Back arrow** ◀. The NASA home page appears.

End Activity

8-1c Accessing a Search Site from the Address Bar

Finding information on the Internet is made easier with search engines, which are available through search sites. **Search sites** are Web sites designed specifically to help you find information on the Web. Some popular search sites are Bing and Google. Most search sites use a **search engine**—a software program—in conjunction with a huge database of information about Web pages to help visitors find Web pages that contain the information they are seeking.

You can use the Address bar to conduct a search using the default search site for Internet Explorer. Unless it has been changed, the default search engine

for Internet Explorer is Bing. To conduct a search, type appropriate **keywords**—one or more words describing what you are looking for—in the Address bar. (Multiple keywords are sometimes called a **search phrase**.) Press the Enter key to begin the search. The default search site opens displaying the **search results**—a list of links to Web pages that contain the keywords. Each result includes a link you can click to display that Web page and a few lines from the Web page that describe the result. Usually, the text of the link is blue and underlined, and the keywords are bold in both the links and the descriptions. Exhibit 8-6 shows search results for the keywords *live green* in the Bing search site.

Exhibit 8-6 Search results for the keywords *live green* in the Bing search site

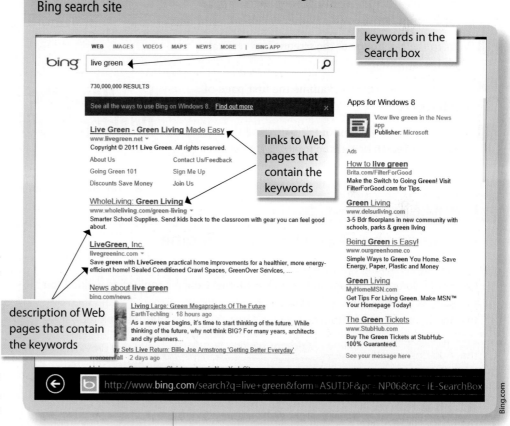

keywords in the Search box

links to Web pages that contain the keywords

description of Web pages that contain the keywords

Bing.com

---

search site A Web site designed to help users search for Web pages that contain keywords.

search engine A software program used by a search site to retrieve Web pages containing the keywords from a search database.

keyword A word typed in a search box on a search site or other Web page to locate information related to that keyword.

search phrase Multiple keywords.

search results A list of links to Web pages that contain the keywords entered in a search engine.

Search the Internet using a search engine.

1 Click in the **Address bar**, type **live green** and then press the **Enter key**. A list of Web pages that contain the keywords *live green* appears in your default search engine. Refer back to Exhibit 8-6 (but keep in mind that your results will not match those shown in Exhibit 8-6 exactly). In most search engines, links to additional pages of results appear at the bottom of the page.

> **Tip:** If the keywords you want to use appear in the Suggestions list below the Address bar, you can click that entry to select it and execute the search.

2 Point to the **right edge of the screen**. The vertical scroll bar appears.

3 Scroll down the page to examine the first page of search results.

4 Scroll back up to the top of the page, and then click in the **Search box** at the top of the page after the keyword *green*.

5 Press the **Spacebar**, type **on a budget** and then press the **Enter key**. The list of results narrows to include only Web sites that contain all of the keywords *live green on a budget*.

6 Scroll down the list on the first page of results, and click a link that interests you. The Web page you clicked loads, replacing the list of results.

7 Use the **Back button** ◀ or the **Back arrow** ◀ on the left edge of the screen to return to the list of search results. The link you clicked is now a different color from the other links to indicate that you visited that Web page.

8 Use the **Back button** ◀ or the **Back arrow** ◀ on the left edge of the screen to return to the NASA home page.

8-2 Using the Internet Explorer Desktop Application

The Internet Explorer desktop application runs on the desktop and is designed to work with a mouse. You can use the Internet Explorer desktop application to perform all of the same tasks that you can perform with the Internet Explorer app.

To start the Internet Explorer desktop application, you need to display the desktop, and then in the taskbar, click the Internet Explorer button ⬛. After it starts, Internet Explorer appears in an application window and displays your home page. This is the same as the home page in the Internet Explorer app. In the Internet Explorer desktop application, the Address bar is at the top. Exhibit 8-7 shows the Bing home page in the Internet Explorer desktop application window.

LEARN MORE

Changing the Default Search Engine

You can set the default search engine for Internet Explorer. You must do this from the Internet Explorer desktop application. In the Internet Explorer application window, on the Address bar, click the Show Address bar AutoComplete arrow ⬛, and then click the Add button at the bottom of the menu. This opens the Internet Explorer Gallery Web site displaying the Add-ons screen with the search providers button selected, as shown in the figure here. Click the search provider you want to use. In the next Web page that appears, click the Add to Internet Explorer button. The Add Search Provider dialog box opens, asking if you want to add this search provider. Click the Make this my default search provider check box to select it, and then click Add.

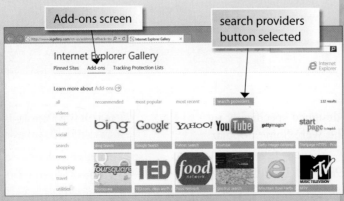

Internet Explorer Gallery page listing search engines

Exhibit 8-7 Web page in the Internet Explorer desktop application

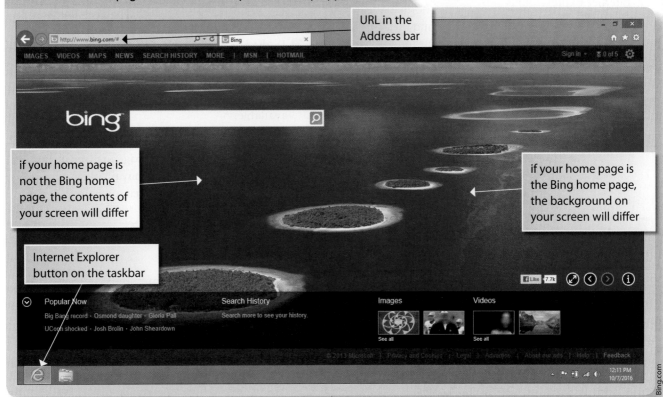

URL in the Address bar

if your home page is not the Bing home page, the contents of your screen will differ

if your home page is the Bing home page, the background on your screen will differ

Internet Explorer button on the taskbar

You display a specific Web page in the Internet Explorer desktop application in the same way as in the Internet Explorer app: You enter its URL in the Address bar, and then press the Enter key or click the Go button. In the Internet Explorer desktop application, the Go button →| appears at the right end of the Address bar. As you type in the Address bar, a list of Web pages whose URLs start with the same characters that were previously visited using the browser or are commonly visited appears in a menu below the Address bar. This is similar to the list that appears in the expanded navigation bar when you type in the Address bar in the Internet Explorer app.

Begin Activity

Start the Internet Explorer desktop application, and go to a specific Web page.

1 Point to the **lower-left corner** of the screen to display the Start screen thumbnail, and then click the **Start screen thumbnail**. The Start screen appears.

2 Click the **Desktop tile**. The desktop appears.

3 On the taskbar, click the **Internet Explorer button** [e]. The Internet Explorer desktop application opens, displaying your home page. If your home page is the Bing home page, your screen will look similar to Exhibit 8-7.

Tip: You can also display a Web page in the Internet Explorer app, display the navigation bar, click the Page tools button [🔧], and then click View on the desktop.

4 If the application window does not fill the screen, click the **Maximize button** [□] in the upper-right corner of the title bar.

5 In the Internet Explorer desktop application, click anywhere in the **Address bar**. The current URL is selected.

6 Type **www.nps.gov**. This is the URL for the home page for the U.S. National Park Service Web site. As you type, a list of Web sites whose URLs contain the same characters you are typing might appear below the Address bar.

7 Press the **Enter key**. Internet Explorer adds *http://* to the URL and then displays the page, in this case, the home page for the U.S. National Park Service Web site.

> **Tip:** You can return to your home page by clicking the Home button 🏠 at the top-right of the application window.

8 In the center of the page, point to **About Us**. The pointer changes to 👆 to indicate that this text is a link, and the URL of the linked page appears above the left end of the status bar. See Exhibit 8-8.

9 Click the **About Us** link. The About Us page loads, and the URL in the Address bar changes to the address for that page.

End Activity

In the Internet Explorer desktop application, the Back and Forward buttons are at the top of the window to the left of the Address bar.

Begin Activity

Go to previously viewed Web pages.

1 To the left of the Address bar, click the **Back button** ◀. The previously viewed Web page—the National Park Service Web site home page—appears on the screen. Now the Forward button is available.

2 To the right of the Address bar, click the **Forward button** ▶. The About Us page loads again. The Forward button is again unavailable (dimmed) because you have not viewed any more pages after the current page.

End Activity

As in the Internet Explorer app, you can type keywords in the Address bar and then press the Enter key to display a list of search results in the default search engine, which is also Bing (unless it was changed).

Exhibit 8-8 Pointing to a link on a Web page in the Internet Explorer desktop application

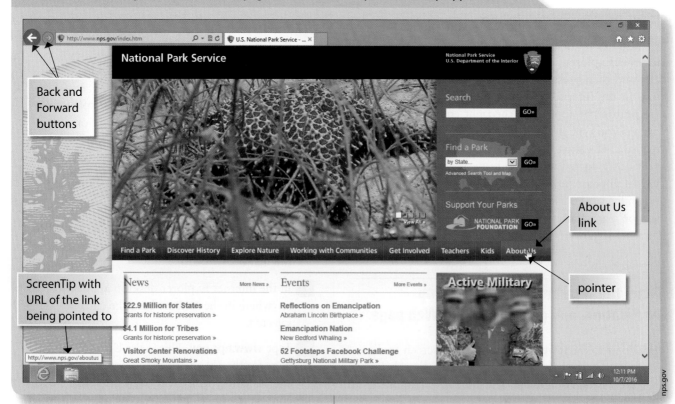

Back and Forward buttons

About Us link

pointer

ScreenTip with URL of the link being pointed to

http://www.nps.gov/aboutus

Changing Your Home Page

You can change your home or start page. You must do this in the Internet Explorer desktop application. First, display the page you want to use as a start page. Near the upper-right corner of the Internet Explorer desktop application window, click the Tools button ⚙, and then click Internet Options to open the Internet Options dialog box with the General tab selected. Under Home page, click Use current to change the start page to the current page, and then click OK to close the dialog box. The start page will be changed in both the Internet Explorer desktop application and in the Internet Explorer app.

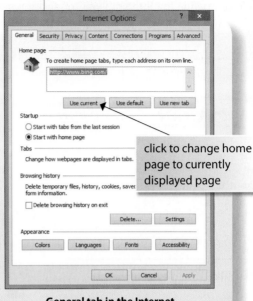

click to change home page to currently displayed page

General tab in the Internet Options dialog box

blank tab to the right of the current tabs and then click the New Tab button 🗋 that is displayed. The new tab that opens lists frequently or recently visited Web pages, which you can click to display that Web page in the new tab. See Exhibit 8-9.

If you want to open a linked Web page in a new tab, you can right-click the link on a Web page, and then click Open link in new tab on the shortcut menu. When you open a new tab by right-clicking a link, the current tab and the new tab create a **tab group**, which is a collection of related tabs.

Exhibit 8-10 shows three tabs open in the browser window. When multiple tabs are open, the tab on top containing the Web page you can see is the current tab. To switch to another tab, you click it. You can close tabs by clicking the Close button ☒ on the right end of the tab. If you are trying to close a tab other than the current tab, point to it to make its Close button visible.

8-3 Using Tabs

Web pages are displayed on **tabs** in both versions of Internet Explorer. You can open multiple tabs to display different Web pages at the same time. Each tab has its own history list.

8-3a Using Tabs in the Internet Explorer Desktop Application

When you start the Internet Explorer desktop application, the start page appears in a tab in the application window. To open a second tab, you point to the small,

Exhibit 8-9 New, blank tab in the Internet Explorer desktop application

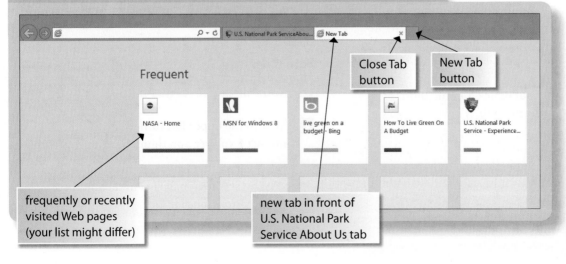

Frequent

Close Tab button

New Tab button

NASA - Home | MSN for Windows 8 | live green on a budget - Bing | How To Live Green On A Budget | U.S. National Park Service - Experience...

frequently or recently visited Web pages (your list might differ)

new tab in front of U.S. National Park Service About Us tab

tab An object that displays a Web page within the Internet Explorer desktop application window or in the Internet Explorer app.

tab group A collection of related tabs.

Exhibit 8-10 Three tabs open in the Internet Explorer desktop application

http://www.usa.gov/About.shtml

U.S. National Park ServiceAbou... | USA.gov: The U.S. Government... | About the USA.gov Website... ✕

Home | FAQs | Site Index | E-mail Your Question | Chat | FREE Publications   Get E-mail Updates | Chan

Esp

USA.gov
Government Made Easy

Search the Government ...   SEARCH

1-800-FED-INFO (333

Services   Blog   Topics   Government Agencies   Contact Government

Home > About USA.gov   Download Adobe

About USA.gov

current tab

USA.gov

the same tab group. This might be difficult to see if the new tab group color is only a slightly darker blue than the first tab.

6 Click the **About the USA.gov Website tab**.

Begin Activity

Use tabs in the Internet Explorer desktop application.

1 To the right of the U.S. National Park Service About Us tab, point to the **small, blank tab**. The New Tab button ⬜ appears on it.

2 Click the **New Tab button** ⬜. A new tab appears in the browser window and displays a list of up to 10 Web sites you spend the most time using. The Address bar is blank. Refer back to Exhibit 8-9. The list of sites on your screen might differ.

> **Tip:** To display tabs you closed during this browsing session, click the Reopen closed tab link. To display all of the tabs you opened the last time you used the Internet Explorer desktop application, click the Reopen last session link.

3 Click in the **Address bar** if necessary, type **www.usa.gov** and then press the **Enter key**. The home page for the USA.gov Web site appears in the new tab.

4 Scroll down to the bottom of the page.

5 Right-click the **About Us link**. On the shortcut menu, click **Open in new tab**. A new tab opens to the right of the USA.gov home page tab. The USA.gov tab and the About the USA.gov Web site tabs are the same color to indicate that they are in

The About the USA.gov page becomes the current tab in the window. Refer to Exhibit 8-10.

7 On the About the USA.gov Website tab, click the **Close Tab button** ✕. The tab closes, and the USA.gov home page is the current tab. Because only one tab is left in the tab group, the USA.gov tab is no longer colored.

8 Right-click the **USA.gov tab**, and then on the shortcut menu, click **Close other tabs**. The USA.gov tab closes, and the U.S. National Park Service About Us tab becomes the current tab.

End Activity

8-3b Using Tabs in the Internet Explorer App

In the Internet Explorer app, tabs appear as thumbnails of the currently open Web pages in the **tab switcher**, which appears at the top of the screen when you right-click the Web page. Exhibit 8-11 shows the tab switcher. In the tab switcher, the current tab has a blue border, and its Web page appears on the screen. To switch to another tab, you click it in the tab switcher, and to close a tab, click the Close Tab button ✕ in the tab in the tab switcher.

Begin Activity

Use tabs in the Internet Explorer app.

1 Point to the **upper-left corner** of the screen. The Internet Explorer app thumbnail appears.

2 Click the **Internet Explorer app thumbnail**. The NASA Web site home page in the Internet Explorer app appears.

tab switcher An area in the Internet Explorer app that displays thumbnails of current or recently visited Web pages for easy navigation between them.

Finding and Using Accelerators

Accelerators are tools that make it easier to find information on the Web without navigating to other Web sites. For example, if you are viewing a Web page about a hotel in a city you plan to visit, you can select the hotel's address and then use an Accelerator to quickly display a map showing the location of the hotel. Instead of copying the address, navigating to the Web page for a mapping service, pasting the address, and then viewing a map, you point to the Accelerator icon ⬈ to display a preview of the map, as shown here. In this case, you perform one step instead of four.

Accelerators are services provided by Web sites, so some sites have them and others do not. The Internet Explorer desktop application comes with a selection of default Accelerators, including Bing Maps and Bing Translator. You can add or remove Accelerators as necessary using the Manage Add-ons dialog box, which you open by clicking the Tools button on the Command bar or Favorites bar, and then clicking Manage add-ons. Accelerators are not available in the Internet Explorer app.

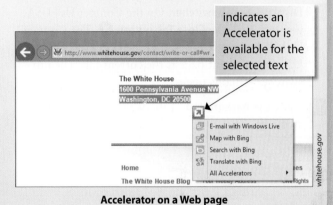

Accelerator on a Web page

Exhibit 8-11 Three tabs in the tab switcher in the Internet Explorer app

New Tab button

Close Tab button

tab switcher

active tab

Tab tools button

NASA.gov, USA.gov

---

3 Right-click the **background** of the Web page. The tab switcher, which shows a tab for the current page, appears at the top of the screen.

4 On the tab switcher, click the **New Tab button** ⬚. A new, blank tab appears briefly in the tab switcher, and then a new, blank page opens with the expanded navigation bar containing tiles of frequently visited and favorite pages. The insertion point is in the Address bar.

5 Type **www.usa.gov** and then press the **Enter key**. The home page for the USA.gov Web site appears in the new tab.

6 Scroll down to the bottom of the page.

7 Right-click the **Contact Us link**. On the shortcut menu, click **Open link in new tab**. The tab switcher appears, displaying a new tab containing the Contact Us page, and then the tab switcher closes. The current tab is still the USA.gov tab.

Tip: You can also press and hold the Ctrl key while you click a link to open the linked page in a new tab.

> **Accelerator** A service on a Web site that make it easier to find information on the Web without navigating to another Web site.

8 Right-click the **background** of the Web page to display the tab switcher. The tab switcher appears with thumbnails of each open Web page. Refer back to Exhibit 8-11.

9 In the tab switcher, click the **Contact Us | USA.gov tab**. The Contact Us Web page becomes the current tab and fills the screen.

10 Display the **tab switcher**. On the Contact Us | USA. gov tab, click the **Close Tab button** ⊗. The Contact Us | USA.gov tab closes, and the USA.gov: The U.S. Government page is the current tab. The tab switcher remains open.

11 Click the **background** of the Web page. The tab switcher closes.

End Activity

8-4 Personalizing Internet Explorer

To make it easier to display the Web pages you view the most frequently, you can personalize Internet Explorer by pinning Web pages to the Start screen or to the taskbar on the desktop. You can also save Web pages as links in a list. If you want to return to a Web page you have visited in the past 20 days and you haven't pinned it or saved it to a list, you can use the history list to find the page.

8-4a Pinning Web Pages

If you visit a Web page frequently, you can pin it to the Start screen or to the taskbar on the desktop application.

When you pin a Web page to the Start screen, it appears as a tile to the right of the tiles already on the screen. Exhibit 8-12 shows two Web pages pinned to the Start screen. Web pages pinned to the Start screen are also listed in the expanded navigation bar that appears when you click in the Address bar. See Exhibit 8-13.

To pin a Web page to the Start screen, first you display it in the Internet Explorer app. On the navigation bar, click the Pin site button 📌, and then on the menu that appears, click Pin to Start. This opens a dialog box that shows the tile as it will look on the Start screen and the name that will appear on the tile. You can type a more meaningful name to replace the name on the tile. See Exhibit 8-14. Click Pin to Start to close the dialog box and pin the Web page.

Exhibit 8-12 Pinned Web pages on the Start screen

tiles for pinned Web pages

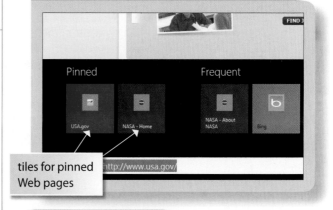

Exhibit 8-13 Pinned Web pages in the expanded navigation bar

tiles for pinned Web pages

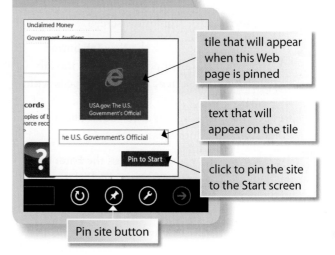

Exhibit 8-14 Dialog box for pinning a Web page to the Start screen

tile that will appear when this Web page is pinned

text that will appear on the tile

click to pin the site to the Start screen

Pin site button

Pin a Web page to the Start screen.

1 In the Internet Explorer app, make sure the home page of the USA.gov site is the active tab, and then scroll to the top of the page.

2 If necessary, right-click a **blank area of the screen** to display the navigation bar and the tab switcher.

3 On the navigation bar, click the **Pin site button** ⊘, and then click **Pin to Start**. A dialog box opens with a tile of the Web page in it and a box with the complete name of the Web page below the tile. Refer back to Exhibit 8-14.

4 Point to the box containing the name of the Web page, and then click the **Clear button** ✕ that appears. The text is removed from the box.

5 Type **USA.gov** and then click **Pin to Start**. The site is pinned to the Start screen.

6 Display the tab switcher, and then click the **NASA – Home tab**. Pin it to the Start screen using the default name of **NASA – Home**.

7 Click the **About Us link**. The About NASA page appears.

8 Return to the **Start screen**, and then scroll right to display the tiles for the pinned sites. Refer back to Exhibit 8-12.

9 Click the **NASA – Home tile** to open the NASA – Home page in the Internet Explorer app in a new tab (the third tab).

10 Close the **NASA – Home tab**. The USA.gov tab (the second tab) becomes the active tab.

11 Click the **Address bar**. The tiles for the pinned sites appear in the expanded navigation bar under the label Pinned to the left of the Frequent tiles. Refer back to Exhibit 8-13.

12 Click the **NASA – Home tile**. The NASA – Home page opens in the active tab, replacing the USA. gov page.

End Activity

You can unpin any site that you no longer need from the Start screen. You can do this in the expanded navigation bar or on the Start screen.

Unpin a Web page from the Start screen.

1 Right-click a **blank area of the screen** to display the Address bar, if necessary. Click in the **Address bar** to display the expanded navigation bar.

2 Under Pinned, right-click the **NASA – Home tile**. On the shortcut menu, click **Remove**. A small dialog box opens containing the NASA – Home tile and an Unpin from Start command.

3 Click **Unpin from Start**. The dialog box closes, and the NASA – Home tile no longer appears under Pinned in the expanded navigation bar.

4 Display the **Start screen**, and then scroll right to display the tile for the USA.gov pinned site. The NASA – Home site tile no longer appears on the Start screen.

5 Right-click the **USA.gov tile**. A check mark appears on the tile to indicate that it is selected, and the Apps bar appears at the bottom of the screen.

6 On the Apps bar, click **Unpin from Start**. The selected tile is removed from the Start screen and will no longer appear on the expanded navigation bar.

End Activity

You can also pin Web pages to the taskbar on the desktop using the Internet Explorer desktop application. First, display the Web page you want to pin on a tab in an Internet Explorer desktop application window. Then, drag the tab to the taskbar until the Web page collapses to a pale rectangle and the Pin to taskbar ScreenTip appears. See Exhibit 8-15. The pinned Web page appears as a button on the taskbar next to the File Explorer and Internet Explorer buttons. Exhibit 8-16 shows a Web page pinned to the taskbar.

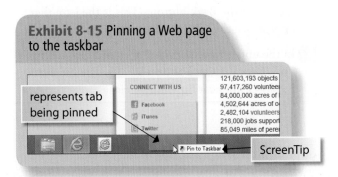

Exhibit 8-15 Pinning a Web page to the taskbar

represents tab being pinned

CONNECT WITH US
Facebook
iTunes
Twitter

121,603,193 objects
97,417,260 volunteel
84,000,000 acres of
4,502,644 acres of o
2,482,104 volunteers
218,000 jobs suppor
85,049 miles of pere

Pin to Taskbar

ScreenTip

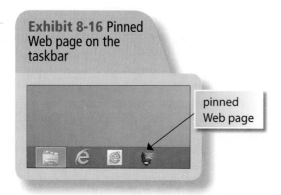

Exhibit 8-16 Pinned Web page on the taskbar

pinned Web page

Begin Activity

Pin a Web page to the taskbar on the desktop.

1 Switch to the **desktop**.

2 In the Internet Explorer application window, point to the **U.S. National Park Service About Us tab**.

3 Press and hold the **mouse button**, and then drag down to the **taskbar** until the Web page collapses to a pale rectangle and the Pin to taskbar Screen-Tip appears. Refer back to Exhibit 8-15.

4 Release the **mouse button**. The tab closes, its icon appears on the taskbar, as shown in Exhibit 8-16. The tab opens in a new Internet Explorer desktop application window. Because this was the only tab open in the Internet Explorer desktop application, the application window closed when the tab closed.

5 On the taskbar, click the **U.S. National Park Service About Us button**. A new Internet Explorer desktop application window opens with the U.S. National Park Service About Us page open in a tab. This window is slightly different than the ordinary Internet Explorer desktop application window: There is no Home button, and the Back and Forward buttons are the same color as the icon to the left of the Back button. (This is the icon that appears on the taskbar when the page is pinned.)

6 In the upper-right corner of the application window, click the **Close button** ✕ . The Internet Explorer application window closes.

End Activity

favorite A shortcut to a Web page saved in a list in the Internet Explorer desktop application or as a tile on the Start screen and on the expanded navigation bar.

To unpin a Web page from the taskbar, right-click the button on the taskbar to open a shortcut menu. See Exhibit 8-17. On the shortcut menu, click Unpin this program from taskbar. Even though the command uses the word "program," it is referring to only the button for the pinned page that you right-clicked.

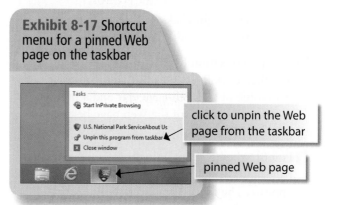

Exhibit 8-17 Shortcut menu for a pinned Web page on the taskbar

Tasks
Start InPrivate Browsing

U.S. National Park ServiceAbout Us
Unpin this program from taskbar
Close window

click to unpin the Web page from the taskbar

pinned Web page

Begin Activity

Unpin a Web page from the taskbar on the desktop.

1 On the taskbar, right-click the **U.S. National Park Service About Us button**. A shortcut menu opens. Refer back to Exhibit 8-17.

2 On the shortcut menu, click **Unpin this program from taskbar**. The shortcut menu closes, and the button is removed from the taskbar.

End Activity

Web pages you pin to the taskbar are not added to the Start screen and vice versa. In other words, if you want a Web page pinned to both the Start screen and the taskbar so that you can easily display that Web page in both the Internet Explorer app and the Internet Explorer desktop application, you need to pin it to both places.

8-4b Saving Web Pages as Favorites

Similar to pinning a Web page to the Start screen, you can save a Web page as a favorite in Internet Explorer. A **favorite** is a shortcut to a Web page saved in a list in the Internet Explorer desktop application or as a tile on the Start screen and on the expanded navigation bar.

To add a Web page as a favorite in the Internet Explorer desktop application, click the View favorites, feeds, and history button ★ in the upper-right corner of the application window to display the Favorites Center, which is shown in Exhibit 8-18. The Favorites Center contains three tabs: Favorites, Feeds, and History. Favorites are listed on the Favorites tab. At the top of the Favorites Center, click Add to Favorites. This opens the Add a Favorites dialog box, which is shown in Exhibit 8-19. You can keep the default name, or you can edit it to something shorter and more understandable.

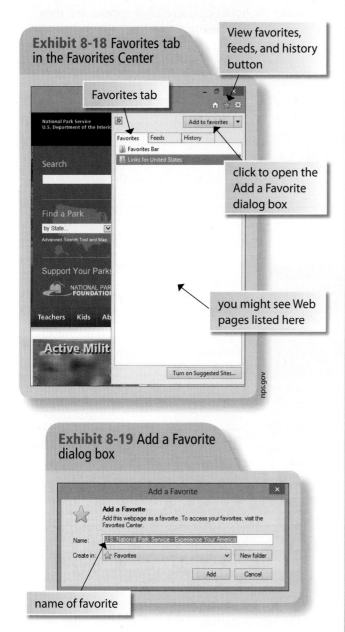

Exhibit 8-18 Favorites tab in the Favorites Center

View favorites, feeds, and history button

Favorites tab

click to open the Add a Favorite dialog box

you might see Web pages listed here

Exhibit 8-19 Add a Favorite dialog box

name of favorite

Begin Activity

Add Web pages as favorites.

1 Start the **Internet Explorer desktop application**.

2 Click in the **Address bar**, type **www.nps.gov** and then press the **Enter key**.

3 Near the upper-right corner of the program window, click the **View favorites, feeds, and history button** ⭐. The Favorites Center opens on top of the browser window.

4 If the Favorites tab is not selected, click the **Favorites tab**. The list of favorites stored on the computer appears. Refer back to Exhibit 8-18.

5 At the top of the Favorites Center, click the **Add to favorites button**. The Add a Favorite dialog box opens. Refer back to Exhibit 8-19. The text in the Name box is the name of the currently displayed Web page, as it appears on the page tab. You can edit this to change the name of the favorite. The Create in box also displays the name of the folder in which the favorite will be stored—the default Favorites folder means that the favorite will be stored in the main Favorites list.

> **Tip:** You can select a different folder by clicking the Create in arrow and choosing another folder, or by creating a new folder by clicking New Folder.

6 In the dialog box, click **Add**. The Add a Favorite dialog box closes, and the home page of the U.S. National Park Service Web site is saved as a favorite.

7 Near the upper-right corner of the application window, click the **View favorites, feeds, and history button** ⭐. The U.S. National Park Service Web page is listed as the last favorite in the Favorites list.

8 Press the **Esc key** to close the Favorites Center without selecting anything.

End Activity

After you have added a Web page as a favorite, you can click its link in the Favorites Center, and that page will load in the current tab.

Begin Activity

Go to a favorite in the Internet Explorer desktop application.

1 Click the **Back button** ← to return to your home page.

2 In the upper-right corner of the application window, click the **View favorites, feeds, and history button** ⭐. The Favorites Center opens with the Favorites tab selected.

3 On the Favorites tab, click the **U.S. National Park Service favorite**. The home page of the U.S. National Park Service Web site loads in the current tab.

End Activity

You can also add favorites in the Internet Explorer app. To add a favorite in the Internet Explorer app, display the Address bar, click the Pin site button ✪, and then on the menu, click Add to favorites. In the Internet Explorer app, the favorites appear in the expanded navigation bar that appears when you click in the Address bar. See Exhibit 8-20.

Exhibit 8-20 Favorites in the expanded navigation bar

Web pages saved as favorites (you might see more or fewer favorites on your screen)

Begin Activity

Save a Web page as a favorite in the Internet Explorer app, and go to it.

1 Switch to the **Internet Explorer app**.

2 Right-click a **blank area of the screen** to display the tab switcher, and then click the **NASA – About NASA tab**. The About NASA Web page appears on the screen.

3 On the navigation bar, click the **Pin site button** ✪. A menu appears.

4 On the menu, click **Add to favorites**. The About NASA Web page is saved as a favorite.

5 Click the **Back button** ◒ or **Back arrow** ◁. The NASA home page appears.

6 Click in the **Address bar**. The navigation bar expands to display Frequent and Favorite Web pages.

7 Under Favorites, point to the **rightmost tile** to make the horizontal scroll bar appear, and then drag the **scroll box** to the right. The two favorites you added—the U.S. National Parks Service home page that you saved as a favorite in the Internet Explorer desktop application and the NASA – About NASA page that you saved as a favorite in the Internet Explorer app—appear as tiles under Favorites. Refer to Exhibit 8-20.

8 Click the **U.S. National Parks Service home page tile**. That Web page appears on the screen in the Internet Explorer app.

End Activity

To help keep your favorites organized, you can delete a favorite if you no longer need it. To do this in the Internet Explorer app, display the expanded navigation bar, right-click the tile under Favorites that corresponds to the Web page you want to delete, and then click Remove on the menu.

Begin Activity

Delete a favorite in the Internet Explorer app.

1 Click in the **Address bar**. The navigation bar expands.

2 Scroll right, if necessary, until you see the **U.S. National Parks Service home page tile**.

3 Right-click the **U.S. National Parks Service home page tile**. On the shortcut menu, click **Remove**. The U.S. National Parks Service home page tile is deleted and no longer appears under Favorites.

End Activity

You can also delete favorites in the Internet Explorer desktop application.

Delete a favorite in the Internet Explorer desktop application.

1 Switch to the **desktop**.

2 In the upper-right corner of the Internet Explorer desktop application window, click the **View favorites, feeds, and history button** ⭐. The Favorites Center opens with the Favorites tab selected. Note that the U.S. National Park Service favorite that you had added in the Internet Explorer desktop application is no longer listed because you removed it as a favorite in the Internet Explorer app. The NASA – About NASA page that you added as a favorite in the Internet Explorer app is listed.

3 In the Favorites Center, right-click the **NASA – About NASA favorite**. On the shortcut menu, click **Delete**. The favorite is deleted.

4 Press the **Esc key** to close the Favorites Center.

8-4c Using Internet Explorer History

Internet Explorer's **history** tracks the Web pages you visit over multiple browsing sessions. The Internet Explorer app and the desktop application share the same browsing history.

In the Internet Explorer desktop application, you can display the complete history by opening the Favorites Center and then clicking the History tab. See Exhibit 8-21. By default, the entries on the History tab are organized into date folders (Today, Yesterday, Two Weeks ago, and so on). Within each date folder, there is a folder for every Web site you visited in either the Internet Explorer desktop application or the Internet Explorer app. Within each site folder, the Web pages you visited appear in alphabetical order. (The suggestions that appear when you start typing a URL in the Address bar of either the Internet Explorer desktop

application or the Internet Explorer app are based on history.) To return to a page in the history, click the Web site's entry in the list for a particular day, and then click the URL to revisit a specific page on that site.

Return to a page in the history in the Internet Explorer desktop application.

1 In the upper-right corner of the Internet Explorer desktop application window, click the **View favorites, feeds, and history button** ⭐. The Favorites Center opens with the Favorites tab selected.

2 In the Favorites Center, click the **History tab**. The History tab becomes the active tab, and a list of date folders appears.

3 Click the **Today link** to expand that folder. A list of Web sites you visited today appears in alphabetical order, with a separate folder for each site. Refer to Exhibit 8-21.

4 In the list, click the **usa (www.usa.gov) folder link**. The list of Web pages in that folder appears. Notice that the Contact Us page appears in this list, even though you viewed it in the Internet Explorer app.

5 Click the **Contact Us | USA.gov link**. The Contact Us page on the USA.gov Web site loads in a new tab.

Exhibit 8-21 History tab in the Favorites Center

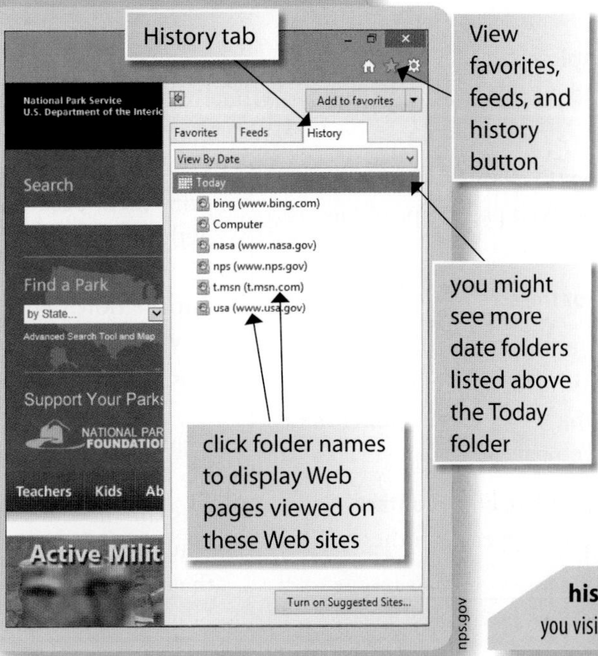

History tab

View favorites, feeds, and history button

you might see more date folders listed above the Today folder

click folder names to display Web pages viewed on these Web sites

In the Internet Explorer app, five or six Web pages in the history appear under Frequent in the expanded navigation bar that appears when you click in the Address bar. You cannot access the complete history in the expanded navigation bar. If you remember the URL for pages in the history that do not appear

history A list that tracks the Web pages you visit over a certain time period.

Deleting the Internet Explorer History

Web pages are kept in Internet Explorer history for 20 days, but you can delete the entire history any time you want. From the Internet Explorer app, display the Charms bar, click the Settings charm, and then click Internet Options at the top to display the Internet Explorer Settings panel. Under Delete Browsing History, click the Delete button. A "Deleting" message appears to the right of the Delete button. After all the browsing history is deleted, the message changes to "Done!" The process of deleting can take a few moments or several minutes. Click a blank area of the Internet Explorer app to close the Internet Explorer Settings panel.

To delete the history from the Internet Explorer desktop application, click the Tools button ⚙ in the upper-right corner of the Internet Explorer desktop application window to open the Tools menu, point to Safety, and then click Delete Browsing History on the submenu that opens. The Delete Browsing History dialog box opens, as shown here. To delete the entire browsing history, make sure all the check boxes except Preserve Favorites website data are selected. Some users prefer to select the Preserve Favorites website data check box so that any data or settings associated with Web pages that are saved as favorites will not be deleted.

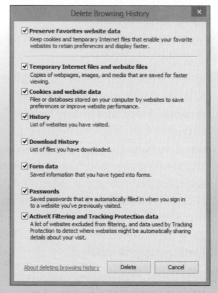

Delete Browsing History dialog box

---

under Frequent, you can start typing it in the Address bar, and the page will appear as one of the suggestions in the expanded navigation bar.

Begin Activity

Return to a page in the history in the Internet Explorer app.

1 Switch to the **Internet Explorer app**. If the navigation bar is not visible and expanded, click the **Address bar**.

2 Under Frequent, click the **U.S. National Park Service About Us tile**. That Web page appears on the screen.

3 Right-click a **blank area of the screen**.

4 Click in the **Address bar**, and then type **con**. The Frequent and Favorites tiles are replaced with suggestions for completing the URL, including the Contact Us | USA.gov Web page.

5 In the expanded navigation bar, click **Contact Us | USA.gov**. That Web page appears on the screen.

End Activity

8-5 Printing Web Pages

You might need to print a Web page occasionally. For example, if you pay for an item on a shopping Web site, you might want to print the receipt. Many Web pages provide a link to a separate printer-friendly version of the page. This version prints only essential information in an appropriate format. Both the Internet Explorer app and desktop application include commands to print Web pages.

It's a good idea to preview the pages before you print them because Web pages are not always designed with printing in mind. For instance, a Web page might be wider than your paper, or it might contain extra information that you don't need printed. If you preview the printout first, you can make some adjustments when you preview the page.

To preview and print a Web page from the Internet Explorer app, display the Charms bar, and then click the Devices charm to open the Devices panel, which lists all the devices connected to the computer. Click your printer name in the list to display the panel for that printer. Exhibit 8-22 shows the panel for the HP Officejet Pro 8600 printer. The printer panel shows the first page of the printout. Depending on your printer,

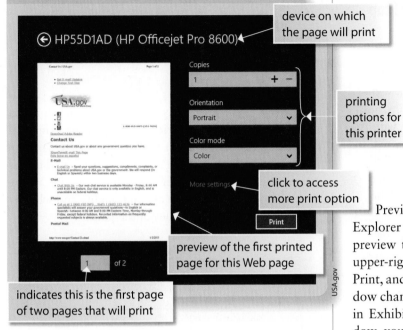

Exhibit 8-22 Devices panel for the HP Officejet Pro 8600 printer in the Internet Explorer app

device on which the page will print

printing options for this printer

click to access more print option

preview of the first printed page for this Web page

indicates this is the first page of two pages that will print

USA.gov

2 Click **the device you want to use** to print. A preview of the Web page as it will print appears. Refer to Exhibit 8-22. Your device may differ.

3 If you are instructed to print, click the **Print button**; the panel closes, and the three pages of the Contact Us | USA Web page print. If your instructor does not want you to print, press the **Esc key** to close the Devices panel.

End Activity

Previewing and printing the Web page in the Internet Explorer desktop application is a two-part process. To preview the page, click the Tools button ⚙ near the upper-right corner of the application window, point to Print, and then click Print Preview. The application window changes to the Print Preview window. As indicated in Exhibit 8-23, which shows the Print Preview window, you can change the orientation from portrait to landscape, display or hide the text that prints at the top and bottom of the page (called headers and footers), and change the print size. (Note that you cannot adjust the headers and footers in the Internet Explorer app.)

you will see other options; in this case, options to change the number of copies printed, change the orientation, and change whether to print the page in color are provided. To preview the rest of the pages in the printout, point to the right side of the preview page, and then click the Forward arrow that appears (or swipe from right to left if you are using a touch screen). To see the same printer preferences available when you click the Preferences button in the Print dialog box in the Internet Explorer desktop application, click More settings in the printer panel.

Begin Activity

Preview and print a Web page in the Internet Explorer app.

1 Display the **Charms bar**, and then click the **Devices charm**. The Devices panel appears and displays a list of devices Internet Explorer can use for printing.

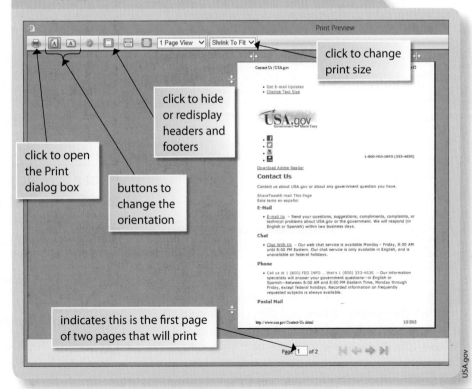

Exhibit 8-23 Print Preview window in the Internet Explorer desktop application

click to change print size

click to hide or redisplay headers and footers

click to open the Print dialog box

buttons to change the orientation

indicates this is the first page of two pages that will print

USA.gov

Display the Print Preview window for a Web page in the Internet Explorer desktop application.

1 Display the **desktop**.

2 In the upper-right corner of the application window, click the **Tools button** ⚙, point to **Print**, and then click **Print Preview**. The Print Preview window opens on top of the Web browser window. Refer back to Exhibit 8-23. The title of the Web page and the page number appear in the header, and the URL and the current date appear in the footer.

3 On the toolbar, click the **Landscape button** 🄰. The orientation of the page in the preview changes to landscape.

4 On the toolbar, click the **Page Setup button** ⚙. The Page Setup dialog box opens. See Exhibit 8-24. Notice that in addition to the options that appear on the toolbar, you can also customize the header and footer or change the margins.

Exhibit 8-24 Page Setup dialog box in the Internet Explorer desktop application

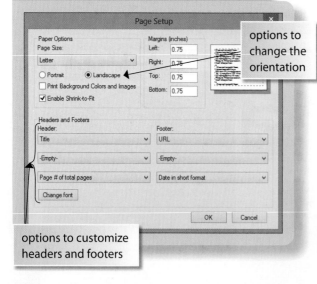

options to change the orientation

options to customize headers and footers

5 In the Headers and Footers section, under Header, click the **–Empty– arrow**, and then click **Custom**. The Custom dialog box opens with the insertion point in the empty box.

6 Type your name, and then click **OK**. The dialog box closes.

7 In the Page Setup dialog box, click **OK**. The Page Setup dialog box closes, and your name appears in the center of the top of the Web page.

When you are ready to print in the Internet Explorer desktop application, you open the Print dialog box. See Exhibit 8-25. In this dialog box, you can select a printer, change the number of pages and copies to print, or change printer preferences specific to the printer you are using, such as print quality and whether to print on one or both sides of the page.

Exhibit 8-25 Print dialog box in the Internet Explorer desktop application

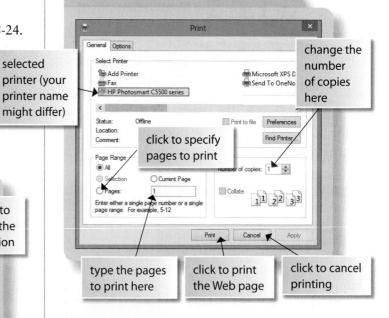

selected printer (your printer name might differ)

change the number of copies here

click to specify pages to print

type the pages to print here

click to print the Web page

click to cancel printing

Print a Web page from the Internet Explorer desktop application.

1 On the toolbar in the Print Preview window, click the **Print button** 🖨. The Print dialog box opens.

2 In the Page Range section, click the **Pages option button**. In the box next to Pages, 1 is selected.

3 Type **2**. Now only the second page will print.

4 If you are instructed to print, click **Print**; the dialog box and the Print Preview window close, the

Contact Us page on the USA.gov Web site appears in the Internet Explorer desktop application window, and page 2 prints. If your instructor does not want you to print, click **Cancel**; the dialog box closes, and the Print Preview window remains open.

5 If the Print Preview window is still open, in the upper-right corner of the Print Preview window, click the **Close button** ❌. The Print Preview window closes, and the Contact Us page on the USA.gov Web site appears in the Internet Explorer desktop application window. The changes you made to the header in the Page Setup dialog box are saved, so you will change the middle part of the header back to Empty.

6 In the upper-right of the application window, click the **Tools button** ⚙, point to **Print**, and then click **Page Setup**. The Page Setup dialog box opens again.

7 In the Headers and Footers section, under Header, click the **Custom arrow**, and then click **-Empty-**.

8 Click **OK**. The Page Setup dialog box closes.

End Activity

Saving a Web Page

You can save a Web page as a file from the Internet Explorer desktop application. To do this, click the Tools button ⚙ in the upper-right corner of the application window, point to File, and then click Save as to open the Save Webpage dialog box shown here. Depending on what portion of the Web page you want to save, you can click the Save as type arrow and choose from four options. The Webpage, complete (*htm,*.html) option saves the entire Web page, including its graphics and other elements that make up the page. This option creates a folder with all of the site's related files, including page elements, such as images and sounds. The Web Archive, single file (*.mht) option saves a "picture" of the current Web page, without any of the page elements. The two other options—Webpage, HTML only (*htm,*.html) and Text File (*.txt)—save just the HTML code or the text from the Web page, respectively, without saving the graphics, frames, or styles on the Web page.

8-6 Closing Internet Explorer

You can close the Internet Explorer desktop application when you are finished using it. If you have only one tab open, you exit the Internet Explorer desktop application the same way you do any other program, using the Close button ❌ on the title bar. However, if more than one tab is open, a dialog box opens, asking if you want to close all the tabs or only the current tab. If you click Close all tabs, the Internet Explorer desktop application closes.

You close the Internet Explorer app in the same way you close any other Windows 8 app: either drag down from the top to the bottom of the screen, or make any other app, including the Desktop app, the active app, display the Switch List, right-click the Internet Explorer app thumbnail, and then click Close on the shortcut menu.

Begin Activity

Close the Internet Explorer desktop application and app.

1 In the upper-right corner of the title bar, click the **Close button** ❌. Because only one tab is open, the Internet Explorer desktop application window closes.

Save Webpage dialog box

2 Point to the **upper-left corner of the screen** to display the Internet Explorer app thumbnail.

3 Right-click the **Internet Explorer app thumbnail**. On the shortcut menu, click **Close**. The Internet Explorer app closes.

End Activity

8-7 Using the Mail App

Email allows you to communicate with other users on a network such as the Internet. If you are like most computer users, you exchange many email messages every day with friends, family, colleagues, and other contacts. You probably also receive newsletters, coupons, offers, and other types of messages from companies and organizations.

Windows 8 includes **Mail**, an app you use to send, receive, and manage email. Using Mail, you can send email to and receive email from anyone in the world who has an email address, regardless of the operating system or type of computer the person is using. Although this section provides steps for using the Mail app, these concepts and activities apply to any email application, including Microsoft Outlook, which comes with Microsoft Office.

8-7a Starting Mail

To use Mail (or any other email program), you need an Internet connection and an email address. Having an email address means you have an email account, which is space on an email server reserved for your messages. You set up an account with an email service provider, which can be an ISP, an employer or school, or a Web service such as Hotmail or Gmail.

The first time you start Mail, you sign in to it with your Microsoft account. Recall that a Microsoft account can be created with any email address; you do not need to use a hotmail.com or live.com email address. Note that if you are signed in to Windows 8 with a Microsoft account, the sign in screen will not be displayed because you will be signed in to Mail with the same Microsoft account used for your Windows 8 sign in.

After you sign in, the main Mail screen opens. The elements on the main Mail screen are labeled in Exhibit 8-26.

ON THE JOB

Writing Effective and Appropriate Email Messages

When you communicate using email, the information you send might be read by users other than the intended recipient(s), especially if you work for a corporation or private institution, so be aware that email is not private. Keep the following guidelines in mind:

▶ Use appropriate language—that is, do not use slang, abbreviations that others might not understand, or profanity. Humor and sarcasm can also be misinterpreted in an email.

▶ Provide meaningful information in the subject line to clearly indicate the contents of the message. Even after people read your message, the subject helps them quickly locate information they might need later.

▶ Keep the content of the message short and related to the topic in the subject line.

▶ State any action that you expect the recipient to take, indicating the timeframe, if appropriate.

▶ Limit the file size of attachments so downloading your message doesn't take too long. Note that most email servers limit the size of the files you can send or receive as attachments.

▶ Check the spelling in the message, and proofread it before you send it.

An email message, like any written document, reflects your ability to communicate clearly and effectively—an important skill in any personal, academic, or professional endeavor. By following these guidelines, you can ensure that recipients of your email messages are not distracted by inappropriate language or tone or confused by typing or grammatical errors.

Mail A Windows 8 app used to send, receive, and manage email.

Exhibit 8-26 Main Mail screen

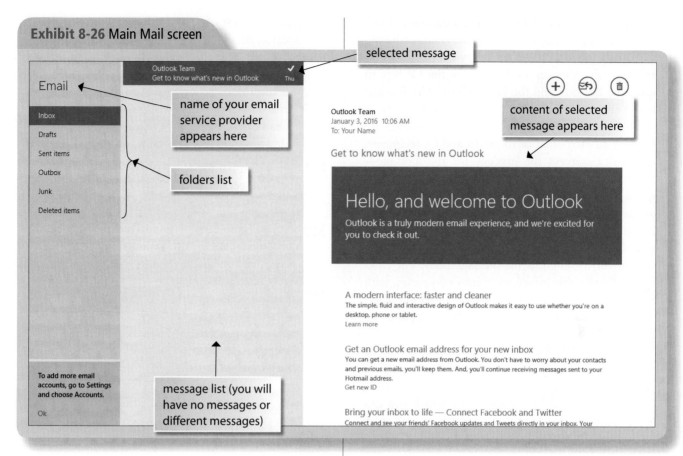

selected message

Email

name of your email service provider appears here

Inbox
Drafts
Sent items
Outbox
Junk
Deleted items

folders list

Outlook Team
Get to know what's new in Outlook   Thu

content of selected message appears here

Outlook Team
January 3, 2016 10:06 AM
To: Your Name

Get to know what's new in Outlook

Hello, and welcome to Outlook

Outlook is a truly modern email experience, and we're excited for you to check it out.

A modern interface: faster and cleaner
The simple, fluid and interactive design of Outlook makes it easy to use whether you're on a desktop, phone or tablet.
Learn more

Get an Outlook email address for your new inbox
You can get a new email address from Outlook. You don't have to worry about your contacts and previous emails, you'll keep them. And, you'll continue receiving messages sent to your Hotmail address.
Get new ID

Bring your inbox to life — Connect Facebook and Twitter
Connect and see your friends' Facebook updates and Tweets directly in your inbox. Your

To add more email accounts, go to Settings and choose Accounts.

Ok

message list (you will have no messages or different messages)

Begin Activity

Start Mail.

1 Display the **Start screen**.

2 Click the **Mail tile**. If this is the first time you started Mail and you are not signed into Windows 8 with a Microsoft account, the Sign in with a Microsoft account screen opens, requesting your Microsoft account information. If you have already set up Mail or are signed into Windows 8 with a Microsoft account, the main Mail screen opens instead of the Sign in with a Microsoft account screen; in that case, skip the rest of this Activity, and go to the section titled "Sending and Receiving Email Using Mail."

Problem? If you do not have a Microsoft account, click the **Sign up for a Microsoft account link**, follow the instructions on the Microsoft Web site to create a Microsoft account, and then repeat Step 2.

3 Enter the Email address associated with your Microsoft account, such as *your_name@ example.com*.

Important: Once you have associated a Windows 8 username and a Microsoft account with the Mail app, that Windows 8 username will remain associated with the app every time you use it.

4 Click the **Password box**, and then type the password for the account.

5 Click the **Sign in button**. If this is the first time you are signing in to Mail, the app connects to your Microsoft account and displays messages received in that account. Refer back to Exhibit 8-26.

End Activity

8-7b Creating and Sending Email Using Mail

An email message looks similar to a memo, with lines for Date, To, From, Cc, and Subject, followed by the body of the message. The Date line shows the date on which you send the message (as set in your computer's clock), and the From line lists your name or email address; these lines are not visible in the window in which you create your email message. You complete the other lines. The To line lists the email addresses of one or more recipients. The Cc line lists the email addresses of anyone who will receive a courtesy copy of the message. Click the Show more link below the Cc box to display the Bcc box and the Priority box. The Bcc line lists the email addresses of anyone who will receive a blind courtesy copy of the message. Bcc recipients are not visible to each other or to the To and Cc recipients. The priority conveys the urgency for the message—high, normal, or low priority. The Subject line provides a quick overview of the message topic, similar to a headline. Focusing on only one topic per email keeps each conversation thread distinct and makes it simpler to find all the messages related to that topic. The main part of the email is the message body. The Mail screen separates this information into two panes, with the sender, recipients, and priority level listed in the left pane and the subject and message in the right pane. See Exhibit 8-27.

When you click the Send button, Mail moves the message from your computer to your email server, which routes it to the recipient. It also keeps a copy of the message in the Sent items folder, which you can open to see all the messages you have sent or replied to.

Begin Activity

Create and send an email message.

1 In the upper-right corner of the screen, click the **New button** ⊕. The screen for composing a new message opens. Refer to Exhibit 8-27.

2 Click in the **To box**, and then type your email address. As you type, if your email appears in a list below the To box, you can click it instead of typing the rest of the address. As soon as you click an email address in the list or click outside the To box, your username will appear instead of your email address in the To box.

Problem? If your name does not appear instead of your email address, you do not have a first and last name set up to display with your Microsoft account. This is not a problem.

3 In the right pane, click **Add a subject**, and then type **Test Message**.

4 Below the subject, click **Add a message**, type **This is a test message.**, press the **Enter key** twice, and then type your name.

5 In the upper-right corner of the screen, click the **Send button** ⊟. The message screen closes, and the main Mail screen appears again. The message is moved to the Outbox folder, and the number 1 appears next to the folder, indicating it contains one unsent message. Then the message is routed to the email server. Unless a problem occurs, you probably will not notice this transmission; it occurs quickly.

Problem? If Mail continues to display the number 1 to the right of the Outbox folder in the Mail pane, right-click the middle of the screen, and then click the **Sync button** on the Apps bar to send the message.

6 In the Mail pane, click **Sent items**. The list of messages that you have sent appears in the left pane.

End Activity

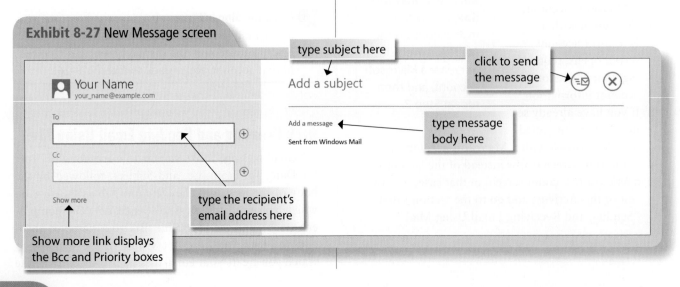

Exhibit 8-27 New Message screen

type subject here

Your Name
your_name@example.com

To

Cc

Show more

Show more link displays the Bcc and Priority boxes

type the recipient's email address here

Add a subject

Add a message

Sent from Windows Mail

click to send the message

type message body here

Correcting Spelling in a Message

Mail includes a built-in spelling dictionary. As you type the text of a message, Mail corrects any words it flags as misspelled according to its dictionary. As shown here, a red wavy line appears under any word that is not in Mail's spelling dictionary. You can right-click the word to display a shortcut menu of spelling suggestions and options to add the word to the dictionary or ignore it.

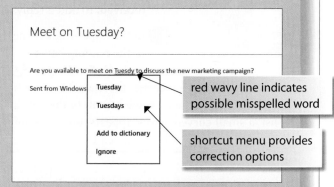

Misspelled word in a Mail message

8-7c Receiving and Reading Email Using Mail

Mail transfers, or downloads, messages addressed to you from your email server to your Inbox whenever you start the program and periodically after that. You can also check for received email by clicking the Sync button on the Apps bar. When the Inbox folder is selected in the left pane, messages downloaded to your Inbox appear in a list in the message list in the center pane on the screen. The subject of messages you have received but have not read yet appears in blue, bold text, and the number of unread messages appears to the right of Inbox in the pane on the left. To read a message, you click it in the list to display its contents in the reading pane on the right.

Begin Activity

Receive and read an email message.

1 In the Mail pane, click **Inbox**. The message list changes to show the list of messages in your Inbox.

Tip: To change how often email is automatically downloaded from the server, display the Charms bar when the Mail app is on the screen, click the Settings charm, click Accounts, and then click your account name to display a panel containing settings for your account.

2 If Test Message does not appear in the message list, right-click a blank area of the screen to display the Apps bar, and then click the **Sync button**. Mail downloads your email messages from the email server, and Test Message appears in the message list. Your Inbox might contain additional email messages.

3 In the message list, click **Test Message**. The content of the selected message appears in the reading pane, and a check mark appears over the time in the message list to indicate that the message is selected. After a few moments, the subject of the message in the message list changes so it is no longer bold to indicate that it has been read.

End Activity

8-7d Replying to and Forwarding Email Messages

Some of the email you receive will ask you to provide information, answer questions, or confirm decisions. Instead of creating a new email message, you can reply directly to a message that you received.

As part of the reply, Mail fills in the To and Subject boxes and includes the text of the original message. If the original message was sent to more than one person, the Reply command creates a response to only the original sender; the Reply all command creates a response to the original sender as well as all of the other recipients.

With both the reply to and forward features, you can add a new message above the original message. Exhibit 8-28 shows a message being replied to.

When you reply to or forward an email, you should place your response at the top of the message above any text from the original message so that the recipients can find it easily. If you respond to questions or insert comments in the original message, you should use a contrasting font color to clearly identify your additions and mention that you have done this in your response at the top of the message.

Exhibit 8-28 Replying to a message

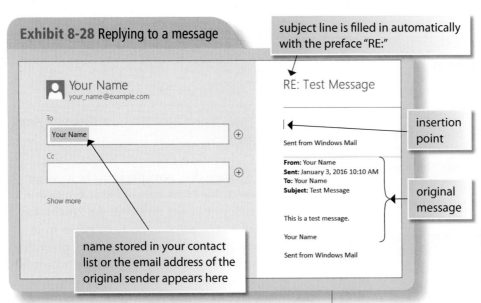

subject line is filled in automatically
with the preface "RE:"

Your Name
your_name@example.com

To
Your Name

Cc

Show more

name stored in your contact
list or the email address of the
original sender appears here

RE: Test Message

Sent from Windows Mail

From: Your Name
Sent: January 3, 2016 10:10 AM
To: Your Name
Subject: Test Message

This is a test message.

Your Name

Sent from Windows Mail

insertion
point

original
message

the person who sent the
original message. In the
subject, *RE:* is inserted
before the original Test
Message subject. The
original message appears
in the bottom portion of
the message body, and the
insertion point is in the
message body above the
original message. Refer
back to Exhibit 8-28.

4 Type **This test message was received.** to add a reply.

5 In the upper-right corner
of the reading pane,
click the **Send button**.

The message screen closes, the main Mail screen
reappears, and the message is sent. In the message
list, a small curved arrow appears above the time,
indicating that you have replied to this message.

End Activity

Begin Activity

Reply to and forward an email message.

1 Make sure **Test Message** is selected in the
message list.

2 In the upper-right corner of the reading pane,
click the **Respond button**. A menu opens with
choices to Reply, Reply all, and Forward.

3 Click **Reply**. In the left pane, your name or email
address appears in the To box because you were

You can also forward a message to someone who
wasn't included on the original message. The Forward
feature creates a copy of the original message subject
and body, but leaves the To, Cc, and Bcc boxes blank.
You can enter the recipient or recipients whom you
want to receive a copy of the message. Exhibit 8-29
shows a message being forwarded.

LEARN MORE

Formatting Message Text

You can format the text of messages you compose to
change the font, font color, and style of the text, as
well as add emoticons. To do this, press and hold the
left mouse button, and then drag the pointer across
the text in the message that you want to format. This
selects the text you dragged across and causes the Apps
bar at the bottom of the screen to appear. As shown
here, the Apps bar in an email message you are composing contains buttons for formatting text including
Font, Bold, Italic, Underline, and Text color. Click one
of the buttons to change the format of the selected
text to the format you clicked. To insert an emoticon
such as a happy face, click in the message area, click
the Emoticons button on the Apps bar to display the

People and faces panel, click a category icon, such as
People or Travel, at the top of the panel, and then
click the emoticon you want to use. Finally, you can
use the More button to format selected paragraphs as
a bulleted or numbered list and to undo or redo the
most recent actions, as shown in the
figure here.

More button opens
additional options

Bulleted list

Numbered list

Undo

Redo

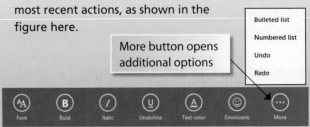

Formatting options on the App bar

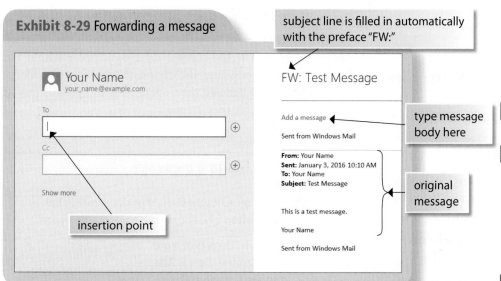

Exhibit 8-29 Forwarding a message

subject line is filled in automatically with the preface "FW:"

Your Name
your_name@example.com

To
[ ] ⊕

Cc
⊕

Show more

insertion point

FW: Test Message

Add a message ← type message body here

Sent from Windows Mail

From: Your Name
Sent: January 3, 2016 10:10 AM
To: Your Name
Subject: Test Message   original message

This is a test message.

Your Name

Sent from Windows Mail

Reply, Reply All, and Forward

It is important to use the Reply and Reply All features appropriately. If not all message recipients need to read your reply, use the Reply feature so that you do not clutter others' Inboxes unnecessarily, and so that you don't inadvertently send a reply to many people when you meant to send it to one person. Likewise, if it's important that everyone who received the original email remain in the "conversation" created by the email chain, be sure to use the Reply All feature so that no one is left out by mistake. When you forward a message, be aware that you might be forwarding private email addresses contained in the header in the original message. Finally, be aware that there is nothing to stop anyone to whom you send, reply, or forward a message from forwarding it on to others, including people you don't know.

Begin Activity

Forward a message.

1 In the message list, select the original **Test Message** if it is not already selected.

2 Click the **Respond button** (⤺), and then click **Forward**. *FW:* is inserted before the subject to indicate it is a forwarded message. As with a reply, the original message appears in the bottom portion of

the message body. The insertion point appears in the To box, which is empty. Refer back to Exhibit 8-29.

3 In the **To box**, type your email address.

4 On the right, click **Add a message** above the copied original message, type **This is an example of a forwarded message.** as the message.

5 Click the **Send button** (⤻). The message screen closes, the main Mail screen appears again, and the message is sent. In the message list, the small curved arrow that had indicated that the message was replied to is replaced by a straight, right-pointing arrow, which indicates that you have forwarded this message.

6 If the reply and the forwarded messages are not in your Inbox, right-click a blank area of the screen. On the Apps bar, click the **Sync button** (⟳).

End Activity

8-7e Deleting Email Messages

After you read and respond to your messages, you can delete any message that you no longer need. When you delete a message from the Inbox, it is not permanently removed from the Inbox; it is moved to the Deleted items folder. Messages remain in the Deleted items folder until you delete that folder's contents. You should delete the contents of this folder periodically; otherwise the Deleted items folder will accumulate a lot of messages you no longer need. When you delete messages from the Deleted items folder, they are permanently removed from your computer. To delete a message from the Inbox or the Deleted items folder, select it in the message list, and then click the Delete button (🗑) in the upper-right corner. If you want to delete all the messages in either folder, click the first message in the message list, press and hold the Shift key, and then click the last message in the message list to select all of the messages. Then when you click the Delete button, all of the selected messages are deleted.

Delete email messages.

1 In the message list, click **Test Message** to select it, if it is not already selected.

2 In the upper-right corner of the screen, click the **Delete button** (🗑). The selected message is moved to the Deleted items folder.

3 In the message list, click **RE: Test Message** to select it, press and hold the **Ctrl key**, and then click **FW: Test Message**. Both messages are selected.

4 Click the **Delete button** (🗑). The selected messages are moved to the Deleted items folder.

5 In the folders list, click the **Sent items folder**. The three messages you sent appear in the message list. The Fw: Test Message is selected because it is at the top of the list as the most recent message sent.

6 Press and hold the **Shift key**, click **Test Message**, and then release the **Shift key**. The three messages are selected.

> **Problem?** If any other messages are selected, click **Test Message** in the message list, press and hold the **Ctrl key**, click the other two **Test Message** messages, and then release the **Ctrl key**.

7 Click the **Delete button** (🗑). The selected messages are moved to the Deleted items folder.

8 In the folders list, click the **Deleted items folder**. The six messages you deleted appear in the message list.

> **Tip:** You can also click the Move button on the Apps bar, and then click the folder to which you want to move the selected messages.

9 In the message list, select the messages you sent and received, and then in the upper-right corner of the screen, click the **Delete button** (🗑). The selected messages in the Deleted items folder are permanently deleted.

10 In the folders list, click the **Inbox folder**. Any messages that are still in your Inbox appear in the message list.

attachment A file that is sent with an email message.

8-7f Working with Attachments

An **attachment** is a file that you send with an email message. The file content does not appear within the message body, and the recipients can save the file to their computer and then open, edit, and print it just as they can a file they created.

Attach a file to a message.

1 In the upper-right corner of the screen, click the **New button** (⊕). A new message screen opens.

2 In the To box, type your email address, click **Add a subject** in the right pane, and then type **First Quarter Sales**.

3 Click **Add a message**, type **Hello,** (including the comma), press the **Enter key** twice, type **The attached workbook contains the sales numbers from the first quarter. Let me know if you have any questions.**, press the **Enter key** twice, and then type your name.

> **Tip:** If the name you are entering as a recipient is listed in your contacts list, the name appears just below the box as you are typing it, and you can click it to add the name as a recipient.

4 Right-click to display the Apps bar. On the Apps bar, click the **Attachments button** (📎). The Files screen appears. See Exhibit 8-30.

5 Click **Files**, and then click the **drive or folder** containing the files you need as you work through the steps in this book. Click folders as needed until you see the files provided with this book.

6 Display the contents of the **Chapter 8 folder** included with this book, display the contents of the **Chapter folder**, and then click the data file **Quarterly Sales**. A check mark appears next to the file, and an icon representing the file appears at the bottom-left of the screen.

7 At the bottom of the screen, click **Attach**. The Files screen closes, and the screen showing the message you are creating reappears. The Quarterly Sales file is listed as an attachment below the subject and above the message. See Exhibit 8-31.

8 Send the message. The message screen closes, and the message is sent, along with the attached file.

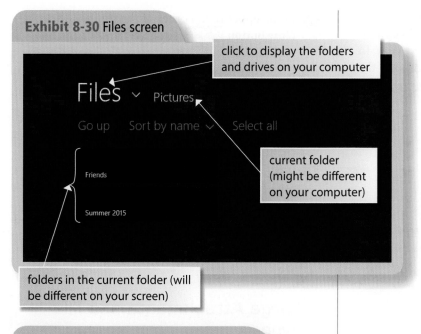

Exhibit 8-30 Files screen

click to display the folders and drives on your computer

Files ∨ Pictures

Go up Sort by name ∨ Select all

current folder (might be different on your computer)

Friends

Summer 2015

folders in the current folder (will be different on your screen)

When you receive a message that contains an attachment, a paperclip appears in the message list above the time that the message was received to indicate that the message includes an attachment. When the message is selected in the list, the file name of the attachment appears below the subject line in the right pane. Exhibit 8-32 shows a message with an attachment selected in the Inbox.

You can choose to open or save the attachment. To open the attachment, you need to make sure the program used to create the attachment is installed on your computer. If the program is not installed, sometimes you can use a text editor, such as WordPad or Notepad, to open and read the attached file.

Exhibit 8-31 Message with an attachment

Your Name
your_name@example.com

To
Your Name

Cc

Show more

First Quarter Sales

Quarterly Sales
.xlsx 10.2 KB

attached file

1 file attached   Send using SkyDrive instead

Hello,

The attached workbook contains the sales numbers from the first quarter. Let me know if you have any questions.

Your Name

Sent from Windows Mail

Exhibit 8-32 Message with an attachment selected in the message list

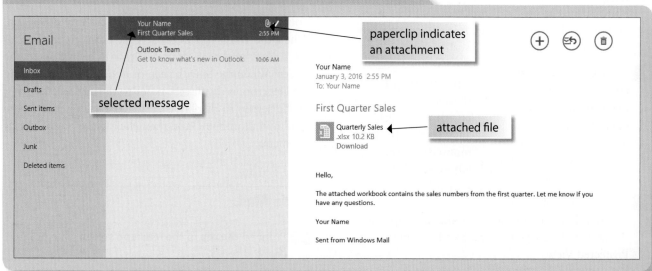

Email

Inbox
Drafts
Sent items
Outbox
Junk
Deleted items

Your Name
First Quarter Sales   2:55 PM

Outlook Team
Get to know what's new in Outlook   10:06 AM

paperclip indicates an attachment

selected message

Your Name
January 3, 2016 2:55 PM
To: Your Name

First Quarter Sales

Quarterly Sales
.xlsx 10.2 KB
Download

attached file

Hello,

The attached workbook contains the sales numbers from the first quarter. Let me know if you have any questions.

Your Name

Sent from Windows Mail

If you open an attachment that causes a Microsoft Office program, such as Word, Excel, or PowerPoint, to open, the attachment is displayed in Protected View. In Protected View, you can read but not edit or save the file. This helps protect your computer from viruses that may be embedded in the attached file.

CAUTION

Check Attachments for Viruses

You should open attached files only after scanning them with antivirus software. Some people spread viruses in email attachments.

Begin Activity

Open a message attachment.

1 If the First Quarter Sales message is not in your Inbox, right-click to display the Apps bar, and then click the **Sync button** ⟳. The First Quarter Sales message appears in the message list, with a paperclip above the time.

2 In the message list, click the **First Quarter Sales message**. The content of the message appears in the pane on the right, and the attached file is listed below the subject with *Download* below it. The icon next to the file name is gray. Refer back to Exhibit 8-32.

3 In the message content, click the attached file **Quarterly Sales.xlsx**. After a moment, the word *Download* disappears, and the icon is now colored blue and green. This indicates that that file has downloaded from the server. It is still attached to the email message.

4 Click **Quarterly Sales. xlsx** again. A menu opens with options to open the attachment, open the attachment with a specific program, or save the attachment.

> **Tip:** If you want to save the attachment, click Save on the shortcut menu that opens when you click the attachment.

5 Click **Open**. The Microsoft Excel application starts on the desktop, and the attached file opens in the Excel window in Protected View.

6 In the upper-right corner of the title bar, click the **Close button** ×. The Excel application window closes.

7 Point to the upper-right corner of the screen to display the Switch List, slide down to display all the open apps in the list, and then click the **Mail app thumbnail**. The main Mail app screen appears again.

8 Delete the **First Quarter Sales message** from the Inbox and Sent items folders, and then delete the message from the Deleted items folder.

End Activity

FYI

Large Attachments and File Types

If you attach a large file to an email message, it might take a long time for your recipient to download your message. Most email servers limit the size of the files you can attach or receive; some allow files no larger than 1 MB although many allow 5 to 10 MB. In addition, some email servers restrict the types of files; for example, some do not allow attachments of executable files, which have.exe file extensions and that a computer can directly run, for security purposes. Check with your correspondents before sending large file attachments to find out about size and file type restrictions.

8-7g Closing Mail

You close Mail the same way you close any other app. When the Mail app is on screen, point to the top of the screen, and then drag down to the bottom of the screen. When the Start screen or another app, including the Desktop, is displayed, point to the upper-left corner of the screen to display the Switch List, right-click the Mail app thumbnail, and then click Close on the shortcut menu.

Begin Activity

Close Mail.

1 Point to **the top of the Mail app screen**. The pointer changes to 🖐.

2 Press and hold the mouse button, drag down to the bottom of the screen until the screen shrinks and follows the pointer to the bottom of the screen.

3 Release the mouse button. The app closes, and the Start screen appears.

End Activity

8-8 Adding Information to the People App

The **People** app is a communication tool in Windows 8 that you use to store information about the people and businesses with whom you communicate. Each person or organization is called a **contact**. Exhibit 8-33 shows the People app with a short list of contacts.

Exhibit 8-33 People app main screen

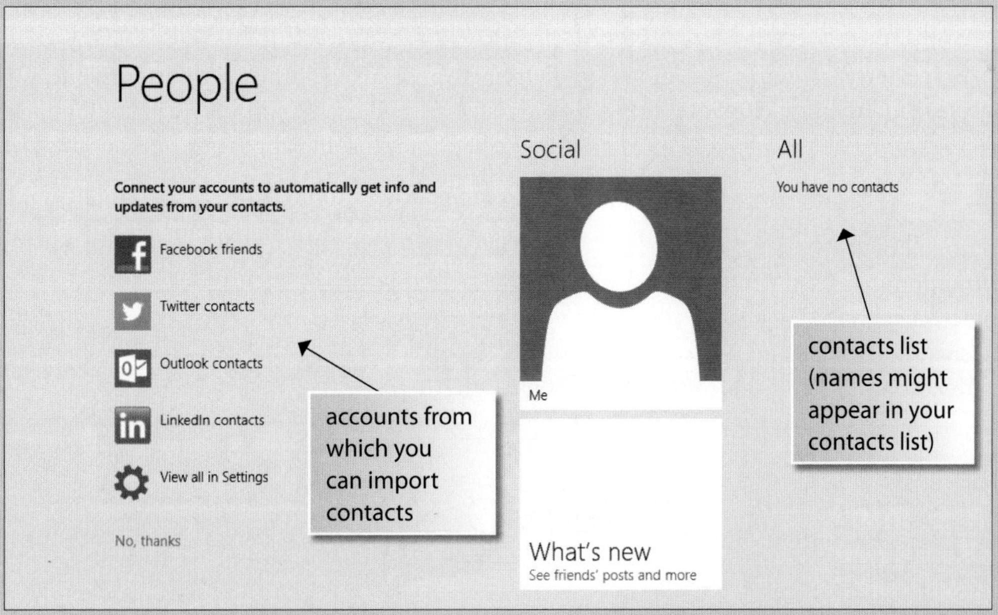

People

Connect your accounts to automatically get info and updates from your contacts.

- Facebook friends
- Twitter contacts
- Outlook contacts
- LinkedIn contacts
- View all in Settings

No, thanks

accounts from which you can import contacts

Social

Me

What's new
See friends' posts and more

All
You have no contacts

contacts list (names might appear in your contacts list)

You store information about each contact, including a name, nickname, company, email addresses, phone and fax numbers, and postal addresses, as well as other information, such as job title, significant other, Web site, and notes. The collected information about a contact is called a **profile**. You can create a new contact and then enter as much information as you want about

that contact on the New contact screen, as shown in Exhibit 8-34.

You can also add contacts to People by importing the information from social networking sites where you maintain contacts, such as Facebook, Google, LinkedIn, Outlook, and Twitter. If you import the same contact information from different sources, the People app detects the duplicate contacts and combines them into a single entry called a linked contact. If you import contact information from your accounts on social networking sites, People maintains a connection to those accounts so it can display updated contact information. If the People tile is a live tile on the Start screen, it also displays updated information as it becomes available.

Begin Activity

Add a contact to the People app.

1 On the Start screen, click the **People tile**. The People app opens, listing any contacts added to the app. Your People window might not contain any contacts. If this is the first time you are starting People, the main screen lists contact sources, including Facebook, Twitter, Exchange, Outlook, and LinkedIn. Refer back to Exhibit 8-33.

2 Right-click **a blank spot** on the screen. On the Apps bar, click the **New button**. The New contact screen in which you can enter basic contact information appears. Refer to Exhibit 8-34.

People A Windows 8 app used to store information about the people and businesses with whom you communicate.

contact Each person or organization with whom you communicate and about whom you store information.

profile The collected information about a contact.

Exhibit 8-34 New contact screen

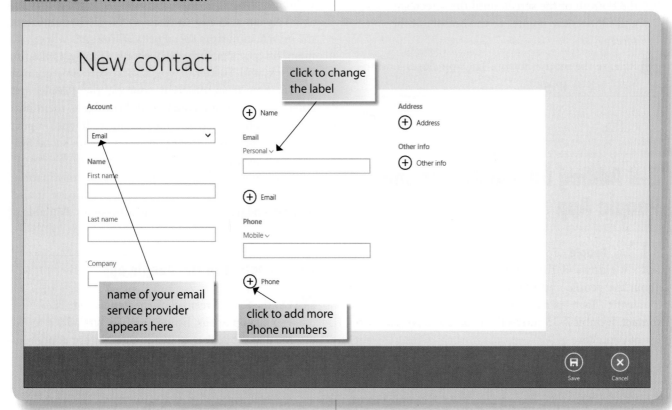

New contact

Account

Email ⌄

Name

First name

Last name

Company

click to change the label

Name

Email
Personal ⌄

Email

Phone
Mobile ⌄

Phone

Address

Address

Other info

Other info

name of your email service provider appears here

click to add more Phone numbers

Save   Cancel

3 Click the **First name box**, type **Kerry** in the First name box, press the **Tab key**, and then type **DeSota** in the Last name box.

4 Under Email, click **Personal** to open a shortcut menu with other email options, and then click **Work**.

Tip: To add additional information for a contact, click the labels with the plus sign next to them.

5 In the Work box, type **kerry_desota@ example.com**. This sets Kerry's work email address as the default email address.

6 Under Phone, click in the **Mobile box**, and then type **978-555-2399**.

Tip: Under Phone, you can click Mobile to open a shortcut menu and select a different phone type.

7 On the Apps bar, click the **Save button**. The new contact screen closes, and the screen containing Kerry DeSota's profile appears. See Exhibit 8-35.

8 Click the **Back button** ⬅ to return to the People screen. The contact you added appears in the All list of contacts.

End Activity

Exhibit 8-35 Profile for a contact

click to return to the People screen

⬅ Kerry DeSota

Email
kerry_desota@example.com
Work

Phone
978-555-2399
Mobile

Email

name of your email service provider appears here

When you select a contact from the People screen, the Contact screen for that contact appears. From there, you can click the Send email link to send that person an email message without starting the Mail app. You can also right-click a blank area of the screen to display the Apps bar with additional actions you can take with the contact. For instance, you can pin a contact to the Start screen, mark a contact as a favorite to appear in a Favorites list on the People screen, link that contact to another contact, or edit the contact's profile. To see additional actions you can take with a contact, right-click the screen to display the Apps bar. See Exhibit 8-36.

Begin Activity

Display the actions for a contact.

1 In the All list, click **Kerry DeSota**. The screen containing the actions you can take for Kerry DeSota appears.

2 Right-click **a blank area** of the screen. The Apps bar appears with buttons corresponding to actions you can take with the contact. Refer to Exhibit 8-36. You can delete contacts if you no longer need them.

3 On the Apps bar, click the **Delete button**. A dialog box appears, asking if you want to delete this contact.

4 In the dialog box, click **Delete**. The Kerry DeSota contact is deleted, and the main screen for the People app reappears.

5 Point to **the top of the screen** so that the pointer changes to 🖐, and then drag down to the bottom of the screen to close the People app.

End Activity

Exhibit 8-36 Screen containing actions you can take with a contact

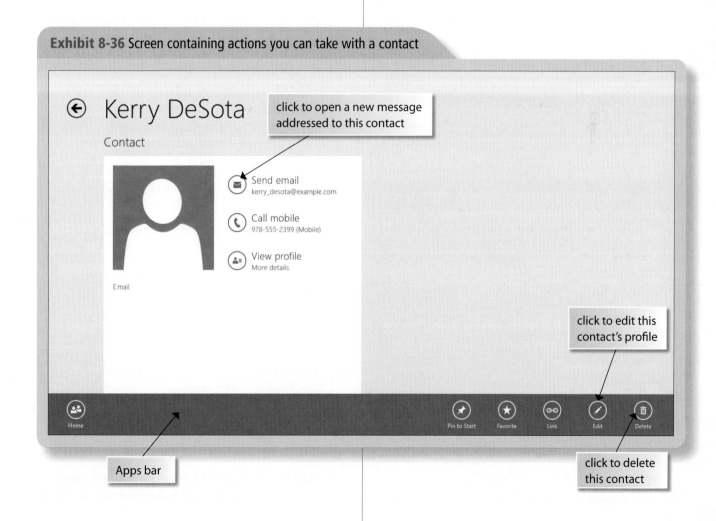

Using the Mail App to Send an Email to a Contact in the People App

When you create an email message in the Mail app, you can click the Add button (a plus sign) next to the To, Cc, or Bcc box to display a list of your contacts in the People app, and then click the name of the person whose email address you want to insert in the box.

Add button in a new message in Mail

Quiz Yourself

1. What are the two definitions of *home page*?

2. How do you conduct a search using the default search engine in Internet Explorer?

3. How is the Internet Explorer desktop application different from the Internet Explorer app?

4. What is a tab?

5. What is the tab switcher?

6. Where do pinned Web pages appear in the Internet Explorer app?

7. Where do pinned Web pages appear in the Internet Explorer desktop application?

8. What is a favorite?

9. What is the history in Internet Explorer?

10. Why is it a good idea to preview a Web page before you print it?

11. What is the difference between replying to an email message and forwarding it?

12. What happens when you delete an email message?

13. What is an attachment?

14. Which Windows 8 app do you use to store information about the people and businesses with whom you communicate?

Practice It

Practice It 8-1

1. Start the Internet Explorer app, type **www.computerhistory.org** in the Address bar, and then press the Enter key.

2. Click the Exhibits link, and then click the Internet History 1962 to 1992 link. Examine this Web page.

3. Use the Back button or the back arrow to return to the home page on the Computer History Museum Web site.

4. Open a new tab, and then go to **www.archive.org**, the Internet Archive Web site.

5. Pin the home page of the Internet Archive site to the Start screen using the name **Internet Archive**.

6. Open any link on the current Web page in a new tab.

7. Open a new tab, and then use the Search charm to conduct a search using **computer history** as the search phrase. In the list of results, click the link to the Computer History page on the Web site www.computersciencelab.com. (If you don't see this result, click another result and then substitute that result in Step 8.)

8. Pin the home page of the Computer History page to the Start screen using the provided name.

9. Close all the tabs except the Computer History Museum home page tab.

10. Use the Internet Archive and Computer History tiles on the Start screen to open the two pages you pinned.

11. Unpin the Internet Archive and Computer History tiles from the Start screen.

12. Print the home page of the Computer History Museum, if you are instructed to print.

13. Close the Internet Explorer app.

14. Start the Internet Explorer desktop application. Maximize the window if it does not already fill the screen.

15. Use the History list to go to the home page of the Computer History Museum, and then save it as a favorite.

16. Use the History list to go to the home page of the Internet Archive Web site.

17. Create a new tab, and then use the History list to go to the other page you viewed on the Internet Archive Web site.

18. Add the two current pages on the Internet Archive Web site as favorites in a folder named **Archive**.

19. In the current tab, use the Favorites list to go to the home page of the Computer History Museum.

20. Display the home page of the Computer History Museum in the Print Preview window, switch the orientation to landscape, and then add your name to the middle portion of the header. If instructed, print page 1.

21. Reset the middle portion of the header to -Empty-, delete the favorites and the favorites folder you added, and then exit the Internet Explorer desktop application.

22. Start the Mail app.

23. Create a new email message. Address it to yourself.

24. Type **Web Sites about Computer History** as the subject.

25. Type the following as the message body:

    Hi,

    The Computer History Museum Web site has several interesting exhibits illustrating the history of computers.

    Your Name

26. Send the email, and then download messages from your server to your Inbox.

27. Reply to the Web Sites about Computer History message, typing the following as the message:

    Thank you for the information.

28. Forward the Re: Web Sites about Computer History message to yourself. Type the following as the message:

    The Internet Archive Web site stores historical, digital collections.

29. Reply to the Fw: Web Sites about Computer History message. Attach the data file **Computer History Sites** located in the Chapter 8/Practice It folder included with this book. Type the following as the message body:

    Please review the attached list.

30. When the message with the attachment arrives in your Inbox, open the attachment in Microsoft Word. Exit Word after reading the document.

31. Move the four messages you received from your Inbox to the Deleted items folder. Move the four messages you sent to the Deleted items folder. Empty the Deleted items folder. Close the Mail app.

32. Start the People app. Add the following person as a new contact:

    First name: John

    Last name: Wynne

    Work email: john_wynne@wynneco.cengage.com

    Mobile phone: 978-555-3209

33. Delete the contact John Wynn. Close the People app.

Practice It 8-2

1. Start Internet Explorer (the Internet Explorer app or the Internet Explorer desktop application), and then go to **www.yelp.com**. If the URL doesn't change to include a large city near your location at the end of it, click in the Search box on the Yelp.com page, type your city and state, and then click Search.

2. Display the Restaurants category in a new tab, and then click a link for a popular restaurant in that category to read reviews of that restaurant.

3. Open a new tab. Go to **www.citysearch.com** in the new tab. If the site doesn't automatically display the Citysearch page for a large city near you, click in the right Search box on the Citysearch page, type your city and state, and then click the appropriate link when it appears.

4. Display the Restaurants category in the current tab, and then click links to find reviews of the same restaurant you read about on Yelp.com. (*Hint*: If you cannot find the same restaurant by clicking links, click in the left Search box on the

Citysearch page, type the restaurant name, and then click the Search button.)

5. Pin the pages with reviews on each site to the Start screen or add them as favorites.

6. Print one review of the restaurant you chose, changing the orientation if needed.

7. Start the People app. Add a friend, classmate, or your instructor as a contact.

8. Start the Mail app. Create a new email message addressed to the person you added as a contact. Type your email address in the Cc box.

9. Type **Restaurant Suggestion** as the subject. Type the following as the message body, replacing the italicized text with the name of the restaurant about which you read reviews and with your name:

   Hi,

   I read a review of *restaurant*, and I think we should meet there for lunch next week.

   Your Name

10. If a friend or classmate sent you the message, reply to it; otherwise, reply to the copy that you sent to yourself. Type **Please see the attached file.** as the message body, and then attach the data file **Restaurant Review Sites** located in the Chapter 8\Practice It folder included with this book.

11. Unpin the Web pages from the Start screen or delete the favorites you added, and then exit Internet Explorer.

12. Delete the messages you sent and received, and then exit Mail.

13. Delete the contact you added to the People app, and then exit People.

On Your Own

On Your Own 8-1

1. Start the Internet Explorer desktop application, and then search for information on Internet hoaxes.

2. Display a result in the current tab, examine the site, and then return to the list of results. Display three more sites in the same manner, returning to the list of results after examining each site.

3. Use the History list to display the home pages of two of the sites you examined in separate tabs. Add these tabs as favorites in a folder named **Hoax Sites**.

4. Close all but one tab, and then search for sites that contain information about Internet scams. Display three results from the results list in new tabs. (Do not display the pages of any Web sites you already visited.) Add these three Web pages as favorites (do not create a folder).

5. Open the Favorites Center, and then open the Organize Favorites dialog box by clicking the Add to favorites button arrow, and then clicking Organize favorites. Use the New Folder command in this dialog box to create a new folder named **Scam Sites**. One at a time, select the three favorites that contain information about Internet scams, and then use the Move command in this dialog box to move these favorites into the new folder. Close the dialog box when you are finished.

6. Start the Mail app, and then create a new message.

7. Address the message to your instructor, and add your email address to the Cc box.

8. Type **Helpful Site** as the subject, and then type the following as the message body, replacing the italicized text with the name of the Web site with information about Internet hoaxes that you liked the best:

   Hi,

   I think the Web site *Hoax Site* contains useful information about avoiding Internet hoaxes.

   Your Name

9. Send the email message.

10. When the message arrives in your Inbox, forward it to your instructor and Cc yourself. Add a sentence identifying the site with the most useful information about Internet scams.

11. Delete the messages you sent and received, and then exit Mail.

12. In the Internet Explorer desktop application, close all but one tab, and then go to the site that you identified as containing useful information about Internet hoaxes.

13. Display the Web page in Print Preview, and then examine the page in landscape orientation.

14. Change the page setup so that your name appears in the middle of the footer.

15. Print the page, if instructed, and then reset the middle area in the footer to -Empty-.

16. Delete the favorites and favorites folder that you created.

17. Delete your browsing history. To do this, start by clicking the Safety button on the Command bar.

18. Exit Internet Explorer.

Chapter 8

ADDITIONAL STUDY TOOLS

IN THE BOOK
▶ Complete end-of-chapter exercises
▶ Study tear-out Chapter Review Card

ONLINE
▶ Complete additional end-of-chapter exercises

▶ Take practice quiz to prepare for tests
▶ Review key term flash cards (online, printable, and audio)
▶ Play "Beat the Clock" and "Memory" to quiz yourself
▶ Watch the videos to learn more about the topics taught in this chapter

Answers to Quiz Yourself

1. *A home page is the page that appears when you start a browser and is also the main page on a Web site.*

2. *To conduct a search using the default search engine, you type keywords in the Address bar, and then press the Enter key to begin the search. The hits are displayed on the search site set for your version of Internet Explorer.*

3. *The Internet Explorer desktop application runs on the desktop; the Internet Explorer app runs as a Windows app.*

4. *A tab is the object on which Web pages are displayed in Internet Explorer.*

5. *The tab switcher is an area in the Internet Explorer app that displays thumbnails of current or recently visited Web pages for easy navigation between them.*

6. *In the Internet Explorer app, pinned Web pages appear on the Start screen and in the expanded navigation bar.*

7. *In the Internet Explorer desktop application, pinned Web pages appear on the taskbar.*

8. *A favorite is a shortcut to a Web page saved in a list in the Internet Explorer desktop application or as a tile on the Start screen and on the expanded navigation bar.*

9. *The history tracks the Web pages you visit in both the Internet Explorer desktop application and the Internet Explorer app, not just during a browsing session, and stores the URLs for those Web pages.*

10. *It is a good idea to preview the pages before you print them because Web pages are not usually designed with printing in mind.*

11. *When you reply to an email message, the email address of the original sender is entered in the To box. When you forward an email message, the To box is left empty so you can add the email address of the person to whom you want to forward the message.*

12. *When you delete an email message, it is moved to the Deleted items folder.*

13. *An attachment is a file that you send with an email message.*

14. *You use the People app to store information about the people and businesses with whom you communicate.*

Introducing Microsoft Office 2013

Pressmaster/Shutterstock.com

Microsoft Office 2013, or **Office**, is a collection of Microsoft applications. The most commonly used applications are Word, Excel, Access, and PowerPoint. Word is used to enter, edit, and format text. Excel is used to enter, calculate, analyze, and present charts of numerical data. Access enables you to enter, maintain, and retrieve related information (or data) in a format known as a database. PowerPoint is used to create a collection of slides that can contain text, charts, pictures, sound, movies, multimedia, and so on. These four Office applications are designed to work together and have common features that work similarly in all of them. Although each Office application is a strong tool individually, their potential is even greater when used together.

Learning Objectives

After studying the material in this chapter, you will be able to:

9-1 Explore common elements of Office application windows

9-2 Use the ribbon

9-3 Select text and use the Mini toolbar

9-4 Undo and redo actions

9-5 Zoom and scroll in application windows

9-6 Work with Office files

9-7 Use the Clipboard

9-8 Get Help

9-9 Close Office applications

Microsoft Office 2013 (Office)
A collection of Microsoft applications.

Microsoft product screenshots used with permission from Microsoft Corporation.

9-1 Exploring Common Elements of Office Application Windows

Each Office application creates different types of files. The files you create in Word are called **documents**, although many people use the term *document* to refer to any file created on a computer. The files you create in Excel are called **workbooks** (commonly referred to as *spreadsheets*). Access files are **databases**, and PowerPoint files are **presentations**.

Signing In and Out of Your Microsoft Account

You can click the Sign in link next to the Minimize button on the title bar to sign in to your Microsoft account.  After you sign in, your username appears in the upper-right corner instead of the Sign in link shown in Exhibits 9-2 and 9-3. If you are signed into Windows 8 with a Microsoft account, you are automatically signed in when you open an Office application. When you are signed in, you can easily save files to your SkyDrive account, which means that you can access them from anywhere or easily share them with others. If you are signed in to your Microsoft account in one Office application, you will be automatically signed into your Microsoft account in all the Office applications.

You can sign out of your Microsoft account if you are signed in only in Office and not with your Windows 8 user account. To do this, click your username in the upper-right corner of the application window and then click Account Settings, or click the FILE tab and then click Account at the bottom left pane. Either method displays the Account screen. Click the Sign out link below your email address under User Information. A dialog box opens warning you that signing out of this account will remove all customizations, and documents and notebooks may no longer sync to the server; click Yes.

Although the file types are different, the Office applications have many common elements and features. To learn about some of the features the applications share, you will start a few Office applications and examine the application windows.

You start Office applications the same way you start any Windows 8 application. If a tile corresponding to the application appears on the Start screen, you can click it. Or, with the Start screen displayed, you can type the first few letters of the application name and then click the application in the list of search results on the Apps screen. The corresponding application starts on the desktop, and its application button appears on the taskbar.

When Word, Excel, Access, and PowerPoint start, the Recent screen in Backstage view appears. **Backstage view** contains commands that allow you to manage application files and options. The only actions available on the Recent screen are to open an existing application file or create a new file. Exhibit 9-1 shows the Recent screen in Backstage view of Word. After you create or open a file, the document, workbook, database, or presentation appears in the application window, ready for you to work.

Begin Activity

Start Office applications and examine the application windows.

1 Make sure your computer is on and the Start screen appears on your monitor.

> **Windows 7 User?** If you are using Windows 7, click the Start button, point to All Programs, click Microsoft Office 2013, and then click Word 2013. Skip Steps 1-3. For Step 6, repeat this except click Excel 2013, and for Step 8, click PowerPoint 2013.

document A Word file.

workbook An Excel file.

database An Access file.

presentation A PowerPoint file.

Backstage view A screen that contains commands to manage application files and options.

OFFICE 2013

Exhibit 9-1 Recent screen in Backstage view in Word

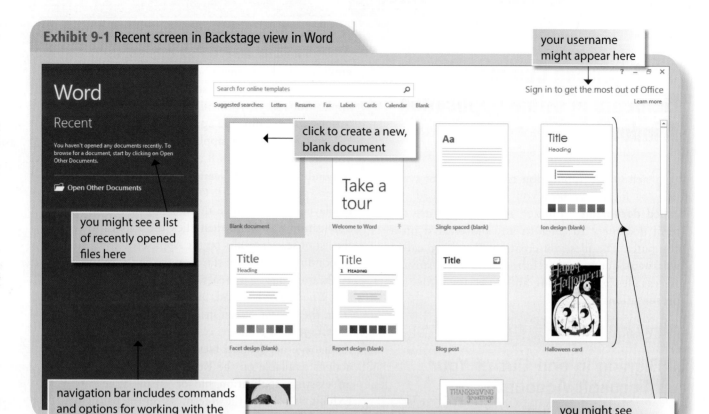

your username might appear here

Word

Recent

You haven't opened any documents recently. To browse for a document, start by clicking on Open Other Documents.

Open Other Documents

you might see a list of recently opened files here

click to create a new, blank document

navigation bar includes commands and options for working with the displayed screen

you might see different thumbnails

2 Type **Word**. The Apps screen appears with Word 2013 in the list of search results.

3 Click **Word 2013**. Word starts on the desktop, and the Recent screen in Backstage view appears. Refer back to Exhibit 9-1. Also, note that a Word button appears on the taskbar.

4 If the application window doesn't fill your screen as shown in Exhibit 9-1, click the **Maximize button** on the title bar.

5 Click the **Blank document tile**. Backstage view closes, and a new, blank document opens. See Exhibit 9-2. The elements labeled in Exhibit 9-2 are found in all of the Office applications.

> **Problem?** If the ribbon is not fully displayed, as shown in Exhibits 9-2 and 9-3, you need to pin it. Refer to the FYI box titled "Pinning and Unpinning the Ribbon" for how to do this.

6 Switch to the **Start screen**, type **Excel**, and then click **Excel 2013** in the list of results on the Apps screen. Excel starts on the desktop with the Recent screen displayed, and an Excel button appears on the taskbar.

7 Click the **Blank workbook tile**. Backstage view closes, and a new, blank workbook opens. See Exhibit 9-3.

8 Switch to the **Start screen**, type **Power**, and then click **PowerPoint 2013** in the list of search results. PowerPoint starts on the desktop with the Recent screen displayed, and a PowerPoint button appears on the taskbar.

> **Tip:** The Recent screen in Access is similar to the Recent screens in the other applications. To start creating a new, blank database, you click the Blank desktop database tile.

9 Click the **Blank Presentation tile**. Backstage view closes, and a new, blank presentation opens. The PowerPoint window contains the same elements labeled in the Word and Excel windows shown in Exhibits 9-2 and 9-3.

10 On the taskbar, click the **Excel button**. The Excel window is the active window and appears on top of the other windows.

End Activity

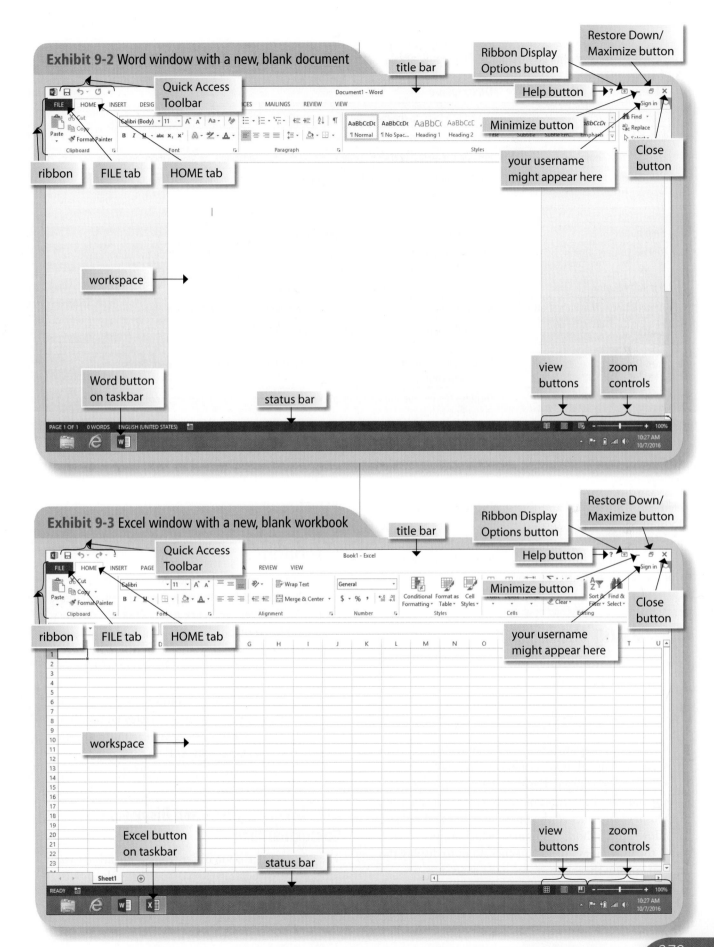

Exhibit 9-2 Word window with a new, blank document

Restore Down/Maximize button

Ribbon Display Options button

title bar

Help button

Quick Access Toolbar

Minimize button

Close button

your username might appear here

ribbon

FILE tab

HOME tab

workspace

Word button on taskbar

status bar

view buttons

zoom controls

Exhibit 9-3 Excel window with a new, blank workbook

Restore Down/Maximize button

Ribbon Display Options button

title bar

Help button

Quick Access Toolbar

Minimize button

Close button

your username might appear here

ribbon

FILE tab

HOME tab

workspace

Excel button on taskbar

status bar

view buttons

zoom controls

Exhibit 9-4 Elements common to Office applications

Element	Description
Ribbon	Provides access to the main set of commands organized by task into tabs and groups
FILE tab	Provides access to Backstage view
Quick Access Toolbar	Provides one-click access to commonly used commands, such as Save, Undo, and Redo
HOME tab	Contains buttons to access the most commonly used commands in each program
Title bar	Contains the name of the open file, the program name, the sizing buttons, the Help button, and the Close button
Help button	Opens the Help window for that application
Ribbon Display Options button	Provides options to display the entire ribbon, display only the tabs, or hide the ribbon until you click the top of the application window
Minimize button	Shrinks the window to its button on the taskbar
Restore Down/Maximize button	Restores the window to its previous size or maximizes the window to fill the screen
Close button	Closes the application window and the open file; if there is only one file open in the application, also exits the program
Status bar	Provides information about the program, open file, or current task as well as the view buttons and zoom controls
Workspace	Displays the file you are working on (Word document, Excel workbook, Access database, or PowerPoint slide)
Zoom controls	Magnifies or shrinks the content displayed in the workspace

As you can see in Exhibits 9-2 and 9-3, many of the elements in the Word and Excel windows are the same. Exhibit 9-4 lists elements common to all of the Office applications. Because these elements are the same in each application, after you have learned one application, it is easy to learn the others.

9-2 Using the Ribbon

Like Windows 8 File Explorer windows, Office applications use a ribbon organized into tabs and groups to provide access to commands. Unlike File Explorer windows, the ribbon is pinned in Office application windows. Remember from Chapter 7 that when an object is pinned, it is permanently displayed, as if it were pinned into place. For the ribbon, this means the commands on the current or active tab are visible even if you have not clicked the tab name. (In File Explorer windows, the ribbon is unpinned, which means you see only the tab names unless you click a tab to display the commands on that tab.)

FYI

Pinning and Unpinning the Ribbon

You can modify the ribbon to unpin it in Office applications. If the ribbon is pinned and you want to hide it unless you click a tab, click the Collapse the Ribbon button at the right end of the ribbon. If the ribbon is unpinned and you want to pin it, click a tab name, and then on the right end of the ribbon, click the Pin the ribbon button to keep the commands on the current tab visible. You can also use the Ribbon Display Options button to the left of the Minimize button on the title bar to collapse, pin, or hide the ribbon.

9-2a Switching Tabs and Displaying Contextual Tabs

The tabs on the ribbon differ from application to application. However, the HOME tab in each application contains commands for the most frequently performed activities, including cutting and pasting, formatting text, and other editing tools. Refer back to Exhibits 9-2 and 9-3 to see the HOME tabs in Word and Excel.

In addition, the INSERT, REVIEW, and VIEW tabs appear on the ribbon in Word, Excel, and PowerPoint, although the commands they include differ from application to application. Exhibit 9-5 shows the INSERT tab selected in the Excel window. Other tabs are application specific, such as the FORMULAS tab in Excel, the DATABASE TOOLS tab in Access, and the SLIDE SHOW tab in PowerPoint. In all applications, the name of the currently selected, or active, tab is colored the same color as the background of the FILE tab. This means it is blue in Word, green in Excel, red in Access, and orange in PowerPoint.

Like the ribbon in File Explorer windows, the ribbon in Office applications contains contextual tabs. Remember that contextual tabs contain commands related to your current task or object. An **object** is anything that can be manipulated as a whole, such as a table, a picture, a shape, a chart, or an equation. Contextual tabs usually appear to the right of the standard ribbon tabs just below a title label. For example, when you click in a table in a Word document, two contextual tabs labeled TABLE TOOLS appear to the right of the VIEW tab, and when you click a text box in PowerPoint, a DRAWING TOOLS FORMAT tab appears (see Exhibit 9-6). **Text boxes** are boxes that contain text. A text box is an example of an object. Contextual tabs disappear when you click elsewhere on the screen, deselecting the object.

Exhibit 9-5 INSERT tab on the ribbon in Excel

Exhibit 9-6 Contextual DRAWING TOOLS FORMAT tab in PowerPoint

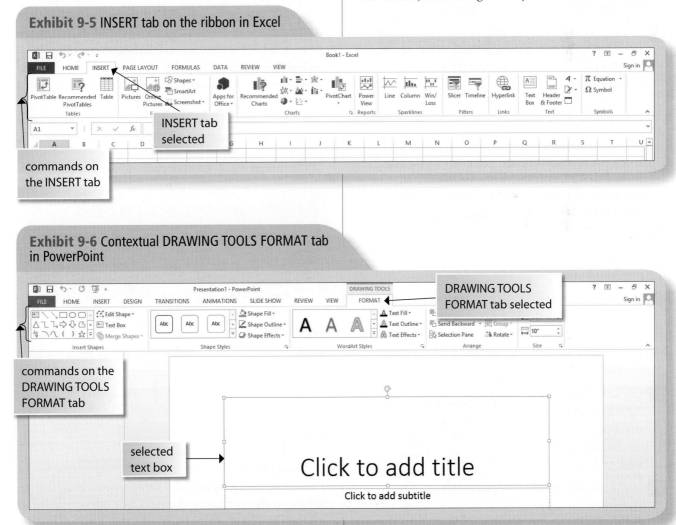

object Anything in a document that can be manipulated as a whole.

text box An object that contains text.

Switch tabs, and display and close a contextual tab.

1 On the ribbon in the Excel window, click the **INSERT tab**. The color of the label *INSERT* on the tab changes to green to indicate that it is selected, and the commands on the INSERT tab appear.

2 Click the **FORMULAS tab**. The color of the label *FORMULAS* on the tab changes to green, and the commands on the FORMULAS tab appear. The FORMULAS tab appears only on the Excel ribbon.

3 On the taskbar, click the **PowerPoint button** . PowerPoint is now the active application.

4 On the ribbon, click the **INSERT tab**. The color of the label *INSERT* on the tab changes to orange, and the commands on the INSERT tab appear. The commands on the INSERT tab on the PowerPoint ribbon are similar to, but not exactly the same as, the commands on the INSERT tab on the Excel ribbon.

5 Click the **SLIDE SHOW tab**. The color of the label *SLIDE SHOW* on the tab changes to orange, and the commands on the SLIDE SHOW tab appear. The SLIDE SHOW tab is unique to PowerPoint.

6 In the center of the window, position the pointer directly on top of the dotted line around *Click to add title* so that the pointer changes to ⬚.

7 With the pointer as ⬚, click the **dotted line**. A solid line appears in place of the dotted line because the text box object is now selected, and the DRAWING TOOLS FORMAT tab appears on the ribbon.

8 Click the **DRAWING TOOLS FORMAT tab** to make it the active tab on the ribbon. Refer back to Exhibit 9-6.

> **Tip:** Sometimes a contextual tab will become the active tab on the ribbon automatically when you select an object.

9 In the middle of the PowerPoint window, click anywhere in the white space outside of the selected text box object. The object is no longer

toggle button A button that you click once to turn a feature on and click again to turn it off.

selected, and the contextual tab disappears from the ribbon. The HOME tab is now the active tab because that was the active tab before you selected the contextual tab.

End Activity

9-2b Using Buttons

As with the ribbon in File Explorer windows, the group names appear at the bottom of the ribbon below the buttons. For the most part, when you click a button in a group on a ribbon tab, something happens in the file. For example, the Clipboard group on the HOME tab in Word, Excel, Access, and PowerPoint includes the Cut, Copy, and Format Painter buttons, which you can click to cut or copy text or objects, or copy formatting.

Some buttons on the ribbon are **toggle buttons**: one click turns the feature on and the next click turns the feature off. While the feature is on, the button remains colored or highlighted to indicate that it is selected. For example, when you click the Bold button **B** in the Font group on the Word HOME tab to select it, the currently selected text is formatted as bold and the Bold button changes so it is colored blue, as shown in Exhibit 9-7. Clicking the Bold button again removes the bold formatting.

Exhibit 9-7 Bold button toggled on in Word

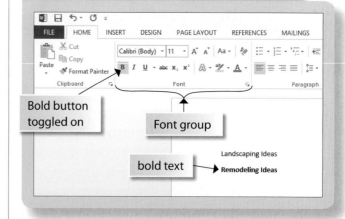

Some buttons have two parts: the top or left part of the button that executes the default command, and an arrow on the bottom or the right that opens a menu of all the commands or options available for that button. When you point to two-part buttons, the part of the button you are pointing to is shaded in a color, and a colored border appears around the other part of the button. In Exhibit 9-8, the pointer is on the Bullets button ⬚ in the Paragraph group on the HOME tab in Word.

Exhibit 9-8 A two-part button

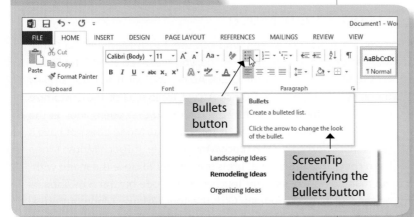

Exhibit 9-8 A two-part button

Bullets button

ScreenTip identifying the Bullets button

Read this before starting the next Activity: In this book, when you need to click the icon part of a two-part button (the top or the left part of the button), the step will instruct you to simply *click the button*. When you need to click the arrow part of a two-part button (below or to the right of the button), the step will instruct you to *click the button arrow*.

Begin Activity

Use buttons on the ribbon.

1 Make **Word** the active application.

2 Type **Landscaping Ideas** and then press the **Enter key**. The text appears in the first line of the document, and the insertion point moves to the second line.

> **Problem?** If you make a typing error, press the Backspace key to delete the incorrect letters and then retype the text.

To use the default command for a two-part button, you click the top or left part of the button—the part of the button with the icon on it. To use a command other than the default, you click the arrow part of the button, and then click one of the commands or options that appear. Exhibit 9-9 shows the options available when you click the arrow part of the Bullets button in the Paragraph group on the HOME tab in Word.

3 On the HOME tab, in the Font group, point to the **Bold button** B. The button changes so that it is shaded blue and its ScreenTip appears.

> **Tip:** Position the pointer on top of a button to see its name and keyboard shortcut (if it has one).

Exhibit 9-9 Options on the Bullets button in Word

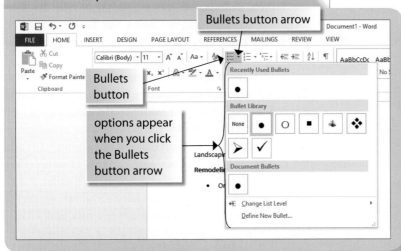

Bullets button arrow

Bullets button

options appear when you click the Bullets button arrow

4 Click the **Bold button** B. The button stays shaded blue to indicate that it is selected.

5 Type **Remodeling Ideas**. The text you typed is in bold. Refer back to Exhibit 9-7.

6 Click the **Bold button** B. The button toggles off and returns to its original color.

Note that some buttons have an arrow on them, but they are not two-part buttons, such as the Line and Paragraph Spacing button in the Paragraph group on the HOME tab in Word. When you point to this type of button, a solid line dividing the button does *not* appear, and clicking any part of this type of button always opens a list of commands or options.

7 Press the **Enter key**, and then type **Organizing Ideas**. The text in the third line is not bold because you toggled the command off before you started typing.

8 On the HOME tab, in the Paragraph group, point to the **Bullets button** ≣, but do not click. The part of the button with the icon is shaded blue, and a line separating the button icon from the arrow indicates that this is a two-part button. Refer back to Exhibit 9-8.

> **Problem?** If the arrow part of the Bullets button is shaded blue, you are pointing to the arrow part of the button. Move the pointer so it is pointing to the left part of the Bullets button.

9 Click the **Bullets button** ≣ (the icon part of the Bullets button). A bullet is added in front of the third line of text and the line is indented.

10 Click in the second line of text, and then click the **Bullets button arrow** ≣ ▾ (the arrow part of the Bullets button). A list of types of bullets appears. Refer back to Exhibit 9-9.

11 In the list, click the **check mark bullet style** ✓. A check mark bullet is added in front of the second line of text, and the line is indented.

12 On the HOME tab, in the Paragraph group, point to the **Line and Paragraph Spacing button** ↕≡ ▾. Although this button has an arrow next to its icon, the arrow part of the button is shaded along with the icon part of the button and there is no line separating the icon from the arrow, so it is not a two-part button.

13 Click the **Line and Paragraph Spacing button** ↕≡ ▾. A list of options opens.

14 On the list, click **3.0**. The spacing after the second line of text—the line the insertion point is currently in—changes to three lines.

End Activity

FYI

Using Touch Mode

If you have a touch screen, you can use Touch Mode in the Office applications. To turn on Touch Mode, you first need to add the Touch/Mouse Mode button to the Quick Access Toolbar if it is not already there. To the right of the Quick Access Toolbar, click the Customize Quick Access Toolbar button ▾. In the menu that opens, look at the Touch/Mouse Mode command. If Touch/Mouse Mode does not have a check mark next to it, click Touch/Mouse Mode. If Touch/Mouse Mode has a check mark next to it, press the Esc key to close the menu without making a selection. The Touch/Mouse Mode button now appears on the Quick Access Toolbar. Click the Touch/Mouse Mode button 👆 to turn on Touch Mode; click it again to turn off Touch Mode. When Touch Mode is on, the ribbon increases in height and the buttons are larger and have more space between them to help you touch only the specific button you want to activate. The figures in this book show the application windows with Touch Mode turned off.

9-2c Using Galleries and Live Preview

A **menu** is a list of commands that appears when you click a button. A **gallery** is a grid that shows visual representations of the options available. When you clicked the Bullets button arrow in the previous Activity, the Bullets gallery and menu appeared (refer back to Exhibit 9-9). The gallery shows the bullet styles you can select. The menu at the bottom contains additional commands for working with bullets.

Galleries can appear when you click a button, such as the gallery on the Bullets button, or they are displayed in a group on the ribbon. An example of a gallery displayed in a group on the ribbon is the gallery in the Styles group on the HOME tab in Word (shown in Exhibit 9-10) and the galleries in the Themes and Variants groups on the DESIGN tab in PowerPoint (shown in Exhibit 9-11). These types of galleries usually have scroll arrows on the right to allow you to shift up or down a row, and a More button ▾ below the scroll arrows that you can click to expand the gallery to see all the options it contains.

In many galleries and on some menus, when you point to an option, **Live Preview** shows the results that would occur in your file if you clicked that option. To continue the bullets example, when you point to a bullet style in the Bullets gallery, a bullet in the style you are pointing to appears before the paragraph in which the insertion point is located. By moving the pointer from option to option, you can quickly see the text formatted with different bullet styles, making it easier to select the style you want.

Exhibit 9-10 Gallery on the HOME tab in Word

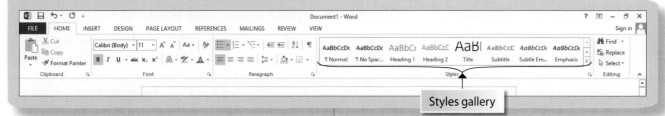

Styles gallery

Exhibit 9-11 Galleries on the DESIGN tab in PowerPoint

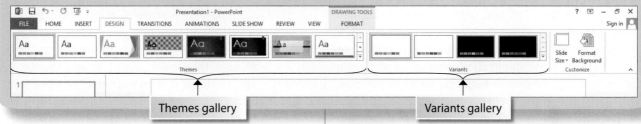

Themes gallery

Variants gallery

Begin Activity

Use galleries and Live Preview.

1 In the Word window, double-click **Landscaping**. The entire word is highlighted with blue to indicate that it is selected.

2 On the HOME tab, in the Font group, click the **Font Size button arrow** $\boxed{11 \; \cdot}$. A menu of font sizes (text sizes) opens.

3 In the menu, point to **26**. Live Preview shows the selected text formatted in the larger size. See Exhibit 9-12.

Exhibit 9-12 Live Preview of a new font size in Word

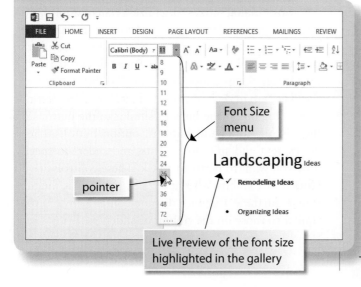

Font Size menu

pointer

Live Preview of the font size highlighted in the gallery

4 Click a blank area of the document to close the gallery without selecting anything.

5 Make **Excel** the active application.

6 Type **Budget** and then press the **Enter key**. The text you typed appears in the first box in column A and the second box in column A has a green border.

7 Click the box containing the word you just typed. The box containing *Budget* now has the green border.

8 On the ribbon, click the **HOME tab** to make it the active tab. In the Font group, click the **Font button arrow** $\boxed{\text{Calibri} \quad \cdot}$ to display the Font gallery.

9 Point to several of the fonts (the design of text) to preview the effect on the text you just typed.

10 In the gallery, click **Algerian**. The gallery closes, and the text you typed is formatted with the Algerian font.

11 Make **Word** the active application. On the HOME tab, in the Styles group, click the **down scroll arrow** $\boxed{\cdot}$ to the right of the Styles gallery. The gallery scrolls down one row.

12 In the Styles group, click the **More button** $\boxed{\cdot}$. The Styles gallery opens so that you can see all of the options in the gallery.

13 Press the **Esc key**. The gallery closes without making a selection.

End Activity

How Buttons, Groups, and Galleries Appear on the Ribbon

The buttons and groups on the ribbon change based on your monitor size, your screen resolution, and the size of the application window. With smaller monitors, lower screen resolutions, and resized application windows, buttons can appear as icons without labels and some groups are condensed into a button that you click to display the commands in the group. The instructions and figures in this book were created using a screen resolution of 1366 × 768 and, unless otherwise specified, the maximized application windows. If you are using a different screen resolution or window size, the buttons on the ribbon might show more or fewer button names, and some groups might be wider or narrower than described in the steps. Some groups might even be reduced to a button; for example, at the lower resolution of 800 × 600, the entire Editing group on the Word HOME tab is collapsed into a single button. If you cannot find a button referenced in the steps, you might need to click the group button first; for example, if the instruction in a step is, "In the Editing group, click the Replace button," you would need to click the Editing button, and then click the Replace button. Also be aware that button icons are shown in this book only when the button name is not visible at the resolution of 1366 × 768. If you cannot find a button in a group on a tab, use the ScreenTips to find the correct button. Using different resolutions also affects the instructions for galleries. At lower resolutions, fewer choices are displayed in a gallery on the ribbon, and at higher resolutions, more choices are displayed. This means that if you are working with a lower resolution and the step instruction says to click a style or button in a gallery on the ribbon and you don't see it, you will need to click the More button first. Likewise, if you are working with a higher resolution, you might not need to click the More button to access the specific style or button in the step; however, you can still follow the step instruction as written.

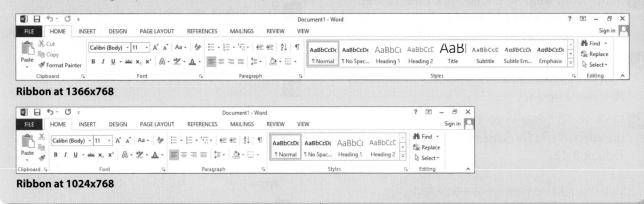

Ribbon at 1366x768

Ribbon at 1024x768

9-2d Using Commands in Dialog Boxes

Some groups on the ribbon tabs have a small button in their lower-right corners called the Dialog Box Launcher ⬓. Most of the time, when you click a Dialog Box Launcher, a dialog box related to that group of buttons opens. A **dialog box** is a window that opens on top of the application window and in which you enter or choose settings for performing a task. For example, the Page Setup dialog box in Excel, shown in Exhibit 9-13, contains options to change how the printed document looks. Some dialog boxes open as a result of you clicking a command on a menu or a button on the ribbon.

Most dialog boxes organize related information into tabs with related options and settings are organized into sections or groups, just as they are on the ribbon. Exhibit 9-13 shows the Page tab selected in the Excel Page Setup dialog box, and Exhibit 9-14 shows the Sheet tab in the same dialog box. You select settings in a dialog box using buttons similar to the buttons on the ribbon, command buttons, option buttons, check boxes, text and spin boxes, lists, and sliders to specify how you want to perform a task. These controls are all labeled in Exhibits 9-13 and 9-14. (Note that the tabs shown in these Exhibits do not contain any buttons similar to those on the ribbon or sliders.)

dialog box A window in which you enter or choose settings for performing a task.

Exhibit 9-13 Page tab in the Page Setup dialog box in Excel

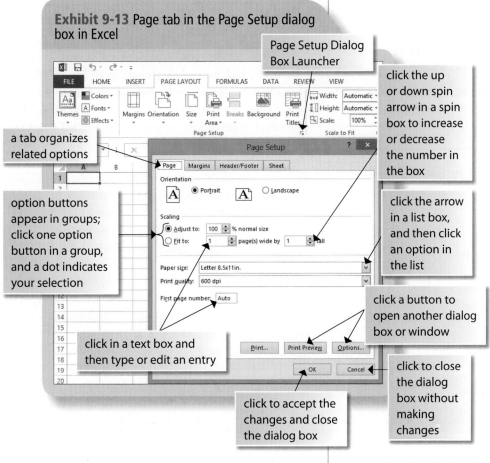

Page Setup Dialog Box Launcher

a tab organizes related options

option buttons appear in groups; click one option button in a group, and a dot indicates your selection

click in a text box and then type or edit an entry

click the up or down spin arrow in a spin box to increase or decrease the number in the box

click the arrow in a list box, and then click an option in the list

click a button to open another dialog box or window

click to close the dialog box without making changes

click to accept the changes and close the dialog box

Exhibit 9-14 Sheet tab in the Page Setup dialog box in Excel

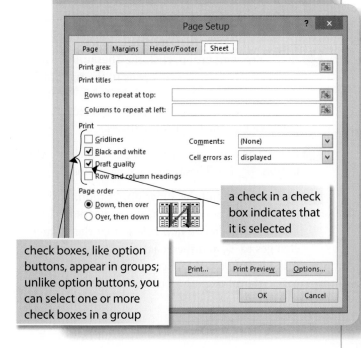

a check in a check box indicates that it is selected

check boxes, like option buttons, appear in groups; unlike option buttons, you can select one or more check boxes in a group

Use commands in a dialog box.

1 Make **Excel** the active application. On the ribbon, click the **PAGE LAYOUT tab** to make it the active tab.

2 In the Page Setup group, click the **Dialog Box Launcher** 🔲. The Page Setup dialog box opens with the Page tab as the active tab in the dialog box. Refer back to Exhibit 9-13.

3 In the Orientation section, click the **Landscape option button**. The black dot moves from the Portrait option button to the Landscape option button, indicating that the Landscape option is now selected. Landscape means that when you print, the page will be wider than it is long.

4 Click the **Paper size arrow**. A list of paper sizes opens. The size that appeared in the box before you clicked the arrow (Letter 8.5×11in.) is selected. A scroll bar appears on the right side of the list because you need to scroll to see the additional choices in the list.

5 Drag the **scroll box** to the bottom of the scroll bar to see some of the additional choices, and then click a blank area of the dialog box to close the list without selecting anything.

6 Click the **Sheet tab** to make it the active tab in the dialog box.

7 In the Print section of the dialog box, click the **Black and white check box**. A check mark appears in the check box, indicating that it is selected.

8 Click the **Draft quality check box**. A check mark appears in this check box as well.

9 Click the **Margins tab** to make it the active tab in the dialog box.

10 Click the **Top up arrow** three times. The value in the Top box changes from .75 to 1.5.

11 In the Bottom box, click after the 5. The insertion point appears in the Bottom box after the 5.

12 Press the **Backspace key** four times, and then type **2**.

13 Click **Cancel**. The dialog box closes without changing the page setup in the workbook.

End Activity

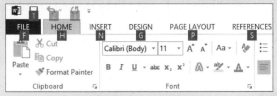
9-2e Open and Close Task Panes

Sometimes when you click a Dialog Box Launcher, a task pane appears instead of a dialog box. A **task pane** is similar to a dialog box, but it appears as a narrow window to the left or right of the workspace. For example, clicking the Thesaurus button in the Proofing group on the REVIEW tabs in Word, Excel, and PowerPoint opens the Thesaurus task pane to the right of the window. Exhibit 9-15 shows the Thesaurus task pane in Excel. In PowerPoint, when a shape or a text box is selected, clicking the Format Shape Dialog Box Launcher in the Drawing group on the HOME tab opens the Format Shape task pane, shown in Exhibit 9-16. Like dialog

task pane A narrow window that appears to the left or right of the workspace in which you can enter or choose settings for performing a task.

boxes, you open some task panes by clicking a command on a menu or a button on the ribbon.

Like in a dialog box, the commands and options available in a task pane vary depending on the purpose of the task pane. Some task panes, like the Format Shape task pane shown in Exhibit 9-16, contain labels and buttons that are similar to tabs in a dialog box. Click each label to display a different, related set of buttons, and click each button to display a different set of commands or options. You can then click the commands with expand arrows (▷) next to them to display the options or commands related to that command. The SHAPE OPTIONS label is selected at the top of the Format Shape task pane in Exhibit 9-16, and the Effects button (☼) is selected as well. The SHADOW commands are expanded.

Task panes can contain all the types of commands available in dialog boxes. The SHADOW options include buttons similar to those on the ribbon and sliders. You can drag a slider to change the value in the associated spin box, you can type a value in the spin box, or you can use the up and down arrows in the spin box.

When you are finished working with a task pane, you can click its Close button ✖ on the title bar to close it.

Begin Activity

Open and close a task pane.

1 On the Excel ribbon, click the **REVIEW tab**. If a green outline does not surround the word *Budget* that you typed earlier, click **Budget**.

2 In the Proofing group, click the **Thesaurus button**. The Thesaurus task pane opens to the right of the workspace. Refer back to Exhibit 9-15. Because the box with the word *Budget* is selected, this task pane contains synonyms for *Budget*.

3 In the Thesaurus task pane title bar, click the **Close button** ✖. The Thesaurus task pane closes.

4 Make **PowerPoint** the active application. Position the pointer directly on top of the dotted line around *Click to add title* so that the pointer changes to ⁺↖, and then click the dotted line. A solid line appears in place of the dotted line indicating that the text box object is now selected.

Exhibit 9-15 Thesaurus task pane in Excel showing synonyms for *Budget*

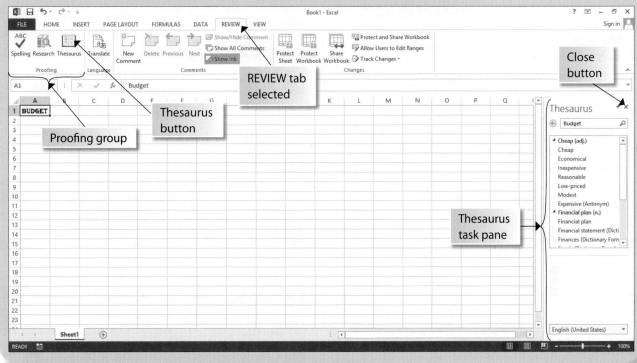

Exhibit 9-16 Format Shape task pane in PowerPoint

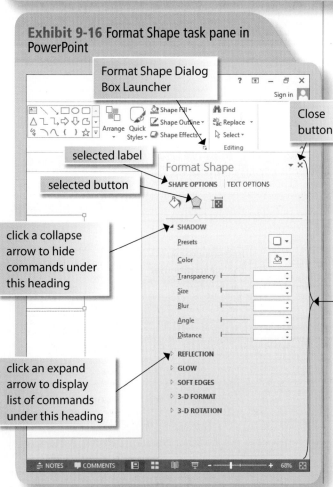

5 On the HOME tab, in the Drawing group, point to the **Dialog Box Launcher** ⬚. The ScreenTip identifies this Dialog Box Launcher as Format Shape.

6 Click the **Format Shape Dialog Box Launcher** ⬚. The Format Shape task pane opens on the right side of the window. The SHAPE OPTIONS label at the top of the task pane is orange, indicating it is selected.

7 In the task pane, click the **Effects button** ◯. The commands in the task pane change to include commands for modifying special effects that can be applied to the selected text box.

8 If the SHADOW list is not expanded, click the **expand arrow** ▷ next to SHADOW. Refer back to Exhibit 9-16.

9 Click the **Transparency spin box up arrow**. Values appear in all of the spin boxes under SHADOW, the slider buttons are positioned on the sliders at a point that reflects the values in the spin boxes, and a shadow effect is applied to the selected text box.

10 Drag the **Distance slider button** to the right until the value in the spin box changes to 115 pt. The shadow of the text in the text box moves farther away from the text.

11 Click the **Presets button** ☐ ▾. Under No Shadow, click the **No Shadow button** ☐. The shadow effect is removed from the text box, the values disappear from the spin boxes, and the slider buttons all return to the left end of the sliders.

12 In the Format Shape task pane title bar, click the **Close button** ✕. The Format Shape task pane closes.

Problem? If you cannot set the Distance value exactly to 115 pt, use the slider button to get as close as possible, and then use the spin arrows to set the value to 115 pt.

End Activity

9-2f Exploring Backstage View

The first tab on the ribbon, in both Office applications and in Windows 8 File Explorer windows, is the FILE tab. Instead of displaying a different set of commands on the ribbon, clicking the FILE tab opens Backstage view. Remember that when you start an Office application, Backstage view offers only the Recent screen. After you open a file, you can access all of the commands available in Backstage view. The left pane in Backstage view is the **navigation bar** and it contains commands you click to display different screens or perform an action. Exhibit 9-17 shows the Info screen in Backstage view in PowerPoint.

Backstage view hides the window containing the open file, including the ribbon. If you need to leave Backstage view and display the commands on a different

tab on the ribbon, you click the Back button ◉ at the top of the navigation bar.

Begin Activity

Explore Backstage view.

1 On the PowerPoint ribbon, click the **FILE tab**. Backstage view in PowerPoint appears, replacing the blank presentation in the workspace. Either the Open or Info screen will be displayed.

2 If the Info screen is not displayed, in the navigation bar, click **Info**. Backstage view displays the Info screen, which contains information about the current file. Refer back to Exhibit 9-17.

3 In the navigation bar, click the **Back button** ◉. Backstage view closes, and the PowerPoint window and ribbon are visible again.

4 Make **Word** the active application, and then click the **FILE tab**. Backstage view in Word appears with the Info screen displayed.

5 In the navigation bar, click the **Back button** ◉. Backstage view closes, and the Word window and ribbon are visible again.

End Activity

navigation bar The left pane in Backstage view.

Exhibit 9-17 Backstage view in PowerPoint with the Info screen displayed

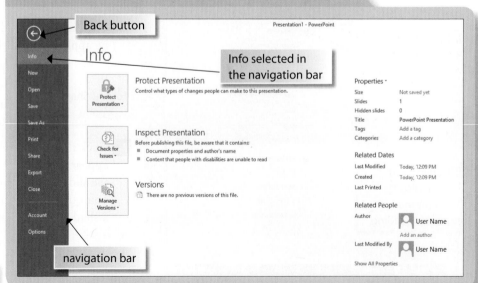

9-3 Selecting Text and Using the Mini Toolbar

As you work with files in Office, you will often need to select text. Once you have selected text, you can modify it or replace it.

9-3a Selecting Text

You can select text using the mouse or the keyboard. To select text using the mouse, click before the first character you want to select, press and hold the mouse button, and then drag over the text. When all of the characters that you want to select are highlighted, release the mouse button. To select text using the keyboard, position the insertion point before the first character you want to select (you can click or use the arrow keys on the keyboard), press and hold the Shift key, and then press the arrow key pointing in the direction in which you want to select text. To combine using the mouse and the keyboard to select text. Click before the first character you want to select, press and hold the Shift key, and then click after the last character you want to select.

In addition, you can select nonadjacent text. To do this, use any method to select the first block of text, press and hold the Ctrl key, and then use the mouse and drag to select as many other blocks of text as you want.

9-3b Using the Mini Toolbar

The **Mini toolbar** contains buttons for the most commonly used formatting commands, such as font, font size, styles, color, alignment, and indents. Exhibit 9-18 shows the Mini toolbar in Word. The exact buttons on the Mini toolbar differ in each application, and all of the commands on the Mini toolbar appear somewhere on the ribbon in that application. The Mini toolbar appears whenever you select text with the mouse or right-click in Word, Excel, or PowerPoint.

If you move the pointer away from text you selected with the mouse, the Mini toolbar fades. Moving the pointer back to the selected text makes the Mini toolbar reappear, but moving the mouse farther away from the selected text makes the Mini toolbar disappear completely. To redisplay it, you need to right-click the selected text or deselect and then reselect the text.

Begin Activity

Select text and use the Mini toolbar.

1 In the Word window, in the first line of text, position the pointer before the letter **I** in the word *Ideas*.

2 Press and hold the mouse button, drag the pointer across the word **Ideas**, and then release the mouse button. The entire word is shaded with gray to indicate that it is selected, and the Mini toolbar appears above and to the right of the selected text.

3 On the Mini toolbar, click the **Bold button** **B**. The Bold button on the Mini toolbar and the Bold button in the Font group on the HOME tab are blue, and the selected text is formatted with bold. Refer back to Exhibit 9-18.

> **Problem?** If the Mini toolbar disappears, you probably moved the pointer away from the selected text. Move the pointer back to the selected text or repeat Steps 1 and 2.

4 Click a blank area of the document to deselect the text.

End Activity

Exhibit 9-18 Mini toolbar in Word

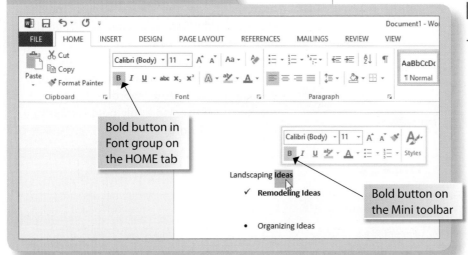

Bold button in Font group on the HOME tab

Bold button on the Mini toolbar

Landscaping Ideas

✓ **Remodeling Ideas**

• Organizing Ideas

Mini toolbar A toolbar with buttons for commonly used formatting commands that appears next to the pointer when you select text with the mouse or you right-click.

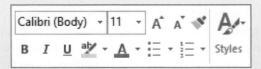
9-4 Undoing and Redoing

If you make a mistake or change your mind about an action as you are working, you can reverse the action by clicking the Undo button 🔄 on the Quick Access Toolbar or by pressing the Ctrl+Z keys. You can continue to click the Undo button or press the Ctrl+Z keys to undo more actions, or you can click the Undo button arrow 🔄▾ and then select as many actions in the list that appears as you want. Exhibit 9-19 shows the Undo button menu in Word with a list of actions on it. You can also Redo an action that you undid by clicking the Redo button ↪ on the Quick Access Toolbar or by pressing the Ctrl+Y keys.

Exhibit 9-19 Undo button menu in Word

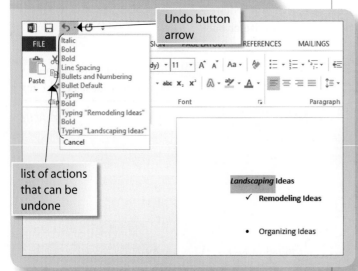

Begin Activity

Undo and redo actions.

1 In the Word window, in the first line of text, double-click **Landscaping** to select it.

2 On the HOME tab on the ribbon, in the Font group, click the **Bold button** B, and then click the **Italic button** I.

3 On the Quick Access Toolbar, point to the **Undo button** 🔄. The ScreenTip identifies the action that will be undone if you click the button, in this case, Undo Italic.

4 Click the **Undo button arrow** 🔄▾. A list of actions that can be undone appears. Refer back to Exhibit 9-19. The list of actions on your screen might differ.

5 On the menu, click **Italic**. The italic formatting is removed from the word *Landscaping*.

6 Click the **Undo button** 🔄. The bold formatting is removed from the word *Landscaping*.

7 On the Quick Access Toolbar, click the **Redo button** ↪. The bold action you just undid is redone, and the word *Landscaping* is bold again.

8 Click a blank area of the document to deselect the text.

End Activity

9-5 Zooming and Scrolling

You can zoom and scroll in the Office applications just like you did when you worked with the Windows 8 Start screen and application windows on the desktop.

9-5a Zooming

Zooming resizes the content in the workspace. You can zoom in to get a closer look at the content of an open document, workbook, or presentation, or of a database report. Likewise, you can zoom out to see more of the content at a smaller size. The Word and Excel figures in this book show the workspace zoomed in to enhance readability.

Exhibit 9-20 VIEW tab and the zoom percentage set to 10% in Word

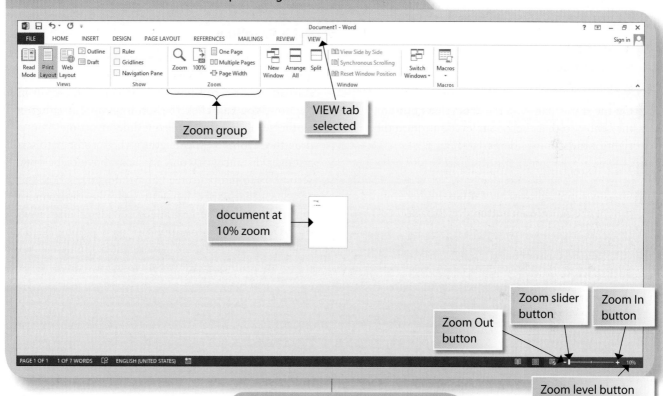

Zoom group

VIEW tab selected

document at 10% zoom

Zoom slider button

Zoom In button

Zoom Out button

Zoom level button indicates the current zoom percentage

Exhibit 9-21 VIEW tab and the Zoom dialog box in Excel

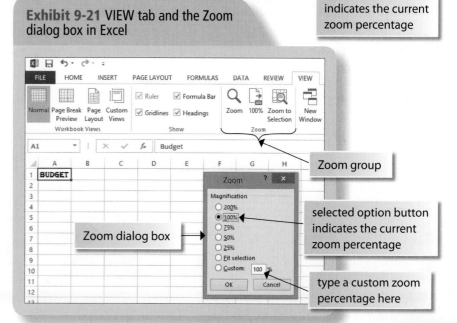

Zoom group

Zoom dialog box

selected option button indicates the current zoom percentage

type a custom zoom percentage here

To change the zoom level, you can drag the Zoom slider button on the Zoom slider at the right end of the status bar or use the buttons in the Zoom group on the VIEW tab on the ribbon. The buttons in the Zoom group on the VIEW tab in each application differ somewhat. Exhibit 9-20 shows the Word window with the VIEW tab selected and a document zoomed to 10%. Exhibit 9-21 shows the Excel window with the VIEW tab selected and the Zoom dialog box open.

Zoom an application window.

1 On the Word status bar, drag the **Zoom slider button** all the way to the left. The percentage on the Zoom level button is 10%, and the document is reduced to its smallest size. Refer back to Exhibit 9-20.

2 Click the **VIEW tab**, as shown in Exhibit 9-20. In the Zoom group, click the **One Page button**. The zoom percentage changes so that the entire page appears in the window.

3 On the VIEW tab, in the Zoom group, click the **Page Width button**. The zoom percentage changes so that the page width fills the window.

4 On the status bar, drag the **Zoom slider button** to the center so that the Zoom level button to the right of the Zoom slider is 100%.

5 Make **Excel** the active application.

6 On the ribbon, click the **VIEW tab**. In the Zoom group, click the **Zoom button**. Refer back to Exhibit 9-21.

7 Click in the **Custom box** after *100*, press the **Backspace key** three times to delete the text in the box, and then type **60**. The Custom option button becomes selected instead of the 100% option button.

8 Click **OK**. The dialog box closes, and the zoom percentage in the Excel window changes to 60%.

9 On the VIEW tab, in the Zoom group, click the **100% button**. The zoom percentage in the Excel window changes to 100%.

9-5b Scrolling

To change which area of the workspace is visible in the application window, you can use the scroll bars. You learned about scroll bars in Chapter 7. To scroll in a window, you can click the scroll arrows at either end of the scroll bar to scroll one line at a time; you can drag the scroll box the length of the scroll bar to scroll a longer distance; or you can click above or below the scroll box to jump a screen at a time.

Scroll bars appear in Office application windows when the workspace is taller or wider than the window. Depending on the application and zoom level, you might see a vertical scroll bar, a horizontal scroll bar, or both. Exhibit 9-22 shows the scroll bars in the Excel window.

Exhibit 9-22 Scroll bars in Excel

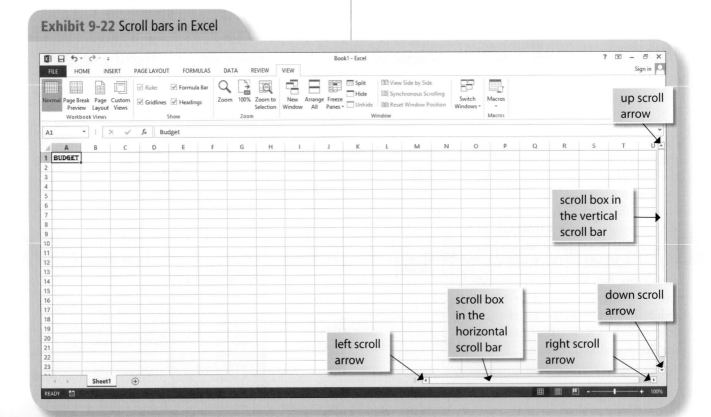

Scroll in an application window.

1 In the Excel window, on the horizontal scroll bar, click the **right scroll arrow** ▶ twice. The worksheet shifts two columns to the right. The first two columns (columns A and B, labeled by letters at the top of the columns) shift out of view and two additional columns shift into view on the right side of the window.

2 On the horizontal scroll bar, drag the **scroll box** all the way to the left. The worksheet shifts left to display columns A and B again.

3 On the vertical scroll bar, click the **down scroll arrow** ▼ three times. The first three rows (rows 1, 2, and 3, labeled by numbers to the left of the rows) scroll up out of view, and three new rows appear at the bottom of the window.

4 On the vertical scroll bar, drag the **scroll box** up to the top of the scroll bar. Rows 1, 2, and 3 scroll back into view.

9-6 Working with Office Files

The most common tasks you perform in any Office application are to create, open, save, and close files. All of these tasks can be done from Backstage view, and the processes for these tasks are basically the same in all Office applications.

9-6a Saving a File for the First Time

As you create and modify an Office file, your work is stored only in the computer's temporary memory. If you were to close the application without saving, turn off your computer, or experience a power failure, your work would be lost. You can save files to the hard drive located inside your computer, an external hard drive, a network storage drive, a portable storage drive such as a USB flash drive, or a folder on a Web site.

To save a file, you can click either the Save button on the Quick Access Toolbar or the Save command in Backstage view. If it is the first time you are saving a file, the Save As screen in Backstage view opens so that you can name the file you are saving and specify a location in which to save it. Exhibit 9-23 shows the Save As screen in Word's Backstage view. To save a file on your computer, you select Computer on the Save As screen. (If you are saving a file to your SkyDrive account, refer to the Web Applications section titled "Saving a File to SkyDrive" at the end of this chapter.) Then on the right, you can select a recently used folder in the Computer list or click the Browse button. Either way, the Save As dialog box opens. The Save As dialog box in Word is shown in Exhibit 9-24. The Save As dialog box looks similar to a File Explorer folder window, and you navigate through it in the same manner so you can choose a location in which to store your file.

When the Save As dialog box opens, there is a suggested file name in the File name box. This is the same as the first few words in the file. The first time you save a file, you need to name it. Remember that file names include a title you specify and a file extension assigned by Office to indicate the file type and that file names can include uppercase and lowercase letters, numbers, hyphens, and spaces in any combination, but not the special characters ? " / \ < > * |. The file extensions for Office 2013 files are *.docx* for Word, *.xlsx*

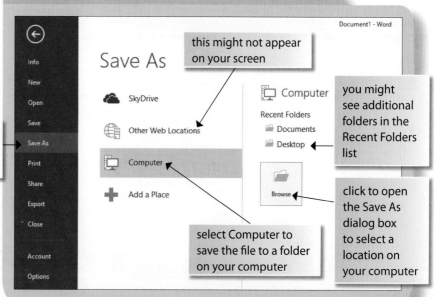

Exhibit 9-23 Save As screen in Word's Backstage view

Exhibit 9-24 Save As dialog box in Word

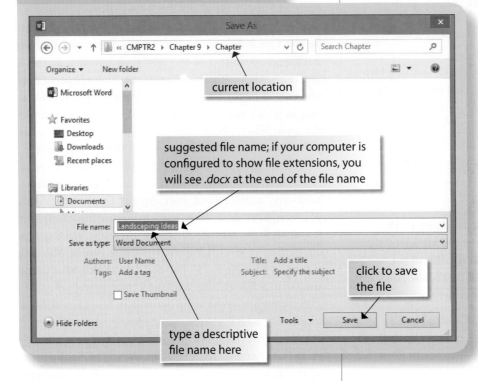

current location

suggested file name; if your computer is configured to show file extensions, you will see *.docx* at the end of the file name

File name: Landscaping Ideas

Save as type: Word Document

type a descriptive file name here

click to save the file

Begin Activity

Save a file for the first time.

1 Make **Word** the active application.

2 On the Quick Access Toolbar, click the **Save button**. Backstage view opens displaying the Save As screen. Refer back to Exhibit 9-23.

3 If necessary, click **Computer**, and then click the **Browse button**. The Save As dialog box opens. Refer back to Exhibit 9-24. The text in the File name box is the suggested file name.

> **Problem?** If you plan to save your files to your SkyDrive account, see the Web Applications section titled "Saving a File to SkyDrive" at the end of this chapter.

for Excel, *.accdb* for Access, and *.pptx* for PowerPoint. File names can include a maximum of 255 characters (including the file extension).

After you save a file, the file name appears in the title bar of the application window. Exhibit 9-25 shows a file name in the Word window title bar. If your computer is configured to show file extensions, you will see the file extension after the file name in the title bar. This book does not show file extensions.

4 Use the techniques you learned in Chapter 7 to navigate to the drive and folder where you plan to store the files you create as you work through these steps.

5 Click in the **File name box**. The suggested file name is selected.

6 Type **Bulleted List Example** in the File name box.

7 Click **Save**. The Save As dialog box and Backstage view close, and the file name you entered for the file appears in the Word window title bar. Refer back to Exhibit 9-25.

End Activity

Exhibit 9-25 File name in the application window title bar

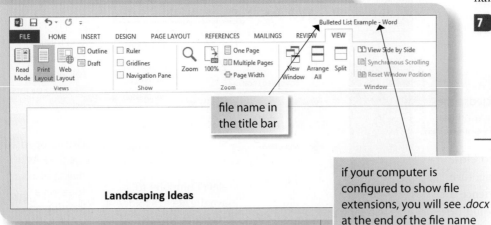

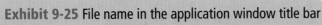

file name in the title bar

if your computer is configured to show file extensions, you will see *.docx* at the end of the file name

Landscaping Ideas

9-6b Saving a File after Making Changes

The saved file includes everything in the document at the time you last saved it. If you make changes to the file, you need to save those changes to the stored version of the file. Until you save the file again, any new edits or additions you make to the document exist only in the computer's memory and are not saved in the file. To save the file again, you click the Save button or use the Save command in Backstage view. Because you already named the document and selected a storage location, the Save As dialog box does not open.

To save a copy of the modified file with a different file name so that the original version remains unchanged, or to save the file to a different location, you can click the FILE tab, and then in the navigation bar, click the Save As command to open the Save As dialog box again. When you do this, the original version of the file remains unchanged and in its original location. Be sure to save frequently as you work so that the file reflects the latest content in case the application or your computer shuts down unexpectedly.

Begin Activity

Modify a file and save your changes.

1. In the Word window, in the third line of the document, click immediately after *Ideas*. The insertion point blinks at the location where you clicked.

2. Press the **Backspace key** five times to delete *Ideas*, and then type **Suggestions**.

3. On the Quick Access Toolbar, click the **Save button** 🖫. The changes you made to the document are saved in the file stored on the drive.

> **Tip:** You can also press the Ctrl+S keys to save the file.

End Activity

9-6c Closing a File

Although you can keep multiple files open at one time, you should close any file you are no longer working on to conserve system resources and prevent changes to the file. You can close a file by clicking the Close command in Backstage view or by clicking the Close button ✕ in the upper-right corner of the title bar. Note, however, that if the file is the only file open in that application, clicking the Close button also exits the application.

If you try to close a file that you have made changes to and you haven't saved the changes, a dialog box, similar to the one shown in Exhibit 9-26, opens, asking whether you want to save your changes. If the file has been saved at least once, clicking Save in this dialog box saves the changes to the file, closes the file, and then exits the application. If the file is not named, clicking Save opens the Save As dialog box so that you can name the file and save it. The application would then close after you click Save in the Save As dialog box. If you don't want to save the file, you click Don't Save.

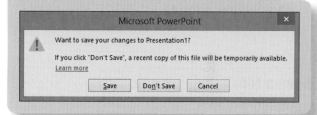

Exhibit 9-26 Dialog box asking if you want to save changes before closing a file

Begin Activity

Close a file.

1. On the Word ribbon, click the **FILE tab**. Backstage view opens.

2. In the navigation bar, click **Close**. Backstage view closes and the document closes, but the Word window stays open.

3. Make **PowerPoint** the active application.

4. In the title bar, click the **Close button** ✕. A dialog box opens, asking if you want to save changes to the file. Refer back to Exhibit 9-26.

5. Click **Don't Save**. The file closes without saving, and the application exits. Word is the active application again.

End Activity

9-6d Opening a File

When you want to view or edit a previously created file, you must first open it. Opening a file transfers a copy of the file from the storage location to the computer's memory and displays it on your screen.

To open a file, display Backstage view, click Open in the navigation bar to display the Open screen, and then click the Browse button to open the Open dialog box. The Open dialog box is very similar to the Save As dialog box.

Protected View

Any file you open that was downloaded from the Internet, accessed from a shared network, or received as an email attachment might open in Protected View. In **Protected View**, you can see the file contents, but you cannot edit, save, or print until you enable editing. To do so, click the Enable Editing button on the Protected View bar. If the Protected View bar is red and the Enable Editing button does not appear on the bar, that means a bigger potential security problem was detected, and something in the file might harm your computer.

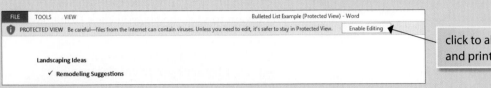

click to allow editing, saving, and printing of the file

Protected View bar in Word

Begin Activity

Open a file.

1 On the Word ribbon, click the **FILE tab** to open Backstage view. Because no files are open, the Open screen appears. Recent Documents is selected, and a list of recently opened documents appears on the right. If the document you want to open is in this list, you can click it to open it. Even though the Bulleted List Example file appears in this list, do not click it so that you can see the Open dialog box.

2 Click **Computer**.

3 In the list on the right, click the **Browse button**. Navigate to the drive and folder in which you saved the file Bulleted List Example.

4 In the list of files, click **Bulleted List Example**, and then click **Open**. The file opens in the Word window.

End Activity

9-7 Using the Clipboard

The **Clipboard** is a temporary storage area in Windows on which text or other objects are stored when you copy or cut them. To **copy** text or an object, you select it, and then use the Copy command to place a copy of it on the Clipboard so that you can paste it somewhere else. If you want to move text from one location and paste it somewhere else, you first need to **cut** it—that is, remove it from the original location and place it on the Clipboard using the Cut command. Once something is on the Clipboard, you can then **paste** it—that is, insert a copy of the text or object on the Clipboard somewhere in the current document or in another document.

9-7a Using the System Clipboard

The system Clipboard is a feature of Windows and is available to all Windows 8 apps and applications. Only one item can be on the system Clipboard at a time. The text or object on the Clipboard stays on the Clipboard until you cut or copy something else or until you shut down your computer. So if you cut text in a Word document and then switch to a File Explorer window and cut a file, the cut file replaces the Word text on the system Clipboard.

Protected View A view of a file in an Office application in which you can see the file contents, but you cannot edit, save, or print them until you enable editing.

Clipboard A temporary storage area in Windows on which text or other objects are stored when you copy or cut them.

copy To duplicate selected text or an object and place it on the Clipboard.

cut To remove selected text or an object from the original location and place it on the Clipboard.

paste To insert a copy of the text or object on the Clipboard in a document.

In all of the Office applications, you can click the Cut button in the Clipboard group on the HOME tab to cut selected text or objects and place them on the system Clipboard, click the Copy button in the same group to copy selected text or objects and place them on the system Clipboard, and click the Paste button to paste the text or objects on the system Clipboard. (Note that the Paste button is a two-part button.) When you press the Delete or Backspace key, the deleted text or object is not placed on the Clipboard.

Begin Activity

Cut, copy, and paste with the system Clipboard.

1 In the third line of text in the Word window, double-click **Suggestions** to select it.

2 On the HOME tab, in the Clipboard group, click the **Copy button**. The selected text remains in the document and is placed on the Clipboard.

3 In the second line of text, click before the word *Ideas*. The text will be pasted at the insertion point.

4 On the HOME tab, in the Clipboard group, click the **Paste button**. The copied text, *Suggestions*, appears between *Remodeling* and *Ideas*. Another button appears below the pasted text; ignore this for now.

5 In the second line of text, double-click **Ideas**.

6 In the Clipboard group, click the **Cut button**. The selected text is removed from the document and replaces the previously copied item on the Clipboard.

7 Make **Excel** the active application, and then click the box to the right of the box containing *BUDGET*.

8 On the ribbon, click the **HOME tab**. In the Clipboard group, click the **Paste button**. The text you cut, *Ideas*, appears in the current box.

End Activity

9-7b Using the Office Clipboard

The Office Clipboard is a special Clipboard available only to Office applications. Unlike the system Clipboard, which can contain only the most recently cut or copied item, the Office Clipboard can hold up to 24 items cut or copied from Office applications. You can then paste these items as needed in any order into any Office document. The last item cut or copied is the first item listed in the Clipboard task pane. Exhibit 9-27 shows the Clipboard task pane open in Word. It contains cut or copied items from Word and Excel files.

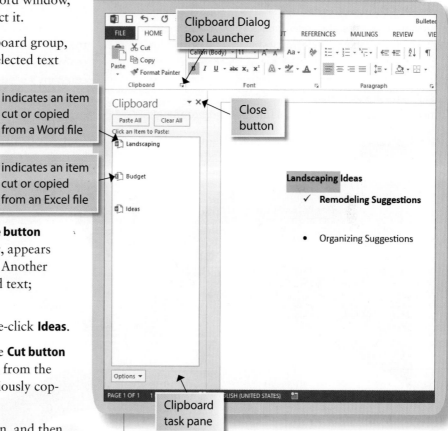

Exhibit 9-27 Clipboard task pane in Word with an item from another Office application

To use the Office Clipboard, you need to activate it by opening the Clipboard task pane in an Office application. If you do not open the Clipboard task pane, the Office Clipboard is not available, and the system Clipboard is used when you cut or copy items. (When the Clipboard task pane is open, the system Clipboard continues to store the latest cut or copied item.) If the Office Clipboard is open in one application, it is available to all of the Office applications.

Integrating Office Applications

Most organizations rely heavily on teams to complete work tasks, and, consequently, team members rely on each other to complete their assigned projects successfully. For example, you might be responsible for providing data for others to analyze or for collecting other team members' data and creating a report. For a team to be effective, it is vital that each member of the team complete his or her piece of the project.

One of the main advantages of Office is **integration**, the ability to share information between applications. Integration ensures consistency and accuracy, and it saves time because you do not have to reenter the same information in several Office applications. It also means that team members can effortlessly share Office files. Team members can create files based on their skills and information that can be used by others as needed. Businesses can take advantage of the integration features of Office every day, as described in the following examples:

- An accounting department can use Excel to create a bar chart illustrating fourth-quarter results for the previous two years and then insert it into a quarterly financial report created in Word. This report could include a hyperlink that employees can click to open the Excel workbook and view the original data.
- An operations department can include an Excel pie chart of sales percentages on a PowerPoint slide, which is part of a presentation to stockholders.
- A marketing department can combine a form letter created in Word with an Access database that stores the names and addresses of potential customers to produce a mailing to promote its company's product.

Andresr/Shutterstock.com

integration The ability to share information between applications.

Use the Office Clipboard.

1 On the HOME tab of the Excel ribbon, in the Clipboard group, point to the **Dialog Box Launcher** ⌐ʟ. The ScreenTip identifies this Dialog Box Launcher as Clipboard.

2 Click the **Clipboard Dialog Box Launcher** ⌐ʟ. The Clipboard task pane opens on the left side of the window and shows items on the Office Clipboard. As you can see, the Office Clipboard already contains the last item you placed on the system Clipboard—the text *Ideas* that you cut from the Word document.

3 Click the box that contains the word *Budget*.

4 On the HOME tab, in the Clipboard group, click the **Copy button**. The text *Budget* appears at the top of the Clipboard task pane.

5 Make **Word** the active application.

6 In the first line of text, double-click **Landscaping** to select it.

7 On the HOME tab, in the Clipboard group, click the **Copy button**.

8 On the HOME tab, in the Clipboard group, click the **Clipboard Dialog Box Launcher** ⌐ʟ. The Clipboard task pane opens with the text you just copied listed at the top of the task pane. Refer back to Exhibit 9-27.

9 In the third line of text in the document, click after *Suggestions*, and then press the **Enter key** twice.

10 In the Clipboard task pane, click **Budget**. The text you copied from the Excel document appears in the Word document.

> **Tip:** To delete an item from the Office Clipboard, point to the item, click the arrow that appears, and then click Delete.

11 In the Clipboard task pane title bar, click the **Close button** ☒.

12 On the Quick Access Toolbar, click the **Save button** 🖫.

deepspacedave/Shutterstock.com; pryzmat/Shutterstock.com

Keyboard Shortcuts for Cut, Copy, and Paste

When you cut, copy, and paste frequently, the keyboard shortcuts for the Cut, Copy, and Paste commands can save you time. To cut selected text or objects, press the Ctrl+X keys. To copy the selected text or objects, press the Ctrl+C keys. To paste the contents of the Clipboard, press the Ctrl+V keys.

9-8 Getting Help

If you don't know how to perform a task or want more information about a feature, you can use the Help window to access Help topics. Each application has its own Help window from which you can find information about all of the Office commands and features as well as step-by-step instructions for using them. The Word Help window is shown in Exhibit 9-28. In the Help window, you can click one of the links, or you can click in the Search help box and type the word or phrase you want help with. To access all of the Help topics, your computer must be connected to the Internet. As shown in Exhibit 9-28, you can also click a More link to start your browser and go to the Support page for the application on Office.com, a Microsoft Web site that contains Help topics and other information and services for use with the Office applications.

Yuri Arcurs/Shutterstock.com

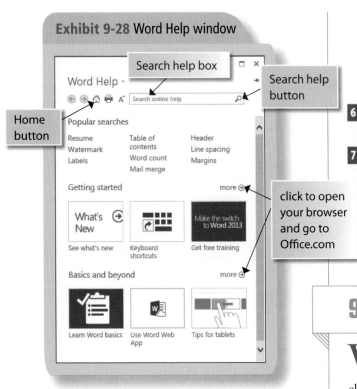

Exhibit 9-28 Word Help window

Search help box

Search help button

Home button

click to open your browser and go to Office.com

window displays a list of topics whose content includes the words you typed in the Search box, in this case, topics whose content contains the phrase *Office Clipboard* or the individual word *Office* or *Clipboard*.

6 Click the **Use the Office Clipboard link**. The topic content is displayed in the Help window.

7 Read the information in the Help window.

8 On the Word Help window title bar, click the **Close button** [X]. The Word Help window closes.

End Activity

9-9 Closing Office Applications

When you finish working with an application, you should close it. You close an application by closing the application window the same way you close any window on the desktop—by clicking its Close button [X] on the title bar. As you saw when you closed the PowerPoint window, when only one file, or no file, is open, clicking the Close button closes the file and closes the application. If more than one file is open in an application, you will need to click the Close button in each file's window to close the application.

Begin Activity

Close Office applications.

1 On the Word window title bar, click the **Close button** [X]. The file closes, and the application closes. The Excel window is the active window on the desktop.

2 In the Clipboard task pane title bar, click the **Close button** [X]. The Clipboard task pane closes.

3 On the Excel window title bar, click the **Close button** [X]. Because you have not saved this file, a dialog box opens asking whether you want to save the changes you made to the workbook.

4 Click **Don't Save**. The file closes without being saved, and the Excel application closes.

End Activity

Begin Activity

Search Help.

1 In the Word title bar, click the **Microsoft Word Help button** [?]. The Word Help window opens. Refer back to Exhibit 9-28.

2 Under the Basics and Beyond heading, click the **Learn Word basics link**. The Basic tasks in Word 2013 topic appears in the Help window.

> **Problem?** If your computer is not connected to the Internet, you will have access only to Basic Help, and your Help window will look different from Exhibit 9-28.

3 Review the information in the window, scrolling down as needed.

4 When you are finished reading the information in the Help window, click the Home button [🏠] at the top of the Word Help window. The start screen (or the Home screen) containing the list of links that appeared when you first started Word Help appears.

5 Click in the **Search help box**, type **Office Clipboard**, and then click the **Search online help button** [🔍] at the right end of the Search help box. The Help

Quiz Yourself

1. What is Backstage view?

2. How is the ribbon organized?

3. What is an object?

4. What is a text box?

5. What is a toggle button?

6. What is Live Preview?

7. What is a dialog box?

8. What is a task pane?

9. When does the Mini toolbar appear?

10. How do you undo your most recent action?

11. Why do you need to save files that you create in Office applications?

12. How do you close a file without exiting the application?

13. Describe the difference between the system Clipboard and the Office Clipboard.

14. How do you open the Help window?

15. How do you exit an Office application?

Practice It

Practice It 9-1

1. Start Word, start Excel, and then start PowerPoint, opening a new, blank file in each application.

2. Make Excel the active application, and then make the DATA tab the active tab.

3. Make PowerPoint the active application, and then click directly on the border of the box around *Click to add subtitle*. Make the DRAWING TOOLS FORMAT tab the active tab on the ribbon. Make the DRAWING TOOLS FORMAT tab disappear from the ribbon.

4. In the PowerPoint window, click in the box labeled *Click to add title*, and then type your first and last name.

5. Select your first name, and then on the HOME tab, in the Font group, click the Bold button.

6. On the HOME tab, in the Font group, use the ScreenTips to identify the Font Color button, and then click the Font Color button arrow to open the Font Color gallery.

7. Use Live Preview to preview several colors, and then change the color of the selected text to Blue (under Standard Colors).

8. In the Font group, click the Font Dialog Box Launcher to open the Font dialog box with the Font tab selected. Click the Font style arrow, and then click Bold Italic. Click after 60 in the Size box, press the Backspace key twice to delete the value, and then type **32**. In the Effects section, select the All Caps check box. Click OK.

9. Select your whole name, and then copy it to the Clipboard.

10. Make Word the active application. Paste your name from the Clipboard. (Note that your name will be pasted as all black text, smaller than in the PowerPoint window, and your first name will not be in all capital letters.)

11. Press the Enter key, type your street address, press the Enter key, and then type your city, state, and ZIP code. Use the mouse to select your name, and then use the Underline button on the Mini toolbar to underline the line of text containing your name. Use the Strikethrough button in the Font group on the HOME tab to draw a line through your name.

12. Undo the actions to strikethrough your name, and make it underlined. Redo the underline action.

13. Scroll down to the bottom of the page in the Word window.

14. Save the Word file to the drive and folder where you are storing your files using the file name **My Contact Info**.

15. Close the My Contact Info file without exiting Word, and then re-open the **My Contact Info** file.

16. Open the Clipboard task pane. (Your name, which you copied from the PowerPoint file, is on the Office Clipboard.) Select the lines containing your street and city, state, and ZIP code, and then copy those lines to the Clipboard.

17. Make Excel the active application, and then open the Clipboard task pane in Excel. Paste your name that you copied from the PowerPoint file. (Note

that your name will look like it did in the Power-Point file.) Press the Down Arrow key, and then paste the address information you copied from the Word document.

18. Use the Zoom slider in Excel to zoom to 150%. Make the VIEW tab the active tab, and then in the Zoom group, click the 100% button.

19. Make PowerPoint the active application. Save the PowerPoint file to the location where you are storing your files using the file name **My Name**.

20. Open the PowerPoint Help window. Search for Help topics that contain the word **themes**, and then read the Help topic "Change the slide design (theme)." Close the Help window.

21. Close PowerPoint, saving changes if asked. Close the Clipboard task pane in the Word window, and then close Word, saving changes if prompted. Close the Clipboard task pane in the Excel window, and then close Excel without saving changes.

Practice It 9-2

1. Start Excel. Open the data file named **Budget** located in the Chapter 9\Practice It folder. (You should have data files if you completed the steps in Chapter 7. If you do not have data files, see your instructor or technical support person, or download them from your CengageBrain account.)

2. Use a button in the Font group on the HOME tab to make the text in the top box bold.

3. Use a button in the Font group on the HOME tab to add a fill color of Green – Accent 6 to the top box.

4. Save the changed file as **Budget Totals** to the drive and folder where you are storing your files.

5. In the chart, click a blank area to the right of the bars to select the chart, and then copy it to the Clipboard.

6. Start Word. Open the data file named **Stockholder** located in the Chapter 9\Practice It folder.

7. Save the file as **Stockholder Letter** to the drive and folder where you are storing your files.

8. Scroll down so you can see the large space between the body of the letter and the signature block, and then click in the middle of this space.

9. Paste the chart you copied. (Note that it will be pasted with orange bars.)

10. Click the chart to select it. Make the CHART TOOLS DESIGN tab the active tab. In the Chart Styles group, click the More button to display all of the chart styles, point to several styles to see the Live Preview, and then click Style 3.

11. Make the PAGE LAYOUT tab the active tab. In the Page Setup group, click the Margins button, and then click Wide to change the margins.

12. In the Page Setup group, click the Dialog Box Launcher to open the Page Setup dialog box. Make the Layout tab the active tab, and then use the Vertical alignment box in the Page section to change the vertical alignment to centered.

13. Close the Stockholder Letter file without closing Word, saving changes when asked.

14. Close both open applications.

On Your Own

On Your Own 9-1

1. Open the PowerPoint data file named **Music** located in the Chapter 9\On Your Own folder. (You should have data files if you completed the steps in Chapter 7. If you do not have data files, see your instructor or technical support person, or download them from your CengageBrain account.)

2. Click anywhere on the bulleted list, and then click directly on top of the dotted-line border.

3. Use the Font button in the Font group on the HOME tab to change the font to Britannic Bold.

4. Use the Text Shadow button in the Font group on the HOME tab to add a shadow effect to the text.

5. Save the file as **Music Categories** to the drive and folder where you are storing your files.

6. Copy the selected text box.

7. Open a new Word document, and then paste the text box you copied into the document.

8. Use the Bullets gallery to change the bullet symbols to open circles.

9. Use the appropriate button on the DESIGN tab to change the page color to Gold, Accent 4. (Note that the page color formatting only appears when you are looking at the document on a computer. It will not appear if you print the document.)

10. Save the file as **Music List** to the drive and folder where you are storing your files.

11. Close Word and PowerPoint.

Chapter 9

ADDITIONAL STUDY TOOLS

IN THE BOOK

▶ Complete end-of-chapter exercises

▶ Study tear-out Chapter Review Card

ONLINE

▶ Complete additional end-of-chapter exercises

▶ Take practice quiz to prepare for tests

▶ Review key term flash cards (online, printable, and audio)

▶ Play "Beat the Clock" and "Memory" to quiz yourself

▶ Watch the videos to learn more about the topics taught in this chapter.

Answers to Quiz Yourself

1. Backstage view contains commands that allow you to manage application files and options.

2. The ribbon is organized into tabs, and each tab is organized into groups.

3. An object is anything in a document that can be manipulated as a whole.

4. A text box is an object that contains text.

5. A toggle button is a button that you click once to turn a feature on and click again to turn it off.

6. Live Preview shows the results that would occur in your file if you clicked an option in a gallery or on a menu.

7. A dialog box is a window in which you enter or choose settings for performing a task.

8. A task pane is a narrow window that appears to the left or right of the workspace in which to enter or choose settings for performing a task.

9. The Mini toolbar appears when you select text with the mouse or right-click in the application window.

10. To undo your most recent action, click the Undo button on the Quick Access Toolbar or press the Ctrl+Z keys.

11. You need to save files that you create in Office applications because as you create and modify an Office file, your work is stored only in the computer's temporary memory. If you exit the application without saving, turn off your computer, or experience a power failure, your work would be lost.

12. To close a file without exiting the application, click the Close command in Backstage view. If more than one file is open in an application, you can also click the Close button in the application window title bar.

13. The system Clipboard contains only the item that was most recently cut or copied and is available to all Windows 8 apps and applications. The Office Clipboard contains up to 24 cut or copied items and is available only to Office applications.

14. To open the Help window in an Office application, click the Help button on the title bar.

15. To exit an Office application, click the Close button in the application window title bar; if more than one file is open, click the Close button in each window's title bar.

Windows 8 and Office 2013: Organize Your Files

1. Develop an organization strategy for storing the files you create and work with. Consider various folder and subfolder structures, and evaluate which one best fits your needs. Plan your approach for naming the files and folders so that you can easily remember their purposes.

2. Use Word to record your plan for organizing the files on your computer.
   a. List the types of files stored on your computer.
   b. Determine where to store the files: on your hard drive or on removable media.
   c. Sketch the folders and subfolders you will use to manage your files. If you choose a hard drive as your storage medium, plan to store your work files and folders in a subfolder of the Documents folder.
   d. Save the file with an appropriate file name, and then close it.

3. Implement your organization strategy:
   a. Create or rename the main and subfolders you want to use for your files.
   b. Move and copy files to the appropriate folders; rename and delete files as necessary.

4. Create a backup copy of your work files by creating a compressed file of the folders and files, and then copying the compressed file to a removable medium, such as a USB flash drive.

5. Use Windows Help and Support to learn about the Sync Center and how to use it.

6. Use Word to record information about what the Sync Center is and when you would use it. Save the file with an appropriate file name in the appropriate folder according to your plan.

7. Open the Sync Center, and then copy and paste an image of the Sync Center window to your document.
   a. Press the Print Screen key to copy an image of the active window on your screen—in this case, the Sync Center window—to the Clipboard.
   b. Make the document about Sync Center the active window.
   c. With the insertion point on a blank line below the text you typed, paste the contents of the Clipboard.
   d. Save the file, and then close it.

Saving a File to SkyDrive

Often the purpose of creating a file is to share it with other people—sending it attached to an email message for someone else to read or use, collaborating with others on the same document, or posting it as a blog for others to review. **SkyDrive** is online storage provided by Microsoft. All you need to access your workspace on SkyDrive is a Microsoft account.

To obtain a Microsoft account, go to **www.skydrive.com**, click the Sign up now link (or something similar), and fill in the requested information. You can also click the Sign in link in the upper-right corner of any Office application or open the Save As screen in Backstage view, click SkyDrive, and then click the Sign up button. When you sign up, you can use an existing email address or you can sign up for a new Hotmail.com or Live.com email address.

When you are working in Word, Excel, and PowerPoint and you are signed into your Microsoft account, the SkyDrive command on the Save As screen in Backstage view has your username in front of it. Click it, and then click the Browse button to open the Save As dialog box with the current location as your SkyDrive. Exhibit 1 shows the Save As dialog box open on the Save As screen in Word's Backstage view. You can also access your SkyDrive by opening a browser window, going to **www.skydrive.com**, and signing in to your Microsoft account from that Web page. (Note that you cannot save to SkyDrive from Backstage view in Access.) On your SkyDrive page, you can click the Upload button at the top to open the Choose File to Upload dialog box, which is very similar to the Save As dialog box.

Important Note: SkyDrive and Office Web Apps are dynamic Web pages and might change over time, including the way they are organized and how actions are performed. The information provided here was accurate at the time this book was published.

Exhibit 1 Save As dialog box open on the Save As screen in Word's Backstage view

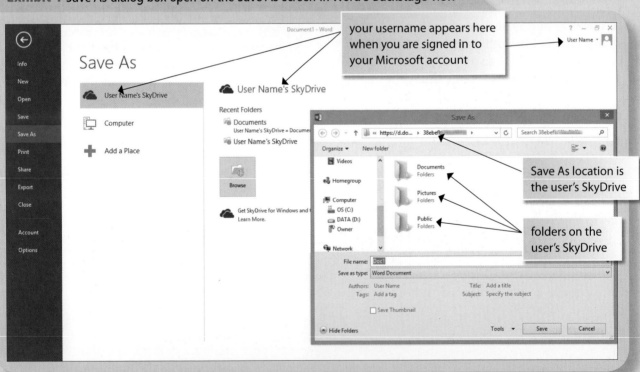

Each of the tiles in your SkyDrive window represents a folder. See Exhibit 2. You can choose to share access to the folders on your SkyDrive. If you do, the people with whom you share the folder can access, view, and download the files stored in those folders. To share a folder, click the folder tile to open the folder, and then on the blue bar at the top, click the Share folder button. A panel opens asking if you're sure you want to share the folder. Click the share this folder link to display another panel. In this panel, you choose how you want to share the link to the folder: you can send the link to the folder via an email message, post the link on Facebook, Twitter, or LinkedIn, or copy the link and paste it anywhere you want. See Exhibit 3. After you make your choice and click the Share folder button, you might see a message in the same panel that tells you that you need to complete a security check. Click the link and then answer the question.

The people you send the link to do not need to be signed in to their Microsoft accounts to access your SkyDrive folder, although you can force them to by checking the appropriate check box in the panel in which you send or copy the link to the folder.

Exhibit 2 Folders on a SkyDrive in a browser window

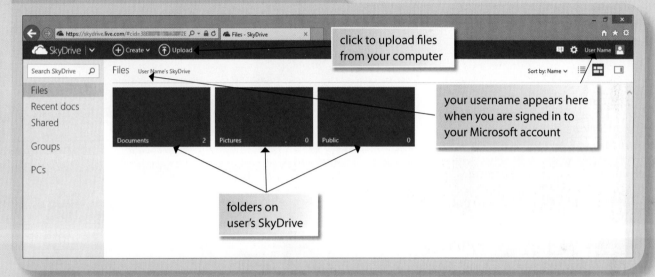

Exhibit 3 Sharing a folder on a SkyDrive

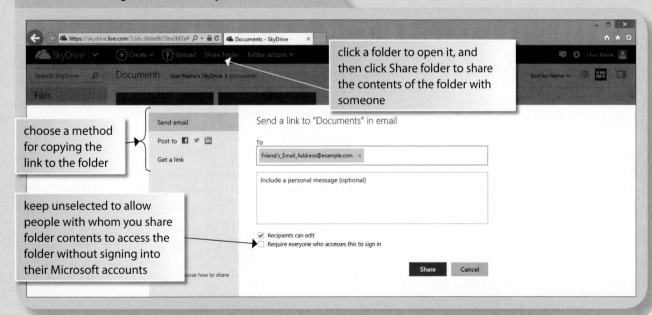

Creating a Document

Monkey Business Images/Shutterstock.com

Microsoft **Word 2013** (or simply **Word**) is a word processing program used to enter, edit, and change the appearance of text. Using Word, you can create all types of documents and make them attractive and easy to read. As part of this process, you often need to enter and edit text and change the way that text and paragraphs look to make the document easier to understand. In addition to entering text in documents, you can create and insert tables and charts in documents and insert photos and drawings created in other programs. Word also has tools so you can check the spelling and grammar in a document. Finally, you can preview and print the documents.

Learning Objectives

After studying the material in this chapter, you will be able to:

10-1 Enter text

10-2 Create documents based on existing documents

10-3 Edit text

10-4 Switch to another open document in Word

10-5 Format text

10-6 Format paragraphs

10-7 Copy formats

10-8 Check spelling and grammar

10-9 Preview and print documents

Microsoft Word 2013 (Word)
Application software used to create and format documents.

10-1 Entering Text

When you work in Word, you can customize the workspace to suit your work style. One thing you can do is show or hide nonprinting characters in your documents. **Nonprinting characters** are characters that do not print and that control the way the document looks. For example, the ¶ character marks the end of a paragraph, and the • character marks the space between words. It is helpful to display nonprinting characters so you can see whether you have typed an extra space, ended a paragraph, and so on.

The first time you start Word, nonprinting characters are not displayed. To show them, you click the Show/Hide ¶ button in the Paragraph group on the HOME tab. If you exit Word and nonprinting characters are displayed, they will appear again the next time you start Word. To hide nonprinting characters, click the Show/Hide ¶ button to toggle it off.

Another helpful tool in Word is the ruler. To display a horizontal ruler along the top of the workspace and a vertical ruler along the left side of the workspace, select the Ruler check box in the Show group on the VIEW tab.

Figures of documents in the Word window in this book show the document window maximized, rulers visible, the zoom level set to 120% (unless specified otherwise), and with nonprinting characters displayed, as shown in Exhibit 10-1.

Begin Activity

Start Word and set up the document window.

1 Start **Word**. Word starts, and the Recent screen appears in Backstage view.

2 Click the **Blank document tile**. A new blank document appears in the Word window.

3 If the Word program window is not maximized, click the **Maximize button** ▢.

Tip: To create a new, blank document when Word is running, click the FILE tab, click New in the navigation bar, and then click Blank document in the right pane.

4 If the rulers are not displayed along the top and left sides of the window, click the **VIEW tab** on the ribbon. In the Show group, click the **Ruler check box** to select it.

5 On the status bar, use the **Zoom slider** and the **Zoom in** ➕ and **Zoom out** ➖ buttons to change the zoom percentage to **120%**.

6 On the ribbon, click the **HOME tab**, if necessary. In the Paragraph group, click the **Show/Hide ¶ button** ¶ if it is not already selected. (When it is selected, it is shaded blue (¶).) Compare your screen to Exhibit 10-1.

End Activity

Now you need to save the document with a name. You will be creating a letter.

Begin Activity

Save a document for the first time.

1 On the Quick Access Toolbar, click the **Save button** 💾. Because this is the first time this document is being saved, the Save As screen opens in Backstage view.

2 With Computer selected, click the **Browse** button. The Save As dialog box opens with the temporary file name selected in the File name box.

Problem? If you are saving your files to your SkyDrive account, click SkyDrive, and then log in to your account if necessary.

3 Type **Letter** to replace the temporary file name in the File name box.

4 Navigate to the drive and folder where you are saving the files you create as you complete the steps in this book.

5 Click **Save**. The dialog box closes, and the file name *Letter* appears in the title bar of the Word window.

End Activity

nonprinting character A character that does not print and that controls the format of a document.

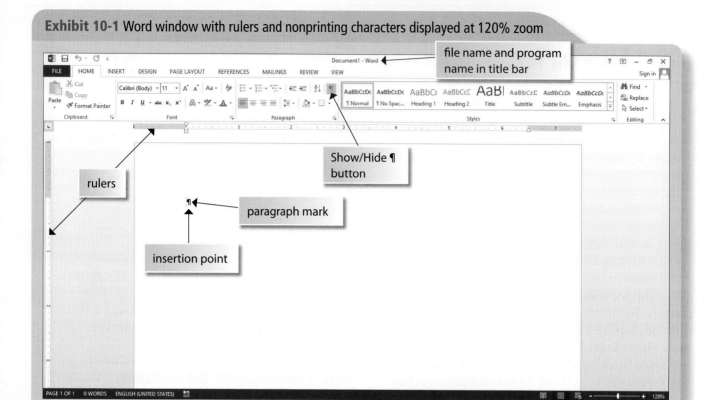

Exhibit 10-1 Word window with rulers and nonprinting characters displayed at 120% zoom

file name and program name in title bar

Show/Hide ¶ button

rulers

paragraph mark

insertion point

10-1a Entering Text

To enter text in a Word document, simply start typing. The characters you type appear at the insertion point. As you type, the text wraps to new lines as needed to accommodate the text. If you make errors as you type, you can press the Backspace key, which deletes the characters and spaces to the left of the insertion point one at a time. You can also press the Delete key, which deletes characters to the right of the insertion point one at a time.

When you press the Enter key, a new paragraph is created. In Word, a "paragraph" can be several lines, one line, a single word, or blank (or empty). For example, the heading for this section, Entering Text, would be a paragraph in a Word document.

Begin Activity

Enter text.

1 Move the **pointer** into the workspace. The pointer changes to I.

2 Type **1117 Parker Ave.** (including the period). The text you typed appears on the screen, and the paragraph mark moves to the right as you type.

3 Press the **Backspace** key four times. The four characters to the left of the insertion point, *Ave.*, are deleted.

4 Type **St.** (including the period).

5 Press the **Left Arrow key** six times. The insertion point moves six characters to the left and is positioned between the *k* and the *e* in *Parker*.

6 Press the **Delete key** twice. The two characters to the right of the insertion point are deleted.

7 Click after **St**. The insertion point appears at the end of the line.

8 Press the **Enter key**. The insertion point moves to a new line, creating a new paragraph.

9 Type **Chicago, IL 60601** and then press the **Enter key**. A third paragraph is created.

End Activity

10-1b Inserting a Date with AutoComplete

When you insert dates, you can take advantage of **AutoComplete**, a feature that automatically inserts dates and other regularly used items. To insert the date with AutoComplete, type the first four characters of all months except May, June, and July. A ScreenTip appears, telling you that you can press the Enter key to insert the month name into the document. See Exhibit 10-2. If you want to type something other than the month name suggested in the ScreenTip, or if you don't want to use the AutoComplete feature, simply continue typing and the ScreenTip will disappear. If you type the current month—and it is not May, June, or July—another ScreenTip appears after you press the Spacebar, instructing you to press the Enter key to insert the current date in the form MMMM dd, yyyy (for example, October 25, 2016). You can press Enter to accept the AutoComplete entry, or you can type any text you want to override the AutoComplete suggestion.

Begin Activity

Insert the date with AutoComplete.

1. Type **Octo** (the first four letters of October). A ScreenTip appears above the letters suggesting *October* as the complete word. Refer to Exhibit 10-2.

2. Press the **Enter key**. The rest of the word *October* is inserted in the document.

3. Press the **Spacebar**. If the current month is October, another ScreenTip appears displaying the current date.

4. Type **25, 2016** and then press the **Enter key**.

End Activity

AutoComplete A feature that automatically inserts dates and other regularly used items.

ON THE JOB

Block Style Business Letters

One of the most common types of documents is a block style business letter. In the block style, each line of text is left-aligned—that is, it starts at the left margin. In other words, the inside address, the date, and the closing are all left-aligned, and the first line of paragraphs is not indented. To show when a new paragraph starts, a blank line is added between each paragraph. The block style is probably the easiest style to use when creating any Word document and has become common in many businesses. The accompanying figure shows the parts of a block style letter.

1117 Park St.
Chicago, IL 60601

→ return address (do not include if letter is printed on letterhead)

October 25, 2016 ← date

Maureen Callahan, Marketing Coordinator
Gillespie Manufacturing
132 South Canal St.
Chicago, IL 60601

← inside address

Dear Ms. Callahan: ← salutation

Larry Cohen told me that you are looking for an assistant. I would like to apply for the position. After working as an intern for Sanford Industries, I have developed strong skills in market research and analysis, and I believe that I would be a valuable asset to your team.

At Sanford Industries I assisted the marketing coordinator in organizing national sales meetings and a convention for our customers. For the convention, I established relationships with vendors and was the primary contact for those vendors at the convention. Based on convention evaluations, attendees scored this convention 20% higher than the previous year's.

In addition to working on the sales meeting and the convention, I were also responsible for the following:

- Verifying radio ad frequency over weekends
- Keeping and distributing the meeting minutes for the team
- Updating existing customer database

I've enclosed a copy of my résumé, which details my coursework and other job experience. I also enclosed the flyer describing Sanford's newest products that I produced for the 2015 Electronics Convention. I look forward to the opportunity to speak with you. You can reach me at the address at the top of this letter, by phone at 312-555-4995, or via email at Thank you for your consideration.

Sincerely, ← complimentary close

← extra space for signature

← signature line

Michael Covais

Enclosures (2) ← indicates the letter has something accompanying it

→ if someone other than the person who signed the letter typed it, the typist's initials go here in all lowercase

Block style business letter

Exhibit 10-2 AutoComplete suggestion for a month name

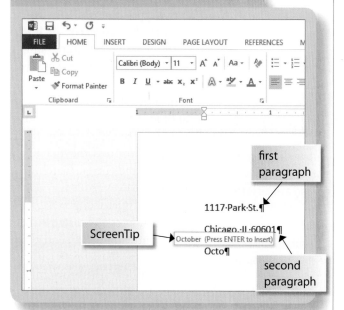

10-1c Correcting Errors as You Type

The **AutoCorrect** feature automatically corrects certain misspelled words and typing errors. For example, if you type *teh* instead of *the*, as soon as you press the Spacebar or the Enter key, AutoCorrect changes it to *the*. AutoCorrect also fixes capitalization errors, including changing the first character in the first word of a sentence to an uppercase letter.

Additionally, printed publications usually include **typographic characters**, which are special characters that are not included on the standard keyboard and that appear in professionally prepared documents. The AutoCorrect feature automatically converts some standard characters into typographic characters as you type. For example, AutoCorrect changes (c) to the standard copyright symbol © as soon as you type the closing parenthesis. Exhibit 10-3 lists some of the other character combinations that AutoCorrect automatically converts to typographic characters.

AutoCorrect A feature that automatically corrects certain misspelled words and typing errors.

typographic character A special character not included on the standard keyboard that appears in professionally prepared documents.

FYI

Inserting the Current Date

You can quickly insert the current date into a document in a variety of formats. Position the insertion point in the location where you want to insert the current date in the document. Click the INSERT tab, and then in the Text group, click the Date & Time button to open the Date and Time dialog box. A variety of date formats are listed in the Available formats box. Click the format you want to use. If you want the current date to appear every time you open the document, select the Update automatically check box. If you want the date to remain unchanged, deselect the Update automatically check box. Click OK to close the dialog box and insert the current date in the format you specified.

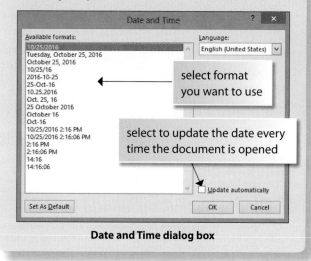

Date and Time dialog box

Exhibit 10-3 Common typographic characters inserted with AutoCorrect

To insert	Type	AutoCorrect converts to
em dash	word--word	word—word
smiley	:) or :-)	☺
copyright symbol	(c)	©
trademark symbol	(tm)	™
registered trademark symbol	(r)	®
ordinal numbers	1st, 2nd, 3rd, etc.	1st, 2nd, 3rd, etc.
fractions	1/2, 1/4	½, ¼
arrows	--> or <--	→ or ←

Use AutoCorrect.

1 Press the **Enter key** to insert a blank paragraph, and then type **DEar**. Make sure you type this word with the two uppercase letters as shown here.

2 Press the **Spacebar**. The incorrect capitalization is automatically corrected.

3 Type **Ms. Callahan:** and then press the **Enter key**.

4 Type **from** and then press the **Spacebar**. The capitalization of the first word in the sentence is corrected.

5 Type **the information on your Web site, i** and then press the **Spacebar**. The capitalization of the word *I* is corrected. In the next step, watch as AutoCorrect corrects the misspelled word *you* when you press the Spacebar.

6 Type **understand that yuo** and then press the **Spacebar**. The misspelled word automatically corrects to *you*.

7 Type **are looking for a Marketing Assistant. I gained experience working at Sanford Industries** (do not type a period).

8 Type **(r)**. As soon as you type the closing parenthesis, the characters *(r)* change to the registered trademark symbol ®, and the symbol is changed to a superscript.

9 Type **.** (a period) to complete the sentence. Compare your screen to Exhibit 10-4.

AutoCorrect also formats Web site addresses that start with *http* and *www* and email addresses as hyperlinks, or links. To indicate that the text is a link, the text is changed to a color and is underlined. When text is formatted as a link, you can click it to open your browser and go to that Web page or open a new email message addressed to the email address you clicked. You rarely want to retain link formatting in printed documents. To remove the link formatting, you right-click the link to display a shortcut menu that includes commands for working with the link. See Exhibit 10-5. Click Remove Hyperlink on the shortcut menu to remove the link formatting.

Exhibit 10-4 AutoCorrected text in document

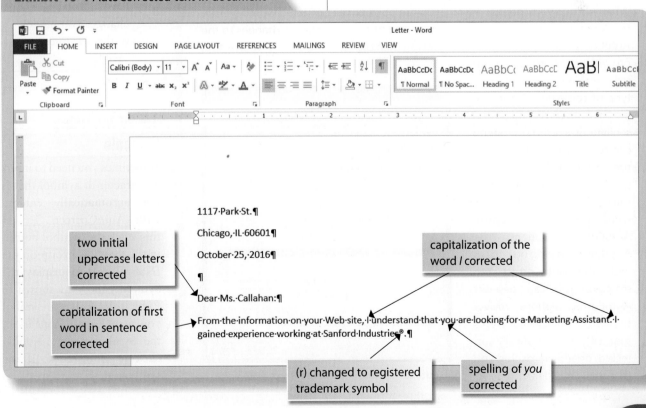

two initial uppercase letters corrected

capitalization of the word *I* corrected

capitalization of first word in sentence corrected

(r) changed to registered trademark symbol

spelling of *you* corrected

1117·Park·St.¶

Chicago,·IL·60601¶

October·25,·2016¶

¶

Dear·Ms.·Callahan:¶

From·the·information·on·your·Web·site,·I·understand·that·you·are·looking·for·a·Marketing·Assistant.··I·gained·experience·working·at·Sanford·Industries®·.¶

Exhibit 10-5 Removing link formatting

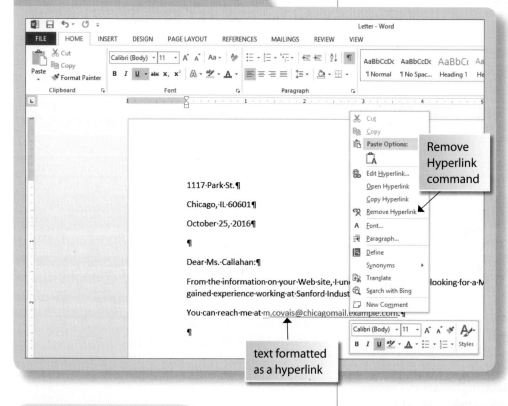

text formatted as a hyperlink

Remove Hyperlink command

Format text as a link and remove the link.

1 Press the **Enter key**, type **You can reach me at m.covais@chicagomail. example.com.** and then press the **Enter key**. AutoCorrect changes the email address you typed to blue and underlined and changes it to a hyperlink.

2 Right-click the **hyperlink**. Refer back to Exhibit 10-5.

3 On the shortcut menu, click **Remove Hyperlink**. The text is changed to ordinary black text and is no longer a hyperlink.

4 On the Quick Access Toolbar, click the **Save button** 🔲. The changes you made to the document are saved.

FYI

Customizing AutoCorrect

When AutoCorrect changes a word, you can point to the corrected word to make the AutoCorrect symbol appear. When you point to the symbol, it changes to the AutoCorrect Options button, which you can then click to undo the AutoCorrection or instruct AutoCorrect to stop making that particular type of correction. For example, if AutoCorrect fixed the spelling of a word, the menu choices would be to change the text back to its original spelling or to stop automatically correcting that specific word. If you click Control AutoCorrect Options, the AutoCorrect dialog box opens with the AutoCorrect tab selected. You can deselect AutoCorrect options, review the list of misspelled words that will be automatically corrected, or add words that you frequently misspell to the list.

AutoCorrect tab in the AutoCorrect dialog box

10-1d Inserting Symbols

Sometimes you need to insert a character or symbol that is not automatically entered with AutoCorrect. To do this, click the Symbol button in the Symbols group on the INSERT tab to display the Symbol gallery, as shown in Exhibit 10-6. If the symbol you want to use appears in the Symbol gallery, simply click it to insert it. If the symbol doesn't appear there, click More Symbols to open the Symbol dialog box, shown in Exhibit 10-7, and then choose the symbol you want in there.

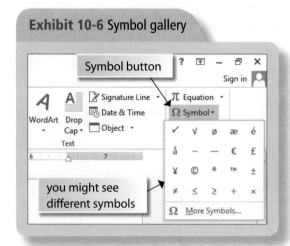

Exhibit 10-6 Symbol gallery

Symbol button

you might see different symbols

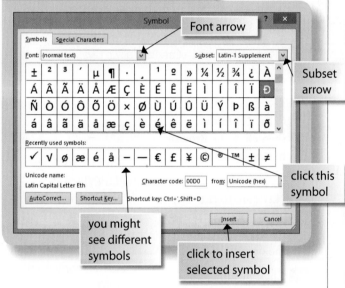

Exhibit 10-7 Symbol dialog box

Font arrow

Subset arrow

click this symbol

you might see different symbols

click to insert selected symbol

Begin Activity

Insert symbols.

1 In the body of the letter, in the first paragraph, click after the period at the end of the second sentence (after ®), and then press the **Spacebar**.

2 Type **I've enclosed a copy of my r**. (Do not type the period.) To finish typing the word *résumé*, you need to use the Symbol dialog box.

3 On the ribbon, click the **INSERT tab**. In the Symbols group, click the **Symbol button**. The Symbol gallery opens. Refer back to Exhibit 10-6.

4 Below the gallery, click **More Symbols**. The Symbol dialog box opens. Refer back to Exhibit 10-7. First you'll examine the types of symbols you can insert.

5 Scroll through the list of symbols to see the types of symbols you can insert.

6 Click the **Font arrow**, scroll to the bottom of the list, and then click **Wingdings**. The symbols change to display the symbols in the Wingdings font.

7 Click the **Special Characters tab**. A list of special characters appears, including the paragraph symbol. Now you'll insert the correct character.

8 Click the **Symbols tab**, click the **Font arrow**, scroll to the top of the Font list, and then click **(normal text)**.

9 Click the **Subset arrow**, and then click **Latin-1 Supplement**. The list scrolls to display the first row in the Latin-1 Supplement subset.

10 Click the **down scroll arrow** three times to scroll the list three rows. Lowercase characters appear in the bottom row. Refer to Exhibit 10-7.

11 In the last row of symbols, click the **é character**, and then click **Insert**. The symbol is inserted in the document.

> **Tip:** If the dialog box is covering the inserted symbol, drag the dialog box by its title bar out of the way.

12 In the dialog box, click **Close**.

13 Type **sum**.

14 On the INSERT tab, in the Symbols group, click the **Symbol button**. The é symbol appears as the first symbol in the gallery now.

15 In the gallery, click the **é symbol**. The gallery closes, and the symbol is inserted in the document.

16 Type a **period**. The last sentence in the first paragraph is now *I've enclosed a copy of my résumé.*

17 Click the blank paragraph at the end of the document, type your name, and then save the document.

18 Click the **FILE tab**, and then click **Close** in the navigation bar to close the document. Word is still open.

End Activity

Moving the Insertion Point

The insertion point indicates where text will be inserted in the document. You can click anywhere in a document to place the insertion point at the location where you clicked. You can also use the keyboard to move the insertion point in the document, which may be faster when your hands are already on the keyboard. Pressing the arrow keys moves the insertion point one character in the direction of the arrow key you pressed. If you combine other keys with the arrow keys, you can move the insertion point quickly to different locations. The table below summarizes the most common keystrokes for moving the insertion point in a document.

Cameramannz/Shutterstock.com; pzAxe/Shutterstock.com

Keystrokes for moving the insertion point

To move insertion point	Press
Left or right one character at a time	Left Arrow key or Right Arrow key
Up or down one line at a time	Up Arrow key or Down Arrow key
Left or right one word at a time	Ctrl+Left Arrow keys or Ctrl+Right Arrow keys
Up or down one paragraph at a time	Ctrl+Up Arrow keys or Ctrl+Down Arrow keys
To the beginning or to the end of the current line	Home key or End key
To the beginning or to the end of the document	Ctrl+Home keys or Ctrl+End keys
To the previous screen or to the next screen	Page Up key or Page Down key
To the top or to the bottom of the document window	Alt+Ctrl+Page Up keys or Alt+Ctrl+Page Down keys

© 2014 Cengage Learning

10-2 Creating Documents Based on Existing Documents

When you create a new document, you can start with a new blank document as you did when you started typing the letter, or you can start with an existing document. For example, if you saved and closed a document, you can re-open that document and continue working on it. If you simply open a document, make changes, and then save the document, the original document is modified. If you want the original document to remain unchanged, you can create a copy of the original document. One way to do this is to open the original document, and then use the Save As command to save it with a new name.

Begin Activity

Open documents and save copies with new names.

1 Click the **FILE tab**. The Open screen in Backstage view appears.

2 Click **Computer**, and then click the **Browse button** to display the Open dialog box.

3 Navigate to the **Chapter 10\Chapter folder** included with the data files.

4 Click **Resume**, and then click **Open**. The Resume document opens in the Word window.

5 Click the **FILE tab**, and then click **Save As** in the navigation pane. The Save As screen appears in Backstage view with Computer selected.

6 Click the **Browse button** to open the Save As dialog box. The current folder is the Chapter 10\Chapter folder, and the file name Resume is selected in the File name box.

7 Type **Resume Final** in the File name box.

Tip: If the document you want to use appears in the Recent Documents list on the Open screen, you can right-click it, and then click Open a copy on the shortcut menu.

8 If necessary, navigate to the drive and folder where you are saving the files you create as you work through these steps.

> **Tip:** Remember to save periodically as you work through the steps in this chapter.

9 Click **Save**. The dialog box closes, and a copy of the Resume document is saved with the name Resume Final.

10 Open the document **Letter2** located in the **Chapter 10\Chapter folder** included with the data files.

11 Save Letter2 as **Cover Letter** in the drive and folder where you are saving the files you create as you work through these steps.

End Activity

10-3 Editing Text

One of the fundamental features of a word processor is the ability to easily edit text without retyping an entire document. When you edit a document, you can type additional text in the document, delete existing text from the document, replace text already in the document, and copy or move text within the document.

10-3a Replacing Selected Text

To replace existing text, you select the text you no longer want and then start typing. The text you type replaces the selected text, no matter how much text is selected. There is no need to press the Delete key to remove the selected text first.

Begin Activity

Replace selected text.

1 In the Cover Letter document, in the body of the letter, in the first sentence in the first paragraph, click before the word *From*, but do not release the mouse button.

2 Drag across the text **From the information on your Web site, I understand** and then release the mouse button. The text you dragged across is selected.

3 Type **L**. The selected text is replaced with the character you typed.

4 Type **arry Cohen told me**. The first sentence now reads *Larry Cohen told me that you are looking for an assistant.*

End Activity

10-3b Using Drag and Drop

You learned how to use the Cut, Copy, and Paste commands in Chapter 9. Another technique for moving and copying text is drag and drop. **Drag and drop** means to select text and then drag the selected text to a new location. As you drag, a vertical line follows the pointer, indicating where the selected text will be placed when you release the mouse button. See Exhibit 10-8. Unlike the Cut

Exhibit 10-8 Text being moved using drag and drop

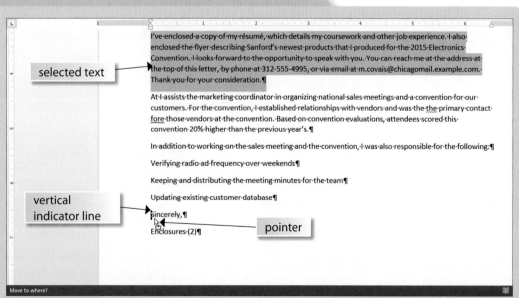

selected text

vertical indicator line

pointer

I've enclosed a copy of my résumé, which details my coursework and other job experience. I also enclosed the flyer describing Sanford's newest products that I produced for the 2015 Electronics Convention. I look forward to the opportunity to speak with you. You can reach me at the address at the top of this letter, by phone at 312-555-4995, or via email at m.covais@chicagomail.example.com. Thank you for your consideration.¶

At I assists the marketing coordinator in organizing national sales meetings and a convention for our customers. For the convention, I established relationships with vendors and was the the primary contact fore those vendors at the convention. Based on convention evaluations, attendees scored this convention 20% higher than the previous year's.¶

In addition to working on the sales meeting and the convention, I was also responsible for the following:¶

Verifying radio ad frequency over weekends¶

Keeping and distributing the meeting minutes for the team¶

Updating existing customer database¶

Sincerely,¶
Enclosures (2)¶

Move to where?

> **drag and drop** A technique for moving or copying selected text or objects to a new location.

or Copy commands, when you use drag and drop, the text you drag is not placed on the Clipboard. If you want to paste the text you dragged to another location, you need to drag it again or use the Cut or Copy command.

Begin Activity

Use drag and drop to move and copy text.

1 Scroll the document until you can see both the second paragraph in the body of the letter and the closing *Sincerely* at the end of the letter.

2 In the body of the letter, move the pointer to the left of the first line of the second paragraph so that the pointer changes to ⌐.

3 Press and hold the mouse button. The first line in the second paragraph is selected.

4 Still pressing the mouse button, drag down until all five lines in the second paragraph are selected, and then release the mouse button.

5 Point to the selected text so that the pointer changes to ▹.

6 Press and hold the mouse button. After a moment, the pointer changes to ▹ and a black vertical line appears within the selected text.

> **Problem?** If you cannot see the pointer or the dotted vertical line, move the pointer slightly to the left or right.

7 Drag down to the closing until the vertical line is positioned before the word *Sincerely*. Refer back to Exhibit 10-8. This shows that the selected text will be positioned before the word *Sincerely*.

8 Release the mouse button. The selected paragraph is now the last paragraph in the body of the letter.

9 In the body of the letter, in the second sentence in the first paragraph, select **Sanford Industries**.

10 Point to the selected text, press and hold the **Ctrl key**, and then press and hold the mouse button. After a moment, the pointer changes to ▹ to

indicate that the text you are dragging is being copied instead of moved.

11 Drag the selected text down to the beginning of the second paragraph in the body of the letter until the vertical indicator line appears between the words *At* and *I*. Release the mouse button, and then release the **Ctrl key**. The text you copied, *Sanford Industries*, appears after the word *At* so that the beginning of the second paragraph is now *At Sanford Industries, I assists*.

> **Problem?** If the selected text moves to the new location instead of being copied there, you released the Ctrl key before the mouse button. Undo your last action, and then repeat Step 11.

End Activity

LEARN MORE

Using Templates

A **template** is a file that contains instructions for changing the appearance of text and graphics, and often sample content, to guide you as you develop your own content. When you open a Word template, you open a copy of the template as an unnamed document, not the template file itself. Word comes with templates that you can access on the New screen in Backstage view. These templates are available from *Office.com*. If you don't see the template you want to use on the New screen, click a template category below the Search box at the top of the screen to display the templates in that category. Or, you can type key words in the Search box to search for templates that have those key words associated with them. After you find the template you want to use, click it, and then in the window that appears, click the Download button.

You can also create custom templates, such as company letterhead or memos, by saving a document as a template. To do this, in the Save As dialog box, click the Save as type arrow, and then click Word Template.

template A file that contains formatting and sometimes sample content.

10-4 Switching to Another Open Document in Word

When more than one document is open in a program window, there are several ways you can switch to the other open document. One way to switch to another open file in a program is to point to the program button on the taskbar to display thumbnails of the open files in that program, and then click the thumbnail. You did this in Chapter 7 when you selected one of two open File Explorer windows. In Word, Excel, and PowerPoint, you can also use the Switch Windows button on the VIEW tab. See Exhibit 10-9.

Exhibit 10-9 Switch Windows button menu

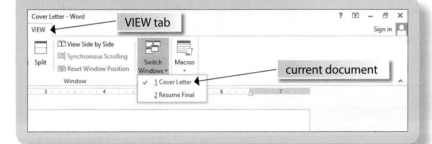

Begin Activity

Switch to another open Word document.

1 On the ribbon, click the **VIEW tab**. In the Window group, click the **Switch Windows button**. The two open documents are listed on the menu that appears. There is a check mark next to Cover Letter because that is the current document. Refer back to Exhibit 10-9.

2 Click **Resume Final**. The menu closes, and the Resume Final document is now the active document.

End Activity

10-5 Formatting Text

Once you have entered the text of a document, you can change how it looks—that is, you can **format** the document. The purpose of formatting is to make the document attractive, emphasize certain points in the document, and make the organization and flow of the document clear to readers. You can format the document by changing the style of the text, adding color to text or as shading behind text, adding borders, and adding and removing space between lines and paragraphs.

To format text, you can either select text that is already entered and then change the format, or you can change the format and then type, and all the text from that point on will retain the new formatting.

10-5a Changing the Font and Font Size

An easy way to change the look of a document is to change the font. A **font** is the design of a set of characters. For example, the font used for the text you are reading right now is Sabon font, and the font used for the heading Changing the Font and Font Size is Eurostile font.

To change the font, select the text you want to change (or position the insertion point at the location where you will type new text), click the Font box arrow in the Font group on the HOME tab, and then select a font. See Exhibit 10-10. The first font listed is the font Word suggests using for headings in the document. The second font listed is the font used for ordinary text in a document, or body text. The list of All Fonts is a complete alphabetical list of all available fonts. Each font name in the list is shown in the font that it names. For example, Arial appears in the Arial font, and Times New Roman appears in the Times New Roman font.

Fonts are measured in **points**, which are units of measurement. One point equals 1/72 of an inch. Text in a book is typically printed in 10- or 12-point type. The font size of this text is 10 points, and the font size of the Changing the Font and Font Size heading is 14 points. To change the font size, click the Font Size box arrow in the Font group on the HOME tab, and then select a size or click in the Font Size box and type the size you want to use.

---

format To change the appearance of a file's content.

font The design of a set of characters.

point The unit of measurement used for type; equal to 1/72 of an inch.

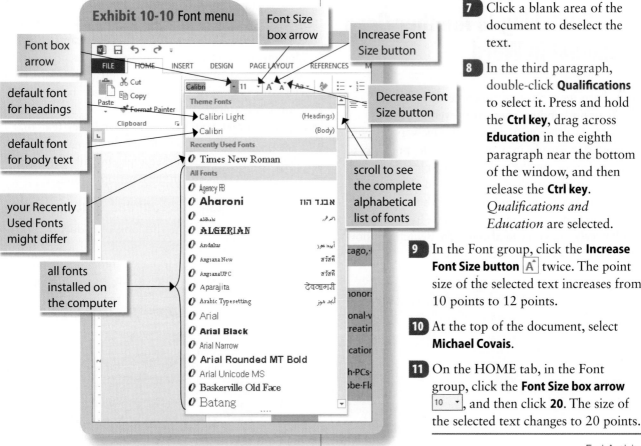

Exhibit 10-10 Font menu

- Font box arrow
- default font for headings
- default font for body text
- your Recently Used Fonts might differ
- all fonts installed on the computer
- Font Size box arrow
- Increase Font Size button
- Decrease Font Size button
- scroll to see the complete alphabetical list of fonts

Theme Fonts
Calibri Light (Headings)
Calibri (Body)
Recently Used Fonts
O Times New Roman
All Fonts
O Agency FB
O **Aharoni** אבגד הוז
O Aldhabi
O **ALGERIAN**
O Andalus أبجد هوز
O AngsanaNew สวัสดี
O AngsanaUPC สวัสดี
O Aparajita देवनागरी
O Arabic Typesetting أبجد هوز
O Arial
O **Arial Black**
O Arial Narrow
O **Arial Rounded MT Bold**
O Arial Unicode MS
O Baskerville Old Face
O Batang

7 Click a blank area of the document to deselect the text.

8 In the third paragraph, double-click **Qualifications** to select it. Press and hold the **Ctrl key**, drag across **Education** in the eighth paragraph near the bottom of the window, and then release the **Ctrl key**. *Qualifications and Education* are selected.

9 In the Font group, click the **Increase Font Size button** $\boxed{A}$ twice. The point size of the selected text increases from 10 points to 12 points.

10 At the top of the document, select **Michael Covais**.

11 On the HOME tab, in the Font group, click the **Font Size box arrow** $\boxed{10}$, and then click **20**. The size of the selected text changes to 20 points.

End Activity

Begin Activity

Change the font and font size.

1 Press the **Ctrl+A keys**. All the text in the document is selected.

2 On the HOME tab, in the Font group, click the **Font box arrow** $\boxed{\text{Calibri (Body)}}$. A list of available fonts appears. Calibri (Body) is shaded blue, indicating that this font is currently applied to the selected text.

3 Point to several fonts, watching the Live Preview of the selected text in the document.

4 Scroll down the list, and then click **Verdana**. The Font gallery closes, and the selected text is formatted in Verdana.

5 With all the text in the document still selected, on the HOME tab, in the Font group, look at the Font Size box $\boxed{11}$ to see that the font size of the selected text is 11 points.

6 On the HOME tab, in the Font group, click the **Decrease Font Size button** $\boxed{A}$. The font size of the selected text changes from 11 points to 10 points.

10-5b Changing Font Styles

To make text stand out, you can change the style of a font, such as by applying bold and italics. To change the style, use the formatting commands in the Font group on the HOME tab. Exhibit 10-11 shows text formatted with bold and italics.

Begin Activity

Change the font style.

1 With *Michael Covais* still selected, press and hold the **Ctrl key**, use the mouse to select **Qualifications** and **Education**, and then release the **Ctrl key**. The three nonsequential paragraphs are selected.

2 On the HOME tab, in the Font group, click the **Bold button** $\boxed{B}$. The button toggles on and changes to $\boxed{B}$, and the selected text is formatted in bold.

3 Scroll down so that you can see the first two paragraphs under Education. In the second line below that heading, select **cum laude**.

4 In the Font group, click the **Italic button** I. The button toggles on, and the selected text is italicized.

5 Scroll down a few more lines, and then select the line that starts with **Internship Sanford Industries**. Format this line so it is **bold**. Refer back to Exhibit 10-11.

End Activity

Exhibit 10-11 Nonadjacent text formatted as bold

Italic button

Bold button

text formatted in bold

Michael·Covais¶

1117·Park·St.·|·Chicago,·IL·60601·|·312-555-4995·|·m.covais@chicagomail.example.com¶

Qualifications¶

Highly·motivated,·honors·graduate·of·Chicago·Booth·School·of·Business·at·the·University·of·Chicago¶

Marketing·professional·with·an·eye·for·detail,·ability·to·build·and·maintain·relationships·with·customers,·and·capability·for·creating·marketing·campaigns¶

Excellent·communication·and·organizational·skills,·and·proficient·in·Spanish¶

Proficient·with·both·PCs·and·Macintosh·computers·and·advanced·user·of·Microsoft·Office,·Adobe·Dreamweaver,·Adobe·Flash¶

Education¶

University·of·Chicago·—·Chicago,·IL¶

BA·*cum·laude*,·Business,·June,·2016¶

Concentration:·Marketing,·Minor:·Spanish¶

Experience¶

text formatted in italics

text formatted in bold

Internship·Sanford·Industries,·September·2015-June·2016¶

PAGE 1 OF 2   6 OF 239 WORDS   ENGLISH (UNITED STATES)

FYI

Formatting Professional Documents

In professional documents, use color and special fonts sparingly. The goal of letters, reports, and other documents is to convey important information, not to dazzle the reader with fancy fonts and colors. Overuse of such elements only serves to distract the reader from the main point.

10-5c Changing Text Color

Another way to emphasize text is to use color. Judicious use of color makes headings or other important text stand out. To apply color to text, click the Font Color button arrow in the Font group on the HOME tab to open the document's color palette. See Exhibit 10-12. The color palette contains a top row of colors labeled Theme Colors. The next five rows under the theme colors are lighter and darker variations of the theme colors. The specific theme colors available might change from one document to another. The row of colors under the Standard Colors label does not change from one document to the next—this row of colors is always available.

Exhibit 10-12 Color palette in the Font Color button gallery

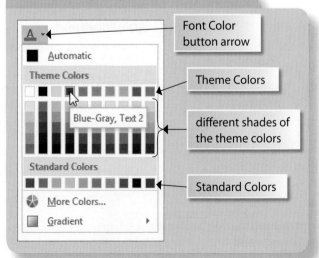

Font Color button arrow

Automatic

Theme Colors

Theme Colors

Blue-Gray, Text 2

different shades of the theme colors

Standard Colors

Standard Colors

More Colors...

Gradient

Change the color of text.

1 Select the **Qualifications** and the **Education headings**.

2 On the HOME tab, in the Font group, click the **Font Color button arrow** [A]. The color palette appears.

3 In the Theme Colors section, in the first row, point to the **orange color**. The ScreenTip that appears identifies this as Orange, Accent 2.

> **Tip:** To restore selected text to the default font, size, and color, click the Clear All Formatting button [🧹] in the Font group on the HOME tab.

4 In the Theme Colors section, in the first row, click the **Blue–Gray, Text 2 color**, using the ScreenTip to identify the color name. The selected headings are now blue.

5 Click a blank area of the document to deselect the headings. Compare your screen to Exhibit 10-13.

End Activity

Exhibit 10-13 Headings formatted with a color

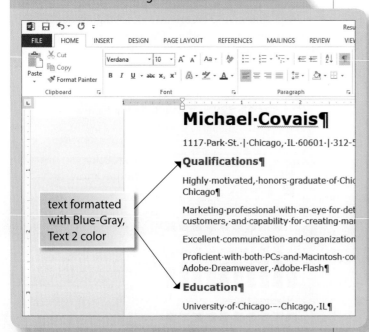

text formatted with Blue-Gray, Text 2 color

paragraph spacing The space above and below a paragraph.

10-6 Formatting Paragraphs

In addition to formatting text, you can also apply formatting to entire paragraphs. For example, you can change the amount of space before or after a paragraph or between the lines within a paragraph, change the alignment of a paragraph from left-aligned to centered, or indent a paragraph.

10-6a Adjusting Paragraph Spacing

Paragraph spacing refers to the space that appears directly above and below a paragraph. Remember, in Word, any text that ends with ¶ (a paragraph mark symbol) is a paragraph. So, a paragraph can be a group of words that is many lines long, a single word, or even a blank line, in which case the only character on the line is a paragraph mark symbol. Paragraph spacing is measured in points. The default setting for paragraph spacing in Word documents is 0 points before each paragraph and 8 points after each paragraph.

To adjust paragraph spacing in Word, you use the Before and After boxes in the Spacing section in the Paragraph group on the PAGE LAYOUT tab. See Exhibit 10-14. You can also use the Add Space Before Paragraph or Remove Space After Paragraph commands on the Line and Paragraph Spacing button menu in the Paragraph group on the HOME tab. See Exhibit 10-15.

Adjust paragraph spacing.

1 Under the Education heading, select the two lines that start with **University of Chicago** and **BA *cum laude***.

2 On the ribbon, click the **PAGE LAYOUT tab**. In the Paragraph group, in the Spacing section, 8 pt appears in the After box, indicating that there is 8 points of space after each of the selected paragraphs. Refer to Exhibit 10-14.

3 In the Paragraph group, in the Spacing section, click the **After box down arrow** twice. The value in the After box changes to 0 pt, and the extra space is removed after the selected paragraphs.

4 Select the **Qualifications** and the **Education headings**.

Exhibit 10-14 Paragraph spacing settings

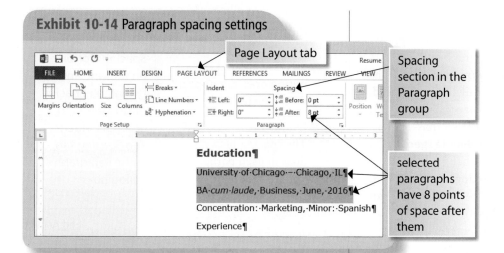

Page Layout tab

Spacing section in the Paragraph group

Education¶

University·of·Chicago·—·Chicago,·IL¶
BA·*cum·laude*,·Business,·June,·2016¶
Concentration:·Marketing,·Minor:·Spanish¶
Experience¶

selected paragraphs have 8 points of space after them

Exhibit 10-15 Line and Paragraph Spacing button menu

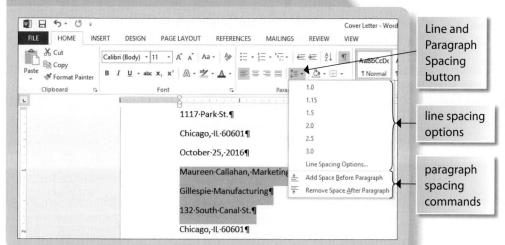

Line and Paragraph Spacing button

line spacing options

1.0
1.15
1.5
2.0
2.5
3.0
Line Spacing Options...
Add Space Before Paragraph
Remove Space After Paragraph

paragraph spacing commands

1117·Park·St.¶

Chicago,·IL·60601¶

October·25,·2016¶

Maureen·Callahan,·Marketing
Gillespie·Manufacturing¶
132·South·Canal·St.¶

Chicago,·IL·60601¶

Tip: When entering text, you can press the Shift+Enter keys to move the insertion point to a new line without starting a new paragraph and therefore create new lines without the paragraph spacing.

9 At the bottom of the menu, click **Remove Space After Paragraph**. The menu closes, and the 8 points of space are removed after each of the selected paragraphs.

10 Click anywhere in the first paragraph (the first line in the return address), and then remove the space after it.

End Activity

5 In the Paragraph group, in the Spacing section, click the **Before box up arrow** twice. The space above the selected paragraph increases to 12 points.

6 Switch to the **Cover Letter document**.

7 Select the first three lines in the inside address (from **Maureen Callahan** through **132 South Canal St.**).

8 On the ribbon, click the **HOME tab**. In the Paragraph group, click the **Line and Paragraph Spacing button** ⬚. A menu of line spacing options appears, with two paragraph spacing commands at the bottom. Refer back to Exhibit 10-15.

FYI

Understanding Spacing Between Paragraphs

When discussing the correct format for letters, many business style guides talk about single spacing and double spacing between paragraphs. In these style guides, "to single space between paragraphs" means creating paragraphs with no extra space between them. Likewise, "to double space between paragraphs" means creating paragraphs with a blank line between them. In many word processors, after you type a paragraph, you press the Enter key once for single spacing and twice for double spacing. With the default paragraph spacing in Word 2013, however, you need to press the Enter key only once to insert a double space after a paragraph. Keep this in mind if you are accustomed to pressing the Enter key twice; otherwise, you will end up with more space than you want between paragraphs.

10-6b Adjusting Line Spacing

Line spacing is the amount of space that appears between lines of text within a paragraph. Word offers a number of preset line spacing options. Paragraphs formatted with the 1.0 setting are called **single spaced**. Single spacing allows the least amount of space between lines—essentially no extra space. Paragraphs formatted with the 2.0 setting are called **double spaced** and have a blank line of space between each line of text in the paragraph. The default line spacing setting is 1.08, which allows a little more space between lines than 1.0 spacing. The 1.08 line spacing setting is designed to make it easier to read text on a computer screen.

Begin Activity

Adjust line spacing.

1 On the HOME tab on the ribbon, in the Editing group, click the **Select button**, and then click **Select All**. All the text in the document is selected.

2 On the HOME tab, in the Paragraph group, click the **Line and Paragraph Spacing button** ‡≡ ▾. Refer back to Exhibit 10-15. None of the line spacing commands have a check mark next

to them. This is because the default line spacing setting for the selected text is 1.08, and this option does not appear on the menu.

3 On the menu, click **1.0**. The spacing between lines in each paragraph is changed to single spacing.

Tip: To see the exact spacing, click Line Spacing Options on the Line and Paragraph Spacing button menu to open the Indents and Spacing tab in the Paragraph dialog box.

End Activity

10-6c Aligning Paragraphs

Normal paragraphs are **left-aligned**—they are flush with the left margin and **ragged**, or uneven, along the right margin. **Right-aligned** paragraphs are aligned along the right margin and ragged along the left margin. Paragraphs that are **centered** are positioned midway between the left and right margins and ragged along both margins. **Justified** paragraphs are flush with both the left and right margins. Text in newspaper columns is often justified. See Exhibit 10-16.

Exhibit 10-16 Paragraph alignments

left alignment
When you go to an interview, don't forget about your appearance. First impressions count, and you want to be able to spend the bulk of the interview discussing your abilities and accomplishments, not trying to overcome a negative first impression.

right alignment
When you go to an interview, don't forget about your appearance. First impressions count, and you want to be able to spend the bulk of the interview discussing your abilities and accomplishments, not trying to overcome a negative first impression.

center alignment
When you go to an interview, don't forget about your appearance. First impressions count, and you want to be able to spend the bulk of the interview discussing your abilities and accomplishments, not trying to overcome a negative first impression.

justified alignment
When you go to an interview, don't forget about your appearance. First impressions count, and you want to be able to spend the bulk of the interview discussing your abilities and accomplishments, not trying to overcome a negative first impression.

line spacing The amount of space between lines of text within a paragraph.

single spaced Line spacing that has no extra space between lines of text in a paragraph.

double spaced Line spacing that has a blank line of text between each line of text in a paragraph.

left-align To align paragraph text along the left margin with ragged edges along the right margin.

ragged Uneven, such as text with an uneven appearance along a margin.

right-align To align paragraph text along the right margin with ragged edges along the left margin.

center To center paragraph text between the left and right margins with ragged edges along both margins.

justify To align paragraph text along both the left and right margins.

Exhibit 10-17 Paragraphs with different alignments

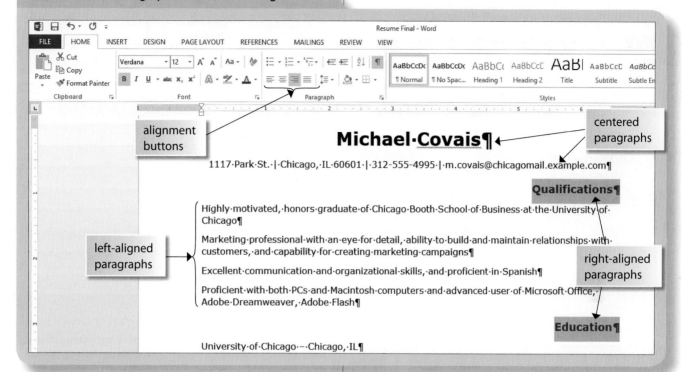

The Paragraph group on the HOME tab includes a button for each of the four types of alignment described in Exhibit 10-16. To align a single paragraph, click anywhere in that paragraph, and then click the appropriate alignment button. To align multiple paragraphs, select the paragraphs, and then click an alignment button.

Begin Activity

Change the alignment of paragraphs.

1. Switch to the **Resume Final document**.

2. At the top of the document, select the first two lines of text (Michael's name and address).

3. On the ribbon, on the HOME tab, locate the Align Left button ☰ in the Paragraph group. It is shaded blue to indicate that it is selected.

4. On the HOME tab, in the Paragraph group, click the **Center button** ☰. The selected paragraphs are centered horizontally on the page.

5. Select the **Qualifications** and the **Education** headings.

6. In the Paragraph group, click the **Align Right button** ☰. The Align Right button toggles on, and the selected paragraphs are right-aligned. Compare your screen to Exhibit 10-17.

7. In the Paragraph group, click the **Align Left button** ☰. The selected headings are left-aligned again.

End Activity

10-6d Using Tabs

A **tab stop** is a location on the horizontal ruler where the insertion point moves when you press the Tab key. Tab stops are useful for aligning small amounts of data in columns and for positioning some of the text on a line so it is centered or right-aligned while leaving the beginning of the line left-aligned. If the Show/Hide ¶ button ¶ is selected, you can see the nonprinting tab character (→) that is inserted when you press the Tab key. A tab is just like any other character you type; you can delete it by pressing the Backspace key or the Delete key.

The default tab stops appear every one-half inch on the horizontal ruler. You can override the default tab stops by setting custom tab stops. The four types of tab stops are Left, Center, Right, and Decimal. (The default tab stops are all Left Tab stops.) Exhibit 10-18

tab stop A location on the horizontal ruler where the insertion point moves when you press the Tab key.

Exhibit 10-18 Tab stop alignment styles

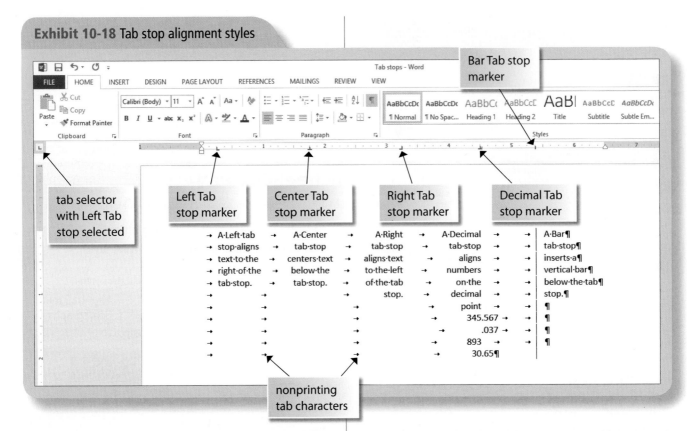

Bar Tab stop marker

tab selector with Left Tab stop selected

Left Tab stop marker

Center Tab stop marker

Right Tab stop marker

Decimal Tab stop marker

nonprinting tab characters

shows the different tab stop styles in a document. Exhibit 10-18 also includes the Bar Tab stop. This is not actually a tab stop—it simply inserts a vertical line (bar) in the document at the location of the stop placed on the ruler.

To set a tab stop, first select a tab stop style using the tab selector, located to the left of the horizontal ruler, and then click on the horizontal ruler where you want to insert the tab stop. The default tab stop style is the Left Tab. When you click the tab selector, you cycle through the four types of tab stops, and then through two markers that can be used to set indents. To return to the Left Tab style, continue clicking the tab selector until it returns to the Left Tab style.

leader line A line that appears between two elements, such as between tabbed text.

When you insert a tab stop (except the Bar Tab stop), all of the default tab stops to its left are removed. This means you press the Tab key only once to move the insertion point to the newly created tab stop, no matter where it is on the ruler. The Left Tab style is selected by default and is probably the tab style you will use most often.

LEARN MORE

Tabs Dialog Box

The Tabs dialog box lets you add a leader line and set tabs at precise positions. A **leader line** is a line or row of dots or dashes that appears in the space between tabbed text. To open the Tabs dialog box, double-click a tab stop on the ruler. To create a tab stop at a precise position, click in the Tab stop position box, and then type the location on the ruler where you want to insert the tab—for example, 4.15. To change the alignment, click an option button in the Alignment section. To set a leader line, click an option button in the Leader section. To change a tab stop, select it in the list, and then modify it as needed. Make sure you click Set to set the tab stop or the changes; clicking OK only closes the dialog box.

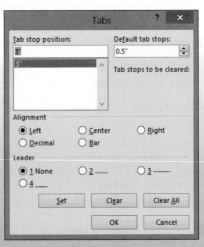

Tabs dialog box

Use tabs.

1 Scroll down so that the paragraph containing *Experience* is at the top of the document window. In the line beginning with *Internship* (below the Experience paragraph), click immediately before the word *Sanford*.

2 Press the **Backspace key** to delete the space, and then press the **Tab key**. A tab symbol (→) appears, and the text after the tab symbol moves so it is aligned at the next default tab stop, which is at the 1-inch mark.

3 With the insertion point in the line that begins with *Internship*, on the horizontal ruler, click the **2-inch mark**. Word inserts a Left Tab stop at that location and removes the default tab stops to its left.

> **Tip:** One way to align columns of text is to separate the text in each row with tabs, and then add the appropriate tab stops.

The text after the tab character shifts to the right and is left-aligned at the 2-inch mark.

4 Press the **Tab key** again. The text shifts right to the next tab stop, which is the default tab stop at 2.5 inches.

5 To the left of the horizontal ruler, click the **tab selector** ⌊. It changes to show the Center Tab style ⊥.

6 Click the **tab selector** ⊥ again. It changes to show the Right Tab style ⌟.

7 On the horizontal ruler, click the **6-inch mark**. A Right Tab stop is added to the ruler at the 6-inch mark, and the text after the second tab symbol shifts left so it is right-aligned at the 6-inch mark.

8 On the ruler, point to the **Right Tab stop**, and then press and hold the mouse button. A dotted vertical line appears. See Exhibit 10-19.

9 Drag the **Right Tab stop** to the right until it is on top of the small triangle marker △ at the 6.5-inch mark on the ruler, and then release the mouse button. The Right Tab stop is repositioned.

10 At the 2-inch mark on the horizontal ruler, drag the **Left Tab stop** down off of the ruler. The Left Tab stop is removed from the ruler. The text after the second tab in the current paragraph moves to the next line. This is because there are two tab characters in the line. The first tab in the line moves the text after it to the tab stop at the right margin, and the second tab in the line moves the text after it to the next tab stop. Because the first tab stop is at the right margin, the text after that tab stop is moved to the next line.

11 Click to the left of *Sanford*, and then press the **Backspace key**. The second tab character is deleted, and the text after the only tab symbol in the line right-aligns properly at the Right Tab stop you inserted.

Exhibit 10-19 Text right-aligned at new Right Tab stop

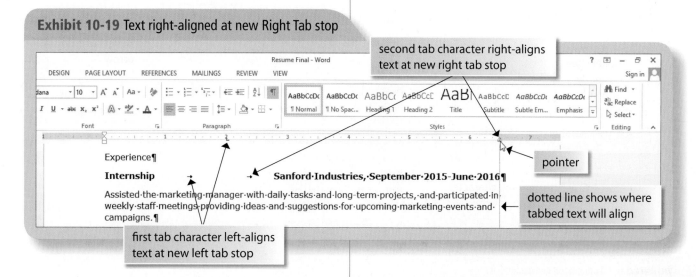

second tab character right-aligns text at new right tab stop

pointer

dotted line shows where tabbed text will align

first tab character left-aligns text at new left tab stop

10-6e Creating a Bulleted List

A **bulleted list** is a group of related paragraphs with a symbol, such as a dot, dash, or other character, that appears to the left of each paragraph. When you create a bulleted list, the bullet symbol is placed at the beginning of the paragraph and a tab character is inserted between the bullet symbol and the text in the paragraph. You can click the Bullets button to create a bulleted list using the default or last-used bullet symbol, or you can click the Bullets button arrow to select a different symbol from the gallery. See Exhibit 10-20.

Begin Activity

Create bulleted lists.

1 Below the Qualifications heading, select the next four paragraphs beginning with **Highly motivated . . .** through **Proficient with both . . .**.

2 On the HOME tab, in the Paragraph group, click the **Bullets button** . The Bullets button toggles on, black circles appear as bullets before each selected paragraph, and the bulleted list is indented.

3 In the Paragraph group, click the **Bullets button arrow** . A gallery of bullet styles opens. Refer back to Exhibit 10-20.

4 In the Bullet Library section of the gallery, point to the bullet styles to see a Live Preview of the bullet styles in the document.

5 In the Bullet Library section, click the **four diamonds shape**. The round bullets are replaced with the four diamonds symbol.

6 Scroll down until you can see the line starting with *Internship*, and then select the four paragraphs beginning with **Developed relationships with . . .** through **Maintained and updated existing customer database**.

7 In the Paragraph group, click the **Bullets button** . The selected paragraph is formatted as a bulleted list with the four diamonds symbol as the bullet character, which is the last symbol you used in the document.

8 Scroll so that the first bulleted item under Qualifications is at the top of the window. Compare your screen to Exhibit 10-21.

Tip: To find additional bullet symbols, click the Bullets button arrow, click Define New Bullet to open the Define New Bullet dialog box, and then click Symbol or Picture.

End Activity

Exhibit 10-20 Bullets gallery

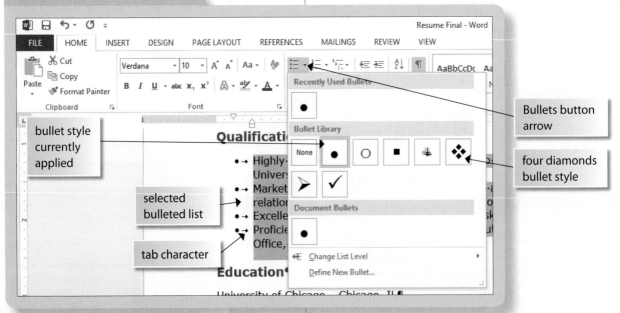

bulleted list A group of related paragraphs with a symbol to the left of each paragraph.

Exhibit 10-21 Résumé after formatting text as bulleted lists

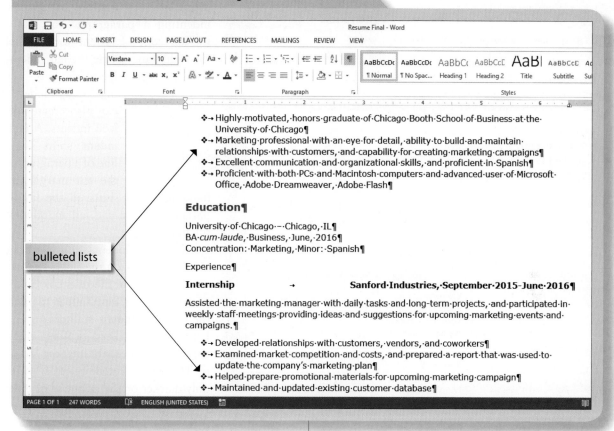

10-6f Creating a Numbered List

For a group of related paragraphs that have a particular order (such as steps in a procedure), you can use numbers instead of bullets to create a **numbered list**. If you insert a new paragraph, delete a paragraph, or reorder the paragraphs in a numbered list, Word adjusts the numbers to make sure they remain consecutive. As with the Bullets button, you can click the Numbering button to apply the default or last-used number style, or you can click the Numbering button arrow to open a gallery of number styles, as shown in Exhibit 10-22.

Begin Activity

Create a numbered list.

1. Switch to the **Cover Letter document**. Scroll so that the salutation *Dear Ms. Callahan:* appears at the top of the document window.

2. In the body of the letter, below the third paragraph, select the three paragraphs starting with **Verifying radio ad frequency . . .** through **Updating existing customer database**.

3. On the HOME tab, in the Paragraph group, click the **Numbering button**. The selected paragraphs are changed to a numbered list.

4. On the HOME tab, in the Paragraph group, click the **Numbering button arrow**. A gallery of numbering formats appears. Refer to Exhibit 10-22.

5. In the gallery, click the numbering style that shows **Arabic numerals followed by a right parenthesis**. The gallery closes, and the style of numbers in the selected paragraphs is changed.

6. In the Paragraph group, click the **Bullets button**. The selected numbered list is changed to a bulleted list with the default bullet symbol.

End Activity

numbered list A group of related paragraphs that have a particular order with sequential numbers to the left of each paragraph.

Exhibit 10-22 Numbering gallery

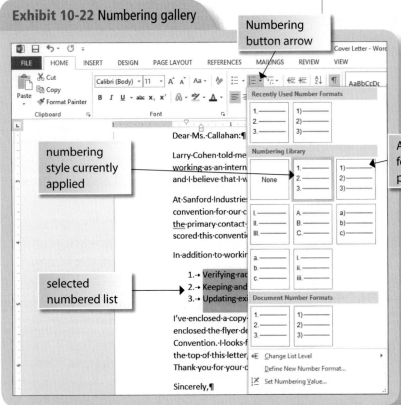

Numbering button arrow

numbering style currently applied

Arabic numerals followed by right parenthesis style

selected numbered list

FYI

Creating Bulleted or Numbered Lists as You Type

To create a bulleted list as you type, click the Bullets button in the Paragraph group on the HOME tab, type the first item in the list, and then press the Enter key. The next paragraph is formatted with the bullet symbol and the Tab character.

To create a numbered list as you type, click the Numbering button in the Paragraph group on the HOME tab, and then start typing. You can use the Auto-Correct feature to create a numbered list. To do this, type the number 1 followed by a period, and then press the Tab key. AutoCorrect formats the paragraph as the first item in a numbered list, and the Numbering button in the Paragraph group on the HOME tab is selected. After you type the first item and then press the Enter key, the number 2 automatically appears in the next paragraph, and the insertion point appears after a Tab character, ready for you to type the second item.

To end both a bulleted and numbered list as you type, press the Enter key twice after you type the last item in the list. This creates a new blank paragraph at the left margin without a bullet or number.

---

first-line indent A paragraph in which the first line is indented from the left margin.

hanging indent A paragraph in which all the lines are indented from the left margin except the first line.

10-6g Indenting a Paragraph

Word offers a number of options for indenting a paragraph. You can shift the left edge of an entire paragraph to the right—increasing the left indent—or shift the right edge to the left—increasing the right indent. You can also create specialized indents. A **first-line indent** shifts the first line of a paragraph from the left margin, and a **hanging indent** shifts all the lines of a paragraph from the left margin except the first line.

To create indents, you can drag the indent markers on the ruler. The marker on the left end of the ruler contains three parts: the First Line Indent marker ▽, the Hanging Indent marker △, and the Left Indent marker ☐. When the three parts are aligned, the marker looks like ⧗. The Right Indent marker △ is the only marker on the right end of the ruler. ScreenTips appear as you point to each marker so that you can drag the correct marker.

To quickly indent an entire paragraph one-half inch, you can also use the Increase Indent button in the Paragraph group on the HOME tab. (Note that if you use the Increase Indent button to indent a bulleted list, it will indent the list one-quarter inch at a time.) To move an indented paragraph back to the left one-half inch, click the Decrease Indent button.

Begin Activity

Change paragraph indents.

1 Switch to the **Resume Final document**. Under the *Internship* line, click anywhere in the paragraph that begins with **Assisted the marketing manager**.

2 On the horizontal ruler, point to the **Left Indent marker** ⬚, which is the rectangle at the bottom of the marker at the left margin on the horizontal ruler ⬚. Use the ScreenTip to make sure you are pointing to the correct section of the marker.

3 While still pointing to the **Left Indent marker** ⬚, press and hold the **mouse button**. A dotted vertical line appears over the document.

4 Drag the **Left Indent marker** ⬚ right to the **.5-inch mark** on the horizontal ruler.

5 Release the **mouse button**. All three sections of the marker move when you drag the Left Indent marker. The entire paragraph containing the insertion point indents from the left one-half inch.

6 Below the *Sales Manager* line (which is the first line below the bulleted list under *Internship*), select the paragraph that begins **Managed staff of five cashiers**.

7 On the HOME tab, in the Paragraph group, click the **Increase Indent button** 🔢. The selected paragraph is indented one-half inch.

8 Under the *Internship* line, select the four items in the bulleted list. On the ruler, notice that the First Line Indent marker is at the .25-inch mark and the Hanging Indent marker is at the .5-inch mark. Paragraphs in bulleted lists are formatted with a hanging indent. The first line of each of the selected paragraphs is indented one-quarter inch, and for the item that is longer than one line, the second line is indented one-half inch.

9 In the Paragraph group, click the **Increase Indent button** 🔢. Because the selected paragraphs are a bulleted list, they are indented one-quarter inch from their original position instead of one-half inch. Now the bullet symbols are aligned with the indented paragraph above the list. Compare your screen to Exhibit 10-23.

10 Scroll down and indent the line that begins *Staffed sales register* one-half inch from the left margin.

> **Tip:** You can also click in the paragraph you want to indent or select multiple paragraphs, click the Dialog Box Launcher in the Paragraph group, and then adjust the settings in the Indentation section.

Exhibit 10-23 Paragraphs indented

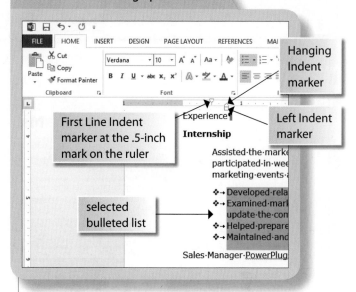

10-6h Adding a Paragraph Border

You can add borders around paragraphs, or you can add only part of a border—for example, a bottom border that appears below the last line of text in a paragraph. You can select different colors and line weights for the border as well, making the border more or less prominent, as needed. To add a border, you click the Borders button arrow to open a menu of border options, as shown in Exhibit 10-24. If you click one of the options in the menu, you add a border using the default style, color, and width, which is a solid ½-point black line. Or you can open the Borders and Shading dialog box and use the commands on the Borders tab as shown in Exhibit 10-25 to create a custom border. Note that you must click the Custom button in the Setting list to apply a custom border; otherwise, the border will be applied to all four sides of the selected text or paragraph.

Begin Activity

Add a paragraph border.

1 Scroll so you can see the top of the page.

2 Select the **Qualifications** and **Education paragraphs**, including the **paragraph marks**.

3 On the HOME tab, in the Paragraph group, click the **Borders button arrow** 🔲. A menu of border options opens. Refer to Exhibit 10-24.

Exhibit 10-24 Borders menu

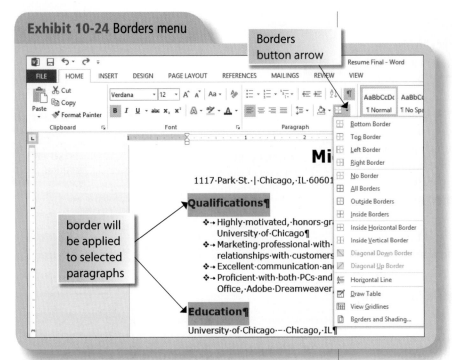

above the selected paragraph. The Borders button now shows the Top Border option.

5 In the Paragraph group, click the **Border button arrow**, and then click **Borders and Shading**. The Borders and Shading dialog box opens with the Borders tab selected. Refer back to Exhibit 10-25. Custom is selected in the Setting list because the border is not applied to all four sides of the paragraph. The Preview section shows the current settings.

6 In the Style list, click the **down scroll arrow** four times, and then click the line style that shows a **thick line above a thin line**.

7 Click the **Color arrow**. The same color palette you used when you changed the font color appears.

8 In the color palette, under Theme Colors, click **Blue–Gray, Text 2**. The selected line style in the Style box and the sample in the Width box change to the dark blue color.

9 Click the **Width arrow**, and then click **1½ pt**. Do not close the dialog box yet; you still need to apply the selected border style.

Exhibit 10-25 Borders tab in the Borders and Shading dialog box

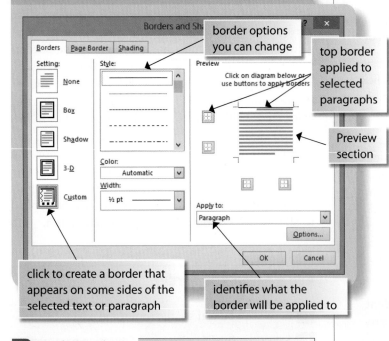

border options you can change

top border applied to selected paragraphs

Preview section

click to create a border that appears on some sides of the selected text or paragraph

identifies what the border will be applied to

10 In the Preview section, click the **top of the paragraph**. The solid black border is replaced with the double-line blue border. Below the Preview section, the Apply to box contains Paragraph, indicating that the border will be applied to the entire paragraph, not just selected text.

> **Problem?** If you click the wrong side, click the border you applied to remove it.

11 Click **OK**. The dialog box closes, and the borders above the Qualifications and Education headings change to the 1½-point, dark blue border you selected.

4 On the Borders menu, click **Top Border**. The menu closes, and a solid line, one-half point wide, black border appears

> **Problem?** If a box appears around either heading, you did not select the paragraph mark before applying the border. Undo the action, and then repeat Steps 2 through 4.

End Activity

Exhibit 10-26 Shading applied to a paragraph

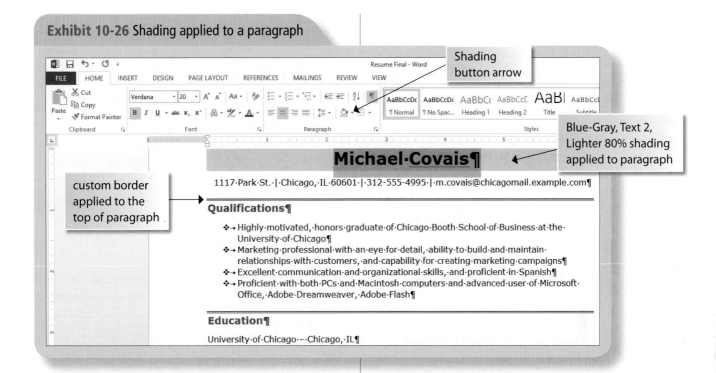

10-6i Adding Paragraph Shading

You can add shading as background color to paragraphs. You can use shading in conjunction with a border for a more defined effect.

Begin Activity

Add shading to a paragraph.

1. At the top of the document, select **Michael Covais** and the **paragraph mark** at the end of the line.

2. On the HOME tab, in the Paragraph group, click the **Shading button arrow** ⬛▾. The color palette appears.

3. In the first row of variants under the Theme Colors, click the **Blue–Gray, Text 2, Lighter 80% color**. The color palette closes, and light blue shading is applied across the width of the page to the paragraph containing Michael's name. Compare your screen to Exhibit 10-26.

> **Problem?** If the shading was applied only behind Stephen's name, you did not select the paragraph mark. Undo the action, and then repeat Steps 1 through 3.

End Activity

10-7 Copying Formats

If you are working with a document that contains a lot of formatting, it can be easier to copy the formatting rather than trying to re-create it on a different block of text. Likewise, if you are pasting text that is formatted differently from the text in the location where you are pasting it, you can control whether the formatting is pasted.

10-7a Using the Format Painter

The **Format Painter** is a tool that allows you to copy formatting from one location to another, such as from one paragraph of text to another. You can use the Format Painter to apply the copied formatting once or over and over again until you toggle it off.

Begin Activity

Use the Format Painter.

1. Select the **Qualifications paragraph**, including the paragraph mark.

> **Format Painter** A tool that is used to copy formatting from one location to another, such as from one block of text to another.

2 On the HOME tab, in the Clipboard group, click the **Format Painter button**, and then move the pointer on top of text in the document (but do not click). The Format Painter button toggles on, and the pointer changes to 🖌️.

3 Below the Education heading and above the *Internship* line, position the pointer to the left of the paragraph containing **Experience** so that it changes to 🖑, and then click. The font and paragraph formatting applied to the *Qualifications* paragraph is copied to the *Experience* paragraph, the Format Painter button toggles off, and the pointer returns to its usual shape.

4 Copy the formatting applied to the **Experience paragraph** to the **Activities paragraph**, which is three lines from the end of the document.

5 Scroll up, and then under the *Experience* heading, select the paragraph beginning with **Internship**, including the paragraph mark. In the Clipboard group, double-click the **Format Painter button**.

6 Below the bulleted list, drag all the way across the line beginning with **Sales Manager**. The formatting from the *Internship* line is copied to this line. Notice on the ruler that the custom Right Tab stop you set was copied as well. Because you double-clicked the Format Painter button, the button is still selected, and the pointer is still 🖌️.

7 Two lines above the *Activities* heading, drag all the way across the line beginning with **Sales Clerk**.

8 In the Clipboard group, click the **Format Painter button**. The Format Painter button toggles off, and the pointer returns to its usual shape. Now you need to add tab characters between the job titles and the companies in the two lines you just applied the copied format to.

9 In the lines beginning with *Sales Manager* and *Sales Clerk*, delete the space before *PowerPlugs*, and insert a tab character in its place.

10 Use the **Format Painter** to copy the formatting of the bulleted list under *Internship* to the three paragraphs under *Sales Manager*, beginning with **Created new training program** . . . through **Developed an electronic scheduling tool** . . . . The paragraph formatting, including the bullet characters and the indent level, is copied to the three paragraphs you selected, and the Format Painter toggles off.

11 Use the **Format Painter** to copy the formatting of the bulleted list under *Qualifications* near the beginning of the document to two paragraphs under the *Activities* paragraph at the end of the document. Compare your document to the one shown in Exhibit 10-27.

Tip: To see the entire document at once, click the One Page button in the Zoom group on the VIEW tab.

End Activity

Organizing a Résumé

You can organize the information in a résumé in many ways. The document you worked on in this chapter is one example. The Resume Final document is organized chronologically. You can also organize a résumé so that your most relevant job experience and skills are listed first. Before creating your own résumé, conduct research so you can decide on the best format. Then you can use the skills you learned in this chapter to format your résumé to best highlight your abilities.

10-7b Using Paste Options

When you paste text or objects in Office programs, you can click the Paste button arrow instead of the Paste button in the Clipboard group on the HOME tab to display a menu of options for pasting the contents of the Clipboard. The buttons on the menu change depending on what you are pasting. The buttons that you will use most often are Keep Source Formatting and Keep Text Only. The Keep Source Formatting button 📋 pastes the contents of the Clipboard in the new location but retains the formatting that the copied or cut item had in its original location. The Keep Text Only button 📋 pastes the contents of the Clipboard using the formatting of the surrounding text in the new location. Another button that commonly appears is the Merge Formatting button 📋, which combines the formatting from the original location with the formatting of the new location. When other buttons are available, they will have similar descriptive names that appear in a ScreenTip when you point to them.

You can point to each button on the Paste button menu to see a Live Preview of the formatted Clipboard

Exhibit 10-27 Completed résumé

Michael Covais

1117 Park St. | Chicago, IL 60601 | 312-555-4995 | m.covais@chicagomail.example.com

Qualifications

❖ Highly motivated, honors graduate of Chicago Booth School of Business at the University of Chicago
❖ Marketing professional with an eye for detail, ability to build and maintain relationships with customers, and capability for creating marketing campaigns
❖ Excellent communication and organizational skills, and proficient in Spanish
❖ Proficient with both PCs and Macintosh computers and advanced user of Microsoft Office, Adobe Dreamweaver, Adobe Flash

Education

University of Chicago – Chicago, IL
BA *cum laude*, Business, June, 2016
Concentration: Marketing, Minor: Spanish

Experience

Internship   **Sanford Industries, September 2015-June 2016**

Assisted the marketing manager with daily tasks and long-term projects, and participated in weekly staff meetings providing ideas and suggestions for upcoming marketing events and campaigns.

❖ Developed relationships with customers, vendors, and coworkers
❖ Examined market competition and costs, and prepared a report that was used to update the company's marketing plan
❖ Helped prepare promotional materials for upcoming marketing campaign
❖ Maintained and updated existing customer database

Sales Manager   **PowerPlugs Electronics, August 2013-September 2015**

Managed staff of five cashiers, providing training, resolving conflicts, and scheduling shifts.

❖ Created new training program to facilitate faster start up and improve customer relations
❖ Awarded Employee of the Month eight times
❖ Developed an electronic scheduling tool for creating weekly employee work hours

Sales Clerk   **PowerPlugs Electronics, August 2011-August 2013**

Staffed sales register during peak store hours.

Activities

❖ American Marketing Association, collegiate member
❖ Chicago Crew Team, four years

Begin Activity

Use paste options.

1 At the top of the document, select **Michael Covais** and the **paragraph mark** at the end of the line.

2 On the HOME tab, in the Clipboard group, click the **Copy button**.

3 Switch to the **Cover Letter document**. At the bottom of the letter, click after the comma after the word *Sincerely*, and then press the Enter key three times.

4 In the Clipboard group, click the **Paste button arrow**. The menu of paste options appears.

5 On the menu, point to the **Keep Source Formatting button** 📋. Michael's name appears in the document with the same formatting it had in the résumé. Refer back to Exhibit 10-28.

6 Point to the **Merge Formatting button** 📋. Live Preview changes the pasted text so it merges the formatting used in the résumé with that of the letter; that is, it changes the text to 11-point Calibri and removes the blue shading but retains the bold formatting.

7 On the Paste Options menu, click the **Keep Text Only button** 📋. The menu closes, and the text is pasted as plain, unformatted text. The Paste Options button 📋 (Ctrl)▾ appears below the lower-right corner of the pasted text.

---

item in the document. See Exhibit 10-28. If you click the Paste button, the contents of the Clipboard is pasted with the default option, which is the first button on the menu. When you paste anything, a Paste Options button 📋 (Ctrl)▾ appears below and to the right of the pasted item. You can click the Paste Options button to display the same menu of buttons that appears on the Paste button menu, and you can click these to change how the pasted item is formatted.

End Activity

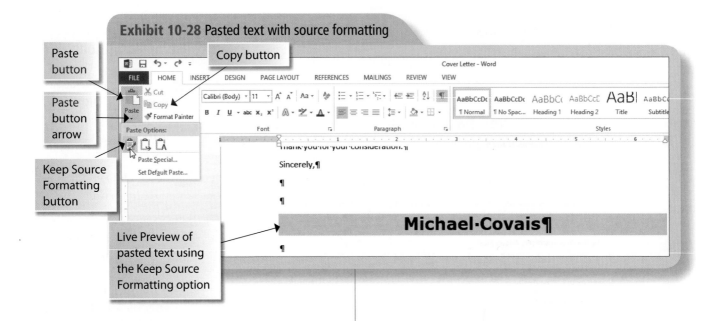

Exhibit 10-28 Pasted text with source formatting

Paste button

Copy button

Paste button arrow

Keep Source Formatting button

Live Preview of pasted text using the Keep Source Formatting option

10-8 Checking Spelling and Grammar

Before you print or send a document, you should always perform a final check of the spelling using the Spelling and Grammar Checker. This is commonly called using the spell checker or **spell checking**. The spell checker continually checks your document against the Office built-in dictionary. If it finds a word that doesn't match the correct spelling in the Office dictionary and was not fixed by AutoCorrect, or if a word, such as a last name, is not in the dictionary, a red, wavy line appears beneath it. A red, wavy underline also appears if the same word appears twice in a row. The context in which words are used can also be checked, so words that are spelled correctly but might be used incorrectly are underlined with a blue, wavy line. For example, if you type *their* when you mean *there*, the word would be flagged. Of course, a computer program can't be 100 percent accurate in determining the correct context, so Word doesn't catch every instance of this type of error. Finally, Word also checks the grammar in a document and flags potential grammatical errors with a blue, wavy underline.

Sometimes grammatical errors are not flagged no matter what is selected in the Grammar Settings dialog box. To ensure an error-free document, you should always read your documents carefully even after using the spelling and grammar tools because nothing beats a human proofread.

To make sure your document will be checked for all types of errors, you need to check the settings in the Word Options dialog box.

Begin Activity

Check the Spelling and Grammar Checker settings.

1. In the Cover Letter document, on the ribbon, click the **FILE tab**. In the navigation bar, click **Options**. The Word Options dialog box opens.

2. In the navigation pane, click **Proofing**. The right pane of the dialog box changes to display options for proofing and correcting documents.

3. Near the bottom of the dialog box, under When correcting spelling and grammar in Word, click the following check boxes, if necessary, to select them:

   - **Check spelling as you type**
   - **Mark grammar errors as you type**
   - **Frequently confused words**
   - **Check grammar with spelling**

Compare your screen to Exhibit 10-29. Now you need to check the grammar settings.

spell check To check a file for spelling and grammatical errors using the Spelling and Grammar Checker.

Exhibit 10-29 Word Options dialog box with Proofing selected

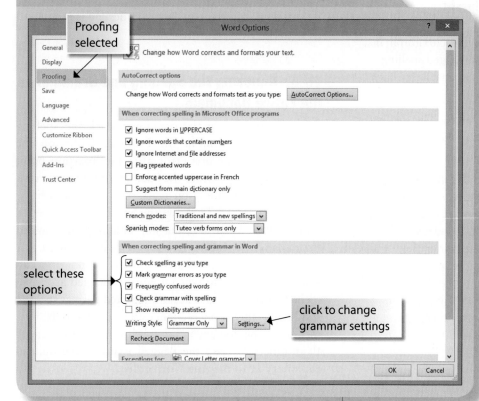

Proofing selected

select these options

click to change grammar settings

unselect any check boxes as needed to match the dialog box shown in Exhibit 10-30.

6 Click **OK**. The Grammar Settings dialog box closes. Click **OK** in the Word Options dialog box to close it.

End Activity

There are three ways to correct misspelled words. You can correct words individually by right-clicking flagged words and then using options on the shortcut menu that opens. You can check the entire document by opening the Spelling task pane. Or, you can simply delete the misspelled word and retype it.

10-8a Checking Flagged Words Individually

You can right-click a word flagged with a colored, wavy underline to open a shortcut menu containing suggestions for alternate spellings or a correction for a grammatical error. It also includes commands for ignoring the misspelled word or grammatical error. See Exhibit 10-31.

4 Make sure **Grammar Only** appears in the box next to Writing Style, and then click **Settings**. The Grammar Settings dialog box opens.

5 Scroll so that you can see all of the options under Grammar. Click the **Subject-verb agreement check box** to select it if it is not already selected. Compare your screen to Exhibit 10-30, and select or

Exhibit 10-30 Grammar Settings dialog box

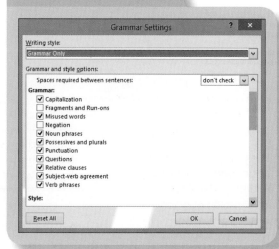

Exhibit 10-31 Shortcut menu for a misspelled word

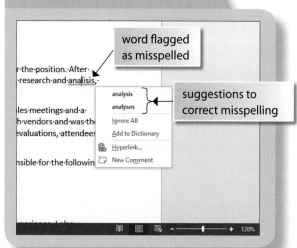

word flagged as misspelled

suggestions to correct misspelling

Check flagged words individually.

1 In the body of the letter, in the first paragraph, in the last sentence, right-click the flagged spelling error **analisis**. A shortcut menu opens. Refer back to Exhibit 10-31.

2 On the shortcut menu, click **analysis**. The spelling of the word is corrected, and the red, wavy underline is removed.

3 In the second paragraph, in the first sentence, right-click the flagged grammar error **assists**. Only one word appears at the top of the shortcut menu as a suggested replacement, *assist*, and this is incorrect.

> **Problem?** If the word *assists* doesn't have a blue, wavy underline, click the word *assists* to make the underline appear, and then repeat Step 3.

4 Click a blank area of the window to close the shortcut menu without selecting anything.

5 Click after the word *assists*, press the **Backspace key**, and then type **ed**. The word is changed to *assisted*, and the blue, wavy underline is removed.

End Activity

10-8b Checking the Spelling and Grammar in the Entire Document

To spell-check the entire document, click the Spelling & Grammar button in the Proofing group on the REVIEW tab. The first error after the insertion point is highlighted, and either the Spelling or Grammar task pane opens, depending on what type of error is highlighted. Exhibit 10-32 shows the Spelling task pane for a misspelled word. Options for handling the flagged error change depending on the type of error found. For example, when a duplicated word is found, you can ignore it or delete it; when a word is flagged as a misspelled word, you can select a suggested correct spelling and then change it once, change all instances of the misspelling in the document, ignore this instance or ignore all instances, or add the flagged word to the built-in dictionary or to the AutoCorrect list.

Exhibit 10-32 Spelling and Grammar task pane showing a misspelled word

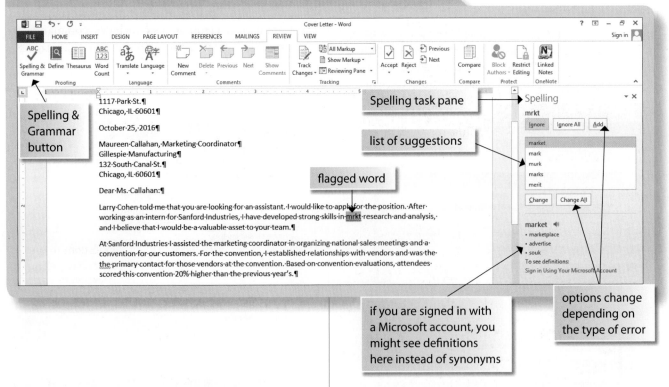

Check the spelling and grammar in the entire document.

1 Press the **Ctrl+Home keys**. The insertion point moves to the beginning of the document.

2 On the ribbon, click the **REVIEW tab**. In the Proofing group, click the **Spelling & Grammar button**. The first flagged word in the document, *mrkt*, is highlighted. The Spelling task pane opens with the correct spelling selected in the list in the task pane. Refer back to Exhibit 10-32.

> **Tip:** You can also click ⬛ on the status bar to open the Spelling task pane. If the button is ⬛, there are no flagged errors.

3 In the task pane, click **Change**. The highlighted word is replaced with the word selected in the task pane, and the next flagged word is highlighted. In this case, the word *the* appears twice in a row. No suggested alternate spellings appear in the Suggestions box because the only choice here is to delete the repeated word or leave it as is.

4 In the task pane, click **Delete**. The repeated word is deleted, and the next flagged word, *fore*, is highlighted. This is a misused word, so the task pane changes to the Grammar task pane. The list of synonyms at the bottom includes synonyms for both the misused word and for the selected correction.

5 Click **Change**. The word is corrected in the document, and the next flagged error is highlighted, which is the sentence that begins with *I looks*. This is a grammar error. An explanation of the grammatical problem appears at the bottom of the task pane. In this case, it describes subject-verb agreement.

> **Problem?** If the word *looks* doesn't have a blue, wavy underline, select the word and the space after it, and then retype it.

6 In the Spelling and Grammar dialog box, click **Change**. The flagged word is corrected, and the next flagged word is highlighted. This is a surname, so it should not be changed.

7 Click **Ignore All**. The word is not changed anywhere it appears in the document. This is the last flagged word in the document, so the Spelling and Grammar dialog box closes, and another dialog box opens telling you that the spelling and grammar check is complete.

> **Problem?** If another word is flagged as misspelled, select the correct spelling in the Suggestions list, and then click the Change button.

8 In the dialog box, click **OK**. The dialog box closes.

FYI

Proofreading Your Document

Although the Spelling and Grammar Checker is a useful tool, it is no substitute for careful proofreading. Always take the time to read your document to check for errors the Spelling and Grammar Checker might have missed. Keep in mind that the Spelling and Grammar Checker cannot pinpoint inaccurate phrases or poorly chosen words. You will have to find those yourself. To produce a professional document, you must read it carefully several times. It's also a good idea to ask one or two other people to read your documents as well; they might catch something you missed.

AlexAranda/Shutterstock.com

10-9 Previewing and Printing Documents

To be sure the document is ready to print, and to avoid wasting paper and time, you should first review it on the Print screen in Backstage view to make sure it will appear as you want when printed. See Exhibit 10-33.

The Print screen contains options for printing the document and a preview displaying a full-page version of the document in the right pane. However, you cannot edit the document from the Print screen; it simply provides a way to look at the document page by page before printing. The Print settings in the left pane allow you to control a variety of print options. For example, you can change the number of copies or which pages to print. If your document has more than one page, you can scroll from page to page by clicking the Next Page ▶ and Previous Page ◀ buttons at the bottom of the preview or dragging the scroll bar to the right of the preview.

Begin Activity

Preview the document.

1 Proof the Cover Letter document one last time, and correct any remaining errors.

2 In the inside address, replace *Maureen Callahan* with your name.

3 Save the Cover Letter document.

4 On the ribbon, click the **FILE tab** to open Backstage view. In the navigation bar, click **Print**. The Print screen appears.

> **Problem?** If the document doesn't appear to fill the preview pane, at the bottom-right corner of the window, click the Zoom to Page button.

5 Review your document, and make sure its overall layout matches the document in Exhibit 10-33. If you notice a problem with paragraph breaks or spacing, click the **Back button** ◀ at the top of the navigation pane, edit the document, and then repeat Step 4.

6 Make sure your printer is turned on and contains paper.

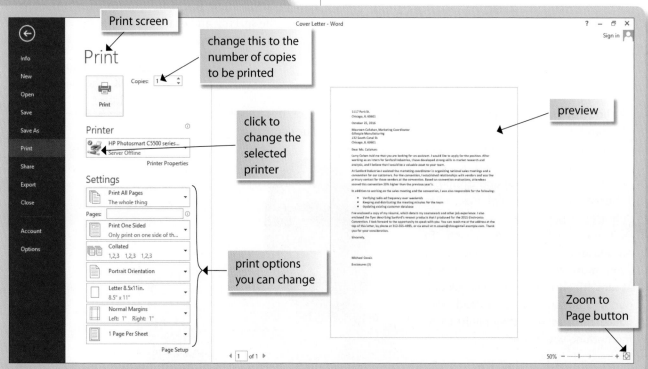

Exhibit 10-33 Print screen in Backstage view

7 In the left pane of the Print screen, click **Print**. Backstage view closes, and the letter prints.

8 On the ribbon, click the **FILE tab**. In the navigation bar, click **Close**. The Cover Letter document closes, and the Resume Final document is the current document.

9 Proof the Resume Final document one last time, and correct any remaining errors.

10 Replace Michael's name at the top of the document with your name, and then save the document.

11 View the Resume Final document on the Print screen in Backstage view.

> **Problem?** If the Resume Final document does not fit on one page, click the 1 Page Per Sheet button near the bottom of the Print screen in Backstage view, point to Scale to Paper Size, scroll down the submenu, and then click Letter 8.5×11in.

12 Print the document, and then close it.

End Activity

Quiz Yourself

1. What are nonprinting characters, and how do you display them?

2. How do you insert symbols that are not included in the AutoCorrect list?

3. When you use drag and drop to move text, can you next use the Paste command to paste that text somewhere else? Why or why not?

4. What is a font?

5. According to the chapter, what is a point?

6. What is the default paragraph spacing in a Word document? What is the default line spacing?

7. What is justified text?

LEARN MORE

Creating an Envelope

Most printers are capable of printing envelopes. To create an envelope, you need to create a document with the address and return address sized and positioned correctly. To do this, click the Envelopes button in the Create group on the MAILINGS tab to open the Envelopes and Labels dialog box with the Envelopes tab selected. Type the recipient's name and address in the Delivery address box, type your return address in the Return address box, load an envelope in the printer, and then print it. If you click Add to Document instead of Print, the envelope will be added as a new page to the current document. Alternatively, if a letter is open in the document window, select the inside address, and then open the Envelopes and Labels dialog box to have the recipient's name and address pasted in the Delivery address box.

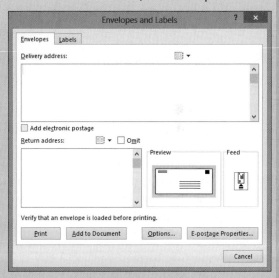

Envelopes tab in the Envelopes and Labels dialog box

8. Where are the default tab stops? What happens to them when you insert a new tab stop?

9. When you create a bulleted or a numbered list, what character is inserted after the bullet symbol or the number, and what type of indent is applied to the paragraph?

10. Describe two ways to indent a paragraph one-half inch from the left margin.

11. What do the buttons on the Paste Options menu do?

12. What tool do you use to copy the format of a block of text to another block of text?

13. What happens when you type text in the Search Document box in the Navigation Pane?

14. How are possible spelling errors, contextual spelling errors, and grammatical errors flagged in a document? (Specify the colors used.)

15. What does the Print screen in Backstage view show?

Practice It

Practice It 10-1

1. Start Word and open a new, blank document. Display the rulers, show nonprinting characters, and then save the blank document as **Complaint Draft**.

2. Type the date **February 18, 2016** using AutoComplete for *February*.

3. Press the Enter key, and then type the following inside address, using the default paragraph spacing and allowing AutoCorrect to change *Cafe* to *Café*:

   Marianne Eklund, Manager

   Corner Café

   403 South Central St.

   Tampa, FL 33604

   Dear Ms. Eklund:

   I am writing to express my disappointment at the service my colleagues and I received at our corporate function to celebrate the launch of our new product EasyGo.

4. After *EasyGo* and before the period, type **(tm)** allowing AutoCorrect to change it to ™.

5. Position the insertion point after the period, and then press the Spacebar. Type **You can reach me at** and then type your email address followed by a period. Press the Enter key, and then type your name.

6. Remove the hyperlink formatting from your email address.

7. Remove the spacing after the first three paragraphs in the inside address.

8. Save and close the document.

9. Open the data file **Complaint** located in the Chapter 10\Practice It folder. Use the Save As command to save the file as **Complaint Letter**. Open the file **Menu** located in the Chapter 10\Practice It folder. Save this file as **Cafe Menu**.

10. Switch to the Cafe Menu document. In the third line, delete the *e* from *Fixe* and use the Symbol button to insert **é** so the word is *Fixé*.

11. Select all the text in the document, change the font to Papyrus, and change the font size to 14 points.

Change the font size of the text in the second paragraph to 12 points.

12. In the first line, make *Corner Café* bold, increase the font size to 20 points, and change the font color to Dark Blue, Text 2.

13. Center-align the first two paragraphs.

14. In the third paragraph, add a Right Tab stop at the 6-inch mark on the ruler, and then drag it to the 6.5-inch mark. Insert a tab character after *Prix Fixé Meal*, and then type **$35.00**.

15. Increase the spacing before and after the third paragraph to 24 points.

16. Select all the text and the paragraph mark in the lines starting with *Appetizer*, *Entrée*, and *Dessert*. Format the lines as bold, and then format them as a numbered list using Arabic numerals followed by a period. Decrease the indent so they are aligned at the left margin. (*Hint*: You will need to drag the Left Indent marker on the ruler.)

17. Format the three paragraphs under *Appetizer*, the four paragraphs under *Entrée*, and the three paragraphs under *Dessert* as bulleted lists using the right-pointing arrowhead in the Bullet Library. Increase the indent so that the bullet character is at the .5-inch mark on the ruler. (*Hint*: You will need to drag the Left Indent marker on the ruler.)

18. Add a custom border to the top and bottom of the paragraph containing *Prix Fixé Meal*. Use the style that appears at the bottom of the Style list without scrolling on the Borders tab in the Borders and Shading dialog box; the Dark Blue, Text 2 color; and a width of 3 points. (*Hint*: Make sure you click the Custom button in the Setting list in the dialog box.)

19. Add Dark Blue, Text 2, Lighter 80% shading to the first paragraph.

20. Copy the formatting of the first paragraph to the last paragraph containing text (*Make your reservation today!*). Change the spacing before the last paragraph containing text to 48 points and after this paragraph to 30 points.

21. Copy the first paragraph to the Clipboard. Switch to the Complaint Letter document. Paste the copied text in the empty paragraph in the second line in the inside address as text only.

22. Select all the text in the document, and then change the line spacing to single spacing.

23. In the body of the letter, in the first paragraph, select *we did not enjoy the evening* and replace it with **instead of the usual delightful service**. At the end of the letter, replace *Your Name* in the closing with your name.

24. In the body of the letter, move the second paragraph (which begins with *Our main course*) after the third paragraph so it becomes the third paragraph. Then copy *Corner Café* from the second sentence in the first paragraph to the end of the last sentence in the first paragraph after *expect from*.

25. In the first paragraph, correct the spelling of the misspelled word *colleagues*. Then check the rest of the document, and make any corrections needed. If a word is flagged but spelled correctly, ignore it.

26. Save the Complaint Letter document, examine it in the preview pane on the Print tab in Backstage view, and then print it. Close the Complaint Letter document.

27. In the Cafe Menu document, add your name in the last, blank paragraph at the end of the document. Save the document.

28. Examine the Cafe Menu document in the preview pane on the Print tab in Backstage view, and then print it. Close the Cafe Menu document.

Practice It 10-2

1. Open a new blank document, and then save the document as **Thank You Letter**.

2. Change the font to Times New Roman, change the font size to 12 points, and change the line spacing to single spaced.

3. Type the following as the return address:

    Baltimore Community Center

    114 27th St.

    Baltimore, MD 21201

4. Press the Enter key, and then add **October 21, 2016** as the date.

5. Press the Enter key, and then type the following as the inside address:

    Daniel Foreman

    Career Counseling

    12 Harborside Rd.

    Baltimore, MD 21201

6. Press the Enter key, type the salutation **Dear Mr. Foreman:** and then press the Enter key.

7. Type the following paragraph: **We are delighted that you will be giving a presentation to our members describing job search strategies. We were hoping that you would address the following questions as part of your presentation:**

8. Press the Enter key, and then type the following questions as separate paragraphs:

    What is the best way to find job listings?

    How do I learn how to network?

    How do I prepare for an interview?

    Do I need to dress in a business suit?

9. Insert a new paragraph after the last question, and then type **Thank you again for your time.** Press the Enter key, and then type the complimentary closing **Sincerely,** (including the comma).

10. Press the Enter key three times, and then type your name.

11. Format the four questions as a numbered list, and then increase the indent so that the numbers are aligned at the .5-inch mark.

12. Format the four questions as bold.

13. Remove the extra space after the first two lines in the return address and after the first three lines in the inside address.

14. Increase the space before the first line in the letter (the first line in the return address) to 30 points.

15. Change the alignment of the return address, the date, and the closing to right-aligned.

16. Check the spelling and grammar in the document, and correct any errors.

17. Save the document, preview and print it, and then close it.

On Your Own

On Your Own 10-1

1. Create a new document based on the Basic Fax Cover template. (*Hint*: You must be connected to the Internet to use templates. Click Fax under the Search box on the New screen to filter the templates to show fax templates.) This template contains placeholders that you click once to select and replace with text.

2. Save the document as **Price Quote**.

3. Next to *To:*, click [Name] to select the placeholder. Type your instructor's name.

4. Next to *From:*, if the name is not your name, select the name, delete it, and then type your name.

5. Next to *Fax:*, replace the placeholder with **617–555–2098**.

6. Next to *Pages:*, replace the placeholder with **2**.

7. Next to *Re:*, type **Remodeling project quote**.

8. Next to *Date:*, click the placeholder, click the arrow that appears, and then click Today below the calendar.

9. Next to *Cc:*, select the placeholder, and then delete it. Then delete Cc:.

10. In the line of check boxes, click the check box next to *For Review* to insert an x in the box.

11. Below the horizontal line, click the placeholder, and then type the following. In the paragraphs containing prices, press the Tab key instead of the Spacebar before the price.

   Per your request, here is my quote for completing your remodeling project:

   5 Windows $1,325.79

   Skylight $399.99

Labor $900.00

Total $2,625.78

Please let me know if you have any questions.

12. Change the size of the text below the horizontal line to 12 points.

13. Format the dollar amounts in bold.

14. Indent all the text under the horizontal line one inch from the left, and then indent the same text one inch from the right.

15. Add shading using the Gray-25%, Accent 2 color behind all the text below the horizontal line. (Note that this document uses a different color palette than the other documents you have created.)

16. Indent the four paragraphs containing prices another half-inch. Notice that the shading is no longer a rectangle behind all the text.

17. Decrease the indent of the four paragraphs containing prices one-half inch.

18. In the four paragraphs containing the prices, set a Left Tab stop at the 1.75-inch mark on the ruler, and set a Decimal Tab stop at the 3.5-inch mark on the ruler. Insert a tab before the first character in each of the four lines containing prices.

19. At the top of the document, click the placeholder asking for your name and address, and then delete it.

20. Save the document, examine it in the preview pane on the Print tab in Backstage view, print it, and then close the document.

Chapter 10

ADDITIONAL STUDY TOOLS

▶ Take practice quiz to prepare for tests

▶ Review key term flash cards (online, printable, and audio)

▶ Play "Beat the Clock" and "Memory" to quiz yourself

▶ Watch the videos to learn more about the topics taught in this chapter

IN THE BOOK

▶ Complete end-of-chapter exercises

▶ Study tear-out Chapter Review Card

ONLINE

▶ Complete additional end-of-chapter exercises

Answers to Quiz Yourself

1. *Nonprinting characters are characters that do not print and that control the format of the document. To display them, click the Show/Hide ¶ button in the Paragraph group on the HOME tab.*

2. *To insert symbols not included in the AutoCorrect list, use the Symbol button in the Symbols group on the INSERT tab.*

3. *When you use drag and drop to move text, you cannot next use the Paste command to paste that text somewhere else because text moved or copied using drag and drop is not placed on the Clipboard.*

4. *A font is the design of a set of characters.*

5. *A point is the unit of measurement used for type equal to 1/72 of an inch.*

6. *The default paragraph spacing in a Word document is zero points before a paragraph and 8 points after it. The default line spacing in a Word document is 1.08.*

7. *Justified text is a type of text alignment in which both sides of the text are aligned along the margins.*

8. *The default tab stops are positioned every half-inch. When you insert a new tab stop, all of the default tab stops before it are deleted.*

9. *When you create a bulleted or a numbered list, a tab character is inserted between the bullet symbol or the number and the text, and the paragraph is formatted with a hanging indent.*

10. *To indent a paragraph one-half inch from the left margin, click the Increase Indent button in the Paragraph group on the HOME tab, or drag the Left Indent marker to the .5-inch mark on the ruler.*

11. *The buttons on the Paste Options menu control the formatting of the pasted text.*

12. *The Format Painter copies the format of a block of text to another block of text.*

13. *When you type text in the Search Document box in the Navigation Pane, all instances of the search text is immediately highlighted in the document.*

14. *Possible spelling errors, contextual spelling errors, and grammatical errors are flagged in a document with wavy underlines: red for spelling errors, blue for possible misused words and grammatical errors.*

15. *The Print screen in Backstage view shows a preview of the document as it will look when it is printed.*

Formatting a Long Document

Yuri Arcurs/Shutterstock.com

Although a shorter document is useful for providing a summary or snapshot view, longer documents are a fact of life in the business world, the government arena, academia, and personal life. Businesspeople and government workers often create long documents for developing business plans, proposing new ideas or products, evaluating current strategies, and explaining new products or approaches. Members of the academic world commonly use long documents when applying for grants, documenting research, submitting journal articles, and even writing books. Word provides many tools for working with longer documents and for making them easier to read.

Learning Objectives

After studying the material in this chapter, you will be able to:

11-1 Find and replace text

11-2 Work with styles

11-3 Work with themes

11-4 Scroll through a long document

11-5 Work with the document outline

11-6 Change the margins

11-7 Insert a manual page break

11-8 Add page numbers, headers, and footers

11-9 Create citations and a list of works cited

11-10 Create footnotes and endnotes

11-1 Finding and Replacing Text

When working with a longer document, you can spend a lot of time reading through the text to locate a particular word or phrase. The Find command provides a faster way to locate a word or phrase. The Find and Replace dialog box makes it simple to replace a word or phrase throughout a document.

11-1a Finding Text

To find specific text in a document, you can use the RESULTS tab in the Navigation pane, which you open by clicking the Find button in the Editing group on the HOME tab. In the Search document box, you type the text for which you are searching. As you type, Word highlights every instance of the search text in the document and displays the corresponding text snippets in the Navigation pane. See Exhibit 11-1. You can click a snippet to go immediately to its location in the document.

Begin Activity

Find text.

1 Open the data file **Proposal** located in the Chapter 11\Chapter folder. Save the document as **Biking Proposal**. Change the zoom percentage to **120%**, if necessary.

2 On the HOME tab, in the Editing group, click the **Find button**. The Navigation pane opens on the left side of the document window with the RESULTS tab selected.

3 At the top of the Navigation pane, click in the **Search document box**, and then type **b**. Every letter *b* in the document is highlighted with yellow.

> **Problem?** If the Search document box contains text, delete it and then repeat Step 3.

4 Continue typing **udgeting** to complete the word *budgeting*. As you continue typing, the highlighting is removed from words that do not match the search text. The two instances of the word *budgeting* are highlighted in the document. Refer to Exhibit 11-1.

5 In the Navigation pane, click the **second snippet**. In the document, the second instance of the word *budgeting* is highlighted with gray shading on top of the yellow highlight.

6 Click in the document window, select the second instance of the word *budgeting*, and then type **Funding**. The text you type replaces the selected instance of *budgeting*, and the snippets in the Navigation pane and the highlighting in the document disappear.

7 In the Navigation pane, click the **Next Search Result button** ▼. The search is performed again, and the remaining instance of *budgeting* is highlighted in the document and listed as a snippet in the Navigation pane.

> **Tip:** Remember to save frequently as you work through the chapter. A good practice is to save after every Activity.

8 In the Navigation pane title bar, click the **Close button** ✕.

End Activity

CAUTION

Using Replace All

Be careful when you use the Replace All command. Say you search for a short word, such as *car*, and replace all instances of *car* with *auto* using the Replace All command. You could end up replacing the text *car* in words such as *careful* and *carry*, resulting in *autoeful* and *autory*.

11-1b Replacing Specific Text

You can replace specific text using the Replace tab in the Find and Replace dialog box, which you open by clicking the Replace button in the Editing group on the HOME tab. On the Replace tab, you type the text you want to locate in the Find what box and the text you want to substitute in the Replace with box. Click Find Next to locate the next instance of the text in the Find what box. Click Replace to replace just that instance, or click Replace All to replace all instances of the text. See Exhibit 11-2.

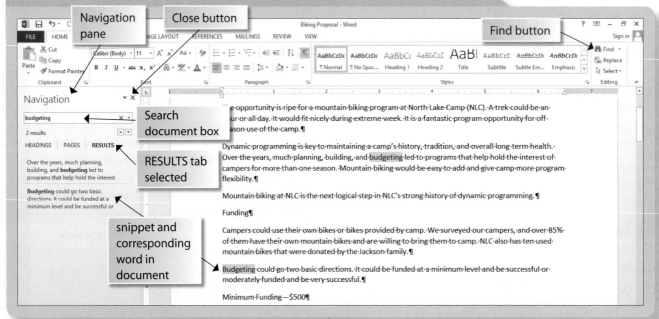

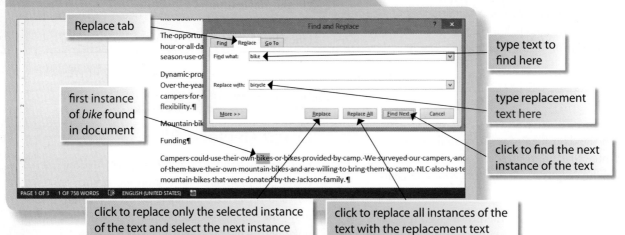

Exhibit 11-2 Replace tab in the Find and Replace dialog box

Begin Activity

Replace specific text.

1 Press the **Ctrl+Home keys**. The insertion point moves to the beginning of the document.

2 On the HOME tab, in the Editing group, click the **Replace button**. The Find and Replace dialog box opens, with the Replace tab selected. The Find what box contains the search text

> **Problem?** If the dialog box displays more options than the one shown in Exhibit 11-2, click Less in the dialog box to collapse it.

you had previously typed in the Search document box in the Navigation pane—*budgeting*.

3 Type **bike**. The selected text in the Find what box is replaced with the text you typed.

4 Click in the **Replace with box**, and then type **bicycle**.

5 Click **Find Next**. The dialog box stays open, and the next instance of *bike* is highlighted in the document. In this instance, the word found is actually *bikes*. Refer back to Exhibit 11-2.

6 In the dialog box, click **Replace**. The selected text in the document changes to *bicycle*, and the next instance of the text *bike* is selected.

7. In the dialog box, click **Replace All**. All instances of the word *bike* in the document are changed to *bicycle*. Another dialog box opens telling you that 11 replacements were made.

8. Click **OK**. The dialog box closes. The Find and Replace dialog box is still open.

9. Click **Close**. The Find and Replace dialog box closes.

10. Save the document.

End Activity

LEARN MORE

Narrowing a Search

You can customize a search to narrow the results. First, open the Find Options dialog box (shown below), and then select the ways you want to narrow the search. For example, you can select the Find whole words only check box to search for complete words, or you can select the Match case check box to find text with the same case (upper or lower) as the search text. To open the dialog box, you can click the Search for more things arrow ⬇ to the right of the Search document box in the Navigation Pane, and then click Options. These same options are also available on the Replace tab in the Find and Replace dialog box when you click the More button to display the Search Options section.

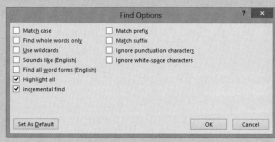

Find Options dialog box

11-2 Working with Styles

A **style** is a named set of formatting instructions, or definitions. All text has a style applied to it. Unless you change to a different style, text is formatted with the Normal style, which, as you have seen, is text formatted as 11-point Calibri in a left-aligned paragraph with line spacing set to 1.08 and 8 points of space after the paragraph.

The Normal style is part of the **Normal template**, which is the template on which all Word documents are based. In Chapter 10, you learned that a template is a file that contains formatting and usually sample content to guide you as you develop your own content. The Normal template does not contain any placeholder text or graphics, but it does include the Normal style and other built-in styles.

Using styles saves time and makes the elements in a document consistent. For example, if you want all the headings in a document to be bold, dark red, 14-point Cambria and centered, you could create a style named Heading that includes all those formatting instructions and apply it to every heading in the document. If you later decide the headings should be 16-point Arial on a shaded blue background, you simply change the style definition, which updates all text that has the Heading style applied to the new style. When you change the text or paragraph formatting of a single instance, such as by applying bold or changing the alignment, you are applying direct formatting. **Direct formatting** overrides the style currently applied, but it does not change the style definition.

There are five types of styles. A **paragraph style** formats an entire paragraph and can include both paragraph- and text-formatting instructions. The Heading style described in the previous paragraph would be a paragraph style. Another commonly used style type is the character style. **Character style** definitions include only text-formatting instructions. A third style type, the **linked style**, behaves as a paragraph or a character style depending on what is selected when you apply the style. If you select only a character or a few words, the style is applied as a character style, and any paragraph formatting included in the style definition is ignored. If you apply a linked style to a paragraph, it is treated as a paragraph style—in other words, it applies both

style A named set of formatting instructions.

Normal template The template on which all Word documents are based.

direct formatting Formatting that overrides the style currently applied.

paragraph style A style type that includes instructions for formatting text and paragraphs.

character style A style type that includes instructions for formatting only text.

linked style A style type that acts as a paragraph style if applied to a paragraph and as a character style if applied to text.

paragraph and text formatting. The other two style types are table and list styles, which are used to format, as the names indicate, tables and lists. Usually, you don't need to worry about identifying the type of a style. Just be sure to correctly select the text to which you want to apply the style.

Style definitions include more than text- and paragraph-formatting instructions and the style type. They also specify which style the style is based on—often the Normal style. Paragraph and linked style definitions also specify which style will be applied to the next paragraph created when you press the Enter key. For paragraphs formatted with the Normal style, the next paragraph created is also formatted with the Normal style. For some styles, such as a style that is intended to format headings, the style for the next paragraph is usually the Normal style or another style created for body text. That makes sense, because you typically want to format only a single paragraph with a heading style.

11-2a Applying a Quick Style

Word comes with many built-in styles. Each built-in style has a name that reflects its suggested use. For example, the Title style is intended for formatting the title at the beginning of a document, and the various Heading styles are intended to format different levels of headings.

The most commonly used styles are listed in the Styles gallery in the Styles group on the HOME tab. Styles that appear in the Styles gallery are called **Quick Styles**. In the Styles gallery, a paragraph symbol (¶) appears next to the names of the Quick Styles that are paragraph styles. Styles without the paragraph symbol next to their names are either character or linked styles.

To apply a Quick Style, select the text or paragraph to which you want to apply the style, and then click the Quick Style name in the Styles gallery. When you apply a style, that style is selected in the Styles gallery.

Quick Style A style that appears in a gallery.

In Exhibit 11-3, the Normal style in the Styles gallery has a blue border, indicating that it is selected; that is, it is the style applied to the currently selected text.

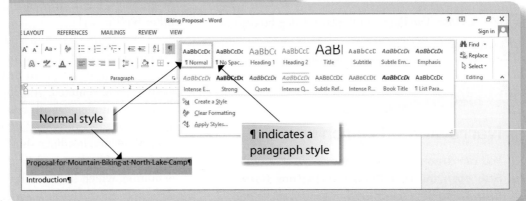

Exhibit 11-3 Quick Styles in the Styles gallery

When you create a new document, only two heading styles, Heading 1 and Heading 2, appear in the Styles gallery. If you apply the Heading 2 style to text, the Heading 3 style is added to the Styles gallery. As you apply each more subordinate heading style, the next level of heading style is added to the gallery.

Begin Activity

Apply Quick Styles.

1. Select the first paragraph in the document (the title line). On the HOME tab, in the Styles group, the Normal style—the default style—is selected.

2. On the HOME tab, in the Styles group, click the **More button**. The Styles gallery opens. Refer back to Exhibit 11-3.

3. Point to several of the styles in the gallery to see the Live Preview of those styles applied to the selected paragraph.

4. Click the **Title style**. The Title style is applied to the selected paragraph. It formats the text as 28-point Calibri Light (Headings) and formats the paragraph with 0 points of space before and after and single-spaced line spacing.

5. Select the **Introduction paragraph** (the second paragraph in the document).

6. In the Styles group, click the **Heading 1 style**. The Heading 1 style formats the selected paragraph as 16-point Calibri Light (Headings), changes the color of the text to Blue, Accent 1, Darker 25%,

removes the space after the paragraph, and changes the space before the paragraph to 12 points.

7 Select the **Funding paragraph** (the fifth paragraph below the title). In the Styles group, only two Heading styles—Heading 1 and Heading 2—are listed in the gallery.

Tip: To apply a style that does not appear in the Styles gallery, open the Styles pane by clicking the Dialog Box Launcher in the Styles group, and then click the style in the list.

8 In the Styles gallery, click the **Heading 2 style**. The selected text is formatted with the Heading 2 style, which is similar to the Heading 1 style, but the size of the text is 13 points and the space before the paragraph is only 2 points. Because you applied the Heading 2 style, the Heading 3 style is now listed in the gallery.

9 Apply Heading Quick Styles to the following paragraphs:

Minimum Funding—$500	Heading 3
Moderate Funding—$4,500	Heading 3
Program Description	Heading 1
Available Land	Heading 2
Possible Routes	Heading 2
North	Heading 3
South	Heading 3
East	Heading 3
West	Heading 3
Potential Issues	Heading 1
Questions	Heading 2
Conclusion	Heading 1

10 Select all of the text in the last paragraph in the Introduction section (starts with **Mountain biking is the…**).

11 In the Styles gallery, click the **More button** ⏷, and then click the **Emphasis style**. The selected text is formatted with the Emphasis style, which applies italic formatting to text. Exhibit 11-4 shows the three pages of the document with the title and heading styles applied.

End Activity

11-2b Modifying a Quick Style

If you want to change some parts of the definition of a Quick Style, you can modify it. To modify a Quick Style, first apply the Quick Style to text or a paragraph, and then change the text or paragraph using direct formatting. Next, right-click the Quick Style name in the Styles gallery, and then on the shortcut menu, click Update *Quick Style Name* to Match Selection (where *Quick Style Name* is the actual name of the style). Exhibit 11-5 shows the shortcut menu for the Heading 1 Quick Style.

Begin Activity

Modify a Quick Style.

1 Select the **Introduction heading paragraph**.

2 Increase the font size of the selected text to **18 points**, and then apply **bold** formatting to the selected text.

3 On the HOME tab, in the Styles group, click the **up scroll arrow** ⏶. The Styles gallery scrolls to display the first row of styles.

4 In the Styles gallery, right-click the selected **Heading 1 style**. A shortcut menu opens. Refer to Exhibit 11-5.

5 On the shortcut menu, click **Update Heading 1 to Match Selection**. The style is redefined to match the formatting changes you made to the Introduction heading, and all the headings with the Heading 1 style applied now match this style.

6 Scroll down to the bottom of page 1, and then click in the **Program Description heading paragraph**. This paragraph has the Heading 1 style applied to it. The changes you made to the style—changing the font size to 18 points and applying bold formatting—were made to this heading as well.

End Activity

FYI

Saving a Style to the Template

Changes to a style definition are saved only with the current document. To make the modified style available to all documents based on the current template (even if it is the Normal template), right-click the Quick Style name, and then click Modify on the shortcut menu to open the Modify Style dialog box. Click the New documents based on this template option button at the bottom of the dialog box, and then click OK.

Exhibit 11-4 Quick Styles applied to the title and headings

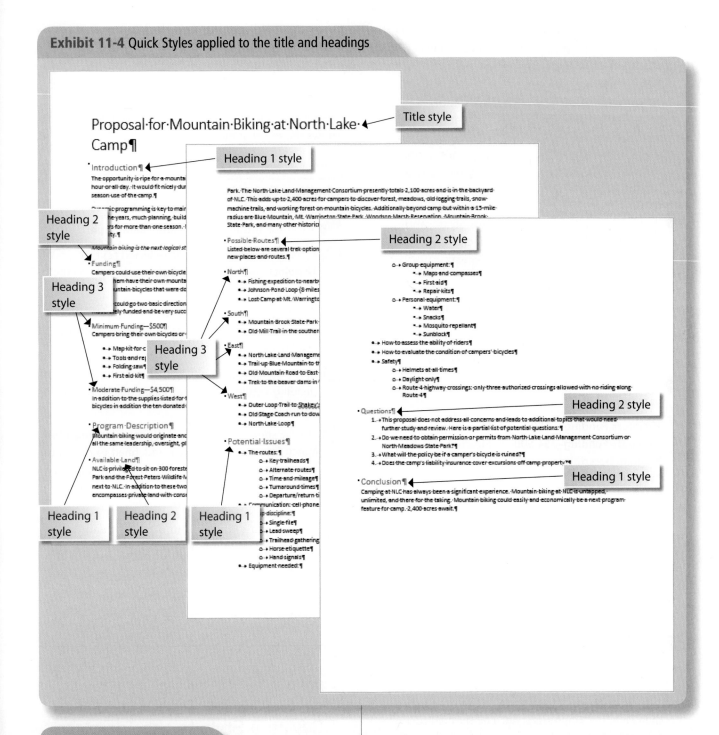

LEARN MORE

Heading Styles

The highest level heading style, Heading 1, is for major headings and applies the most noticeable formatting, with a larger font than the other heading styles. (In heading styles, the highest level has the lowest number.) The Heading 2 style is for headings subordinate to the highest level headings; it applies slightly less prominent formatting than the Heading 1 style. When you apply a heading style, the font labeled (Headings) in the Font list is applied to the text.

Heading 1
Heading 2
Heading 3

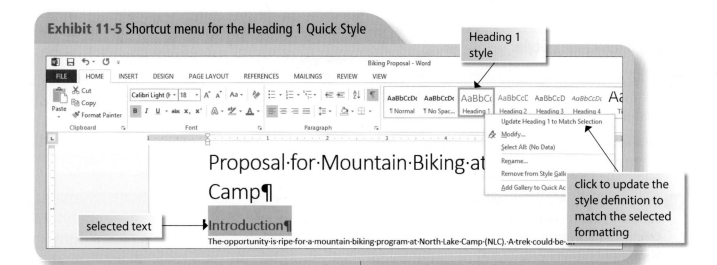

Heading 1 style

selected text

click to update the style definition to match the selected formatting

11-2c Creating a New Quick Style

You might need to create a new style for a document. The easiest way to create a new Quick Style is to format text in the way that you want, and then create the style based on the formatted text. To do this, select the formatted text, click the More button in the Styles group, and then click Create a Style to open the Create New Style from Formatting dialog box, which is shown in Exhibit 11-6. You can name and save the style from this dialog box.

New Quick Styles are created as linked styles. If you want to change the style to another type of style, in the Create New Style from Formatting dialog box, click Modify to open a larger version of the Create New Style from Formatting dialog box, which is shown in Exhibit 11-7. Click the Style type arrow, and then select the style type from the list.

Exhibit 11-6 Small Create New Style from Formatting dialog box

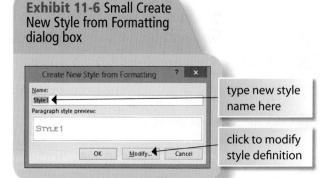

type new style name here

click to modify style definition

Exhibit 11-7 Large Create New Style from Formatting dialog box

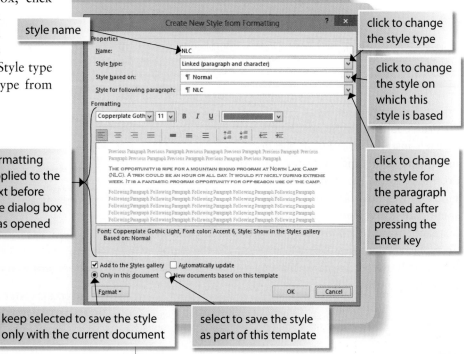

style name

click to change the style type

click to change the style on which this style is based

formatting applied to the text before the dialog box was opened

click to change the style for the paragraph created after pressing the Enter key

keep selected to save the style only with the current document

select to save the style as part of this template

Create a new Quick Style.

1 At the beginning of the document, in the first paragraph under the Introduction heading, select **NLC**.

2 Change the font of the selected text to **Copperplate Gothic Light**. Change the color to **Green, Accent 6, Darker 25%**.

3 In the Styles group, click the **More button** ⨪. Below the gallery, click **Create a Style**. A small Create New Style from Formatting dialog box opens with the temporary style name selected in the Name box. Refer back to Exhibit 11-6.

4 In the Name box, type **NLC**.

5 Click **Modify**. The larger Create New Style from Formatting dialog box opens. Refer back to Exhibit 11-7.

6 Click the **Style type arrow**, and then click **Character**.

7 Click **OK**. The dialog box closes, and the new Quick Style is added to the Styles gallery after the Normal style.

8 In the first paragraph under the Funding heading, select **NLC**.

9 In the Styles group, click the **NLC style**. The new style is applied to the selected text. See Exhibit 11-8.

You could apply the new NLC style to each instance of NLC in the document, one at a time. A faster way to do this is to use the Replace tab in the Find and Replace dialog box. This is the same dialog box you used when you replaced all the instances of the text *bike* with *bicycle* in the document. To replace formatting, click More to expand the dialog box, and then specify the formatting you want to use. See Exhibit 11-9.

Exhibit 11-8 Custom style applied to text

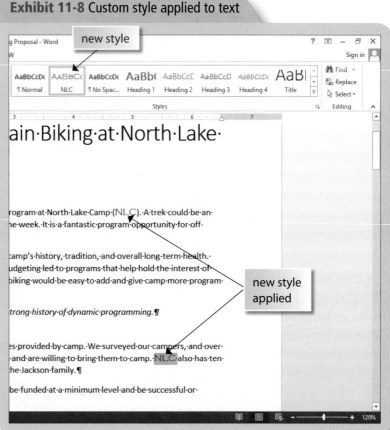

new style

new style applied

Exhibit 11-9 Expanded Find and Replace dialog box with style applied to replacement text

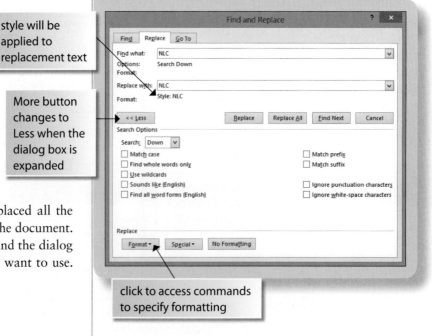

style will be applied to replacement text

More button changes to Less when the dialog box is expanded

click to access commands to specify formatting

Replace formatting.

1 In the Editing group, click the **Replace button**. The Find and Replace dialog box opens. Because *NLC* was selected before you opened the dialog box, *NLC* appears in the Find what box.

2 Click in the **Replace with box**, delete **bicycle** if necessary, and then type **NLC**.

3 At the bottom of the dialog box, click **More**. The dialog box expands to show additional options, and the More button you just clicked changes to Less.

4 With the insertion point in the Replace with box, click **Format** at the bottom of the dialog box. On the menu, click **Style**. The Replace Style dialog box opens.

5 In the list, select **NLC**, and then click **OK**. The Replace Style dialog box closes, and *Style: NLC* appears under the Replace with box. Refer back to Exhibit 11-9.

6 Click **Replace All**. A dialog box opens telling you that 10 replacements were made.

7 Click **OK** in the dialog box that tells you that 10 replacements were made. All instances of *NLC* formatted with the Normal style are replaced with *NLC* formatted with the NLC style.

> **Problem?** If the dialog box that opens tells you that fewer replacements were made and asks if you want to continue searching from the beginning, click **Yes**, and then continue with Step 7.

8 In the Find and Replace dialog box, click **Close**.

11-3 Working with Themes

You can alter the look of the document by changing the document's theme. A **theme** is a coordinated set of colors, fonts, and effects. Created by professional designers, themes ensure that a document has a polished, coherent look. Twenty-one themes are included

FYI

Modifying the Style Based On and Style for Following Paragraph Settings

Part of a style definition is the style on which the style is based. When you create a new style based on the formatting of selected text, the new style retains a connection to the original style. If you modify the original style, these changes will also be applied to the new style. For example, suppose you need to create a new style that will be used exclusively for formatting the heading *Budget* in all reports. You could start by selecting text formatted with the Heading 1 style, change the font color of the selected text to purple, and then save the formatting of the selected text as a new style named Budget. If you then modify the Heading 1 style—perhaps by adding italics—the text in the document that is formatted with the Budget style will also have italics, because it is based on the Heading 1 style. This connection between a new style and the style on which it is based enforces a consistent look among styles, helping to create a document with a coherent design. If, on the other hand, you don't want the new style to change when the style it is based on changes, open the larger Create from New Style Formatting dialog box, click the Style based on arrow, and then click Normal or (no style).

When you create a new paragraph or linked style, the style for the next paragraph created when you press the Enter key is that new style. To change this, open the larger version of the Create New Style from Formatting dialog box, as described above, click the Style for following paragraph arrow, and then select the style you want.

in Office, and many more are available in the templates stored on Office.com. The default theme for new documents is the Office theme.

Every theme assigns one font to headings and one to body text. These two theme fonts are always listed at the top of the Fonts menu with the labels *(Headings)* and *(Body)*. You have already seen this when you opened the Fonts menu to apply a different font to text and

> **theme** A coordinated set of colors, fonts, and effects.

when you examined the fonts applied to documents. Some themes use one font for headings and another for body text; other themes use the same font for both elements. In the Office theme, the heading font is Calibri Light, and the body font is Calibri. If you change the theme, the theme fonts in the Font list change to match the fonts for the new theme.

This is the Office theme's heading font, Calibri Light.
This is the Office theme's body font, Calibri.
This is the Wood Type theme's heading font, Rockwell Condensed.
This is the Wood Type theme's body font, Rockwell.

When you type text in a new document, the text is formatted with the body text font. If you change the theme, text formatted with the theme fonts changes to the new theme's fonts. Text formatted with a non-theme font will not change.

Each theme also has a color palette. You saw the colors associated with the Office theme when you changed the color of text and the color of paragraph borders and shading. The Theme Colors are the coordinated colors of the current theme. This set of colors changes from theme to theme. Exhibit 11-10 shows the color palettes for the Office, Banded, and Wood Type themes. If you change the theme, text or objects formatted with a theme color will change based on the new theme's color palette. Text or objects formatted with one of the Standard Colors, or another color you select after clicking More Colors, will not change.

The Theme Colors are coordinated to look good together, so if you are going to use multiple colors in a document (perhaps for paragraph shading and font color), it's a good idea to stick with the Theme Colors.

11-3a Changing the Theme

You change the theme using the Themes gallery, which you open by clicking the Themes button in the Themes group on the DESIGN tab. See Exhibit 11-11. Select the theme you want in the gallery. The new theme is applied to the entire document, and the colors and fonts change to match the colors and fonts of the new theme.

Begin Activity

Change the document's theme.

1 Scroll to the beginning of the document so that you can see the second line of the first paragraph formatted with the Title style, the Introduction heading formatted with the Heading 1 style, the Funding heading formatted with the Heading 2 style, and the Minimum Funding—$500 paragraph formatted with the Heading 3 style.

2 Select the **Minimum Funding—$500 heading**. On the HOME tab, in the Font group, click the **Font Color button arrow**. The color selected in the color palette is in the fifth column, last row in the theme colors. This is the Accent 1 color, the Darker 50% shade.

3 Press the **Esc key** to close the palette. On the ribbon, click the **DESIGN tab**. In the Document Formatting group, point to the **Themes button**. The ScreenTip indicates that Office is the current theme.

Exhibit 11-10 Theme color palettes

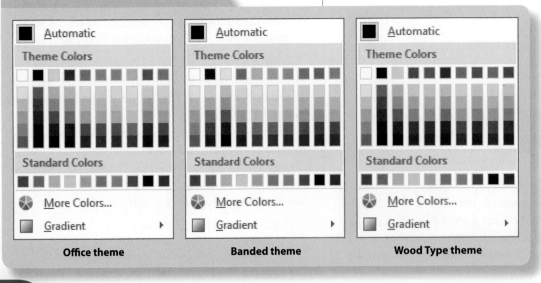

Office theme　　Banded theme　　Wood Type theme

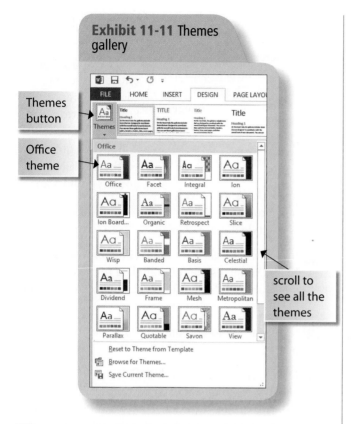

Exhibit 11-11 Themes gallery

Themes button

Office theme

scroll to see all the themes

retained. Text formatted with the NLC style is now gray because you used a theme color in the style definition. You can see the revised NLC style in the paragraphs under the Introduction and Funding headings.

Tip: To create a style that uses a theme font that doesn't change if the theme is changed, use the font in the alphabetical list rather than the theme fonts at the top of the Fonts list.

11 In the first line under the Introduction heading, select **NLC**. In the Font group, click the **Font Color button arrow** 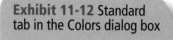. The selected color is in the same position in the palette as the theme color you selected when you created the style; but now it is a shade of gray, not green. (The font is unchanged because you did not select the theme font when you created the style.)

12 At the bottom of the color palette, click **More Colors**. The Colors dialog box opens with the Custom tab selected.

13 Click the **Standard tab**, and then click the same **dark green color** that is selected in Exhibit 11-12.

4 Click the **Themes button**. The Themes gallery opens. Refer back to Exhibit 11-11.

5 In the gallery, point to the **Facet theme** to see a Live Preview in the document. The fonts in the document change, and the color of the text formatted with the Heading styles changes.

6 Point to several other themes, and then click the **Basis theme**. The fonts and colors in the document change to those used in the Basis theme.

7 On the ribbon, click the **HOME tab**. In the Font group, click the **Font box arrow** Calibri (Body). The Font gallery opens. The font for both headings and body text is Corbel.

8 Press the **Esc key** to close the Font list. Select the **Minimum Funding—$500 heading**, if necessary.

9 In the Font group, click the **Font Color button arrow** A . The color palette opens. The Theme Colors in the palette are the Basis theme colors. The selected color for the Introduction heading is still in the fifth column, last row of the theme colors. This is still the Accent 1, Darker 50% color.

10 Press the **Esc key** to close the color palette, and then scroll through the document. The changes you made to the Heading 1 style definition are

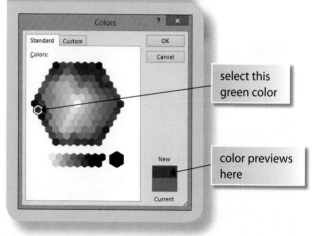

Exhibit 11-12 Standard tab in the Colors dialog box

select this green color

color previews here

14 Click **OK**. The selected text is reformatted with the dark green color.

15 In the Styles group, right-click the **NLC style**, and then click **Update NLC to Match Selection**. The style definition is updated. All the text with that style applied changes color to match the new definition.

16 In the Font group, click the **Font Color button arrow** 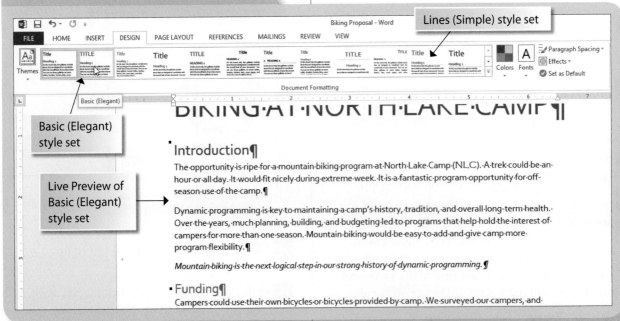. The custom color you selected appears in a new Recent Colors row below the Standard Colors row.

17 Press the **Esc key** to close the color palette.

End Activity

11-3b Changing the Style Set

A **style set** is a set of Quick Styles. If you change the style set, the Quick Style definitions are changed. Because you are changing the style definitions, any changes you made to a Quick Style will not be retained. Also, any custom styles you create will not be redefined. You can change the style set before or after you apply styles. Exhibit 11-13 shows the Live Preview of the Basic (Elegant) style set applied to the Biking Proposal document.

Begin Activity

Change the Style Set.

1 On the ribbon, click the **DESIGN tab**. In the Document Formatting group, point to the **first style set** in the gallery. This is always the current style set.

2 Point to the **second style set** in the gallery. Its ScreenTip identifies it as the Basic (Elegant) style set. The Live Preview shows the changes to the titles and headings. The paragraphs formatted with the Heading 1 style are no longer bold and text formatted with the NLC style did not change. Refer to Exhibit 11-13.

> **Tip:** To change the paragraph and line spacing of the entire document, click the Paragraph Spacing button in the Document Formatting group on the DESIGN tab, and then select an option.

3 In the gallery, click the **Lines (Simple) style set**. The Lines (Simple) style set is applied to the document, and all the text formatted with the Title and Headings styles changes.

4 Select the **Minimum Funding—$500 heading**, if necessary.

5 On the ribbon, click the **HOME tab**. In the Font group, click the **Font Color button arrow** 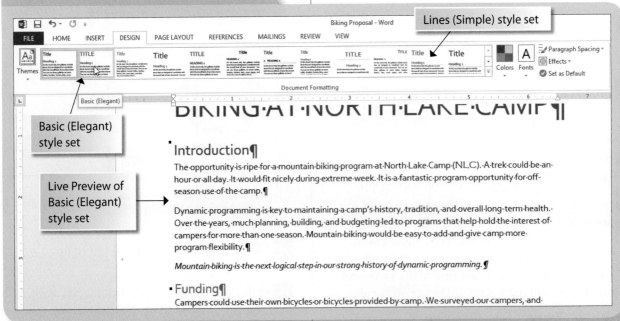. The color palette hasn't changed—it's still the Banded theme color palette—but the selected color for the heading is in a different position in the palette—it's now the Text 1, Lighter 25% color.

End Activity

Exhibit 11-13 Style sets on the DESIGN tab

style set A group of Quick Styles.

Customizing the Normal Template

The combination of themes and style sets provides an almost dizzying number of choices. You can select a theme; change the theme fonts, colors, or effects; change the style set; change the paragraph and line spacing; and redefine or create new styles to create a document quickly formatted with a distinctive look. If you come up with a combination you want to save and use when you create new documents—in other words, if you want to save changes to the Normal template—click the Set as Default button in the Document Formatting group on the DESIGN tab.

11-3c Modifying a Theme

Once you have chosen a theme and a style set, you can change any of the elements that make up the theme, including the color palette, the theme fonts, the style of the effects, and the default paragraph spacing. To change the theme fonts, you select from font sets on the Fonts button menu in the Document Formatting group on the DESIGN tab. To change the theme colors, select from the palettes in the Document Formatting group. See Exhibits 11-14 and 11-15.

Exhibit 11-14 Fonts button menu

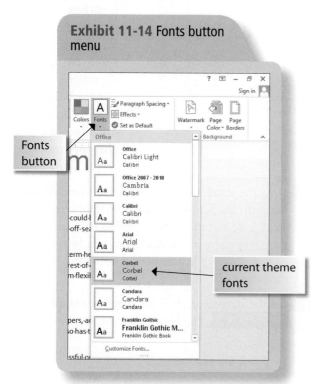

Fonts button

current theme fonts

Exhibit 11-15 Colors button menu

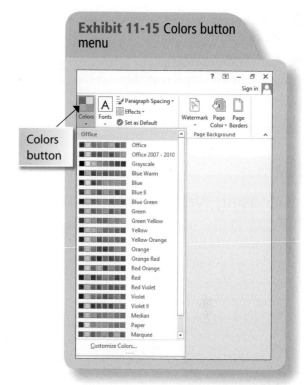

Colors button

Begin Activity

Modify the theme fonts and colors.

1 On the ribbon, click the **DESIGN tab**. In the Document Formatting group, click the **Fonts button**. The Fonts menu opens, listing sets of coordinated fonts for headings and body text. The Corbel font set is shaded blue to indicate that it is the current font set. Refer back to Exhibit 11-14.

> **Problem?** If the Corbel font set is not shaded blue, don't worry about it.

2 Point to several of the font sets to see the Live Preview.

3 Scroll down, and then click the **Century Gothic–Palatino Linotype font set**. Those fonts (Century Gothic for the headings and Palatino Linotype for the body text) are applied to the document.

4 In the Document Formatting group, click the **Colors button**. Refer back to Exhibit 11-15. Scroll down the list to see that none of these palettes is selected. The palettes in the list are provided in addition to the palettes used by the themes. The only theme palette that appears in this gallery is the Office theme color palette. (To use the color palettes of any of the other themes, you need to apply that theme.)

5 Point to several of the palettes to see the Live Preview.

6 Click the **Green color palette**. The elements in the document formatted with theme colors change to the corresponding theme colors of the Green color palette.

End Activity

Creating New Theme Fonts and Colors

If none of the theme font sets suits your needs, you can select the theme fonts you want. Click the Customize Fonts command on the Fonts button menu in the Document Formatting group on the DESIGN tab. In the Create New Theme Fonts dialog box, select a heading and a body text font, and type a name for the new theme font set in the Name box. Click Save.

You can also customize theme colors. Click the Customize Colors command on the Colors button menu in the Document Formatting group on the DESIGN tab. In the Create New Theme Colors dialog box, select a color for each theme element listed, and then type a name for the new color set in the Name box. Click Save.

In both cases, the new, custom font set and theme color set will be listed at the top of their respective menus.

Create New Theme Fonts dialog box

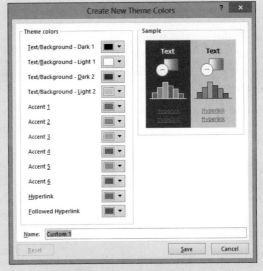

Create New Theme Colors dialog box

11-4 Scrolling Through a Long Document

One way to move among the pages in a multiple-page document is to drag the scroll box in the vertical scroll bar. As you drag, a ScreenTip appears, identifying the current page number. If paragraphs are formatted with the built-in heading styles, the first heading on the page also appears in the ScreenTip. (Pressing the Page Up and Page Down keys scrolls the document one screen at a time unless the document is displayed at One Page zoom.)

Another way to move to another page in the document is to use the PAGES tab in the Navigation pane. To open the Navigation pane, you can click the page count indicator button at the left end of the status bar; you can select the Navigation pane check box in the Show group on the VIEW tab; or you can click the Find button in the Editing group on the HOME tab. After you open the Navigation pane, you need to click the PAGES tab to see thumbnails of the pages in the document in a scrollable list. See Exhibit 11-16. You click a thumbnail to instantly move to that page in the document.

Begin Activity

View different pages in a multiple-page document.

1 In the vertical scroll bar, point to the **scroll box**, and then press and hold the mouse button. A ScreenTip appears identifying the page as page 1. The first heading on the page, *Introduction*, also appears in the ScreenTip.

2 Drag the **scroll box** slowly down the vertical scroll bar until the ScreenTip identifies the current page as page 3, and then release the mouse button. Page 3 appears in the document window, and the page number indicator on the status bar identifies the page as Page 3 of 3.

3 On the status bar, click the **page count indicator** PAGE 3 OF 3. The Navigation pane opens.

Exhibit 11-16
PAGES tab in the
Navigation pane

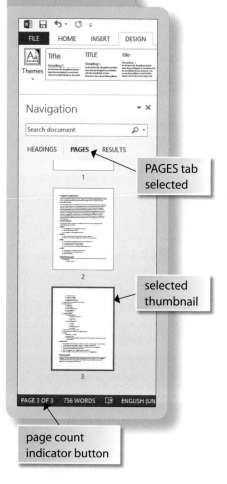

PAGES tab
selected

selected
thumbnail

page count
indicator button

Document Statistics

The word count indicator, which lists the number of words in the document, is located next to the page count indicator on the status bar. When text is selected, the number of words in the selection is identified followed by the total number of words, such as 57 OF 756 WORDS. To see more statistics, click the word count indicator or click the Word Count button in the Proofing group on the REVIEW tab to open the Word Count dialog box. The Word Count dialog box lists the number of pages, words, characters with and without spaces, paragraphs, and lines in the document or selected text.

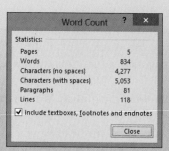

Word Count dialog box

11-5 Working with the Document Outline

Reviewing a document's outline can help you manage a document's overall organization. It lets you see, at a glance, the hierarchy of the document headings. Paragraphs formatted with the Heading 1 style are the highest level headings. Paragraphs formatted with the Heading 2 style are subordinate to Heading 1 paragraphs. In an outline, subordinate headings—or subheadings—are indented below the Heading 1 paragraphs. Each successive level of heading styles (Heading 3, Heading 4, and so on) is indented farther to the right.

When you work with an outline, you can move topics to other locations in the outline, or you can change the level of headings. Moving a heading to a higher level in the outline—for example, changing a Heading 2 paragraph into a Heading 1 paragraph—is called **promoting** the heading. Moving an item lower in the outline is called **demoting** the heading. If you used the built-in heading styles to format the headings in your document, when you promote or demote a heading, the next higher or lower level of heading style is automatically applied to the paragraph.

There are two ways to work with a document outline: in the Navigation pane and in Outline view.

4 In the Navigation pane, click the **PAGES tab**, if necessary. Thumbnails of the pages in the document appear in the Navigation pane. The blue border around the page 3 thumbnail indicates it is the current page. Refer back to Exhibit 11-16.

5 Point to the Navigation pane. A vertical scroll bar appears.

6 In the Navigation pane, scroll to the top of the list, and then click the **page 1 thumbnail**. The document scrolls to page 1.

7 At the top of the Navigation pane, click the **Close button** ⊠. The Navigation pane closes.

End Activity

promote To move an item to a higher level in an outline.

demote To move an item to a lower level in an outline.

11-5a Using the Navigation Pane

To work with a document outline, you use the HEADINGS tab in the Navigation pane. When you click a heading in the Navigation pane, the document scrolls to display that heading at the top of the document window. You can also promote and demote headings in the Navigation pane. When you change the level of a heading, subheadings are promoted or demoted one level as well. Headings with subheadings have either a Collapse arrow ◢ or an Expand arrow ▷ next to them in the Navigation pane. You can also drag a heading up or down in the Navigation pane to position it in a new location in the outline. When you do this, any subheadings and body text under the heading move to the new location with the heading you drag. See Exhibit 11-17.

Exhibit 11-17 HEADINGS tab in the Navigation pane while moving a heading

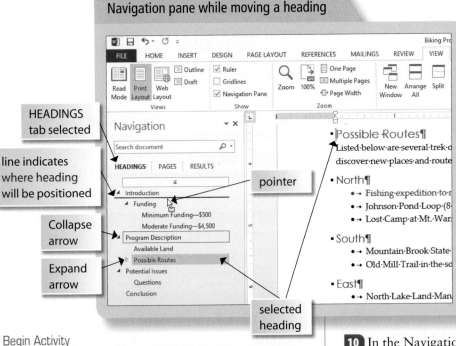

HEADINGS tab selected

line indicates where heading will be positioned

pointer

Collapse arrow

Expand arrow

selected heading

Begin Activity

Change the outline in the Navigation pane.

1 On the ribbon, click the **VIEW tab**. In the Show group, click the **Navigation Pane check box**. The Navigation pane opens.

2 At the top of the Navigation pane, click the **HEADINGS tab**. The document headings are displayed in the Navigation pane.

3 In the Navigation pane, click the **Possible Routes heading**. The document scrolls to display that heading at the top of the document window with the insertion point at the beginning of the heading.

4 In the Navigation pane, next to the Possible Routes heading, click the **Collapse arrow** ◢. The headings formatted as Heading 3 headings under the Possible Routes heading disappear, and the arrow next to the Possible Routes heading changes to an Expand arrow ▷.

5 In the Navigation pane, point to the **Program Description heading**. A box appears around the heading.

6 Drag the **Program Description heading** up, but do not release the mouse button. As you drag the heading, the pointer changes to ▨, which is the same pointer you saw when you used the drag-and-drop technique, and a horizontal line appears indicating the position of the heading when you release the mouse button. Refer to Exhibit 11-17.

7 When the horizontal line is positioned above *Funding* and below *Introduction*, as shown in Exhibit 11-17, release the mouse button. The Program Description heading and all the subheadings under it are moved to the new position in the document.

8 In the Navigation pane, click the **Questions heading**.

9 On the ribbon, click the **HOME tab**. In the Styles group, the Heading 2 style is selected.

10 In the Navigation pane, right-click the **Questions heading**. On the shortcut menu, click **Promote**. The heading moves to the left in the Navigation pane so it aligns below the other headings formatted with the Heading 1 style. In the Styles group on the HOME tab, the style applied to this heading is now Heading 1.

11 In the Navigation pane, click the **Close button** ✕ to close it.

End Activity

11-5b Using Outline View

Outline view displays the various heading levels in a document as an outline in the document window instead of in a pane. If you create an outline in Outline view, the built-in heading styles are applied automatically. Working with the outline in Outline view is similar to viewing the structure of a document in the Navigation pane. However, in Outline view, you can see the body text below the headings if you want.

In Outline view, outline symbols appear to the left of each paragraph. See Exhibit 11-18. The plus sign symbol ⊕ appears next to headings that have subheadings or body text below the heading. The minus sign symbol ⊖ appears next to headings that do not have any subordinate text. A small gray circle ◎ next to a paragraph indicates the text is body text and not a heading. A horizontal line below a heading indicates that there is body text below that heading.

Exhibit 11-18 Outline view with three levels of headings displayed

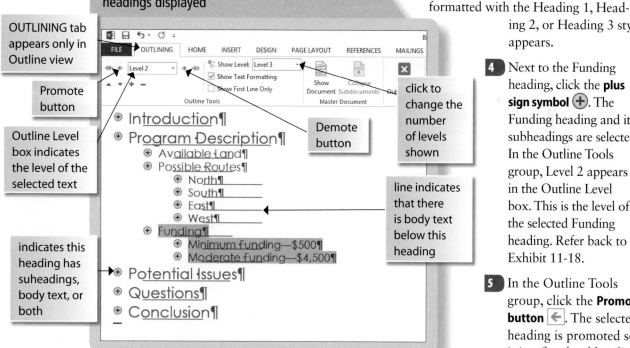

When you click the outline symbol next to a heading, you select the heading and all of its subordinate text, or a section. To move a section after you select it, you can drag it or click the Move Up or Move Down button in the Outline Tools group on the OUTLINING tab, which is visible only in Outline view. You can also use buttons on the OUTLINING tab to promote or demote headings or to demote text from a heading to body text.

Begin Activity

Change the outline in Outline view.

1 On the ribbon, click the **VIEW tab**. In the Views group, click the **Outline button**. The document switches to Outline view, and a new tab, OUTLINING, appears on the ribbon and is the active tab.

2 If necessary, change the zoom level to **120%** to match the figures in this section.

3 On the OUTLINING tab, in the Outline Tools group, click the **Show Level box arrow**, and then click **Level 3**. Scroll to the top of the window. Now only text formatted with the Heading 1, Heading 2, or Heading 3 style appears.

Tip: If the formatting applied to headings makes the text difficult to read in Outline view, click the Show Text Formatting check box in the Outline Tools group on the OUTLINING tab to deselect it and show all the text as black.

4 Next to the Funding heading, click the **plus sign symbol** ⊕. The Funding heading and its subheadings are selected. In the Outline Tools group, Level 2 appears in the Outline Level box. This is the level of the selected Funding heading. Refer back to Exhibit 11-18.

5 In the Outline Tools group, click the **Promote button** ←. The selected heading is promoted so it is a first-level heading, and its subheadings are promoted to second-level headings. In the Outline Tools group, Level 1 now appears in the Outline Level box.

6 Next to the Funding heading, point to the **plus sign symbol** ⊕, press and hold the mouse button, and then drag down, but do not release the mouse button. As you drag, a horizontal line appears, indicating the position of the heading, and the pointer changes to ↕.

Tip: You can also click the Move Up button ▲ and the Move Down button ▼ in the Outline Tools group to move paragraphs in an outline.

7 When the horizontal line is above the Questions heading, release the mouse button. The Funding heading and its subheads move to just above the Questions heading. See Exhibit 11-19.

8 On the OUTLINING tab, in the Close group, click the **Close Outline View button** to close Outline view.

End Activity

11-6 Changing the Margins

Margins are the blank areas at the top, bottom, left, and right sides of the page between the text and the edge of the page. The default settings for documents are one-inch margins on all sides. See Exhibit 11-20. This is fine for most documents. But sometimes you might want to change the margins. For example, you might want to provide additional space to allow readers to take notes. To change the margins, click the Margins button in the Page Setup group on the PAGE LAYOUT tab to display the menu, as shown in Exhibit 11-21. You can choose from the predefined margins on the menu, or you can click the Custom Margins command to open the Margins tab in the Page Setup dialog box to select your own settings. See Exhibit 11-22. After you create custom margin settings, the most recent set appears as an option at the top of the menu.

Exhibit 11-19 Final outline of Biking Proposal document

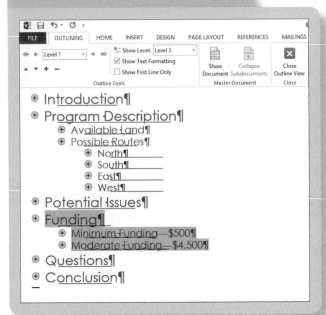

Exhibit 11-20 One-inch margins in document

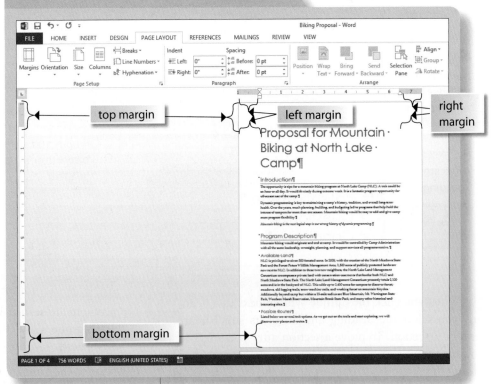

margin The blank area above or below text, or to the left or right of text between the text and the edge of the page.

Change the page margins.

1 Press the **Ctrl+Home keys** to move the insertion point to the beginning of the document.

2 On the ribbon, click the **VIEW tab**. In the Zoom group, click the **One Page button**. The current page of the document, page 1, appears completely in the Word window, and you can easily see the margins. Refer back to Exhibit 11-20.

3 On the ribbon, click the **PAGE LAYOUT tab**. In the Page Setup group, click the **Margins button**. The Margins menu opens. Refer back to Exhibit 11-21.

4 Click **Wide**. The menu closes, and the margins in the document are changed to the Wide setting, which keeps the one-inch margin at the top and bottom but changes both the left and right margins to two inches.

5 In the Page Setup group, click the **Margins button**. At the bottom of the menu, click **Custom Margins**. The Page Setup dialog box opens with the Margins tab selected. Refer back to Exhibit 11-22. The current margin settings are displayed in the boxes in the Margins section at the top of the Margins tab. The value in the Top box is selected.

6 Press the **Tab key** twice to select the value in the **Left box**, and then type **1.5**.

7 In the Right box, click the **down arrow** five times to change the value to 1.5".

8 Click **OK**. The margins are changed to the custom settings.

9 Change the zoom level back to **120%**.

End Activity

FYI

Working with Custom Margins

If you need to use a specific custom margin for all your documents, on the Margins tab of the Page Setup dialog box, click the Set As Default button. Keep in mind that most printers cannot print to the edge of the page. If you create custom margins that are too narrow for your printer, a dialog box opens warning you of this and advising you to change the margin settings.

Exhibit 11-21
Margins menu

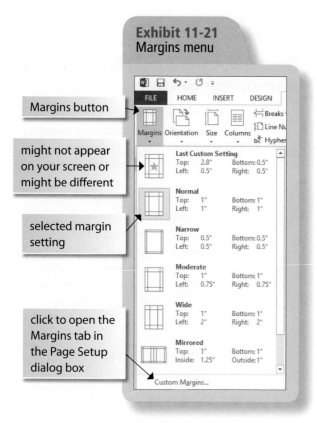

- Margins button
- might not appear on your screen or might be different
- selected margin setting
- click to open the Margins tab in the Page Setup dialog box

Exhibit 11-22 Page Setup dialog box with the Margins tab selected

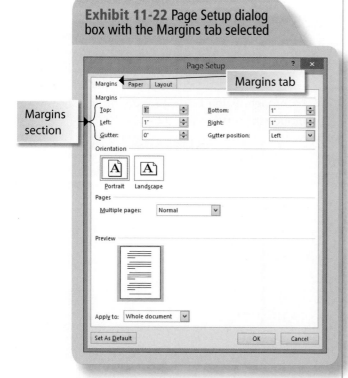

- Margins section
- Margins tab

11-7 Inserting a Manual Page Break

As you add text to a document, **automatic page breaks** (sometimes called **soft page breaks**) are inserted. You can create a new page manually by inserting a **manual page break** (sometimes called a **hard page break**). To insert a manual page break, use the Page Break button in the Pages group on the INSERT tab. When nonprinting characters are displayed, manual page breaks appear as a dotted line with the words *Page Break* in the center of the line. See Exhibit 11-23.

Exhibit 11-23 Manual page break in document

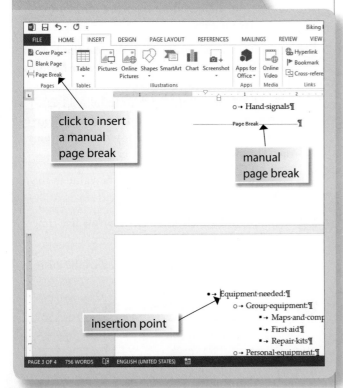

click to insert a manual page break

manual page break

insertion point

automatic page break (soft page break) A page break that is created when content fills a page and a new page is created automatically.

manual page break (hard page break) A page break that you insert to force content after the break to appear on a new page.

widow The last line of a paragraph that appears by itself at the top of a page.

orphan The first line of a paragraph left at the bottom of a page before the page break.

LEARN MORE

Controlling Page Breaks with Paragraph Settings

When you apply a built-in heading style to a paragraph, you also apply settings that prevent awkward page breaks. One of these settings is widow and orphan control. A **widow** is the last line of a paragraph that appears by itself left at the top of a page, and an **orphan** is the first line of a paragraph left at the bottom of a page before the page break. You also apply "Keep" settings. When the Keep with next setting is applied to a paragraph, the paragraph never appears at the bottom of a page. It is connected to the next paragraph, and the page will break before the paragraph with the Keep with next setting. The Keep lines together setting doesn't allow a soft page break to appear within the paragraph. And the Page break before setting inserts a soft page break before the paragraph. Unfortunately, when you change style sets, these settings are not always retained with the Heading style definitions. To adjust these settings, right-click the Quick Style in the Styles gallery, and then click Modify to open the Modify Style dialog box. At the bottom of the dialog box, click Format, and then click Paragraph to open the Paragraph dialog box. Click the Line and Page Breaks tab, and then click the desired check boxes in the Pagination section. Click OK in both open dialog boxes to redefine the style to include the settings you chose.

Line and Page Breaks tab in the Paragraph dialog box

To insert a manual page break.

1 Scroll so that you can see the bottom of page 2 and the top of page 3, and then click before the word *Equipment* in the bulleted item *Equipment needed*.

2 On the ribbon, click the **INSERT tab**. In the Pages group, click the **Page Break button**. A manual page break is inserted before the insertion point, and the Equipment needed bulleted item moves to the top of the next page. Refer back to Exhibit 11-23.

11-8 Adding Page Numbers, Headers, and Footers

To add page numbers in a document, you use a page number field. A **field** is a placeholder for variable information that includes an instruction to insert the specific information. A page number field inserts the correct page number on each page. Usually, page numbers appear in the top or bottom margin. You can also insert page numbers in the side margins; although for business or academic documents, it's customary to place them at the top or bottom of a document.

When you insert a page number field, the document switches to Header and Footer view. A **header** is text that appears at the top of every page in a document; a **footer** is text that appears at the bottom of every page. In this book, the chapter number and title appear in the footer. In Header and Footer view,

the body of the document is dimmed, indicating that it cannot be edited, and you can type only in the header or footer area.

11-8a Inserting Page Numbers

To add page numbers to a document, click the Page Number button in the Header & Footer group on the INSERT tab. On the menu that opens, point to the position on the page where you want to insert the page number to open a menu of page number styles. See Exhibit 11-24. You can choose to insert the page number in the header or footer area, in the left or right margin, or at the current position of the insertion point.

Add page numbers.

1 If necessary, click anywhere on page 3 to position the insertion point.

Exhibit 11-24 Gallery of page number styles

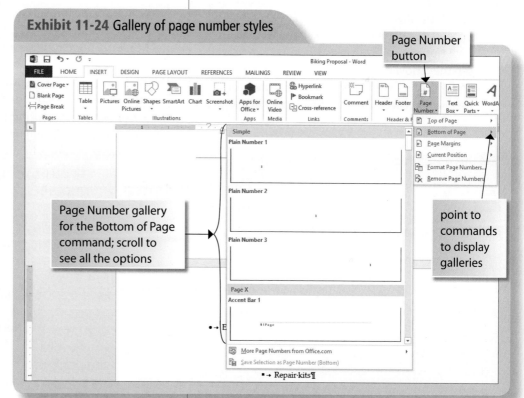

field In Word, a placeholder for variable information that includes an instruction to insert the specific information.

header Text that appears at the top of every page.

footer Text that appears at the bottom of every page.

2 On the ribbon, click the **INSERT tab**, if necessary. In the Header & Footer group, click the **Page Number button** to open the Page Number menu.

Tip: To remove page numbers from a document, click the Remove Page Numbers command on the Page Number button menu.

3 Point to **Bottom of Page**. A gallery of page number styles opens. Refer back to Exhibit 11-24.

4 Scroll down and examine the styles of page number that you can insert.

5 Scroll back to the top of the list, and then click the **Plain Number 3 style**. The document switches to Header and Footer view, and the page number for the current page (page 3) appears right-aligned in the footer area. The page number has a gray background, indicating that it is a field and not simply a number that you typed. (The field might not be shaded on your screen.) The HEADER & FOOTER TOOLS DESIGN tab appears on the ribbon.

Problem? If you see {PAGE * MERGEFORMAT} instead of a page number, click the **FILE tab**, click **Options**, click **Advanced**, scroll down to see the "Show document content" section, and then click the **Show field codes instead of their values check box** to deselect it. Click **OK**.

6 If necessary, click the **HEADER & FOOTER TOOLS DESIGN tab** to make it the active tab. See Exhibit 11-25.

7 On the HEADER & FOOTER TOOLS DESIGN tab, in the Close group, click the **Close Header and Footer button**. Header and Footer view closes, and the HEADER & FOOTER TOOLS DESIGN tab no longer appears on the ribbon.

End Activity

Format page numbers

To change the numbering style for a page number or to specify a number to use as the first page number, click the Page Number button in the Header & Footer group on the HEADER & FOOTER TOOLS DESIGN tab, and then click Format Page Numbers.

11-8b Adding a Header and Footer

You can insert a simple header or footer in Header and Footer view, which you switch to by double-clicking in the header or footer area, or by clicking the Header or Footer button in the Header & Footer group on the INSERT tab and clicking Edit Header or Edit Footer. You then type the header or footer text directly in the header or footer area, formatting the text as you would any other text in a document. You can also insert a formatted header or footer by using the Header and Footer buttons in the Header & Footer group on the INSERT tab or on the HEADER & FOOTER TOOLS DESIGN tab, and then click a style in the gallery of headers and footers that opens.

Many of the styles in the Header

Exhibit 11-25 Page number inserted in footer

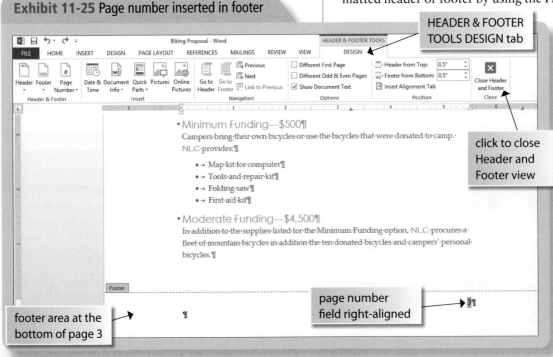

HEADER & FOOTER TOOLS DESIGN tab

click to close Header and Footer view

footer area at the bottom of page 3

page number field right-aligned

and Footer galleries include page numbers and graphic elements such as horizontal lines or shaded boxes. Some also include content controls. A **content control** is a placeholder for text you insert; it can store a specific type of text, such as a date or a document property. A **property** is identifying information about a file that is saved with the file, such as the author's name and the date the file was created. Information entered in a content control associated with a property will appear in any other content control that is associated with that property. For example, if you enter the company name in a Company content control in the header, and the Company content control also appears in the footer, the company name that you typed in the header will appear automatically in the footer. Some content controls are associated with properties that appear automatically in the content control. For example, the registered user's name is saved as the document author property every time you create a document, so that name will appear in a content control that displays the author name.

Most of the content controls that appear in headers and footers are text placeholders. You click the text placeholder once to make it active, and then type the text to replace the placeholder. Date content controls are formatted so that you can click an arrow to display a calendar and then select a date from the calendar. You can delete a content control that you don't want to use.

Headers and footers have a Center Tab stop at the 3.25-inch mark and a Right Tab stop at the 6.5-inch mark. These tab stops center and right-align text based on the Normal margins. If you change the margin settings, consider changing the tab settings to better align the header or footer text. If the Right Tab stop is outside of the right margin, the second tab stop is at the right margin instead of at 6.5-inch mark.

When a header or footer area is active, the HEADER & FOOTER TOOLS DESIGN tab is available on the ribbon, and tabs identifying the header and footer areas appear in the left margin. Exhibit 11-26 shows a header with content controls and a footer with a page number.

Exhibit 11-26 Footer and header in document

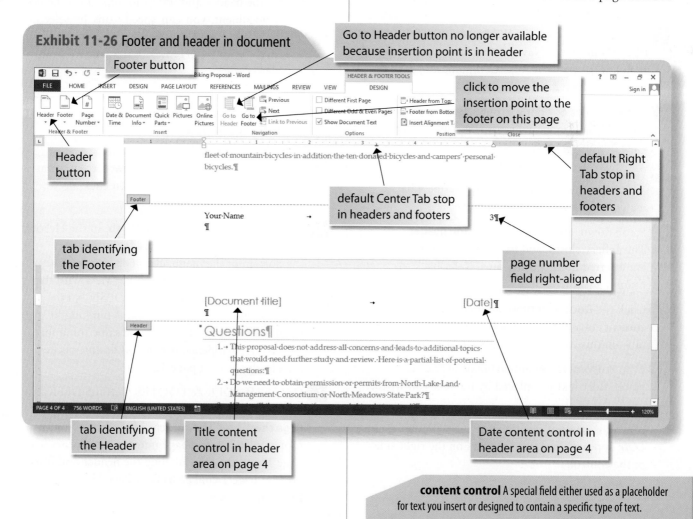

content control A special field either used as a placeholder for text you insert or designed to contain a specific type of text.

property Identifying information about a file that is saved with the file.

Create a footer.

1 On page 2, double-click in the **footer area**. The document switches to Header and Footer view, and the HEADER & FOOTER TOOLS DESIGN tab appears on the ribbon and is the active tab. The insertion point is positioned before the page number field in the footer area, ready for you to begin typing.

2 Type your name.

3 On the ribbon, click the **HOME tab**. In the Paragraph group, click the **Align Left button** ☰. The text in the footer is now left-aligned.

4 With the insertion point between your name and the page number field, press the **Tab key** twice. The page number moves to the 5.5-inch mark on the ruler, aligning the text with the Right Indent marker at the 5.5-inch mark.

5 On the ribbon, click the **HEADER & FOOTER TOOLS DESIGN tab**. In the Navigation group, click the **Go to Header button**. The insertion point moves to the header on page 2.

6 In the Header & Footer group, click the **Header button**. The Header gallery opens, similar to the Page Number gallery.

7 Point to several of the header styles. The Screen-Tips name the header style and describe what is included in that particular header.

8 Scroll down, and then click the **Grid header**. The gallery closes, and two content controls are inserted in the header area. Refer back to Exhibit 11-26.

9 Click the **Document title content control**. The entire content control becomes selected and the Title tab—in this case, with the label *Title*—appears.

10 Type **Proposal for Mountain Biking at NLC**. The placeholder text is replaced by the text you typed.

11 Click the **Date content control**. The entire content control is selected, and the title tab with the label *Date* appears. An arrow appears on the right side of the control.

12 Click the **arrow**. At the bottom of the calendar that appears, click **Today**. The calendar closes, and today's date replaces the placeholder text in the Date content control.

> **Tip:** You can click the arrows to the right and left of the month name to scroll to other months.

13 Click the **Date title tab**. The entire control is selected.

14 Press the **Delete key**. The Date content control is deleted.

15 Double-click in the document area. Header and Footer view closes.

When you insert a page number or a header or footer, it appears on every page in the document. If you don't want the header and footer to appear on the first page of a document, you can specify this by selecting the Different First Page check box in the Options group on the HEADER & FOOTER TOOLS DESIGN tab.

Remove the header and footer from the first page of the document.

1 Change the view to **One Page view**, scroll so that you can see all of page 1, and then click anywhere on page 1.

2 On the ribbon, click the **INSERT tab**. In the Header & Footer group, click the **Header button**. At the bottom of the menu, click **Edit Header**. The view changes to Header & Footer view with the HEADER & FOOTER TOOLS DESIGN tab selected, and the insertion point is blinking in the header on page 1. This is the same thing that would have happened if you had double-clicked in the Header area of page 1.

3 On the HEADER & FOOTER TOOLS DESIGN tab, in the Options group, click the **Different First Page check box**. The content of the header and footer, including the page number, disappears from page 1, and the tabs labeling the header and footer area on page 1 change to First Page Header and First Page Footer.

4 Scroll down to see page 2, and confirm that the header and footer still appear on the page.

5 Close Header and Footer view. Change the zoom back to **120%**.

End Activity

LEARN MORE

Preformatted Cover Pages

A document's cover page typically includes the title and the name of the author. Some people also include a summary of the report on the cover page; this is commonly referred to as an abstract. In addition, you might include the date, the name and possibly the logo of your company or organization, and a subtitle. A cover page should not include the document header or footer. You can create your own cover page, or you can use one of the preformatted cover pages included with Word. To use a preformatted cover page, click the Cover Page button in the Pages group on the INSERT tab, and then click a cover page in the gallery. The cover page includes content controls in which you can enter the document title and author, the date, and so on.

11-9 Creating Citations and a List of Works Cited

When you write a research paper, you should always cite your sources. A **source** is anything you use to research your topic, including books, magazines, Web sites, and movies. Every time you quote or refer to a source within the research paper itself, you need to include a **citation**, a formal reference to the work of others, usually as a parenthetical reference to the author and page number of a source. A citation should include enough information to identify the quote or referenced material so that the reader can easily locate the source in the accompanying works cited list.

Every source you cite needs to be listed in a **list of works cited**, sometimes called **references** or a **bibliography**. In common usage, the list of works cited, references, and the bibliography are the same thing: a list of the sources cited in a document. Sometimes, the list of works cited and the bibliography are different, where the list of works cited is a list only of the works cited in the document, and the bibliography is a complete list of all the sources consulted when researching a topic, even sources that are not cited in the document. Sometimes, this complete list of sources is called a *complete bibliography* or a *complete list of works cited*, and the shorter list of works actually cited is called a *works consulted list* or a *selected bibliography*.

The exact form for citations and the list of works cited varies, depending on the style guide you are using and the type of material you are referencing. People in different fields use different style guides, with each style guide designed to suit the needs of a specific discipline. For example, journalists commonly use the Associated Press (AP) style, which focuses on the concise writing style common in magazines and newspapers. Researchers in the social and behavioral sciences use the American Psychological Association (APA) style, which is designed to help readers scan an article quickly for key points and emphasizes the date of publication in citations. Other scientific and technical fields have their own specialized style guides. In the humanities, the Modern Language Association (MLA) style is widely used. Refer to the style guide you are using to see exactly what information you need to include in citations and the list of works cited, as well as how to format this information. Note that some style guides require both a list of works cited and a complete bibliography.

In Word documents, you can specify the style you want to use from a list of 12 styles. Then, when you insert citations and create the list of works cited, they are formatted appropriately for the selected style. You can change the style you select at any time, and if any citations already exist, or if the list of works cited is already created, they are reformatted using the new style.

Begin Activity

Select a style for the citations and list of works cited.

1 On the ribbon, click the **REFERENCES tab**.

2 In the Citations & Bibliography group, click the **Style box arrow**, and then click **MLA Seventh Edition** in the list of styles.

End Activity

source Anything you use to research your topic.

citation A formal reference to the work of others.

list of works cited, references, or bibliography A list of sources cited in a document or consulted while researching a topic.

Formatting a Research Paper Using MLA Style

MLA Handbook for Writers of Research Papers, published by The Modern Language Association of America, contains instructions for formatting a research document and citing the sources used in research conducted for a paper using the MLA style. The MLA guidelines were developed, in part, to simplify the process of transforming a manuscript into a journal article or a chapter of a book. The style calls for minimal formatting; the simpler the formatting in a manuscript, the easier it is to turn the text into a published document. The MLA guidelines were also designed to ensure consistency in documents, so that all research papers look alike. Therefore, no special formatting is applied to the text in an MLA style research paper. Headings should be formatted like the other text in the document, with no bold or heading styles.

Compared to style guides for technical fields, the MLA style is flexible about the form and location of citations, making it

---

MLA STYLE CHECKLIST

✓ Font is standard and easy to read (such as Times New Roman or Calibri) and at a standard size (such as 12 points)

✓ No extra space before or after all paragraphs in the document

✓ All lines double-spaced

✓ Text is aligned left (with a ragged right), and there is only one space after periods and other punctuation marks

✓ All margins are one inch

✓ First line of each body paragraph is one-half inch from the left margin, even the first paragraph after headings

✓ A page number, preceded by your last name, appears in the upper-right corner of each page; if requested, do not include the page number on the first page

✓ List of works cited is titled *Works Cited*

✓ Works Cited list begins on a new page

✓ Paragraphs in the Works Cited list are formatted with a hanging indent

✓ Include a title page only if requested; otherwise, include your name, instructor's name, course name, and the date as the first four lines in the document, followed by the title, which is centered horizontally

✓ Title of the paper and Works Cited title do not use any special formatting except to be centered horizontally on the page

✓ Works Cited list is arranged alphabetically by author (consult the *MLA Handbook* for more detailed instructions)

© 2014 Cengage Learning

MLA Style Checklist

---

easy to include citations without disrupting the natural flow of the writing. In this style, citations of other writers take the form of a brief parenthetical entry, with a complete reference to each item included in the alphabetized bibliography at the end of the research paper. Typically, though, you insert an MLA citation at the end of a sentence in which you quote or refer to material from a source. For books or journals, the citation usually includes the author's last name and a page number. However, if the sentence containing the citation already includes the author's name, you only need to include the page number in the citation. For detailed guidelines, consult the current edition of *MLA Handbook for Writers of Research Papers*, which includes many examples.

11-9a Creating a New Source and Inserting a Citation

To create a new source and insert a citation to it, click the Insert Citation button in the Citations & Bibliography group on the REFERENCES tab, and then click Add New Source to open the Create Source dialog box. See Exhibit 11-27. In the dialog box, you choose the type of source—book, Web site, sound recording, and so on—and the dialog box changes to contain the appropriate boxes for gathering the information about the source type you selected according to the style guide you selected prior to opening this dialog box. When you close the dialog box, the citation will be inserted in the style you chose inside a Citation content control. For example, if you chose the MLA style, the author's last name will be inserted between parentheses. In Exhibit 11-27, Book is selected in the Type of Source box, and the boxes shown in the dialog box collect the information needed to document the source when the source is a book and the style is MLA.

Exhibit 11-27 Create Source dialog box

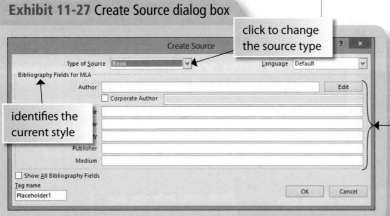

Begin Activity

Create a new source, and insert a citation.

1 On page 1, below the Available Land heading, place the insertion point immediately before the period at the end of the third sentence (after *North Meadows State Park*).

2 On the REFERENCES tab, in the Citations & Bibliography group, click the **Insert Citation button**, and then click **Add New Source**. The Create Source dialog box opens. Refer back to Exhibit 11-27.

3 Click the **Type of Source arrow**, scroll down one line, and then click **Web site**. The boxes in the dialog box

change to collect the information needed when the source is a Web site and the style is MLA.

4 Click in the **Author box**, and then type **Alan Freeman**.

5 Click in the **Name of Web Page box**, and then type **Protected Land in the North Lake Area**.

Tip: Web sites don't always provide all the information used to create a citation; include as much information as you can.

6 Click in the **Year box**, and then type **2011**.

7 Click in the **Year Accessed box**, and then type **2016**. Click in the **Month Accessed box**, and then type **May**. Click in the **Day Accessed box**, and then type **5**.

8 Click in the **Medium box**, and then type **Web**.

9 Click **OK**. The dialog box closes, and *(Freeman)* is inserted at the insertion point.

10 Click anywhere on the **(Freeman) citation**. The Citation content control is now visible.

11 Locate the Funding heading on page 3. In the first paragraph under the Funding heading, position the insertion point at the end of the second sentence before the period (after *bring them to camp*).

12 On the REFERENCES tab, in the Citations & Bibliography group, click the **Insert Citation button**. The source you just added is listed on the Insert Citation menu.

13 Click **Add New Source**.

14 Click the **Type of Source arrow**, and then click **Report**. The boxes in the dialog box change to collect the information needed when the source is a report using MLA style.

15 Below the Author box, click the **Corporate Author check box** to select it. Click in the empty box to the right of the Corporate Author label, and then type **North Lake Camping Committee**.

16 Add the following information:

Title:	**2015 Report on Survey Results**
Year:	**2015**
City:	**Elliot**
Medium:	**Print**

17 Click **OK**. The dialog box closes, and the citation is inserted.

End Activity

11-9b Inserting a Citation to an Existing Source

If you need to insert a citation to a source you have already added to your source list, you simply select the source from the Insert Citation menu. Exhibit 11-28 shows two sources listed on the menu.

Exhibit 11-28 Insert Citation menu with sources

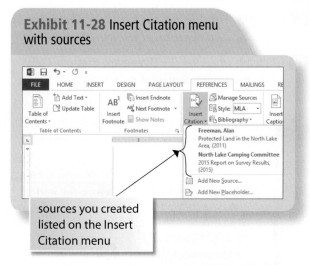

sources you created listed on the Insert Citation menu

Begin Activity

Insert a citation to an existing source.

1 Under the Funding heading on page 3, in the second paragraph, place the insertion point immediately before the last period in the paragraph.

2 On the REFERENCES tab, in the Citations & Bibliography group, click the **Insert Citation button**. The two sources you added are listed at the top of the menu. Refer back to Exhibit 11-28.

3 Click **North Lake Camping Committee**. The citation is inserted at the insertion point.

End Activity

11-9c Using the Source Manager

The Current List is the list of sources associated with the current document. The Master List is available for use with any document created using the same user account on that computer. Both the Master List and the Current List are accessible via the Source Manager dialog box, which you open by clicking the Manage Sources button in the Citations & Bibliography group on the REFERENCES tab. See Exhibit 11-29. You can use the Source Manager dialog box to copy sources from one list to the other, delete and edit existing sources, or create new sources without adding a citation in the document. Sources in the Current List that have a check mark next to them are cited in the document; those without a check mark are not cited.

Exhibit 11-29 Source Manager dialog box

list of sources stored on the computer

source in Master List that doesn't appear in Current List (this source will not appear on your screen)

you might see additional sources in the Master List on your screen

check mark indicates that the source is cited in the document

list of sources in the current document

new source added but not cited

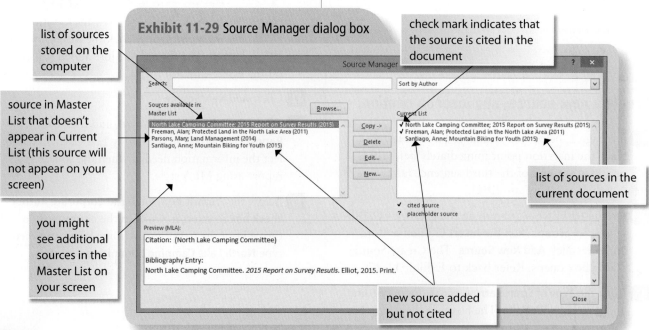

Use the Source Manager dialog box.

1 On the REFER-ENCES tab, in the Citations & Bibliography group, click the **Manage Sources button**. The Source Manager dialog box opens with the Master List of sources on the left and the Current List on the right.

2 Click **New**. The Create Source dialog box opens.

3 Click the **Type of Source arrow**, and then click **Book**.

4 Add the following information:
Author: **Anne Santiago**
Title: **Mountain Biking for Youth**
Year: **2015**
City: **Boston**
Publisher: **Holmes Press**
Medium: **Print**

5 Click **OK**. The Create Source dialog box closes, and the book you added appears in both the Master List and the Current List. In the Current List, there is no check mark next to it, indicating that the book is not cited in the document. Refer back to Exhibit 11-29.

6 Click **Close**. The Source Manager dialog box closes.

11-9d Editing a Citation

If you need to add additional information to the cita-tion, such as a page number, click the citation to display the Citation content control, click the Citation Options arrow that appears, and then click Edit Citation to open the Edit Citation dialog box. Exhibit 11-30 shows a selected citation content control and the Edit Citation dialog box. If your style guide allows it, you can also use the Edit Citation dialog box to remove,

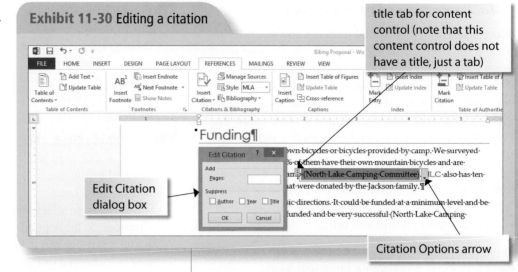

Exhibit 11-30 Editing a citation

title tab for content control (note that this content control does not have a title, just a tab)

Edit Citation dialog box

Citation Options arrow

or suppress, the author's name from the citation by selecting the Author check box in the Edit Citation dialog box, so that only the page number appears in the citation. Because Word will replace the suppressed author name with the title of the source, you need to suppress the title as well by selecting the Title check box in the Edit Citation dialog box.

Edit a citation to include the page number.

1 Under the Funding heading on page 3, in the first paragraph, click the **North Lake Camping Committee citation**. The content control containing the citation appears.

2 Click the **Citation Options arrow**, and then click **Edit Citation**. The Edit Citation dialog box opens with the insertion point in the Pages box. Refer back to Exhibit 11-30.

3 Type **7**, and then click **OK**. The dialog box closes, and the citation changes to include the referenced page number from the report.

> **Tip:** To delete a citation, click the citation to display the content control, click the title tab (the tab with the three dots) on the left side of the content control, and then press the Delete key.

4 In the second paragraph under the Funding head-ing, modify the North Lake Camping Committee citation to include the page reference **12**.

11-9e Generating a List of Works Cited

To create a list of works cited for a document, click the Bibliography button in the Citations & Bibliography group on the REFERENCES tab, and then click one of the options in the list. See Exhibit 11-31. This creates a field that lists all the works in the Current List in the Source Manager dialog box. If you select the Works Cited, References, or Bibliography style in the gallery, the appropriate title is inserted along with the field inside a content control. If you select Insert Bibliography at the bottom, the list of sources in the Current List in the Source Manger is inserted as a field without a content control and title.

Exhibit 11-31 Bibliography button menu

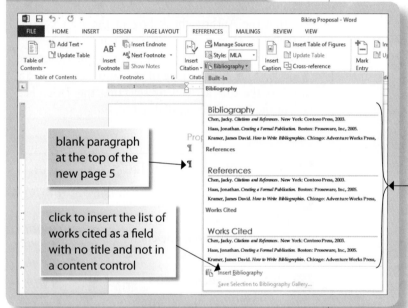

blank paragraph at the top of the new page 5

click to insert the list of works cited as a field with no title and not in a content control

The format of the entries in the list of works cited matches the style selected in the Style box in the Citations & Bibliography group on the REFERENCES tab. Because the list is a field, you can update the list later to reflect changes to the source list.

Begin Activity

Generate the bibliography.

1 Press the **Ctrl+End keys**. The insertion point moves to the end of the document.

2 Insert a **manual page break**. A new page 5 is created.

3 On the REFERENCES tab, in the Citations & Bibliography group, click the **Bibliography button**. The Bibliography menu opens. Refer to Exhibit 11-31.

4 Click **Works Cited**. The list of works cited is inserted below the Works Cited heading in the style selected in the Style box in the Citations & Bibliography group on the REFERENCES tab—in this case, in the MLA style. The text is formatted in the body font, and the Works Cited heading is formatted with the Heading 1 style. Compare your screen to Exhibit 11-32.

click one of the styles to insert a title and the list of works cited in a content control

Tip: If no sources appear in the Current List when you try to create a list of works cited, a message is inserted telling you that there are no sources in the current document.

End Activity

11-9f Modifying a Source

To modify information about a source, you need to open the Edit Source dialog box for that source. To do this, click a citation to that source in the document to display the content control, click the Citation Options arrow on the content control, and then click Edit Source; or in the Source Manager dialog box, select the source in either the Master List or the Current List, and then click Edit. After you are finished editing the source, if the source is listed in both the Master List and the Current List, a dialog box opens prompting you to update both lists. In almost all cases, you should click Yes to ensure that the source information is correct in all places it is stored on your computer.

Begin Activity

To edit a source in the research paper.

1 On page 1, in the paragraph under the Available Land heading, click the **Freeman citation**.

2 On the content control, click the **Citation Options arrow**, and then click **Edit Source**. The Edit Source

Exhibit 11-32 Works Cited content control in document

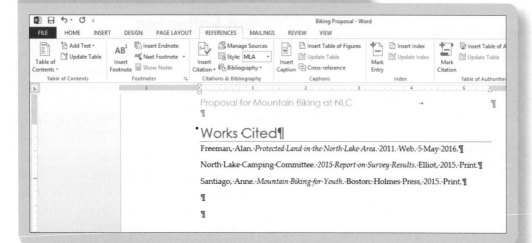

Click **Yes**. The dialog box closes, and the source is modified, although the citation remains unchanged.

End Activity

11-9g Updating the List of Works Cited

Because the list of works cited is a field, you can update the bibliography to reflect new or edited sources. If you created the list of works cited using the Insert Bibliography command, to update the field, you need to right-click it, and then on the shortcut menu, click Update Field. If you used one of the styles in the gallery and the list of works cited is in a content control, click the list to display the content control (see Exhibit 11-33), and then on the title tab, click the Update Citations and Bibliography button.

Begin Activity

Update the list of works cited.

1. On page 5, click anywhere in the list of **works cited**. The list itself is highlighted in gray, indicating that it is a field and not regular text. The content control containing the list is also visible. Refer to Exhibit 11-33.

2. On the title tab, click the **Update Citations and Bibliography button**. The date change that you made to the Freeman citation appears in the Works Cited list.

End Activity

---

dialog box opens. It is identical to the Create Source dialog box, but, obviously, contains all the information you already entered for this source. The name in the Author box displays the last name first, just as it would appear in a list of works cited.

3. Click in the **Month box**, and then type **August**.

4. Click **OK**. A dialog box opens asking if you want to update the master source list and the current document.

Acknowledging Your Sources

A research paper is a way to explore the available information about a subject and then present this information, along with your own understanding of the subject, in an organized and interesting way. Acknowledging all the sources of the information presented in your research paper is essential. If you don't do this, you might be subject to charges of plagiarism, or trying to pass off someone else's thoughts as your own. Plagiarism is an extremely serious accusation, which has academic consequences ranging from failing an assignment to being expelled from school. To ensure that you cite all your sources, create citations in your document as you type it. It is very easy to forget to go back and cite all sources correctly after you have finished typing a paper. Forgetting to cite a source could lead to accusations of plagiarism and all of the consequences that entails.

silver-john/Shutterstock.com

Exhibit 11-33 Works Cited displayed in a content control

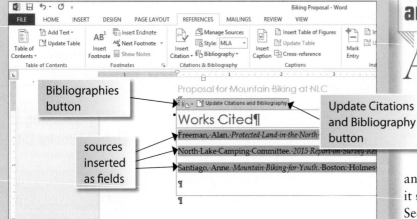

Bibliographies button

sources inserted as fields

Update Citations and Bibliography button

Converting a List of Works Cited to Static Text

You should always double-check the format of the citations and the list of works cited to make sure that they are formatted correctly in the style prescribed by the style guide you are using. Style guides are updated from time to time, or your company or instructor might require you to use a modified style. If you need to adjust the style of the list, you can select the text and paragraphs as usual and add formatting, but if you then update the list, the formatting will revert to the selected style. When you are sure that you are finished updating the list, click the list to display the content control, click the Bibliographies button in the content control title tab, and then click Convert bibliography to static text to convert the list from a field that can be updated automatically to static text—that is, text that cannot be updated automatically. Then you can modify the format of the list as desired. For example, you can change the format of titles from underlined to italics or modify the indent.

footnote An explanatory comment or reference that appears at the bottom of a page.

reference marker A small, superscript number to the right of text that corresponds to the footnote or endnote.

endnote An explanatory comment or reference that appears at the end of a section or at the end of a document.

11-10 Creating Footnotes and Endnotes

A **footnote** is an explanatory comment or reference that appears at the bottom of a page. When you create a footnote, Word inserts a small, superscript number called a **reference marker** in the text and in the bottom margin of the page and positions the insertion point next to it so you can type the text of the footnote. See Exhibit 11-34. **Endnotes** are similar, except that the text of an endnote appears at the end of a section or at the end of the document, and the reference marker is a lowercase Roman numeral unless you change it.

Exhibit 11-34 Insertion point in a new footnote

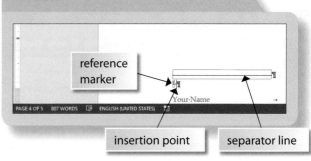

reference marker

insertion point

separator line

Word automatically manages the reference markers for you, keeping them sequential from the beginning of the document to the end, no matter how many times you add, delete, or move footnotes or endnotes. For example, if you move a paragraph containing footnote 4 so that it falls before the paragraph containing footnote 1, Word renumbers all the footnotes in the document to keep them sequential.

Begin Activity

Add a footnote.

1 On page 4, under the Questions heading, position the insertion point after the question mark after question number 4.

2 On the REFERENCES tab, in the Footnotes group, click the **Insert Footnote button**. A superscript 1 is inserted as a reference marker at the insertion point, and the same reference marker—the superscript number 1—appears in the bottom margin below a separator line. The insertion point is next to the number in the bottom margin, ready for you to type the text of the footnote. Refer back to Exhibit 11-34.

3 Type **If we need to increase our liability insurance, this will affect the budget.**

4 In the footnote, double-click directly on the reference marker (the superscript number 1). The document scrolls to the location of the reference marker in the text.

5 Scroll up to page 3. In the bulleted list, position the insertion point after the last, first-level bulleted item, *Safety*.

6 On the REFERENCES tab, in the Footnotes group, click the **Insert Footnote button**. A superscript 1 is again inserted as a reference marker, and the insertion point moves to the new footnote.

7 Type **We might want to have each participant sign a contract agreeing to these terms.**

8 On the REFERENCES tab, in the Footnotes group, click the **Next Footnote button**. The document scrolls, and the footnote you typed previously on page 4 appears. This footnote has been renumbered to 2 because it appears in the document after the footnote you added on page 2.

9 Save the document, and then close it.

End Activity

FYI

Citations in Footnotes or Endnotes

Footnotes and endnotes can contain any information you think might be useful to your readers. Citations, however, are only used to list specific information about a book or other source you refer to or quote from in the document. Many style guides require citations to be inline and appear in parentheses at the end of the sentence containing the information from the source. You can also display citations in footnotes or endnotes. This style is used in some nonfiction books. To insert a citation in a footnote or endnote, insert the footnote or endnote, and then insert the citation using the usual method.

Quiz Yourself

1. What happens when you use the Replace All command?

2. What style is applied to text if you do nothing to change it?

3. What is the template on which all Word documents are based?

4. How is a linked style different from a paragraph or character style?

5. How do you apply a Quick Style to text already in a document?

6. What is a theme?

7. What happens when you apply a different style set to a document?

8. What happens when you promote a paragraph in an outline?

9. How do you move a heading up or down in a document in both the Navigation pane and in Outline view?

10. What is the default setting for margins in a new document?

11. Explain the difference between an automatic and a manual page break.

12. What do you actually insert when you use the Page Number command to insert page numbers in a document?

13. Define *header* and *footer*.

14. What is a content control?

15. What is a source?

16. Why do you need to cite your sources?

17. What is included in the list of works cited when you use the Bibliography command to create the list?

18. What is the difference between a footnote and an endnote?

Practice It

Practice It 11-1

1. Open the data file **Dams** located in the Chapter 11\ Practice It folder. Save the document as **Embankment Dams**.

2. Replace all instances of the word *cement* with **concrete**.

3. Find the phrase *Portland concrete*. Replace that instance of *concrete* with **cement**.

4. Apply the Title Quick Style to the first paragraph.

5. Apply the Heading 1 Quick Style to the following paragraphs: History, Overview, Aswan Dam, Largest Embankment Dam: Itaipu Dam, and Problems.

6. Apply the Heading 2 Quick Style to the following paragraphs: Types of Dams and Construction.

7. Apply the Heading 3 Quick Style to the following paragraphs: Slope and Permeability.

8. At the beginning of the document, select the History heading paragraph, change its size to 18 points, and underline it. Then update the definition of the Heading 1 Quick Style to match the formatting of the History paragraph.

9. At the beginning of the document, select the first paragraph under the History heading, change the line spacing to single-spacing, and change the space after the paragraph to 12 points. Then create a new paragraph Quick Style based on this paragraph named **Body**, and apply this new style to all the body text in the document.

10. Change the theme to the Retrospect theme.

11. Change the theme colors to the Paper color palette, and then change the theme fonts to the Constantia-Franklin Gothic Book font set.

12. Change the style set to the Word 2013 (B&W) style set.

13. In the Navigation pane, promote the Types of Dams heading to a Level 1 heading, and then move the History heading down so it follows the Types of Dams heading.

14. In Outline view, promote the Construction heading and its subheadings one level so that the Construction heading is a Level 1 heading. Then move the Construction heading and its subheadings up to precede the Aswan Dam heading.

15. Change the left and right margins to 1.5 inches.

16. At the end of the document, create a manual page break to create a new, blank page 4.

17. Use the Plain Number 2 page number style to insert a page number in the center of the footer area.

18. Insert the Filigree header from the Header gallery. In the Document title content control, type **Embankment Dams**. In the other content control— the Author content control—type your name, replacing the user name that's there, if necessary.

19. Don't show the headers and footers on page 1.

20. Change the style for citations and the list of works cited to the APA style.

21. On page 1, in the first paragraph under the History heading, delete the highlighted text *[citation]*, and then insert the following citation:

Type of Source:	**Book**
Author:	**R. L. Simmons**
Title:	**Dam Building Deconstructed**
Year:	**2009**
City:	**Boston**
Publisher:	**Anston Press**

22. On page 2, in the first paragraph under the Aswan Dam heading, replace the highlighted text *[citation]* with the following citation:

Type of Source:	**Web site**
Name of Web Page:	**Modern Dams**
Name of Web Site:	**Science of Building**
Year:	**2016**
Month:	**June**
Day:	**4**
URL:	

http://www.scienceofbuilding.example.org/dams/ modern.html

23. On page 3, in the second paragraph under the Problems heading, replace the highlighted text *[citation]* with a citation to *Dam Building Deconstructed* by R. L. Simmons.

24. Add the page reference **45** to the Simmons citation on page 3, and then add the page reference **15** to the Simmons citation on page 1.

25. On page 4, generate a list of works cited using the built-in Bibliography style.

26. Create the following source without inserting a citation to it:

Type of Source:	**Book**
Author:	**Sam Blackwater**
Title:	**Dams on the Missouri**
Year:	**2012**
City:	**New York**
Publisher:	**Messier Publishing**

27. Update the bibliography to include the new source.

28. On page 2, after the fourth sentence in the paragraph under the Permeability heading, insert the following footnote: **Sheet piling could be used, but it is much more costly.** Then, on page 1, under the History heading, after the last sentence in the first paragraph, insert the following footnote: **This dam no longer exists, and the reservoir is now a desert.**

29. Save and close the document.

Practice It 11-2

1. Open the data file **Constitution** located in the Chapter 11\Practice It folder. Save the document as **New Constitution**.

2. Replace all four instances of the word *organization* with the word **structure**.

3. Apply the Title Quick Style to the first paragraph, reduce the font size of the text in this paragraph to 22 points, and then update the Title Quick Style definition to match this change.

4. Apply the Heading 1 Quick Style to the following paragraphs: Introduction, A New Direction, Evolving Issues, Money Problems, Lack of Protection, States' Rights Concerns, and Conclusion.

5. Adjust the outline as follows:

   Introduction

   Evolving Issues

       States' Rights Concerns

       Money Problems

       Lack of Protection

   A New Direction

   Conclusion

6. Change the theme to Integral, and then change the theme color palette to Grayscale.

7. At the beginning of the document, change the size of the text in the first paragraph under the Introduction heading to 12 points, change the line spacing to 1.5, and then create a new linked Quick Style named **Extra Spacing**. Apply this style to all of the body text in the document.

8. Change the size of the text in a paragraph formatted with the Heading 1 style to 20 points, and then update the Heading 1 Quick Style definition to match this formatting. Change the size of the text in a paragraph formatted with the Heading 2 style to 16 points, and then update the Heading 2 Quick Style to match this formatting.

9. Change the top and bottom margins to 1.3 inches, and the left margin to 1.5 inches.

10. Replace the first instance of the highlighted text *[citation]* (under the States' Rights Concerns heading) with a citation to the following using the Turabian style:

Type of Source:	**Web site**
Author:	**G. S. Franklin**
Name of Web Page:	**The Constitution: The Beginning**
Name of Web Site:	**Illustrated History**
Year:	**2016**
Month:	**February**
Day:	**24**
URL:	

http://www.illustratedhistory.example.net/ constitution/beginning.html

11. Replace the second instance of the highlighted text *[citation]* (under the Lack of Protection heading) with a citation to the following using the Turabian style:

Type of Source:	**Book**
Author:	**Mary P. Benton**
Title:	**Shay's Rebellion: A Second Revolution**
Year:	**2013**
City:	**Sacramento**
Publisher:	**Four Square Press**

12. Replace the third instance of the highlighted text *[citation]* (under the A New Direction heading) with a citation to the Web page authored by G.S. Franklin.

13. At the end of the document, create a new page, and insert a list of works cited using the built-in Bibliography style.

14. Create the following source without inserting a citation to it:

Type of Source:	**Journal Article**
Author:	**Devon Washington**
Title:	**Dissecting the Articles**
Journal Name:	**Journal of U.S. History**
Year:	**2015**
Pages:	**13–16**

15. Update the list of works cited.

16. Add your name left-aligned in the header.

17. On page 1, after the last sentence in the first paragraph under the Introduction heading, insert the following footnote: **All amendments to the Articles of Confederation required a super majority.**

18. Save and close the document.

On Your Own

On Your Own 11-1

1. Open the data file **Lab** located in the Chapter 11\ On Your Own folder. Save the document as **Lab Report**.

2. Change the style set to Black & White (Classic).

3. Apply the Heading 1 Quick Style to the first paragraph (*Introduction*). Use the Font dialog box to change the format of this text to Small caps instead of All caps. (*Hint*: On the HOME tab, in the Font group, click the Dialog Box Launcher.) Center the paragraph, and then change the space before the paragraph to 24 points. Update the Heading 1 Quick Style to match this formatting.

4. Apply the redefined Heading 1 Quick Style to the following paragraphs: Purpose, Materials and Methods, Results, and Discussion.

5. Move the section titled Purpose so it is the first section in the document.

6. Use the Cover Page button in the Pages group on the INSERT tab to insert the Sideline cover page. On the cover page, type your course name in the

Company content control. In the Title content control, type **Mitosis and the Cell Cycle**. In the Author content control, add your name. In the Date content control, add the current date. Delete the Subtitle content control.

7. Change the color of the text on the title page to Black. Remove the border from the left of your course name, the title, and the empty row below the title in the table.

8. Using the APA style, add the following sources without inserting citations. (*Hint*: Show all the fields in the Create Source dialog box.)

Type of Source:	**Book**
Author:	**Carolyn Edwards, John Griffin, Sandra Suleki**
Title:	**Biology Basics**
Year:	**2015**
City:	**New York**
Publisher:	**Kenfield Books**

Type of Source:	**Article in a Periodical**
Author:	**Jeremy Walsh, M.D.**
Title:	**Mitosis Myths**
Periodical Title:	**Science for Today**
Year:	**2016**
Month:	**January**
Pages:	**35–42**

9. On a new page at the end of the document, create a list of works cited titled *Works Cited*.

10. Edit the Biology Basics source to include an edition number of 5, and then update the list of works cited. (*Hint*: Select the Show All Bibliography Fields check box in the Edit Source dialog box.)

11. Insert the Grid footer. Insert the Blank header, and then replace the placeholder with your name. Do not show the header and footer on the title page.

12. In the paragraph under Materials and Methods, position the insertion point after the sentence that ends with *paper towel* (the fifth sentence). Insert the following as an endnote: **It was carefully done so that cover slip would not move laterally and ruin the slide.**

Chapter 11

ADDITIONAL STUDY TOOLS

IN THE BOOK
▶ Complete end-of-chapter exercises
▶ Study tear-out Chapter Review Card

ONLINE
▶ Complete additional end-of-chapter exercises

▶ Take practice quiz to prepare for tests
▶ Review key term flash cards (online, printable, and audio)
▶ Play "Beat the Clock" and "Memory" to quiz yourself
▶ Watch the videos to learn more about the topics taught in this chapter

Answers to Quiz Yourself

1. *When you use the Replace All command, all instances of the text in the Find what box are replaced with the text in the Replace with box.*

2. *The style applied to text if you do nothing to change it is the Normal style.*

3. *The template on which all Word documents are based is the Normal template.*

4. *A character style affects only selected text. A paragraph style affects the entire paragraph. But you can apply a linked style only to selected text or to an entire paragraph.*

5. *To apply a Quick Style to text already in a document, first select the text or paragraph, and then click the Quick Style in the Styles gallery on the HOME tab.*

6. *A theme is a coordinated set of colors, fonts, and effects.*

7. *When you apply a different style set to a document, the Quick Style definitions are changed to match those of the new style set.*

8. *When you promote a paragraph in an outline, the paragraph is moved up to a higher level in the outline.*

9. *To move a heading up or down in a document in both the Navigation Pane and in Outline view, click it to select it (in Outline view, click its outline symbol), and then drag it to its new position.*

10. *The default setting for margins in a new document is one inch all around.*

11. *An automatic page break is created when you fill a page with text and a new page is automatically created. A manual page break is created when you use the Page Break command to force text after the break to a new page.*

12. *When you use the Page Number command to insert page numbers in a document, you actually insert a field.*

13. *A header is text that appears at the top of every page in a document. A footer is text that appears at the bottom of every page in a document.*

14. *A content control is a placeholder for text you insert or designed to contain a specific type of text, such as a date.*

15. *A source is anything you use to research your topic.*

16. *You need to cite your sources to avoid charges of plagiarism or trying to pass off someone else's thoughts as your own.*

17. *When you use the Bibliography command to create the list of works cited, you insert every source in the Current List in the Source Manager dialog box, even if the source is not cited.*

18. *A footnote appears at the foot or bottom of a page, and an endnote appears at the end of a document.*

Enhancing a Document

StockLite/Shutterstock.com

W ord documents can contain much more than text. Elements such as tables, illustrations, graphical headlines, and formatted headings can be used to enhance documents. Some documents (including this book) are formatted in multiple columns. Other documents have decorative borders around the entire page.

Word provides many tools for creating these elements. Tables allow you to organize information in rows and columns. Sections allow you to format parts of a document in different ways. You can add images stored on Office.com to your document, and WordArt allows you to create eye-catching headlines. Building blocks allow you to create formatted text and graphical elements to reuse in many documents, which helps to give related documents a consistent look.

These enhancements can be used in any kind of document, though you'll commonly see them in flyers and newsletters.

Learning Objectives

After studying the material in this chapter, you will be able to:

12-1 Organize information in tables

12-2 Change the page orientation

12-3 Divide a document into sections

12-4 Insert and modify graphics

12-5 Wrap text around graphics

12-6 Move graphics

12-7 Add text effects and WordArt text boxes

12-8 Work with columns

12-9 Work with building blocks

12-1 Organizing Information in Tables

A **table**, a grid of horizontal rows and vertical columns, is a useful way to present information that is organized into categories. For example, you can use a table to organize contact information for a list of clients. For each client, you could include the following information: first name, last name, street address, city, state, and ZIP code.

Tables are organized into columns and rows. The box at the intersection of a column and a row is a **cell**. The row at the top of the table, called the **header row**, typically contains the labels for the columns so you know what type of data appears in each column.

12-1a Creating a Table

When you create a table in Word, you specify how many rows and columns to include in the table. You do this with the Table button in the Tables group on the INSERT tab. When you click the Table button, you can drag across the grid that appears to select the number of columns and rows to include in the table, as shown in Exhibit 12-1. You can also click the Insert Table command to open the Insert Table dialog box in which you can specify the number of columns and rows.

Create a table.

1. Open the data file **Table** located in the Chapter 12\Chapter folder. Save the document as **Class Table**.

2. If necessary, change the zoom to **120%** and display the **nonprinting characters**.

3. In the body of the letter, position the insertion point in the second paragraph (the blank paragraph).

4. On the ribbon, click the **INSERT tab**. In the Tables group, click the **Table button**. A table grid opens, with a menu at the bottom.

5. Point to the **grid** to highlight two columns and five rows. (The outline of a cell turns orange when it is highlighted.) As you move the pointer across the grid, Word indicates the size of the table (columns by rows) at the top of the grid. A Live Preview of the table structure appears in the document. Refer to Exhibit 12-1.

6. When **2×5 Table** appears at the top of the grid, click the **grid**. An empty table with two columns and five rows is inserted in the document, and the insertion point is in the upper-left cell. The two columns are the same widths. Because nonprinting characters are displayed, each cell contains an end-of-cell mark, and each row contains an end-of-row mark. The TABLE TOOLS DESIGN and LAYOUT contextual tabs appear on the ribbon. See Exhibit 12-2.

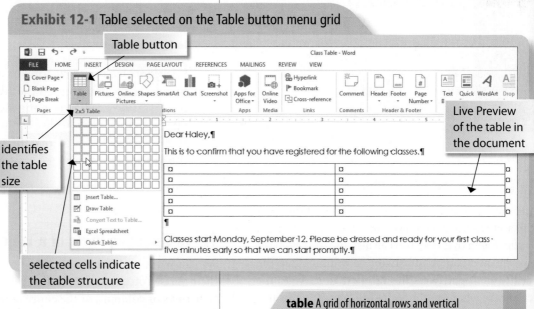

Exhibit 12-1 Table selected on the Table button menu grid

> **table** A grid of horizontal rows and vertical columns.
>
> **cell** The intersection of a column and a row.
>
> **header row** The top row in a table that contains the column labels.

Exhibit 12-2 Blank table with two columns and five rows

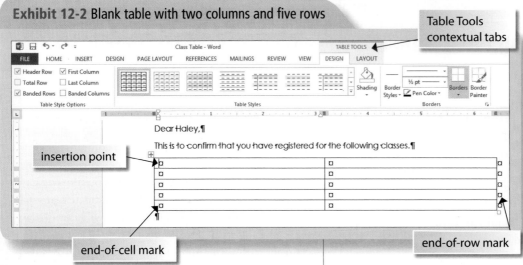

Table Tools contextual tabs

insertion point

end-of-cell mark

end-of-row mark

LEARN MORE

Creating a Quick Table

A **Quick Table** is a table template that contains sample text and formatting. To insert a Quick Table, point to the Quick Tables command on the Table button menu, and then scroll through the gallery of Quick Tables that appears. You can insert a calendar, a simple list, tables with subheads, and other types of formatted tables. You can then replace the text in the Quick Table with your own text.

ITEM	NEEDED
Books	1
Magazines	3
Notebooks	1
Paper pads	1
Pens	3
Pencils	2
Highlighter	2 colors
Scissors	1 pair

12-1b Entering Data in a Table

To enter data in a table, simply move the insertion point to a cell and type. You can move the insertion point to a cell by clicking in that cell. You can also use the keyboard to move the insertion point between cells. To move to the next cell to the right, press the Tab key. To move to the next cell to the left, press the Shift+Tab keys. You can also press the arrow keys to move between cells. If the data

Quick Table A table template with sample text and formatting.

takes up more than one line in the cell, Word automatically wraps the text to the next line and increases the height of that cell as well as all of the cells in that row.

Begin Activity

Enter data into a table.

1 With the insertion point in the upper-left cell in the table, type **Class**. As you type, the end-of-cell mark moves to the right to accommodate the text.

2 Press the **Tab key** to move the insertion point to the next cell to the right.

3 Type **Time** and then press the **Tab key**. Because the insertion point was in the last column, it moves to the first cell in the next row.

4 Type the following information in the table, pressing the **Tab key** to move from cell to cell:

Tap	5–6
Ballet	6–7
Jazz	6–7:30
Modern	6–8

> **Problem?** If a new row appears at the bottom of your table, you pressed the Tab key when the insertion point was in the last cell in the table. On the Quick Access Toolbar, click the **Undo button** to remove the extra row from the table.

End Activity

12-1c Selecting Parts of a Table

As you work with tables, you need to be able to select their parts. You can select a cell, a row or column, multiple rows or columns, or the entire table. To select parts of a table from the ribbon, position the insertion point in a cell, click the Select button in the Table group on the TABLE TOOLS LAYOUT tab, and then click the appropriate command—Select Cell, Select Column, Select Row, or Select Table. See Exhibit 12-3.

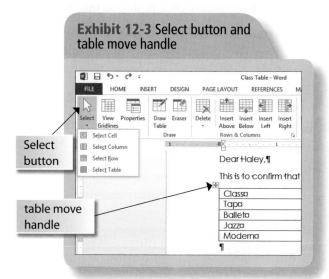

Exhibit 12-3 Select button and table move handle

Select button

table move handle

You can also use the pointer to select parts of a table. To select an entire row, point to the row in the left margin so that the pointer changes to ⇗, and then click to select that row; to select a column, point just above the top of a column so the pointer changes to ⬇, and then click. You can also drag to select adjacent rows, columns, or cells, or use the Shift or Ctrl key while clicking to select adjacent and nonadjacent cells, rows, or columns. Finally, you can click the table move handle ⊞ above the upper-left corner of the table to select the entire table. To deselect a cell or table, click anywhere else in the document.

Begin Activity

Select parts of a table.

1 Move the pointer to the **left of the top row** in the table so it changes to ⇗, and then click. The top row is selected.

Tip: Press the Shift key as you select additional rows or columns to select adjacent rows or columns; use the Ctrl key to select nonadjacent rows or columns.

2 Point to the **top of the first column** so that the pointer changes to ⬇, and then click. The first column is selected.

Problem? If you have a hard time making the pointer change to ⬇, point above the table, and then slowly move the pointer down on top of the column.

3 Point to the table so that the **table move handle** ⊞ appears above the upper-left corner of the table.

4 Click the **table move handle** ⊞. The entire table is selected.

5 Click any **cell** in the table to deselect the table and place the insertion point in that cell.

End Activity

12-1d Inserting a Row or Column

You can modify the structure of a table by adding or removing rows and columns. To insert a row or column, move the pointer to the left of a row divider or above a column divider to display an Insert Control. Exhibit 12-4 shows an Insert Control for a column. Click the Insert Control ⊕ to insert a row above or a column to the left of the Control. You can also use the Insert Above, Insert Below, Insert Left, or Insert Right buttons in the Rows & Columns group on the TABLE TOOLS LAYOUT tab.

Exhibit 12-4 Commands to insert rows and columns

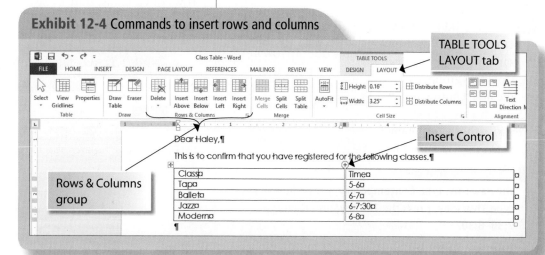

TABLE TOOLS LAYOUT tab

Insert Control

Rows & Columns group

Insert rows and columns in a table.

1 Point above the column border between the Class and Time columns. The Insert Control ⊕ appears. Refer back to Exhibit 12-4.

2 Click the **Insert Control** ⊕. A new column is inserted to the left of the Insert Control—between the Class and Time columns. The overall width of the table did not change. The original two columns decreased in width, making all three columns the same width.

3 In the new column, click in the **top cell**, and then type **Day**.

4 Press the **Down Arrow key**. The insertion point moves down one row.

5 Type the following information in the new column, pressing the **Down Arrow key** to move from cell to cell:

Monday
Monday
Thursday
Wednesday

6 Make sure the insertion point is in the **second cell in the last row**.

7 Click the **TABLE TOOLS LAYOUT tab** if necessary. In the Rows & Columns group, click the **Insert Above button**. A new row is inserted above the row containing the insertion point.

Tip: To create a new bottom row in a table, place the insertion point in the rightmost cell in the bottom row, and then press the Tab key.

8 Click in the **first cell in the new row**, type **Contemporary**, press the **Tab key**, type **Thursday**, press the **Tab key**, and then type **7:30–8:30**.

9 Position the insertion point anywhere in the **last column**.

10 In the Rows & Columns group, click the **Insert Right button**. A new column is inserted to the right of the Time column, and all the columns are resized.

11 In the new column, click in the **top cell**, and then type **Price**. Compare your screen to Exhibit 12-5.

Exhibit 12-5 Table with new columns and new row

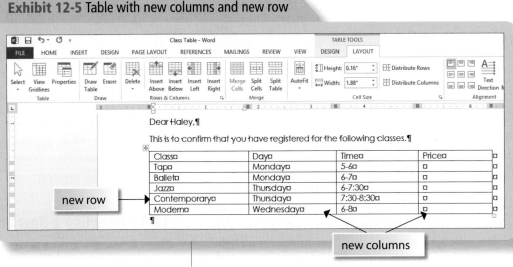

new row

new columns

12-1e Deleting a Row, Column, or Table

To delete the structure of a row, column, or the entire table—including its contents—you click in the row or column you want to delete—or anywhere in the table if you want to delete the whole table—and then click the Delete button in the Rows & Columns group on the TABLE TOOLS LAYOUT tab. This opens the menu of commands shown in Exhibit 12-6. To delete multiple rows or columns, start by selecting all the rows or columns you want to delete.

Exhibit 12-6 Delete button menu

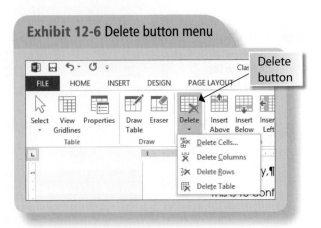

Delete button

Sorting Rows in a Table

You can sort a table based on the contents of one of the columns in alphabetical, numerical, or chronological order. For example, you could sort the table you just created based on the contents of the Class column. When you sort, you can choose to sort either in ascending (alphabetical or lowest to highest) or descending (reverse alphabetical or highest to lowest) order. You can also sort a table based on more than one column. For example, if a table included a list of items purchased at several stores, you could sort the table first on the store names, and then on the item names so that the list would be alphabetized by store name and then by item name within each store. To sort a table, select the table, and then click the Sort button in the Data group on the TABLE TOOLS LAYOUT tab to open the Sort dialog box (shown here).

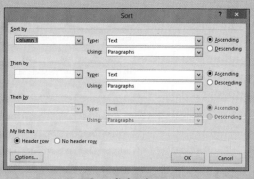

Sort dialog box

Begin Activity

Delete a row and a column.

1 Position the insertion point anywhere in the **Jazz row** in the table.

2 On the TABLE TOOLS LAYOUT tab, in the Rows & Columns group, click the **Delete button**. The Delete menu opens, displaying options for deleting cells, columns, rows, or the entire table. Refer back to Exhibit 12-6.

3 Click **Delete Rows**. The Jazz row is deleted.

> **Tip:** To delete the contents of a cell, row, column, or table, select the parts of the table containing the contents you want to delete, and then press the Delete key.

4 Position the insertion point anywhere in the **Price column**.

5 In the Rows & Columns group, click the **Delete button**, and then click **Delete Columns**. The Price column is deleted. The width of the three remaining columns does not change and the table no longer fills the width of the page.

End Activity

12-1f Changing Column Widths

Columns that are too narrow or too wide for the material they contain can make a table hard to read. When the insertion point is positioned in a table, Move Table Column markers appear on the horizontal ruler above each column border to indicate the column widths. See Exhibit 12-7. You can make column widths adjust automatically to accommodate the widest entry in the column. To adjust the width of all the columns at once to match their widest entries, click the AutoFit button in the Cell Size group on the TABLE TOOLS LAYOUT tab, and then click AutoFit Contents. To adjust the width of a single column to fit its widest entry, double-click its right column border. To change a column's width to a specific width, drag the column's right border to a new position, as shown in Exhibit 12-7, or type a measurement in the Width box in the Cell Size group on the TABLE TOOLS LAYOUT tab.

Exhibit 12-7 Identifying and changing column widths in tables

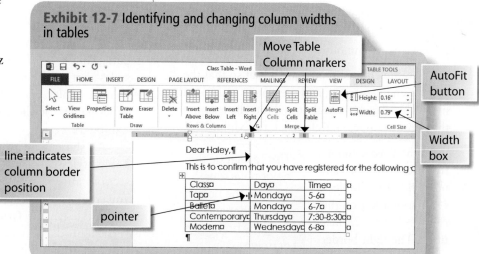

Don't Select Text Before Resizing Columns

When you adjust the width of a table column, make sure that none of the text or cells in the table is selected. If a cell is selected when you change the column width, only the width of the selected cell will be changed.

Begin Activity

Change the width of columns in a table.

1 Click anywhere in the **table**, if necessary. On the ruler, Move Table Column markers indicate the width of each column. Refer back to Exhibit 12-7. (Note that your table will not yet look like the table shown in Exhibit 12-7.)

2 Point to the **Time column right border** so that the pointer changes to ┿‖┿.

3 Double-click the **Time column right border**. The column border moves left so that the Time column is just wide enough to accommodate the widest entry in the column.

> **Tip:** To make the entire table span the page width, click the AutoFit button in the Cell Size group on the TABLE TOOLS LAYOUT tab, and then click AutoFit Window.

4 On the TABLE TOOLS LAYOUT tab, in the Cell Size group, click the **AutoFit button**. A menu opens.

5 On the menu, click **AutoFit Contents**. All the columns in the table adjust so that each is just wide enough to accommodate its widest entry.

6 Point to the **Class column right border** so that the pointer changes to ┿‖┿, and then press and hold the mouse button. A vertical dotted line the length of the window appears. Refer back to Exhibit 12-7.

7 Drag the **Class column right border** to the right until the Move Table Column marker on the ruler is at the 1.25-inch mark. The right border of the middle column

> **Tip:** To change the height of a row, point to the bottom row border and drag the border up or down.

did not move, so the middle column is now too narrow.

8 Drag the **Time column right border** to the right until the Move Table Column marker on the ruler is at the 3.5-inch mark on the ruler.

9 Drag the **Day right column border** to the right to the 2.5-inch mark on the ruler.

End Activity

Using AutoFit in Tables

The default setting for tables in Word is for the table width to be the same width as the page, for text to wrap within cells, and for the columns to automatically resize as you enter text. This means that if you enter text in a cell with a natural breaking point, such as between words, the text will wrap within the cell. But if there is no natural breaking point, the column will widen to accommodate the long entry and the other columns will become narrower to keep the total width of the table the same. You can control this behavior using the commands on the AutoFit button menu in the Cell Size group on the TABLE TOOLS LAYOUT tab. The first command, AutoFit Contents, changes the column widths to just fit the contents of each cell, including shrinking the width of empty columns. The second command, AutoFit Window, returns the table to the default behavior. The third command, Fixed Column Width, causes the column widths to stay the same no matter how wide an entry is.

12-1g Formatting Tables with Table Styles

You have already used styles to format text and paragraphs. Word also includes a variety of built-in styles that you can use to add borders, shading, and color to tables. You select a table style from the Table Styles gallery on the TABLE TOOLS DESIGN tab. See Exhibit 12-8.

As shown in Exhibit 12-8, the first row in the Table Styles gallery contains styles in the Plain Tables section, and below that is the Grid Tables section. If you scroll the list of styles, you see the List Tables section. Styles in the Grid Tables section include visible vertical borders between the columns; styles in the List Tables section do not.

Exhibit 12-8 Table Styles gallery

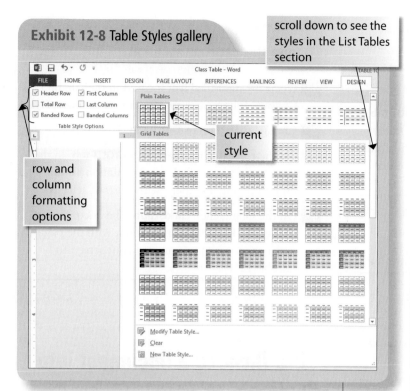

scroll down to see the styles in the List Tables section

current style

row and column formatting options

3 In the Table Style Options group, click the **First Column check box** to deselect it. The bold formatting is removed from the first column in the table.

End Activity

FYI

Fine-tuning Table Styles

After you apply a table style to a table, you might like the look of the table but find that it no longer effectively conveys the information or is not quite as easy to read. To solve this problem, you can, of course, apply a different style to the table. You can also customize the table formatting by using the Shading and Borders buttons on the TABLE TOOLS DESIGN tab. Remember that built-in styles and shading and border colors that you choose from the Theme Colors in the color palette will change if you change the theme.

When you apply a style to a table, you can select or deselect the check boxes in the Table Style Options group on the TABLE TOOLS DESIGN tab to format additional rows and columns with the table style. For example, you can specify that the first and last rows—the header and total rows—and the first and last columns be formatted differently from the rest of the rows and columns in the table. Some styles format the rows in alternating colors, called **banded rows**, while others format the columns in alternating colors, called **banded columns**.

Begin Activity

Apply a table style.

1 On the ribbon, click the **TABLE TOOLS DESIGN tab**. In the Table Styles group, click the **More button** ⎘. The Table Styles gallery opens. Refer back to Exhibit 12-8. The first style in the Plain Tables section is selected.

2 Scroll down to display the styles in the List Tables section. Click the **List Table 1 Light – Accent 3 style** (use the ScreenTips to locate this style). The Table Styles gallery closes, and the table is formatted with the style you selected.

12-1h Aligning Tables and Text in Tables

You can change the alignment of the entire table on the page, and you can change the alignment of text in cells. To change the alignment of the table on the page, align it the same way you align a paragraph by using the paragraph alignment buttons in the Paragraph group on the HOME tab. To change the alignment of text in cells, use the alignment buttons in the Alignment group on the TABLE TOOLS LAYOUT tab.

Begin Activity

Align a table and the text in a table.

1 Click the **table move handle** ⊕ to select the entire table.

> **Tip:** You can also click the Select button in the Table group on the TABLE TOOLS LAYOUT tab, and then click Select Table.

banded rows/banded columns Formatting that displays alternate rows (or columns) in a table with different fill colors.

2 On the ribbon, click the **HOME tab**. In the Paragraph group, click the **Center button** ≡. The table is centered horizontally on the page.

3 Select the **Time column**.

4 On the ribbon, click the **TABLE TOOLS LAYOUT tab**. In the Alignment group, click the **Align Top Center button** ≡. All the text in the Time column is centered in the cells. Compare your table to the one shown in Exhibit 12-9.

End Activity

Exhibit 12-9 Final formatted table

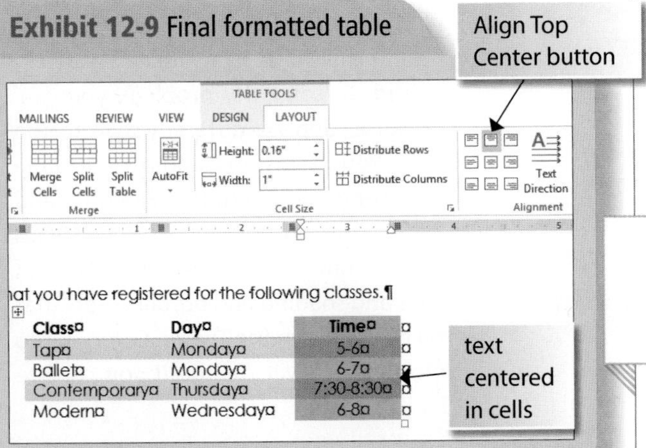

text centered in cells

12-2 Changing the Page Orientation

You can set the **orientation**—the way a page is turned—for the pages in a document. A page set to **portrait orientation** is taller than it is wide. This orientation, most commonly used for letters, reports, and other formal documents, is the usual orientation for most Word documents. **Landscape orientation** is a page that is wider than it is tall. You can easily change the orientation of a document using the Orientation button in the Page Setup group on the PAGE LAYOUT tab.

orientation The way a page is turned.

portrait orientation The layout of a page taller than it is wide.

landscape orientation The layout of a page wider than it is tall.

section A part of a document that can have its own page-level formatting and properties.

section break A formatting mark in a document that indicates the start of a new section.

Begin Activity

Change the page orientation.

1 Open the data file **Flyer** located in the Chapter 12\ Chapter folder. Save the document as **Dance Flyer**.

2 Change the zoom to **One Page**.

3 On the ribbon, click the **PAGE LAYOUT tab**. In the Page Setup group, click the **Orientation button**. The Orientation menu opens with Portrait selected.

4 On the menu, click **Landscape**. The document changes to landscape orientation, with the page wider than it is tall. Compare your screen to Exhibit 12-10.

End Activity

12-3 Dividing a Document into Sections

A **section** is a part of a document that can have its own page-level formatting and properties. For example, you can format one section in a document with 1-inch margins and portrait orientation, and the next section with 2-inch margins and landscape orientation. Each section in a document can also have different headers and footers, or a new section can restart the page numbering.

Every document has at least one section. To divide a document into multiple sections, you insert a **section break**. The four types of section breaks are:

▶ **Next Page**—inserts a section break, and forces a new page to start after the section break.

▶ **Continuous**—inserts a section break without starting a new page.

▶ **Even Page**—inserts a section break, and forces a new page to start on the next even-numbered page.

▶ **Odd Page**—inserts a section break, and forces a new page to start on the next odd-numbered page.

If you delete a section break, the formatting from the section below the deleted section break is applied to the section above the deleted section break. The formatting information for the last section in a document, or in a document with no section breaks, is contained in the last paragraph mark in the document.

Exhibit 12-10 Document in landscape orientation

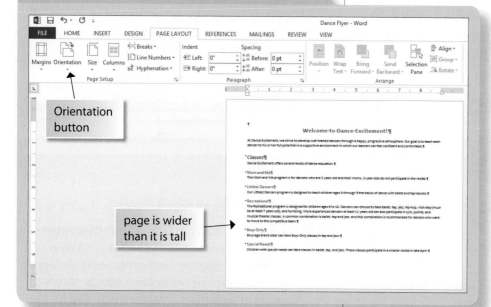

Orientation button

page is wider than it is tall

Insert a section break.

1 Change the zoom to **120%**.

2 Scroll down to the bottom of page 3. Place the insertion point to the left of *Dance Excitement* above the address.

3 On the ribbon, click the **PAGE LAYOUT tab**, if necessary. In the Page Setup group, click the **Breaks button**. The Breaks menu opens. Refer to Exhibit 12-11.

12-3a Inserting a Section Break

You use the Breaks button in the Page Setup group on the PAGE LAYOUT tab to select the type of section break you want to insert. See Exhibit 12-11. The Page Breaks section of the menu includes options for controlling how the text flows from page to page. The Section Breaks section includes the four types of section breaks.

When nonprinting characters are displayed, a section break is indicated by a double dotted line with the words *Section Break* in the center of it, followed by the type of section break. See Exhibit 12-12.

4 In the Section Breaks section, click **Next Page**. A section break is inserted, and the text after the insertion point moves to the top of the new page 4. Refer to Exhibit 12-12.

Tip: To delete a section break, click the line representing the break, and then press the Delete key.

5 On page 4, below the address, place the insertion point before the Faculty heading. Insert another **Next Page section break**. The Faculty heading and the text after it move to page 5. There are now three sections in the document.

End Activity

Exhibit 12-11 Breaks button menu

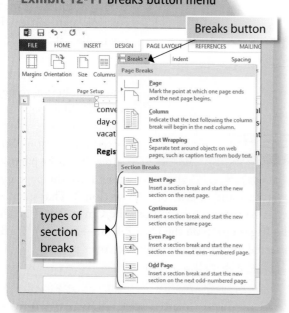

Breaks button

types of section breaks

FYI

Viewing Section Breaks in Draft View

If the section break appears at the end of a line, you might not be able to see it. If you switch to Draft view, section breaks appear all the way across the screen. Draft view displays the text of the document without showing its layout. To switch to Draft view, click the Draft button in the Views group on the VIEW tab. To switch back to Print Layout view, click the Print Layout button in the Views group on the VIEW tab or click the Print Layout button on the status bar.

Exhibit 12-12 Next Page section break

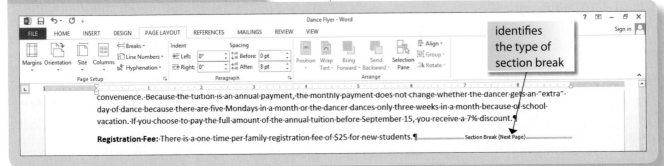

identifies the type of section break

12-3b Formatting a Section Differently from the Rest of the Document

Once you have inserted a section break, you can format each section separately. When you change the page-level formatting of a section, the other sections in the document remain unchanged. See Exhibit 12-13.

Exhibit 12-13 Sections formatted with different orientations

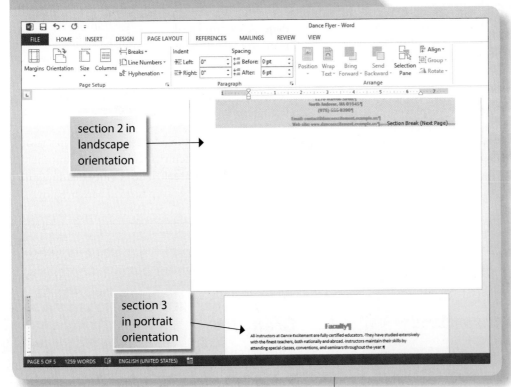

section 2 in landscape orientation

section 3 in portrait orientation

Begin Activity

Format a section.

1 Change the zoom to **60%**. Scroll so that you can see the section break on page 4 and the top of page 5.

2 Click **anywhere on page 5** (which is in section 3).

3 On the PAGE LAYOUT tab, in the Page Setup group, click the **Orientation button**, and then click **Portrait**. Section 3, which consists of page 5, changes to portrait orientation. Section 1, which consists of pages 1–3, and section 2, which consists of page 4, remain in landscape orientation. Compare your screen to Exhibit 12-13.

End Activity

12-3c Adding Different Headers and Footers in Sections

One advantage of dividing a document into sections is that the headers and footers in each section can differ. For example, if the document includes a cover page, and you want the page numbering to begin on the first page after the cover page, you can insert a section break after the cover page, and then have the page numbers start and appear only in section 2. That's actually what happens when you use the Cover Page button in the Pages group on the INSERT tab—a section break is inserted automatically after the cover page.

Add different headers and footers in sections.

1 Change the zoom to **120%**, and make sure the insertion point is still on page 5.

2 On the ribbon, click the **INSERT tab**. In the Header & Footer group, click the **Footer button**, and then below the gallery, click **Edit Footer**. The insertion point moves to the footer area on page 5. On the left, the Footer area is labeled Footer –Section 3–, and on the right, the footer is labeled Same as Previous.

3 Type your name.

4 Scroll up to see the bottom of page 4. The footer area on this page is labeled Footer –Section 2–, and your name appears here as well. See Exhibit 12-14.

End Activity

The Same as Previous tab on headers and footers in sections means that the header or footer in that section is linked to the previous section. The Same as Previous tab does not appear in section 1 because there is no previous section to link to. To unlink the sections, make sure the insertion point is in the header or footer that you want to unlink, and then deselect the Link to Previous button in the Navigation group on the HEADER & FOOTER TOOLS DESIGN tab.

Unlink section headers and footers.

1 Scroll down, and make sure the insertion point is still in the footer area for section 3.

2 On the HEADER & FOOTER TOOLS DESIGN tab, in the Navigation group, click the **Link to Previous button**. The button is no longer selected, and the Same as Previous tab on the footer disappears.

3 Scroll up so you can see the top of page 5 and the bottom of page 4. Notice that the section 3 header area on page 5 still contains the Same as Previous tab because the headers in the two sections are still linked.

4 On page 4, click after your name in the footer, press the **Tab key** twice, and then type **DRAFT**. The text is right-aligned at the default Right Tab stop in the headers and footers—the 6.5-inch mark. Because the page has landscape orientation, the right margin is at the 9-inch mark.

5 Drag the **Right Tab stop** on top of the Right Indent marker at the 9-inch mark on the ruler.

6 Scroll down so you can see the footer on page 5. The footer on page 5 is unchanged and does not include the word *DRAFT* because you unlinked the footer in section 3 from the footer in the previous section.

7 Double-click anywhere in the document outside the header or footer areas. Header and Footer view closes.

End Activity

Exhibit 12-14 Footer and header in different sections

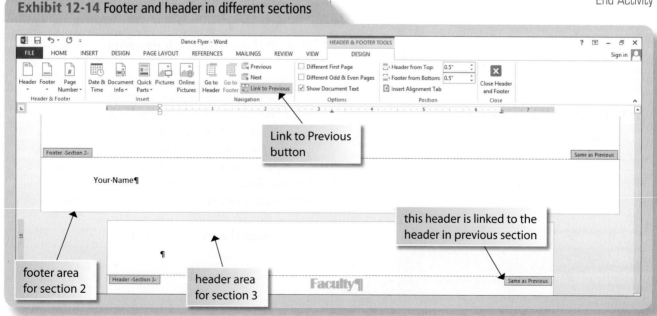

Creating Odd and Even Pages

Most professionally produced books and reports are printed on both sides of the paper and then bound. When you open a bound book or report, odd-numbered pages appear on the right, and even-numbered pages appear on the left. The margin on the inside of each page, where the pages are bound together, is called the gutter. Often, the headers and footers for odd-numbered pages are different from the headers and footers for the even-numbered pages. For instance, the page numbers might appear on the outside edge of the footer. So, page numbers appear on the right side of the footer on odd-numbered pages, and they appear on the left side of the footer on even-numbered pages.

You can set up the pages in a multiple-page document with odd and even pages. After you insert a header or footer, select the Different Odd & Even Pages check box in the Options group on the HEADER & FOOTER TOOLS DESIGN tab. To increase the width of the gutter to allow for binding, click the Margins button in the Page Setup group on the PAGE LAYOUT tab, and then click Custom Margins to open the Page Setup dialog box with the Margins tab selected. Change the measurement in the Gutter box.

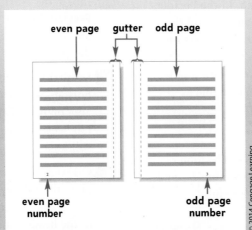

Odd and even page layout

© 2014 Cengage Learning

12-4 Inserting and Modifying Graphics

A **graphic** is a picture, shape, design, graph, chart, or diagram. You can include many types of graphics in your documents, including photographs, drawings, and graphics created using other programs. You can also create graphics using drawing tools in Word.

A graphic is an example of an **object**. An object is anything in a document or other file that can be treated as a whole. For example, a table is an object. Objects can be added, deleted, moved, formatted, and resized.

12-4a Inserting Online Pictures

You can add pictures stored on Web sites to documents. To do this, click the Online Pictures button in the Illustrations group on the INSERT tab. This opens the Insert Pictures dialog box, shown in Exhibit 12-15. You can choose to search for an image on Office.com or use the Bing search engine to search for images across the Internet. Office.com is a Microsoft Web site that contains resources for Microsoft Office users. The images stored on Office.com are often called *clip art*, which just means images stored in collections so that you can easily locate and use them.

After selecting where you want to search (Office.com or the Internet using the Bing search engine), click in the Search box next to your choice, and then type keywords. When you use the Bing search engine, you get the same results that you would get if you were to type keywords in the Search box on the Bing home page.

Images stored on Office.com have keywords directly associated with them. For example, images of a car might be associated with the keywords *car* and *racing*; images of a car moving down a road might be associated with the additional keywords *road* and *driving*. If you search using just the keyword *car*, the image of the car moving down a road will appear in your results, along with images of cars not on a road and images of cars without drivers. The more keywords you use, the narrower (more specific) your search results will be.

graphic A picture, shape, design, graph, chart, or diagram.

object Anything in a document or other file that can be treated as a whole.

Exhibit 12-15 Insert Pictures dialog box to insert online pictures

search button

Insert Pictures

[ ] Office.com Clip Art
Royalty-free photos and illustrations

[ ] Bing Image Search
Search the web   Search Bing

type keywords here to search on Office.com

Sign in with your Microsoft account to insert photos and videos from Flickr, SkyDrive, and other sites.

Begin Activity

Insert an online picture.

1 Place the insertion point on page 1 to the left of the first word in the *Welcome to Dance Excitement!* paragraph.

2 On the ribbon, click the **INSERT tab**. In the Illustrations group, click the **Online Pictures button**. The Insert Pictures dialog box opens. Refer to Exhibit 12-15.

3 Click in the **Office.com Clip Art search box**, if necessary. Type **ballet slippers tutus**, and then click the **Search button** 🔍. After a moment, images that match these keywords appear in the dialog box.

4 Click the **photograph of the ballerina's feet colored blue**, and then click **Insert**. The photo is placed in the line at the current location of the insertion point.

Problem? If you don't see the photo described in Step 4 and shown in Exhibit 12-16, click a different photo. (Do not click an image that looks like a drawing.) If no results appear, search again, but use only the keyword **ballet**.

5 Change the zoom to **70%** so you can see the whole photo. See Exhibit 12-16.

End Activity

12-4b Examining a Selected Object

To work with or delete an object, you first need to select the object. When most objects are selected, a **selection box** surrounds the object. In Exhibit 12-16, the photo is selected. The small squares at each corner of the selection boxes and in the center of each side are **sizing handles** that you can drag to change the size of the selected object. For some selected objects, like the photo you inserted, a circle appears above the top-middle sizing handle of the selected object. This is the **rotate handle**, which you can drag to rotate the object in either direction.

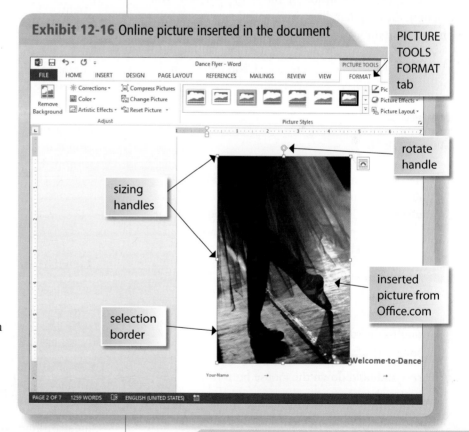

Exhibit 12-16 Online picture inserted in the document

PICTURE TOOLS FORMAT tab

rotate handle

sizing handles

selection border

inserted picture from Office.com

selection box The box that surrounds an object when it is selected.

sizing handle A small square that appears at the corner or on the side of a selection box.

rotate handle A small circular handle on a selected object that you can drag to rotate the object in either direction.

When an object is selected, a contextual tab appears on the ribbon with options for formatting, editing, moving, and resizing that object. For tables, as you have already seen, the two TABLE TOOLS contextual tabs appear. When you select most images, the PICTURE TOOLS FORMAT tab appears (refer back to Exhibit 12-16). However, some images are treated as drawings, so the DRAWING TOOLS FORMAT tab appears when they are selected. The PICTURE TOOLS FORMAT tab and the DRAWING TOOLS FORMAT tab contain similar commands.

12-4c Cropping a Picture

If you want to cut off part of a graphic, you can **crop** it. For example, you could crop an illustration of an ice cream cone by cropping off the cone, leaving only the ice cream itself. To crop a photo, select it, and then click the Crop button in the Size group on the PICTURE TOOLS FORMAT tab. When the Crop button is selected, crop handles appear just inside of the sizing handles. You can drag the crop handles to crop off those parts of the photo. See Exhibit 12-17.

The Crop button appears only on the PICTURE TOOLS FORMAT tab. There is no Crop button on the DRAWING TOOLS FORMAT tab.

Begin Activity

Crop a photo.

1. On the ribbon, click the **PICTURE TOOLS FORMAT tab**, if necessary. In the Size group, click the **Crop button**. The Crop button is selected, and black crop handles appear inside the sizing handles on the photo's selection border.

2. Scroll the document so you can see the top of the photo and the sizing and crop handles on the sides of the photo.

3. Point to the **top-middle crop handle**. The pointer changes to ⌐.

4. Press and hold down the mouse button. The pointer changes to +.

5. Drag down to just below the ballerina's bended knee, and then release the mouse button.

6. Scroll up so that you can see the uncropped portion of the photo. The top portion of the photo that will be cropped off is shaded gray.

7. Change the zoom to **120%**, and then drag the **bottom-middle crop handle** up to about 1/8 inch below the foot on the left.

8. Drag the **right-middle crop handle** to the left to about 1/8 inch to the right of the foot on the right.

9. Drag the **left-middle crop handle** to the right to about 1/4 inch to the left of the leg on the left. Refer back to Exhibit 12-17. Adjust the crop, if necessary, to match the Exhibit.

10. On the PICTURE TOOLS FORMAT tab, in the Size group, click the **Crop button**. The Crop button is deselected, and the crop handles and the cropped portions of the photo disappear.

End Activity

Problem? If the entire photo moves, release the mouse button, click the **Undo button** ↺ on the Quick Access Toolbar, and then repeat Steps 3–5, pausing slightly before dragging the crop handle.

Tip: You can also drag the photo inside the crop area to reposition it.

crop To cut off part of a graphic.

Exhibit 12-17 Cropped photo

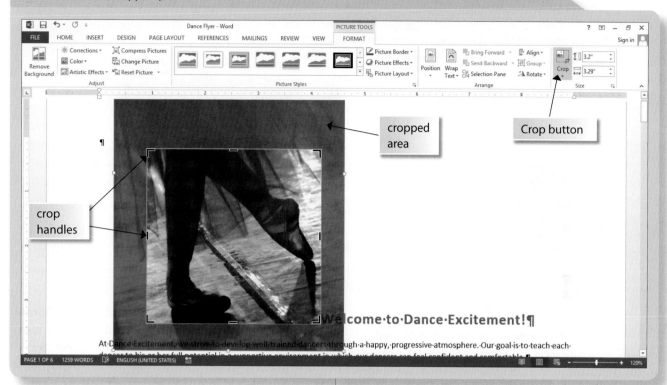

12-4d Resizing a Picture

You can change the size of graphics you insert. The easiest way to do this is to drag the sizing handles. You can also change a graphic's measurements using the Shape Height and Shape Width boxes in the Size group on the PICTURE TOOLS or DRAWING TOOLS FORMAT tab.

Pictures and other objects that cause the PICTURE TOOLS FORMAT tab to appear when selected have their aspect ratios locked by default. **Aspect ratio** specifies an object's height relative to its width. When you resize a graphic with its aspect ratio locked, dragging a corner sizing handle or changing one dimension in the Size group on the PICTURE TOOLS FORMAT tab changes the other dimension by the same percentage. However, dragging one of the sizing handles in the middle of the graphic's border overrides the locked aspect ratio setting and resizes the object only in the direction you drag. Generally, you do not want to override the aspect ratio setting when resizing photos because the images will be distorted.

Begin Activity

Resize a picture.

1 On the selected photo, point to the **upper-right sizing handle**. The pointer changes to ↗.

2 Press and hold the mouse button. The pointer changes to +.

3 Drag the **sizing handle** down and to the left. As you drag, the overall size of the photo shrinks.

4 When the photo is approximately **1.5-inches square**, release the mouse button. Use the measurements in the Shape Height and Shape Width boxes in the Size group on the PICTURE TOOLS FORMAT tab as a guide. See Exhibit 12-18.

Problem? If the photo flipped so it is facing the other way, you dragged the pointer past the photo. Click the **Undo button** ↶ on the Quick Access Toolbar, and then repeat Steps 1–4, making sure you do not drag the pointer past the photo.

End Activity

---

aspect ratio An object's height relative to its width.

Exhibit 12-18 Resized picture

picture measurements

12-4e Formatting a Picture

Like text and tables, pictures can have a style applied to them. A picture style can consist of a border, a shape, or an effect such as a shadow, reflection, or three-dimensional effect. To apply a style to a picture, select a style in the Picture Styles gallery on the PICTURE TOOLS FORMAT tab. If you want to modify part of the style definition, you can use the Picture Border and Picture Effects buttons in the Picture Styles group on the PICTURE TOOLS FORMAT tab.

Begin Activity

Format a picture.

1 On the PICTURE TOOLS FORMAT tab, in the Picture Styles group, click the **More button** ⯆.

2 Point to the various styles, and observe the Live Preview of the picture styles on the photo.

3 In the Picture Styles gallery, click the **Simple Frame, Black style**. The gallery closes, and the style you selected is applied. This style applies a 3-point, black border and a small drop shadow effect. You can adjust this style by using the buttons in the Picture Styles group.

Tip: If file size is a concern, select a picture, click the Compress Pictures button in the Adjust group on the PICTURE TOOLS FORMAT tab, and then select a lower resolution.

4 In the Picture Styles group, click the **Picture Border button arrow**, point to **Weight**, and then click **¼ pt**. The border thickness is changed to ¼ point. See Exhibit 12-19.

End Activity

LEARN MORE

Removing a Photo's Background

Remove Background

One specialized technique for editing photos allows you to remove the background of a photo, leaving only the foreground image. For example, you can edit a photo of a bird in the sky to remove the sky, leaving only the image of the bird. To edit a photo to remove the background, use the Remove Background button in the Adjust group on the PICTURE TOOLS FORMAT tab. Removing a photo's background can be tricky, especially if you are working on a photo with a background that is not clearly differentiated from the foreground image. For example, you might find it difficult to remove a white, snowy background from a photo of an equally white snowman.

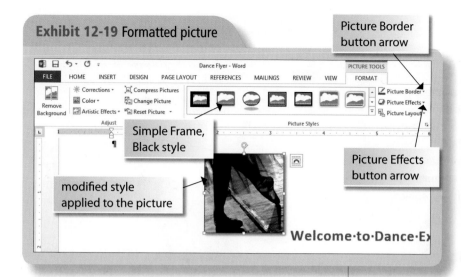

Exhibit 12-19 Formatted picture

Picture Border button arrow

Simple Frame, Black style

modified style applied to the picture

Picture Effects button arrow

- ▶ **Behind Text**—text flows over the graphic.

- ▶ **In Front of Text**—text flows behind the graphic.

To change the wrap properties of an object, select the graphic, and then click the Layout Options button that appears next to the upper-right corner of the selected graphic to open a menu of wrap options. See Exhibit 12-20. Select the wrap option you want to use. These same options are available on the Wrap Text button menu in the Arrange group on the PICTURE TOOLS FORMAT tab.

12-5 Wrapping Text Around Graphics

Graphic objects in a document can be either inline or floating. An **inline object** (often called an **inline graphic**) is located in a specific position in a line of text in the document, and the object moves along with the text. For example, if you type text to the left of an inline object, the object moves right to accommodate the new text. You can drag the object to another position in the document, but it appears in a line of text wherever you drop it. When you format a paragraph that contains an inline object, the inline object is also formatted. For example, if you right-align the paragraph, the inline graphic will be right-aligned with the paragraph. The photo you inserted is an inline object.

A **floating object** (often called a **floating graphic**) can be positioned anywhere in the document, and the text will flow—wrap—around the object or float on top of or behind text. The wrap settings for graphics are:

- ▶ **Square**—text flows around the straight edges of an object's border.

- ▶ **Tight**—text flows around the contours of the object itself.

- ▶ **Through**—text flows around the contours of the object itself and also fills any open spaces in the graphic.

- ▶ **Top and Bottom**—text stops at the top border of an object and resumes below the bottom border.

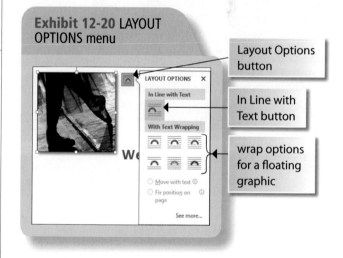

Exhibit 12-20 LAYOUT OPTIONS menu

Layout Options button

In Line with Text button

wrap options for a floating graphic

Begin Activity

Change a graphic's text wrap properties.

1 Click the **photo** to select it, if necessary.

2 Click the **Layout Options button** . The LAYOUT OPTIONS menu opens. Refer to Exhibit 12-20.

3 On the menu, click the **Square option**. The text in the document wraps around the photo on both sides, and the Square option on the menu is now shaded blue to indicate that it is selected.

End Activity

inline object (inline graphic) A graphic that is positioned in a line of text and moves along with the text.

floating object (floating graphic) A graphic that can be positioned anywhere in a document.

Understanding Anchors

All floating graphics are attached, or anchored, to a paragraph. If you move the paragraph to which a floating graphic is anchored, the graphic will move also. If you cut the paragraph to the Clipboard, the graphic is cut as well. When nonprinting characters are displayed, an anchor icon appears next to the paragraph to which the floating graphic is anchored. You can anchor a floating graphic to another paragraph if you want. If you drag a floating graphic to a new position on the page, the anchor moves as well, and the graphic is anchored to a new paragraph close to its new location.

However, unless you lock the anchor, if you move the graphic, it will be anchored to another paragraph. To lock a floating graphic's anchor to a specific paragraph, click More Layout Options on the Wrap Text button menu, click the Position tab, and then select the Lock anchor check box.

Stephen Coburn/Shutterstock.com

12-6 Moving Graphics

To move a graphic, you drag it to its new position. If the graphic is an inline graphic, you can drag it to its new position in any line of text. The same pointer and vertical indicator line that you saw when you dragged selected text appears.

When you drag a floating graphic, the graphic follows the pointer, and the text flows around it as you drag. As you drag floating graphics, green horizontal and vertical lines called **alignment guides** appear to help you align the object with the text and other objects on the page and with the margins. See Exhibit 12-21. You can drop the graphic anywhere on the page. You might need to make small adjustments in the graphic's position if the text doesn't wrap as you expect.

alignment guide A green horizontal or vertical line that appears when you drag a floating object in a Word document to help you position the object.

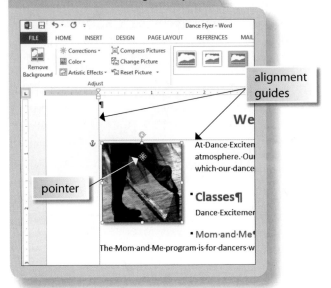

Begin Activity

Move graphics.

1 Point to the **photo** so that the pointer changes to 🔀.

2 Drag the **photo** to the left and down so that the green vertical alignment guides indicate that the left edge of the photo aligns with the left margin and the top edge of the photo aligns with the top of the paragraph below the *Welcome to Dance Excitement!* heading. Refer back to Exhibit 12-21.

End Activity

Using the Position Button

The Position button in the Arrange group on the PICTURE TOOLS FORMAT tab is a shortcut to formatting a graphic as a floating graphic with the Square wrapping option and moving the graphic to a specific position on the page (top left, top middle, top right, and so on). For example, to position a graphic in the lower-right corner of the page and wrap the text around the top and left sides of the graphic, click the Position button, and then click the style in the bottom right of the gallery.

12-7 Adding Text Effects and WordArt Text Boxes

Text effects are special formatting effects, such as an outline, a shadow, reflection, or glow effect, you can apply to text. A **text box** is a container that contains text. Like the photo you inserted, text boxes are objects that have a selection border, sizing handles, and a rotate handle. **WordArt** is a term used to describe formatted, decorative text in a text box.

12-7a Applying Text Effects

To apply text effects to text, click the Text Effects and Typography button 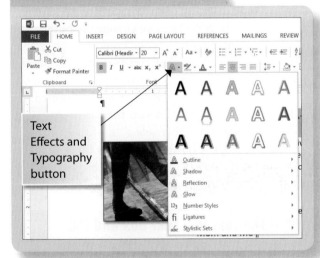 in the Font group on the HOME tab. The menu that opens includes a gallery of styles you can apply and a list of effect categories that contain submenus. See Exhibit 12-22. When you apply text effects, you are treating each character more like a shape that has an outline and an inside—a fill—color. To change the inside color, you simply change the font color.

Exhibit 12-22 Text Effects and Typography button menu

Begin Activity

Format text with text effects.

1 On page 1, select all of the text in the second paragraph (*Welcome to Dance Excitement!*).

2 On the ribbon, click the **HOME tab**. In the Font group, click the **Text Effects and Typography button**. A menu of styles and categories of effects opens. Refer to Exhibit 12-22.

3 In the gallery of styles, click the **Gradient Fill – Orange, Accent 4, Outline – Accent 4 style**. The style is applied to the selected text.

4 Click the **Text Effects and Typography button**, and then point to **Outline**. In the color palette in the submenu, the Orange, Accent 4 color is selected. This is the outline color that is part of the style you applied to the text.

5 Point to **Shadow**. In the submenu, No Shadow is selected as part of the style you applied.

6 In the Outer section, click the **Offset Diagonal Bottom Right shadow**. The shadow is applied to the text.

7 In the Font group, click the **Font Color button arrow**, and then click the **Red, Accent 2, Darker 25% color**. The color of the text changes to the dark red color.

End Activity

12-7b Inserting WordArt Text Boxes

To insert a text box, you use the Text Box button in the Text group on the INSERT tab. After you create a text box, you can apply WordArt styles and other formatting to it. To insert a text box that has a WordArt style applied to it, use the WordArt button in the Text group on the INSERT tab. When you click this button, a gallery of styles opens, as shown in Exhibit 12-23. This is the same gallery of styles as on the Text Effects button menu. However, when you insert WordArt, you don't simply format text; you create a text box containing text formatted with the style you choose.

Exhibit 12-23 WordArt button menu

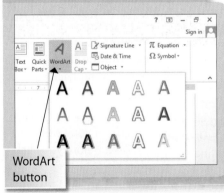

text effects Special formatting effects that you can apply to text.

text box An object that contains text.

WordArt Formatted, decorative text in a text box.

When you insert a WordArt text box, it contains placeholder text *Your text here*, as shown in Exhibit 12-24. You can also select text in the document, and then use the WordArt button to create WordArt from the selected text.

Exhibit 12-24 WordArt text box inserted

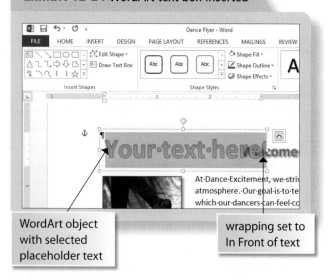

WordArt object with selected placeholder text

wrapping set to In Front of text

Text boxes and WordArt that you create from selected text are inserted as floating objects with the wrapping set to Square. When you create a WordArt text box without first selecting text, the wrapping is set to In Front of Text.

Begin Activity

Insert a WordArt text box.

1. On page 1, place the insertion point in the empty first paragraph (above the *Welcome to Dance Excitement!* paragraph).

2. On the ribbon, click the **INSERT tab**. In the Text group, click the **WordArt button**. The gallery of WordArt styles appears. Refer back to Exhibit 12-23.

3. In the gallery, click the **Gradient Fill – Orange, Accent 4, Outline – Accent 4 style**. A text box is inserted with the placeholder text *Your text here*. The placeholder text is selected. Refer back to Exhibit 12-24. Because the wrap-

> **Tip:** If you select text before you click the WordArt button, the WordArt text box will contain the selected text.

ping is set to In Front of Text, you can see the text in the document behind the text box.

4. Type **Dance Excitement**.

End Activity

The DRAWING TOOLS FORMAT tab appears on the ribbon when a text box is selected. This tab is similar to the PICTURE TOOLS FORMAT tab. Most of the commands in the WordArt Styles group format the text in the text box. The styles in the styles gallery are the same styles you saw when you created the WordArt. The commands in the Shape Styles group format the text box itself.

You can format the text in a text box just as you would any text in a document using the commands in the Font group on the HOME tab, including adding text effects. In addition, text in a text box can be formatted with 3D effects and transformed into waves, circles, and other shapes. Exhibit 12-25 shows the Transform submenu on the Text Effects button menu. The menu of text effects contains the same options that appear on the Text Effects and Typography button menu in the Font group on the HOME tab plus two additional options: 3-D Rotation and Transform. These last two options are available only for text boxes.

You can also format the object itself—the container holding the text. You can change the outline and fill color (the inside color) of the container, or apply a style or the same effects that you can apply to photos. When the insertion point is in a text box, the border is a dashed line. When the entire text box is selected, the border is a solid line. When you format the text in a text box, you need to either select all of the text in the text box, or click the border of the text box to make it a solid line and to select the entire text box.

Begin Activity

Format the text in a text box and the text box.

1. Point to the **WordArt text box border** so that the pointer changes to ⛶, and then click the border. The border changes to a solid line, and the text box is selected.

2. On the DRAWING TOOLS FORMAT tab, in the WordArt Styles group, click the **Text Outline button arrow**. The color palette opens.

Exhibit 12-25 Commands on the DRAWING TOOLS FORMAT tab

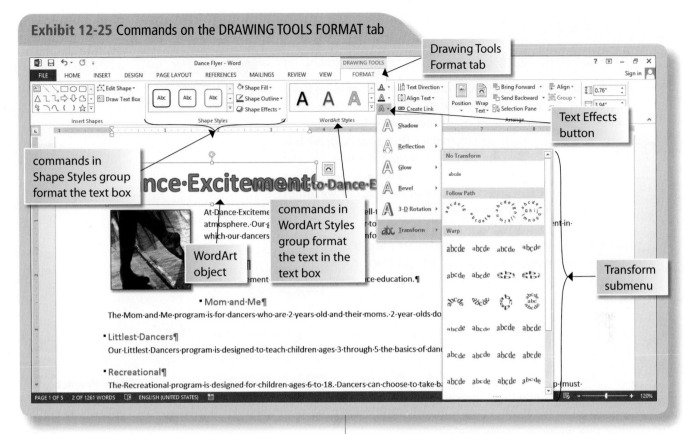

commands in Shape Styles group format the text box

WordArt object

commands in WordArt Styles group format the text in the text box

Drawing Tools Format tab

Text Effects button

Transform submenu

3 In the color palette, click the **Red, Accent 3, Darker 50% color**. The outline of the text in the text box changes to dark red.

4 In the WordArt Styles group, click the **Text Fill button arrow** ![A], and then click the **Red, Accent 3 color**. This is the same as changing the font color.

5 In the WordArt Styles group, click the **Text Effects button** ![A], and then point to **Transform**. The gallery of transform effects appears. Refer back to Exhibit 12-25.

6 Point to several of the transform effects to see the Live Preview on the WordArt.

7 In the Warp section, click the **Chevron Up effect**. The text is formatted in the shape you selected.

8 In the Shape Styles group, click the **Shape Fill button arrow**. In the color palette, click the **White,**

Tip: If you deselect a text box with a transform or 3D effect applied and then click it to edit the text, the effect is removed temporarily.

Background 1 color. The text box shape is filled with white, and you can no longer see the text behind it. Compare your screen to Exhibit 12-26.

End Activity

Exhibit 12-26 Formatted WordArt text box

You can resize text boxes in the same manner as photos: you drag the sizing handles or use the Shape Height and Shape Width boxes in the Size group on the DRAWING TOOLS FORMAT tab. The aspect ratio for text boxes is not locked, so changing one dimension will not automatically change the other. When a text box is selected, Left and Right Indent markers on the ruler indicate the margins inside the text box.

More About Text Boxes

You can insert text boxes containing ordinary text—that is, text that is not WordArt. To do this, click the Text Box button in the Text group on the INSERT tab. Click one of the styles in the gallery to insert a formatted text box containing placeholder text, or click Draw Text Box to insert an empty text box. You can format the text in a text box just as you would any text. You can also format the text box itself by adding or changing the fill color or the color or weight of the border. Text boxes are inserted as floating objects. Click the first style to insert a text box containing placeholder text formatted with the Normal style, or click another style to insert a text box formatted with colors and borders. If the text you want to place in the text box is already in the document, you can select it first and then create a text box that contains the text you selected.

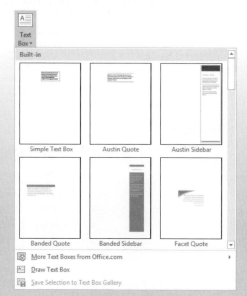

Text Box gallery

Unlike photos, text boxes are inserted as floating objects so you can position them anywhere on the page. Text boxes created using the WordArt button have the In Front of Text wrapping option applied.

Begin Activity

Resize a text box, change its wrapping option, and move it.

1 On the DRAWING TOOLS FORMAT tab, in the Size group, click in the **Shape Width box**. The current measurement is selected.

2 Type **6**, and then press the **Enter key**. The WordArt text box is resized to 6 inches wide.

3 In the Size group, click in the **Shape Height box**, type **1**, and then press the **Enter key**. The height of the WordArt text box is resized to 1 inch.

4 Click the **Layout Options button** 🖼, and then click the **Top and Bottom option**.

5 Point to the **solid line text box border** so that the pointer changes to ⬌.

6 Drag the **WordArt text box** to the right above the *Welcome to Dance Excitement!* paragraph, and use the green alignment guides to align the top of the WordArt text box with the top margin and to horizontally center the text box. Compare your screen to Exhibit 12-27.

End Activity

Exhibit 12-27 Resized and repositioned WordArt text box

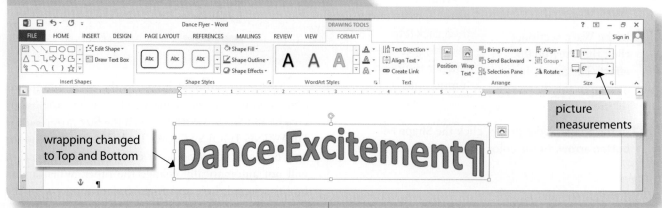

12-8 Working with Columns

Columns allow the eye to take in a lot of text and to scan quickly for interesting information. Formatting text in multiple columns also allows you to fit more text on a page than if the text were in only one column.

12-8a Creating Columns

You can format an entire document or only a section of a document in columns. To format the current section (or an entire document if it does not contain any section breaks) in columns, click the Columns button in the Page Setup group on the PAGE LAYOUT tab, and then select a command on the Columns menu, shown in Exhibit 12-28. Selecting Two or Three formats the section in the corresponding number of columns of equal width. Selecting Left or Right formats the section in two columns of unequal width with the narrower column on the side identified by the command. The command One formats the section in one column (the normal setting for ordinary documents).

To create columns with any other format, adjust the width between columns, add a line between columns, format the entire document in columns when it contains section breaks, or insert a Continuous section break automatically and format the text after the section break in columns, click the More Columns command to open the Columns dialog box.

Exhibit 12-28 Columns button menu

Columns button

See Exhibit 12-29. The buttons in the Presets section correspond to the commands on the Columns button menu. At the bottom of the dialog box, the Apply to box indicates what part of the document will be formatted with this column setting—the current section, the entire document, or from the insertion point forward.

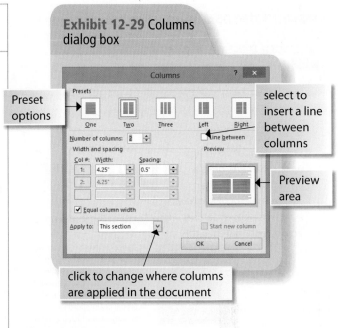

Exhibit 12-29 Columns dialog box

Preset options

select to insert a line between columns

Preview area

click to change where columns are applied in the document

Begin Activity

Format a document in columns.

1. Below the WordArt text box, place the insertion point before the word *Welcome*.

2. On the ribbon, click the **PAGE LAYOUT tab**. In the Page Setup group, click the **Columns button**. The Columns menu opens. Refer to Exhibit 12-28.

3. Click **Two**. All the text in section 1 after the insertion point is formatted in two columns.

4. Scroll down and view pages 4 and 5. These pages, which are in sections 2 and 3, are still formatted in one column.

5. Scroll to the beginning of the document. Make sure the insertion point is still positioned before the word *Welcome*.

6. In the Page Setup group, click the **Columns button**, and then click **More Columns**. The Columns dialog box opens. Refer to Exhibit 12-29. In the Apply to box, *This section* appears, indicating that the settings you select in this dialog box will apply only to the text in the current section.

7. Above the Preview section, click the **Line between check box** to select it. A vertical line appears in the Preview area separating the two columns.

Exhibit 12-30 Document formatted in two columns

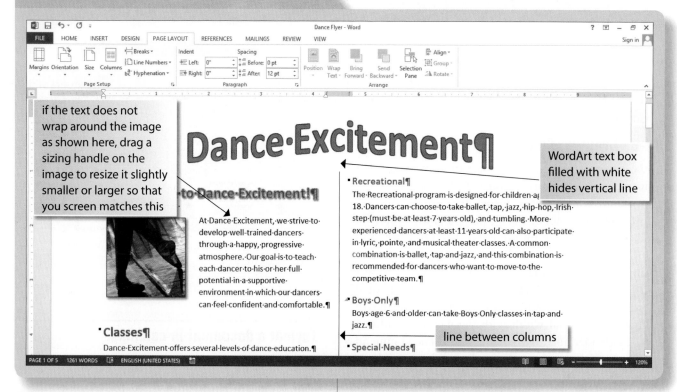

if the text does not wrap around the image as shown here, drag a sizing handle on the image to resize it slightly smaller or larger so that you screen matches this

Dance·Excitement¶

...to·Dance·Excitement!¶

At·Dance·Excitement,·we·strive·to·develop·well-trained·dancers·through·a·happy,·progressive·atmosphere.·Our·goal·is·to·teach·each·dancer·to·his·or·her·full·potential·in·a·supportive·environment·in·which·our·dancers·can·feel·confident·and·comfortable.¶

▪ **Classes¶**

Dance·Excitement·offers·several·levels·of·dance·education.¶

▪ **Recreational¶**

The·Recreational·program·is·designed·for·children·ag [...] 18.·Dancers·can·choose·to·take·ballet,·tap,·jazz,·hip-hop,·Irish·step·(must·be·at·least·7·years·old),·and·tumbling.·More·experienced·dancers·at·least·11·years·old·can·also·participate·in·lyric,·pointe,·and·musical·theater·classes.·A·common·combination·is·ballet,·tap·and·jazz,·and·this·combination·is·recommended·for·dancers·who·want·to·move·to·the·competitive·team.¶

▪ **Boys·Only¶**

Boys·age·6·and·older·can·take·Boys·Only·classes·in·tap·and·jazz.¶

▪ **Special·Needs¶**

WordArt text box filled with white hides vertical line

line between columns

PAGE 1 OF 5   1261 WORDS   ENGLISH (UNITED STATES)   120%

---

8 Click **OK**. The Columns dialog box closes. A vertical line is inserted between the two columns.

9 Scroll up so you can see the WordArt text box. The vertical line behind the text box is not visible because you filled the text box with white. Compare your screen to Exhibit 12-30.

End Activity

FYI

Inserting a Page Border

A page border adds interest to a document by decorating/embellishing the edges/boundary of a page. On the DESIGN tab, in the Page Background group, click the Page Borders button. The Borders and Shading dialog box opens with the Page Border tab selected. Select any of the line styles in the Style list, or click the Art arrow and then select a graphic to use as the border. If you are working with a document that contains section breaks, make sure the Apply to box contains the correct setting (Whole document or This section).

12-8b Balancing Columns

Balancing columns—that is, making the columns on pages in a section the same length—creates a professional-looking document. To automatically balance columns, you insert a Continuous section break at the end of the last column on the last page in the section. The columns will remain balanced no matter how much material you add or remove from either column.

If you want a column to end at a specific point, or you want to manually balance the columns, insert a column break using the Breaks button in the Page Setup group on the PAGE LAYOUT tab.

Begin Activity

Balance columns.

1 Scroll down so that you can see the end of the second column on page 3. (The last paragraph starts with *Registration Fee.*)

2 In the second column, in the last line, place the insertion point between the paragraph mark and the dotted line that indicates the Next Page section break you inserted earlier.

3 On the PAGE LAYOUT tab, in the Page Setup group, click the **Breaks button**. The Breaks menu opens.

Exhibit 12-31 Final flyer

section 1 formatted in two columns and landscape orientation

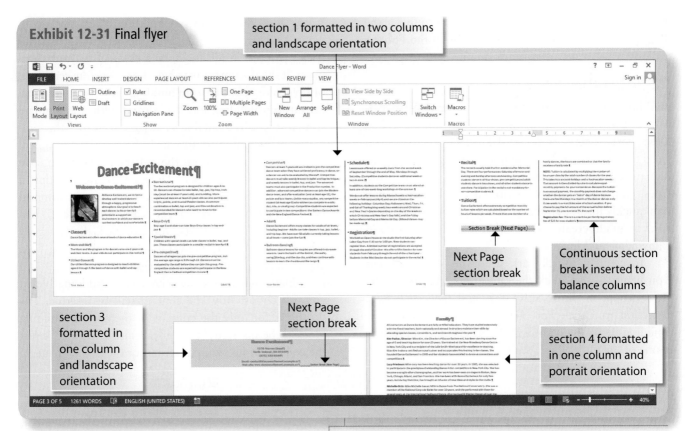

Next Page section break

Continuous section break inserted to balance columns

section 3 formatted in one column and landscape orientation

Next Page section break

section 4 formatted in one column and portrait orientation

4 In the Section Breaks section, click **Continuous**. A Continuous section break is inserted at the insertion point, and the columns on the last page are balanced. Now there are two section breaks in a row; the Continuous section break you just inserted is immediately followed by the Next Page section break you inserted before the address on page 4. Section 1 is everything before the Continuous section break, section 2 is essentially blank because nothing appears between the two section breaks, section 3 is page 4, and section 4 is page 5.

5 Scroll down so you can see the footer on page 3 and the header on page 4.

6 On page 3, double-click in the footer area. The tab on the footer identifies the footer as section 1, and the header on page 4 is identified as section 3.

7 Double-click anywhere outside the footer or header area.

8 On the ribbon, click the **VIEW tab**. In the Zoom group, click the **Multiple Pages button**.

9 Change the zoom to **40%**. Compare your screen to Exhibit 12-31.

End Activity

12-9 Working with Building Blocks

Building blocks are parts of a document that are stored and reused. Word has many predesigned building blocks for a wide variety of items, including cover pages, calendars, numbering, text boxes, and more. You used building blocks when you added formatted headers and footers. You can create custom building blocks as well.

Building blocks are stored in galleries. For example, the predesigned choices listed on the Header button menu are building blocks stored in the Headers gallery. If you save a custom building block to another gallery, it will be available when you access that gallery along with the built-in building blocks in that gallery. For example, if you create a custom footer and then save it to the Footers gallery, you can click the

Shutterstock 58277284

building block A part of a document that is stored and reused.

Footer button in the Header & Footer group on the INSERT tab to see your custom footer in the Footers gallery.

12-9a Creating Quick Parts

Building blocks that are stored in the Quick Parts gallery in the Text group on the INSERT tab are called **Quick Parts**. There are no predefined Quick Parts; you need to create these. For example, you might make your signature block for a letter ("Sincerely," several blank lines, your name, and your title) a Quick Part so you can quickly insert that text without typing it every time. Or, you might create a Quick Part that contains a company name and logo.

To create a Quick Part, select the formatted text you want to save, click the Quick Parts button in the Text group on the INSERT tab, and then click Save Selection to Quick Part Gallery. In the Create New Building Block dialog box that opens, you can type the name of the Quick Part. See Exhibit 12-32.

When you create a custom building block in a document, it is stored in the Building Blocks template so that it can be used in all documents created on your computer. If the document was based on a custom template, or if you create the custom building block in a template, the custom building block is stored with the template so that it will be available to anyone who uses the template on any computer to which the template is copied.

You can also choose the gallery in which to save a custom building block. Unless you are creating a specialty custom building block, such as a customized header, the Quick Parts gallery is a good choice. To further organize Quick Parts, you can click the Category arrow in the Create New Building Block dialog box, and then click Create New Category.

Finally, when you save the custom building block, you can choose how the content will be inserted. The default is for only the content of the custom building block to be inserted, but you can also choose to insert the content in its own paragraph or on its own page.

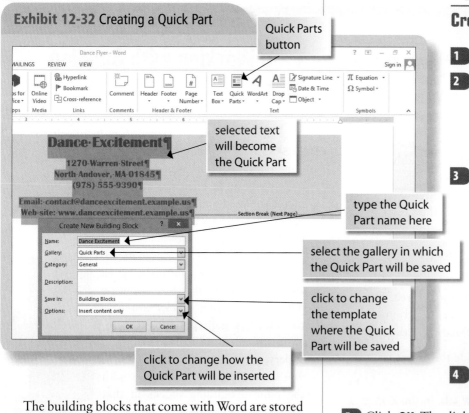

Exhibit 12-32 Creating a Quick Part

Quick Parts button

selected text will become the Quick Part

type the Quick Part name here

select the gallery in which the Quick Part will be saved

click to change the template where the Quick Part will be saved

click to change how the Quick Part will be inserted

The building blocks that come with Word are stored in the global Building Blocks template, which is available to all Word documents created on the computer.

Quick Part A building block stored in the Quick Parts gallery.

Begin Activity

Create Quick Parts.

1 Change the zoom to **120%**.

2 On page 4, select all of the text from **Dance Excitement** through the **paragraph mark after the Web site address**. Do *not* select the section break.

3 On the ribbon, click the **INSERT tab**. In the Text group, click the **Quick Parts button**, and then click **Save Selection to Quick Part Gallery**. The Create New Building Block dialog box opens. Refer to Exhibit 12-32. The building block will be saved in the Quick Parts gallery and in the Building Blocks template.

4 In the Name box, type **Contact Info**.

5 Click **OK**. The dialog box closes, and the formatted contact information is saved as a custom building block.

End Activity

12-9b Inserting Quick Parts

After you create a Quick Part, it appears on the Quick Parts button menu as shown in Exhibit 12-33, and it is available for you to insert into other documents. To insert a Quick Part, click the Quick Parts button in the Text group on the INSERT tab, and then click the Quick Part on the menu.

Exhibit 12-33 Quick Parts menu

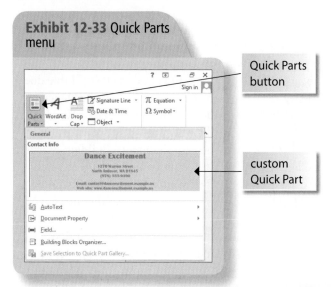

Quick Parts button

custom Quick Part

Begin Activity

Insert a Quick Part.

1 Switch to the **Class Table** document. Position the insertion point at the beginning of the document (before the word *August*).

2 On the ribbon, click the **INSERT tab**. In the Text group, click the **Quick Parts button**. The Quick Part you created, Contact Info, appears on the Quick Parts menu. Refer to Exhibit 12-33.

3 Click the **Contact Info Quick Part**. The menu closes, and the contact information is inserted in

Tip: Right-click a Quick Part on the Quick Parts menu to open a shortcut menu containing additional ways to insert the Quick Part.

its own paragraph at the insertion point. Compare your screen to Exhibit 12-34.

4 In the closing of the letter, replace *Kim Parker* with your name.

5 Save and close the document.

End Activity

CAUTION

Avoid Using Theme Fonts and Colors for Quick Parts

Because you usually want formatted text that you save as a Quick Part to be inserted with the same formatting every time, make sure the formatted text is not formatted with theme fonts or colors or styles with definitions that include theme elements.

Exhibit 12-34 Quick Part inserted in a document

Contact Info Quick Part

12-9c Managing Building Blocks

The Building Blocks Organizer dialog box lists all of the building blocks in the global Building Blocks template and in the current template. See Exhibit 12-35. In the Building Blocks Organizer dialog box, you can sort the building blocks by their names, gallery location, categories, or template location. You can also use the Building Blocks Organizer to insert a building block, edit the properties of a building block, or delete a building block.

Exhibit 12-35 Building Blocks Organizer dialog box

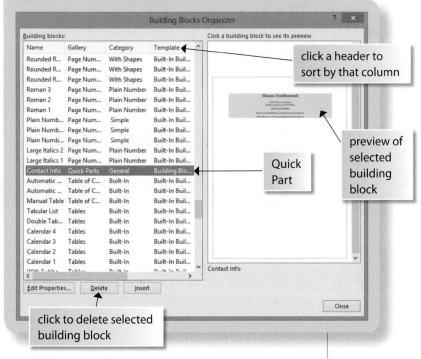

click a header to sort by that column

preview of selected building block

Quick Part

click to delete selected building block

Begin Activity

Use the Building Blocks Organizer and delete Quick Parts.

1. On the INSERT tab, in the Text group, click the **Quick Parts button**, and then click **Building Blocks Organizer**. The Building Blocks Organizer dialog box opens.

2. Click the **Name column header**. The list is sorted in alphabetical order by name.

3. Click the **Gallery column header**. The list is sorted in alphabetical order by gallery.

4. Scroll down until you see the entry in the Quick Parts gallery, and then click the **Contact Info building block**. The selected building block appears in the preview pane. Refer to Exhibit 12-35.

Tip: To open the Building Blocks gallery with a Quick Part selected in the Building blocks list in the dialog box, right-click the Quick Part on the Quick Parts menu, and then on the shortcut menu, click Organize and Delete.

5. Below the Building blocks list, click **Delete**. A dialog box opens, asking if you are sure you want to delete the selected building block.

6. Click **Yes**. The dialog box closes, and the Contact Info custom building block is deleted from the computer.

7. At the bottom of the dialog box, click **Close**. The Building Blocks Organizer dialog box closes.

8. Save and close the Class Table document, save and close the Dance Flyer document, and then exit Word. A dialog box opens asking if you want to save changes to Building Blocks. If you had not deleted the Quick Part you created and you wanted to save it for use in the future, you would click Save. Because you deleted the Quick Part, it doesn't matter if you save changes to the Building Blocks template.

9. Click **Don't Save**. The dialog box closes, and Word exits.

End Activity

Quiz Yourself

1. In a table, what is the intersection of a column and a row called?

2. When a table is formatted with banded rows, what does it mean?

3. Explain the difference between portrait and landscape orientation.

4. What is a section?

5. How many sections does a document have if it does not contain a section break?

6. What is a sizing handle?

7. What happens to a photo when you crop part of it?

8. What is WordArt?

9. Explain the difference between an inline graphic and a floating graphic.

10. When you click one of the options on the Columns button menu, what part of the document is the column formatting applied to?

11. How do you balance columns without inserting manual column breaks?

12. What is a building block?

13. Where are Quick Parts stored?

14. How do you insert a Quick Part?

15. Describe the Building Blocks Organizer.

Practice It

Practice It 12-1

1. Use the Open command in Backstage view to open the data file **Newsletter** located in the Chapter 12\Practice It folder. (Do not double-click the file in a File Explorer window to open it.) Open the Save As dialog box. Notice that the Save as type is a Word Template so the Quick Part you will create will be included in your solution file. Type **Library Newsletter** in the File name box. Click Save.

2. In the blank paragraph at the end of the document, insert a table with two columns and five rows.

3. Enter the following data in the table:

Area	Purchase
Technology	New computers for Teen Center
Book acquisitions	Books and magazine subscriptions
Murals	Paint and supplies
Bulletin boards	Maps and posters

4. Insert a new last column, and then type **Date** in the first row in the new column.

5. Insert a new second column, and then enter the following data:

Budget
$5500
$4200
$250
$125

6. Insert a new row above the Murals row with the following data in the first three cells:

Supplies
$300
Book rack, book plates, maps, and posters

7. Delete the row containing *Bulletin boards* and the column labeled *Date*.

8. AutoFit all of the columns.

9. Increase the width of the first column to 1.5 inches, AutoFit the Budget column, and then increase the width of the Purchase column so the right border is at the 5-inch mark on the ruler. (*Hint*: Make sure no text in the table is selected before resizing the columns.)

10. Format the table with the Grid Table 4 – Accent 3 table style. Apply special formatting to the header row, remove special formatting from the first column, and use banded rows.

11. Center the table horizontally on the page, and then center the column labels *Area* and *Purchase* in their cells.

12. Format all the text after the date in the third line of the document in two columns. Include a line between the two columns.

13. Balance the columns by inserting a Continuous section break before the Donations heading at the end of the second paragraph. (Don't worry about the position of the table.) Then insert a Next Page section break before the Donations heading, which has moved to the bottom of the first column.

14. Change the formatting of the last section in the document (the section containing the Donations heading and the table) so that it is one column and in landscape orientation.

15. Insert a column break before the Recommendations Bulletin Board heading.

16. On page 2, use the Edit Header command on the Header button menu to insert a header, and then unlink the header on page 2 from the previous section.

17. In the header on page 2, type your name so that it is left-aligned, type **Newsletter** aligned under the Center Tab stop, and then type **page 2** aligned under the Right Tab stop. Move the Right Tab stop to the 9.25-inch mark on the ruler, and then move the Center Tab stop to the 4.5-inch mark.

18. At the top of page 1, in the paragraph under the Spine Label Replacement heading, place the insertion point before *Replacing*, and then insert an online picture from Office.com. Use the keywords **book stack**, and insert a photo of a stack of books.

Make sure you select a photo, not a drawing, and select one that has a background (that is, not just a stack of books on a white background).

19. Crop the photo tightly around the stack of books, and then resize the cropped photo so it is approximately 1-inch high.

20. Format the photo using the Bevel Rectangle picture style, and then apply a 5 Point soft edge (using the Soft Edges submenu on the Picture Effects button menu).

21. Change the photo to a floating graphic using the Square wrapping option. Drag it so that it is positioned to the left of the first paragraph under the Spine Label Replacement heading and so that according to the green alignment guides, the top edge is aligned with the top of the paragraph and the left edge is aligned with the left margin.

22. Place the insertion point in the blank, first paragraph at the beginning of the document. Insert a WordArt text box using the Fill – White, Outline, Accent 1, Shadow style. Type **Portland Library Friends** as the text in the text box.

23. Change the fill color of the text in the WordArt text box to Brown, Accent 3, and change the Text Outline color of the text in the WordArt text box to White, Background 1. (Make sure the entire text box is selected.)

24. Apply the Deflate transform effect to the WordArt, and then increase the curve of the Deflate transform effect slightly. Reposition the WordArt text box so it is centered above the Newsletter title and so the *y* in *Library* is almost touching the second *t* in *Newsletter*.

25. Save the entire paragraph containing *Newsletter* (including the paragraph mark) as a Quick Part named **Title** in the Library Newsletter template. (Make sure Library Newsletter appears in the Save in box in the Create New Building Block dialog box.)

26. Save the document.

Practice It 12-2

1. Open the data file **Notice** located in the Chapter 12\Practice It folder. Save the document as **Trip Notice**.

2. Format the paragraphs between the Driving Directions heading and the Alternate Transportation Options heading in three columns.

3. Insert a column break at the bottom of the first column before the From the North/South/East heading.

4. Insert another column break at the bottom of the second column before the From the West/Southwest heading.

5. In the blank first paragraph, insert a WordArt text box using one of the styles in the last row. Type **Kidz Klub Adventure** as the text in the text box.

6. Change the fill of the text in the text box to Dark Purple, Text 2. Change the color of the outline of the text in the text box to Light Blue, Background 2.

7. Apply the Arch Up transform effect in the Follow Path section of the gallery to the WordArt text box.

8. Center the WordArt above the top line of text in the document. Make sure the vertical alignment guide shows that the text box is center-aligned and a horizontal alignment guide shows that the top of the text box is aligned with the top margin.

9. At the beginning of the first paragraph below the date, insert a photo of a butterfly from Office.com. Use one that does not have a background.

10. Crop the photo if necessary, and change the text wrapping to Square. Position the photo to the left of the two paragraphs below the date. Resize the photo so it is the same height as the two paragraphs.

11. Add your name as a left-aligned footer.

12. Save the document, and then close it.

On Your Own

On Your Own 12-1

1. Use the Open command in Backstage view to open the data file **Brochure** located in the Chapter 12\On Your Own folder. (Do not double-click the file in a File Explorer window to open it.) Save the file as **Auction Brochure** leaving the Save as type set to Word Template so the Quick Part you will create will be included in your solution file.

2. Change the orientation of the document to Landscape.

3. Select all the text in the document except for the first paragraph containing *Auction*, and then convert the selected text into a table with three columns. (*Hint*: Use the Convert Text to Table command on the Table button menu. Adjust the number of columns to 3, and make sure the Paragraphs option button is selected in the Separate text at section.)

4. Add a new row to the top of the table with the labels **Package**, **Value**, and **Description**.

5. Change the Theme Colors to Paper, and then apply the Grid Table 4 – Accent 1 table style to the table. Format the header row and the first column with special formatting, and use banded rows. Adjust the formatting of text in specific cells in the first row and first column if necessary so they are consistent.

6. Adjust the column widths so that the first column is 2 inches wide, the second column is AutoFit, and the third column stretches to the right margin.

7. Center all the text in the Value column using the Align Center command. Center all the text in the Package column using the Align Center Left command.

8. Select the first paragraph (containing *Auction*), including the paragraph mark, and convert it to a WordArt text box using the Gradient Fill – Gray style. Apply the Perspective Diagonal Upper Left shadow effect to the text in the text box.

9. Position the WordArt as a floating graphic above the table and approximately aligned with the left edge of the table.

10. Use the keyword **auction** to search for an online picture on Office.com, and choose an image.

11. Crop off part of the image if it would look better.

12. Change the wrap properties of the image to Tight. Position it in the upper-right corner of the document. Change the zoom to One Page, and then reduce its size as needed so that it fits above the table and the table stays on one page.

13. Save the WordArt as a Quick Part in the Auction Brochure template. Name the Quick Part **Auction Heading**.

14. Save the document, and then close it.

Chapter 12

ADDITIONAL STUDY TOOLS

IN THE BOOK
▶ Complete end-of-chapter exercises
▶ Study tear-out Chapter Review Card

ONLINE
▶ Complete additional end-of-chapter exercises

▶ Take practice quiz to prepare for tests
▶ Review key term flash cards (online, printable, and audio)
▶ Play "Beat the Clock" and "Memory" to quiz yourself
▶ Watch the videos to learn more about the topics taught in this chapter

Answers to Quiz Yourself

1. The intersection of a column and a row is a cell.

2. When a table is formatted with banded rows, every other row is shaded.

3. Portrait orientation describes a page taller than wide. Landscape orientation describes a page wider than tall.

4. A section is a part of a document that has its own page-level formatting and properties.

5. If a document does not contain a section break, it contains one section.

6. Sizing handles are the small squares at each corner of the selection boxes and in the center of each side of the selection boxes that you can drag to change the size of the selected object.

7. When you crop part of a photo, you cut off the part that you crop.

8. WordArt is formatted, decorative text that is treated as an object.

9. An inline graphic is a graphic that is positioned in a line of text and moves along with the text. A floating graphic is a graphic that can be positioned anywhere in a document.

10. When you click one of the options on the Columns button menu, the column formatting is applied to the current section.

11. To balance columns without inserting manual column breaks, insert a Continuous section break at the end of the last column.

12. A building block is a part of a document that is stored and reused.

13. Quick Parts are stored in the Quick Parts gallery.

14. To insert a Quick Part, select it on the Quick Parts button menu.

15. The Building Blocks Organizer lists all the Quick Parts in the current template and stored on the computer. You can select a building block in the list and delete it in the Building Blocks Organizer.

Word: Create a Flyer

1. Plan a flyer for an upcoming event, such as a sale. Identify the content you will include on the flyer, such as at least five items for sale, a description of each item, the original cost of each item, the sale price for each item, and the location, date, and time of the sale (for this project, you can use real or fictional data). Decide how the document should be organized and formatted.

2. Create a new document for the flyer.

3. Enter the text for the flyer.

4. Use a WordArt text box to create an attractively formatted title for the flyer. Be sure to use a descriptive title that accurately describes the content of your flyer.

5. Create a table that has at least four rows and three columns. Enter descriptive column headers for each column, and then enter appropriate data in each row.

6. Format the table with a style. Make sure it is clear and easy to read.

7. Include at least one image from Office.com to add interest to the flyer. Use appropriate keywords to find images related to your flyer's content.

8. Position, size, and orient the image attractively on the flyer.

9. Change the style set of the flyer to anything other than the default style set. Change the theme of the flyer to any theme other than the Office theme.

10. Use Quick Styles to format some of the text on the flyer, such as the date and time.

11. Modify the formatting of the text with Quick Styles applied so that the text looks better in your flyer, and then update the definitions of the Quick Styles with the new formatting.

12. Format the rest of the flyer by changing fonts, font sizes, font colors, borders, and so forth as needed to make the flyer attractive and easy to read.

13. Change the margins and page orientation as needed to fit the flyer on one page.

14. Format the flyer for your printer. Include headers and footers that display the file name, your name, and the date on which the flyer is printed.

15. Use the spell checker to check the spelling and grammar of the document, and then proofread it.

16. Preview the document in Backstage view to be sure that it will print as expected, and then print it.

17. Save the document, and then close it.

Using the Word Web App

The Office Web Apps are free versions of the Office programs that are available to anyone with a free Microsoft account. The Web Apps do not make all of the features of the full version of the program installed on your computer available. You do not need to have Microsoft Office 2013 programs installed on your computer to access and use Office Web Apps.

There are two ways to work with files using the Word Web App: You can view a file in View mode, or you can edit it in Edit mode. In View mode, you are limited to using the Find command and changing the zoom level. In Edit mode, you can enter and edit text, apply basic direct font and paragraph formatting and Quick Styles, use the spell checker, and insert tables and pictures. (Note that in the Word Web App, to search for online pictures stored on Office.com, you need to use the Clip Art button.) Exhibit 1 shows a document in View mode in the Word Web App. Exhibit 2 shows the same document in Edit mode.

Exhibit 1 Document in the Word Web App in View mode

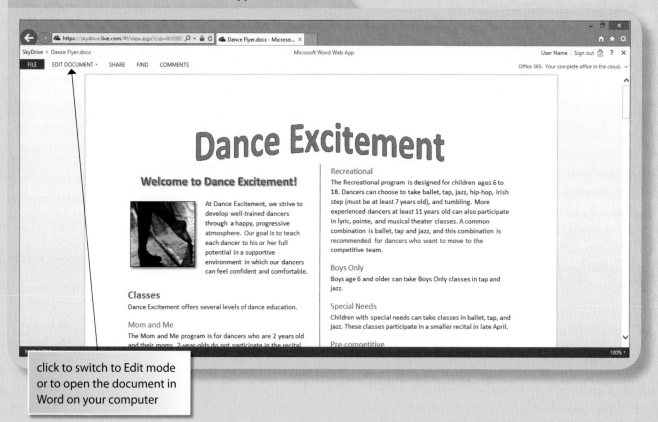

click to switch to Edit mode or to open the document in Word on your computer

Exhibit 2 Document in the Word Web App in Edit mode

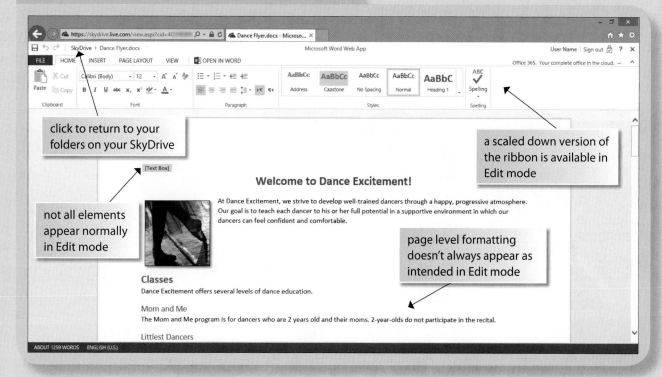

click to return to your folders on your SkyDrive

a scaled down version of the ribbon is available in Edit mode

not all elements appear normally in Edit mode

page level formatting doesn't always appear as intended in Edit mode

To use the Word Web App to view or edit a document, the document must be stored on your SkyDrive or someone else must have shared it with you on their SkyDrive. Open the folder on SkyDrive containing the document you want to view or edit, and then click it to open it in View mode. To edit the document, click the EDIT DOCUMENT button to the right of the FILE tab. To create a new document in the Word Web App (or a new Excel, PowerPoint, or OneNote document), click the Create button at the top of the window in SkyDrive, and then click Word document. See Exhibit 3.

Exhibit 3 Create menu in SkyDrive

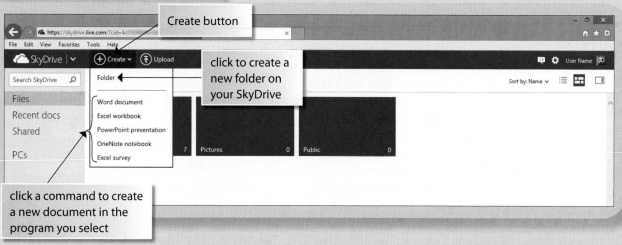

Create button

click to create a new folder on your SkyDrive

click a command to create a new document in the program you select

Creating a Workbook

Dmitriy Shironosov/Shutterstock.com

A spreadsheet is group of values and other data organized into rows and columns. Companies use spreadsheets to track budgets and inventory and to help create a plan for future business. You can use a spreadsheet to create a personal budget or to balance a checkbook. You can create a spreadsheet using **Microsoft Excel 2013** (or just **Excel**), which is used to enter, analyze, and present quantitative data. By using Excel and taking advantage of the powerful calculations it can perform, you can automate tasks that would otherwise take many hours. You can also format the data in a worksheet. Formatting can transform a plain workbook filled with numbers and text into a powerful presentation that captures the user's attention and adds visual emphasis to the points you want to make.

Learning Objectives

After studying the material in this chapter, you will be able to:

13-1 Understand spreadsheets and Excel

13-2 Enter and format data

13-3 Edit cell content

13-4 Work with columns and rows

13-5 Work with cells and ranges

13-6 Enter simple formulas and functions

13-7 Preview and print a workbook

Microsoft Excel 2013 (Excel) A computer application used to enter, analyze, and present quantitative data.

Microsoft product screenshots used with permission from Microsoft Corporation.

13-1 Understanding Spreadsheets and Excel

Exhibit 13-1 shows a cash flow report in a spreadsheet. The spreadsheet records the estimated and actual cash flow for the month of June. Each line, or row, displays a different value, such as the starting cash balance or cash sales for the month. Each column displays the budgeted or actual numbers or text that describes those values.

Exhibit 13-1 Spreadsheet data in Excel

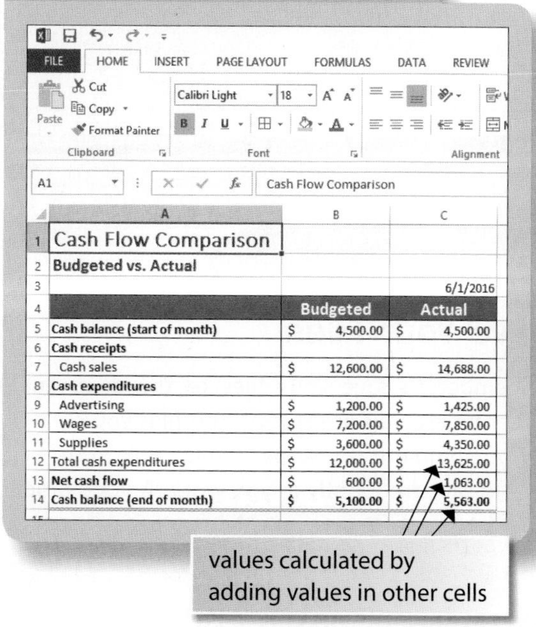

values calculated by adding values in other cells

The total cash expenditures in row 12 in the spreadsheet, the net cash flow in row 13, and the closing cash balance for the month in row 14 are not entered directly but are calculated from other numbers in the spreadsheet. For example, the total cash expenditure is equal to the sum of expenditures on advertising, wages, and supplies in rows 9 through 11.

13-1a Parts of the Excel Window

In addition to the common elements found in all Office 2013 applications, including the title bar, ribbon, scroll bars, and status bar, the Excel window contains features that are unique to Excel, as shown in Exhibit 13-2.

Excel stores spreadsheets in files called **workbooks**. The workbook that is currently being used is the active workbook. The name of the workbook appears in the title bar of the Excel window. Each workbook is made up of individual **sheets**. Each sheet is identified by a sheet name, which is displayed in its sheet tab. Excel supports two kinds of sheets: worksheets and chart sheets. A **worksheet** contains data laid out in a grid of rows and columns. A **chart sheet** contains a visual representation of spreadsheet data. Charts can also be embedded within worksheets, so you can view both the data and the charts in one sheet.

Each workbook can contain multiple worksheets and chart sheets. You can add sheets to a workbook as needed. This capability enables you to better organize data and focus each worksheet on one area of data. For example, a sales report workbook might have a different worksheet for each sales region and another worksheet that summarizes the results from all the regions. A chart sheet might contain a chart that graphically compares the sales results from all of the regions.

Worksheets are laid out in rows and columns. Row headers identify each row with a number, ranging from 1 to 1,048,576. Column headers identify each column with a letter. The first 26 are columns A through Z. After Z, the next column headers are labeled AA, AB, AC, and so forth until you reach the last possible column, which is labeled XFD.

Rows and columns intersect in a single **cell**; all data entered in a worksheet is placed in cells. Each cell is identified by a **cell reference**, which indicates its column and row location. For example, the cell reference B6 indicates the cell located where column B intersects row 6.

> **workbook** An Excel file that stores a spreadsheet.
>
> **sheet** An individual page in a workbook that is either a worksheet or a chart sheet.
>
> **worksheet** A sheet that contains data laid out in a grid of rows and columns.
>
> **chart sheet** A sheet that contains a visual representation of spreadsheet data.
>
> **cell** The location in a worksheet where a row and column intersect.
>
> **cell reference** The row and column location of a specific cell.

Exhibit 13-2 Parts of the Excel window

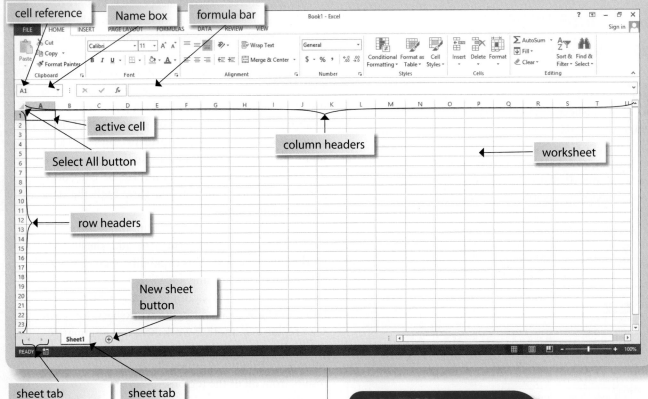

cell reference · Name box · formula bar

active cell · column headers · worksheet · Select All button · row headers · New sheet button · sheet tab scrolling buttons · sheet tab

Begin Activity

Start Excel, and save a workbook.

1. Start **Excel**. The Recent screen opens in Backstage view.

2. Click the **Blank workbook tile**. The Excel window opens, displaying a blank worksheet in an untitled workbook. Refer back to Exhibit 13-2.

3. If the Excel window is not maximized, click the **Maximize button** ☐.

4. Change the zoom level of the worksheet to **120%**.

5. On the Quick Access Toolbar, click the **Save button** 🖫. Because this is the first time you are saving the workbook, the Save As screen appears.

6. Save the workbook as **ModArte Inventory**.

End Activity

active cell The selected cell in a worksheet.

Name box The location where the active cell reference is displayed.

CAUTION

Save Your Files

Remember to save your files to the drive and folder where you are storing the files you create as you complete the steps in this book. Also, be sure to save frequently as you work. A good practice is to save after every Activity.

13-1b Moving the Active Cell

The cell in which you are currently working is the **active cell**. Excel distinguishes the active cell by outlining it with a green box. In Exhibit 13-2, cell A1 is the active cell. The cell reference for the active cell appears in the **Name box** located in the upper-left corner of the worksheet.

You can click a cell to make it the active cell, or you can press the arrow keys to move from one cell to another. Exhibit 13-3 identifies the keys you can use to move around a worksheet. You can also move directly to a specific cell by typing its cell reference in the Name box, and then pressing the Enter key. Scrolling the worksheet does not change the location of the active cell.

Exhibit 13-3 Excel navigation keys

Press	To move the active cell
Arrow keys	Up, down, left, or right one cell
Home	To column A of the current row
Ctrl+Home	To cell A1
Ctrl+End	To the last cell in the worksheet that contains data
Enter	Down one row or to the start of the next row of data
Shift+Enter	Up one row
Tab	One column to the right
Shift+Tab	One column to the left
Page Up, Page Down	Up or down one screen
Ctrl+Page Up, Ctrl+Page Down	To the previous or next sheet in the workbook

© 2014 Cengage Learning

Begin Activity

Move the active cell.

1 Point to the **worksheet area**. The pointer changes to ✛. A1 is in the Name box because cell A1 is the active cell. The column header for column A and the row header for row 1 are shaded and the text is green to help you locate the active cell.

2 Click **cell A5**. Cell A5 now has a green box around it to indicate that it is the active cell, the cell reference in the Name box changes to A5, and the row header for row 5 is shaded and contains green text instead of the row header for row 1.

3 Press the **Tab key**. The active cell moves one cell to the right to cell B5.

4 Press the **Page Down key**. The active cell moves down one full screen.

5 Click in the **Name box**. The active cell reference in the Name box is selected.

6 Type **D4**. The cell reference you typed replaces the selected reference.

7 Press the **Enter key**. Cell D4 is now the active cell.

8 Press the **Ctrl+Home keys**. The active cell returns to the first cell in the worksheet, cell A1.

End Activity

13-1c Inserting and Deleting a Sheet

New workbooks contain one worksheet named Sheet1. If you need more worksheets, you can add them. When you add a new worksheet, it is named with the next consecutive sheet number, such as Sheet2. You can also delete unneeded worksheets that were added to the workbook.

Begin Activity

Insert and delete worksheets.

1 To the right of the Sheet1 sheet tab, click the **New sheet button** ⊕. A new worksheet named Sheet2 is inserted to the right of the last sheet tab.

2 Click the **New sheet button** ⊕. A new worksheet named Sheet3 is inserted to the right of the last sheet tab.

3 Right-click the **Sheet3 sheet tab**. On the shortcut menu, click **Delete**. The Sheet3 worksheet is deleted.

End Activity

13-1d Switching Between Sheets

The sheet currently displayed in the workbook window is the **active sheet**. Its sheet tab has a green border on the bottom, and the sheet name is in bold, green text. The sheet tabs for inactive sheets do not have a bottom border, and the sheet name is in normal black text. An inactive sheet becomes active when you click its sheet tab. In Exhibit 13-4, Sheet1 is the active sheet.

For workbooks that contain more sheet tabs than can be displayed at the same time in the workbook window, you can scroll through the sheet tabs using the sheet tab scrolling buttons to the left of the first sheet tab (refer again to Exhibit 13-4).

Exhibit 13-4 Active and inactive sheets

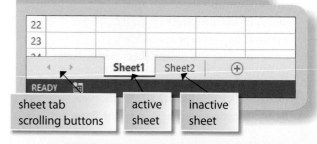

sheet tab scrolling buttons

active sheet

inactive sheet

active sheet The sheet currently displayed in the workbook window.

Switch the active sheet.

1 Click the **Sheet1 sheet tab**. The Sheet1 worksheet becomes the active sheet. Refer back to Exhibit 13-4.

2 Click the **Sheet2 sheet tab** to make the second worksheet active.

3 In Sheet2, change the zoom to **120%**.

13-1e Renaming a Sheet

The default worksheet names, Sheet1, Sheet2, and so on, are not very descriptive. You can rename sheets with more meaningful names so that you know what they contain. The width of the sheet tab will adjust to the length of the name you enter. Exhibit 13-5 shows Sheet1 renamed.

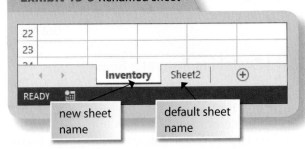

Exhibit 13-5 Renamed sheet

new sheet name

default sheet name

Begin Activity

Rename sheets.

1 Double-click the **Sheet1 sheet tab**. The sheet name is selected in the sheet tab.

2 Type **Inventory**, and then press the **Enter key**. The text you type replaces the selected sheet name and the width of the sheet tab expands as you type to accommodate the longer sheet name. Refer back to Exhibit 13-5.

> **Tip:** Sheet names cannot exceed 31 characters, including blank spaces.

3 Double-click the **Sheet2 sheet tab**, type **Documentation** and then press the **Enter key**. The

newly named Documentation worksheet is now the active sheet.

13-1f Moving and Copying a Sheet

You can change the placement of the sheets in a workbook. A good practice is to place the most important sheets at the beginning of the workbook (the leftmost sheet tabs) and less important sheets toward the end (the rightmost tabs).

The quickest way to move a sheet is to drag its sheet tab to the new location. As you drag a sheet tab, the pointer changes to ⬚, which indicates where the sheet tab will be dropped when you release the mouse button. See Exhibit 13-6. This technique is called drag and drop because you are dragging the sheet tab and dropping it in a new location. To copy rather than move a sheet, press and hold the Ctrl key as you drag and drop the sheet tab. The copy is placed where you drop the sheet tab; the original sheet remains in its initial position.

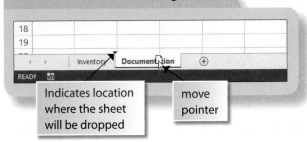

Exhibit 13-6 Sheet tab being moved

Indicates location where the sheet will be dropped

move pointer

Begin Activity

Move a sheet.

1 Click the **Documentation sheet tab**, but don't release the mouse button. The pointer changes to ⬚, and a small black triangle appears in the upper-left corner of the sheet tab. Refer back to Exhibit 13-6.

2 Drag left until the small black triangle is at the left edge of the Inventory sheet tab.

3 Release the mouse button. The Documentation worksheet is now the first sheet in the workbook.

Effective Workbook Design

Effective workbooks are carefully planned and designed. An effective workbook should clearly identify its goal and present information in a well-organized format.

To develop a good workbook, you should determine the workbook's purpose, content, and organization before you start entering data. It is often helpful to use a planning analysis sheet, which includes a series of questions that help you think about the purpose of the workbook and how to achieve the desired results. You should also create a list of the sheets you plan to use in the workbook, making note of each sheet's purpose.

After you know what the workbook should include and how it should be organized, you are ready to create it. Follow this basic process to build a complete and accurate workbook that you and others can easily use:

1. Insert a documentation sheet.
Describe the workbook's purpose and organization. Include the name of the workbook author, the date the workbook was created, and any additional information that others can use to track the workbook to its source.

2. Enter all of the data (both values and labels).
Add text to indicate what the values represent and, if possible, where they originated. Other users might want to view the source of your data.

3. Enter formulas for calculated values.
Use formulas to calculate results rather than entering the results of the calculations. For more complex calculations, provide documentation explaining them.

4. Test the workbook.
Try out a variety of sample values to weed out any errors in your calculations. Edit the data and formulas to correct any errors.

5. Distribute the final workbook.
Be sure to save the final version and create a backup copy when the project is completed. You can store and share the workbook's contents in a variety of ways—online, as a printed copy, or as a PDF file (a special file that preserves the formatting of the worksheet but does not allow it to be edited), among others.

Planning Analysis Sheet—Order Form

What problems do I want to solve?
- I need to have contact information for each customer.
- I need to identify the item and quantity ordered for my customers.
- I need to record the price per item.
- I need to determine how much revenue I am generating.

What data do I need?
- Each customer's name and contact information
- The date each customer order was placed
- The item and quantity each customer ordered

What calculations do I need to enter?
- The total charge for each order
- The total number of items ordered for all orders
- The total revenue generated from all orders

What form should my solution take?
- The customer orders should be placed in a grid with each row containing data on a different customer.
- Information about each customer should be placed in separate columns.
- The last column should contain the total charge for each customer.
- The last row should contain the total number of items ordered and the total revenue from all customer orders.

13-2 Entering and Formatting Data

You enter data by typing it into the active cell. When you finish typing, you need to press the Enter or Tab key or click the Enter button ☑ to complete the data entry and move to the next cell in the worksheet. As you enter data into the worksheet, it appears in both the active cell and in the formula bar. The **formula bar** displays the contents of the active cell, which can be data or, as you'll see later, the underlying formulas used to create a calculated value.

LEARN MORE

Entering Data

Text you type is not entered into the worksheet until you accept it. The easiest way to accept data is to press the Enter key, the Tab key, or an arrow key. You can also click the Enter button ☑, which appears between the formula bar and the Name box.

ethylalkohol/Shutterstock.com

13-2a Entering Text

Text data is a combination of letters, numbers, and symbols that form words and sentences. When you enter text data into a cell, the text is left-aligned unless you change it.

When creating a worksheet, you should make sure its intent and content are clear to others. One way to do this is to create a documentation sheet, which documents why you created the workbook and what it contains. It is also a good way to relay the workbook's purpose and content to others with whom you share the workbook. The documentation sheet shown in Exhibit 13-7 includes text data with the company name (ModArte), the worksheet's author, the current date, and the worksheet's purpose.

formula bar A bar used to enter, edit, or display the contents of the active cell.

text data Any combination of letters, numbers, and symbols that form words and sentences.

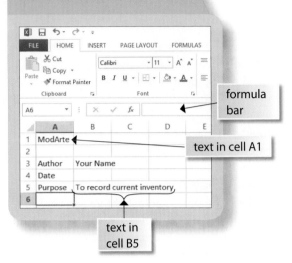

Exhibit 13-7 Documentation sheet with text data

Begin Activity

Enter text.

1 In the Documentation worksheet, in cell A1, type **ModArte**. As you type, the text appears in both cell A1 (the active cell) and in the formula bar.

2 Press the **Enter key**. The text is entered, and the active cell moves down one cell to cell A2.

3 Press the **Enter key** to move the active cell down one cell to cell A3.

4 Type **Author** and then press the **Tab key**. The text is entered, and the active cell moves one cell to the right to cell B3.

5 Type your name, and then press the **Enter key**. The text is entered, and the active cell moves one cell down and to the left to cell A4.

6 Type **Date** and then press the **Tab key**. The text is entered, and the active cell moves one cell to the right to cell B4, where you will later enter the date you created the workbook.

7 Click **cell A5** to make it the active cell, type **Purpose** and then press the **Tab key**. The active cell moves one cell to the right to cell B5.

8 Type **To record current inventory** and then press the **Enter key**. Refer back to Exhibit 13-7.

9 Click the **Inventory sheet tab** to make it the active sheet. Cell A1 is the active cell.

10 Type **Inventory Date** and then press the **Enter key**. The label is entered in the cell, and cell A2 is the active cell. Although it looks like the text you typed extends into cell B1, it is all in cell A1.

11 Enter the following column labels in row 2, pressing the **Tab key** after each entry:

> **Tip:** To place text on separate lines within the same cell, press the Alt+Enter keys to create a line break within the cell.

cell A2:   **Artist**
cell B2:   **Title**
cell C2:   **Inventory**
cell D2:   **Unit Cost**
cell E2:   **Inventory Value**

12 Click **cell A3**, the start of the next row where you want to begin entering the customer data.

13 Type **Dali** in cell A3, press the **Tab key** to move to the next cell, type **The Disintegration of the Persistence of Memory** in cell B3, and then press the **Enter key**. You have entered the first artist and title and moved the active cell to cell A4.

14 Enter the following text in **cells A4** through **B7**. Compare your screen to Exhibit 13-8:

cell A4:   **Kandinsky**   cell B4:   **The Bridge**
cell A5:   **Picasso**   cell B5:   **Woman with a Blue Hat**
cell A6:   **Rothko**   cell B6:   **White Center**
cell A7:   **van Gogh**   cell B7:   **Sunflowers on Gold**

End Activity

Exhibit 13-8 Text data entered in cells

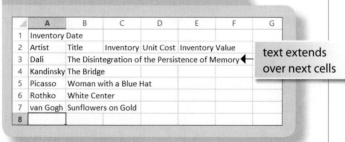

text extends over next cells

13-2b Formatting Text

Formatting text involves changing fonts, font sizes, font styles, and color. These text formatting options are the same as those you worked with in Word. They are available in the Font group on the HOME tab. Remember that fonts and colors are organized into theme and non-theme fonts and colors, so if you want to format text with a font or a color that will not change when the theme is changed, use a non-theme font and color.

Begin Activity

Format text.

1 Make the **Documentation worksheet** the active sheet. Click cell A1.

2 On the HOME tab, in the Font group, click the **Font box arrow** Calibri.

3 At the top of the Font list, click **Calibri Light (Headings)**. The company name in cell A1 changes to the Calibri Light font, the default headings font in the current theme.

4 In the Font group, click the **Font Size box arrow** 11, and then click 24. The company name changes to 24 points.

5 In the Font group, click the **Bold button** B. The company name is formatted in bold.

6 In the Font group, click the **Font Color button arrow** A to display the theme and standard colors.

7 In the Standard Colors section, click the **Dark Blue color**. Remember to use the ScreenTip to identify the correct color. The company name changes to dark blue. Compare your screen to Exhibit 13-9.

End Activity

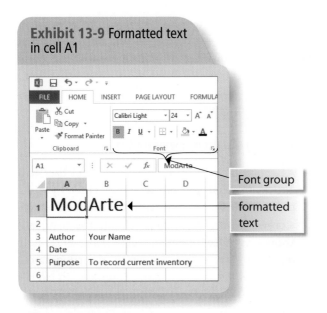

Exhibit 13-9 Formatted text in cell A1

13-2c Entering Dates

Date data is commonly recognized formats for date and time values. When you enter a date in a cell, such as April 15, 2016, Excel interprets it as a date and not as text and formats it appropriately. You can enter dates in any of the standard formats, including the following

date formats (as well as many others), and Excel recognizes each format as representing the same date:

▶ **4/6/2016**   ▶ **April 6, 2016**

▶ **4/6/16**   ▶ **6-Apr-16**

▶ **4-6-2016**

In Excel, dates are actually numbers that are formatted to appear as text. This allows you to perform calculations with dates, such as determining the elapsed time between two dates. Date and time data are right-aligned in the cell by default.

No matter how you enter dates, Excel alters the date format to one of two default formats. If you use numbers separated by slashes or hyphens, Excel displays the date with the four-digit year value. For example, if you enter the date 4/6/16, Excel changes it to 4/6/2016. If you use text for the month, for example, April 6, 2016, Excel converts the date to the format 6-Apr-16.

Begin Activity

Enter dates.

1 Make the **Inventory worksheet** the active sheet, and then click **cell B1**. Although it looks like cell B1 contains the text *Date*, you can see in the formula bar that the cell is empty.

date data Text or numbers in commonly recognized formats for date values.

2 Type **March 22, 2016** and then press the **Tab key**. The date you typed appears in cell B1 but is reformatted as 22-Mar-16. Now that there is data in cell B1, the excess text in cell A1 cannot flow over cell B1.

3 Click **cell B1**. In the formula bar, the value in the cell is 3/22/2016.

4 Make the **Documentation worksheet** the active sheet.

5 Click **cell B4**, type today's date, and then press the **Enter key**. The date appears in one of the two default date formats, depending on the format in which you entered the date.

End Activity

13-2d Formatting Dates

Because Excel stores dates and times as numbers and not as text, you can apply different formats without affecting the date and time value. The format that is applied when you enter a date using numbers and slashes, *mm/dd/yyyy*, is the Short Date format. The Long Date format displays the day of the week and the full month name in addition to the day of the month and the year. To change a date format to the Short or Long Date format, you use the Number Format box arrow in the Number group on the HOME tab, as shown in Exhibit 13-10.

Begin Activity

Format dates.

1 Make the **Inventory worksheet** the active sheet, and then click **cell B1**, if necessary. On the HOME tab, in the Number group, the Number Format box displays Custom.

2 In the Number group, click the **Number Format box arrow** to display commonly used number formats. Refer to Exhibit 13-10.

3 Click **Short Date**. The date format is changed to the Short Date number format, 3/22/2016.

End Activity

13-2e Entering Numbers

Number data is any numerical value that can be used in a mathematical calculation. In Excel, numbers can be integers such as 378, decimals such as 1.95, or negatives such as –5.2. Excel treats a currency value such as $87.25 as the number 87.25 and a percentage such as 95% as the decimal number 0.95. By default, numbers are right-aligned in cells.

Begin Activity

Enter number data.

1 Click **cell C3**, type **28**, and then to the left of the formula bar, click the **Enter button** ✓. The inventory quantity for the Dali print is entered in cell C3. In the Format Number box in the Number group on the HOME tab, General is selected. Now that cell C3 contains data, the excess text from cell B3 cannot flow over cell C3.

2 Click **cell D3**, type **$4.81**, and then to the left of the formula bar, click the **Enter button** ✓. In the formula bar, the value is 4.81, without the dollar sign. In the Number Format box, Currency is selected. The Currency format was automatically applied because you typed the dollar sign.

Exhibit 13-10 Available formats in Number Format menu

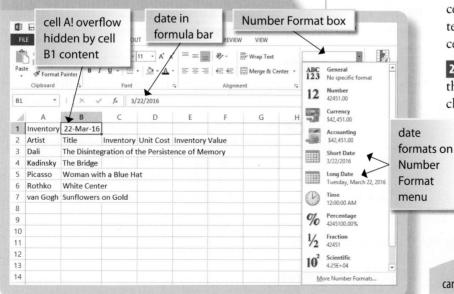

> **number data** Any numerical value that can be used in a mathematical calculation.

3 Click **cell C4**, type **17**, press the **Tab key**, type **5.10** in **cell D4**, and then to the left of the formula bar, click the **Enter button** ✓. The value you typed in cell D4 is changed to 5.1, without the zero.

4 Enter the following inventory values and unit costs into **cells C5** through **D7**, but do not type the dollar sign for the unit costs. Then compare your screen to Exhibit 13-11:

cell C5:	**34**	cell D5:	**6.14**
cell C6:	**6**	cell D6:	**8.92**
cell C7:	**29**	cell D7:	**4.12**

End Activity

Exhibit 13-11 Number data entered in a worksheet

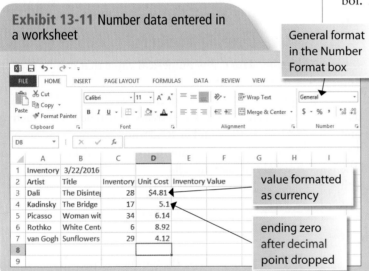

13-2f Formatting Numbers

You can format values using a number format, which displays the values in a way that makes them easier to understand and interpret. As you have already seen with the Currency value in cell D3, changing the number format has absolutely no effect on the value stored in the workbook. Excel formats numbers in the General format, which, for the most part, displays values exactly as they are typed by the user. To make numbers easier to interpret, you can:

▶ Set how many digits appear to the right of the decimal point.

▶ Add commas to act as a thousands separator for large values.

▶ Include currency symbols to identify the monetary unit being used.

▶ Display percentages using the % symbol.

The most common number formats are Accounting, Currency, Number, and Percentage. The Accounting format adds a dollar sign (or the currency symbol you select) at the left edge of the cell, inserts a comma as a thousands separator, sets two decimal places, aligns numbers by their decimal points one space from the right end of the cell, and encloses negative numbers in parentheses. The Currency format is similar to the Accounting format except the currency symbol is placed directly to the left of the number, numbers are aligned at the right edge of the cell, and negative values are indicated by a negative sign to the left of the number. The Comma Style button formats selected cells in the Accounting format but without a currency symbol. The Number format is used for general numbers, and includes two decimal places and negative signs. Percentage format changes the value to the decimal equivalent in hundreds, adds the % symbol after the number, and removes all decimal places. For example, if you enter 1 in a cell and then apply the Percentage format, the value will be changed to 100%.

Whatever format is applied to a number, you can change the number of decimal places displayed. When you decrease the number of decimal places shown, the values are rounded using standard rounding practices: If the number is five or higher, the value is rounded up and the number to its left is increased by one. If the number is four or lower, the value is rounded down and the number to its left remains the same. These options are all available in the Number group on the HOME tab.

Begin Activity

Format numbers.

1 Click **cell D4**. On the HOME tab, in the Number group, the Number Format box identifies these numbers as having the General number formats.

2 In the Number group, click the **Comma Style button** ▾. The value now shows the ending zero because the Comma format shows two digits to the right of the decimal point. If this number was greater than 999, it would now also include a comma as a thousands separator. The Number Format box identifies the cell as having the Accounting format.

3 In the Number group, click the **Accounting Number Format button** $. $ symbol is added to the unit cost value.

4 In the Number group, click the **Decrease Decimal button**. One decimal place is removed.

5 In the Number group, click the **Increase Decimal button** to redisplay the currency with two decimal places.

6 On the HOME tab, in the Clipboard group, double-click the **Format Painter button**, and then click cell D3. The Accounting format is copied from cell D4 to cell D3. The Format Painter is still selected.

7 Click **cells D5**, **D6**, and **D7**, and then in the Clipboard group, click the **Format Painter button** to deselect it. All the number values in column D are formatted with the Accounting format. Compare your screen to Exhibit 13-12.

End Activity

> **Tip:** To select other currency symbols, click the Accounting Number Format button arrow $ in the Number group on the Home tab, and then click a currency symbol.

Exhibit 13-12 Numbers formatted with Accounting format

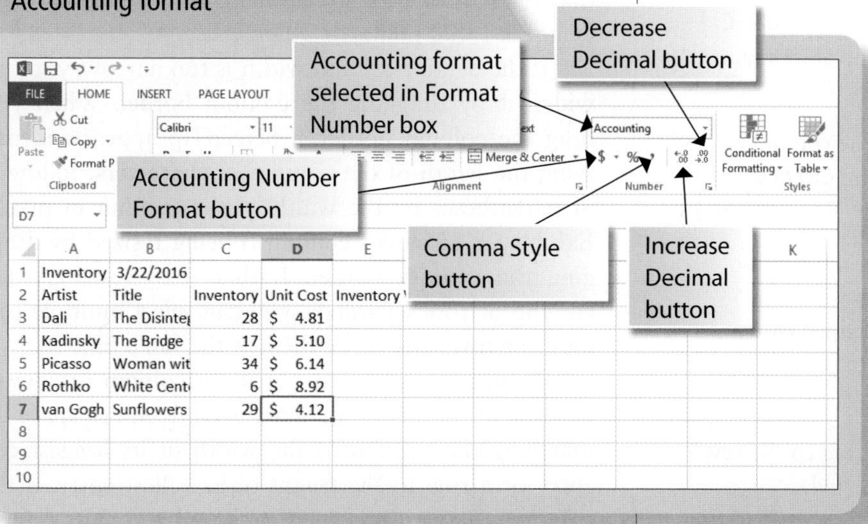

13-3 Editing Cell Content

As you work, you might make mistakes that you want to correct or undo, or you might need to replace a value based on more current information. You could simply make the cell active and then type the new entry or clear the value in the cell and then type the correct value. If you need to edit only a portion of an entry rather than change the entire contents of a cell, you can edit the contents of a selected cell in the formula bar, or you can do one of the following to edit the cell contents directly in the cell:

▶ Double-click the cell.

▶ Select the cell, click anywhere in the formula bar, and then click in the cell.

▶ Select the cell, and then press the F2 key.

When editing content directly in a cell, some of the keyboard shortcuts work differently because now they apply only to the text within the selected cell. For example, pressing the Home key moves the insertion point to the beginning of the cell's content, and pressing the Left Arrow key or the Right Arrow key moves the insertion point backward or forward through the cell's content.

Begin Activity

Edit cell content.

1 Double-click **cell D6**. The formatting disappears from the cell and the insertion point is blinking in the cell.

2 Press the **Right Arrow key** as many times as necessary to move the insertion point to the end of the cell, after the 2.

3 Press the **Backspace key** twice to delete 92, type **86**, and then press the **Enter key**. The unit cost value in cell D6 changes to $8.86.

> **Problem?** If you make a mistake as you edit, press the **Esc key** or click the **Cancel button** ✕ on the formula bar to cancel the changes you made while editing.

End Activity

13-4 Working with Columns and Rows

You can modify a worksheet to make it easier to read and include more data. To do this, you can change the column widths and row heights, insert columns and rows, and delete columns and rows.

13-4a Selecting Columns and Rows

In order to work with columns and rows, you need to know how to select them. To select a column, you click its column header. Likewise, to select a row, you click its row header. To select adjacent columns or rows, you can drag across the column or row headers, or you can click the first header, press and hold the Shift key, and then click the last header. To select nonadjacent columns or rows, press and hold the Ctrl key as you click the column or row headers. Finally, you can select all the columns and rows in a worksheet by clicking the Select All button in the upper-left corner of the worksheet.

Begin Activity

Select columns and rows.

1. Click the **column A column header**. The entire column is selected.

2. Press and hold the **Shift key**, click the **column C column header**, and then release the **Shift key**. Columns A through C are selected.

3. Press and hold the **Ctrl key**, click the **column F column header**, and then release the **Ctrl key**. Columns A through C and column F are selected.

4. Click the **column A column header**, but do not release the mouse button. Without releasing the mouse button, drag to the **column B column header**, and then release the mouse button. Both columns A and B are selected.

5. Click the **row 2 header**, and then drag to the **row 7 header**. Rows 2 through 7 are selected.

6. Click anywhere in the worksheet to deselect the rows.

End Activity

AutoFit In Excel, to resize a column by matching its width to the width of its longest cell entry or resize a row to the height of its tallest cell entry.

13-4b Changing Column Widths and Row Heights

The default sizes of the columns and rows in a worksheet might not always accommodate the information you need to enter. For example, on the Inventory sheet, the text in cell E2 is so long that it seems to overflow into cell F2. When you enter more text than can fit in a cell, the additional text is visible in the adjacent cells as long as they are empty. If the adjacent cells also contain data, Excel displays only as much text as fits into the cell, cutting off the rest of the text entry. For example, all of the titles in cells B3 through B7 are cut off because the adjacent cells in column C contain data. The complete text is still entered in the cell; it's just not displayed. To make the cell content easier to read or fully visible, you can resize the columns and rows in the worksheet.

Column widths are expressed in terms of either the number of characters the column can contain or the size of the column in pixels. A pixel is a single point, or the smallest colorable area, on a computer monitor or printout. The default column width allows you to type about eight or nine characters in a cell before that entry is either cut off or overlaps the adjacent cell. The default column width is 8.43 characters or 64 pixels. Of course, if you decrease the font size of characters, you can fit more text within a cell. Row heights are expressed in points—the same unit of measurement that is used for font sizes—or pixels. The default row height is 15.00 points or 20 pixels.

If the default column width is too narrow, you can widen it by dragging the column border. When you drag the column border, a ScreenTip appears, identifying the width of the column in characters, followed in parentheses by the width of the column in pixels. Exhibit 13-13 shows column B being resized by dragging the column border. Rather than resizing each column or row separately, you can select multiple columns or rows and resize them at the same time.

Another option is to AutoFit a column or row to its content. **AutoFitting** eliminates any empty space by matching the column to the width of its longest cell entry or a row to the height of its tallest entry. If the column is blank, Excel restores the column to its default width. The simplest way to AutoFit a column is to double-click its right border. To AutoFit a row, double-click its bottom border.

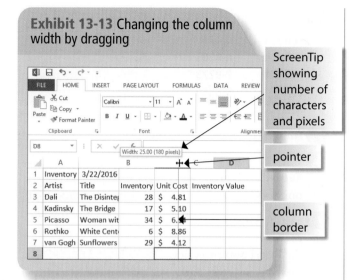

Exhibit 13-13 Changing the column width by dragging

ScreenTip showing number of characters and pixels

pointer

column border

Finally, you can use the commands on the Format button menu in the Cells group on the HOME tab to resize columns and rows. Exhibit 13-14 shows the Format button menu. The top five commands on this menu, in the Cell Size section, provide options for adjusting column width and row height.

Exhibit 13-14 Format button menu

Format button

commands for resizing rows and columns

If you enter an integer with more digits than can fit in a cell, the column width automatically widens to accommodate the number. If you resize a column narrower after you enter a number and the number no longer fits in the cell, you see ###### in the cell instead of the number. You can display the entire number by increasing the column width. If you enter a decimal value in a cell and it is too wide to fit in the cell, the

decimal places are rounded so that the number fits. You can still see the complete number in the formula bar.

Begin Activity

Change column widths.

1 Point to the **right border** of the column B column heading. The pointer changes to ↔.

2 Drag to the right until the ScreenTip identifies the width of the column as **25 characters**, but do not release the mouse button. Refer back to Exhibit 13-13.

> **Tip:** You can also click the Format button in the Cells group on the HOME tab, click Column Width, and then type the width you want in the Column Width dialog box.

3 Release the mouse button. The width of column B expands to 25 characters, and all of the titles in column B except the title in cell B3 fit and are now visible.

4 Point to the **right border** of the column A column header. When the pointer changes to ↔, double-click. The width of column A AutoFits to 13.57 characters, which displays all of the text in cell A1, the widest entry in the column.

5 Select **column C** and **column D**.

6 Drag the **right border** of the column D column header to the right until the column width changes to **12 characters**, and then release the mouse button. Both of the selected columns are now 12 characters wide.

7 Select **column E**. On the HOME tab, in the Cells group, click the **Format button**. A menu of commands opens. Refer back to Exhibit 13-14.

8 Click **AutoFit Column Width**. The width of the selected column—column E—Auto Fits to its content.

9 Click anywhere in the worksheet to deselect the column.

End Activity

13-4c Inserting a Column or Row

You can insert a new column or row anywhere within a worksheet. When you insert a new column, the existing columns shift to the right, and the new column has the same width as the column directly to its left. When you insert a new row, the existing rows shift down, and the new row has the same height as the row above it. You can insert a column or row using the Insert button in the Cells group on the HOME tab, and then selecting the appropriate command on the menu. Exhibit 13-15 shows the Insert button menu. If you select a row or column first, you can click the Insert button instead of opening the menu. If a column is selected, clicking the button inserts a new column; if a row is selected, clicking the button inserts a new row.

Exhibit 13-15 Insert button menu

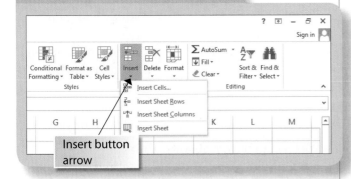

Insert button arrow

Begin Activity

Insert columns and rows.

1 Click **cell C1**. On the HOME tab, in the Cells group, click the **Insert button arrow**. The Insert button menu opens. Refer back to Exhibit 13-15.

2 Click **Insert Sheet Columns**. The menu closes and a new column C is inserted into the worksheet, shifting the columns to the right of the new column. The new column has the same width as the column to its left, column B.

3 Click **cell C2**, type **Item Number** and then press the **Enter key**. The new column label is entered, and cell C3 is the active cell.

clear To remove data from cells but leave the blank cells in the worksheet.

delete To remove both the data and the cells from a worksheet.

4 Enter the following data in **cells C3** through **C7**:

cell C3:	**D-1287**
cell C4:	**K-0283**
cell C5:	**P-9273**
cell C6:	**R-5392**
cell C7:	**V-3028**

5 AutoFit the contents of **column C**.

6 Click the **row 2 row header**. The entire second row is selected.

7 On the HOME tab, in the Cells group, click the **Insert button**. A new row 2 is inserted, and the remaining rows shift down. Compare your screen to Exhibit 13-16.

Tip: The Insert Options button that appears when you insert a column or row lets you choose how the inserted column or row is formatted.

End Activity

Exhibit 13-16 New column and row added to worksheet

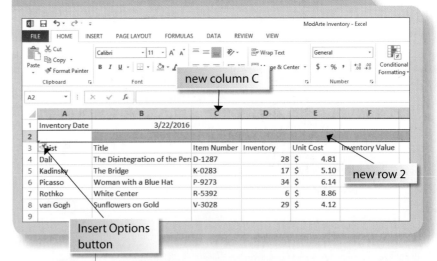

13-4d Clearing or Deleting a Row or Column

Adding new data to a workbook is common, as is removing old or erroneous data. You can remove data in two ways: clearing and deleting.

▶ **Clearing**—Removes data from a worksheet but leaves the blank cells

▶ **Deleting**—Removes both the data and the cells from the worksheet

When you delete a column, the columns to the right shift left to fill the vacated space. Similarly, the rows below a deleted row shift up to fill the vacated space. Deleting a column or row has the opposite effect of inserting a column or row.

You can delete entire columns or rows by selecting them, and then clicking the Delete button in the Cells group on the HOME tab. To clear data from a column or row without deleting the column or row itself, select the columns or rows with data to clear, and then press the Delete key.

You'll first clear data from the worksheet and then delete the row that contained the data. Usually, you would do this in one step by simply deleting the row, but this activity highlights the difference between clearing and deleting.

Begin Activity

Clear a row and delete a row.

1 Click the **row 7 row header**. Row 7 is selected.

2 Press the **Delete key**. The values are cleared from row 7, and row 7 remains selected.

3 On the HOME tab, in the Cells group, click the **Delete button**. Row 7 is deleted, and the rows below it shift up.

End Activity

13-5 Working with Cells and Ranges

A group of cells is called a **cell range** or **range**. Ranges can be either adjacent or nonadjacent. An adjacent range is a single rectangular block of cells. All of the artist data entered in cell A3 through cell A7 is an adjacent range because it forms one rectangular block of cells. A nonadjacent range consists of two or more distinct adjacent ranges. In Exhibit 13-17, the artist data in cell A3 through cell A7 are an adjacent range, and the inventory and unit costs in cell D3 through cell E7 together are another adjacent range. The two selected ranges are nonadjacent ranges.

Just as a cell reference indicates the location of an individual worksheet cell, a **range reference** indicates the location and size of a range. For adjacent ranges, the range reference specifies the locations of the upper-left and lower-right cells in the rectangular block separated by a colon. The range reference for nonadjacent ranges separates each adjacent range reference by a semicolon. In Exhibit 13-17, the range in column A is referenced as A3:A7, and the range in columns D and E is referenced as D3:E7. The selected non-adjacent range in Exhibit 13-17 is referenced as A3:A7;D3:E7.

Exhibit 13-17 Nonadjacent range A3:A7;D3:E7 selected

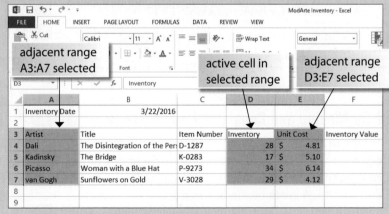

cell range (**range**) A group of cells.

range reference The location and size of a range.

13-5a Selecting a Range

You select adjacent and nonadjacent ranges of cells by dragging the pointer over the cells. Selecting a range enables you to work with all of the cells in the range as a group. This means you can do things like move the cells, delete them, or clear their contents at the same time.

Begin Activity

Select ranges.

1 Click **cell A1**, but do not release the mouse button. This cell will be the cell in the upper-left corner of the range A1:F7.

> **Tip:** You can enter a range reference in the Name box to select that range in the worksheet.

2 Drag the pointer to **cell F7**, and then release the mouse button. The cells you drag over are shaded (except cell A1) and surrounded by a green box. Cell F7 is the cell in the lower-right corner of the adjacent range A1:F7. The first cell you clicked, cell A1, remains white to indicate that it is the active cell in the worksheet.

3 Click any cell in the worksheet to deselect the range.

4 Select the adjacent **range A3:A7**.

5 Press and hold the **Ctrl key**, select the adjacent **range D3:E7**, and then release the **Ctrl key**. All of the cells in the nonadjacent range A3:A7;D3:E7 are selected. Refer back to Exhibit 13-17.

6 Click any cell in the worksheet to deselect the nonadjacent range.

End Activity

13-5b Moving and Copying a Cell or Range

One way to move a cell or range is to select it, position the pointer over the bottom edge of the selection, and then drag the selection to a new location, as shown in Exhibit 13-18. A green box indicates where the selected range will be dropped. You can also use drag and drop to copy a cell or range by pressing the Ctrl key as you drag the selected range to its new location.

Drag and drop can be a difficult and awkward way to move or copy a selection, particularly if the worksheet is large and complex. In those situations, it is often more efficient to use the Cut or Copy and

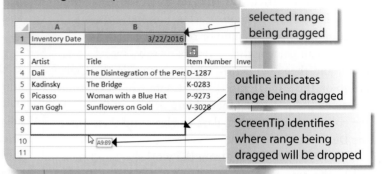

Exhibit 13-18 Range being moved with drag and drop

- selected range being dragged
- outline indicates range being dragged
- ScreenTip identifies where range being dragged will be dropped

Paste commands. When you cut or copy a range, the selected cells are surrounded by a blinking border, indicating that the selection is stored on the Clipboard. The blinking border remains until you paste a cut range or start entering data in another cell. After the blinking border disappears, the selection is no longer stored on the Clipboard and you cannot paste it.

To make pasting a range easier, you can select only the upper-left cell of the range in the new location rather than the exact range where you want to paste. Excel will paste the entire range on the Clipboard with the same pattern of cells in the new location. Be aware that the pasted data will overwrite any data already in those cells.

Begin Activity

Move a range and a cell.

1 Select the **range A1:B1**.

2 Move the pointer over the bottom border of the selected range so that the pointer changes to ⬩.

3 Press and hold the **left mouse button** to change the pointer to ⬩.

4 Drag the selection down eight rows, but do not release the mouse button. A ScreenTip appears, indicating the new range reference for the selected cells—A9:B9. Refer back to Exhibit 13-18.

5 When the ScreenTip displays the range A9:B9, release the mouse button. The selected cells move to the new location.

> **Tip:** If the new location is not visible, drag the selected range to the edge of the worksheet in the direction you want to scroll.

Exhibit 13-19 Cells inserted within a range

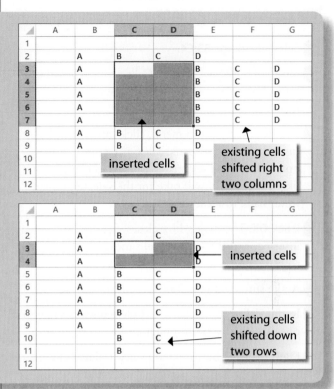

selected range

selected range

inserted cells

existing cells shifted right two columns

inserted cells

existing cells shifted down two rows

6 Make sure the **range A9:B9** is selected.

7 On the HOME tab, in the Clipboard group, click the **Cut button**. The selected range is surrounded by a blinking border, which indicates that its contents are stored on the Clipboard.

8 Click **cell A1**. This cell is the upper-left corner of the range where you want to paste the data.

9 In the Clipboard group, click the **Paste button**. Excel pastes the contents of the range A9:B9 into the range A1:B1. The blinking border disappears, and the Paste button is grayed out as visual clues that the Clipboard is now empty.

End Activity

13-5c Inserting and Deleting a Cell or Range

If you click the Insert button in the Cells group on the HOME tab while one cell is selected, a cell is inserted and the selected cell and the cells below it move down one row. If you select a range and then click the Insert button, the selected range shifts down when the selected range is wider than it is long, and shifts right when the selected range is longer than it is wide, as illustrated in Exhibit 13-19.

If you click the Insert button arrow, you can use the Insert Cells command on the menu to open the Insert dialog box shown in Exhibit 13-20. This allows you to specify whether you want to shift the existing cells right or down, or whether to insert an entire row or column. The selected option is Excel's best guess of which way you want the current cells to shift.

If you no longer need a specific cell or range in a worksheet, you can delete those cells and any content they contain. To delete a range, select the range, and then click the Delete button in the Cells group on the HOME tab. As with deleting a row or column, cells adjacent to the deleted range either move up or left to fill in the vacancy left by the deleted cells. To specify how the adjacent cells shift, or if you want to delete the entire row or column, click the Delete button arrow, and then click Delete Cells to open the Delete dialog box, which is similar to the Insert dialog box.

Exhibit 13-20 Insert dialog box

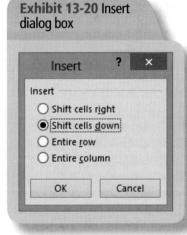

Insert and delete ranges.

1 Select the **range B3:C4**.

2 On the HOME tab, in the Cells group, click the **Insert button arrow** to open the Insert button menu.

3 On the Insert button menu, click **Insert Cells**. The Insert dialog box opens. The Shift cells down option button is selected because this is the most likely action you will take for the selected range. Refer back to Exhibit 13-20.

4 Click **OK**. The dialog box closes, four cells are inserted, and the selected cells move down two rows.

5 Make sure the **range B3:C4** is still selected.

6 In the Cells group, click the **Delete button arrow** to open the Delete button menu.

7 On the Delete button menu, click **Delete Cells**. The Delete dialog box opens. The Shift cells up option button is selected by default.

8 Click **OK**. The dialog box closes, the selected cells are deleted, and the cells below the selected cells move up two rows.

End Activity

13-5d Wrapping Text Within a Cell

You can force text that extends beyond a cell's border to fit within the cell. First, make the cell with text that is cut off the active cell. Then, click the Wrap Text button in the Alignment group on the HOME tab. As shown in Exhibit 13-21, the row height increases as needed to wrap all the text within the cell. You can click the Wrap Text button again to turn off the text wrapping within the active cell.

Begin Activity

Wrap text within a cell.

1 Make **cell B4** the active cell. The title of the Dali print extends past the right border of cell B4.

> **formula** A mathematical expression that returns a value.
>
> **operator** A mathematical symbol used to combine values.

Exhibit 13-21 Cell with text wrapping

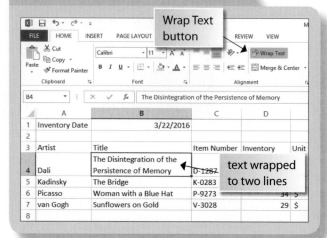

2 On the HOME tab, in the Alignment group, click the **Wrap Text button**. The button is selected, the text in cell B4 wraps to a second line so that the entire title is visible, and the row height increases so you can see both lines of text within cell B4. Refer back to Exhibit 13-21.

End Activity

13-6 Entering Simple Formulas and Functions

Up to now, you have entered only text, numbers, and dates in the worksheet. However, the main reason for using Excel is to display values calculated from data. For example, the workbook has all the data needed to determine the total inventory ModArte has in stock and the value of the current inventory. Such calculations are added to a worksheet using formulas and functions.

13-6a Entering a Formula

A **formula** is a mathematical expression that returns a value. In most cases, this is a number, although it can also be text or a date. Every Excel formula begins with an equal sign (=) followed by an expression that describes the operation to be done. A formula is written using **operators** that combine different values, returning a single value that is then displayed in the cell. The most commonly used operators are arithmetic operators that perform addition, subtraction, multiplication, division, and exponentiation. For example, the following formula uses the + operator to add 5 and 7, returning a value of 12:

$$=5+7$$

Most formulas in Excel contain references to cells that store numbers rather than the specific values. For example, the following formula returns the result of adding the values in cells A1 and B2:

$$=A1+B2$$

If the value 5 is stored in cell A1 and the value 7 is stored in cell B2, this formula would also return a value of 12. Exhibit 13-22 describes the different arithmetic operators and provides examples of formulas.

or click the next cell reference. Exhibit 13-23 shows a formula typed in cell F4 that references cells D4 and E4. After a formula has been entered into a cell (by pressing the Enter or Tab key or clicking the Enter button ✓), the cell displays the *results* of the formula and not the formula itself.

Exhibit 13-23 Formula with two cell references

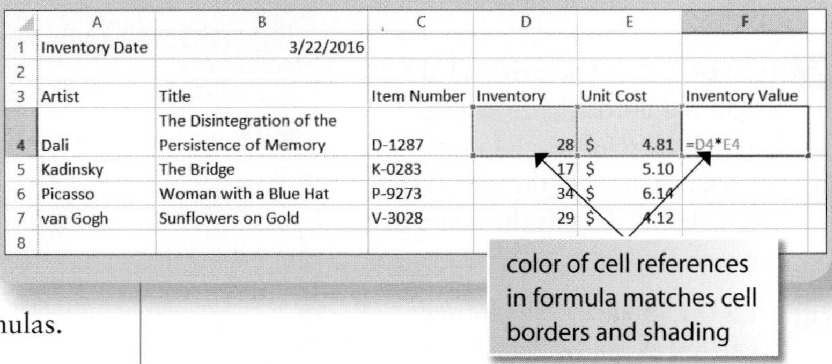

	A	B	C	D	E	F
1	Inventory Date	3/22/2016				
2						
3	Artist	Title	Item Number	Inventory	Unit Cost	Inventory Value
4	Dali	The Disintegration of the Persistence of Memory	D-1287	28	$ 4.81	=D4*E4
5	Kadinsky	The Bridge	K-0283	17	$ 5.10	
6	Picasso	Woman with a Blue Hat	P-9273	34	$ 6.14	
7	van Gogh	Sunflowers on Gold	V-3028	29	$ 4.12	
8						

color of cell references in formula matches cell borders and shading

Exhibit 13-22 Arithmetic operators

Operation	Arithmetic Operator	Example	Description
Addition	+	=10+A1	Adds 10 to the value in cell A1
		=B1+B2+B3	Adds the values in cells B1, B2, and B3
Subtraction	−	=C9−B2	Subtracts the value in cell B2 from the value in cell C9
		=1−D2	Subtracts the value in cell D2 from 1
Multiplication	*	=C9*B9	Multiplies the values in cells C9 and B9
		=E5*0.06	Multiplies the value in cell E5 by 0.06
Division	/	=C9/B9	Divides the value in cell C9 by the value in cell B9
		=D15/12	Divides the value in cell D15 by 12
Exponentiation	^	=B5^3	Raises the value of cell B5 to the third power
		=3^B5	Raises 3 to the value in cell B5

© 2014 Cengage Learning

To enter a formula in a cell, start by typing an equal sign. This indicates that you are entering a formula rather than data. If you are using numbers in the formula, type the first number. If you are using a cell reference, you can type the cell reference or click the cell you want to reference to add that reference to the formula. The latter technique reduces the possibility of error caused by typing an incorrect cell reference. When you add a cell reference to a formula, the reference is colored blue and a blue border appears around the corresponding cell in the worksheet. Then you type the operator you want to use, and then you type the next number or cell reference

Begin Activity

Enter formulas.

1 Make **cell F4** the active cell. You will enter a formula to calculate the inventory value of the Dali print.

2 In cell F4, type = to begin the formula. The equal sign indicates that you are entering a formula rather than data.

Tip: Remember, formulas always begin with = (an equal sign).

3 After the equal sign, type D so that the formula so far is =D. A list of Excel function names starting with the letter D appears below the cell. You can ignore this for now; you'll learn more about Excel functions shortly.

4 Type **4** so that the formula so far is =D4. The function list closes because no function name begins with *D4*. Cell D4 is surrounded by a light blue box and shaded to visually indicate which cell you are referencing in the formula. The corresponding cell reference D4 in the formula you are typing is colored the same light blue. Cell D4 contains the current inventory of the Dali print.

5 Type ***** to enter the multiplication operator.

6 Type **E4**. Cell E4 is surrounded by a light red border and shading, and the cell reference E4 in the formula changes to the same light red. Cell E4 contains the unit cost for each Dali print.

7 Press the **Enter key**. The formula is entered in cell F4, which now displays the calculated value $134.68. The result is displayed as currency because cell E4, referenced in the formula, contains a currency value.

8 In **cell F5**, type = to begin the formula.

9 Click **cell D5**. The cell reference is inserted into the formula. At this point, any cell you click changes the cell reference used in the formula. The cell reference isn't "locked" until you type an operator.

10 Type ***** to enter the multiplication operator. The cell reference for cell D5 is "locked" in the formula, and the next cell you click will be inserted after the operator.

11 Click **cell E5** to enter its cell reference in the formula.

12 To the left of the formula bar, click the **Enter button** ✓ to enter the formula. Cell F5 displays the value $86.70, which is the total value of the "The Bridge" inventory. In the formula bar, the formula appears, not the result. Compare your screen to Exhibit 13-24.

13 Click in the **formula bar**. The cell displays the formula again, the colored boxes appear around each cell referenced in the formula, and the cell refer-

ences in the formula bar are colored with the same colors so that you can quickly match the cell references with their locations in the worksheet.

14 Press the **Esc key** to remove the focus from the formula bar and redisplay the calculated value in cell F4.

End Activity

Exhibit 13-24 Formula and formula result

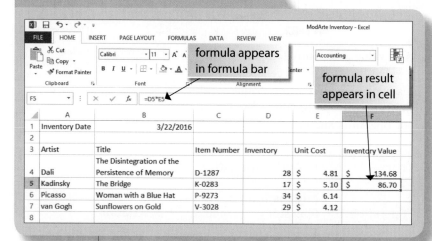

13-6b Copying and Pasting Formulas

Sometimes, you need to repeat the same formula for several rows of data. Rather than retyping the formula, you can copy the formula and then paste it into the remaining rows. Pasting a formula is different from pasting a value. When you paste a copied or cut formula, Excel adjusts the cell references used in the formula to reflect the new location of the formula in the worksheet. For example, if a formula in cell C3 contains a cell reference to cell B1, it contains a cell reference to the cell two cells above and one cell to the left of the cell containing the formula. You could copy this formula and then paste it into cell E5, and the cell reference in the formula would automatically change to cell D3, the cell that is two cells above and one cell to the left of the cell containing the formula. Excel does this automatically because you want to replicate the actions of a formula rather than duplicate the specific value the formula generates. In Exhibit 13-25, the formula =D4*E4 was copied from cell F4 and pasted in cell F6. When it was pasted, it was changed to =D6*E6.

Exhibit 13-25 Formula copied and pasted

> cell references adjusted in formula copied from cell F4 and pasted in cell F6

	A	B	C	D	E	F	G
1	Inventory Date		3/22/2016				
2							
3	Artist	Title			it Cost	Inventory Value	
4	Dali	The Disintegration of the Persistence of Memory	D-1287	28	4.81	$ 134.68	
5	Kadinsky	The Bridge	K-0	17	5.10	$ 86.70	
6	Picasso	Woman with a Blue Hat	P-9		6.14	$ 208.76	
7	van Gogh	Sunflowers on Gold	V-3		4.12		
8							

F6 · fx =D6*E6

> this cell contains the formula =D4*E4

> result of the pasted formula

(Ctrl)

Begin Activity

Copy and paste formulas.

1 Make **cell F4** the active cell. This cell contains the formula to copy.

2 On the HOME tab, in the Clipboard group, click the **Copy button**. The formula is copied to the Clipboard. A blinking box surrounds cell F4, indicating that you can paste the cell contents.

3 Click **cell F6**. This is the cell in which you want to paste the formula.

4 In the Clipboard group, click the **Paste button**. Excel pastes the formula into the selected cell. Notice in the formula bar that the formula has changed from =D4*E4 to =D6*E6. Refer back to Exhibit 13-25.

5 Make **cell F7** the active cell, and then paste the contents of the Clipboard into the cell. You can paste the formula without recopying because the blinking box still surrounds the cell whose contents you copied to the Clipboard. The formula is adjusted again to =D7*E7.

6 Press the **Esc key** to remove the blinking box from cell F7.

> **Tip:** It's a good idea to check the cell references in a copied formula to ensure the cell references changed as you expected.

End Activity

LEARN MORE

Viewing Worksheet Formulas

In some cases you might want to view the formulas used to develop the workbook. For example, if you encounter unexpected results and you want to examine the underlying formulas. When you display the formulas in a worksheet instead of the resulting values, the columns containing formulas temporarily widen so that you can see the entire formulas. To view the formulas, click the Show Formulas button in the Formula Auditing group on the FORMULAS tab.

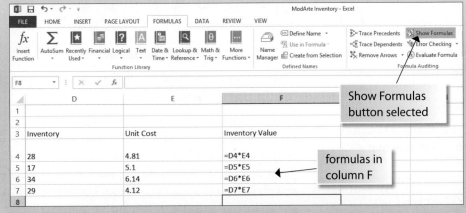

	D	E	F
1			
2			
3	Inventory	Unit Cost	Inventory Value
4	28	4.81	=D4*E4
5	17	5.1	=D5*E5
6	34	6.14	=D6*E6
7	29	4.12	=D7*E7
8			

> Show Formulas button selected

> formulas in column F

Worksheet showing formulas

13-6c Entering a Function

In addition to cell references and operators, formulas can also contain functions. A **function** is a named operation that replaces the action of an arithmetic expression. Functions are used to simplify formulas. For example, to add the values in the range A1:A9, you could enter the long formula:

**=A1+A2+A3+A4+A5+
A6+A7+A8+A9**

> **function** A named operation that replaces the action of an arithmetic expression.

Or, you could use the SUM function:

=SUM(A1:A9)

In both cases, Excel adds the values in cells A1 through A9, but the SUM function is faster and simpler to enter and less prone to a typing error. You should always use a function, if one is available, in place of a long, complex formula.

There are many ways to enter a function in a worksheet. One way is to type it. Because a function is part of a formula, type an equal sign to start the formula, and then type the function name. For the SUM function, the next thing you need to type is the range whose values you want to add. These values are placed between parentheses. Exhibit 13-26 shows the SUM function in cell D8 that adds the values in the range D4:D7.

Exhibit 13-26 SUM function in cell F8

D8	:	×	✓	f_x	=SUM(D4:D7		

⊿	A	B	C	D	E
1	Inventory Date		3/22/2016		
2					
3	Artist	Title	Item Number	Inventory	ScreenTip
4	Dali	The Disintegration of the Persistence of Memory	D-1287	28	$ 4.81
5	Kadinsky	The Bridge	K-0283	17	$ 5.10
6	Picasso	Woman		34	$ 6.14
7	van Gogh	Sunflow	SUM function entered in cell	29	$ 4.12
8				=SUM(D4:D7)	
9				SUM(number1, [number2], ...)	

Begin Activity

Enter a function.

1 Make **cell D8** the active cell.

2 Type = to begin the formula.

3 Type **SUM** to enter the function name. As when you entered the formula, a list of functions opens listing functions that begin with the letters you typed.

4 Type (. The list of functions closes, and a ScreenTip appears, showing how the SUM function should be written.

AutoSum A feature that inserts the SUM, AVERAGE, COUNT, MIN, or MAX function

5 Select the **range D4:D7**. The function changes to include the cells you selected, and a blinking blue box surrounds the selected range. The values to calculate the total inventory are stored in the range D4:D7.

> **Tip:** You can also type a range reference directly in a function.

6 Type) to complete the function. The blinking box changes to solid blue, the range reference in the function changes to blue text, and the complete function, =SUM(D4:D7), appears in cell D8. Refer back to Exhibit 13-26.

7 Press the **Tab key** to enter the function. The calculated value of the SUM function appears in cell D8, indicating that the total inventory is 108 prints.

End Activity

FYI

Excel Functions

Excel supports over 300 different functions from the fields of finance, business, science, and engineering. For example, the PMT function calculates the amount of the loan payments based on an interest rate and a payment schedule; and the CONVERT function converts a number in one unit of measurement system to another unit of measurement. Functions are not limited to numbers. Excel also provides functions that work with text and dates, such as LOWER, which converts all the characters in a cell to lowercase letters, or NETWORKDAYS, which calculates the number of workdays between two dates.

Function Library

13-6d Using AutoSum

A quick and easy way to enter commonly used functions is with the AutoSum feature. **AutoSum** inserts one of five common functions and a range reference that Excel determines by examining the layout of the data and choosing the most likely range. For example, if you use AutoSum with the SUM function in a cell that is below a column of numbers, Excel assumes that you want to summarize the values in the column. Similarly, if you use AutoSum with the SUM function in a cell to the right of a row of values, Excel assumes you want to summarize the values in that row. If the range reference is incorrect, you can change it.

To use AutoSum with the SUM function, click the AutoSum button in the Editing group on the HOME tab or click the AutoSum button in the Function Library group on the FORMULAS tab.

Begin Activity

Use AutoSum.

1 Make **cell F8** the active cell.

2 On the HOME tab, in the Editing group, click the **AutoSum button**. The SUM function with the range reference F4:F7 is entered in cell F8.

> **Tip:** To change the range reference, drag the square in any corner of the selected range, select a different range in the worksheet, or type a different range reference directly in the formula.

3 Press the **Enter key** to accept the formula. The total inventory value, $549.62, is displayed in cell F8.

End Activity

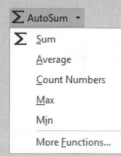
ON THE JOB

Creating Effective Formulas

You can use formulas to quickly perform calculations on business, science, and engineering data. To use formulas effectively, keep in mind the following:

▶ **Keep formulas simple.**
Use functions in place of long, complex formulas whenever possible. For example, use the SUM function instead of entering a formula that adds individual cells. This makes it easier to confirm that the formula is accurate.

▶ **Do not place important data in formulas.**
The worksheet displays only formula results rather than the actual formulas with that important data. For example, the formula =0.05*A5 calculates a 5% sales tax on a price in cell A5, but hides the 5% tax rate. Instead, you should enter the tax rate in another cell, such as cell A4, with

an appropriate label and use the formula =A4*A5 to calculate the sales tax. Readers can then see the tax rate as well as the resulting sales tax.

▶ **Break up formulas to show intermediate results.**
Complex calculations should be split so that the different parts of the computation are easily distinguished and understood. For example, the formula =SUM(A1:A10)/SUM(B1:B10) calculates the ratio of two sums but hides the two sum values. Instead, enter each SUM function in a separate cell, such as cells A11 and B11, and use the formula =A11/B11 to calculate the ratio. Readers can see both sums and the value of their ratio in the worksheet and better understand the final result.

Exhibit 13-27 Worksheet displayed in Page Layout view

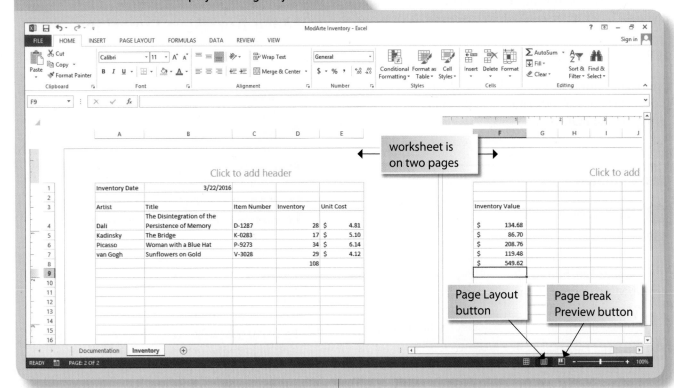

13-7 Previewing and Printing a Workbook

When you have finished the final edit of the work-book, you might want to print a hard copy. However, before you print the workbook, you should preview it to ensure that it will print correctly.

13-7a Changing Worksheet Views

You can view a worksheet in three ways. **Normal view**, which you have been using, simply shows the contents of the sheet. **Page Layout view**, shown in Exhibit 13-27, shows how the sheet will look when printed. **Page Break**

Normal view The Excel view that shows the contents of the current sheet.

Page Layout view The Excel view that shows how the current sheet will look when printed.

Page Break Preview The Excel view that displays the location of page breaks within the worksheet.

Preview, shown in Exhibit 13-28, displays the location of page breaks within the worksheet. This is particularly useful when a worksheet will span several printed pages and you want to control what content appears on each page. The view buttons are located on the right edge of the status bar. You can also change the view by clicking the appropriate button in the Workbook Views group on the VIEW tab.

Exhibit 13-28 Worksheet displayed in Page Break Preview

	A	B	C	D	E	F
1	Inventory Date		3/22/2016			
2						
3	Artist	Title	Item Number	Inventory	Unit Cost	Inventory Value
4	Dali	The Disintegration of the Persistence of Memory	D-1287	28	$ 4.81	$ Page134.68
5	Kadinsky	The Bridge	K-0283	17	$ 5.10	$ 86.70
6	Picasso	Woman with a Blue Hat	P-9273	34	$ 6.14	$ 208.76
7	van Gogh	Sunflowers on Gold	V		$ 4.12	$ 119.48
8						$ 549.62
9						
10						

indicates page break

Begin Activity

Change worksheet views.

1 On the right end of the status bar, click the **Page Layout button** 📄. The page layout of the worksheet appears in the workspace. The data appears on two pages. Refer back to Exhibit 13-27.

2 On the status bar, click the **Page Break Preview button** 🔲. The view switches to Page Break Preview, which shows only those parts of the current worksheet that will print. A dotted blue line separates one page from another.

3 Change the zoom level to **120%** so that you can more easily read the contents of the worksheet. Refer back to Exhibit 13-28.

4 Make the **Documentation worksheet** the active sheet. The Documentation worksheet is still in Normal view.

5 Make the **Inventory worksheet** the active sheet.

6 On the status bar, click the **Normal button** 🔲. The worksheet returns to Normal view. The dotted black line between columns E and F indicates where a page break will be placed when the worksheet is printed.

End Activity

13-7b Changing the Orientation

You can adjust the worksheet so that it prints on a single page. The simplest way to accomplish this is to change the page orientation. By default, Excel displays pages in portrait orientation, where the page is taller than it is wide. In many cases, however, you will want to print the page in landscape orientation, where the page is wider than it is tall.

Begin Activity

Change the page orientation.

1 On the ribbon, click the **PAGE LAYOUT tab**.

2 In the Page Setup group, click the **Orientation button**.

3 On the menu, click **Landscape**. The page orientation changes to landscape, and the dotted line moves to between columns I and J to indicate the new page break. The Inventory worksheet content now fits on one page.

End Activity

13-7c Previewing and Printing a Workbook

You can print the contents of a workbook using the Print screen in Backstage view. As shown in Exhibit 13-29, the Print screen provides options for choosing what and how to print. For example, you can specify the number of copies to print and which printer to use. You can print only the selected cells, the active sheets, or all of the worksheets in the workbook that contain data. The

Exhibit 13-29 Print screen in Backstage view

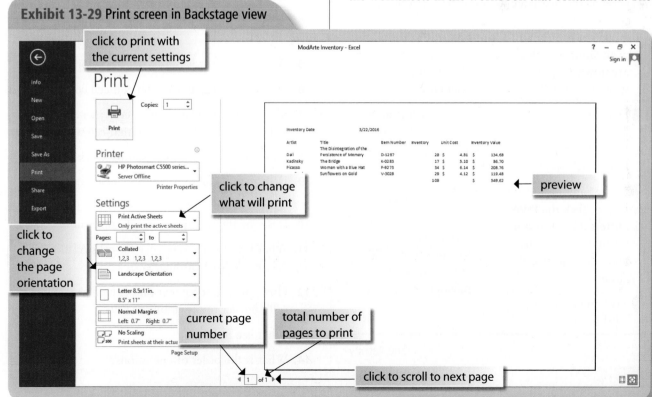

printout includes only the data in the worksheet. The other elements in the worksheet, such as the row and column headings and the gridlines around the cells, do not print. You also see a preview of the workbook so you can check exactly how the printed pages will look with the settings you selected before you print.

Begin Activity

Preview and print a workbook.

1 On the ribbon, click the **FILE tab**. In the navigation bar, click **Print**. The Print screen appears in Backstage view. Refer back to Exhibit 13-29.

2 At the top of the left column, in the Copies box, make sure 1 appears so that only one copy of the workbook will print.

3 If the printer to which you want to print is not already listed in the Printer button, click the **Printer button**, and then click the desired printer.

4 In the Settings group, click the **Print Active Sheets button**, and then click **Print Entire Workbook**. The preview changes to show the Documentation worksheet as the first page to be printed of two pages, and at the bottom, the page number indicator changes to show that there are now two pages to print. The Documentation worksheet is still in portrait orientation.

> **Tip:** You can also choose to print only the selected cells, the active sheet (or sheets), or all the worksheets in the workbook that contain data.

5 Below the preview, click the **Next Page button** ▶. The second page—the Inventory worksheet in landscape orientation—appears in the preview. Refer back to Exhibit 13-29.

6 At the top of the Print screen, click the **Print button**. The workbook is sent to the printer, and Backstage view closes.

> **Problem?** If you don't want to print the workbook, click the **Back button** ← at the top of the navigation bar.

7 Save and close the workbook.

End Activity

Scaling a Printout

You can scale a worksheet to force the contents to fit or fill a page when printed. To scale something means to change its size proportionally. To scale a worksheet, click the PAGE LAYOUT tab, and then use one of the commands in the Scale to Fit group. Click the Width or Height arrow, and then click the number of pages on which you want the printout to fit. Change the percentage in the Scale box to specify a custom percentage. You can also scale a printout by clicking the No Scaling button on the Print screen in Backstage view, and then clicking an option on the menu.

Quiz Yourself

1. What is the difference between a workbook and a worksheet?

2. What is the cell reference for the cell located in the fourth column and seventh row of a worksheet?

3. List two ways of identifying the active cell in the worksheet.

4. List the three types of data you can enter into a worksheet.

5. Why would you want to format a worksheet?

6. In what two places can you edit cell content?

7. What happens when text entered in a cell is too long to be fully displayed in that cell?

8. Explain how the AutoFit feature works.

9. Describe the difference between clearing data and deleting data.

10. Describe the two types of cell ranges in Excel.

11. What is the range reference for cells A1 through A5 and cells F1 through G5?

12. How can you force text that extends beyond a cell's border to fit within the cell?

13. What is a formula?

14. What is the order of operations?

15. Write the formula that adds the values in cells C4 and E9 and then divides the sum by the value in cell A2.

16. What is a function? Why are functions used?

17. What formula would you enter to add the values in cells C4, C5, and C6? What function would you enter to achieve the same result?

18. What view shows how the sheet will look when printed?

Practice It

Practice It 13-1

1. Create a new, blank workbook, and then save the workbook as **Card Shoppe**.

2. Insert a new worksheet in the workbook.

3. Rename the Sheet1 worksheet as **Customer Orders**. Rename the Sheet2 worksheet as **Documentation**.

4. Move the Documentation worksheet so it is the first sheet in the workbook.

5. In the Documentation worksheet, enter the following data in the cells specified:
   cell A1: **Card Shoppe**
   cell A3: **Author:**   cell B3: your name
   cell A4: **Date:**   cell B4: the current date
   cell A5: **Purpose:**   cell B5: **To track customer orders for Card Shoppe**

6. Format cell A1 so the text is 20-point Calibri Light (Headings) and Dark Red.

7. In the Customer Orders worksheet, enter the following labels in the cells specified:
   cell A1:   **Last Name**
   cell B1:   **First Name**
   cell C1:   **Cards**
   cell D1:   **Price per Card**
   cell E1:   **Total Charge**

8. In the Customer Orders worksheet, enter the following customer names:
   cell A2: **Nolan**   cell B2: **Jack**
   cell A3: **Morton**   cell B3: **Eva**
   cell A4: **Kramer**   cell B4: **Frank**
   cell A5: **Gardner**   cell B5: **Zoey**
   cell A6: **Rasnick**   cell B6: **Suzanne**

9. In the Customer Orders worksheet, enter the following order quantities and charges:
   cell C2: **24**   cell D2: **2.99**
   cell C3: **9**   cell D3: **3.49**
   cell C4: **2**   cell D4: **3.99**
   cell C5: **8**   cell D5: **3.99**
   cell C6: **35**   cell D6: **2.49**

10. Format the values in the range D2:D6 in the Accounting format.

11. Edit the contents of cell C1 to **Number of Cards**. Edit the contents of cell C2 to **17**.

12. Insert a new column A.

13. Enter the following data into the new column A:
    cell A1:   **Order Date**
    cell A2:   **Sept. 30, 2016**
    cell A3:   **Oct. 4, 2016**
    cell A4:   **Oct. 8, 2016**
    cell A5:   **Oct. 9, 2016**
    cell A6:   **Oct. 17, 2016**

14. Format the dates in the range A2:A6 in the Short Date format.

15. Set the width of columns A, B, and C to 15 characters. AutoFit the contents of columns D, E, and F.

16. Clear the data from row 4, and then delete the row.

17. Select the range A1:F5. Use drag and drop or cut and paste to move the selected range to range A4:F8.

18. In cell A1, enter **Customer Orders**. In cell A2, enter **September 29 to October 17**.

19. Wrap the text in cell A2.

20. In cell F5, enter a formula that multiplies the number of cards in cell D5 by the price per card in cell E5 to calculate the total charge for the customer in row 5.

21. Copy the formula in cell F5, and then paste it into cells F6, F7, and F8.

22. In cell D9, enter the SUM function to add the total number of cards ordered.

23. In cell F9, use AutoSum to enter the SUM function to calculate the total charge for all of the customer orders.

24. View the worksheet in Page Layout view and Page Break Preview. Return to Normal view.

25. Change the page orientation of the Customer Orders worksheet to landscape.

26. Print the entire workbook.

27. Save the workbook, and then close it.

Practice It 13-2

1. Open the data file **Timber** located in the Chapter 13\Practice It folder. Save the workbook as **Timber Paper**.

2. At the top of the Sheet1 worksheet, insert three new rows.

3. In cell A1, enter the text **Timber Paper Company Income Statement***. (The asterisk is a footnote reference to the note in cell A29.)

4. In cell A2, enter the text **For the years ending December 31, 2014 through December 31, 2016**.

5. In the range C6:E7, enter the following net sales and cost of sales:

cell C6:	**21320**
cell C7:	**6433**
cell D6:	**16529**
cell D7:	**5968**
cell E6:	**14045**
cell E7:	**4604**

6. In the range C11:E14, enter the following expenses:

cell C11:	**2019**
cell C12:	**3267**
cell C13:	**633**
cell C14:	**620**
cell D11:	**1822**
cell D12:	**2618**
cell D13:	**507**
cell D14:	**511**
cell E11:	**1724**
cell E12:	**2267**
cell E13:	**474**
cell E14:	**347**

7. In the nonadjacent range C18:E18;C20:E20; C24:E24, enter the following values for Other Income, Income Taxes, and Shares:

cell C18:	**421**
cell D18:	**374**

cell E18:	**298**
cell C20:	**1506**
cell D20:	**1237**
cell E20:	**1016**
cell C24:	**3611**
cell D24:	**3001**
cell E24:	**2849**

8. Format the values you entered in the range C6:E7;C11:E14;C18:E18;C20:E20 in the Accounting format with no decimal places. Format the values in the range C24:E24 in the Comma Style format with no decimal places.

9. Expand column A to 17 characters, and then AutoFit column B.

10. In the range C8:E8, enter a formula to calculate the gross margin for each year, where the gross margin is equal to the net sales minus the cost of sales.

11. In the range C15:E15, enter the SUM function to calculate the total operating expenses for each year, where the total operating expenses equal the sum of the four expense categories.

12. In the range C17:E17, enter a formula to calculate the operating income for each year, where operating income is equal to the gross margin minus the total operating expenses.

13. In the range C19:E19, enter a formula to calculate the pretax income for each year, where pretax income is equal to the operating income plus other income.

14. In the range C22:E22, enter a formula to calculate the company's net income for each year, where net income is equal to the pretax income minus income taxes.

15. In the range C25:E25, enter a formula to calculate the earnings per share for each year, where earnings per share is equal to the net income divided by the number of shares. Format the results with the Accounting format and two decimal places.

16. AutoFit columns C, D, and E.

17. Edit the contents of cell A18 to capitalize the word *income*.

18. Rename the Sheet1 worksheet as **Income Statement**.

19. Insert a new sheet, rename the worksheet as **Documentation**, and then move it to the beginning of the workbook.

20. In the Documentation worksheet, enter the following text and values:
    cell A1: **Timber Paper Company**
    cell A3: **Author:**   cell B3: your name
    cell A4: **Date:**   cell B4: the current date
    cell A5: **Purpose:**   cell B5: **To create an income statement for Timber Paper Company for 2014 through 2016**

21. Format the company name in cell A1 so it is 20-point Arial Black and Green, Accent 6, Darker 50%. Format the date in cell B4 with the Long Date format.

22. View both worksheets in Page Layout view, making sure each worksheet fits on one page in portrait orientation.

23. Print the entire workbook.

24. Save the workbook, and then close it.

On Your Own

On Your Own 13-1

1. Open the data file **Sunny** located in the Chapter 13\ On Your Own folder. Save the workbook as **Sunny Day Pizza**.

2. Rename the Sheet1 worksheet as **Sales History**.

3. Insert 12 rows at the top of the Sales History worksheet. (*Hint:* Select rows 1 through 12 before using the Insert command.)

4. Increase the width of column A to 23 characters and increase the width of columns B through F to 14 characters.

5. Copy the contents of the range B13:F13. Paste the contents of the Clipboard in the range B7:F7.

6. In the range A8:A11, enter the following data:
   cell A8: **Total Pizzas Served**
   cell A9: **Average per Month**

cell A10: **Maximum**
cell A11: **Minimum**

7. Select the range B26:F26, and then use AutoSum to calculate the sum of the pizzas served in each of the five restaurants.

8. Drag and drop the calculated values that are in the range B26:F26 to the range B8:F8. Notice that the formulas still show the original results because the cell references in the function did not change when you moved the range.

9. Select the range B26:F26, and then use AutoSum to calculate the average number of pizzas served in each of the five restaurants. (*Hint:* Click the Auto-Sum button arrow to access additional functions.)

10. Drag and drop the calculated values that are in the range B26:F26 to the range B9:F9.

11. Select the range B26:F26, and then use AutoSum to calculate the maximum number of pizzas served in each of the five restaurants. Move the calculated values in the range B26:F26 to the range B10:F10.

12. Select the range B26:F26, and then use AutoSum to calculate the minimum number of pizzas served in each of the five restaurants. Move the calculated values in the range B26:F26 to the range B11:F11.

13. In the Sales History worksheet, enter the following data:
    cell A1: **Sunny Day Pizza**
    cell A2: **Sales Report**
    cell A3: **Year**   cell B3: **2016**
    cell A4: **Total Pizzas Served**

14. In cell B4, use the SUM function to add the values in the range B8:F8.

15. Insert a new worksheet. Rename the worksheet as **Restaurant Directory**.

16. In the Restaurant Directory worksheet, enter the following data:
    cell A1: **Sunny Day Pizza**
    cell A2: **Restaurant Directory**

17. In the range A4:D9, enter the following data:

Restaurant	Manager	Location	Phone
1	Anthony Quinlan	58 Oak Drive	555–3585
2	Ada Nunez	4514 Prescott Avenue	555–3728
3	Christina Seward	525 Simpson Street	555–4093
4	Hazel Breton	3654 Orchard Lane	555–7831
5	Eileen Jones	1087 Summit Boulevard	555–6117

18. Format the labels in row 4 as bold.

19. Set the widths of columns A through D so that all of the data is visible. (*Hint:* Column A should be wide enough to display the Restaurant heading but not fit the contents in cells A1 and A2. You can AutoFit the rest of the columns to their contents.)

20. Insert a new worksheet in the workbook. Rename the inserted sheet as **Documentation**. Move the Documentation worksheet to be the first sheet in the workbook.

21. In the Documentation worksheet, enter appropriate data to record the company name, yourself as the author, the current date, and the purpose of the workbook.

22. View each sheet in the workbook in Page Layout view, and change the page orientation or scale each worksheet as needed so that it fits on a single page. (*Hint:* The Scale commands are on the PAGE LAYOUT tab or on the Print screen.)

23. Print the entire workbook.

24. Save the workbook, and then close it.

Chapter 13

ADDITIONAL STUDY TOOLS

IN THE BOOK
▶ Complete end-of-chapter exercises
▶ Study tear-out Chapter Review Card

ONLINE
▶ Complete additional end-of-chapter exercises

▶ Take practice quiz to prepare for tests
▶ Review key term flash cards (online, printable, and audio)
▶ Play "Beat the Clock" and "Memory" to quiz yourself
▶ Watch the videos to learn more about the topics taught in this chapter

Answers to Quiz Yourself

1. A workbook is an Excel file, which stores a spreadsheet. A worksheet is an individual page or sheet in a workbook that contains data laid out in a grid of rows and columns.

2. The cell reference for the cell located in the fourth column and seventh row of a worksheet is D7.

3. The active cell is outlined with a green border and its cell reference appears in the Name box.

4. The three types of data you can enter into a worksheet are text, dates and times, and numbers.

5. You format a worksheet to make it easier to read and understand the data.

6. You can edit cell content in the formula bar or directly in the cell.

7. When text entered in a cell is too long to be fully displayed in that cell, Excel displays only as much text as fits into the cell, cutting off the rest of the text entry; although the complete text is still entered in the cell, it is not displayed.

8. The AutoFit feature eliminates any empty space by matching the column to the width of its longest cell entry or the height of a row to its tallest cell entry.

9. Clearing removes data from a worksheet but leaves the blank cells. Deleting removes both the data and the cells from the worksheet.

10. An adjacent range is a single rectangular block of cells. A nonadjacent range consists of two or more distinct adjacent ranges.

11. The range reference for cells A1 through A5 and cells F1 through G5 is: A1:A5;F1:G5.

12. To force text that extends beyond a cell's border to fit within the cell, make the cell with cut-off text the active cell, and then click the Wrap Text button in the Alignment group on the HOME tab.

13. A formula is a mathematical expression that returns a value.

14. The order of operations is a set of predefined rules used to determine the sequence in which operators are applied in a calculation—first, exponentiation (^); second, multiplication (*) and division (/); and third, addition (+) and subtraction (−).

15. The formula that adds the values in cells C4 and E9 and then divides the sum by the value in cell A2 is =(C4+E9)/A2.

16. A function is a named operation that replaces the action of an arithmetic expression. Functions are used to simplify formulas, reducing what might be a long expression into a compact statement.

17. The formula to add the values in cells C4, C5, and C6 is =C4+C5+C6. The function that achieves the same result is =SUM(C4:C6).

18. Page Layout view shows how the sheet will look when printed.

Excel 2013

Working with Formulas and Functions

Monkey Business Images/Shutterstock.com

Learning Objectives

After studying the material in this chapter, you will be able to:

14-1 Use relative, absolute, and mixed cell references in formulas

14-2 Enter functions

14-3 Use AutoFill

14-4 Work with date functions

14-5 Work with the PMT financial function

14-6 Format cells and ranges

Most Excel workbooks are created to record and analyze data. Formulas and functions make it simpler and more accurate to perform this analysis. To do this effectively, you enter data in cells in a worksheet and then reference those cells in formulas that perform calculations on that data, such as adding a column of numbers as part of a budget. Referencing cells prevents errors that could occur if you retype data. Referencing cells also means that you can change data in one place and the new data is automatically used in calculations that reference that data.

Some functions provide a shorter way to enter common formulas, such as the SUM function for adding numbers, the AVERAGE function for calculating the average value of a group of numbers, and so forth. Other functions perform complex calculations based on the data you enter. For example, Excel has a function you can use to determine loan payments based on the parameters you enter.

14-1 Using Relative, Absolute, and Mixed Cell References in Formulas

O ne of the most powerful aspects of Excel is being able to copy formulas between cells. This allows you to enter a formula one time and then use that same formula throughout a workbook. When you paste the formula, sometimes you will want the cell references in the formula to change according to the new location in the spreadsheet. Other times, you will want the cell references to stay the same as they were in the original formula. You can control whether cell references change by how you enter them.

Begin Activity

Use cell references in a formula.

1 Open the data file **Turner** located in the Chapter 14\Chapter folder. Save the workbook as **Turner Budget**.

2 In the **Documentation worksheet**, enter your name in **cell B3** and the date in **cell B4**.

3 Make the **Budget worksheet** the active sheet. Set the zoom to **120%**, if necessary, and then review its contents.

4 Select the **range B9:C9**.

5 On the HOME tab, in the Editing group, click the **AutoSum button**. The SUM function is inserted in both cells, and the estimated income is calculated for the school and summer months. Compare your screen to Exhibit 14-1.

> **Tip:** Remember to save frequently as you work through the chapter. A good practice is to save after every Activity.

End Activity

Exhibit 14-1 Monthly income estimates

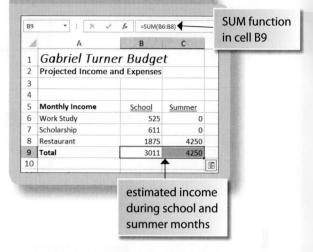

SUM function in cell B9

estimated income during school and summer months

14-1a Using Relative References

So far, you have used relative cell references in formulas. A **relative reference** is always interpreted in relation, or relative, to the location of the cell containing the formula. For example, when you entered the formula in cell B9 to sum the income for the school months, Excel interprets the cell references in that formula relative to the location of cell B9. In other words, Excel interprets the formula =SUM(B6:B8) as adding the values entered in the three cells directly above cell B9.

If the formula is moved or copied to other cells, Excel uses this same interpretation of the cell references. You saw this in Chapter 13 when you copied the formula that calculated the value of the inventory value of a print and then pasted the copied formula into other cells in the column to calculate the values of the inventory of the rest of the prints.

Exhibit 14-2 illustrates how a relative reference in a formula changes when the formula is copied to another group of cells. In this figure, the formula =A2 entered in cell C5 displays 10, which is the value entered in cell A2. When pasted to a new location, each of the pasted formulas contains a reference to a cell that is three rows up and three rows to the left of the current cell's location.

relative reference A cell reference that is interpreted in relation to the location of the cell containing the formula.

Exhibit 14-2 Formulas using relative references

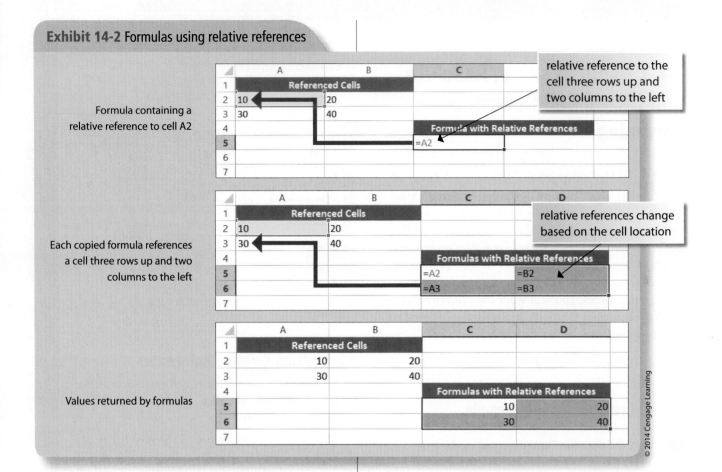

Formula containing a relative reference to cell A2

relative reference to the cell three rows up and two columns to the left

Each copied formula references a cell three rows up and two columns to the left

relative references change based on the cell location

Values returned by formulas

© 2014 Cengage Learning

Begin Activity

Use relative references in formulas.

1 Scroll down to view the **range A26:M34**. This range lists the estimated monthly expenses by category for the coming year.

2 In **cell B34**, enter the formula **=SUM(B26:B33)**. Cell B34 displays 9025, the total value of all the cells in the range B26:B33. January's estimated expenses are $9,025.

> **Tip:** You can type the SUM function or use the AutoSum button.

3 Copy the formula in **cell B34** to the Clipboard. You can copy cell contents to more than one cell at once.

4 Select the **range C34:M34**. On the HOME tab, in the Clipboard group, click the **Paste button**. The formula in cell B34 is pasted in each of the cells in the selected range to calculate the estimated monthly expenses for the rest of the year. Compare your screen to Exhibit 14-3.

5 Review the total expenses for each month. Notice that January and August are particularly expensive months because the expenses include both tuition and the purchase of books for the upcoming semester.

6 Click each cell in the **range B34:M34** and review the formula entered in the cell. The formulas all calculate the sums of the values in the cells above them, so the cell references are different in each formula. For example, the formula =SUM(C26:C33) was inserted in cell C34, the formula =SUM(D26:D33) was inserted in cell D34, and so forth.

End Activity

Exhibit 14-3 Total monthly expenses

	C34	▾	⋮	×	✓	f_x	=SUM(C26:C33)								

	A	B	C	D	E	F	G	H	I	J	K	L	M
21	Income / Expenses	Jan	Feb	Mar	Apr	May	Jun	Jul	Aug	Sep	Oct	Nov	Dec
22	Work Study												
23	Scholarship												
24	Restaurant												
25	**Total**												
26	Rent	660	660	660	660	660	660	660	660	660	660	660	660
27	Food	285	285	285	285	285	285	285	285	285	285	285	285
28	Utilities	115	105	90	85	70	75	80	75	70	70	90	105
29	Phone/Internet	115	115	115	115	115	115	115	115	115	115	115	115
30	Clothes	50	50	50	50	150	50	50	250	50	50	150	50
31	Tuition	6575	0	0	0	0	1350	0	5900	0	0	0	0
32	Books & Supplies	1005	0	0	0	0	275	0	775	0	0	0	0
33	Travel/Entertainment	220	160	170	520	170	190	920	550	155	225	315	385
34	**Total**	9025	1375	1370	1715	1450	3000	2110	8610	1335	1405	1615	1600
35	**Net Cash Flow**												

monthly totals

Reduce Data Entry

A good practice when designing a workbook is to enter values in separate cells in one location of the worksheet, and then reference the appropriate cells in formulas throughout the worksheets. This reduces the amount of data entry when you need to use the same data in more than one location. It also makes changing a data value faster and more accurate, because all the formulas based on that cell are updated to reflect the new value.

wrangler/Shutterstock.com

14-1b Using Absolute References

Cell references that remain fixed when a formula is copied to a new location are called **absolute references**. In Excel, absolute references have a $ (dollar sign) before each column and row designation. For example, B8 is a relative reference to cell B8, but $B$8 is an absolute reference to cell B8. When you copy a formula that contains an absolute reference to a new location, the reference does not change.

Exhibit 14-4 shows an example of how copying a formula with an absolute reference results in the same cell reference being pasted in different cells regardless of their location. In this figure, the sales tax of different purchases is calculated and displayed. All items

have the same 5 percent tax rate, which is stored in cell A2, applied to the purchase. The sales tax and the total cost of the first item are calculated in cells C2 and D2, respectively. When those formulas are copied and pasted to the remaining purchases, the relative references in the formulas change to point to the new location of the purchase cost; the sales tax rate continues to point to cell A2, regardless of the cell in which the formula is pasted.

Begin Activity

Use absolute references in formulas.

1 In **cell B22**, enter =$B$6. This formula contains an absolute reference to cell B6, which contains the monthly work study income for the school months.

2 In **cell B23**, enter =$B$7. This formula contains an absolute reference to cell B7, which contains the monthly scholarship income for the school months.

3 In **cell B24**, enter =$B$8. This formula contains an absolute reference to cell B8, which contains the monthly restaurant income for the school months.

4 In **cell B25**, enter =SUM(B22:B24). This formula adds the monthly work study, scholarship, and restaurant income during the school months.

> **absolute reference** A cell reference that remains fixed when copied to a new location; includes a $ in front of both the column letter and row number.

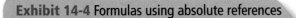

Exhibit 14-4 Formulas using absolute references

Formula containing an absolute reference to the sales tax rate in cell A2

| C2 | | : | × | ✓ | *fx* | =B2*$A$2 |

	A	B	C	D
1	*Sales Tax*	Purchase	Sales Tax	Total
2	*0.05*	24.95	=B2*$A$2	=B2+C2
3		122.35		
4		199.81		
5		45.4		
6		4		
7				

relative references to cells B2 and C2

relative reference to cell B2

absolute reference to cell A2

Each copied formula references the same cell (cell A2)

| C2 | | : | × | ✓ | *fx* | =B2*$A$2 |

	A	B	C	D
1	*Sales Tax*	Purchase	Sales Tax	Total
2	*0.05*	24.95	=B2*$A$2	=B2+C2
3		122.35	=B3*$A$2	=B3+C3
4			=B4*$A$2	=B4+C4
5			=B5*$A$2	=B5+C5
6				
7				

relative references change based on the cell location

relative reference changes based on the cell location

absolute reference remains unchanged in the formula

Values returned by the formulas

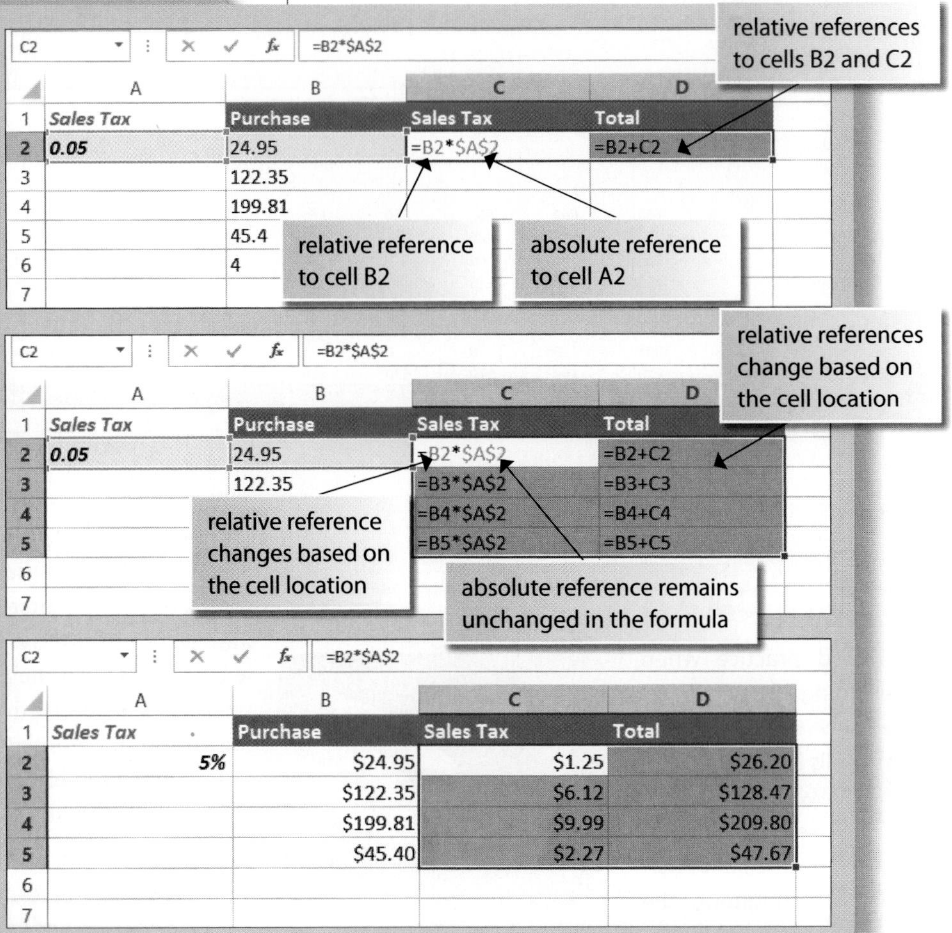

| C2 | | : | × | ✓ | *fx* | =B2*$A$2 |

	A	B	C	D
1	*Sales Tax*	Purchase	Sales Tax	Total
2		5%	$24.95	$1.25	$26.20
3			$122.35	$6.12	$128.47
4			$199.81	$9.99	$209.80
5			$45.40	$2.27	$47.67
6					
7					

5 Copy the formulas in the **range B22:B25**, and paste them into the **range C22:F25;J22:M25**. February through May and September through December show the estimated income for the school months. Compare your screen to Exhibit 14-5.

6 Click each cell in the **range C22:F24;J22:M24**, and verify that the copied formulas contain the absolute cell references =$B$6, =$B$7, and =$B$8.

Instead of entering an absolute reference in a cell by typing dollar signs, you can type just the column letter and row number, and then press the F4 key to change the reference to an absolute reference. Pressing the F4 key adds a dollar sign in front of both the column letter and row number to change both references to absolute. If you continue to press the F4 key, first the

End Activity

Exhibit 14-5 Results of formulas with absolute references

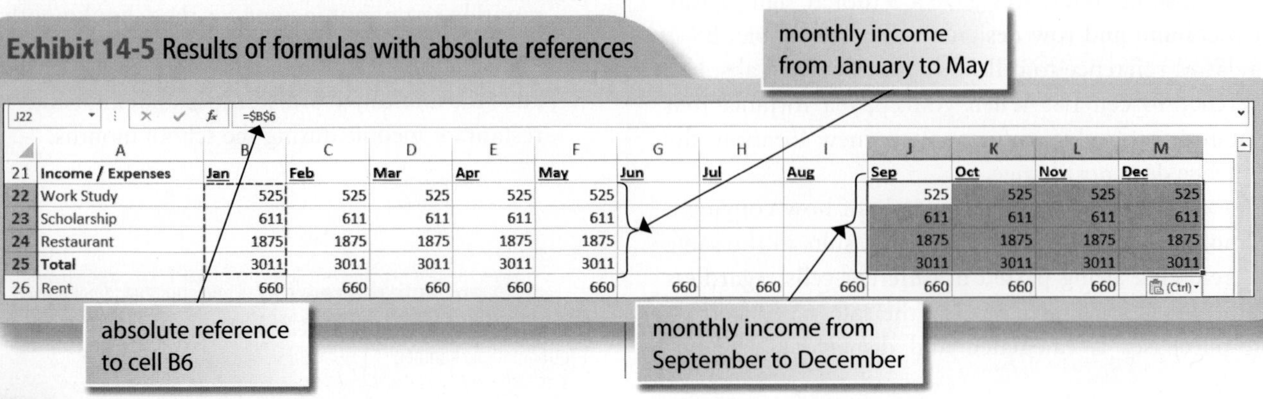

| J22 | | : | × | ✓ | *fx* | =$B$6 |

	A	B	C	D	E	F	G	H	I	J	K	L	M
21	Income / Expenses	Jan	Feb	Mar	Apr	May	Jun	Jul	Aug	Sep	Oct	Nov	Dec
22	Work Study	525	525	525	525	525				525	525	525	525
23	Scholarship	611	611	611	611	611				611	611	611	611
24	Restaurant	1875	1875	1875	1875	1875				1875	1875	1875	1875
25	Total	3011	3011	3011	3011	3011				3011	3011	3011	3011
26	Rent	660	660	660	660	660	660	660	660	660	660	660	

monthly income from January to May

absolute reference to cell B6

monthly income from September to December

Anette Linnea Rasmussen/Shutterstock.com

dollar sign is removed from in front of the column letter, then the dollar sign is added back in front of the column reference, but it is removed from in front of the row reference, then the dollar signs are removed completely.

Begin Activity

Enter absolute references using the F4 key.

1 In **cell G22**, type **=C6** and then press the **F4 key**. Cell C6 contains the income from work study during the summer months. The cell reference changes to =$C$6, an absolute reference.

> **Problem?** If the cell reference did not change to an absolute reference, press the **F Lock key**, and then press the **F4 key** again. If the cell reference still does not change, retype it by typing the dollar signs.

2 Press the **F4 key** again. The reference changes to =C$6.

3 Press the **F4 key** again to change the reference to =$C6.

4 Press the **F4 key** again to change the reference to =C6.

5 Press the **F4 key** once more to change the reference back to =$C$6. Press the **Enter key**.

6 In **cell G23**, enter **=$C$7**.

7 In **cell G24**, enter **=$C$8**.

8 In **cell G25**, enter the formula **=SUM(G22:G24)**. This formula adds the work study, scholarship, and restaurant income during the summer months to calculate a total of 4250.

9 Copy the **range G22:G25** to the Clipboard. Paste the copied formulas into the **range H22:I25**. The total income is added for the months of June through August.

End Activity

14-1c Using Mixed References

When you pressed the F4 key the second and third time in the previous Activity, you created cell references that contained both a relative reference and an absolute

reference. This is called a **mixed reference**. In a mixed reference, the reference to the part of the reference with the dollar sign in front of it is absolute, and the reference to the part of the reference without the dollar sign in front of it is relative. For example, in the mixed reference A$2, the column reference is relative and the row reference is absolute, and in the mixed reference $A2, the column reference is absolute and the row reference is relative. When you copy and paste a formula with a mixed reference to a new location, the absolute portion of the cell reference remains fixed and the relative portion shifts.

Exhibit 14-6 shows an example of using mixed references to complete a multiplication table. The first cell in the table, cell B3, contains the formula =$A3*B$2, which multiplies the first column entry (A3) by the first row entry (B2), returning 1. When this formula is copied to another cell, the absolute portions of the cell references remain unchanged and the relative portions of the references change. For example, if the formula is copied to cell E6, the first mixed cell reference changes to $A6 because the column reference is absolute and the row reference is relative, and the second cell reference changes to E$2 because the row reference is absolute and the column reference is relative. The result is that cell E6 contains the formula =$A6*E$2 and returns 16. Other cells in the multiplication table are similarly modified so that each entry returns the multiplication of the row and column headings.

Begin Activity

Enter formulas with mixed references.

1 Make the **Car Savings Plan worksheet** the active sheet.

2 In **cell B5**, enter **=$A5*B$4**. This formula uses mixed references to calculate the amount of savings generated by saving $50 per month (cell B4) for 12 months (cell A5). The calculated value $600 is displayed. The value is formatted as Currency because the value in cell B4 is formatted as Currency.

> **mixed reference** A cell reference that contains both an absolute reference and a relative reference.

Exhibit 14-6 Multiplication table using mixed references

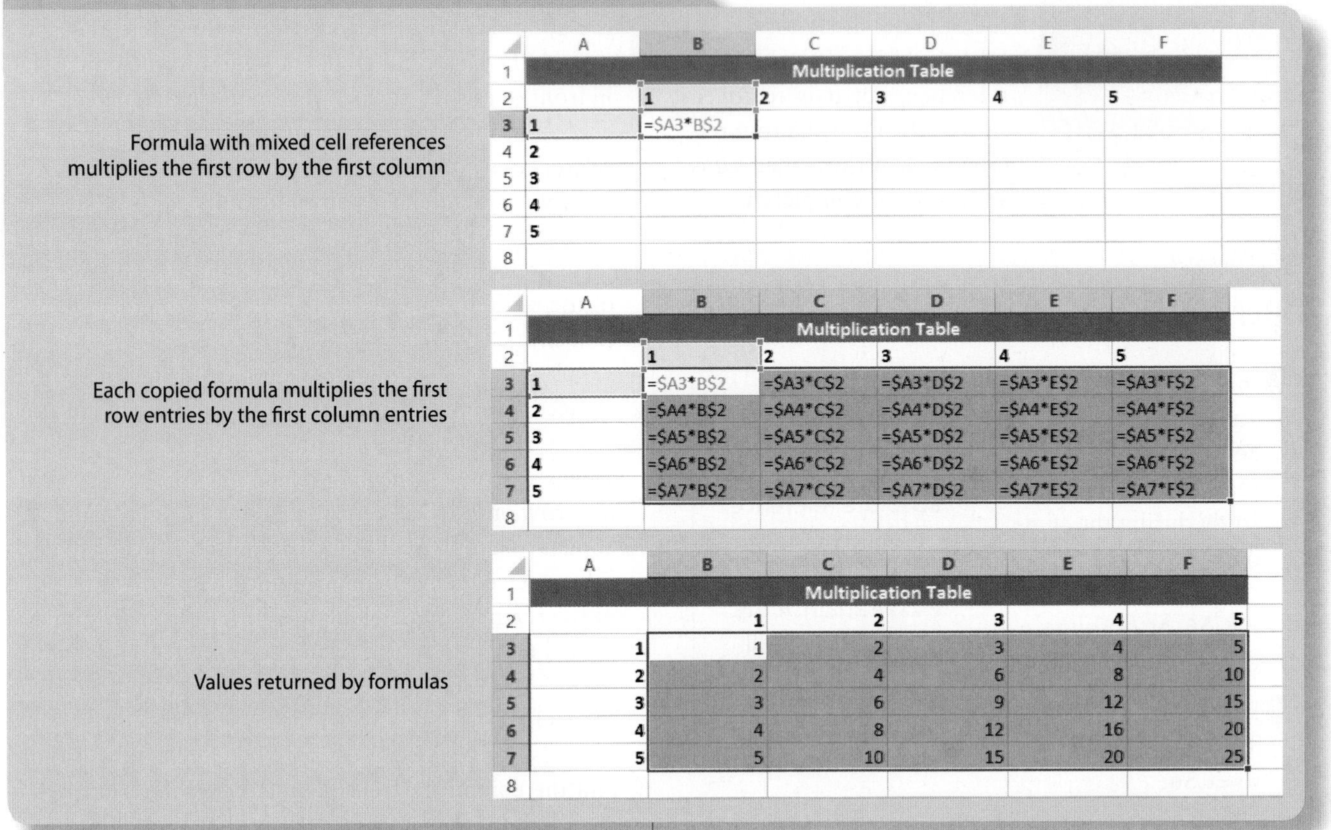

Formula with mixed cell references multiplies the first row by the first column

	A	B	C	D	E	F
1			Multiplication Table			
2		1	2	3	4	5
3	1	=$A3*B$2				
4	2					
5	3					
6	4					
7	5					
8						

Each copied formula multiplies the first row entries by the first column entries

	A	B	C	D	E	F
1			Multiplication Table			
2		1	2	3	4	5
3	1	=$A3*B$2	=$A3*C$2	=$A3*D$2	=$A3*E$2	=$A3*F$2
4	2	=$A4*B$2	=$A4*C$2	=$A4*D$2	=$A4*E$2	=$A4*F$2
5	3	=$A5*B$2	=$A5*C$2	=$A5*D$2	=$A5*E$2	=$A5*F$2
6	4	=$A6*B$2	=$A6*C$2	=$A6*D$2	=$A6*E$2	=$A6*F$2
7	5	=$A7*B$2	=$A7*C$2	=$A7*D$2	=$A7*E$2	=$A7*F$2
8						

Values returned by formulas

	A	B	C	D	E	F
1			Multiplication Table			
2		1	2	3	4	5
3	1	1	2	3	4	5
4	2	2	4	6	8	10
5	3	3	6	9	12	15
6	4	4	8	12	16	20
7	5	5	10	15	20	25
8						

3 Copy the formula in **cell B5** to the Clipboard. You need to paste this formula into the range B6:B7 and the range C5:G7. Instead, you can select the cell that contains the formula you are copying as part of the range you will paste to.

4 Select the **range B5:G7**, and then in the Clipboard group, click the **Paste button**. The pasted formulas calculate total savings over 12, 24, and 36 months for deposits ranging from $50 to $200 per month.

5 Click the **Esc key** to remove the contents of the Clipboard. Compare your screen to Exhibit 14-7.

End Activity

formula uses mixed cell references to multiply each column value by each row value

Exhibit 14-7 Completed car savings plan

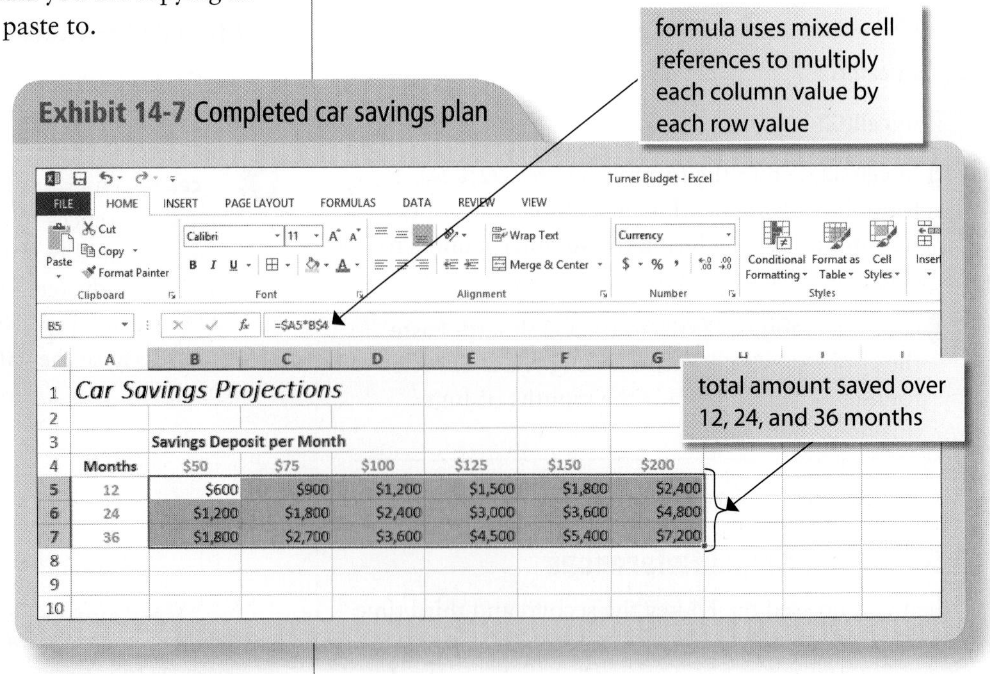

total amount saved over 12, 24, and 36 months

B5 → =$A5*B$4

	A	B	C	D	E	F	G
1	Car Savings Projections						
2							
3		Savings Deposit per Month					
4	Months	$50	$75	$100	$125	$150	$200
5	12	$600	$900	$1,200	$1,500	$1,800	$2,400
6	24	$1,200	$1,800	$2,400	$3,000	$3,600	$4,800
7	36	$1,800	$2,700	$3,600	$4,500	$5,400	$7,200
8							
9							
10							

When to Use Relative, Absolute, and Mixed References

An important part of effective formula writing is using the correct type of cell reference. Keep in mind the following when choosing whether to use relative, absolute, or mixed cell references:

▶ **Relative references**—use relative references, such as L17, when you want to repeat the same formula with cells in different locations on your worksheet. Relative references are commonly used when copying a formula that sums a column of numbers or that calculates the cost of several items by multiplying the item cost by the quantity being purchased.

▶ **Absolute references**—use absolute references, such as $L$17, when you want different formulas to refer to the same cell. This usually occurs when a cell contains a constant value, such as a tax rate, that will be used in formulas throughout the worksheet.

▶ **Mixed references**—mixed references, such as $L17 and L$17, are seldom used other than when creating tables of calculated values such as a multiplication table in which the values of the formula or function can be found in the initial rows and columns of the table.

14-2 Entering Functions

Remember from Chapter 13 that a function is a named operation that replaces the action of an arithmetic expression. Every function follows a set of rules, or **syntax**, which specifies how the function should be written. The general syntax of Excel functions is

FUNCTION(argument1,argument2,...)

where *FUNCTION* is the name of the function, and *argument1*, *argument2*, and so forth are **arguments**, which are the numbers, text, or cell references used by the function to return a value. When you use multiple arguments within a function, they are separated by a comma.

You have already worked with the SUM function with one argument. For that function, the function name is SUM, and the range reference that appears between the parentheses is the single argument.

Not all functions have arguments. Some functions have **optional arguments**, which are not required for the function to return a value but can be included to provide more control over how Excel calculates the returned value. If an optional argument is not included, Excel assumes a default value for it. This chapter shows optional arguments within square brackets along with the argument's default value:

FUNCTION(argument1[,argument2=value2,. ..])

In this function, *argument1* is required, *argument2* is an optional argument, and *value2* is the default value used for *argument2*. Optional arguments are always placed last in the argument list.

The hundreds of available Excel functions are organized into the 13 categories described in Exhibit 14-8.

The SUM function is one of the most commonly used Math & Trig functions. Exhibit 14-9 describes the SUM function as well as some of the other common Math, Trig, and Statistical functions used in workbooks.

For example, the AVERAGE function calculates the average value from a collection of numbers. The syntax of the AVERAGE function is

AVERAGE(number1[,number2,number3,...])

where *number1*, *number2*, *number3*, and so forth are either numbers or cell references to numbers. The formula

=AVERAGE(1,2,5,8)

uses the AVERAGE function to calculate the average of 1, 2, 5, and 8, returning the value 4.

You can replace the values used as arguments with cell references. So, if the range A1:A4 contains the values 1, 2, 5, and 8, the following formula also returns 4:

=AVERAGE(A1:A4)

syntax A set of rules.

argument The numbers, text, or cell references used by a function to return a value.

optional argument An argument that is not required for the function to return a value but provides more control over how the returned value is calculated.

Exhibit 14-8 Excel function categories

Category	Description
Compatibility	Functions available in earlier versions of Excel that have been replaced with new functions that provide the same actions
Cube	Functions that retrieve data from multidimensional databases involving online analytical processing (OLAP)
Database	Functions that retrieve and analyze data stored in databases
Date & Time	Functions that analyze or create date and time values and time intervals
Engineering	Functions that analyze engineering problems
Financial	Functions that have financial applications
Information	Functions that return information about the format, location, or contents of worksheet cells
Logical	Functions that return logical (true-false) values
Lookup & Reference	Functions that look up and return data matching a set of specified conditions from a range
Math & Trig	Functions that have math and trigonometry applications
Statistical	Functions that provide statistical analyses of a set of data
Text	Functions that return text or evaluate text
Web	Functions that provide information on Web-based connections

© 2014 Cengage Learning

Exhibit 14-9 Common Math, Trig, and Statistical functions

Function	Category	Description
AVERAGE(*number1*[,*number2*, *number3*,...]),	Statistical	Calculates the average of a collection of numbers, where *number1*, *number2*, and so forth are either numbers or cell references. Only *number1* is required. For more than one cell reference or to enter numbers directly into the function, use the optional arguments *number2*, *number3*, and so forth.
COUNT(*value1*[,*value2*, *value3*,...])	Statistical	Counts how many cells in a range contain numbers, where *value1*, *value2*, and so forth are text, numbers, or cell references. Only *value1* is required. For more than one cell reference or to enter numbers directly into the function, use the optional arguments *value2*, *value3*, and so forth.
COUNTA(*value1*[,*value2*, *value3*,...])	Statistical	Counts how many cells are not empty in ranges *value1*, *value2*, and so forth, or how many numbers are listed within *value1*, *value2*, and so forth.
INT(*number*)	Math & Trig	Displays the integer portion of a number, *number*.
MAX(*number1*[,*number2*, *number3*,...])	Statistical	Calculates the maximum value of a collection of numbers, where *number1*, *number2*, and so forth are either numbers or cell references.
MEDIAN(*number1*[,*number2*, *number3*,...])	Statistical	Calculates the median, or middle, value of a collection of numbers, where *number1*, *number2*, and so forth are either numbers or cell references.
MIN(*number1*[,*number2*, *number3*,...])	Statistical	Calculates the minimum value of a collection of numbers, where *number1*, *number2*, and so forth are either numbers or cell references.
RAND()	Math & Trig	Returns a random number between 0 and 1.
ROUND(*number*,*num_digits*)	Math & Trig	Rounds a number to a specified number of digits, where *number* is the number you want to round and *num_digits* specifies the number of digits to round the number.
SUM(*number1*[,*number2*, *number3*,...])	Math & Trig	Adds a collection of numbers, where *number1*, *number2*, and so forth are either numbers or cell references.

© 2014 Cengage Learning

14-2a Inserting a Function Using the Insert Function Dialog Box

The Insert Function dialog box allows you to search for a function and organizes the functions by category. To open the Insert Function dialog box, you can click the Insert Function button to the left of the formula bar or in the Function Library group on the FORMULAS tab. Exhibit 14-10 shows the Insert Function dialog box with the SUM function selected in the Select a function box.

Exhibit 14-10 SUM function selected in the Insert Function dialog box

- type a description of the function you want to find
- click to select a different function category
- selected function
- link to the Help topic about this function
- syntax and description of the SUM function

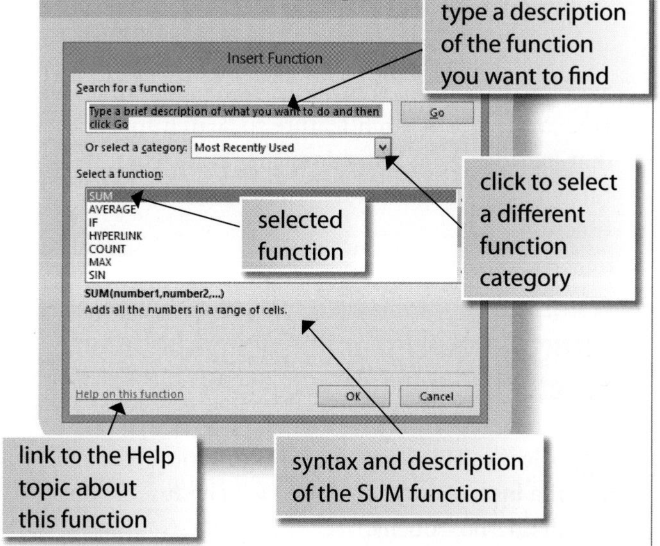

After you select a function, the Function Arguments dialog box opens, listing all of the arguments associated with that function. (If you know the function's category and name, you can select that function by clicking the appropriate category button in the Function Library group on the FORMULAS tab, and then clicking the function you want to open the Function Arguments dialog box for that function.) In the Function Arguments dialog box, required arguments are in bold type; optional arguments are in normal type. Exhibit 14-11 shows the Function Arguments dialog box for the SUM function with a range reference entered in the Number1 box as the first argument.

To add cell references as arguments, you can type the cell reference in the argument box, or you can click in the argument box in the dialog box, and then click the cell or range reference in the worksheet. When

Exhibit 14-11 Function Arguments dialog box for the SUM function

- required argument is in bold
- optional argument is in regular type
- description of the selected argument
- link to the Help topic about the function
- Collapse Dialog Box button
- value that will be returned by the function
- value that will be displayed in the active cell

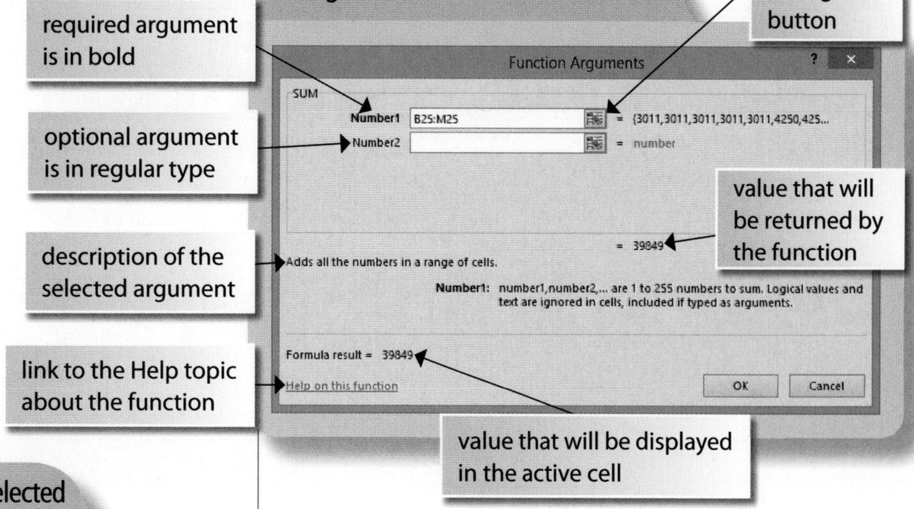

you do this, the Function Arguments dialog box collapses to show only the selected argument box. See Exhibit 14-12.

Begin Activity

Insert the SUM function using the Insert Function dialog box.

1 Make the **Budget worksheet** the active sheet. Select **cell B12**.

2 To the left of the formula bar, click the **Insert Function button** f_x. The Insert Function dialog box opens with the text in the Search for a function box selected. Most recently used appears in the Or select a category box.

> **Tip:** Click the Or select a category arrow, and then click a category to change the list of functions displayed in the Select a function dialog box.

3 In the Select a function box, click **SUM**. The syntax and a description of the SUM function appear below the Select a function box. Refer back to Exhibit 14-10.

4 Click **OK**. The Function Arguments dialog box opens, listing all of the arguments associated with the SUM function. Depending on the surrounding data, the Number1 box sometimes shows Excel's best guess of the range you want to sum. In this case, the insertion point is blinking in the Number1 box.

Exhibit 14-12 Function Arguments dialog box collapsed

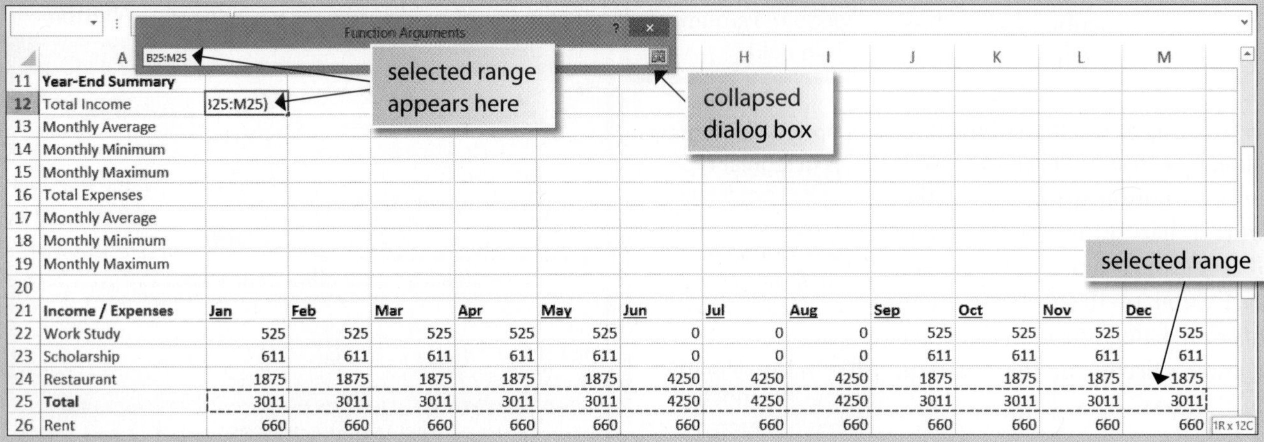

selected range appears here

collapsed dialog box

selected range

	A	Jan	Feb	Mar	Apr	May	Jun	Jul	Aug	Sep	Oct	Nov	Dec	
11	Year-End Summary							H	I	J	K	L	M	
12	Total Income													
13	Monthly Average													
14	Monthly Minimum													
15	Monthly Maximum													
16	Total Expenses													
17	Monthly Average													
18	Monthly Minimum													
19	Monthly Maximum													
20														
21	Income / Expenses	Jan	Feb	Mar	Apr	May	Jun	Jul	Aug	Sep	Oct	Nov	Dec
22	Work Study	525	525	525	525	525	0	0	0	525	525	525	525
23	Scholarship	611	611	611	611	611	0	0	0	611	611	611	611
24	Restaurant	1875	1875	1875	1875	1875	4250	4250	4250	1875	1875	1875	1875
25	Total	3011	3011	3011	3011	3011	4250	4250	4250	3011	3011	3011	3011
26	Rent	660	660	660	660	660	660	660	660	660	660	660	660

5 Click **any cell** in the worksheet. The selected cell has a blinking border to indicate it is selected for the formula, and the cell reference appears in the Number1 box in the Function Arguments dialog box.

6 Click **cell B25**, but do not release the mouse button. B25 appears in the Number1 box.

7 Drag to select the **range B25:M25**, but do not release the mouse button. As you drag, the dialog box collapses to show just its title bar and the Number1 box. Refer back to Exhibit 14-12.

8 Release the mouse button. The dialog box expands to its full size and the range reference B25:M25 appears as the value of the Number1 argument. The values of the cells in the range reference are listed to the right of the Number1 box, and the result of the function appears in the bottom-left of the dialog box. Refer back to Exhibit 14-11.

9 Click **OK**. The formula =SUM(B25:M25) is entered in cell E10, as shown in the formula bar. The calculated value 39849, which is the estimated total annual income, appears in the cell.

Problem? If the dialog box is blocking cell B25 or you cannot see row 25 because the worksheet is scrolled, drag the dialog box out of the way by its title bar or use the vertical scroll bar to scroll row 25 into view.

End Activity

If you don't see the function you want to use in the Select a function list in the Insert Function dialog box, you can use the search feature to search for a function that performs a particular calculation. This is helpful when you don't know the category or name of a function.

Begin Activity

Insert the MIN function using the Insert Function dialog box.

1 Select **cell B14**. To the left of the formula bar, click the **Insert Function button** f_x. The Insert Function dialog box opens.

2 In the Search for a function box, type **Display the smallest number in a set of values** and then click **Go**. The list of functions in the Select a function box changes to functions that match the phrase you typed.

Tip: To learn more about the function selected in the Select a function box, click the Help on this function link.

3 In the Select a function box, click **MIN** if it is not already selected, and then click **OK**. The Function Arguments dialog box appears with the arguments for the MIN function. The reference for the range B12:B13 is selected in the Number1 box.

4 With the range reference in the Number1 box selected, select the **range B25:M25** in the worksheet. The range you selected replaces the selected reference in the Number1 box.

5 Click **OK**. The dialog box closes, and the formula =MIN(B25:M25) is entered in cell B14, which displays 3011—the lowest estimated income for any month of the year.

End Activity

One of the categories available in the Insert Functions dialog box is the Most Recently Used category. This category lists the most recently used functions, sorted in order of recent use, in the Select a function box.

Begin Activity

Insert recently used functions with the Insert Function dialog box.

1 Select **cell B16**, and then, to the left of the formula bar, click the **Insert Function button** f_x. The Insert Function dialog box appears with the Most Recently Used category selected. The MIN function followed by the SUM function appear at the top of the Select a function box because these are the two functions you have used most recently.

> **Problem?** If Most Recently Used is not the current category, click the **Or select a category arrow**, and then click **Most Recently Used**.

2 In the Select a function box, click **SUM**, and then click **OK**. The Function Arguments dialog box for the SUM function appears.

3 In the worksheet, select the **range B34:M34**. The range with the estimated monthly expenses appears in the Number1 box.

> **Tip:** Click the Collapse Dialog Box button to shrink the Function Arguments dialog box to its title bar and the currently selected argument box. The button changes to the Expand Dialog Box button, which you can click to restore the dialog box.

4 In the Function Arguments dialog box, click **OK**. The formula =SUM(B34:M34) is inserted in cell B16, which displays 34610—the total projected expenses for the upcoming year. Compare your screen to Exhibit 14-13.

End Activity

Exhibit 14-13 Values after entering the SUM and MIN functions

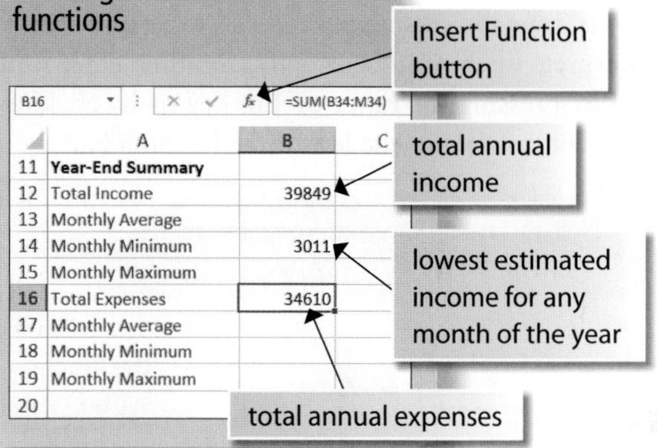

- Insert Function button
- total annual income
- lowest estimated income for any month of the year
- total annual expenses

14-2b Typing a Function in a Cell

After you become familiar with a function, it can be faster to type the function directly in a cell rather than using the Insert Function dialog box, as you did in Chapter 13 when you typed the SUM function in a cell. As with any formula, first type = (an equal sign). Then start typing the function name. As you type, a list of functions that begin with the letters you typed appears. As shown in Exhibit 14-14, when you type A, the list shows all of the functions starting with the letter A; when you type AV, the list shows only those functions starting with the letters AV, and so forth. This helps to ensure that you are entering a legitimate Excel function name. If you don't know what a specific function does, you can select the function in the list to display a ScreenTip with a description of that function.

Exhibit 14-14 Functions list in the worksheet

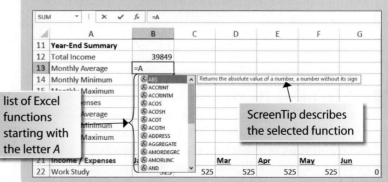

- list of Excel functions starting with the letter A
- ScreenTip describes the selected function

To insert a function in the active cell, press the Tab key or double-click the function name in the list to insert the function name and the opening parenthesis. You could also continue typing it and then type the opening parenthesis. After the opening parenthesis is added, a ScreenTip appears showing the function's syntax. See Exhibit 14-15. To add the first argument, you can select a cell or range or type the appropriate reference or argument. After you enter all the arguments, type the closing parenthesis to ensure that Excel interprets the formula correctly, and then enter it in the cell by pressing the Enter or Tab key or by clicking the Enter button ✓ to the left of the formula bar.

Exhibit 14-15 Function in cell with ScreenTip showing the syntax

SUM	▼	⋮	×	✓	*f*x	=AVERAGE(

	A	B	C
11	**Year-End Summary**		
12	Total Income	39849	
13	Monthly Average	=AVERAGE(	
14	Monthly Minimum	AVERAGE(**number1**, [number2], ...)	
15	Monthly Maximum		

ScreenTip shows the function syntax

next argument to be entered is in bold

Begin Activity

Type functions in cells.

1 Select **cell B13**.

2 Type **=A**. As you type a formula, a list with function names starting with the letter A opens. Refer back to Exhibit 14-14.

Tip: You can also start entering a function in a cell by clicking a category button in the Function Library group on the FORMULAS tab and then clicking the function you want to use.

3 Type **V**. The list shows only those functions starting with the letters *AV*.

4 Click **AVERAGE** to select the name of the function you want to use. A ScreenTip appears, describing the selected function.

5 Press the **Tab key**. The AVERAGE function with its opening parenthesis is inserted into cell B13, and a ScreenTip shows the syntax for the function. At this point, you can either type the range reference or select the range with your mouse. Refer back to Exhibit 14-15.

6 Select the **range B25:M25**. The range reference is added to the formula.

7 Type **)** (the closing parenthesis), and then press the **Enter key**. The formula =AVERAGE(B25:M25) is entered in cell B13, which displays 3320.75—the average estimated monthly income.

Tip: To avoid typing errors, it is often better to use your mouse to enter range references.

Problem? If #NAME? appears in the cell, you probably mistyped the function name. Edit the formula to correct the misspelling.

8 In **cell B15**, type **=M**, double-click **MAX** to insert the function, drag to select the **range B25:M25**, type **)** and then press the **Enter key**. The number 4250—the highest estimated income for any month of the year—appears in cell B15.

9 Enter the following functions, using any method and using the **range B34:M34** as the argument. When you are finished, compare your screen to Exhibit 14-16.

cell B17	**AVERAGE**
cell B18	**MIN**
cell B19	**MAX**

End Activity

Exhibit 14-16 Year-end summary values

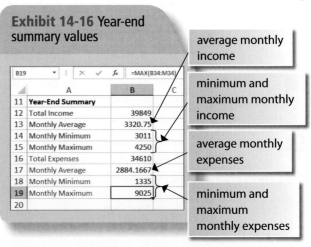

B19	▼	⋮	×	✓	*f*x	=MAX(B34:M34)

	A	B	C
11	**Year-End Summary**		
12	Total Income	39849	
13	Monthly Average	3320.75	
14	Monthly Minimum	3011	
15	Monthly Maximum	4250	
16	Total Expenses	34610	
17	Monthly Average	2884.1667	
18	Monthly Minimum	1335	
19	Monthly Maximum	9025	
20			

average monthly income

minimum and maximum monthly income

average monthly expenses

minimum and maximum monthly expenses

14-2c Editing Data Used in a Formula

Formulas provide the greatest flexibility for working with data that changes. By entering data values in cells and then referencing those cells in formulas, you can quickly change a value and immediately see the new formula results. This allows you to use Excel to change one or more values in a spreadsheet and then immediately see how those changes affect calculated values. For example in the Budget worksheet, if you change any of the values entered in the range B6:C8, the values that contain formulas that reference those cells—B22:M24—are changed. This causes the values in the cells that reference those cells—B25:M25—to change, and therefore the values in any cells that contain references to those cells to change. Exhibit 14-17 illustrates this.

Exhibit 14-17 How the revised income projection affects the calculated values

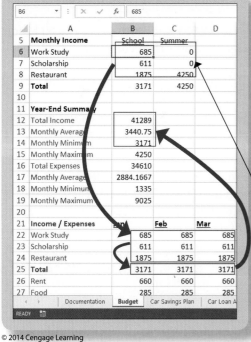

changing projected work study income affects values in row 22, row 25, and the range B12:B19

© 2014 Cengage Learning

Begin Activity

Edit data used in a formula.

1 Make **cell B6** the active cell. You will change the monthly income earned from work study during the school months.

2 Type **685**, and then click the **Enter button** ✓. Refer back to Exhibit 14-17. (You will need to scroll to see all the cells shown in the Exhibit.)

End Activity

14-3 Using AutoFill

AutoFill copies content and formats from a cell or range into an adjacent cell or range. The cell contents can be text, values, or formulas. AutoFill can also extend a series of numbers, patterned text, and dates into the adjacent selection.

14-3a Using the Fill Handle to Copy Cell Contents

After you select a cell or range, the **fill handle** ■ appears in the lower-right corner of the selection. See Exhibit 14-18. When you drag the fill handle over an adjacent range, AutoFill copies the content and formats from the original cell into the adjacent range.

> **AutoFill** An Excel feature that copies content and formats from a cell or range into an adjacent cell or range.
>
> **fill handle** A box in the lower-right corner of a selected cell or range that you drag over an adjacent cell or range to copy the content and formatting from the original cells into the adjacent range.

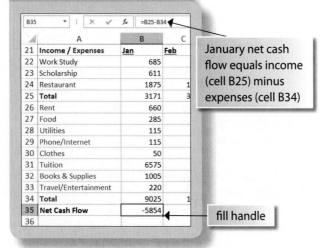

January net cash flow equals income (cell B25) minus expenses (cell B34)

fill handle

Begin Activity

Enter a formula to calculate net cash flow.

1 In **cell B35**, type the formula **=B25–B34**. This formula subtracts total expenses from total income for January.

Tip: Net cash flow is equal to the amount of money earned after paying expenses.

2 To the left of the formula bar, click the **Enter button** ✓. The result, –5854, indicates a projected shortfall for January. This is due to the cost of tuition and books that occur in that month.

End Activity

Now that you entered a formula in cell B35, you can use the fill handle to quickly copy the formula to the range C35:M35. After you release the mouse button, the contents of the cell whose fill handle you dragged are pasted into the cells over which you dragged. See Exhibit 14-19.

Begin Activity

Use a cell's fill handle to copy the cell contents.

1 Make sure **cell B35** is the active cell. The fill handle appears in the lower-right corner of the cell.

2 Point to the **fill handle** ■ in the lower-right corner of the cell. The pointer changes to ✚.

3 Click the **fill handle** ■, and without releasing the mouse button, drag over the **range C35:M35**. A green border appears around the range.

4 Release the mouse button. The selected range is filled with the formula in cell B35. The Auto Fill Options button 🔳 appears below the lower-right corner of the selected range. Refer to Exhibit 14-19.

Exhibit 14-19 Formulas pasted with AutoFill

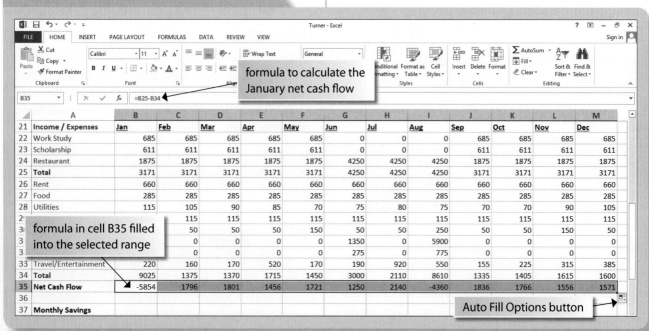

formula to calculate the January net cash flow

formula in cell B35 filled into the selected range

Auto Fill Options button

5 Review the monthly net cash flows to confirm that AutoFill correctly copied the formula into the selected range. These calculations provide a picture of how the net cash flow varies from month to month. Only in January and August, when tuition payments for the semesters are due, do expenses exceed income.

End Activity

You can also drag the fill handle of a selected range. After you release the mouse button, the contents of each cell are copied to the corresponding cells in the same row or column.

Begin Activity

Use a range's fill handle to copy the range contents.

1 In **cell B38**, enter **=E7** to retrieve the balance in the savings account at the beginning of the year.

2 In **cell B39**, enter **=B25** to retrieve the January total income.

3 In **cell B40**, enter **=B34** to retrieve the January total expenses. These relative references will change when you copy the formula to other months.

4 In **cell B41**, type **=**, click **cell B38**, type **+**, click **cell B39**, type **–** (a minus sign), and then click **cell B40**. This formula calculates the ending balance for the savings account, which is equal to the starting balance plus any deposits (the total monthly income) minus the withdrawals and transfers (the total monthly expenses). Cell B41 displays 1646, which is the projected balance in the savings account at the end of January.

5 Select the **range B38:B41**, and then drag the **fill handle** ■ over the **range C38:C41** to calculate the ending balance for February.

6 In **cell C38**, change the formula to **=B41**. Now the February starting balance for the savings account is based on the January ending balance.

7 Select the **range C38:C41**, and then drag the **fill handle** ■ over the **range D38:M41**. The formulas and formatting from February are copied into the remaining months of the year.

8 In **cell F7**, enter **=M41**. The formula displays the ending balance of the savings account in December—14179.

End Activity

Using the Auto Fill Options Button

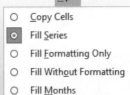

By default, AutoFill copies both the content and the formatting of the original range to the selected range. However, sometimes you might want

Auto Fill Options button menu

to copy only the content or only the formatting. The Auto Fill Options button that appears after you release the mouse button lets you specify what is copied. As shown here, clicking this button provides a list of AutoFill options. The Copy Cells option copies both the content and the formatting. The Fill Series option continues the pattern of data. The Fill Formatting Only option copies the formatting into the selected cells but not any content. The Fill Without Formatting option copies the content but not the formatting. The last option uses the Flash Fill feature to copy content from other cells into one cell based on the pattern you set.

14-3b Creating a Series

AutoFill can also be used to create a series of numbers, dates, or text based on a pattern. To create a series of numbers, you enter the initial values in the series in a selected range and then use AutoFill to complete the series. Exhibit 14-20 shows how AutoFill can be used to insert the numbers from 1 to 10 in a selected range. The first few numbers in the range were entered to establish the pattern for AutoFill to use—in this case, consecutive positive integers 1 through 3 in range A1:A3. Then, you select the range, and drag the fill handle over the cells where you want the pattern continued; in this case, the fill handle was dragged over the range A4:A10. Excel fills in the rest of the series.

Exhibit 14-20 AutoFill extends a sequence

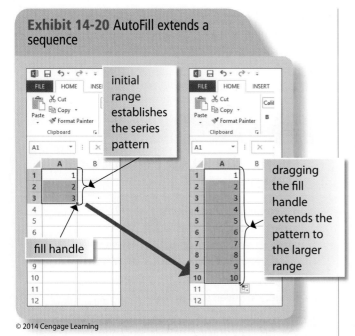

initial range establishes the series pattern

fill handle

dragging the fill handle extends the pattern to the larger range

© 2014 Cengage Learning

AutoFill can extend a wide variety of series, including dates and times and patterned text. Exhibit 14-21 shows examples of some series that AutoFill can generate. For example, a text pattern that includes text and a number, such as Region 1, Region 2, and so on, can be extended using AutoFill. In each case, you must provide enough information for AutoFill to identify the pattern.

Exhibit 14-21 AutoFill applied to values, dates and times, and patterned text

Type	Initial pattern	Extended series
Values	1, 2, 3	4, 5, 6, …
	2, 4, 6	8, 10, 12, …
Dates and times	Jan	Feb, Mar, Apr, …
	January	February, March, April, …
	14-Jan, 14-Feb	14-Mar, 14-Apr, 14-May, …
	12/30/2016	12/31/2016, 1/1/2017, 1/2/2017, …
	12/31/2016, 1/31/2017	2/28/2017, 3/31/2017, 4/30/2017, …
	Mon	Tue, Wed, Thu, …
	Monday	Tuesday, Wednesday, Thursday , …
	11:00AM	12:00PM, 1:00PM, 2:00PM, …
Patterned text	1st period	2nd period, 3rd period, 4th period, …
	Region 1	Region 2, Region 3, Region 4, …
	Quarter 3	Quarter 4, Quarter 1, Quarter 2, …
	Qtr3	Qtr4, Qtr1, Qtr2, …

AutoFill can recognize some patterns from only a single value, such as *Jan* or *January* to create a series of month names or abbreviations, or *Mon* or *Monday* to create a series of the days of the week.

As you drag a fill handle over a range, a ScreenTip appears showing you how AutoFill will fill the series. For example, if a cell contains Jan, the common abbreviation for January, the next cell will be filled with Feb, the abbreviation for February. See Exhibit 14-22.

Exhibit 14-22 ScreenTip when AutoFilling month abbreviations

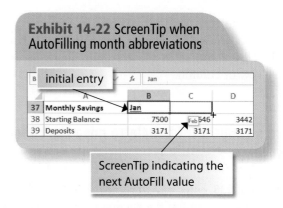

initial entry

ScreenTip indicating the next AutoFill value

Begin Activity

Use AutoFill to enter a series.

1 In **cell B37**, enter **Jan**. (Do not enter the period.) This is the first value in the series.

2 Select **cell B37** if necessary. On the HOME tab, in the Font group, click the **Bold button** B, and then click the **Underline button** U. The text in cell B37 is formatted as bold and underlined.

3 Drag the **fill handle** ■ over **cell C37**, but do not release the mouse button. A ScreenTip shows the month abbreviation for the next cell in the series. In this case, it shows Feb for cell C37. Refer back to Exhibit 14-22.

4 Continue dragging over the **range D37:M37**, and then release the mouse button. AutoFill enters the three-letter abbreviations for each remaining month of the year. It also copied the bold and underline formatting applied to cell B37. Compare your screen to Exhibit 14-23.

End Activity

© 2014 Cengage Learning

Exhibit 14-23 Month series completed with AutoFill

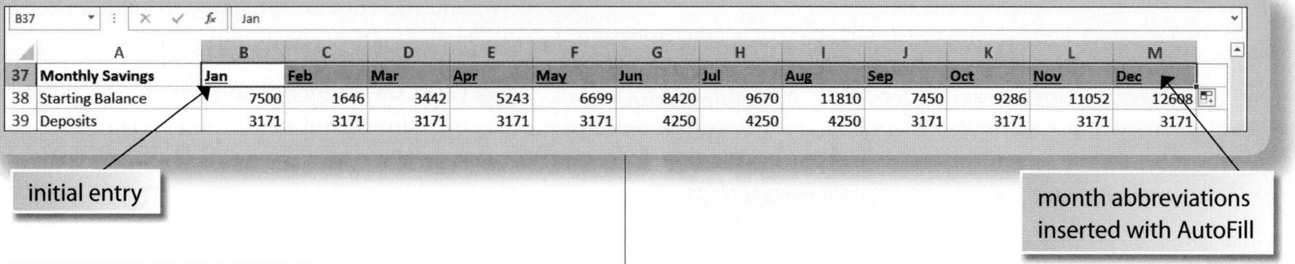

	A	B	C	D	E	F	G	H	I	J	K	L	M
37	Monthly Savings	Jan	Feb	Mar	Apr	May	Jun	Jul	Aug	Sep	Oct	Nov	Dec
38	Starting Balance	7500	1646	3442	5243	6699	8420	9670	11810	7450	9286	11052	12698
39	Deposits	3171	3171	3171	3171	3171	4250	4250	4250	3171	3171	3171	3171

B37 ▾ : × ✓ ƒx | Jan

initial entry

month abbreviations inserted with AutoFill

© 2014 Cengage Learning

FYI

Creating a Series with a Complex Pattern

For more complex patterns, you can use the Series dialog box. To do so, enter the first value of the series in a worksheet cell, select the entire range that will contain the series, click the Fill button in the Editing group on the HOME tab, and then click Series. The Series dialog box opens. You can use the Series dialog box to specify a linear or growth series for numbers; a Date series for dates that increase by day, weekday, month, or year; or an AutoFill series for patterned text. With numbers, you can also specify the step value (indicating how much each number increases over the previous entry) and a stop value (to specify the endpoint for the entire series).

Series dialog box

14-4 Working with Date Functions

A **date function** is a function that inserts or calculates dates and times. Exhibit 14-24 describes seven of the date functions supported by Excel. You can use these functions to help with scheduling or to determine on what days of the week certain dates occur.

Perhaps the most commonly used date function is the TODAY function, which displays the current date. The syntax of the TODAY function is:

=TODAY()

Exhibit 14-24 Date and time functions

Function	Description
DATE (*year*,*month*,*day*)	Creates a date value for the date represented by the *year*, *month*, and *day* arguments
DAY(*date*)	Extracts the day of the month from the *date* value
MONTH(*date*)	Extracts the month number from the *date* value where 1=January, 2=February, and so forth
YEAR(date)	Extracts the year number from the *date* value
WEEKDAY (*date*[,*return_type*])	Calculates the day of the week from the *date* value, where 1=Sunday, 2=Monday, and so forth; to choose a different numbering scheme, set the optional *return_type* value to "1" (1=Sunday, 2=Monday, ...), "2" (1=Monday, 2=Tuesday), or "3" (0=Monday, 1=Tuesday, ...)
NOW( )	Displays the current date and time
TODAY( )	Displays the current date

The TODAY function doesn't have any arguments. If you enter the TODAY function using the Insert Function dialog box, the Function Arguments dialog box that opens informs you of this. See Exhibit 14-25. Notice that Volatile appears next to Formula result. This means that the result will change—in this case, it will always show the current date.

The NOW function, which displays both the current date and the current time, also does not have any arguments. The syntax of the NOW function is:

=NOW()

date function A function that inserts or calculates dates and times.

Exhibit 14-25 Function Arguments dialog box for the TODAY function

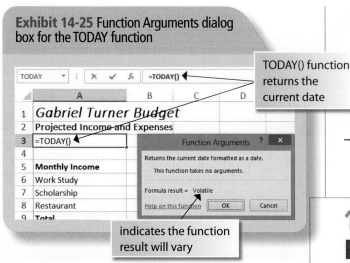

TODAY() function returns the current date

indicates the function result will vary

3 In the date functions list, click **TODAY**. The TODAY function is entered in cell A3, and the Function Arguments dialog box appears. Refer to Exhibit 14-25.

4 Click **OK**. The Function Arguments dialog box closes, and the formula =TODAY() is entered into cell A3.

End Activity

Note that both functions require open and close parentheses even though there are no arguments to place inside them.

The values returned by the TODAY and NOW functions are updated automatically whenever you reopen the workbook or enter a new calculation.

Begin Activity

Enter a date function.

1 Select **cell A3**.

2 On the ribbon, click the **FORMULAS tab**. In the Function Library group, click the **Date & Time button**. A menu of date functions opens.

14-5 Working with the PMT Financial Function

A **financial function** is a function related to monetary calculations, such as loans and payments. Excel provides a wide range of financial functions. Exhibit 14-26 describes some of Excel's financial functions that are often used to develop budgets. These financial functions are the same as those widely used in business and accounting to perform various financial calculations, such as depreciation of an asset, the amount of interest paid on an investment, and the present value of an investment.

FYI

Excel Dates and Times as Numeric Values

Although dates and times entered into a cell usually are displayed as text, they are actually stored by Excel as numbers measuring the interval between the specified date and time and January 1, 1900 at 12:00 a.m. For example, the date May 1, 2016 is stored as 42,491, which is the number of days between January 1, 1900 and May 1, 2016. Times are stored as fractional parts of one day. The time 6:00 a.m. is stored as 0.25 because that represents one-fourth of a 24-hour day (starting the day from 12:00 a.m.). Similarly, the date and time of May 1, 2016 at 6:00 a.m. is stored as 42,491.25.

Excel stores dates and times as numbers to make it easier to calculate time intervals. For example, to calculate the difference between one date and another, you subtract the earlier date from the later date. If you subtract the date and time of April 30, 2016 at 12:00 a.m. from May 1, 2016 at 6:00 p.m., Excel displays 1.75—or one and three-quarters of a day. You can always view the actual date and time by selecting the cell that contains the date/time entry and applying the General number format or by switching the workbook window to Formula view.

HomeStudio/Shutterstock.com

financial function A function related to monetary calculations, such as loans and payments.

Exhibit 14-26 Financial functions for loans and investments

Function	Description
FV(*rate,nper,pmt*[,*pv*=0][,*type*=0])	Calculates the future value of an investment, where *rate* is the interest rate per period, *nper* is the total number of periods, *pmt* is the payment in each period, *pv* is the present value of the investment, and *type* indicates whether payments should be made at the end of the period (0) or the beginning of the period (1)
PMT(*rate,nper,pv*[,*fv*=0][,*type*=0])	Calculates the payments required each period on a loan or investment, where *fv* is the future value of the investment
IPMT(*rate,per,nper,pv*[,*fv*=0][,*type*=0])	Calculates the amount of a loan payment devoted to paying the loan interest, where *per* is the number of the payment period
PPMT(*rate,per,nper,pv*[,*fv*=0][,*type*=0])	Calculates the amount of a loan payment devoted to repaying the principal of a loan
PV(*rate,nper pmt*[,*fv*=0][,*type*=0])	Calculates the present value of a loan or investment based on periodic, constant payments
NPER(*rate,pmt,pv*[,*fv*=0][,*type*=0])	Calculates the number of periods required to repay a loan or investment
RATE(*nper,pmt,pv*[,*fv*=0][,*type*=0])	Calculates the interest rate of a loan or investment based on periodic, constant payments

© 2014 Cengage Learning

14-5a Understanding Loan Factors

One commonly used financial function is the **PMT function**, which is used to calculate a payment schedule required to completely repay a loan. The cost of a loan to the borrower is largely based on three factors: the principal, the time required to repay the loan, and the interest. **Principal** is the amount of money being loaned.

The length of time required to repay the loan is usually specified as the number of payments. To calculate the number of payments, you need to know the length of the loan in years and the number of payments required per year, and then you multiple these numbers. For example, a 10-year loan that is paid monthly—that is, 12 times per year—has 120 payments (10 years × 12 months per year). If that same 10-year loan is paid quarterly—that is, four times per year—it has 40 payments (10 years × 4 quarters per year). The length of time between each payment is the **payment period**, or just **period**.

Interest is the amount added to the principal by the lender. Think of interest as a kind of "user fee" because the borrower is paying for the right to use the lender's money for a length of time. Generally, the interest rate is expressed at an annual percentage rate, or APR. For example, an 8 percent APR means that the annual interest rate on a loan is 8 percent of the amount owed to the lender. To calculate how much interest a borrower owes each payment period—the interest rate per period—the annual interest rate is divided by the number of payments per year (often monthly or quarterly).

So, if the 8 percent annual interest rate is paid monthly, the resulting monthly interest rate is $1/12$ of 8 percent, which is about 0.67 percent per month. If payments are made quarterly, then the interest rate per quarter would be $1/4$ of 8 percent, which is 2 percent per quarter.

14-5b Entering the PMT Function

To calculate the costs associated with a loan, you need the following information:

- Annual interest rate
- Number of payments or payment periods per year
- Length of the loan
- Principal amount

With this information, you can use the PMT function to determine the loan payments for a specific amount. The syntax of the PMT function is

$$\text{PMT}(rate, nper, pv[, fv=0][, type=0])$$

where *rate* is the interest rate for each payment period, *nper* is the total number of payments required to repay

PMT function A financial function that calculates the monthly payment required to repay a loan.

principal The amount of money being loaned.

payment period (period) The length of time between each loan payment.

interest The amount added to the principal by the lender.

the loan, and *pv* is the present value of the loan or the principal. The optional argument *fv* is the future value of the loan. Because the intent with most loans is to repay them completely, the future value is equal to 0 by default. The optional *type* argument specifies when the interest is charged on the loan, either at the end of the payment period (type=0)—for example, at the end of every month—or at the beginning of the payment period (type=1). The default is type=0.

For example, if you borrowed $10,000 to buy a car, you could use the PMT function to calculate your monthly payment over a five-year period, payable monthly, at an annual interest rate of 9 percent. The APR is 9 percent; therefore the rate argument—the interest rate per period—is 9 percent divided by 12 monthly payments, which is 0.75 percent per month. The nper argument—the total number of payments or payment periods—is equal to the number of years (five) multiplied by the number of payments per year (12), or 60. The pv argument—the principal—is $10,000. Because the loan will be repaid completely and payments will be made at the end of the month, you can accept the default values for the fv and type arguments. The resulting PMT function

=PMT(0.75,60,10000)

returns a value of –$207.58, which means you would need to pay $207.58 every month for five years before the loan and the interest are completely repaid. The value is negative because the payment is an expense to the borrower. Essentially, the loan is money the borrower subtracts from his or her funds to repay the loan.

Of course, one of the benefits of using Excel is that you can have Excel calculate the interest rate per period (the rate argument) and the number of payments or payment periods (the nper argument). To do this, you could use formulas as the arguments and rewrite the PMT function as:

=PMT(0.09/12,5*12,10000)

Another way to do this is to set up a worksheet in which you directly enter the values you know—the annual interest rate (APR), the number of payments per year, the number of years of the loan, and the loan amount—into cells, and then add formulas to calculate the interest rate per period and the number of payments. Then you can reference the cells containing the calculated rate and number of payments and the cell containing the loan amount as the arguments in the PMT function.

Begin Activity

Set up a worksheet to use the PMT function to calculate a monthly payment.

1 Make the **Car Loan Analysis worksheet** the active sheet.

2 Make **cell B3** the active cell. On the HOME tab, in the Number group, click the **Percent Style button** %. Now you can type the percentage as a whole number rather than a decimal number.

3 Type **6**, and then press the **Enter key**. 6% appears in cell B3. This is the annual interest rate for the loan.

4 In **cell B4**, enter **12** as the number of payments per year. This is because the loan needs to be paid monthly.

5 In **cell B5**, enter the formula **=B3/B4** to calculate the interest per period. This is the rate argument for the PMT function. The calculated value is 0.50 percent per month. The formula result did not pick up the percentage formatting from cell B3.

6 Make **cell B5** the active cell. On the HOME tab, in the Number group, click the **Percent Style button** %. The value is formatted as a percentage and appears as 1%. This is because the percent format does not show any decimal places. Any calculations that reference this value will use the true value in the cell—0.5%—so you don't need to change the format. However, it is confusing to someone looking at the worksheet, so you will change the format to show one decimal place.

7 In the Number group, click the **Increase Decimal button**. The value in cell B5 changes to 0.5%. This is the correct interest rate per period.

> **Tip:** To see a more precise interest rate per period for loans, continue clicking the Increase Decimal button to add at least three decimal places.

8 In **cell B6**, enter **5**. This is the length of the loan in years.

9 In **cell B7**, enter the formula **=B4*B6** to multiply the number of payments per year by the number of years. This calculates the total number of monthly payments—60.

10 In **cell B8**, enter **20000** for the amount of the loan. To make it easier to read, this value should be formatted as Currency.

11 Select **cell B8**, if necessary. On the HOME tab, in the Number group, click the **Number Format box arrow** General ▾, and then click **Currency**.

End Activity

Once you have set up the worksheet, you can add the PMT function. Instead of typing the values of the arguments directly in the function, you will reference the corresponding cells in the worksheet. Exhibit 14-27 shows the Function Arguments dialog box for the PMT function with cell references instead of values in the boxes that contain the arguments.

Begin Activity

Insert the PMT function to calculate a monthly payment.

1 Select **cell B10**. To the left of the formula bar, click the **Insert Function button** *fx*. The Insert Function dialog box opens. In the Or select a category box, Date & Time appears because that was the last function category you used.

2 Click the **Or select a category box arrow**, and then click **Financial**. Financial functions appear in the Select a function box.

3 Scroll down the alphabetical list until you see the PMT function, click **PMT**, and then click **OK**. The Function Arguments dialog box for the PMT

function opens. Refer to Exhibit 14-27. The PMT function requires three arguments—rate, nper, and pv—and you can add two optional arguments—fv and type. The insertion point is in the Rate box.

4 In the worksheet, click **cell B5**, the cell that contains the interest rate per month.

5 Click in the **Nper box**, and then click **cell B7**, the cell that contains the total number of monthly payments required to repay the loan. (*Nper* stands for *Number Per.*)

6 Click in the **Pv box**, and then click **cell B8**, the cell that contains the present value of the loan. In cell B10, the complete formula =PMT(B5,B7,B8) appears. Refer to Exhibit 14-27.

7 Click **OK**. The value $386.66 appears in cell B10. The cell picked up the Currency formatting from the pv value in cell B8. The number is in parentheses and colored red because that is how Currency formatting formats negative numbers. Compare your screen to Exhibit 14-28.

8 Double-click **cell B10**. Instead of the calculated result, the function appears in cell B10. Notice that each cell reference listed as an argument is a different color, and the cells referenced have colored borders and shading that correspond to the colors of the cells' references in the function.

9 Press the **Esc key** to exit Edit mode.

End Activity

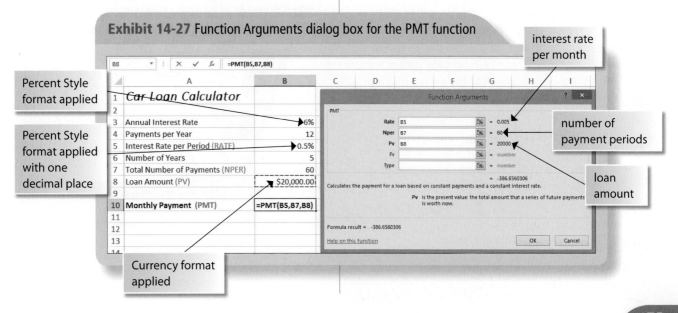

Exhibit 14-27 Function Arguments dialog box for the PMT function

Percent Style format applied

Percent Style format applied with one decimal place

Currency format applied

interest rate per month

number of payment periods

loan amount

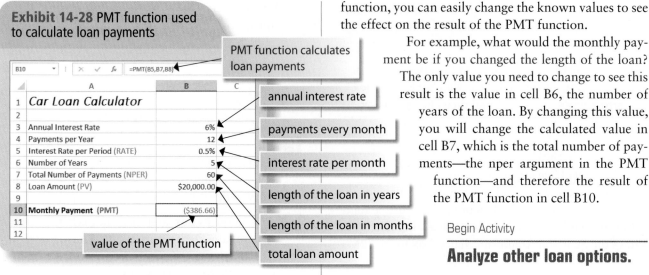

Exhibit 14-28 PMT function used to calculate loan payments

PMT function calculates loan payments

annual interest rate

payments every month

interest rate per month

length of the loan in years

length of the loan in months

total loan amount

value of the PMT function

14-5c Performing What-If Analysis

One key benefit of Excel is its ability to do a **what-if analysis**, which lets you examine how changing values entered directly in a worksheet, such as the interest rate, the length of the loan, or the amount borrowed, affect the calculated values. By setting up a worksheet with these values and then using cell references in the

function, you can easily change the known values to see the effect on the result of the PMT function.

For example, what would the monthly payment be if you changed the length of the loan? The only value you need to change to see this result is the value in cell B6, the number of years of the loan. By changing this value, you will change the calculated value in cell B7, which is the total number of payments—the nper argument in the PMT function—and therefore the result of the PMT function in cell B10.

Begin Activity

Analyze other loan options.

1. Click **cell B6**, type **3**, and then press the **Enter key**. By reducing the number of years from five to three, the amount of the monthly payment increases to $608.44.

2. In **cell B8**, change the value to **18,000**. For this smaller loan, the monthly payment drops to $547.59 per month.

End Activity

LEARN MORE

Using Functions to Manage Personal Finances

Excel has many financial functions to manage personal finances. The following list can help you determine which function to use for the most common personal finance calculations:

▶ To determine how much an investment will be worth after a series of monthly payments at some future time, use the FV (future value) function.

▶ To determine how much you need to spend each month to repay a loan or mortgage within a set period of time, use the PMT (payment) function.

▶ To determine how much of your monthly loan payment is used to pay the interest, use the IPMT (interest payment) function.

▶ To determine how much of your monthly loan payment is used for repaying the principal, use the PPMT (principal payment) function.

▶ To determine the largest loan or mortgage you can afford given a set monthly payment, use the PV (present value) function.

▶ To determine how long it will take to pay off a loan with constant monthly payments, use the NPER (number of periods) function.

wacpan/Shutterstock.com

what-if analysis An examination of how changing values entered directly in a worksheet affect calculated values.

14-6 Formatting Cells and Ranges

A workbook often contains several cells that store the same type of data. For example, each worksheet might have a cell that contains the sheet title, or a range of financial data might have several cells containing summary totals. A good design practice is to apply the same format to worksheet cells that contain the same type of data.

You can format the appearance of individual cells by modifying the alignment of text within the cell, indenting cell text, or adding borders of different styles and colors to individual cells or ranges.

14-6a Using the Format Cells Dialog Box

The buttons in the Font and Alignment groups on the HOME tab provide access to the most common formatting choices. Using these buttons has the same effect as in Word. As you have already seen, you can also use the buttons in the Number group to format cell values.

If you need to make more formatting changes to cell contents, you can open the Format Cells dialog box. The Format Cells dialog box, shown in Exhibit 14-29, has the following six tabs, each focusing on a different set of formatting options:

► **Number**—options for formatting the appearance of numbers, including dates and numbers treated as text such as telephone or Social Security numbers.

► **Alignment**—options for how data is aligned within a cell.

► **Font**—options for selecting fonts, font sizes, font styles, underlining, font colors, and font effect.

► **Border**—options for adding and removing cell borders as well as selecting a line style and color.

► **Fill**—options for creating and applying background colors and patterns to cells.

► **Protection**—options for locking or hiding cells to prevent other users from modifying their contents.

Begin Activity

Use the Format Cells dialog box.

1 Switch to the **Budget worksheet**, and then select the **range B6:C9**. These cells are formatted with the General number format.

2 On the HOME tab, in the Number group, click the **Accounting Number Format button** $. Dollar signs appear along the left edges of the selected cells, and two decimal places appear after each value. Notice that the values of zero in cells C6 and C7 are displayed as a dollar sign followed by a hyphen. This is how a zero value is displayed in the Accounting Number format.

3 In the Number group, click the **Decrease Decimal button**. The numbers after the decimal point are removed. A standard accounting practice is to display a currency symbol in only the first and Total entries within a column of values.

4 Select the **range B7:C8**. To remove the dollar sign from the cells in the middle of the range, you need to open the Format Cells dialog box.

5 In the Number group, click the **Dialog Box Launcher**. The Format Cells dialog box opens with the Number tab displayed. Custom is selected in the Category box. This is because you changed the standard formatting of the Accounting Number format.

> **Tip:** You can also open the Format Cells dialog box by right-clicking a cell or selected range, and then clicking Format Cells on the shortcut menu.

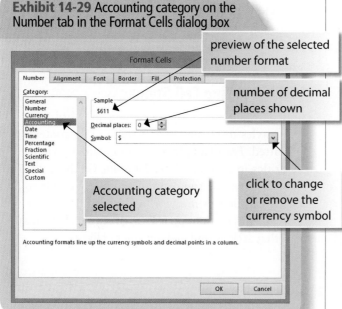

Exhibit 14-29 Accounting category on the Number tab in the Format Cells dialog box

- preview of the selected number format
- number of decimal places shown
- Accounting category selected
- click to change or remove the currency symbol

6 In the Category box, click **Accounting**. The dialog box shows the current options for the Accounting format—in this case, zero decimal places and a dollar sign as the symbol. Refer back to Exhibit 14-29.

7 Click the **Symbol arrow**, click **None**, and then click **OK**. The dollar sign is removed from the selected cells.

> **Tip:** You could also click the Comma Style button in the Number group on the HOME tab to format cells with the Accounting format with no currency symbol.

8 Select the **non-adjacent range B23:M24;B27:M33**.

9 Open the **Format Cells dialog box**. In the Category list, click **Accounting**.

10 Click the **Decimal places box down arrow** twice to change the value in the box to zero.

11 Click the **Symbol box arrow**, and then click **None**.

12 Click **OK**. The selected cells are formatted with the Accounting Number format with no symbol and zero decimal places.

13 Select the **nonadjacent range B22:M22;B25:M26; B34:M34;B39:M40**. Apply the **Accounting Number Format** with a **dollar sign** and **zero decimal places**.

End Activity

If you enter an integer with more digits than can fit in a cell, the column width automatically widens to accommodate the number. However, if you enter a decimal value in a cell and it is too wide to fit in the cell, the decimal places are rounded so that the number fits. And if you resize a column narrower after you enter a number and the number no longer fits in the cell, or if you apply a format that makes the number larger, such as adding decimal places, and the number no longer fits in the cell, ###### appears in the cell instead of the number. The number is still in the cell as it was entered or formatted, and you see the complete number in the formula bar. You can also display the entire number by increasing the column width or changing the number format.

Format additional cells with the Accounting format.

1 Select the **nonadjacent range B35:M35;B38:M38;B41:M41**.

2 On the HOME tab, in the Number group, click the **Accounting Number Format button** $. The Accounting format is applied to the range. In several of the selected cells, including cell B35, ######## appears instead of the value.

3 In the Number group, click the **Decrease Decimal button** twice. The decimal places are removed, and the numbers fit in the column. Notice that the values in several of the cells, including cell B35, are within parentheses. This is how the Accounting format displays negative values.

> **Tip:** If pound signs (#) appear in a cell, you can increase the column width to display a value.

4 Select the **nonadjacent range B12;B16;E7:F7**. Apply the **Accounting format** with a **dollar sign** and **zero decimal places**.

5 Select the **nonadjacent range B13:B15;B17:B19**. In the Number group, click the **Comma Style button**. The Accounting format with no symbol is applied.

6 In the Number group, click the **Decrease Decimal button** twice. Compare your screen to Exhibit 14-30. You will need to scroll to see all the rows on your screen.

End Activity

14-6b Applying Cell Styles

Similar to styles you apply to text in Word, you can apply styles to change how a cell and its contents are formatted. For example, you can create a style to display titles in a bold, white, 20-point Calibri font on a blue background. You can then apply that style to any cell with a title in the workbook. As in Word, if you revise the style, the appearance of any cell formatted with that style is updated automatically.

Exhibit 14-30 Budget worksheet with formatted numbers

	A	B	C	D	E	F	G	H	I	J	K	L	M
5	Monthly Income	School	Summer		Savings Account								
6	Work Study	$ 685	$ -		Starting	Ending							
7	Scholarship	611	-		$ 7,500	$ 14,179							
8	Restaurant	1,875	4,250										
9	Total	$ 3,171	$ 4,250										
10													
11	Year-End Summary												
12	Total Income	$ 41,289											
13	Monthly Average	3,441											
14	Monthly Minimum	3,171											
15	Monthly Maximum	4,250											
16	Total Expenses	$ 34,610											
17	Monthly Average	2,884											
18	Monthly Minimum	1,335											
19	Monthly Maximum	9,025											
20													
21	Income / Expenses	Jan	Feb	Mar	Apr	May	Jun	Jul	Aug	Sep	Oct	Nov	Dec
22	Work Study	$ 685	$ 685	$ 685	$ 685	$ 685	$ -	$ -	$ -	$ 685	$ 685	$ 685	$ 685
23	Scholarship	611	611	611	611	611	-	-	-	611	611	611	611
24	Restaurant	1,875	1,875	1,875	1,875	1,875	4,250	4,250	4,250	1,875	1,875	1,875	1,875
25	Total	$ 3,171	$ 3,171	$ 3,171	$ 3,171	$ 3,171	$ 4,250	$ 4,250	$ 4,250	$ 3,171	$ 3,171	$ 3,171	$ 3,171
26	Rent	$ 660	$ 660	$ 660	$ 660	$ 660	$ 660	$ 660	$ 660	$ 660	$ 660	$ 660	$ 660
27	Food	285	285	285	285	285	285	285	285	285	285	285	285
28	Utilities	115	105	90	85	70	75	80	75	70	70	90	105
29	Phone/Internet	115	115	115	115	115	115	115	115	115	115	115	115
30	Clothes	50	50	50	50	150	50	50	250	50	50	150	50
31	Tuition	6,575	-	-	-	-	1,350	-	5,900	-	-	-	-
32	Books & Supplies	1,005	-	-	-	-	275	-	775	-	-	-	-
33	Travel/Entertainment	220	160	170	520	170	190	920	550	155	225	315	385
34	Total	$ 9,025	$ 1,375	$ 1,370	$ 1,715	$ 1,450	$ 3,000	$ 2,110	$ 8,610	$ 1,335	$ 1,405	$ 1,615	$ 1,600
35	Net Cash Flow	$ (5,854)	$ 1,796	$ 1,801	$ 1,456	$ 1,721	$ 1,250	$ 2,140	$ (4,360)	$ 1,836	$ 1,766	$ 1,556	$ 1,571
36													
37	Monthly Savings	Jan	Feb	Mar	Apr	May	Jun	Jul	Aug	Sep	Oct	Nov	Dec
38	Starting Balance	$ 7,500	$ 1,646	$ 3,442	$ 5,243	$ 6,699	$ 8,420	$ 9,670	$ 11,810	$ 7,450	$ 9,286	$ 11,052	$ 12,608
39	Deposits	3,171	3,171	3,171	3,171	3,171	4,250	4,250	4,250	3,171	3,171	3,171	3,171
40	Withdrawals	9,025	1,375	1,370	1,715	1,450	3,000	2,110	8,610	1,335	1,405	1,615	1,600
41	Ending Balance	$ 1,646	$ 3,442	$ 5,243	$ 6,699	$ 8,420	$ 9,670	$ 11,810	$ 7,450	$ 9,286	$ 11,052	$ 12,608	$ 14,179

LEARN MORE

Copying and Pasting Formats

The Paste Options button in Excel is similar to the Paste Options button in Word. However, in Excel, it includes many more options than in Word. For example, you can paste values with and without formatting, you can choose to paste calculated results instead of a formula, or you can paste values and retain the column width from the source cells. As in Word, you can access these options by clicking the Paste button arrow in the Clipboard group on the HOME tab, or you can paste cell contents in the worksheet and then click the Paste Options button that appears below the lower-right corner of the range where you pasted the items.

In Excel, you can also use the Paste Special command on the Paste button menu to control how content is pasted from the Clipboard. When you click Paste Special, the Paste Special dialog box opens, in which you can choose how to paste the copied range.

Paste Options button menu

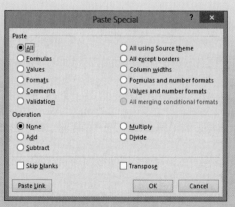

Paste Special dialog box

Excel has a variety of built-in styles to format worksheet titles, column and row totals, and cells with emphasis. These are available in the Cell Styles gallery shown in Exhibit 14-31, which you access by clicking the Cell Styles button in the Styles group on the HOME tab. Some styles are based on the workbook's current theme and may change if the theme is changed.

5 Select the **nonadjacent cells A5;A11;A21;A37**.

6 Apply the **Accent6 style** to the selected cells. The selected cells are formatted with the same style applied to the range E5:F5.

7 Select the **nonadjacent range B25:M25;B41:M41**.

8 In the Styles group, click the **Cell Styles button**. In the Good, Bad and Neutral section, click the **Good style**. Each cell in the selected range is formatted with the selected style— green text on a light green background.

9 Select the **range B34:M34**.

10 In the Styles group, click the **Cell Styles button**. In the Good, Bad and Neutral section, click the **Bad style**. The expense values are formatted differently from the income values with red text on a light red background.

11 Click **any cell** in the worksheet to deselect the range. Compare your screen to Exhibit 14-32.

Exhibit 14-31 Cell Styles gallery

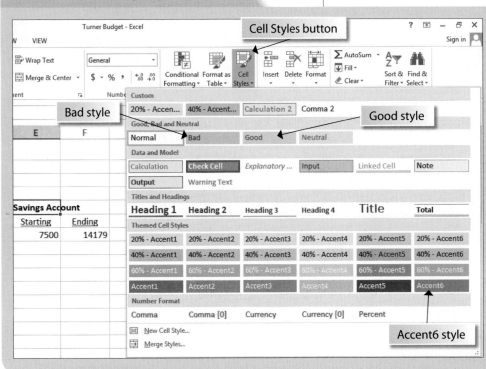

Begin Activity

Apply cell styles.

1 In the **Budget worksheet**, select **cell E5**.

2 On the HOME tab, in the Styles group, click the **Cell Styles button**. The Cell Styles gallery opens. Refer to Exhibit 14-31.

3 Point to several styles in the Cell Styles gallery to see the Live Preview of the style on cell E5.

4 In the Themed Cell Styles section, click the **Accent6 style**. The gallery closes, and the text in cell E5 is formatted as 11-point, white text, and the cell is filled with a green background. The text overflows into cell F5. You cannot see the text because it is now formatted as white, and cell F5 is filled with white, not green. You'll fix this shortly.

End Activity

14-6c Aligning Cell Content

Text in a cell is horizontally left-aligned by default, and numeric values (including dates) are right-aligned. The default vertical alignment for cell contents is bottom-aligned. You might want to change these alignments to make the cell content more readable or visually appealing. In general, you should center column titles and left-align other cell text and align numbers within a column by the decimal point. The buttons to set these alignment options are located in the Alignment group on the HOME tab. Exhibit 14-33 describes the actions of these buttons.

Exhibit 14-32 Budget worksheet with cell styles applied

	A	B	C	D	E	F	G	H	I	J	K	L	M
24	Restaurant	1,875	1,875	1,875	1,875	1,875	4,250	4,250	4,250	1,875	1,875	1,875	1,875
25	**Total**	$ 3,171	$ 3,171	$ 3,171	$ 3,171	$ 3,171	$ 4,250	$ 4,250	$ 4,250	$ 3,171	$ 3,171	$ 3,171	$ 3,171
26	Rent	$ 660	$ 660	$ 660	$ 660	$ 660	$ 660	$ 660	$ 660	$ 660	$ 660	$ 660	$ 660
27	Food	285	285	285	285	285	285	285	285	285	285	285	285
28	Utilities	115	105	90	85	70	75	80	75	70	70	90	105
29	Phone/Internet	115	115	115	115	115	115	115	115	115	115	115	
30	Clothes	50	50	50	50	150	50	50	250	50	50	150	
31	Tuition	6,575	-	-	-	-	1,350	-	5,900	-	-	-	-
32	Books & Supplies	1,005					275		775				
33	Travel/Entertainment	220	160	170	520	170	190	920	550	155	225	315	385
34	**Total**	$ 9,025	$ 1,375	$ 1,370	$ 1,715	$ 1,450	$ 3,000	$ 2,110	$ 8,610	$ 1,335	$ 1,405	$ 1,615	$ 1,600
35	**Net Cash Flow**	$ (5,854)	$ 1,796	$ 1,801	$ 1,456	$ 1,721	$ 1,250	$ 2,140	$ (4,360)	$ 1,836	$ 1,766	$ 1,556	$ 1,571
36													
37	Monthly Savings	Jan	Feb	Mar	Apr	May	Jun	Jul	Aug	Sep	Oct	Nov	Dec
38	Starting Balance	$ 7,500	$ 1,646	$ 3,442	$ 5,243	$ 6,699	$ 8,420	$ 9,670	$ 11,810	$ 7,450	$ 9,286	$ 11,052	$ 12,608
39	Deposits	3,171	3,171	3,171	3,171	3,171	4,250	4,250	4,250	3,171	3,171	3,171	3,171
		9,025	1,375	1,370	1,715	1,450	3,000	2,110	8,610	1,335	1,405	1,615	1,600
		$ 1,646	$ 3,442	$ 5,243	$ 6,699	$ 8,420	$ 9,670	$ 11,810	$ 7,450	$ 9,286	$ 11,052	$ 12,608	$ 14,179

Bad style · Good style · Accent6 style

Documentation | **Budget** | Car Savings Plan | Car Loan Analysis | (+)

READY | AVERAGE: $2,884 | COUNT: 12 | SUM: $34,610 | 120%

Exhibit 14-33 Alignment buttons

Button	Name	Description
▤	Top Align	Aligns the cell content with the cell's top edge
▤	Middle Align	Centers the cell content vertically within the cell
▤	Bottom Align	Aligns the cell content with the cell's bottom edge
▤	Align Left	Aligns the cell content with the cell's left edge
▤	Center	Centers the cell content horizontally within the cell
▤	Align Right	Aligns the cell content with the cell's right edge
▤	Decrease Indent	Decreases the size of the indentation used in the cell
▤	Increase Indent	Increases the size of the indentation used in the cell
▤	Orientation	Rotates the cell content to any angle within the cell
▤	Wrap Text	Forces the cell text to wrap within the cell borders
▤	Merge & Center	Merges the selected cells into a single cell, and centers the content horizontally within the merged cell

© 2014 Cengage Learning

Begin Activity

Align cell content.

1 Select **cell B3** if it is not already the active cell.

2 On the HOME tab, in the Alignment group, click the **Align Left button** ▤. The date is left-aligned in the cell. This makes the header information on the worksheet easier to read.

3 Select the **range B21:M21;B37:M37**.

4 In the Alignment group, click the **Center button** ▤. The selected column labels are centered.

> **Tip:** For cells taller than the height of their contents, you can change the vertical alignment from the default bottom-alignment so the contents are middle- or top-aligned.

5 Select the **non-adjacent range A9;A25;A34:A35;A41**. These cells all contain calculated totals.

6 In the Alignment group, click the **Align Right button** ▤. The selected labels are right-aligned in their cells.

End Activity

14-6d Indenting Cell Content

Sometimes you want a cell's content indented a few spaces from the cell's left edge. This is particularly useful for entries that are considered subsections of a worksheet. For example, the monthly deposits and withdrawals in rows 39 and 40 of the Budget worksheet can be considered a subsection. They would be easier to identify if the labels were indented a few spaces. Each time you click the Increase Indent button in the Alignment group on the HOME tab, you increase the indentation by roughly one character space. To decrease or remove an indentation, click the Decrease Indent button.

Begin Activity

Indent cell content.

1 Select the **range A39:A40**.

2 On the HOME tab, in the Alignment group, click the **Increase Indent button**. twice. The contents of the selected cells indent to the right two character spaces.

3 In the Alignment group, click the **Decrease Indent button**. Each label moves left one character space. See Exhibit 14-34.

End Activity

Exhibit 14-34 Aligned and indented text

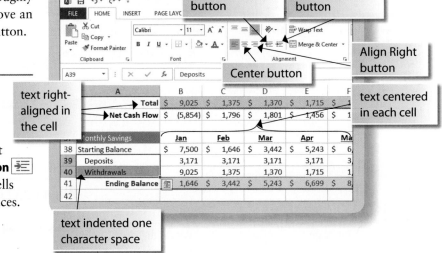

LEARN MORE

Aligning Numbers

Generally, you don't want to change the horizontal alignment of numbers from the default of right-aligned. If you are looking at a column of numbers, it is helpful to align the numbers so that, visually, each digit in a number aligns with the digits in the corresponding places in the numbers above and below it. For example, consider the following list of numbers:

12
1250
1
125

It is much easier to understand the relative values of the numbers in this list if they are right-aligned:

    12
  1250
     1
   125

Likewise, columns of numbers that contain a decimal point are easier to understand if they are aligned on their decimal point. For example, the values

12.125
12.5
12.75

are easier to understand if they appear as

12.125
12.5
12.75

or as

12.125
12.500
12.750

If you are working with a list of values that have varying numbers of digits after the decimal point, you should open the Number tab in the Format Cell dialog box to change the number of decimal places to fit the largest number of digits that you want to appear in the list. That way, the numbers will all have the same number of digits after the decimal point so that when they are right-aligned, they will appear to be aligned on the decimal points.

Rotating Cell Content

Text and numbers are usually displayed within cells horizontally. However, you can rotate cell text to save space or to provide visual interest to a worksheet. This is commonly used as a way to label narrow columns or identify rows in a category. For example, the Budget worksheet you are working on could be reorganized to include category labels in a merged cell to the left of each category that are rotated in the merged cells so that they read vertically from bottom to top, as shown in the illustration. You can choose from the following Orientation options, which you access by clicking the Orientation button in the Alignment group on the HOME tab:

▶ **Angle Counterclockwise**—rotates cell content to a 45-degree angle to the upper-right corner of the merged cell.

▶ **Angle Clockwise**—rotates cell content to a 45-degree angle to the lower-right corner of the merged cell.

| Angle Counterclockwise |
| Angle Clockwise |
| Vertical Text |
| Rotate Text Up |
| Rotate Text Down |
| Format Cell Alignment |

Orientation button menu

▶ **Vertical Text**—rotates cell content to appear stacked from the top of the cell to the bottom.

▶ **Rotate Text Up**—rotates cell content 90 degrees counterclockwise so that text is placed sideways in the cell and read from the bottom of the cell to the top.

▶ **Rotate Text Down**—rotates cell content 90 degrees clockwise so that text is placed sideways in the cell and read from the top of the cell to the bottom.

After you rotate cell content, you may need to resize the column width or row height to eliminate excess space or add more space so that the cell contents are completely visible.

14-6e Merging Cells

Merging combines two or more cells into one cell. You can merge cells horizontally and vertically. When you merge cells, only the content from the upper-left cell in the range is retained, and the cell reference for the merged cell is the original upper-left cell reference. For example, if you merge cells A1 and A2, the merged cell reference is cell A1, and if you merge cells A1, A2, B1, and B2, the merged cell reference is still cell A1.

To merge selected cells and center the content, use the Merge button in the Alignment group on the HOME tab. If you click the Merge button arrow, you can choose from the following merge options:

▶ **Merge & Center**—merges the range into one cell, and horizontally centers the content.

▶ **Merge Across**—merges each of the rows in the selected range across the columns in the range.

▶ **Merge Cells**—merges the range into a single cell, but does not horizontally center the cell content.

▶ **Unmerge Cells**—reverses a merge, returning the merged cell back into a range of individual cells.

After you merge a range into a single cell, you can change the alignment of its content.

Begin Activity

Merge and center cells.

1 Select the **range E5:F5**.

2 On the HOME tab, in the Alignment group, click the **Merge & Center button**. The range E5:F5 merges into one cell. The merged cell reference is E5, and the text is centered within the merged cell. The formatting from cell E5 is applied to the new merged cell.

Tip: After merging cells with formatting, you might need to reapply formatting or the cell style.

3 Click **any other cell** in the worksheet to deselect the merged cell. The merged cell is formatted with the Accent6 cell style from cell E5. Compare your screen to Exhibit 14-35.

End Activity

merge To combine two or more cells into one cell.

Exhibit 14-35 Merged cells

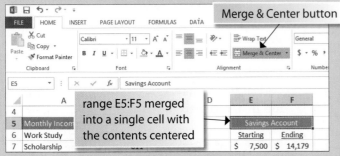

range E5:F5 merged into a single cell with the contents centered

Exhibit 14-36 Borders button menu

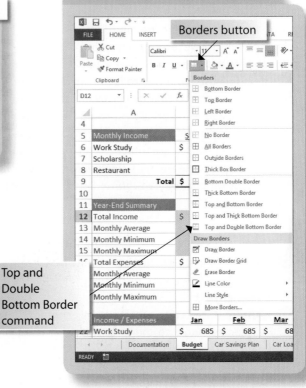

Top and Double Bottom Border command

14-6f Adding Cell Borders

Sometimes you want to include lines along the edges of cells to improve the readability of the rows and columns of data. One way to do this is by adding a border to a cell or range. A **border** is a line you add along an edge of a cell. You can add borders to the left, top, right, or bottom of a cell or range; around an entire cell; or around the outside edges of a range. A standard accounting practice is to add a single top border and a double bottom border to the total rows to clearly differentiate them from financial data. You can also specify the thickness of and the number of lines in the border. All of these border options are available from the Borders button in the Font group on the HOME tab, as shown in Exhibit 14-36.

Borders are different from the gridlines that surround the cells in each worksheet. **Gridlines** are the lines that divide the columns and rows on the worksheet and define the structure of the worksheet. When a worksheet is printed, the gridlines are not printed unless you specify that they should be. Borders are always printed.

Begin Activity

Add cell borders.

1 Select the **range B9:C9**. This row shows the total monthly income during school and summer.

2 On the HOME tab, in the Font group, click the **Borders button arrow** ⊞ ▾ to display a list of available borders and options. Refer back to Exhibit 14-36.

border A line added along an edge of a cell.

gridlines Lines that divide columns and rows in a worksheet and define the structure of the worksheet.

3 Click **Top and Double Bottom Border**. The borders on the selected cells change to black lines. Notice that the Borders button changed to ⊞ to match the selection you just made.

Tip: You can use the Total cell style to make cell text bold and add colored top and double bottom borders to selected cells.

4 Select the **nonadjacent range B25:M25;B34:M34;B41;M41**. These rows show the total monthly income, expenses, and account balance.

5 In the Font group, click the **Borders button** ⊞. The selected cells now have a single top border and a double bottom border, following standard accounting practice.

6 Select the **range A1:C1**.

7 On the HOME tab, in the Font group, click the **Borders button arrow** ⊞ ▾, and then click **More Borders**. The Format Cells dialog box opens with the Border tab displayed. See Exhibit 14-37.

8 In the Line section, in the Style box, click the **thick line** (the sixth line in the second column).

Exhibit 14-37 Border tab in the Format Cells dialog box

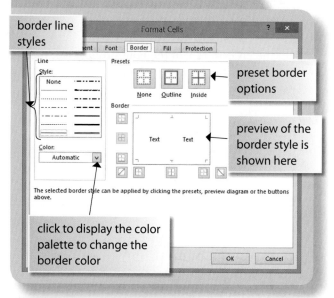

border line styles

preset border options

preview of the border style is shown here

click to display the color palette to change the border color

9 In the Line section, click the **Color arrow** to display the color palette. Click the **Green, Accent 6, Darker 50% color**.

10 In the Border section, click the **bottom border** of the preview. A thick dark green bottom border appears in the preview.

11 Click **OK**. The dialog box closes, and the selected cells have a thick, dark green bottom border.

End Activity

14-6g Changing Cell Background Color

Another way to distinguish sections of a worksheet is by formatting the cell background. You can change the color of cells by adding background colors, also known as **fill colors** because you are filling the cell with colors.

ON THE JOB

Using Color to Enhance a Workbook

When used wisely, color can enhance any workbook. However, when used improperly, color can distract the user, making the workbook more difficult to read. As you format a workbook, keep in mind the following tips:

▶ **Use colors from the same theme within a workbook.** This helps to maintain a consistent look and feel across the worksheets. If the built-in themes do not fit your needs, you can create a custom theme.

▶ **Use colors to differentiate types of cell content and to direct users where to enter data.** For example, you can format a worksheet so that formula results appear in cells without a fill color and users enter data in cells with a light gray fill color.

▶ **Use pleasing color combinations.** Although somewhat subjective, keep in mind that some color combinations are difficult to read.

▶ **Print the workbook on both color and black-and-white printers.** This extra step helps to ensure that the printed copy is readable in both versions.

▶ **Understand your printer's limitations and features.** Colors that look good on your monitor might not look as good when printed.

▶ **Be sensitive to your audience.** About 8 percent of all men and 0.5 percent of all women have some type of color blindness and might not be able to see the text when certain color combinations are used. Red-green color blindness is the most common, so avoid using red text on a green background or green text on a red background.

fluidworkshop/Shutterstock.com

fill color A color added to cells or shapes.

You already added fill colors when you used the styles to format the category labels and the total rows. If you don't like any of the styles with fill colors in the Cell Styles gallery, you can select any background color you like by clicking the Fill Color button arrow in the Font group on the HOME tab.

If you add a dark fill color to cells, black text can be harder to read than text formatted with a light or white font color. The Accent6 cell style that you applied to the category labels in the Budget worksheet changed the font color in these cells to white as part of the style. If you change the fill color of cells using the Fill Color button, you might then need to change the font color in those cells.

Begin Activity

Change the fill color.

1 Select the **range E6:F7**.

2 On the HOME tab, in the Font group, click the **Fill Color button arrow** to display the color palette.

3 In the Theme Colors section, click the **Gold, Accent 4, Lighter 60% color**. The background color of the cells is now light gold, hiding the gridlines. Compare your worksheet to Exhibit 14-38.

4 Save the workbook, and then close it.

End Activity

Exhibit 14-38 Final Budget worksheet with border and fill colors

	A	B	C	D	E	F	G	H	I	J	K	L	M
1	Gabriel Turner Budget												
2	Projected Income and Expenses												
3	4/6/2016												
4													
5	Monthly Income	School	Summer		Savings Account								
6	Work Study	$ 685	$ -		Starting	Ending							
7	Scholarship	611	-		$ 7,500	$ 14,179							
8	Restaurant	1,875	4,250										
9	Total	$ 3,171	$ 4,250										
10													
11	Year-End Summary												
12	Total Income	$ 41,289											
13	Monthly Average	3,441											
14	Monthly Minimum	3,171											
15	Monthly Maximum	4,250											
16	Total Expenses	$ 34,610											
17	Monthly Average	2,884											
18	Monthly Minimum	1,335											
19	Monthly Maximum	9,025											
20													
21	Income / Expenses	Jan	Feb	Mar	Apr	May	Jun	Jul	Aug	Sep	Oct	Nov	Dec
22	Work Study	$ 685	$ 685	$ 685	$ 685	$ 685	$ -	$ -	$ -	$ 685	$ 685	$ 685	$ 685
23	Scholarship	611	611	611	611	611	-	-	-	611	611	611	611
24	Restaurant	1,875	1,875	1,875	1,875	1,875	4,250	4,250	4,250	1,875	1,875	1,875	1,875
25	Total	$ 3,171	$ 3,171	$ 3,171	$ 3,171	$ 3,171	$ 4,250	$ 4,250	$ 4,250	$ 3,171	$ 3,171	$ 3,171	$ 3,171
26	Rent	$ 660	$ 660	$ 660	$ 660	$ 660	$ 660	$ 660	$ 660	$ 660	$ 660	$ 660	$ 660
27	Food	285	285	285	285	285	285	285	285	285	285	285	285
28	Utilities	115	105	90	85	70	75	80	75	70	70	90	105
29	Phone/Internet	115	115	115	115	115	115	115	115	115	115	115	115
30	Clothes	50	50	50	50	150	50	50	250	50	50	150	50
31	Tuition	6,575	-	-	-	-	1,350	-	5,900	-	-	-	-
32	Books & Supplies	1,005	-	-	-	-	275	-	775	-	-	-	-
33	Travel/Entertainment	220	160	170	520	170	190	920	550	155	225	315	385
34	Total	$ 9,025	$ 1,375	$ 1,370	$ 1,715	$ 1,450	$ 3,000	$ 2,110	$ 8,610	$ 1,335	$ 1,405	$ 1,615	$ 1,600
35	Net Cash Flow	$ (5,854)	$ 1,796	$ 1,801	$ 1,456	$ 1,721	$ 1,250	$ 2,140	$ (4,360)	$ 1,836	$ 1,766	$ 1,556	$ 1,571
36													
37	Monthly Savings	Jan	Feb	Mar	Apr	May	Jun	Jul	Aug	Sep	Oct	Nov	Dec
38	Starting Balance	$ 7,500	$ 1,646	$ 3,442	$ 5,243	$ 6,699	$ 8,420	$ 9,670	$ 11,810	$ 7,450	$ 9,286	$ 11,052	$ 12,608
39	Deposits	3,171	3,171	3,171	3,171	3,171	4,250	4,250	4,250	3,171	3,171	3,171	3,171
40	Withdrawals	9,025	1,375	1,370	1,715	1,450	3,000	2,110	8,610	1,335	1,405	1,615	1,600
41	Ending Balance	$ 1,646	$ 3,442	$ 5,243	$ 6,699	$ 8,420	$ 9,670	$ 11,810	$ 7,450	$ 9,286	$ 11,052	$ 12,608	$ 14,179
42													

1. Explain the difference between a relative reference, an absolute reference, and a mixed reference.

2. What are the relative, absolute, and mixed cell references for cell H9?

3. What is the general syntax of all Excel functions?

4. In a function, what is an argument?

5. Describe how to type a function directly in a cell.

6. What is AutoFill?

7. How do you use the fill handle?

8. Describe how to use AutoFill to create a series of numbers.

9. What is a date function?

10. Which date function returns the current date?

11. What is the PMT function?

12. What is the syntax of the PMT function?

13. Most interest rates are presented as an annual interest rate. How do you determine the interest rate per month?

14. Write the formula to determine the monthly payment for a $50,000 loan with an annual interest rate of 4 percent that will be repaid in three years.

15. Why does the PMT function return a negative value?

16. Why would you use a cell style?

17. Unless you change the alignment, how is text aligned within a cell, and how are values aligned within a cell?

18. If the range A1:C5 is merged into a single cell, what is the cell reference of this merged cell?

19. What is a border?

20. What is a fill color? When would you use fill colors?

21. Where can you access all of the formatting options for worksheet cells?

Practice It

Practice It 14-1

1. Open the data file **Car** located in the Chapter 14\ Practice It folder. Save the workbook as **Car Loan**.

2. In the Documentation worksheet, enter your name in cell B3. Enter the TODAY function in cell B4 to display the current date. Left-align the date.

3. Make the Budget worksheet the active sheet. In cell B12, enter **Jan**.

4. In the range C12:M12, use AutoFill to replace the month numbers with the abbreviations *Feb* through *Dec*.

5. In cell B19, use the SUM function to calculate total January expenses in the range B14:B18.

6. In cell B20, enter a formula that subtracts the total January expenses from the total January income to calculate the net cash flow for January.

7. Copy the formulas in the range B19:B20 to the range C19:M20.

8. In cell B3, enter the SUM function to calculate the total monthly income for the entire year in the range B13:M13.

9. In cell C3, enter the AVERAGE function to calculate the average monthly income for the year.

10. In cell D3, enter the MAX function to calculate the maximum monthly income for the year.

11. In cell E3, enter the MIN function to calculate minimum monthly income for the year.

12. Select the range B3:E3, and then copy the formulas in the selected range to the range B4:E10 to complete the Year-End Summary table. Note that cell C8 will show the value #DIV/0!, indicating that Excel cannot calculate the average car payment because you can't divide by zero. This will be resolved when you enter payment values.

13. Format cells I3 and I5 with the Percent Style, and show two decimal places.

14. In the range I3:I8, enter the following data:

cell I3	**4.68**
cell I4	**12**
cell I5	**=I3/I4**
cell I6	**3**
cell I7	**=I6*I4**
cell I8	**15000**

15. In cell I9, enter the PMT function to calculate the monthly payment required to repay the loan.

16. In cell B18, enter the formula **=I9** to display the results of the PMT function for the January car payment.

17. Edit the formula in cell B18 to use an absolute reference.

18. Copy the formula in cell B18 into the range C18:M18. Verify that the values in the range B18:M18 match the monthly payment for car loan. (Note that the calculations in the worksheet are updated to reflect the car payments.)

19. Format the numbers in the nonadjacent range B3:E3;B9:E10;B13:M13; B19:M20 with the Accounting format with no decimal places.

20. Format the nonadjacent range B4:E8;B14:M18 with the Accounting format with no decimal places and no currency symbol.

21. Format the range I8:I9 with the Accounting format with no decimal places.

22. Apply the Accent6 cell style to cells A2, G2, and G9 and the range B12:M12.

23. Apply the following cell styles to the ranges specified:

    range B13:M13   40% - Accent6
    range B19:M19   40% - Accent2
    range B20:M20   40% - Accent5

24. Select the range C1:E1. Merge and center the cells, and then apply the Linked Cell cell style to the range.

25. Select the range G2:I2, and then merge and center the cells.

26. Select the range G9:H9, merge and center the cells, and then right-align the text in the merged cell.

27. Center the text in the range B2:E2 and the range B12:M12.

28. Select the range A14:A18, and then indent the text one space.

29. Add a Top and Double Bottom Border to the range B13:M13 and the range B19:M19.

30. Apply the Gold, Accent 4, Lighter 60% fill color to cell I9.

31. In cell I3, change the annual interest rate to **4.12%**. In cell I6, change the total years of the loan to **5**.

32. Save the workbook, and then close it.

Practice It 14-2

1. Open the data file **Online** located in the Chapter 14\Practice It folder. Save the workbook as **Online Backup Services**.

2. In the Documentation worksheet, enter your name in cell B3, and enter the TODAY function in cell B4. Left-align the date in cell B4.

3. In the Price Comparison worksheet, use AutoFill to enter the labels Month 1, Month 2, and so forth in the range B12:M12 and the range B17:M17.

4. Format the nonadjacent range B8:C10;F8:G10;J8:K10 as Currency. Format the nonadjacent range B13:N15;B18:N20 as Currency also.

5. Add the following formulas:

    cell C8   a formula to display the setup cost value from cell B8

    cell C9   a formula that multiplies an absolute reference to the monthly timeframe in cell B5 by the monthly cost in cell B9

    cell C10   a formula that multiplies an absolute reference to the number of gigabytes to back up in cell B3 by an absolute reference to the yearly timeframe in cell B4 and by the annual cost per gigabyte in cell B10

6. Copy the formulas in the range C8:C10 to the range G8:G10 and the range K8:K10 to calculate the costs for vendors 2 and 3.

7. In cell B13, enter a formula to add the setup cost, the monthly cost, and the annual cost per gigabyte for the first vendor. Enter similar formulas in cells B14 and B15 to calculate the Month 1 cost for the first year for the second and third vendors.

8. In the range C13:C15, enter formulas to retrieve the monthly cost for the corresponding vendor. Be sure to use an absolute reference to the cell in each formula so you can copy the formulas.

9. Copy the formulas in the range C13:C15 to the range D13:M15.

10. In the range B18:B20, enter formulas to add the monthly cost and the annual cost per gigabyte for the corresponding vendor to calculate the first month cost for each additional year.

11. In the range C18:C20, enter formulas using absolute values to retrieve the monthly cost for the corresponding vendor. Copy the formulas in the range C18:C20 to the range D18:M20.

12. In the range N13:N15;N18:N20, use the SUM function to total the first year and additional year costs for each vendor.

13. Merge the following cells, leaving them left-aligned: range D8:E8, range D9:E9, range D10:E10, range H8:I8, range H9:I9, and range H10:I10. (*Hint*: Click the Merge Cells option on the Merge & Center button menu.)

14. Format the following ranges as directed:

range A7:C7;A13;A18	Accent4 cell style
range A8:C10,B13:N13; B18:N18	40% - Accent4 cell style
range D7:G7;A14;A19	Accent6 cell style
range D8:G10;B14:N14; B19:N19	40% - Accent6 cell style
range H7:K7;A15;A20	Accent5 cell style
range H8:K10;B15:N15; B20:N20	40% - Accent5 cell style

15. Center the labels in the range A12:N12;A17:N17.

16. Add a thick border outline around the range A3:B5, and add thin borders between the cells inside this range.

17. Save the workbook, and then close it.

On Your Own

On Your Own 14-1

1. Open the data file **Clear** located in the Chapter 14\On Your Own folder. Save the workbook as **Clear Lake Jazz**.

2. In the Documentation worksheet, enter your name in cell B3, and enter the NOW function in cell B4. Left-align the date.

3. In the Fundraising worksheet, enter the three-letter month abbreviations (Jan, Feb, and so on) for each year (rows 12, 25, 37) in columns C through N. For example, for 2015, enter the month abbreviations in the range C12:N12.

4. Right-align the text in the range F3:F9.

5. In the range G3:G9, enter the loan conditions, and use the PMT function to calculate the monthly payment required to repay a $1,000,000 loan (principal) in 30 years at an annual rate of 3.46% that is paid monthly. Format the cells appropriately.

6. In cell C16, enter a formula with an absolute reference that retrieves the principal of the loan you used in the PMT function.

7. For each year, in the Loan Payment row, enter a formula in each month with an absolute reference to the loan payment returned by the PMT function.

8. For each year, use the SUM function to calculate total income per month and total expenses per month.

9. In column O, use the SUM function to calculate the total annual income and expense for each entry (individual donations, major donors, grants, loan, total income, construction expenses, loan payments, and total expenses).

10. For each year, enter a formula to calculate the net cash flow per month.

11. In cell C23, enter a formula that adds the starting cash available (retrieved using an absolute reference to cell C3) and the January net cash flow (retrieved from cell C22) to calculate the January 2015 cash available.

12. In cell D23, enter a formula that adds the cash available from the previous month and the net cash flow for the current month. Copy this formula to the remaining months of the current year, and then copy the 2015 cash available formulas to the other two years. Edit the January 2016 and 2017 cash available formulas to add the cash available from the last month of the previous year to the net cash flow for the current month.

13. Merge the range A12:A23, and then rotate the text up and middle-align it. Repeat for the range A25:A35 and the range A37:A47.

14. Change the theme to the Ion Boardroom theme. (*Hint*: The command is on the PAGE LAYOUT tab.)

15. Format the numeric values using standard accounting practices, and do not show decimal places except in the cell containing the PMT function.

16. Apply cell styles to the merged cells in column A to fill the merged cells with different colors. Apply a dark cell style using a color different from the colors you used for the merged cells in column A to the range E9:F9 and a cell style using the same color but a lighter shade to cell G9.

17. Add a thick border around the range E3:G9.

18. Use a cell style to apply standard accounting borders to the numeric values in the two rows

for each year that calculate totals. Indent the row labels for the two total rows for each year.

19. Center the month column labels, and make them bold.

20. Save the workbook, and then close it.

Chapter 14

ADDITIONAL STUDY TOOLS

IN THE BOOK

▶ Complete end-of-chapter exercises

▶ Study tear-out Chapter Review Card

ONLINE

▶ Complete additional end-of-chapter exercises

▶ Take practice quiz to prepare for tests

▶ Review key term flash cards (online, printable, and audio)

▶ Play "Beat the Clock" and "Memory" to quiz yourself

▶ Watch the videos to learn more about the topics taught in this chapter

Answers to Quiz Yourself

1. *A relative reference is a cell reference that is interpreted in relation to the location of the cell containing the formula. An absolute reference is a cell reference that remains fixed when copied to a new location; it includes $ in front of both the column letter and row number. A mixed reference is a cell reference that contains an absolute row reference or an absolute column reference, such as $A2 or A$2.*

2. *For cell H9, the relative reference is H9, the absolute reference is $H$9, and the mixed reference is either $H9 or H$9.*

3. *The general syntax of all Excel functions is FUNCTION(argument1,argument2,...) where FUNCTION is the name of the function, and argument1, argument2, and so forth are arguments.*

4. *In a function, arguments are the numbers, text, or cell references used by the function to return a value.*

5. *To type a function directly in a cell, first type an equal sign. As you begin to type a function name, a list of functions that begin with the letters you typed appears. To insert a function in the active cell, press the Tab key or double-click its function name. You can then either select a cell or range or type the appropriate reference or argument. When the function is complete, you enter it into the cell as usual.*

6. *AutoFill is an Excel feature that copies content and formats from a cell or range into an adjacent cell or range. AutoFill can also extend a series of numbers, patterned text, and dates into the adjacent selection.*

7. *After you select a cell or range, the fill handle appears in the lower-right corner of the selection. When you drag the fill handle over an adjacent range, AutoFill copies the content and formats from the original cell into the adjacent range.*

8. To create a series of numbers with AutoFill, you enter the initial values in the series, such as the first few consecutive integers, in a selected range to establish the pattern for AutoFill to use, select the range, and then drag the fill handle over the cells where you want the pattern continued.

9. A date function is a function that inserts or calculates dates and times.

10. The TODAY function returns the current date.

11. The PMT function is a financial function that calculates the monthly payment required to repay a loan.

12. The syntax of the PMT function is
PMT(rate,nper,pv[,fv=0][,type=0])
where rate is the interest rate for each payment period, nper is the total number of payment periods required to repay the loan, pv is the present value of the loan or the amount that needs to be borrowed, fv is the future value of the loan, and type specifies when the interest is charged on the loan.

13. To determine the interest rate per month, divide the annual interest rate by 12.

14. The formula to determine the monthly payment for a $50,000 loan with an annual interest rate of 4 percent that will be repaid in three years is:
=PMT(0.04/12,3*12,50000)

15. The PMT function returns a negative value because the payment is an expense to the borrower.

16. A cell style lets you apply the same collection of formatting options to multiple cells within the workbook, ensuring consistency throughout the workbook.

17. Unless you change the alignment, text is aligned with the left and bottom borders of a cell and values are aligned with the right and bottom borders of a cell.

18. If the range A1:C5 is merged into a single cell, the cell reference of this merged cell is A1.

19. A border is a line you add along an edge of a cell.

20. A fill color is a background color that is added to worksheet cells. Fill colors are useful for differentiating parts of a worksheet or highlighting data.

21. You can access all the formatting options for worksheet cells in the Format Cells dialog box.

Creating an Advanced Workbook

Kzenon/Shutterstock.com

Excel has a variety of tools to help you create more advanced workbooks and analyze the data in them. One common skill you need when creating a workbook is translating an equation into an Excel formula. The formula may be simple or complex, and it can include cell references as well as numbers. You can create formulas that change what is displayed in the cell based on other data in the worksheet. You can highlight cells to locate trends or unusual data. After a worksheet's content is set, you can hide data you don't want others to see. You can also fine-tune how the worksheet will print.

Learning Objectives

After studying the material in this chapter, you will be able to:

15-1 Make a workbook user-friendly

15-2 Flash Fill a range

15-3 Enter formulas with multiple calculations

15-4 Fix error values

15-5 Work with the IF logical function

15-6 Create a nested IF function

15-7 Highlight cells with conditional formatting

15-8 Hide rows and columns

15-9 Format a worksheet for printing

15-1 Making a Workbook User-Friendly

Every workbook should be accessible to its intended users. When a workbook is user-friendly, anyone who needs to enter data in the workbook or interpret its results can understand the workbook's contents, including any jargon or unusual terms, what is being calculated, and how the equations make those calculations.

Documenting the contents of a workbook helps to avoid errors and confusion, and makes a workbook easier for other people to understand. For workbooks that include many calculations, it is helpful to explain the formulas and terms used in the calculations. Such documentation also can serve as a check that the equations are accurate.

Begin Activity

Review a user-friendly workbook.

1 Open the data file **Getaway** located in the Chapter 15\ Chapter folder. Save the workbook as **Getaway Travel**.

> **Tip:** Remember to save frequently as you work through the chapter. A good practice is to save after every Activity.

2 In the Documentation worksheet, enter your name in **cell B3** and the current date in **cell B4**.

3 In **cell B4**, left-align the date.

4 If necessary, change the zoom to **120%**, and then review the contents of the worksheets. The purpose of this workbook is to calculate total trip cost and package discount percentage for popular travel destinations. The Trip Comparison worksheet lists the agency's service fees and calculates the total costs with fees for air and hotel purchased separately and as a package. All information is clearly labeled.

5 In **cell B5**, enter **To calculate total trip cost and package discount percentage for popular travel destinations and to label sale destinations**.

End Activity

15-2 Using Flash Fill

Flash Fill enters text based on patterns it finds in the data. Usually, you need to enter at least one value and then start typing the next value for Flash Fill to suggest content. Exhibit 15-1 shows Atlanta, Georgia entered in cell A12 and Flash Fill–generated content for the rest of column A based on the pattern used for cell A12—the city name from column B, a comma, and then the state name from column D. To accept the suggested content, press the Enter key. If you don't want to accept the suggested content, continue typing. You can also press the Esc key to make the suggested content disappear.

Exhibit 15-1 Text being entered with Flash Fill

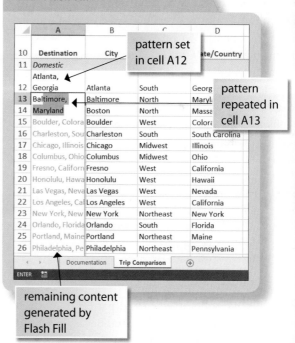

After you accept Flash Fill entries, the Flash Fill Options button appears to the right of the first cell containing suggested content. If you click the Flash Fill Options button, the menu that opens provides options to undo Flash Fill, accept the suggestions, and select all the changed cells.

> **Flash Fill** An Excel feature that enters text based on patterns that it finds in the data.

EXCEL 2013

Creating an Excel Table

When a range contains related data, such as the trip comparison data, you can format it as an Excel table. An **Excel table** is a range of data that is treated as a distinct object in a worksheet. An Excel table makes it easier to identify, manage, and analyze related data. For example, you can quickly sort the data, filter the data to show only those rows that match specified criteria, and add formulas to an entire column. In addition, the entire table is formatted using a single table style, which specifies formats for the entire table, including font color, fill color, and borders. Formatting a table with a table style is more efficient than formatting individual cells in the table. Excel tables can include optional elements such as a header row that contains titles for the different columns in the table and a total row that contains formulas summarizing the values in the table's data. They can also have banded rows, which format every other row in the table with a fill color, making the data easier to read. If you later add or delete a row from the table, the banded rows are adjusted to maintain the alternating row colors. You can create more than one Excel table in a worksheet.

When you create an Excel table, arrows appear next to each column label. You can click an arrow to change the way the data in the table is displayed by sorting it or hiding rows that contain certain data. If you scroll the table above the column headings, the text of the header row replaces the letters in the column headers, making it easier to track which columns you are viewing.

When you add a formula in one cell of a table, the formula is automatically entered in the other cells in that column. You can also enter summary functions for each column in the Total row. When you click in the Total row, an arrow button appears. When you click the arrow button, a list of the most commonly used functions opens—SUM, AVERAGE, COUNT, MIN, and MAX.

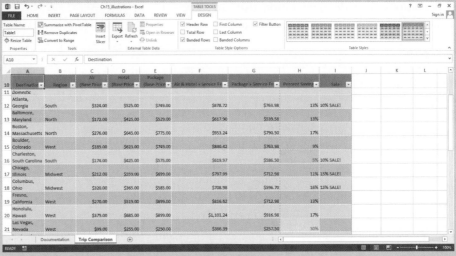

Excel table

Flash Fill works best when the pattern is clearly recognized from the values in the data. Be sure to enter the data pattern in the column or row right next to the related data. The data used to generate the pattern must be in a rectangular grid and cannot have blank rows or columns. Also, Flash Fill enters text, not formulas. If you edit or replace an entry originally used by Flash Fill, the content generated by Flash Fill will not be updated.

Excel table A range of data that is treated as a distinct object in a worksheet.

Begin Activity

Use Flash Fill to enter text.

1 Make the **Trip Comparison worksheet** the active worksheet.

2 Select **cell A12**, type **Atlanta, Georgia** to begin the pattern, and then press the **Enter key**.

3 In cell **A13**, type **Bal**. As soon as you type the first letter, Flash Fill generates the remaining entries in the column based on the pattern you used in cell A12. Refer back to Exhibit 15-1.

4 Press the **Enter key** to accept the suggested entries. The columns specifying City and State/Country are no longer needed now that the destinations appear in column A.

5 Delete the **nonadjacent range B10:B34;D10:D34**. The duplicate data is removed from the worksheet, and the remaining data shifts to the left to fill the space.

6 Scroll down, and if any of the rows did not change to a row height of 30, double-click or drag the bottom row border to change the row height to 30 points.

End Activity

15-3 Entering Formulas with Multiple Calculations

In Chapter 14, you created simple formulas to perform a single calculation. Formulas can also be used to perform multiple calculations. If a formula contains more than one arithmetic operator, Excel performs the calculation using the same order of operations you might already have seen in math classes. The **order of operations** is a set of predefined rules used to determine the sequence in which operators are applied in a calculation:

- First, exponentiation (^) is calculated.

- Second, multiplication (*) and division (/) are calculated in any order.

- Third, addition (+) and subtraction (−) are calculated.

For example, the formula

$$=3+4*5$$

returns 23 because multiplication occurs before addition, even though it appears second in the expression. So first, the operation 4*5 is performed to return 20, and then the addition operation is performed to add 3 to that value to return 23.

To change the order of operations, you can enclose parts of the formula within parentheses. Any expression within a set of parentheses is calculated before the rest of the formula. So, the formula

$$=(3+4)*5$$

first calculates the value of the expression inside the parentheses—in this case, adding 3+4 to return 7. This result is then multiplied by 5 to return 35.

Note that formulas containing more than one multiplication and division operation and formulas containing more than one addition and subtraction operation return the same result no matter what order you perform the operations. For example, the formula

$$=4*10/8$$

returns 5 whether you first multiply 4*10 to get 40 and then divide by 8 to get a final result of 5 or you first divide 10 by 8 to get 1.25, and then multiply this value by 4.

The order of operations has a big impact on how Excel calculates the results of a formula. As you can see in Exhibit 15-2, including or moving parentheses within a formula can greatly affect the results.

Exhibit 15-2 Results of formulas using different orders of operations

Formula	Result
=50+10*5	100
=(50+10)*5	300
=50/10−5	0
=50/(10−5)	10
=50/10*5	25
=50/(10*5)	1

© 2014 Cengage Learning

An important skill you need when creating a workbook is translating an equation into an Excel formula. In the Trip Comparison worksheet in the Getaway Travel workbook, you need to create a formula to calculate the cost of purchasing an airline ticket and hotel room separately. The total cost is the airfare plus the cost of the hotel added to the service fee that Getaway Travels adds to each transaction. The service fee differs depending on the type of service and the cost. To book airfare and hotel rooms, they charge a 3.5% fee. The equation to calculate the total air and hotel cost is:

(Air + Hotel) x Service Fee + Air + Hotel

order of operations A set of predefined rules used to determine the sequence in which operators are applied in a calculation—first, exponentiation (^); second, multiplication (*) and division (/); and third, addition (+) and subtraction (−).

To convert this equation into an Excel formula, you need to replace Air and Hotel with their corresponding base prices for each destination, and Service Fee with the service fee percentage for Air & Hotel. The service fee is stored in cell B4 in the worksheet. For the first destination—Atlanta, Georgia—the Air and Hotel base prices are stored in cells C12 and D12, respectively. The resulting Excel formula is:

=(C12+D12)*B4+C12+D12

Following the order of operations, Excel will first add the base prices in cells C12 and D12, and then multiply the total base price by the service fee percentage in cell B4. The resulting service fee is then added to the base prices in cells C12 and D12. This is shown in Exhibit 15-3.

2 Type =(, click **cell C12**, type +, click **cell D12**, and then type). This first part of the formula adds the base price of airfare to Atlanta to the hotel cost in Atlanta. To calculate the service fee, you need to multiply that sum by the Air & Hotel service fee percentage.

3 Type * to insert the multiplication sign, and then click **cell B4** to select the Air & Hotel service fee. Finally, to calculate the total price for the customer, you need to add the service fee, which will be calculated by the operations currently in the cell, to the sum of the airfare and the hotel cost.

> **Tip:** To be certain you obtain the results you want, use parentheses to indicate which operation in a formula should be calculated first.

4 Type +, click **cell C12**, type +, and then click **cell D12**. Refer back to Exhibit 15-3.

5 Press the **Enter key**. The total cost for the service fee plus the cost of airfare and hotel in Atlanta is $878.72.

End Activity

Exhibit 15-3 Formula using the order of operations

	A	B	C	D			G
3	Service Fees						
4	Air & Hotel	3.50%					
5	Package<$500	3.00%					
6	Package>=$500	2.00%					
7							
8							
9	Trip Comparison (3 days, 2 nights)						
10	Destination	Region	Air (Base Price)	Hotel (Base Price)	Package (Base Price)	Air & Hotel + Service Fee	Pa... Service Fee
11	*Domestic*						
12	Atlanta, Georgia	South	$324.00	$525.00	$749.00	=(C12+D12)*B4+C12+D12	

parentheses tell Excel to perform the addition calculation first

then multiply that result by cell B4

then add the values in cells C12 and D12

Begin Activity

Enter a formula using the order of operations and a constant.

1 Select **cell F12**. You need to create a formula to calculate the total price of airfare and hotel in Atlanta by first calculating the service fee and then adding that result to the sum of the airfare and the hotel cost.

constant A value in a formula that doesn't change.

FYI

Using Constants in Formulas

A **constant** is a value in a formula that doesn't change. A constant can be entered directly in a formula or placed in a separate worksheet cell and referenced in the formula. The location you select depends on the constant being used, the purpose of the workbook, and the intended audience. In the Trip Comparison worksheet, the service fees in the range B4:B6 are constants. Placing constants in separate cells that you reference in the formulas can help users better understand the worksheet because no values are hidden within the formulas. Also, when a constant is entered in a cell, you can add explanatory text next to each constant to document how it is being used in the formula. On the other hand, you don't want a user to inadvertently change the value of a constant and throw off all the formula results. You need to evaluate how important it is for other people to immediately see the constant and whether the constant requires any explanation for other people to understand the formula.

Usually, if you reference a cell that contains a constant, you should use an absolute reference. Then, if you copy the formula containing the reference, the reference to the cell containing the constant will not change.

15-4 Fixing Error Values

If some part of a formula is preventing Excel from returning a calculated value, Excel flags the possible error with an **error indicator** (a small green triangle) that appears in the upper-left corner of the cell. When the cell containing the error is the active cell, the Error Checking button ◈ appears to the left of the cell. Some errors cause an error value to appear instead of the formula results. An **error value** is a message indicating the type of error in the cell. Error values begin with a pound sign (#) followed by an error name that indicates the type of error. Exhibit 15-4 describes common error values that you might see instead of the results from formulas and functions.

To obtain more information about the source of the error, you can point to the Error Checking button ◈ to display a ScreenTip with a description of the possible error. Exhibit 15-5 shows a worksheet with errors in several cells.

Exhibit 15-5 Formula with error value message and ScreenTip

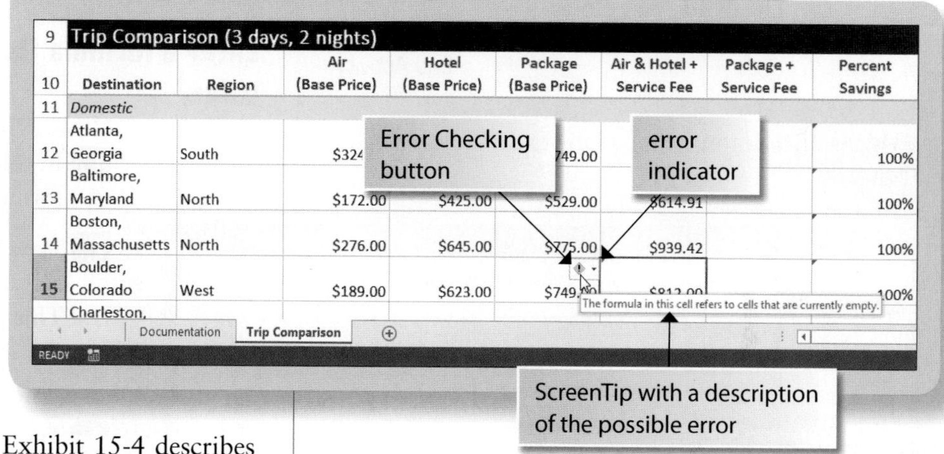

Error Checking button

error indicator

ScreenTip with a description of the possible error

Exhibit 15-4 Error value messages

Error Value	Description
#DIV/0!	The formula or function contains a number divided by 0.
#NAME?	Excel doesn't recognize text in the formula or function, such as when the function name is misspelled.
#N/A	A value is not available to a function or formula, which can occur when a workbook is initially set up prior to entering actual data values.
#NULL!	A formula or function requires two cell ranges to intersect, but they don't.
#NUM!	Invalid numbers are used in a formula or function, such as text entered in a function that requires a number.
#REF!	A cell reference used in a formula or function is no longer valid, which can occur when the cell used by the function was deleted from the worksheet.
#VALUE!	The wrong type of argument is used in a function or formula. This can occur when you reference a text value for an argument that should be strictly numeric.

© 2014 Cengage Learning

Error values appear based on the error-checking rules selected in the Excel Options dialog box. For example, one rule checks for formulas that refer to empty cells. If the rule is selected, an error value appears when a formula uses a cell that is blank. If the rule is not selected, a formula that uses a blank cell does not result in an error value.

Begin Activity

Verify the Error Checking settings.

1 On the ribbon, click the **FILE tab**. In the navigation bar, click **Options**. The Excel Options dialog box opens.

2 In the navigation bar of the dialog box, click **Formulas**. The Formulas tab in the Excel Options dialog box appears.

Tip: You can also click the Error Checking button ◈ next to a cell with an error indicator, and then click Error Checking Options to open the Formulas tab in the Excel Options dialog box.

error indicator A small green triangle that appears in the upper-left corner of the cell with a possible error.

error value A message that appears in a cell that indicates some part of a formula is preventing Excel from returning a calculated value.

3 In the Error Checking section, click the **Enable background error checking check box** to select it if it is not already selected.

4 In the Error checking rules section, click any check boxes that are not selected. Now all types of errors will be flagged. Compare your screen to Exhibit 15-6.

5 Click **OK**. The dialog box closes.

End Activity

Exhibit 15-6 Formulas tab in the Excel Options dialog box

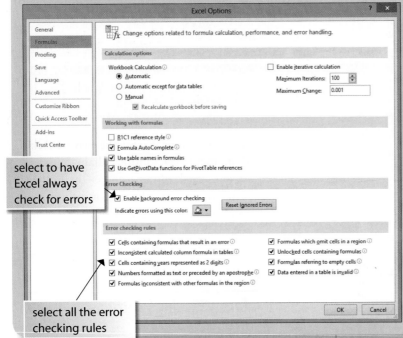

The next Activity is to show you examples of errors identified by Excel. The cells under the Percent Savings column heading are intended to show the percent savings a customer receives by purchasing the package instead of airfare and hotel separately. To calculate the percent savings, you subtract the package cost—which is the lower cost, in this case—from the value in the Air & Hotel + Service Fee column—the higher cost, and then divide the resulting value by the package cost. The formula to accomplish this for Atlanta is:

=(F12–G12)/F12

Following the order of operations, the formula first subtracts the total package price (located in cell G12) from the total air and hotel price (located in cell F12),

and then divides the results by the total air and hotel price (located in cell F12).

At the moment, there is nothing in the Package + Service Fee column. You will add this calculation shortly. For now, you will enter the formula in cell H12 to calculate the percent savings, and then you will copy this formula. Then you will copy the formula in cell F12.

Begin Activity

Enter a formula that produces an error value.

1 In **cell H12**, type = to begin the formula.

2 Type **(**, click **cell F12**, type **–** (a minus sign), click **cell G12**, and then type **)**. This part of the formula subtracts the complete package price from the complete price of airfare plus hotel.

3 Type **/** to insert the division sign, and then click **cell F12**. This completes the formula =(F12–G12)/F12. Dividing the difference between the two prices by the package price calculates the percentage difference between the two prices.

4 To the left of the formula bar, click the **Enter button** ✓. The result of the formula appears as $1.00 because the formula picked up the Currency formatting from cell F12. This value should be formatted as a percentage.

5 On the HOME tab, in the Number group, click the **Percent Style button** %. The result of the formula appears as 100%. This is because there is no value in cell G12.

6 To the left of cell H12, point to the **Error Checking button** ◈. The ScreenTip identifies the error. In this case, the formula refers to cells that are currently empty. Generally, you don't want formulas to reference cells that do not contain a value. However, this error will be resolved once you add the formula to cell G12.

> **Tip:** Click the Error Checking button ◈ to open a menu with options to help you resolve the error.

7 Drag the **fill handle** from cell H12 down through the **range H13:H15**. Each cell in the range the formula was copied to displays #DIV/0!, indicating a divide by zero error. The formulas in the range H13:H15 are trying to divide by the values in the range F13:F15. Currently, these cells are empty. To fix this, you will copy the formula in cell F12 to the range F13:F15.

8 Copy the formula in **cell F12** to the **range F13:15**. The values in the range H13:H15 all change to 100% because you are no longer trying to divide by zero. However, cell F15 contains a small green triangle in the upper-left corner, indicating an error.

11 Copy the formula in **cell F12** to the **range F13:F15**, and then click each cell to verify that the formulas contain an absolute reference to cell B4. Compare your screen to Exhibit 15-7.

12 Copy the formula in **cell F15** to the nonadjacent **range F16:F28;F30:F34**.

End Activity

Exhibit 15-7 Cells with corrected formula

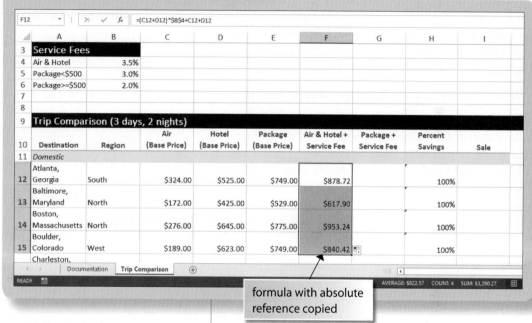

formula with absolute reference copied

9 Select **cell F15**, and then point to the **Error Checking button** . The ScreenTip indicates that you are referencing an empty cell. Refer back to Exhibit 15-5. In the formula bar, the formula is =(C15+D15)*B7+C15+D15. Cell B7 is the empty cell. The original formula in cell F12 should have used an absolute reference to cell B4. Although cells F13 and F14 do not contain the green triangle that indicates an error, the formulas in these cells are also incorrect because they reference cells B5 and B6 instead of cell B4.

10 Select **cell F12**. In the formula bar, click **B4**, press the **F4 key** to change the reference to an absolute reference, and then press the **Enter key**.

FYI

Showing Decimal Places in Percentages

The number of decimal places you show in a percentage (or any other number) depends on how exactly you need to see that value. When you are considering an interest rate for a loan, it is important to show enough decimal places in the interest rate percentage so that the number is not rounded. The Percent Savings column in the Trip Comparison worksheet, however, is intended to be a marketing tool to give people an idea of how much they will save by purchasing the package instead of booking airfare and hotel separately. Adding decimal places to the percentages in this column would not make this clearer.

15-5 Working with the IF Logical Function

A **logical function** is a function that works with statements that are either true or false. Consider a statement such as *cell A5=3*. If cell A5 is equal to 3, this statement is true; if cell A5 is not equal to 3, this statement is false.

Excel supports many different logical functions, one of which is the IF function. The **IF function** is a logical function that returns one value if a statement is true and returns a different value if that statement is false. The syntax of the IF function is

IF(*logical_test*[,*value_if_true*][,*value_if_false*])

where *logical_test* is a statement that is either true or false, *value_if_true* is the value returned by the IF function if the statement is true, and *value_if_false* is the value returned by the function if the statement is false. For example, the following formula tests whether the value in cell A1 is equal to the value in cell B1:

=IF(A1=B1,100,50)

If it is, the formula returns 100; otherwise, it returns 50.

If the values of 100 and 50 are stored in cells C1 and C2, you can use the cell references in the IF function arguments instead of the values. The resulting formula

=IF(A1=B1,C1,C2)

returns the value of cell C1 if the value in cell A1 equals the value in cell B1; otherwise, it returns the value of cell C2.

The IF function also works with text. When you include text in an argument, you need to enclose it in double quotation marks. For example, the following formula tests whether the value of cell A1 is equal to YES—in other words, if cell A1 contains the text *YES*.

=IF(A1="YES","DONE","")

If the value of cell A1 is equal to YES, the formula returns the text *DONE*; otherwise, it returns nothing as indicated by the two sets of double quotation marks. You can also use calculations as the *value_if_true* and *value_if_false* arguments. For example, in the function

=IF(A1="YES",(B1*B2), "No")

if cell A1 contains YES, the formula returns the result of multiplying cell B1 by cell B2; otherwise, it returns the text *No*.

The = symbol in the logical test argument is a comparison operator. A **comparison operator** is a symbol that indicates the relationship between two values. Exhibit 15-8 describes the comparison operators that can be used in the logical test argument in a logical function.

Exhibit 15-8 Comparison operators

Operator	Relationship	Example	Description
=	Equal to	A1=B1	Tests whether the value in cell A1 *is equal to* the value in cell B1
>	Greater than	A1>B1	Tests whether the value in cell A1 *is greater than* the value in cell B1
<	Less than	A1<B1	Tests whether the value in cell A1 *is less than* the value in cell B1
>=	Greater than or equal to	A1>=B1	Tests whether the value in cell A1 *is greater than or equal to* the value in cell B1
<=	Less than or equal to	A1<=B1	Tests whether the value in cell A1 *is less than or equal to* the value in cell B1
<>	Not equal to	A1<>B1	Tests whether the value in cell A1 *is not equal to* the value in cell B1

© 2014 Cengage Learning

Although you could type the formula with the IF function directly in a cell, the Function Arguments dialog box for the IF function, shown in Exhibit 15-9, makes it simpler to enter each part of the formula.

logical function A function that works with statements that are either true or false.

IF function A logical function that tests a condition and then returns one value if the condition is true and another value if the condition is false.

comparison operator A symbol that indicates the relationship between two values.

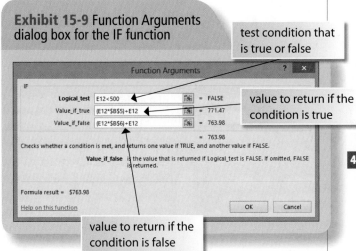

Exhibit 15-9 Function Arguments dialog box for the IF function

test condition that is true or false

value to return if the condition is true

value to return if the condition is false

In the Trip Comparison worksheet, you need to calculate the total cost of packages in column G. The total cost is the package price plus the service fee. The service fee is 3 percent if the package price is less than $500 and 2 percent if the cost of the package is $500 or more. You can use an IF function to make this calculation in one formula. For Atlanta, the logical test is whether the value in cell E12 is less than $500. The *value_if_true* argument is a calculation that multiplies the package price in cell E12 by the service fee percentage in cell B5, which contains the service fee for packages that cost less than $500. The *value_if_false* argument is a calculation that multiplies the package price in cell E12 by the service fee percentage in cell B6, which contains the service fee for packages that cost $500 or more. This results in the following formula:

=IF(E12<500,(E12*$B$5)+E12,(E12*$B$6)+E12)

The references to the cells containing the services fees are absolute so that when you copy the formulas, the references won't change.

Begin Activity

Insert an IF function.

1 Select **cell G12**. To calculate the service fee for the package, you first need to know whether the cost of the package is less than $500.

2 On the ribbon, click the **FORMULAS tab**. In the Function Library group, click the **Logical button**, and then click **IF** in the list of logical functions. The Function Arguments dialog box for the IF function opens, and the IF function and its parentheses appear in cell G12. The insertion point is in the Logical_test box in the dialog box. The logical

test for this function is whether the price of the Atlanta package is less than $500.

3 Click **cell E12**, and then type **<500**. This creates the equation *E12<500*. Next, you need to enter the calculation to be performed if the condition in the Logical_test box is true—that is, if the value in cell E12 is less than $500.

4 Click in the **Value_if_ true box**, type **(**, click **cell E12**, type *****, and then click **cell B5**. You're going to copy this formula, so you need to change the reference to cell B5 to an absolute reference.

Tip: When you type the IF function directly in a cell, remember that the *value_if_true* argument comes before the *value_if_ false* argument.

5 Press the **F4 key**, type **)+**, and then click **cell E12**. The final formula of *(E12*$B$5)+E12* multiplies the service fee percentage for packages that cost less than $500 (cell B5) by the base package price (cell E12) to determine the service fee, and then adds the calculated fee to the base price of the package (cell E12). Note that you do not need to add the parentheses around the multiplication operation because it would be performed first anyway; however, using the parentheses makes it easier to understand the formula. Now you need to enter the calculation to be performed if the condition in the Logical_test box is false—in other words, if the package price is $500 or more.

6 Click in the **Value_if_false box**, type **(**, click **cell E12**, type *****, click **cell B6**, press the **F4 key**, type **)+**, and then click **cell E12**. The final formula of *(E12*$B$6)+E12* multiplies the service fee percentage for packages that cost $500 or more (cell B6) by the base package price (cell E12) to determine the service fee, and then adds the calculated fee to the base price of the package (cell E12). Refer back to Exhibit 15-9.

7 Click **OK**. The value $763.98 is displayed in cell G12. Because the package price for Atlanta is $749, which is more than $500, the value_if_false calculation was performed—the package price was multiplied by 2 percent in cell B6 and the resulting service fee was added to the base package price to calculate the total package price. Compare your screen to Exhibit 15-10.

8 Copy the **range G12:H12** to the **nonadjacent range G13:H28;G30:H34**. Now that there are formulas in column G, the cells in column H that contain the formula to calculate the percent savings no longer contain the green error indicator triangle.

End Activity

Exhibit 15-10 Package price plus service fee calculated

| G12 | | ✕ ✓ fx | =IF(E12<500,(E12*$B$5)+E12,(E12*$B$6)+E12) | | | |

IF function calculates the package price plus the corresponding service fee

	A	B	C	D	E
3	**Service Fees**				
4	Air & Hotel	3.5%			
5	Package<$500	3.0%			
6	Package>=$500	2.0%			
7					
8					
9	**Trip Comparison (3 days, 2 nights)**				

formula returns the price for the package plus a 2% service fee

	Destination	Region	Air (Base Price)	Hotel (Base Price)	Package (Base Price)	Air & Hotel + Service Fee	Package + Service Fee	Percent Savings
10								
11	*Domestic*							
12	Atlanta, Georgia	South	$324.00	$525.00	$749.00	$878.72	$763.98	13%
13	Baltimore, Maryland	North	$172.00	$425.00	$529.00	$617.90		100%
14	Boston, Massachusetts	North	$276.00	$645.00	$775.00	$953.24		100%
15	Boulder, Colorado	West	$189.00	$623.00	$749.00	$840.42		0%
	Charleston,							

percentage updated

Documentation   **Trip Comparison**   ⊕

FYI

Using Logical Functions to Make Decisions

When creating a budget, it is common to want to transfer money into a savings account when the net cash flow is greater than a predetermined amount. With Excel, you need a formula that can "choose" whether to transfer the funds. You can build this kind of decision-making capability into a formula through the use of a logical function. For example, you can use an IF function for each month to test whether the net cash flow for that month is greater than a certain amount, such as $400. If it is, the IF function can indicate that you should transfer some of the extra money into a savings account. On the other hand, if the net cash flow is less than the specified amount, no money transfer is indicated.

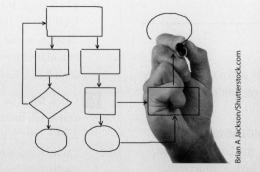

nest To place one item, such as a function, inside another.

15-6 Creating a Nested IF Function

Functions can also be placed inside another function, or **nested**. If a formula contains several functions, Excel starts with the innermost function and then moves outward. For example, the following formula first calculates the average of the values in the range A1:A100 using the AVERAGE function, then extracts the integer portion of that value using the INT function, and then tests whether cell A5 is equal to that value:

=IF(A5=INT(AVERAGE(A1: A100)),"Average","")

If cell A5 is equal to the integer portion of the result of the AVERAGE function, the formula returns the text Average; otherwise, it returns no text. You can use multiple IF functions to test for several conditions. In the Trip Comparison worksheet, the Sale column should contain text that indicates which packages are currently on sale. Trips to the South are on sale for 10% off, trips to the Midwest are on sale for 15% off, and international trips are on sale for 20% off. You can create a nested IF function to add the correct text to each cell.

Begin Activity

Create a nested IF function.

1 In **cell I12**, type **=IF(** to start the function. First you need to enter the first condition to check if the content of cell B12 is South. When you enter text as a condition, you need to enclose it in quotation marks.

2 Click **cell B12**, type =, type **"South"**, and then type **,** (a comma). The formula in the formula bar is now =IF(B12="South",. Next you need to enter the value-if-true. If the region is categorized as South, there is a 10% discount with the current sale.

3 Type **"10% SALE!"** and then type **,** (a comma). The next part of an IF function is the value-if-false. In this case, if the first condition—checking to see if South appears in cell B12—is false, you want to check to see if the value in the cell equals Midwest. This means the value-if-false calculation will be a second IF statement.

4 Type **IF(** to start the second IF statement, click **cell B12**, type =, type **"Midwest"**, and then type **,** (a comma). This is the second condition that will be tested. Now you need to type the value-if-true for this second IF statement.

5 Type **"15% SALE!"**, and then type **,** (a comma). The value-if-false for the second IF statement will be a third IF statement.

6 Type **IF(B12= "International",""" 20% SALE!"**, and then type **,** (a

comma). Now you need to type the value-if-false for the third IF statement.

7 Type **""** (two quotation marks with nothing between them). This specifies to Excel not to insert any text in the cell. The result of this nested IF is that if the value in cell B12 is not South, not Midwest, and not International, nothing will be entered in the cell.

8 Type **)))** to add the closing parentheses for all three IF statements.

9 To the left of the formula bar, click the **Enter button** ✓. The text *10% SALE!* appears in cell I12, the cell containing the nested IF functions, because cell B12 contains South. Compare your screen to Exhibit 15-11.

10 Copy the **cell I12** to the nonadjacent range **I13:I28;I30:I34**.

End Activity

Exhibit 15-11 Nested IF function

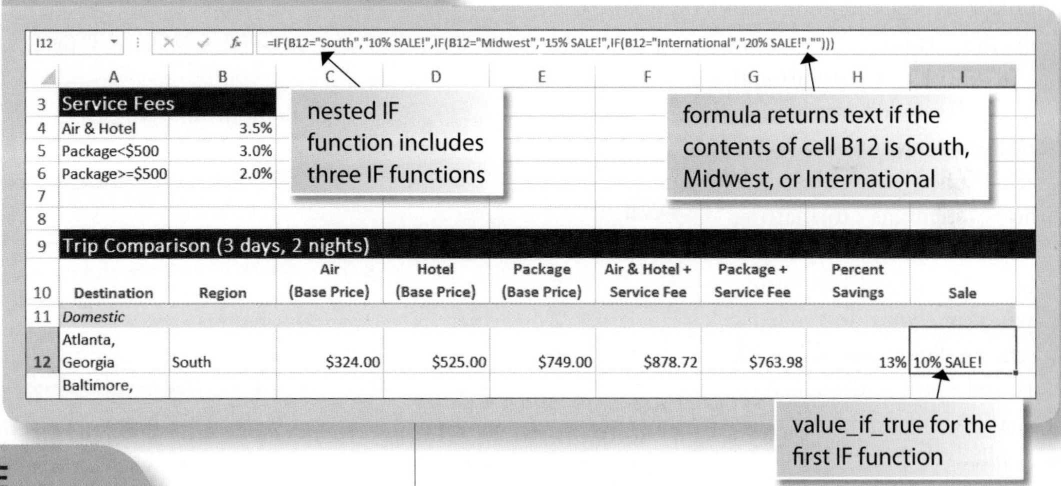

Formula bar: =IF(B12="South","10% SALE!",IF(B12="Midwest","15% SALE!",IF(B12="International","20% SALE!","")))

nested IF function includes three IF functions

formula returns text if the contents of cell B12 is South, Midwest, or International

	A	B	C	D	E	F	G	H	I
3	Service Fees								
4	Air & Hotel	3.5%							
5	Package<$500	3.0%							
6	Package>=$500	2.0%							
7									
8									
9	Trip Comparison (3 days, 2 nights)								
10	Destination	Region	Air (Base Price)	Hotel (Base Price)	Package (Base Price)	Air & Hotel + Service Fee	Package + Service Fee	Percent Savings	Sale
11	Domestic								
12	Atlanta, Georgia	South	$324.00	$525.00	$749.00	$878.72	$763.98	13%	10% SALE!
	Baltimore,								

value_if_true for the first IF function

LEARN MORE

Parenthesis Pairs

One challenge of nested functions or formulas is to make sure that you include all of the parentheses. You can check this by counting the number of left parentheses and making sure that number matches the number of right parentheses. Excel will also display each level of nested parentheses in a different color to make it easier to match the opening and closing parentheses in the formula. If the number of parentheses doesn't match, Excel will not accept the formula and will offer a suggestion for rewriting the formula so that the number of left and right parentheses does match.

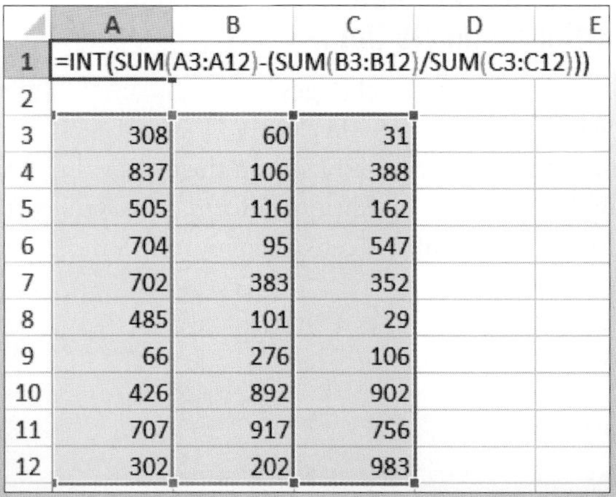

	A	B	C	D	E
1	=INT(SUM(A3:A12)-(SUM(B3:B12)/SUM(C3:C12)))				
2					
3	308	60	31		
4	837	106	388		
5	505	116	162		
6	704	95	547		
7	702	383	352		
8	485	101	29		
9	66	276	106		
10	426	892	902		
11	707	917	756		
12	302	202	983		

Matching parenthesis pairs

15-7 Highlighting Cells with Conditional Formatting

Conditional formatting applies formatting only when a cell's value meets a specified condition. This can help you analyze data. For example, conditional formatting is often used to highlight important trends and values of interest.

With conditional formatting, the format applied to a cell depends upon the value or content of the cell. For example, conditional formatting can format negative numbers as red and positive numbers as black. Conditional formatting is dynamic—if the cell's value changes, the cell's format also changes as needed. Each type of conditional formatting has a set of rules that defines how the formatting should be applied and under what conditions the format will be changed.

To apply a conditional format, you need to create a conditional formatting rule that specifies the type of condition (such as formatting cells greater than a specified value), the type of formatting when that condition occurs (such as light red fill with dark red text), and the cell or range to which the formatting is applied.

15-7a Highlighting a Cell Based on Its Value

Cell highlighting changes a cell's font color or background fill color or both based on the cell's value. Excel provides built-in conditional formatting rules that allow you to highlight cells that meet specific criteria.

Exhibit 15-12 describes some of the ways that cells can be highlighted with conditional formatting.

To apply conditional formatting to cells, you first select the range that you want to highlight. Click the Conditional Formatting button in the Styles group on the HOME tab to display the conditional formatting options shown in Exhibit 15-13.

Exhibit 15-12 Highlighting rules

Rule	Highlights
Greater Than	Cells that are greater than a specified number
Less Than	Cells that are less than a specified number
Between	Cells that are between two specified numbers
Equal To	Cells that are equal to a specified number
Text That Contains	Cells that contain specified text
A Date Occurring	Cells that contain a specified date
Duplicate Values	Cells that contain duplicate or unique values
Top 10%	Cells that contain the values in the top 10 percent
Bottom 10%	Cells that contain the values in the bottom 10 percent

© 2014 Cengage Learning

Exhibit 15-13 Conditional Formatting button menu

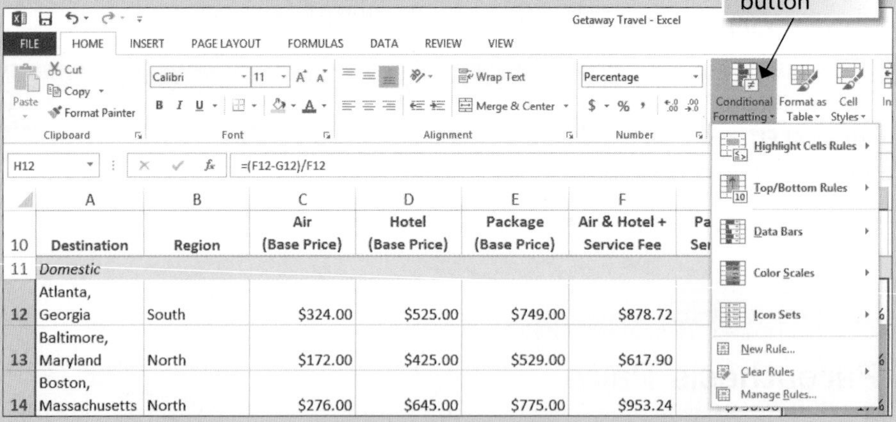

To apply one of the built-in cell highlighting rules, point to Highlight Cells Rules or Top/Bottom Rules to display the available options, and then click the type of condition you want to create for the rule, such as Greater Than. A dialog box opens so you can specify the formatting to use for that condition. Exhibit 15-14 shows the Greater Than dialog box.

conditional formatting Formatting that is applied to a cell only when the cell's value meets a specified condition.

Exhibit 15-14 Greater Than dialog box

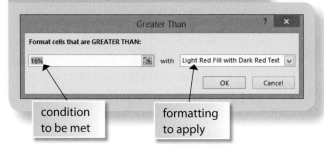

10 Click the **with arrow**, and then click **Green Fill with Dark Green Text**. The three cells containing the highest percentages are filled with light green and contain dark green text.

11 Click **OK**, and then scroll down. The cells with the three highest percentages—cells H21, H27, and H32—are filled with green and contain dark green text. Because this rule affects the same cells affected by the rule you previously applied, none of the cells are shaded yellow any longer.

12 Make sure the **range H12:H34** is still selected. In the Styles group, click the **Conditional Formatting button**, point to **Top/Bottom Rules**, and then click **Bottom 10 Items**. The Bottom 10 Items dialog box, which is similar to the Greater Than dialog box, opens with 10 in the left box and Light Red Fill with Dark Red Text in the with box.

13 Select the **10** in the left box, and then type **3**, and then click **OK**.

14 Select **any cell in column H** to deselect the range, and then scroll down. The three cells containing the lowest percentages are filled with light red and contain dark red text. The cells containing the three highest values are still shaded green. Exhibit 15-15 shows rows 16 through 27 after applying the conditional formatting.

End Activity

Begin Activity

Highlight cells with conditional formatting.

1 Select the **range H12:H34**.

2 On the ribbon, click the **HOME tab**. In the Styles group, click the **Conditional Formatting button**. Refer back to Exhibit 15-13.

3 Point to **Highlight Cells Rules**. A submenu lists the available highlighting rules.

4 Click **Greater Than**. The Greater Than dialog box opens. The default condition specifies that cells in the selected range with a value greater than 16% will be filled with a light red fill and the text formatted as dark red. Refer back Exhibit 15-14.

5 Delete the current entry in the Format cells that are GREATER THAN box, and then type **20%**.

6 Click the **with arrow**, and then click **Yellow Fill with Dark Yellow Text**. All cells in the selected range with a value greater than 20% will be highlighted with yellow text on a yellow background.

7 Click **OK** to apply the highlighting rule, and then scroll down. Only cells H21 and H32 are highlighted.

8 Make sure the **range H12:H34** is still selected. In the Styles group, click the **Conditional Formatting button**, point to **Top/Bottom Rules**, and then click **Top 10 Items**. The Top 10 Items dialog box, which is similar to the Greater Than dialog box, opens. The number 10 in the left box in the dialog box specifies the number of items to highlight.

9 Select the **10** in the left box, and then type **3**.

15-7b Clearing a Conditional Formatting Rule

If you no longer want to highlight cells using the conditional formatting, you can remove, or clear, the current highlighting rule. You can clear all of the rules from a selected range or an entire worksheet. These commands are available by clicking the Conditional Formatting button and then pointing to Clear Rules. If you want to delete only some of the conditional formatting rules, you need to use the Conditional Formatting Rules Manager dialog box shown in Exhibit 15-16. To open this dialog box, click the Conditional Formatting button, and then click Manage Rules.

If conflicting conditional formats are applied to the same range of cells, rules listed higher in the dialog box take precedence. For example, in Exhibit 15-16, the Top 3 rule is applied instead of the Cell Value >0.2 rule.

Exhibit 15-15 Cells highlighted with conditional formatting

red highlights cells with the bottom three values

green highlights cells with the top three values

	A	B	C	D	E	F	G	H	I
16	Charleston, South Carolina	South	$174.00	$425.00	$575.00	$619.97	$586.50	5%	10% SALE!
17	Chicago, Illinois	Midwest	$212.00	$559.00	$699.00	$797.99	$712.98	11%	15% SALE!
18	Columbus, Ohio	Midwest	$320.00	$365.00	$585.00	$708.98	$596.70	16%	15% SALE!
19	Fresno, California	West	$270.00	$519.00	$699.00	$816.62	$712.98	13%	
20	Honolulu, Hawaii	West	$379.00	$685.00	$899.00	$1,101.24	$916.98	17%	
21	Las Vegas, Nevada	West	$99.00	$255.00	$250.00	$366.39	$257.50	30%	
22	Los Angeles, California	West	$429.00	$688.00	$957.00	$1,156.10	$976.14	16%	
23	New York, New York	Northeast	$179.00	$735.00	$875.00	$945.99	$892.50	6%	
24	Orlando, Florida	South	$204.00	$425.00	$550.00	$651.02	$561.00	14%	10% SALE!
25	Portland, Maine	Northeast	$287.00	$295.00	$575.00	$602.37	$586.50	3%	
26	Philadelphia, Pennsylvania	Northeast	$218.00	$618.00	$699.00	$865.26	$712.98	18%	
27	Phoenix, Arizona	Southwest	$258.00	$279.00	$433.00	$555.80	$445.99	20%	
	Seattle,								

Documentation **Trip Comparison** ⊕

Exhibit 15-16 Conditional Formatting Rules Manager dialog box

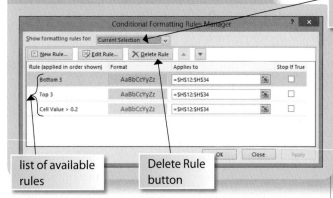

shows the rules for column H, which is currently selected

list of available rules

Delete Rule button

Begin Activity

Clear a conditional formatting rule.

1 On the HOME tab, in the Styles group, click the **Conditional Formatting button**, and then click **Manage Rules**. The Conditional Formatting Rules Manager dialog box opens, listing the three rules you created for the selected range. Refer to Exhibit 15-16.

2 Click the **Top 3 rule** to select it.

3 Near the top of the dialog box, click the **Delete Rule button**. The rule is deleted from the list.

4 Click **OK**. The dialog box closes, and the green shading is removed from the cells containing the highest three percentages. Now that the Top 3 rule is deleted, the effect of the first rule you created is visible again, and cells H21 and H32 are shaded yellow.

Tip: To clear all of the conditional formatting rules from a range or worksheet, click the Conditional Formatting button, point to Clear Rules, and then click the appropriate Clear command in the submenu.

End Activity

Using Conditional Formatting Effectively

Conditional formatting is an excellent way to highlight important trends and data values. It can also help isolate and highlight potential problems. However, it should be used judiciously. An overuse of conditional formatting can obscure the data values you want to emphasize. You will need to make decisions about what to highlight and how it should be highlighted. Keep in mind the following tips as you consider the best ways to effectively communicate your findings to others:

▶ **Document the conditional formats you use.** If a bold, green font means that a sales number is in the top 10 percent of all sales, include that information in a legend in the worksheet. The legend should identify each color used in the worksheet and what it means, so others know why certain cells are highlighted.

▶ **Don't clutter data with too much highlighting.** Limit highlighting rules to one or two per data set. Highlights are designed to draw attention to points of interest. If you use too many, you will end up highlighting everything—and, therefore, nothing.

▶ **Use color sparingly in worksheets with highlights.** It is difficult to differentiate a highlight color from a regular fill color. This is especially true when fill colors are used in every cell.

▶ **Consider alternatives to conditional formats.** If you want to highlight the top 10 sales regions, it might be more effective to simply sort the data with the best-selling regions at the top of the list.

31.51	$945.38
29.91	$897.27
31.06	$931.67
32.04	$961.09
32.28	$968.37
32.34	$970.29
31.79	$953.70
30.95	$928.44
30.91	$927.25
31.78	$953.46
32.81	$984.22
33.70	$1,011.02
34.91	$1,047.20
34.83	$1,044.93

Stephen Aaron Rees/Shutterstock.com

Remember that the goal of highlighting is to provide a strong visual clue of important data or results. Careful use of conditional formatting helps readers to focus on the important points you want to make rather than be distracted by secondary issues and facts.

Using the Quick Analysis Tool to Add or Remove Conditional Formatting

The **Quick Analysis tool** provides access to some of the most commonly used formatting and analysis tools, including conditional formatting. Whenever you select a range of data, the Quick Analysis button ▤ appears next to the lower-right corner of the range. Click the Quick Analysis button to open the Quick Analysis tool. The FORMATTING section includes Greater Than, Text Contains, and Top 10% conditional formatting. Click the conditional formatting you want to apply to open the corresponding dialog box, and then set the options as usual. Click Clear Format to remove the conditional formatting from the selected range.

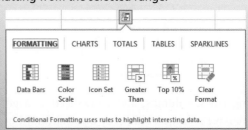

FORMATTING section in the Quick Analysis tool

> **Quick Analysis tool** A button that appears next to a selected range that provides access to commonly used formatting and analysis tools.

15-8 Hiding Rows and Columns

Sometimes a worksheet contains so much data that it doesn't fit in the worksheet window. One way to manage the contents of a large worksheet is to selectively hide (and later unhide) rows and columns containing extraneous information. This allows you to focus your attention on only a select few data points. You can also hide rows or columns before printing if you don't want others to see the contents of those rows or columns or be distracted by their content. For example, before printing the Trip Comparison worksheet for customers, you might want to hide the rows containing the service fee percentages. The values are not important for marketing purposes, as long as the service fee is disclosed to the customer somewhere. You can tell rows or columns are hidden because the numbers or letters are no longer consecutive, and a double border appears between the rows or columns. Exhibit 15-17 shows rows 2 through 9 hidden in the Trip Comparison worksheet.

Begin Activity

Hide and unhide worksheet data.

1 Select **row 2** through **row 9**.

2 On the HOME tab, in the Cells group, click the **Format button**, and then point to **Hide & Unhide**. A submenu opens, listing the commands for hiding and unhiding the selected rows, columns, or sheet.

> **Tip:** You can also hide or unhide a row or column by right-clicking the selected row or column header and clicking Hide or Unhide on the shortcut menu.

3 On the submenu, click **Hide Rows**. Rows 2 through 9 are hidden, and the row numbers in the worksheet jump from row 1 to row 10. Notice that the trip comparison data does not change even though its formulas use data from the hidden rows. Refer to Exhibit 15-17.

4 Drag to select **row 1** and **row 10**, which are the rows before and after the hidden rows.

5 In the Cells group, click the **Format button**, point to **Hide & Unhide**, and then click **Unhide Rows**. Rows 2 through 9 reappear.

6 Hide **row 3** through **row 8**.

End Activity

Exhibit 15-17 Rows hidden in the worksheet

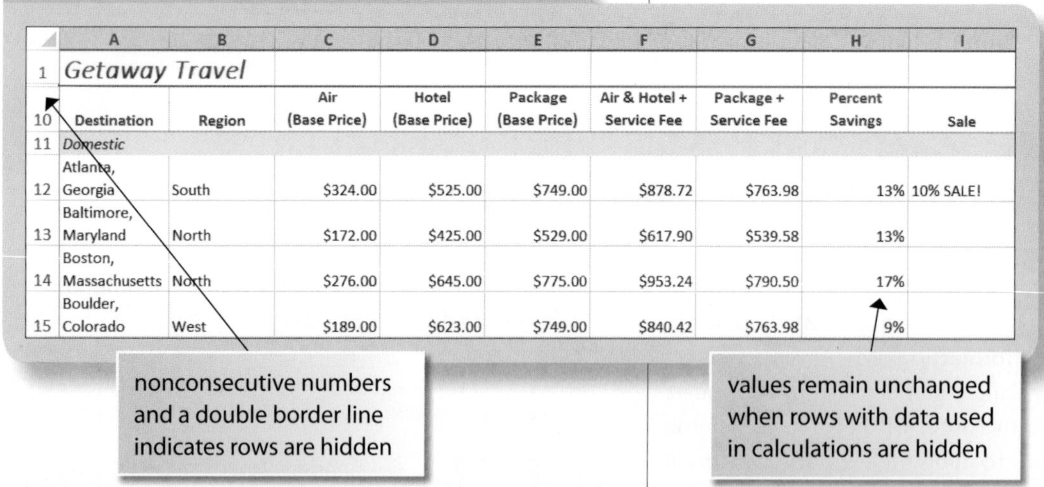

	A	B	C	D	E	F	G	H	I
1	*Getaway Travel*								
10	Destination	Region	Air (Base Price)	Hotel (Base Price)	Package (Base Price)	Air & Hotel + Service Fee	Package + Service Fee	Percent Savings	Sale
11	*Domestic*								
12	Atlanta, Georgia	South	$324.00	$525.00	$749.00	$878.72	$763.98	13%	10% SALE!
13	Baltimore, Maryland	North	$172.00	$425.00	$529.00	$617.90	$539.58	13%	
14	Boston, Massachusetts	North	$276.00	$645.00	$775.00	$953.24	$790.50	17%	
15	Boulder, Colorado	West	$189.00	$623.00	$749.00	$840.42	$763.98	9%	

nonconsecutive numbers and a double border line indicates rows are hidden

values remain unchanged when rows with data used in calculations are hidden

Hiding rows, columns, and worksheets is a good way to manage a large volume of information, but it should never be used to hide data that is crucial to understanding a workbook. Note that hiding a row or column does not affect the other formulas in the workbook. Formulas still show the correct value even if they reference a cell in a hidden row or column.

Designing Workbooks for Readability and Appeal

Designing a workbook requires the same care as designing any written document or report. A well-formatted workbook is easier to read and establishes a sense of professionalism with readers. Do the following to improve the organization and appearance of your workbooks:

▶ **Clearly identify each worksheet's purpose.** You can do this by including descriptive column and row titles as well as labels to identify other important aspects of the worksheet. Also, use a descriptive sheet name for each worksheet.

▶ **Don't crowd a worksheet with too much information.** Each worksheet should deal with only one or two topics. Place extra topics on separate sheets. Readers should be able to interpret each worksheet with a minimal amount of horizontal and vertical scrolling.

▶ **Place the most important information first in the workbook.** Position worksheets summarizing your findings near the front of the workbook. Position worksheets with detailed and involved analysis near the end as an appendix.

▶ **Use consistent formatting throughout the workbook.** If negative values appear in red on one worksheet, format them in red on all sheets. Also, be consistent in the use of thousands separators, decimal places, and percentages.

JetKat/Shutterstock.com

▶ **Pay attention to the formatting of the printed workbook.** Make sure your printouts are legible with informative headers and footers. Check that the content of the printout is scaled correctly to the page size and that page breaks divide the information into logical sections.

Excel provides many formatting options. However, keep in mind that too much formatting can be intrusive, overwhelm data, and make the document difficult to read. A well-formatted workbook seamlessly conveys data to the reader. If the reader is spending time thinking about how the workbook looks, it means he or she is not thinking about the data.

15-9 Formatting a Worksheet for Printing

Igor Kolos/Shutterstock.com

You should take as much care in formatting the printed output as you do in formatting the contents of the electronic file. Excel has a variety of print settings that you can use to specify what prints and how it appears on the printed pages. Print settings can be applied to an entire workbook or to individual sheets.

15-9a Inserting and Removing Page Breaks

Often the contents of a worksheet do not fit onto a single page. By default, Excel prints as much of the content that fits on a single page without resizing the content and then inserts **automatic page breaks** to continue printing the remaining worksheet content on successive pages. This can result in page breaks that leave a single column or row on a separate page or split worksheet content in awkward places such as within range of related data. Automatic page breaks appear as dotted blue lines in Page Break Preview. See Exhibit 15-18.

automatic page break A page break Excel inserts when no more content will fit on the page.

Exhibit 15-18 Worksheet with automatic page breaks

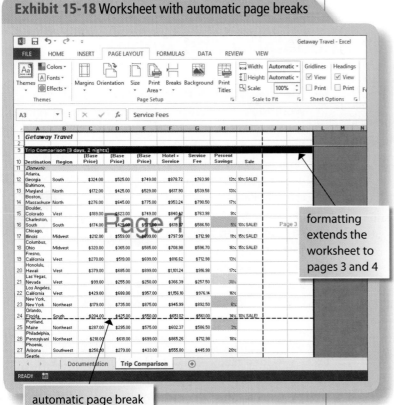

formatting extends the worksheet to pages 3 and 4

automatic page break

One way to fix this problem is to scale the printout by reducing the font size to fit on a single sheet of paper. However, if you have more than one or two columns or rows to fit onto the page, the resulting text is often too small to read comfortably. A better fix is usually to split the worksheet into logical segments, which you can do by inserting **manual page breaks** that specify where the page breaks occur. A page break is inserted directly above and to the left of a selected cell, directly above a selected row, or to the left of a selected column. Remember that automatic page breaks appear as dotted blue lines in Page Break Preview. Manual page breaks appear as solid blue lines.

Begin Activity

Move and insert page breaks.

1 On the status bar, click the **Page Break Preview button** 🔲. The worksheet switches to Page Break Preview. The worksheet's contents do not fit on a

single page, and the trip comparison data breaks across pages.

2 On the ribbon, click the **PAGE LAYOUT tab**. In the Page Setup group, click the **Orientation button**, and then click **Landscape**. The page orientation changes to landscape, making each page wide enough to display all of the columns in each table. There is a page 3 and a page 4 in the preview because the range J9:K9 is filled with the same color as the rest of the cells in row 9. This formatting appears because you deleted cells in the worksheet below row 9 after using the Flash Fill feature, and the rest of the cells below row 9 shifted left. The solid blue line to the right of column K indicates the manual page break. Refer back to Exhibit 15-18.

3 Position the pointer on top of the **solid blue line** so that it changes to ↔, and then drag the line to the left to position it between columns I and J. Pages 3 and 4 no longer are included in the preview.

4 Select **cell A29**.

5 On the PAGE LAYOUT tab, in the Page Setup group, click the **Breaks button**, and then click **Insert Page Break**. A solid blue line appears above row 29. Compare your screen to Exhibit 15-19.

6 On the ribbon, click the **FILE tab**. In the navigation bar, click **Print**. The preview on the Print screen shows the first page of the current worksheet.

7 Below the preview, click the **Next Page button** ▶. The second page of the worksheet containing the rest of the domestic data appears. Notice that the column headings in row 10 do not appear on this page.

Tip: You can set the gridlines or the row and column headings to print by clicking the Print check boxes in the Sheet Options group on the PAGE LAYOUT tab.

Tip: To remove a manual page break, click the cell below or to the right of the page break, click the Breaks button, and then click Remove Page Break.

manual page break A page break you insert to specify where a page break occurs.

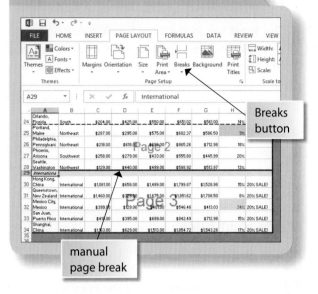

Exhibit 15-20 Print area set in Page Break Preview

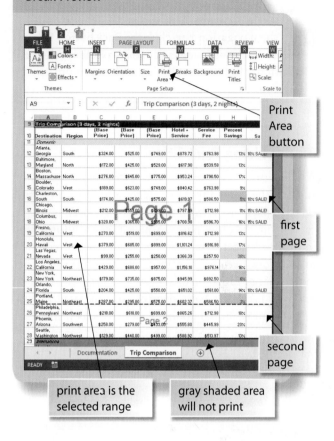

8. Click the **Next Page button** ▶. The third page of the worksheet appears. The international trip comparison data is on the third page.

9. In the navigation bar, click the **Back button** ← to close Backstage view and redisplay the worksheet with the PAGE LAYOUT tab selected on the ribbon.

End Activity

15-9b Setting the Print Area

By default, all cells in the active worksheet containing text, formulas, or values are printed. The region of the active sheet that is sent to the printer is known as the **print area**. To print part of a worksheet, you can define the print area, overriding the default setting. A print area can cover an adjacent or nonadjacent range in the current worksheet. The rest of the worksheet content is gray to indicate that it will not be part of the printout. See Exhibit 15-20.

The easiest way to set the print area is in Page Layout view or Page Break Preview. For example, to print only the trip comparison in the Monthly Sales worksheet, you could set the print area to cover that range while in Page Break Preview.

Begin Activity

Set and clear the print area.

1. Select the **range A9:I28**. This range includes the header row containing Trip Comparison and the data for domestic travel only.

2. On the PAGE LAYOUT tab, in the Page Setup group, click the **Print Area button**, and then click **Set Print Area**. The print area changes to cover only the selected range A9:I28.

3. Select **cell A9**. Any worksheet content that is not included in the print area is shaded gray to indicate that it will not be part of the printout. Refer back to Exhibit 15-20.

4. On the ribbon, click the **FILE tab**. In the navigation bar, click **Print**. On the Print screen, below the preview, the page numbers indicate that now only two pages will print.

> **print area** The region of the active sheet that is sent to the printer.

5 Below the preview, click the **Next Page button** ▷. The second page of the worksheet containing the rest of the domestic data appears.

6 In the navigation bar, click the **Back button** ⬅ to close Backstage view and redisplay the worksheet with the PAGE LAYOUT tab selected on the ribbon.

End Activity

15-9c Adding Print Titles

A good practice is to include descriptive information such as the company name, logo, and worksheet title on each page of a printout in case a page becomes separated from the other pages. You can repeat information in the worksheet by specifying which rows or columns in the worksheet act as **print titles**. If a worksheet contains a large range of data, you can print the column and row labels on every page of your printout by designating those initial columns and rows as print titles. You do this on the Sheet tab in the Page Setup dialog box. See Exhibit 15-21.

Exhibit 15-21 Sheet tab in the Page Setup dialog box

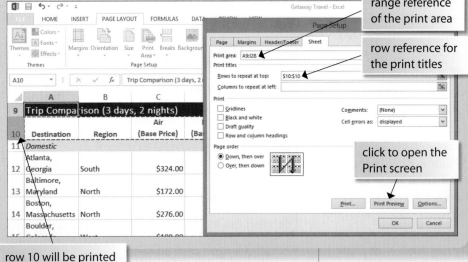

range reference of the print area

row reference for the print titles

click to open the Print screen

row 10 will be printed on every page

FYI

Print Options on the Sheet Tab

The Sheet tab in the Page Setup dialog box provides other print options, such as printing the gridlines or row and column headings. You can also print the worksheet in black and white or in draft quality. For a multiple page printout, you can specify whether the pages are ordered by going down the worksheet and then across, or across first and then down.

Begin Activity

Create print titles.

1 Switch to **Normal view**.

2 On the **PAGE LAYOUT** tab, in the Page Setup group, click the **Print Titles button**. The Page Setup dialog box opens with the Sheet tab selected.

3 In the Print titles section, click in the **Rows to repeat at top box**.

4 Click in the worksheet, and then select **row 10**. The row reference $10:$10 appears in the Rows to repeat at top box, indicating that the print title range starts and ends with row 10. A blinking border appears around row 10 in the worksheet, indicating that the contents of these rows will be repeated on each page of the printout. Refer back to Exhibit 15-21.

5 At the bottom of the dialog box, click **Print Preview**. The dialog box closes, and the Print screen appears in Backstage view.

6 Below the preview, click the **Next Page button** ▷. The second page of the worksheet containing the rest of the domestic data appears. The column headings from row 10 appear at the top of the page. Compare your screen to Exhibit 15-22.

print title Information from a workbook that appears on every printed page.

Exhibit 15-22 Print titles added to the printout

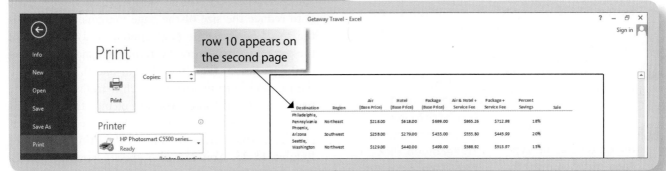

row 10 appears on the second page

Destination	Region	Air (Base Price)	Hotel (Base Price)	Package (Base Price)	Air & Hotel + Service Fee	Package + Service Fee	Percent Savings	Sale
Philadelphia, Pennsylvania	Northeast	$218.00	$618.00	$699.00	$865.26	$712.98	18%	
Phoenix, Arizona	Southwest	$258.00	$279.00	$435.00	$555.80	$445.99	20%	
Seattle, Washington	Northwest	$129.00	$440.00	$499.00	$588.92	$515.97	13%	

7 In the navigation bar, click the **Back button** ⬅ to close Backstage view and redisplay the worksheet with the PAGE LAYOUT tab selected on the ribbon.

End Activity

15-9d Creating Headers and Footers

Another way to repeat information on each printed page is with headers and footers, as you did in Word. You can add headers and footers that contain helpful and descriptive text usually not found within the worksheet, such as the workbook's author, the current date, the workbook file name, and page numbers.

The header and footer each have a left section, a center section, and a right section. Within each section, you type the text you want to appear or insert elements such as the worksheet name or the current date and time. These header and footer elements are dynamic; if you rename the worksheet, for example, the name is automatically updated in the header or footer.

Begin Activity

Insert a header and a footer.

1 On the status bar, click the **Page Layout button** 📖.

2 Scroll so that you can see the top margin of the worksheet, and then point to **Click to add header**. A light border surrounds the entire header section, and a dark border surrounds the middle section of the header.

3 Click the **left section** of the header. The dark border appears around the left section, the insertion point appears in the left section, and the HEADER & FOOTER TOOLS DESIGN tab appears on the ribbon.

4 On the ribbon, click the **HEADER & FOOTER TOOLS DESIGN tab**, if necessary.

5 In the left section of the header, type **File name:** and then press the **Spacebar**.

6 On the HEADER & FOOTER TOOLS DESIGN tab, in the Header & Footer Elements group, click the **File Name button**. The code &[File], which displays the file name of the current workbook, is added to the left section of the header.

7 Click the **right section** of the header. In the left section, the &[File] code is replaced with the workbook file name, *Getaway Travel*.

8 In the Header & Footer Elements group, click the **Current Date button**. The code &[Date] is added to the right section of the header. See Exhibit 15-23.

Exhibit 15-23 Header with content

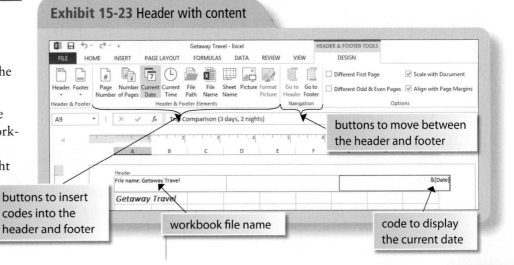

buttons to move between the header and footer

buttons to insert codes into the header and footer

workbook file name

code to display the current date

9 On the HEADER & FOOTER TOOLS DESIGN tab, in the Navigation group, click the **Go to Footer button**. The worksheet scrolls so you can see the footer, and the insertion point is in the right section of the footer.

10 Type **Prepared by:**, press the **Spacebar**, and then type your name.

> **Tip:** To quickly enter commonly used header or footer text, in the Header & Footer group, click the Header or Footer button, and then click the text you want.

11 In the footer, click in the **center section**. Type **Page** and then press the **Spacebar**.

12 In the Header & Footer Elements group, click the **Page Number button**. The code &[Page] is added after the text in the center section of the footer.

13 Press the **Spacebar**, type **of** and then press the **Spacebar**.

14 In the Header & Footer Elements group, click the **Number of Pages button**. The text *Page &[Page] of &[Pages]* appears in the center section of the footer. Compare your screen to Exhibit 15-24.

> **Problem?** If the footer shows a different page number, the active cell in your worksheet is in another location.

15 Click the **FILE tab**, and then in the navigation bar, click **Print**. The header and footer you added appear in the preview.

End Activity

15-9e Setting the Page Margins

Another way to fit a large worksheet on a single page is to reduce the size of the page margins. A margin is the space between the page content and the edges of the page. In a new worksheet, the page margins are set to 0.7 inches on the left and right and 0.75 inches on the top and bottom with 0.3-inch margins around the page header and footer. You can change these margins as needed by selecting from a set of predefined margin sizes, which are available on the Print screen. See Exhibit 15-25. You can also specify your own margins. For example, you might need narrower margins to fit all of the columns on a page or wider margins to accommodate the page binding. You use the Margins tab in the Page Setup dialog box to set custom margins. See Exhibit 15-26.

Begin Activity

Set the page margins.

1 On the Print screen, click the **Normal Margins button**. A menu opens with a list of predefined margins. Refer to Exhibit 15-25.

> **Tip:** You can also set the margins by clicking the Margins button in the Page Setup group on the PAGE LAYOUT tab.

2 Click **Wide**. The menu closes, and the margins are changed to set 1-inch margins around the printed content with 0.5-inch margins above the header and below the footer. The size of the margins around the page increases but does not affect how the content fits on the pages. In the preview, notice that the Sale column no longer fits on page 1 and the preview now consists of four pages.

3 Click the **Wide Margins button**, and then click **Custom Margins**. The Page Setup dialog box opens with the Margins tab selected. Refer to Exhibit 15-26.

Exhibit 15-24 Footer with content

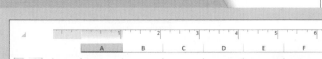

current page and total number of pages

your name appears here

Exhibit 15-25 Normal Margins menu on the Print screen

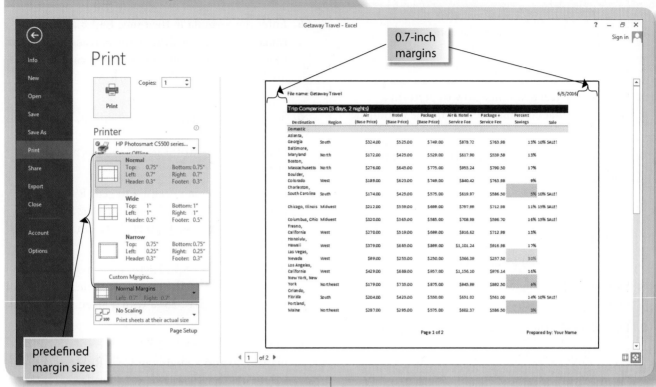

predefined margin sizes

Exhibit 15-26 Margins tab in the Page Setup dialog box

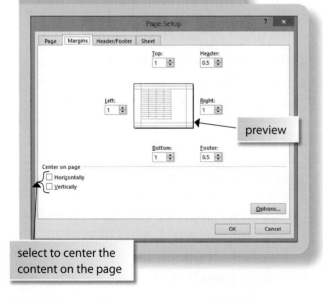

preview

select to center the content on the page

4 Click the **Left down arrow**. The value in the Left box changes from 1 to 0.75.

5 Change the value in the **Right box** to **0.75**.

6 Click **OK**. The dialog box closes, and the margins in the preview are adjusted. The Sale column again fits on page 1.

7 Print the worksheet, if requested, or click the **Back button** ⬅ to close Backstage view and return to Page Layout view.

End Activity

LEARN MORE

Centering Content on the Page

Worksheet content is printed on pages starting from the left and top margins. This can leave a lot of empty space on the right and top sides of the pages. To center the content on the page, click the Dialog Box Launcher in the Page Setup group on the PAGE LAYOUT tab to open the Page Setup dialog box, click the Margins tab, and then select the Horizontally and Vertically check boxes to center the content of the current sheet on the page. Refer to Exhibit 15-26.

Quiz Yourself

1. Why should you document the contents of a workbook?

2. What does Flash Fill do?

3. How does Excel determine how to perform a calculation that contains more than one arithmetic operator?

4. What is an error value, and when does it appear?

5. What is the IF function?

6. Write the formula that tests whether the value in cell S2 is equal to the value in cell P7 and then returns 75 if it is, but otherwise returns 150.

7. What is conditional formatting?

8. How would you highlight the top 10 values in the range A1:C20?

9. How does clearing a conditional formatting rule affect the cell contents?

10. Why would you hide some rows or columns in a worksheet?

11. Why would you define a print area?

12. Describe the difference between automatic and manual page breaks.

13. What are print titles?

14. Describe how to add the workbook file name in the center section of the footer on every page of a printout.

Practice It

Practice It 15-1

1. Open the data file **Tool** located in the Chapter 15\ Practice It folder. Save the workbook as **Tool Barn**.

2. In the Documentation worksheet, enter your name in cell B3 and the date in cell B4.

3. Use Flash Fill to enter the first and last names of the staff in the range B7:B11.

4. Make the Model Comparison worksheet the active sheet. Determine the formula to subtract the units sold in 2015 from the units sold in 2016 to calculate the increase in sales, and then divide that increase by the units sold in 2015 to calculate the percent increase in units sold for each model. Remember the order of operations.

5. Enter the formula in the range E4:E8 and the range E12:E16 to calculate the percent increase in units sold for each model. Make sure these ranges are formatted with Percent style and no decimal places.

6. Select the nonadjacent range C9:D9;C17:D17, and then enter formulas to calculate the total units sold per year for gas chainsaws and electric chainsaws.

7. Copy the formula in cell E4 to cells E9 and E17, pasting only the formula and number formatting. (*Hint*: Use the Paste Options button after pasting the formula.)

8. In the range E4:E8;E12:E16, use conditional formatting to add a Highlight Cells Rule to cells with values greater than 25% with a green fill and dark green text.

9. In the range E4:E8;E12:E16, use conditional formatting to add a Highlight Cells Rule to cells with values less than 0% with a red border.

10. Make the Monthly Sales worksheet the active sheet. In the range D5:D16;J5:J16, enter the SUM function to calculate the total units sold for all chainsaws by month.

11. In the range B17:D17;H17:J17, use the SUM function to add the total of each column.

12. Hide column D, and then hide column J.

13. In cell E5, enter a formula to calculate the total of all gas and electric chainsaws sold in January 2015.

14. In cell E6, enter a formula to calculate the total of all gas and electric chainsaws sold in February 2015, and then add that to the total chainsaws sold in January 2015 (cell E5).

15. Copy the formula in cell E6 to the range E7:E16. Copy the formulas in the range E5:E16 to the range K5:K16.

16. Unhide columns D and J.

17. In cell F5, enter an IF function that tests whether the number of all chainsaws sold in January 2016 is greater than the number of chainsaws sold in January 2015. If it is, the formula should return the text **"UP"**; otherwise, it should return no text. (*Hint*: Enter **" "** to specify no text.)

18. Copy the formula in cell F5 to the range F6:F16.

19. View the worksheet in Page Break Preview.

20. Set the print area to the range A3:K17. Set the print titles to repeat row 1 at the top of each page. Insert a page break between column E and column F.

21. For the Model Comparison and Monthly Sales worksheets, create headers and footers that display your name in the center section of the header, display the sheet name in the left section of the footer, display the workbook file name in the center section of the footer, and display the current date in the right section of the footer.

22. Save the workbook, and then close it.

Practice It 15-2

1. Open the data file **TalkWell** located in the Chapter 15\Practice It folder. Save the workbook as **TalkWell Mobile Phones**.

2. In the Documentation worksheet, enter your name in cell B3 and the date in cell B4.

3. In the Mobile Phone Sales worksheet, enter a formula in cell C5 that adds the sales of all phones in January in Region 1.

4. Copy the formula in cell C5 to the range C5:G16 to find the total sales for each month in each region.

5. Use conditional formatting to highlight the top 10 items in the nonadjacent range C19:G30;C33:G44;C47:G58 with a red border. (*Hint*: Select the nonadjacent range, and then apply the conditional formatting.)

6. Use conditional formatting to highlight the top 10% of cells in the range C5:G16 with a light red fill with dark red text.

7. Enter a formula in cell C3 that adds the total sales in Region 1 and then divides that amount by the total sales in all regions. Format the results as a percentage with no decimal places.

8. Copy the formula in cell C3 to the range D3:G3 to find the percentage of total sales for each region. (*Hint*: Make sure you used an absolute reference in the formula you copied.)

9. In cell C2, use an IF function to test whether the percentage of total sales in 2016 for Region 1 is greater than or equal to 15%. If it is, the formula returns **"Good Sales"**; otherwise, it leaves the cell blank.

10. Copy the IF function to the range D2:G2.

11. View the Mobile Phone Sales worksheet in Page Layout view. Set the margins to Wide, and set the page orientation to landscape.

12. View the Mobile Phone Sales worksheet in Page Break Preview. Insert manual page breaks at cells A18 and A32.

13. Repeat rows 1 and 2 of the worksheet on every printed page.

14. Insert page breaks to print each table of data on a separate page.

15. Center each page both horizontally and vertically on the paper.

16. Display your name in the center header, display the file name in the left footer, display **Page** *page number* **of** *number of pages* in the center footer, and then display the current date in the right footer.

17. Save the workbook, and then close it.

On Your Own

On Your Own 15-1

1. Open the data file **Singleton** located in the Chapter 15\On Your Own folder. Save the workbook as **Singleton Rentals**.

2. In the Documentation worksheet, enter your name in cell B3 and the date in cell B4.

3. In the Yearly Rates worksheet, in the % Increase column, enter formulas to calculate what percentage the income increased between 2015 and 2016 and what percentage the vacancies increased between 2015 and 2016. Remember the order of operations.

4. Format the results appropriately, using symbols and an appropriate number of decimal places.

5. In the range G6:G13, use IF functions to test whether the corresponding cells in column F are positive. If they are, display the contents of cell H1; if not, display the contents of cell I1.

6. Edit cell H1 to **Up**, and edit cell I1 to **Down**.

7. Hide columns H and I in the worksheet.

8. In the Monthly Rates worksheet, hide the Units Vacant in 2015 and the Units Vacant in 2016 data.

9. In the Net Increase data, use conditional formatting to highlight the top 10% of vacancies, the bottom 10% of vacancies, and the values equal to zero.

10. Unhide the Units Vacant in 2015 and the Units Vacant in 2016 data.

11. Clear the Cell Value = 0 rule from the worksheet.

12. Format the Units Vacant in 2015 data as a table. Select the range A6:I18. On the HOME tab, in the Styles group, click the Format as Table button, and then click Table Style Medium 6 table style. Click OK in the Format As Table dialog box to accept the defaults. Notice the banded rows formatting that was added to the table.

13. On the TABLE TOOLS DESIGN tab, in the Table Style Options group, click the Total Row check box. For each cell in the range B19:I19, click the arrow button to display a list of the available functions, and then click Sum.

14. Add descriptive headers and footers to each worksheet, being sure to include your name, the current date, and the file name.

15. View each worksheet in Page Layout view or Print Preview, and then change the print area, margins, orientation, print titles, and page breaks as needed to ensure that the printout is easily read and interpreted.

16. Save the workbook, and then close it.

Chapter 15

ADDITIONAL STUDY TOOLS

IN THE BOOK
▶ Complete end-of-chapter exercises
▶ Study tear-out Chapter Review Card

ONLINE
▶ Complete additional end-of-chapter exercises

▶ Take practice quiz to prepare for tests
▶ Review key term flash cards (online, printable, and audio)
▶ Play "Beat the Clock" and "Memory" to quiz yourself
▶ Watch the videos to learn more about the topics taught in this chapter

Answers to Quiz Yourself

1. You should document the contents of a workbook to make it accessible to its intended users, avoid errors and confusion, and make it easier for others to understand.

2. Flash Fill enters text based on patterns it finds in the data.

3. If a formula contains more than one arithmetic operator, Excel performs the calculation using the order of operations—first, exponentiation (^); second, multiplication (*) and division (/); and third, addition (+) and subtraction (−).

4. An error value is a message indicating that some part of a formula is preventing Excel from returning a calculated value. An error value appears instead of the formula results.

5. The IF function is a logical function that returns one value if a statement is true and returns a different value if that statement is false.

6. The formula that tests whether the value in cell S2 is equal to the value in cell P7, and then returns 75 if it is, but returns 150 otherwise is =IF(S2=P7,75,150).

7. Conditional formatting is formatting that is applied to a cell only when the cell's value meets a specified condition.

8. To highlight the top 10 values in the range A1:C20, first select the range, then click the Conditional Formatting button in the Styles group on the HOME tab, point to Highlight Cells Rules, point to Top/Bottom Rules, and then click Top 10. Select the format, and then click OK.

9. Clearing a conditional formatting rule doesn't affect the contents of the cells.

10. You might hide some rows or columns in a worksheet to remove extraneous information from view.

11. You would define a print area to specify what part of a worksheet should be printed.

12. Excel prints as much of the content that fits on a single page without resizing the content and then inserts automatic page breaks to continue printing the remaining worksheet content on successive pages. A manual page break is one you insert to specify exactly where the page break occurs.

13. Print titles are information from a workbook that appears on every printed page.

14. To add the workbook file name in the center section of the footer on every page of a printout, switch to Page Layout view, scroll down until you see the footer, click in the center section of the footer, and then click the File Name button in the Header & Footer Elements group on the Header & Footer Tools Design tab.

Inserting and Formatting Charts

OrnaYdur/Shutterstock.com

Charts provide a way to illustrate numbers. Because many people are overwhelmed by tables of numbers, you can use charts to show trends or relationships in data that are easier to see than by looking at the actual numbers. In Excel, you can choose from a variety of charts to create the type of chart that best illustrates the data. Each chart can be formatted to highlight specific data and to include chart elements that help others understand the data. Charts can be included on a worksheet or in a chart sheet devoted to that chart. You can also create mini charts that appear near or within cells with data. With all of these options, you can easily develop workbooks and reports that are effectively illustrated with attractive and helpful charts.

Learning Objectives

After studying the material in this chapter, you will be able to:

16-1 Create a chart

16-2 Move and resize a chart

16-3 Modify a chart

16-4 Create an exploded pie chart

16-5 Create a column chart

16-6 Create a line chart

16-7 Edit chart data

16-8 Insert and format sparklines

16-9 Insert and modify data bars

Microsoft product screenshots used with permission from Microsoft Corporation.

16-1 Creating a Chart

A chart, or **graph**, is a visual representation of a set of data values. Charts show trends or relationships that may not be readily apparent from numbers alone. For example, it can be difficult to identify in which range of months a mutual fund performed exceptionally well simply looking at numbers, whereas a chart can make that relationship easy to see.

Begin Activity

Review chart data.

1 Open the data file **Minneapolis** located in the Chapter 16\Chapter folder. Save the workbook as **Minneapolis Real Estate**.

2 In the **Documentation worksheet**, enter your name in **cell B3** and the date in **cell B4**.

3 Left-align the date in **cell B4**.

4 Review the contents of each worksheet.

End Activity

The Summary Report worksheet will summarize data and facts about Minneapolis real estate. The Historical Prices worksheet lists real estate prices from 2012 through 2016. The Metro Population worksheet lists the populations of Minnesota cities. The Structure Types worksheet shows the breakout of Minneapolis structure types compared to the entire United States. The Population History worksheet shows population changes in Minnesota cities between 1985 and 2015. Much of this numerical data would be easier to understand as charts.

16-1a Selecting a Data Source

Each chart has a **data source**, which is the range that contains the data to display in the chart. A data source includes one or more **data series**, which is the set of values represented in a chart. The data series includes one or more **categories**, which are the sets of values that represent the data for the same item. The **category values** provide descriptive labels for each data series, and the **data series values** contain the actual numbers plotted on the chart.

Category values are usually located in the first column or first row of the data source. The data series values are usually placed in subsequent columns or rows. However, you can select category and data series values from anywhere within a workbook.

The data source shown in Exhibit 16-1 includes two columns. The category values are located in the first column, and the one and only data series is located in the second column. The first row of this data source contains labels that identify the category values (City) and the data series (Production Goal).

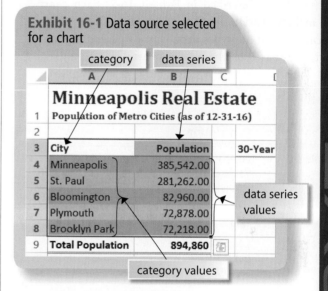

Exhibit 16-1 Data source selected for a chart

Begin Activity

Select the data source for a chart.

1 Make the **Metro Population worksheet** the active sheet.

> **chart (graph)** A visual representation of a set of data values.
>
> **data source** The range that contains the data to display in a chart.
>
> **data series** A set of values represented in a chart.
>
> **category** A set of values that represent data for one item in a chart.
>
> **category values** The row or column of a data source that provides the descriptive labels for each data series.
>
> **data series values** The actual numbers plotted on a chart.

2 Select the **range A3:B8**. The data source in this range has one data series, named Population, that includes one category, named City. The category values in the range A4:A8 list the different cities. The data series values in the range B4:B8 contain the population numbers to be charted. Refer back to Exhibit 16-1.

End Activity

16-1b Selecting a Chart Type

You can create a wide variety of charts from a selected data source. Excel includes 53 charts organized into the 10 chart types described in Exhibit 16-2. Each chart type includes variations of the same chart type, which are called chart subtypes. You can also create custom chart types based on the built-in charts.

Exhibit 16-2 Excel chart types

Chart type	Description
Column	Compares values from different categories. Values are indicated by the height of the columns.
Line	Compares values from different categories. Values are indicated by the height of the line.
Pie	Compares relative values of different categories to the whole. Values are indicated by the size of the pie slices.
Bar	Compares values from different categories. Values are indicated by the length of the bars.
Area	Compares values from different categories. Similar to the line chart except that areas under the lines contain a fill color.
X Y (Scatter)	Shows the patterns or relationship between two or more sets of values.
Stock	Displays stock market data, including the high, low, opening, and closing prices of a stock.
Surface	Compares three sets of values in a three-dimensional chart.
Radar	Compares a collection of values from several different data sets.
Combo	Combines two or more data types to make the data easy to visualize, especially when the data is widely used.

© 2014 Cengage Learning

You should select the type of chart that makes the data easiest to interpret. For example, a pie chart provides the best way to show the breakout of the population data you selected. A **pie chart** is a chart in the shape of a circle divided into slices like a pie. Each pie slice represents one data series value and shows that value as a percentage of the whole. The larger the value, the larger the pie slice. When you chart the population data, each slice will represent the percentage of the total population from one of the five metro cities in Minnesota. The data source for a pie chart should include only the category values and the data series values, not any row or column totals because Excel will treat those totals as another category to be plotted on the chart. In this case, you will not include the Total Population row as part of the data source, because it is not a population category and should not be included in a pie chart.

16-1c Inserting a Pie Chart

The chart types are available in the Charts group on the INSERT tab. To create a chart from the selected data source, you click the button that corresponds to the type of chart you want to insert, which opens a gallery of chart subtypes. You can point to each subtype in the gallery to see a Live Preview of the selected data source in that chart subtype. Exhibit 16-3 shows the Pie charts gallery. Just click a chart subtype to insert that chart in the worksheet.

When you create or select a chart, two CHART TOOLS tabs appear on the ribbon. The DESIGN tab provides commands to set the chart's overall design, including changing the chart type, and to work with individual elements of the chart such as the chart's title. The FORMAT tab provides commands to change the appearance of graphic shapes in the chart such as the chart's border or markers placed in the chart. When you select a cell or another object that is not a chart, the CHART TOOLS tabs disappear until you reselect the chart.

Three buttons appear to the right of the selected chart. The Chart Elements button ⊞ is used to add, remove, or change elements displayed in the chart. The Chart Styles button 🖉 sets the style and color scheme of the chart. The Chart Filters button ▼ lets you edit the data displayed in the chart.

pie chart A chart in the shape of a circle divided into slices like a pie that shows the data values as a percentage of the whole.

Choosing the Right Chart Type

Excel supports a wide variety of charts. Deciding which type of chart to use requires evaluating the data and determining the ultimate purpose or goal of the chart. Consider how the data will appear with each type of chart before making a final decision.

▶ Pie charts are generally most effective when there are six or fewer slices, when each slice is large enough to view, and when the relative sizes of the different slices can be easily distinguished.

▶ Column or bar charts work well for data that includes more than six categories or whose values are close together.

▶ Line charts are best for categories that follow a sequential order. Be aware, however, that the time intervals must be a constant length if used in a line chart. Line charts will distort data that occurs in irregular time intervals, making it appear that the data values occurred at regular intervals when they did not.

▶ Pie, column, bar, and line charts assume that numbers are plotted against categories. In science and engineering applications, you will often want to plot two numeric values against one another. For that data, use scatter charts, which show the patterns or relationship between two or more sets of values. Scatter charts are also useful for data recorded at irregular time intervals.

If you still cannot find the right chart to meet your needs, you can create a custom chart based on the built-in chart types. Third-party vendors also sell software to allow Excel to create charts not built into the software.

cubens 3d/Shutterstock.com

Exhibit 16-3 Pie charts gallery

Insert Pie or Doughnut Chart button

data source

Begin Activity

Insert a pie chart.

1 On the ribbon, click the **INSERT tab**.

2 In the Charts group, click the **Insert Pie or Doughnut Chart button** 🥧▾. The Pie charts gallery opens. Refer back to Exhibit 16-3.

3 Point to the different pie chart subtypes.

4 In the 2-D Pie section, click **Pie** (the first pie chart). The pie chart is inserted in the Metro Population worksheet; three buttons appear next to the chart and two CHART TOOLS tabs appear on the ribbon. Compare your screen to Exhibit 16-4.

End Activity

16-1d Selecting Chart Elements

Chart elements are individual parts of a chart such as the chart area, the chart title, the plot area, data markers, and a legend. See Exhibit 16-5. The **chart area** contains the chart and all of the other chart elements. The **chart title** is a descriptive label or name for the chart. The **plot area** is the part of the chart that contains the graphical representation of the data series. Each value in a data series is represented

chart element An individual part of a chart.

chart area The area that contains the chart and all of the other chart elements.

chart title A descriptive label or name for the chart.

plot area The part of the chart that contains the graphical representation of the data series.

Exhibit 16-4 Pie chart inserted into the worksheet

CHART TOOLS tabs appear when the chart is selected

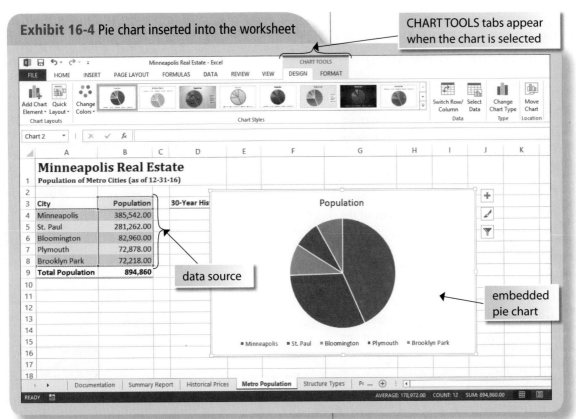

by a **data marker** such as a pie slice. A **legend** is a rectangular area that indicates the data markers associated with the data series. You can choose which of these elements to include in the chart as well as where each element is placed and how each element looks.

Before you can work with a chart element, you must select it. The simplest way to select a chart element is to click it. To ensure that you are clicking the right element, point to the element and check that the correct element name appears in the ScreenTip. The name of the selected element appears in the Chart Elements box located in the Current Selection group on the CHART TOOLS FORMAT tab. You can also use this box to select chart elements. Click the Chart Elements box arrow, and then select the appropriate chart element in the list. A selection box with sizing handles, which you use to reposition or resize the element, surrounds the selected element. See Exhibit 16-6.

Exhibit 16-5 Chart elements

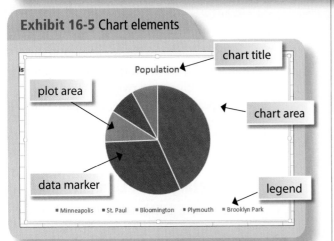

Exhibit 16-6 Current Selection list

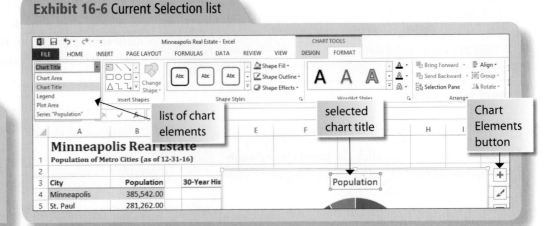

data marker
An object in a chart that represents a value in a data series, such as a pie slice or column.

legend A rectangular area that indicates the data markers associated with the data series.

Selecting a Recommended Chart

The Quick Analysis tool provides a list of recommended charts for the selected data source. After you select the range you want to use as a chart's data source, the Quick Analysis button 📖 appears in the lower-right corner of the selected range. Click the Quick Analysis button 📖, and then click CHARTS to display a list of recommended charts. You can point to the different charts to see how the data would appear in the chart style. If you want to use a chart style, click that option. If not, you can click the More Charts button to open the Insert Chart dialog box, which has two tabs: The Recommended Charts tab shows the different types of charts that Excel has determined are most appropriate for the data. The All Charts tab provides access to all of the different chart types and subtypes. You can also open the Insert Chart dialog box with the Recommended Charts tab displayed by clicking the Recommended Charts button in the Charts group on the INSERT tab.

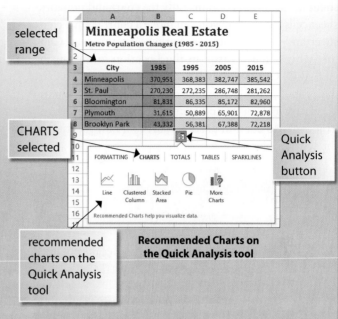

selected range

CHARTS selected

Quick Analysis button

recommended charts on the Quick Analysis tool

Recommended Charts on the Quick Analysis tool

Begin Activity

Select chart elements.

1 Point to an empty area of the selected chart. The pointer changes to ✛ and the ScreenTip *Chart Area* appears, indicating that the pointer is over the chart area.

2 In the chart area above the pie chart, point to **Population**. The ScreenTip *Chart Title* appears, indicating that the pointer is over the chart title.

3 Click **Population**. A selection box appears around the chart title, indicating that it is selected.

4 On the ribbon, click the **CHART TOOLS FORMAT tab**. In the Current Selection group, notice that *Chart Title* appears in the Current Selection box.

> **Problem?** If you don't see the CHART TOOLS FORMAT tab, the chart is not selected. In the Metro Population worksheet, click any part of the **chart** to select it, and then repeat Step 4.

5 Click the **Current Selection box arrow** to display a list of elements in the current chart. Refer back to Exhibit 16-6.

6 In the Current Selection list, click **Plot Area**. The selection box surrounds the pie chart.

7 Select the **chart area**.

End Activity

16-2 Moving and Resizing a Chart

Each chart you create is inserted as an embedded chart in the worksheet that contains its data source. An **embedded chart** is an object in a worksheet. For example, the pie chart is embedded in the Metro Population worksheet. The advantage of an embedded chart is that you can display the chart alongside its data source or any text or graphics that can explain the chart's meaning and purpose. However, an embedded chart might cover worksheet cells that hide data and formulas. To avoid hiding data, you can move an embedded chart to a different sheet in the workbook, you can reposition it on the worksheet, or you can resize the chart.

embedded chart A chart that is an object in a worksheet.

16-2a Moving a Chart to a Different Sheet

You can move an embedded chart to a different worksheet in the workbook, or you can move it to a **chart sheet** (a sheet that contains only the chart and no worksheet cells). Likewise, you can move a chart from a chart sheet and embed it in any worksheet you select. Click the Move Chart button in the Location group on the CHART TOOLS DESIGN tab to open the Move Chart dialog box, which provides options for moving charts between worksheets and chart sheets. See Exhibit 16-7. You can also cut and paste a chart to a new location in the workbook.

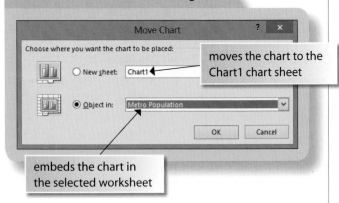

Exhibit 16-7 Move Chart dialog box

moves the chart to the Chart1 chart sheet

embeds the chart in the selected worksheet

Begin Activity

Move an embedded chart to another sheet.

1 On the ribbon, click the **CHART TOOLS DESIGN tab**.

2 In the Location group, click the **Move Chart button**. The Move Chart dialog box opens. Refer back to Exhibit 16-7.

3 Click the **Object in box arrow** to display a list of worksheets in the active workbook, and then click **Summary Report**.

4 Click **OK**. The embedded pie chart moves from the Metro Population worksheet to the Summary Report worksheet and remains selected.

> **Tip:** To move a chart to a chart sheet, in the Move Chart dialog box, click the New sheet option button, type a name for the chart sheet in the box, and then click OK.

End Activity

chart sheet A sheet in a workbook that contains only a chart and no worksheet cells.

Creating a Chart Sheet

Chart sheets are helpful for detailed charts that need more space to be seen clearly or when you want to show a chart without any worksheet text or data. Some reports require large expansive charts rather than compact graphs to provide more detail and make them easier to view and share. In those situations, you may want to devote an entire sheet to a graph rather than embed it within a worksheet. To create a larger version of a chart that covers an entire sheet, you move the chart to a chart sheet. Chart sheets do not contain worksheet cells.

To move an embedded chart to a chart sheet, first select the chart in the worksheet. On the CHART TOOLS DESIGN tab, in the Location group, click the Move Chart button. In the Move Chart dialog box that opens, click the New sheet option button, type a name for the chart sheet in the box, and then click OK. The chart is moved to a new chart sheet with the name you specified. You can format the chart in the chart sheet using the same tools and commands as you use to format a chart embedded in a worksheet. You can rename and move the chart sheet the same way as you rename and move a worksheet.

16-2b Repositioning and Resizing a Chart

An embedded chart might cover other data in the worksheet or be placed in an awkward location. You can reposition and resize the embedded chart to better fit on the worksheet. To do so, first select the chart. A selection box, which you use to reposition or resize the object, surrounds the chart. To reposition the chart, drag the selection box to a new location in the worksheet. To resize the chart, drag a sizing handle on the selection box to change the object's width and height. See Exhibit 16-8.

Begin Activity

Reposition and resize a chart.

1 Point to an **empty part of the chart** until the pointer changes to and the ScreenTip Chart Area appears.

Exhibit 16-8 Pie chart repositioned and resized

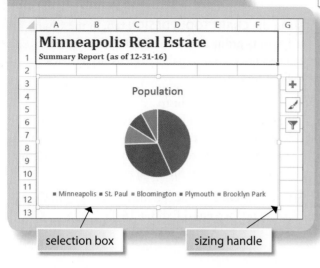

selection box

sizing handle

2 Click the **chart area**, drag to the left until the chart's upper-left corner is in cell A3, and then release the mouse button. The chart moves to a new location.

> **Problem?** If the chart resizes or other chart elements move, undo your last action, and then repeat Steps 1 through 3, being sure to drag the pie chart from the chart area.

3 Point to the **sizing handle** in the lower-right corner of the chart until the pointer changes to ⬉.

> **Tip:** To maintain the aspect ratio of the chart as you resize it, hold down the Shift key as you drag the sizing handle.

4 Drag the **sizing handle** up to cell F12. The chart resizes to cover the range A3:F12 and remains selected. (It's okay if the chart extends into the next row or column.) Refer to Exhibit 16-8.

End Activity

16-3 Modifying a Chart

After you create a chart, you can change its style and layout. You can also choose which chart elements to include with the chart and change how each element is formatted. This flexibility enables you to create a chart that best conveys its data. It also lets you create a chart with a look and feel that suits your intended readers.

16-3a Changing the Chart Style

When you create a chart, the chart is formatted with the default chart style for that chart type. For example, the default pie chart style applies a solid color to each slice. You can modify the appearance of a chart by applying a different **chart style** to the chart.

The chart styles are located in the Chart Styles gallery, which is available on the CHART TOOLS DESIGN tab or by clicking the Chart Styles button ⬚ next to the selected chart. See Exhibit 16-9. There are both two-dimensional and three-dimensional chart styles. The 3-D chart styles provide the illusion of depth and distance, which makes the charts appear to stand out on the page and add visual interest. Live Preview shows how each of the selected charts will look with the different chart styles.

Exhibit 16-9 Chart Styles gallery for pie charts

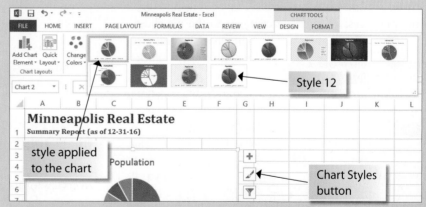

Style 12

style applied to the chart

Chart Styles button

For even more control over how a chart looks, you can select and format individual elements. To apply formatting to an individual chart element, double-click that chart element to open a pane with format options specific to the selected element.

> **chart style** A style that formats an entire chart at one time.

Change the chart style.

1 Make sure the **pie chart** is selected.

2 On the **CHART TOOLS DESIGN tab**, in the Chart Styles group, click the **More button** ⊽. The Chart Styles gallery opens. Refer back to Exhibit 16-9.

> **Tip:** You can also click the Chart Styles button 🖌 next to the selected chart to access the chart styles.

3 Point to different styles in the gallery. Live Preview shows the impact of each chart style on the pie chart's appearance.

4 Click **Style 12**. Each pie slice is now connected to the next slices without a white border between them.

16-3b Changing a Chart Layout

Chart layouts provide different options for displaying and arranging chart elements. These layouts specify which chart elements are displayed and how they are formatted. The chart layouts include some of the most common ways of displaying different charts. Each chart type has its own collection of layouts. For a pie chart, the chart layout you choose may hide or display the chart title, display a chart legend or place legend labels in the pie slices, and add percentages to the pie slices.

The chart layouts are available by clicking the Quick Layout button in the Chart Layouts group on the CHART TOOLS DESIGN tab. See Exhibit 16-10.

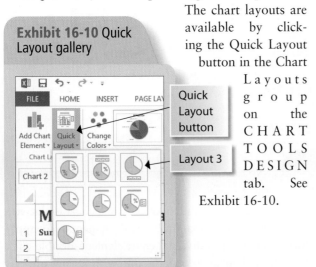

Exhibit 16-10 Quick Layout gallery

chart layout An option for displaying and arranging chart elements.

Change the chart layout.

1 On the **CHART TOOLS DESIGN tab**, in the Chart Layouts group, click the **Quick Layout button**. The Quick Layout gallery opens. Refer back to Exhibit 16-10.

2 In the first row, point to **Layout 3** (the third layout). Live Preview shows the impact of the layout on the pie chart's appearance. The chart title is removed from the chart, and the pie chart resizes to fill the space.

3 Click **Layout 3** to change the chart's layout. Compare your screen to Exhibit 16-11.

Exhibit 16-11 Pie chart with new chart style and layout

16-3c Positioning and Formatting a Chart Title

The chart title provides a description of a chart or an overview of its purpose. It is one of the chart elements that can be included in a pie chart. You can add or remove the chart title by clicking the Chart Elements button ➕ next to the selected chart, and then clicking the Chart Title check box. See Exhibit 16-12. When you create a chart, Excel uses the data series label as the chart title. You can edit or replace this default chart title. You can also format the text of the chart title just like you can format any text.

Exhibit 16-12 Chart title updated and formatted

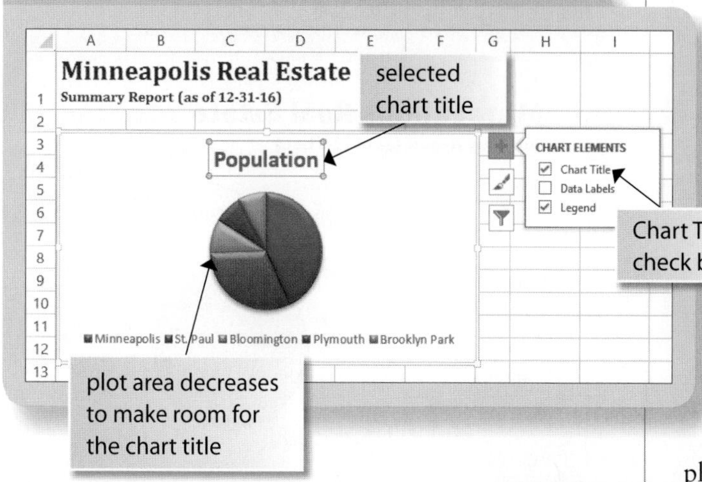

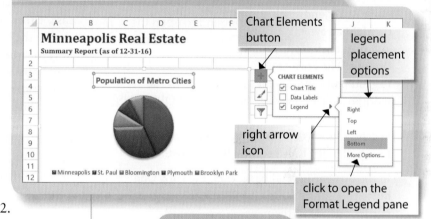

- selected chart title
- Chart Title check box
- plot area decreases to make room for the chart title

Elements button ⊞ next to the selected chart to open the CHART ELEMENTS menu, point to Legend to display the right arrow ▶ next to the Legend option, click the right arrow ▶, and then click one of the placement options—Right, Top, Left, or Bottom. Live Preview shows the legend placement when you point to an option. See Exhibit 16-13.

If you click More Options, the Format Legend pane opens at the right side of the workbook window. The Format pane provides additional options for formatting the selected element's appearance. In this case, because the legend is selected, the page is labeled "Format Legend" and includes options for formatting the legend's fill, border, effects (shadow, glow, and soft edges), placement, and text. See Exhibit 16-14.

Begin Activity

Replace and position a chart title.

1 Click the **Chart Elements button** ⊞ next to the selected chart. A menu with the available chart elements for the selected chart appears. Notice that only the Legend check box is selected, as this is the only element currently on the chart.

2 Click the **Chart Title check box**. The chart title is added to the chart and a selection box appears around the chart title. Refer back to Exhibit 16-12.

3 In the **chart title**, click after *Population*, press the **Spacebar**, and then type **of Metro Cities**.

> **Tip:** You can replace all of the title text in the selected selection box by typing and then pressing the Enter key.

4 Click the border of the **chart title selection box** to select the entire box.

5 Change the font size to **12 points**. The chart title reduces in size, and the pie chart increases in size to fill the extra space.

End Activity

16-3d Positioning the Chart Legend

The chart legend identifies each of the data series in the chart. With a pie chart, the legend shows the color used for each slice and its corresponding category value. In this case, the category values are the different cities. You can choose where to position the legend. Click the Chart

Exhibit 16-13 Legend options in the Chart Elements button menu

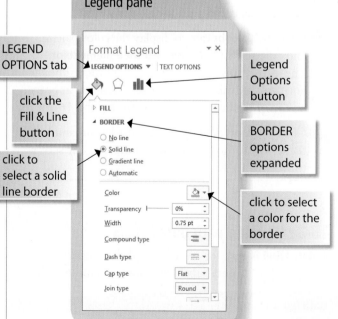

- Chart Elements button
- legend placement options
- right arrow icon
- click to open the Format Legend pane

Exhibit 16-14 Format Legend pane

- LEGEND OPTIONS tab
- Legend Options button
- click the Fill & Line button
- click to select a solid line border
- BORDER options expanded
- click to select a color for the border

Position the chart legend.

1 Next to the selected chart, click the **Chart Elements button** ⊞. The CHART ELEMENTS menu appears next to the chart.

2 Point to **Legend** to display the right arrow ▶ next to the Legend option.

3 Click the **right arrow** ▶ to display the placement options. Refer back to Exhibit 16-13.

4 Click **Left**. The legend moves to the left side of the chart.

5 If necessary, click the **Chart Elements button** ⊞ next to the selected chart.

6 On the CHART ELEMENTS menu, point to **Legend**, click the **right arrow** ▶, and then click **More Options**. The Format Legend pane appears on the right side of the workbook window with the LEGEND OPTIONS tab selected. On the LEGEND OPTIONS tab, the Legend Options button ▥ is selected, and the LEGEND OPTIONS section is expanded.

> **Tip:** You can also double-click the legend to open the Format Legend pane.

7 In the Format Legend pane, click the **Fill & Line button** ◇, and then click **BORDER** to display the border options in the pane.

8 Click the **Solid line option button**. The additional line options in the pane are now available.

9 Click the **Color button** to display the color palette, and then select the **Orange, Accent 6 theme color**. The legend now has a dark orange border, although you can't see this because the selection box appears on top of the border. Refer back to Exhibit 16-14.

10 Click the **chart area** to deselect the legend and better see the formatted border. Compare your screen to Exhibit 16-15.

16-3e Working with Data Labels

A **data label** is text for an individual data marker, such as a pie slice. A data label can show a value or other

data label Text for an individual data marker.

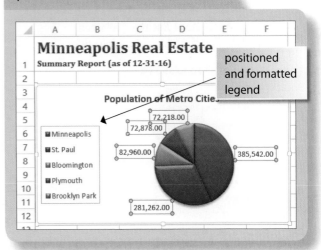

Exhibit 16-15 Chart legend positioned and formatted

descriptive text. When you use a chart layout that shows data labels, each label is placed where it best fits—in this case, either on the pie slice or along its side. You can change the label placement so that all data labels appear next to their pie slices. Labels placed outside of the pie might appear far from their slices. In those cases, Excel adds leader lines to connect each data label to its corresponding data marker. A leader line is not used when enough space exists in the chart area to place a label next to its slice. The data label placement options are available on the Data Labels submenu OF CHART ELEMENTS menu. Additional data label options are available in the Format Data Labels pane. See Exhibit 16-16.

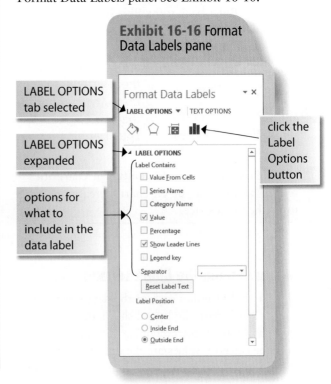

Exhibit 16-16 Format Data Labels pane

Format data labels.

1 Click the **Chart Elements button** [+] next to the selected chart, and then click **Data Labels**. The data labels are added to each pie slice.

2 Point to **Data Labels**, click the **right arrow** [▶], and then click **Outside End**. This option sets the data labels outside the pie chart.

3 Point to **Data Labels**, click the **right arrow** [▶], and then click **More Options**. The pane on the right changes to the Format Data Labels pane.

> **Tip:** You can also open the Format pane by double-clicking a chart element.

4 Click the **LABEL OPTIONS tab** if it is not already selected.

5 Click the **Label Options button** [▮▮] if it is not already selected, and then click **LABEL OPTIONS** below the buttons to expand that section. Refer back to Exhibit 16-16. In the Label Contains section, the Value and the Show Leader Lines check boxes are already checked because these are the default data label options. These options set the data labels to display as the values in the data source and use leader lines when needed to connect the labels with their corresponding pie slices.

6 In the Label Contains section, click the **Value check box** to deselect it. The value data labels are removed from the chart.

7 Click the **Percentage check box**. The data values are displayed as percentages of the whole. Even though the Show Leader Lines check box is selected, the lines don't appear on the chart because the chart area has enough space to place the labels close to their slices.

8 In the Format Data labels pane, click **LABEL OPTIONS** to collapse that section. Click **NUMBER** to expand that section and display options related to formatting numbers.

9 Click the **Category box arrow**, and then click **Percentage**. The data labels appear as percentages on the outer edges of the slices. Compare your screen to Exhibit 16-17.

Exhibit 16-17 Formatted data labels

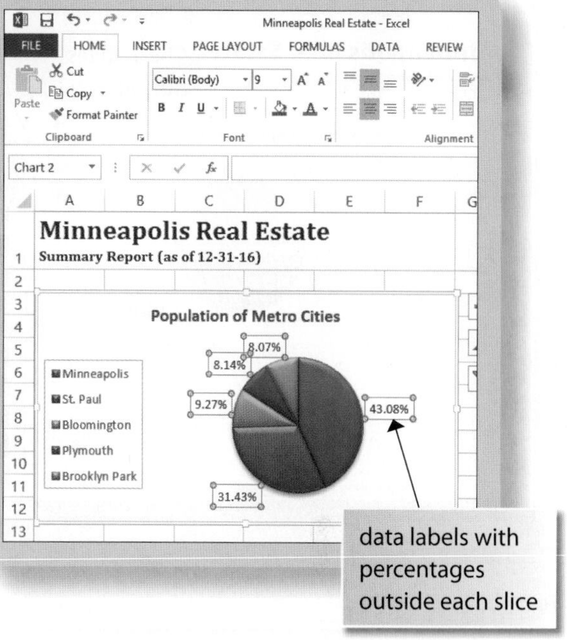

data labels with percentages outside each slice

16-3f Changing the Color of a Data Series

The data series is the range of values plotted on the chart. The values in each data series are plotted as a single unit on a chart. Usually, you use one color for an entire data series. However, in a pie chart, you want each slice to have a different color or a distinct shade of the same color so that the slices are easy to distinguish.

Pie slice colors should be as distinct as possible to avoid confusion. Using distinct colors is especially important for adjacent slices. Depending on the printer quality or the monitor resolution, similarly colored slices might be difficult to distinguish. You can change all of the pie slice colors at once by clicking the Chart Styles button [🖉] next to the selected chart, clicking COLOR at the top of the menu, and then clicking the set of colors you want to use. See Exhibit 16-18.

You can also change the color of each slice in a pie chart individually. To select an individual slice, you first click the pie chart slices to select the entire data series, and then you click the specific slice you want to select. The Format pane changes to the Format Data Point pane, and you can use the FILL options in the pane to select the fill you want to use for the selected slice. See Exhibit 16-19. You can also use the Fill Color button in the Font group on the HOME tab to change the fill color.

Exhibit 16-18 Pie chart color options

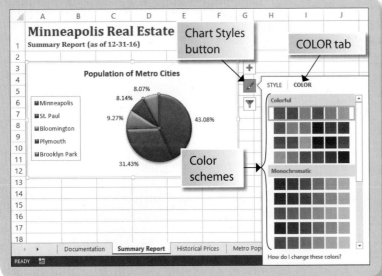

Begin Activity

Change the color of a data series.

1 Next to the selected chart, click the **Chart Styles button** 🖌, and then click **COLOR** at the top of the menu. The available color schemes appear in the gallery. Refer back to Exhibit 16-18.

2 Point to the different color sets to see a Live Preview of the selection on the pie chart, and then click **Color 3**. The slices and the legend colors change color to reflect the selected color scheme.

3 Click the **pie chart** to select the entire data series (you will see the ScreenTip *Series "Population" Point . . .* followed by whichever point you clicked on the pie chart).

4 Click the dark purple **Brooklyn Park slice**, which represents 8.07 percent of the pie. Only that value, or slice, is selected. The pane to the right of the worksheet window changes to the For-mat Data Point pane.

5 Click the **Fill & Line button** 🖌 to display the fill and border options.

6 Click **Fill** to expand the list of fill options in the pane.

7 Click the **Solid fill option button**. Click the **Color button** to display the color palette, and then select the **Olive Green, Accent 3 theme color**. The Brooklyn Park slice and legend marker change to olive green. Each pie slice now has a distinct color. Refer back to Exhibit 16-19.

> **Tip:** You can also use the Fill Color button in the Font group on the HOME tab to change the font color of a selected data series or data point.

8 In the Format Data Point pane, click the **Close button** ☒. The task pane closes.

End Activity

Exhibit 16-19 Format Data Point pane and Pie slices with new colors

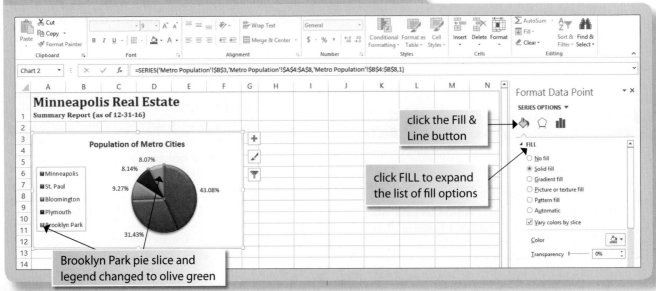

16-4 Creating an Exploded Pie Chart

Pie slices do not need to be fixed within the pie. An **exploded pie chart** moves one slice away from the others as if someone were taking the piece away from the pie. Exploded pie charts are useful for emphasizing one category above all of the others. For example, to emphasize how much of a state's population is located in a specific city, you could explode that single slice, moving it away from the other slices in the pie. See Exhibit 16-20.

Exhibit 16-20 Exploded pie chart

To explode a pie slice, select that slice from the pie chart and then drag the slice away from the pie. You can also explode multiple slices by selecting each slice and dragging them away. To explode all of the slices, select the entire pie and drag the pointer away from the pie's center. Each slice will be exploded and separated from the others. Although you can explode more than one slice, the resulting pie chart is rarely effective as a visual aid to the reader.

Begin Activity

Create an exploded pie chart.

1 Click the **pie chart**. The entire data series is selected as indicated by the sizing handles on each pie slice.

2 Click the light red **Minneapolis slice** to select that slice.

3 Drag the selected **Minneapolis slice** to the right approximately one-half inch. The slice is separated from the rest of the pie chart. Refer to Exhibit 16-20.

End Activity

16-5 Creating a Column or Bar Chart

A **column chart** displays values in different categories as columns; the height of each column is based on its value. A **bar chart** is a column chart turned on its side so that the length of each bar is based on its value. Each data series has columns or bars of the same color.

Column and bar charts apply to a wider range of data than pie charts. For example, you can show how a set of values changes over time, such as housing prices over several years. You can also include several data series in a column or bar chart, such as the populations of five cities over several years. The values from different data series are displayed in columns side by side. Pie charts usually show only one data series.

16-5a Inserting a Column Chart

The process for creating a column chart is the same as for creating any other chart. First, you select the data source. Then, you select the type of chart you want to create. After the chart is embedded in the worksheet, you can move and resize the chart as well as change the chart's design, layout, and format.

Begin Activity

Create a column chart.

1 Make the **Structures Types worksheet** the active sheet. Select the **range A3:C12**.

2 On the ribbon, click the **INSERT tab**. In the Charts group, click the **Insert Column Chart button** 📊▼. The gallery shows the different column charts you can create.

> **exploded pie chart** A pie chart where one slice is moved away from the pie.
>
> **column chart** A chart that displays values in different categories as columns so that the height of each column is based on its value.
>
> **bar chart** A column chart that is turned on its side so that the length of each bar is based on its value.

3 In the 2-D Column section, click the **Clustered Column chart** (the first chart). The column chart is inserted in the active worksheet, and the CHART TOOLS DESIGN tab is selected on the ribbon.

4 On the CHART TOOLS DESIGN tab, in the Location group, click the **Move Chart button**. The Move Chart dialog box opens.

5 Click the **Object in box arrow**, click **Summary Report**, and then click **OK**. The column chart moves to the Summary Report worksheet and is still selected.

6 In the Summary Report worksheet, drag the selected column chart down so its upper-left corner is in **cell A14**.

7 Drag the **lower-right sizing handle** until the chart covers the **range A14:F27**. The chart is resized smaller. Compare your screen to Exhibit 16-21.

End Activity

Pie Chart or Column Chart?

Column and bar charts are better than pie charts when the number of categories is large or the categories are close in value. It is easier to compare height or length than area. When data includes more than six categories, a pie chart cannot display the categories effectively. Instead, you should create a column chart to display the data. Below, the same data is shown as a pie chart and as a column chart. As you can see, it is more difficult to determine which pie slice has the largest area and by how much. This is much simpler to determine with the column chart.

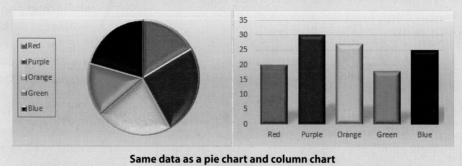

Same data as a pie chart and column chart

16-5b Formatting a Column Chart

The process for formatting a chart is the same for each type of chart, although the specific formats and options available reflect the current chart type. The CHART TOOLS DESIGN tab provides a gallery of column chart layouts and a gallery of column chart styles and access to the individual chart elements you can include on the column chart. The CHART TOOLS FORMAT tab provides options to change the appearance of a column chart by formatting these chart elements.

You have already seen how to add and remove chart elements, change the chart color scheme, and change the color of one value in a data series. You can also format an entire data series at once. For example, in a column chart, you can change the amount of space between the columns or change the way the columns look by changing their inside color (or fill). One option is to fill the columns with a gradient—shading in which one color blends into another or varies from one shade to another. To format a data series in a column chart, double-click any column in the series you want to change to open the Format Data Series pane. You can then click the Series Options button to display the tab on which you can adjust the amount of space between the columns. See Exhibit 16-22. To change the fill color of columns, you click the Fill & Line button in the Format Data Series pane.

Exhibit 16-21 Column chart of structure types

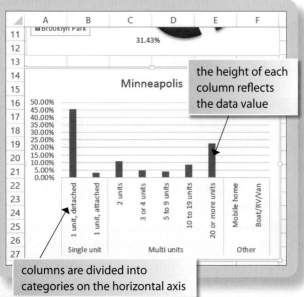

the height of each column reflects the data value

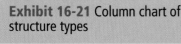
columns are divided into categories on the horizontal axis

Exhibit 16-22 Format Data Series pane

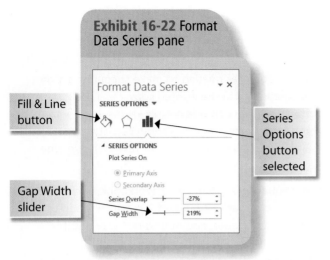

Fill & Line button

Series Options button selected

Gap Width slider

Begin Activity

Format a column chart.

1 In the column chart, click the **chart title** to select it.

2 Change the font size of the chart title to **12 points**.

3 Enter **Structure Types** as the new chart title.

4 In the column chart, double-click **any column**. All of the columns for the data series in the chart are selected, and the Format Data Series pane opens.

5 Click the **Series Option button** if it is not already selected. The Series Options are displayed in the Format pane. Refer back to Exhibit 16-22.

6 Drag the **Gap Width slider** to the left until the value in the Gap Width box is **50%**. The gap between adjacent columns is reduced, and the columns become wider to fill the space.

> **Problem?** If you cannot drag the Gap width slider to exactly 50%, select the value in the Gap Width box below the slider, type **50**, and then press the **Enter key**.

7 In the Format Data Series pane, click the **Fill & Line button**. If the fill options are not expanded, click **FILL**.

8 Click the **Gradient fill option button** to fill the columns with a gradually changing mix of colors.

9 Click the **Direction button** to display a gallery of gradient directions. Click **Linear Up** (the second option in the second row). The columns are filled with a gradient that blends to the top. Compare your screen to Exhibit 16-23.

End Activity

Exhibit 16-23 Formatted column chart

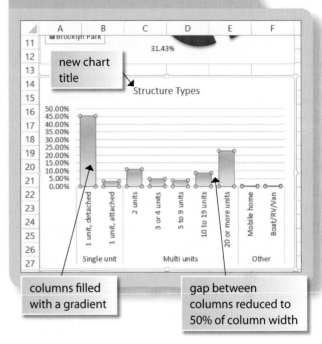

new chart title

columns filled with a gradient

gap between columns reduced to 50% of column width

FYI

Formatting a Data Point

In a pie chart, each slice or data marker has a different format. In a column chart, all of the columns usually have the same format because the columns are distinguished by height, not color. However, you can format individual columns in a data series to highlight a particular value. For example, you can change the color of one column, as shown here. You can also modify the appearance of the data markers in a column chart using any of the standard formatting options, including fonts, sizes, colors, and bold.

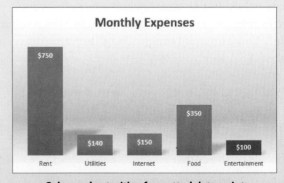

Column chart with a formatted data point

Communicating Effectively with Charts

Studies show that people interpret information more easily in a graphic form than in a tabular format. As a result, charts can help communicate the real story underlying the facts and figures you present to colleagues and clients. A well-designed chart can illuminate the bigger picture that might be hidden by viewing only the numbers. However, poorly designed charts can mislead readers and make it more difficult to interpret data.

To create effective and useful charts, keep in mind the following tips as you design charts:

▶ **Keep it simple.** Do not clutter a chart with too many graphic elements. Focus attention on the data rather than on decorative elements that do not inform.

▶ **Focus on the message.** Design the chart to highlight the points you want to convey to readers.

▶ **Limit the number of data series.** Most charts should display no more than four or five data series. Pie charts should have no more than six slices.

▶ **Choose colors carefully.** Display different data series in contrasting colors to make it easier to distinguish one series from another. Modify the default colors as needed to make them distinct on the screen and in the printed copy.

▶ **Limit the chart to a few text styles.** Use a maximum of two or three different text styles in the same chart. Having too many text styles in one chart can distract attention from the data.

Remember, everything in a workbook, including worksheets and charts, should inform the reader in the simplest, most accurate, and most direct way possible.

StockLite/Shutterstock.com

16-5c Changing the Axis Scale

Chart data is plotted along axes. The **vertical (value) axis** shows the range of values from all of the data series plotted on the chart. The **horizontal (category) axis** shows the category values from each data series. The range of values, or **scale**, of an axis is based on the values in the data source.

The scale usually ranges from 0 through the maximum value. If the scale includes negative values, it ranges from the minimum value through the maximum value. You can modify the scale of the vertical axis to make it easier to read.

The labels on the vertical (value) axis identify intervals along the axis. For example, an axis whose scale is 0 through 50 might have labels identifying intervals every five units, as in 0, 5, 10, 15, 20, and so on. You can change this interval by changing the units. For example, you could specify that the axis labels appear every 10 units, as in 0, 10, 20, and so on. Keep in mind that more labels at smaller intervals, but fewer labels at larger intervals could make the chart less informative.

By default, no titles appear next to the axes. This is fine when the axis labels are self-explanatory. Otherwise, you can add descriptive axis titles. In general, you should avoid adding extra chart elements such as axis titles when that information is easily understood from other parts of the chart.

The axis options are available in the Format Axis pane. See Exhibit 16-24. The label Auto next to some options indicates that Excel set automatic values based on the values represented in the chart. The Bounds section indicates the minimum and maximum values that appear on the selected axis. The Units section indicates the intervals at which the values appear in the chart.

---

vertical (value) axis The axis along the side of the chart that shows the range of values from all of the data series plotted on the chart.

horizontal (category) axis The axis along the bottom of the chart that shows the category values from each data series.

scale The range of values along an axis.

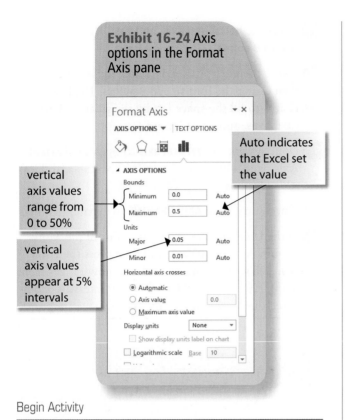

Exhibit 16-24 Axis options in the Format Axis pane

vertical axis values range from 0 to 50%

vertical axis values appear at 5% intervals

Auto indicates that Excel set the value

5 In the Format Axis pane, click AXIS OPTIONS to collapse that section, and then click **NUMBER** to expand the NUMBER section. In the Category box, Percentage is selected. This is the current format of the numbers on the vertical axis.

6 In the Decimal places box, select **2**, type **0**, and then press the **Enter key**. The percentages now show only integers. The percentages on the vertical axis range from 0 percent to 50 percent in 10 percent intervals with no decimal places. The vertical axis is still selected.

7 On the ribbon, click the **HOME tab**, and then change the font size to **8 points**. The values displayed in the vertical axis are smaller, leaving more room for the data series.

8 On the horizontal axis, click **any of the labels**. A selection box appears around all the labels on the horizontal axis.

9 Change the font size of the text on the horizontal axis to **8 points**. Compare your screen to Exhibit 16-25.

10 Close the **Format Axis pane**.

End Activity

Begin Activity

Change the axis scale and title.

1 In the column chart, click **any value on the vertical axis** (the list of percentages). The Format Data Series pane changes to the Format Axis pane.

Tip: If no pane is open, double-click a chart element to open its corresponding pane.

2 If they are not already selected, click the **AXIS OPTIONS tab**, and then the **Axis Options button** 📊. Refer back to Exhibit 16-24.

3 If the Axis Options section is not expanded, click **AXIS OPTIONS**. Note that in the Bounds section, the minimum value of the axis is set to 0 and the maximum value is set to 0.5, or 50 percent. This matches the values listed on the vertical axis. In the Units section, 0.05 appears in the Major box, indicating that the values on the vertical axis will appear every five percentage points.

4 In the Units section, select the current value in the Major box, type **0.10**, and then press the **Enter key**. The values on the vertical axis change from showing 5 percent intervals to 10 percent intervals.

vertical axis scale ranges from 0% to 50% in 10% intervals

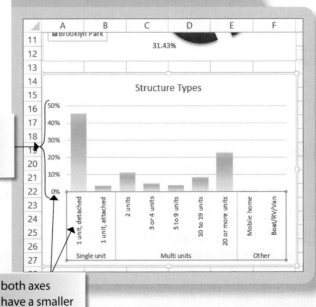

Exhibit 16-25 Formatted chart axes

both axes have a smaller font size

16-6 Creating a Line Chart

A line chart displays data values using a connected line rather than columns or bars. Line charts are typically used when the data consists of values drawn from categories that follow a sequential order at evenly spaced intervals, as with historical data in which the data values are recorded periodically such as monthly, quarterly, or yearly. Each data series has a different line color. Line charts are also commonly used instead of column charts when there are many data points across several data series. For example, when there are 40 data points across three data series, a column chart of this data would be difficult to read and interpret, whereas a line chart more clearly conveys this data.

16-6a Inserting and Formatting a Line Chart

The process for creating a line chart is the same as for creating pie charts and column charts, though the specific options available differ a bit. A data marker for a line chart can appear with or without the connecting line.

Begin Activity

Create and format a line chart.

1 Make the **Historical Prices worksheet** the active sheet. Select the **range A3:D56**.

2 On the ribbon, click the **INSERT tab**. In the Charts group, click **Insert Line Chart button**. In the 2-D Line section, click the **Line chart**. A line chart is embedded in the Historical Prices worksheet.

3 Move the line chart to the **Summary Report worksheet**. Reposition and resize the chart to cover the **range H3:M13**.

> **Problem?** If you don't see the chart on the Summary Report worksheet, scroll the worksheet down.

4 In the line chart, replace the **chart title** with **Price History**.

5 Change the font size of the chart title to **12 points**.

6 Click the **vertical axis** to select it, and then change its font size to **8 points**.

7 Select the **horizontal axis**, and then change its font size to **8 points**.

8 Below the horizontal axis, select the **legend**, and then change its font size to **8 points**. The line chart resizes to fill the space left by the smaller chart title, axes, and chart legend.

9 Double-click the **vertical axis** to open the Format Axis pane with the AXIS OPTIONS tab and the Axis Options button selected.

10 If necessary, click **AXIS OPTIONS** to expand that list.

11 In the Units section, select the value in the Minimum box, type **100000**, and then press the **Enter key**. The scale of the vertical axis now ranges from $100,000 to $400,000 in $50,000 intervals. Compare your screen to Exhibit 16-26.

End Activity

Exhibit 16-26 Formatted line chart

vertical axis scale ranges from $100,000 to $400,000 in $50,000 intervals

line chart with three data series

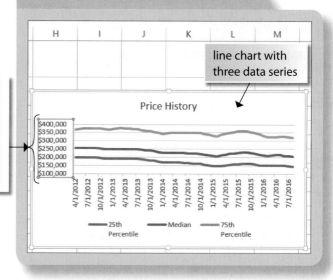

16-6b Editing the Axis Scale and Labels in a Line Chart

When a chart involves large numbers, the axis labels can take up a lot of the available chart area and be difficult to read. You can simplify the chart's appearance by displaying units of measure more appropriate to the data values. For example, you can display the value 20 to represent 20,000 or 20,000,000. This is particularly useful when space is at a premium, such as in an embedded chart confined to a small area of the worksheet. In Exhibit 16-27, the vertical axis in the

line chart A chart that displays data values using a connected line rather than columns or bars.

Exhibit 16-27 Rescaled vertical axis

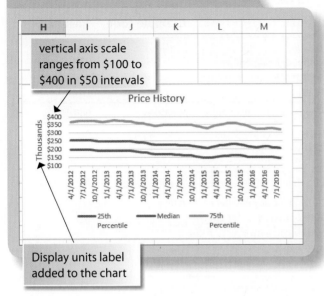

vertical axis scale ranges from $100 to $400 in $50 intervals

Display units label added to the chart

Price History chart on the left is scaled from $100,000 to $400,000 in intervals of $50,000. The chart on the right is easier to read and understand because the display unit is Thousands allowing the vertical axis to be scaled from $100 through $400 in intervals of $50. When you select the display units, such as Thousands, you can choose to show the display unit in a label next to the axis.

LEARN MORE

Creating a Combination Chart

A **combination chart** combines two or more chart types in a single graph, such as a column chart and a line chart. To create a combination chart, first select the data series in an existing chart that you want to appear as another chart type. Then, on the CHART TOOLS DESIGN tab, in the Type group, click the Change Chart Type button, click the chart type you want to apply to the selected series, and then click OK. The selected series changes to the new chart type on the chart, leaving the other data series in its original format.

Begin Activity

Change the scale of the vertical axis.

1 Make sure the vertical axis is still selected, and the Format Axis pane is still open displaying the AXIS OPTIONS section. In the Format Axis pane, the value in the Display units box is None, and the Show display units label on chart check box is not selected.

2 In the Format Axis pane, click the **Display units box arrow**, and then click **Thousands**. The values on the vertical axis change from $100,000 to $400,000 in intervals of $50,000 to $100 through $400 in intervals of $50. The Show display units label on chart check box is now selected and the display units label *Thousands* was added, indicating that the values are expressed in units of 1,000. Refer back to Exhibit 16-27.

End Activity

In addition to numbers, a scale can be based on dates, as the horizontal axis is in the Price History line chart. As with numerical scales, you can set the minimum and maximum dates to use in the scale's range. You can also set the major and minor units as days, months, or years to use for the scale's interval. This is helpful when the data source includes exact dates, but the chart trends only need to show years. Also as with numeric scales, you can specify the intervals.

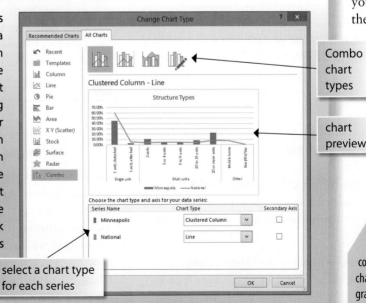

Combo chart types

chart preview

select a chart type for each series

Change Chart Type dialog box

combination chart A chart that combines two or more chart types in a single graph, such as a column chart and a line chart.

Exhibit 16-28 shows the Format Axis pane with the Axis Options button selected for an axis that shows dates. You can change it from showing four months per year—currently specified by the unit 3 months in the Major row in the Units section—to any other interval and unit you specify. For example, if the axis is divided into too many units, you could specify that labels identify markers every two years.

Exhibit 16-28
Horizontal axis options in the Format Axis pane

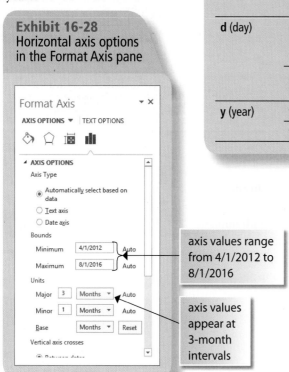

To change the way a time or date unit is displayed, you need to change the format code. Format codes use the letters m, d, and y to signify month, day, and year. Examples of format codes are shown in Exhibit 16-29.

Begin Activity

Edit axis scale and labels.

1 In the chart, double-click the **horizontal axis**. The Format Axis pane changes to show the options for the dates on the horizontal axis. Refer back to Exhibit 16-28.

2 In the Format Axis pane, in the Units section, select the value in the Major box, and then type **2**.

3 Click the **Major box arrow** (the box currently contains Months), and then click **Years**. The units on

Exhibit 16-29 Examples for format codes

Code	Description	Example code	Result
m (month)	m = one digit for months January through September, two digits for October through December	m/d/yy	4/1/16
	mm = two digits for all months	mm/dd/yy	04/01/16
	mmm = standard three-letter text abbreviation for month names	mmm d, yyyy	Apr 1, 2016
	mmmm = full text month name	mmmm d, yyyy	April 1, 2016
d (day)	d = one digit for day numbers 1 through 9, two digits for day numbers 10 and above	m/d/yy	4/1/16
	dd = two digits for all day numbers	mmmm dd, yyyy	April 01, 2016
y (year)	yy = two digits for all years	m/d/yy	4/1/16
	yyyy = four digits for all years	mm/dd/yyyy	04/01/2016

the horizontal axis change to indicate every two years. Because you are using years as the labels, the months and days in the labels are not needed.

4 In the Format Axis pane, click **AXIS OPTIONS** to collapse this section, and then click **NUMBER** to expand that section. In the Category box, Date is selected. In the Format Code box, *m/d/yyyy* appears, indicating the dates will be displayed in the format 4/1/2016.

5 In the Format Code box, change the code to **yyyy**, and then to the right of the Format Code box, click **Add**. The format of the dates on the horizontal axis changes to display only the year. Compare your screen to Exhibit 16-30.

6 Close the Format Axis pane.

End Activity

16-6c Adding and Formatting an Axis Title

An axis title is descriptive text that appears next to the axis values. An axis title can provide additional information that is not covered in the chart title. It can include information about the source of the data and the units in which the data is measured. You can choose how the axis title appears on the chart by clicking the Chart Elements button, pointing to Axis Titles, clicking the right arrow button ▶, and then selecting an option on the Axis Titles submenu.

Exhibit 16-30 Axis label based on the format code

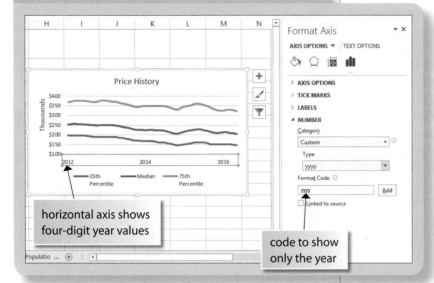

horizontal axis shows four-digit year values

code to show only the year

Begin Activity

Add and format an axis title.

1 To the right of the line chart, click the **Chart Elements button** [+]. The Axis Titles check box is not selected.

2 Point to **Axis Titles**, and then click the **right arrow** [▶]. Options for adding the Primary Horizontal and Primary Vertical titles appear on the submenu.

3 Click the **Primary Vertical check box**. A title is added to the vertical axis above the units label.

4 Replace **Axis Title** with **Prices in Thousands**. The descriptive title is entered.

5 Change the font size of the axis title to **8 points**. With the added axis title, there is no need for the display units label.

6 Click **Thousands** (the units label), and then press the **Delete key**.

End Activity

LEARN MORE

Custom Number and Date Formats

You can create custom formats for all types of numbers. One application of a custom format is to add text to a number, which is often used to include the units of measure alongside the value, such as 10k to indicate 10,000, 20k to indicate 20,000, and so forth. To add text to a value, you use the custom format

value"text"

where value is the number format applied to the value, and text is the text to include next to the value. The text must be placed within quotation marks. For example, the format to display integers with a comma as a thousands separator is

#,##0

The # sign is a placeholder for a number; the 0 indicates that a 0 will appear if there is not a number in that position. To change this to a format that displays the letter k at the end of the value, the custom format would be

#,##0"k"

FYI

Overlaying Chart Titles and Legends

You can overlay chart titles and legends in the chart area, which means they are placed on top of the chart. Overlaying these elements makes more space for the plot area because the chart does not resize to make room for that element. An overlaid chart element floats in the chart area and is not fixed to a particular position. This means that you can drag the chart element to a new location. This is helpful because when you overlay a chart element, it might overlap some of the chart contents. After you overlay an element, you might want to format it to make it easier to read. To overlay a chart title, click the Chart Elements button, point to Chart Title, click the right arrow button, and then click Centered Overlay. To overlay a legend, double-click the legend to open the Format Legend pane, and then select the Show the legend without overlapping the chart check box in the LEGEND OPTIONS section in the Legend Options.

16-6d Adding Gridlines

Gridlines extend the values of the major or minor units across the plot area. By default, horizontal gridlines appear on line charts and column charts. Each gridline is aligned with a major unit on the vertical axis. You can change the gridlines so that they appear for only the minor units, appear for both the major and minor units, or do not appear at all. The horizontal axis has these same gridline options. You select which gridlines to add to a chart with the Gridlines submenu on Chart Elements button menu. See Exhibit 16-31. Gridlines are similar to borders in that you can change their color and design style as well as add drop shadows or glowing color effects. The other options are available in the Format pane.

Begin Activity

Add gridlines to a chart.

1 To the right of the line chart, click the **Chart Elements button** ⊞, point to **Gridlines**, and then click **right arrow** ▶. The available gridlines appear in the submenu. The Primary Major Horizontal check box is selected. This corresponds to the

FYI

Understanding the Series Function

If you select a chart's series, the formula displayed in the formula bar uses the SERIES function. The SERIES function describes the content of a chart data series, and has the syntax

=SERIES(name, categories, values, order)

where *name* is the name that appears in the chart, *categories* are the labels that appear on the horizontal axis of the chart, *values* are the values that Excel plots for the data series, and *order* is the order in which the series appears in the chart. For example, a data series might be represented by the following SERIES function:

=SERIES(Sheet1!$D$1,Sheet1!$A$2:$A$9, Sheet1!$D$2:$D$9,3)

In this function, the name of the series is in cell D1 in the Sheet1 worksheet, the labels are in the range A2:A9 in the Sheet1 worksheet, the data values are in the

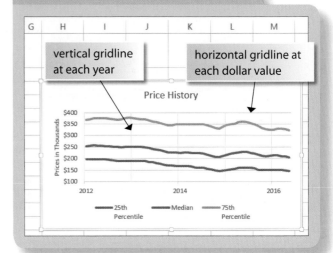

Exhibit 16-31 Gridlines added to the line chart

horizontal gridlines to the right of each dollar value in the line chart.

2 Click the **Primary Minor Vertical check box**. Faint vertical gridlines appear on the chart to indicate every year. Refer to Exhibit 16-31.

End Activity

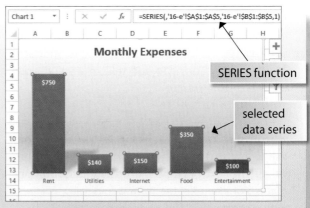

SERIES function for the selected data series

range D2:D9 in the Sheet1 worksheet, and the series is the third data series in the chart.

Although you can edit the SERIES function within the formula bar to make quick changes to your chart, the function is tied to an existing chart. It cannot be used within a worksheet cell or referenced from another Excel formula.

gridlines Lines that extend the values of the major or minor units across the plot area of a chart.

16-7 Editing Chart Data

Chart data can be edited and revised at any time. You do this by modifying the data range that the chart is based on, not by directly modifying the data in the chart. The change can be as simple as updating a specific value within the data source. Or it can be as involved as adding another data series to the chart.

16-7a Changing a Data Value or Label

Charts remain linked or connected to their data sources, even if they appear in different worksheets. If you change any value or label in the data source, the chart is automatically updated to show the new content. As a result, you can immediately see how changing one or more values affects the chart.

Begin Activity

Change a chart's data source.

1 In the **pie chart**, examine the Brooklyn Park pie slice. The data label for the slice indicates that it is 8.07% of the whole pie.

2 Make the **Metro Population worksheet** the active sheet.

3 In **cell B8**, change the value to **68610**.

4 Make the **Summary Report worksheet** the active sheet. The pie chart has been updated with the new data value, and the data label now indicates that the Brooklyn Park slice is 7.70% of the whole. Because the pie slices show percentages, not the actual data values, all the slices were updated to their new percentages.

End Activity

16-7b Adding a Data Series to an Existing Chart

You can modify a chart by adding a new data series. The new data series appears in the chart with a different set of data markers in the same way that the line chart you created had different data markers for each of the three different series. You modify a chart from the Select Data Source dialog box. See Exhibit 16-32. The left side lists the data series displayed in the chart. The right side lists the horizontal axis labels associated with each data series. You can add, edit, or remove any of these data series from the chart.

LEARN MORE

Chart Filters

You can apply chart filters to limit what data in the chart's data source is displayed in the chart. Click the Chart Filters button next to the selected chart to display a list of the data series and category values used in the chart. Click the corresponding check boxes to deselect them and then click Apply to hide the original data from the chart. The chart is recalculated to show only the checked categories or series. Filtering is helpful when you want to focus on only a subset of the original data.

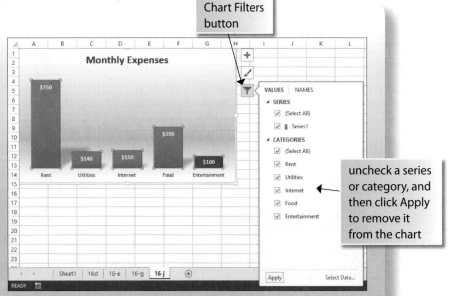

Chart Filters button menu

Exhibit 16-32 Select Data Source
dialog box

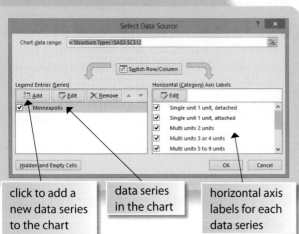

click to add a new data series to the chart

data series in the chart

horizontal axis labels for each data series

Begin Activity

Add a data series to an existing chart.

1 Click the **Structure Types column chart** to select it.

2 On the ribbon, click the **CHART TOOLS DESIGN tab**. In the Data group, click the **Select Data button**. The Select Data Source dialog box opens. Refer back to Exhibit 16-32.

3 Click the **Add button**. The Edit Series dialog box opens. In this dialog box, you specify the name of the new data series and its range of data values.

4 With the insertion point in the Series name box, click the **Structure Types sheet tab**, and then click **cell D3**, which is the cell containing the series name.

5 Press the **Tab key** to move the insertion point to the Series values box. In the worksheet, select the **range D4:D12**. See Exhibit 16-33.

Exhibit 16-33 Edit Series
dialog box

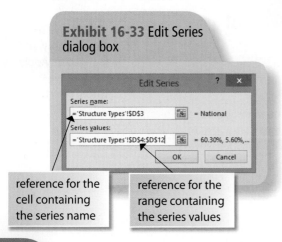

reference for the cell containing the series name

reference for the range containing the series values

6 Click **OK**. The Edit Series dialog box closes, and the Select Data Source dialog box reappears. The National data series is added to the list of data series in the chart.

7 Click **OK**. The National structure type values appear as red columns in the chart, next to the blue columns that indicate the Minneapolis structure types. Now that this chart contains more than one data series, the legend should be displayed.

8 To the right of the column chart, click the **Chart Elements button** ⊞, and then click the **Legend** check box. The legend is added to the right of the chart.

9 On the chart's selection box, drag the **middle-right sizing handle** to the right to expand the width of the chart to cover column H.

10 Drag the **chart** down one row so that the chart is positioned in the range A15:H28. Compare your screen to Exhibit 16-34.

End Activity

Exhibit 16-34 Column chart with
added data series

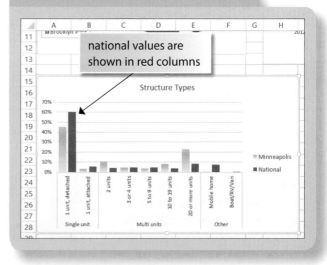

national values are shown in red columns

16-7c Modifying Lines and Data Markers

You can change the appearance of the lines and data markers in a line chart. You do this with the Marker Options in the Format Data Series pane. See Exhibit 16-35. For example, you can remove the lines connecting categories when they have no meaning. You can also change the shape and size of the marker itself, such as changing square markers to horizontal line markers at each data point.

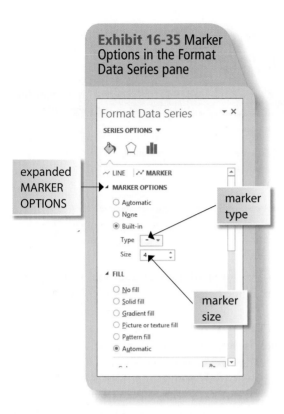

Exhibit 16-35 Marker Options in the Format Data Series pane

expanded MARKER OPTIONS

marker type

marker size

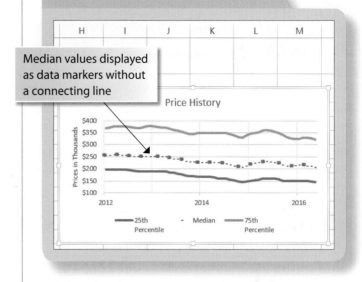

Exhibit 16-36 Line chart with lines and data markers

Median values displayed as data markers without a connecting line

Begin Activity

Modify lines and data markers.

1 In the **Price History line chart**, double-click the **red Median data series line** to select it. The Format Data Series pane appears.

2 In the Format Data Series pane, click the **Fill & Line button** ⬙. The options change to show the LINE tab selected and the LINE options expanded.

3 Click the **No line option button**. The line is removed from the chart and the MARKER tab appears in the Format Data Series pane.

4 In the Format Data Series pane, click the **MARKER tab**, and then click **MARKER OPTIONS** to expand that section.

5 Click the **Built-in option button**. You can now select the type and size of the marker.

6 Click the **Type box arrow**, and then click the **short horizontal line** (the sixth marker in the list).

7 Click the **Size down arrow** so 4 appears in the Size box. The Median values appear on the chart as data markers without a line. Compare your screen to Exhibit 16-36.

End Activity

16-8 Inserting and Formatting Sparklines

A **sparkline** is a chart that is displayed entirely within a cell. The goal of a sparkline is to convey a large amount of graphical information within a very small space. They don't include chart elements such as legends, titles, gridlines, or axes. You can create three types of sparklines:

▶ A line sparkline for highlighting trends

▶ A column sparkline for column charts

▶ A win/loss sparkline for highlighting positive and negative values

Exhibit 16-37 shows examples of each type of sparkline. The line sparklines show the sales history of each department and all four departments for a computer manufacturer. The sparklines show the recent temperature averages for four cities. Temperatures above 0°C are in blue columns; temperatures below 0°C are in red columns that extend downward. Finally, the win/loss sparklines reveal a snapshot of the season results for four sports teams. Wins are displayed in blue; losses are in red.

sparkline A graph that is displayed entirely within a cell.

Exhibit 16-37 Examples of sparklines

	A	B	C
1	Sales by Department		
2	(sales in millions)		
3	Department	Current	1-Year
4	Tablets	$ 29.40	
5	Printers	13.25	
6	Monitors	13.55	
7	Peripherals	11.75	
8	All Departments	$ 67.95	

line sparklines

	A	B	C
1	Temperature Record		
2	City	Yearly	Monthly
3	Seattle	37.7 °C	
4	Buenos Aires	54.0 °C	
5	Moscow	14.3 °C	
6	Melbourne	47.4 °C	

column sparklines

	A	B	C
1	Team	Record	Season
2	Cutler Tigers	10-2	
3	Apsburg Hawks	8-4	
4	Central City Spartans	6-6	
5	Liddleton Lions	3-9	

win/loss sparklines

Sparklines can be inserted anywhere within the workbook and can represent data from several rows or columns. To create a set of sparklines, you specify a data range containing the data you want to graph, and then you select a location range where you want the sparklines to appear in the Create Sparklines dialog box. See Exhibit 16-38. Note that the cells in which you insert the sparklines need not be blank. Sparklines are added as part of the cell background and do not replace any cell content.

The SPARKLINE TOOLS DESIGN tab provides options for formatting the appearance of sparklines. Sparklines can show data markers to identify the high and low points, negative points, first and last point, and all points. Just select the check boxes for the markers you want to display in the Show group. As with other charts, the Style gallery in the Style group provides

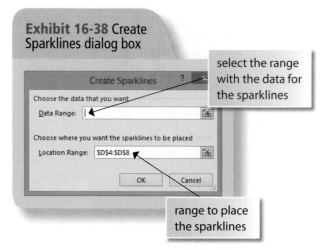

Exhibit 16-38 Create Sparklines dialog box

select the range with the data for the sparklines

range to place the sparklines

built-in styles for sparklines. In addition, you can specify the sparkline color and the marker color, which are also available in the Style group. The only other feature you can add to a sparkline is an axis, which for sparklines is simply a horizontal line that separates positive values from negative values. Click the Axis button in the Group group, and then click Show Axis. To remove sparklines from the worksheet, select the sparkline or sparklines to delete. On the SPARKLINE TOOLS DESIGN tab, in the Group group, click the Clear button.

Begin Activity

Insert and format sparklines.

1 Make the **Metro Population worksheet** the active sheet. Select the **range D4:D8**.

2 On the ribbon, click the **INSERT tab**. In the Sparklines group, click the **Line button**. The Create Sparklines dialog box opens with the insertion point in the Data Range box. The location range is already entered because you selected it before opening the dialog box. Refer back Exhibit 16-38.

3 With the insertion point in the Data Range box, click the **Population History sheet tab**, and then select the **range B4:E8** to enter the range that contains the data to chart.

> **Problem?** If you don't see the Population History sheet tab, to the left of the sheet tabs, click the **Next sheet button** ▶ as many times as needed to scroll the sheet tabs.

4 Click **OK**. The dialog box closes, and the Metro Population sheet tab is the current tab again. Sparklines are inserted into each cell in the selected location range D4:D8. The SPARKLINE TOOLS DESIGN tab appears on the ribbon and is the active tab.

5 On the SPARKLINE TOOLS DESIGN tab, in the Show group, click the **High Point check box** and the **Low Point check box** to display markers for the high and low points within each sparkline.

> **Tip:** On the SPARKLINE TOOLS DESIGN tab, in the Style group, click the Sparkline Color button to change the sparkline color and click the Marker Color button to change the data marker color.

6 On the SPARKLINE TOOLS DESIGN tab, in the Style group, click the **More button** ⏷. In the Style gallery, in the second row, click **Sparkline Style Accent 1, Darker 25%.** The line changes to a darker blue and the markers change to a darker red. Compare your screen to Exhibit 16-39.

End Activity

Sparkline Groups

Sparklines can be grouped or ungrouped. Grouped sparklines share a common format. Ungrouped sparklines can be formatted individually. When you create sparklines, all of the sparklines in the location range are part of a single group. Clicking any cell in the location range selects all of the sparklines in the group. Similarly, any formatting you apply affects all the sparklines in the group. This ensures that all the sparklines for related data are formatted consistently.

You can differentiate one sparkline in a group by formatting that sparkline differently. First, select the individual sparkline you want to format. Then, on the SPARKLINE TOOLS DESIGN tab, in the Group group, click the Ungroup button. The selected sparkline is split from the rest of the sparklines in the group. Finally, apply a unique format to the selected sparkline. To regroup the sparklines, select all of the cells in the location range containing sparklines, and then click the Group button in the Group group.

Exhibit 16-39 Sparklines with data markers

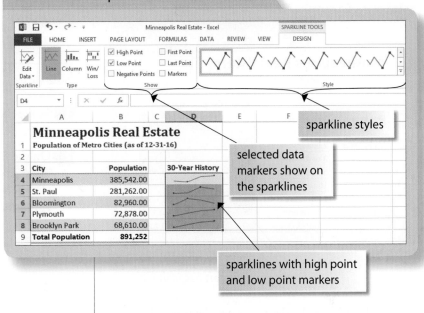

sparkline styles

selected data markers show on the sparklines

sparklines with high point and low point markers

16-9 Inserting and Modifying Data Bars

A **data bar** is conditional formatting that adds a horizontal bar to the background of a cell containing a number. When applied to a range of cells, the data bars have the same appearance as a bar chart with each cell containing one bar. The lengths of data bars are based on the values in the selected range. Cells with larger values have longer bars; cells with smaller values have shorter bars. See Exhibit 16-40. Data bars are dynamic, which means that if one cell's value changes, the lengths of the data bars in the selected range are automatically updated. When data bars are used with negative values, the data bars originate from the center of the cell with negative bars extending to the left and positive bars extending to the right.

> **data bar** Conditional formatting that adds a horizontal bar to a cell's background that is proportional.

Exhibit 16-40 Data bars added to the Structure Types worksheet

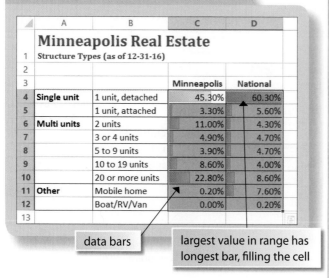

	A	B	C	D
1	**Minneapolis Real Estate** Structure Types (as of 12-31-16)			
2				
3			Minneapolis	National
4	**Single unit**	1 unit, detached	45.30%	60.30%
5		1 unit, attached	3.30%	5.60%
6	**Multi units**	2 units	11.00%	4.30%
7		3 or 4 units	4.90%	4.70%
8		5 to 9 units	3.90%	4.70%
9		10 to 19 units	8.60%	4.00%
10		20 or more units	22.80%	8.60%
11	**Other**	Mobile home	0.20%	7.60%
12		Boat/RV/Van	0.00%	0.20%
13				

data bars

largest value in range has longest bar, filling the cell

The lengths of the data bars are determined based on the values in the selected range. The cell with the largest value contains a data bar that extends across the entire width of the cell, and the lengths of the other bars in the selected range are determined relative to that bar. In some cases, this means that the longest data bar overlaps the cell's data value, making it difficult to read. You can modify the length of the data bars by altering the conditional formatting rule in the Edit Formatting Rule dialog box. See Exhibit 16-41.

Exhibit 16-41 Edit Formatting Rule dialog box

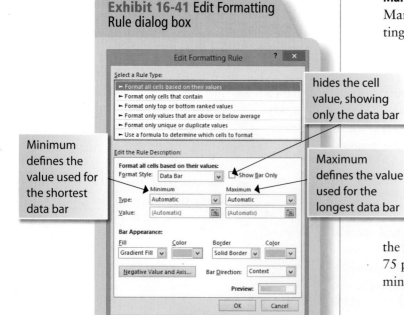

Minimum defines the value used for the shortest data bar

hides the cell value, showing only the data bar

Maximum defines the value used for the longest data bar

Data bars are always placed in the cells containing the value they represent, and each cell represents only a single bar.

Begin Activity

Add data bars.

1 Make the **Structure Types worksheet** the active sheet. Select the **range C4:D12**.

2 On the HOME tab, in the Styles group, click the **Conditional Formatting button**, and then point to **Data Bars** to display the Data Bars gallery.

> **Tip:** You can also click the Quick Analysis button ▣ and then click Data Bars in the FORMATTING section to format the selected range with the solid blue data bars.

3 In the Gradient Fill section, click the **Orange Data Bar style**. The data bars are added to the selected cells. Refer back to Exhibit 16-40. These data bars present essentially the same information as the column chart you created earlier. However, the data bars have the advantage of being compact and integrated with the values in the Structure Types data.

4 On the HOME tab, in the Styles group, click the **Conditional Formatting button**, and then click **Manage Rules**. The Conditional Formatting Rules Manager dialog box opens. In the Show formatting rules for box, Current Selection appears.

5 Click **Edit Rule**. The Edit Formatting Rule dialog box opens. Refer back to Exhibit 16-41. You want to modify the data bar rule to proportionally reduce the lengths of the data bars.

6 In the Type row, click the **Maximum box arrow**, and then click **Number**.

7 In the Value row, click in the **Maximum box**, and then replace the value with **0.75**. The rule now sets the maximum value for the data bar to 0.75, or 75 percent. All data bar lengths will then be determined relative to this value.

8 Click **OK** in each dialog box. The longest data bar now spans three-fourths of the cell width. Compare your screen to Exhibit 16-42.

9 Save the workbook, and then close it.

End Activity

Exhibit 16-42 Edited data bars

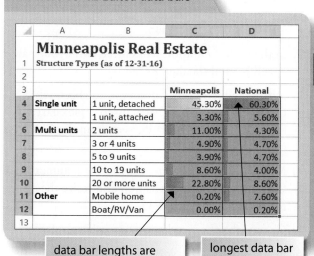

data bar lengths are expressed relative to a maximum value of 75%

longest data bar covers less than three-fourths of the cell

Quiz Yourself

1. What is the difference between a data source and a data series?

2. What is the difference between the chart area and the plot area?

3. In what two locations can you place a chart?

4. If a data series contains values divided into 10 categories, would this data be better displayed as a pie chart or a column chart? Why?

5. What is a column chart, and how is a bar chart different?

6. Why would you change the scale of a chart axis?

7. What are major units and minor units?

8. When should you use a line chart instead of a column chart?

9. What is a combination chart? Describe how to create a combination chart.

10. What does it mean to overlay a chart title or legend?

11. How do you update a chart after editing the chart data?

12. How do you add a data series to an already existing chart?

13. What are sparklines? Describe the three types of sparklines.

14. What are data bars?

15. How do data bars differ from sparklines?

Practice It

Practice It 16-1

1. Open the data file **Hot** located in the Chapter 16\ Practice It folder. Save the workbook as **Hot Springs Resorts**.

2. In the Documentation worksheet, enter your name in cell B3 and the date in cell B4.

3. In the Usage Data worksheet, select the range B4:E4;B17:E17. Insert a pie chart using the Pie chart type in the 2-D Pie section in the gallery.

4. Move the embedded pie chart to the Summary Charts worksheet. Reposition and resize the chart to cover the range A3:F14.

5. Change the chart style of the pie chart to Style 7.

6. Change the chart layout of the pie chart to Layout 2.

7. Change the chart title to **Total Annual Usage**. Change the font size of the chart title to 12 points.

8. Position the legend to the left of the pie chart. Change the border color of the legend to a solid line using the Gray-25%, Background 2 theme color.

9. Change the data labels to appear on the outside end of the pie chart.

10. In the Usage Data worksheet, select the range A4:E16. Insert a column chart using the 3-D Clustered Column chart type in the 3-D Column section in the gallery.

11. Move the embedded column chart to the Summary Charts worksheet. Reposition and resize the embedded column chart to cover the range A16:M32.

12. Change the chart style of the column chart to Style 6.

13. Change the chart layout of the column chart to Layout 3.

14. Change the chart title to **Amenities Usage By Month**. Set the font size of the chart title to 12 points.

15. Add a primary vertical axis title to the column chart. Enter **Attendance** as the vertical axis title.

16. Change the vertical axis scale of the column chart so that the maximum is **900**. (*Hint*: In the AXIS OPTIONS, change the Maximum value in the Bounds section.)

17. In the Usage Data worksheet, change the month labels in the range A5:A16 to the full month names. Change the value in cell E5 to **96**. In the Summary Charts worksheets, make sure the charts are updated to reflect the full month names and the new totals.

18. In the Usage Data worksheet, select the range A4:A16;F4:F16. Insert a line chart using the Line chart type in the 2-D Line section in the gallery.

19. Move the embedded line chart to the Summary Charts worksheet. Reposition and resize the embedded column chart to cover the range G3:M14.

20. Change the chart style of the column chart to Style 7. Remove the legend from the line chart.

21. Change the chart title to **Total Monthly Usage**. Set the font size of the chart title to 12 points.

22. Change the axis scale of the line chart to a minimum bounds of 750 and a maximum bounds of 2,150 with a major unit of 250.

23. In the Usage Data worksheet, in the range G5:G16, insert line sparklines based on the data range B5:E16.

24. On the sparklines, show the high point and low point markers.

25. Change the sparkline style to Sparkline Style Accent 1, Darker 25%.

26. Select the range F5:F16, and then insert data bars using the Blue Data Bar option in the Solid Fill section of the gallery.

27. Save the workbook, and then close it.

Practice It 16-2

1. Open the data file **World** located in the Chapter 16\Practice It folder. Save the workbook as **World Steel Production**.

2. In the Documentation worksheet, enter your name in cell B3 and the date in cell B4.

3. In the Production by Country worksheet, select the range A5:A10;N5:N10. Insert a pie chart using the Pie chart in the 2-D Pie section in the Charts gallery.

4. Move the embedded pie chart to the Summary Charts worksheet. Reposition and resize the chart to cover the range A4:F15.

5. Change the chart style of the pie chart to Style 6.

6. Change the chart layout of the pie chart to Layout 6.

7. Enter **Total Steel Production by Country** as the chart title. Change the font size of the chart title to 12 points.

8. Position the legend at the left of the pie chart. Change the border color of the legend to a solid line in the Gray-25%, Background 2, Darker 50% theme color.

9. In the Production by Country worksheet, select the range A4:M10. Insert a column chart using the Clustered Column chart in the 2-D Column section in the gallery.

10. Move the embedded column chart to the Summary Charts worksheet. Reposition and resize the embedded column chart to cover the range A17:K33.

11. Change the chart style of the column chart to Style 7.

12. Change the chart title to be Centered Overlay. Change the chart title to **Steel Production by Country and Month**. Set the font size of the chart title to 12 points.

13. Change the fill color of the plot area to a gradient fill. Change the fill direction to Linear Right.

14. In the column chart, change the Asia data series to a line. (*Hint*: Select the Asia data series. On the Chart Tools Design tab, in the Type group, click the Change Chart Type button. In the Change Chart Type dialog box, on the All Charts tab, in the Combo group, click the Clustered Column – Line on Secondary Axis option, and then click OK.)

15. In the Summary Charts worksheet, in the merged cell H6, insert a line sparkline based on the data range B11:M11 in the Production by Country worksheet.

16. On the sparkline, show the high point and low point markers.

17. Change the sparkline style to Sparkline Style Colorful #1.

18. Change the sparkline type to Column. (*Hint*: On the Sparkline Tools Design tab, in the Type group, click the Column button.)

19. Save the workbook, and then close it.

On Your Own

On Your Own 16-1

1. Open the data file **Portlandia** located in the Chapter 16\On Your Own folder. Save the workbook as **Portlandia Skies**.

2. In the Documentation worksheet, enter your name in cell B3 and the date in cell B4.

3. In the Weather worksheet, based on the data in the range A4:M8, insert an appropriate chart (such as a column chart, line chart, or bar chart). Move the embedded chart to a chart sheet named **Average Days Chart**.

4. Format the chart using an appropriate chart layout and chart style.

5. Insert an appropriate chart title for the chart, and then change the font size as needed.

6. Add appropriate axis titles, and change the font sizes as needed.

7. Position the legend appropriately, and change its font size, border color, fill color, and so forth as desired.

8. Change the axis scale as needed to eliminate blank areas of the chart.

9. Add vertical gridlines to the major units in the chart.

10. Format the plot area to use an attractive fill.

11. Change the data series as needed so that each data series uses a distinct data marker fill and line color.

12. In the Weather worksheet, edit the text in cell A6 to **Partly Cloudy**.

13. In the Weather worksheet, based on the data in the range A4:A8;N4:N8, insert a pie chart. Reposition and resize the chart attractively on the Weather worksheet.

14. Format the pie chart attractively, using the chart layout, chart style, chart title, legend, and data labels of your choice.

15. In the Weather worksheet, in the cells of your choice, insert a line or column sparkline for each of the following data: Clear (range B5:M5), Partly Cloudy (range B6:M6), Cloudy (range B7:M7), and Rainy (range B8:M8). Format the sparklines appropriately and enter labels to identify each sparkline.

16. In the Weather worksheet, insert data bars in the range N5:N8.

17. Save the workbook, and then close it.

Chapter 16

ADDITIONAL STUDY TOOLS

IN THE BOOK
▶ Complete end-of-chapter exercises
▶ Study tear-out Chapter Review Card

ONLINE
▶ Complete additional end-of-chapter exercises

▶ Take practice quiz to prepare for tests
▶ Review key term flash cards (online, printable, and audio)
▶ Play "Beat the Clock" and "Memory" to quiz yourself
▶ Watch the videos to learn more about the topics taught in this chapter

Answers to Quiz Yourself

1. A data source is the range that contains the data being displayed in a chart. A data source is a collection of one or more data series, which is a range of values that is plotted as a single unit on a chart.

2. The chart area contains the chart and all of the other chart elements. The plot area is the part of the chart that contains the graphical representation of the data series.

3. You can place a chart in a worksheet as an embedded chart or you can place a chart into a chart sheet, which contains only the chart and no worksheet cells.

4. A data series that contains values divided into 10 categories would be better displayed as a column chart because a pie chart is more effective with six or fewer categories.

5. A column chart displays values in different categories as columns; the height of each column is based on its value. A bar chart is a column chart turned on its side so that the length of each bar is based on its value.

6. You would change the scale of a chart axis to make the chart easier to read.

7. Major units identify the main intervals on a chart axis. Minor units identify smaller intervals between the major units.

8. You should use a line chart instead of a column chart when the data consists of values drawn from categories that follow a sequential order at evenly spaced intervals, as with historical data in which the data values are recorded periodically such as monthly, quarterly, or yearly.

9. A combination chart combines two or more chart types in a single graph, such as a column chart and a line chart. To create a combination chart, first select the data series in an existing chart that you want to appear as another chart type. Then, on the CHART TOOLS DESIGN tab, in the Type group, click the Change Chart Type button, click the chart type you want to apply to the selected series, and then click OK.

10. Overlaying a chart title or legend means they are placed on top of the chart in the chart area.

11. A chart is automatically updated when its data source is edited.

12. To add a data series to an existing chart, select the chart, click the Select Data button in the Data group on the CHART TOOLS DESIGN tab, click the Add button in the Select Data Source dialog box, click in the Series name box in the Edit Series dialog box, select the range with the new data series. Click OK in each dialog box.

13. A sparkline is a graph that is displayed within a cell. The three types of sparklines are line sparklines, column sparklines, and win/loss sparklines.

14. A data bar is conditional formatting that adds a horizontal bar to the background of a cell containing a number.

15. Data bars differ from sparklines in that the bars are always placed in the cells containing the value they represent and each cell represents only a single bar from the bar chart. By contrast, a column sparkline can be inserted anywhere within the workbook and can represent data from several rows or columns.

Excel: Create a Budget

1. Plan a budget workbook. Identify the workbook's purpose or goal. Figure out the data you need to collect and enter in the workbook (for this project, you can use real or fictional data). Determine what calculations you need to enter in the workbook. Decide how the workbook should be organized and formatted.

2. Create a new workbook for the financial data. Use the first worksheet as a documentation sheet that includes your name, the date on which you start creating the workbook, and a brief description of the workbook's purpose. Format the worksheet appropriately.

3. Use a second worksheet to create the budget. Enter appropriate labels to identify the data the budget will include. Include a section to enter values that remain consistent from month to month, such as monthly income and expenses. You can then reference these cells in formulas.

4. In the budget worksheet, enter the data on which the budget will be based. Be sure to enter realistic earnings for each month of the year and realistic expenses for each month. Apply appropriate number formats and styles to the values.

5. In the budget worksheet, enter formulas and functions to calculate the total earnings each month, the average monthly earnings, and the total earnings for the entire year. Also, calculate the total expenses for each month, the average monthly expenses, and the total expenses for the year.

6. Calculate the monthly net cash flow (the value of total income minus total expenses).

7. Use the cash flow values to track the savings throughout the year. Use a realistic amount for savings at the beginning of the year. Use the monthly net cash flow values to add or subtract from this value. Project the end-of-year balance in savings under your proposed budget.

8. Format the budget worksheet by changing fonts, font sizes, font colors, borders, cell styles, fill colors, and so forth as needed to make the worksheet attractive, ensure it is easy to read and interpret, and has a uniform appearance.

9. Use conditional formatting to automatically highlight negative net cash flow months.

10. Insert a pie chart that compares the monthly expenses for the categories.

11. Insert a column chart that charts all of the monthly expenses regardless of the category.

12. Insert a line chart or sparkline that shows the change in the savings balance throughout the 12 months of the year.

13. Insert new rows at the top of the worksheet and enter titles that describe the worksheet's contents.

14. Use a third worksheet to plan for a major purchase, such as a car or a computer. Determine the amount of the purchase and the current annual interest rate charged by your local bank. Provide a reasonable length of time to repay the loan, such as five years for a car loan or 20 to 30 years for a home loan. Use the PMT function to determine how much you would have to spend each month on the payments for your purchase. You can do these calculations in a separate worksheet.

15. Add the loan information to the monthly budget and evaluate the impact of the purchase of this item on the budget. Examine other possible loans and evaluate their impact on the budget. If the payment exceeds the budget, reduce the estimated price of the item being purchased until you determine an affordable monthly payment.

16. Format the worksheets for your printer. Include headers and footers that display the workbook file name, the workbook's author, and the date on which the report is printed. If the report extends across several pages, repeat appropriate print titles on all of the pages, set page breaks and orientation as needed, and include page numbers and the total number of pages on every printed page.

17. Save the workbook, and then close it.

Working with the Excel Web App

Similar to the Word Web App, you can use the Excel Web App to view or edit Excel workbooks on SkyDrive. See Exhibit 1. When you edit a workbook in the Excel Web App, you can apply basic formatting, perform calculations, and create charts. You can use a limited number of functions. However, the FORMULAS tab and the Function Arguments dialog box are not available.

Exhibit 1 Excel workbook open in Excel Web App

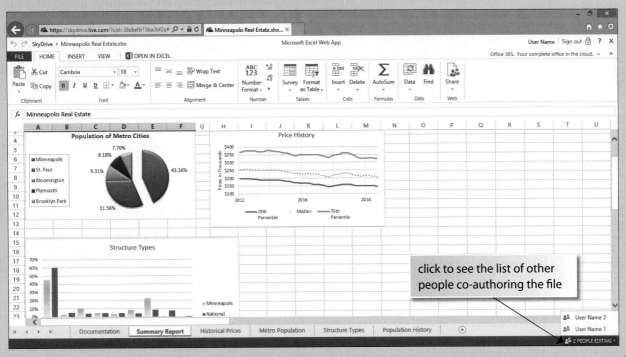

The Web Apps for all three Office applications—Word, Excel, and PowerPoint—allow co-authoring, a feature that allows you to edit a document, workbook, or presentation stored in a SkyDrive folder at the same time as a colleague. To allow someone to co-author a workbook, you must share the file with that person as described in the Web Applications section at the end of Chapter 9.

After you have given someone editing privileges for a file, you and that person can each open the file in the Web App. If either of you edits the workbook, the other will see the edit moments later. When you co-author a file, the number of people currently co-authoring appears at the bottom of the window, and you can click this to see a list of their names or email addresses. Refer again to Exhibit 1.

The Excel Web App provides a template for creating Excel surveys. To use this feature, click the Survey button in the Tables group on the INSERT tab in the Excel Web App, and then click New Survey. A window opens in which you can create questions. You click in the Enter your first question here box to open a dialog box in which you can create questions. Type the question in the top box. The default response type is Text. You can click the Response Type box arrow to choose from the response types shown in Exhibit 2. Some of the response types change the bottom part of the dialog box. For example, if you select Choice, a box appears in which you list the three choices from which respondents must select their answers. To distribute the survey, click Share Survey after you finish creating the questions, a new window opens with the custom Web address in it. Copy this and then paste it in an email message or to a social media site, or paste it in any other location where your respondents can access it. Although you need a Microsoft account in order to create the survey, people responding to the survey do not need one in order to complete the survey.

Exhibit 2 Window that opens when you create a new survey

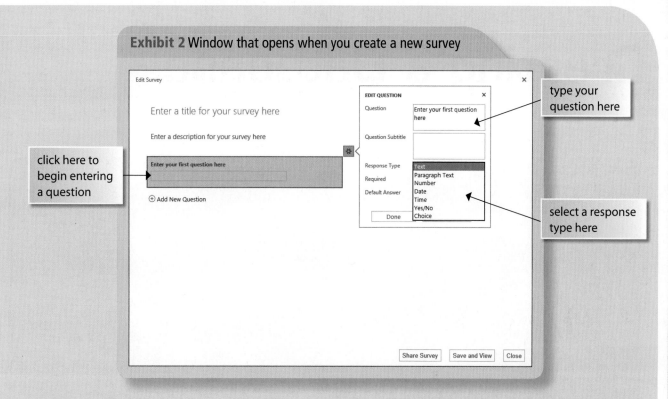

As people submit their completed surveys, the responses are automatically tabulated in the Excel survey worksheet that is created and stored in the open workbook on your SkyDrive when you create the survey. The responses are tabulated whether the workbook is open or closed. See Exhibit 3.

Exhibit 3 Four responses to a survey

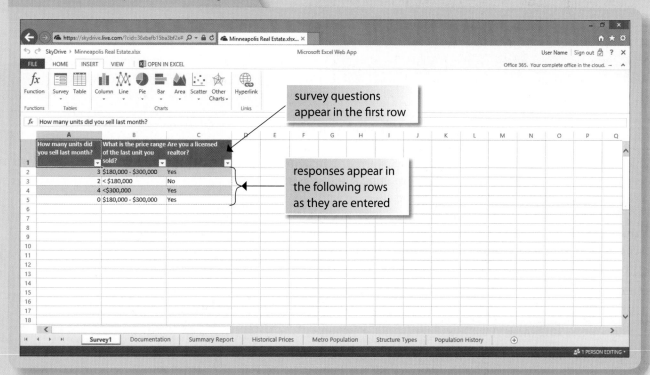

Creating a Database

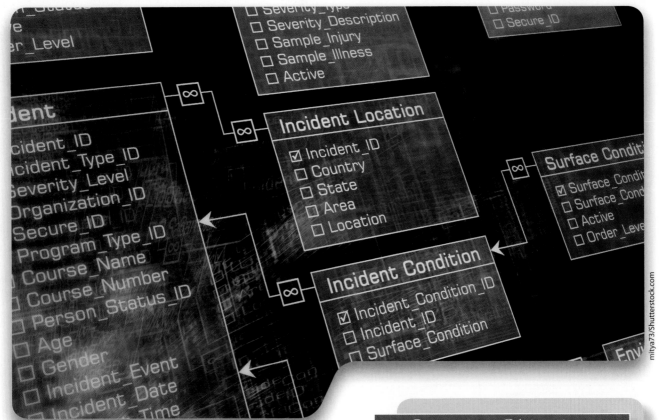

mitya73/Shutterstock.com

Data is a valuable resource to any business. Important data for many businesses includes customers' names and addresses and contract amounts and dates. Organizing, storing, maintaining, retrieving, and sorting this type of data are critical activities that enable a business to find and use information effectively.

Microsoft Access 2013 (or simply **Access**) is used to enter, maintain, and retrieve related data. Businesses often use Access to maintain such data as information about customers, contracts, and invoices, as well as information about assets and inventory.

Learning Objectives

After studying the material in this chapter, you will be able to:

17-1 Understand database concepts

17-2 Create a database

17-3 Work in Datasheet view

17-4 Work with fields and properties in Design view

17-5 Modify a table's structure

17-6 Close and open objects and databases

17-7 Create simple queries, forms, and reports

17-8 Compact and repair a database

Microsoft Access 2013 (Access) A computer application used to enter, maintain, and retrieve related data in a format known as a database.

Microsoft product screenshots used with permission from Microsoft Corporation.

17-1 Understanding Database Concepts

A database is an organized collection of related information. For example, a database containing information about a business might be called BusinessInfo, and a database containing information about personal finances, such as stock portfolio information, might be called MyFinances.

Each piece of data in a database—that is, a single characteristic or attribute of a person, place, object, event, or idea—is stored in a **field**. For example, a database named BusinessInfo that contains information about a business's customers might include fields that contain the following customer data: ID number, first name, last name, company name, street address, city, state, ZIP code, and phone number.

A **table** is a collection of related fields. Exhibit 17-1 shows a table with the following fields that contain information about customers: CustomerID, LastName, FirstName, and Phone.

The content of a field is the **field value**. In Exhibit 17-1, the field values in the first row for CustomerID, LastName, FirstName, and Phone are, respectively: 1; Sanders; Lily; and (408) 555-3999.

Each row in a table contains all the fields about a single person, place, object, event, or idea, and this is called a **record**. The table shown in Exhibit 17-1 contains five records.

A database that contains more than one related table is a **relational database**. In a relational database, the tables are related to each other using a **common field**, which is simply a field that appears in more than one table. For example, a relational database that included the table of customer information shown in Exhibit 17-1 might also contain a table named Contract that stores data about customer contracts and a table named Invoice that stores data that is used to create customer invoices. To track

the information for each customer, each of the three tables needs to have at least one field in common.

In a relational database, each record in a table must be unique. To ensure that each record in a table is unique, at least one field in each table is designated as the primary key. A **primary key** is a field, or a collection of fields, whose value uniquely identifies each record in a table. No two records can contain the same value for the primary key field. For example, a table named Customer might have, in addition to FirstName and LastName fields for customer names, a CustomerID field. The CustomerID field would be the primary key field. Usually a field such as the CustomerID field is designated as the primary key because no two customers will have the same Customer ID number. Two customers might, however, have the same last name, so you would not select the LastName field as the table's primary key because the last name alone might not uniquely identify each record in the table.

Exhibit 17-1 A database table

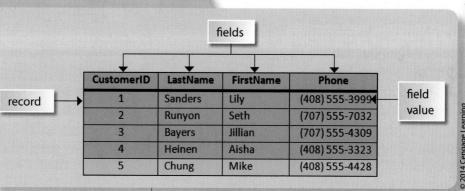

fields

record

CustomerID	LastName	FirstName	Phone
1	Sanders	Lily	(408) 555-3999
2	Runyon	Seth	(707) 555-7032
3	Bayers	Jillian	(707) 555-4309
4	Heinen	Aisha	(408) 555-3323
5	Chung	Mike	(408) 555-4428

field value

© 2014 Cengage Learning

field A part of a database that contains a single characteristic or attribute of a person, place, object, event, or idea.

table In Access, a collection of related fields.

field value The content of a field.

record All the fields in a table about a single person, place, object, event, or idea; that is, a row in a table.

relational database A database that contains a collection of related tables.

common field A field that appears in more than one table.

primary key A field, or a collection of fields, whose value uniquely identifies each record in a table.

FYI

Database Management Systems

A **database management system (DBMS)** is software used to create and maintain a database, control the storage of databases on disk, and facilitate the creation, manipulation, and reporting of data. A **relational database management system (relational DBMS)** is a DBMS that is used to create and maintain relational databases. Most database management systems, including Access, are relational database management systems. Specifically, a relational DBMS:

- Allows you to create database structures containing fields, tables, and table relationships
- Lets you easily add new records, change field values in existing records, and delete records
- Contains a built-in query language, which lets you obtain immediate answers to the questions you ask about your data
- Contains a built-in report generator, which lets you produce professional-looking, formatted reports from your data
- Protects databases through security, control, and recovery facilities

A relational DBMS allows multiple users to share the same data. For example, the BusinessInfo database in the earlier example contains only one copy of the Customers, Contracts, and Invoices tables, and all users can access those tables when they need information.

Finally, a DBMS can handle massive amounts of data and can be used to create relationships among multiple tables.

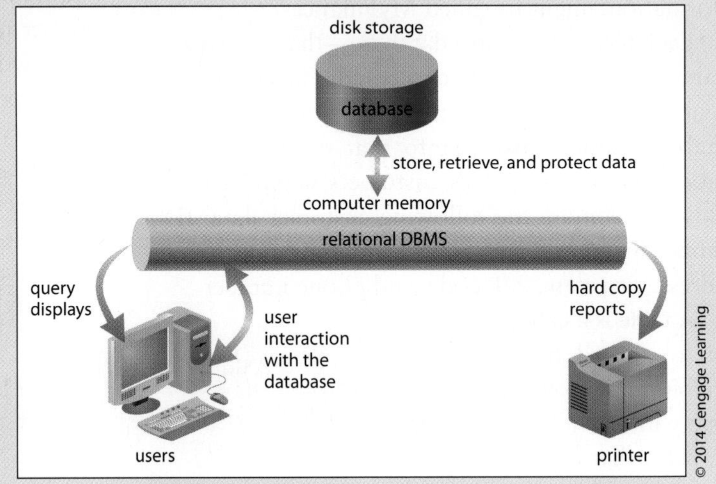

Relational database management system

To form a relationship between two tables—that is, to connect two tables—the two tables must contain a common field, and the common field must be the primary key in at least one of the tables being related. This is how the database knows which record in one table is related to which record or records in the other table or tables.

When the primary key from one table is included in another table, it is called a **foreign key**. In the Contracts table, the CustomerID field is a foreign key. Although a table may have only one primary key, it can have many foreign keys.

foreign key A field in a table that is a primary key in another table and that is included to form a relationship between the two tables.

database management system (DBMS) Software used to create databases and manipulate the data in them.

relational database management system (relational DBMS) A database management system in which data is organized as a collection of related tables.

Exhibit 17-2 shows the relationship between three tables in a database. CustomerID, which is the primary key in the Customers table, is included in the Contracts table so that we can identify the contracts for each customer. The CustomerID field is not the primary key in the Contracts table because a customer might have signed more than one contract. ContractNumber, which is the primary key in the Contracts table, is included in the Invoices table so that each invoice is associated with a specific contract. ContractNumber is not the primary key in the Invoices table because one contract might result in several invoices being created.

17-2 Creating a Database

After you create or open a database, the Navigation Pane appears along the left side of the Access window and displays all of the tables, reports, and other objects in the database. The Navigation Pane is the main control center for opening and working with database objects.

Exhibit 17-2 Database relationship between tables

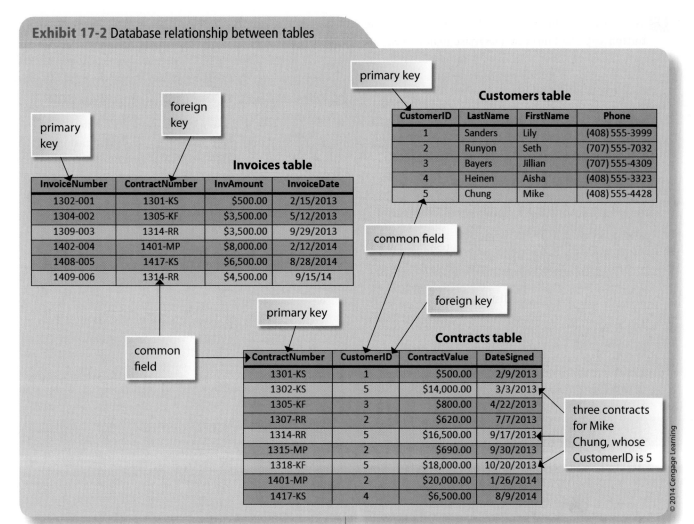

Invoices table

InvoiceNumber	ContractNumber	InvAmount	InvoiceDate
1302-001	1301-KS	$500.00	2/15/2013
1304-002	1305-KF	$3,500.00	5/12/2013
1309-003	1314-RR	$3,500.00	9/29/2013
1402-004	1401-MP	$8,000.00	2/12/2014
1408-005	1417-KS	$6,500.00	8/28/2014
1409-006	1314-RR	$4,500.00	9/15/14

Customers table

CustomerID	LastName	FirstName	Phone
1	Sanders	Lily	(408) 555-3999
2	Runyon	Seth	(707) 555-7032
3	Bayers	Jillian	(707) 555-4309
4	Heinen	Aisha	(408) 555-3323
5	Chung	Mike	(408) 555-4428

Contracts table

ContractNumber	CustomerID	ContractValue	DateSigned
1301-KS	1	$500.00	2/9/2013
1302-KS	5	$14,000.00	3/3/2013
1305-KF	3	$800.00	4/22/2013
1307-RR	2	$620.00	7/7/2013
1314-RR	5	$16,500.00	9/17/2013
1315-MP	2	$690.00	9/30/2013
1318-KF	5	$18,000.00	10/20/2013
1401-MP	2	$20,000.00	1/26/2014
1417-KS	4	$6,500.00	8/9/2014

three contracts for Mike Chung, whose CustomerID is 5

© 2014 Cengage Learning

Any open table, report, or other object appears in the right pane with a tab that displays its name. You can open more than one object at a time and click the tabs to switch between them.

CAUTION

Save Your Files

Remember to save your files to the drive and folder where you are storing the files you create as you complete the steps in this book.

Begin Activity

Create a new, blank database.

1 Start **Access**. Access starts, and the Recent screen appears in Backstage view.

2 Click the **Blank desktop database tile**. A dialog box opens. See Exhibit 17-3.

Tip: To create a database that contains objects matching those found in common databases, such as databases that store data about contacts or events, type keywords in the Search box at the top of the Recent screen to find an appropriate template.

Exhibit 17-3 Blank desktop database dialog box

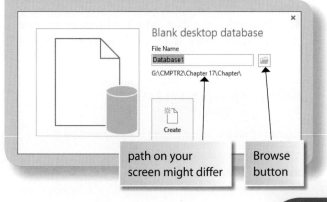

path on your screen might differ

Browse button

3 To the right of the File Name box, click the **Browse button** 🗁. The File New Database dialog box, which is similar to the Save As dialog box in other programs, opens.

4 Navigate to the **Chapter 17\Chapter folder** or to the drive and folder in which you store the files you create in this book.

5 In the File name box, change the file name to **Solar**.

6 Click **OK**. The dialog box closes, and Solar.accdb appears in the File Name box. The file extension .accdb identifies the file as an Access database.

7 Click the **Create button**. Access creates the new database, saves it to the specified drive, and then opens an empty table named Table1 in Datasheet view. The Table1 table is listed in the Navigation Pane. See Exhibit 17-4.

8 If the Access program window is not maximized, click the **Maximize button** 🗖.

End Activity

LEARN MORE

Understanding the Access 2007 – 2013 File Format

Access 2013 uses the .accdb file extension, which is the same file extension used for databases created with Microsoft Access 2007 and Microsoft Access 2010. All database files with the .accdb file extension can be used in Access 2007, Access 2010, and Access 2013.

17-3 Working in Datasheet View

To create your database, you need to design a table and enter data into it. One way to create and work with tables is to work in Datasheet view.

Datasheet view The Access view that shows a table's contents as a datasheet.

datasheet Rows and columns in which a table's contents are displayed.

data type The type of data that can be entered for a field.

Datasheet view shows the table's contents as a datasheet. A **datasheet** displays the table's contents in rows and columns, similar to a Word table or an Excel worksheet. In Access, each column is a field, and each row is a record. In Datasheet view, you can create fields and enter records, much like you enter data in a Word table or an Excel worksheet. When you first create a new database, an empty table opens in Datasheet view. Refer to Exhibit 17-4.

When you create a table, keep in mind that you should divide all information into its smallest useful part. For example, instead of including a person's full name in one field, separate the first name and the last name into separate fields. When you name a field, you should choose a name that describes the purpose or contents of the field so you and other users can quickly tell what the field stores. For example, you might use CustomerID, FirstName, LastName, and Phone as field names. A field name must be unique within a table, but it can be used again in another table in the same database.

In Access, each field must be assigned a data type. A **data type** specifies the type of data that may be entered for that field—such as text, numbers, currency, and dates and times. For example, a field that will store invoice dates will be assigned the Date/Time data type, limiting users to entering only dates and/or times in the field. Exhibit 17-5 describes the most commonly used data types.

17-3a Creating a Table in Datasheet View

When you create a table in Datasheet view, you first need to create the empty table structure. A blank table is created automatically when you start Access and create a new database, as was shown in Exhibit 17-4. If you need to create a new, blank table in Datasheet view, click the Table button in the Tables group on the CREATE tab.

After creating a blank table, you need to add fields to it. To define a new field, you assign a data type and enter a field name. Clicking the Click to Add column heading in the table opens a list of data types. See Exhibit 17-6. Click a data type to assign it to the new field. After you select a data type, you can type the field name.

If a field name is not completely visible in a datasheet because the column is too narrow, you can resize the column using the same techniques you used for columns in Word tables and Excel worksheets: you can double-click the column border to AutoFit the contents or drag a column border to change the column width to any size you want.

Exhibit 17-4 Access window with an empty table in Datasheet view

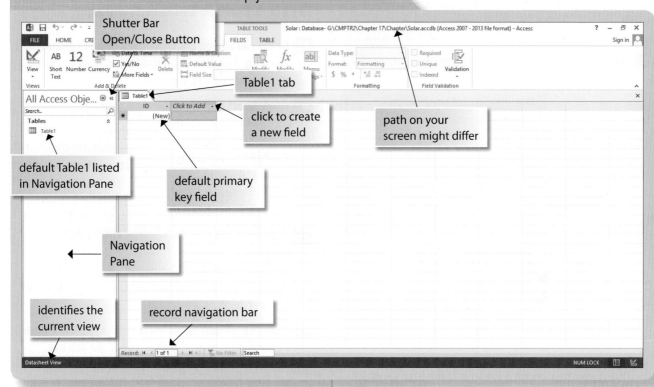

- Shutter Bar Open/Close Button
- Table1 tab
- click to create a new field
- path on your screen might differ
- default Table1 listed in Navigation Pane
- default primary key field
- Navigation Pane
- identifies the current view
- record navigation bar

Exhibit 17-5 Common data types

Data type	Description	Field size	Use for
Short Text	Letters, digits, spaces, and special characters	0 to 255 characters; default is 255	Names, addresses, descriptions, and numbers not used in calculations
Long Text	Letters, digits, spaces, and special characters	1 to 65,535 characters; exact size is determined by entry	Long comments and explanations
Number	Positive and negative numbers that can contain digits, a decimal point, commas, and a plus or minus sign	1 to 15 digits	Fields that will be used in calculations, except those involving money
Date/Time	Dates and times from January 1, 100 to December 31, 9999	8 bytes	
Currency	Monetary values	Accurate to 15 digits on the left side of the decimal point and to 4 digits on the right side	
AutoNumber	Unique integer created by Access for every record; can be sequential or random numbering	9 digits	The primary key in any table
Yes/No	Values that are yes or no, on or off, and true or false	1 character	Fields that indicate the presence or absence of a condition, such as whether an invoice has been paid
Hyperlink	Text used as a hyperlink address	Up to 65,535 characters total	A link to a file or Web page, a location within a file or Web page, another field

© 2014 Cengage Learning

Exhibit 17-6 Field being added to a datasheet

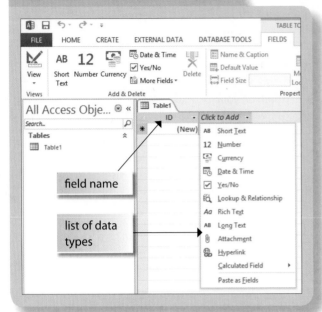

field name

list of data types

When you first create a table in Datasheet view, the first field in the datasheet is named ID and is identified as the primary key for the table. This field is assigned the AutoNumber data type, which will add a unique number, beginning with 1, to the ID field as you enter each record in the table. If you want, you can rename the primary key field, change its data type, and then type your own values for the primary key.

FYI

Planning a Table

Before creating a table, you should plan what data it will store and how that data will be organized. For example, a table to track information about a company's contracts might be organized based on the plan shown here. As shown in the plan, data about contracts will be stored in four fields, including fields to contain the contract ID, customer ID, contract value, and date the contract was signed. The ContractID field will be the primary key for the table because each contract is assigned a unique contract number. The CustomerID field is a foreign key that connects the information about contracts to customers. The customer data will be stored in a separate table.

Field	Purpose
ContractID	Unique number assigned to each contract; will serve as the table's primary key
CustomerID	Unique number assigned to each customer; common field that will be a foreign key to connect the Customer table
ContractValue	Dollar amount for the contract
DateSigned	Date on which the contract was signed

Plan for a table to track a company's contracts

Begin Activity

Create a table in Datasheet view.

1 In the datasheet, click the **Click to Add column heading**. The list of available data types appears. Refer back to Exhibit 17-6.

2 Click **Short Text** to select the type of data to store in the field. A new field is added to the table, and its placeholder name, Field1, is selected in the column heading.

> **Tip:** You can also add a field by clicking the appropriate data type button in the Add & Delete group on the TABLE TOOLS FIELDS tab.

3 Type **FirstName** as the field name, and then press the **Enter key**. The list of available data types appears for the next field so you can quickly add another field.

4 Select **Short Text** as the data type, type **LastName** as the field name, and then press the **Tab key**. The list of available data types appears for the next field.

5 Select **Date & Time** as the data type, type **Since** as the field name, and then press the **Tab key**. The list of available data types appears for the next field.

> **Tip:** To change a data type in Datasheet view, click the field whose data type you want to change, click the Data Type arrow in the Formatting group on the TABLE TOOLS FIELDS tab, and then click the new data type.

6 Right-click the field name **Since**. On the shortcut menu, click **Rename Field**. The Since field name is selected.

7 Type **CustomerSince** and then press the **Tab key**. The list of available data types appears for the next field.

8 Right-click the field name **ID**. On the shortcut menu, click **Rename Field**. The ID field name is selected.

9 Type **CustomerID** and then press the **Tab key**.

10 Double-click the **CustomerSince column heading right border** to widen the column to fit the contents.

> **Problem?** If a menu opens, you clicked the arrow on the CustomerSince column heading. Click the arrow again to close the menu, and then repeat Step 10.

End Activity

17-3b Saving a Table

A table is not stored in the database until you save it. When you save a table, you are saving its structure—the number of fields, the field names, the column widths in the datasheet, and so on. The first time you save a table, you should give it a descriptive name that identifies the information it contains. To save the table, you click the Save button on the Quick Access Toolbar.

If you store your database on a removable drive, such as a USB drive, you should never remove the drive while the database file is open. If you do, Access will encounter problems that might damage the database when it tries to save the database.

Begin Activity

Save and name a table.

1 On the Quick Access Toolbar, click the **Save button** 🔲. The Save As dialog box opens with the default table name Table1 selected in the Table Name box.

> **Tip:** You can also use the Save and Save As commands in the navigation bar in Backstage view.

2 In the Table Name box, type **Customers** and then click **OK**. The Customers table is saved in the database, and the table name is updated in the Navigation Pane and on the table's tab. Compare your screen to Exhibit 17-7.

End Activity

Exhibit 17-7 Table saved with a new name

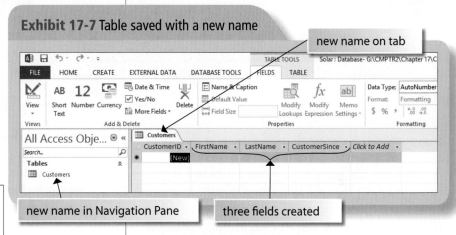

new name on tab

new name in Navigation Pane

three fields created

LEARN MORE

Saving a Database

Unlike other Office programs, you do not need to save the database after you add or delete records. Access automatically saves changes to the active database when you change or add a record or close the database. Clicking the Save button saves the design and format of an Access object, such as a table. For example, if you add or delete fields, or change the width of a column in a datasheet, you need to save these changes.

17-3c Entering Records

After you create the structure of a table by naming fields and assigning data types, you can enter records. To enter records in a table datasheet, you type the field values below the column headings for the fields. When you start typing a value in a field, a pencil symbol 🖉 appears in the row selector at the beginning of the row for the new record. The pencil symbol indicates that the record is being edited. See Exhibit 17-8.

One way a datasheet differs from Word tables and Excel worksheets is that when you add a record to a table, you can enter it only in the next available row. You cannot insert a row between existing records for

Exhibit 17-8 First field value entered

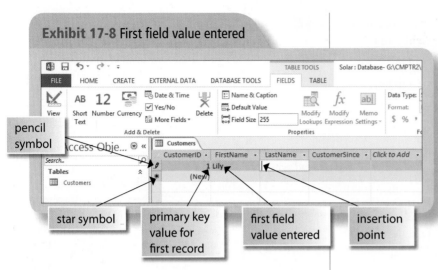

Labels pointing to the exhibit: pencil symbol, star symbol, primary key value for first record, first field value entered, insertion point

the new record. A star symbol ✳ appears at the beginning of the next available row for a new record.

If you mistype a field value or need to change it, you can correct it. Click in the field to position the insertion point, use the Backspace key or Delete key to delete incorrect text, type the correct text, and then press the Tab key or the Enter key. Note that you cannot edit the values in a field that has the AutoNumber data type.

Begin Activity

Enter records in a table.

1 In the first row of the datasheet, click in the **First-Name column**. The FirstName column header is highlighted, and the insertion point appears in the FirstName column for the first record, ready for you to enter the field value.

2 Type **Lily** and then press the **Tab key**. The field value is entered, and the insertion point moves to the LastName column for the first record. Access assigns the first primary key value. Refer to Exhibit 17-8.

3 Type **Wilson** and then press the **Tab key**. Access enters the field value and moves the insertion point to the CustomerSince column.

4 Type **2/25/16** and then press the **Tab key**. The year changes to 2016 even though you entered only the final two digits of the year because the Customer-Since field has the Date/Time data type, which formats dates with four-digit years. The first record is entered into the table, and the insertion point appears in the Customer-ID field for the second record. The pencil symbol is removed from the first row because the record in that row is no longer being edited.

> **Problem?** If you see another date format for the CustomerSince field, your Windows date setting is different. Continue with Step 5; this difference will not cause any problems.

5 Press the **Enter key** to move to the FirstName field in the second row, type **Carlos**, press the **Enter key** to move to the LastName field, type **Rosario**, press

Stephen Firmender/Shutterstock.com; © 2014 Cengage Learning

LEARN MORE

Naming Tables and Fields

Each table in a database and each field in a single table must have a unique name. Be sure to use descriptive names that indicate what the field or table stores. For example, you might use Customer as a table name and CustomerID, FirstName, and LastName as field names because these names describe their contents.

In addition, when naming fields, keep in mind the following guidelines:

▶ A field name can have up to 64 characters, including letters, numbers, spaces, and special characters, except for a period (.), exclamation mark (!), accent grave (`), and square brackets ([ ]).

▶ A field name cannot begin with a space.

▶ Capitalize the first letter of each word in a field name that combines multiple words (for example, Invoice-Date).

▶ Use standard abbreviations, such as Num for Number, Amt for Amount, and Qty for Quantity.

▶ Avoid using spaces in field names (even though Access allows them) because they can cause errors when you perform other tasks.

HELLO my name is

FirstName LastName

the **Enter key** to move to the CustomerSince field, type **4-2-16**, and then press the **Enter key**. The second record is entered, the number 2 was assigned to the CustomerID field in the second row, and the third row is active, ready for a new record. Again, the CustomerSince date you entered was changed to match the Date/Time format.

6 Press the **Tab key** to move to the FirstName field in the third row, enter **Jillian** as the first name, **Connor** as the last name, and **6/15/2016** as the CustomerSince date.

7 Click the field containing **Connor**. The insertion point appears in the field.

8 Use the same editing techniques you've used in Word and Excel to change the name to **Bayers**.

9 Enter the following data for the fourth and fifth records:

FirstName	LastName	CustomerSince
Aisha	Heinen	10-5-15
Mike	Chung	6/13/2016

End Activity

> **Problem?** If you enter a value in the wrong field, a menu might open with options for addressing the problem. If this happens, click the **Enter new value option** to highlight the field with the incorrect value, and then type the correct value.

17-4 Working with Fields and Properties in Design View

Each field in a table is defined by a variety of attributes, or characteristics, called properties. A **property** describes one characteristic of a field. A field name and its data type are properties.

The properties for a field depend on the field's data type. In addition to the field name and the data type, the following are common additional properties for different fields:

▶ **Description**—an optional property for describing a field; usually used only when the field name is not descriptive enough or the field has a special function such as a primary key.

▶ **Field Size**—the maximum storage size for Short Text, Long Text, Number, and AutoNumber fields.

▶ **Format**—describes how the value is displayed; for example, with the Date/Time data type, you can choose an existing format or enter a custom format using the same custom codes as you used in Excel.

▶ **Decimal Places**—the number of decimal places that are displayed to the right of the decimal point in a field defined with the Number or Currency data type.

▶ **Caption**—the field name as it will appear in database objects, such as in the table in Datasheet view. For example, you might use the field name CustNum in the table's design but set the Caption property to display Customer Number as the field's caption to enhance readability in datasheets and forms.

▶ **Default Value**—the value automatically entered in a field. For example, if every customer in a Customers table live in a certain state, you might set the Default Value property for the State field to the state's abbreviation.

> **property** One characteristic or aspect of a field, such as its name or data type.

The field name and data type properties are available on the ribbon on the TABLE TOOLS FIELDS tab in Datasheet view, but more properties are available in Design view. **Design view** shows a listing of a table's fields and field properties. See Exhibit 17-9. A table design grid in the top portion of the window lists the field names and data types. The table design grid also includes a description of each field. At the bottom of the window in Design view, the Field Properties pane lists the additional properties available for the field currently selected in the table design grid, and the Help box displays information about the currently selected property. In Design view, you can create and modify fields, but you cannot enter records.

To switch between Datasheet view and Design view, you can use the View button on the ribbon. This button appears in three places on the ribbon. It appears in the Views group on the HOME tab; in Datasheet view, it appears in the Views group on the TABLE TOOLS FIELDS tab; and in Design view, it appears in the Views group on the TABLE TOOLS DESIGN tab. The icon on the View button changes to reflect the view that you will switch to; that is, in Datasheet view, the icon

shows that clicking it will switch you to Design view, and vice versa in Design view. If you can switch to more than one view, you can click the View button arrow to display a menu of available views. You can also use buttons on the status bar to switch among views, similar to the view buttons on the status bars in Word and Excel.

17-4a Changing Field Properties in Design View

When you first create a field, most properties are assigned default values. You can change these values to match the field's content or purpose. To do this, you change the values in the Field Properties pane in Design view. Often you can change a property by typing the new value in the property's box. For some properties, when you click the box in the Field Properties pane, an arrow appears at the right end of the box. This indicates that in addition to typing the new value, you can click the arrow and then choose from a list of predesigned formats or values for that property. Generally, it's a good idea to create the structure of a table and change field properties before you enter any data so that values you have already entered do not change unexpectedly when a property changes.

Exhibit 17-9 Table in Design view

Design view The Access view that shows the underlying structure of a database object and allows you to modify that structure.

Field Size Property for Number Fields

When you use the Number data type to define a field, you should set the Field Size property based on the largest value you expect to store in that field. Access processes smaller data sizes faster, using less memory, so you can optimize the database's performance and its storage space by selecting the correct field size for each field. Number fields have the following Field Size property settings:

▶ **Byte**—stores whole numbers (numbers with no fractions) from 0 to 255 in one byte

▶ **Integer**—stores whole numbers from −32,768 to 32,767 in two bytes

▶ **Long Integer** (default)—stores whole numbers from −2,147,483,648 to 2,147,483,647 in four bytes

▶ **Single**—stores positive and negative numbers to precisely seven decimal places and uses four bytes

▶ **Double**—stores positive and negative numbers to precisely 15 decimal places and uses eight bytes

▶ **Replication ID**—establishes a unique identifier for replication of tables, records, and other objects in databases created using Access 2003 and earlier versions and uses 16 bytes

▶ **Decimal**—stores positive and negative numbers to precisely 28 decimal places and uses 12 bytes

---

Begin Activity

Change field properties in Design view.

1 On the status bar, click the **Design View button** 📝. The table switches to Design view. Refer back to Exhibit 17-9. The table design grid lists the fields you entered in Datasheet view. The Field Properties pane lists the available properties for the selected CustomerID field, and a description of the selected property (field name) appears in the Help box.

2 In the table design grid, in the Field Name column, click **FirstName**. The field is selected in the table design grid, and its properties appear in the Field Properties pane.

3 In the Field Properties pane, select the value in the **Field Size box**, and then type **20**. This is the maximum number of characters allowed for a customer's first name. The description in the Help box changed to describe the currently selected property.

> **Tip:** To change a field property in Datasheet view, use the buttons in the Formatting group on the TABLE TOOLS FIELDS tab.

4 In the table design grid, in the Field Name column, click **CustomerSince**. The properties for the CustomerSince field appear in the Field Properties pane. A Date/Time field does not have a Field Size property, so that property is not listed.

5 In the Field Properties pane, click in the **Format box**. An arrow appears at the right end of the Format box.

6 Click the **Format box arrow**. A list of date formats opens. These are similar to the data formats you used in Excel.

7 In the list, click **Long Date**. The format is changed.

8 On the Quick Access Toolbar, click the **Save button** 💾 to save the changes to the design of the Customers table. Because you reduced the Field Size property of the FirstName field from 255 characters to 20 characters, a dialog box appears, indicating that some data may be lost because the field size was decreased. If you click Yes and any value in the FirstName field contains more than 20 characters, any characters after the twentieth will be deleted. In this case, none of the values in the FirstName field in your table have more than 20 characters.

9 Click **Yes**. The table is saved.

10 On the TABLE TOOLS DESIGN tab, in the Views group, click the **View button**. The table returns to Datasheet view. The date no longer fits in the CustomerSince column because the Long Date format that you selected as the field's Format property displays many more characters than the default Short Date format.

11 Double-click the **Customer-Since column header right border** to widen the column to fit the contents. The dates in that field now appear in the Long Date format. Compare your screen to Exhibit 17-10. Note that the property change to the FirstName field is not apparent because none of the names entered have more than 20 characters.

12 Save the **Customers table**.

End Activity

Exhibit 17-10 Records with the Long Date format

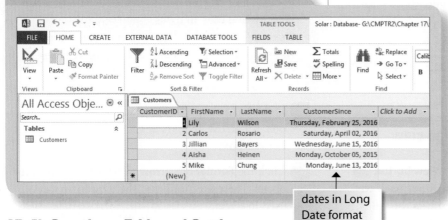

dates in Long Date format

17-4b Creating a Table and Setting Properties in Design View

Because you can set additional properties for fields in Design view, it can be a good idea to create a table in Design view. Then, after you have named all the fields and modified the field properties, you can switch to Datasheet view to enter records. To create a new, blank table in Design view, switch to Design view immediately after creating a new database. Or, if a table already exists and you need to create a new one, click the Table Design button in the Tables group on the CREATE tab. You can also create a table in Datasheet view and then switch to Design view, but you must save the table before switching views.

When you first create a table in Design view, the insertion point appears in the table design grid in the first row's Field Name box, ready for you to begin defining the first field in the table. To name a field, type it in the Field Name box. To assign a data type to a field, click in the Data Type box, click the arrow that appears, and then select the data type. See Exhibit 17-11.

Begin Activity

Create a table in Design view.

1 On the ribbon, click the **CREATE tab**. In the Tables group, click the **Table Design button**. The view switches to Design view, and a new, blank table named Table1 is created. This table will contain contract data, and its first field will contain the unique number that identifies each contract.

2 In the table design grid, in the Field Name column, in the first row, type **ContractID** and then press the **Tab key** to select the Data Type box. The default data type, Short Text, appears highlighted in the Data Type box, which now also contains

---

FYI

Input Mask Property

The Input Mask property can be used to display data in a specific format. For example, you might use the Input Mask property to format a field that stores phone numbers with the area code enclosed in parentheses and a dash to separate the other seven digits. In this case, the user would simply type the digits of the phone number, and the input mask would format the field value using the input mask. If you decide at a later time to change the display of the phone numbers, you need to change only the Input Mask property for the field, and all of the phone numbers would immediately use the new formatting.

If you add an input mask to a field, you need to keep the big picture in mind. For instance, if the customer list for a company includes international customers, an input mask that restricts a phone number field to the format (000) 0000000 would cause problems because other countries use different formats to display their phone numbers, and some use a different number of digits.

HannaMonika/Shutterstock.com

Exhibit 17-11 New table in Design view after entering the first field name

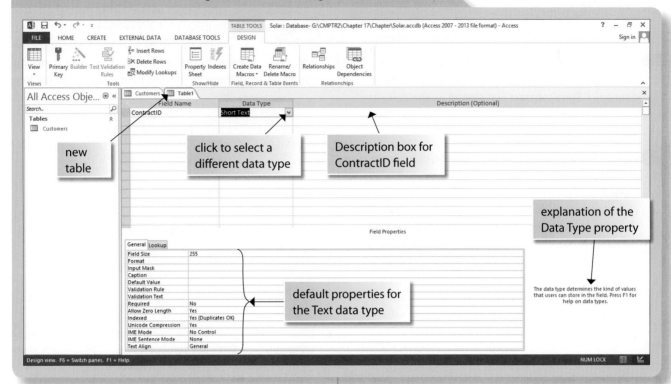

an arrow, and the field properties for a Text field appear in the Field Properties pane. Refer to Exhibit 17-11. The Help box provides an explanation for the current property, Data Type. Contract ID numbers at this company are always two digits that identify the year, followed by two numbers that identify the actual contract number, a hyphen, and the initials of the salesperson at the company who completed the contract. Therefore, the default Short Text data type is appropriate.

3 Press the **Tab key** to accept Short Text as the data type and to move the insertion point to the Description box.

4 In the Description box, type **Primary key**. The description you entered will appear on the status bar when you view the table in Datasheet view. (Note that specifying Primary key as the Description property does not set the current field as the primary key; you will set the primary key shortly.)

5 In the Field Properties pane, change the **Field Size property** to **7**.

6 In the Field Properties pane, click in the **Caption box**, and then type **Contract Number**. This value is what will appear in Access objects, including

tables. When you look at a table in Datasheet view, you will see this caption as the field name for this field instead of ContractID.

> **Tip:** You can press the F6 key to move the insertion point from the table design grid to the Field Properties pane.

7 Click in the **second row** in the table design grid, type **CustomerID** as the field name, and then press the **Tab key**. Short Text is selected as the data type.

8 Click the **Short Text box arrow**, and then click **Number** to specify the data type.

9 Press the **Tab key**, and then type **Foreign key** as the description. In the Field Properties pane, click in the **Caption box**, and then type **Customer ID** as the Caption property. The CustomerID field is the field that will connect (relate) the Contracts table to the Customers table you already created. The related field in the Customers table is also named CustomerID, and it has the AutoNumber data type. The data type of a foreign key must be compatible with the data type of the primary key in the original table.

10 In the table design grid, in the **third row**, enter **ContractValue** as the field name, **Currency** as the data type, **Total value of the contract** as the description, and **Contract Value** as the Caption property.

11 In the table design grid, in the **fourth row**, enter **DateSigned** as the field name, **Date/Time** as the data type, **Date contract was signed** as the description, **Short Date** as the Format property, and **Date Signed** as the Caption property.

12 In the table design grid, in the **fifth row**, enter **Signed** as the field name, **Yes/No** as the data type, and **Signed?** as the Caption property. This field can have only two values: Yes (the contract was signed) or No (it hasn't been signed yet). In the Default Value box, the value is No. Until the contract is signed, No will be entered as the default value in the Signed field in all new records. Because the default appearance for the Yes/No data type is a check box, this means the check box will be unchecked for new records. Compare your screen to Exhibit 17-12.

End Activity

Exhibit 17-12 New table in Design view

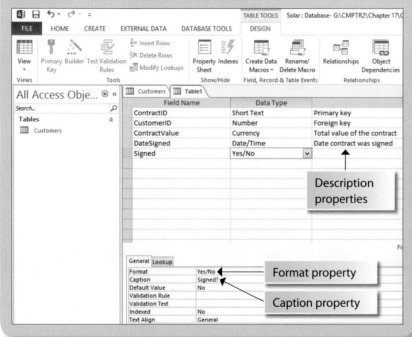

17-4c Specifying the Primary Key

You can choose which field to use as the primary key in Design view. See Exhibit 17-13. The Primary Key button in the Tools group on the TABLE TOOLS DESIGN tab is a toggle. Click the button to remove the key symbol if you want to specify a different field as the primary key.

Exhibit 17-13 Field selected as the primary key

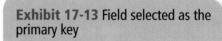
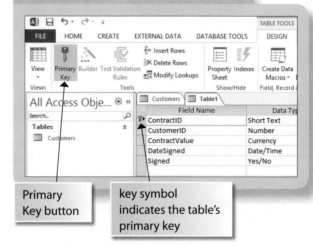

Primary Key button

key symbol indicates the table's primary key

Begin Activity

Specify a primary key.

1 In the table design grid, click in the **ContractID row** to make it the current field.

2 On the TABLE TOOLS DESIGN tab, in the Tools group, click the **Primary Key button**. A key symbol 🔑 appears in the row selector for the ContractID row, indicating that the ContractID field is the table's primary key. Refer to Exhibit 17-13.

End Activity

17-4d Saving the Table Design and Entering Records

After you design a table, you need to save it. To enter records into the new table, you need to switch to Datasheet view. You can use the Save button, or you can let Access remind you to save the table when you switch to Datasheet view.

Changing the Default Primary Key Field

When you create a new table in Datasheet view, Access creates the ID field as the table's default primary key. You can rename the ID field to better reflect the contents of the field you want to use for the primary key. Right-click the ID field, click Rename Field on the shortcut menu, type a new name, and then click in the next row.

The renamed primary key field still retains the properties of the default field, including its data type. The default ID primary key field is assigned the AutoNumber data type. For primary keys that contain a mix of letters and numbers, such as contract numbers, select the Short Text data type. However, you can also change the data type. In Datasheet view, you use the Data Type box for changing the data type. On the FIELDS tab, in the Formatting group, click the column, click the Data Type box arrow, and then click the new data type.

Ingvar Bjork/Shutterstock.com

Begin Activity

Save the table design and enter records.

1 On the TABLE TOOLS DESIGN tab, in the Views group, click the **View button**. A dialog box opens telling you that you must first save the table.

2 Click **Yes**. The Save As dialog box opens with Table1 selected in the Table Name box.

3 Type **Contracts** and then click **OK**. The Contracts table is added to the Tables list in the Navigation Pane, and the Contracts table is displayed in Datasheet view.

4 Double-click the right borders of each column in the datasheet to AutoFit the widths.

5 In the first row of the datasheet, type **1404-RR** as the contract number, and then press the **Tab key**.

6 Type **5** as the customer ID, press the **Tab key**, type **620** as the contract value,

and then press the **Tab key**. The contract value amount is displayed with a dollar sign and two decimal places to match the default format for the Currency data type even though you didn't type them. To the right of the Date Signed field, a calendar icon appears.

7 In the Date Signed field, type **1/16/16** and then press the **Tab key**. The Signed? field is selected.

> **Tip:** To use the mouse to enter the date, click the calendar icon and then select the date.

8 Press the **Spacebar**. A check mark appears in the check box.

9 Press the **Tab key** to move to the second record. Compare your screen to Exhibit 17-14.

10 Save the Contracts table.

> **Tip:** You can press the Tab key to leave a Yes/No check box unchecked. To use the mouse to select the check box, click it.

End Activity

Exhibit 17-14 Record entered in the Contracts table

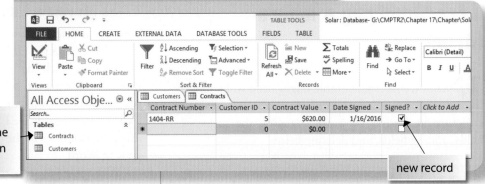

Contracts table in the Navigation Pane

new record

Guidelines for Designing Databases

Cybrain/Shutterstock.com

To design a database, you need to determine the fields, tables, and relationships needed to satisfy the data and processing requirements for an organization. Keep in mind the following guidelines:

▶ **Identify the fields needed to produce the required information.** Be sure to consider and include both the obvious and not so obvious data.

▶ **Divide each piece of data into its smallest useful part.** Individual units make the data more useful and flexible. For example, a person's complete name should be stored in two fields rather than one field.

▶ **Group related fields into tables.** Each table should have one focus. For example, fields related to invoices could be grouped into an Invoices table, and the fields related to customers could be grouped into a Customers table.

▶ **Determine each table's primary key.** Often, one of the fields in the table naturally serves the function of a primary key. For some tables, two or more fields might be needed to function as the primary key. In these cases, the primary key is called a **composite key**. For example, a school grade table would use a combination of student number and course code to serve as the primary key. For other tables, no single field or combination of fields can uniquely identify a record in a table. In these cases, you need to add a field whose sole purpose is to serve as the table's primary key.

▶ **Include a common field in related tables.** You use the common field to connect one table logically with another table. For example, the Contracts and Customers tables both include the CustomerID field as a common field; the CustomerID field. You can use the CustomerID value for a customer and search the Contracts table for all records with that CustomerID value. Likewise, you can determine which customer has a particular contract by searching the Customers table to find the record with the same CustomerID value as the corresponding value in the Contracts table.

▶ **Avoid data redundancy and inconsistent data.** When you store the same data in more than one place, **data redundancy** occurs. With the exception of using common fields to connect tables, data redundancy wastes storage space and can cause inconsistencies.

▶ **Determine the properties of each field.** You need to identify the properties, or characteristics, of each field so that the DBMS knows how to store, display, and process the field values. These properties include the field's name, maximum number of characters or digits, description, valid values, and other field characteristics.

17-5 Modifying a Table's Structure

Even a well-designed table might need to be modified. Some changes you can make to a table's structure in Design view are changing the order of fields, adding fields, and deleting fields.

composite key A primary key that requires two or more fields to uniquely identify each record in a table.

data redundancy Data stored in more than one place.

17-5a Moving a Field in Design View

To move a field in Design view, you first need to select the field's row in the table design grid. To select a field in Design view, click the box to the left of the row (sometimes called a record selector or row selector). After a row is selected, you can drag it up or down to its new location in the grid. See Exhibit 17-15. This is similar to dragging headings in the Navigation pane or in Outline view in Word.

Although you can move fields in Datasheet view by dragging a field's column heading to a new location, doing so rearranges only the display of the table's fields; the table structure is not changed. To move a field

Exhibit 17-15 Field being moved in the table structure

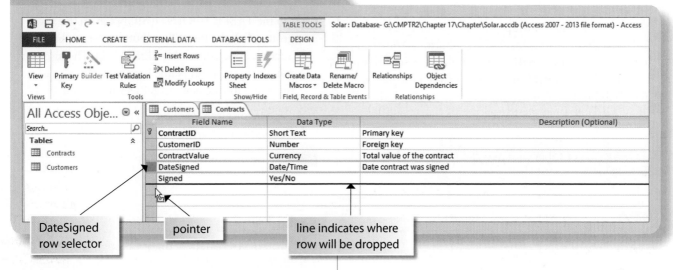

permanently, you must display the table in Design view. After you modify the table's structure, be sure to save the table.

Begin Activity

Move a field in a table.

1 Display the Contracts table in **Design view**.

2 In the table design grid, point to the **DateSigned row selector**. The pointer changes to ➡. Click the **DateSigned row selector** to select the row.

3 Press and hold the mouse button while pointing to the **DateSigned row selector**. The pointer changes to ⬚. Drag down until the dark line indicating the drop location for the field appears below the Signed field. Refer back to Exhibit 17-15.

4 Release the mouse button. The DateSigned field now appears below the Signed field in the table.

5 Save the Contracts table, and then click the **Customers tab** to display the Customers table.

6 Display the Customers table in **Design view**.

7 Move the **LastName Field** above the FirstName field.

8 Save the **Customers table**, and then switch to **Datasheet view**

to confirm that the LastName field appears to the left of the FirstName field.

End Activity

17-5b Adding a Field

You can add a new field to a table at any time. If the field will be the last field in the table, you can add the field the same way as when you add fields to a new table. If you decide the field belongs in a different location, you can always move it to its proper position.

You can also insert a new field between existing fields. In Datasheet view, select the field to the left of where you want the new field to be inserted. Then, in the Add & Delete group on the TABLE TOOLS FIELDS tab, click the button for the data type of the field you want to insert. Exhibit 17-16 shows a new field inserted to the right of the FirstName field in Datasheet view.

Exhibit 17-16 Table with new field in Datasheet view

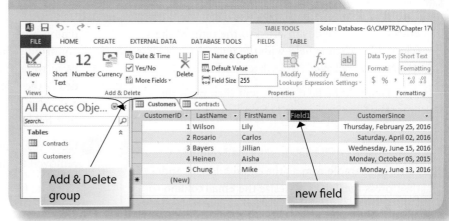

You can also insert new fields between other fields in Design view. In the table design grid, select the row below where you want the new field to be inserted. Then, in the Tools group on the TABLE TOOLS DESIGN tab, click the Insert Rows button. You then enter the field name, data type, optional description, and any additional field properties for the new field as usual. Exhibit 17-17 shows a new field inserted above the Email field in Design view.

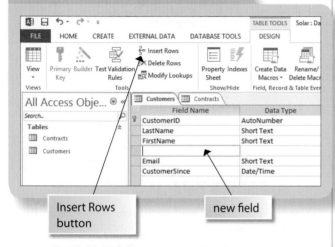

Exhibit 17-17 Table with new field in Design view

Insert Rows button

new field

Keep in mind that the new field does not contain data for any existing records. If you want to add data to the new field in existing records, you need to go back to each existing record in Datasheet view, click in the column for that record, and type the new data.

Begin Activity

Add a field to a table.

1 In Datasheet view for the Customers table, click the **FirstName column header** to select the field.

2 On the ribbon, click the **TABLE TOOLS FIELDS tab**. In the Add & Delete group, click the **Short Text button**. A new field is inserted to the right of the selected FirstName field with the temporary field name Field1 selected. Refer back to Exhibit 17-16.

3 Type **Email** as the field name, and then press the **Enter key**. The CustomerID field value for the first record is selected.

4 In the first record, click in the **Email column**, type **lwilson@example.com** as the email address, and then press the **Tab key**. Resize the **Email column** to fit the widest value.

5 Switch the table to **Design view**. In the table design grid, in the Field Name column, click **Email**.

6 On the TABLE TOOLS DESIGN tab, in the Tools group, click the **Insert Rows button**. A new, blank row appears above the current Email field. The insertion point is in the Field Name box, ready for you to type the name for the new field. Refer to Exhibit 17-17.

7 Type **InvoiceItem** as the field name, and keep the **Data Type** as **Short Text**.

8 Save the Customers table.

End Activity

17-5c Deleting a Field

After you have created a table, you might need to delete a field. When you delete a field, you also delete all the values for that field from the table. So, before you delete a field, make sure that you really want to do so and that you choose the correct field to delete. You can delete one field at a time, or you can select and delete a group of fields at the same time.

You can delete fields in either Datasheet view or Design view. In Datasheet view, select the field to delete, and then click the Delete button in the Add & Delete group on the TABLE TOOLS FIELDS tab. In Design view, click the Field Name box for the field to delete, and then click the Delete Rows button in the Tools group on the TABLE TOOLS DESIGN tab.

Begin Activity

Delete a field from a table.

1 In the table design grid, in the Field Name column, click **InvoiceItem** to make it the current field.

2 On the TABLE TOOLS DESIGN tab, in the Tools group, click the **Delete Rows button**. A dialog box appears, confirming that you want to permanently delete the selected field and all of the data in that field.

> **Tip:** You can also select the column header in Datasheet view and then click the Delete button in the Add & Delete group on the TABLE TOOLS FIELDS tab.

3 Click **Yes**. The selected InvoiceItem field is removed from the Customers table.

4 Save the Customers table.

End Activity

17-6 Closing and Opening Objects and Databases

Unlike other programs, you need to open and close the tables and other objects in a database. A database can be open but have all its objects closed.

17-6a Closing a Table

When you are done working with a table, you should close it. You close the selected table by clicking the Close button ☒ in the upper-right corner of the pane. Note that the ScreenTip for the Close button shows the name of the tab that will close as part of the button name, such as Close 'Table1'. If you changed the table structure but didn't save it, a dialog box appears reminding you to save. It is a good idea to work in an object and then save and close it as you go.

Begin Activity

Close a table.

1 If it is not already selected, click the **Customers tab**.

2 In the upper-right corner of the pane, to the right of the tabs, click the **Close 'Customers' button** ☒. The Customers table closes, and the Contracts table is displayed.

3 Right-click the **Contracts tab**. On the shortcut menu, click **Close**. The Contracts table closes, and the main portion of the Access window is now blank because no table or other database object is open.

> **Problem?** If a dialog box appears asking if you want to save the changes to the layout of the Contracts table, click **Yes**.

End Activity

17-6b Closing a Database

When you are done working with a database, you should close it. To close an open database without closing the Access program, click the FILE tab to display Backstage view, and then click Close in the navigation bar. You can also close Access, which also closes the database.

Begin Activity

Close an existing database.

1 On the ribbon, click the **FILE tab**. Backstage view appears with the Info screen displayed.

2 In the navigation bar, click **Close**. The Solar database closes, and the blank Access window appears.

End Activity

17-6c Opening a Database

You open an existing database from Backstage view by clicking Open in the navigation bar and then using the Open dialog box to navigate to and open the database.

Begin Activity

Open an existing database.

1 Open the data file **Solar17** located in the Chapter 17\Chapter folder. The Solar17 database opens. This database contains three objects: the Contracts, Customers, and Invoices tables.

2 Click the **FILE tab**. In the navigation bar, click **Save As** to display the Save As screen.

3 Under File Types, make sure **Save Database As** is selected.

4 Under Save Database As on the right, make sure **Access Database** is selected.

5 Click the **Save As button**. The Save As dialog box opens.

6 Save the database as **SolarPower17** to the location where you are saving your files.

> **Problem?** If the Security Warning bar appears, click the **Enable Content** button to close it. If the Security Warning dialog box opens asking if you want to make this file a Trusted Document, click **Yes** to prevent the Security Warning bar from appearing again, or click **No** to have the Security Warning bar appear the next time you open the database.

End Activity

17-6d Opening a Table

All of the tables (as well as any query, form, or report) in a database are listed in the Navigation Pane. You open a table or other object by double-clicking its name in the Navigation Pane.

Begin Activity

Open a table.

1 In the Navigation Pane, double-click **Customers** to open the Customers table in Datasheet view. Examine the fields in the Customers table.

> **Tip:** You can click the Shutter Bar Open/Close Button 《 to hide the Navigation Pane and display more of the datasheet.

2 In the Navigation Pane, double-click **Contracts** to open the Contracts table in Datasheet view. Examine the fields in the Contracts table.

3 Open the **Invoices table**, and then examine the fields in the Invoices table. See Exhibit 17-18.

4 Close the **Customers** and **Contracts tables**.

End Activity

17-6e Moving Around a Datasheet

You move around a datasheet using many of the same techniques you learned when you worked with Word tables and Excel worksheets. You can click in a field to make it the active field, or you can use the Tab key or the arrow keys to move to a different field. Access databases can contain thousands of records. When a table contains many records, only some of the records are visible on the screen at one time. You can use the navigation buttons on the record navigation bar, shown in Exhibit 17-19, to move through the records and to see the number of the current record as well as the total number of records in the table.

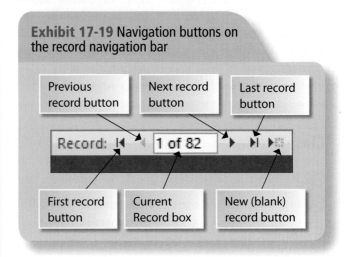

Exhibit 17-19 Navigation buttons on the record navigation bar

Begin Activity

Move around a datasheet.

1 In the Invoices table, click anywhere in the **second record** except in the Paid field (this would change the value of the check box). On the record navigation bar, the Current Record box shows that record 2 is the current record and there are 82 records in the table.

2 On the record navigation bar, click the **Next record button** ▶. The third record is now highlighted, identifying

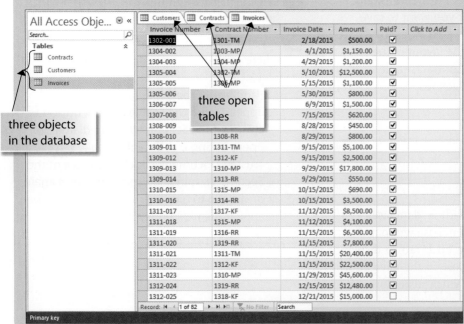

Exhibit 17-18 Three tables open in the database

it as the current record, and the Current Record box changed to display 3 of 82 to indicate that the third record is the current record.

3 Click the **Last record button** ▶|. The last record in the table, record 82, is now the current record.

4 In the vertical scroll bar, drag the **scroll box** to the top of the bar. Although the first records are now visible, record 82 is still the current record, as indicated in the Current Record box.

5 On the record navigation bar, click the **Previous record button** ◀. Record 81 is now the current record.

6 On the record navigation bar, click in the **Current Record box**, press the **Backspace key** twice to delete 81, type **1**, and then press the **Enter key**. The first record is selected.

7 On the record navigation bar, click the **New (blank) record button** ▶꘎. The first field in the next available blank record (record 83) is selected.

8 On the record navigation bar, click the **First record button** |◀. The first record is now the current record and is visible on the screen.

End Activity

LEARN MORE

Navigation Pane

The Navigation Pane lists all of the objects in the open database in separate groups. Icons identify the different types of database objects, making it simple to distinguish between them. You can click the arrow on the title bar of the Navigation Pane to display a menu with

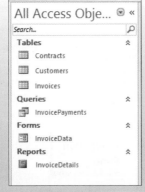

Navigation Pane

options for various ways to group and display objects in the Navigation Pane. In addition, you can use the Search box to enter text to find in the listed objects. For example, you could search for all objects that contain the word **Invoice** in their names. Note that Access searches for objects only in the categories and groups currently displayed in the Navigation Pane.

17-7 Creating Simple Queries, Forms, and Reports

The data in a database becomes even more useful when you can extract specific information and display it in a format that is easy to read and understand. You can do this by creating simple queries, forms, and reports based on the tables and other queries in a database.

17-7a Creating a Simple Query

A **query** is a question about the data stored in a database. When you create a query, you specify which fields to use to answer the question. Then Access displays only the records that fit, so you don't have to navigate through the entire database. In the Invoices table, for example, you might create a query to display only the invoice numbers and the invoice dates.

You can use the Simple Query Wizard to create a query based on the records and fields in a table. (A *wizard* is a series of dialog boxes that takes you step-by-step through a process.) After you start the Simple Query Wizard, you select the table or another query on which to base the new query, and then you select which fields to include in the query. Exhibit 17-20 shows the dialog box in the Simple Query Wizard in which you make these selections.

Exhibit 17-20 First Simple Query Wizard dialog box

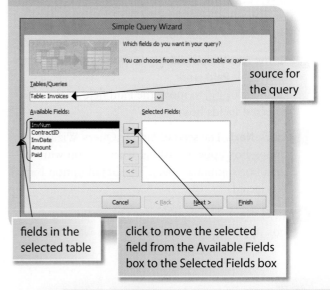

query A question about the data stored in a database.

If values in one of the selected fields can be used in calculations, such as the Amount field, the next dialog box that appears asks whether you want a detail or summary query. The default is a **detail query**, which shows every field of every record.

Query results are not stored in the database. However, the query design is stored in the database with the name you specified. You can redisplay the query results at any time by opening the query again.

Begin Activity

Create a query using the Simple Query Wizard.

1 On the ribbon, click the **CREATE tab**. In the Queries group, click the **Query Wizard button**. The New Query dialog box opens with Simple Query Wizard selected in the list.

2 Click **OK**. The first Simple Query Wizard dialog box opens. Table: Invoices is selected in the Tables/Queries box, and the fields in the Invoices table are listed in the Available Fields box. The first field in the list is selected. Refer back to Exhibit 17-20.

3 Click the **Tables/Queries box arrow**. All three objects in the database are listed. The Invoices table is selected because it was the selected table in the Navigation Pane before you started the Simple Query Wizard.

4 Click **Table: Invoices**.

5 With InvNum selected in the Available Fields box, click [>]. The InvNum field moves to the Selected Fields box.

> **Tip:** You can also double-click a field to move it from the Available Fields box to the Selected Fields box.

6 In the Available Fields box, click **Paid**, and then click [>] to move the Paid field to the Selected Fields box.

7 Click **Next**. The second Simple Query Wizard dialog box appears, asking whether you want a detail or summary query. The Detail option button is selected.

8 Click **Next**. The final Simple Query Wizard dialog box appears, asking what title you want to use for

the query. The suggested query title is based on the name of the table you are using.

9 In the What title do you want for your query? box, change the suggested name to **InvoicePayments**. Near the bottom of the dialog box, the Open the query to view information option button is selected.

10 Click **Finish**. The query results appear on a new tab named InvoicePayments in Datasheet view, and the query is added to the Navigation Pane. Compare your screen to Exhibit 17-21. The query lists all the records but shows only the InvNum and Paid fields as you specified in the first dialog box in the Simple Query Wizard.

11 Close the **InvoicePayments query**.

> **Problem?** If a dialog box opens asking if you want to save the changes to the layout of the query, you changed the query layout in some way, such as by resizing a column. If the change is intentional, click **Yes**; otherwise, click **No**.

End Activity

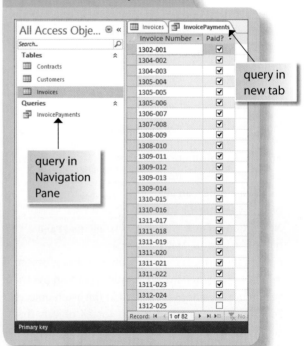

Exhibit 17-21 Query results

---

detail query A query that shows every field of every record as defined by the query criteria.

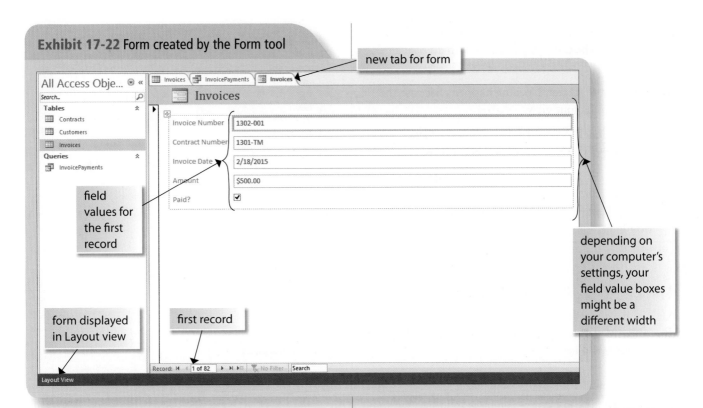

Exhibit 17-22 Form created by the Form tool

new tab for form

All Access Obje... ⊙ «
Search...
Tables ⊗
  Contracts
  Customers
  Invoices
Queries ⊗
  InvoicePayments

Invoices

Invoice Number	1302-001
Contract Number	1301-TM
Invoice Date	2/18/2015
Amount	$500.00
Paid?	☑

field values for the first record

depending on your computer's settings, your field value boxes might be a different width

form displayed in Layout view

first record

Record: 1 of 82 ▶ ▶| No Filter Search

Layout View

17-7b Creating a Simple Form

You use a **form** to enter, edit, and view records in a database. Although you can perform these same functions with tables and queries, forms can present data in customized and helpful ways. In a simple form, the fields from the table or query on which the form is based are displayed one record at a time, allowing you to focus on the values for one record. Each field name appears on a separate line with its field value for the current record displayed in a box to the right. You use the navigation buttons at the bottom of the form to move between records.

To quickly create a form containing all of the fields in a table (or query), you use the Form tool. The table or other database object on which you are basing the form must be selected in the Navigation Pane when you select the Form tool.

When you first create a form, it opens in Layout view. See Exhibit 17-22. You use **Layout view** to make design changes to the form.

Begin Activity

Create a simple form.

1 In the Navigation Pane, click the **Invoices table**, if necessary, to select it.

2 On the CREATE tab, in the Forms group, click the **Form button**. Because the Invoices table is

open and nothing else is selected in the Navigation Pane, a simple form showing every field in the Invoices table is created. Refer to Exhibit 17-22. The name on the tab is the same as the table name on which the form is based, and the fields in the form display the Caption properties set for the fields. The field values for the first record appear in the form, and a border appears around the value for the first field in the form, Invoice Number, indicating that it is selected. The form is in Layout view.

Tip: You can also select a query in the Navigation Pane to create the form based on the query you select.

3 On the record navigation bar, click the **Next record button** ▶. The values for the second record in the Invoices table appear in the form.

4 On the record navigation bar, click the **New (blank) record button** ▶. A blank form is created, and 83 of 83 appears in the Current Record box on the record navigation bar.

form A database object used to enter, edit, and view records in a database.

Layout view The Access view in which you can make design changes to database objects such as forms and reports.

5 Next to the Invoice Number field name, click the **empty field box**. It is highlighted with an orange border.

6 Type any character. Nothing happens because the form is in Layout view.

7 On the Quick Access Toolbar, click the **Save button** 💾. The Save As dialog box opens.

8 In the Form Name box, type **InvoiceData** and then click **OK**. The form's tab now displays the name InvoiceData, and the form is added to the Navigation Pane.

End Activity

17-7c Entering Data in a Form

After you create a form, you can use it to enter data in the table. To do this, you need to switch from Layout view to Form view.

Begin Activity

Enter data in a form.

1 On the FORM LAYOUT TOOLS DESIGN tab, in the Views group, click the **View button**. The form appears in Form view. The insertion point is blinking in the first field, Invoice Number.

2 Type **1412-056** and then press the **Tab key**. The insertion point moves to the next field.

3 Enter the following data, pressing the **Tab key** after entering each field value:

Contract Number	**1414-TM**
Invoice Date	**12/18/16**
Amount	**6000**
Paid	**No**

Compare your screen to Exhibit 17-23.

4 Close the **InvoiceData form**, saving if requested. The Invoices table is displayed in Datasheet view.

End Activity

When you add data using one object, such as a form, and the table you added the data to is open, you need to refresh the table before you can see the data you added using the form in the datasheet.

> **report** A database object that shows a formatted printout or screen display of the contents of the table or query objects on which the report is based.

Exhibit 17-23 Form with new data

Begin Activity

Refresh data.

1 On the record navigation bar, click the **Last record button** ▶|. There are still only 82 records in the datasheet; the record you entered using the form isn't included.

2 On the HOME tab, in the Records group, click the **Refresh All button**. The datasheet is refreshed, and the first record is selected.

3 Display the last record in the datasheet. The datasheet now contains 83 records; the record you added using the form is the last record.

4 Close the **Invoices table**.

End Activity

17-7d Creating a Simple Report

A **report** is a formatted printout or screen display of the contents of one or more tables or queries. A report shows each field in a column with the field values for each record in a row, similar to a datasheet. However, the report has a more visually appealing format for the data—column headings are in a different color, borders appear around each field value, a graphic of a report is included in the upper-left corner of the report, and the current day, date, and time appear in the upper-right corner. Dotted horizontal and vertical lines mark the edges of the page and show where text will be printed on the page. Exhibit 17-24 shows a simple report created from the Invoices table.

You can use the Report tool to quickly create a report based on all of the fields from a selected table or query. The Report tool also generates summaries and totals in the report automatically.

Begin Activity

Create a simple report using the Report tool.

1 In the Navigation Pane, click the **Invoices table**.

2 On the ribbon, click the **CREATE tab**. In the Reports group, click the **Report button**. A simple report showing every field in the Invoices table is created. Refer to Exhibit 17-24. The name on the tab is Invoices, because the report is based on the Invoices table. The report opens in Layout view. On the ribbon, the REPORT LAYOUT TOOLS tabs appear and the DESIGN tab is selected.

End Activity

17-7e Formatting a Report

The report is displayed in Layout view. In Layout view, you can change the format of the report. One way is to resize columns to better fit the data and ensure that all values will be printed. Also note that the page area, the area that will print, is defined by the dotted lines. Anything outside of the page area will not be printed.

Begin Activity

Format a report.

1 In the Paid? column, click **any field value**. The field you clicked has a dark orange border; the rest of the field values in the Paid? column are highlighted with lighter orange boxes.

2 In the Paid? column, point to the **right border** of any field value. The pointer changes to ↔.

3 Drag the right border of any field value in the **Paid? column** until the column is just wide enough to fit the Paid? column heading. The column is now narrower, better fitting the values. Compare your screen to Exhibit 17-25.

End Activity

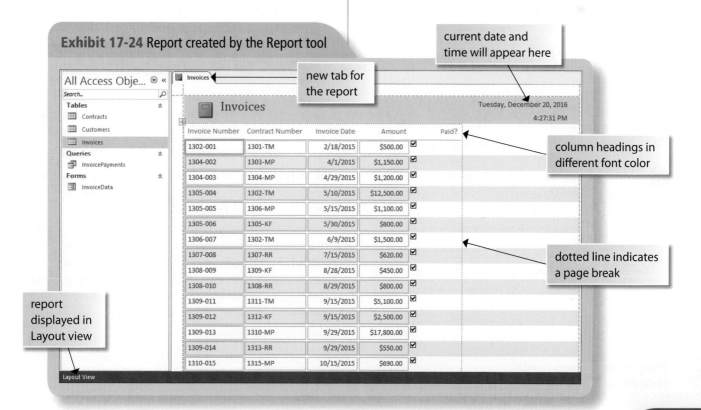

Exhibit 17-24 Report created by the Report tool

Exhibit 17-25 Report after resizing columns

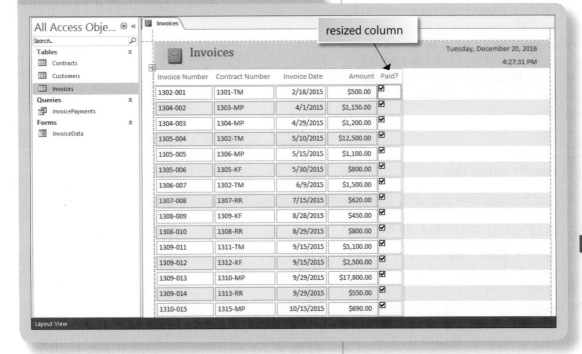

Reports are generally intended to be printed and distributed. When a table or query on which a report is based includes a field that can be used in calculations, the total of this field is calculated and displayed at the end of the report below a horizontal rule. If this field is not useful in your report, you can delete it.

A page number field also appears at the bottom of each page in a report. If you don't like the placement of a page number field, you can drag it to a new position.

Exhibit 17-26 shows the calculated field and the page number field at the end of the Invoices report.

Begin Activity

Delete a calculated field in a report.

1 Scroll to the bottom of the report. A calculated Amount Total field containing a total dollar amount was added at the bottom of the Amount column. Refer to Exhibit 17-26.

2 Click the **Amount Total field** ($1,052,510.00), and then press the **Delete key**. The field is deleted from the report, and the report scrolls back to the top of the page.

3 Scroll to the bottom of the report, click the **field above the page number field** (with one border as a solid line), and then press the **Delete key**.

4 Scroll back down to the bottom of the page. The stray blank line was deleted.

5 Click the **page number field**. An orange box appears around the field.

6 Point to the **selected page number field** so that the pointer changes to ⛶. Drag the **page number field** to the left as far as it will go.

7 On the ribbon, click the **REPORT LAYOUT TOOLS FORMAT tab**. In the Font group, click the **Align Left button** ≡. The text in the selected field is left aligned.

End Activity

17-7f Viewing a Report in Print Preview

In Layout view, the report doesn't show how many pages the report includes. To see this, you need to switch to Print Preview. **Print Preview** shows exactly how the report will look when printed. When you switch to Print Preview, the ribbon changes to include only the PRINT PREVIEW tab, which includes tools and options for printing the report as well as for changing the page size, the page layout, and how the report is displayed in Print Preview. Exhibit 17-27 shows the report at One Page zoom in Print Preview.

Print Preview The Access view that shows exactly how a report will look when printed.

Exhibit 17-26 Calculated field and page number field at the end of the report

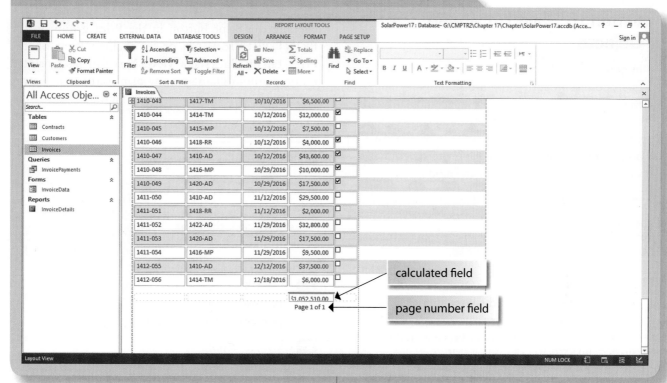

Exhibit 17-27 First page of the report in Print Preview

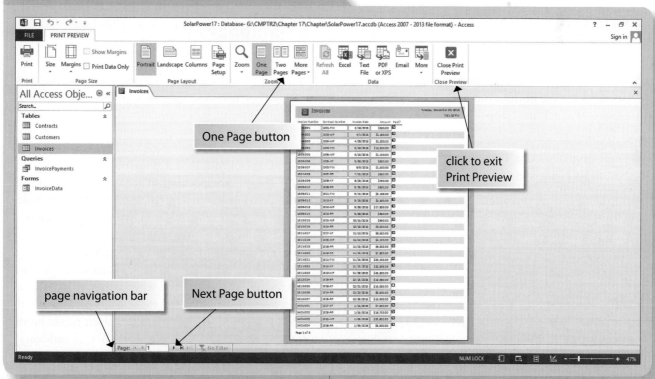

Begin Activity

View a report in Print Preview.

1 On the REPORT LAYOUT TOOLS DESIGN tab, in the Views group, click the **View button arrow**, and then click **Print Preview**. The first page of the report is displayed in Print Preview, and the PRINT PREVIEW tab replaces all of the other tabs on the ribbon.

2 On the PRINT PREVIEW tab, in the Zoom group, click the **One Page button** (even if it is already selected). Refer back to Exhibit 17-27.

3 On the page navigation bar, click the **Next Page button** ▶ twice. The second and then the third page of the report are displayed in Print Preview.

4 Change the zoom level to **100%**, and then scroll down to see the bottom of the third page of the report. "Page 3 of 3" appears at the bottom of the page.

5 On the Quick Access Toolbar, click the **Save button** 🖫. The Save As dialog box opens.

6 Save the report as **InvoiceDetails**. The tab displays the new report name, and the report appears in the Navigation Pane.

End Activity

17-7g Printing a Report

A report is often printed and then distributed to others to review. Although table and query datasheets can be printed, they are usually used for viewing and entering data; reports are generally used for printing the data in a database. You can change the print settings in the Print dialog box, which you open by clicking the Print button in the Print group on the PRINT PREVIEW tab or by clicking Print on the Print tab in Backstage view. You can also print a report without changing any print settings using the Quick Print option in Backstage view.

Begin Activity

Print a report.

1 On the PRINT PRE-VIEW tab, in the Print group, click the **Print button**. The Print dialog box opens.

2 Click **OK**. The dialog box closes, and the report prints with the default print settings.

3 Close the report.

> **Tip:** You can also click the **FILE tab**, click **Print** in the navigation bar, and then click **Print** on the Print screen.

End Activity

17-8 Compacting and Repairing a Database

Each time you open and work in a database, the size of the database increases. In addition, when you delete records or when you delete or replace database objects—such as queries, forms, and reports—the space they occupied does not become available for other records or objects until you compact the database. As illustrated in Exhibit 17-28, **compacting** a database rearranges the data and objects in a database to decrease its file size, making more space available and letting you open and close the database more quickly.

When you compact a database, Access repairs the database at the same time. In many cases, Access detects that a database is damaged when you try to open it and gives you the option to compact and repair it at that time. For example, the data in a database might become damaged, or corrupted, if you close Access suddenly by turning off your computer. If you think your database might be damaged because it is behaving unpredictably, you can use the Compact & Repair Database option to fix it.

compact To rearrange data and objects in a database to decrease its file size.

Exhibit 17-28 Compacting a database

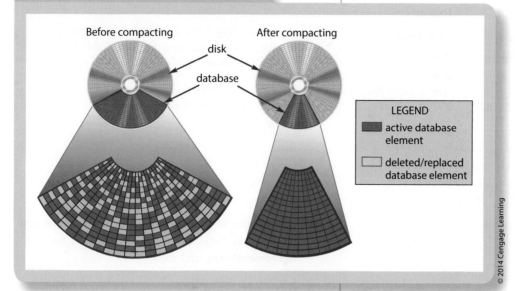

Before compacting   After compacting

disk

database

LEGEND

active database element

deleted/replaced database element

© 2014 Cengage Learning

Begin Activity

Compact and repair a database.

1 On the ribbon, click the **FILE tab**. Backstage view opens with the Info screen displayed.

2 Click the **Compact & Repair Database button**. Backstage view closes, and the database is compacted and repaired.

3 Close the database.

Tip: To compact and repair a database every time you close the file, click the FILE tab, click Options, click Current Database, and then select the Compact on Close check box.

End Activity

Quiz Yourself

1. What is a field?

2. What is a record?

3. How are tables related in a relational database?

4. Explain the difference between a primary and a foreign key.

5. What does the Data Type property do?

6. Describe how the data in a table is displayed in Datasheet view.

7. Describe how a table's contents appear in Design view.

8. When you create a new table in Datasheet view, which field does Access create, by default, as the primary key field for the new table and what are its default field name and data type?

9. In Datasheet view, what do the pencil symbol and the star symbol at the beginning of a record represent?

10. What is a property?

11. What does the Caption property do?

12. What is a query?

13. What is a form?

14. What is a report?

15. When you create a form using the Form tool, in which view does the form open?

16. What happens when you compact a database?

Practice It

Practice It 17-1

1. Start Access, and create a new, blank database named **Clients**.

2. Add the following fields to the table in the order shown, leaving the first field named ID:

Short Text	**Company**
Short Text	**FirstName**
Short Text	**LastName**
Short Text	**Phone**
Date/Time	**CustomerSince**

3. Resize the CustomerSince column width so it fits the column name.

4. Save the table as **Customers**.

5. Enter the following records in the Customers table:

	Record 1	Record 2
Company	**Bangor Lighting**	**High Estate Realtors**
FirstName	**Brian**	*your first name*
LastName	**Martin**	*your last name*
Phone	**207-555-6869**	**207-555-3132**
CustomerSince	**1/10/2015**	**11/29/2016**

6. Resize columns in the datasheet so that all the field values are completely displayed and the widest value just fits, and then save the table.

7. Switch to Design view. For each field, set the following field size or format and caption:

	Field Size/Format	Caption
Company	**150**	
FirstName	**20**	**First Name**
LastName	**25**	**Last Name**
CustomerSince	**Long Date**	**Customer Since**

8. Add a new field as the last field in the Customers table with the field name **CallPM**, the Yes/No data type, a Format property of Yes/No, and a Caption property of **Call after 8?**. Make sure the Default Value property is No.

9. Add the following descriptions to the Description property for each of the fields listed below:

ID	**Primary key**
CallPM	**Indicates whether client has given permission for us to call after 8:00 pm**

10. Save the table, and then switch the table to Datasheet view. Resize the Customer Since column to its best fit.

11. In the Call after 8? column, select the check boxes for both records.

12. Save the table, and then close the database.

13. Open the data file **Snow17** located in the Chapter 17\Practice It folder. Save the database as **SnowRemoval17**.

14. In the ServiceAgreement table, set the AgreementNum field to be the primary key, and then save and close the table.

15. In Design view for the Invoices table, move the Paid field so it follows the InvAmt field, and then save and close the table.

16. In Design view for the Clients table, add a new Short Text field named **Email** between the Phone and Street fields, and then save and close the table.

17. Create a query named **AllAmounts** that includes the AgreementNum and Amount fields from the ServiceAgreement table. Save and close the query.

18. Create a form based on the ServiceAgreement table, and then enter the following as a new record in the form:

Agreement #	**1624**
Client ID	**22**
Amount	**1700**
Date Signed	**12/22/16**

19. Display the ServiceAgreement table to see the new record, and then close the table. Save the form as **AgreementForm**, and then close it.

20. Create a report based on the ServiceAgreement table. Resize each field so it is slightly wider than the longest entry (either the field name itself or an entry in the field).

21. At the bottom of the report, delete the calculated Amount Total field and the field that contains the horizontal rule. Then drag the page number field as far left as possible, and left-align the contents of that field.

22. Display the report in Print Preview, and then print it.

23. Save the report as **AgreementReport**, and then close it.

24. Compact and repair the database.

25. Close the database.

Practice It 17-2

1. Start Access, and create a new, blank database named **Classes**.

2. Add the following fields to the table in the order shown, leaving the first field named ID:

Short Text	**ClassName**
Yes/No	**Juniors**
Currency	**Cost**
Number	**Length**

3. Save the table as **Class**.

4. Enter the following records in the Class table:

	Record 1	Record 2
ClassName	**Clay Discovery**	*your first and last names*
Juniors	**Yes**	**No**
Cost	**75**	**100**
Length	**45**	**60**

5. Resize columns in the datasheet so that the widest value in each field just fits, and then save the table.

6. Switch to Design view, and then for the ClassName field, change the Field Size property to **45** and the Caption property to **Class Name**.

7. Add a new field as the last field in the Class table with the field name **Level**, the Short Text data type, a Description property of **Beginning, Intermediate**, or **Advanced**, a Field Size property of **20**, and a Caption property of **Class Level**. Set the Default Value property to **Beginning**.

8. Add the following descriptions to the Description property for each of the fields listed below:

ID	**Primary key**
Juniors	**Does the class allow teen participation?**
Length	**Class duration in minutes**

9. Save the table, and then close the database.

10. Open the data file **Art17** located in the Chapter 17\Practice It folder. Save the database as **ArtClasses17**.

11. In the Classes table, specify that the following classes accept juniors: 123-PA, 204-DR, 205-DR, 392-CL, 394-CL, and 410-PH.

12. In Design view, move the Cost field so it follows the Length field. Delete the Level field. Save and close the table.

13. Create a query named **ClassCost** based on the Classes table that includes the ClassName, Cost, and Length fields (in that order). Close the query.

14. Create a form based on the Classes table, and then enter the following as a new record in the Classes table using the form.

Class ID	**414-PH**
Class Name	**Darkroom III**
Juniors	**No**
Length	**120**
Cost	**300**

15. After entering the record, save the form as **ClassInfo** and then close it.

16. Open the Classes table in Datasheet view to see the new record.

17. Create a report based on the Classes table. Resize each field so it is slightly wider than the longest entry (either the field name itself or an entry in the field).

18. Delete the total field and the horizontal rule that was added at the bottom. Align the page number field so its right edge is aligned with the right edge of the rightmost field. Change the alignment of the text in the page number field so it is right-aligned.

19. Display the report in Print Preview, and then print it.

20. Save the report as **ClassList**, and then close it.

21. Close all open objects, and then compact and repair the database.

22. Close the database.

On Your Own

On Your Own 17-1

1. Open the data file **DonationTable17** located in the Chapter 17\On Your Own folder. Save the database as **DonationTable17Edited**.

2. Open the Donations table, and then switch to Design view.

3. Rename the ID field as **AgencyID**.

4. Set the DonationID field as the primary key.

5. Set appropriate values for the DonationID field's Description, Field Size, and Caption properties. (*Hint*: To determine the field size of the DonationID field, look at the records in the datasheet.)

6. Change the Field Size and Caption properties for the rest of the fields (use the Medium Date format for the DonationDate field, leave the Description field size at 255, use **Pickup?** as the caption for Pickup, and make sure the default value for Pickup is No). Save the table.

7. In Datasheet view, resize the columns as needed so that all of the columns are just wide enough to display the widest values. Save the table, and then close it.

8. In the Navigation Pane, select the Donations table. Copy the Donations table to the Clipboard.

9. Open the data file **Donations17** located in the Chapter 17\On Your Own folder. Save the database as **DonationsList17**.

10. In DonationsList17, paste the contents of the Clipboard. In the Paste Table As dialog box that opens, change the table name to **Donations**, make sure the Structure and Data option button is selected, and then click OK.

11. Open the Agencies table, and then delete the Fax and Notes fields from the table. Save and close the table.

12. Use the Simple Query Wizard to create a query that includes all the fields in the Donors table except the DonorID field. Save the query as **DonorPhoneList**.

13. Sort the query results by the Last Name column. (*Hint*: Make the Last Name column the current field, and then click the appropriate button on the HOME tab in the Sort & Filter group.)

14. Adjust column widths in the datasheet as needed, and then save and close the query.

15. Create a form based on the Donors table.

16. In the new form, navigate to record 8. In Form view, change the first name to your first initial and your last name (for example, *JSmith*).

17. In Layout view, change the font style of each of the labels (DonorID, First Name, Last Name, and Phone) to bold.

18. Print the form for the current record only.

19. Save the form as **DonorInfo**, and then close it.

20. Create a report based on the Donors table.

21. In Layout view, resize each field so it is slightly wider than the longest entry (either the field name itself or an entry in the field).

22. At the bottom of the report, make adjustments as necessary so that there are no extra fields and so that the page number is left-aligned.

23. Save the report as **DonorList**.

24. Display the report in Print Preview, and verify that the fields and page number fit within the page area. Print the report, and then close it.

25. Compact and repair the database, and then close it.

26. Open the **DonationTable17Edited** database, compact and repair it, and then close it.

Chapter 17

ADDITIONAL STUDY TOOLS

IN THE BOOK

▶ Complete end-of-chapter exercises

▶ Study tear-out Chapter Review Card

ONLINE

▶ Complete additional end-of-chapter exercises

▶ Take practice quiz to prepare for tests

▶ Review key term flash cards (online, printable, and audio)

▶ Play "Beat the Clock" and "Memory" to quiz yourself

▶ Watch the videos to learn more about the topics taught in this chapter

Answers to Quiz Yourself

1. A field is a single characteristic of a person, place, object, event, or idea.

2. A record is all the fields about a single person, place, object, event, or idea collected in a row in a table.

3. Tables in a relational database are related through common fields.

4. The primary key, whose values uniquely identify each record in a table, is called a foreign key when it is placed in a second table to form a relationship between the two tables.

5. The Data Type property restricts the type of data that can be entered in a field.

6. In Datasheet view, a table's contents are displayed in rows and columns.

7. In Design view, you see the structure of a table, including field names, data types, and properties, but no data.

8. When you create a new table in Datasheet view, the first field is the primary key field. It is named ID, and its data type is AutoNumber.

9. The pencil symbol indicates that the record is being edited. The star symbol indicates the next row available for a new record.

10. A property is one characteristic or aspect of a field, such as its name or data type.

11. The Caption property is what appears in tables and other objects in place of the field name.

12. A query is a question about the data stored in a database.

13. A form is a database object used to enter, edit, and view records in a database.

14. A report is a database object that shows a formatted printout or screen display of the table or query objects on which the report is based.

15. When you create a form with the Form tool, the form opens in Layout view.

16. When you compact a database, you rearrange data and objects in a database to decrease its file size and repair any errors.

Maintaining and Querying a Database

Andresr/Shutterstock.com

Designing and creating a database is just the beginning. Once the database structure is developed, the ongoing work of record keeping begins. Data is constantly changing. People regularly get new phone numbers and email addresses. Invoices are sent and then paid. Customer activity is ongoing, and tracking this accurately leads to developing new strategies for promoting services. So, no matter what kind of information the database contains—customer, contract, invoice, or asset data, to name just a few—the information must be accurate and current to be of value. This requires continual and diligent entering and updating of records.

Database records can also be used to monitor and analyze other aspects of the business by creating and using queries to retrieve information from the database. Queries can also be saved so anyone can run the queries at any time, modify them as needed, or use them as the basis for designing new queries to meet additional information requirements.

Microsoft product screenshots used with permission from Microsoft Corporation.

Learning Objectives

After studying the material in this chapter, you will be able to:

18-1 Maintain database records

18-2 Work with queries in Design view

18-3 Sort and filter data

18-4 Define table relationships

18-5 Create a multitable query

18-6 Add criteria to a query

18-7 Create a copy of a query

18-8 Add multiple criteria to queries

18-9 Create a calculated field

18-10 Use a property sheet

18-11 Use functions in a query

18-1 Maintaining Database Records

A database is only as useful and accurate as the data it contains. Maintaining a database involves adding new records, updating the field values of existing records, and deleting outdated records to keep the database current and accurate.

18-1a Editing Field Values

Records often need to be edited to update or correct a field value. For example, information, such as a phone number or email address, might have changed, or the original record might have been entered inaccurately, and as a result, it contains an error. To replace a field value, you select it in the table datasheet and then type the new entry. To edit a field value, position the insertion point in the field value, and use standard editing techniques to delete and insert text as needed.

FYI

Navigate and Edit Fields

The F2 key is a toggle that you use to switch between navigation mode and editing mode. In navigation mode, Access selects an entire field value. The entry you type while in navigation mode replaces the highlighted field value. In editing mode, you can insert or delete characters in a field value. You can use the mouse or the keyboard to move the location of the insertion point, as you have done in Word and Excel.

deepspacedave/Shutterstock.com

Begin Activity

Move around the datasheet, and modify records.

1 Open the data file **Solar18** located in the Chapter 18\Chapter folder. Save the database as **SolarPower18**.

2 In the Navigation Pane, double-click the **Customers table**. The table opens in Datasheet view. In the first record, the field value for the first field—the Customer ID field—is selected.

3 Press the **Ctrl+End keys**. The last field—the Email field—in the last record—record 35—in the Customers table is selected.

4 Press the **Up Arrow key**. The Email field value for record 34, the second to last record, is now selected.

5 Press the **Shift+Tab keys**. The Phone field value for record 34 is selected.

6 Click at the end of the field value to position the insertion point to the right of the phone number. Press the **Backspace key** to delete the 0, type **1** as the new final digit of the phone number, and then press the **Enter key**. The Phone field value is updated.

> **Tip:** Remember that changes to field values are saved when you move to a new field or another record or when you close the table.

7 Press the **Home key**. The Customer ID field value for record 34 is now selected.

8 Press the **Ctrl+Home keys**. The Customer ID field value for the first record is selected.

9 Press the **Down Arrow key** twice, and then press the **Tab key** to select the Last Name field value for the third record.

10 Type **Hamilton**. Press the **Tab key** to select the First Name field value for the third record, type **Derek**, and then press the **Tab key** to move to the next field.

End Activity

18-1b Finding and Replacing Data

As a database grows, the number of records becomes numerous—too numerous to scroll and search for a specific record that you need to update or delete. Instead of scrolling the table datasheet to find the field value you need to change or delete, you can use the Find and Replace dialog box to locate a specific field value in a table, query datasheet, or form. See

Exhibit 18-1. In the Find and Replace dialog box, you specify the value you want to find, where to search for that value, and whether to locate all or part of a field value. You also can choose to search up or down from the currently selected record. If you want to substitute a different field value, you can enter that value on the Replace tab.

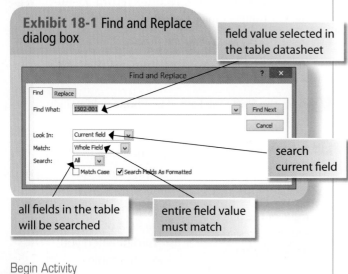

Exhibit 18-1 Find and Replace dialog box

field value selected in the table datasheet

search current field

all fields in the table will be searched

entire field value must match

Begin Activity

Find data.

1 Open the **Invoices table** in Datasheet view. The Invoice Number field value for the first record is selected. This is the field you want to search.

2 On the HOME tab, in the Find group, click the **Find button**. The Find and Replace dialog box opens with the value in the Find What box selected. This value is the Invoice Number field value for the first record in the Invoices table. Refer back to Exhibit 18-1.

3 In the Find What box, type **1606-033** to replace the selected value. You want to find the record for invoice number 1606-033.

4 Click **Find Next**. The datasheet scrolls to the record for invoice number 1606-033 (record number 63) and selects the Invoice Number field value.

5 In the Find and Replace dialog box, click **Cancel**. The Find and Replace dialog box closes.

6 For invoice number 1606-033, click in the **Amount box**, and then edit the value to **$13,750.00**.

7 Close the **Invoices table**.

End Activity

18-1c Deleting a Record

Deleting a record removes all of the field values for that record from the database. Before you delete a record, you must select the entire row for the record in the datasheet. Then, you can delete the selected record using the Delete button in the Records group on the HOME tab or the Delete Record command on the shortcut menu. Keep in mind that the deletion of a record is permanent and cannot be undone.

Begin Activity

Delete a record.

1 In the Customers table, find the record for the customer with the last name **Velazquez**.

2 Click **the row selector** to select the entire record for the customer with the last name Velazquez.

3 On the HOME tab, in the Records group, click the **Delete button**. A dialog box appears, confirming that you want to delete the record and reminding you that you cannot undo this deletion.

4 Click **Yes**. The dialog box closes, and the record is removed from the table.

5 Close the **Customers table**.

End Activity

CAUTION

AutoNumbered Field Values

Each value generated by a field is unique. When you use the AutoNumber data type to define the primary key field, the AutoNumber data type ensures that all primary key field values are unique. When you delete a record that has an AutoNumber field, the corresponding value is also deleted and cannot be reused. After deleting a record with an AutoNumber field, you might see gaps in the numbers used for the field values.

18-2 Working with Queries in Design View

In Chapter 17, you used the Simple Query Wizard to create a query based on one table. You can also create queries in Design view. When you do this, you are constructing a query by example. **Query by example** (**QBE**) retrieves the information that precisely matches the example you provide of the information being requested. Queries can be based on one table, on multiple tables, on other queries, or on a combination of tables and queries. For example, you might use a query to find records in the Customers table for only those customers who have unpaid invoices as recorded in the Invoices table.

Designing Queries vs. Using a Query Wizard

More specialized, technical queries, such as finding duplicate records in a table, are best created using a Query Wizard. A Query Wizard prompts you for information by asking a series of questions and then creates the appropriate query based on your answers. You used the Simple Query Wizard to display only some of the fields in the Invoice table. The other Query Wizards can create more complex queries. For common, informational queries, it is often easier to design the query yourself than to use a Query Wizard.

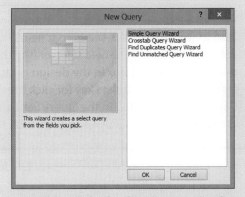

New Query dialog box listing query wizards

18-2a Designing a Select Query

Most questions about data are general queries in which you specify the fields and records you want to select. These common requests for information, such as "Which customers are located in Berkeley?" or "How many invoices have been paid?", are select queries. A **select query** is a query in which you specify the fields and records you want Access to select. The answer to a select query is returned in a query datasheet.

When you design a query in Design view, you specify which fields to include in the query. To begin, you click the Query Design button in the Queries group on the CREATE tab. This opens a new Query window in Design view with the Show Table dialog box open. See Exhibit 18-2.

Exhibit 18-2 Show Table dialog box

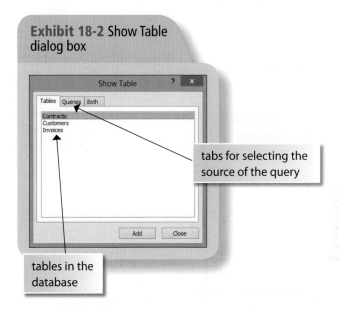

tabs for selecting the source of the query

tables in the database

In this dialog box, click the table and query names of the tables and queries on which you are basing your query, and then click Add to add the field lists from those tables and queries to the top portion of the Query window. The bottom portion of the Query window contains the **design grid**, which is the area to which you add the fields and record-selection criteria for your query. Each column in the design grid contains specifications about a field being used in the query. Exhibit 18-3 shows the field list from the Customers table added to the top portion of the Query window and the CustomerID field added to the design grid. In the design grid, the field name appears in the Field box, and the table name that contains the field appears in the Table box. The selected Show check box indicates that the field will be displayed in the datasheet after you run the query.

query by example (**QBE**) A query that retrieves the information that precisely matches the example you provide of the information being requested.

select query A query in which you specify the fields and records you want Access to select.

design grid The bottom portion of the Query window in Design view to which you add the fields and record-selection criteria for a query.

Exhibit 18-3 Field added to the design grid

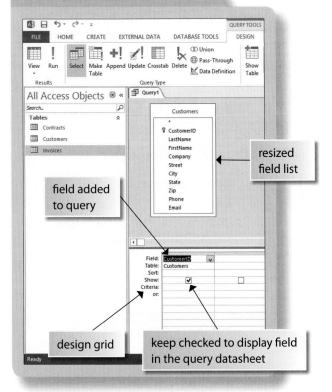

resized field list

field added to query

design grid

keep checked to display field in the query datasheet

Begin Activity

Design a select query.

1 On the ribbon, click the **CREATE tab**. In the Queries group, click the **Query Design button**. The Query window opens in Design view. The Show Table dialog box opens with the Tables tab selected. The three tables in the database are listed on the Tables tab. Refer back to Exhibit 18-2.

2 In the list, click **Customers**, and then click **Add**. The field list for the Customers table is added to the Query window.

> **Problem?** If the wrong table is added to the Query window, execute Step 3 first. Next, right-click **the table name** in the field list in the Query window, and then click **Remove Table**. To add the correct table to the Query window, click the **Show Table button** in the Query Setup group on the QUERY TOOLS DESIGN tab to redisplay the Show Table dialog box, and then repeat Steps 2 and 3.

recordset The result of a query, which is a set of records that answers the question.

3 In the Show Table dialog box, click **Close**. The Show Table dialog box closes.

4 Point to the **bottom border** of the Customers field list to change the pointer to ↕, and then drag the **bottom border** of the Customers field list down until the vertical scroll bar in the field list disappears and all of the fields are visible. (Email is the last field in the list.)

5 In the Customers field list, double-click **CustomerID**. The field is placed in the Field box in the first column of the design grid. Refer back to Exhibit 18-3.

> **Tip:** You can also drag a field from the field list to a column in the design grid to add the field to the query.

6 In the Customers field list, click **Company**, and then drag Company down to the **second column Field box** in the design grid. When the pointer changes to ⬚, release the mouse button. The Company field is placed in the Field box in the second column in the design grid.

7 Add the **FirstName**, **LastName**, **City**, **Email**, and **Phone** fields to the third through seventh columns in the design grid.

> **Problem?** If you accidentally add the wrong field to the design grid, select that field's column by clicking the **field selector** (the thin bar above the Field box in the design grid), and then press the **Delete key** (or click the **Delete Columns button** in the Query Setup group on the QUERY TOOLS DESIGN tab).

End Activity

Query results appear in a query datasheet. To see the query results in a query datasheet, click the View or Run button in the Results group on the QUERY TOOLS DESIGN tab. The result of a query is also referred to as a **recordset** because the query produces a set of records that answers your question. Exhibit 18-4 shows the query results for the query you created based on the Customers table.

Although a query datasheet looks like a table datasheet, a query datasheet is temporary. Its contents are based on the criteria specified in the query design grid. In contrast, a table datasheet shows the permanent data in a table. Data in a query datasheet is not duplicated; it

Exhibit 18-4 Query datasheet with query results

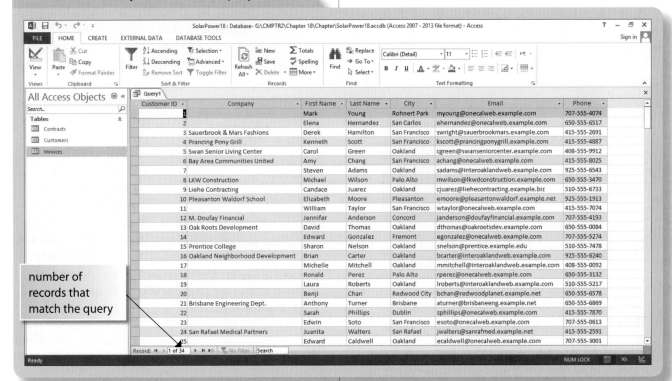

number of records that match the query

is the same data that is contained in the table datasheet displayed in a different way. If you update data in a query datasheet, the data in the underlying table will be updated with those changes.

Begin Activity

Run and save a query.

1 On the ribbon, on the QUERY TOOLS DESIGN tab, in the Results group, click the **Run button**. The query runs, and the results are displayed in Datasheet view. The fields you added to the design grid appear in the datasheet in the same order as in the design grid. The records are displayed in order based on the values in the primary key field, Customer ID. A total of 34 records are displayed in the datasheet. Refer back to Exhibit 18-4.

2 On the Quick Access Toolbar, click the **Save button** 💾. The small Save As dialog box opens.

3 In the Query Name box, type **CustomerContact**, and then click **OK**. The query name appears on the tab for the query object and also in the Queries group in the Navigation Pane.

End Activity

18-2b Modifying a Query

If the results of a query are not what you expected or require, you can make changes to the query. For example, you can hide a field's values in the query results, change the order in which the fields appear in the query results, or add fields to or remove fields from the query.

Sometimes, you might want to hide a field in a query's results. For example, if a query lists all customers who live in San Francisco, you don't need to see the City field listing the same value—San Francisco—for every record. To hide a field in the query results, click the Show check box in that field's column in the design grid to deselect it.

Keep in mind that hiding a field's values does not remove the field from the query design. To delete a field from the query design, click in its column and then click the Delete Columns button in the Query Setup group on the QUERY TOOLS DESIGN tab.

If you want the fields to appear in a different order in the query results, you can change the order of the fields in the design grid. To move a field, first select the field's column in the design grid. The thin bar above each column in the design grid is the **field selector**, and

field selector The thin bar above each column in the design grid in a Query window that you click to select the entire field.

you click the field selector to select the entire column in the design grid. After a field is selected, you can drag it left or right and drop it when the vertical line is in the location where you want the field to be inserted, as shown in Exhibit 18-5.

Exhibit 18-5 Selected field being moved in the design grid

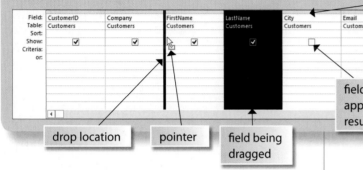

Begin Activity

Modify a query.

1 On the HOME tab, in the Views group, click the **View button**. The CustomerContact query switches to Design view.

2 In the design grid, in the Show row for the City column, click the **Show check box**. The Show check box is no longer selected, indicating that the City field will still be included in the query but will not appear in the results.

3 Point to the **LastName field selector** so that the pointer changes to ↓, and then click. The entire field is selected.

4 Point to the **LastName field selector** so that the pointer is ↖, and then drag the selected field to the left until the vertical line to the left of the FirstName field is highlighted. Refer back to Exhibit 18-5.

5 Release the mouse button. The LastName field moves to the left of the FirstName field.

6 In the design grid, click in the **Email column**. On the QUERY TOOLS DESIGN tab, in the Query

sort The process of rearranging records in a specified order or sequence.

sort field The field used to determine the order of records in the datasheet.

filter A set of restrictions placed on records in a datasheet or form to temporarily isolate a subset of the records.

Setup group, click the **Delete Columns button**. The Email field is removed from the query design.

> **Tip:** You can also click a field selector to select that column and then press the Delete key to delete a field from a query design.

7 On the QUERY TOOLS DESIGN tab, in the Results group, click the **Run button**. The results of the modified query are displayed in the query datasheet. Notice that the City field is hidden, the Last Name field values appear to the left of the First Name field values, and the Email field is no longer included in the query results.

End Activity

18-3 Sorting and Filtering Data

The records in the query datasheet are listed in order by the field values in the primary key field for the table. Sometimes, however, you will want to display the records in a specific order, such as in alphabetical order by city. Other times, you will want to display a subset of the records, such as only the records for a certain city. To make these changes, you can sort and filter the data.

Sorting is the process of rearranging records in a specified order or sequence. For example, you might sort customer information by the Last Name field to more easily find specific customers, or you might sort contracts by the Contract Value field to monitor the financial aspects of a business. When you sort data in a query, only the records in the query datasheet are rearranged; the records in the underlying tables remain in their original order.

To sort records, you must select the **sort field**, which is the field used to determine the order of records in the datasheet. You sort records in either ascending (increasing) or descending (decreasing) order, as described in Exhibit 18-6.

A **filter** is a set of restrictions you place on the records in a datasheet or form to temporarily isolate a subset of the records. A filter lets you view different

Exhibit 18-6 Sort results for different data types

Data type	Ascending sort results	Descending sort results
Short Text, Long Text*	A to Z	Z to A
Number	Lowest to highest numeric value	Highest to lowest numeric value
Date/Time	Oldest to most recent date	Most recent to oldest date
Currency	Lowest to highest numeric value	Highest to lowest numeric value
AutoNumber	Lowest to highest numeric value	Highest to lowest numeric value
Yes/No	Yes (check mark in check box) then no values	No then yes values

*Note that Long Text fields are sorted on only the first 255 characters

© 2014 Cengage Learning

subsets of displayed records so that you can focus on only the data you need. Unless you save the object with a filter applied, the filter is not available the next time you open the object.

18-3a Sorting in Datasheet View

In Datasheet view, you can click the arrow ▼ on a column heading in the datasheet to open a menu of options for sorting and filtering field values. Exhibit 18-7 shows the menu that appears when you click the arrow on the Last Name column heading. The first two commands sort the values in the current field in ascending or descending order. You can also click the Ascending and Descending buttons in the Sort & Filter group on the HOME tab to sort the data based on the current field. When records are sorted, an arrow appears on the right side of the column heading, indicating the sort order. If you sort in ascending order, the arrow points up. If you sort in descending order, the arrow points down.

Begin Activity

Use AutoFilter to sort data.

1 In the CustomerContact datasheet, click the **Last Name column heading arrow** ▼. A menu opens. Refer to Exhibit 18-7.

2 On the menu, click **Sort A to Z**. The records are rearranged in ascending alphabetical order by last name, as indicated by the up arrow on the right side of the Last Name column heading.

Tip: You can also use the Ascending and Descending buttons in the Sort & Filter group on the HOME tab to sort records based on the selected field in a datasheet.

End Activity

18-3b Sorting Multiple Fields in Design View

Sometimes you need to sort using more than one field. The first field you sort by is the primary sort field, the second field you sort by is the secondary sort field, and so on. For example, you might sort a list of customers alphabetically by city. To make it easier to locate a specific name within a city, you can then sort alphabetically by Last Name within each city. In this case, City is the primary sort field, and Last Name is the secondary sort field.

Exhibit 18-7 Menu that appears when you click a column heading arrow

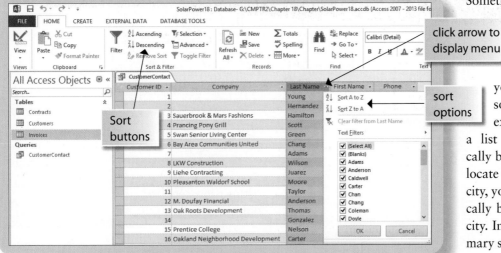

You can select as many as 10 different sort fields. For example, you might sort invoices based on whether they are paid or unpaid. Then you could sort each group of invoices by the invoice date. And finally, you could sort the invoices for each date by the invoice amount.

To sort by two fields in Datasheet view, first apply a sort to the secondary field, and then apply a sort to the primary field. For queries, you can also sort fields in Design view. In Design view, the leftmost sort field in the design grid is the primary sort field, and each remaining sort field is applied from left to right. Exhibit 18-8 shows a query with two sort fields specified.

Exhibit 18-8 Query with two sort fields

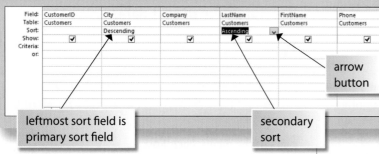

leftmost sort field is primary sort field

secondary sort

arrow button

Begin Activity

Sort multiple fields in Design view.

1 On the HOME tab, in the Views group, click the **View button**. The CustomerContact query switches to Design view. You will sort the query results in reverse alphabetical order by city and then within each city, in alphabetical order by last name.

2 In the design grid, in the City field, click the **Show check box** to select it. The field will again be displayed in the query results.

3 Move the **City field** to the left of the Company field. The City field will appear to the left of the Company field in the query results. This will be the primary sort field.

4 In the design grid, click in the **City column Sort box**. An arrow button appears at the right end of the City column Sort box.

5 Click the **City column Sort box arrow button** to display the sort options, and then click **Descending**. The City field now has a descending sort order. Because the City field is a Short Text field, the field values will be displayed in reverse alphabetical order.

6 Click the **LastName Sort box**, click the **arrow button**, and then click **Ascending**. The Last-Name field, which will be the secondary sort field because it appears to the right of the primary sort field (City) in the design grid, now has an ascending sort order. Refer back to Exhibit 18-8.

7 On the QUERY TOOLS DESIGN tab, in the Results group, click the **Run button**. In the query datasheet, the records appear in descending order based on the values in the City field. Records with the same City field value appear in ascending order by the values in the Last Name field. Compare your screen to Exhibit 18-9.

Exhibit 18-9 Query datasheet sorted on two fields

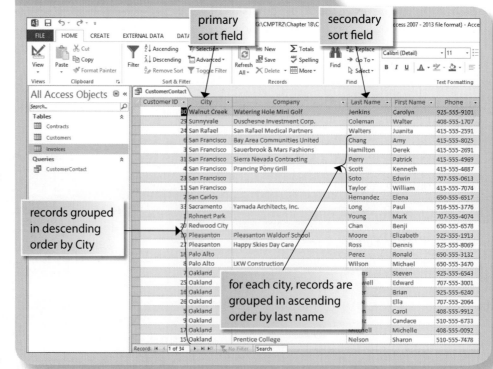

primary sort field

secondary sort field

records grouped in descending order by City

for each city, records are grouped in ascending order by last name

8 Save the **CustomerContact query**. All the design changes—including the selection of the sort fields—are saved with the query.

End Activity

18-3c Filtering Data

There are several methods you can use to filter data.

▶ **Common filters**—filters the datasheet based on a field value. They are listed on the menu that appears when you click the arrow on the column heading in Datasheet view.

▶ **Filter by selection**—filters the datasheet based on a selected field value in a datasheet or form. Exhibit 18-10 shows the Selection menu when San Francisco is selected in the City field. The commands on the menu change depending on the data type of the selected field. In this case, you can choose to display records with a City field value that equals the selected value (in this case, San Francisco); does not equal the value; contains the value somewhere within the field; or does not contain the value somewhere within the field.

▶ **Filter by form**—changes the datasheet to display blank fields so that you can choose a value for any blank field to apply a filter that selects only those records containing that value.

When a datasheet has been filtered, *Filtered* appears on the status bar and a Filtered button appears to the right of the navigation buttons. Also, as shown in Exhibit 18-11, the arrow on the column heading for the filtered field changes to a filter icon. To remove the filter and redisplay all the records, click the Toggle Filter button in the Sort & Filter group on the HOME tab.

Exhibit 18-10 Selection menu to filter the City field with San Francisco selected

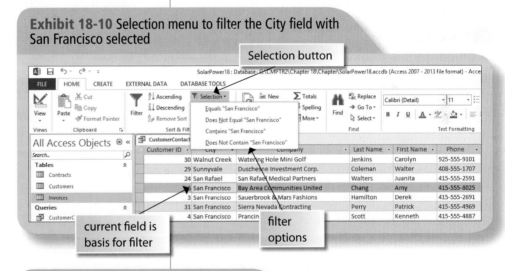

current field is basis for filter

filter options

Selection button

Exhibit 18-11 Query datasheet with filter

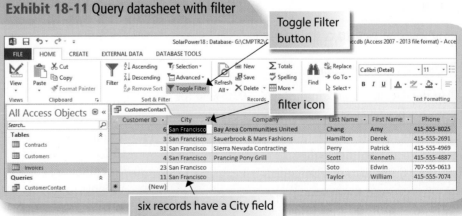

Toggle Filter button

filter icon

six records have a City field value of San Francisco

Filter records by selection.

1 In the CustomerContact query datasheet, locate the first occurrence of a City field containing the value **San Francisco**, and then click anywhere within that field value.

2 On the HOME tab, in the Sort & Filter group, click the **Selection button**. A menu opens with options for the type of filter to apply. Refer back to Exhibit 18-10. You want to display all the records whose City field value equals San Francisco.

3 In the Selection menu, click **Equals "San Francisco"**. The filtered results appear in the datasheet, and the filter icon appears in the column heading for the City field. Only six records have a City field value of San Francisco. Refer back to Exhibit 18-11.

4 On the HOME tab, in the Sort & Filter group, click the **Toggle Filter button**. The filter is removed, and all 34 records are redisplayed in the query datasheet.

5 Close the **CustomerContact query**. A dialog box appears, asking if you want to save changes to the design of the query which now includes the filter you just created.

6 Click **No** to close the query without saving the changes.

You can apply more than one filter to a datasheet. When you apply the second filter, that filter is applied only to the records displayed as a result of applying the first filter.

Apply two filters to a datasheet.

1 Open the **Invoices table**.

2 In the datasheet, click in the **Invoice Date field** for any record.

3 On the HOME tab, in the Sort & Filter group, click the **Selection button**. In the Selection menu, click **Between**. The Between Dates dialog box opens.

4 In the Oldest box, type **1/1/2016**. In the Newest box, type **12/31/2016**.

5 Click **OK**. The filter is applied to the query datasheet, which now shows the 85 records of invoices dated 2016.

6 In the datasheet, click in the **Amount field for the first record**.

7 On the HOME tab, in the Sort & Filter group, click the **Selection button**. The menu that opens contains commands to display values related to the value in the selected field.

8 Click the **Selection button** again to close the menu. In the datasheet, click the **Amount column heading arrow**, and then point to **Number Filters**. The same commands that appeared on the Selection menu are on this menu, but no value appears next to the commands.

9 On the submenu, click **Greater Than**. The Custom Filter dialog box opens.

10 Click in the **Amount is greater than or equal to box**, type **100,000**, and then click **OK**. The datasheet now shows only one record—one invoice dated 2016 with an amount of at least $100,000.

11 On the HOME tab, in the Sort & Filter group, click the **Toggle Filter button**. The filters are removed.

12 Close the **Invoices table** without saving the changes to the design.

18-4 Defining Table Relationships

One of the most powerful features of a relational database management system is its ability to define relationships between tables. You use a common field to relate one table to another. The process of relating tables is often called joining tables. When you join tables that have a common field, you can use data from them as if they were one larger table. For example, you can join the Customers and Contracts tables by using the CustomerID field in both tables as the common field. Then you can use a query, a form, or a report to display selected data from each table, even though the data is contained in two separate tables. See Exhibit 18-12.

Exhibit 18-12 One-to-many relationship and query

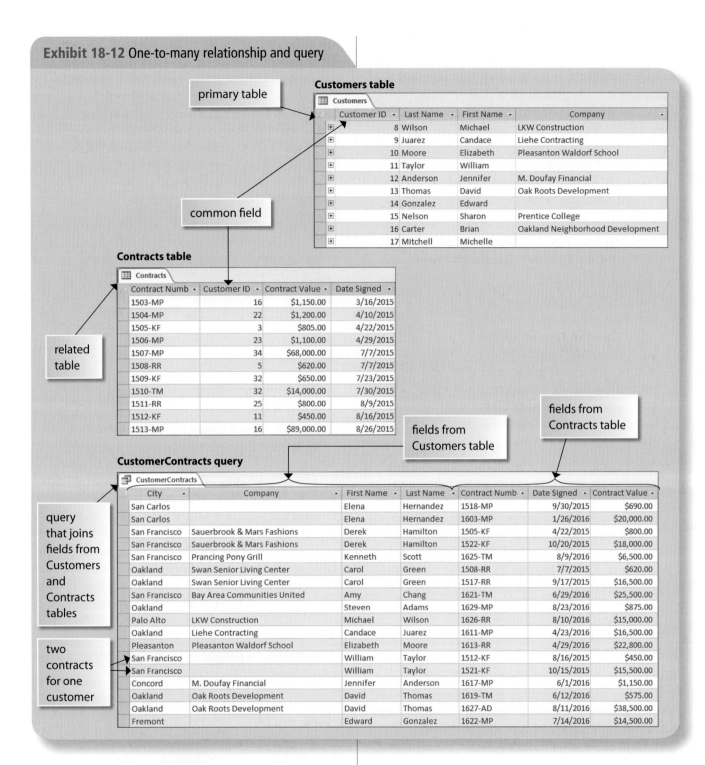

Customers table

primary table

common field

Contracts table

related table

fields from Customers table

fields from Contracts table

CustomerContracts query

query that joins fields from Customers and Contracts tables

two contracts for one customer

A **one-to-many relationship** exists between two tables when one record in the first table matches zero, one, or many records in the second table, and when each record in the second table matches at most one record in the first table. For example, as shown in Exhibit 18-12, customer 16 has two contracts in the Contracts table. Every contract has a single matching customer (the "one" side of the relationship), and a customer can have zero, one, or many contracts (the "many" side of the relationship).

The two tables that form a relationship are referred to as the primary table and the related table. The

one-to-many relationship A connection between two tables when one record in the primary table matches zero, one, or many records in the related table, and when each record in the related table matches at most one record in the primary table.

primary table is the "one" table in a one-to-many relationship. In Exhibit 18-12, the Customers table is the primary table because there is only one customer for each contract. The **related table** is the "many" table. In Exhibit 18-12, the Contracts table is the related table because a customer can have zero, one, or many contracts.

Referential integrity is a set of rules to maintain consistency between related tables when data in a database is updated. The referential integrity rules are:

- You cannot add a record to a related table unless a matching record already exists in the primary table, preventing the possibility of **orphaned records**.

- You cannot change the value of the primary key in the primary table if matching records exist in a related table. However, you can select the Cascade Update Related Fields option, which updates the corresponding foreign keys when you change a primary key field value, eliminating the possibility of inconsistent data.

- You cannot delete a record in the primary table if matching records exist in the related table. However, you can select the Cascade Delete Related Records option to delete the record in the primary table as well as all records in the related table that have matching foreign key field values. This option is rarely used because it often leads to related records being unintentionally deleted from the database.

18-4a Defining a One-to-Many Relationship Between Tables

When tables have a common field, you can define a relationship between them in the Relationships window. To create a relationship, first add the field list for each table in the relationship to the Relationships window. To form the relationship, drag the common field

from the primary table to the related table. The Edit Relationships dialog box, shown in Exhibit 18-13, then opens so you can select the relationship options for the two tables. To enforce referential integrity, select that check box. To override the rule that prevents you from changing the value of a primary key in the primary table, select the Cascade Update Related Fields option.

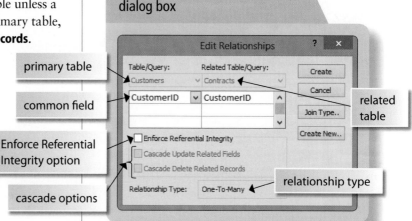

Exhibit 18-13 Edit Relationships dialog box

After you close the Edit Relationships dialog box, the relationship is defined. In the window, the relationship is shown with a line—called a join line—connecting the two tables. See Exhibit 18-14. The "1" above the end of the join line attached to the primary table and the infinity symbol above the end of the join line attached to the related table indicate that the relationship is set to enforce referential integrity.

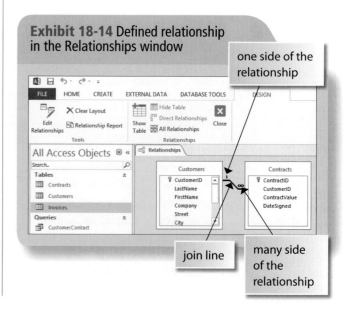

Exhibit 18-14 Defined relationship in the Relationships window

primary table The "one" table in a one-to-many relationship.

related table The "many" table in a one-to-many relationship.

referential integrity A set of rules to maintain consistency between related tables when data in a database is updated.

orphaned record A record in a related table that has no matching record in the primary table.

Define a one-to-many relationship between tables.

1 On the ribbon, click the **DATABASE TOOLS tab**. In the Relationships group, click the **Relationships button**. The Relationships window opens.

2 On the RELATIONSHIP TOOLS DESIGN tab, in the Relationships group, click the **Show Table button**. The Show Table dialog box opens, listing the three tables in the database on the Tables tab.

3 In the Show Table dialog box, double-click **Customers**. The Customers table's field list is added to the Relationships window.

4 Double-click **Contracts**. The Contracts table's field list is added to the Relationships window.

5 Click **Close**. The Show Table dialog box closes.

6 In the Customers field list, click **CustomerID**, and then drag it to **CustomerID** in the Contracts field list. The Edit Relationships dialog box opens. Refer back to Exhibit 18-13.

> **Tip:** If fields are hidden in a table field list, you can drag the bottom of the field list down until the vertical scroll bar disappears and all of the fields are visible.

7 Click the **Enforce Referential Integrity check box** to select it. The two cascade options become available.

8 Click the **Cascade Update Related Fields check box** to select it.

9 Click **Create**. The Edit Relationships dialog box closes, and the one-to-many relationship between the two tables is defined. The completed relationship appears in the Relationships window, with the join line connecting the common field of CustomerID in each table. Refer back to Exhibit 18-14. In this relationship, Customers is the primary table and Contracts is the related table.

10 On the Quick Access Toolbar, click the **Save button** 🔲 to save the layout in the Relationships window.

11 Close the **Relationships window**.

End Activity

18-4b Working with Related Data in a Subdatasheet

After you define a one-to-many relationship between tables with a common field, the primary table in the relationship contains a **subdatasheet** that displays the records from the related table. Exhibit 18-15 shows the subdatasheet for the second record in the Customers table. When you open the primary table, the subdatasheet for each record in the primary table is collapsed until you expand it by clicking the expand button [+].

If you did not select the option to cascade deletions to related records when you created a relationship between two tables, you cannot delete a record in a primary table that has matching records in a related table. If you want to delete a record from the primary table, you first must delete the related records in the related table. Although you could open the related table and then find and delete the related records, a simpler way is to delete the related records from the primary table's subdatasheet, which deletes the records from the related table.

Exhibit 18-15 Subdatasheet with related records

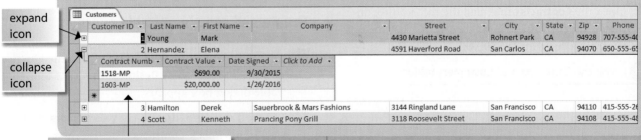

expand icon

collapse icon

subdatasheet containing related records from the Contracts table

subdatasheet A datasheet that displays the records from a related table in the primary table's datasheet.

Begin Activity

Work with related data in a subdatasheet.

1 Open the **Customers table** in Datasheet view. Because this is the primary table in a relationship, expand buttons ⊞ appear next to each record.

2 To the left of Customer ID 2, click the **expand button** ⊞. The subdatasheet for this customer appears, listing the related records from the Contracts table, and the expand icon changes to a collapse icon ⊟. Refer back to Exhibit 18-15.

3 Select the entire row for **Customer ID 2**. On the HOME tab, in the Records group, click the **Delete button**. A dialog box opens, indicating that you cannot delete the record because the Contracts table contains records that are related to the current customer. This occurs because you enforced referential integrity and did not select the option to cascade deletions to related records.

4 Click **OK** to close the dialog box.

5 If necessary, to the left of Customer ID 2, click the **collapse button** ⊟. The subdatasheet for that record collapses.

6 Display the **Customer ID 3 subdatasheet**. Two related records from the Contracts table for this customer appear in the subdatasheet.

7 In the subdatasheet, for Contract Number 1505-KF, edit the Contract Value field value to **$800.00**.

8 Collapse the **Customer ID 3 subdatasheet**.

9 Open the **Contracts table**, find the record for Contract Number **1505-KF**, and then verify that the contract value is now $800.00.

10 Close the **Contracts** and **Customers tables**.

End Activity

multitable query A query based on more than one table.

18-5 Creating a Multitable Query

A **multitable query** is a query based on more than one table. To create a query that retrieves data from multiple tables, the tables must have a common field. Because you established a relationship between the Customers (primary) and Contracts (related) tables based on the common CustomerID field that exists in both tables, you can now create a query to display data from both tables at the same time. The one-to-many relationship between two tables is shown in the Query window with a join line, which is the same way the relationship is indicated in the Relationships window. Exhibit 18-16 shows a multitable query created using the Customers and Contracts tables in Design view.

Exhibit 18-16 Multitable query

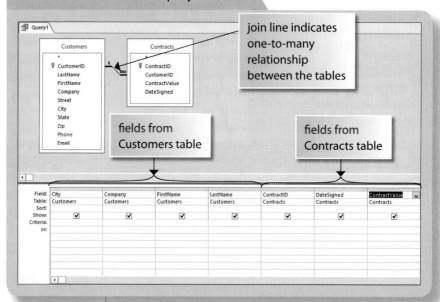

Begin Activity

Create and run a multitable query.

1 On the ribbon, click the **CREATE tab**. In the Queries group, click the **Query Design button**. The Show Table dialog box appears.

2 On the Tables tab, double-click **Customers**, and then double-click **Contracts**. The field lists for the Customers and Contracts tables appear in the Query window with a join line indicating the one-to-many relationship between the tables.

3 In the Show Table dialog box, click **Close**. The dialog box closes.

4 Resize the **Customers field list** so that all the fields in the table are displayed.

5 In the Customers field list, double-click **City** to place this field in the first column of the design grid.

6 Add the following fields from the Customers field list to the design grid: **Company**, **FirstName**, and **LastName**.

7 Add the following fields from the Contracts field list to the design grid: **ContractID**, **DateSigned**, and **ContractValue**. Refer back to Exhibit 18-16.

8 On the QUERY TOOLS DESIGN tab, in the Results group, click the **Run button**. The query runs, and the results appear in Datasheet view. The selected fields from both the Customers table and the Contracts table appear in the query datasheet. Compare your screen to Exhibit 18-17. The records are displayed in order according to the values in the CustomerID field because it is the primary key field in the primary table, even though this field is not included in the query datasheet.

9 Save the query as **CustomerContracts**, and then close it.

End Activity

18-6 Adding Criteria to a Query

You can refine a query to display only selected records by specifying criteria. **Criteria** are conditions for selecting records. For example, you could create a query that displays customer names and invoice numbers for all customers, and add a criterion to select only those records with unpaid invoices. You specify criteria in a field's Criteria box in the design grid in the Query window.

To add criteria to a query, you need to create expressions to specify the conditions. To do this, you use one of the operators shown in Exhibit 18-18. You add a condition in the Criteria box in the appropriate column in the design grid. When you do this, the field value in each record is compared to the value you enter after the comparison operator, and only those records for which that condition is true are displayed in the query results. For example, if you type *San Francisco* in the Criteria box in the City column in the design grid, when you run the query, only those records in the Customers table with the value *San Francisco* in the City field would be displayed. (Note that this example uses the Equals to comparison operator, but you do not need to type it.) Similarly, if you type <> *San Francisco* in the Criteria box, the query results would include all the records except for the ones with *San Francisco* in the City field. Exhibit 18-19 shows a query that includes the Paid field and will include only records where the paid field is equal to No—that it, the check box in the Paid field is not selected.

fields from Customers table

fields from Contracts table

Exhibit 18-17 Results of a multitable query

City	Company	First Name	Last Name	Contract Numb	Date Signed	Contract Value
Rohnert Park		Mark	Young	1501-TM	2/9/2015	$500.00
Rohnert Park		Mark	Young	1502-TM	3/3/2015	$14,000.00
San Carlos		Elena	Hernandez	1518-MP	9/30/2015	$690.00
San Carlos		Elena	Hernandez	1603-MP	1/26/2016	$20,000.00
San Francisco	Sauerbrook & Mars Fashions	Derek	Hamilton	1505-KF	4/22/2015	$800.00
San Francisco	Sauerbrook & Mars Fashions	Derek	Hamilton	1522-KF	10/20/2015	$18,000.00
San Francisco	Prancing Pony Grill	Kenneth	Scott	1625-TM	8/9/2016	$6,500.00
Oakland	Swan Senior Living Center	Carol	Green	1508-RR	7/7/2015	$620.00
Oakland	Swan Senior Living Center	Carol	Green	1517-RR	9/17/2015	$16,500.00
San Francisco	Bay Area Communities United	Amy	Chang	1621-TM	6/29/2016	$25,500.00
Oakland		Steven	Adams	1629-MP	8/23/2016	$875.00
Palo Alto	LKW Construction	Michael	Wilson	1626-RR	8/10/2016	$15,000.00
Oakland	Liehe Contracting	Candace	Juarez	1611-MP	4/23/2016	$16,500.00
Pleasanton	Pleasanton Waldorf School	Elizabeth	Moore	1613-RR	4/29/2016	$22,800.00
San Francisco		William	Taylor	1512-KF	8/16/2015	$450.00
San Francisco		William	Taylor	1521-KF	10/15/2015	$15,500.00
Concord	M. Doufay Financial	Jennifer	Anderson	1617-MP	6/1/2016	$1,150.00
Oakland	Oak Roots Development	David	Thomas	1619-TM	6/12/2016	$575.00
Oakland	Oak Roots Development	David	Thomas	1627-AD	8/11/2016	$38,500.00
Fremont		Edward	Gonzalez	1622-MP	7/14/2016	$14,500.00
Oakland	Prentice College	Sharon	Nelson	1616-AD	5/20/2016	$205,000.00
Oakland	Oakland Neighborhood Development	Brian	Carter	1503-MP	3/16/2015	$1,150.00
Oakland	Oakland Neighborhood Development	Brian	Carter	1513-MP	8/26/2015	$89,000.00
Oakland		Michelle	Mitchell	1516-RR	9/11/2015	$550.00
Oakland		Michelle	Mitchell	1605-RR	2/22/2016	$14,500.00

Record: 1 of 54   No Filter   Search

criteria Conditions that determine which records are selected in a query.

Exhibit 18-18 Operators for creating criteria in Access

Operator	Description	Example
=	Equal to (optional; default operator)	"Hall"
<>	Not equal to	<>"Hall"
<	Less than	<#1/1/99#
<=	Less than or equal to	<=100
>	Greater than	>"C400"
>=	Greater than or equal to	>=18.75
Between …	Between two values	Between 50
And …	(inclusive)	And 325
In ()	In a list of values	In ("Hall", "Seeger")
Like	Matches a pattern that includes wildcards	Like "706*"

© 2014 Cengage Learning

Exhibit 18-19 Criteria added to the design grid

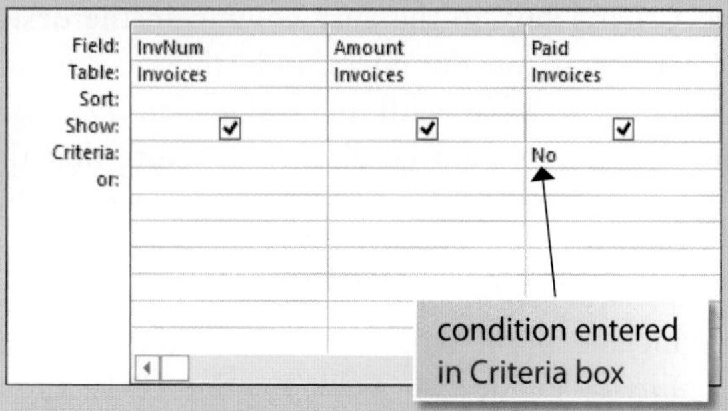

Field:	InvNum	Amount	Paid
Table:	Invoices	Invoices	Invoices
Sort:			
Show:	☑	☑	☑
Criteria:			No
or:			

condition entered in Criteria box

Begin Activity

Create queries with one criterion.

1 Create a new query in Design view.

2 Add the **Invoices table** to the Query window.

3 Add the following fields from the Invoices table to the design grid: **InvNum**, **Amount**, and **Paid**.

4 In the design grid, click in the **Paid field Criteria box**, and then type **No**. This tells Access to retrieve only the records for unpaid invoices. As soon as you type the letter *N*, a menu appears with options for entering various functions for the criteria. You don't need to enter a function, so you can close this menu.

5 Press the **Esc key** to close the menu. You must close the menu so that you don't enter a function, which would cause an error. The query results will now

show only customers with unpaid invoices. Refer back to Exhibit 18-19.

6 Save the query as **InvoicesUnpaid**.

7 Run the query. The query datasheet displays the field values for only the 15 records that have a Paid field value of No. Compare your screen to Exhibit 18-20.

8 Close the **InvoicesUnpaid query**.

Exhibit 18-20 Query results showing only unpaid invoices

InvoicesUnpaid

Invoice Number	Amount	Paid?
1512-028	$15,000.00	☐
1601-006	$3,000.00	☐
1606-029	$1,150.00	☐
1609-056	$875.00	☐
1610-065	$6,500.00	☐
1610-067	$7,500.00	☐
1611-076	$29,500.00	☐
1611-077	$2,000.00	☐
1611-078	$9,800.00	☐
1611-079	$4,000.00	☐
1611-080	$14,325.00	☐
1611-081	$32,800.00	☐
1611-082	$17,500.00	☐
1611-083	$9,500.00	☐
1612-084	$37,500.00	☐
*		☐

LEARN MORE

Formatting a Datasheet

You can format a datasheet using many of the same features you learned in Word and Excel. For example, you can change the font, font size, and font color using the buttons in the Text Formatting group on the HOME tab. You can also change the alternate row color in a datasheet by using the Alternate Row Color button in the Text Formatting group on the HOME tab.

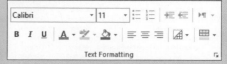

Text Formatting group on the HOME tab

18-7 Creating a Copy of a Query

When the design of the query you need to create next is similar to an existing query, you can create a copy of the query and then rename the copy. This process is faster than creating a new query from scratch. You can copy and paste the query in the Navigation Pane, or you can use the Save As command to save a copy of the query design.

Begin Activity

Create copies of database objects.

1 In the Navigation Pane, in the Queries group, right-click **InvoicesUnpaid**, and then on the shortcut menu, click **Copy**.

2 At the bottom of the Navigation Pane, right-click an empty area, and then on the shortcut menu, click **Paste**. The Paste As dialog box opens with Copy Of InvoicesUnpaid selected in the Query Name box.

3 In the Query Name box, type **InvoicesUnpaidFees** as the name for the new query, and then press the **Enter key**. The dialog box closes, and the new query appears in the Queries section of the Navigation Pane.

4 In the Navigation Pane, double-click the **CustomerContracts query** to open, or run, the query. The query datasheet opens.

5 Switch to **Design view**. You are saving a copy of the query design, not the query results.

6 On the ribbon, click the **FILE tab**. In the navigation bar, click **Save As**. The Save As screen appears.

7 Under File Types, click **Save Object As**, and then click the **Save As button**. A small Save As dialog box opens, similar to the Save dialog box that appears when you save a table or query. In the As box, Query is selected.

8 In the Save 'CustomerContracts' to box, type **TopContractValues** as the new query name.

9 Click **OK**. The new query is saved with the name you specified and appears in the Navigation Pane.

Once you've create a copy of a query, you can open the copy and modify the existing design just as you would modify any query. You can modify the TopContractValues query design to list only those contracts with a value of $25,000 or more. Exhibit 18-21 shows the comparison operator greater than or equal to in the expression >=25000 in the ContractValue column. The query results will contain only records with a value of $25,000 or more in the ContractValue field.

Exhibit 18-21 Criteria entered for the ContractValue field

Field:	Company	FirstName	LastName	ContractID	DateSigned	ContractValue
Table:	Customers	Customers	Customers	Contracts	Contracts	Contracts
Sort:						
Show:	☑	☑	☑	☑	☑	☑
Criteria:						>=25000
or:						

new condition entered

Begin Activity

Create a query with a comparison operator.

1 In the design grid, delete the **City field**.

2 In the design grid, click in the **ContractValue field Criteria box**, and then type **>=25000**. The condition specifies that a record will be selected only if its ContractValue field value is $25,000 or greater. Refer back to Exhibit 18-21.

Problem? If a dialog box opens indicating that you entered an expression containing invalid syntax, you might have typed a comma in the amount. Commas are not allowed in selection criteria for Currency fields. Click **OK** to close the dialog box, and then delete the comma from the ContractValue Criteria box.

3 Run the query. The query datasheet displays the selected fields for only those 20 records with a ContractValue field value that is greater than or equal to $25,000. Compare your screen to Exhibit 18-22.

4 Save the **TopContractValues query**, and then close the query.

End Activity

End Activity

Company	First Name	Last Name	Contract Numb	Date Signed	Contract Value
Chen Builders	Marie	Patterson	1507-MP	7/7/2015	$68,000.00
Oakland Neighborhood Development	Brian	Carter	1513-MP	8/26/2015	$89,000.00
Jack's Café	Ella	Doyle	1514-TM	9/3/2015	$25,500.00
San Rafael Medical Partners	Juanita	Walters	1515-KF	9/4/2015	$25,000.00
	Edward	Caldwell	1520-RR	10/15/2015	$32,500.00
	Edward	Caldwell	1523-RR	11/7/2015	$39,000.00
Greenleaf Builders	Stephanie	Henderson	1601-KF	1/12/2016	$30,800.00
Chen Builders	Marie	Patterson	1602-TM	1/16/2016	$34,000.00
	Edward	Caldwell	1604-RR	2/18/2016	$138,000.00
Greenleaf Builders	Stephanie	Henderson	1608-MP	3/26/2016	$165,000.00
Sierra Nevada Contracting	Patrick	Perry	1612-AD	4/29/2016	$37,000.00
Prentice College	Sharon	Nelson	1616-AD	5/20/2016	$205,000.00
Sierra Nevada Contracting	Patrick	Perry	1618-RR	6/4/2016	$46,000.00
Bay Area Communities United	Amy	Chang	1621-TM	6/29/2016	$25,500.00
Happy Skies Day Care	Dennis	Ross	1623-RR	7/26/2016	$37,250.00
	Ronald	Perez	1624-MP	7/30/2016	$35,000.00
Oak Roots Development	David	Thomas	1627-AD	8/11/2016	$38,500.00
	Edward	Caldwell	1628-AD	8/17/2016	$50,000.00
	Edward	Caldwell	1630-AD	9/2/2016	$41,000.00
Yamada Architects, Inc.	Paul	Long	1631-AD	9/9/2016	$132,000.00

18-8 Adding Multiple Criteria to Queries

Some queries require more than one criterion. To create these more complex queries that have multiple criteria, you need to combine two or more conditions. You can specify that the records meet all of the conditions you define or one or the other of the conditions. When you want the records in the query results to meet all of your conditions, you use the **And operator**. For example, you might want to display all the records that have a City field value of *Oakland* and have a ContractValue field value greater than $25,000. When you want the records in the query results to meet at least one of the specified conditions, you use the **Or operator**. For example, you could create a query that displays all records that have a City field value of *Oakland* or have a ContractValue field value greater than $25,000.

And operator The operator used to select records only if all of the specified conditions are met.

Or operator The operator used to select records if at least one of the specified conditions is met.

18-8a Using the And Logical Operator

To create a query with the And logical operator, you specify all of the conditions in the same Criteria row of the design grid. The query will then display records only if all of the conditions are met. If even one condition is not met, the record is not included in the query results. Exhibit 18-23 shows two conditions in the Criteria row in the design grid. The query results for this query will display only records that have a value of Oakland in the City field and a value greater than $25,000 in the ContractValue field.

Begin Activity

Use the And logical operator in a query.

1. Create a new query in Design view.

2. Add the **Customers table** and **Contracts table** to the Query window.

3. Add the following fields from the Customers field list to the design grid: **Company**, **FirstName**, **LastName**, and **City**.

4. Add the following fields from the Contracts field list to the design grid: **ContractValue** and **DateSigned**.

5. In the design grid, click in the **City field Criteria box**, type **Oakland** and then press the **Tab key**. The first condition is entered, and the insertion point moves to the ContractValue field Criteria box. Notice that quotation marks were added around the condition because the City field is a Short Text field.

Exhibit 18-23 Query with And logical operator

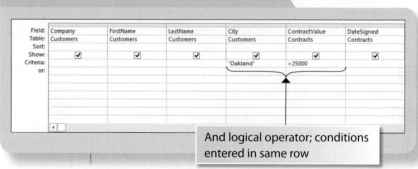

And logical operator; conditions entered in same row

6 In the **ContractValue field Criteria box**, type **>25000** and then press the **Tab key**. The second condition is entered. Refer back to Exhibit 18-23. Because both conditions appear in the same Criteria row, both conditions must be met for a record to appear in the query results.

7 Run the query. The query datasheet includes only the 11 records for customers who meet both conditions: a City field value of Oakland and a ContractValue field value greater than $25,000. Compare your screen to Exhibit 18-24.

8 Save the query as **TopOaklandCustomers** and then close the query.

End Activity

Exhibit 18-24 Query results listing records with the city equal to Oakland and a contract value greater than $25,000

Company	First Name	Last Name	City	Contract Value	Date Signed
Chen Builders	Marie	Patterson	Oakland	$68,000.00	7/7/2015
Oakland Neighborhood Development	Brian	Carter	Oakland	$89,000.00	8/26/2015
Jack's Café	Ella	Doyle	Oakland	$25,500.00	9/3/2015
	Edward	Caldwell	Oakland	$32,500.00	10/15/2015
	Edward	Caldwell	Oakland	$39,000.00	11/7/2015
Chen Builders	Marie	Patterson	Oakland	$34,000.00	1/16/2016
	Edward	Caldwell	Oakland	$138,000.00	2/18/2016
Prentice College	Sharon	Nelson	Oakland	$205,000.00	5/20/2016
Oak Roots Development	David	Thomas	Oakland	$38,500.00	8/11/2016
	Edward	Caldwell	Oakland	$50,000.00	8/17/2016
	Edward	Caldwell	Oakland	$41,000.00	9/2/2016

18-8b Using the Or Logical Operator

To create a query with the Or logical operator, you specify each condition in a different Criteria row. The query will display records if any of the conditions are met. Exhibit 18-25 shows one condition in the Criteria row in the design grid and a second condition in the "or" row. The query results for this query will display records that have a value of less than $10,000 in the ContractValue field and a value in the DateSigned field between January 1, 2016 and March 31, 2016.

Exhibit 18-25 Query window with the Or logical operator

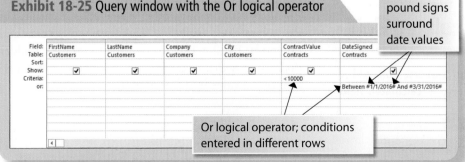

pound signs surround date values

Or logical operator; conditions entered in different rows

Begin Activity

Use the Or logical operator in a query.

1 Create a new query in Design view.

2 Add the **Customers table** and the **Contracts table** to the Query window.

3 Add the following fields from the Customers field list to the design grid: **FirstName**, **LastName**, **Company**, and **City**.

4 Add the following fields from the Contracts field list to the design grid: **ContractValue** and **DateSigned**.

5 Click in the **ContractValue field Criteria box**, type **<10000** and then press the **Tab key**. The first condition—to select contracts with amounts less than $10,000—is specified, and the Criteria box for the DateSigned field is selected.

6 Press the **Down Arrow key** to select the DateSigned field "or" box. Entering a condition in the "or" box creates a query using the Or logical operator.

7 In the **DateSigned field or box**, type **Between 1/1/2016 And 3/31/2016** and then press the **Tab key**. The second condition—to select contracts when the DateSigned field value is between 1/1/2016 and 3/31/2016—is specified.

8 In the design grid, point to the top of the **DateSigned right column border** so that the pointer changes to ✛, and then double-click to resize the DateSigned column so that the entire condition is visible. Refer back to Exhibit 18-25. Note that Access automatically places pound signs (#) around date values in the condition to distinguish them from the operators.

> **Problem?** To make the pointer change shape, make sure you point to the top of the column border next to the field selector.

9 In the design grid, click in the **DateSigned field Sort box**, click the **arrow button** ⌄, and then click **Descending**. The query results will appear in descending order by DateSigned to create a logical order in which to analyze the data.

10 Run the query. The query results include the selected fields for the 27 records that meet one or both of the following conditions: a ContractValue field value of less than $10,000 or a DateSigned field value between 1/1/2016 and 3/31/2016. The records in the query datasheet appear in descending order based on the values in the DateSigned field. Compare your screen to Exhibit 18-26.

11 Save the query as **SmallOrQ1Contracts** and then close the query.

End Activity

18-9 Creating a Calculated Field

To perform a calculation in a query, you add a calculated field to the query. A **calculated field**

> **calculated field** A field that displays the results of a mathematical expression.

Exhibit 18-26 Results of query using the Or logical operator

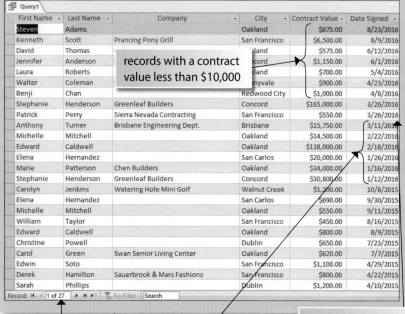

27 records meet one or both conditions

records with a contract value less than $10,000

records with a signed contract date between 1/1/2016 and 3/31/2016

record with a contract value less than $10,000 and a signed contract date between 1/1/2016 and 3/31/2016

displays the results of a mathematical expression. When you run a query that contains a calculated field, Access evaluates the expression in the calculated field and displays the resulting value in the query datasheet, form, or report.

To enter an expression for a calculated field, you type it in an empty Field box in the design grid. You can also use the Expression Builder to enter the expression. Expression Builder is an Access tool that makes it easy for you to create a mathematical expression. When you click the Builder button in the Query Setup group on the QUERY TOOLS DEISGN tab, the Expression Builder dialog box opens. In the dialog box, the Expression Categories box lists the fields from the query so you can include them in the expression, and the Expression Elements box contains other elements you can use in the expression, including functions, constants, and operators. Exhibit 18-27 shows the Expression Builder dialog box with an expression in it to calculate five percent of the value in the Amount field.

Exhibit 18-27 Expression Builder
dialog box

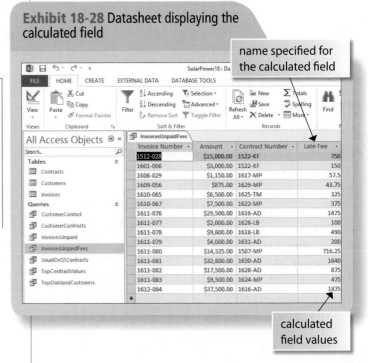

expression

other elements you can use in the expression

selected field used in expression

Begin Activity

Create a query with a calculated field.

1 Open the **InvoicesUnpaidFees query**, and then switch to **Design view**. This is the copy of the InvoicesUnpaid query.

2 Add the **ContractID field** from the **Invoices table field list** to the fourth column in the design grid.

3 Click the **Paid field Show check box** to remove the check mark. The query name indicates that the data is for unpaid invoices, so you don't need to include the Paid field values in the query results.

4 Save the **Invoices UnpaidFees query**.

5 Click the **blank Field box** to the right of the ContractID field. This field will contain the calculated expression.

> **Tip:** A query must be saved and named in order for its fields to be listed in the Expression Categories box of the Expression Builder.

6 On the QUERY TOOLS DESIGN tab, in the Query Setup group, click the **Builder button**. The Expression Builder dialog box opens. The insertion point is in the large box at the top of the dialog box, ready for you to enter the expression.

7 In the Expression Categories box, double-click **Amount**. The field name is added to the expression box and placed within brackets and followed by a space.

8 Type ***** (an asterisk) to enter the multiplication operator, and then type **.05** for the constant. The expression you entered for the calculated field will multiply the Amount field values by .05 (which represents a five percent late fee). Refer back to Exhibit 18-27.

9 Click **OK**. The Expression Builder dialog box closes, and the expression is added to the design grid in the Field box for the calculated field as *Expr1: [Amount]*0.05*. The text before the colon will appear as the field name in the query results.

10 At the beginning of the expression, select **Expr1**, and then type **Late Fee** to specify a more descriptive name for the field. Be sure to leave the colon after the field name; it is needed to separate the calculated field name from the expression. The complete expression is *Late Fee: [Amount]*0.05*.

11 Run the query. The query datasheet contains the specified fields and the calculated field with the column heading Late Fee. Compare your screen to Exhibit 18-28.

End Activity

Exhibit 18-28 Datasheet displaying the calculated field

name specified for the calculated field

calculated field values

18-10 Using a Property Sheet

In the query results for the InvoicesUnpaidFees query, the amounts listed in the Late Fee column are not formatted as currency. You can specify a format for a calculated field, just as you can for any field, by modifying its properties. As you have seen, when you work with tables, some of the field properties appear in the Field Properties pane at the bottom of the window in Design view. You can see additional properties by opening the Property Sheet. When you are working with queries, you need to open the Property Sheet to adjust any of the field properties. Exhibit 18-29 shows the Property Sheet for the calculated field in the InvoicesUnpaidFees query.

Exhibit 18-29 Property Sheet for the calculated field

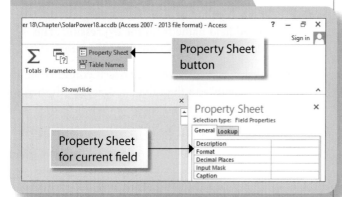

Begin Activity

Format a calculated field.

1 Switch the InvoicesUnpaidFees query to **Design view**.

2 In the design grid, click the **Late Fee calculated field Field box**.

3 On the QUERY TOOLS DESIGN tab, in the Show/Hide group, click the **Property Sheet button**. The Property Sheet for the calculated field appears on the right side of the Query window. Refer back to Exhibit 18-29.

> **Tip:** You can also right-click a field in the design grid, and then click Properties on the shortcut menu to open the Property Sheet for that field.

4 In the Property Sheet, click the **Format box**, click the **arrow button** to display a list of available formats, and then click **Currency**. The Format property is set to Currency, which displays values with a dollar sign and two decimal places.

5 In the Property Sheet, click the **Close button** ✕. The Property Sheet closes.

6 Run the query. The amounts in the Late Fee calculated field are now displayed with dollar signs and two decimal places.

7 Save the **InvoicesUnpaidFees query**, and then close it.

End Activity

CAUTION

Calculated Fields

The Calculated Field data type, which is available only for tables in Datasheet view, lets you store the result of an expression as a field in a table. However, database experts caution against storing calculations in a table for the following reasons:

▶ **Storing calculated data in a table consumes space and increases the size of the database.** The preferred approach is to use a calculated field in a query; with this approach, the result of the calculation is not stored in the database—it is produced only when you run the query—and it is always current.

▶ **Using the Calculated Field data type provides limited options for creating a calculation.** A calculated field in a query provides more functions and options for creating expressions.

▶ **Including a field in a table whose value is dependent on other fields in the table violates database design principles.** To avoid problems, create a query that includes a calculated field to perform the calculation you want, instead of creating a field in a table that uses the Calculated Field data type.

18-11 Using Functions in a Query

You can use a table or query datasheet to perform calculations, such as sums, averages, minimums, and maximums, on the displayed records. To do this, you use functions to perform arithmetic operations on selected records in a database. These are the same functions that are available in Excel. Exhibit 18-30 lists the most frequently used functions.

Exhibit 18-30 Frequently-used functions

Function	Determines
Average	Average of the field values for the selected records
Count	Number of records selected
Maximum	Highest field value for the selected records
Minimum	Lowest field value for the selected records
Sum	Total of the field values for the selected records

© 2014 Cengage Learning

18-11a Using the Total Row in a Datasheet

To perform a calculation using a function in a table or query datasheet, you can add a Total row at the bottom of the datasheet. In the Total row, you can then choose one of the functions for a field in the datasheet, and the results of the calculation will be displayed in the Total row for that field. Exhibit 18-31 shows the menu that appears when you click a field in a Total row.

Exhibit 18-31 Menu of functions in the Total row

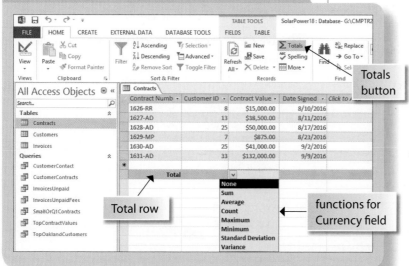

You can add or remove the Total row from the datasheet by clicking the Totals button in the Records group on the Home tab; this button works as a toggle to switch between the display of the Total row and the results of any calculations in the row, and the display of the datasheet without this row.

Begin Activity

Use the Total row.

1 Open the **Contracts table** in Datasheet view.

2 On the HOME tab, in the Records group, click the **Totals button**. A Total row appears at the bottom of the datasheet.

3 Scroll to the bottom of the datasheet to view the last records in the datasheet and the Total row.

4 In the Total row, click in the **Contract Value column**, and then click the **arrow button** that appears on the left side of the field to display a menu of functions. Refer back to Exhibit 18-31. The available functions depend on the data type of the current field. In this case, the menu provides functions for a Currency field.

5 On the menu, click **Sum**. Access adds all the values in the Contract Value column and displays the total $1,555,310.00 in the Total row for the column.

6 On the HOME tab, in the Records group, click the **Totals button**. The Total row disappears from the datasheet.

7 Close the **Contracts table** without saving the changes to the table's layout.

End Activity

18-11b Creating Queries with Functions

Functions can operate on the records that meet a query's selection criteria. You specify a function for a specific field, and the appropriate operation applies to that field's values for the selected records. For example, you can use the Minimum, Average, and Maximum functions for the ContractValue field to display the minimum, average, and maximum of all the contract amounts in the Contracts table. For each calculation you want to perform on the same field, you need to add the field to the design grid.

After you run the query, the query datasheet uses a default column name that includes the function and the field name, such as MinOfContractValue, for the field. You can change the datasheet column name to a more descriptive or readable name by entering that name in the Field box followed by a colon and the field name, such as Minimum Contract Value: ContractValue. See Exhibit 18-32.

Exhibit 18-32 Total row inserted in the design grid

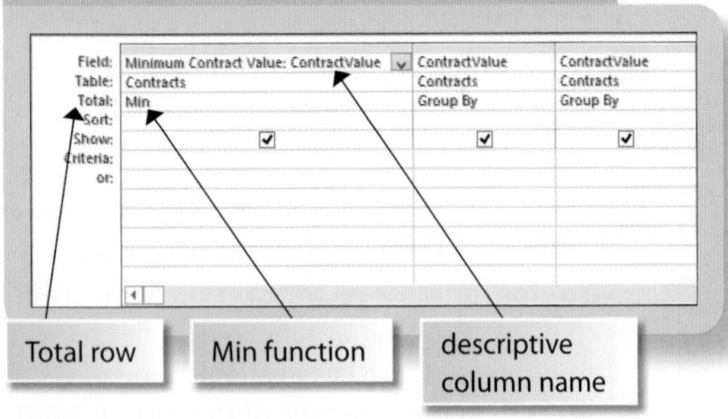

Field:	Minimum Contract Value: ContractValue	ContractValue	ContractValue
Table:	Contracts	Contracts	Contracts
Total:	Min	Group By	Group By
Sort:			
Show:	☑	☑	☑
Criteria:			
or:			

Total row   Min function   descriptive column name

Begin Activity

Create a query with functions.

1 Create a new query in **Design view**.

2 Add the **Contracts table** to the Query window.

3 In the Contracts field list, double-click **Contract-Value** three times to add three copies of the field to the design grid.

4 On the QUERY TOOLS DESIGN tab, in the Show/Hide group, click the **Totals button**. The Total row appears between the Table and Sort rows in the design grid. The default function Group By appears in the Total boxes.

5 In the design grid, click in the **first ContractValue column Total box**, click the **arrow button** ⌄, and then click **Min** to specify the function to use for the field. This function will calculate the minimum amount of all the ContractValue field values.

6 Click in the **first ContractValue column Field box**, and then press the **Left** or **Right Arrow key** to position the insertion point to the left of ContractValue. Type

Minimum Contract Value: (including the colon), and then press the **Spacebar**. The Field box now contains *Minimum Contract Value: ContractValue*.

> **Tip:** Be sure to type the colon following the name or the query will not work correctly.

7 In the design grid, resize the first column so you can see all of the text in the Field box. Refer back to Exhibit 18-32.

8 Click in the **second ContractValue column Total box**, click the **arrow button** ⌄, and then click **Max**. This function will calculate the maximum amount of all the ContractValue field values.

9 Click in the **second ContractValue Field box**, position the insertion point to the left of Contract-Value, type **Maximum Contract Value:** and then press the **Spacebar**.

10 Click in the **third ContractValue column Total box**, click the **arrow button** ⌄, and then click **Avg**. This function will calculate the average of all the ContractValue field values.

11 Click in the **third ContractValue Field box**, position the insertion point to the left of ContractValue, type **Average Contract Value:** and then press the **Spacebar**.

12 Run the query. The query datasheet includes one record with the results of the three calculations. These calculations are based on all of the records selected for the query—in this case, all 54 records in the Contracts table.

13 Resize all of the columns to their best fit so that the column names are fully displayed. Compare your screen to Exhibit 18-33.

14 Save the query as **ContractValueStats**, and then close the query.

End Activity

Exhibit 18-33 Result of query using functions

18-11c Creating Calculations for Groups of Records

In addition to calculating statistical information on all or selected records in selected tables, you can calculate statistics for groups of records. For example, you can determine the number of customers in each city or the average contract amount by city. The **Group By operator** divides the selected records into groups based on the values in the specified field. Those records with the same value for the field are grouped together, and the datasheet displays one record for each group. Functions, which appear in the other columns of the design grid, provide statistical information for each group.

Begin Activity

Create a query with the Group By operator.

1. Create a copy of the **ContractValueStats query**. Name the copy **ContractValueStatsByCity**.

2. Open the **ContractValueStatsByCity query**, and then switch to **Design view**.

3. On the QUERY TOOLS DESIGN tab, in the Query Setup group, click the **Show Table button**. The Show Table dialog box appears.

4. Add the **Customers table** to the Query window, and then close the **Show Table dialog box**.

5. In the Customers field list, drag the **City field** to the **first column in the design grid**. The City field appears in the first column, and the existing fields shift to the right. In the City field Total box, Group By appears.

6. Run the query. The query results include 15 records—one for each City group. Each record contains the City field value for the group and the results of each calculation using the Min, Max, and Avg functions. The summary statistics represent calculations based on the 54 records in the Contracts table. Compare your screen to Exhibit 18-34.

7. Save the **ContractValueStatsByCity query**, and then close it.

Exhibit 18-34 Records grouped by City

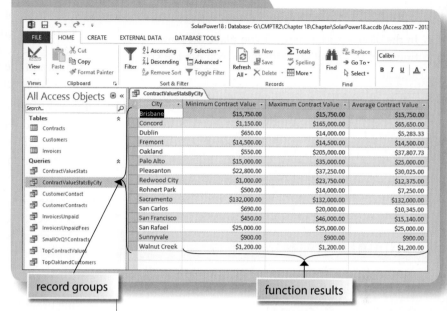

record groups

function results

8. Compact and repair the SolarPower18 database, and then close the database. Do not save the contents of the Clipboard.

End Activity

Quiz Yourself

1. In Datasheet view, what is the difference between navigation mode and editing mode?

2. Describe the field list and the design grid in the Query window in Design view.

3. What is a select query?

4. How are a table datasheet and a query datasheet similar? How are they different?

5. Describe how records are organized when you select multiple sort fields.

6. What is a filter?

7. When does a one-to-many relationship exist between tables?

8. What is referential integrity?

9. How do you create a multitable query?

10. What is a condition, and when do you use it?

> **Group By operator** An operator that divides selected records into groups based on the values in the specified field.

11. In the design grid, where do you place the conditions for two different fields when you use the And logical operator?

12. In the design grid, where do you place the conditions for two different fields when you use the Or logical operator?

13. How do you perform a calculation in a query?

14. How do you calculate statistical information, such as sums, averages, minimums, and maximums, on the records displayed in a table datasheet or selected by a query?

15. Explain what the Group By operator does.

Practice It

Practice It 18-1

1. Open the data file **Snow18** located in the Chapter 18\Practice It folder. Save the database as **SnowRemoval18**.

2. Open the Clients table in Datasheet view. For Client ID 1, change the field values in the First Name and Last Name columns to your first and last names.

3. Find the record with the Company field value of **Hanford Fashion**. Change the Phone field value to **207-555-6243**. Close the Clients table.

4. Open the ServiceAgreements table, find the record for Agreement # **1636**, and then delete the record. Close the ServiceAgreements table.

5. Create a query in Design view based on the Clients table. Include the following fields in the query: Company, FirstName, LastName, and Phone. Save the query as **ClientPhoneList**, and then run the query.

6. Modify the ClientPhoneList query in Design view to sort the query results in ascending order by the Company field and then in ascending order by the LastName field. Save the modified query, run the query, and then close it.

7. Create a one-to-many relationship between the primary Clients table and the related ServiceAgreements table based on the ClientID field. Enforce referential integrity, and select the Cascade Update Related Fields check box.

8. Create a one-to-many relationship between the primary ServiceAgreements table and the related Invoices table based on the AgreementNum field. Enforce referential integrity, and select the Cascade Update Related Fields check box. Save the layout in the Relationships window, and then close the window.

9. Open the ServiceAgreements table in Datasheet view, find the record for Agreement # **1616**, display the subdatasheet, change the record for invoice number 1611-071 to unpaid by clicking the Paid? check box, and then close the table.

10. Create a query in Design view based on the ServiceAgreements and Invoices tables. Select the AgreementNum, AgreementAmt, and ServiceType fields from the ServiceAgreements table, and then select the InvNum and InvAmt fields from the Invoices table. Sort the query results in descending order based on the AgreementAmt. Select only those records for business customers by entering **Commercial** in the ServiceType Criteria box. Do not display the ServiceType field values in the query results. Save the query as **BusinessAgreements**, run the query, and then close it.

11. Create a query in Design view that lists all unpaid invoices that are dated between 1/1/2016 and 12/31/2016. Include the following fields from the Invoices table in the query: InvNum, InvAmt, InvDate, and Paid. Sort the InvDate field in ascending order. Do not show the Paid field in the query results. Save the query as **UnpaidInvoices**, run the query, and then close it.

12. Create a query in Design view that lists clients located in Bangor or service agreements for less than $1,000. Include the Company, City, FirstName, and LastName fields from the Clients table and the AgreementNum and AgreementAmt fields from the ServiceAgreements table. Sort the query in ascending order by the City field and then in descending order by the AgreementAmt field. Save the query as **BangorOrSmallAgreements**, run the query, and then close it.

13. Create a copy of the UnpaidInvoices query. Name the copy **UnpaidInvoicesCashDiscount**. Open the UnpaidInvoicesCashDiscount query in Design view, and then add a calculated field to the fourth column in the design grid that calculates a six percent discount based on the InvAmt field values. (*Hint*: Multiply the InvAmt field by 0.06.) Change

the field's column name to **Cash Discount** and format it correctly. Save the query, and then run it.

14. In Design view for the UnpaidInvoicesCashDiscount query, modify the format of the Cash Discount field so that it uses the Currency format. Run the query, and then save and close the query.

15. Create a query in Design view that calculates the minimum, maximum, and average agreement amounts for all service agreement amounts using the field names Lowest, Highest, and Average, respectively. Save the query as **AgreementStats**. Run the query.

16. Create a copy of the AgreementStats query. Name the copy **AgreementStatsByCity**. Modify the AgreementStatsByCity query so that the records are grouped by the City field in the Clients table. Sort the query in ascending order by the City field. The City field should appear first in the query datasheet. Save the query, run the query, and then close it.

17. Compact and repair the SnowRemoval18 database, and then close it.

Practice It 18-2

1. Open the data file **Art18** located in the Chapter 18\Practice It folder. Save the database as **ArtClasses18**.

2. In the Instructors table, for Instructor ID CC-1201, change the value in the First Name and Last Name columns to your first and last names.

3. In the Instructors table, find the record with the last name of **Weigel**, and then change the value in the Hire Date column to **8/12/2014**. Close the Instructors table.

4. Create one-to-many relationships between the primary Instructors table and the related Classes table using the InstructorID field, and between the primary Classes table and the related Students table using the ClassID field. In each relationship, enforce referential integrity, and select the option to cascade updates to related fields. Save and close the Relationships window.

5. In the Instructors table, find the record with the Instructor ID DR-9123, delete the related record in the subdatasheet for this instructor, and then

delete the record for this instructor. Close the Instructors table.

6. Create a query in Design view based on the Students table that includes the LastName, FirstName, and Phone fields. Sort the query in ascending order by LastName. Save the query as **StudentPhoneNumbers**, and then run the query.

7. In the StudentPhoneNumbers query results, change the phone number for Christa Harris to **740-555-0878**. Close the query.

8. Create a query in Design view based on the Instructors and Classes tables. Add the LastName and InstructorID fields from the Instructors table. Add the ClassID, ClassName, Juniors, Length, and Cost fields from the Classes table. Sort in ascending order on the LastName field, and then sort in ascending order by the ClassID field. Save the query as **ClassesByInstructor**, and then run it.

9. Create a copy of the ClassesByInstructor query named **JuniorsClasses**. Modify the JuniorsClasses query to display all classes taught by instructors who allow teens (juniors) to participate. Do not include the Juniors field in the query results. Save the query, and then run it.

10. Create a copy of the JuniorsClasses query named **JuniorsClassesLowCost**. Modify the JuniorsClassesLowCost query to display only those classes taught by instructors who allow teens (juniors) to participate and that cost $100 or less. Do not include the Juniors field values in the query results. Save the query, and then run it.

11. In the JuniorsClassessLowCost query datasheet, calculate the total cost of the classes selected by the query. Save and close the query.

12. Compact and repair the ArtClasses18 database, and then close it.

On Your Own

On Your Own 18-1

1. Open the data file **Donations18** located in the Chapter 18\On Your Own folder. Save the database as **DonationsList18**.

2. In the Donors table, for Donor ID 2016-001, change the First Name field value to your first

name, and change the Last Name field value to your last name.

3. Create one-to-many relationships between the primary Agencies table and the related Donations table, and between the primary Donors table and the related Donations table. For each relationship, enforce referential integrity, and cascade updates to related fields. Save and close the Relationships window.

4. In the Donors table, delete the record for Donor ID 2016-028. (Be sure to delete the related record first.)

5. Create a query based on the Agencies table that includes the Agency, FirstName, LastName, and City fields. Save the query as **AgenciesByCity**, and then run it.

6. Modify the AgenciesByCity query design so that it sorts records in ascending order first by City and then in ascending order by Agency. Save and run the query.

7. In the AgenciesByCity query datasheet, change the contact for the Carpenter After-School Center to **Mary Sheehan**. Close the query.

8. Create a query in Design view that displays the DonorID, FirstName, and LastName fields from the Donors table, and the Description and DonationValue fields from the Donations table for all donations with a value over $100. Sort the query in descending order by DonationValue. Save the query as **BigDonors**, and then run the query.

9. Create a copy of the BigDonors query named **BigCashDonors**. Modify the BigCashDonors query to display only records with cash donations of more than $100. Do not include the Description field values in the query results. In the query datasheet, calculate the sum of the cash donations. Save and close the query.

10. Create a query in Design view that displays the Agency field from the Agencies table, and the DonationID, DonationDate, and Description fields from the Donations table. Save the query as **TrailsDonations**, and then run the query.

11. Use the Selection button in the Sort & Filter group on the HOME tab to filter the TrailsDonations query datasheet to display only the records for donations to Eastern Wyoming Trails.

12. Format the TrailsDonations query datasheet to use an alternate row color of the Red, Accent 2, Lighter 80% theme color. (*Hint*: Use the Alternate Row Color button in the Text Formatting group on the HOME tab to select the row color.) Resize the columns to best fit the complete field names and values. Save the TrailsDonations query.

13. Create a copy of the TrailsDonations query named **FurnitureOrHousewares**. Modify the FurnitureOrHousewares query to display donations of furniture or housewares and to list the Agency ID instead of the Agency name. Sort the records in ascending order first by Description and then in ascending order by AgencyID. Run the query, adjust the column widths, save the query, and then close it.

14. Create a query in Design view that displays the DonorID, Agency, Description, and DonationValue fields for all donations that require a pickup. Do not display the Pickup field in the query results. Save the query as **PickupCharge**. Create a calculated field named **Net Donation** that displays the results of subtracting $10.50 from the Donation-Value field values. Display the results in ascending order by DonationValue. Format the calculated field with the Currency format. Run the query, resize the columns in the query datasheet to their best fit, save the query, and then close it.

15. Create a query in Design view based on the Donations table that displays the sum, average, and count of the DonationValue field for all donations. (*Hint*: Use the Count function to count the number of rows.) Enter appropriate column names for each field. Format the sum and average values as Currency. Save the query as **DonationStats**, and then run the query. In the query datasheet, resize the columns to their best fit, save the query, and then close it.

16. Create a copy of the DonationStats query named **DonationStatsByAgency**. Modify the Donation-StatsByAgency query to display the sum, average, and count of the DonationValue field for all donations grouped by Agency, with Agency appearing as the first field. Sort the records in descending order by the donation total. Save the query, run the query, and then close it.

17. Compact and repair the DonationsList18 database, and then close it. (Do not save the contents of the Clipboard.)

Chapter 18

ADDITIONAL STUDY TOOLS

IN THE BOOK

▶ Complete end-of-chapter exercises

▶ Study tear-out Chapter Review Card

ONLINE

▶ Complete additional end-of-chapter exercises

▶ Take practice quiz to prepare for tests

▶ Review key term flash cards (online, printable, and audio)

▶ Play "Beat the Clock" and "Memory" to quiz yourself

▶ Watch the videos to learn more about the topics taught in this chapter

Answers to Quiz Yourself

1. *In navigation mode, the entire field value is selected, and anything you type replaces the field value; in editing mode, you can insert or delete characters in a field value based on the location of the insertion point.*

2. *The field list contains the table name at the top of the list and the table's fields listed in the order in which they appear in the table; the design grid displays columns that contain specifications about a field you will use in the query.*

3. *A select query is a general query in which you specify the fields and records you want Access to select.*

4. *A table datasheet and a query datasheet look the same, appearing in Datasheet view, and can be used to update data in a database. A table datasheet shows the permanent data in a table, whereas a query datasheet is temporary and its contents are based on the criteria you establish in the design grid.*

5. *Each additional sort field organizes the records within the higher-level sort.*

6. *A **filter** is a set of restrictions you place on the records in an open datasheet or form to temporarily isolate a subset of the records.*

7. *A one-to-many relationship exists between two tables when one record in the primary table matches zero, one, or many records in the related table, and when each record in the related table matches at most one record in the primary table.*

8. *Referential integrity is a set of rules to maintain consistency between related tables when data in a database is updated.*

9. *The process for creating a multitable query is similar to creating a query with one table. First, the tables must have a common field with an established relationship. Then, you open the tables in the Query window and add fields from any of the field lists for the open tables to the design grid.*

10. *A condition is a criterion, or rule, that determines which records are selected. You specify a condition as part of a query to refine the query to display only selected records.*

11. *In the design grid, when you use the And logical operator, you place the conditions for two different fields in the same Criteria row.*

12. *In the design grid, when you use the Or logical operator, you place the two different fields in different Criteria rows.*

13. *To perform a calculation in a query, you add a calculated field to the query, which displays the results of an expression (a combination of database fields, constants, and operators).*

14. *To calculate statistical information, such as sums, averages, minimums, and maximums, on the records displayed in a table datasheet or selected by a query, you use functions to perform arithmetic operations on selected records in a database.*

15. *The Group By operator divides selected records into groups based on the values in a field.*

Creating Forms and Reports

Dmitriy Shironosov/Shutterstock.com

Forms, which can be based on a table or query, provide a simpler, more intuitive layout for displaying, entering, and changing data. Forms can also display data from two or more tables at the same time, offering a more complete picture of the information in the database. For example, a form might show data about customers and their associated contracts, which are stored in separate tables.

Reports provide a formatted printout or screen display of the data in a database. For example, a database might include a formatted report of customer and contract data that staff can use for market analysis and strategic planning for selling services to customers. With reports, you can format information in a professional manner, making the report appealing and easy to use.

Learning Objectives

After studying the material in this chapter, you will be able to:

19-1 Create a form using the Form Wizard

19-2 Modify a form's design in Layout view

19-3 Find data using a form

19-4 Create a form based on related tables

19-5 Preview and print selected form records

19-6 Create a report using the Report Wizard

19-7 Modify a report's design in Layout view

19-1 Creating a Form Using the Form Wizard

You have already used the Form tool to create a simple form to enter, edit, and view records in a database. The Form tool creates a form automatically, using all the fields in the selected table or query. You can also create a form using the Form Wizard, which guides you through the process of creating a form. In the Form Wizard dialog boxes, you select the tables or queries on which to base the form, choose which fields to include in the form, and specify the order in which the selected fields should appear in the form. See the first dialog box in Exhibit 19-1. You then select a form layout, which can be Columnar, Tabular, Datasheet, and Justified. The Tabular and Datasheet layouts display the fields from multiple records at one time. The Columnar and Justified layouts display the fields from one record at a time. See the center dialog box in Exhibit 19-1. Finally, you enter a title for the form and choose whether to open the form in Form view so you can work with data or in Design view so you can modify the form's design. See the third dialog box in Exhibit 19-1.

Begin Activity

Create a form using the Form Wizard.

1 Open the data file **Solar19** located in the Chapter 19\Chapter folder. Save the database as **SolarPower19**.

2 In the Navigation Pane, select the **Customers table**.

3 On the ribbon, click the **CREATE tab**. In the Forms group, click the **Form Wizard button**. The first Form Wizard dialog box opens. The Customers table is selected in the Tables/Queries box, and the fields from the Customers table are listed in the Available Fields box. Refer to the first dialog box shown in Exhibit 19-1.

4 Click >> to move all the fields to the Selected Fields box.

5 In the Selected Fields box, click **Phone**, and then click < to move the Phone field back

Exhibit 19-1 Dialog boxes in the Form Wizard

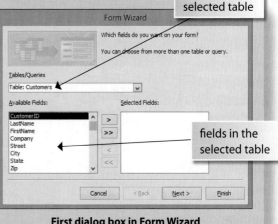

First dialog box in Form Wizard

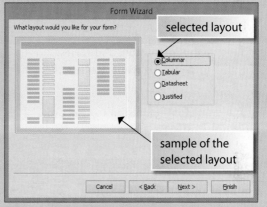

Second dialog box in Form Wizard

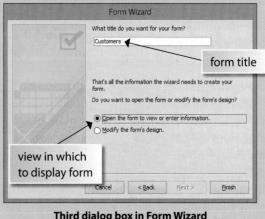

Third dialog box in Form Wizard

to the Available Fields box. In the Selected Fields box, the Email field is selected. The next field you add will be added below the selected Email field.

6 With the Phone field selected in the Available Fields box, click [>]. The Phone field is added back to the Selected Fields box below the Email field.

7 Click **Next** to display the second Form Wizard dialog box, which provides the available layouts for the form: Columnar, Tabular, Datasheet, and Justified. A sample of the selected layout appears on the left side of the dialog box. Refer back to the second dialog box shown in Exhibit 19-1.

8 Click the **Tabular option button**, and review the corresponding sample layout. Review the **Datasheet** and **Justified** layouts.

9 Click the **Columnar option button** to select that layout for the form.

10 Click **Next**. The third and final Form Wizard dialog box shows the Customers table's name as the default form title. *Customers* is also the default name that will be used for the form object. Refer back to the third dialog box shown in Exhibit 19-1.

11 In the "What title do you want for your form" box, edit the form name to **CustomerInfo**.

12 Click **Finish**. The CustomerInfo form opens in Form view, displaying the field values for the first record in the Customers table. The form

> **Tip:** You can close the Navigation Pane to display more of the Form window.

title appears on the object tab, as the object name in the Navigation Pane, and as a title on the form itself. The Columnar layout places the captions for each field on the left and the field values in boxes on the right. The width of the field value boxes is based on the size of the field. Compare your screen to Exhibit 19-2.

End Activity

Exhibit 19-2 CustomerInfo form in Form view

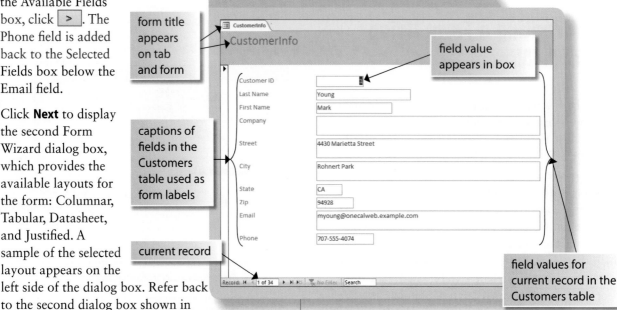

form title appears on tab and form

field value appears in box

captions of fields in the Customers table used as form labels

current record

field values for current record in the Customers table

19-2 Modifying a Form's Design in Layout View

After you create a form, it opens in Form view. If you need to improve its appearance or to make the form easier to use, you need to switch to Layout view. In Layout view, you can see a record in the form and change its layout at the same time, which lets you easily see the results of any design changes you make. You can continue to make changes, undo modifications, and rework the design in Layout view to achieve the look you want for the form. For example, you might change the font, font size, or font color of the labels; add a picture; or modify other form elements such as the type of line used for the field value boxes. You can make all of these changes in Layout view. To make one of these changes, you must select an object. In Layout view, a solid orange outline identifies the currently selected object on the form.

Keep in mind that some changes to the form design must be done in Design view, which gives you a more detailed view of the form's structure.

19-2a Applying a Theme to a Form

You can quickly change the look of a form by applying a different theme, which determines the design scheme for the colors and fonts used in the form. Forms are originally formatted with the Office theme, but you can apply a different theme in Layout view. The theme you select is applied to all of the objects in the database unless you specify to apply the theme to the current object only or to all matching objects, such as all forms. To change the theme, you use the Themes button in the Themes group on the FORM LAYOUT TOOLS DESIGN tab, as shown in Exhibit 19-3.

Exhibit 19-3 Form in Layout view

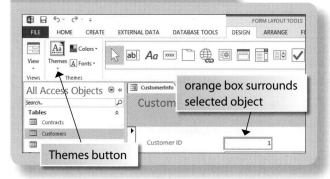

Themes button

orange box surrounds selected object

Begin Activity

Apply a theme to a form.

1 Display the form in **Layout view**. The FORM LAYOUT TOOLS tabs appear on the ribbon, and the Field List pane appears, listing available fields in the form.

2 On the ribbon, click the **FORM LAYOUT TOOLS DESIGN tab**. The field value box for the Customer ID field is selected, as indicated by the orange border. Refer back to Exhibit 19-3.

LEARN MORE

Working with Themes

Themes provide a quick way to format the objects in a database consistently. You can choose to apply a theme to the current object or to all matching objects, such as all forms in the database. You can also choose to make a theme the default theme for the database, which means any existing objects and any new objects you create in the database will be formatted with the selected theme. Instead of clicking a theme in the Themes gallery, you right-click the theme and then click the option you want on the shortcut menu.

When you apply a theme to all matching objects in the database or make the theme the default for the database, Access applies that theme to both new and existing objects in the database. Although this

3 In the Themes group, click the **Themes button**. The Themes gallery appears, showing the available themes for the form.

4 In the Themes gallery, right-click the **Ion Boardroom theme**. A shortcut menu appears with options for applying the theme to all matching objects, applying the theme to this object only (the CustomerInfo form), or making the theme the default for all objects in the database.

5 On the shortcut menu, click **Apply Theme to This Object Only**. The gallery closes, and the Customer-Info form is formatted with the Ion Boardroom theme. Compare your screen to Exhibit 19-4.

End Activity

Exhibit 19-4 Form with theme applied

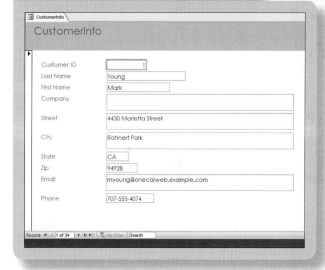

approach ensures design consistency, it can also introduce formatting problems with existing objects.

A better approach is to select the Apply Theme to This Object Only option on the short-cut menu for a theme in the Themes gallery, for each existing form and report. If the new theme causes problems for that form or report, you can simply reapply the previous theme to return the object to its original design.

Shortcut menu for a theme

19-2b Changing the Form Title's Text and Appearance

A form's title should be descriptive and indicate the form's purpose. To make the form's purpose clearer, you can edit or replace the form's current title. You can also format it to change its appearance. For example, you can make text bold, italic, and underlined; change the font, font color, and font size; and change the alignment of text. These options are located in the Font group on the FORM LAYOUT TOOLS FORMAT tab.

Begin Activity

Change the appearance of a form title.

1 Click the **CustomerInfo form title**. An orange box surrounds the title, indicating it is selected.

2 Click between the letters *r* and *I* to position the insertion point in the title text, and then press the **Spacebar**. The form title is now *Customer Info*, and the title appears on two lines.

3 Press the **Down Arrow key** to move the insertion point to the end of the title, and then type **rmation**. The form title is now *Customer Information*.

4 Click in the **main form area** to deselect the title. Click **Customer Information** to reselect the title. The orange outline appears around the title.

5 On the ribbon, click the **FORM LAYOUT TOOLS FORMAT tab**. In the Font group, click the **Font Color button arrow** , and then click the **Purple, Accent 6, Darker 50% theme color**. The color is applied to the form title. Compare your screen to Exhibit 19-5.

End Activity

control An item in a form, report, or other database object that you can manipulate to modify the object's appearance.

control layout A set of controls grouped together in a form or report so that you can manipulate the set as a single control.

Exhibit 19-5 Form title with new color applied

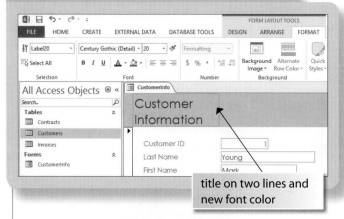

title on two lines and new font color

19-2c Adding a Logo to a Form

A logo can be used to provide color and visual interest in a form. A logo is one of many controls you can use in a form. A **control** is an item in a form, report, or other database object that you can manipulate to modify the object's appearance. The controls you add and modify in Layout view are available on the FORM LAYOUT TOOLS DESIGN tab in the Controls group and the Header/Footer group.

When you add a logo or other control to a form, it is placed in a **control layout**, which is a set of controls grouped together in a form or report so that you can manipulate the set as a single control. Exhibit 19-6 shows a logo inserted on the CustomerInfo form in its control layout. The dotted outline indicates the control layout is selected. You can remove a control from the control layout so you can move the control independently of the control layout.

Begin Activity

Add a picture to a form.

1 On the ribbon, click the **FORM LAYOUT TOOLS DESIGN tab**. In the Header/Footer group, click the **Logo button**. The Insert Picture dialog box opens.

2 Click the data file **Panels** located in the Chapter 19\ Chapter folder, and then click **OK**. A picture of solar panels appears on top of the form title. A solid orange outline surrounds the picture, indicating it is selected, and a dotted outline surrounds the control layout. Refer to Exhibit 19-6.

Exhibit 19-6 Form with picture

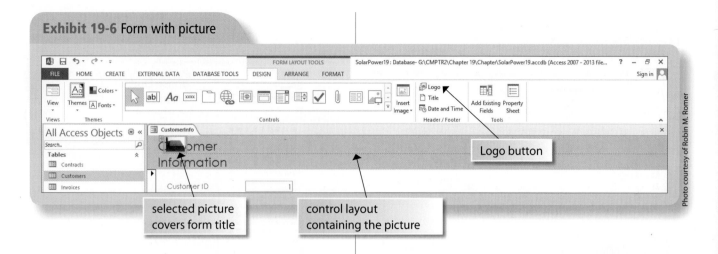

Logo button

selected picture covers form title

control layout containing the picture

Photo courtesy of Robin M. Romer

3 Right-click the **selected picture** to display the shortcut menu, point to **Layout**, and then click **Remove Layout**. The picture is removed from the control layout.

4 Drag the **picture** to the right of the title so that it does not block any part of the form title.

5 Drag a **corner of the orange box** to enlarge the picture to fit within the shaded title area. Compare your screen to Exhibit 19-7.

End Activity

Exhibit 19-7 Form with repositioned and resized picture

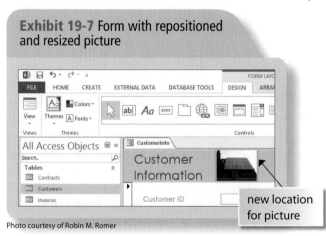

new location for picture

Photo courtesy of Robin M. Romer

19-2d Changing the Lines in a Form

Each field value in the form is displayed in a field value box. The field value boxes are made up of solid lines, which, depending on the theme, might overshadow the field values and make them difficult to read. Fortunately, the lines are another type of control that you can modify in Layout view. The Control Formatting group on the FORM LAYOUT TOOLS FORMAT tab provides options for changing the thickness, type, and color of any line in a form. (See Exhibit 19-8.) You can change the line type for each field value box in the form one at a time. Or, you can select all of the field value boxes and apply a new line type to all of them at the same time.

Begin Activity

Change the lines in a form.

1 Click the **Customer ID field value box**, which contains the field value 1. An orange outline appears around the field value box to indicate it is selected.

2 On the ribbon, click the **FORM LAYOUT TOOLS FORMAT tab**. In the Control Formatting group, click the **Shape Outline button**. The Shape Outline gallery opens with options for changing the line color, line thickness, and line type.

3 Point to **Line Type** to display a submenu with line formats, and then click the **Dots line type**. Refer to Exhibit 19-8.

4 Click a **blank area of the main form** to deselect the field value box. The Customer ID field value box is now a dotted line.

Chapter 19: Creating Forms and Reports **625**

Exhibit 19-8 Line Type submenu

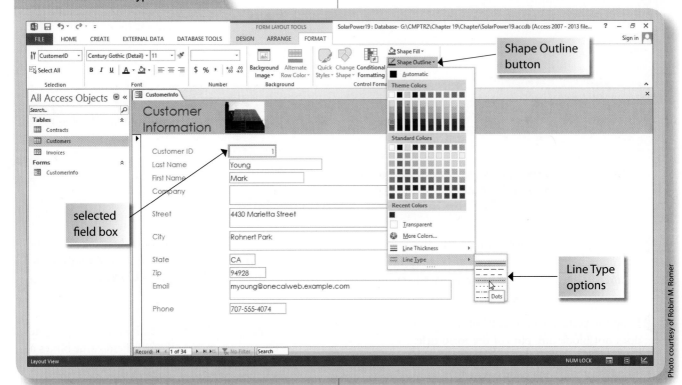

5 Click the **Last Name field value box**, press and hold the **Shift key**, click each remaining field value box below the Last Name field value box, and then release the **Shift key**. All of the field value boxes except the Customer ID field value box are selected.

6 On the FORM LAYOUT TOOLS FORMAT tab, in the Control Formatting group, click the **Shape Outline button**, and then point to **Line Type**.

7 Click the **Dots line type**, and then click a **blank area of the main form**. The line type for each box is now dotted.

8 Save the form.

End Activity

19-3 Finding Data Using a Form

You can use the Find and Replace dialog box to search for data in a form. As you did when using the Find and Replace dialog box to search a datasheet,

you choose a field to base the search on by making that field the current field, and then you enter the value you want to match. The record you want to view is then displayed in the form.

19-3a Searching for a Partial Value

Instead of searching for an entire field value, you can search for a record that contains part of the value anywhere in that field. Performing a partial search such as this is often easier than matching the entire field value and is useful when you don't know or can't remember the entire field value. For example, you can search for part of a company's name.

To search fields for values, use the Find and Replace dialog box as shown in Exhibit 19-9. When you open this dialog box, the default is to search in the current field, so you should click in the field in which you want to search before you open the dialog box. Another default is that the entire field must match the search text unless you change the option in the Match box to Any Part of Field.

Use an Effective Form Design

A form, like any written document, should convey information clearly and effectively. By producing a well-designed and well-written form, you can ensure that other people will be able to work productively and efficiently. As you create a form:

▶ **Consider how the form will be used.** The form's design should accommodate the needs of the people who will use the form to view, enter, and maintain data. For example, if a database form matches an existing paper form, use the same fields in the same order as those on the paper form so users can use the Tab key to move from one field to the next in the database form to enter the necessary information from the paper form.

▶ **Include a meaningful title.** The form should clearly identify its purpose, and a descriptive title ensures that users immediately know what the form is intended for.

▶ **Use correct spelling and grammar.** The text in a form should not contain any spelling or grammatical errors. This not only creates a professional image but also keeps users focused on the task at hand—entering or reviewing data.

▶ **Enhance the form's appearance.** A visually appealing form is user-friendly and can improve the form's readability, helping to prevent data entry errors.

▶ **Use a consistent design.** Use similar elements—titles, pictures, fonts, and so on—in each form in a database to provide a cohesive appearance. A mix of styles and elements in a database could lead to problems when working with the forms.

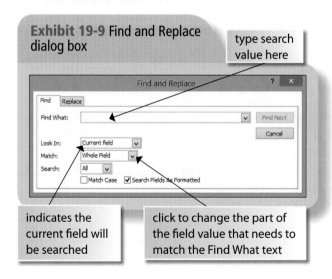

Exhibit 19-9 Find and Replace dialog box

type search value here

indicates the current field will be searched

click to change the part of the field value that needs to match the Find What text

Begin Activity

Search for a partial value.

1 Display the form in **Form view**.

2 Click in the **Email field value box** to select Email as the current field and as the field to search.

3 On the HOME tab, in the Find group, click the **Find button**. The Find and Replace dialog box opens. The Look In box shows that the current field (in this case, Email) will be searched. Refer to Exhibit 19-9.

4 In the Find What box, type **parry** to search for records that contain the text *parry* in the email address.

5 Click the **Match arrow** to display the list of matching options, and then click **Any Part of Field** to find records that contain the text *parry* in any part of the Email field.

Tip: Unless you select the Match Case check box, Access will find any record containing the search text with any combination of uppercase and lowercase letters.

6 Click **Find Next**, and then drag the Find and Replace dialog box by its title bar so you can see the field value boxes in the form. The CustomerInfo form now displays record 31, which is the record for Patrick Perry. The text *parry* is selected in the Email field value box because you searched for this word.

7 Click in the **form area** to make the form active. The Find and Replace dialog box remains open and the text *parry* is still selected in the Email field.

8 Type **perry** to replace the selected text in the Email field. The contact's email address is now correct.

End Activity

19-3b Searching with Wildcards

Instead of entering an exact value to find when you search for text with the Find and Replace dialog box, you can use wildcards. A **wildcard character** is a placeholder you use when you know only part of a value or when you want to start or end with a specific character or match a certain pattern. Exhibit 19-10 lists wildcard characters.

Exhibit 19-10 Wildcard characters

Wildcard Character	Purpose	Example
*	Match any number of characters. It can be used as the first and/or last character in the character string.	th* finds the, that, this, therefore, and so on
?	Match any single alphabetic character.	a?t finds act, aft, ant, apt, and art
[]	Match any single character within the brackets.	a[fr]t finds aft and art but not act, ant, and apt
!	Match any character not within brackets.	a[!fr]t finds act, ant, and apt but not aft and art
-	Match any one of a range of characters. The range must be in ascending order (a to z, not z to a).	a[d-p]t finds aft, ant, and apt but not act and art
#	Match any single numeric character.	#72 finds 072, 172, 272, 372, and so on

© 2014 Cengage Learning

For example, you might want to view the records for customers with phone numbers beginning with the area code 707. You could search for any field containing the digits 707 in any part of the field, but this search would also find records with the digits 707 in other parts of the phone number. To find only those records with the 707 area code, you can use the * wildcard character.

wildcard character A placeholder you use when you know only part of a value, or when you want to start or end with a specific character or match a certain pattern.

Begin Activity

Search with a wildcard character.

1 In the CustomerInfo form, scroll down, and then click in the **Phone field value box**. This is the field you want to search.

2 Click the **Find and Replace dialog box** to make it active. The Look In box setting is still Current field, which is now the Phone field; this is the field that will be searched.

3 Click in the Find What box to select **parry**, and then type **707***.

4 Click the **Match arrow**, and then click **Whole Field**. Because you are using a wildcard character in the search value, you want to search the whole field.

5 Click **Find Next**. The search process starts from the point of the previously displayed record in the form, which was record 31, and then finds records in which any field value in the Phone field begins with 707. Record 1 is the first record found for a customer with the area code 707. The search process cycled back through the beginning of the records in the underlying table.

6 Click **Find Next**. Record 12 is the next record found for a customer with the area code 707.

7 Continue to click **Find Next** to find each record for a customer with the area code 707 until a dialog box appears, indicating that the search is finished.

8 Click **OK** to close the dialog box.

9 Click **Cancel** to close the Find and Replace dialog box.

End Activity

19-3c Maintaining Table Data Using a Form

Maintaining data using a form in Form view is often easier than using a datasheet because you can focus on all the changes for one record at one time. For example, you can add a new record to the table. Exhibit 19-11 shows the CustomerInfo form in Form view after clicking the New button in the Records group on the HOME tab or the New (blank) record button on the record navigation bar. In Form view, you can also edit the field values for a record or delete a record from the underlying table. If you know the number of the record you want to edit or delete, you can enter the number in the Current Record box to move to that record.

Exhibit 19-11 Form for a new record

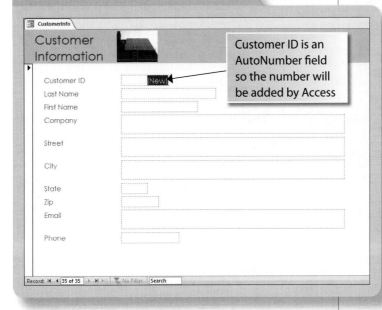

Begin Activity

Maintain table data using a form.

1 In the status bar at the bottom of the form, click in the **Current Record box**, delete **26**, type **8** and then press the **Enter key**. Record 8 (LKW Construction) is now current.

2 In the Street field value box, double-click **4457** to select the entry, and then type **8274**. The address is updated.

3 On the HOME tab, in the Records group, click the **New button**. Record 35, the next available new record, becomes the current record. All field value boxes are empty, and the insertion point is positioned in the Customer ID field value box. Refer back to Exhibit 19-11.

4 Press the **Tab key**, and then type your last name in the Last Name field.

5 Press the **Tab key**, and type your first name in the First Name field.

6 Press the **Tab key** seven times to move the insertion point to the Phone field, and then press the **Tab key** once more. A new record 36, the next available new record, becomes the current record, and the record for Customer ID 35 is saved in the Customers table.

7 Close the **CustomerInfo form**.

End Activity

19-4 Creating a Form Based on Related Tables

You can create a form that displays the data from two tables at the same time, such as when you want to review the data for each customer and the customer's contracts at the same time. A form based on two tables requires the tables to have a defined relationship. For example, defining a relationship between a Customers (primary) table and a Contracts (related) table enables you to create a form based on both tables. When you use related tables in a form, the form includes a main form and a subform. A **main form** displays the data from the primary table. A **subform** displays the data from the related table. Access uses the defined relationship between the tables to join them automatically through the common field that exists in both tables.

19-4a Creating a Form with a Main Form and a Subform

When creating a form based on two tables, first you choose the primary table and select the fields to include in the main form. Then you choose the related table and select the fields to include in the subform.

To create a form and a subform, you use the Form Wizard. If you select fields from two tables in the first dialog box, a new second dialog box appears, as

> **main form** The part of a form that displays data from the primary table in a defined relationship.
>
> **subform** The part of a form that displays data from a related table in a defined relationship.

shown in Exhibit 19-12. In this dialog box, you choose whether to create a main form with a subform or a linked form. In a linked form, only the main form fields are displayed, and a button with the subform's name on it appears on the main form. You can click this button to display the associated subform records.

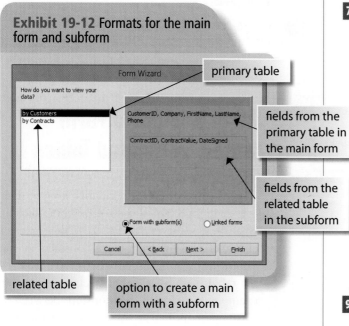

Exhibit 19-12 Formats for the main form and subform

primary table

fields from the primary table in the main form

fields from the related table in the subform

related table

option to create a main form with a subform

Begin Activity

Create a form with a main form and a subform.

1 On the ribbon, click the **CREATE tab**. In the Forms group, click the **Form Wizard button**. The first Form Wizard dialog box opens.

2 If necessary, click the **Tables/Queries arrow**, and then click **Table: Customers**.

3 Move the following fields from the Available Fields box to the Selected Fields box: **CustomerID, Company, FirstName, LastName,** and **Phone**.

> **Tip:** You can double-click a field to move it between the Available Fields box and the Selected Fields box.

4 Click the **Tables/Queries arrow**, and then click **Table: Contracts**. The fields from the Contracts table appear in the Available Fields box.

5 Move all the fields in the Contracts table to the Selected Fields box. The table name (Contracts) is included in the CustomerID field name to distinguish it from the same field (CustomerID) in the Customers table.

6 Move the **Contracts.CustomerID** field back to the Available Fields box.

7 Click **Next**. The second Form Wizard dialog box appears. The Form with subform(s) option button is selected. The left box shows the order in which the data will be displayed—first data from the primary Customers table, and then data from the related Contracts table. The preview on the right shows how the form will appear—fields from the Customers table at the top in the main form and fields from the Contracts table at the bottom in the subform. Refer back to Exhibit 19-12.

8 Click **Next**. The third Form Wizard dialog box opens, in which you choose the subform layout. The Tabular layout displays subform fields as a table. The Datasheet layout displays subform fields as a table datasheet.

9 Click the **Datasheet option button** if it is not already selected, and then click **Next**. The fourth Form Wizard dialog box opens, in which you choose titles for the main form and the subform.

10 In the **Form box**, click to the right of the last letter, press the **Backspace** key to delete the *s*, and then type **Contracts**. The main form name is now *CustomerContracts*.

11 In the **Subform box**, delete the space between the two words so that the subform name is *Contracts-Subform*.

12 Click **Finish**. The completed form opens in Form view formatted with the Office theme. The main form displays the fields from the first record in the Customers table in a columnar format. The records in the main form appear in primary key order by Customer ID. Customer ID 1 has two related records in the Contracts table, which appear in the subform in the datasheet format. Compare your screen to Exhibit 19-13.

End Activity

Exhibit 19-13 Main form with subform in Form view

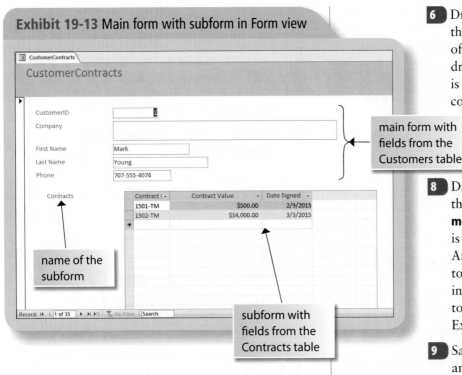

main form with fields from the Customers table

name of the subform

subform with fields from the Contracts table

19-4b Modifying a Main Form and Subform in Layout View

You can modify a form with a main form and a subform, just as you can a form based on one table. For example, you can edit the form title, resize the subform, and resize columns to fully display their field values. You can make these types of changes in Layout view or Design view.

Begin Activity

Modify a main form and subform in Layout view.

1 Display the **CustomerContracts form** in **Layout view**.

2 In the shaded title area at the top of the form, select and then edit the **Customer-Contracts form title** so that the title in the form is **Customer Contracts**.

3 Click a **blank area** of the main form to deselect the title.

4 Click the **subform** to select it. An orange outline surrounds the subform.

5 Resize each column in the subform datasheet to its best fit.

6 Drag the **left edge of the subform** to the left to align it with the left edge of the field value boxes, and then drag its **right edge** to the left until it is just to the right of the Date Signed column.

7 Scroll down so that you can see the bottom of the subform.

8 Drag the **top edge of the form** down three rows. Then drag the **table move handle** ⊕ up until the pointer is to the right of the label Contracts. After you release the mouse button, you can see the entire subform in the window without needing to scroll. Compare your screen to Exhibit 19-14.

9 Save the **CustomerContracts form**, and then switch to **Form view**.

End Activity

Exhibit 19-14 Modified form in Layout view

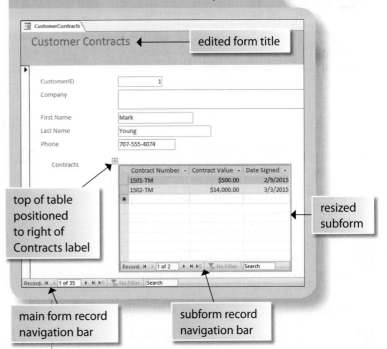

edited form title

top of table positioned to right of Contracts label

resized subform

main form record navigation bar

subform record navigation bar

19-4c Displaying Records in a Main Form and a Subform

A form with a main form and subform includes two sets of navigation buttons. The navigation buttons at the bottom of the Form window select records from the primary table in the main form. The navigation buttons at the bottom of the subform select records from the related table in the subform. The subform navigation buttons may not be visible until you scroll to the bottom of the main form. If you enter data in the main form, the primary table is updated. If you enter data in the subform, the related table is updated.

LEARN MORE

Main Form and Subform Names

The main form name (CustomerContracts, in this case) appears on the object tab and as the form title. The subform name (Contracts, in this case) appears to the left of the subform. Access displays only the table name for the subform, but uses the complete object name, ContractsSubform, in the Navigation Pane. The subform designation is necessary in a list of database objects, so that you can distinguish the Contracts subform from other objects, such as the Contracts table. The subform designation is not needed in the CustomerContracts form; only the table name is required to identify the table containing the records in the subform.

Begin Activity

Navigate main form and subform records.

1 On the record navigation bar at the bottom of the main Form window, click the **Last record button** ▶|. Record 35 in the Customers table (your information) becomes the current record in the main form. The subform shows that this customer currently has no contracts.

2 Click the **Previous record button** ◀. Record 34 in the Customers table (for Chen Builders) becomes the current record in the main form. The subform shows that this customer has two contracts.

3 On the record navigation bar at the bottom of the main Form window, in the Current Record box, select **34**, type **25** and then press the **Enter key**. Record 25 in the Customers table (for LKW Construction) becomes the current record in the main

form. The subform shows that this customer has six contracts. The first contract is selected.

4 In the subform, on the record navigation bar, click the **Next record button** ▶. The second contract in the subform, ContractNumber 1520-LB, is selected in the subform.

5 On the record navigation bar in the subform, click the **Last record button** ▶|. Contract Number 1630-AD in the Contracts table becomes the current record in the subform.

End Activity

19-5 Previewing and Printing Selected Form Records

When you print a form, Access prints as many form records as can fit on a printed page. If only part of a form record fits on the bottom of a page, the remainder of the record prints on the next page. You can choose to print all pages or a range of pages. In addition, you can print only the currently selected form record. Before printing, you should always preview the form using Print Preview to see how it will look when printed, as shown in Exhibit 19-15.

Begin Activity

Preview the form.

1 On the ribbon, click the **FILE tab**. In the navigation bar, click **Print**. The Print screen has three options: Quick Print, Print, and Print Preview.

2 Click **Print Preview**. The Print Preview window opens, showing the records for the CustomerContracts form. Each record appears in its own form, and shading distinguishes one record from the next. Refer to Exhibit 19-15.

3 On the ribbon, on the PRINT PREVIEW tab, in the Close Preview group, click the **Close Print Preview button**. Print Preview closes, and you return to the CustomerContracts form in Form view with the record for LKW Construction still displayed in the main form.

End Activity

Exhibit 19-15 Form records displayed in Print Preview

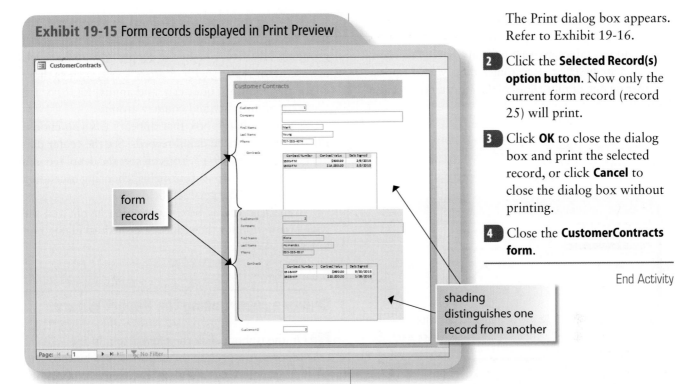

form records

shading distinguishes one record from another

You can print the data of a single record. To do this, you need to open the Print dialog box from the Print screen in Backstage view. See Exhibit 19-16. You can also open the Print dialog box by clicking the Print button in the Print group on the PRINT PREVIEW tab; however, the option to print only selected records does not appear in the Print dialog box when you use this method.

Exhibit 19-16 Print dialog box

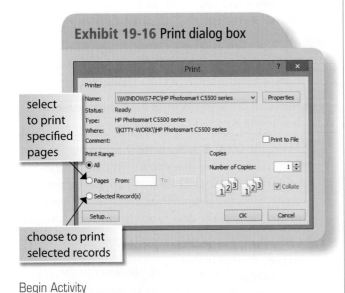

select to print specified pages

choose to print selected records

Begin Activity

Print the current record.

1 On the ribbon, click the **FILE tab**. In the navigation bar, click **Print**. On the Print tab, click **Print**.

The Print dialog box appears. Refer to Exhibit 19-16.

2 Click the **Selected Record(s) option button**. Now only the current form record (record 25) will print.

3 Click **OK** to close the dialog box and print the selected record, or click **Cancel** to close the dialog box without printing.

4 Close the **CustomerContracts form**.

End Activity

19-6 Creating a Report Using the Report Wizard

A report is a formatted printout of the contents of one or more tables or queries in a database. You can design your own reports, or you can use the Report Wizard to create them. The Report Wizard guides you through the process of creating a report. You choose which fields to display from tables and queries as well as how to group and sort the records in the report, the page orientation, and the report's title. As with a form, you can change the report's design after you create it.

19-6a Creating a Report

When you create a report with the Report Wizard, you first choose the table or query on which to base the report and then select the fields you want to include in the report. You can select fields from more than one table as long as the tables are related, such as the Customers and Contracts tables.

In the Report Wizard, the second dialog box lets you choose whether to show the data in the report grouped by table or ungrouped. See the first dialog box in Exhibit 19-17. A grouped report places the data from the first table in one group followed by the related records. For example, each customer record will appear in its own group followed by the related contract records for that customer. An example of an ungrouped report would be a report of records from the Customers and Contracts tables in order by ContractID. Each contract and its associated customer data would appear together on one or more lines of the report, not grouped by table.

Exhibit 19-17 Dialog boxes in the Report Wizard

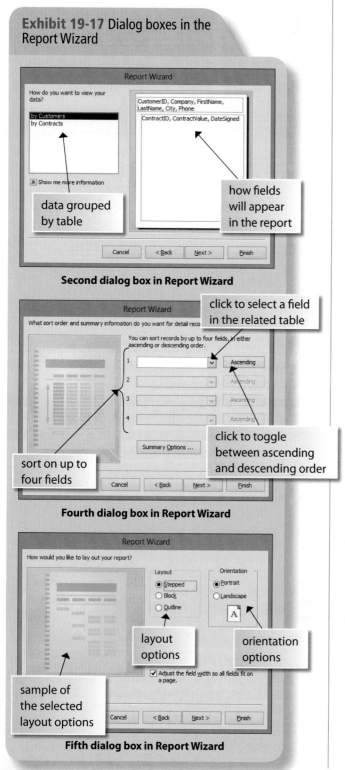

Second dialog box in Report Wizard

data grouped by table

how fields will appear in the report

click to select a field in the related table

sort on up to four fields

click to toggle between ascending and descending order

Fourth dialog box in Report Wizard

layout options

orientation options

sample of the selected layout options

Fifth dialog box in Report Wizard

Whether the report is grouped or ungrouped, the next dialog box in the Report Wizard lets you select grouping levels to add to the report. Grouping levels are useful for reports with multiple levels, such as those containing monthly, quarterly, and annual totals, or for those containing city and country groups.

The next dialog box that appears lets you choose the sort order for the detail records. See the center dialog box in Exhibit 19-17. You can sort the detail records for the report by up to four fields, choosing ascending or descending order for each field.

In the next dialog box, you select a layout and the page orientation for the report. See the third dialog box in Exhibit 19-17.

Begin Activity

Create a report using the Report Wizard.

1 On the ribbon, click the **CREATE tab**. In the Reports group, click the **Report Wizard button**. The first Report Wizard dialog box opens. As with the first Form Wizard dialog box, you select the table or query and then add fields to use in the report.

2 If necessary, click the **Tables/Queries arrow**, and then click **Table: Customers**.

3 Move the following fields from the Available Fields box to the Selected Fields box: **CustomerID**, **Company**, **FirstName**, **LastName**, **City**, and **Phone**. The fields will appear in the report in the order you select them.

4 Click the **Tables/Queries arrow**, and then click **Tables: Contracts**. The fields from the Contracts table appear in the Available Fields box.

5 Move all of the fields from the Available Fields box to the Selected Fields box.

6 Move the **Contracts.CustomerID** field from the Selected Fields box back to the Available Fields box. The CustomerID field will appear on the report with the customer data, so you do not need to include it in the detail records for each contract.

7 Click **Next**. The second Report Wizard dialog box appears, in which you select whether the report is grouped by table or ungrouped. Refer to the first dialog box shown in

Tip: You can display tips for creating reports and examples of reports by clicking the Show me more information button.

Exhibit 19-17. You will leave the report grouped by the Customers table.

8 Click **Next**. The third Report Wizard dialog box opens, in which you can choose additional grouping levels. Two grouping levels are shown: one for a customer's data, and the other for a customer's contracts.

9 Click **Next**. The fourth Report Wizard dialog box opens, in which you can choose the sort order for the detail records. The records from the Contracts table for a customer represent the detail records for the report. Refer back to the second dialog box shown in Exhibit 19-17.

10 Click the **1 arrow**, and then click **DateSigned**. The Ascending option is selected, so the contracts will be shown in chronological order.

11 Click **Next**. The fifth Report Wizard dialog box opens, in which you choose a layout and page orientation for the report. Refer back to the third dialog box shown in Exhibit 19-17.

12 In the Layout section, click the **Outline option button** to select the Outline layout.

13 In the Orientation section, click the **Landscape option button**. This page orientation provides more space across the page to display longer field values.

14 Click **Next**. The sixth and final Report Wizard dialog box opens. The report title you enter in this dialog box also serves as the name for the report object in the database.

15 In the box for the title, edit the title to **CustomersAnd-Contracts**. You entered the report name as one word so that the report object is named appropriately. You will edit the title in the report later.

16 Click **Finish**. The Report Wizard creates the report, saves the report as an object in the database, and opens the report in Print Preview.

End Activity

Create a Report Based on a Query

You can create a report based on one or more tables or queries. When you base a report on a query, you can use criteria and other query features to retrieve only the information you want to display in the report. Experienced Access users often create a query just so they can create a report based on that query. When planning a report, consider creating a query first and then basing the report on that query to produce the exact results you want to see in the report.

19-6b Previewing a Report

In Print Preview, you can check the overall layout of the report, as well as zoom in to read the text. This enables you to find any formatting problems or other issues and make the necessary corrections. Exhibit 19-18 shows the CustomersAndContracts report in Print Preview zoomed in.

Exhibit 19-18 Close-up view of the report

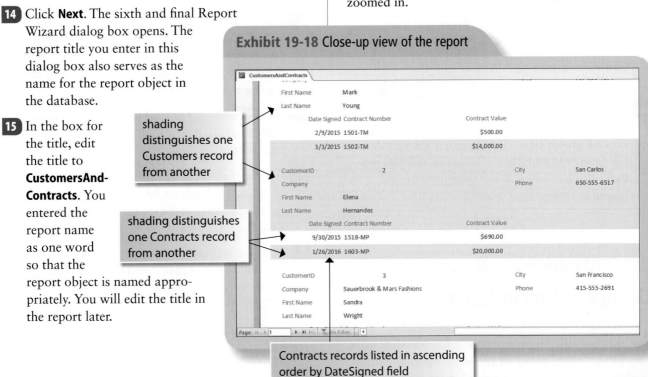

shading distinguishes one Customers record from another

shading distinguishes one Contracts record from another

Contracts records listed in ascending order by DateSigned field

Preview a report.

1 On the ribbon, on the PRINT PREVIEW tab, in the Zoom group, click the **Zoom button arrow**, and then click **Fit to Window**. The entire first page of the report is displayed in Print Preview.

2 Click the **center of the report**. The display changes to show a close-up view of the report. Refer back to Exhibit 19-18. Shading distinguishes one customer's record from the next, as well as one contract record from the next within a group of each customer's contract records. The detail records for the Contracts table fields appear in ascending order based on the values in the DateSigned field. Because the DateSigned field is used as the sort field for the contracts, it appears as the first field in this section, even though you used the Report Wizard to select the fields in a different order.

3 Scroll to the bottom-left corner of the first page, reading the report as you scroll. Notice the current date at the left edge of the bottom of the first page of the report; the Report Wizard included this as part of the report's design.

4 Scroll to the right, and view the page number at the right edge of the footer.

5 Click the report to zoom back out, and then use the navigation buttons to review the 12 pages of the report.

> **Problem?** If you see blank pages every other page as you navigate the report, the text of the page number might not be completely within the page border. You'll fix this problem shortly.

6 On the PRINT PRE-VIEW tab, in the Close Preview group, click the **Close Print Preview button**. The report is displayed in Design view.

19-7 Modifying a Report's Design in Layout View

You modify a report's design in Layout view or in Design view. Many of the same options that are available for forms are also provided for reports.

19-7a Changing a Report's Appearance

You can change the text of the report title as well as the font and color of text in a report to enhance its appearance. The same themes available for forms are also available for reports. You can choose to apply a theme to the current report object only, or to all reports in the database. When you point to a theme in the Themes gallery, a ScreenTip displays the names of the database objects that use the theme. You can also add a picture to a report for visual interest or to identify a particular section of the report.

Change a report's appearance.

1 Display the report in **Layout view**. The REPORT LAYOUT TOOLS tabs appear on the ribbon.

2 On the REPORT LAYOUT TOOLS DESIGN tab, in the Themes group, click the **Themes button**, right-click the **Ion Boardroom theme**, and then click **Apply Theme to This Object Only**. The gallery closes, and the theme is applied to the report.

3 At the top of the report, select the report title **CustomersAndContracts**, and then edit the text to **Customers and Contracts**.

4 Click in the **report** to deselect the report title, and then select the **report title** again.

5 On the ribbon, click the **REPORT LAYOUT TOOLS FORMAT tab**. In the Font group, click the **Font Color button arrow** [A], and then click the **Purple, Accent 6, Darker 50% theme color**. The color is applied to the report title.

6 On the ribbon, click the **REPORT LAYOUT TOOLS DESIGN tab**. In the Header/Footer group, click the **Logo button**.

7 Double-click the data file **Panels** located in the Chapter 19\Chapter folder. The picture is inserted in the upper-left corner of the report, partially covering the report title.

8 Drag the selected **picture** to the right of the report title within the shaded title area. Compare your screen to Exhibit 19-19.

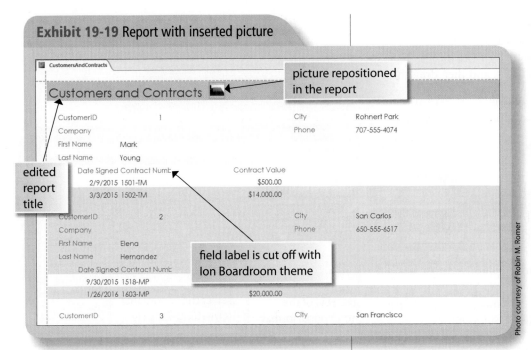

Exhibit 19-19 Report with inserted picture

- picture repositioned in the report
- edited report title
- field label is cut off with Ion Boardroom theme

19-7b Resizing Fields and Field Values in a Report

After you apply a new theme to a report, you should check the report to be sure that the theme's design didn't cause spacing issues or text to be cut off. For example, the larger font used by the Ion Boardroom theme has caused the Contract Number field label to be truncated. Working in Layout view, you can resize and reposition labels and fields to improve the appearance of the report or to address the problem of some field values not being completely displayed. To select and resize multiple fields, you press the Shift key as you select the different fields. You should also check the page number in the footer to make sure it fits completely on the page.

Begin Activity

Resize field labels and field value boxes.

1 In the report, click the first **Contract Number field label** to select it. When you select a field label in Layout view, all of the labels for that field are selected in the report. Any changes you make to a single selected field will also be made to the other labels for that field.

2 Resize the **Contract Number field label** until the entire field label is visible. The change is made throughout the report.

3 Find the record for **Customer ID 16**, Oakland Neighborhood Development.

4 In the record for Customer ID 16, click the **City field label**, press and hold the **Shift key**, and then click the **Phone field label**. Both field labels are selected and can be resized.

5 Drag the **left edge** of either selected field label to the right until the black outlines indicating the width of the labels are approximately 1.5 inches wide. The City and Phone field labels for the entire report are now smaller, moving them closer to their values. Compare your screen to Exhibit 19-20.

Exhibit 19-20 Report with resized field labels and field value boxes

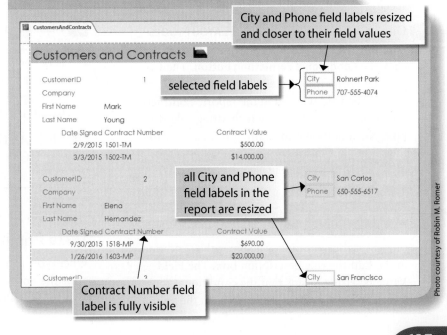

- City and Phone field labels resized and closer to their field values
- selected field labels
- all City and Phone field labels in the report are resized
- Contract Number field label is fully visible

6 Scroll the report to the bottom and to the right, and view the page number text. If the page number in the footer is not completely within the page border, select the footer text, and then drag the **orange box** to the left until the page number text is within the page border.

End Activity

19-7c Using Conditional Formatting in a Report

You can add conditional formatting to a report or form. As when you used conditional formatting in Excel, special formatting is applied to field values that meet the condition or conditions you set. For example, you might use conditional formatting in a report to format contract amounts that are greater than or equal to $20,000 in a bold, red font.

Begin Activity

Use conditional formatting in a report.

1 Scroll down to the bottom of the report. In the record for Customer ID 33, click the **Contract Value field value**. An orange outline appears around

Tip: You must select a field *value box*, and not the field *label*, before applying a conditional format.

the field value box, and a lighter orange outline appears around the other Contract Value field value boxes in the report. The conditional formatting you specify will affect all the values for the field.

2 On the ribbon, click the **REPORT LAYOUT TOOLS FORMAT tab**. In the Control Formatting group, click the **Conditional Formatting button**. The Conditional Formatting Rules Manager dialog box opens. The field selected in the report, ContractValue, appears in the Show formatting rules for box. No conditional formatting rules are set for the selected field.

3 In the dialog box, click the **New Rule button**. The New Formatting Rule dialog box opens. The selected rule type specifies that Access will check field values in the selected field to determine if they meet the condition. You enter the condition in the Edit the rule description box. The Field Value Is setting means that the conditional format you specify will be applied only when the value

for the selected ContractValue field meets the condition. See Exhibit 19-21.

Exhibit 19-21 New Formatting Rule dialog box

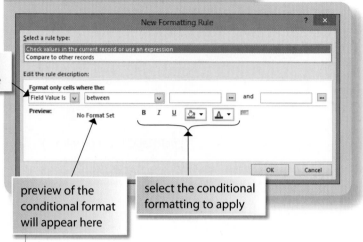

specify the condition here

preview of the conditional format will appear here

select the conditional formatting to apply

4 On the box that contains the word *between*, click the **arrow**, and then click **greater than or equal to**.

5 Press the **Tab key** to move to the next box, and then type **20000**. The condition is set to format cells where the field value is greater than or equal to 20,000.

6 In the Preview section, click the **Font color button arrow**, and then click the **Red standard color**.

7 In the Preview section, click the **Bold button**. Any field value that meets the condition will be formatted in bold, red text.

8 Click **OK**. The new rule you specified appears in the Rule section of the Conditional Formatting Rules Manager dialog box as *Value >= 20000*. The Format section on the right shows the conditional formatting (red, bold font) that will be applied based on this rule. See Exhibit 19-22.

9 Click **OK**. The conditional formatting is applied to the ContractValue field values. Compare your screen to Exhibit 19-23.

End Activity

19-7d Printing a Report

When you print a report, you can specify whether to print the entire report or select pages to print. You do this from the Print dialog box.

Begin Activity

Exhibit 19-22 Conditional Formatting Rules Manager dialog box

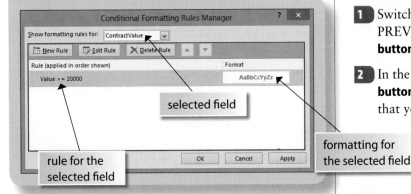

rule for the selected field

selected field

formatting for the selected field

Print a report.

1 Switch to Print Preview. On the PRINT PREVIEW tab, in the Print group, click the **Print button**. The Print dialog box opens.

2 In the Print Range section, click the **Pages option button**. The insertion point is in the From box so that you can specify the range of pages to print.

3 In the From box, type **1**, press the **Tab key** to move to the To box, and then type **1**. These settings specify that only page 1 of the report will be printed.

Exhibit 19-23 Print Preview of report with conditional formatting

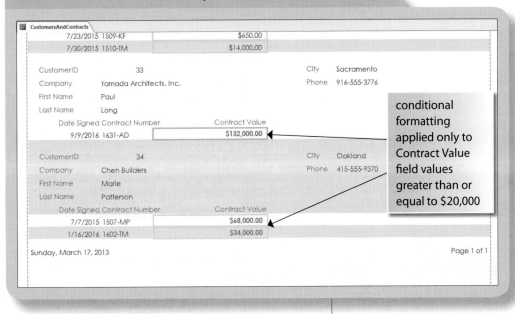

conditional formatting applied only to Contract Value field values greater than or equal to $20,000

4 Click **OK** to print the first page of the report, or click **Cancel** to close the Print dialog box without printing.

5 Save the **Customers-And-Contracts report**, and then close it.

6 Compact and repair the **Solar-Power19 database**, and then close the database.

End Activity

CAUTION

Preview Reports Before Printing

Before printing a report, be sure to review the report in Print Preview so you can find and correct any formatting problems or other issues. You can also determine where the pages will break and make adjustments as needed. It is particularly important to preview a report after you have changed its design to ensure new problems have not occurred in the report. This approach ensures that the final printed report looks exactly the way you want it to, and also saves time and resources because you won't need to reprint the report because an unexpected formatting error occurred.

Quiz Yourself

1. Describe the difference between creating a form using the Form tool and creating a form using the Form Wizard.

2. How do you apply a theme to an existing form?

3. What is a control?

4. What is a wildcard character?

5. Which wildcard character matches any single alphabetic character?

6. In a form that contains a main form and a subform, what data is displayed in the main form and what data is displayed in the subform?

7. Describe the navigation buttons used to move through a form containing a main form and a subform.

8. Describe how to print only the current record displayed in a form.

9. What are detail records?

10. Describe how to resize a field in a report.

11. When working in Layout view for a report, how do you select multiple fields in the report?

12. How do you apply conditional formatting to a report?

Practice It

Practice It 19-1

1. Open the data file **Snow19** located in the Chapter 19\Practice It folder. Save the database as **SnowRemoval19**.

2. Use the Form Wizard to create a form based on the Clients table. Select all fields for the form, use the Columnar layout, and specify the title **ClientContactInfo** for the form.

3. Display the form in Layout view, and then apply the Organic theme to the ClientContactInfo form only.

4. Edit the form title so that it appears as **Client Contact Info** (three words). Change the font color of the form title to the Blue-Gray, Accent 3, Darker 50% theme color.

5. Insert the data file **Shovel** located in the Chapter 19\Practice It folder as a logo in the ClientContactInfo form. Remove the picture from the control layout, move the picture to the right of the form title, and then resize it to be the same height as the shaded title area.

6. Change the line type for all of the field value boxes to Dots.

7. Switch to Form view, and use the Client Contact Info form to update the Clients table as follows:

   a. Use the Find command to search for **pony** anywhere in the Company field to display the record for the Pony Grill (Client ID 19). Change the Street field value in this record to **8930 Saddle Brook Way**.

   b. Add a new record with your first and last names in the First Name and Last Name fields.

8. Save and close the form.

9. Use the Form Wizard to create a form containing a main form and a subform based on the Clients and ServiceAgreements tables. Select all fields from the Clients table for the main form, and select AgreementNum, AgreementDate, and AgreementAmt from the ServiceAgreements table for the subform. Use the Datasheet layout. Specify the title **ClientAndServiceAgreements** for the main form and **ServiceAgreementsSubform** for the subform.

10. Change the form title text to **Client Service Agreements**.

11. Resize all columns in the subform to their best fit. Save and close the ClientAndServiceAgreements form.

12. Use the Report Wizard to create a report based on the primary ServiceAgreements table and the related Invoices table. Select all the fields from the ServiceAgreements table, and select the InvNum, InvDate, InvAmt, and Paid fields from the Invoices table. Do not specify any additional grouping levels, and sort the detail records by the Paid field in descending order. Choose the Outline layout and Landscape orientation. Specify the title **InvoicesByAgreement** for the report.

13. Display the report in Layout view. Change the report title text to **Invoices by Agreement**.

14. Apply the Organic theme to the InvoicesByAgreement report only.

15. Change the color of the report title text to the Blue-Gray, Accent 3, Darker 50% theme color.

16. Resize the Service Type label so it is about half the width it used to be, and resize the Amount field value box so the value in it is right-aligned with the values in the ClientID and DateSigned field value boxes.

17. Apply conditional formatting so that the Invoice Date field values less than 1/1/2016 are bold with a background color of Light Green.

18. Preview each page of the report, verifying that all the fields fit on the page. If necessary, return to Layout view and make changes so the report prints within the margins of the page and so that all field names and values are completely displayed.

19. Save the InvoicesByAgreement report, print only page 3 of the report, and then close the report.

20. Compact and repair the SnowRemoval19 database, and then close it.

Practice It 19-2

1. Open the data file **Art19** located in the Chapter 19\Practice It folder. Save the database as **ArtClasses19**.

2. Use the Form Wizard to create a form based on the Students table. Select all the fields for the form and the Columnar layout. Specify the title **StudentData** for the form.

3. Apply the Integral theme to the StudentData form only.

4. Edit the form title so that it appears as **Student Data** (two words), and change the font color of the form title to the Teal, Accent 6, Darker 50% theme color.

5. Use the Find command to display the record for Marcus Elam, and then change the Address field value for this record to **304 Forest Avenue**.

6. Use the StudentData form to add a new record to the Students table using the Student ID **ZA7584**, the Class ID **395-CL**, and your first and last names in the First Name and Last Name fields.

7. Save and close the StudentData form.

8. Use the Form Wizard to create a form containing a main form and a subform. Select all the fields from the Instructors table for the main form, and select the ClassID, ClassName, and Juniors fields from the Classes table for the subform. Use the Datasheet layout. Specify the title **ClassesByInstructor** for the main form and the title **ClassesSubform** for the subform.

9. Change the form title text for the main form to **Classes by Instructor**.

10. Change the line type for all the field value boxes except for the Full Time? check box to Dots.

11. Resize columns in the subform to their best fit, and then move through the records in the main form and until you see the class name Clay Hand-building and Sculpture, and then resize the Class Name column to fit that class name.

12. Save and close the ClassesByInstructor form.

13. Use the Report Wizard to create a report based on the primary Classes table and the related Students table. Select all fields from the Classes table, and select the FirstName, LastName, and BirthDate fields from the Students table. Do not select any additional grouping levels, and sort the detail records in ascending order by LastName. Choose the Outline layout and Landscape orientation. Specify the title **StudentClasses** for the report.

14. Apply the Slice theme to the StudentClasses report only.

15. Edit the report title so that it appears as **Student Classes** (two words); and change the font color of the title to the Dark Blue, Accent 1, Darker 50% theme color.

16. In Layout view, make the Length and Cost field label boxes about half as wide as their current widths, then change the width of the Cost field value box so the value in it is right-aligned with the value in the Length field value box above it. Make sure the page number is completely within the page border, moving the control as needed.

17. Insert the data file **Paint** located in the Chapter 19\Practice It folder as a logo in the report. Move the picture to the right of the report title, and resize it larger to fit the space.

18. Apply conditional formatting so that any Cost field value greater than 200 appears as bold and with the text color as Maroon 5.

19. Preview the entire report to confirm that it is formatted correctly. If necessary, return to Layout view, and make changes so that all field labels and field values are completely displayed. When you are finished, save the report, print the first page, and then close the report.

20. Compact and repair the ArtClasses19 database, and then close it.

On Your Own

On Your Own 19-1

1. Open the data file **Donations19** located in the Chapter 19\On Your Own folder. Save the database as **DonationsList19**.

2. Use the Form Wizard to create a form based on the Donations table. Select all the fields for the form and the Columnar layout. Specify an appropriate title for the form.

3. Apply a different theme to the form only.

4. Edit the form title as needed so that spaces separate each word. Change the font color of the form title to a color that is easy to read with the theme you applied to the form.

5. Use the appropriate buttons in the Font group on the FORM LAYOUT TOOLS FORMAT tab to underline the form title and make it bold. Resize the title, as necessary, so that all of the title text appears on the same line.

6. Use the form to update the Donations table. Search for records that contain the word **small** anywhere in the Description field. Find the record with the field value Small appliances (and the Donation ID 2126), and then change the Donation Value for this record to **120.00**. Save and close the form.

7. Use the Form Wizard to create a form containing a main form based on the Donors table and a subform based on the Donations table that lists the DonorID numbers, each donor's first and last

names, a description of the donation, and the donation value. Use the Datasheet layout, and specify appropriate titles for the main form and the subform.

8. Apply the same theme you applied in Step 3 to this form only.

9. Edit the form title so that each word is separated by a space and uses correct capitalization. Change the font color of the title to the same color you used in Step 4.

10. Use the appropriate button in the Font group on the FORM LAYOUT TOOLS FORMAT tab to apply a background color of your choice to all the field value boxes in the main form.

11. Use the appropriate button in the Control Formatting group on the FORM LAYOUT TOOLS FORMAT tab to change the outline of all the main form field value boxes to a line thickness of three points.

12. Resize each column in the subform to its best fit. Navigate through the records in the main form to find the value *Garden equipment* in the subform, and then resize the Description as necessary. Save the form.

13. Use the Report Wizard to create a report based on the primary Agencies table and the related Donations table that shows the agency name, the agency phone number, the donation and donor ID numbers, the donation date, the description of the donation, and the donation value. In the third Report Wizard dialog box, add DonorID as an additional grouping level. Sort the detail records in descending order by DonationValue. Choose the Outline layout and Portrait orientation. Specify the name **AgencyDonations** for the report.

14. Apply the same theme you applied in Step 3 to this report only.

15. Edit the report title appropriately, and then change the font color of the report title to the same color you used in Step 4.

16. Resize the field labels and field value boxes for the donation value, donation ID, donation date, and description to fully display their values and so that the field values stay aligned under the labels.

17. Insert the data file **CharityLogo** located in the Chapter 19\On Your Own folder in the report. Place the picture appropriately in the report. Resize it larger to fill the space.

18. Apply conditional formatting to the Donation Value field to format values of $250 or greater with formatting different from the rest of the values.

19. Preview the report to confirm that it is formatted correctly and all field labels and field values are fully visible. Save the report, print one page that shows the conditional formatting you applied, and then close the report.

20. Compact and repair the DonationsList19 database, and then close it.

Chapter 19
ADDITIONAL STUDY TOOLS

IN THE BOOK
▶ Complete end-of-chapter exercises
▶ Study tear-out Chapter Review Card

ONLINE
▶ Complete additional end-of-chapter exercises

▶ Take practice quiz to prepare for tests
▶ Review key term flash cards (online, printable, and audio)
▶ Play "Beat the Clock" and "Memory" to quiz yourself
▶ Watch the videos to learn more about the topics taught in this chapter

Answers to Quiz Yourself

1. The Form tool creates a form using all the fields in the selected table or query. The Form Wizard allows you to choose some or all of the fields in the selected table or query, choose fields from other tables and queries, and display fields in any order on the form.

2. To apply a theme to a form, display the form in Layout view, click the Themes button in the Themes group on the Design tab, and then click the theme in the displayed gallery to apply it to all objects or right-click the theme and choose to apply it to the current object only.

3. A control is an item on a form, report, or other database object that you can manipulate to modify the object's appearance.

4. A wildcard character is a placeholder you use when you know only part of a value or when you want to start or end with a specific character or match a certain pattern.

5. The question mark (?) wildcard character matches any single alphabetic character.

6. The main form displays the data from the primary table, and the subform displays the data from the related table.

7. The navigation buttons in the subform are used to navigate and display records from the related table in the subform. The navigation buttons in the Form window are used to navigate and display records from the primary table in the main form.

8. To print only the current record displayed in a form, you open the Print dialog box, click the Selected Record(s) option button, and then click OK.

9. Detail records are the field values for the records from the related table when you create a report based on two tables that are joined in a one-to-many relationship.

10. To resize a field on a report, display the report in Layout view, click the field you want to resize to select it, and then drag an edge of the orange outline surrounding the field to the size you want.

11. When working in Layout view for a report, hold down the Shift key as you click different fields to select multiple fields on the report.

12. To apply conditional formatting to a report, display the report in Layout view, select the field value box for the field you want to format conditionally, click the Conditional Formatting button in the Control Formatting group on the Report Layout Tools tab, click the New Rule button in the Conditional Formatting Rules Manager dialog box, specify the condition and formatting in the New Formatting Rule dialog box, and then click OK in each dialog box.

Access: Create a Database

1. Plan a database to track data for an organization, an event, or a project (either real or fictional). Determine how many tables you need and what data will go into each table. Identify the layout of the columns (fields) and rows (records) for each table. Determine the field properties you need for each field.

2. Create a new database to contain the data you want to track.

3. Create at least two tables in the database that can be joined through a one-to-many relationship.

4. Define the properties for each field in each table. Include a mix of data types for the fields (for example, do not include only Text fields in each table).

5. Specify a primary key for each table.

6. Define the necessary one-to-many relationships between the tables in the database with referential integrity enforced.

7. Enter at least 10 records in each table.

8. Create three to four queries based on single tables and multiple tables. The queries should include some or all of the following: exact match conditions, comparison operators, and logical operators.

9. For some of the queries, use sorting and filtering techniques to display the query results in various ways. Save these queries with the sort and/or filter applied.

10. Create at least one calculated field in one of the queries.

11. Use at least one function to produce a summary statistic based on the data in at least one of the tables.

12. Create at least one form for each table in the database. Enhance each form's appearance with pictures, themes, line colors, and so on.

13. Create at least one form with a main form and subform based on related tables in the database. Enhance the form's appearance appropriately.

14. Create at least one report based on each table in the database. Enhance each report's appearance with pictures, themes, color, and so on.

15. Apply conditional formatting to the values in at least one of the reports.

16. Compact and repair the database, and then close it.

Creating a Presentation

Clara/Shutterstock.com

Microsoft PowerPoint 2013 (or simply **PowerPoint**) is a powerful presentation graphics program used to create slides that can contain text, charts, pictures, sound, movies, and so on. Files created in PowerPoint are called **presentations**. PowerPoint presentations consist of slides, which are similar to pages in a document. You can show these presentations as slide shows on a computer monitor, project them onto a screen, share them over the Internet, or publish them to a Web site. You can also create documents from the presentation by printing the slides, outlines, or speaker notes.

Learning Objectives

After studying the material in this chapter, you will be able to:

20-1 Create a presentation

20-2 Rearrange text and slides and delete slides

20-3 Add speaker notes

20-4 Run a slide show

20-5 Add animations

20-6 Add transitions

20-7 Add footers and headers to slides and handouts

20-8 Review, preview, and print a presentation

Microsoft PowerPoint 2013 (PowerPoint) A presentation graphics program used to create a collection of slides that can contain text, charts, pictures, sound, movies, multimedia, and so on.

presentation A file created in PowerPoint.

20-1 Creating a Presentation

When you create a blank presentation in PowerPoint, the presentation appears in Normal view. See Exhibit 20-1. **Normal view** displays slides one at a time in the Slide pane and displays thumbnails of all the slides in the Slides tab. The **Slide pane** shows how the text and graphics on the current slide will look during a slide show. The **Slides tab** shows a column of numbered slide thumbnails. If the NOTES button on the status bar is selected, the Notes pane appears below the Slide pane. The **Notes pane** contains notes for the presenter to refer to when delivering the presentation.

As you create presentations, you will work extensively with these different panes and tabs. They provide you the flexibility to work with and view the presentation in a variety of ways, enabling you to create the most effective presentation for conveying the slide show's purpose and goals to the intended audience.

Begin Activity

Start PowerPoint.

1 Start **PowerPoint**. The recent screen appears in Backstage view.

2 Click the **Blank Presentation tile**. A new, blank presentation appears in the PowerPoint window.

3 If the PowerPoint program window is not maximized, click the **Maximize button** ☐. Your screen should look like Exhibit 20-1.

4 On the Quick Access Toolbar, click the **Save button** 🖫. Because this is the first time this presentation has been saved, the Save As screen appears.

5 Save the presentation as **Gourmet**.

End Activity

20-1a Creating a Title Slide

The first slide in a PowerPoint presentation is usually the **title slide**, which typically contains the title of the presentation and a subtitle, often the presenter's name. The blank title slide contains two objects called text placeholders. A **placeholder** is a region of a slide reserved for inserting text or graphics. A **text placeholder** is a placeholder designed to contain text. Text placeholders usually display text that describes the purpose of the placeholder and instructs you to click so that you can start typing in the placeholder. The larger text placeholder on the title slide is designed to hold the presentation title, and the smaller text placeholder is designed to contain a subtitle. Once you enter text into a text placeholder, it is no longer a placeholder and becomes an object called a **text box**.

> **CAUTION**
>
> ## Save Your Files
>
> Remember to save your files to the drive and folder where you are storing the files you create as you complete the steps in this book. Also, be sure to save frequently as you work. A good practice is to save after every Activity.

Normal view The PowerPoint view that displays slides one at a time in the Slide pane and thumbnails of all the slides in the Slides tab.

Slide pane The area of the PowerPoint window that displays the currently selected slide as it will look during the slide show.

Slides tab The area of the PowerPoint window that shows a column of numbered slide thumbnails so you can see a visual representation of several slides at once.

Notes pane The area of the PowerPoint window that contains notes for the presenter to refer to when delivering the presentation.

title slide The first slide in a presentation; typically contains the presentation title and a subtitle.

placeholder A region of a slide reserved for inserting text or graphics.

text placeholder A placeholder designed to contain text.

text box An object that contains text.

Exhibit 20-1 Blank presentation in the PowerPoint window in Normal view

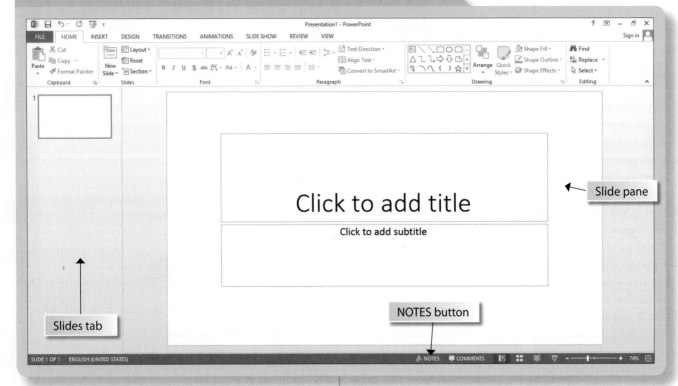

To add text to a text placeholder, you click in it, and then type. When you click in a placeholder, the placeholder text disappears, and the insertion point, which indicates where text will appear when you start typing, appears as a blinking line in the center of the placeholder. This means the placeholder is active, and any text you type will appear in the placeholder. In addition, a contextual tab, the DRAWING TOOLS FORMAT tab, appears on the ribbon. See Exhibit 20-2.

Begin Activity

Add text to text placeholders.

1 Click anywhere in the **Click to add title box**, which is the title text placeholder. The title text placeholder text disappears, and the insertion point appears in the box. Refer to Exhibit 20-2.

Problem? If the insertion point appears as a thin, blue rectangle with the Mini toolbar above and to the right of it, ignore this, and continue with Step 2.

layout A predetermined way of organizing the objects on a slide.

2 Type **Gourmet Delivered** as the title.

3 Click a blank area of the slide. The border of the title text placeholder disappears, and the text you typed appears in place of the placeholder text. The thumbnail in the Slides tab also contains the text you typed.

4 Click in the **Click to add subtitle box**, which is the subtitle text placeholder.

5 Type your first and last name, and then click anywhere else on the slide except in the title text box.

End Activity

20-1b Adding a New Slide and Choosing a Layout

After the title slide, you need to add additional slides to the presentation. When you add a new slide, the slide is formatted with a **layout**, which is a predetermined way of organizing the objects on a slide, including title text and other content (bulleted lists, photographs, charts, and so forth). PowerPoint provides nine built-in layouts, as described in Exhibit 20-3. All layouts, except the Blank layout, include placeholders to help you create a presentation.

Exhibit 20-2 Title text placeholder active on the title slide

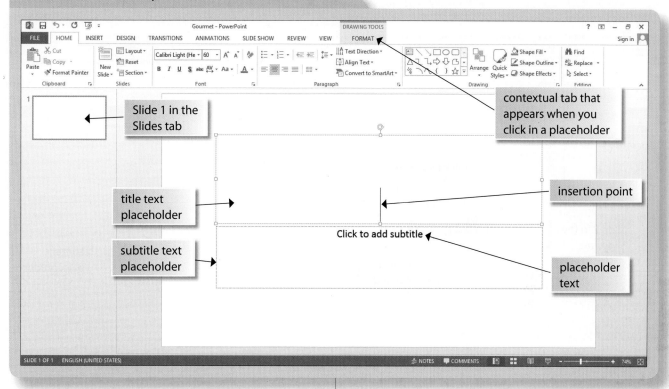

Exhibit 20-3 Built-in layouts in PowerPoint

Layout	Description
Title Slide	Contains the presentation title and a subtitle; is usually used as the first slide in a presentation
Title and Content	Contains either a bulleted list or a graphic in addition to the slide title
Section Header	Contains a section title and text that describes the presentation section
Two Content	The same as the Title and Content layout, but with two side-by-side content placeholders, each of which can contain a bulleted list or a graphic
Comparison	The same as the Two Content layout, but includes text placeholders above the content placeholders to label the content
Title Only	Includes only a title text placeholder for the slide title
Blank	Does not contain any placeholders
Content with Caption	Contains a content placeholder, a title text placeholder to identify the slide or the content, and a text placeholder to describe the content; suitable for photographs or other graphics that need an explanation
Picture with Caption	Similar to the Content with Caption layout, but with a picture placeholder instead of a content placeholder

© 2013 Cengage Learning

Slides can include several types of placeholders, but the most common are text and content placeholders. You have already seen text placeholders on the title slide. Most layouts include a title text placeholder to contain the slide title. A **content placeholder** is intended to contain the slide content, which can be text or a graphic object, such as a table, a chart, a diagram, a picture, clip art, or a video. If you click in a content placeholder and then add text, the content placeholder is no longer a placeholder and becomes a text box. Exhibit 20-4 shows a slide with the Title and Content layout applied.

content placeholder A placeholder designed to hold any type of slide content—text, a graphic, or another object.

Exhibit 20-4 New slide with the Title and Content layout

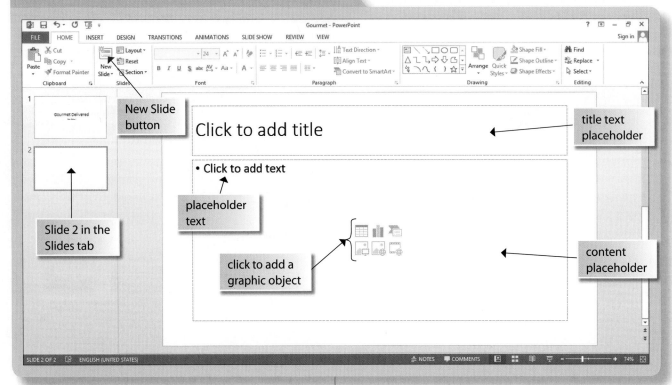

To insert a new slide, you use the New Slide button in the Slides group on the HOME tab. If you are inserting a new slide after the title slide and you click the New Slide button, the new slide is created using the Title and Content layout. Otherwise, the new slide is created using the same layout as the current slide. If you want to choose a different layout, click the New Slide button arrow, and then select the layout you want to use from the menu that opens. Exhibit 20-5 shows the layouts on the New Slide button arrow.

You can also change the layout of a slide after it is created. To do this, click the Layout button in the Slides group on the HOME tab, and then select the layout you want to use.

Begin Activity

Create new slides, and change the layout.

1 On the HOME tab, in the Slides group, click the **New Slide button**. A new Slide 2 appears in the Slide pane and in the Slides tab with the Title and Content layout applied. Refer back to Exhibit 20-4. The content placeholder contains placeholder text that you can click to insert your own text and six icons that you can click to insert the specific item identified by each icon.

2 In the Slide pane, click anywhere in the **title text placeholder**, and then type **About Our Company**.

3 On the HOME tab, in the Slides group, click the **New Slide button arrow**. The New Slide gallery opens, displaying the nine layouts available. Refer to Exhibit 20-5.

Exhibit 20-5 Layouts on the New Slide button menu

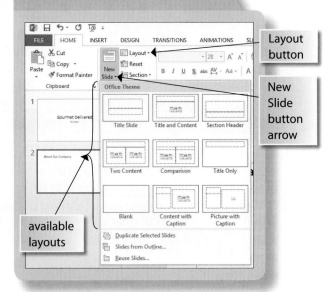

4 In the gallery, click the **Two Content layout**. Slide 3 is created with the Two Content layout, which consists of three placeholders: the title text placeholder and two content placeholders side by side.

5 In the Slide pane, click anywhere in the **title text placeholder**, and then type **Contact Us**.

6 On the HOME tab, in the Slides group, click the **Layout button**. The same gallery of layouts you saw on the New Slide gallery appears.

7 In the gallery, click the **Title and Content layout**. The layout of Slide 3 changes to the layout you selected.

End Activity

20-1c Moving Between Slides in Normal View

As you work on a presentation, you will need to move from one slide to another. In Normal view, you can click a slide thumbnail in the Slides tab to display that slide in the Slide pane. You can also use the scroll bar in the Slide pane to scroll from slide to slide, or click the Next Slide ▼ or Previous Slide ▲ buttons at the bottom of the vertical scroll bar in the Slide pane.

Begin Activity

Move from one slide to another.

1 In the Slides tab, click the **Slide 1 thumbnail**. The title slide appears in the Slide pane.

2 In the Slide pane, drag the **scroll box** to the bottom of the scroll bar. As you drag, a ScreenTip appears, identifying the slide that will appear when you release the mouse button.

3 Release the mouse button. Slide 3 ("Contact Us") appears in the Slide pane.

4 At the bottom of the scroll bar, click the **Previous Slide button** ▲. Slide 2 ("About Our Company") appears in the Slide pane.

End Activity

20-1d Working with Lists

Often, text on a slide is in the form of bulleted lists to emphasize important points to the audience. Items in a list can appear at different levels. A **first-level item** is a main item in a list; a **second-level item**—sometimes

called a **subitem**—is an item beneath and indented from a first-level item. Usually, the font size—the size of the text—in subitems is smaller than the size used for text in the level above.

A **bulleted list** is a list of "paragraphs" (words, phrases, sentences, or paragraphs) with a special symbol such as a dot, dash, circle, box, star, or other character to the left of each paragraph. A bulleted item is one paragraph in a bulleted list. If the symbol to the left of each item in a list is a number, the list is referred to as a **numbered list**. And if no symbol appears, the list is referred to as an **unnumbered list**.

To add a bulleted list to a slide, click the placeholder text in a content placeholder. When you do this, the placeholder text disappears, the insertion point appears in its place, and a light gray bullet symbol appears. See Exhibit 20-6. Notice that on the HOME tab, in the Font group, in the Font Size box, the font size of this first-level bullet is 28 points.

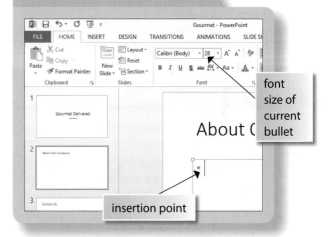

Exhibit 20-6 Insertion point in the content placeholder

After you type the text of a bulleted item, press the Enter key to move the insertion point to the next line. This creates a new bulleted item. If you don't type anything next to a bullet, the bullet will not appear on the slide.

first-level item A main item in a list.

second-level item (subitem) An item beneath and indented from a first-level item.

bulleted list A list of paragraphs with a special symbol to the left of each paragraph.

numbered list A list of paragraphs with a sequential numbers to the left of each paragraph.

unnumbered list A list of paragraphs that do not have any symbol to the left of each paragraph.

Begin Activity

Create a bulleted list.

1 In **Slide 2** ("About Our Company"), in the content placeholder, click the placeholder text, "Click to add text".

2 Type **Gourmet meals prepared specially for you** and then press the **Enter key**. A new bullet that is lighter than the first bullet appears. It will darken as soon as you start typing text.

3 Type **Meals are ready for** and then press the **Enter key**. A third bullet is added to the slide.

End Activity

You can change a first-level bulleted item into a subitem, and you can change a subitem into a first-level bulleted item. Moving an item to a higher level, such as changing a second-level bullet to a first-level bullet, is called **promoting** the item. Moving an item lower in the outline, such as changing a first-level bullet to a second-level bullet, is called **demoting** the item. Exhibit 20-7 shows the insertion point next to a subitem below a first-level item.

Exhibit 20-7 Subbullet created

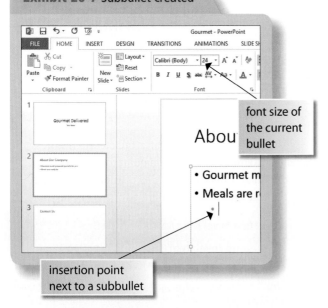

font size of the current bullet

insertion point next to a subbullet

promote To move an item to a higher level in an outline.

demote To move an item to a lower level in an outline.

Begin Activity

Add subitems to a bulleted list.

1 Press the **Tab key**. The new bullet is demoted and indented to become a subitem. The subitem is a faint dash. The font size of the subitem is 24 points, which is smaller than the font size used in the first-level bullets on the slide. Refer back to Exhibit 20-7.

> **Tip:** To change the font size of both first-level items and subitems at the same time, click the text box border and then use the Increase Font Size A or Decrease Font Size A button in the Font group on the HOME tab.

2 Type **Serving** and then press the **Enter key**. A second subitem is created.

3 Type **Heating** and then press the **Enter key** to create a third subitem.

4 Type **Freezing** and then press the **Enter key** to create a fourth subitem.

5 Press the **Shift+Tab keys**. The subitem is promoted and changes to a first-level bullet.

6 Type **Select from a variety of menus** as the bullet text.

7 Click a blank area of the slide outside the content text box. The dashed line border of the text box disappears.

End Activity

Sometimes, you will want to create a new line within a bulleted item without creating a new bullet. This is helpful when you include an address as a bullet item and want to split the address on two lines of the same bullet. To create a new line, press the Shift+Enter keys. This moves the insertion point to the next line without creating a new paragraph.

Begin Activity

Create a new line without creating a new bullet.

1 Display **Slide 3** ("Contact Us") in the Slide pane. Click to the right of the bullet in the content placeholder, and then type **Phone:** as the bullet text.

2 Press the **Shift+Enter keys**. The insertion point moves to the next line without creating a new bullet.

3 Type **912–555–3800** and then press the **Enter key**. A new bullet is created.

4 Type **Address:** and then press the **Shift+Enter keys**.

5 Type **101 West Bayside Ave.** and then press the **Shift+Enter keys**. Type **Savannah, GA 31401**. The address is entered on two lines under the Address bullet without creating new bullets.

6 Save the presentation, and then close it.

End Activity

> **Tip:** To change a bulleted list into a numbered list, select the bulleted items, and then click the Numbering button in the Paragraph group on the HOME tab; to change it to a list without any bullets, click the Bullets button to deselect it.

20-1e Using AutoFit

As you add text to a content placeholder, **AutoFit** makes adjustments if you add more text than will fit in the placeholder. First it reduces the spacing between lines, and then it reduces the font size of the text. AutoFit is turned on by default. When you start typing the next bullet, you will see AutoFit adjust the text to make it fit. If AutoFit adjusts the text in a text box, the AutoFit Options button appears in the Slide pane below and to the left of the placeholder. You can click the AutoFit Options button and select an option on the menu to control the way AutoFit works. See Exhibit 20-8. If you select the option to turn off AutoFit for a text box, you can turn it back on later.

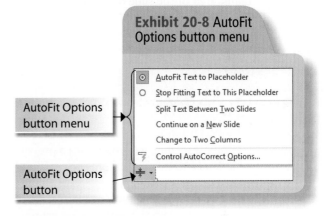

Exhibit 20-8 AutoFit Options button menu

AutoFit Options button menu

- AutoFit Text to Placeholder
- Stop Fitting Text to This Placeholder
- Split Text Between Two Slides
- Continue on a New Slide
- Change to Two Columns
- Control AutoCorrect Options...

AutoFit Options button

Begin Activity

Use the AutoFit feature.

1 Open the data file **Expansion** located in the Chapter 20\Chapter folder. Save the file as **Expansion Goals**.

2 On Slide 1 (the title slide), click in the subtitle text box, and then type your name.

3 Display **Slide 2** ("About Our Company") in the Slide pane.

4 In the last bulleted item, click after the word *available*, and then press the **Enter key**. A new first-level bullet is created.

5 Type **M**. After you type the first character in this new bullet, the line spacing in the text box tightens up slightly, and the AutoFit Options button appears next to the lower-left corner of the text box.

> **AutoFit** A PowerPoint feature that automatically changes the line spacing and the font size of text if you add more text than will fit in a placeholder.

6 Click the **AutoFit Options button** ⬓. The AutoFit Options button menu appears. The default option, AutoFit Text to Placeholder, is selected. Refer back to Exhibit 20-8.

7 Click anywhere on the slide to close the AutoFit Options button menu without changing the selected default option.

> **Tip:** You can also press the Esc key to close a menu without selecting a command or option.

8 In the last bulleted item, click immediately after *M*, and then type **enus change seasonally** to complete the bulleted item.

9 Click a blank area of the slide to deselect the list.

End Activity

20-1f Changing Themes

Plain white slides with a common font (such as black Times New Roman or Calibri) often fail to hold an audience's attention. Audiences expect more interesting color schemes, fonts, graphics, and other effects. You can easily change the fonts and color used for the background, title text, body text, accents, and graphics in a presentation as well as the style used in a presentation by changing the theme. In a presentation, the Headings theme font is used for the slide titles and the Body theme font is used for text in content placeholders. Some PowerPoint themes include graphics as part of the slide background. In PowerPoint, each theme has several variants with different coordinating colors and sometimes slightly different backgrounds. A theme and its variants are called a **theme family**. To see the available themes, click the More button in the Themes group in the DESIGN tab. See Exhibit 20-9.

Planning a Presentation

As you prepare a presentation, consider a few key questions to help you plan what to say. Being able to answer these questions will help you create a presentation that successfully delivers its message or motivates the audience to take an action.

▶ **What is the purpose of the presentation?**

In other words, what action or response do you want the audience to have? If you are making a sales pitch, you want the audience to buy what you are selling. If you are delivering good or bad news, you want the audience to hear the message clearly and take action based on the facts you provide.

Goal !?!

▶ **Who is the audience?**

Think about the needs and interests of the audience, as well as any decisions they will make as a result of what you have to say. Make sure what you choose to say to the audience is relevant to their needs, interests, and decisions, or it will be forgotten.

viviamo/Shutterstock.com

Monkey Business Images/Shutterstock.com

▶ **How much time do you have for the presentation?**

Consider the amount of time available. Make sure you pace yourself as you speak. You don't want to spend too much time on the introduction and end up having to eliminate some of your closing remarks because you run out of time. This diminishes the effectiveness of the entire presentation and weakens its impact on the audience.

Arber/Shutterstock.com

▶ **Will the audience benefit from printed output?**

Some presentations are effectively delivered with on-screen visuals. Others require printed support materials because there is too much information to be displayed on the screen. In other cases, you want the audience to have something to take with them to help remember what you said.

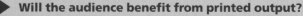

theme family A theme and its variants.

Exhibit 20-9 Themes on the DESIGN tab

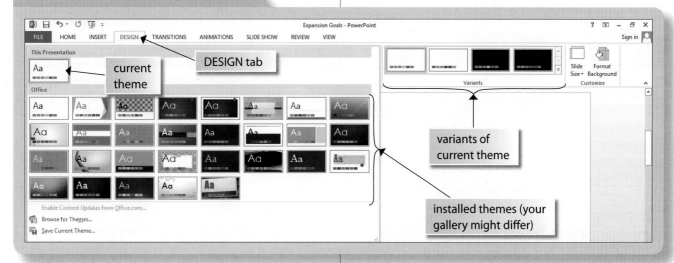

By default, new, blank presentations have the Office theme applied. PowerPoint comes with several installed themes, and many more themes are available online at Office.com. In addition, you can use a custom theme stored on your computer or network. When you apply a different theme, be aware that some themes use a font size much smaller than 28 points for first-level items in a bulleted list. For some fonts, a smaller font size is fine because the font itself is much larger.

Choose Appropriate Themes

The theme you choose for a presentation should reflect the content and the intended audience. For example, if you are presenting a new curriculum to a group of elementary school teachers, you might choose a theme that uses bright, primary colors. If you are presenting a marketing plan to a mutual fund company, you might choose a theme that uses dark colors formatted in a way that conveys sophistication.

Begin Activity

Change the theme.

1 On the ribbon, click the **DESIGN tab**. In the Themes group, the first theme displayed in the group is always the currently applied theme.

2 In the Themes group, point to the **first theme**, which has an orange highlight around it. A Screen-Tip identifies the theme, which, in this case, is the Office Theme. After the currently applied theme, the rest of the available themes are listed.

3 In the Themes group, click the **More button**. The Themes gallery opens. Refer back to Exhibit 20-9.

4 Point to several of the themes to see the Live Preview on Slide 2.

5 Using the ScreenTips, locate the **Vapor Trail theme**, and then click it. The design and colors of the slides in the presentation change to those of the default variant of the Vapor Trail theme.

> **Problem?** This theme might be named Vapor on your computer. If you don't see either theme, select another theme to use.

6 In the Variants group, point to each variant to see the Live Preview. Note that the ScreenTips are the same as the theme name.

7 In the Variants group, click the **fourth variant**. The background and font colors change to match the ones used in this variant. Compare your screen to Exhibit 20-10.

End Activity

Exhibit 20-10 Fourth variant of the Vapor Trail theme applied to the presentation

20-1g Modifying Text and Changing Bullet Levels in Outline View

Outline view displays the outline of the entire presentation in the Outline tab, which is similar to the Slides tab. See Exhibit 20-11. Slide titles appear at the top level in the outline, and the slide content—that is, the bulleted lists—are indented below the slide titles. When you view the outline in the Outline tab, you see only the text of the slide titles and the text in content placeholders; you do not see any graphics on the slides or any text that is not in a content placeholder.

You can modify the text of a slide in the Outline tab in Outline view as well as in the Slide pane. You also promote and demote items in the Outline tab using the same techniques you use in the Slide pane. Any changes you make in the Outline tab appear on the slide in the Slide pane.

If you need to move bulleted items from one slide to another, or change a bulleted item to a new slide title, it can be easier to do this in Outline view than in Normal view.

Begin Activity

Modify text in the Outline tab.

1 On the ribbon, click the **VIEW tab**. In the Presentation Views group, click the **Outline View button**. The presentation is displayed in Outline view, and you see the outline of the presentation in the Outline tab. Because Slide 2 is displayed in the Slide pane, all of the text on Slide 2 is selected in

Outline view The PowerPoint view that displays slides one at a time in the Slide pane and the text of the slides in the Outline tab.

the Outline tab. Also, the Notes pane now appears below the Slide pane. Refer back to Exhibit 20-11.

2 In the Outline tab, scroll down until **Slide 4** ("Competition") is at the top of the Outline tab. Slide 2 ("About Our Company") still appears in the Slide pane.

3 In the Outline tab, click anywhere on the text in **Slide 4** ("Competition"). Slide 4 appears in the Slide pane.

4 In the Outline tab, in the fourth first-level bullet in Slide 4 ("Competition"), click immediately before the word *Less*, and then press the **Enter key**. A new line is created above the current bulleted item in both the Outline tab and the Slide pane, and the last three bulleted items move down.

5 Press the **Up Arrow key**. The insertion point moves up to the new line, and the bullet appears in the new line.

6 Type **Advantages**. The text you typed appears in the Outline tab and in the Slide pane.

7 In the Outline tab, in Slide 5 ("5-Year Goals"), point to the bullet to the left of *All-organic options* so that the pointer changes to ⊹, and then click. The All-organic options bulleted item and its subitem are selected.

> **Problem?** If the pointer does not change to ⊹, move the pointer a little to the left of the bullet symbol.

8 On the ribbon, click the **HOME tab**. In the Paragraph group, click the **Increase List Level button**. The selected first-level bulleted item is demoted—it is indented and becomes a second-level

Exhibit 20-11 Presentation outline in the Outline tab

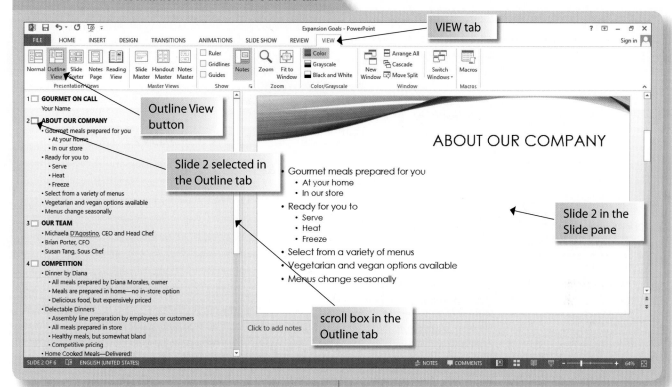

bulleted item—and its subitem becomes a third-level bulleted item.

9 In the Outline tab, in Slide 5 ("5-Year Goals"), click the **Gluten-free options bullet** to select the entire bulleted item.

10 On the HOME tab, in the Paragraph group, click the **Decrease List Level button** 📑. The selected third-level bulleted item is promoted to the second level.

11 In the Outline tab, in Slide 4 ("Competition"), click the **Advantages bullet**.

12 On the HOME tab, in the Paragraph group, click the **Decrease List Level button** 📑. The selected first-level bulleted item is promoted to a slide title for a new Slide 5, and the three bulleted items below it are now first-level bulleted items on the new Slide 5. Compare your screen to Exhibit 20-12.

End Activity

Problem? If the subitem is not indented as a third-level item, you selected only the All-organic options item without selecting its subitem. Skip Steps 9 and 10.

20-2 Rearranging Text and Slides, and Deleting Slides

In addition to changing the level of bulleted items on slides, you can move bulleted items to new positions on slides or from one slide to another, and you can rearrange the slides themselves. To move bulleted items from one position to another, you must work in the Outline tab or in the Slide pane. To move slides from one position to another, you can work in the Slides or Outline tab in Normal view or in Slide Sorter view. **Slide Sorter view** displays all the slides in the presentation as thumbnails to provide you with a visual overview of the presentation.

20-2a Moving Bulleted Items

Bulleted items should be placed in a logical order, such as most to least important, alphabetically, or chronologically. You can move a bulleted item to a new position in the outline by using drag and drop. You drag the bulleted item by its bullet. As you drag, a horizontal

> **Slide Sorter view** The PowerPoint view that displays all the slides in a presentation as thumbnails to provide a visual overview of the presentation.

Exhibit 20-12 New slide created by promoting text

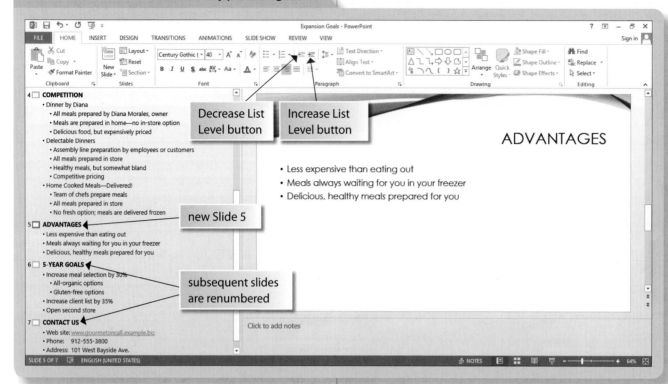

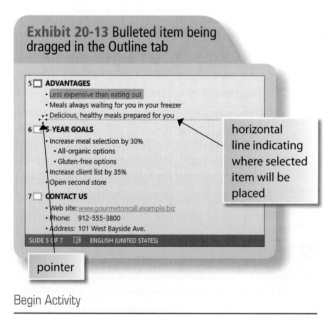

Exhibit 20-13 Bulleted item being dragged in the Outline tab

line follows the pointer to show you where the bulleted item will be positioned after you release the pointer. See Exhibit 20-13.

Begin Activity

Move bulleted items.

1 If Slide 5 ("Advantages") is not the current slide, in the Outline tab, click the **Slide 5 slide icon** ☐. Slide 5 is displayed in the Slide pane.

2 In the Outline tab, in the Slide 5 text, point to the **Less expensive than eating out bullet** so that the pointer changes to ⊕.

3 Press and hold the **mouse button**, and then drag the **bulleted item** down until the horizontal line indicating the position of the item you are dragging appears below the Delicious, healthy meals prepared for you bullet on Slide 5. Refer back to Exhibit 20-13.

> **Tip:** You can also use the Cut, Copy, and Paste commands to move text or slides.

4 With the horizontal line positioned below the Delicious, healthy meals prepared for you bullet, release the **mouse button**. The bulleted item you dragged is now the last bulleted item on Slide 5, both in the Outline tab and in the Slide pane.

5 In the Slide pane, point to the **Delicious, healthy meals prepared for you bullet** so that the pointer changes to ⊕.

6 Drag the **Delicious, healthy meals prepared for you bulleted item** up until the horizontal line indicating the new

> **Problem?** If the Mini toolbar is in the way, locate the line by looking to the right of the Mini toolbar.

position of the bullet is above the first bulleted item on the slide, and then release the mouse button. The Delicious, healthy meals prepared for you bullet is now the first bulleted item on Slide 5 in both the Slide pane and in the Outline tab.

End Activity

20-2b Rearranging Slides

As you develop a presentation, you might want to change the order in which the slides appear. You can drag slides to reposition them in the Outline tab in Outline view by dragging a slide by its slide icon. You can also rearrange slides in the Slides tab in Normal view and in Slide Sorter view. See Exhibit 20-14. In the Slides tab in Normal view and in Slide Sorter view, you move a slide by dragging its thumbnail.

Begin Activity

Rearrange slides.

1 In the Outline tab, drag the **Slide 6 slide icon** ☐ (the slide titled "5-Year Goals") up until the horizontal line indicating the new position of the slide appears just above the slide title for Slide 5 ("Advantages"). The slide titled "5-Year Goals" is now Slide 5 and the slide titled "Advantages" is now Slide 6.

2 On the status bar, click the **Slide Sorter button** ⊞. The presentation appears in Slide Sorter view. An orange border appears around the Slide 5 thumbnail, indicating that the slide is selected.

3 If necessary, change the zoom level to **90%** so you can see four slides in the first row and three slides in the second row. Refer back to Exhibit 20-14.

4 Drag the **Slide 3 thumbnail** (the "Our Team" slide) down to position it between the Slide 6 ("Advantages") and the Slide 7 ("Contact Us") thumbnails. As you drag, the other slides move out of the way. The slide titled "Our Team" is now Slide 6.

5 Double-click the **Slide 6 thumbnail** (the "Our Team" slide). The presentation appears in the previous view—in this case, Outline view—with Slide 6 in the Slide pane.

6 On the status bar, click the **Normal button** ▣. The slide thumbnails appear in the Slides tab, and the Notes pane is now visible below the Slide pane.

7 In the Slides tab, click **any slide thumbnail** so that you can change the zoom of the Slides tab. Otherwise, the Slide pane will change zoom instead.

8 On the ribbon, click the **VIEW tab**. In the Zoom group, click the **Zoom button**. The Zoom dialog box opens.

9 Click in the **Percent box**, delete the value in it, type **48** and then click **OK**. The Slides tab zooms to 48%.

End Activity

Exhibit 20-14 Slide Sorter view

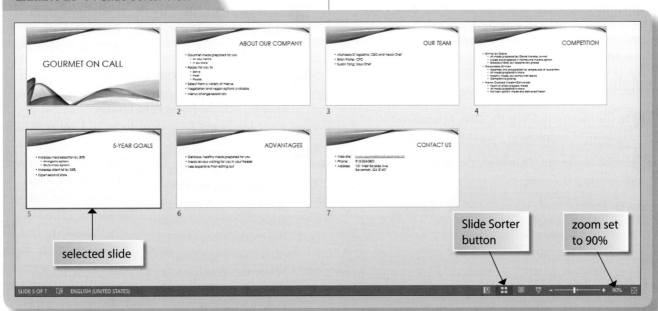

selected slide

Slide Sorter button

zoom set to 90%

Duplicating Slides

As you create a presentation, you might want to create a slide that is similar to another slide. Starting with a copy of a slide that already exists can save time. To duplicate a slide, right-click the slide thumbnail in the Slides tab in Normal view, and then click Duplicate Slide on the shortcut menu. You can also use the ribbon to duplicate one or multiple slides. In the Slides group on the HOME tab, click the New Slide button arrow, and then click Duplicate Selected Slides. If you select more than one slide before you use the Duplicate Selected Slides command, all of the selected slides will be duplicated.

original *duplicated*

filmfoto/Shutterstock.com

20-2c Deleting Slides

As you develop a presentation, you will sometimes need to delete slides. You can delete slides in the Slides and Outline tabs in Normal view and in Slide Sorter view. To delete a slide, right-click the thumbnail in the Slides tab or Slide Sorter view, and then click Delete Slide on the shortcut menu. You can also click its thumbnail in the Slides tab or Slide Sorter view or click the slide icon in the Outline tab, and then press the Delete key. It is a good idea to verify that you are deleting the correct slide by first displaying it in the Slide pane.

Begin Activity

Delete a slide.

1 In the Slides tab, click the **Slide 3 thumbnail**. Slide 3 ("Competition") appears in the Slide pane.

2 In the Slides tab, right-click the **Slide 3 thumbnail**.

speaker notes Notes that appear in the Notes pane to remind the speaker of points to make when the particular slide appears during the slide show.

Notes Page view The PowerPoint view that displays each slide in the top half of the presentation window and the speaker notes for that slide in the bottom half.

3 On the shortcut menu, click **Delete Slide**. Slide 3 is deleted. The slide titled "5-Year Goals" is now Slide 3 and appears in the Slide pane.

End Activity

20-3 Adding Speaker Notes

Speaker notes help the speaker remember what to say when a particular slide appears during the presentation. You use the Notes pane to add and display speaker notes. In Normal view, you can open the Notes pane below the Slide pane by clicking the NOTES button on the status bar. See Exhibit 20-15. Click the NOTES button again to close the Notes pane. If you use Outline view, the Notes pane appears automatically when you switch to Outline view.

You can switch to **Notes Page view** to display each slide in the top half of the presentation window and the speaker notes for that slide in the bottom half. See Exhibit 20-16. You can also print notes pages with a picture of and notes about each slide.

Begin Activity

Create a note and view slides in Notes Page view.

1 Make sure **Slide 3** ("5-Year Goals") is displayed in the Slide pane.

2 Click in the **Notes pane**.

3 Type **Pass out marketing plan.** as the note. Refer to Exhibit 20-15.

> **Problem?** If the Notes pane is not visible, click the **NOTES button** on the status bar.

4 On VIEW tab, in the Presentation Views group, click the **Notes Page button**. Slide 3 is displayed in Notes Page view. Refer to Exhibit 20-16.

5 At the bottom of the vertical scroll bar, click the **Next Slide button** ⬇. Slide 4 ("Advantages") appears in Notes Page view. The notes placeholder appears below the slide because this slide does not contain any speaker notes.

> **Tip:** In Normal view and in Notes Page view, you can also press the Page Up key to move to the previous slide or the Page Down key to move to the next slide.

Exhibit 20-15 Speaker note on Slide 3

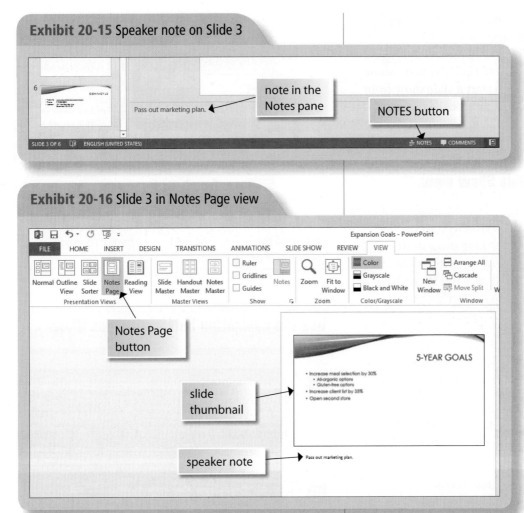

Exhibit 20-16 Slide 3 in Notes Page view

Show view and Presenter view. As the presenter, you need to advance the slide show, which means you need to do something to display the next slide. To advance the slide show, you can click anywhere on the slide that is currently displayed, or you can use the keyboard by pressing the Spacebar, the Enter key, the Right Arrow key, or the Page Down key. You can also use the keyboard to move to the previous slide by pressing the Left Arrow key, the Page Up key, or the Backspace key. If you right-click the currently displayed slide during a slide show, a shortcut menu that contains commands to jump to specific slides opens. Finally, you can also use buttons on a toolbar that appears in the lower-left corner of the currently displayed slide in Slide Show view or below the currently displayed slide in Presenter view.

After you display the last slide in a slide show, the screen changes to black with a small note at the top that tells you that you have reached the end of the slide show. To end the slide show—that is, to remove the black screen and return to the view from which you started—advance the slide show once more. You can also end a slide show at any time by pressing the Esc key or by right-clicking the slide and then clicking End Show on the shortcut menu.

6 At the bottom of the vertical scroll bar, click the **Next Slide button** ⬇ twice to display Slide 6 ("Contact Us"). This slide has a speaker note.

7 On the VIEW tab, in the Presentation Views group, click the **Normal button**. Slide 6 appears in the Slide pane in Normal view. You can clearly see the speaker note in the Notes pane.

8 On the status bar, click the **NOTES button**. The Notes pane closes.

End Activity

20-4 Running a Slide Show

After you have created and proofed your presentation, you should view it as a slide show to see how it will appear to your audience. You can do this in Slide

20-4a Using Slide Show View

Slide Show view displays one slide after another so that each slide fills the entire screen with no toolbars or other

> **Slide Show view** The PowerPoint view that displays one slide after another so that each slide fills the entire screen with no toolbars or other Windows elements visible on the screen and displays special effects applied to the text and graphics on each slide or to the slide itself.

Windows elements visible on the screen. It also displays special effects applied to the text and graphics on each slide or to the slide itself. To start a slide show from the current slide in Slide Show view, click the Slide Show button 🖳 on the status bar. To start a slide show from the first slide in the presentation, click the Start From Beginning button 🖳 on the Quick Access Toolbar.

Begin Activity

Run a slide show in Slide Show view.

1 On the Quick Access Toolbar, click the **Start From Beginning button** 🖳. The slide show starts from the beginning, and Slide 1 fills the screen in Slide Show view.

> **Tip:** To start the slide show from the current slide, click the Slide Show button 🖳 on the status bar.

2 Click anywhere on the screen to advance the slide show. Slide 2 ("About Our Company") appears on the screen.

3 Press the **Spacebar** to display the next slide. Slide 3 ("5-Year Goals") appears on the screen.

4 Press the **Enter key** to display the next slide. Slide 4 ("Advantages") appears on the screen.

5 Press the **Left Arrow key** to redisplay the previous slide. Slide 3 ("5-Year Goals") reappears.

6 Right-click anywhere on the screen. On the short-cut menu, click **See All Slides** to display all the slides in the presentation, similar to Slide Sorter view.

7 Click the **Slide 6** ("Contact Us") **thumbnail**. Slide 6 ("Contact Us") appears on the screen.

8 Right-click anywhere on the screen. On the short-cut menu, click **Last Viewed**. The most recently viewed slide prior to the current slide—Slide 3 ("5-Year Goals")—reappears.

End Activity

In Slide Show view, if you move the pointer on the slide, a faint row of buttons appears in the lower-left corner of the slide. See Exhibit 20-17. You can use these buttons to navigate the slide show.

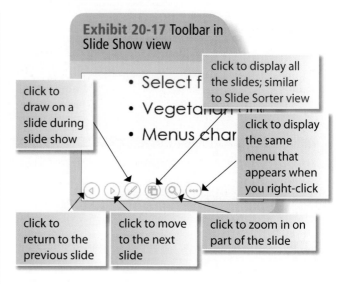

Exhibit 20-17 Toolbar in Slide Show view

click to draw on a slide during slide show

click to display all the slides; similar to Slide Sorter view

click to display the same menu that appears when you right-click

click to return to the previous slide

click to move to the next slide

click to zoom in on part of the slide

Begin Activity

Use the navigation buttons in Slide Show view.

1 Move the **pointer** without clicking. A faint row of buttons appears in the lower-left corner. Refer back to Exhibit 20-17. (The buttons in Exhibit 20-17 were enhanced so you can see them more clearly. They will be very faint on your screen.)

2 Click the **Zoom into the slide button** 🔍. The pointer changes to ⊕, and three-quarters of the slide is darkened.

3 Move the pointer to the title text **5-Year Goals**, watching as the bright rectangle follows it, and then click. The view zooms so that the part of the slide inside the bright rectangle fills the screen, and the pointer changes to 🖐.

> **Tip:** You can also use Reading view if you want to be able to resize the window containing the slide show.

4 Point to the lower-left corner of the screen, press and hold the mouse button to change the pointer to 🖐, and then drag up and to the right to pull another part of the zoomed-in slide into view.

5 Press the **Esc key** to zoom back out to see the whole slide.

Exhibit 20-18 Slide 3 in Presenter view

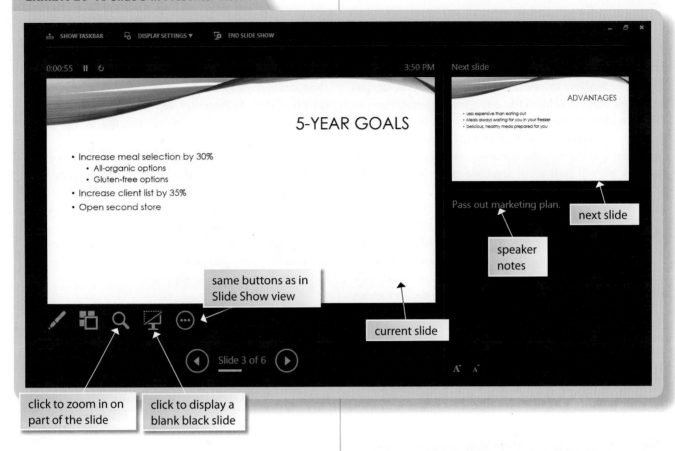

SHOW TASKBAR   DISPLAY SETTINGS ▼   END SLIDE SHOW

0:00:55 ❚❚ ↻   3:50 PM   Next slide

5-YEAR GOALS

• Increase meal selection by 30%
  • All-organic options
  • Gluten-free options
• Increase client list by 35%
• Open second store

ADVANTAGES
• Less expensive than eating out
• Meals always waiting for you in your freezer
• Delicious, healthy meals prepared for you

Pass out marketing plan.

next slide

speaker notes

same buttons as in Slide Show view

current slide

◀ Slide 3 of 6 ▶

A˄ A˅

click to zoom in on part of the slide

click to display a blank black slide

6 Move the pointer so you can see the faint row of buttons in the lower-left corner, and then click the **Advance to the next slide button** ⊳. Slide 4 ("Advantages") appears.

7 Press the **Right Arrow key** twice to advance two slides. The next two slides, Slide 5 ("Our Team") followed by Slide 6 ("Contact Us"), appear.

8 Click anywhere on the screen. A black screen with a message that this is the end of the slide show appears.

9 Use any method to advance the slide show. Slide Show view closes, and the presentation appears in Normal view with Slide 1 in the Slide pane.

End Activity

20-4b Using Presenter View

Presenter view, which was designed to make it easier to display a slide show using a second monitor or a projection screen, shows the current slide in the left pane, the next slide in the right pane, and other helpful controls and information in other areas of the screen, including speaker notes and a timer showing how long the slide show has been running. The slide in the left pane is the slide that fills the screen in Slide Show view on the second monitor or projection screen and is what the audience sees. See Exhibit 20-18.

If your computer is connected to a projector or second monitor, and you start a slide show in Slide Show view, Presenter view automatically starts on the computer, and Slide Show view appears on the second monitor or projection screen. If, for some reason, you don't want to use Presenter view in that circumstance, you can switch to Slide Show view. If you want to practice using Presenter view when your computer is not connected to a second monitor or projector, you can switch to Presenter view from Slide Show view.

Presenter view The PowerPoint view that shows the current slide, the next slide, speaker notes, a timer showing how long the slide show has been running, and other helpful controls and information; designed to make it easier to display a slide show using a second monitor or a projection screen.

Displaying a Blank Slide During a Slide Show

Sometimes during a presentation, the audience has questions about the material, and you want to pause the slide show to respond to their questions. Or, you might want to refocus the audience's attention on you instead of on the visuals on the screen. In these cases, you can display a blank slide (either black or white). When you do this, the audience, with nothing else to look at, will shift all of their attention to you. Some presenters plan to use blank slides and insert them at specific points during their slide shows. If you did not create blank slides in your presentation file, but during your presentation you feel you need to display a blank slide, you can easily do this in Slide Show or Presenter view by pressing the B key to display a blank black slide or the W key to display a blank white slide. To remove the black or white slide and redisplay the slide that had been on the screen before you displayed the blank slide, press any key on the keyboard or click anywhere on the screen. In Presenter view, you can also use the Black or unblack slide show button 🖾 to toggle a black slide on or off.

An alternative to redisplaying the slide that had been displayed prior to the blank slide is to click the Advance to the next slide button ⓓ or ⬤. This can be more effective than redisplaying the slide that was onscreen before the blank slide because, after you have grabbed the audience's attention and prepared them to move on, you won't lose their focus by displaying a slide they have already seen.

Begin Activity

Run a slide show in Presenter view.

1 Display **Slide 2** ("About Our Company") in the Slide pane.

2 On the status bar, click the **Slide Show button** 🖵. Clicking this button starts the slide show from the current slide, so Slide 2 appears in Slide Show view.

3 Right-click anywhere on the slide. On the shortcut menu, click **Show Presenter View**. The presentation switches to Presenter view. Slide 2 ("About Our Company")—the current slide—appears in the left pane. Because there are no speaker notes for this slide, No Notes appears in the right pane below the next slide preview.

4 Click anywhere on **Slide 2**. The next slide, Slide 3 ("5-Year Goals") appears in the left pane. The speaker note that you added to this slide (*Pass out marketing plan.*) appears in the right pane below the next slide preview. Refer back to Exhibit 20-18.

5 Below the current slide, click the **Advance to the next slide button** ⓓ. Slide 4 ("Advantages") appears in the left pane.

6 At the top of the screen, click the **END SLIDE SHOW button**. Presenter view closes, and the slide you started with, Slide 2 ("About Our Company"), appears in the Slide pane in Normal view.

End Activity

20-5 Adding Animations

Animations are special effects applied to an object, such as a graphic or a bulleted list, that make the object move or change. Animations add interest to a slide show and draw attention to the text or object being animated.

Animation effects are grouped into the following four types in the Animations gallery (see Exhibit 20-19):

▶ **Entrance**—text and objects animate as they appear on the slide; one of the most commonly used animation types.

▶ **Emphasis**—the appearance of text and objects already visible on the slide changes or the text or objects move in place.

▶ **Exit**—text and objects leave the screen before the slide show advances to the next slide.

▶ **Motion Paths**—text and objects move following a path on a slide.

---

animation A special effect applied to an object that makes the object move or change.

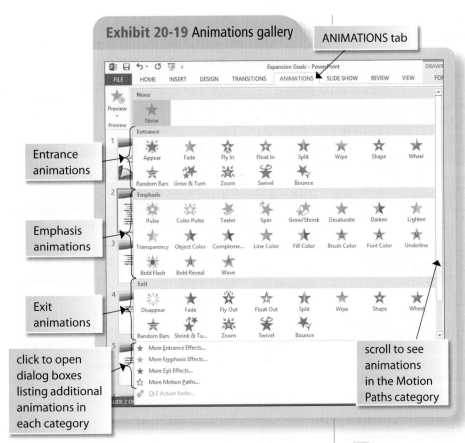

Exhibit 20-19 Animations gallery

ANIMATIONS tab

Entrance animations

Emphasis animations

Exit animations

click to open dialog boxes listing additional animations in each category

scroll to see animations in the Motion Paths category

indicating they are not available. This is because nothing is selected on the slide.

3 In the Slide pane, click anywhere on the **title text**. A dotted line appears around the border of the title text box, and the animations in the Animation group are now available. All of the animations currently visible in the Animation group are entrance animations.

4 In the Animation group, point to the **Fly In animation**. The animation previews in the Slide pane and the slide title flies in from the bottom of the slide.

5 In the Animation group, click the **More button**. The Animation gallery opens. Refer back to Exhibit 20-19.

6 In the Emphasis section, click the **Underline animation**. The gallery closes, and the animation previews in the Slide pane by underlining the slide title from left to right. An animation sequence icon with the number 1 in it appears next to the upper-left corner of the title text box.

7 On the ANIMATIONS tab, in the Preview group, click the **Preview button**. The emphasis animation applied to the slide title previews on the slide again.

8 On the status bar, click the **Slide Show button**. Slide 2 appears in Slide Show view.

9 Advance the slide show. The animation you applied—the emphasis Underline animation—occurs, and the slide title is underlined.

10 Right-click a blank area of the slide. On the shortcut menu, click **End Show**.

Unless you change the behavior, animations are set to start On Click, which means when you advance the slide show—that is, when you click the screen or press the Spacebar, Enter key, or Right Arrow key.

After you apply an animation to an object on a slide, an animation sequence icon appears near the upper-left corner of the object. The number in the icon indicates the order of the animation when you advance the slide show. In other words, the item labeled with the number 1 animation sequence icon animates first, the item labeled with the number 2 animation sequence icon animates second, and so on.

20-5a Animating a Text Box

To animate a text box, you click anywhere in it, and then click an animation in the Animation group on the ANIMATIONS tab.

Begin Activity

Animate a slide title.

1 Make sure **Slide 2** ("About Our Company") is displayed in the Slide pane.

2 On the ribbon, click the **ANIMATIONS tab**. The animations in the Animation group are grayed out,

End Activity

20-5b Animating Bulleted Lists

When you apply an animation to text, it affects all of the text in the text box. When you animate a bulleted list, sequential animation sequence numbers appear next to each bulleted item. If an item has subitems, the same animation sequence number that appears next to the first-level item appears next to the subitems. See Exhibit 20-20. This means that each first-level bulleted item along with its subitems is animated one at a time.

Exhibit 20-20 Animation sequence icons for a bulleted list with subbullets

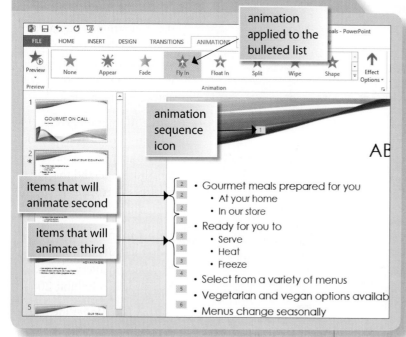

6 Advance the slide show twice more to make the next two first-level bullets and their subitems fly onto the screen.

7 Press the **Esc key** to end the slide show.

End Activity

20-5c Changing Animation Effects

Most animations have effects that you can modify. For example, the Fly In and Wipe animations can animate text or objects to fly in or wipe from different directions. In addition, you can change the sequence effects for objects made up of multiple items, such as a bulleted list. The default sequence for bulleted lists is for items to appear By Paragraph. This means that each first-level item and its subitems animates one at a time when you advance the slide show. You can change this so that the entire list animates at once as one object, or so that each first-level item animates at the same time but as separate objects.

The animation effects that you can modify appear on the Effect Options menu that appears when you click the Effect Options button in the Animation group on the ANIMATIONS tab. Exhibit 20-21 shows the Direction options for the Fly In animation and the Sequence options for a bulleted list.

Begin Activity

Animate a bulleted list.

1 On **Slide 2** ("About Our Company"), click anywhere in the bulleted list to make the text box active.

2 On the ANIMATIONS tab, in the Animation group, click the **Fly In animation**. Each first-level bulleted item flies in from the bottom along with its subitems. The numbered animation sequence icons next to each item indicate the order of the animations. Refer back to Exhibit 20-20.

3 On the status bar, click the **Slide Show button** . Slide 2 appears in Slide Show view with only the slide title visible.

4 Advance the slide show. The first animation—the Underline animation—occurs.

5 Advance the slide show again. The first bulleted item and its subitems fly onto the screen.

Begin Activity

Change animation effects.

1 On **Slide 2** ("About Our Company"), click anywhere on the **bulleted list**, if necessary. In the Animation group, Fly In is selected.

2 In the Animation group, click the **Effect Options button**. The menu of options that you can change for the selected Fly In animation and the selected bulleted list object appears. Refer to Exhibit 20-21.

3 Click **From Left**. The animation previews and the bulleted items fly in from the left, one first-level bulleted item at a time.

4 In the Animation group, click the **Float In animation**. The animation previews and the bulleted items float in one first-level item at a time.

Exhibit 20-21 Animation applied to a title

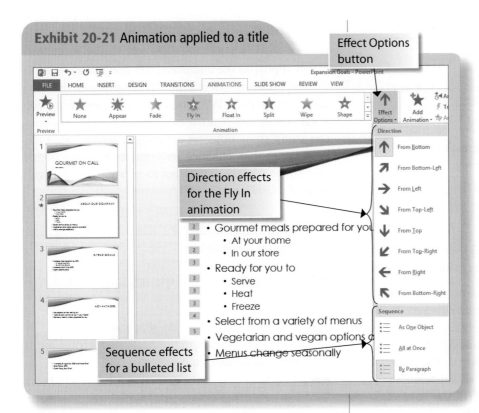

Effect Options button

Direction effects for the Fly In animation

Sequence effects for a bulleted list

20-5d Using the Animation Painter

For consistency, you will usually want to apply the same animation to all the slide titles in the presentation. You can display each slide in the Slide pane and repeat the same procedure to apply the same animation to each slide title. A faster and more accurate method is to use the **Animation Painter** to copy an animation from one object to another. To do so, you click the animated object, click the Animation Painter button in the Advanced Animation group on the ANIMATIONS tab, click the slide containing the object you want to animate, and then click that object. If you want to copy the animation to multiple objects, double-click the Animation Painter button. You can then click as many objects as you want, and the Animation Painter will remain selected and active until you click it again or press the Esc key to turn it off.

5 In the Animation group, click the **Effect Options button**. The sequence options are the same because a bulleted list is still the object being animated, but the Float animation has only two direction options available.

6 Click **Float Down**.

7 Click the **Effect Options button**. At the bottom of the menu, the three sequence options for a bulleted list are listed.

8 Click **As One Object**. All the bulleted items float in from the top at the same time. A single animation sequence icon appears next to the bulleted list indicating that the entire list will animate as one object.

9 Apply the **Wipe animation**, and then change the effect to **From Left**. The default sequence option, By Paragraph, is applied automatically when you applied the new animation.

10 Click the **title text**. In the Animation group, click the **Effect Options button**. The Underline animation has no effects you can modify, and the title text box has only one sequence option—As One Object.

11 Press the **Esc key** to close the menu without making a selection.

End Activity

FYI

Selecting Appropriate Animations

When you choose an animation, keep the purpose of the presentation and the intended audience in mind. Flashy or flamboyant animations are acceptable for informal, fun-oriented presentations but are not appropriate in formal business, technical, or educational presentations. These types of presentations should be more conservative. Although you want to capture the audience's attention, you should not select an animation that appears frivolous, such as one that makes the text bounce or spin onto the screen.

Animation Painter A tool in PowerPoint that you can use to copy an animation from one object to another.

Use the Animation Painter.

1 On Slide 2 ("About Our Company"), click anywhere on the **bulleted list**.

2 In the Advanced Animation group, click the **Animation Painter button**. The button changes to orange to indicate that it is selected.

3 Move the pointer onto the slide. The pointer changes to ⩓ 🖌 indicating that the Animation Painter is active.

4 In the Slides tab, click the **Slide 3 thumbnail**. Slide 3 ("5-Year Goals") appears in the Slide pane.

5 In the Slide pane, click anywhere on the **bulleted list**. The Wipe animation with the From Left direction effect and then By Paragraph sequence effect is copied from the bulleted list on Slide 2 and applied to the bulleted list on Slide 3. The Animation Painter button is no longer selected, and the pointer returns to its default shape. The border still appears around the bulleted list, indicating that it is selected.

6 On the ANIMATIONS tab, in the Advanced Animation group, double-click the **Animation Painter button**.

7 Display **Slide 4** ("Advantages") in the Slide pane. In the Slide pane, click the **bulleted list**. The copied animation is applied to the bulleted list on Slide 4, but this time, the Animation Painter button remains selected, and the pointer is still ⩓ 🖌.

8 Apply the copied animation to the bulleted list on Slide 5.

9 On the ANIMATIONS tab, in the Advanced Animation group, click the **Animation Painter button**. The button is deselected, and the pointer returns to its usual shape.

> **Tip:** You can also press the Esc key to deselect the Animation Painter button.

End Activity

transition The manner in which the next slide appears on the screen in place of the previous slide during a slide show.

20-5e Removing an Animation

If you animate a slide title, make sure you consider how it will appear to the audience. You don't want to leave them wondering what type of information the next slide will contain. As you create a presentation, you might decide to remove an animation. For example, too many animations on a slide can distract an audience rather than enhance your message. If you decide that you don't want an object to be animated, you can remove its animation.

Remove an animation.

1 Display **Slide 2** ("About Our Company") in the Slide pane.

2 In the Slide pane, click the **title text**. On the ANIMATIONS tab, in the Animation group, the Underline animation is selected.

3 On the ANIMATIONS tab, in the Animation group, click the **More button** ⯆.

4 At the top of the gallery, click the **None animation**. The gallery closes, and the Underline animation is removed from the title text on Slide 2.

End Activity

20-6 Adding Transitions

A **transition** is the manner in which the next slide appears on the screen in place of the previous slide during a slide show. The default is for one slide to disappear and the next slide to immediately appear on the screen. You can make the transitions more interesting by using commands in the Transition to This Slide group on the TRANSITIONS tab. You can modify transitions in Normal or Slide Sorter view.

Transitions are organized into three categories: Subtle, Exciting, and Dynamic Content. Dynamic Content transitions are a combination of the Fade transition for the slide background and a different transition for the slide content. If slides have the same background, it looks like the slide background stays in place and only the slide content moves. Like animations, you can modify transitions using the Effect Options button. Each transition has different effects that you can apply. Exhibit 20-22 shows the Transitions gallery in the Transition to This Slide group on the TRANSITIONS tab.

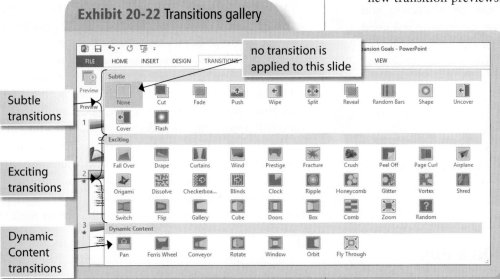

Exhibit 20-22 Transitions gallery

Add transitions to the slides.

1 On the ribbon, click the **TRANSITIONS tab**. In the Transition to This Slide group, click the **Push transition**. The Push transition is applied to the current slide, and you see a preview of the Push transition in the Slide pane.

2 On the TRANSITIONS tab, in the Preview group, click the **Preview button**. The transition is again previewed in the Slide pane.

3 In the Transition to This Slide group, click the **More button** ⬇. The gallery of transitions opens. Refer back to Exhibit 20-22.

4 In the first row in the Exciting section, click the **Peel Off transition** to apply the Peel Off transition to the current slide. The transition previews by peeling Slide 1 from the lower-right corner of the screen to the upper-left corner.

5 In the Transition to This Slide group, click the **Effect Options button**. The Peel Off transition has only two effects from which you can choose.

6 Click **Right**. The transition previews by peeling Slide 1 from the lower-left corner of the screen to the upper-right corner.

7 In the Transition to This Slide group, click the **Cover transition**. The Cover transition replaces the Peel Off transition for the current slide, and the new transition previews.

8 In the Transition to This Slide group, click the **Effect Options button**. The Cover transition has many effects from which you can choose.

9 Click **From Top-Left**. Currently, the transition is applied only to Slide 2.

10 On the TRANSITIONS tab, in the Timing group, click the **Apply To All button**. The Cover transition with the From Top-Left effect is applied to all of the slides in the presentation.

11 Display **Slide 6** ("Contact Us") in the Slide pane.

12 In the Transition to This Slide group, click the **More button** ⬇, and then click the **Switch transition** in the Exciting section. The Switch transition is applied only to the current slide, Slide 6, and a preview of the Switch transition appears.

13 Display **Slide 4** ("Advantages") in the Slide pane. On the status bar, click the **Slide Show button** 🖵. Slide 4 transitions onto the screen with the Cover transition and the From Top-Left effect.

14 Advance the slide show four times to animate and display all of the content on Slide 4 and transition to Slide 5 ("Our Team") with the Cover transition.

15 Advance the slide show four more times to animate and display all of the content on Slide 5 and transition to Slide 6 ("Contact Us") with the Switch transition.

16 End the slide show.

20-7 Adding Footers and Headers

Sometimes it can be helpful to have information on each slide such as the title of the presentation or the company name. It can also be helpful to have the slide number and the date displayed on each slide. In common usage, a footer is any text that appears at the bottom of every page in a document or every slide in a presentation. However, in PowerPoint, a **footer** is specifically the text that appears in a Footer text box designated for this purpose. This text box can appear anywhere on the slide; in some themes the footer appears at the top of slides.

For notes pages and **handouts**—printouts of the slides—you can also add text in a header text box. Similar to a footer, in PowerPoint, a **header** is text that appears in a Header text box. The Header text box appears in the top-left corner of handouts and notes pages.

footer In PowerPoint, text that appears in a Footer text box, which can appear anywhere on a slide depending on the theme, or at the bottom of handouts and notes pages.

handout A printout of the slides in a presentation.

header In PowerPoint, text that appears at the top of handouts and notes pages in a document.

20-7a Inserting Footers, Slide Numbers, and the Date on Slides

To add a footer, the slide number, and the date to slides, you need to open the Slide tab on the Header and Footer dialog box by clicking the Header & Footer button in the Text group on the INSERT tab. See Exhibit 20-23. When you add this information, you can choose to add it only to the current slide or to all the slides. There is also a Preview area in the dialog box that shows where the footer, slide number, and date will appear on the slide.

Often, presenters do not want the footer, slide number, and date to appear on the title slide. You can specify that these elements appear on all slides except the title slide by selecting the Don't show on title slide check box. When you do this, any slide other than Slide 1 must be displayed in the Slide pane.

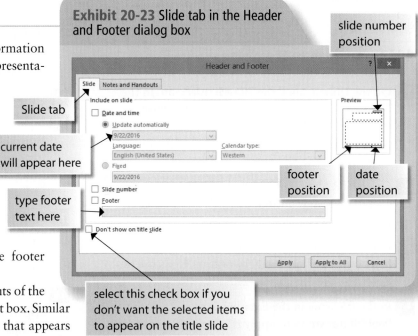

Exhibit 20-23 Slide tab in the Header and Footer dialog box

Begin Activity

Insert footers, slide numbers, and the date on slides.

1 On the ribbon, click the **INSERT tab**. In the Text group, click the **Header & Footer button**. The Header and Footer dialog box opens with the Slide tab on top. In the upper-right corner of the dialog box, the Preview box shows a preview slide with rectangles that identify where the footer, date, and slide number will appear. Their exact positions change depending on the current theme. Refer back to Exhibit 20-23.

Tip: Clicking the Date & Time button or the Slide Number button also opens the Header and Footer dialog box.

2 Click the **Footer check box** to select it. In the Preview box, the rectangle at the lower-left of the slide turns black to indicate that the footer will appear on the slides.

3 Click in the **Footer box**, and then type **Gourmet Delivered**.

4 Click the **Slide number check box** to select it. The rectangle at the upper-right of the Preview box turns black to indicate that the slide number will appear in this location on each slide.

5 Click the **Date and time check box**. The rectangle at the lower-right of the Preview box turns black, and the options under this check box darken so you can choose one of them.

6 If necessary, click the **Update automatically option button**. The current date will appear on the slides every time the presentation is opened.

7 Click the **Don't show on title slide check box** to select it.

Tip: To have a specific date always appear on the slides, select the Fixed option button on the Slide tab in the Header and Footer dialog box, and then type a date in the Fixed box.

8 Click **Apply to All**. The dialog box closes, and all the slides except the title slide contain the footer and today's date at the bottom of the slides and the slide number in the upper-right corner of the slides.

9 Display Slide 6 ("Contact Us") in the Slide pane, if necessary. Compare your screen to Exhibit 20-24.

10 Display **Slide 1** (the title slide) in the Slide pane. Verify that the footer, slide number, and date do not appear on the slide.

End Activity

Exhibit 20-24 Footer, date, and slide number on Slide 6

CONTACT US

slide number

- Web site: www.gourmetoncall.example.biz
- Phone: 912-555-3800
- Address: 101 West Bayside Ave.
  Savannah, GA 31401

footer

date

Gourmet Delivered

9/22/2016

20-7b Inserting Headers and Footers on Notes Pages and Handouts

If you plan to print notes for your reference or distribute handouts to the audience, you might want to add information to the header and footer in these printouts. The footer that appears on the slides does not appear on the notes pages or the handouts. You need to open the Notes and Handouts tab in the Header and Footer dialog box to set the options for both headers and footers on notes and handouts. The page number appears in the footer of notes and handouts by default.

Begin Activity

Add a header and footer to the notes pages and handouts.

1 Display **Slide 2** ("About Our Company") in the Slide pane.

2 On the INSERT tab, in the Text group, click the **Header & Footer button**. The Header and Footer dialog box opens with the Slide tab on top.

3 Click the **Notes and Handouts tab**. In addition to the Date and time and Footer check boxes, this tab contains a Page number check box instead of a Slide number check box, as well as a Header check box and a box in which to type a header. The Page number check box is selected by default, and the thick black border around the box in the lower-right corner of the preview indicates that this is where the page number will appear. Note that the footer you added to the slides does not appear in the Footer box on the Notes and Handouts tab.

4 Click the **Header check box** to select it. A thick border appears around the placeholder in the upper-left corner of the Preview. That is where the header will appear.

5 Click in the **Header box**, and then type **Business Expansion Plans**.

6 Click the **Footer check box**, click in the Footer box, and then type **Presentation to Investors**.

7 Click **Apply to All**. The dialog box closes, and all notes pages and handouts that you print will now contain the header and footer you typed, as well as the page number in the footer.

8 Save the presentation.

End Activity

20-8 Reviewing, Previewing, and Printing a Presentation

After you complete your presentation, you should always check the spelling in your presentation, proofread it, and view it in Slide Show or Presenter view to make sure everything works as expected.

20-8a Checking and Reviewing a Presentation

You should always check the spelling in a presentation and proofread it for errors. Using the spell checker in PowerPoint is similar to using the spell checker in Word—click the Spelling button, examine any flagged words, and decide whether to change the word or ignore

the suggested correction. After you check the spelling, you should run the slide show to verify that all of your animations and transitions work as you expect and to review the contents of each slide.

Begin Activity

Check and review the presentation.

1 On the ribbon, click the **REVIEW tab**. In the Proofing group, click the **Spelling button**.

2 If there are spelling errors, the Spelling dialog box opens. In that case, decide how to handle each word that is flagged because it was not found in the PowerPoint dictionary, just as you would in a Word document. If there aren't any spelling errors, or after you correct all the spelling errors, a dialog box opens, telling you that the spelling check is complete.

3 Click **OK**.

4 Display **Slide 1** (the title slide) in the Slide pane.

5 On the status bar, click the **Slide Show button** 🖵. The slide show starts in Slide Show view.

6 Advance through the slide show. If you see any problems while you are watching the slide show, press the **Esc key** to exit the slide show and return to Normal view, make the necessary corrections, and then return to Slide Show view.

7 Switch to **Slide Sorter view**.

8 Change the zoom level to **120% zoom** so that the slide thumbnails are as large as possible but still all appear within the Slide Sorter window. Compare your presentation to Exhibit 20-25.

9 Save the presentation.

End Activity

20-8b Displaying the Print Screen

PowerPoint provides several ways to print the slides in your presentation. You access the print options from the Print screen in Backstage view. See Exhibit 20-26. In the Settings section, you can click the Full Page Slides button to choose from the following options for printing the presentation:

▶ **Full Page Slides**—prints each slide full size on a separate piece of paper; speaker notes are not printed.

Exhibit 20-25 Completed presentation in Slide Sorter view

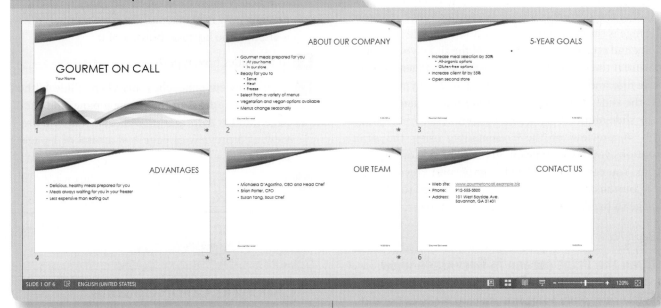

Exhibit 20-26 Print screen in Backstage view

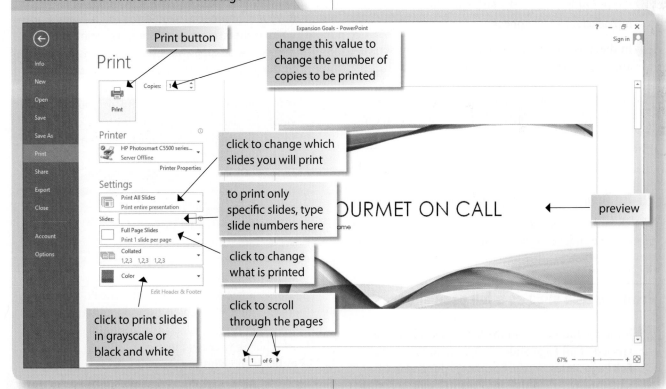

▶ **Notes Pages**—prints each slide as a notes page, with the slide at the top of the page and speaker notes below the slide, similar to how a slide appears in Notes Page view.

▶ **Outline**—prints the text of the presentation as an outline.

▶ **Handouts**—prints the presentation with one, two, three, four, six, or nine slides on each piece of paper. When printing three slides per page, the slides appear down the left side of the page and lines for notes appear to the right of each slide. When printing four, six, or nine slides, you can choose whether to order the slides from left to right in rows (horizontally) or from top to bottom in columns (vertically).

You can also click the Print All Slides button to specify whether you will print all the slides, selected slides, the current slide, or a custom range. Custom Range is selected automatically if you click in the Slides box and type the slide numbers of the slides you want to print. If the slides you want to print are sequential, type the first and last slide numbers separated by a hyphen. If the slides you want to print are not sequential, type the slide numbers separated by commas.

A preview of the presentation using the print options you select appears on the right side of the Print tab. You can click the Next Page ⯆ and Previous Page ⯅ buttons at the bottom of the preview to scroll from page to page, or you can drag the scroll bar.

Begin Activity

Open the Print screen in Backstage view.

1 Display **Slide 1** (the title slide) in the Slide pane, if necessary.

2 On the ribbon, click the **FILE tab**. The Info screen in Backstage view appears.

3 In the navigation bar, click **Print**. The Print screen appears in Backstage view. The Print screen contains options for printing the presentation, and a preview of the first slide or page as it will print with the currently selected options. Refer to Exhibit 20-26.

End Activity

20-8c Printing Full Page Slides

The default option for printing a presentation is to print all the slides as full page slides, one slide per page.

Begin Activity

Print the title slide as a full page slide.

1 If the second button in the Settings section is not labeled "Full Page Slides," click it, and then click **Full Page Slides**. At the bottom of the preview pane, the page number information indicates that you are viewing Slide 1 of 6 slides to print.

2 In the Settings section, click the **Print All Slides button**. You can print all the slides, selected slides, the current slide, or a custom range. In this case, you want to print just the title slide as a full page slide, not all six slides.

3 Click **Custom Range**. The menu closes, and the insertion point is blinking in the Slides box. The preview now is blank, and the page number information at the bottom shows 0 of 0.

4 In the Slides box, type **1**.

5 In the preview pane, click anywhere. Slide 1 (the title slide) appears in the preview pane, and the page number information indicates that you are viewing a preview of page 1 of a total of 1 page to print.

6 At the top of the Print section, click the **Print button**. Backstage view closes, and Slide 1 prints.

End Activity

LEARN MORE

Choosing Color Options

You can choose whether to print a presentation in color, grayscale, or black and white. Obviously, if your computer is connected to a black and white printer, the presentation will print in black and white or grayscale even if Color is selected in the bottom button in the Settings section. If you plan to print in black and white or grayscale, you should change this setting so you can see what the slides will look like without color and to make sure they are legible. You can do this using the VIEW tab on the ribbon or the Print screen in Backstage view. To do this from the VIEW tab, click the Grayscale or Black and White button in the Color/Grayscale group. To do this from the Print screen, click the Color button, and then click Grayscale or Pure Black and White. The preview will change to show the presentation in grayscale or black and white.

joingate/Shutterstock.com

20-8d Printing Handouts

If you print a presentation as handouts, you can fit multiple slides on a page. To choose the number of slides per page, click the Full Page Slides button, and then select one of the options in the Handouts section. See Exhibit 20-27.

Exhibit 20-27 Print options menu on the Print screen

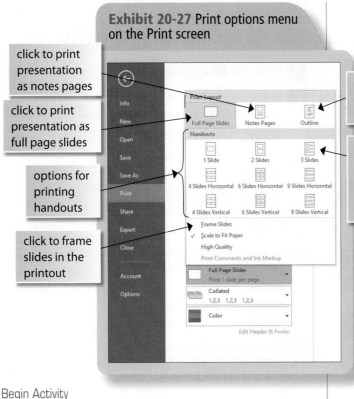

click to print presentation as notes pages

click to print presentation as full page slides

options for printing handouts

click to frame slides in the printout

click to print presentation as an outline

click to print 3 slides per page with lines next to each slide for notes

4 In the Settings section, click the **6 Slides Horizontal button**. The Frame Slides command now has a check mark next to it because the default for handouts is to frame the slides. You can click this command at any time to toggle it on or off.

5 Click a blank area of the screen to close the open menu.

6 Below the Custom Range button, click in the **Slides box**, and then press the **Delete** or **Backspace key** to delete the 1. The button above the Slides box changes from Custom Range to Print All Slides, and all six slides appear on the page in the preview, arranged in order in three rows from left to right.

7 At the top of the Print section, click the **Print button**. Backstage view closes, and the handout prints.

End Activity

Begin Activity

Print handouts.

1 On the ribbon, click the **FILE tab**. In the navigation bar, click **Print**. The Print screen appears in Backstage view.

2 In the Settings section, click the **Full Page Slides button**. A menu opens with choices for printing the presentation. At the bottom of the menu, Frame Slides does not have a check mark next to it because the default for Full Page Slides, the currently selected option, is to not frame the slides on the page. Refer back to Exhibit 20-27.

Tip: To print full page slides with a border around them, click the Full Page Slides button in the Settings section, and then click Frame Slides.

3 In the Handouts section, click **6 Slides Horizontal**. The preview changes to show Slide 1 smaller and in the upper-left corner of the page.

Tip: If you select 3 Slides to print handouts as three slides per page, the slides print with horizontal lines to the right of each slide to make it easier for someone to take notes.

20-8e Printing Notes Pages

You can print the slides as notes pages to include any speaker notes. Click the second button under Settings, and then click Notes Pages. Then you can scroll through the preview to see which slides contain notes. If you want to print only the slides that contain notes, click in the Slides box, and then type the slide numbers.

Begin Activity

Print slides containing speaker notes.

1 Open the **Print screen** in Backstage view.

2 In the Settings section, click the **6 Slides Horizontal button**. The button is labeled "6 Slides Horizontal," one of the options for printing handouts, because that was the last printing option selected.

3 In the Print Layout section of the menu, click **Notes Pages**. The menu closes, and the preview shows Slide 1 as a notes page. You will verify that Slides 3 and 6 contain speaker notes.

4 Below the preview, click the **Next Page button** ▶ twice to display Slide 3 ("5-Year Goals") in the preview, and then click the **Next Page button** ▶ three more times to display Slide 6 ("Contact Us"). These slides contain speaker notes.

5 In the Settings section, click in the **Slides box**, type **3,6** to specify the slides to print, and then click a blank area of the Print screen. Only the two specified pages will print.

6 Scroll through the preview to confirm that Slides 3 and 6 will print.

7 Click the **Print button**. Slides 3 and 6 print as notes pages.

End Activity

20-8f Printing the Presentation as an Outline

You can also print the presentation as an outline. The printout matches the text you see in the Outline tab in Normal view.

Begin Activity

Print the presentation as an outline.

1 Open the **Print screen** in Backstage view.

2 In the Settings section, click the **Notes Pages button**, and then click **Outline**. Slides 3 and 6 appear as an outline in the preview pane.

3 Click the **Custom Range button**, and then click **Print All Slides**. The entire outline appears in the preview.

4 At the top of the Print section, click the **Print button**. Backstage view closes, and the outline prints.

5 Close the presentation.

> **Tip:** If an outline is a bit longer than one page, you can click the Outline button, and then click Scale to Fit Paper to try to force the outline to fit on one page.

End Activity

FYI

Are Handouts Necessary?

Before taking the time to create handouts for a presentation, consider when to provide the audience with handouts and whether the audience will find value in having them. Many speakers provide printed copies of their presentation slides to the audience at the beginning of their presentation. This usually reduces the need for the audience to take notes on each slide as it is presented. However, sometimes the audience starts to read the handouts as soon as they are distributed, getting ahead of the speaker. The audience may also stop listening to the speaker because they are focused more intently on the printed text. And as they turn the pages, the rustle of paper can be distracting to the speaker and other audience members. To avoid this problem, first decide if handouts are truly necessary.

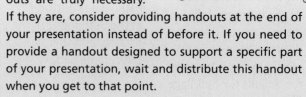

Granite/Shutterstock.com

If they are, consider providing handouts at the end of your presentation instead of before it. If you need to provide a handout designed to support a specific part of your presentation, wait and distribute this handout when you get to that point.

1. Which view displays the slide thumbnails or presentation outline in a tab on the left, the slides in a Slide pane, and speaker notes below the Slide pane?

2. What is a placeholder?

3. What is a text box?

4. What is a layout?

5. What does AutoFit do?

6. What is included in a theme family?

7. What happens when you demote a slide title one level?

8. How can you move a slide from one position to another?

9. How do you create speaker notes?

10. After you have created and proofed your presentation, why should you view it as a slide show?

11. Describe Slide Show view.

12. Describe Presenter view.

13. What is an animation?

14. What tool can you use to copy animation from one object to another?

15. What is a transition?

16. In PowerPoint, what is a footer?

17. When you add a footer and slide number to slides, how do you prevent them from appearing on the title slide?

18. What are the four ways you can print the content of a presentation?

Practice It

Practice It 20-1

1. Start PowerPoint, and then save the new, blank presentation as **Bookstore Plan**.

2. In Slide 1, add the title **Best Books**, and add your name as the subtitle.

3. Add a new Slide 2 using the Title and Content layout.

4. Add the slide title **A Bookstore for Booklovers** and then add the following first-level bulleted items:

   - **Independent bookseller**
   - **Skilled staff**
   - **Events**

5. Below the Events bullet item, add the following second-level bulleted items:

   - **Author signings**
   - **Book launch parties**
   - **Book clubs**

6. Add a new Slide 3 using the Comparison layout, and then add the slide title **Contact Us**.

7. Change the layout of Slide 3 ("Contact Us") to Title and Content.

8. In the content placeholder on Slide 3, add the first-level bulleted item **Address**, add a second-level bulleted item **400 Oak St.**, and then add **Philadelphia, PA 19107** on a new line without creating a new subitem.

9. Save the presentation, and then close it. Open the data file **Bookstore** located in the Chapter 20\Practice It folder. Save the presentation as **Bookstore Growth**.

10. Display Slide 6 ("A Bookstore for Booklovers"). Below the first-level item "Skilled staff," add the following subitems, allowing the text to AutoFit in the text box:

    - **Genre specialists**
    - **Invested in the community**

11. Display Slide 2 ("About Us") in the Slide pane, and then change the theme of the presentation to the Berlin theme. Apply the third variant.

12. Display the Outline tab. In the Outline tab on Slide 6, add **New Ideas** as a new, first-level bulleted item before the "Add pastries to coffee shop" item.

13. In the Outline tab, on Slide 6, promote the "New Ideas" bulleted item so it becomes a new Slide 7.

14. On the new Slide 7 ("New Ideas"), create a third bulleted item, and then type **"Staff Picks" list**. Drag the "Staff Picks" lists bulleted item up so it appears as the first item in the list above the Add pastries to coffee shop bulleted item.

15. In the Outline tab, on Slide 4 ("Why a New Store?"), under the Sales have risen steadily first-level bulleted item, demote the At least 12% increase each quarter bulleted item to a subitem. If necessary, promote the Marked increase after coffee shop opened bulleted item back to a second-level bulleted item.

16. Rearrange the slides so that Slide 2 ("About Us") becomes Slide 6, Slide 5 ("A Bookstore for Booklovers") becomes Slide 2, Slide 3 ("Contact Us") becomes Slide 7, and Slide 6 ("New Ideas") becomes Slide 5.

17. Delete Slide 4 ("Join Us for the Party!").

18. On Slide 2 ("A Bookstore for Booklovers"), animate the slide title using the Bold Reveal animation in the Emphasis category.

19. On Slide 2 ("A Bookstore for Booklovers"), animate the bulleted list using the Wipe animation in the Entrance category to the bulleted lists. Change the direction effect to From Top.

20. Copy the animation applied to the bulleted list on Slide 2 to the bulleted lists on Slides 3 through 5.

21. On Slide 2 ("A Bookstore for Booklovers") remove the animation applied to the title text.

22. Apply the Pan transition in the Dynamic Content category to all of the slides. Apply the Cover transition in the Subtle category to only Slides 1 (the title slide) and 2 ("A Bookstore for Booklovers").

23. On Slide 4 ("New Ideas"), add **We solicited ideas from both staff and customers.** as a speaker note. On Slide 6 ("Contact Us"), add **Mention that the Web site is being redesigned.** as a speaker note.

24. Add the footer **Best Books New Store Proposal** to all the slides except the title slide, and then display the current date (set to update automatically) and the slide number on all the slides except the title slide.

25. On the notes and handouts, add **Best Books** as a header and **New Store Presentation** as a footer.

26. Check the spelling in the presentation, making any corrections necessary. Review each slide in the presentation.

27. View the entire slide show. Make sure the animations and transitions work as you expect, and look carefully at each slide and check the content. If you see any errors or formatting problems, press the Esc key to end the slide show, fix the error, and then start the slide show again from the current slide.

28. Save the presentation. Print the title slide as a full page slide. Print the entire presentation as handouts, six slides per page, and as an outline. Print Slides 4 and 6 as notes pages.

29. Close the presentation.

Practice It 20-2

1. Open the data file **Customer** located in the Chapter 20\Practice It folder. Save the presentation as **Customer Presentation**.

2. In the title slide, add **OfficePro** as the title, press the Enter key, and then type **Cleaning Specialists**. Add your name as the subtitle.

3. Delete Slide 3 ("Our Cleaning Staff").

4. Move Slide 6 ("Weekly Services") so it becomes Slide 3.

5. On Slide 3 ("Weekly Services"), at the end of the bulleted list, add **Clean stairs and elevators** as a new first-level bulleted item.

6. On Slide 3, add **Remember to pause for questions from the audience.** as the speaker note.

7. On Slide 2 ("Daily Services"), at the end of the bulleted list, add **Clean and disinfect restrooms** as a new first-level bulleted item.

8. On Slide 2 ("Daily Services"), in the second first-level bulleted item, make the word *Sinks* a new first-level bullet, and then demote the bulleted items "Sinks" and "Toasters" to second-level bullets so that four second-level bulleted items now appear under "Clean kitchen and lounge area including."

9. On Slide 4 ("Specialized Services"), drag the bulleted items to the following order:

   - Air duct cleaning
   - Sanitizing all lavatory fixtures, sinks, partitions, walls, etc.
   - Carpet cleaning
   - Pressure washing
   - Stripping and refinishing

10. Animate the bulleted lists on Slides 2 through 5 with the Shape entrance animation using the Plus Shapes effect.

11. On Slide 6 ("For More Information"), animate the bulleted list using the Fly In entrance animation. Change the sequence effect so that the entire list animates as one object.

12. Add the Push transition to all of the slides except the title slide.

13. Display the footer text **Presentation for New Clients** as well as the slide number and the current date (set to update automatically) on all of the slides except the title slide.

14. Apply the Frame theme, and then apply the third variant.

15. Check the spelling throughout the presentation, and then view the slide show. If you see any errors, press the Esc key to end the slide show, correct the error, and then start the slide show again from the current slide. Save the presentation.

16. Preview the presentation in grayscale, and then in pure black and white. If you have a color printer, switch back to color so the presentation will print in color.

17. Print the title slide as a full page slide, print Slides 2 through 6 as a handout with six slides per page arranged vertically, and then print Slide 3 as a notes page.

18. Close the presentation.

On Your Own

On Your Own 20-1

1. Open the data file **Sales** located in the Chapter 20\ On Your Own folder. Save the presentation as **Sales Presentation**.

2. In the title slide, add **Mike's Mini Golf and More** as the presentation title, and then add your name as the subtitle.

3. On Slide 2 ("Price Packages"), add **Mention that these packages can be customized.** as the speaker note.

4. On Slide 2, move the Birthday Basics bulleted item and its subitems to be first in the list.

5. On Slide 2, change the last three bulleted items into subitems under The Fundraiser bulleted item.

6. On Slide 3 ("Mini Golf"), add **Variety of pitch speeds** as the fourth subitem under "Batting Cages."

7. On Slide 3 ("Mini Golf"), change the Batting Cages bulleted item into a new Slide 4 with its four subitems as first-level bullets on the new Slide 4. Keep the other bulleted items on Slide 3. (*Hint:* Make sure the bulleted list on the new Slide 4 consists of four first-level items.)

8. On Slide 6 ("Arcade"), promote the Current Classics subitem so it becomes a first-level bulleted item with three subitems.

9. Move Slide 5 ("Customer Comments") so that it becomes Slide 6.

10. Add a new Slide 6 using the Title and Content layout with the slide title **Go Carts** and the following three first-level bulleted items:

   - **Two tracks**
   - **Helmets provided**
   - **Minimum age: 13**

11. Under the Two tracks bulleted item, add the following subitems. (*Hint:* AutoCorrect changes the two hyphens to an em dash—a typographic character—after you press the Spacebar after the word following the second dash.)

   - **Twist and Turn--lots of curves**
   - **Slick--go really fast**

12. Change the theme to the Retrospect theme and its second variant.

13. Change the theme fonts to the Arial theme fonts. (*Hint:* On the DESIGN tab, in the Variants group click the More button, and then point to Fonts.)

14. In all of the bulleted lists and in the list on Slide 7, increase the point size of the text in the first-level items to 24 points and the point size of the text in the second-level items to 20 points.

15. Animate the bulleted lists on Slides 2 through 6 using the Grow & Turn animation. Change the sequence effect so the lists animate as one object.

16. Animate the list on Slide 7 ("Customer Comments") using the Appear animation. Keep the default sequence effect to animate the items one at a time.

17. Add the Checkerboard transition to Slide 1 (the title slide), add the Fracture transition to Slide 8 ("Contact Us"), and add the Gallery transition to the rest of the slides (Slides 2 through 7).

18. Change the speed of the Gallery transition applied to Slides 2 through 7 so it takes two seconds instead of 1.6 seconds. (*Hint*: Use the Duration box in the Timing group on the TRANSITIONS tab.)

19. Display the slide number and current date (set to update automatically) on all slides, including the title slide. Add your name as a header on the notes and handouts.

20. Check the spelling in the presentation, and view the slide show. If you see any errors, press the Esc key to end the slide show, correct the error, and then start the slide show again from the current slide. Save the presentation.

21. Preview the presentation in grayscale and then in pure black and white. If you have a color printer, switch back so the presentation will print in color.

22. Print the presentation as handouts with four slides per page arranged horizontally. Print Slide 2 ("Price Packages") as a notes page. Print the presentation outline on one page. (If the outline does not fit on one page even after selecting Scale to Fit Paper, print it on two pages.)

23. Close the presentation.

Chapter 20

ADDITIONAL STUDY TOOLS

IN THE BOOK
▶ Complete end-of-chapter exercises
▶ Study tear-out Chapter Review Card

ONLINE
▶ Complete additional end-of-chapter exercises

▶ Take practice quiz to prepare for tests
▶ Review key term flash cards (online, printable, and audio)
▶ Play "Beat the Clock" and "Memory" to quiz yourself
▶ Watch the videos to learn more about the topics taught in this chapter

Answers to Quiz Yourself

1. The view that displays the slide thumbnails or presentation outline in a tab on the left, the slides in a Slide pane, and speaker notes below the Slide pane is Normal view.

2. A placeholder is a region of a slide, or a location in an outline, reserved for inserting text or graphics.

3. A text box is a container that holds text.

4. A layout is a predetermined way of organizing the objects on a slide including title text and other content (bulleted lists, photographs, charts, and so forth).

5. AutoFit automatically changes the line spacing and the font size of the text in a text box if you add more text than will fit.

6. A theme family includes a theme and its variants.

7. When you demote a slide title one level, it becomes a first-level bulleted item.

8. To move a slide from one position to another, you can drag its thumbnail in the Slides in Normal view or in Slide Sorter view.

9. To create speaker notes, click in the Notes pane, and then type.

10. After you have created and proofed your presentation, you should view it as a slide show to see how it will appear to your audience.

11. Slide Show view displays one slide after another so that each slide fills the entire screen with no toolbars or other Windows elements visible on the screen and displays special effects applied to the text and graphics on each slide or to the slide itself.

12. Presenter view displays each slide in a small window that floats on top of the program window, and you can display each slide, one after the other in the small window to see how it will appear during the slide show.

13. An animation is a special effect applied to an object that makes the object move or change.

14. The Animation Painter is the tool you can use to copy animation from one object to another.

15. A transition is a special effect that changes the way an entire slide appears during a slide show.

16. In PowerPoint, a footer is text that appears in a Footer text box, which can appear anywhere on a slide depending on the theme, or at the bottom of handouts and notes pages.

17. To prevent a footer and slide number from appearing on the title slide, select the Don't show on title slide check box in the Header and Footer dialog box.

18. You can print a presentation as full page-sized slides, handouts, notes pages, and an outline.

PowerPoint 2013

Enhancing a Presentation

iofoto/Shutterstock.com

W̲e live in a highly visual society. Most people are exposed to multimedia daily and expect to have information conveyed visually as well as verbally. In many cases, a graphic is more effective than words for communicating an important point. For example, if a sales force has reached its sales goals for the year, a graphic of a person summiting a mountain can convey a sense of exhilaration.

PowerPoint allows you to incorporate many types of graphics and multimedia in slide shows. You can insert tables and charts, clip art and pictures stored on a computer or network, and video and music. You can use animation to make the slides come alive with movement. Judicious use of graphics and multimedia elements can clarify a point for audience members and help them remember it later. Of course, the audience needs to see a slide show to appreciate the graphic content. The Broadcast feature in PowerPoint allows you to deliver a slide show live over the Internet to anyone with a browser.

Microsoft product screenshots used with permission from Microsoft Corporation.

Learning Objectives

After studying the material in this chapter, you will be able to:

21-1 Work with slide masters

21-2 Insert graphics

21-3 Create SmartArt diagrams

21-4 Apply animations to graphics

21-5 Modify animation timings

21-6 Add video to a slide

21-7 Compress pictures and media

21-8 Present online

21-1 Working with Slide Masters

The **slide master** stores theme fonts, colors, elements, and styles, as well as text and other objects that appear on all the slides in the presentation. Slide masters ensure that all the slides in the presentation have a similar appearance and contain the same elements. A slide master is associated with a theme. The **theme Slide Master** is the primary slide master, and text, graphics, and formatting on the theme Slide Master appear on all slides in the presentation. Changes made to the theme Slide Master affect all of the slides in the presentation. Each theme Slide Master has an associated **layout master** for each layout in the presentation. If you modify a layout master, the changes affect only slides that have that layout applied. For example, the Title Slide Layout master is used by slides with the Title Slide Layout applied, and the Title and Content Layout master is used by slides with the Title and Content Layout applied.

You already know how to modify the look of documents, worksheets, database forms and reports, and presentations by applying a different theme and changing the theme colors and fonts. If you want to make additional changes to the overall look of slides, it is a good idea to make this type of change in the slide masters rather than on the individual slides. For example, if you want to change the color of bullets in bulleted lists or add a graphic to every slide in a presentation, you should do this in the slide master to keep the look of the slides in the presentation consistent.

You can modify slide masters by changing the size and design of text in the content placeholders, adding or deleting graphics, changing the background, and making other modifications.

21-1a Working in Slide Master View

The components of a slide layout include not only the title and content placeholders but also background graphics and text boxes for the footer, slide number, and date, as well as any other objects included as part of the design. Exhibit 21-1 shows a slide with the Title and Content layout applied for a presentation whose theme—the Wisp theme—includes background graphics. The slide contains a title text box, a bulleted list that was created in the content placeholder, a Footer text box at the bottom of the slide, and the Slide Number text box on top of the orange shape to the left of the title text placeholder. It also contains three graphics—the thin vertical rectangle on the left edge of the slide, curvy shapes meant to look like strands of tall grass, and the orange shape to the left of the title text placeholder. Note that the Date text box is not displayed. Exhibit 21-2 shows the theme Title and Content Layout master, which is the layout master for the slide shown in Exhibit 21-1.

To view the slide masters, you need to switch to **Slide Master view**. In Slide Master view, the largest thumbnail in the pane on the left is the slide master associated with the current theme.

Begin Activity

Work in Slide Master view.

1. Open the data file **Wildlife** located in the Chapter 21\Chapter folder. Save the file as **Wildlife Sanctuary**.

2. Add your name as the subtitle.

3. Display **Slide 5** ("Keep Nature Natural") in the Slide pane. Examine the elements on the slide. Refer to Exhibit 21-1.

4. On the ribbon, click the **VIEW tab**. In the Master Views group, click the **Slide Master button**. In the Slides tab, drag the scroll box to the top. The presentation is displayed in Slide Master view. Refer to Exhibit 21-2.

> **Tip:** You can also press and hold the Shift key and click the Normal button 🔲 on the status bar to switch to Slide Master view.

---

slide master A slide that contains theme elements and styles, as well as text and other objects that appear on all the slides in the presentation.

theme Slide Master The primary slide master for a presentation.

layout master A slide master for a specific layout in a presentation.

Slide Master view The PowerPoint view that displays the slide masters.

Exhibit 21-1 Title and Content layout applied to Slide 5

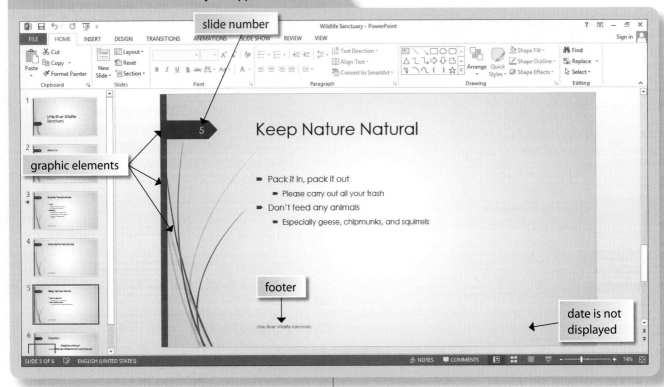

Exhibit 21-2 Title and Content Layout master in Slide Master view

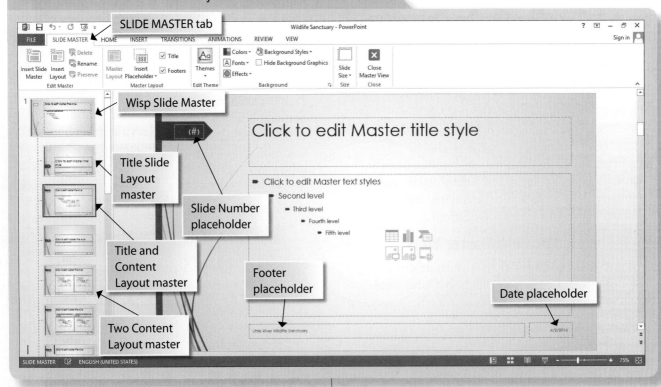

5 In the Slides tab, point to the **selected layout thumbnail** (the one with the orange border). The ScreenTip identifies it as the Title and Content Layout and informs you that this layout is used by Slides 5 and 6.

6 In the Slides tab, click the **Title Slide Layout master**. The Title Slide Layout master appears in the Slide pane. The Title Slide Layout master contains the elements that appear on the title slide—the title text placeholder and the subtitle text placeholder. It also contains the same three graphics that appeared on the Title and Content Layout master, although the orange shape is in a different position than on the Title and Content Layout master.

7 In the Slides tab, point to the **top thumbnail**, which is slightly larger than the other thumbnails. This is the theme Slide Master; the ScreenTip identifies it as the Wisp Slide Master and informs you that it is used by Slides 1 through 6. The theme Slide Master includes the name of the theme as the first part of the Slide Master name.

8 Click the **Wisp Slide Master** to display it in the Slide pane. The Slide Master has the thin vertical rectangle on the left edge and the curvy shapes but not the orange shape. Any graphics that appear on the theme Slide Master appear on all the slides in the same position as on the Slide Master. The orange shape does not appear on the Wisp Slide Master because it appears in a different position on the Title Slide layout master than on the Title and Content Layout master.

Tip: Remember to save frequently as you work through the chapter. A good practice is to save after every Activity.

End Activity

LEARN MORE

Handouts and Notes Masters

In addition to the slide masters, each presentation has a **handouts master** that contains the elements that appear on all the printed handouts and a **notes master** that contains the elements that appear on the notes pages. To display these masters, click the appropriate buttons in the Master Views group on the VIEW tab.

21-1b Modifying Text Placeholders in the Slide Master

You can adjust the size and position of text placeholders on slide masters. You can also delete placeholders if you want. When a text box is active, its border is a dotted line. To select a text box, you click the text box border to change it to a solid line. To change the size of a text placeholder, you drag the sizing handles, the same way you drag sizing handles to resize pictures in a Word document. To move a text box, you drag the selected text box by its border, as shown in Exhibit 21-3.

Exhibit 21-3 Dragging a text box

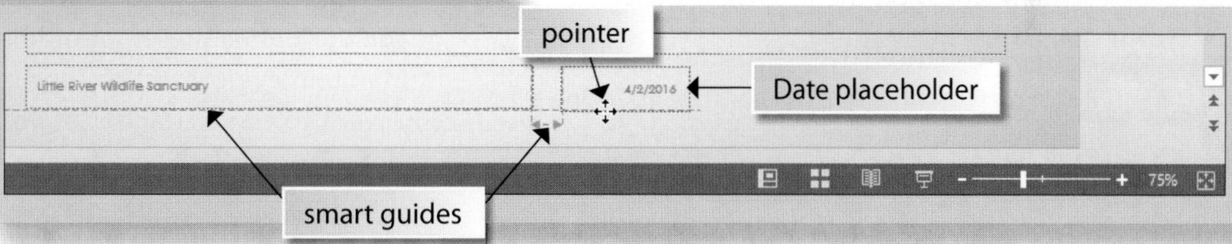

When you drag an item on slides to reposition them, dashed orange lines and arrows called **smart guides** appear, to help you align the object. These guides are similar to the alignment guides that appear when you position a floating object in a Word document.

You can also change the formatting of all the text in a text box when the entire text box is selected. For example, you can change the font or the font size.

handouts master A master that contains the elements that appear on printed handouts.

notes master A master that contains the elements that appear on the notes pages.

smart guide A dashed, orange line or arrow that appears when you drag an object on a slide to help you position the object.

Rehearsing Your Presentation

VladKol/Shutterstock.com

Unless you create a presentation that is intended for a user to watch without a presenter, the content of a slide show is only one part of a presentation. The other part is you—the presenter. Presenters who try to stand up and "wing it" in front of a crowd usually reveal this amateur approach the moment they start speaking—by looking down at their notes, rambling off topic, or turning their back on the audience to read from the slides displayed on the screen.

To avoid being seen as an amateur, you need to rehearse your presentation. Even the most knowledgeable speakers rehearse to ensure they know how the topic flows, what the main points are, how much time to spend on each slide, and where to place emphasis. Experienced presenters understand that while practice may not make them perfect, it will certainly make them better.

Where you practice isn't that important. You can talk to a mirror, a video camera, your family, or a group of friends. Watching your performance often reveals the weaknesses you don't want the audience to see and that your friends or family may be unwilling or unable to identify. Whatever you choose to do, the bottom line is this: If you practice, you will improve.

As you rehearse, focus on the following steps:

▶ **Practice speaking fluently.** Be sure to speak in an easy, smooth manner, and avoid using nonwords and fillers. Nonwords consist of *ums*, *ahs*, *hms*, and other such breaks in speech. Fillers are phrases that don't add any value yet add length to sentences, such as *like* or *you know*. Both can dilute a speaker's message because they are not essential to the meaning of what's being spoken. At best, they can make you sound unprofessional. At worst, they can distract the audience and make your message incomprehensible.

▶ **Work on your tone of voice.** When delivering a presentation, you usually want to speak passionately, with authority, and with a smile. If you aren't excited about your presentation, how will your audience feel? By using your voice to project energy, passion, and confidence, your audience will automatically pay more attention to you. Smile and look directly at audience members and make eye contact. If your message is getting across, they will instinctively affirm what you are saying by returning your gaze, nodding their heads, or smiling. However, be careful not to overdo it. Speaking too loudly or using an overly confident or arrogant tone will quickly turn off an audience and make them stop listening altogether.

▶ **Decide how to involve the audience.** If you involve audience members in your presentation, they will pay closer attention to what you have to say. When an audience member asks a question, be sure to affirm him or her before answering. For example, you could respond with "That's a great question" or "Thanks for asking. Here's what my research revealed." An easy way to get the audience to participate is to start with a question and invite responses, or to stop partway through to discuss a particularly important point. Also, remember to repeat the question to the audience in case other audience members were not able to hear the original question.

▶ **Be aware of your body language.** Although the content of your presentation plays a role in your message delivery, it is your voice and body language during the presentation that make or break it. Maintain eye contact to send the message that you want to connect and that you can be trusted. Stand up straight to signal confidence. Conversely, avoid slouching (which can convey laziness, lack of energy, or disinterest) and fidgeting or touching your hair (which can signal nervousness). Resist the temptation to glance at your watch; you don't want to send a signal that you'd rather be someplace else. Finally, be aware of your hand movements. The best position for your hands is to place them comfortably by your side, in a relaxed position. As you talk, you can use hand gestures to help make a point, but be careful not to overdo it.

▶ **Check your appearance.** An audience's first impression of a speaker is also based on appearance. Before a single word is spoken, the audience sizes up the way the presenter looks. You want to look professional and competent. Make sure your appearance is neat, clean, and coordinated, and that you dress in appropriate clothing.

Adding Placeholders and Creating a Custom Layout

Although each theme comes with nine layouts, you might find that none of them meets your needs. You already know how to customize an existing layout by resizing, moving, and deleting the placeholders. In addition, you can add placeholders to an existing layout master, or you can create a completely new layout master.

To insert a new placeholder, switch to Slide Master view. Click the Insert Placeholder button arrow in the Master Layout group on the SLIDE MASTER tab, select a placeholder type, and then click or drag on the slide, similar to creating a text box.

To create a new layout master, click the Insert Layout button in the Edit Master group on the SLIDE MASTER tab. A new layout identical to the Title Only Layout master is created. To create a custom layout that doesn't include any of the elements of the current slide master, click the Insert Slide Master button instead of the Insert Layout button. When you create a new layout, the default name is Custom Layout Layout. To change the name of the new layout, right-click it, and then click Rename Layout on the shortcut menu. In Normal view, the new layout will be available on the New Slide button menu and on the Layout button menu.

Begin Activity

Modify text placeholders in the Slide Master.

1 In Slide Master view, with the **Wisp Slide Master** selected, click the **Footer placeholder** at the bottom of the Slide pane.

2 Drag the **right-middle sizing handle** to the left to resize the placeholder box so it is about five inches wide.

> **Tip:** Use the Shape Width box in the Size group on the DRAWING TOOLS FORMAT tab to help you size the box.

3 Click the **Date placeholder border** so that it changes to a solid line, and then position the pointer on the selected border. The pointer changes to ⁺⬚.

4 Drag the **Date placeholder** to the left to position it about one-quarter inch to the right of the Footer placeholder. As you drag, smart guides appear to help you keep the top and bottom borders of the Date placeholder aligned with the borders of the Footer placeholder. Refer back to Exhibit 21-3.

5 Drag the **Slide Number placeholder** from the left of the title text placeholder to the bottom of the slide, and use the smart guides to right-align it with the right edge of the content placeholder and horizontally with the other two placeholders.

6 With the **Slide Number placeholder** selected, press and hold the **Shift key**, click the **Date placeholder**

border, click the **Footer placeholder border**, and then release the **Shift key**. The three placeholders are selected.

7 On the ribbon, click the **HOME tab**. In the Font group, click the **Font Size button arrow** ⬚, and then click **11**.

8 In the Font group, click the **Font Color button arrow** ⬚, and then click the **Black, Text 1 color**. The text in the placeholders is now 11 points and black.

9 Click the **content placeholder border**. In the Font group, the Font Size button indicates that the text is 12+ points. This means that in the selected text box, the text that is the smallest is 12 points, and there is some text that is a larger point size.

10 In the Font group, click the **Increase Font Size button** ⬚ three times. Each level of bulleted text in the content placeholder increases by two or four points each time you click the button. Now the font size of the smallest text in the content placeholder is 18 points. (If you used the Font Size button arrow to change the font size, all of the bulleted items would have been changed to the same point size.)

11 Click anywhere in the **first-level bulleted item**. The Font Size box indicates that this text is 28 points.

12 Click the **content placeholder border**. In the Font group, click the **Font Color button** ⬚. The last color applied, Black, Text 1, is applied to all of the text in the content placeholder. Compare your screen to Exhibit 21-4.

Exhibit 21-4 Graphic selected on the Title and Content Layout master

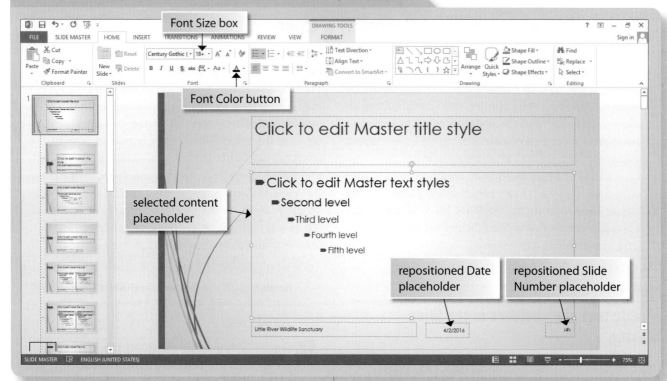

13 Display the **Title and Content placeholder** in the Slide pane. The changes you made on the Wisp Slide Master are reflected on the Title and Content placeholder in the Slide pane.

14 Display the **Two Content Layout master** in the Slide pane. Slides 2, 3, and 4 use the Two Content layout. The size and color of the text has been changed to match the changes you made on the Wisp Slide Master, but the Slide Number placeholder is still positioned to the left of the title text placeholder.

15 On the Two Content Layout master, drag the **Slide Number placeholder** to the bottom-right of the slide.

End Activity

21-1c Deleting a Graphic from the Slide Master

Many themes contain graphics in the Slide Master or on individual layout masters. Often the graphics are attractive elements of the slide design. However, sometimes you might want to delete a graphic because it doesn't fit well with your content or you would rather use something else. You can do this in Slide Master

view. To delete a graphic, you first need to click it to select it. Exhibit 21-5 shows the orange shape graphic on the Two Content Layout master selected.

Exhibit 21-5 Graphic selected on the Two Content Layout master

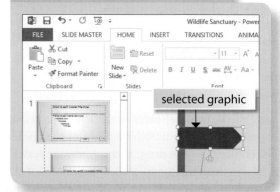

Begin Activity

Delete a graphic from the Slide Master.

1 On the Two Content Layout master, in the Slide pane, click the **orange shape** to the left of the title placeholder to select it. Refer back to Exhibit 21-5.

2 Press the **Delete key**. The graphic is deleted.

3 Display the **Title and Content Layout master** in the Slide pane, and then delete the graphic to the left of the title placeholder.

4 Display the **Title Slide Layout master** in the Slide pane. The Slide Number placeholder is still positioned to the left of the title text placeholder. This doesn't need to be adjusted because the slide number is not displayed on the title slide.

5 Click the **orange shape**, and then press the **Delete key**. The orange shape is deleted from the slide.

Problem? If the Slide Number placeholder was deleted instead of the orange shape, you clicked the placeholder's border instead of clicking the shape behind the placeholder. On the Quick Access Toolbar, click the **Undo button**, and then repeat Step 5, taking care to select the shape.

End Activity

LEARN MORE

Adding Graphics to the Slide Master

You can also add graphics to the slide master. For instance, you might want a company logo to appear on every slide, or you might want a colored line to appear below the slide titles. To add clip art or a picture to the theme Slide Master or to specific layout masters, you must use the Online Pictures or Pictures button in the Images group on the INSERT tab.

21-1d Modifying the Slide Background

You can customize the background of slides in a presentation. To change the slide background, click the Background Styles button in the Background group on the SLIDE MASTER tab to display the Background Styles gallery. See Exhibit 21-6. This gallery contains backgrounds that use four of the colors from the theme

color palette. Some of the styles have gradients applied. A **gradient** is shading in which one color blends into another or varies from one shade to another.

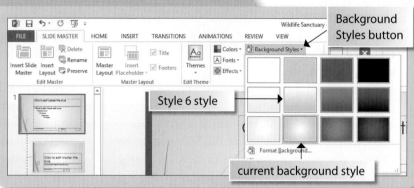

Exhibit 21-6 Background Styles gallery

Begin Activity

Modify the slide background.

1 Display the **Wisp Slide Master** in the Slide pane.

2 On the ribbon, click the **SLIDE MASTER tab**. In the Background group, click the **Background Styles button**. A gallery of styles opens. Refer back to Exhibit 21-6.

> **Tip:** To access more choices for customizing the background, click Format Background below the gallery to open the Format Background task pane.

3 In the gallery, click the **Style 6 style**. The background style is applied to all of the layout masters.

End Activity

21-1e Closing Slide Master View

When you are finished modifying the slide master, you need to close Slide Master view and return to Normal view. You should always examine the slides in Normal view after you make changes to the slide master to make sure they look as you expected them to.

---

gradient Shading in which one color blends into another or varies from one shade to another.

Close Slide Master view and examine the results of the changes.

1 On the SLIDE MASTER tab, in the Close group, click the **Close Master View button**. Slide Master view closes, and the presentation appears in Normal view with Slide 5, which has the Title and Content layout applied, in the Slide pane. The changes you made in Slide Master view are visible on the slide.

> **Tip:** You can also click the Normal button 🔲 on the status bar to close Slide Master view.

2 Display **Slide 2** ("About Us") in the Slide pane. This slide has the Two Content layout applied. The changes made in Slide Master view are visible on this slide as well.

3 Display **Slide 1** (the title slide) in the Slide pane. The changes you made to the Title Layout master are visible on this slide.

Selecting Appropriate Font Colors

When you select font colors for use on slides or when you modify the slide background, make sure your text is easy to read on the slide during a slide show. Font colors that work well are dark colors on a light background, or light colors on a dark background. Avoid red text on a blue background or blue text on a green background (and vice versa) unless the shades of those colors are in strong contrast. These combinations might look good up close on your computer monitor, but they are almost totally illegible to an audience watching your presentation on a screen in a darkened room. Also avoid using red/green combinations, which color-blind people find illegible.

Color combinations

© 2014 Cengage Learning

21-2 Inserting Graphics

Remember that a graphic is a picture, shape, design, graph, chart, or diagram. You can include many types of graphics in your presentation: clip art; graphics created using other programs; scanned photographs, drawings, and cartoons; other picture files stored on your computer or network; or graphics you create using drawing tools in PowerPoint.

When you insert a graphic in a PowerPoint slide (or an Excel worksheet), you do not have to set text-wrapping options; graphics are always floating graphics in PowerPoint slides and Excel worksheets. To reposition a graphic on a slide, drag it to its new position. In PowerPoint, objects "snap to" or align with an invisible grid when they are moved. This usually helps you align objects on a slide. If a graphic jumps from one location to another as you drag it and you can't position it exactly where you want it, press and hold the Alt key as you drag it. The Alt key temporarily disables the feature that forces objects to snap to the grid.

21-2a Inserting a Picture File

You can insert graphics stored on your computer on a slide. If a slide has an empty content placeholder, as shown in Exhibit 21-7, you can click the Pictures button in the content placeholder. This opens the Insert Picture dialog box, which is similar to the Open dialog box. To insert an image stored on Office.com, you would click the Online Pictures button in the content placeholder.

Add a graphic from a file using a button in the content placeholder.

1 Display **Slide 2** ("About Us") in the Slide pane. This slide has the Two Content layout applied. Refer to Exhibit 21-7.

2 On the right side of the slide, in the content placeholder, click the **Pictures button** 🖼. The Insert Picture dialog box opens. This dialog box is similar to the Open and Save As dialog boxes.

Exhibit 21-7 Slide 2 with the Two Content layout applied

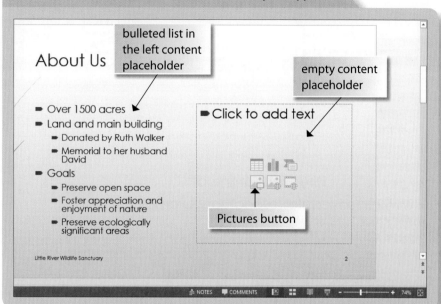

bulleted list in the left content placeholder

empty content placeholder

About Us

Click to add text

- Over 1500 acres
- Land and main building
  - Donated by Ruth Walker
  - Memorial to her husband David
- Goals
  - Preserve open space
  - Foster appreciation and enjoyment of nature
  - Preserve ecologically significant areas

Pictures button

Little River Wildlife Sanctuary

2

NOTES   COMMENTS   74%

4 Display **Slide 3** ("Explore the Sanctuary") in the Slide pane, and then insert the picture data file **Hikers** located in the Chapter 21\Chapter folder in place of the content placeholder.

5 Display **Slide 4** ("Glass-Bottomed Canoe"), and then insert the picture data file **Canoe** located in the Chapter 21\Chapter folder in place of the content place-holder on the left.

End Activity

If a slide does not have an empty content placeholder, you can insert a picture using the Pictures button in the Images group on the INSERT tab.

If you need to resize a picture on a slide, you can drag its sizing handles. Remember to drag the corner sizing handles to maintain the aspect ratio of the picture so that the image does not become distorted.

3 Click the picture data file **Landscape** located in the Chapter 21\Chapter folder, and then click **Insert**. The dialog box closes, and the picture replaces the content placeholder on the slide. The PICTURE TOOLS FORMAT tab appears on the ribbon and is the active tab. Compare your screen to Exhibit 21-8.

Exhibit 21-8 Picture inserted in the content placeholder on Slide 2

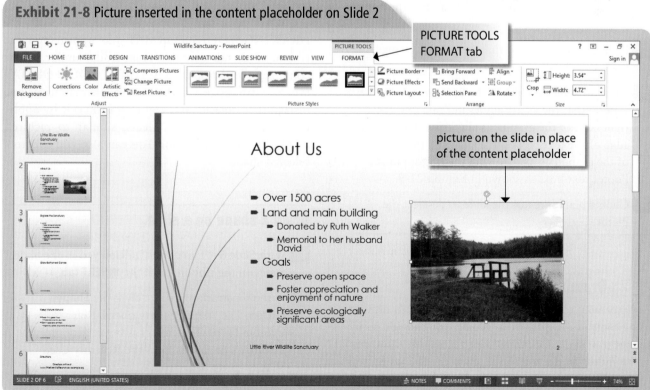

PICTURE TOOLS FORMAT tab

picture on the slide in place of the content placeholder

About Us

- Over 1500 acres
- Land and main building
  - Donated by Ruth Walker
  - Memorial to her husband David
- Goals
  - Preserve open space
  - Foster appreciation and enjoyment of nature
  - Preserve ecologically significant areas

Little River Wildlife Sanctuary

2

SLIDE 2 OF 6   ENGLISH (UNITED STATES)   NOTES   COMMENTS   74%

Photo courtesy of Katherine T. Pinard

Add a graphic from a file using the ribbon, and reposition it.

1 Display **Slide 6** ("Directions") in the Slide pane.

2 On the ribbon, click the **INSERT tab**. In the Images group, click the **Pictures button**. The Insert Picture dialog box opens.

3 Click the picture data file **Goose** located in the Chapter 21\ Chapter folder, and then click **Insert**. The dialog box closes, and the picture of the goose appears in the center of Slide 6.

4 Point to the bottom-right-corner sizing handle so that the pointer changes to ⬉. Drag the sizing handle down and to the right to resize the picture so it is approximately two inches high. After you release the mouse button, look at the measurement in the Height box in the Size group on the PICTURE TOOLS FORMAT tab, and then click the Height box up or down arrows as needed to change the value in the box to two inches.

5 Point to the picture so that the pointer changes to ⬌.

6 Drag the **goose picture** to the bottom-right of the slide so that the smart guides indicate that the right edge of the graphic is aligned with the right edge of the text box on the slide and the bottom of the graphic is aligned with the bottom of the Footer text box, as shown in Exhibit 21-9.

7 Click a blank area of the slide to deselect the picture.

21-2b Drawing a Shape

Another way to add a graphic to a slide is to draw it using tools available in PowerPoint. You can add many shapes to a slide, including lines, rectangles, stars, and many more. To draw a shape, click the Shapes button in the Illustrations group on the INSERT tab or in the

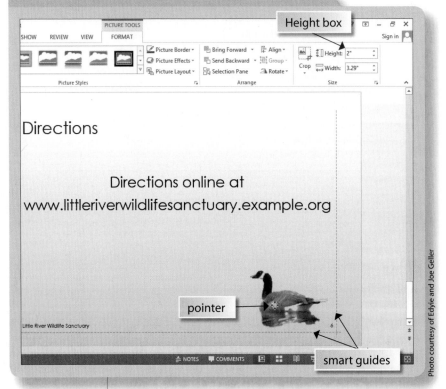

Exhibit 21-9 Picture repositioned using smart guides

Photo courtesy of Edyie and Joe Geller

Drawing group on the HOME tab to display the Shapes gallery, as shown in Exhibit 21-10. (There is no icon in the content placeholders to insert a shape.) Click a shape in the gallery, and then click and drag on the slide to draw the shape.

When a drawn shape is selected on a slide, the DRAWING TOOLS FORMAT tab appears on the ribbon. This tab contains commands similar to the commands found on the PICTURE TOOLS FORMAT tab. You can resize a shape in the same manner as you resize other objects. You can also format it by applying styles, borders, and effects, similar to pictures, and by filling it with color. You can also add text to a selected shape.

Draw a shape on a slide.

1 With **Slide 6** ("Directions") displayed in the Slide pane, on the ribbon, click the **INSERT tab**.

2 In the Illustrations group, click the **Shapes button**. The Shapes gallery opens. Refer to Exhibit 21-10. The gallery is organized into nine categories of shapes, plus the Recently Used Shapes group at the top.

Exhibit 21-10 Shapes gallery

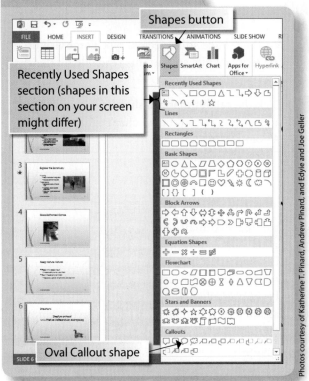

Shapes button

Recently Used Shapes section (shapes in this section on your screen might differ)

Oval Callout shape

Photos courtesy of Katherine T. Pinard, Andrew Pinard, and Edyie and Joe Geller

3 In the Callouts section, click the **Oval Callout shape**. The gallery closes, and the pointer changes to +.

4 In the Slide pane, point to a blank area about four inches above and to the left of the picture of the goose. Press and hold the mouse button, and then drag down and to the right. As you drag, an oval callout shape is drawn. Release the mouse button when the shape is approximately 1.5 inches high and 2.5 inches wide. The callout shape appears on the slide, and the DRAWING TOOLS FORMAT tab becomes the active tab on the ribbon. A selection box and sizing handles appear around the shape, and a yellow diamond-shaped adjustment handle appears on the bottom point of the shape that you can drag to change the way a shape looks without changing its size.

5 On the DRAWING TOOLS FORMAT tab, in the Size group, adjust the values in the **Shape Height** and **Shape Width** boxes so that the shape is 1.5 inches high and 2.5 inches wide, if necessary.

Tip: To draw a circle, square, or equilateral triangle, hold the Shift key while you drag the pointer after selecting the Oval, Rectangle, or Isosceles Triangle shape, respectively.

6 Drag the **yellow adjustment handle** to the right so that the point of the callout shape is directed toward to the picture of the goose.

7 Drag the **callout shape** to position it to the left of and a little above the picture of the goose. Compare your screen to Exhibit 21-11.

End Activity

Exhibit 21-11 Adjusted and resized callout shape

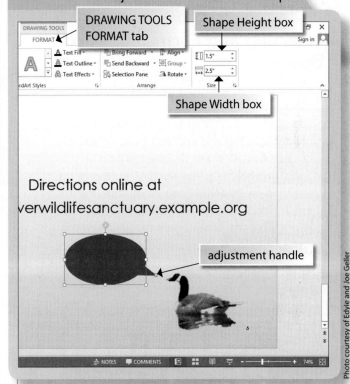

DRAWING TOOLS FORMAT tab

Shape Height box

Shape Width box

adjustment handle

Photo courtesy of Edyie and Joe Geller

LEARN MORE

Inserting Tables on a Slide

To insert a table on a slide, click the Insert Table button ⊞ in a content placeholder to open a dialog box in which you specify the number of columns and rows you want to insert. You can also click the Table button in the Tables group on the INSERT tab to insert a table using the same grid you used in Word. After you insert a table, the steps for working with the table are the same as working with a table in a Word document.

21-2c Adding Text to a Shape

To add text to a shape, select it, and then type. The text will be inserted at 18 points in the Body font of the selected theme. The text will wrap in the shape automatically. If you type more text than the shape can hold, you can resize the shape or change the font size to make it fit. The color of the text is black or white, depending on the fill color of the shape.

Add text to a shape.

1 With the shape still selected, type **Come visit us!**. The text is white so that it is readable on the dark background.

2 Click the **callout shape dashed line border** to select the entire shape, and then change the font size to **24 points**.

21-2d Formatting Graphics

You can apply formatting to any object on a slide. As you have seen, when a picture is selected on a slide, the PICTURE TOOLS FORMAT tab appears on the ribbon, and when a shape is selected on a slide, the DRAWING TOOLS FORMAT tab appears. The commands on the two tabs are very similar. For example, you can apply a style, add or change the border or outline, and add special effects. Exhibit 21-12 shows the callout shape selected and the DRAWING TOOLS FORMAT tab on the ribbon. Some formatting tools are available only to one or the other type of object. For example, the Remove Background tool is available only to pictures, and the Fill command is available only to shapes. The **fill** is the formatting of the area inside a shape.

Exhibit 21-12 Drawn shape with a style applied and the border modified

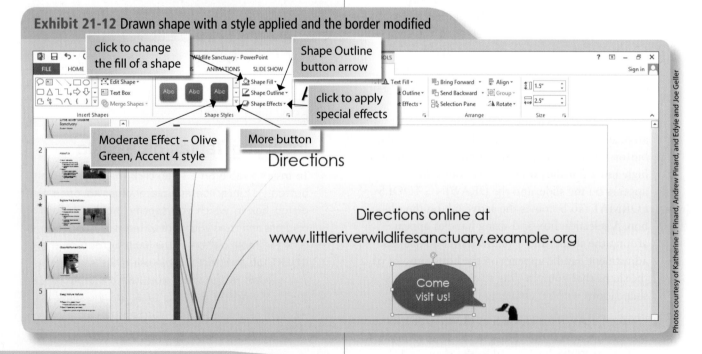

Photos courtesy of Katherine T. Pinard, Andrew Pinard, and Edyie and Joe Geller

fill The formatting of the area inside a shape.

Format drawings and pictures on slides.

1 If necessary, on **Slide 6** ("Directions"), select the **callout shape**.

2 On the ribbon, click the **DRAWING TOOLS FORMAT tab**. In the Shape Styles group, an orange border appears around one of the styles. When you draw a shape, this default style is applied.

3 In the Shape Styles group, click the **More button**. The Shape Styles gallery opens.

4 In the gallery, click the **Moderate Effect – Olive Green, Accent 4 style**, using the ScreenTips to locate this style. The style is applied to the callout shape.

5 In the Shape Styles group, click the **Shape Outline button arrow**. On the menu, point to **Weight**, and then click **2¼ pt**. The weight of the shape border increases to 2¼ points. Refer back to Exhibit 21-12.

6 Display **Slide 4** ("Glass-Bottomed Canoe"). On Slide 4, select the picture. The PICTURE TOOLS FORMAT tab appears on the ribbon.

7 On the ribbon, click the **PICTURE TOOLS FORMAT tab**. In the Picture Styles group, click the **Drop Shadow Rectangle style**. The style is applied to the picture.

8 Format the pictures on **Slide 3** ("Explore the Sanctuary") and **Slide 2** ("About Us") in the Slide pane with the **Drop Shadow Rectangle style**.

If photos you want to use in a presentation are too dark or require other fine-tuning, you can use PowerPoint's photo correction tools. You can use options on the Corrections button menu to sharpen a blurry image or soften details in a photo or adjust the brightness and contrast to change the difference between dark and light areas in the photo. See Exhibit 21-13. You can also use the options on the Color button menu to adjust the color saturation, which is the amount or intensity of color in a photo, and the color tone, which is the amount of reds and yellows or blues and greens, in a photo. See Exhibit 21-14.

Exhibit 21-13 Corrections button menu

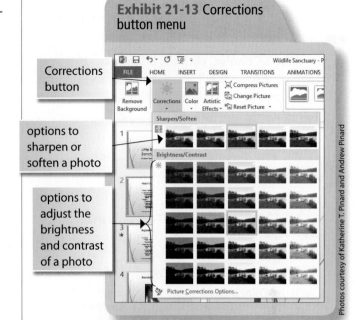

Corrections button

options to sharpen or soften a photo

options to adjust the brightness and contrast of a photo

Photos courtesy of Katherine T. Pinard and Andrew Pinard

Exhibit 21-14 Color button menu

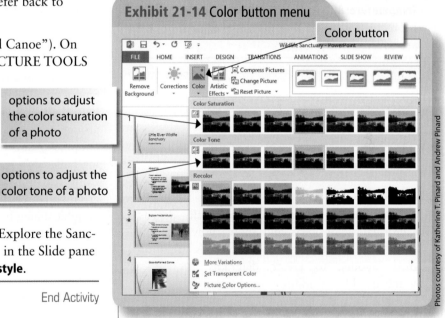

Color button

options to adjust the color saturation of a photo

options to adjust the color tone of a photo

Photos courtesy of Katherine T. Pinard and Andrew Pinard

Edit a photo.

1 On **Slide 2** ("About Us"), select the **photo**. On the ribbon, click the **PICTURE TOOLS FORMAT tab**, if necessary.

2 In the Adjust group, click the **Corrections button**. A menu opens showing options for sharpening and softening the photo and adjusting the brightness and the contrast. Refer back to Exhibit 21-13.

3 Under Sharpen, click the **Sharpen: 25% style**. The image is sharpened slightly so it is more in focus.

4 Click the **Corrections button** again, and then under Brightness/Contrast, click the **Brightness: -20% Contrast: +20% style**. The brightness of the photo decreases, and the contrast increases.

5 In the Adjust group, click the **Color button**. A menu opens with options for adjusting the saturation and tone of the photo's color. Refer back to Exhibit 21-14.

6 Under Color Saturation, click the **Saturation: 200% style**. The colors in the photo are more intense.

> **Tip:** If you make changes to photos and then change your mind, you can click the Reset Picture button in the Adjust group on the PICTURE TOOLS FORMAT tab.

7 Click the **Color button**, and then under Color Tone, click the **Temperature: 8800 K**. More reds and yellows are added to the photo.

End Activity

21-3 Creating SmartArt Diagrams

A **diagram** is an illustration that visually depicts information or ideas and shows how they are connected. You can use **SmartArt**, diagrams with pre-designed layouts, to create diagrams easily and quickly. In addition to shapes, SmartArt diagrams usually include text to help describe or label the shapes. You can create the following types of diagrams using SmartArt:

▶ **List**—shows a list of items in a graphical representation.

> **diagram** An illustration that visually depicts information or ideas and shows how they are connected.
>
> **SmartArt** A diagram with a predesigned layout.

▶ **Process**—shows a sequence of steps in a process.

▶ **Cycle**—shows a process that has a continuous cycle.

▶ **Hierarchy** (including **organization charts**)—shows the relationship between individuals or units within an organization.

▶ **Relationship** (including **Venn diagrams**, **radial diagrams**, and **target diagrams**)—shows the relationship between two or more elements.

▶ **Matrix**—shows information in a grid.

▶ **Pyramid**—shows foundation-based relationships.

▶ **Picture**—provides a location for a picture or pictures.

There is also an Office.com category, which, if you are connected to the Internet, displays additional SmartArt diagrams available on Office.com. You also might see an Other category, which contains SmartArt diagrams previously downloaded from Office.com.

21-3a Creating a SmartArt Diagram

To create a SmartArt diagram, you can click the Insert SmartArt Graphic button in a content placeholder, or you can click the SmartArt button in the Illustrations group on the INSERT tab to open the Choose a SmartArt Graphic dialog box. You can also convert an existing bulleted list into a SmartArt diagram by using the Convert to SmartArt Graphic button in the Paragraph group on the HOME tab. The Choose a SmartArt Graphic dialog box is shown in Exhibit 21-15. To filter the diagram layouts shown, click a category in the list on the left.

Exhibit 21-15 Choose a SmartArt Graphic dialog box

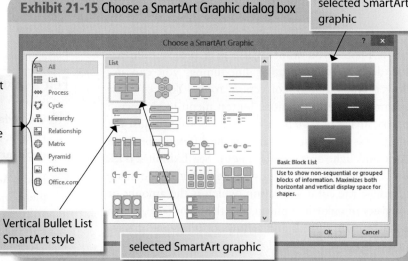

preview of the selected SmartArt graphic

click a SmartArt category to filter the list of diagrams in the center pane

Vertical Bullet List SmartArt style

selected SmartArt graphic

Create a SmartArt diagram.

1 Display **Slide 5** ("Keep Nature Natural") in the Slide pane, and then click the bulleted list.

2 On the HOME tab, in the Paragraph group, click the **Convert to SmartArt Graphic button**. A gallery of SmartArt diagram types opens.

3 Below the gallery, click **More SmartArt Graphics**. The gallery closes, and the Choose a SmartArt Graphic dialog box opens. Refer back to Exhibit 21-15.

4 In the center pane, click the **Vertical Bullet List SmartArt diagram**. A preview and description of the selected diagram appear in the right pane.

5 Click **OK**. The dialog box closes, and the bulleted list on the slide is replaced with a Vertical Bullet List SmartArt diagram with the text from the bulleted list in the diagram. The SMARTART TOOLS

> **Tip:** If there is no text on a slide, you can click the Insert SmartArt button in the content placeholder on a slide, or you can click the SmartArt button in the Illustrations group on the INSERT tab.

DESIGN tab is the active tab on the ribbon. You might see a text pane labeled Type your text here to the left of the diagram.

6 If the text pane is not visible, on the SMART-ART TOOLS DESIGN tab, in the Create Graphic group, click the **Text Pane button**. The button is selected, and the text pane appears to the left of the SmartArt diagram. Compare your screen to Exhibit 21-16. The SmartArt diagram consists of colored rectangles that contain the text from the first-level bullets in the original list with the second-level bullets from the original list below each one. The border around the diagram defines the borders of the entire Smart-Art diagram object.

End Activity

21-3b Modifying a SmartArt Diagram

A SmartArt diagram is a larger object composed of smaller objects. You can modify the diagram by adding or deleting shapes, modifying the text by changing the font format, and changing the way the shapes look. You can also modify the diagram as a whole. Exhibit 21-17 shows the SmartArt diagram after a new shape was added to it.

Exhibit 21-16 Vertical Bullet List SmartArt diagram on Slide 5

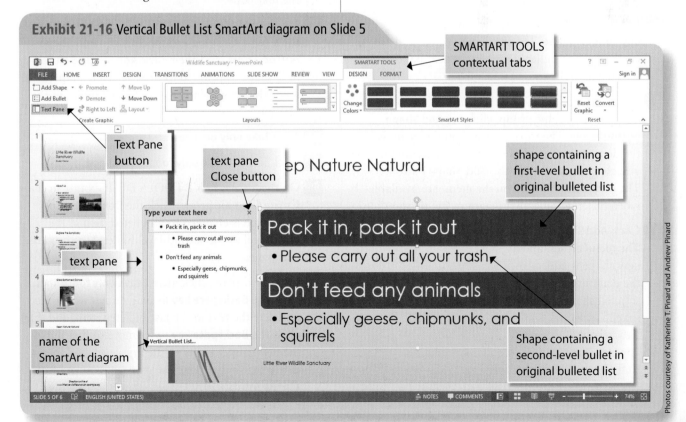

Photos courtesy of Katherine T. Pinard and Andrew Pinard

Exhibit 21-17 New shape added to the SmartArt diagram

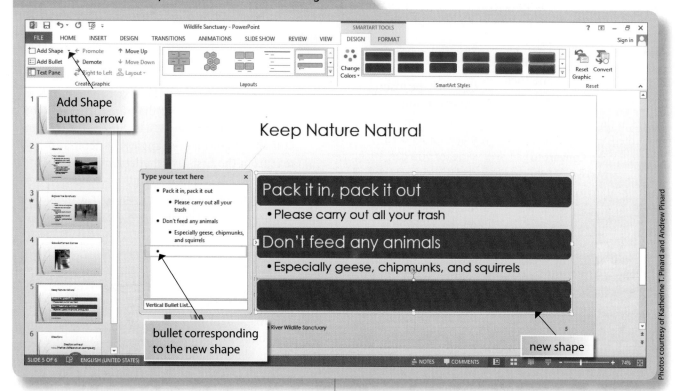

Photos courtesy of Katherine T. Pinard and Andrew Pinard

Begin Activity

Modify a SmartArt diagram.

1 In the SmartArt diagram, click the **Don't feed any animals shape**. The shape is selected, and the corresponding bulleted item in the text pane is selected as well.

2 On the SMARTART TOOLS DESIGN tab, in the Create Graphic group, click the **Add Shape button arrow**. The top command on the menu is the default command that would be executed if you clicked the icon on the Add Shape button. The commands in gray on the menu are available when different SmartArt diagrams are on the slide.

3 Click **Add Shape After**. The menu closes, and a new shape is added to the diagram below the selected shape. The new shape is selected, and a corresponding bullet appears in the text pane. Refer back to Exhibit 21-17.

> **Tip:** You can work in the text pane using the same skills you use to work with a bulleted list on a slide.

4 Type **Leave only footprints**. The text appears in the new shape and next to the corresponding bullet in the text pane.

5 On the SMARTART TOOLS DESIGN tab, in the Create Graphic group, click the **Add Shape button arrow**, and then click **Add Shape Before**. A new shape appears above the selected shape, and a new bullet appears above the last bullet in the text pane.

6 Type **Take only pictures**.

7 Click in the **Leave only footprints shape**.

8 On the SMARTART TOOLS DESIGN tab, in the Create Graphic group, click the **Demote button**. The shape is changed to a bulleted item at the same level as the second-level bulleted items in the text pane.

9 In the text pane, click after **Leave only footprints**, press the **Backspace key** as many times as needed to delete the text in the last bulleted item, and then press the **Backspace key** twice more to first move the now empty bullet to the first-level, and then delete that bullet. The last shape is removed from the diagram.

10 In the text pane or in the diagram, click after the text **Take only pictures**. Type **;** (a semicolon), press the **Spacebar**, and then type **leave only footprints**.

11 In the upper-right corner of the text pane, click the **Close button** ❌. The text pane closes.

End Activity

21-3c Formatting a SmartArt Diagram

As with any object, you can add formatting to a SmartArt diagram using the commands on the contextual SMARTART TOOLS tabs. To quickly change the colors and look of a SmartArt diagram, you can use the Change Colors button and the options in the SmartArt Styles gallery on the SMARTART TOOLS DESIGN tab. See Exhibit 21-18.

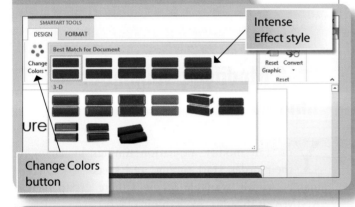

Exhibit 21-18 SmartArt gallery and Change Colors button

Begin Activity

Format a SmartArt diagram.

1 Click the **SmartArt diagram border**, if necessary, to select the SmartArt diagram.

2 On the SMARTART TOOLS DESIGN tab, in the SmartArt Styles group, click the **More button** ⤓. A gallery of styles available for the diagram opens. Refer to Exhibit 21-18.

3 In the gallery, in the Best Match for Document section, click the **Intense Effect style**. The style of the graphic changes to the one you chose.

4 In the SmartArt Styles group, click the **Change Colors button**. A gallery of color options opens.

5 In the gallery, scroll down, and then in the Accent 5 section, click the **Colored Fill – Accent 5 style**. The gallery closes, and the colors in the SmartArt diagram change to the style you selected. Compare your screen to Exhibit 21-19.

End Activity

Exhibit 21-19 Formatted SmartArt diagram

21-4 Applying Animations to Graphics

When you animated text in Chapter 20, you actually animated the text boxes, which are objects. You can animate any object on a slide, including photos, shapes, and SmartArt diagrams. Because a SmartArt diagram is composed of more than one object, when you animate a SmartArt diagram, you can change the sequence effects, similar to the sequence effects you can change for a bulleted list. However, when you animate a photo or a shape, because they are single objects, there are no sequence effects that you can change.

Begin Activity

Apply animations to graphics.

1 On **Slide 5** ("Keep Nature Natural"), click the **SmartArt diagram** to select it, if necessary. On the ribbon, click the **ANIMATIONS tab**.

2 In the Animation group, click the **Wipe animation**, which is an entrance animation. The animation previews, and the diagram wipes onto the slide from the bottom. A single animation sequence icon appears next to the SmartArt diagram.

3 In the Animation group, click the **Effect Options button**. The Wipe animation has four direction effects and five sequence effects from which you can choose.

4 Click **From Left**. The animation previews again, this time wiping the diagram in from the left.

5 Click the **Effect Options button** again. Because the SmartArt diagram is composed of multiple objects, Sequence effects are available, similar to the Sequence effects for bulleted lists.

6 Click **One by One**. Each shape in the diagram animates one at a time. Now there are five animation sequence icons next to the diagram.

7 Display **Slide 3** ("Explore the Sanctuary") in the Slide pane, and then click the bulleted list. Animation sequence icons appear next to the items in the bulleted list, and the entrance animation Fly In is selected in the Animation group on the ANIMATIONS tab.

8 Click the **photo** to select it. In the Animation group, click the **Shape button**. The animation previews and the photo fades in from the outside to the center in a circle shape. The animation sequence icon that appears next to the photo contains a 3.

9 In the Animation group, click the **Effect Options button**. The Shape animation has two types of effects you can modify—the direction from which the object will fade in and the shape of the fade. There are no Sequence effects available because the photo is a single object.

10 Under Shapes, click **Plus**. The shape fades in from the outside to the center in a plus shape.

11 In the Preview group, click the **Preview button**. The Hiking bulleted item and its subitems flies on, followed by the Canoeing item, and then the photo fades in.

End Activity

21-5 Modifying Animation Timings

You can modify animation timings by changing their order, start timing, and speed. These commands are all available in the Timing group on the ANIMATIONS tab. See Exhibit 21-20.

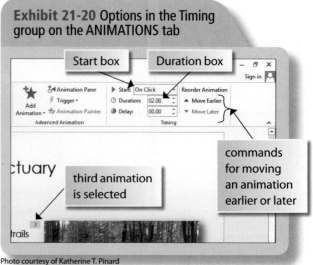

Exhibit 21-20 Options in the Timing group on the ANIMATIONS tab

Start box

Duration box

third animation is selected

commands for moving an animation earlier or later

Photo courtesy of Katherine T. Pinard

21-5a Modifying the Order of Animations

If objects on a slide do not animate in the order you want, you can change the order of the animations. To see the current order, display the slide in the Slide pane, click the ANIMATIONS tab, and then examine the numbers in the animation sequence icons. Items labeled with lower number animation sequence icons animate before items labeled with higher number animation sequence icons. To change the animation order, click the object or the animation sequence icon associated with the item whose animation order you want to change. In the Timing group on the ANIMATIONS tab, click the Move Earlier or Move Later button under the Reorder Animation label.

Begin Activity

Modify the order of animations.

1 On **Slide 3** ("Explore the Sanctuary"), click the **photo** to select it. The number 3 in the animation sequence icon indicates that this object will be the third object animated on the slide when you do something to advance the slide show.

2 In the Timing group, click the **Move Earlier button**. Refer back to Exhibit 21-20. The animation sequence number next to the photo changes to a 1, and the numbers next to the bulleted list items change to 2 and 3. Now the photo will animate first.

3 Click the **bullet symbol next to Hiking**. The first-level item and all its subitems are selected. All of the animation sequence icons next to these items are selected as well.

4 On the ANIMATIONS tab, in the Timing group, click the **Move Earlier button**. The animation sequence numbers next to the Hiking item and its subitems change to 1, and the number next to the photo changes to 2.

5 On the status bar, click the **Slide Show button** 🖥. Slide 3 appears in Slide Show view.

6 Press the **Spacebar**. The Hiking bulleted item and its subitems fly in from the left.

7 Press the **Spacebar** again. The photo of people hiking fades in.

8 Press the **Spacebar** one more time. The Canoeing bulleted item and its subitems fly in from the left.

9 Press the **Esc key** to end the slide show.

End Activity

21-5b Modifying the Start Timing of an Animation

Animations can occur when you do something to advance the slide show, or they can occur automatically. When an object animates when you advance the slide show, its start timing is set to On Click. When an object animates automatically, its start timing is set to With Previous or After Previous. When you apply an animation to a bulleted list that contains subitems, as is the case with Slide 2, the subitems animate at the same time as their first-level bullet. This is because their start timing is set to With Previous.

You can change the start timing for animations. First, select the animated bulleted item or object whose start timing you want to change, and then click the Start arrow in the Timing group on the ANIMATIONS tab to change whether an animation starts when you advance the slide show (On Click), at the same time as when the previous item animates (With Previous), or automatically after the previous item animates (After Previous).

The numbers in the animation sequence icons increase by one for each item that is set to animate On Click. When an animation is set to start With Previous or After Previous, the animation sequence number does not increase. On Slide 3 ("Explore the Sanctuary"), the Hiking first-level bulleted item is animated when you advance the slide show. The animation sequence icons next to its subitems also have a number 1 on them because their start timing is set to With Previous. The animation sequence number is the same as the first-level bulleted item because you don't need to do anything to advance the slide show to animate this item since it will animate with the previous item. If an item is labeled with an animation sequence icon containing the number 0 (zero), the default behavior was changed, and that item will animate at the same time as or immediately after the slide transitions onto the screen.

Begin Activity

Change the start timing of animations.

1 On **Slide 3** ("Explore the Sanctuary"), next to the Hiking bulleted item, click the **animation sequence icon 1**. On the ANIMATIONS tab, in the Timing group, On Click appears in the Start box, indicating that the Hiking bulleted item will animate when you do something to advance the slide show.

2 Next to the first subitem under Hiking, click the **animation sequence icon 1**. In the Start box, With Previous appears, indicating that the subitem will animate with the first-level item when you advance the slide show.

3 Click the **photo**. The animation sequence icon next to the photo contains a 2. In the Start box, On Click appears.

4 Click the **Start box arrow**, and then click **With Previous**. The animation sequence number next to the photo changes to 1, the same number as the animation sequence numbers next to the Hiking item and its subitems.

5 On the status bar, click the **Slide Show button** 🖵, and then press the **Spacebar**. The Hiking item and its subitems fly in from the left, and the photo fades in at the same time.

6 Right-click the slide, and then on the shortcut menu, click **See All Slides**. Thumbnails of all the slides appear.

7 Click the **Slide 5** ("Keep Nature Natural") **thumbnail** to display it in Slide Show view, and then press the **Spacebar** five times to display each of the five items in the diagram. Each shape wipes in one at a time.

8 Press the **Esc key** to end the slide show. The two subitems in the diagram should animate with their first-level items.

9 In the diagram, click **Please carry out all your trash**. The five animation sequence icons are all selected. To change the start timing of a single item in the list, you need to select the specific animation sequence icon connected to the item.

10 Click the **animation sequence icon 2**. In the Timing group, click the **Start box arrow**, and then click **With Previous**. The animation sequence icon associated with the Please carry out all your trash subitem changes to a 1 to indicate that it will animate at the same time as the other item numbered 1. The two animation sequence icons numbered 1 are stacked one on top of each other.

11 Click the **animation sequence icon 3**. In the Timing group, click the **Start box arrow**, and then click **With Previous**.

12 On the status bar, click the **Slide Show button** 🖵. Slide 5 appears in Slide Show view.

13 Press the **Spacebar**. The first shape and its subitem wipe onto the screen.

14 Press the **Spacebar** again to animate the second first-level shape and its subitem.

15 Press the **Spacebar** a third time to display the last shape.

16 Press the **Esc key** to end the slide show.

End Activity

21-5c Changing the Speed of Animations

You can adjust the speed of animations. To change the speed of an animation, you change the time in the Duration box in the Timing group on the ANIMATIONS tab. To make an animation go faster, decrease the time in the Duration box; to make it go slower, increase the time.

Begin Activity

Change the speed of animations.

1 Display **Slide 3** ("Explore the Sanctuary") in the Slide pane, and then click the **photo** to select it.

2 On the ANIMATIONS tab, in the Timing group, click the **Duration down arrow** four times. The Shape animation applied to the photo will now take one second to complete instead of two.

3 On the status bar, click the **Slide Show button** 🖵, and then press the **Spacebar**. The photo fades in more quickly than before.

4 End the slide show.

End Activity

LEARN MORE

Changing the Speed of Transitions

A Duration box appears in the Timing group on the TRANSITIONS tab to allow you to change the speed of transitions in the same way you change the duration of an animation. As with animations, you decrease the value in the Duration box to make the transition faster, and increase the value to slow it down.

21-6 Adding Video

You can insert digital video in slides or in slide masters. PowerPoint supports various file formats, but the most commonly used are the MPEG-4 format, the Windows Media Audio/Video format, and the Audio Visual Interleave format, which appears in Explorer windows as the Video Clip file type. After you insert a video, you can modify it by changing the length of time the video plays, changing playback options, and applying formats and styles.

21-6a Inserting a Video on a Slide

You can insert a video clip in two different ways. You can use the Video button in the Media group on the INSERT tab, or you can click the Insert Video button in a content placeholder to display the Insert Video dialog box, shown in Exhibit 21-21. You can choose to insert a video from a file or from the Web. When you insert video from the Web, you can search for a video using the Bing search engine, or, if you have the embed code from a Web site such as YouTube, you can paste the embed code in the From a Video Embed Code box.

Exhibit 21-21 Insert Video dialog box

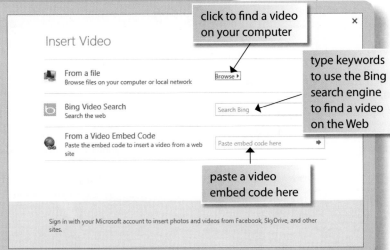

Begin Activity

Insert a video on a slide.

1 Display **Slide 4** ("Glass-Bottomed Canoe") in the Slide pane.

2 In the content placeholder on the right, click the **Insert Video button**. The Insert Video dialog box opens.

3 Next to From a file, click **Browse**. Another Insert Video dialog box opens. This dialog box is similar to the Open and Save As dialog boxes.

Tip: You can also click the Video button arrow in the Media group on the INSERT tab, and then click Video on My PC to open the Insert Video dialog box.

4 Click the movie data file **Canoe Video** located in the Chapter 21\Chapter folder, and then click **Insert**. The movie is inserted in place of the content placeholder. The VIDEO TOOLS contextual tabs appear on the ribbon, and the VIDEO TOOLS FORMAT tab is the active tab. Compare your screen to Exhibit 21-22.

5 On the play bar below the movie, click the **Play button** ▶, and then watch the video, which is approximately 23 seconds long. Note that this video has no sound.

End Activity

21-6b Formatting a Video

Videos can be formatted just like pictures. For example, you can crop the sides of a video or resize it by dragging the sizing handles. Be careful if you resize a video; you want to maintain the aspect ratio so you don't distort the image. You can also apply a style or special effects to a video.

Begin Activity

Format a video.

1 On **Slide 4** ("Glass-Bottomed Canoe"), if necessary, click the **video** to select it, and then click the **VIDEO TOOLS FORMAT tab**.

2 In the Size group, click the **Crop button**. Crop the black area from the top, bottom, and sides of the video, and then in the Size group, click the **Crop button** to deselect it.

3 Drag the **upper-left-corner sizing handle** up and to the left until the left edge of the video is touching the right edge of the photo.

Exhibit 21-22 Video inserted on Slide 4

4 Drag the **video** down and right to center it in the area to the right of the photo.

5 On the VIDEO TOOLS FORMAT tab, in the Video Styles group, click the **Video Effects button**.

6 On the menu, point to **Reflection**. In the Reflection Variations section, click the **Half Reflection, touching style**. A reflection appears below the video. Compare your screen to Exhibit 21-23.

7 On the play bar below the movie, click the **Play button** ▶. The video plays in the reflection as well as in the main video window.

End Activity

21-6c Trimming a Video

If a video is too long, or if it contains parts you don't want to show during the slide show, you can trim the clip from within PowerPoint. To do this, click the Trim Video button in the Editing group on the VIDEO TOOLS PLAYBACK tab to open the Trim Video dialog box. See Exhibit 21-24. Drag the green and red sliders to indicate where you want the video to start and stop.

Exhibit 21-23 Cropped, resized video with a reflection style applied

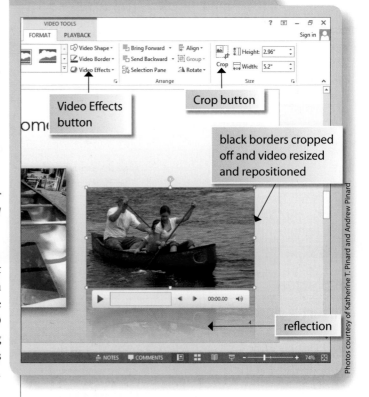

Exhibit 21-24 Trim Video dialog box

Photo courtesy of Katherine T. Pinard

drag the green Start Time slider to specify the point at which the video will start playing

drag the red End Time slider to specify the point at which the video will stop playing

Begin Activity

Trim a video.

1 On **Slide 4** ("Glass-Bottomed Canoe"), if necessary, click the **video** to select it, and then click the **VIDEO TOOLS PLAYBACK tab**.

2 In the Editing group, click the **Trim Video button**. The Trim Video dialog box opens. Refer back to Exhibit 21-24.

3 On the bar below the video, drag the **green Start Time slider** to the right to approximately the 8-second mark. The time in the Start Time box changes to match the time point where you dragged the slider. The video will now start playing at this point.

4 Drag the **red End Time slider** to the left to approximately the 19.5-second mark. The time in the End Time box changes to match the time point where you dragged the slider. The video will stop playing at this point.

5 Click **OK**. You can watch the trimmed video in Normal view.

6 On the play bar, click the **Play button** ▶. The trimmed video—now about 11.5 seconds long—plays.

End Activity

21-6d Changing Video Playback Options

You can change several options for how a video plays. For example, you can set a video to play automatically when the slide appears during a slide show or wait until you click the video's play button. You can also set a video to loop continuously until the next slide is displayed or to fill the screen while it is playing, covering the other objects on the slide. Video playback options are described in Exhibit 21-25, and the Video Options group on the VIDEO TOOLS PLAYBACK tab is shown in Exhibit 21-26.

Exhibit 21-25 Video playback options

Video Option	Function
Volume	Change the volume of the video from high to medium or low or mute it.
Start	Change how the video starts, either when the presenter advances the slide show (On Click) or automatically when the slide appears during the slide show.
Play Full Screen	When selected, the video fills the screen during the slide show.
Hide While Not Playing	When selected, the video does not appear on the slide when it is not playing; make sure the video is set to play automatically if this option is selected.
Loop until Stopped	When selected, the video will play continuously until the next slide appears during the slide show.
Rewind after Playing	When selected, the video will rewind after it plays so that the first frame or the poster frame appears again.

© 2014 Cengage Learning

Exhibit 21-26 Video Options group on the VIDEO TOOLS PLAYBACK tab

VIDEO TOOLS PLAYBACK tab

Start box

select to rewind after playing

Fade settings

Video Options group

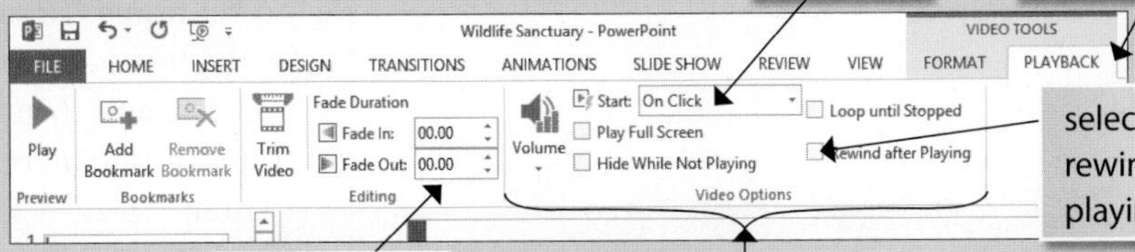

Change video playback options.

1 On **Slide 4** ("Glass-Bottomed Canoe"), if necessary, click the **video** to select it.

2 Click the **VIDEO TOOLS PLAYBACK tab**. Refer back to Exhibit 21-26.

3 In the Video Options group, click the **Rewind after Playing check box** to select it. Now the video will rewind to the beginning after playing in the slide show.

4 In the Video Options group, click the **Start box arrow**, and then click **Automatically**. Now the video will play automatically when the slide is displayed during a slide show.

5 On the status bar, click the **Slide Show button** 🖵. Slide 4 appears in Slide Show view, and the video plays. The way the video started and stopped is a little bit abrupt.

6 End the slide show.

7 On the VIDEO TOOLS PLAYBACK tab, in the Editing group, click the **Fade In box up arrow** twice and then click the **Fade Out box up arrow** twice to change the values in both boxes to **00.50**, or one-half second.

8 Play the slide show from the current slide. Now there is a brief, one-half second fade at the start and end of the video.

9 Press the **Esc key** to end the slide show.

End Activity

> **Tip:** To play the movie so that it fills the entire screen, select the Play Full Screen check box in the Video Options group on the VIDEO TOOLS PLAYBACK tab.

LEARN MORE

Changing the Video Volume

You can also set the volume options for video. To do this, click the Volume button in the Video Options group on the VIDEO TOOLS PLAYBACK tab to select from Low, Medium, High, or Mute. You can make more precise adjustments using the Volume control on the right end of the video's play bar.

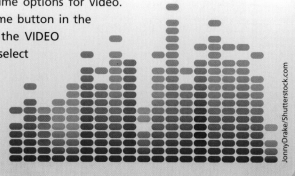

JonnyDrake/Shutterstock.com

FYI

Understanding Video and Audio Animation Effects

When you insert video and audio clips, media animation effects are applied to the clip automatically, and the Start setting of these animation effects (shown on the ANIMATIONS tab) is tied to the Start setting of the media clip (shown on the VIDEO TOOLS or AUDIO TOOLS PLAYBACK tab). When you insert a media clip, the default Start setting is On Click. A Play animation is also automatically applied to the clip, and it too is set to start On Click. If you insert audio or video on a slide that contains other animations, and the animations and media do not play as you expect during a slide show, remember to check the ANIMATIONS tab to see if the Play animation settings are in conflict with the settings on the PLAYBACK tab.

21-6e Setting a Poster Frame

A **poster frame**, sometimes called a **preview frame**, is the image that appears before the video starts playing. The default poster frame for a video is the first frame of the video. You can change this so that any frame from the video or any image stored in a file is the poster frame. To set the poster frame to a specific frame in the video, click the playbar at the point the frame appears, and then click the Poster Frame button in the Adjust group on the VIDEO TOOLS FORMAT tab. See Exhibit 21-27. Click Current Frame to set the poster frame to the currently displayed frame.

Exhibit 21-27 Setting a poster frame

Begin Activity

Set the poster frame for a video.

1 On **Slide 4** ("Glass-Bottomed Canoe"), click the **video** to select it, if necessary.

2 On the ribbon, click the **VIDEO TOOLS FORMAT tab**.

3 In the Slide pane, point to the play bar so that you see a ScreenTip identifying the time at the point where the pointer is positioned.

4 Move the pointer until it is at approximately the 4-second mark, and then click. The gray indicator in the play bar moves back to the 4-second mark.

5 On the ribbon, click the **VIDEO TOOLS FORMAT tab**. In the Adjust group, click the **Poster Frame button**. A menu opens.

6 On the menu, click **Current Frame**. The menu closes, and a note appears in the play bar indicating that this will be the poster frame.

7 On the status bar, click the **Slide Show button**. Slide 4 appears in Slide Show view, and the video plays. When the video is finished, it rewinds and displays the poster frame again.

8 Press the **Esc key** to end the slide show.

End Activity

LEARN MORE

Adding a Sound Clip to a Slide

To add a sound clip to a slide, use the Audio button in the Media group on the INSERT tab. You can add audio from a file on your computer, search for an audio clip on Office.com, or record new audio. When you add an audio clip, a sound icon appears in the middle of the slide with a play bar below it. The options for changing how the sound plays during the slide show appear on the AUDIO TOOLS PLAYBACK tab. In addition, the Audio Styles group contains the Play in Background button. When you select this, the Play Across Slides, Loop until Stopped, and Rewind after Playing check boxes in the Audio Options group become selected. The audio clip will play continuously as you display the rest of the slides in the presentation.

mikeledray/Shutterstock.com

Photos courtesy of Katherine T. Pinard and Andrew Pinard

21-7 Compressing Pictures and Media

When you save a presentation that contains photos, PowerPoint automatically compresses the photos to a resolution of 220 pixels per inch (ppi). (For comparison, photos printed in magazines are typically 300 ppi.) Compressing photos reduces the size of the presentation file, although it also reduces the quality of the photos. To change the compression settings, select a photo, and then in the Adjust group on the PICTURE TOOLS FORMAT tab, click the Compress Pictures button to open the Compress Pictures dialog box. See Exhibit 21-28.

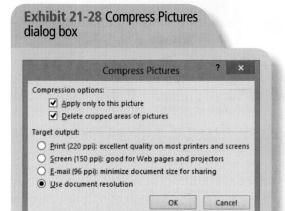

Exhibit 21-28 Compress Pictures dialog box

If you insert additional photos or crop a photo after you apply the new compression settings to all the slides, you will need to apply the new settings to the new photos. Photo compression is not permanent until you close the file. This means if you compress photos to a lower resolution and then change your mind and want to decompress them to the default resolution, you can do this as long as you have not closed the file. Once the compression settings are permanently applied, you cannot change your mind because the extra information has been discarded.

Begin Activity

Modify the compression of pictures.

1 On **Slide 4** ("Glass-Bottomed Canoe"), click the **photo** to select it.

2 On the ribbon, click the **PICTURE TOOLS FORMAT tab.**

3 In the Adjust group, click the **Compress Pictures button.** The Compress Pictures dialog box opens. Refer back to Exhibit 21-28.

4 Click the **E-mail (96 ppi) option button.** This setting compresses the photos to the smallest possible size. At the top of the dialog box under Compression options, the Delete cropped areas of pictures check box is already selected. This option is not applied to cropped photos until you open this dialog box and then click the OK button to apply it. To make the presentation file size as small as possible, leave this selected. The Apply only to this picture check box is also selected; to apply the settings to all the photos in the file, you need to deselect it.

5 Click the **Apply only to this picture check box** to deselect it.

6 Click the **OK button.** The dialog box closes, and the compression settings are applied to all the photos in the presentation.

End Activity

FYI

Keeping Photos Uncompressed

Suppose you are a photographer and want to create a presentation to show your photos. In that case, you would want to display them at their original, uncompressed resolution. To do this, you need to change a setting in the PowerPoint Options dialog box before you add photos to slides. Click the FILE tab to open Backstage view, click Options in the navigation bar to open the PowerPoint Options dialog box, click Advanced in the navigation bar, and then locate the Image Size and Quality section. To keep images at their original resolution, click the Do not compress images in file check box to select it. Note that you can also change the default compression setting for photos in this dialog box—you can increase the compression or choose to automatically discard cropped portions of photos. These changes affect only the current presentation.

As with pictures, you can compress media files. If you need to send a file via email or you need to upload it, you should compress media files to make the final PowerPoint file smaller. To do this, click the FILE tab to display the Info screen in Backstage view, and then click the Compress Media button. See Exhibit 21-29.

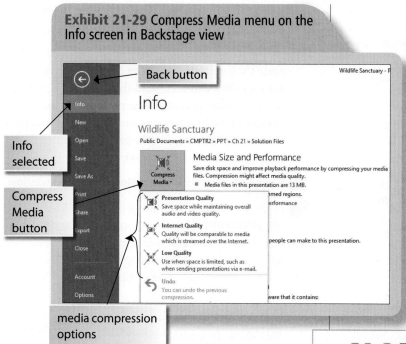

Exhibit 21-29 Compress Media menu on the Info screen in Backstage view

Back button

Wildlife Sanctuary - P

Info

Info selected

Info

Wildlife Sanctuary

Public Documents » CMPTR2 » PPT » Ch 21 » Solution Files

Compress Media button

Compress Media ▾

Media Size and Performance

Save disk space and improve playback performance by compressing your media files. Compression might affect media quality.
■ Media files in this presentation are 13 MB.

...med regions.

Presentation Quality
Save space while maintaining overall audio and video quality.

...performance

Internet Quality
Quality will be comparable to media which is streamed over the Internet.

...people can make to this presentation.

Low Quality
Use when space is limited, such as when sending presentations via e-mail.

Undo
You can undo the previous compression.

...ware that it contains:

media compression options

The more you compress files, the smaller the final presentation file will be, but also the lower the quality. When you compress videos, any parts of videos that you trimmed off will be deleted, similar to deleting the cropped portions of photos.

Begin Activity

Compress media.

1 Click the **FILE tab**. Backstage view appears, displaying the Info screen.

2 Click the **Compress Media button**. A menu opens listing your compression choices. Refer back to Exhibit 21-29.

3 Click **Low Quality**. The menu closes, and a dialog box opens listing the video file in the presentation, with a progress bar appearing next to it in the Status column to show you the progress of the compression. After the file is compressed, the progress bar is replaced by a message indicating that compression for the file is complete and stating how much the video file size was reduced. The

Tip: If the Info screen in Backstage view contains an Optimize Media button as well as the Compress Media button, click the Optimize Media button first to prevent any potential problems playing the video on the slide.

Cancel button at the bottom changes to the Close button.

4 Click the **Close button**. Next to the Compress Media button on the Info screen, the bulleted list tells you that the presentation's media was compressed to Low Quality and that you can undo the compression if the results are unsatisfactory.

5 At the top of the navigation bar, click the **Back button** ⬅. Slide 4 ("Glass-Bottomed Canoe") appears in the Slide pane.

6 Save the presentation.

End Activity

21-8 Presenting Online

You can broadcast a presentation over the Internet, and anyone with the URL for the presentation and a browser can watch it. When you present online, you send the presentation to a special Microsoft server that is made available for this purpose. (If you have access to a SharePoint server, you can send the presentation to that server instead.) To start an online presentation, click the Present Online button in the Start Slide Show group on the SLIDE SHOW tab. After clicking CONNECT in the dialog box that appears, a unique Web address is created. This Web address is displayed in a dialog box, as shown in Exhibit 21-30. The dialog box contains commands

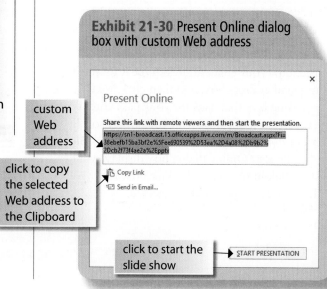

Exhibit 21-30 Present Online dialog box with custom Web address

Present Online

Share this link with remote viewers and then start the presentation.

custom Web address

https://sn1-broadcast.15.officeapps.live.com/m/Broadcast.aspx?Fi=8Bebefb15ba3bf2e%5Fee690539%2D53ea%2D4a08%2Db9b2%2Dcb2f73f4ae2a%2Epptx

click to copy the selected Web address to the Clipboard

Copy Link

Send in Email...

click to start the slide show

START PRESENTATION

for you to copy the Web address or to start your email program and send the address via email. While you run your presentation on your computer in Slide Show view, remote audience members can view it on their computers in a Web browser at the same time using the Web address that you provide.

To use this feature, you need a Microsoft ID (or access to a SharePoint server), and you need to be connected to the Internet.

Note: You must have a Microsoft ID to complete the Activities in this section. If you don't have a Microsoft ID, go to www.skydrive.com, and then click Sign up, click the Sign in link in the upper-right corner of the PowerPoint window, or refer to the first Learn More box in Chapter 7.

Begin Activity

Start a broadcast.

1 On the ribbon, click the **SLIDE SHOW tab**. In the Start Slide Show group, click the **Present Online button**. The Present Online dialog box opens.

2 Click **CONNECT**. The dialog box changes to show that you are connecting to Office Presentation Services.

> **Problem?** A warning might appear in the dialog box stating that the media needs to be optimized. You can ignore the warning for this set of steps.

If you are not signed in to PowerPoint with a Microsoft ID, the next dialog box that opens asks for your email address. You need to enter the email address associated with your Microsoft ID. If you are signed in to PowerPoint with your Microsoft ID, the next dialog box displays your custom link—in this case, skip Step 3.

3 If asked for your email address, type it in the Type your email address box, and then click **Next**. In the next dialog box that asks for your password, type the password associated with your Microsoft ID account in the Password box, and then click **Sign In**. The Present Online dialog box displays your custom link in the Share this link box. Refer back to Exhibit 21-30. The link is selected.

4 Click **Copy Link**. The link is copied to the Clipboard.

5 Start your email program or log in to your Web-based email service, create a new message, and then paste the copied link into the body of the email message. You can then send the link to people you want to invite to your online presentation. If anyone clicks the link before you start the presentation, the message *Waiting for the presentation to begin...* will appear in the browser window.

6 Switch back to the **PowerPoint application window**.

7 In the Present Online dialog box, click **START PRESENTATION**. The dialog box closes, and the slide show starts and begins broadcasting. Anyone who clicked the link you copied and sent will see your slides as you advance through the slide show.

8 Press the **Esc key** to end the slide show. The slide show appears in Normal view with the PRESENT ONLINE tab selected on the ribbon. Although the slide show ended, the online presentation has not.

9 On the PRESENT ONLINE tab, in the Present Online group, click the **End Online Presentation button**. A dialog box opens, warning that everyone viewing this presentation will be disconnected.

> **Tip:** If you need to invite people after closing the Present Online dialog box that contains the custom Web address, click the Send Invitations button in the Present Online group on the PRESENT ONLINE tab to reopen it.

10 In the dialog box, click **End Online Presentation** to confirm that you want to end the online presentation. The dialog box closes, and the PRESENT ONLINE tab is removed from the ribbon. The last slide displayed during the broadcast disappears from the browser window of anyone still watching the broadcast, and the message *The presentation has ended.* appears in its place.

11 Close the presentation.

End Activity

Saving a Presentation for Distribution

PowerPoint lets you save presentations in several formats that allow others to view the presentation but does not allow them to make any changes to it. Each method produces a different type of file for you to distribute. Before distributing a presentation, you should consider checking it for hidden or private information. To do this, click the Check for Issues button on the Info tab in Backstage view, and then click Inspect Document.

▶ **Video**—you can save a presentation as a video in the MPEG-4 format. After you have created the video, you can play it in Windows Media Player or any other video player. To save the presentation as a video, click Export in the navigation tab in Backstage view, and then click Create a Video.

▶ **Picture Presentation**—you can save a presentation as a picture presentation, which saves each slide as an image file in the JPEG format and then places that image on a slide in a new presentation so that it fills the entire slide. This format prevents other people from modifying it or copying complex animations, backgrounds, or other features. To save a presentation as a picture presentation, on the Export screen in Backstage view, click Change File Type, and then click PowerPoint Picture Presentation under Presentation File Types.

▶ **Individual Image Files**—you can save slides as individual image files. To do this, on the Export screen in Backstage view, click Change File Type, and then click PNG Portable Network Graphics or JPEG File Interchange Format under Image File Types. You can save only the current slide or all the slides.

▶ **PowerPoint Show**—you can save a presentation as a PowerPoint Show file, which causes the presentation to open only in Slide Show view. To save a presentation as a PowerPoint Show, on the Export screen in Backstage view, click Change File Type, and then click PowerPoint Show under Presentation Files Types.

▶ **Portable Document Format (PDF)**—you can save a presentation as a PDF file and then open it using Adobe's free Reader software. When you save a presentation as a PDF file, each slide becomes a page in the PDF file. To do this, on the Export screen in Backstage view, click Create PDF/XPS Document.

▶ **Package Presentation for CD**—you can package a presentation for CD, which saves all the files needed to run the presentation in a folder or to a CD. If you package a presentation to a CD, when the CD is inserted in the computer and starts running, the user is offered the opportunity to download Viewer, a free program that allows you to run a slide show but not edit it. You can also search the Microsoft Web site for this program and install it on any computer that does not already have PowerPoint installed on it. To package a presentation for CD, on the Export screen in Backstage view, click Package Presentation for CD.

Quiz Yourself

1. What is the difference between the theme Slide Master and a layout master?

2. Describe the two ways you can add a picture stored in a file on your computer to a slide.

3. How do you add a shape to a slide?

4. How do you add text to a shape on a slide?

5. What is a diagram?

6. Describe how to convert a bulleted list into a SmartArt diagram.

7. How do you modify animation effects?

8. How do you modify an animation so that it starts automatically at the same time as the previous animation?

9. How do you change the speed of an animation?

10. What happens during playback when you add a reflection effect to a video?

11. How do you shorten a video's playback?

12. What is a poster frame?

13. How do you increase the compression of all the photos in a presentation?

14. What happens when you present a presentation online?

Practice It

Practice It 21-1

1. Open the data file **Geese** located in the Chapter 21\Practice It folder. Save the presentation as **Geese Problem**.

2. Switch to Slide Master view.

3. Display the Wood Type Slide Master in the Slide pane.

4. In the lower-right corner, delete the blue circle. (*Hint:* Click near the top of the circle so that the selection border that appears is taller than the Date placeholder to the left.)

5. Select the Slide Number placeholder (in the same position as the blue circle was, to the right of the Date placeholder), the Date placeholder, and the

Footer placeholder. Change the font color of the text in all three placeholders to Black, Text 1.

6. Increase the font size of the text in the content placeholder so that the text of the first-level bulleted item is 24 points. (Make sure the rest of the text increases in size as well.) Click the second-level bullet to select all of the subitem text, and then change the color of the subitems to Black, Text 1, Lighter 25%.

7. On the Two Content Layout master, increase the font size of the first-level bulleted items in both content placeholders to 24 points. (Make sure the rest of the text increases in size as well.)

8. On the Title Slide Layout master, delete the blue circle.

9. Apply the Style 2 background style to all the slides.

10. On the Wood Type Slide Master, draw a Bevel shape (in the Basic Shapes section of the Shapes gallery) in the upper-right corner of the slide about one-half inch high and 3.5 inches wide. Type **Macon Road Neighborhood Association** in the bevel shape. Change the font size of the text to 12 points, and then resize the shape so it is 0.3 inches high and 3.5 inches wide. Position the shape so there is about one-eight inch between its top and right edges and the top and right edges of the slide.

11. Apply the Light 1 Outline, Colored Fill – Black, Dark 1 shape style to the bevel shape.

12. Position the Slide Number placeholder below the bevel shape. Use the smart guides to align the top of the Slide Number placeholder with the top of the title text placeholder and the right edge of the Slide Number placeholder with the right edge of the bevel shape.

13. Close Slide Master view.

14. Display Slide 5 ("Possible Solutions") in the Slide pane. In place of the content placeholder on the right, insert the picture data file **Barrier** located in the Chapter 21\Practice It folder. Apply the Simple Frame, White style to the picture, and then sharpen the photo by 50%.

15. Display Slide 6 ("West Bend River: Alternative Nesting Site"). In place of the content placeholder on the right, insert the picture data file **Geese**

Photo located in the Chapter 21\Practice It folder. Apply the Simple Frame, White style to the picture, increase the color saturation by 200%, and increase the contrast by 20%.

16. Display Slide 4 ("Causes") in the Slide pane. Convert the bulleted list on the slide to the Converging Radial SmartArt diagram (located in the Relationship category).

17. Add a new shape after the People feed shape in the SmartArt diagram. Add the words **Cut grass** to the shape.

18. Change the colors of the diagram to the Dark 1 Outline style (in the Primary Theme Colors section on the Change Colors menu). Change the style of the SmartArt diagram to the Cartoon style.

19. Animate the SmartArt diagram with the Fade entrance animation. Change the Sequence effect to One by One, and change the duration to one-half second.

20. On Slide 5 ("Possible Solutions"), animate the photo with the Split entrance animation and the Vertical Out effect. Change the order of the animations on Slide 5 so that the photo is the second item to animate.

21. Change the Start timing of the photo animation to With Previous so it animates with the Build shoreline barriers item.

22. Display Slide 3 ("Listen!") in the Slide pane. Insert the video data file **Geese Video** located in the Chapter 21\Practice It folder.

23. Crop the black borders of the sides of the video. Apply the Half Reflection, 4 pt offset reflection style to the video.

24. Set the video to rewind after playing.

25. Trim the video so it ends at approximately the 8-second mark.

26. Use the frame at approximately the 4.5-second mark as the poster frame.

27. Compress all the photos in the presentation to 96 ppi. Compress the media using the Low Quality setting.

28. On Slide 1, add your name in the line below the word by in the subtitle. Save the presentation.

29. Broadcast the presentation, and then close it.

Practice It 21-2

1. Open the data file **Round Lake** located in the Chapter 21\Practice It folder. Save the file as **Round Lake Resort**.

2. On the Ion Slide Master, make the following modifications:

   a. Modify the title text so the text is bold.

   b. Change the width of the title text placeholder so it is the same width as the content placeholder.

   c. Delete the green rectangle shape below the Slide Number placeholder.

   d. Change the font size of the text in the content placeholder so the text in the first-level bulleted item is 28 points and the text in the fifth-level bulleted item is 18 points.

3. On the Title Slide Layout master, modify the title text placeholder so that the text size is 66 points.

4. On the Two Content Layout master, modify both content placeholders so the text in the first-level bulleted item is 24 points and the text in the fifth-level bulleted item is 16 points.

5. In Normal view, add your name as the subtitle on Slide 1.

6. On Slide 2 ("Why Build at Round Lake?"), insert the video data file **Lake** located in the Chapter 21\ Practice It folder.

7. Crop the black edges from the video. Change the size of the video so it is four inches high, maintaining the aspect ratio, and then position the video so it is centered in the area to the right of the bulleted list and its top edge is aligned with the top edge of the bulleted list.

8. Trim the video so that it starts at approximately the 4-second mark and ends at the 18-second mark.

9. Set the video to start automatically, and then set a one-half-second fade.

10. Change the volume of the video to Low. Set the video to loop until stopped and to rewind after playing.

11. Apply the Beveled Perspective Left video style to the video.

12. On Slide 2, insert a rectangle shape below the video that is the same width as the video and about one-quarter-inch high.

13. Add the text **Property Today** to the rectangle.

14. Format the rectangle using the Subtle Effect – Lime, Accent 1 shape style.

15. On Slide 4 ("Benefits"), insert an online picture of a photo of canoes and chairs near water or an attractive lake and trees. Adjust the sharpness, brightness and contrast, saturation, and tone of the photo. Apply the Bevel Perspective Left, White effect to the picture. Use a command on the Picture Border button menu to remove the border.

16. On Slide 5 ("Plan"), convert the bulleted list to a Basic Bending Process SmartArt diagram.

17. After the Submit proposal to council shape, add a new shape containing the text **Begin lake cleanup**.

18. Change the color of the SmartArt diagram to Colored Outline – Accent 4 (in the Accent 4 section). Change the style to the Moderate Effect SmartArt style.

19. Animate the SmartArt diagram with the Lighten emphasis animation. Modify the SmartArt animation so that the shapes lighten one by one, and then change the speed of the SmartArt animations to one-quarter second.

20. On Slide 6 ("Round Lake Resort"), insert the picture data file **Logo** located in the Chapter 21\ Practice It folder. Resize the logo so it is 3.5 inches high, maintaining the aspect ratio. Center the logo in the space in the center of the slide.

21. Compress all the photos in the presentation to 96 ppi. Compress the media to Low Quality. Save the presentation.

22. Broadcast the presentation, and then close it.

On Your Own

On Your Own 21-1

1. Open the data file **Landmarks** located in the Chapter 21\On Your Own folder. Save the file as **Landmarks Quiz**.

2. Add the following as a footer on all slides except the title slide: **Click the correct answer.** (including the period).

3. On the Banded Slide Master, drag the left-middle sizing handle to the right to change the width of the title text placeholder to approximately 9.5 inches wide, keeping the right edge of the title text placeholder aligned with the right edge of the content placeholder. Change the font size of the text in the Footer placeholder to 28 points, and format it as bold.

4. On the Banded Slide Master, change the size of the Footer placeholder box to 1.65 inches high and 1.75 inches wide. Position the Footer placeholder box so it is centered between the left edge of the title text placeholder and the left edge of the slide. Change the alignment of the text in the Footer placeholder so that it is left-aligned. (*Hint*: Use the Align Left button in the Paragraph group on the HOME tab.)

5. On the Two Content Layout master, change the font size of the text in the content placeholder on the left so that the size of the text in the first-level bulleted items is 28 points and the size of the text in the fifth-level bulleted items is 20 points.

6. In the content placeholders on Slides 2, 3, and 4, use the Online Picture button in the content placeholders to insert photos of the following from Office.com:

   - Slide 2 ("Question 1"): the Arc de Triomphe

   - Slide 3 ("Question 2"): a single statue on Easter Island

   - Slide 4 ("Question 3"): the Parthenon

7. On Slides 2, 3, and 4, resize the photos, maintaining the aspect ratio, so they are no more than four inches wide and as tall as possible so that they still fit in the gray area of the slide. Position them so that the top edge of each is aligned with the top edge of the bulleted list on the slide and the right edge is aligned with the right edge of the title text box. Apply the Drop Shadow Rectangle style to each photo.

8. On Slides 2, 3, and 4, change the second, third, and fourth bullet symbols to a lettered list from A to C, and remove the bullet symbol from the first bulleted item.

9. On Slide 2 ("Question 1"), draw a rectangle, and then resize it to 1.5 inches high and 1.3 inches wide. Center this rectangle between the second lettered item and the photo. Use the Shape Outline button to remove its outline, and then use the Shape Fill button to fill it with the Lime, Accent 2 color.

10. Copy the rectangle to the Clipboard. Paste copies of the rectangle to the right of the first and third lettered items. The three rectangles should align vertically in the space between the text and the photo.

11. Select all three rectangles, and then copy them to Slides 3 and 4. On both slides, position the rectangles to the right of each lettered list item.

12. On Slide 2, add the text **Incorrect** to the first two rectangles, and then add the text **Correct** to the third rectangle. Change the font size of the text in all three rectangles to 20 points, and format it as bold.

13. On Slide 3, add the text **Correct** to the middle rectangle, and then add the text **Incorrect** to the top and bottom rectangles. Format the text in the rectangles to match the formatting of the text in the rectangles on Slide 2.

14. On Slide 4, add the text **Correct** to the bottom rectangle, and then add the text **Incorrect** to the top two rectangles. Make the text in all three rectangles bold.

15. On Slide 4, draw another rectangle, and then resize it so it is .6 inches high and 1.4 inches wide. Change its outline to No Outline. Leave its fill as yellow.

16. Position the yellow rectangle so it is on top of one of the green rectangles, hiding it completely. Copy the yellow rectangle to the Clipboard, and then paste the copied rectangle twice. Position the copied rectangles on top of the other two green rectangles on the slide.

17. Select the three yellow rectangles, and then apply the exit animation Wipe. (Make sure you choose the Wipe animation in the Exit section, not in the Entrance section.) Change the direction of the animation to From Top.

18. Copy the selected three rectangles to the Clipboard. Display Slide 3 in the Slide pane, paste the copied rectangles, and then position the pasted rectangles on top of the three green rectangles. Do the same on Slide 2.

19. On Slide 2, draw a Rounded Rectangle approximately 1.5 inches high and 4.5 inches wide on top of the letter A and the first item in the lettered list. Draw another Rounded Rectangle approximately one inch high and 4.5 inches wide on top of the letter B and the second item in the lettered list, and then draw a third Rounded Rectangle on top of the letter C and the third item in the lettered list.

20. On Slide 2, select the top yellow rectangle. On the ANIMATIONS tab, set the Rounded Rectangle surrounding the first lettered item as the trigger for this animation. (*Hint*: Use the Trigger button in the Advanced Animation group on the ANIMATIONS tab. Select the Rounded Rectangle with the lowest number in the list.) Set the Rounded Rectangle surrounding the second lettered item as the trigger for the middle yellow rectangle. (Select the Rounded Rectangle with the second lowest number in the list.) Set the Rounded Rectangle surrounding the third lettered item as the trigger for the bottom yellow rectangle. (Select the Rounded Rectangle with the highest number in the list.)

21. Click the yellow rectangle to the right of the first lettered item. Use the Shape Fill command to fill it with the same color as the slide background. (*Hint*: Use the Eyedropper command.)

22. With the rectangle still selected, use the Format Painter to copy its formatting to the other two yellow rectangles on the slide.

23. Right-click the top Rounded Rectangle, and then click Format Shape to open the Format Shape task pane. In the task pane, click FILL. Change the Transparency to 100%. In the task pane, click LINE, and then change the outline to No line.

24. With the transparent Rounded Rectangle still selected, use the Format Painter to copy its formatting to the other two Rounded Rectangles on the slide.

25. On Slides 3 and 4, repeat Steps 21 through 24 to change the fill of the yellow rectangles to the same color as the slide background and to create transparent rectangles on the lettered items that serve as triggers for the animations applied to the green rectangles.

26. On Slide 5 ("Presented by"), draw a rectangle large enough to cover *Click the correct answer.* to the left of the slide title. Change its fill and outline so you cannot see the rectangle.

27. On Slide 5, add your name as a bulleted item, and then save the presentation.

28. Run the presentation in Slide Show view. On Slides 2, 3, and 4, click each lettered item to see the answers. Close the presentation when you're finished.

Chapter 21

ADDITIONAL STUDY TOOLS

IN THE BOOK

▶ Complete end-of-chapter exercises

▶ Study tear-out Chapter Review Card

ONLINE

▶ Complete additional end-of-chapter exercises

▶ Take practice quiz to prepare for tests

▶ Review key term flash cards (online, printable, and audio)

▶ Play "Beat the Clock" and "Memory" to quiz yourself

▶ Watch the videos to learn more about the topics taught in this chapter

Answers to Quiz Yourself

1. The theme Slide Master is the primary slide master for a presentation. A layout master is a slide master for a specific layout in a presentation.

2. To add a picture stored in a file on your computer to a slide, you can use the Pictures button in a content placeholder, or you can use the Pictures command in the Images group on the INSERT tab.

3. To add a shape to a slide, select the shape on the Shapes button menu, and then drag on the slide.

4. To add text to a shape, select the shape, and then type.

5. A diagram is an illustration that visually depicts information or ideas and shows how they are connected.

6. To covert a bulleted list to a SmartArt diagram, select a bulleted list, and then click the Convert to SmartArt button in the Paragraph group on the HOME tab.

7. To modify animation effects, select the animated object, click the Effect Options button in the Animation group on the ANIMATIONS tab, and then select the effect you want to change.

8. To modify an animation so that it starts automatically at the same time as the previous animation, change the Start setting to With Previous.

9. To change the speed of an animation, increase the value in the Duration box in the Timing group on the ANIMATIONS tab to slow down the animation, or decrease the value in the Duration box to speed up the animation.

10. When a reflection effect is applied to a video, the video plays in the reflection during playback.

11. To shorten a video's playback, use the Trim Video command.

12. A poster frame is the image that appears in a video object before the video starts playing.

13. To increase the compression of photos in a presentation, select a photo, click the Compress Pictures button in the Adjust group on the PICTURE TOOLS FORMAT tab, and then select the new compression setting in the dialog box that opens; to apply the new settings to all the photos in the presentation, deselect the check box that specifies the settings will be applied only to the selected picture.

14. When you present a presentation online, the presentation is sent to a special Microsoft server, and a unique Web address is created. People who have the Web address can watch the presentation in their browser windows as you run the slide show.

PowerPoint: Prepare a Presentation

1. Plan a presentation about a topic of your choosing. For example, you can create a presentation to train others how to do a job; convey information about a person, place, or thing; influence others to buy or do something; or create a slide show of photographs around a specific topic, event, or person. Develop the basic outline of the presentation, and decide what content will go on each slide.

2. Create a new PowerPoint presentation, and apply an appropriate theme. Make sure you choose a theme that is relevant to your presentation and intended audience.

3. On Slide 1, add an appropriate title for the presentation. Add your name as a subtitle.

4. On the theme Slide Master, add a digital image that is related or relevant to the presentation you are creating.

5. Look at each layout master, and make sure the digital image is appropriately placed on it. If not, remove the digital image from the theme Slide Master, and then add it and position it appropriately on each layout master.

6. Create a presentation based on your plan.

7. Where needed, create bulleted lists to provide details or information about the topic.

8. Add clip art or graphics to illustrate your points. Use at least one SmartArt diagram. (*Hint*: Examine the diagrams in the Picture category.)

9. On at least one slide, insert a shape, such as a rectangle, triangle, circle, arrow, or star.

10. If appropriate, add video and audio clips. Trim the clips as needed, and set appropriate playback and formatting options.

11. On at least one slide, do not use a bulleted list; use only an image, clip art, a video, SmartArt, or another graphic element, with animation if appropriate. Make sure the effect during the slide show conveys your planned spoken message.

12. Examine the presentation outline. Are you using too many words? Can any of your bulleted lists be replaced with a graphic?

13. Re-evaluate the theme you chose. Do you think it is still appropriate? Does it fit the content of the presentation? If not, apply a different theme, or modify the colors or fonts.

14. Add appropriate transitions and animations. Remember that the goal is to keep audience members engaged without distracting them.

15. Check the spelling, including contextual spelling, of the presentation, and then proofread it.

16. Rehearse the presentation. Consider your appearance, and decide on appropriate clothing to wear. Practice in front of a mirror and friends or family. If possible, create a video of yourself giving the presentation. Notice and fine-tune your body language, tone of voice, and fluency to fully engage your audience.

Working with the PowerPoint Web App

As with the Word and Excel Web Apps, you can use the PowerPoint Web App to view or edit PowerPoint presentations stored on a SkyDrive account. When you open a presentation in the PowerPoint Web App in View mode, it appears in the browser window similar to the way it looks in Reading view. See Exhibit 1. If you use the buttons on the navigation bar, when you scroll through the presentation, you will see the presentation as it appears in Slide Show view with a few exceptions. Some transitions and animations are not supported and video clips might be distorted.

Exhibit 1 Presentation in View mode in the PowerPoint Web App

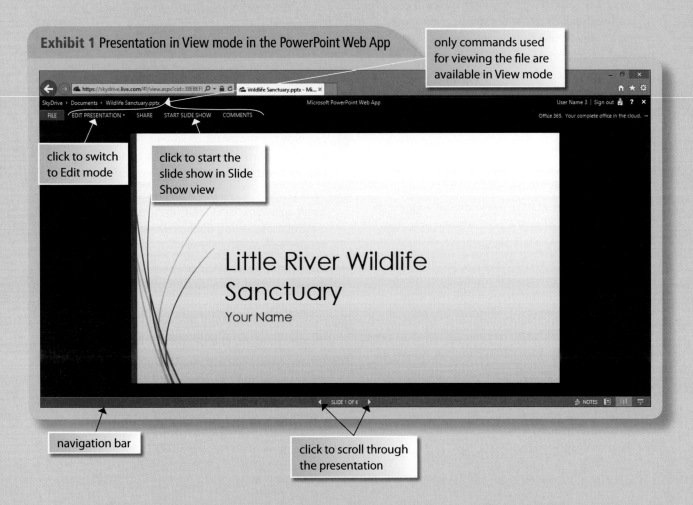

If you open a presentation in the PowerPoint Web App in Edit mode, you can add and delete slides; format text; insert pictures, clip art, and SmartArt; and create hyperlinks. See Exhibit 2. You can only insert objects on slides that contain an empty content placeholder.

From both View mode and Edit mode, you can switch to Slide Show view. (Note that if your pop-up blocker is set to block most pop-ups, you might need to allow pop-ups from the Windows Live Web site.) See Exhibit 3. As you can see, Slide Show view in the PowerPoint Web App looks very similar to the way a presentation looks in a browser window during a broadcast. The same limitations apply in this view as for a broadcast. However, as with Edit mode, if your presentation contains audio clips, the presentation might not display at all in Slide Show view. Note that in Slide Show view in the PowerPoint Web App, you can click the mouse button or press the appropriate keys to advance the slide show, but you cannot right-click to access the shortcut menu. Also, the Slide Show toolbar contains only the Next Slide and Previous Slide buttons.

Exhibit 2 Presentation in Edit mode in the PowerPoint Web App

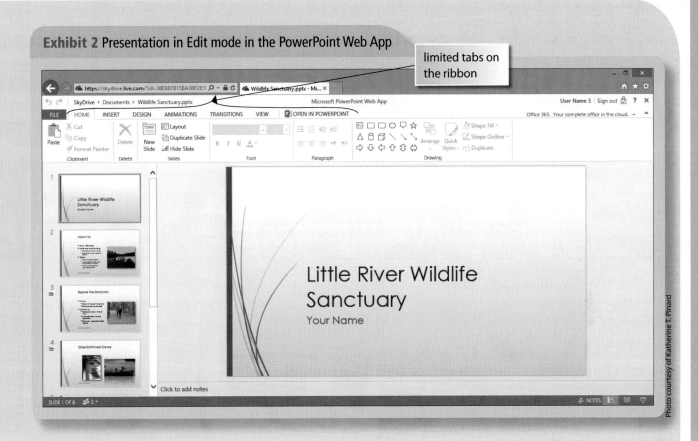

Exhibit 3 Presentation in Slide Show view in the PowerPoint Web App

Photo courtesy of Katherine T. Pinard

Integrating Word, Excel, Access, and PowerPoint

EDHAR/Shutterstock.com

Collaboration and teamwork have become the norm. Individuals are often asked to prepare or focus on a specific aspect of a project, report, or event. They research, create, and analyze the information, and then develop the related files needed for the final product. In many cases, they use one type of application to create the documents. The different files are then integrated to create an in-depth and complete product, with each part of the file having been created in the program that best fits that data. This process allows each person to use his or her expertise and as a team create a stronger, better final product.

The integration capabilities of Microsoft Office allow team members to share files and data easily. In addition to copying and pasting among different programs, you can embed a file of one type in a file of another type; link files so that when the original file changes, the changes appear in the file linked to it; and import and export data from one file format to another.

Microsoft product screenshots used with permission from Microsoft Corporation.

Learning Objectives

After studying the material in this chapter, you will be able to:

22-1 Understand object linking and embedding (OLE)

22-2 Import and export data

22-3 Use the Object command to insert text from a file

22-4 Copy and paste among Office programs

22-5 Create PowerPoint slides from a Word outline

22-6 Create form letters with mail merge

22-1 Object Linking and Embedding

Office 2013 supports **object linking and embedding** (**OLE**), a way of transferring and sharing objects between programs. Remember that an object is anything that can be manipulated as a whole; in other words, it is the specific information that you want to share between programs and can be anything from a chart or a table to a picture, video, sound clip, or almost anything else you can create on a computer. The program used to create the object you want to integrate into another program is the **source program**; the file that initially contains the object is the **source file**. The program used to create the file where you want to insert the object is called the **destination program**; the file where you want to insert the object is called the **destination file**.

The ability to integrate Microsoft Office documents allows people to share info and create complex docs even if they're not in the same location, an important consideration in our global society.

When you **embed** an object, a copy of the object along with a link to the source program become part of the destination file, and you can edit the object using the source program's commands. There is no connection between an embedded object and its source file, which means that changes made to the object in the source file do not appear in the destination file. You must have access to the source program to edit an embedded object; you do not need access to the source file.

When you **link** an object, a direct connection is created between the source and destination files. The object exists in only one place—the source file—but the link displays the object in the destination file as well. You must have access to the source file if you want to make changes to the linked source object. If you edit a linked object in the source file, the link ensures that the changes appear in the destination file. If you edit a linked object in the destination file, the changes do not appear in the source file. The next time the link is updated, the changes made in the destination file will be overwritten with the linked data from the source file.

Both linking and embedding involve inserting an object into a destination file; the difference lies in where their respective objects are stored. The advantage of embedding an object instead of linking it is that the source file and the destination file can be stored separately. You can use the source program commands to make changes to the object in the destination file, and the source file will be unaffected. The disadvantage is that the destination file size is somewhat larger than it would be if the object was simply pasted as a picture or text, or if it was linked. The advantage of linking an object instead of embedding it is that the object remains identical in the source and destination files, and the destination file size does not increase as much as if the object were embedded. The disadvantage is that the source and destination files must be stored together. When you need to copy information from one program to another, consider which option is the best choice for your needs.

Exhibit 22-1 illustrates the difference between linking and embedding. Exhibit 22-2 summarizes embedding and linking and compares their advantages and disadvantages.

object linking and embedding (OLE) A way of transferring and sharing objects between programs.

source program The program used to create an object.

source file The file that contains an object that you want to integrate into another file.

destination program The program used to create the file where you want to insert an object created in a different file.

destination file The file into which you want to insert an object created in another file.

embed To copy an object along with a link to the source program in a destination file.

link To establish a direct connection between a source file and a destination file.

Exhibit 22-1 Embedding contrasted with linking

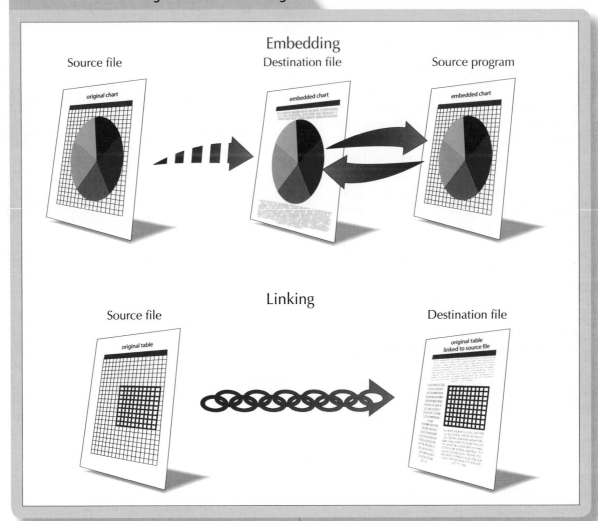

Embedding

Source file   Destination file   Source program

original chart   embedded chart   embedded chart

Linking

Source file   Destination file

original table   original table linked to source file

Exhibit 22-2 Comparing integration methods

	Embedding	**Linking**
Description	Displays and stores an object in the destination file.	Displays an object in the destination file along with the source file's location; stores the object in the source file.
Use if you want to	Include the object in the destination file, and edit the object using the source program without affecting the source file.	Edit the object in the source file and have the changes appear in the destination file.
Advantages	The source file and destination file can be stored separately. You can use source program commands to make changes to the object in the destination file.	The destination file size remains fairly small. The source file and the object in the destination file remain identical.
Disadvantages	The destination file size increases to reflect the addition of the object from the source file.	The source and destination files must be stored together.

Sharing Information

Dmitriy Shironosov/Shutterstock.com

Most organizations rely heavily on teams to complete work tasks. Consequently, team members rely on each other to complete their assigned projects successfully. For example, you might be responsible for providing data for others to analyze, or for collecting other team members' data and creating a report. When a team works together to complete a project, each member of the team must complete his or her part of the project. If even one person fails to do this, the entire project is affected. Learning the different roles team members play, how they complement each other for efficient task completion, and how to lead and motivate a team toward goal achievement can mean the difference between professional success and failure. As you work in different Microsoft Office programs, keep in mind that you might need to share your work with others on your team, at school, or in a professional environment. Take the time to make sure your work is complete and ready to be shared with others, and that it can be imported or exported, as needed, for use in other programs.

22-1a Creating an Embedded Excel Chart in Word or PowerPoint

If you want to embed a chart in a Word document or PowerPoint slide, and the chart or the data to create it does not already exist in a separate Excel file, you can create the chart from within the Word or PowerPoint file. To do this, in either program, click the Chart button in the Illustrations group on the INSERT tab to open the Insert Chart dialog box. After you select the type of chart you want to create, a spreadsheet with sample data opens, and a chart based on the sample data and the chart style you selected appears in the document or slide.

Begin Activity

Create an embedded chart in a Word document.

1 Open the Word data file **EcoBrochure** located in the Chapter 22\Chapter folder. Save the document as **EcoFlooring Brochure**.

2 At the bottom of page 1, after *Prepared by:*, type your name. If necessary, change the zoom to **120%**.

3 On page 2, delete the **yellow highlighted text**. The insertion point is in the now empty paragraph.

4 On the ribbon, click the **INSERT tab**. In the Illustrations group, click the **Chart button**. The Insert Chart dialog box opens. Column is selected in the list of chart types.

5 Click **OK**. The dialog box closes, a column chart with sample data appears in the document and a spreadsheet with sample data appears above it. Colored borders appear around the cells that are included in the chart. Compare your screen to Exhibit 22-3.

> **Tip:** You can also create an embedded chart in a PowerPoint slide using the Chart button in the Illustrations group on the INSERT tab, or by clicking the Insert Chart button in a Content placeholder.

End Activity

Once you insert the chart, you can modify the sample data in the spreadsheet so that it contains your data. The chart will adjust as you edit the spreadsheet.

Exhibit 22-3 Spreadsheet and column chart with sample data in Word window

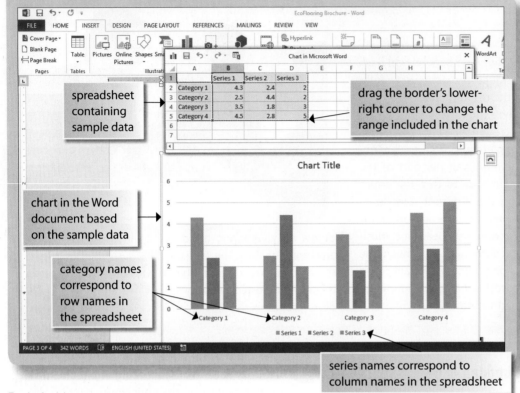

spreadsheet containing sample data

chart in the Word document based on the sample data

category names correspond to row names in the spreadsheet

drag the border's lower-right corner to change the range included in the chart

series names correspond to column names in the spreadsheet

Begin Activity

Modify data in a spreadsheet.

1 In the spreadsheet, click **cell A2**, type **Ash** and then press the **Down Arrow key**. The text you type replaces the place-holder text in the cell and below the first set of columns in the chart in the Word window.

2 In **cell A3**, type **Bamboo**, and then press the **Down Arrow key**.

3 In **cell A4**, type **Beech**, and then press the **Down Arrow key**.

4 In **cell A5**, type **Cherry birch**, and then press the **Down Arrow key**. Cell A6, which doesn't contain placeholder text, is selected.

5 In **cell A6**, type **Hevea**, and then press the **Down Arrow key**. The colored borders in the spreadsheet expand to row 6, and a new label is added to the

Tip: If the data on which a chart will be based exists in an Excel worksheet, you can copy the data to the Excel worksheet that opens when you click the Chart button in the Word or PowerPoint file.

6 In the **range A7:A10**, type the following:

Kempas
Maple
Oak
Walnut

7 In the Chart in Microsoft Word window, click **cell B2**, type **3.8** and then press the **Enter key**. The first green column in the chart shortens to the 3.8 mark.

8 In the **range B3:B10**, enter the following values:

6.1
3.1
3.1
4.3
5.6
2.9
4.2
3.6

9 In the spreadsheet, drag the **lower-right blue border corner** to the left two columns so that the blue border surrounds the range B2:B10. The blue and yellow columns in the chart in the Word window disappear.

10 In the spreadsheet, click the **Close button** ☒. The spreadsheet closes. In the Word document, the chart is selected, and the CHART TOOLS DESIGN tab is selected.

11 To the right of the chart, click the **Chart Elements button** ➕, and then click the **Legend check box** to deselect it. The legend is removed from the chart.

12 In the chart, click the **Series 1 title**, and then type **Janka Rating for Common Woods** as the new title. Compare your screen to Exhibit 22-4.

13 Save the document.

End Activity

Exhibit 22-4 Completed column chart in Word document

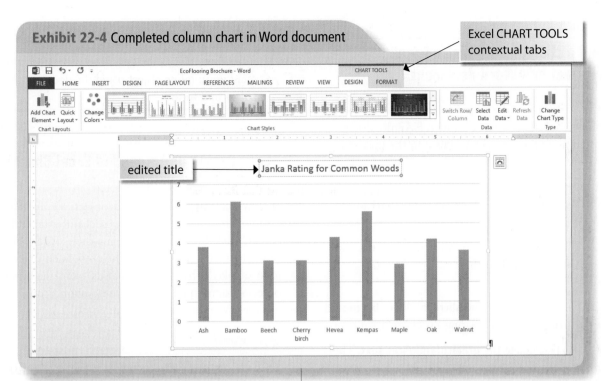

Excel CHART TOOLS contextual tabs

edited title → Janka Rating for Common Woods

22-1b Embedding a Chart Created in an Excel Worksheet in Word or PowerPoint

If a chart already exists in an Excel worksheet, you can copy it from there and then embed it in the document or slide. You can then use Excel commands to modify the chart from within the document or slide. Your changes, however, will not appear in the original file.

Remember that when you use the Paste command, you have access to several options to paste the object in different ways. If you click the Paste button arrow instead of clicking the Paste button, a menu with Paste Options buttons appears. You can point to each button to see a Live Preview of the pasted object. Exhibit 22-5 shows the Live Preview when a chart is on the Clipboard and you are pointing to the Use Destination Theme & Embed Workbook button. For most objects, you can choose whether to keep the source file formatting or use the destination

file formatting. For some objects, such as pasting an Excel chart into a Word document, you can also choose to embed or link the object or paste it as a picture. Remember, if you click the Paste button, you can change the way an object is pasted by clicking the Paste Options button that appears below and to the right of the pasted object to access the same menu of options.

Exhibit 22-5 Paste button menu with Paste Options and Live Preview of the chart

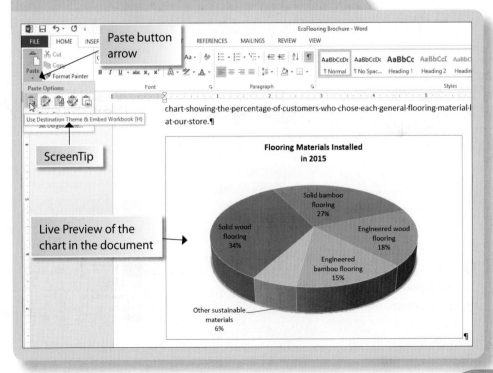

Paste button arrow

ScreenTip

Live Preview of the chart in the document

Embed a chart created in an Excel worksheet in a Word document.

1 Open the Excel data file **EcoMaterials** located in the Chapter 22\Chapter folder. Save the document as **EcoFlooring Materials**. On the taskbar, a Microsoft Excel button ⊞ appears next to the Microsoft Word button.

2 In the Excel worksheet, click the **pie chart** to select it.

3 On the HOME tab, in the Clipboard group, click the **Copy button**. The chart is copied to the Clipboard.

4 On the taskbar, click the **Microsoft Word button** 🗗 to return to the EcoFlooring Brochure document.

5 On page 2, delete the **green highlighted text**. The insertion point is in the now empty paragraph.

6 On the HOME tab, in the Clipboard group, click the **Paste button arrow**. A menu of Paste options appears.

7 In the Paste button menu, point to the **Use Destination Theme & Embed Workbook button** 🗐 (the first button). The chart appears in the document at the insertion point using the theme colors and fonts in the Word document file. Refer back to Exhibit 22-5. This is the default option.

> **Tip:** The same options appear on the Paste button arrow in the PowerPoint window when an Excel chart has been copied to the Clipboard.

8 In the Paste button menu, point to the **Keep Source Formatting & Embed Workbook button** 🗐 (the second button). The chart changes to use the theme colors and fonts from the source file.

> **Tip:** To change the default paste option, click Set Default Paste on the Paste menu, and then make your selections in the Cut, copy, and paste section of the Advanced page of the Word Options dialog box that opens.

9 In the Paste button menu, point to the other three buttons, noting the change in the chart in the document and

reading their ScreenTips, and then click the **Use Destination Theme & Embed Workbook button** 🗐 (the first button). The chart is pasted in the document as an inline object using the document theme colors and fonts.

22-1c Editing an Embedded Excel Chart in Word or PowerPoint

When you edit an embedded object within the destination program, the changes affect only the embedded object; the original object in the source program remains unchanged. To edit the embedded object, click it to display tabs and commands from the embedded object's source program on the ribbon. You can then use these to modify the embedded object.

Edit an embedded chart in a Word document.

1 In the Word document, click the **embedded pie chart**. The selection box and handles appear around the chart object, and the Excel CHART TOOLS contextual tabs appear on the Word ribbon.

2 On the HOME tab, in the Paragraph group, click the **Center button** ☰. The paragraph containing the inline chart object is formatted so it is centered horizontally.

3 To the right of the pie chart, click the **Chart Styles button** 🖌, and then click the **Style 6 style**.

4 In the Chart Styles menu, click the **COLOR tab**. Under Monochromatic, click the **Color 5 color scheme**. The colors used in the pie chart are changed to shades of green instead of shades of yellow.

5 On the ribbon, click the **CHART TOOLS DESIGN tab**. In the Data group, click the **Edit Data button**. The spreadsheet for the embedded pie chart appears above the chart.

6 In the spreadsheet, in **cell B5**, change the value to **31**. In **cell B6**, change the value to **30**. The chart in the Word document changes to reflect the new data.

7 In the spreadsheet, click the **Close button** ☒. The spreadsheet closes.

8 Switch to the **Excel window**. Notice the values in cells B5 and B6 in the EcoFlooring Materials workbook are unchanged.

9 Close the **EcoFlooring Materials workbook**.

10 In the **EcoFlooring Brochure document**, switch to **One Page view**, and then scroll through the document.

11 Save the document, and then close it.

End Activity

22-1d Linking an Excel Chart to a Word Document or PowerPoint Presentation

If a chart exists in an Excel worksheet and you think you might update it in the future, you can link it to a Word document or PowerPoint slide instead of embedding it. Then when you modify the Excel file, the changes will appear in the destination file. To link an Excel chart to a Word document or PowerPoint presentation, copy the chart in the Excel file, and then use one of the Link buttons on the Paste button menu. You must leave the Excel workbook open while you paste, or the Paste button menu will offer only options to embed the chart or paste it as an image.

Begin Activity

Link an Excel worksheet to a PowerPoint presentation.

1 Open the PowerPoint data file **EcoPresentation** located in the Chapter 22\Chapter folder. Save the presentation as **EcoFlooring Presentation**.

2 On the title slide, add your name as the subtitle.

3 Open the Excel workbook **EcoGrowth** located in the Chapter 22\Chapter folder. Save the workbook as **EcoFlooring Growth**.

4 Select the **column chart**, and then copy it to the Clipboard.

5 Switch to the PowerPoint presentation **EcoFlooring Presentation**, and then display **Slide 2** ("Growth Chart") in the Slide pane.

6 On the HOME tab, in the Clipboard group, click the **Paste button arrow**. The same buttons that appeared when you embedded the Excel chart in the Word document appear.

7 Click the **Use Destination Theme & Link Data button**. The chart object is pasted into the slide and is linked to the Excel workbook.

8 Resize the **chart** to fill the space below the slide title. Compare your screen to Exhibit 22-6.

End Activity

LEARN MORE

Embedding Excel Worksheet Data in Word and PowerPoint

When you copy worksheet data, the first two buttons on the Paste button menu are Keep Source Formatting and Use Destination Styles. Selecting either of these two buttons pastes the data as an ordinary table. The table is not embedded; it was converted to a Word or PowerPoint table. You can then format the table using the usual methods. If you want to embed worksheet data in either a Word document or a PowerPoint slide instead of pasting it as a table or linking it to the Excel worksheet, you need to use the Paste Special command. To do this, click the Paste button arrow, and then click Paste Special to open the Paste Special dialog box. With the Paste option button selected, click Microsoft Excel Worksheet Object in the As list, and then click OK. The table is placed into the document or the slide with a selection box and sizing handles around it. You cannot edit the data in an embedded table as you do an ordinary Word or PowerPoint table. Instead, you double-click the embedded table to access Excel editing commands. When you double-click the embedded table, instead of the worksheet appearing in a separate Excel window, a copy of the entire workbook from which you copied the table appears within a dashed line border and the Excel ribbon tabs completely replace the Word or PowerPoint ribbon tabs.

Paste Special dialog box

Exhibit 22-6 Linked Excel chart in a PowerPoint slide

Excel CHART TOOLS contextual tabs

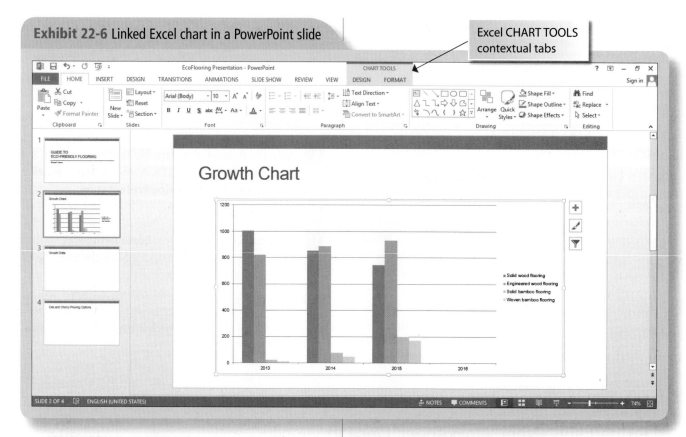

22-1e Linking Excel Worksheet Data to Word or PowerPoint

When you copy Excel worksheet data and then click the Paste button arrow in a Word document, two of the buttons on the menu are Link commands. However, if you use these buttons to link data from cells in an Excel worksheet to a Word document, the link will not always be maintained after you close the Word document. When you copy Excel worksheet data and then click the Paste button arrow in a PowerPoint presentation, none of the buttons on the menu are Link commands. To create a stable link in a Word document or to create a link in a PowerPoint slide, you need to use the Paste Special command to open the Paste Special dialog box. In the Paste Special dialog box, click the Paste link option button. The As list changes to include link options including Microsoft Excel Worksheet Object, as shown in Exhibit 22-7. Then, just like with a linked chart, you can edit the source file, and the edits will appear in the destination file.

Exhibit 22-7 Paste Special dialog box with Paste link options

Paste link option button

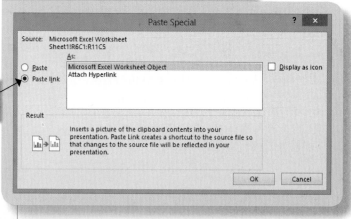

Begin Activity

Link Excel worksheet data to a PowerPoint slide.

1 Switch to the Excel workbook **EcoFlooring Growth**.

2 Select the **range A6:E11**, and then copy it to the Clipboard.

3 Switch to the PowerPoint presentation **EcoFlooring Presentation**, and then display **Slide 3** ("Growth Data") in the Slide pane.

4 On the HOME tab, in the Clipboard group, click the **Paste button arrow**. Point to each Paste Options button, watching the worksheet change on the slide and reading the ScreenTip. The set of buttons on the Paste button menu are different than the sets of Paste buttons you have seen until now. None of the buttons on the Paste button menu allow you to link the worksheet data.

5 On the menu, click **Paste Special**. The Paste Special dialog box opens. The Paste option button is selected, and a list of format options for the copied worksheet data appears.

> **Tip:** With the Paste option button selected, keep Microsoft Excel Worksheet Object selected in the As list to embed the worksheet in the slide.

6 Click the **Paste link option button**. Microsoft Excel Worksheet Object appears in the As list. Refer back to Exhibit 22-7.

7 In the As list, click **Microsoft Excel Worksheet Object**, and then click **OK**. The dialog box closes, and the worksheet data appears on the slide.

8 Resize the **worksheet object** to fill the space below the slide title. Compare your screen to Exhibit 22-8.

End Activity

22-1f Updating Linked Objects When the Destination File Is Open

When an object is linked from a source file to a destination file, you can edit the information in the source file, and the changes will appear in the destination file. If both files are open, the changes appear instantaneously. Sometimes linked data does not automatically update, even if both files are open. If the linked object is a chart, you can click the Refresh Data button in the Data group on the CHART TOOLS DESIGN tab. If the linked object is a worksheet, right-click the linked object in the destination file to open a shortcut menu, and then click Update Link.

Begin Activity

Update linked objects.

1 In the PowerPoint presentation, display **Slide 2** ("Growth Chart") in the Slide pane, and then select the **linked chart**.

Exhibit 22-8 Linked Excel worksheet data on a PowerPoint slide

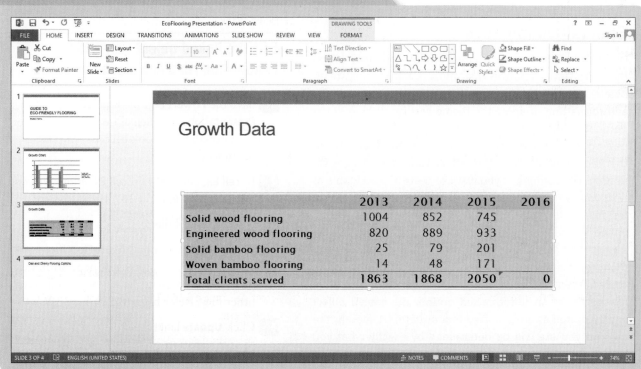

2 On the ribbon, click the **CHART TOOLS DESIGN tab**. In the Data group, click the **Edit Data button**. The original worksheet from which you copied the data, EcoFlooring Growth, becomes the active window.

3 In the Excel window, click **cell E7**, type **613** and then press the **Enter key**. A bar is added to the chart in the Excel worksheet.

4 Switch to the **Power-Point window**. The new bar containing the data on solid wood flooring for 2016 was added to the chart on Slide 2.

5 Display **Slide 3** ("Growth Data") in the Slide pane. The value you typed in the source file appears in the table on Slide 3.

> **Problem?** If the chart did not update, click the **chart** in the slide, and then on the CHART TOOLS DESIGN tab, in the Data group, click the **Refresh Data button**.

> **Problem?** If the table did not update, right-click the **table**, and then on the shortcut menu, click **Update Link**.

End Activity

Paste Options vs. the Paste Special Dialog Box

Using one of the buttons on the Paste button menu (or on the Paste Options button that appears after you paste an object) allows you to choose to keep the source file theme and formatting or apply the theme and formatting in the destination file, in addition to letting you choose between pasting, embedding, and linking. Using the commands in the Paste Special dialog box offers additional choices for pasting. For example, if you want to paste an Excel table as text, you can choose to paste it as formatted or unformatted text; and if you want to paste a table or chart as an image, you can choose from a few additional file types. You cannot, however, choose to use the source or destination theme formatting. If you choose a formatted option, the copied object will be pasted with the source file formatting; if you choose an unformatted option, the copied object will be pasted as unformatted text or data. Ultimately, the method you use will be determined by exactly what you want to appear in your destination document.

22-1g Updating Linked Objects When the Destination File Is Closed

When you link objects to a file, they are set to update automatically or manually. When you open a destination file that contains a linked object that is set to update automatically, a dialog box opens asking if you want to update the linked data. See Exhibit 22-9. If the linked object is set to be updated manually, no dialog box appears when you open the file, but you can refresh the data or update the link.

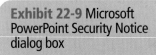

Exhibit 22-9 Microsoft PowerPoint Security Notice dialog box

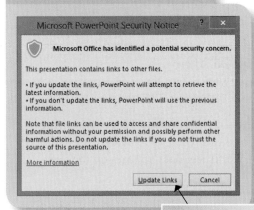

click to update data in the destination file with new data from the source file

Begin Activity

Edit the linked object when the destination files are closed.

1 Save the PowerPoint file **EcoFlooring Presentation**, and then close it. The EcoFlooring Growth workbook becomes the active document.

2 In **cell E8**, enter **974**, in **cell E9**, enter **279**, and then in **cell E10**, enter **387**.

3 Save the Excel file.

4 Open the PowerPoint file **EcoFlooring Presentation**. A dialog box opens notifying you that the presentation contains links to other files. Refer back to Exhibit 22-9.

5 Click **Update Links**. The dialog box closes and the presentation opens.

6 Display **Slide 3** ("Growth Data") in the Slide pane. The worksheet data is updated with the new values.

7 Display **Slide 2** ("Growth Chart") in the Slide pane. The new columns do not appear above the 2016 label in the chart.

8 Click the **chart** to select it. On the ribbon, click the **CHART TOOLS DESIGN tab**. In the Data group, click the **Refresh Data button**. Three bars are added to the 2016 data. Compare your screen to Exhibit 22-10.

9 Save the **EcoFlooring Presentation file**.

10 Close the Excel workbook **EcoFlooring Growth**.

> **Problem?** If the table did not update, right-click the **table**, and then on the shortcut menu, click **Update Link**.

End Activity

Exhibit 22-10 Updated linked chart in the PowerPoint presentation

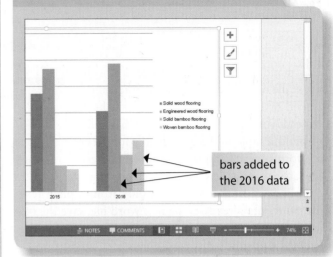

bars added to the 2016 data

Using the Links Dialog Box

By default, linked objects are supposed to update automatically; however, sometimes this is not the case. To see if a link is set to update automatically or manually, you can open the Links dialog box. To do this, click the FILE tab in the destination file to display the Info screen in Backstage view. At the bottom on the right, in the Related Documents section, click the Edit Links to Files link. The Links dialog box opens listing all the links in the file. To change the update setting for a link, click the appropriate setting at the bottom of the dialog box.

You can also use the Links dialog box to change the location of a linked object's source file. For example, if you send a file containing a linked object to a colleague, you need to send the source file as well if you want your colleague to have the ability to edit the linked object and have changes appear in both the destination and the source files. Your colleague likely will not have the same folder structure as you do and, therefore, will need to identify the new location (that is, the file path) of the source file. To do this, in the list of links in the Links dialog box, click the link whose location has changed, click Change Source, and then navigate to the new location of the source file.

Finally, you can break a link in the Links dialog box. This is a good idea if you plan to send the file to someone who will not have access to the linked object's source file. After you break a link, users who open the destination file will not get a message asking if they want to update the links—an impossible task if the users do not have access to the source file. To break a link, select the link in the list in the dialog box, and then click Break Link.

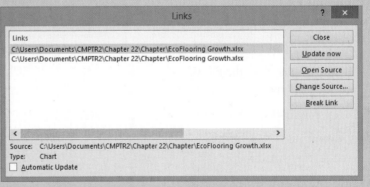

Links dialog box in PowerPoint

22-2 Importing and Exporting Data

You might want to use Access commands to analyze data stored in a list in a text file or an Excel worksheet. You cannot embed or link data in an Access datasheet. Instead, you can import data from these files to build a table in Access. Then, you can create forms, reports, queries, and other Access objects based on the tables. You cannot import data directly from a Word file, only from a plain text file. So if data already exists in a Word file, save the file as a plain text file using the Save as type arrow in the Save As dialog box.

22-2a Importing an Excel List into an Access Table

You can only import data that is in the form of a list—a series of paragraphs or worksheet rows that contain related data, such as product names and prices or client names and phone numbers. Before you import the list, you should check the format of the data. The first row of data will become the field names in the new table, so it is important that every column have a heading. Each row of data becomes a record in the database, so there should not be any rows above the column heads and there should not be any blank rows.

Begin Activity

Import an Excel list to a table in a new database.

1 Open the Excel data file **EcoTypes**, located in the Chapter 22\ Chapter folder. Save the file as **EcoFlooring Types**.

2 Delete **rows 1–4**.

3 In **cell A1**, enter **Species**. Compare your screen to Exhibit 22-11.

4 Save and close the file.

End Activity

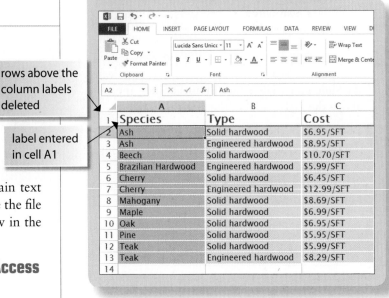

Exhibit 22-11 Worksheet prepped to import into Access

rows above the column labels deleted

label entered in cell A1

Once you have prepared the worksheet, you can start Access and import the data into an existing table or to a new table. To do this, you click the Excel button in the Import & Link group on the EXTERNAL DATA tab to open the Get External Data – Excel Spreadsheet dialog box. See Exhibit 22-12.

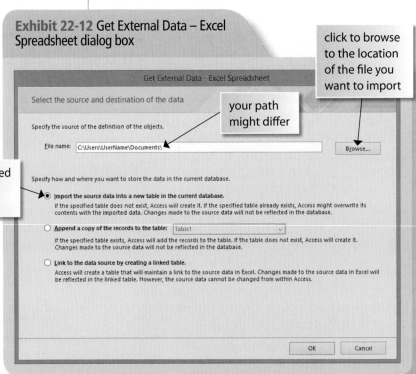

Exhibit 22-12 Get External Data – Excel Spreadsheet dialog box

click to browse to the location of the file you want to import

your path might differ

data will be imported into a new table in the database

You need to click Browse to select the file to import. To import the data into a new table in the database, keep the *Import the source data into a new table in the current database* option button selected. After you click OK, the Import Spreadsheet Wizard starts. The first dialog box in the wizard previews the data from the worksheet you are importing in a table in the dialog box. See Exhibit 22-13. If the first row in the worksheet contains headings, you need to select the First Row Contains Column Headings check box so that the headings will become the field names in the Access table. After you make this specification, click Next in the next two dialog boxes to accept the defaults. In the last wizard dialog box, you can specify the name for the Access table.

Exhibit 22-13 First dialog box in the Import Spreadsheet Wizard

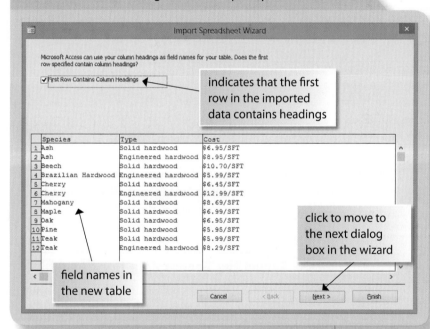

Begin Activity

Import Excel data to an Access table.

1. Create a new Access database named **EcoFlooring-Types**.

2. On the ribbon, click the **EXTERNAL DATA tab**. In the Import & Link group, click the **Excel button**. The Get External Data – Excel Spreadsheet dialog box opens. Refer back to Exhibit 22-12.

3. In the dialog box, click **Browse**. The File Open dialog box opens.

4. Navigate to the location where you are storing your files, click **EcoFlooring Types**, and then click **Open**. EcoFlooring Types.xlsx and its path are listed in the File name box in the Get External Data – Excel Spreadsheet dialog box. The *Import the source data into a new table in the current database* option button is selected, so the data will be imported into a new table in the database.

5. Click **OK**. The first dialog box in the Import Spreadsheet Wizard opens. The first row in the Excel worksheet contains column headings, so you need to select that option.

> **Tip:** If the workbook contains more than one worksheet, another dialog box will open asking you to confirm the worksheet to import.

6. If it is not already selected, click the **First Row Contains Column Headings check box**. Refer to Exhibit 22-13.

7. Click **Next**. In the second dialog box in the wizard, you could specify information about the fields you are importing, including the data type of each field.

8. Click **Next** to accept the default field names and other information. The next dialog box in the wizard lets you assign a primary key to the data. The Let Access add primary key option button is selected. Because the worksheet you are importing does not contain information you can convert to a primary key, you will let Access add one to the table.

9. Click **Next** to let Access add a primary key. The final dialog box in the Import Spreadsheet Wizard opens. The text in the Import to Table box is selected, and the *I would like a wizard to analyze my table after importing the data* check box is deselected.

10. In the Import to Table box, type **Types** and then click **Finish**. The Get External Data – Excel Spreadsheet dialog box appears again, displaying the Save Import Steps screen. If you were going to import this table again, you could save the choices

you made when you went through the wizard. You don't need to do that in this case, so you'll leave the Save import steps check box unchecked.

11 In the dialog box, click **Close**. The new table appears in the Navigation Pane.

12 In the Navigation Pane, double-click **Types** to open the Types table. The Excel data has been imported into the new Access table, and the column headings are converted to field names and the row data to records. Compare your screen to Exhibit 22-14.

13 Close both tables.

End Activity

Exhibit 22-14 Excel data imported into an Access table

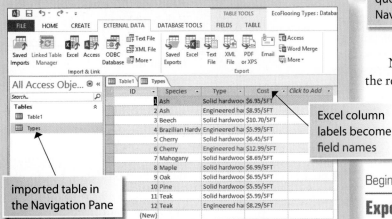

Excel column labels become field names

imported table in the Navigation Pane

22-2b Exporting Access Data to a Word File

Recall from your work with Access that you use a query to extract information from a database. The query results are stored in a datasheet. You can export the query results to a new text document or Excel worksheet.

Begin Activity

Create a query.

1 Create a query named **OakCherry** that lists only the records with a species of oak or cherry, and

Rich Text Format (RTF) A text format that preserves the formatting and layout of data.

shows the Species, Type, and Cost fields for those records.

2 Run the query, and then widen the **Type column** to fit the widest entry. See Exhibit 22-15.

End Activity

Exhibit 22-15 Results of the OakCherry query

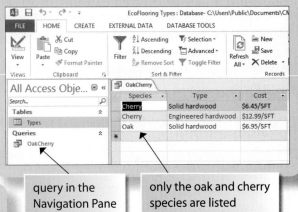

query in the Navigation Pane

only the oak and cherry species are listed

Now that the query is created, you can export the results to a text file. To export to a text file, you can choose the Text file type, which creates a document with unformatted text, or **Rich Text Format** (**RTF**), a text format that preserves the layout of data.

Begin Activity

Export the Access data to a Word file.

1 In the Navigation Pane, click the **OakCherry query** to select it.

2 On the ribbon, click the **EXTERNAL DATA tab**. In the Export group, click the **More button**, and then click **Word**. The Export – RTF File dialog box opens. It is similar to the dialog box that opened when you imported data from Excel. In the File name box, the path is to the

> **Tip:** If you don't need to preserve the layout of your data, export the table or query to a plain text file by clicking the Text File button in the Export group on the EXTERNAL DATA tab.

location where you are storing your files, and the file name of the new file is OakCherry.rtf.

3. In the File name box, change the file name **OakCherry.rtf** to **Oak Cherry Table.rtf** (leave the rest of the file path as is). Under Specify export options, the first check box is selected and you cannot click it to remove the check mark. With this check box selected, the formatting and layout of the data in the query datasheet will be preserved. You cannot change it because you are exporting to an RTF document, so the layout and formatting will remain as originally designed.

> **Problem?** If you can't see the last character because the path is too long, click anywhere in the File name box, and then press and hold the **Right Arrow key** until the insertion point moves to the end of the file name.

4. Click the **Open the destination file after the export operation is complete check box** to select it. Now the new file will open automatically after you close this dialog box.
5. Click **OK**. Access converts the query results into an RTF file and opens the new file in Word.
6. Close the **Word file.** The Export – RTF File dialog box is still open in Access with the Save Export Steps screen displayed. As in the Save Import Steps screen you saw earlier, you can click the Save export steps check box, and then save the steps you took to export the query. You don't need to do this.
7. Click **Close**. The dialog box closes.

End Activity

FYI

Saving Import and Export Steps in Access

If you know you will be importing data to or exporting data from a database more than once, it is a good idea to save the steps you took using the Import or Export Wizard. To do this, click the Save import steps or Save export steps check box in the corresponding screen in the Get External Data or Export dialog boxes. When you select this check box, the dialog box changes to display boxes that allow you to name the saved operation and add a description to remind you of the details of the operation. After you have saved a set of import or export steps, you can access them by clicking the EXTERNAL DATA tab, and then clicking the Saved Imports button in the Import group or the Saved Exports button in the Export group. When you do, the Manage Data Tasks dialog box opens. You can then click the Saved Imports or Saved Exports tab to see each list of saved operations. To run the selected operation, click Run in the dialog box.

22-3 Using the Object Command in Word, Excel, and PowerPoint

The Object button in the Text group on the INSERT tab in Word, Excel, and PowerPoint allows you to insert the contents of one file into another file. If you use the Object command and then click the Create from File tab, you can select a file and then choose to embed or link that file. If you do this, the entire file is inserted as an object in the destination file. Note that in Word, you can also use the Text from File command on the Object button menu to insert only the text of another text file into the destination document.

Begin Activity

Insert the text of a file into a different Word file.

1. Open the Word data file **EcoLetter**, located in the Chapter 22\Chapter folder. Save it as **EcoFlooring Letter**. Change the zoom to **120%**.
2. In the body of the letter, delete the **yellow highlighted text.**

3 On the ribbon, click the **INSERT tab**. In the Text group, click the **Object button arrow**, and then click **Text from File**. The Insert File dialog box opens.

> **Tip:** You could also open the RTF file in a Word window, copy the table, and then paste it into the destination document.

4 Navigate to the folder where you are storing the files you create, click **Oak Cherry Table**, and then click **Insert**. The Query results are inserted into the document as a table.

5 Click anywhere in the **table**.

6 On the ribbon, click the **TABLE TOOLS DESIGN tab**. In the Table Style Options group, select the **Header Row check box**, and deselect the **Banded Rows** and **Banded Columns check boxes**.

7 Apply the **List Table 7 Colorful – Accent 1 table style** (the green style in the last row under List Tables in the Table Styles gallery).

8 Select the **table**, and then center the table horizontally.

9 Delete **one of the blank paragraphs** below the table. Compare your screen to Exhibit 22-16.

10 In the closing at the end of the letter, replace *Aaron Greenburg* with your name, and then save the document.

End Activity

22-4 Copying and Pasting Among Office Programs

If you want to use Access data in a PowerPoint slide, you cannot export it directly to a slide. You can, however, use Copy and Paste commands to copy data from a datasheet, and then paste it to a PowerPoint slide as a table.

Begin Activity

Copy and paste Access data to a PowerPoint slide.

1 Switch to the Access database **EcoFlooringTypes**. The OakCherry query is still open.

2 To the left of the Species column heading, click the **selector box**. All the records in the query results datasheet are selected.

3 On the ribbon, click the **HOME tab**. In the Clipboard group, click the **Copy button**. The selected query results are copied to the Clipboard.

4 Switch to the PowerPoint file **EcoFlooring Presentation**. Display **Slide 4** ("Oak and Cherry Flooring Options") in the Slide pane.

5 In the Slide pane, click in the **blank area below the title**.

6 On the HOME tab, in the Clipboard group, click the **Paste button arrow**, point to each button to see its effect, and then click the **Use Destination Theme button**. PowerPoint inserts the query results in a table on the slide.

> **Tip:** Remember that you can use the Office Clipboard to collect text and objects from various files so that you can paste them later.

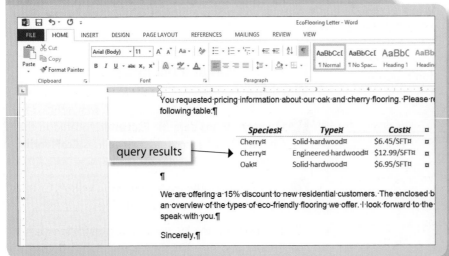

Exhibit 22-16 Query results inserted as a table in the brochure

7 In the table, click in the **first row** (containing *OakCherry*).

8 On the ribbon, click the **TABLE TOOLS LAYOUT tab**. In the Rows & Columns group, click the **Delete button**, and then click **Delete Rows**. The first row in the table is deleted.

9 Click the **table border** to select the entire table. Change the font size of the table text to **28 points**.

10 Specify that the **Header row** is to be treated differently. Apply the **Themed Style 1 – Accent 1 table style**.

11 AutoFit each column in the table. Center the table vertically in the area under the slide title, keeping the left edge aligned with the left edge of the title text. Compare your screen to Exhibit 22-17.

Exhibit 22-17 Formatted data from the Access query on the PowerPoint slide

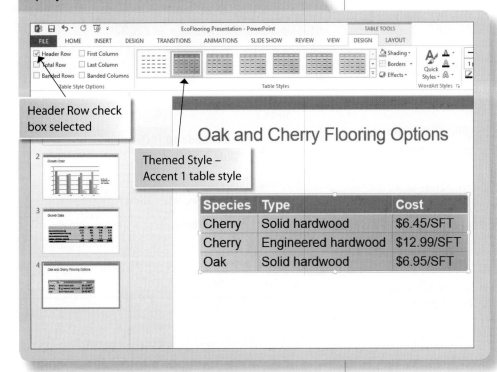

Header Row check box selected

Themed Style – Accent 1 table style

Oak and Cherry Flooring Options

Species	Type	Cost
Cherry	Solid hardwood	$6.45/SFT
Cherry	Engineered hardwood	$12.99/SFT
Oak	Solid hardwood	$6.95/SFT

12 Save the presentation.

13 Switch to the Access database **EcoFlooring Types**, close the **OakCherry query**, saving changes if prompted, and then exit Access.

End Activity

22-5 Creating PowerPoint Slides from a Word Outline

If you have an outline in a Word document, you can use that outline to create PowerPoint slides. When you create slides from a Word outline, PowerPoint uses the heading styles in the Word document to determine how to format the text. Each paragraph formatted with the Heading 1 style becomes the title of a new slide, each paragraph formatted with the Heading 2 style becomes a first level bulleted item on a slide, and so on.

When you create slides from an outline, PowerPoint inserts them after the current slide. If the document containing the outline is formatted with a theme different from the theme applied to the presentation, you might need to reset the slides to force them to use the theme formatting in the presentation. When you reset slides, you reset the position, size, and formatting of the slide placeholders to match the settings in the slide masters.

Begin Activity

Create PowerPoint slides from a Word outline.

1 Open the Word data file **EcoOutline** located in the Chapter 22\Chapter folder.

2 Switch to **Outline view**. Examine the structure of the document. Close the **EcoOutline document**.

3 Switch to the PowerPoint file **EcoFlooring Presentation**. Display **Slide 1** (the title slide) in the Slide pane.

4 On the HOME tab, in the Slides group, click the **New Slide button arrow**, and then click **Slides from Outline**. The Insert Outline dialog box opens.

5 Navigate to the **Chapter 22\Chapter folder**, click **EcoOutline**, and then click **Insert**. PowerPoint inserts and formats the text of the Word outline to create Slides 2 through 9.

Exhibit 22-18 Final presentation in Slide Sorter view

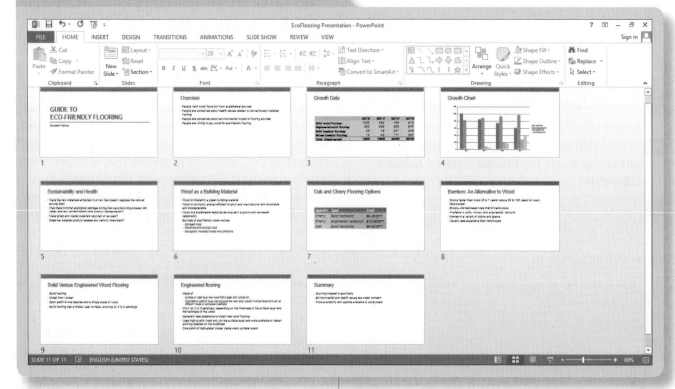

6 Display **Slide 9** in the Slide pane. Slide 9 does not contain any text because there was a blank paragraph at the end of the Word outline.

7 In the Slides tab, right-click the **Slide 9 thumbnail**, and then click **Delete Slide**. The blank slide is deleted.

8 Display **Slide 8** ("Summary") in the Slide pane. The slide text is a different color and style than the text on the other slides. This is because the document containing the outline was formatted with a different theme than the presentation.

9 Press and hold the **Shift key**, and then scroll up in the Slides tab and click the **Slide 2 thumbnail**. Slides 2 through 8 are selected.

10 On the HOME tab, in the Slides group, click the **Reset button**. The slides are reformatted with the theme used in the presentation.

11 Rearrange the slides in the presentation as follows:

- Move **Slide 10** ("Growth Data") so it becomes **Slide 3**.

- Move the new **Slide 10** ("Growth Chart") so it becomes **Slide 4**.

- Move **Slide 11** ("Oak and Cherry Flooring Options") so it becomes **Slide 7**.

12 Switch to **Slide Sorter view**. Change the zoom level to **80%**. Compare your screen to Exhibit 22-18.

13 Save the presentation, and then close the presentation and exit PowerPoint.

End Activity

22-6 Creating Form Letters with Mail Merge

A **form letter** is a Word document that contains standard paragraphs of text and a minimum of variable text, such as the names and addresses of the letter's recipients. The **main document** of a form letter

form letter A Word document that contains standard paragraphs of text and a minimum of variable text.

main document A document that contains the text and other information that you want to keep the same in each form letter.

Exhibit 22-19 Plan for the form letter

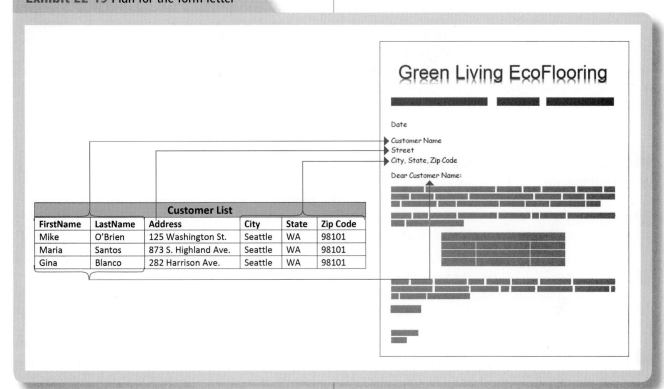

Customer List					
FirstName	**LastName**	**Address**	**City**	**State**	**Zip Code**
Mike	O'Brien	125 Washington St.	Seattle	WA	98101
Maria	Santos	873 S. Highland Ave.	Seattle	WA	98101
Gina	Blanco	282 Harrison Ave.	Seattle	WA	98101

contains the text and other information (including punctuation, spaces, and graphics) that you want to keep the same in each letter. It also includes **merge fields**, which contain instructions for replacing the field placeholder with the variable information that changes from one letter to another. The variable information is contained in a **data source**, which can be a Word table, an Access database, or some other source. When you **merge** the main document with the data source, Word replaces the merge fields with the appropriate information from the data source. See Exhibit 22-19. The term **mail merge** is used when you are merging a main document with a list of addresses from a data source.

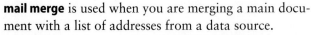
JoLin/Shutterstock.com

The first step in completing the mail merge is to specify the type of document you want to create, such as a form letter, mailing labels, or envelopes. Next, you select the main document, which Word also calls the **starting document**. Then, you select recipients from the data source. When you use an Access database as the data source for a mail merge, you select a table or query defined in the database as the actual data source.

After you have identified the main document and the data source, you insert the merge fields into the main document. Finally, you preview the main document, make any needed changes, and merge the main document and the data source to produce customized form letters.

To perform a mail merge, you can use buttons on the MAILINGS tab on the ribbon or you can use the Mail Merge Wizard, which appears in a task pane to the right of the Word window. The Mail Merge wizard is helpful; but if you work from left to right on the MAILINGS tab, you should have no trouble creating a main document with the correct merge fields, and then performing the merge.

merge field A field that contains instructions to be replaced with the variable information that changes from one letter to another.

data source In a mail merge, a file that contains the variable information for form letters.

merge To combine a main document with a data source.

mail merge To merge a main document with a list of addresses from a data source.

starting document The main document in a Word mail merge.

22-6a Selecting a Main Document and Data Source

The main document of a mail merge can be a new or an existing Word document. In this case, the starting document is the letter to potential customers. You will begin by starting Word and opening the main document, and selecting the list of recipients.

Begin Activity

Select the main document and data source for a mail merge.

1 If necessary, on the taskbar, click the **Word button** to display the **EcoFlooring Letter**. Scroll to the top of the document.

2 On the ribbon, click the **MAILINGS tab**. Notice that only a few buttons on the Mailings tab are available. The other buttons will become available as you set up the mail merge.

3 In the Start Mail Merge group, click the **Start Mail Merge button**. A menu opens with Normal Word Document selected. You want to merge a letter, but you can also create email messages, envelopes, labels, or a directory of all the names in the data source.

> **Tip:** To be guided step-by-step through the mail merge process, click the Start Mail Merge button in the Start Mail Merge group on the MAILINGS tab, and then click Step by Step Mail Merge Wizard.

4 Click **Letters** to specify that you want to merge a letter. The next step is to select the recipients of the letter. You want to select recipients from an existing list in an Access database.

5 In the Start Mail Merge group, click the **Select Recipients button**, and then click **Use an Existing List**. The Select Data Source dialog box opens, displaying a list of possible data sources.

6 Navigate to the **Chapter 22\Chapter folder**, click the Access file **Contacts**, and then click **Open**. Because the data source is an Access database, the Select Table dialog box opens

listing all the tables in the selected database (this database contains one table and one query). You need to choose a table or query in the selected database as the data source. If the database contained only one table, the Select Table dialog box would not open; instead, the Mail Merge Recipients dialog box would open immediately after you selected the database.

7 Click the **Customer table** to select it, and then click **OK**. The dialog box closes and the Edit Recipient List button, as well as several others, is now available on the ribbon.

End Activity

You can edit the recipient list before completing the merge. To do this, click the Edit Recipient List button in the Start Mail Merge group on the MAILINGS tab to open the Mail Merge Recipients dialog box. See Exhibit 22-20. In this dialog box, you can narrow the list by deselecting records individually. You can also sort the list or filter it to include only records that meet specific criteria of recipients. To sort the list by a single column, you can click the column heading arrow and then click one of the Sort commands. To filter the list, click the Filter link at the bottom of the dialog box to open the Filter and Sort dialog box. In this dialog box, you select the field on which you want to filter, select the comparison operator, and then fill in the text in which to compare the field value. See Exhibit 22-21.

Exhibit 22-20 Mail Merge Recipients dialog box

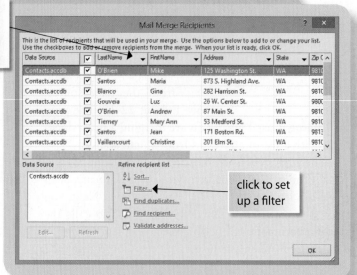

click a column head to sort the table by that column

click to set up a filter

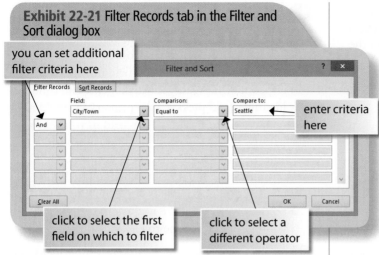

Exhibit 22-21 Filter Records tab in the Filter and Sort dialog box

you can set additional filter criteria here

enter criteria here

click to select the first field on which to filter

click to select a different operator

Begin Activity

Edit the recipient list.

1 In the Start Mail Merge group, click the **Edit Recipient List button**. The Mail Merge Recipients dialog box opens. Refer back to Exhibit 22-20.

2 At the bottom of the dialog box, click the **Filter link**. The Filter and Sort dialog box opens with the Filter Records tab selected.

3 Click the **Field arrow**, and then click **City/Town**. The Comparison and Compare to boxes in the first row are now available. Equal to appears in the Comparison box, and the insertion point is blinking in the Compare to text box.

4 In the Compare to text box, type **Seattle**. Refer back to Exhibit 22-21.

5 Click **OK**. The Filter and Sort dialog box closes and only the addresses for customers in Seattle are displayed in the Mail Merge Recipients dialog box.

6 Click **OK** to close the Mail Merge Recipients dialog box.

End Activity

22-6b Inserting the Merge Fields

As noted earlier, a merge field is a special instruction that tells Word where to insert the variable information from the data source into the main document. For example, right now the letter does not have an inside address (the address for the recipient) at the top, as business letters usually do, so you will insert a merge field to tell Word what information to pull from the data source. For Caitlin's letter, you will insert the Address block and Greeting line merge fields. You then will check the merge fields to make sure they correspond with the fields in the Customer table.

The Address Block merge field inserts each recipient's first and last names, address, city and state in a single merge field. It can also include the recipient's company name. When you click the Address Block button in the Write & Insert Fields group on the MAILINGS tab, the Insert Address Block dialog box opens, as shown in Exhibit 22-22.

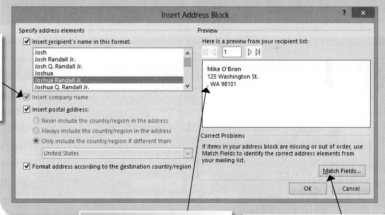

Exhibit 22-22 Insert Address Block dialog box

option is not available because the data source does not include a Company field

City/Town field was not correctly indentified in the Address Block merge field

click to match fields in the data source with predetermined fields in the Address Block

You use this dialog box to choose the format of the recipient's name and to specify whether to include the company name and country in the address. The Preview box on the right shows you a preview of how the address block will look with data from your recipient list. The default format of first and last name is selected in the list on the left. Word tries to match fields in a recipient list with predetermined fields in the Address Block, but sometimes you need to explicitly identify a field. If Word cannot match the fields, you need to click

Match Fields to open the Match Fields dialog box. See Exhibit 22-23. On the left are the fields Word expects in the Address Block. On the right are the fields in the data source. Click an arrow in the list on the right and select the correct field in the list.

Exhibit 22-23 Match Fields dialog box

click to match the City/Town field in the data source to the City field in the Address Block

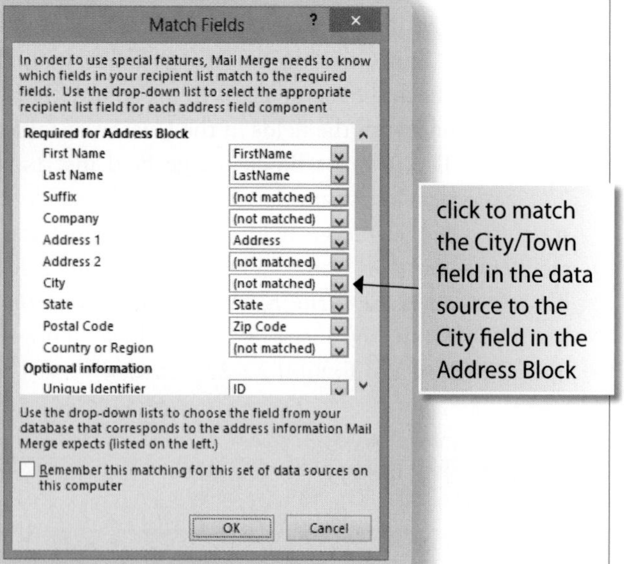

Begin Activity

Insert merge fields into a main document.

1 Below the date in the letter, click in the **blank paragraph**. This is where the recipient's name and address will appear.

2 On the MAILINGS tab, in the Write & Insert Fields group, click the **Address Block button**. The Insert Address Block dialog box opens. Refer back to Exhibit 22-22. In this case, Word did not find a match for the City field in the Address Block.

> **Tip:** Click the Insert Merge Field button to insert merge fields individually instead of a block of fields, as with the Address Block and Greeting Line field.

3 In the Correct Problems section of the dialog box, click **Match Fields**. The Match Fields dialog box opens. Refer back to Exhibit 22-23. You want Word to match the City field in the Address Block with the City/Town field in the Access table.

4 Click the **City arrow**, and then click **City/Town**.

5 Click **OK**. A dialog box opens warning that if you match a field in your data source with the built-in Unique Identifier field, that field might be available to people who read your document. The Unique Identifier field picks up the primary key field in the table. If the primary key field in your Access database contained confidential data such as Social Security numbers, you would click the No button, change the Unique Identifier field to "(not matched)," and then close the Match Fields dialog box. However, you are not using the ID field in your letter, so it is fine to click the Yes button.

6 Click **Yes**. The warning dialog box and the Match Fields dialog box close. The Preview area in the Insert Address Block dialog box now displays the city as part of the address.

7 Click **OK** to close the Insert Address Block dialog box. The Address block merge field appears in the main document between double chevrons (« »). Now that there is a merge field in the letter, a few more buttons on the Mailings tab are available.

> **Problem?** If the Address block merge field appears between curly braces and includes additional text, such as {ADDRESSBLOCK \f}, Word is displaying field codes. Click the **FILE tab**, click **Options** in the navigation bar, click **Advanced** in the navigation pane, scroll down the list on the right, and then, in the Show document content section on the right, deselect the **Show field codes instead of their values check box**.

End Activity

Next you need to insert a greeting line to personalize the salutation. When you click the Greeting Line button in the Write & Insert Fields group on the MAILINGS tab, the Insert Greeting Line dialog box opens. See Exhibit 22-24. The Greeting line format and the Preview at the bottom of the dialog box show how Word will insert the salutation. The Greeting line for invalid recipient names box shows how the greeting will appear if a name is missing from the data source.

Exhibit 22-24 Insert Greeting Line dialog box

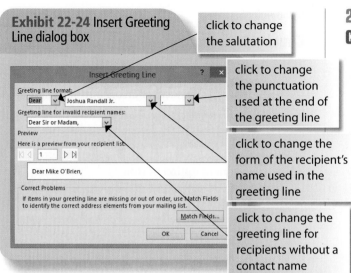

click to change the salutation

click to change the punctuation used at the end of the greeting line

click to change the form of the recipient's name used in the greeting line

click to change the greeting line for recipients without a contact name

Begin Activity

Insert the Greeting Line merge field.

1 In the salutation, delete **Dear Sustainable Partner:** (including the colon).

2 On the MAILINGS tab, in the Write & Insert Fields group, click the **Greeting Line button**. The Insert Greeting Line dialog box opens. Refer to Exhibit 22-24. The Greeting line format and the Preview at the bottom of the dialog box show that Word will insert as the salutation *Dear* followed by the recipient's entire name, and then a comma.

3 In the Greeting line format section (next to Joshua Randall Jr.), click the **third arrow**, and then click : (the colon). The change is reflected in the Preview section. You can accept the other options in the Greeting Line dialog box—to begin the salutation with *Dear* and to use *Dear Sir or Madam* for records in the Contacts table that do not include a contact name.

4 Click **OK**. Word inserts the Greeting Line merge field in the main document.

5 Save the document.

End Activity

22-6c Previewing the Mail Merge and Checking for Errors

With the starting document and merge fields in place, you're ready to perform the mail merge. But first you should preview the merge. To do this, click the Preview Results button in the Preview Results group on the MAILINGS tab. If the Address Block merge field is inserted in a paragraph that has extra space after it, the results will show the inside address with space between each line. See Exhibit 22-25. To fix this, you need to change the format of the paragraph containing the Address Block merge field.

Begin Activity

Preview a merged document and fix the Address Block paragraph formatting.

1 On the MAILINGS tab, in the Preview Results group, click the **Preview Results button**. The first merged form letter appears with Mike O'Brien as the first recipient. This is the first letter, as indicated by the "1" in the Preview Results group. Refer back to Exhibit 22-25. Notice that each line in the inside address has a space after it. To fix this, you'll turn off the preview and then format the Address Block merge field.

Exhibit 22-25 Preview of mail merge

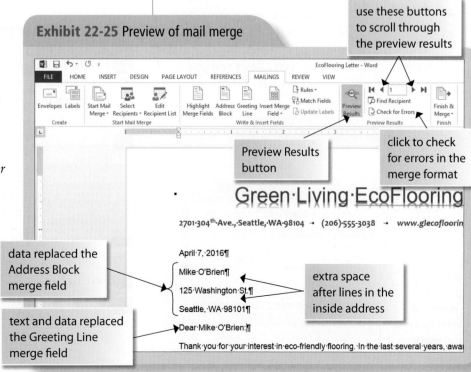

use these buttons to scroll through the preview results

Preview Results button

click to check for errors in the merge format

data replaced the Address Block merge field

extra space after lines in the inside address

text and data replaced the Greeting Line merge field

2 In the Preview Results group, click the **Preview Results button**. The preview turns off and you see the merge fields again.

3 Click the **Address Block merge field**.

4 On the ribbon, click the **HOME tab**. In the Paragraph group, click the **Line and Paragraph Spacing button** [≡▾], and then click **Remove Space After Paragraph**. The extra space after the paragraph is removed.

5 Position the insertion point at the end of the Address Block line, and then press the **Enter key**. This inserts a single blank line (a paragraph formatted with no extra space after it) between the last line of the inside address and the salutation.

6 On the ribbon, click the **MAILINGS tab**. In the Preview Results group, click the **Preview Results button**. Mike O'Brien's information appears in the letter properly formatted.

7 In the Preview Results group, click the **Next Record button** ▶ to preview the next recipient. The letter to Maria Santos appears.

End Activity

It is also a good idea to use the Check for Errors command to check the main document for errors. When you select this command, a dialog box opens in which you choose to simulate the merge and list the errors in a new document or to complete the merge, reporting each error as it is found in a new document after the merge is completed. See Exhibit 22-26. The option that simulates the merge is the safest as it allows you to easily modify the main document to correct the errors.

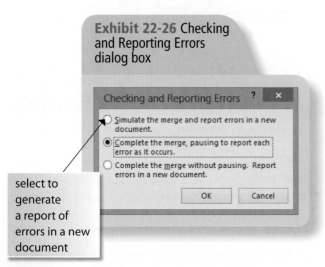

Exhibit 22-26 Checking and Reporting Errors dialog box

Checking and Reporting Errors

○ Simulate the merge and report errors in a new document.

● Complete the merge, pausing to report each error as it occurs.

○ Complete the merge without pausing. Report errors in a new document.

OK   Cancel

select to generate a report of errors in a new document

Begin Activity

Check a main document for errors.

1 On the MAILINGS tab, in the Preview Results group, click the **Check for Errors button**. The Checking and Reporting Errors dialog box opens. Refer to Exhibit 22-26.

2 Click the **Simulate the merge and report errors in a new document option button**.

3 Click **OK**. After a moment, another dialog box opens reporting that no mail merge errors were found.

4 Click **OK** to close the dialog box.

End Activity

22-6d Finishing the Mail Merge

After you have inserted all of the merge fields, previewed the merge, and checked the document for errors, you can finish the merge. To do this, you click the Finish & Merge button in the Finish group on the MAILINGS tab. On the menu that opens, you can choose to print the form letters, send them as email messages, or save the completed letters to a new document so that you can print them later. If you merge the letters to a new Word document, you can proofread the final letters before printing all of them.

Begin Activity

Finish a mail merge.

1 On the MAILINGS tab, in the Finish group, click the **Finish & Merge button**, and then click **Edit Individual Documents**. The Merge to New Document dialog box opens.

2 If it is not already selected, click the **All option button**, and then click **OK**. A new document opens with the temporary name "Letters" followed by a number. This 12-page document contains one letter for each contact who lives in Seattle.

3 Scroll through the merged document to see the merged addresses and salutations.

4 Save the document as **Merged Letters**.

5 Close the document. The Main Letter document is the current document again.

6 On the MAILINGS tab, in the Preview Results group, click the **Preview Results button** to toggle it off.

7 Save the document, and then close it.

End Activity

LEARN MORE

Performing a Mail Merge with an Email Message

You can make the most of your email correspondence by merging your Outlook Contacts with an email message. To do this, you click E-Mail Messages on the Start Mail Merge button, click the Select Recipients button, and then click Choose from Outlook Contacts.

Using the Mail Merge Recipients dialog box, you can filter the contacts to include only those people to whom you want to send your message. After you compose

U.P.images_vector/Shutterstock.com

your message, click the Finish & Merge button, and then click Send E-mail Messages. This opens the Merge to E-mail dialog box in which you can type the subject for your email message. After you click OK, Word creates new email messages addressed to each person in your recipients list and places them in your Outlook Outbox, ready to send the next time you send email messages.

Quiz Yourself

1. What is OLE?

2. What is the difference between embedding an object and linking an object?

3. When an object is embedded, how many copies of the object exist?

4. If an Excel chart is linked to a Word document, which is the source program?

5. What happens if you make changes to a linked object in the destination file?

6. How do you use Excel data in an Access table without using the Copy and Paste commands?

7. What does RTF stand for?

8. How do you insert text from a text file into another Word file without using the Copy and Paste commands?

9. How can you use data from an Access datasheet in a PowerPoint slide without first exporting it to another file format?

10. Describe the slide or slides that PowerPoint would create from a Word outline that has one Level 1 paragraph and three Level 2 paragraphs.

11. After importing a Word outline, how do you change the format of a slide so that it matches the theme used in the presentation?

12. In a mail merge, what is a merge field?

13. What is the file that contains the variable information to be used in a mail merge called?

Practice It

Practice It 22-1

1. Open the Word data file **SandbarFlyer** located in the Chapter 22\Practice It folder. Save the document as **Sandbar CC Flyer**.

2. In the fourth paragraph, replace the yellow highlighted text with an embedded pie chart that you create from within the Word document. Use the following as data for the chart:

Biology	1145
Business	359
Chemistry	471
English	1612
Hospitality & Tourism	549

3. In the chart object in the Word document, change the chart title to **Distribution of Majors 2013–2015**. Add data labels to the center of the pie slices that identify the percentage of each slice.

4. Open the Excel data file **SandbarNumber** located in the Chapter 22\Practice It folder. Save the workbook as **Sandbar CC Number**.

5. In the worksheet, copy the column chart to the Clipboard.

6. In the Word document Sandbar CC Flyer, delete the green highlighted text, and then insert the chart as an embedded object using the destination theme.

7. Edit the data in the embedded worksheet that contains the column chart so that Business in 2015 is **610** and Hospitality and Tourism in 2015 is **250**.

8. Resize both charts so they are as wide as the paragraphs in the document, and then change their height to approximately 2.6 inches. Make more adjustments as needed so that all the text and the two charts fit on one page.

9. Open the PowerPoint data file **SandbarPresentation** located in the Chapter 22\Practice It folder. Add your name as the subtitle, and then save the presentation as **Sandbar CC Presentation**.

10. Link the column chart in the Excel file Sandbar CC Number to Slide 2 ("Number of Students Chart") in the PowerPoint file Sandbar CC Presentation using the destination theme. Resize the chart to fill the space on the slide.

11. Link the worksheet data in the Excel file Sandbar CC Number to Slide 3 ("Number of Students") in the PowerPoint file Sandbar CC Presentation.

12. Edit the data in the Excel file Sandbar CC Number so that Business in 2015 is **610**. Update the chart and datasheet in the PowerPoint presentation if necessary.

13. Save the PowerPoint file, and then close it.

14. Edit data in the Excel file so that Hospitality and Tourism in 2015 is **250**.

15. Re-open the PowerPoint file **Sandbar CC Presentation**. Examine both Slides 2 and 3, and manually update the links if necessary.

16. Open the Excel data file **SandbarCourses** located in the Chapter 22\Practice It folder. Save the document as **Sandbar CC Courses**.

17. Prepare the worksheet to be imported into Access by deleting the rows above the column labels and adding the label **Dept.** above the data in column A.

18. Save the workbook, and then close it.

19. Open the Access database named **Sandbar** located in the Chapter 22\Practice It folder. Save it as **SandbarCC**.

20. Import the Excel file Sandbar CC Courses into it to create a new table named **Course**. Make sure you indicate that the first row contains headers, and let Access set the primary key.

21. Create a query named **Business** that lists only classes in the Business department. Resize columns as needed.

22. Export the query results to a Word Rich Text File named **Business Courses**.

23. Open the Word data file **SandbarLetter** located in the Chapter 22\Practice It folder. Save the document as **Sandbar CC Letter**.

24. In the empty paragraph in the body of the letter, insert the text of the Word file **Business Courses** in the Word document Sandbar CC Letter. Format the table with the Grid Table 4 – Accent 6 table style with the Header Row treated differently and the Banded Rows option set. Center the table horizontally, and delete one of the empty paragraphs below the table.

25. In the SandbarCC Access file, copy the Business query results to the Clipboard, and then paste them using the destination theme to Slide 4 ("Business Courses") in the PowerPoint file Sandbar CC Presentation. Remove the first row in the pasted table, and then change the font size of the text in the table to 24 points. Apply the table style Medium Style 1 – Accent 1 with the Header Row treated differently, AutoFit the column, and then center the table in the blank area on the slide.

26. Import the Word outline stored in the file **SandbarOutline** in the Chapter 22\Practice It folder so that the slides created from the outline appear after Slide 4 ("Business Courses") in the PowerPoint file Sandbar CC Presentation.

27. Reset the new Slides 5–10, and then delete the blank Slide 10.

28. In the PowerPoint file Sandbar CC Presentation, move Slide 5 ("Student Population") so that it becomes Slide 2.

29. In the Word file Sandbar CC Letter, select the Letters main document type.

30. Select the Access file SandbarCC as the data source. Select the Student table.

31. Edit the recipient list by filtering it so that only students with an interest in Business are included in the mail merge.

32. Insert the Address Block and Greeting Line merge fields at the beginning of the document below the date. Match fields as needed. In the Greeting Line merge field, use Dear as the salutation, choose just the first name as the name to be used in the greeting line, and choose a comma at the end of the line.

33. Preview the document. Adjust the spacing after the Address Block merge field as needed.

34. Check the document for errors by simulating the merge.

35. Complete the merge by merging all the records to a new file. (There should be six letters.) Save the file as **Sandbar CC Merged Letters**.

36. Close the merged document Sandbar CC Merged Letters. Turn the Preview off in the document Sandbar CC Letter, and then save and close the Sandbar CC Letter document.

37. Close all open files, saving if prompted.

Practice It 22-2

1. Open the Excel data file **SpaServices** located in the Chapter 22\Practice It folder. Save the workbook as **Salon Isle Services**.

2. Open the PowerPoint data file **SpaPresentation** located in the Chapter 22\Practice It folder. Enter your name as the subtitle. Save the presentation as **Salon Isle Presentation**.

3. Embed the chart in the Excel file Salon Isle Services in Slide 2 ("Comparison of Prices") of the PowerPoint file Salon Isle Presentation using the destination theme. Apply the Style 9 style (on the CHART TOOLS DESIGN tab) to the embedded chart object.

4. In the embedded chart, change the price in cell C5 to **$55** and change the price in cell C7 to **$50**.

5. In the Excel file Salon Isle Services, copy Sheet1 to a new worksheet. In the new worksheet, delete the chart, and then prepare the data on Sheet1 (2) to be exported to an Access table. (*Hint*: Make sure a label appears in every cell in column A for all rows that contain data.) Label column B **Service** and column C **Price**.

6. Save and close the Excel file Salon Isle Services.

7. Create a new Access database named **SalonIsle**.

8. In the Access database SalonIsle, import the data from Sheet1 (2) in the Excel file Salon Isle Services to a new table named **Services**. Make sure you indicate that the first row contains headers, and let Access set the primary key. (*Hint*: Make sure you select Sheet1 (2) in the first dialog box in the Import Spreadsheet Wizard.)

9. Create a query named **Hair** that lists the service and price for all services of the type Hair, but do not show the Type field. Resize columns as needed in the query results. (*Hint*: If you get only one result, close the query, delete the query and the Services table, and then repeat Step 8, making sure you add row labels.)

10. Export the results of the query to a Rich Text File named **Hair Services**.

11. In the PowerPoint file Salon Isle Presentation, create new slides after Slide 2 by importing the outline in the Word data file **SpaOutline**, located in the Chapter 22\Practice It folder. Reset the imported slides. Move Slide 2 ("Comparison of Prices") so it becomes Slide 4, and then move Slide 7 (a blank slide) so it becomes Slide 5.

12. Add the title **Hair Services** to Slide 5, and then change the layout to Title Only.

13. Use the Object button in the Text group on the Insert tab to embed the **Hair Services** file into Slide 5.

14. Double-click the embedded table to open a Word window in the Slide, select all the text and data in the table, and then increase the font size of all the text in the table to 20 points. Format the table with the Grid Table 3 – Accent 2 table style, and then AutoFit each column. Click a blank area of the slide, and then resize the object vertically so it fits on the slide and the text is not distorted. Position the table so it is visually centered in the blank area on the slide. (The table object will not be centered.)

15. Change the layout of Slides 2 and 3 to the Two Content layout. On each slide, move the last first-level bulleted item and its subitems to the content placeholder on the right. Change the size of the text in the bulleted lists on Slide 2 and 3 so the first-level items are 24 points and the second level

items are 20 points. (*Hint:* On Slide 2, you need to adjust these individually.)

16. Change the font size of the text in the bulleted lists on Slides 6 and 7 to 24 points.

17. Close all open files, saving when prompted.

On Your Own

On Your Own 22-1

1. Open the Excel data file **ZooNumbers** located in the Chapter 22\On Your Own folder. Save the workbook as **Zoo Visitor Numbers**.

2. Open the PowerPoint data file **ZooPresentation** located in the Chapter 22\On Your Own folder. Add your name as the subtitle, and then save the presentation as **Zoo Slide Show**.

3. In the Excel file Zoo Visitor Numbers, copy the column chart to the Clipboard.

4. Link the copied chart to Slide 2 ("Number of Visitors") using the destination theme. Resize the chart object to fill the slide.

5. In the Excel file Zoo Visitor Numbers, add the following data as the number of visitors in 2015: **648, 1411, 173,** and **80**.

6. Save the changes to the Excel file Zoo Visitor Numbers, and then update the chart in the Power-Point file Zoo Slide Show if needed.

7. Open the Word data file **ZooLetter** located in the Chapter 22\On Your Own folder. Save the document as **Zoo Customer Letter**.

8. In the Excel file Zoo Visitor Numbers, copy the column chart to the Clipboard.

9. In the Word document Zoo Customer Letter, delete the yellow highlighted text, and then link the copied chart to the document using the destination theme. Resize the chart so that it is approximately 2.5 inches high and the same width as the paragraphs.

10. In the Excel file Zoo Visitor Numbers, change the number of Adult visitors in 2015 to **710** and then change the number of Children who visited in 2015 to **1500**. Save the file.

11. Open the Excel data file **ZooAnimals** located in the Chapter 22\On Your Own folder. Save the workbook as **Zoo Animals by Type**.

12. Prepare the Excel file Zoo Animals by Type file for importing into Access. Add **Species** as the column A label. Save and close the file.

13. Create a new Access database named **ZooData**. Import the Excel file Zoo Animals by Type to a new table named **Animals**.

14. Create four queries, each listing all the animals in one species. Do not show the Species field. Save each query with the name of the species included. Resize columns as needed in the query results.

15. Open the Office Clipboard, and then copy the query results for each of the four queries to the Office Clipboard.

16. Paste each query into the appropriate slide in the PowerPoint file Zoo Slide Show using the Text Only paste option. (*Hint:* Select the Keep Text Only option after you paste the objects. On each slide, delete the Type bulleted item, increase the size of the items in the list to 24 points, and left-align the list text box with the title text box.

17. Use the Word file Zoo Customer Letter to create a form letter using the Access file ZooVisitors as the data source.

18. Edit the recipient list by sorting the customers alphabetically by last name.

19. Insert the Address Block and Greeting Line merge fields, matching fields if necessary. In the Greeting Line merge field, change the form of the name to the first name, and change the form of greeting line for records with an invalid recipient name to **Dear Guest,**.

20. In the body of the letter, replace the green high-lighted text with the Date_Visited merge field.

21. Preview the merged document, and then correct any spacing issues.

22. In the closing, replace *Karl Croston* with your name.

23. Turn the preview off, merge only the first and second letter of the mail merge to a new document, and then save the new document as **Zoo Letters**.

24. Close all open documents, saving when prompted.

Chapter 22

ADDITIONAL STUDY TOOLS

IN THE BOOK
▶ Complete end-of-chapter exercises
▶ Study tear-out Chapter Review Card

ONLINE
▶ Complete additional end-of-chapter exercises

▶ Take practice quiz to prepare for tests
▶ Review key term flash cards (online, printable, and audio)
▶ Play "Beat the Clock" and "Memory" to quiz yourself
▶ Watch the videos to learn more about the topics taught in this chapter

Answers to Quiz Yourself

1. *OLE is a way of transferring and sharing objects between programs.*

2. *Embedding stores a copy of the object in the destination file, and any changes made to the source file do not appear in the destination file; linking stores the object in the source file and displays it in the destination file, and any changes to the object in the source file appear in the destination file.*

3. *When an object is embedded, two copies of the object exist, one in the source file and one in the destination file.*

4. *If an Excel chart is linked to a Word document, the source program is Excel.*

5. *If you make changes to a linked object in the destination file, the changes you make appear in the destination file; however, if you update the linked object, the data in the source file will overwrite the changes you made to the linked object in the destination file.*

6. *To use Excel data in an Access table without using the Copy and Paste commands, prepare the Excel worksheet so that there are no blank rows and no rows above the column headings, and then import the worksheet into Access.*

7. *RTF stands for Rich Text Format.*

8. *To insert text from a text file into another Word file without using the Copy and Paste commands, use the Text from File command on the Object menu.*

9. *To use data from an Access datasheet in a PowerPoint slide without first exporting it to another file format, copy the data on the datasheet, and then paste it onto the slide.*

10. *If you create PowerPoint slides from a Word outline that has one Level 1 paragraph and three Level 2 paragraphs, the outline will create one slide with a title and three first-level bulleted items.*

11. *After importing a Word outline, to change the format of a slide so that it matches the theme used in the presentation, select the slides whose format need to be changed, and then click the Reset button in the Slides group on the HOME tab.*

12. *In a mail merge, a merge field contains instructions for replacing the field placeholder with the variable information that changes from one letter to another.*

13. *The file that contains the variable information to be used in a mail merge is called the data source.*

Index

< (left angle bracket), 500, 606
> (right angle bracket), 500, 606
_ (paragraph symbol), 311
! (exclamation point), 628
(hash mark), 478, 628
* (asterisk), 441, 628
+ (plus sign), 441
- (minus sign), 441, 628
/ (forward slash), 17, 441
= (equal sign), 500, 606
? (question mark), 628
@ (at symbol), 16, 17, 150
[] (square brackets), 628
^ (caret), 441
· (space character), 311
. (dot or period), 17, 225

A

absolute references, 457–459, 461
accelerators, 249
Access, 556–639. *See also* database(s);
    database tables; form(s); queries;
    report(s)
    copying and pasting data to
      PowerPoint slides, 736–737
    file format, 560
    saving import and export steps, 735
accounting software, 100, 101
active cell, moving, 424–425
active sheet, 425
    switching, 425–426
active window, 208
addition operator (+), 441
Address bar, 212
    accessing search sites, 243–244
    navigating using, 218
Align Left button, 481
Align Right button, 481
aligning
    cell content, 480–481
    numbers, 482
    paragraphs, 326–327
    tables, 393–394
    text in tables, 393–394
alignment guides, 404
alphanumeric keys, 54
Alternate key, 54

ALU (arithmetic logic unit), 40
American National Standards
    Institute (ANSI), 121
American Psychological Association
    (APA) style, 373
American Recovery and Reinvestment
    Act, 192
analog signals, 114
anchors, floating objects, 404
And operator, 608–609
Android, 87
Angle Clockwise button, 483
Angle Counterclockwise button, 483
animation(s), slides, 664–668
    Animation Painter, 667–668
    applying to graphics, 700
    appropriate, selecting, 667
    audio, 706
    changing animation effects,
      666–667
    copying, 667
    order, 701
    removing, 668
    speed, 702
    timings, 700–702
    video, 706
Animation Painter, 667–668
ANSI (American National Standards
    Institute), 121
antennae, 133
antispyware software, 171
antivirus software, 171
AP (Associated Press) style, 373
APA (American Psychological
    Association) style, 373
app(s)
    closing, 229–230
    snapping, 210
    starting, 204–207
    switching between open windows
      and running apps, 209–211
appeal, workbooks, 509
appearance, rehearsing
    presentations, 686
application(s)
    cloud, 6
    desktop, 205
    starting, 204–207

application service providers
    (ASPs), Internet community
    members, 141
application software, 88–102
    business, 93–95
    categories, 88–91
    database, 93, 94–95. *See also*
      Access
    multimedia, 95–98
    presentation graphics, 93, 95. *See*
      also PowerPoint
    spreadsheet, 93, 94. *See also* Access
    system software vs., 88
    word processing, 93, 94. *See also*
      Word
application windows, 207
architectures, networks, 109–110, 111
area charts, 522
arguments, functions, 461
arithmetic logic unit (ALU), 40
arithmetic operators, 441
ARPANET, 139
arrow(s), buttons, 282–283
arrow keys, 54
ASPs (application service
    providers), Internet community
    members, 141
Associated Press (AP) style, 373
asterisk (*)
    multiplication operator, 441
    wildcard character, 628
asynchronous transmission, 115
at symbol (@), email addresses, 16,
    17, 150
attachments, email, 266–268
audience involvement, rehearsing
    presentations, 686
audio
    adding sound clips to slides, 707
    animation effects, slides, 706
audio capture software, 97
audio editing software, 97
audio input, 61–63
audio output, 71–72
audio ports, 39
AutoComplete
    inserting dates in documents,
      313–314
    worksheets, 429

definition, 3
desktop, 7
embedded, 5
energy efficiency, 12
environmental concerns, 23, 25–26
hardware. *See* hardware
health issues, 22–23
heat generated, 23
history, 8
impact on daily life, 2
Internet appliances, 10
mainframe, 11
midrange servers (minicomputers),
    10–11
mobile devices. *See* mobile devices
network, 9
notebook (laptop), 9
PCs, 7, 9–10
platforms, 7
portable. *See* portable computers
primary operations, 3, 4
professionals, 4–5
protecting, 19
sabotage. *See* computer sabotage
setting up, 148
software. *See* software
supercomputers, 11–12
system unit. *See* system unit
tablet, 9
types, 5–12
users, 4
uses, 2
workspace design, 24
zombie, 167–168
computer chips, 32. *See also* central
    processing unit (CPU)
computer crime, 163
computer ethics, 21
Computer Fraud and Abuse Act of
    1984, 191
Computer Matching and Privacy
    Protection Act, 192
computer networks. *See* Internet;
    network(s)
computer professionals, 4–5
computer sabotage, 167–171
    botnets, 167–168
    data, program, or Web site
        alteration, 170
    DoS attacks, 170, 171
    malware, 168–170
    protecting against, 170–171
Computer Science Network
    (CSNET), 139
computer vision syndrome, 22

computer-aided design (CAD)
    software, 100
computer-monitoring software, 186
concentrators, 133
conditional formatting, reports,
    638, 639
conditional formatting, worksheets,
    504–507
    clearing rules, 505–506, 507
    effective use, 507
connecting to the Internet, 142–148
    choosing connection type, 144–147
    selecting device type, 143–144
    selecting ISPs, 148
    setting up computer, 148
constants, formulas, 496
contact(s)
    adding to People app, 269–271
    definition, 269
    displaying actions, 271
    profiles, 269
    sending email to, 272
contact information,
        presentations, 653
content controls, 371
content placeholders, 649
    adding graphics from files using,
        690–691
Content with Caption layout, 649
contextual tabs, 282
Continuous section breaks, 394
control(s), forms, 624
Control key, 54
control layouts, forms, 624
control unit, 40–41
controller chipsets, 38
conventional dial-up Internet access,
    144–145
cooling components, 35
COPA (Child Online Protection Act),
    190, 192
COPPA (Children's Online Privacy
    Protection Act), 192
Copy command, keyboard
    shortcut, 301
copying. *See also* copying and
    pasting; duplicating
    animations, 667
    cell contents, using fill handle,
        468–469
    cell ranges, 438, 439
    files, 221–222, 223–224
    folders, 221–222, 223–224
    formats in documents, 335–338
    queries, 607
    records, from another database, 565

system Clipboard, 298–299
    text, drag and drop, 319–320
    worksheets, 426
copying and pasting
    Access data to PowerPoint slides,
        736–737
    formulas, 442–443
    worksheet cell formats, 479
copyright, 19–20
corporate information, online, 158
correcting errors. *See* error correction
cost, Internet, 143
COUNT function, 445, 462
Count function, 613
COUNTA function, 462
cover pages, preformatted, 373
CPOs (chief privacy officers), 189
CPU. *See* central processing unit (CPU)
crime, 163
criteria
    adding to queries, 605–606
    multiple, queries, 608–610
cropping pictures, 400–401
CRT monitors, 63
CSNET (Computer Science
    Network), 139
CTS (carpal tunnel syndrome), 22
cube functions, 462
Currency data type, 561
custom date formats, 541
custom margins, 367
custom number formats, 541
customizing
    AutoCorrect, 316
    File Explorer windows, 216
    Normal template, 361
Cut command, keyboard
    shortcut, 301
cutting, system Clipboard, 298–299
cyberbullying, 177
cybercrime, 163
cyberstalking, 177
cyberterrorism, 164
Cycle diagrams, 696
cylinders, hard disks, 43, 44

D

data, 3–4
    backing up, 46, 227
    digital representation, 31
    reading from optical discs, 46
    words, 34
    writing to optical discs, 46, 47, 48
data bars, 547–549
data files, 218

mouse. *See* mice
moving. *See also* navigating; positioning
  active cell, 424–425
  bulleted items on slides, 657–659
  cell ranges, 438–439
  charts, 525–527
  fields in Design view, 572–573
  files, 221–223
  folders, 221–223
  graphics in documents, 404
  insertion point, 318
  page breaks in worksheets, 510–511
  system files, 213
  text boxes, 408
  windows, 209
  worksheets, 426
moving text
  drag and drop, 319–320
  keyboard shortcut, 301
MS-DOS, 83
multi-channel RAM, 35
multi-core CPUs, 33
multifunction devices (MFDs), 71
multimedia, application software, 95–98
multimedia networking, 108
multimedia projectors, 68
multimedia software, 98
multiplexers, 133
multiplication operator (*), 441
multiprocessing, 79–80
multitable queries, 604–605
multitasking, 79
music input systems, 62–63

N

#N/A error value, 497
name(s), main forms and subforms, 632
Name box, 424
#NAME? error value, 497
naming
  database tables, 564
  fields, 564
  files, 224–226
narrowing searches, 351
NAS (network attached storage), 50
National Information Infrastructure Protection Act, 191
navigating
  datasheets, 576–577
  fields, 591
  to folders, 215–218

main forms, 632
  to previously viewed page in history, 256
  between slides in Normal view, 651
  to specific Web pages, Internet Explorer desktop application, 245–246
  subforms, 632
  to Web pages, 239–241
navigation bar, 290
navigation buttons, 212
Navigation pane, 213, 577
  outlines, 364
NCs (network computers), 9
nested functions, 502–503
nested IF function, 502–503
netbooks, 9
network(s), 12–18. *See also* Internet
  accessing, 14–16
  architectures, 109–110, 111
  communications protocols, 121–122
  coverage area, 110, 112–113
  data transmission. *See* data transmission
  definition, 107
  hardware, 130–134
  media, 117–121
  networking standards, 122–130
  sharing folders, 110
  size, 110, 112–113
  topologies, 109
  wired, 107, 109
  wireless, 107, 109, 168
network adapters, 130
network attached storage (NAS), 50
network computers (NCs), 9
network interface cards (NICs), 130
network operating systems, 81–82
network ports, 39
networking, multimedia, 108
networking applications, 108
networking media, 117–121
  wired, 117–118
  wireless, 118–121
Next Page section breaks, 394
NFSNET, 139
NICs (network interface cards), 130
Nigerian letter fraud scheme, 175
nonprinting characters, 311
nonremovable batteries, 33
nonunique fields, 599
Normal style, 351
Normal template, 351
  customizing, 361

Normal view
  navigating between slides, 651
  presentations, 647
  worksheets, 446
not equal to operator (<>), 500, 606
note taking software, 100
notebook computers, 9
notes masters, 685
notes page(s)
  footers, 671–672
  headers, 671–672
  printing, 675–676
Notes Page view, 660–661
Notes pane, 647
notification area, 203
NOW function, 471, 472
#NULL! error value, 497
#NUM! error value, 497
number data, 431–433
  aligning, 482
  entering in worksheets, 431–432
  formatting, 432–433
  numbers, 432–433
Number data type, 561
number fields, Field Size property, 567
number formats, custom, 541
numbered lists, 331–332
  slides, 651
numeric keypad, 54
numeric values, dates and times as, 472

O

object(s), 281. *See also* graphics
  definition, 398
  inline, 403
  selecting, 399–400
Object command, 735–736
object linking and embedding (OLE), 721–731
  destination file, 721, 722
  destination program, 721, 722
  editing embedded Excel charts, 726–727
  embedding Excel charts in Word or PowerPoint files, 723–726, 727
  linking Excel worksheets to Word or PowerPoint files, 727–729
  Links dialog box, 731
  modifying embedded data in spreadsheets, 724–725
  Paste Options button vs. Paste Special dialog box, 730
  source file, 721, 722
  source program, 721, 722

Learning Objectives

1-1	Explain what computers do
1-2	Identify types of computers
1-3	Describe computer networks and the Internet
1-4	Understand how computers impact society

Digital Backpack

Practice It: Practice It 1-3—Discuss the pros and cons of using technology in your daily life.

On Your Own: On Your Own 1-2—Discuss your opinion about campus gossip sites.

Quiz: Take the practice quiz to prepare for tests.

Key Terms: Review the key term flash cards (online, printable, and audio).

Games: Play *Beat the Clock* and *Memory* to quiz yourself.

Videos: Watch the videos to learn more about the topics taught in this chapter.

Infographic

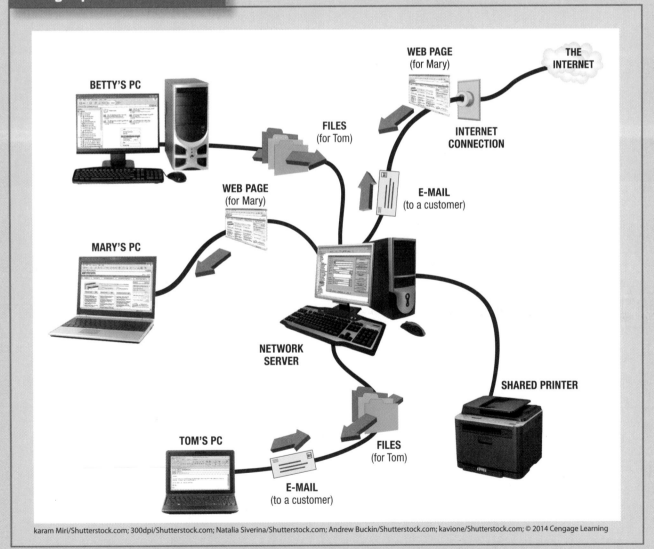

karam Miri/Shutterstock.com; 300dpi/Shutterstock.com; Natalia Siverina/Shutterstock.com; Andrew Buckin/Shutterstock.com; kavione/Shutterstock.com; © 2014 Cengage Learning

reviewcard

Visit CourseMate for **CMPTR**[2] at www.cengagebrain.com
for additional study tools!

Quick Reference Tools

Primary Operations of a Computer

- Input—entering data into the computer
- Processing—performing operations on the data
- Output—presenting the results
- Storage—saving data, programs, or output

Data vs. Information

- Data are unorganized facts input into a computer.
- Information is data that has been processed into a meaningful form.
- The computer processes data into information.

Types of Computers

- An embedded computer is a tiny computer designed to perform specific tasks for a product.
- A mobile device is a small communications device that has built-in computing or Internet capability.
- A personal computer (PC) is a small computer designed for use by one person at a time.
- A midrange server is a computer used to host programs and data for a small network.
- A mainframe computer is a powerful computer many large organizations use to manage large amounts of centralized data.
- A supercomputer is the most powerful and most expensive type of computer available.

Computers and Societal Issues

- Intellectual property rights include three main types: copyrights, trademarks, and patents.
- Common physical conditions from computer use include eyestrain, blurred vision, fatigue, headaches, backaches, and wrist and finger pain. Repetitive stress injuries (RSIs) include carpal tunnel syndrome and DeQuervain's tendonitis.
- Ergonomics is the science of fitting a work environment to the people who work there.
- Green computing refers to using computers in an environmentally friendly manner, including reducing the use of natural resources such as energy and paper, and proper disposal of e-waste.

Computer Networks

- A network is a collection of computers and other devices that are connected to enable users to share hardware, software, and data, as well as to communicate electronically.
- Networks are used in the home, small offices, schools, large corporations, and public locations such as coffeehouses, bookstores, and libraries.
- The Internet is the largest and most well-known computer network in the world; it is technically a network of networks.

The Internet and the World Wide Web

- The Internet refers to the physical structure of that network.
- The World Wide Web (Web or WWW) refers to one resource that is available through the Internet.
- A group of Web pages belonging to one person or organization is called a Web site.
- Web pages are stored on computers called Web servers that are continually connected to the Web.
- Web servers can be accessed by anyone with a Web-enabled device and an Internet connection.

Key Definitions

Go to your CMPTR² CourseMate site for a full list of key terms and definitions.

cloud computing To use data, applications, and resources stored on computers accessed over the Internet rather than on users' computers.

domain name A text-based Internet address used to uniquely identify a computer on the Internet.

input The process of entering data into a computer; can also refer to the data itself.

Internet The largest and most well-known computer network, linking millions of computers all over the world.

network Computers and other devices that are connected to share hardware, software, and data.

output The process of presenting results of processing; can also refer to the results themselves.

processing Performing operations on data that has been input into a computer to convert that input to output.

storage The operation of saving data, programs, or output for future use.

Web server A computer continually connected to the Internet that stores Web pages accessible through the Internet.

Learning Objectives

2-1	Understand how data is represented to a computer
2-2	Identify the parts inside the system unit
2-3	Explain how the CPU works
2-4	Describe different types of storage systems
2-5	Identify and describe common input devices
2-6	Identify and describe common output devices

Digital Backpack

Practice It: Practice It 2-3—Research and recommend a new personal printer to purchase.

On Your Own: On Your Own 2-2—Discuss the benefits and drawbacks of online/cloud storage services.

Quiz: Take the practice quiz to prepare for tests.

Key Terms: Review the key term flash cards (online, printable, and audio).

Games: Play *Beat the Clock* and *Memory* to quiz yourself.

Videos: Watch the videos to learn more about the topics taught in this chapter.

Infographic

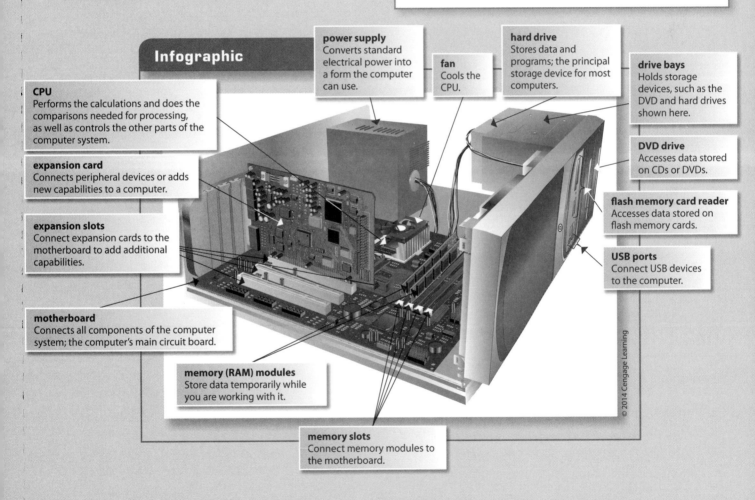

power supply
Converts standard electrical power into a form the computer can use.

fan
Cools the CPU.

hard drive
Stores data and programs; the principal storage device for most computers.

drive bays
Holds storage devices, such as the DVD and hard drives shown here.

DVD drive
Accesses data stored on CDs or DVDs.

CPU
Performs the calculations and does the comparisons needed for processing, as well as controls the other parts of the computer system.

expansion card
Connects peripheral devices or adds new capabilities to a computer.

expansion slots
Connect expansion cards to the motherboard to add additional capabilities.

motherboard
Connects all components of the computer system; the computer's main circuit board.

memory (RAM) modules
Store data temporarily while you are working with it.

memory slots
Connect memory modules to the motherboard.

flash memory card reader
Accesses data stored on flash memory cards.

USB ports
Connect USB devices to the computer.

© 2014 Cengage Learning

Quick Reference Tools

Bits and Bytes

- Digital computers are binary, understanding two states represented by 0 and 1 (on and off).
- A bit is the smallest unit of data a binary computer can recognize, represented by a 0 or a 1.
- Eight bits are referred to as a byte.
- A file is a named collection of bytes that represent virtually any type of data.

The System Unit

- The system unit houses the processing hardware for the computer, as well as other devices.
- The system unit includes the motherboard, power supply, central processing unit, memory, expansion slots and cards, buses, ports, and connectors.
- Most computers support Plug and Play, meaning the computer automatically configures new devices upon installation and computer boot up.

The CPU

- A typical CPU includes an arithmetic/logic unit (ALU), a floating point unit (FPU), a control unit, a prefetch unit, a decode unit, a bus interface unit, registers, and an internal cache memory.
- A system clock, located on the motherboard, synchronizes all of a computer's operations.
- The machine cycle: (1) Fetch the instruction from cache or RAM; (2) Decode the instructions into a form the ALU or FPU can understand; (3) Execute the instructions; and (4) Store the data or results in registers or RAM.

Storage Systems

- Storage systems provide nonvolatile storage, making it possible to save programs, data, and processing results for later use.
- Storage systems include a storage medium (the hardware where data is stored) and a storage device (the hardware where a storage medium is inserted to be read from or written to).
- Storage devices include hard drives, optical discs, flash memory, remote storage (network or online/cloud storage), smart cards, and storage servers.

Input Devices

- An input device is any piece of equipment used to enter data into the computer.
- Common input devices are keyboards, pointing devices, touch devices, scanners, and readers.
- Images, video, and audio input are becoming more common and accessible.

Output Devices

- An output device presents the results of processed data from the computer to the user.
- The most common output devices are computer screens, data projectors, printers, and audio speakers.

Key Definitions

Go to your CMPTR² CourseMate site for a full list of key terms and definitions.

bit The smallest unit of data that a binary computer can recognize.

byte Eight bits grouped together.

central processing unit (CPU or **processor)** The chip located on the motherboard of a computer that performs the processing for a computer.

circuit board A thin board containing computer chips and other electronic components.

flash memory Nonvolatile chips that can be used for storage by a computer or a user.

memory Chips located inside the system unit used to store data and instructions while it is working with them.

monitor A display device for a desktop computer.

mouse A common pointing device that the user slides along a flat surface to move the pointer on the screen.

port A connector on the exterior of the system unit case that is used to connect an external hardware device.

ROM (read-only memory) Nonvolatile chips on the motherboard that permanently store data or programs.

Universal Serial Bus (USB) A versatile bus architecture widely used for connecting peripherals.

USB flash drive Flash memory media integrated into a self-contained unit that plugs into a USB port.

Learning Objectives

3-1	Explain system software and operating systems
3-2	Identify operating systems for personal computers
3-3	Identify operating systems for mobile devices and larger computers
3-4	Describe common types of application software
3-5	Describe application software used for business
3-6	Describe application software used for working with multimedia
3-7	Describe other types of application software

Digital Backpack

Practice It: Practice It 3-3—Consider the advantages and disadvantages of installed versus Web-based applications.

On Your Own: On Your Own 3-2—Discuss the impact of open source software on commercial software companies and software quality.

Quiz: Take the practice quiz to prepare for tests.

Key Terms: Review the key term flash cards (online, printable, and audio).

Games: Play *Beat the Clock* and *Memory* to quiz yourself.

Videos: Watch the videos to learn more about the topics taught in this chapter.

Infographic

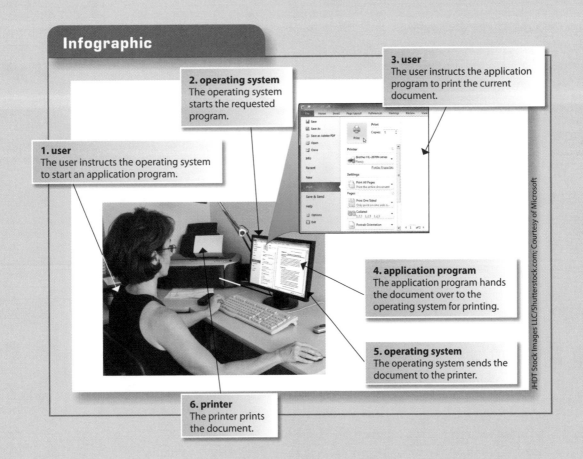

1. user
The user instructs the operating system to start an application program.

2. operating system
The operating system starts the requested program.

3. user
The user instructs the application program to print the current document.

4. application program
The application program hands the document over to the operating system for printing.

5. operating system
The operating system sends the document to the printer.

6. printer
The printer prints the document.

JHDT Stock Images LLC/Shutterstock.com; Courtesy of Microsoft

Quick Reference Tools

System Software and Operating Systems

- System software includes the operating system and utility programs that control a computer system and enable application software to run.
- The operating system is loaded into memory during the boot process and serves as the intermediary between the user and the computer and between application programs and the hardware.
- Most operating systems today use a graphical user interface (GUI).

Operating Systems for Personal Computers

- Many operating systems are designed for personal computers or for network servers.
- The original operating system was DOS; the most widely used today are Windows, Windows Server, Windows Home Server, Mac OS, Mac OS Server, UNIX, and Linux.

Operating Systems for Mobile Devices

- Notebook, netbook, and other portable personal computers typically use the same operating systems as desktop computers.
- Common operating systems for mobile devices include Windows Phone, Windows Embedded, Android, iOS, BlackBerry OS, HP webOS, and Symbian OS.

Other Application Software

- Multimedia application software includes graphics software, audio capture and editing software, video editing and DVD authoring software, and audio and video media players.
- Special purpose software includes desktop publishing software; educational, entertainment, and reference software; note-taking software, CAD and design software; accounting and personal finance software; and project management, collaboration and remote access software.

Application Software

- Application software can be open source, commercial, shareware, freeware, or public domain.
- Mobile devices usually require mobile software.
- Software can be installed on a computer or run directly from the Internet as Web-based software.

Business Application Software

- Related software programs can be sold bundled as a software suite.
- Office suites include word processing, spreadsheet, database, and presentation software.
- Common office software suites include Microsoft Office, Corel WordPerfect Office, Apple iWork, OpenOffice.org, and Google Docs.

Key Definitions

Go to your CMPTR² CourseMate site for a full list of key terms and definitions.

application software The programs that allow you to perform specific tasks on a computer.

boot process The actions taken by programs built into the computer's hardware to start the operating system.

device driver (driver) A small program used to communicate with a peripheral device, such as a monitor, printer, portable storage device, or keyboard.

multiprocessing A processing technique in which multiple processors or multiple processing cores in a single computer each work on a different job.

operating system A collection of programs that manages and coordinates the activities taking place within the computer.

parallel processing A processing technique in which multiple processors or multiple processing cores in a single computer work together to complete one job more quickly.

shareware program A software program that is distributed on the honor system; typically available free of charge but may require a small registration fee.

software license A permit that specifies the conditions under which a buyer can use the software.

software suite Related software programs, such as a group of graphics programs, utility programs, or office-related software, that are sold bundled together.

system software Programs such as the operating system and utility programs that control a computer and its devices, and enable application software to run on the computer.

virtual memory A memory management technique frequently used by operating systems that uses a portion of the computer's hard drive as additional RAM.

Windows The predominant operating systems for personal computers.

review card

CHAPTER 4
Computer Networks
Networks and the Internet

Learning Objectives

4-1	Explain what networks are
4-2	Identify network characteristics
4-3	Understand how data is transmitted over a network
4-4	Describe common types of network media
4-5	Identify protocols and networking standards
4-6	Describe networking hardware

Digital Backpack

Practice It: Practice It 4-3—Create a wired home network scenario.

On Your Own: On Your Own 4-2—Discuss possible solutions to the problem of interference with wireless devices and who should be responsible for fixing the problem.

Quiz: Take the practice quiz to prepare for tests.

Key Terms: Review the key term flash cards (online, printable, and audio).

Games: Play *Beat the Clock* and *Memory* to quiz yourself.

Videos: Watch the videos to learn more about the topics taught in this chapter.

Infographic

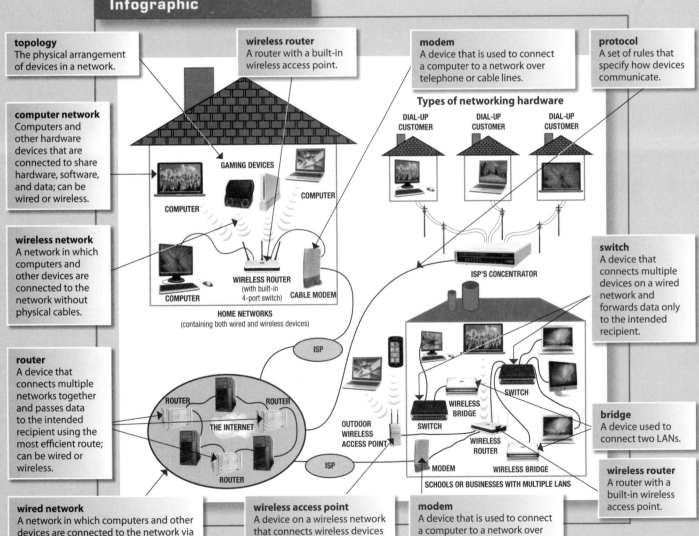

topology
The physical arrangement of devices in a network.

computer network
Computers and other hardware devices that are connected to share hardware, software, and data; can be wired or wireless.

wireless network
A network in which computers and other devices are connected to the network without physical cables.

router
A device that connects multiple networks together and passes data to the intended recipient using the most efficient route; can be wired or wireless.

wired network
A network in which computers and other devices are connected to the network via physical cables.

wireless router
A router with a built-in wireless access point.

modem
A device that is used to connect a computer to a network over telephone or cable lines.

protocol
A set of rules that specify how devices communicate.

switch
A device that connects multiple devices on a wired network and forwards data only to the intended recipient.

bridge
A device used to connect two LANs.

wireless router
A router with a built-in wireless access point.

wireless access point
A device on a wireless network that connects wireless devices to that network.

modem
A device that is used to connect a computer to a network over telephone or cable lines.

Types of networking hardware

DIAL-UP CUSTOMER · DIAL-UP CUSTOMER · DIAL-UP CUSTOMER

ISP'S CONCENTRATOR

COMPUTER · GAMING DEVICES · COMPUTER · COMPUTER

WIRELESS ROUTER (with built-in 4-port switch) · CABLE MODEM

HOME NETWORKS (containing both wired and wireless devices)

ISP · THE INTERNET · ROUTER · ROUTER · ROUTER · ISP

OUTDOOR WIRELESS ACCESS POINT · SWITCH · WIRELESS BRIDGE · SWITCH · WIRELESS ROUTER · MODEM · WIRELESS BRIDGE

SCHOOLS OR BUSINESSES WITH MULTIPLE LANS

Quick Reference Tools

Common Network Topologies

- **Star network** is a network in which all networked devices connect to a central device through which all network transmissions are sent.
- **Bus network** is a network that uses a central cable to which all network devices connect.
- **Mesh network** is a network that uses a number of different connections between network devices so that data can take any of several possible paths from source to destination.

Common Network Architectures

- **Client-server networks** include both clients (computers and other devices on the network that request and use network resources) and servers (computers that are dedicated to processing client requests).
- **Peer-to-peer (P2P) networks** include computers that work at the same functional level and provide users direct access to the network devices.

Connecting to a Wi-Fi Hotspot

- To connect to a **Wi-Fi hotspot**, click the icon representing your wireless network connection in the notification area, click the network to which you want to connect in the list that appears, and then click Connect.

Sharing Folders

- Do not enable sharing for folders you want to keep private from others on your network.

Serial Transmission Types

- **Synchronous transmission** organizes data into groups or blocks of data, which are transferred at regular, specified intervals.
- **Asynchronous transmission** sends data when it is ready to be sent, without being synchronized.
- **Isochronous transmission** sends data at the same time as other related data with the different types of data delivered at the proper speed for their applications.

Common Protocols for Internet Applications

- **TCP/IP (Transmission Control Protocol/Internet Protocol)** is used to transfer data over the Internet.
- **HTTP (Hypertext Transfer Protocol)** and **HTTPS (Secure Hypertext Transfer Protocol)** are used to display Web pages.
- **FTP (File Transfer Protocol)** is used to transfer files over the Internet.
- **SMTP (Simple Mail Transfer Protocol)** and **POP3 (Post Office Protocol)** are used to deliver email over the Internet.

Key Definitions

Go to your CMPTR² CourseMate site for a full list of key terms and definitions.

bandwidth (throughput) The amount of data that can be transferred in a given time period.

Bluetooth A networking standard for very short-range wireless connections.

client A computer or other device on a network that requests and uses network resources.

client-server network A network that includes both clients and servers.

download To retrieve files from a server to a client.

Ethernet (802.3) The most widely used standard for wired networks.

network interface card (NIC) A network adapter in the form of an expansion card.

protocol A set of rules to be followed in a specific situation.

server A computer that is dedicated to processing client requests.

TCP/IP A networking protocol that uses packet switching to facilitate the transmission of messages; the protocol used with the Internet.

upload To transfer files from a client to a server.

wide area network (WAN) A network that connects devices located in a large geographical area.

Wi-Fi (802.11) A widely used networking standard for medium-range wireless networks.

Wi-Fi hotspot A location that provides wireless Internet access to the public.

WiMAX (802.16) An emerging wireless networking standard that is faster and has a greater range than Wi-Fi.

reviewcard
CHAPTER 5
Introducing the Internet and Email
Networks and the Internet

Learning Objectives

5-1	Understand how the Internet evolved
5-2	Set up your computer to use the Internet
5-3	Understand how to search the Internet for information
5-4	Understand how email evolved
5-5	Describe common Internet communication methods and activities

Digital Backpack

Practice It: Practice It 5-3—Consider the ethics of paid or sponsored blog posts.

On Your Own: On Your Own 5-2—Evaluate the pros and cons of allowing defendants and witnesses to participate remotely in court proceedings.

Quiz: Take the pr actice quiz to prepare for tests.

Key Terms: Review the key term flash cards (online, printable, and audio).

Games: Play *Beat the Clock* and *Memory* to quiz yourself.

Videos: Watch the videos to learn more about the topics taught in this chapter.

Infographic

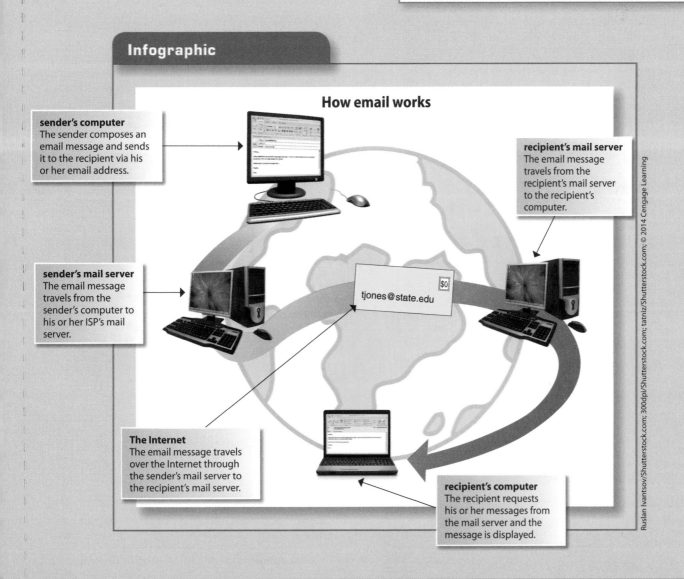

How email works

sender's computer
The sender composes an email message and sends it to the recipient via his or her email address.

recipient's mail server
The email message travels from the recipient's mail server to the recipient's computer.

sender's mail server
The email message travels from the sender's computer to his or her ISP's mail server.

tjones@state.edu

$0

The Internet
The email message travels over the Internet through the sender's mail server to the recipient's mail server.

recipient's computer
The recipient requests his or her messages from the mail server and the message is displayed.

Ruslan Ivantsov/Shutterstock.com; 300dpi/Shutterstock.com; tatniz/Shutterstock.com; © 2014 Cengage Learning

Quick Reference Tools

Evolution of the Internet

- ARPANET was created in 1969 and provided the exchange of written information.
- Over the next decade, hundreds of college and university networks were connected to ARPANET.
- In 1989, Tim Berners-Lee proposed the World Wide Web as a way to organize information.
- The Mosaic Web browser, released in 1993, provided a graphical user interface, allowing users to display images.
- The Web is the most widely used part of the Internet today.
- Internet2 is a research and development tool to help create revolutionary Internet technologies.

Today's Internet Community

- The Internet community includes users, Internet service providers (ISPs), Internet content providers, application service providers (ASPs), infrastructure companies, hardware and software companies, governments, and Internet organizations.
- Each network connected to the Internet is privately owned and individually managed.

Common Internet Activities

- The most common Internet activities are browsing and email.
- Online communication includes instant messaging (IM), text messaging, blogs, microblogs, podcasts, Voice over Internet Protocol (VoIP), Web conferences, and Webinars.
- Online communities include social networking sites and wikis.
- Other activities include online entertainment, e-commerce, and e-portfolios.

Using the Mail App

- Search sites are Web sites designed to help users find information on the Web.
- Most search sites use a search engine (a software program) along with a database of information about Web pages to help users find Web pages.
- Search site databases are updated regularly using small automated programs (called spiders or webcrawlers).
- To conduct a search, you type appropriate keywords into the search box on a search site; its search engine uses those keywords to return hits to Web pages that match your search criteria.
- Almost everything on the Internet is copyrighted. Be sure to get the content owner's permission.

Connecting to the Internet

- First, select the type of device to access the Internet, such as a personal computer, a mobile phone, or a television.
- Second, choose the type of connection to access the Internet, such as dial-up, cable, DSL, etc.
- Third, select an ISP.
- Fourth, set up your computer (varies based on the computer, connection type, and ISP).

Use Internet Explorer

- You can send email messages from any Internet-enabled device to any email address.
- The sent message travels from your computer, through a network, to your mail server.
- The message continues through the Internet to the recipient's mail server, which stores the email message until it is retrieved.
- The server then forwards the message to the recipient's computer.

Key Definitions

Go to your CMPTR² CourseMate site for a full list of key terms and definitions.

ARPANET The predecessor of the Internet, named after the Advanced Research Projects Agency (ARPA), which sponsored its development.

DSL (Digital Subscriber Line) Fast, direct Internet access via standard telephone lines.

e-commerce Online financial transactions.

e-portfolio A collection of an individual's work accessible via the Web.

mobile wireless Internet access Internet access via a mobile phone network.

search engine A software program used by a search site to retrieve matching Web pages from a search database.

social networking site A site that enables a community of individuals to communicate and share information.

Wi-Fi hotspot A location that provides wireless Internet access to the public.

Visit CourseMate for **CMPTR²** at www.cengagebrain.com for additional study tools!

review card

CHAPTER 6
Computer, Network, and Internet Security and Privacy
Networks and the Internet

Learning Objectives

6-1	Explain network and Internet security concerns
6-2	Identify and protect against unauthorized access and use
6-3	Identify and protect against computer sabotage
6-4	Identify and protect against online theft, online fraud, and other dot coms
6-5	Describe and protect against cyberstalking and other personal safety concerns
6-6	Assess personal computer security and identify precautions
6-7	Identify privacy concerns
6-8	Discuss current security and privacy legislation

Digital Backpack

Practice It: Practice It 6-3—Research risks related to using a W-Fi hotspot and identify precautions you can take.

On Your Own: On Your Own 6-2—Consider the ethics of including instruction on writing computer viruses in computer classes.

Quiz: Take the practice quiz to prepare for tests.

Key Terms: Review the key term flash cards (online, printable, and audio).

Games: Play *Beat the Clock* and *Memory* to quiz yourself.

Videos: Watch the videos to learn more about the topics taught in this chapter.

Infographic

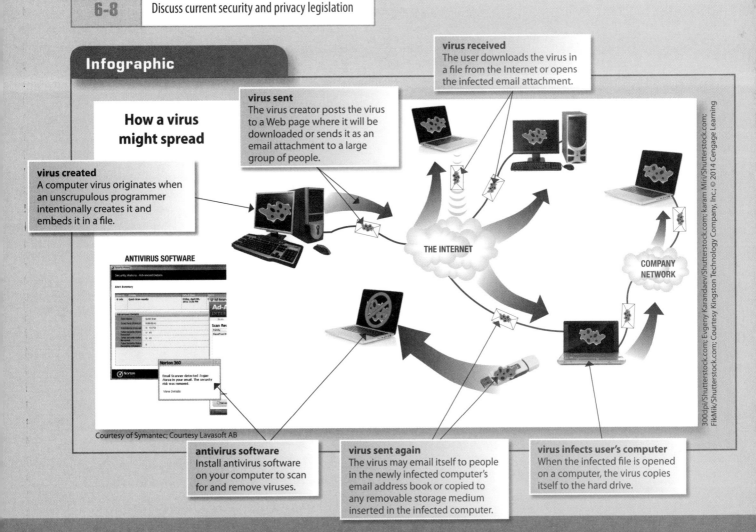

How a virus might spread

virus created
A computer virus originates when an unscrupulous programmer intentionally creates it and embeds it in a file.

virus sent
The virus creator posts the virus to a Web page where it will be downloaded or sends it as an email attachment to a large group of people.

virus received
The user downloads the virus in a file from the Internet or opens the infected email attachment.

THE INTERNET

COMPANY NETWORK

ANTIVIRUS SOFTWARE

Courtesy of Symantec; Courtesy Lavasoft AB

antivirus software
Install antivirus software on your computer to scan for and remove viruses.

virus sent again
The virus may email itself to people in the newly infected computer's email address book or copied to any removable storage medium inserted in the infected computer.

virus infects user's computer
When the infected file is opened on a computer, the virus copies itself to the hard drive.

3000pi/Shutterstock.com; Evgeny Karandaev/Shutterstock.com; karam Miri/Shutterstock.com; FlkMik/Shutterstock.com; Courtesy Kingston Technology Company, Inc.; © 2014 Cengage Learning

Visit CourseMate for **CMPTR²** at www.cengagebrain.com
for additional study tools!

Quick Reference Tools

Network and Internet Security

- Computer crime (or cybercrime) includes any illegal act involving a computer.
- Hacking is a threat to individuals and businesses, and to governments as cyberterrorism.
- Unauthorized use of a Wi-Fi network occurs with war driving and Wi-Fi piggybacking.
- Some criminals intercept communications to gain access to data, files, email, and other content.

Computer Sabotage and Dot Cons

- Computer sabotage leads to lost productivity, lost sales, and higher labor costs.
- Computer sabotage occurs via botnets; computer viruses and malware; denial of service (DoS) attacks, and alteration of data, programs, or Web sites.
- Dot cons include data, information, or identity theft; phishing and pharming; online auction fraud, and other Internet scams.

Personal Computer Security

- Common security concerns are hardware theft, loss, or damage; system failures due to hardware or software problems; computer virus, natural disaster, sabotage, or terrorist attack.
- To protect against hardware loss or damage and system failures, you can lock doors and equipment, encrypt files, install security software, and use firewalls, encryption, and VPNs.

Privacy Concerns

- Personal information can be located in many different databases, leading to electronic profiling.
- Most businesses and Web sites that collect personal information have a privacy policy.
- Spam can be countered with spam or junk mail filters, and opting in or out of marketing lists.
- Legal electronic surveillance uses computer monitoring software, video surveillance, employee monitoring, and presence technology.

Personal Safety Concerns

- Cybercrime can be physically dangerous, especially for children.
- Common online harassment includes cyberbullying and cyberstalking.
- Online pornography involving minors is illegal; many believe that the Internet is making it easier for sexual predators to meet and target children.

Security Legislation

- New legislation is passed periodically to address the latest computer crimes, but it is difficult for the legal system to keep pace with the rate at which technology changes.
- Domestic and international jurisdictional issues arise because many computer crimes affect businesses and people located in areas other than the one in which the criminal is located.

Key Definitions

Go to your CMPTR² CourseMate site for a full list of key terms and definitions.

antivirus software Software used to detect and eliminate computer viruses and other types of malware.

cyberbullying Children or teenagers bullying other children or teenagers via the Internet.

cyberstalking Repeated threats or harassing behavior between adults carried out via email or another Internet communications method.

cyberterrorism An attack launched by terrorists via the Internet.

electronic profiling Using electronic means to collect a variety of in-depth information about an individual, such as name, address, income, and buying habits.

encryption A method of scrambling the contents of an email message or a file to make it unreadable if an unauthorized user intercepts it.

firewall A collection of hardware and/or software that protects a computer or computer network from unauthorized access.

phish To use spoofed email message to gain credit card numbers and other personal data to be used for fraudulent purposes.

surge suppressor A device that protects a computer system from damage due to electrical fluctuations.

virus A software program installed without the user's knowledge that is designed to alter the way a computer operates or to cause harm to the computer system.

review card

CHAPTER 7
Exploring Windows 8 and Managing Files
Windows 8

Learning Objectives

7-1	Use the Windows 8 Start screen and desktop
7-2	Work with windows on the desktop
7-3	Switch between open windows and running apps
7-4	Work with the Windows 8 file system
7-5	Work with files
7-6	Delete files and work with the Recycle Bin
7-7	Close apps and windows
7-8	Get help
7-9	Shut down Windows

Digital Backpack

Practice It: Practice It 7-3—Create a compressed copy of your files for this course on removable media.

On Your Own: On Your Own 7-2—Build a logical folder structure for your course work and organize your files into folders and subfolders.

Quiz: Take the practice quiz to prepare for tests.

Key Terms: Review the key term flash cards (online, printable, and audio).

Games: Play *Beat the Clock* and *Memory* to quiz yourself.

Videos: Watch the videos to learn more about the topics taught in this chapter.

Infographic

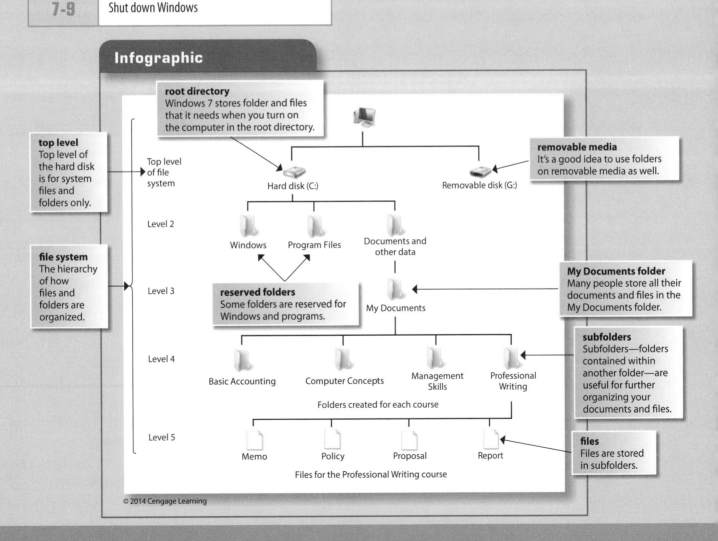

root directory
Windows 7 stores folder and files that it needs when you turn on the computer in the root directory.

top level
Top level of the hard disk is for system files and folders only.

file system
The hierarchy of how files and folders are organized.

removable media
It's a good idea to use folders on removable media as well.

reserved folders
Some folders are reserved for Windows and programs.

My Documents folder
Many people store all their documents and files in the My Documents folder.

subfolders
Subfolders—folders contained within another folder—are useful for further organizing your documents and files.

files
Files are stored in subfolders.

Top level of file system

Hard disk (C:)   Removable disk (G:)

Level 2 — Windows   Program Files   Documents and other data

Level 3 — My Documents

Level 4 — Basic Accounting   Computer Concepts   Management Skills   Professional Writing
Folders created for each course

Level 5 — Memo   Policy   Proposal   Report
Files for the Professional Writing course

© 2014 Cengage Learning

Quick Reference Tools

Starting Windows 8

- If the lock screen appears, click anywhere on the screen or press any key.
- If the Welcome screen appears and lists only the previous user's name, click the Back button.
- On the Welcome screen, click your user name, type your password if you have one, and then press the Enter key.
- If the Start screen does not appear, press the Windows key, click Sign out, and then repeat previous bullet.

Using Windows Help and Support

- On the Start screen, type help, and then click Help and Support.
- In the Help window, click a link to get basic information or find more information on the Microsoft Web site.
- Click the Browse Help link, click a category, click a subcategory if needed, and then click a topic.
- In the Search box, type a word or phrase about the topic you want to find, and then click the Search Help button.

Navigating Windows

- Point to the upper-left corner of the screen, and then click a thumbnail on the Switch List.
- Press and hold the Alt key and press and release the Tab key to select a thumbnail.

Windows 8 File System

- At the top of the hierarchy is the root directory, which usually is drive C.
- Folders can contain subfolders.
- Libraries recognize files and folders by category.

Folders and Files

- To create a folder, on the Quick Access Toolbar, click the New folder button.
- To move a file or folder into a folder, drag the file or folder on top of another folder.
- To copy a file or folder, press and hold the Ctrl key as you drag the file or folder on top of another folder.
- To delete a file or folder, right-click the file or folder, and then click Delete.
- Each part of the file path is separated by a backslash: G:\Chapter 7\Chapter\File Name.docx

Ending a Windows Session

- Display the Charms bar, click the Settings charm, then click the Power button in the Settings panel.
- Sign out to close all programs and sign out of Windows 8 but leave the computer on.
- Log off to close all programs, log off Windows 8, and leave the computer running.
- Sleep to keep the current session in memory and put the computer in a low-power state.
- Shut down to close all open programs, shut down Windows, and turn off your computer.

Key Definitions

Go to your CMPTR² CourseMate site for a full list of key terms and definitions.

active window The window to which the next keystroke or command is applied.

Charms bar A bar that appears on the right edge of the Start screen that contains commands for interacting with Windows 8.

desktop The work area for using applications designed to run in Windows and where you manage files and folders.

double-click To click the left mouse button twice in quick succession.

drag To position the pointer on top of an item, and then press and hold the left mouse button while moving the pointer.

point To position the pointer directly on top of an item.

right-click To click the right mouse button and immediately release it.

shortcut A very small file that points to the location of the actual folder or file.

shortcut menu A menu that lists actions you can take with the item you right-clicked.

Start screen The screen in Windows 8 where you can access programs and features of your computer.

status bar A banner at the bottom of a window that displays information or messages about the task you are performing or the selected item.

tile A rectangle on the Start screen that represents an application or another resource.

window A rectangular work area on the desktop that contains a program, text, files, or other data.

review card

Learning Objectives

8-1	Use the Internet Explorer app
8-2	Use the Internet Explorer desktop application
8-3	Use tabs in both the Internet Explorer app and the desktop application
8-4	Personalize Internet Explorer
8-5	Print Web pages
8-6	Close the Internet Explorer app and desktop application
8-7	Use the Mail app
8-8	Add information to the People app

Digital Backpack

Practice It: Practice It 8-3—Use Internet Explorer to locate travel quotes, and then use the Mail app to share your findings.

On Your Own: On Your Own 8-2—Use Internet Explorer and Google to search for information on the Web, and then use the Mail app to share your findings.

Quiz: Take the practice quiz to prepare for tests.

Key Terms: Review the key term flash cards (online, printable, and audio).

Games: Play *Beat the Clock* and *Memory* to quiz yourself.

Videos: Watch the videos to learn more about the topics taught in this chapter.

Infographic

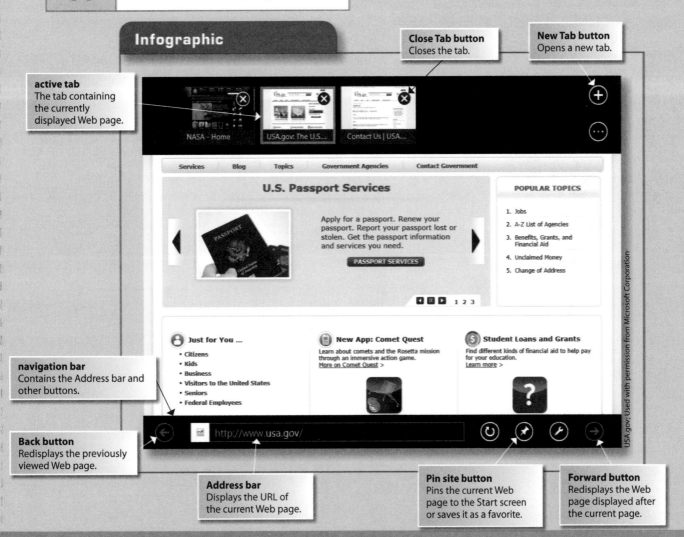

Close Tab button
Closes the tab.

New Tab button
Opens a new tab.

active tab
The tab containing the currently displayed Web page.

navigation bar
Contains the Address bar and other buttons.

Back button
Redisplays the previously viewed Web page.

Address bar
Displays the URL of the current Web page.

Pin site button
Pins the current Web page to the Start screen or saves it as a favorite.

Forward button
Redisplays the Web page displayed after the current page.

USA.gov: Used with permission from Microsoft Corporation

Quick Reference Tools

Use the Internet Explorer App

- To start the Internet Explorer app, on the Start screen, click the Internet Explorer tile.
- To display a Web page, right-click the screen to display the Address bar, at the bottom of the screen, click in the Address bar, type the URL of the Web page, and then press the Enter key.
- To display a page previously visited during the current session, click the Back button to the left of the Address bar or point to the left side of the screen and then click the Back arrow.
- To open a new tab, right-click the screen, and then in the tab switcher, click the New Tab button.
- To pin a Web page to the Start screen, right-click the screen to display the Address bar, click the Pin site button, click Pin to Start, and then click Pin to Start in the dialog box.
- To save a Web page as a favorite, right-click the screen to display the Address bar if necessary, click the Pin site button, and then click Add to favorites.

Use the Internet Explorer Desktop Application

- To start the Internet Explorer desktop application, on the desktop, on the status bar, click the Internet Explorer button.
- To display a Web page, at the top of the window, click in the Address bar, type the URL of the Web page, and then press the Enter key.
- To display a page previously visited during the current session, click the Back button to the left of the Address bar.
- To open a new tab, point to the blank tab to the right of the tabs, and then click the new Tab button.
- To pin a Web page, drag the tab to the taskbar.
- To save a Web page as a favorite, click the View favorites, feeds, and history button, click the Favorites tab if necessary, click the Add to favorites button, and then click Add.

Use the Mail App

- To start Mail, on the Start screen, click the Mail tile.
- To create a new email message, in the upper-right corner of the screen, click the New button.
- To reply to a message, select it, in the upper-right corner of the screen, click the Respond button, and then click Reply or Reply all.
- To forward a message, select it, in the upper-right corner of the screen, click the Respond button, and then click Forward.

Use the People App

- To start the People app, on the Start screen, click the People tile.
- To create a new contact, right-click the screen to display the Apps bar, and then on the Apps bar, click the New button.
- To delete a contact, right-click the screen to display the Apps bar, on the Apps bar click the Delete button, and then click Delete in the dialog box.

Key Definitions

Go to your CMPTR² CourseMate site for a full list of key terms and definitions.

attachment A file that is sent with an email message.

favorite A shortcut to a Web page saved in a list in the Internet Explorer desktop application or as a tile on the Start screen and on the expanded navigation bar.

history A list that tracks the Web pages you visit over a certain time period.

keyword A word typed in a search box on a search site or other Web page to locate information related to that keyword.

load To copy a Web page from a server to a computer.

profile The collected information about a contact.

search engine A software program used by a search site to retrieve Web pages containing the keywords from a search database.

search phrase Multiple keywords.

search results A list of links to Web pages that contain the keywords entered in a search engine.

tab An object that displays a Web page within the Internet Explorer desktop application window or in the Internet Explorer app.

tab group A collection of related tabs.

tab switcher An area in the Internet Explorer app that displays thumbnails of current or recently visited Web pages for easy navigation between them.

Learning Objectives

9-1	Explore common elements of Office application windows
9-2	Use the ribbon
9-3	Select text and use the Mini toolbar
9-4	Undo and redo actions
9-5	Zoom and scroll in application windows
9-6	Work with Office files
9-7	Use the Clipboard
9-8	Get Help
9-9	Close Office applications

Digital Backpack

Practice It: Practice It 9-3—Complete a presentation with a checklist of camping supplies.

On Your Own: On Your Own 9-2—Identify the programs used to complete event planning tasks.

Quiz: Take the practice quiz to prepare for tests.

Key Terms: Review the key term flash cards (online, printable, and audio).

Games: Play *Beat the Clock* and *Memory* to quiz yourself.

Videos: Watch the videos to learn more about the topics taught in this chapter.

Infographic

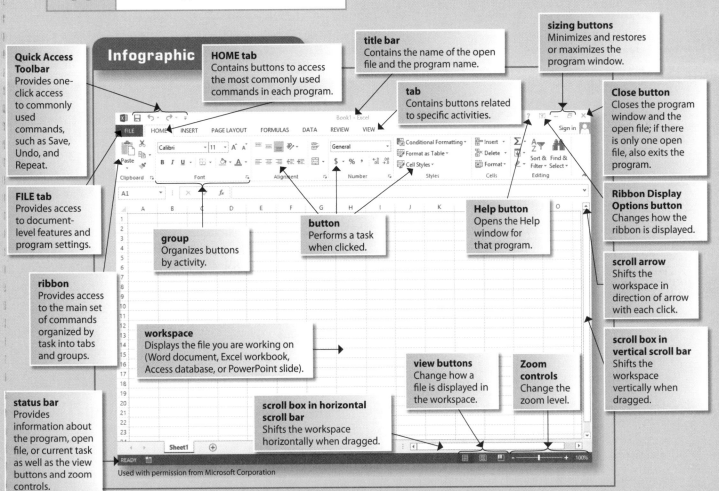

sizing buttons
Minimizes and restores or maximizes the program window.

title bar
Contains the name of the open file and the program name.

Quick Access Toolbar
Provides one-click access to commonly used commands, such as Save, Undo, and Repeat.

HOME tab
Contains buttons to access the most commonly used commands in each program.

tab
Contains buttons related to specific activities.

Close button
Closes the program window and the open file; if there is only one open file, also exits the program.

FILE tab
Provides access to document-level features and program settings.

group
Organizes buttons by activity.

button
Performs a task when clicked.

Help button
Opens the Help window for that program.

Ribbon Display Options button
Changes how the ribbon is displayed.

ribbon
Provides access to the main set of commands organized by task into tabs and groups.

scroll arrow
Shifts the workspace in direction of arrow with each click.

workspace
Displays the file you are working on (Word document, Excel workbook, Access database, or PowerPoint slide).

scroll box in vertical scroll bar
Shifts the workspace vertically when dragged.

status bar
Provides information about the program, open file, or current task as well as the view buttons and zoom controls.

scroll box in horizontal scroll bar
Shifts the workspace horizontally when dragged.

view buttons
Change how a file is displayed in the workspace.

Zoom controls
Change the zoom level.

Used with permission from Microsoft Corporation

Quick Reference Tools

Identify buttons

- Position the pointer on top of a button to see a ScreenTip with its name and keyboard shortcut (if it has one).

Use the Mini toolbar

- The Mini toolbar appears when you select text using the mouse or when you right-click.
- Click buttons on it just as you click buttons on the ribbon.
- If it disappears, move the mouse toward it or right-click.

Contextual tabs

- Remember that contextual tabs appear only when an object is selected.

Save vs. Save As

- The Save command saves the file using the same file name and in the same location.
- The Save As command saves a copy of the file; you can type a new name and choose a new location.

Select Text

- To select text using the mouse, click before the first character, press and hold the mouse button, and then drag over the text.
- To select text using the keyboard, position the insertion point before the first, press and hold the Shift key, and then press the arrow key pointing in the direction you want to select.
- To select text using the mouse and the keyboard, click before the first character, press and hold the Shift key, and then click after the last character.
- To select nonadjacent text, select the first block of text, press and hold the Ctrl key, and then drag to select other blocks of text.

Use Live Preview

- Select text that you want to format.
- Point to an option in a gallery to see a live preview of the option.
- Click the option to apply it to the selected text.

Key Definitions

Go to your CMPTR² CourseMate site for a full list of key terms and definitions.

Backstage view A screen that contains commands to manage application files and options.

database An Access file.

dialog box A window in which you enter or choose settings for performing a task.

document A Word file.

gallery A menu or grid that shows visual representations of the options available for a button.

integration The ability to share information between programs.

Live Preview A feature that shows the results that would occur if you clicked the option to which you are pointing in a gallery.

Microsoft Office 2013 (Office) A collection of Microsoft programs.

Mini toolbar A toolbar with buttons for commonly used formatting commands that appears next to the pointer when text is selected using the mouse or when you right-click.

navigation bar The left pane in Backstage view.

object Anything in a document that can be manipulated as a whole.

Protected View A view of a file in an Office program in which you can see the file contents, but you cannot edit, save, or print them until you enable editing.

presentation A PowerPoint file.

task pane A narrow window that appears to the left or right of the workspace in which you can enter or choose settings for performing a task.

toggle button A button that you click once to turn a feature on and click again to turn it off.

workbook An Excel file.

Learning Objectives

10-1	Enter text
10-2	Create documents based on existing documents
10-3	Edit text
10-4	Switch to another open document in Word
10-5	Format text
10-6	Format paragraphs
10-7	Copy formats
10-8	Check spelling and grammar
10-9	Preview and print documents

Digital Backpack

Practice It: Practice It 10-3—Create and format a Word document using an existing document.

On Your Own: On Your Own 10-2—Modify text, review page layout, and print a Word document.

Quiz: Take the practice quiz to prepare for tests.

Key Terms: Review the key term flash cards (online, printable, and audio).

Games: Play *Beat the Clock* and *Memory* to quiz yourself.

Videos: Watch the videos to learn more about the topics taught in this chapter.

Infographic

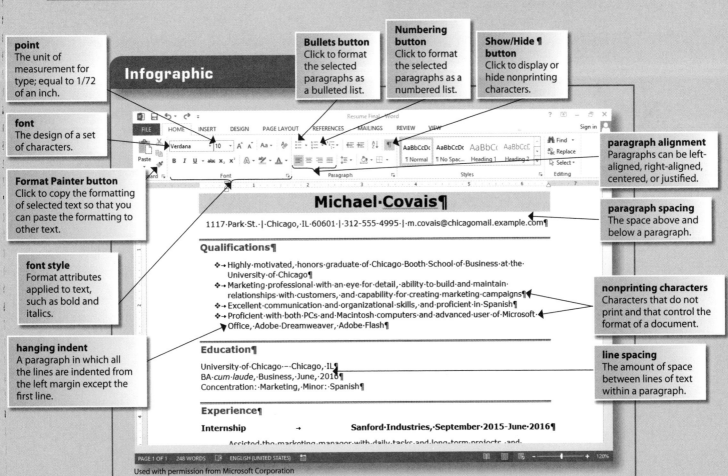

point
The unit of measurement for type; equal to 1/72 of an inch.

font
The design of a set of characters.

Format Painter button
Click to copy the formatting of selected text so that you can paste the formatting to other text.

font style
Format attributes applied to text, such as bold and italics.

hanging indent
A paragraph in which all the lines are indented from the left margin except the first line.

Bullets button
Click to format the selected paragraphs as a bulleted list.

Numbering button
Click to format the selected paragraphs as a numbered list.

Show/Hide ¶ button
Click to display or hide nonprinting characters.

paragraph alignment
Paragraphs can be left-aligned, right-aligned, centered, or justified.

paragraph spacing
The space above and below a paragraph.

nonprinting characters
Characters that do not print and that control the format of a document.

line spacing
The amount of space between lines of text within a paragraph.

Used with permission from Microsoft Corporation

Quick Reference Tools

Create a Document

- To enter text, type in a document, pressing the Enter key only to start a new paragraph.
- To insert a date with AutoComplete, press the Enter key when the date appears in a ScreenTip.
- To insert a symbol, click the Symbol button in the Symbols group on the INSERT tab, and then click More Symbols. Click a symbol, click Insert, and then click Close.
- To save a document with a new name, click Save As in Backstage view, and then click the Browse button or the folder name. In the Save As dialog box, type a new file name, and then click Save.

Copy Formats

- To copy the format of text and apply it to other text, select the text. On the HOME tab, in the Clipboard group, click the Format Painter button, and then click or select the text you want to format.
- To copy text and keep its formatting, click the Paste button in the Clipboard group on the HOME tab, and then click the Keep Source Formatting button.

Edit Text

- To replace text, select it and type.
- To move text, drag selected text to a new location.

Format Text and Paragraphs

- You can format text by changing the font, size, style, and color.
- You can format paragraphs by changing the line spacing; paragraph spacing, alignment, borders, and shading; and by creating bulleted and numbered lists.
- To create a tab stop, click the tab selector to select a tab style, and then click on the horizontal ruler to add a tab stop.
- To create first-line, hanging, right, and left paragraph indents, use the indent markers on the horizontal ruler.

Check Spelling and Grammar

- Misspelled words have a red wavy underline. Contextual spelling errors have a blue wavy underline. Grammar errors also have a blue wavy underline.
- Right-click a flagged word, and then click the correction on the shortcut menu.
- To check spelling in the entire document, on the REVIEW tab, in the Proofing group, click the Spelling & Grammar button.

Preview and Print a Document

- Click the FILE tab, and then in the navigation bar, click Print.
- In the right pane, review the preview.
- In the left pane, set the print options.
- Click the Print button.

Key Definitions

Go to your CMPTR² CourseMate site for a full list of key terms and definitions.

AutoCorrect A feature that automatically corrects certain misspelled words and typing errors.

first-line indent A paragraph in which the first-line is indented from the left margin.

format To change the appearance of a file and its content.

leader line A line that appears between two elements, such as between tabbed text.

line spacing The amount of space between lines of text within a paragraph.

single spaced Line spacing that has no extra space between lines of text in a paragraph.

spell check To check a file for spelling and grammatical errors using the Spelling and Grammar Checker.

tab stop (tab) A location on the horizontal ruler where the insertion point moves when you press the Tab key.

template A file that contains formatting and sometimes sample content.

Learning Objectives

11-1	Find and replace text
11-2	Work with styles
11-3	Work with themes
11-4	Scroll through a long document
11-5	Work with the document outline
11-6	Change the margins
11-7	Insert a manual page break
11-8	Add page numbers, headers, and footers
11-9	Create citations and a list of works cited
11-10	Create footnotes and endnotes

Digital Backpack

Practice It: Practice It 11-3—Create a Word document using styles and themes and work with the document outline.

On Your Own: On Your Own 11-2—Modify the style set, insert page numbers, and create citations.

Quiz: Take the practice quiz to prepare for tests.

Key Terms: Review the key term flash cards (online, printable, and audio).

Games: Play *Beat the Clock* and *Memory* to quiz yourself.

Videos: Watch the videos to learn more about the topics taught in this chapter.

Infographic

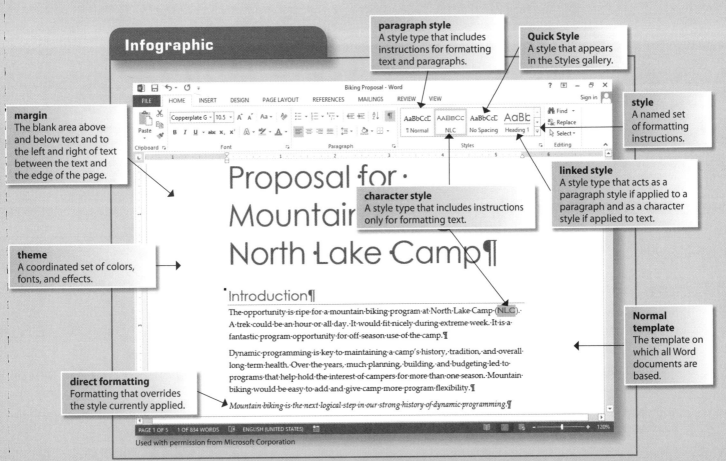

paragraph style
A style type that includes instructions for formatting text and paragraphs.

Quick Style
A style that appears in the Styles gallery.

style
A named set of formatting instructions.

margin
The blank area above and below text and to the left and right of text between the text and the edge of the page.

linked style
A style type that acts as a paragraph style if applied to a paragraph and as a character style if applied to text.

character style
A style type that includes instructions only for formatting text.

theme
A coordinated set of colors, fonts, and effects.

Normal template
The template on which all Word documents are based.

direct formatting
Formatting that overrides the style currently applied.

Used with permission from Microsoft Corporation

Quick Reference Tools

Use Styles

- The five types of styles are paragraph, character, linked, table, and list.
- To apply a Quick Style, on the HOME tab, in the Styles group, click the More button, and then click a style in the Quick Styles gallery.
- To create a new Quick Style, select the text with the formatting you want, in the Quick Styles gallery, click Create a Style, type a style name, and then click OK.

Apply a Theme

- To change the theme, on the DESIGN tab, in the Document Formatting group, click the Themes button, and then click a theme.
- You can modify the theme fonts and colors using the corresponding buttons in the Document Formatting group on the DESIGN tab.

Set Margins, Page Breaks, Headers, and Footers

- You can set how much blank space appears around the edges of the page by changing the page margins.
- To start a new page, you can insert a manual page break.
- To add page numbers to a document, on the INSERT tab, in the Header & Footer group, click the Page Number button, and then click a page number style.
- To add text as a header or footer, double-click in the header or footer area, type text and format it as needed, and then click in the document area.

Review the Document Outline

- You can view a document's structure in the Navigation pane and then browse by the document's headings or by thumbnails of the pages.
- In the Navigation pane, when browsing by heading, you can collapse or expand, promote or demote, and move headings.
- Outline view shows the document's heading levels as an outline. You can promote or demote and move headings to reorganize the document.

Create Footnotes or Endnotes

- On the REFERENCES tab, in the Footnotes group, click the Insert Footnote button or the Insert Endnote button, and then type the note text.

Create Lists of Citations

- On the REFERENCES tab, in the Citations & Bibliography group, click the Style box arrow, and then click a style, such as MLA Seventh Edition.
- To enter a new source, in the Citations & Bibliography group, click the Insert Citation button, click Add New Source, enter source information, and then click OK.
- To insert a citation to an existing source, click the Insert Citation button, and then click the source.
- To generate a bibliography, click the Bibliography button, and then select a format.

Key Definitions

Go to your CMPTR² CourseMate site for a full list of key terms and definitions.

automatic page break (soft page break) A page break that is created when content fills a page and a new page is created automatically.

content control A special field used as a placeholder for text you insert or designed to contain specific type of text.

demote To move an item to a lower level in an outline.

endnote An explanatory comment or reference that appears at the end of a section or at the end of a document.

field In Word, a placeholder for variable information that includes an instruction to insert the specific information.

footer Text that appears at the bottom of every page.

footnote An explanatory comment or reference that appears at the bottom of a page.

header Text that appears at the top of every page.

manual page break (hard page break) A page break that you insert to force content after the break to appear on a new page.

promote To move an item to a higher level in an outline.

style set A group of Quick Styles.

review card

CHAPTER 12
Enhancing a Document
Word 2013

Learning Objectives

12-1	Organize information in tables
12-2	Change the page orientation
12-3	Divide a document into sections
12-4	Insert and modify graphics
12-5	Wrap text around graphics
12-6	Move graphics
12-7	Add text effects and WordArt text boxes
12-8	Work with columns
12-9	Work with building blocks

Digital Backpack

Practice It: Practice It 12-3—Add a table and graphics to enhance a Word document.

On Your Own: On Your Own 12-2—Modify the formatting, page orientation, and layout and then print the document.

Quiz: Take the practice quiz to prepare for tests.

Key Terms: Review the key term flash cards (online, printable, and audio).

Games: Play *Beat the Clock* and *Memory* to quiz yourself.

Videos: Watch the videos to learn more about the topics taught in this chapter.

Infographic

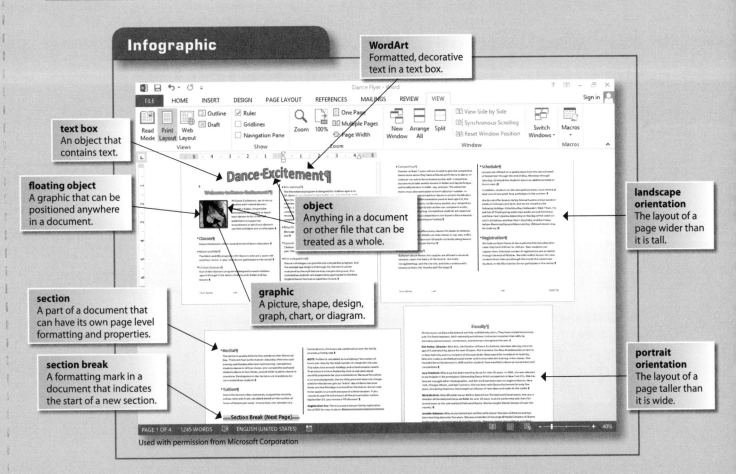

WordArt
Formatted, decorative text in a text box.

text box
An object that contains text.

floating object
A graphic that can be positioned anywhere in a document.

object
Anything in a document or other file that can be treated as a whole.

landscape orientation
The layout of a page wider than it is tall.

section
A part of a document that can have its own page level formatting and properties.

graphic
A picture, shape, design, graph, chart, or diagram.

section break
A formatting mark in a document that indicates the start of a new section.

portrait orientation
The layout of a page taller than it is wide.

Used with permission from Microsoft Corporation

Visit CourseMate for **CMPTR²** at www.cengagebrain.com for additional study tools!

Quick Reference Tools

Organize Information in Tables

- To create a table, on the INSERT tab, in the Tables group, click the Tables button, and then click the box in the grid that represents the lower-right corner of the table.
- To insert or delete rows and columns, click in the appropriate row or column, and then on the TABLE TOOLS LAYOUT tab, in the Rows & Columns group, click the corresponding button.
- To format a table, on the TABLE TOOLS DESIGN tab, in the Table Styles group, click the More button, and then click a table style.

Add Section Breaks and Columns

- The four types of section breaks are Next Page, Continuous, Even Page, and Odd Page.
- You can format each section separately.
- To insert a section break, on the PAGE LAYOUT tab, in the Setup group, click the Breaks button, and then click a section break.
- To format a document in columns, on the PAGE LAYOUT tab, in the Page Setup group, click the Columns button, and then click a column option.
- To balance text in columns, insert a continuous section break.

Change Page Orientation

- On the PAGE LAYOUT tab, in the Page Setup group, click the Orientation button, and then click an orientation.

Add Graphics

- To insert online pictures, on the INSERT tab, in the Illustrations group, click the Online Pictures button. In the Insert Pictures dialog box, type a keyword in the Office.com Clip Art box, and then click the search button. Click an image, and then click Insert.
- To resize a graphic, drag a sizing handle on the selection box.
- To crop a photo, on the PICTURE TOOLS FORMAT tab, in the Size group, click the Crop button, drag a crop handle, and then click the Crop button again.
- To format a picture, on the PICTURE TOOLS FORMAT tab, in the Picture Styles group, use the appropriate buttons.

Add WordArt Text Boxes

- To insert a WordArt text box, on the INSERT tab, in the Text group, click the WordArt button, select a style, and then type text.
- To format WordArt, on the DRAWING TOOLS FORMAT tab, click the appropriate buttons to change the styles, size, etc.
- To change the text wrap option, click the Layout Options button next to the graphic, and then select a wrap option.

Create Quick Parts

- To create a building block, select the text. On the INSERT tab, in the Text group, click the Quick Parts button, and then click Save Selection to Quick Part gallery.

Key Definitions

Go to your CMPTR² CourseMate site for a full list of key terms and definitions.

aspect ratio The proportion of an object's height to its width.

building block A part of a document that is stored and reused.

cell The intersection of a column and a row in a table.

crop To cut off part of a graphic.

graphic A picture, shape, design, graph, chart, or diagram.

object Anything in a document that can be treated as a whole.

orientation The way a page is turned.

Quick Part A building block stored in the Quick Parts gallery.

selection box The box that surrounds an object when it is selected.

sizing handle A small circle that appears at the corner of a selection box or a square that appears on the side of a selection box.

table A grid of horizontal rows and vertical columns.

text box An object that contains text.

reviewcard

CHAPTER 13
Creating a Workbook
Excel 2013

Learning Objectives

13-1	Understand spreadsheets and Excel
13-2	Enter and format data
13-3	Edit cell content
13-4	Work with columns and rows
13-5	Work with cells and ranges
13-6	Enter simple formulas and functions
13-7	Preview and print a workbook

Digital Backpack

Practice It: Practice It 13-3—Enter data in cells and format an Excel worksheet, working with columns, rows, and cells.

On Your Own: On Your Own 13-2—Work with formulas and functions and print an Excel worksheet.

Quiz: Take the practice quiz to prepare for tests.

Key Terms: Review the key term flash cards (online, printable, and audio).

Games: Play *Beat the Clock* and *Memory* to quiz yourself.

Videos: Watch the videos to learn more about the topics taught in this chapter.

Infographic

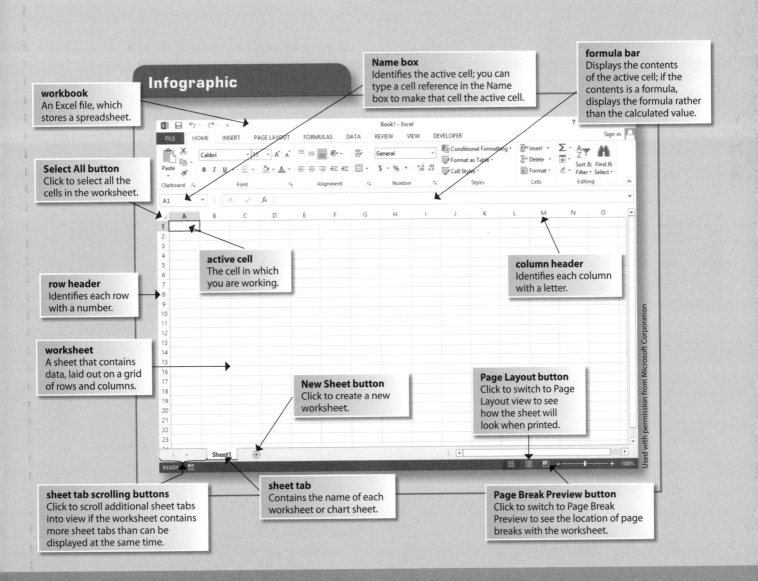

workbook
An Excel file, which stores a spreadsheet.

Select All button
Click to select all the cells in the worksheet.

row header
Identifies each row with a number.

worksheet
A sheet that contains data, laid out on a grid of rows and columns.

Name box
Identifies the active cell; you can type a cell reference in the Name box to make that cell the active cell.

formula bar
Displays the contents of the active cell; if the contents is a formula, displays the formula rather than the calculated value.

active cell
The cell in which you are working.

column header
Identifies each column with a letter.

New Sheet button
Click to create a new worksheet.

Page Layout button
Click to switch to Page Layout view to see how the sheet will look when printed.

sheet tab scrolling buttons
Click to scroll additional sheet tabs into view if the worksheet contains more sheet tabs than can be displayed at the same time.

sheet tab
Contains the name of each worksheet or chart sheet.

Page Break Preview button
Click to switch to Page Break Preview to see the location of page breaks with the worksheet.

Used with permission from Microsoft Corporation

Quick Reference Tools

Create a Workbook

- To move the active cell, click a new cell, use a keyboard shortcut, or type the cell reference in the Name box, and then press the Enter key.
- To insert a sheet, click the New sheet button.
- To switch between sheets, click the sheet tab.
- To delete a sheet, right-click the sheet tab, and then on the shortcut menu, click Delete.
- To rename a sheet, double-click the sheet tab, type the new name, and then press the Enter key.
- To move a sheet, drag its sheet tab. To copy a sheet, press and hold the Ctrl key while dragging.

Work with Columns and Rows

- To select a column or row, click its header.
- To select adjacent columns or rows, drag across multiple columns or rows.
- To select nonadjacent columns or rows, press and hold the Ctrl key while clicking headers.
- To insert a column or row, on the HOME tab, in the Cells group, click the Insert button arrow, and then click the item you want to insert.
- To delete a column or row, select it, and then on the HOME tab, in the Cells group, click the Delete button.

Work with Ranges

- To move a range, select it and drag it by its border.
- To insert a range, select the size of the range to insert. On the HOME tab, in the Cells group, click the Insert button arrow, and click Insert Cells.
- To delete a range, select it, and then on the HOME tab, in the Cells group, click the Delete button arrow, and click Delete Cells.

Enter Simple Formulas and Functions

- To enter a formula, type = and then the formula.
- To enter the SUM function, type =SUM and then type the range between parentheses.
- To enter an AutoSum function, on the HOME tab, in the Editing group, click the AutoSum button arrow, and then click a function.

Format Data

- To format text, on the HOME tab, in the Font group, use the buttons to change fonts, font sizes, font styles, and colors.
- To format dates, on the HOME tab, in the Number group, click the Number Format box arrow, and then click a date format.
- To format numbers, on the HOME tab, in the Number group, use the buttons to add commas, currency symbols, and percent signs, and change the number of decimal places.

Preview and Print a Workbook

- To preview the printed workbook, click the FILE tab, and then in the navigation bar, click Print.
- To view formulas in a worksheet, on the FORMULAS tab, in the Formula Auditing group, click the Show Formulas button.
- To change the page orientation, on the PAGE LAYOUT tab, in the Page Setup group, click the Orientation button, and then click an option.

Key Definitions

Go to your CMPTR² CourseMate site for a full list of key terms and definitions.

adjacent range A single rectangular block of cells.

AutoSum A feature that inserts the SUM, AVERAGE, COUNT, MIN, or MAX function.

cell range (range) A group of cells.

cell reference The row and column location of a specific cell.

formula A mathematical expression that returns a value.

function A named operation that replaces the action of an arithmetic expression.

Microsoft Excel 2013 (Excel) A computer application used to enter, analyze, and present quantitative data.

nonadjacent range Two or more distinct adjacent ranges.

Normal view The Excel view that shows the contents of the current sheet.

operator A mathematical symbol used to combine values.

Page Layout view The Excel view that shows how the current sheet will look when printed.

range reference The location and size of a range.

Learning Objectives

14-1	Use relative, absolute, and mixed cell references in formulas
14-2	Enter functions
14-3	Use AutoFill
14-4	Work with date functions
14-5	Work with the PMT financial function
14-6	Format cells and ranges

Digital Backpack

Practice It: Practice It 14-3—Create an Excel worksheet that includes absolute, relative, and mixed formulas.

On Your Own: On Your Own 14-2—Modify worksheet data to include formulas and functions and prepare a worksheet for printing.

Quiz: Take the practice quiz to prepare for tests.

Key Terms: Review the key term flash cards (online, printable, and audio).

Games: Play *Beat the Clock* and *Memory* to quiz yourself.

Videos: Watch the videos to learn more about the topics taught in this chapter.

Infographic

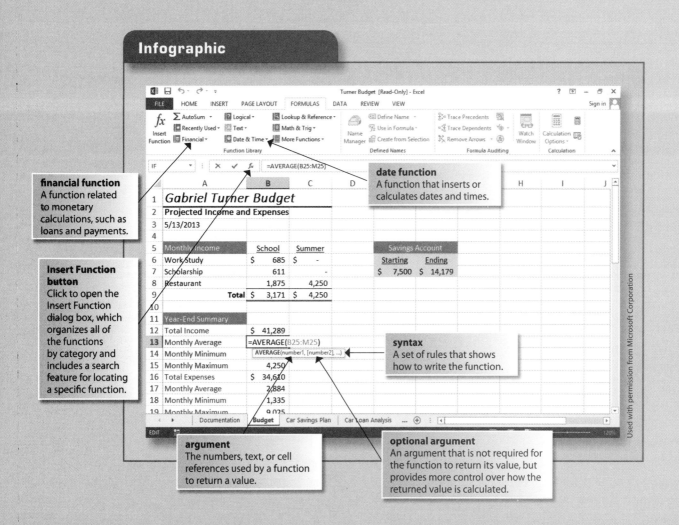

financial function
A function related to monetary calculations, such as loans and payments.

Insert Function button
Click to open the Insert Function dialog box, which organizes all of the functions by category and includes a search feature for locating a specific function.

date function
A function that inserts or calculates dates and times.

syntax
A set of rules that shows how to write the function.

argument
The numbers, text, or cell references used by a function to return a value.

optional argument
An argument that is not required for the function to return its value, but provides more control over how the returned value is calculated.

Used with permission from Microsoft Corporation

Quick Reference Tools

Enter a Function Using the Insert Function Dialog Box

- To open the Insert Function dialog box, to the left of the formula bar, click the Insert Function button.
- To enter a function by searching for it using the Insert Function dialog box, in the Insert Function dialog box, in the Search box, type keywords, and then click Go.
- To enter a function by using the list of recently used functions in the Insert Function dialog box, click the Or select a category arrow, click Most Recently Used, and then in the Select a function list, click the function name.

Enter a Function by Typing It in a Cell

- Type = (an equal sign), type the first letter or two of the function you want to insert, click the function name in the list that appears, double-click the function name, select the range or enter, and then type) (closing parenthesis).

Function Syntax

- *FUNCTION(argument1[,argument2=value2,...])*

Use Date Functions

- To display the current date, type =TODAY().
- To display the current date and time, type =NOW().
- To insert a date function using the Date & Time button, on the FORMULAS tab, in the Function Library group, click the Date & Time button, and then click TODAY or NOW in the date functions list.

Use AutoFill

- Select a cell or range, and then drag the fill handle to the right or down.

Use the PMT Function

- *PMT(rate,nper,pv[,fv=0][,type=0])*

Key Definitions

Go to your CMPTR² CourseMate site for a full list of key terms and definitions.

absolute reference A cell reference that remains fixed when copied to a new location; includes $ in front of both the column letter and row number.

argument The numbers, text, or cell references used by a function to return a value.

AutoFill An Excel feature that copies content and formats from a cell or range into an adjacent cell or range.

comparison operator A symbol that indicates the relationship between two values.

date function A function that inserts or calculates dates and times.

fill handle A box in the lower-right corner of a selected cell or range that you drag over an adjacent cell or range to copy the content and formatting from the original cells into the adjacent range.

financial function A function related to monetary calculations, such as loans and payments.

IF function A logical function that tests a condition and then returns one value if the condition is true and another value if the condition is false.

mixed reference A cell reference that contains an absolute row reference or an absolute column reference, such as $A2 or A$2.

nest To place one item inside another, such as a function.

optional argument An argument that is not required for the function to return a value, but provides more control over how the returned value is calculated.

order of precedence A set of predefined rules used to determine the sequence in which operators are applied in a calculation—first exponentiation ($\wedge$), second multiplication (*) and division (/), and third addition (+) and subtraction (−).

PMT function A financial function that calculates the monthly payment required to pay back a loan.

principal The amount of money being loaned.

relative reference A cell reference that is interpreted in relation to the location of the cell containing the formula.

syntax A set of rules.

what-if analysis An examination of how changing values entered directly in a worksheet affect calculated values.

Learning Objectives

15-1	Make a workbook user-friendly
15-2	Flash Fill a range
15-3	Enter formulas with multiple calculations
15-4	Fix error values
15-5	Work with the IF logical function
15-6	Create a nested IF function
15-7	Highlight cells with conditional formatting
15-8	Hide rows and columns
15-9	Format a worksheet for printing

Digital Backpack

Practice It: Practice It 15-3— Format Excel data in cells and ranges and create a table.

On Your Own: On Your Own 15-2—Create an Excel worksheet with conditional formatting and hidden worksheet data.

Quiz: Take the practice quiz to prepare for tests.

Key Terms: Review the key term flash cards (online, printable, and audio).

Games: Play *Beat the Clock* and *Memory* to quiz yourself.

Videos: Watch the videos to learn more about the topics taught in this chapter.

Infographic

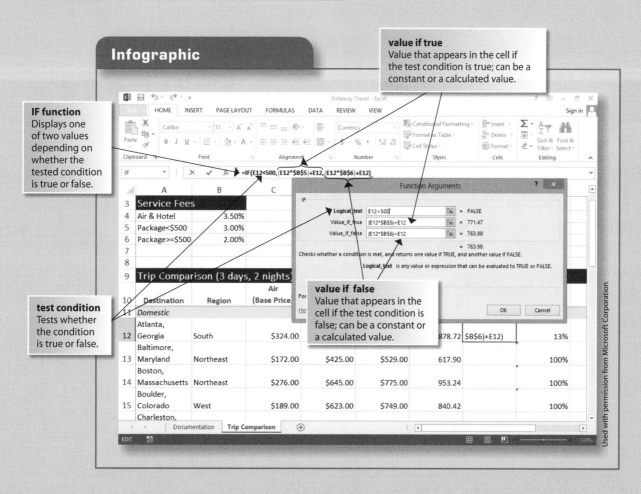

value if true
Value that appears in the cell if the test condition is true; can be a constant or a calculated value.

IF function
Displays one of two values depending on whether the tested condition is true or false.

test condition
Tests whether the condition is true or false.

value if false
Value that appears in the cell if the test condition is false; can be a constant or a calculated value.

Used with permission from Microsoft Corporation

Quick Reference Tools

Create Complex Formulas

- Calculations in formulas are performed based on the order of operations— exponentiation (^); multiplication (*) and division (/); addition (=) and subtraction (–).

- To change the order of operations, enclose parts of the formula within parentheses. Any expression within a set of parentheses is calculated before the rest of the formula.

- Constants are entered directly in a formula or placed in a separate worksheet cell and referenced in the formula.

Hide Worksheet Data

- To hide worksheet data, select the row or column to hide, on the HOME tab, in the Cells group, click the Format button, point to Hide & Unhide, and then click Hide Rows or Hide Columns.

- To unhide worksheet data, select the rows or column on either side of the hidden rows and columns, on the HOME tab, in the Cells group, click the Format button, point to Hide & Unhide, and then click Unhide Rows or Unhide Columns.

Error Value Messages

- Error values messages indicate the type of error that occurred in a cell.

- To obtain more information about an error, click a cell containing an error, and then point to the Error Checking button that appears to display a ScreenTip containing a description of the error.

Use Conditional Formatting

- To apply conditional formatting, select a range, on the HOME tab, in the Styles group, click the Conditional Formatting button, select a rule, and then refine the rule in the dialog box that opens.

- To clear a conditional formatting rule, click the Conditional Formatting button, click Manage Rules, select the rule, and then click Delete Rule.

IF Functions and Nested IFs

- The IF function returns one value if a statement is true and a different value if the statement is false.

- IF function syntax is: IF(*Logical_test*[,*value_if_true*][,*value_if_false*]).

- Functions can be nested inside another function. If a formula contains more than one function, the innermost function is calculated first, then the next most innermost function, and so on.

Format a Worksheet for Printing

- To insert a manual page break, click the row below the page break location, click the Page Break Preview button on the status bar, click the PAGE LAYOUT tab on the ribbon, in the Page Setup group, click the Breaks button, and then click Insert Page Break.

- To set the print area, select the range to print, click the PAGE LAYOUT tab on the ribbon, in the Page Setup group, click the Print Area button, and then click Set Print Area.

Key Definitions

Go to your CMPTR² CourseMate site for a full list of key terms and definitions.

automatic page break A page break Excel inserts when no more content will fit on the page.

conditional formatting Formatting that is applied to a cell only when the cell's value meets a specified condition.

conditional formatting rule A list of the condition, the type of formatting applied when the condition occurs, and the cell or range to which the formatting is applied.

Excel table A range of data that is treated as a distinct object in a worksheet.

Flash Fill An Excel feature that enters text based on patterns that it finds in the data.

manual page break A page break you insert to specify where a page break occurs.

order of operations A set of predefined rules used to determine the sequence in which operators are applied in a calculation—first exponentiation (^); second multiplication (*)_ and division (/); and third, addition (+) and subtraction (-)

print area The region that is sent to the printer from the active sheet.

print title Information from a workbook that appears on every printed page.

Learning Objectives

16-1	Create a chart
16-2	Move and resize a chart
16-3	Modify a chart
16-4	Create an exploded pie chart
16-5	Create a column chart
16-6	Create a line chart
16-7	Edit chart data
16-8	Insert and format sparklines
16-9	Insert and modify data bars

Digital Backpack

Practice It: Practice It 16-3—Create and modify different charts and edit chart data.

On Your Own: On Your Own 16-2—Edit chart data and insert and modify sparklines and data bars.

Quiz: Take the practice quiz to prepare for tests.

Key Terms: Review the key term flash cards (online, printable, and audio).

Games: Play *Beat the Clock* and *Memory* to quiz yourself.

Videos: Watch the videos to learn more about the topics taught in this chapter.

Infographic

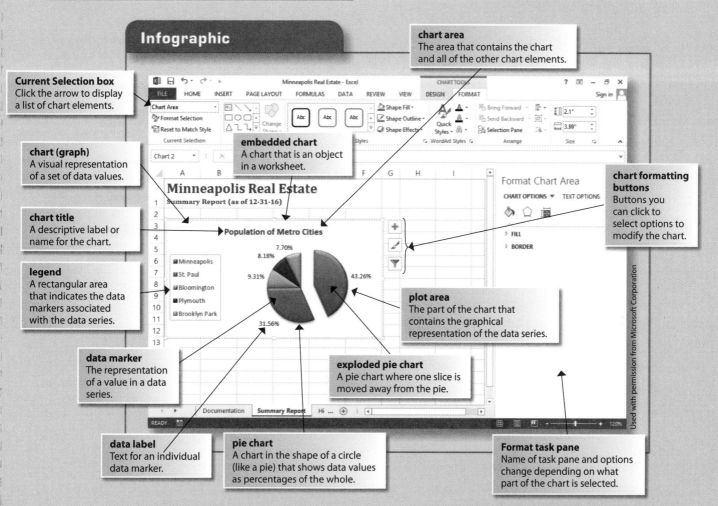

chart area
The area that contains the chart and all of the other chart elements.

Current Selection box
Click the arrow to display a list of chart elements.

chart (graph)
A visual representation of a set of data values.

embedded chart
A chart that is an object in a worksheet.

chart formatting buttons
Buttons you can click to select options to modify the chart.

chart title
A descriptive label or name for the chart.

legend
A rectangular area that indicates the data markers associated with the data series.

plot area
The part of the chart that contains the graphical representation of the data series.

data marker
The representation of a value in a data series.

exploded pie chart
A pie chart where one slice is moved away from the pie.

data label
Text for an individual data marker.

pie chart
A chart in the shape of a circle (like a pie) that shows data values as percentages of the whole.

Format task pane
Name of task pane and options change depending on what part of the chart is selected.

Quick Reference Tools

Create a Chart

- To create a chart, select the data source range, on the INSERT tab, in the Charts group, click the chart type, and then click the style.

Change a Chart's Location

- To move a chart to another sheet, select the chart area, on the CHART TOOLS DESIGN tab, in the Location group, click the Move Chart button; in the Move Chart dialog box, click the Object in box arrow, click the worksheet to move the chart to, and then click OK.
- To move a chart on a sheet, drag it to a new location.

Formatting a Chart

- To change the chart style, on the CHART TOOLS DESIGN tab, in the Chart Styles group, select a style.
- To change the chart layout, on the CHART TOOLS DESIGN tab, in the Chart Layouts group, click the Quick Layout button, and then select a layout.
- To add data labels, click the Chart Elements button to the right of the chart, point to Data Labels, click the right arrow, and then select an option.
- To change the color of a data series, double-click a data marker, in the Format Data Point pane, click the Fill & Line button, click FILL to expand the list, click the Solid fill option button, click the Color button, and then click a color.

Create an Exploded Pie Chart

- To create an exploded pie chart, select the pie chart, click a pie slice, and then drag the slice away from the chart.

Modify an Axis

- To change the axis scale, double-click a value on the axis, click the AXIS OPTIONS tab in the Format Axis pane, click AXIS OPTIONS to expand the list, and then in the Units section, make changes.
- To add an axis title, click the Chart Elements button to the right of the chart, point to Axis Titles, click the right arrow, click the title to add, replace the placeholder text with the title.
- To add gridlines, click the Chart Elements button to the right of the chart, point to Gridlines, click the right arrow, click a checkbox.

Insert Sparklines

- To insert sparklines, select the range, on the INSERT tab, in the Sparklines group, click the Line button, in the Create Sparklines dialog box, in the Data Range box, select the range to chart, and then click OK.

Insert Data Bars

- To insert data bars, select the range, on the HOME tab, in the Styles group, click the Conditional Formatting button, point to Data Bars, and then select a style in the gallery.

Key Definitions

Go to your CMPTR² CourseMate site for a full list of key terms and definitions.

category A set of values that represent data for one item in a chart.

category values The first column of the data range, which are the groups or categories to which the series values belong.

chart (graph) A visual representation of a set of data values.

combination chart A chart that combines two or more chart types in a single graph, such as a column chart and a line chart.

data bar Conditional formatting that adds a horizontal bar to a cell's background that is proportional in length to the cell's value.

data source The range that contains the data to display in a chart.

data series A set of values represented in a chart.

horizontal (category) axis The horizontal axis that shows the category values from each data series.

legend A rectangular area that indicates the data markers associated with the data series.

scale The range of values along an axis.

sparkline A graph that is displayed within a cell.

vertical (value) axis The vertical axis that shows the range of series values from all of the data series plotted on the chart.

reviewcard

Learning Objectives

17-1	Understand database concepts
17-2	Create a database
17-3	Work in Datasheet view
17-4	Work with fields and properties in Design view
17-5	Modify a table's structure
17-6	Close and open objects and databases
17-7	Create simple queries, forms, and reports
17-8	Compact and repair a database

Digital Backpack

Practice It: Practice It 17-3—Create an Access database and modify a table's structure.

On Your Own: On Your Own 17-2—Work in Datasheet view and Design view, and compact and repair a database.

Quiz: Take the practice quiz to prepare for tests.

Key Terms: Review the key term flash cards (online, printable, and audio).

Games: Play *Beat the Clock* and *Memory* to quiz yourself.

Videos: Watch the videos to learn more about the topics taught in this chapter.

Infographic

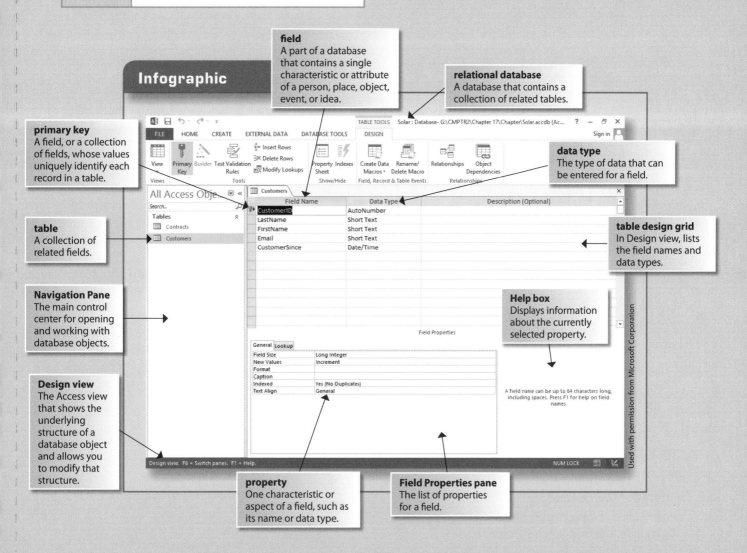

field
A part of a database that contains a single characteristic or attribute of a person, place, object, event, or idea.

relational database
A database that contains a collection of related tables.

primary key
A field, or a collection of fields, whose values uniquely identify each record in a table.

data type
The type of data that can be entered for a field.

table
A collection of related fields.

table design grid
In Design view, lists the field names and data types.

Navigation Pane
The main control center for opening and working with database objects.

Help box
Displays information about the currently selected property.

Design view
The Access view that shows the underlying structure of a database object and allows you to modify that structure.

property
One characteristic or aspect of a field, such as its name or data type.

Field Properties pane
The list of properties for a field.

Used with permission from Microsoft Corporation

Quick Reference Tools

Create a Table

- To create a table in Datasheet view, on the CREATE tab, in the Tables group, click the Table button; in the table, click Click to Add, click a data type, and then type a field name; click in the row below the field name, and then type data.

- To create a table in Design view, on the CREATE tab, in the Tables group, click the Table Design button; in the table design grid, type a field name, and then press the Enter key; click the arrow that appears in the Data Type column, and then click a data type.

Change Field Properties in Design View

- In the table design grid, click a field name, in the Field Properties pane, click in the box to the right of the property, type a new property, or click the arrow that appears, and then select the new property.

Create and Use a Simple Form

- To select a table on which to base the form, select it in the Navigation Pane.

- To create the form, on the CREATE tab, in the Forms group, click the Form button.

- To insert data using the form, on the FORM LAYOUT TOOLS DESIGN tab, in the Views group, click the View button, and then enter data in the form.

Create a Simple Query

- To start the Simple Query Wizard, on the CREATE tab, in the Queries group, click the Query Wizard button, select Simple Query Wizard, and click OK.

- To select an object, click the Tables/Queries arrow, and then click the object.

- To select a field, click it in the Available Fields list, and then click the > button to move the selected field to the Selected Fields box.

- To name and finish the wizard, click Next twice, in the What title do you want for your query box, type the query name, and then click Finish.

Specify the Primary Key

- In Design view, click a field name, and then on the TABLE TOOLS DESIGN tab, in the Tools group, click the Primary Key button.

Create a Simple Report

- To select an object on which to base the report, select it in the Navigation Pane.

- To create the report, on the CREATE tab, in the Reports group, click the Report button.

- To change column widths in the report, drag a column border.

- To view a report in Print Preview, on the REPORT LAYOUT TOOLS DESIGN tab, in the Views group, click the View button arrow, and then click Print Preview.

- To print a report, on the PRINT PREVIEW tab, click the Print button, and then click OK in the Print dialog box.

Key Definitions

Go to your CMPTR² CourseMate site for a full list of key terms and definitions.

common field A field that appears in more than one table.

composite key A primary key that requires two or more fields to uniquely identify each record in a table.

data redundancy Data stored in more than one place.

database management system (DBMS) Software used to create databases and manipulate the data in them..

Datasheet view The Access view that shows a table's contents as datasheet.

foreign key A field in a table that is a primary key in another table and that is included to form a relationship between the two tables.

form A database object used to enter, edit, and view records in a database.

Layout view The Access view in which you can make design changes to database objects such as forms and reports, and see the effects of those changes immediately.

primary key A field, or a collection of fields, whose value uniquely identifies each record in a table.

query A question about the data stored in a database.

record All the fields in a table about a single person, place, object, event, or idea; that is, a row in a table.

report A database object that shows a formatted printout or screen display of the contents of the table or query objects on which the report is based.

review card

CHAPTER 18
Maintaining and Querying a Database
Access 2013

Learning Objectives

18-1	Maintain database records
18-2	Work with queries in Design view
18-3	Sort and filter data
18-4	Define table relationships
18-5	Create a multitable query
18-6	Add criteria to a query
18-7	Create a copy of a query
18-8	Add multiple criteria to queries
18-9	Create a calculated field
18-10	Use a property sheet
18-11	Use functions in a query

Digital Backpack

Practice It: Practice It 18-3—Create, run, and modify a query for an Access database and then sort and filter data in a query.

On Your Own: On Your Own 18-2—Define record selection criteria for queries and use functions in a query.

Quiz: Take the practice quiz to prepare for tests.

Key Terms: Review the key term flash cards (online, printable, and audio).

Games: Play *Beat the Clock* and *Memory* to quiz yourself.

Videos: Watch the videos to learn more about the topics taught in this chapter.

Infographic

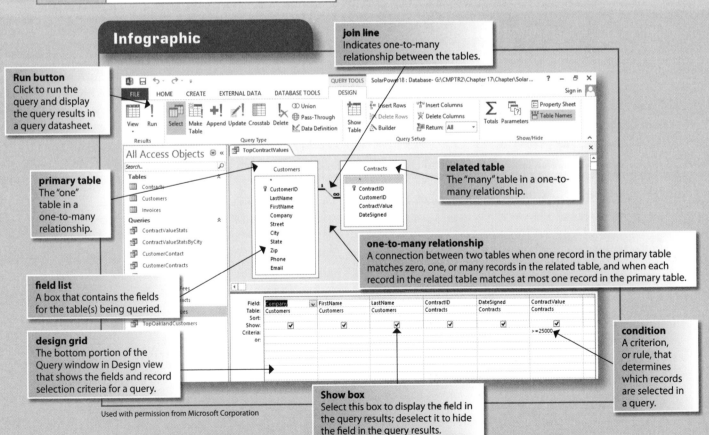

join line
Indicates one-to-many relationship between the tables.

Run button
Click to run the query and display the query results in a query datasheet.

primary table
The "one" table in a one-to-many relationship.

related table
The "many" table in a one-to-many relationship.

one-to-many relationship
A connection between two tables when one record in the primary table matches zero, one, or many records in the related table, and when each record in the related table matches at most one record in the primary table.

field list
A box that contains the fields for the table(s) being queried.

design grid
The bottom portion of the Query window in Design view that shows the fields and record selection criteria for a query.

Show box
Select this box to display the field in the query results; deselect it to hide the field in the query results.

condition
A criterion, or rule, that determines which records are selected in a query.

Used with permission from Microsoft Corporation

Quick Reference Tools

Design a Select Query

- To open a new Query window in Design view, on the CREATE tab, in the Queries group, click the Query Design button.
- To select tables to include in the query, in the Show Table dialog box, in the Tables list, click the table name, and then click Add.
- To add a field to the design grid, in the field list, double-click it.

Sort Multiple Fields in Design View

- To choose the first field on which to sort, in Query Design view, in the design grid, in the field column of the field you want to sort on, click in the Sort row, click the arrow button, and then click the sort order.
- To choose the second field on which to sort, in the field column to the right of the first sort field, click in the Sort row, click the arrow button, and then click the sort order.

Run a Query

- To run a query, in Design view, on the QUERY TOOLS DESIGN tab, in the Results group, click the Run button.

Define a One-to-Many Relationship

- To open the Relationships window, on the DATABASE TOOLS tab, in the Relationships group, click the Relationships button.
- To add tables to the Relationships window, on the RELATIONSHIP TOOLS DESIGN tab, in the Relationships group, click the Show Table button, and then in the Show Table dialog box, double-click the table name.
- To establish a relationship in the Relationship window, in the table field list on the left, click the common field, and then drag it to the table field list on the right.
- To enforce referential integrity, in the Edit Relationship dialog box, select the Enforce Referential Integrity check box.
- To update foreign key values in the related table whenever a primary key value in the primary table changes, select the Cascade Update Related Fields check box to select it.
- To create the relationship, in the Relationship window, click Create.

Create a Query with a Calculated Field

- To open the Expression Builder dialog box, in Query Design view, in the design grid, click in the Field box in which you want to create an expression, and then on the Query Tools design tab, in the Query Setup group, click the Builder button.
- To build the expression, use the expression elements and common operators, or type the expression directly in the expression box.

Key Definitions

Go to your CMPTR² CourseMate site for a full list of key terms and definitions.

And operator The operator used to select records only if *all* of the specified conditions are met.

calculated field A field that displays the results of an expression (a combination of database fields, constants, and operators).

Group By operator An operator that divides selected records into groups based on the values in the specified field.

Or operator The operator used to select records if *at least one* of the specified conditions is met.

orphaned record A record in a related table that has no matching record in the primary table.

query by example (QBE) A query that retrieves the information that precisely matches the example you provide of the information being requested.

referential integrity A set of rules to maintain consistency between related tables when data in a database is updated.

select query A query in which you specify the fields and records you want Access to select.

sort field The field used to determine the order of records in the datasheet.

subdatasheet A datasheet in which records from a related table are displayed in the primary table.

Learning Objectives

19-1	Create a form using the Form Wizard
19-2	Modify a form's design in Layout view
19-3	Find data using a form
19-4	Create a form based on related tables
19-5	Preview and print selected form records
19-6	Create a report using the Report Wizard
19-7	Modify a report's design in Layout view

Digital Backpack

Practice It: Practice It 19-3—Create a report using the Report Wizard and modify report design in Layout view.

On Your Own: On Your Own 19-2—Create a form with a main form and a subform and then print form records.

Quiz: Take the practice quiz to prepare for tests.

Key Terms: Review the key term flash cards (online, printable, and audio).

Games: Play *Beat the Clock* and *Memory* to quiz yourself.

Videos: Watch the videos to learn more about the topics taught in this chapter.

Infographic

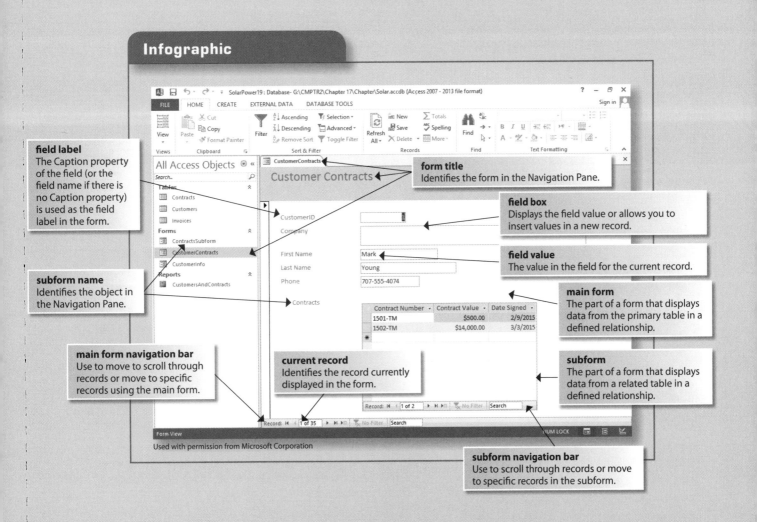

field label
The Caption property of the field (or the field name if there is no Caption property) is used as the field label in the form.

subform name
Identifies the object in the Navigation Pane.

main form navigation bar
Use to move to scroll through records or move to specific records using the main form.

form title
Identifies the form in the Navigation Pane.

field box
Displays the field value or allows you to insert values in a new record.

field value
The value in the field for the current record.

main form
The part of a form that displays data from the primary table in a defined relationship.

current record
Identifies the record currently displayed in the form.

subform
The part of a form that displays data from a related table in a defined relationship.

subform navigation bar
Use to scroll through records or move to specific records in the subform.

Used with permission from Microsoft Corporation

Quick Reference Tools

Create a Form Using the Form Wizard

- To start the Form Wizard, on the CREATE tab, in the Forms group, click the Form Wizard button.
- To select the object on which to base the form, click the Tables/Queries arrow, and then click the object.
- To move fields from the Available Fields box to the Selected Fields box, click the fields, and then click the > button.
- To complete the wizard, click Next twice, in the third Form Wizard dialog box, in the Form box, type the form name, and then click Finish.

Apply a Theme to a Form

- To open the Themes gallery, open the form in Layout view, and then on the FORM LAYOUT TOOLS DESIGN tab, in the Themes group, click the Themes button.
- To apply a theme to all objects, in the Themes gallery, click the theme you want to apply.
- To apply a theme to the current object only, right-click the theme you want to apply, and then on the shortcut menu, click Apply Theme to This Object Only.
- To apply a theme to all matching objects, right-click the theme you want to apply, and then on the shortcut menu, click Apply Theme to All Matching Objects.

Preview and Print Selected Form Records

- To preview a form, click the FILE tab, click Print, and then click Print Preview.
- To print the current records, click the Selected Record(s) option button. To print specific records, click the Pages option button.

Find Data in a Form or Datasheet

- To open the Find and Replace dialog box, in Form view, select the field you want to search, and then on the Home tab, in the Find group, click the Find button.
- To specify the field value you want to find, in the Find and Replace dialog box, in the Find What box, type the field value.
- To specify the matching options, in the Find and replace dialog box, click the Match arrow, and then click the option you want.
- To search for the next match to the value in the Find What box, click Find Next.

Create a Main Form and a Subform

- To start the Form Wizard, on the CREATE tab, in the Forms group, click the Form Wizard button.
- To select the object on which to base the main form, click the Tables/Queries arrow, and then click the object.
- To move fields from the Available Fields box to the Selected Fields box, click the fields, and then click the > button.
- To select the related object, click the Tables/Queries arrow again, click the related object, and then move the appropriate fields to the Selected Fields box.
- To complete the wizard, click Next three times, type the form and subform names in the appropriate boxes, and then click Finish.

Use Conditional Formatting in a Report

- To open the Conditional Formatting Rules Manager dialog box, in Layout view, click the field to format, click the REPORT LAYOUT TOOLS FORMAT tab, in the Control Formatting group, click the Conditional Formatting button.
- To create a rule, click the New Rule button.

Key Definitions

Go to your CMPTR² CourseMate site for a full list of key terms and definitions.

control An item on a form, report, or other database object that you can manipulate to modify the object's appearance.

control layout A set of controls grouped together in a form or report so that you can manipulate the set as a single control.

main form The part of a form that displays data from the primary table in a defined relationship.

subform The part of a form that displays data from a related table in a defined relationship.

wildcard character A placeholder you use when you know only part of a value or when you want to start or end with a specific character or match a certain pattern.

Learning Objectives

20-1	Create a presentation
20-2	Rearrange text and slides and delete slides
20-3	Add speaker notes
20-4	Run a slide show
20-5	Add animations
20-6	Add transitions
20-7	Add footers and headers to slides and handouts
20-8	Review, preview, and print a presentation

Digital Backpack

Practice It: Practice It 20-3—Create a PowerPoint presentation that includes animations and transitions.

On Your Own: On Your Own 20-2—Modify a PowerPoint presentation, prepare speaker notes and handouts, and print a presentation.

Quiz: Take the practice quiz to prepare for tests.

Key Terms: Review the key term flash cards (online, printable, and audio).

Games: Play *Beat the Clock* and *Memory* to quiz yourself.

Videos: Watch the videos to learn more about the topics taught in this chapter.

Infographic

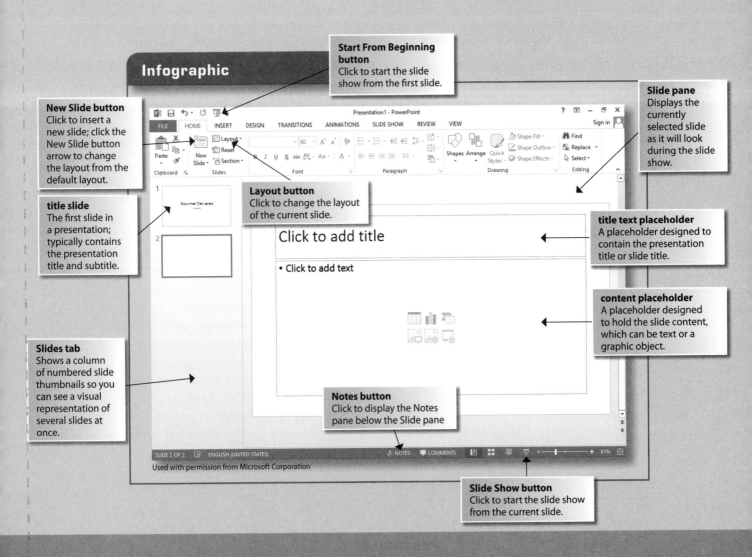

Start From Beginning button
Click to start the slide show from the first slide.

New Slide button
Click to insert a new slide; click the New Slide button arrow to change the layout from the default layout.

Slide pane
Displays the currently selected slide as it will look during the slide show.

title slide
The first slide in a presentation; typically contains the presentation title and subtitle.

Layout button
Click to change the layout of the current slide.

title text placeholder
A placeholder designed to contain the presentation title or slide title.

content placeholder
A placeholder designed to hold the slide content, which can be text or a graphic object.

Slides tab
Shows a column of numbered slide thumbnails so you can see a visual representation of several slides at once.

Notes button
Click to display the Notes pane below the Slide pane

Slide Show button
Click to start the slide show from the current slide.

Used with permission from Microsoft Corporation

Quick Reference Tools

Run a Slide Show

- To start a slide show from the current slide, click the Slide Show button on the status bar.
- To start a slide show from the first slide, on the Quick Access Toolbar, click the Start From Beginning button.
- To move forward in a slide show, click the left mouse button; or press the Spacebar, the Enter key, the Left Arrow key, or the Page Down key; to move backward in a slide show, press the Right Arrow key or the Page Up key.

Print the Presentation

- To display options for printing the presentation, click the FILE tab, and then in the navigation bar, click Print.
- To select the type of printout, click the Full Page Slides button, and then click Full Page Slides, Notes Pages, Outline, or one of the options under Handouts.
- To print non-sequential slides, type the slide numbers in the Slides box on the Print screen separated by commas.

Add Transitions

- To apply a transition, on the TRANSITIONS tab, in the Transition to This Slide group, click the transition you want to use.
- To apply a transition to all the slides, on the TRANSITIONS tab, in the Timing group, click the Apply to All button.

Animate Objects

- Click the object, and then on the ANIMATIONS tab, in the Animation group, click an animation.
- To change an animation effect, click the Effect Options button in the Animation group on the ANIMATIONS tab, and then cilck an effect.
- To remove an animation, click the None animation in the Animation group on the ANIMATIONS tab.

Add Footers to Slides

- To add a footer to the slides, on the INSERT tab, in the Text group, click the Header & Footer button.
- To remove the footer from the title slide, select the Don't show on title slide check box on the Slide tab in the Header and Footer dialog box.

Add Speaker Notes

- To display the Notes pane, click the NOTES button on the status bar.
- To add speaker notes, click in the Notes pane, and then type the note.

Key Definitions

Go to your CMPTR² CourseMate site for a full list of key terms and definitions.

animation A special effect applied to an object that makes the object move or change.

bulleted list A list of paragraphs with a special symbol to the left of each paragraph.

content placeholder A placeholder designed to hold any type of slide content—text, a graphic, or another object.

demote To move an item to a lower level in an outline.

first-level item A main item in a list.

handout A printout of the slides in a presentation.

layout A predetermined way of organizing the objects on a slide.

Microsoft PowerPoint 2013 (PowerPoint) A presentation graphics program used to create a collection of slides that can contain text, charts, pictures, sound, movies, multimedia, and so on.

placeholder A region of a slide reserved for inserting text or graphics.

presentation A file created in PowerPoint.

promote To move an item to a higher level in an outline.

second-level item (subitem) An item beneath and indented from a first-level item.

speaker notes Notes that appear in the Notes pane to remind the speaker of points to make when the particular slide appears during the slide show.

text box A container that holds text.

text placeholder A placeholder designed to contain text.

transition A special effect that changes the way a slide appears on the screen in Slide Show or Reading view.

CHAPTER 21
Enhancing a Presentation
PowerPoint 2013

Learning Objectives

21-1	Work with slide masters
21-2	Insert graphics
21-3	Create SmartArt diagrams
21-4	Apply animations to graphics
21-5	Modify animation timings
21-6	Add video to a slide
21-7	Compress pictures and media
21-8	Present online

Digital Backpack

Practice It: Practice It 21-3—Enhance a PowerPoint presentation using graphics, media, and animations.

On Your Own: On Your Own 21-2—Create a slide master and broadcast a PowerPoint presentation.

Quiz: Take the practice quiz to prepare for tests.

Key Terms: Review the key term flash cards (online, printable, and audio).

Games: Play *Beat the Clock* and *Memory* to quiz yourself.

Videos: Watch the videos to learn more about the topics taught in this chapter.

Infographic

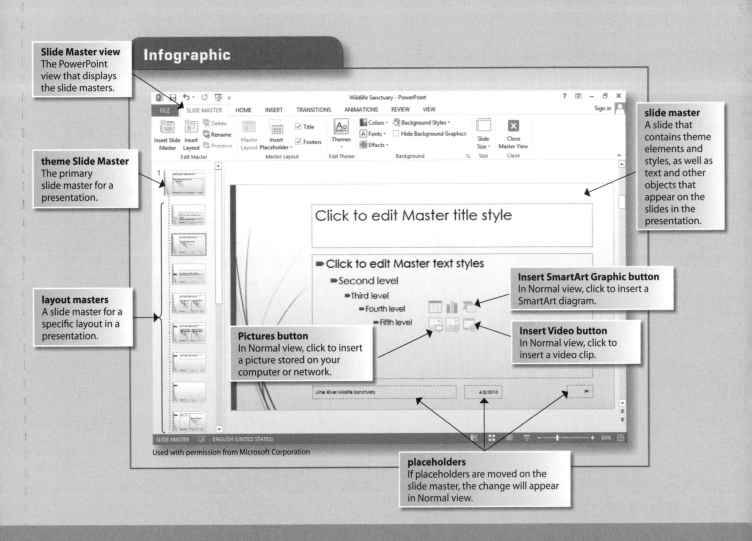

Slide Master view
The PowerPoint view that displays the slide masters.

theme Slide Master
The primary slide master for a presentation.

layout masters
A slide master for a specific layout in a presentation.

slide master
A slide that contains theme elements and styles, as well as text and other objects that appear on the slides in the presentation.

Insert SmartArt Graphic button
In Normal view, click to insert a SmartArt diagram.

Pictures button
In Normal view, click to insert a picture stored on your computer or network.

Insert Video button
In Normal view, click to insert a video clip.

placeholders
If placeholders are moved on the slide master, the change will appear in Normal view.

Used with permission from Microsoft Corporation

Quick Reference Tools

Word with Slide Masters

- For each theme in a presentation, the slide master includes the theme Slide Master and a layout master for each layout.
- To modify the slide master, switch to Slide Master view.
- In Slide Master view, you can modify the placeholders, fonts, colors, and slide background, and you can insert and remove graphics.

Add Video to a Slide

- Insert a video by using the Insert Video button in a content placeholder or by using the Video button in the Media group on the INSERT tab.
- Format video by changing options such as changing the way a clip starts and its volume. You can also trim an audio or video clip, and set a poster frame for a video clip.

Insert Graphics and SmartArt Diagrams

- To insert a picture, click the Pictures button in a content placeholder or click the Pictures button in the Illustrations group on the INSERT tab.
- To insert a shape, click the Shapes button in the Illustrations group on the INSERT tab.
- To create SmartArt, click the Insert SmartArt Graphic button in a content placeholder or the SmartArt button in the Illustrations group on the INSERT tab.
- To convert a bulleted list into SmartArt, click the Convert to SmartArt button in the Paragraph group on the HOME tab.

Customize Animations

- Use the Move Earlier and Move Later buttons in the Timing group on the ANIMATIONS tab to change the order of animations on a slide.
- To change how an animation starts, click the Start box arrow in the Timing group on the ANIMATIONS tab, and then select an option.
- To change the speed of an animation, change the time in the Duration box in the Timing group on the ANIMATIONS tab.

Present Online

- Use the Present Online feature to deliver a presentation over the Internet.
- Send custom link to the presentation.

Compress Pictures and Media

- Pictures are compressed to 220 ppi by default.
- To compress pictures further, select a picture, click the PICTURE TOOLS FORMAT tab, and then in the Adjust group, click the Compress Pictures button. Select a compression option, deselect the Apply only to this picture check box, and then click OK.
- To compress media, click the FILE tab, click the Compress Media button on the Info screen, and then click one of the quality options.

Key Definitions

Go to your CMPTR² CourseMate site for a full list of key terms and definitions.

diagram An illustration that visually depicts information or ideas and shows how they are connected.

fill The formatting of the area inside a shape.

gradient Shading in which one color blends into another or varies from one shade to another.

handouts master A handout that contains the elements that appear on printed handouts.

layout master A slide master for a specific layout in a presentation.

notes master A note that contains the elements that appear on the notes pages.

poster frame (preview frame) In a video object, the image that appears before the video starts playing.

slide master A slide that contains theme elements and styles, as well as text and other objects that appear on the slides in the presentation.

SmartArt A diagram with a predesigned layout.

theme Slide Master The primary slide master for a presentation.

Learning Objectives

22-1	Understand object linking and embedding (OLE)
22-2	Import and export data
22-3	Use the Object command to insert text from a file
22-4	Copy and paste among Office programs
22-5	Create PowerPoint slides from a Word outline
22-6	Create Form Letters with Mail Merge

Digital Backpack

Practice It: Practice It 22-3—Create an embedded Excel chart in a Word document and PowerPoint presentation and import Excel data into an Access table.

On Your Own: On Your Own 22-2—Use a Word outline to create a PowerPoint presentation and link Excel data to a slide.

Quiz: Take the practice quiz to prepare for tests.

Key Terms: Review the key term flash cards (online, printable, and audio).

Games: Play *Beat the Clock* and *Memory* to quiz yourself.

Videos: Watch the videos to learn more about the topics taught in this chapter.

Infographic

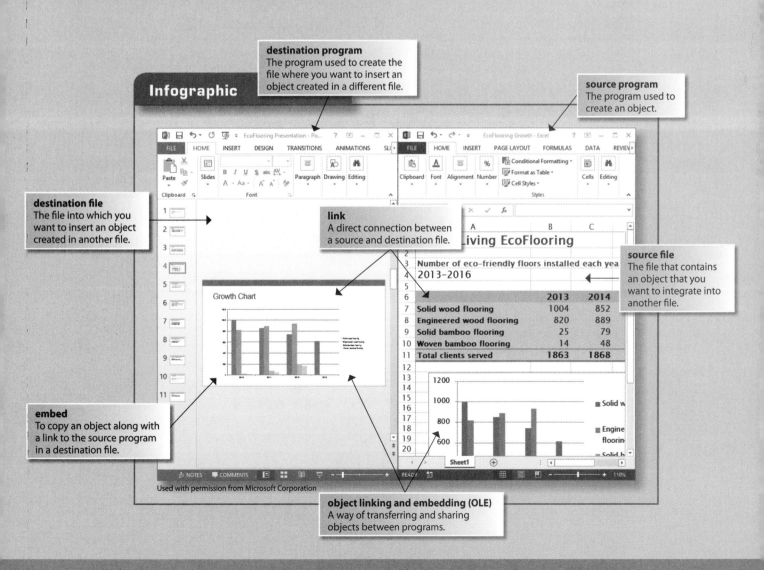

destination program
The program used to create the file where you want to insert an object created in a different file.

source program
The program used to create an object.

destination file
The file into which you want to insert an object created in another file.

link
A direct connection between a source and destination file.

source file
The file that contains an object that you want to integrate into another file.

embed
To copy an object along with a link to the source program in a destination file.

object linking and embedding (OLE)
A way of transferring and sharing objects between programs.

Used with permission from Microsoft Corporation

Quick Reference Tools

Object Linking and Embedding

- The program used to create the object you want to integrate into another file is the source program and the file that contains the object is the source file.
- The program used to create the file where you want to insert the object is the destination program and the file in which you will insert the object is the destination file.
- To embed an object means to paste it along with a link to the source program.
- To link an object means to create a connection between the source and destination file.

Import to and Export from Access

- You can import data into an Access table from another program as long as the data is in the form of a list.
- You can export data from an Access table to an Excel file, a Rich Text file, or a plain text file, and others.

Insert Objects

- Use the Object command to insert the contents of one file into another file.

Create PowerPoint Slides from a Word Outline

- When you create a PowerPoint presentation from a Word outline, paragraphs formatted with the Heading 1 style become slide titles, paragraphs formatted with the Heading 2 style become first-level bullets, and so on.
- Slides created from a Word outline are inserted after the current slide.
- You might need to reset slides created from a Word outline to apply the theme and slide master formatting correctly.

Create Form Letters with Mail Merge

- Use Mail Merge to merge data from a data source with a letter to create personalized form letters.
- If the column labels in the data source don't match the Word field names, you can use the Match Fields command to manually match the fields.
- Preview the merge before printing to make sure the correct data is inserted and that paragraph spacing is correct.

Copy and Paste Between Programs

- Use the Copy and Paste commands to copy an object from one file to another. Use the Office Clipboard.

Key Definitions

Go to your CMPTR² CourseMate site for a full list of key terms and definitions.

data source A file that contains the variable information for form letters.

destination file The file into which you want to insert an object created in another file.

destination program The program used to create the file where you want to insert an object created in a different file.

embed To copy an object along with a link to the source program in a destination file.

form letter A Word document that contains standard paragraphs of text and a minimum of variable text.

link To establish a direct connection between a source and destination file.

mail merge To merge a main document with a list of addresses from a data source.

main document A document that contains the text and other information that you want to keep the same in each form letter.

merge field A field that contains instructions to be replaced with the variable information that changes from one letter to another.

merge To combine a main document with a data source.

object linking and embedding (OLE) A way of transferring and sharing objects between programs.

Rich Text Format (RTF) A text format that preserves the formatting and layout of data.

source file The file that contains an object that you want to integrate into another file.

source program The program used to create an object.

starting document The main document in a Word mail merge.

review**card**

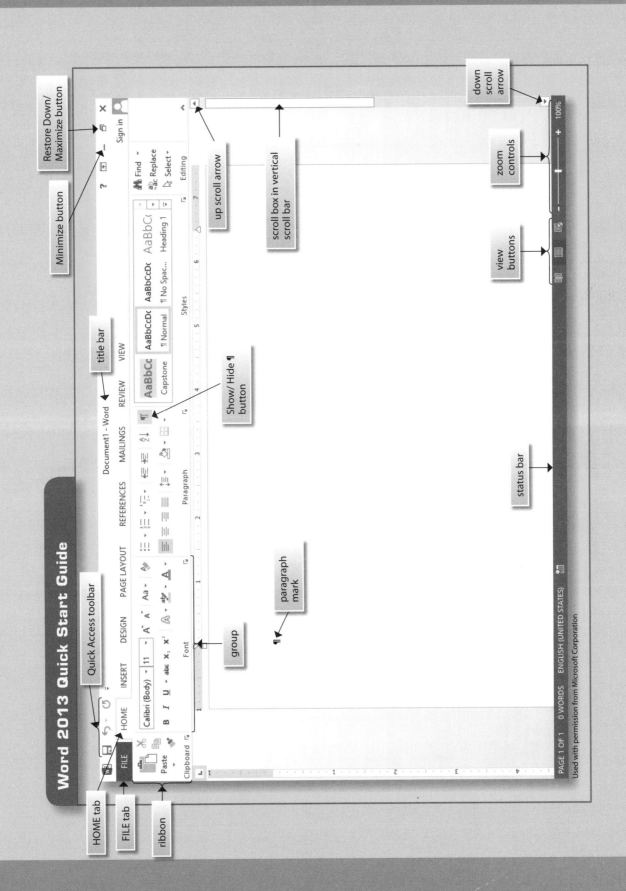

Word 2013 Quick Start Guide

- Restore Down/Maximize button
- Minimize button
- title bar
- Quick Access toolbar
- HOME tab
- FILE tab
- ribbon
- group
- paragraph mark
- Show/Hide ¶ button
- up scroll arrow
- scroll box in vertical scroll bar
- down scroll arrow
- zoom controls
- view buttons
- status bar

Used with permission from Microsoft Corporation

Excel 2013 Quick Start Guide

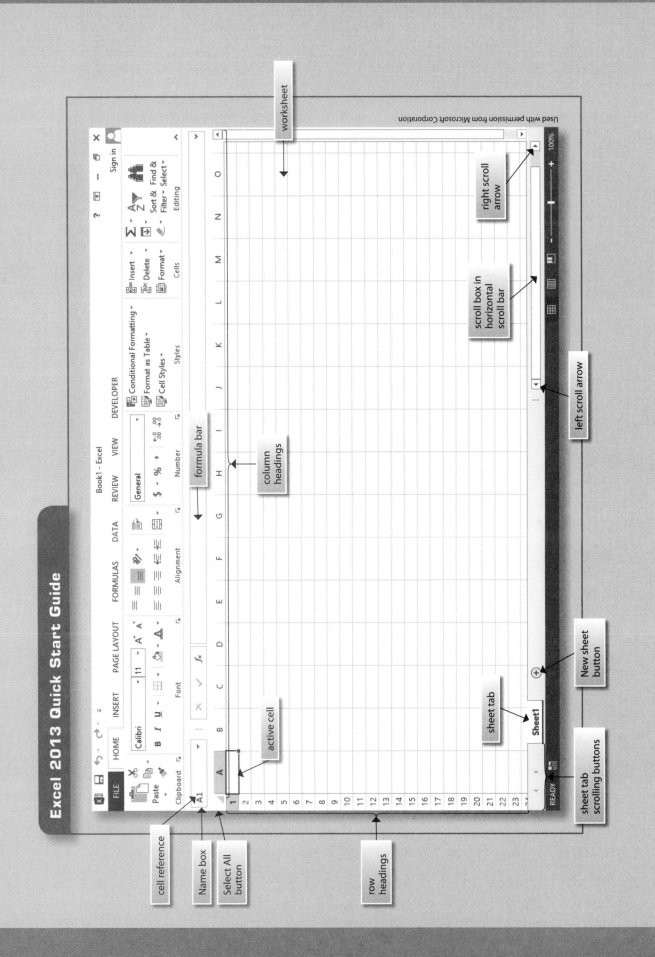

Used with permission from Microsoft Corporation

- worksheet
- right scroll arrow
- scroll box in horizontal scroll bar
- left scroll arrow
- New sheet button
- sheet tab
- sheet tab scrolling buttons
- row headings
- Select All button
- Name box
- cell reference
- active cell
- formula bar
- column headings

reviewcard

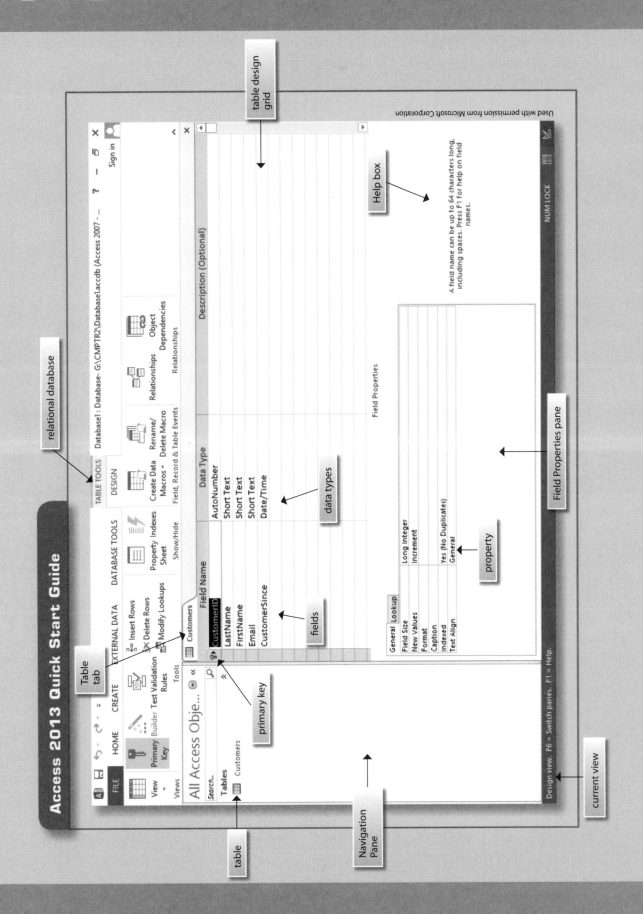

Access 2013 Quick Start Guide

relational database

table design grid

Help box

A field name can be up to 64 characters long, including spaces. Press F1 for help on field names.

Field Properties pane

data types

property

fields

Table tab

primary key

Navigation Pane

table

current view

Used with permission from Microsoft Corporation

Visit CourseMate for **CMPTR²** at www.cengagebrain.com
for additional study tools!

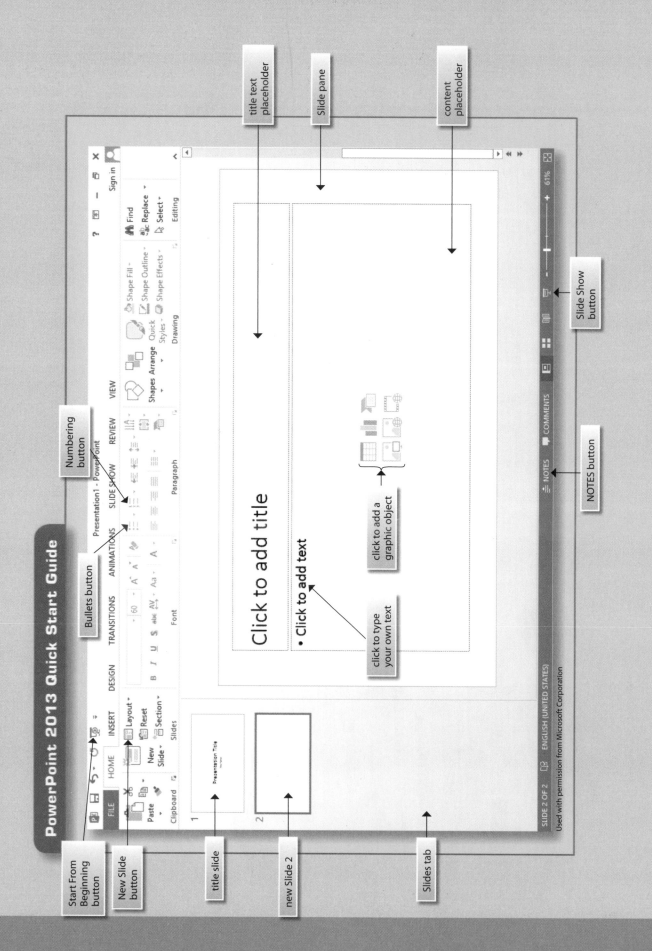

PowerPoint 2013 Quick Start Guide

Start From Beginning button

New Slide button

Bullets button

Numbering button

title text placeholder

Slide pane

content placeholder

Slide Show button

NOTES button

title slide

new Slide 2

Slides tab

click to type your own text

click to add a graphic object

Click to add title

Click to add text

Visit CourseMate for **CMPTR²** at www.cengagebrain.com for additional study tools!